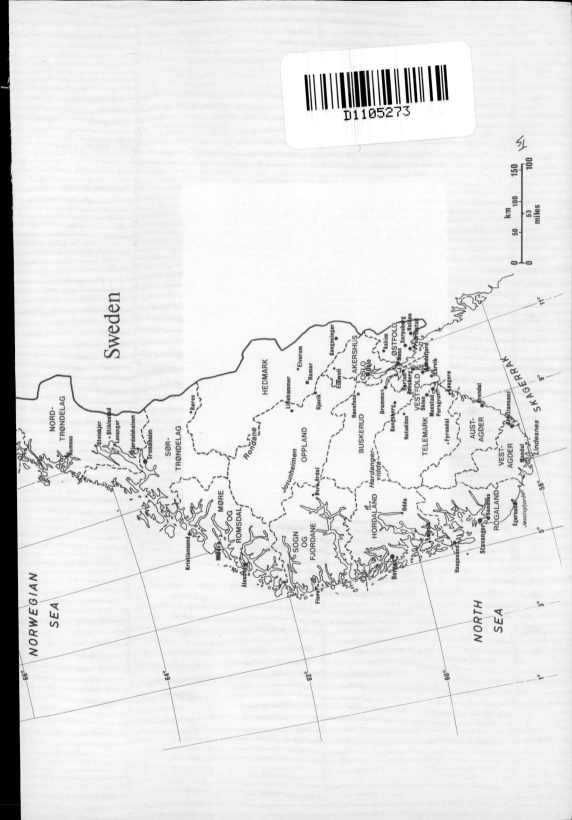

QUISLING

To Anne and Jon Olav

ODDVAR K. HOIDAL

QUISLING

A STUDY IN TREASON

NORWEGIAN UNIVERSITY PRESS

Norwegian University Press (Universitetsforlaget AS), 0608 Oslo 6
Distributed world-wide excluding Scandinavia by
Oxford University Press, Walton Street, Oxford OX2 6DP

London   New York   Toronto
Delhi   Bombay   Calcutta   Madras   Karachi
Kuala Lumpur   Singapore   Hong Kong   Tokyo
Nairobi   Dar es Salaam   Cape Town
Melbourne   Auckland

and associated companies in
Beirut   Berlin   Ibadan   Mexico City   Nicosia

An abridged Norwegian version of this book was published by
Universitetsforlaget in the autumn of 1988.

Jacket design: Åsmund Lindal
Front cover photo: National Archives of Norway
Photo editor: Marianne Gran

British Library Cataloguing in Publication Data

Hoidal, Oddvar K.
   Quisling: a study in treason.
   1. Norway. Politics. Quisling, Vidkun, 1988–1945
   I. Title
   948.1'041'0924

ISBN 82–00–18400–5

Printed in Norway
by Verbum/Aase Grafiske

Preface

This study is the result of a period of research and writing which originated in the early 1970s, while background reading and some gathering of material extended back even further. The first draft was completed in the spring of 1983. Since then my primary effort has been devoted to editing a manuscript of considerable size in order to reduce it to manageable proportions. The reader should therefore recognize that while the results of some books and articles that have appeared since the initial draft was finished have been incorporated into the study, no systematic research has been conducted since May 1983.

Many persons on both sides of the Atlantic have furnished valuable support toward making the study a reality. Mrs. Agnes Peterson, Curator of the Central and Western European Collections at the Hoover Institution, Stanford University, provided the initial stimulus toward beginning the project. Professor Magne Skodvin of the University of Oslo's Historical Institute generously made available documents from his collection, gave learned advice, and assisted in securing access to sources of information. Parliamentary Archivist Tor Kindingsland of the Norwegian *Storting* helped to make my stay in the Parliamentary Archive a memorable professional experience. The head of Oslo University Library's manuscript collection, Sverre Flugsrud, aided in finding key documents during the period when the Quisling Archive was still located at the University Library. The University Library's head librarian, Gunnar Christie Wasberg, gave permission for me to have direct access to original copies of the Library's newspaper collection from the 1930s and 1940s, thereby eliminating the mental torpor that inevitably accompanies prolonged use of microfilm viewers. Director Knut Haugland and his assistants at the Norwegian Resistance Museum (Norges Hjemmefrontmuseum), Oslo, provided all possible aid during my research stay, as did National Archivist Dagfinn Mannsåker and his staff at the National Archive. Oslo's Institute for Social Science Research made available needed office space for the initial planning and writing of the study. During two periods of extended writing I had need to draw upon the library resources of Norway's public library system. The professional librarians who assisted me on these occasions provided invaluable help. Therefore, a personal word of appreciation to Birgit Aalstad and her staff at Brumunddal Folkebibliotek and to Eldbjørg Skjerve at Ringebu Folkebibliotek. Finally, special thanks to Ole Kristian Grimnes, senior lecturer at the University of Oslo's Historical Institute for

8

his careful reading of the manuscript and for his critical comments. Any errors of fact and interpretation that remain – which are inevitable in a work of this size – are of course my own.

I was fortunate to receive a Fulbright research grant and two San Diego State University Foundation research grants during the course of researching and writing the study. The United States Educational Foundation in Norway was most helpful in making housing arrangements in Oslo. I would also like to thank San Diego State University's College of Arts and Letters for financial support in the manuscript's editorial preparation. Mrs. Barbara Schloss performed rapid and thorough service in typing the first chapters of the manuscript, which was completed with the able assistance of Mrs. Mary Pedersen and Mrs. Madeleine Scott. Dr. Jimmy Hwang of SDSU's Social Science Research Laboratory provided valuable technical expertise whenever the intricacies of computer technology needed to be mastered fully.

The book's most persistent, and most treasured, critic is my wife, Anne Kløvnes Hoidal, who actively participated in its entire period of maturation. It is therefore dedicated to her and to our son, for the many happy times we shared during the years when it was shaped.

O.K.H.
San Diego, California
August 1987

Contents

Introduction

Vidkun Quisling occupies a unique position in modern history. With the possible exceptions of Trygve Lie and Fridtjof Nansen, he is the only Norwegian political figure to gain an international reputation in the twentieth century. Because of the notoriety that he received for his collaboration with the Germans during World War II, his name became synonymous with the word traitor. The epithet proved to be lasting. Long after the general public has forgotten the specific details of his activity during World War II, the term "quisling" continues to be applied to persons accused of treasonable cooperation with an outside power. As a derisory expression, his name has become a permanent part of political vocabulary.

Despite this recognition of his name, he has yet to receive coverage in an authoritative political biography. No standard work exists, not even in his native country. Books that have appeared in Norway have either been very brief, or they have restricted their contents only to a portion of his life.[1]

Two books on Quisling are available in English. The first to appear was Ralph Hewins' biography, *Quisling: Prophet Without Honour*.[2] Issued in 1965, this title aroused more controversy in Norway than any other book published on a historical subject since the end of the war. The reaction was understandable because the biography was an unabashed apologia for Quisling. Its author, an English journalist, sought whenever possible to portray his subject in a favorable light. However, the book's critics have been able to demonstrate its inadequacies. Not only because of its lack of balance, but more importantly because of its inaccuracies, distortions, and omissions, it failed to establish itself as a revisionist study of any significant value. The second work appeared six years later. Written by an English academic, Paul M. Hayes, it sought to provide a more objective account. Throughout the book, entitled *Quisling: The Career and Political Ideas of Vidkun Quisling, 1887–1945*,[3] one notes the author's attempt to provide a balanced portrayal. Expert historians in Norway, however, have generally commented that Hayes at times lacked a full understanding of Norwegian society and body politics when writing the book, sometimes resulting in errors or questionable conclusions. Furthermore, he on occasion made use of unreliable sources.[4] The best study currently available on Quisling's early career is Hans Dietrich Loock's *Quisling, Rosenberg und Terboven: Zur Vorgeschichte und Geschichte der nationalsozialistischen Revolution in Norwegen*.[5] The book's coverage ends, however, in September 1940, which means that the greater part of Quisling's activity during the occupation is not included. The Norwegian fascist leader also was not the sole focus of Loock's attention in this work. Quisling shared the spotlight with the major German protagonists who were responsible for shaping Germany's course in the invasion and occupation of Norway.

In order to understand fully Quisling's actions as a collaborator during World War II, it is necessary to have a total perspective of his involvement in Norwegian politics. Such a perspective has not yet been provided. From the end of World War II to the present, his motives have often been misinterpreted because of the apparent inconsistencies that he exhibited during different periods in his life. In order to explain the many seeming contradictions that he presented, already during his postwar treason trial the concept of viewing him as a "puzzle" ("*gåte*") arose. The idea of regarding Quisling as a "puzzle" has endured since that time.

Superficially this concept may appear to be quite plausible. It seems to give if not an explanation, then at least a perspective from which to view the many contrasting features that he displayed. To mention only a few of the more sensational: the difference between his humanitarian relief activity and his later disregard for human life; his vehement anti-socialism and anti-communism, contrasted with his initial attempt to become involved in politics through these two movements, plus his original admiration for the Bolshevik Revolution; his denunciation of the socialists for allegedly being treasonous because of their earlier close contact with the Soviet Union, compared with his own willingness to accept money and support from the Third Reich; his strongly expressed nationalism, which stood in obvious conflict with his willingness to surrender his country to the Germans; his early ascetic lifestyle, which contrasted with the grand manner in which he lived during the war; and his deep concern and affection for his wife, which differed greatly from his treatment of the woman in his first marriage, who according to all available evidence was abandoned when he committed bigamy.

These differing forms of behavior certainly seem to be paradoxical. However, the key to gaining insight into his actions is not as problematic as one may initially assume. He did have a many-faceted personality. Like most persons with a modicum of intelligence, he operated at several levels. Again like most individuals, he was also capable of changing his views and his values during the course of a lifetime. But while his character was complex, it is not difficult to understand. It is necessary to place his actions within the context of his entire life, in particular if comprehension is to be gained concerning how it was possible for him to play the role of an arch-collaborator during World War II. If this is done, then the various acts that he committed, which appear to be irreconcilable when viewed singly or when compared only with another seemingly contradictory fact, become intelligible. For only when the entire scope of his career is observable do the individual aspects become part of a meaningful pattern. Because he did believe, as the contents of this book will reveal, that he had a special mission to fulfill.

This study seeks to provide a complete and thorough account of Vidkun Quisling's life, with its focus concentrated on the changing nature of the position he occupied in Norwegian politics. In order to gain a full understanding of the role he played in politics, equal weight is given to the prewar decade as well as to the occupation period. This is done because his experiences in the 1930s provide valuable insight into his behavior during the German occupation.

The book is not intended to be solely a monograph which restricts its narrative at all times to Quisling's person. A study of his life requires that consideration be given to the society in which he lived and operated. Whenever required, he is therefore placed within the broader context of Norwegian historical development.

It is hoped that the following account of Quisling's life will provide greater understanding of this figure whose name arouses general recognition, but whose true motives and actions are shrouded in the mist of notoriety and sensationalism that has become associated with him.

CHAPTER I

Early Years
1887–1929

I am of the Nordic race, and my father's family has resided in Telemark for centuries.

Vidkun Quisling,
Studentene fra 1905

The roots of Norway's most controversial modern political figure go back to an isolated rural district in southeastern Norway. Fyresdal is a long valley located in the west-central portion of the province of Telemark. Like much of Telemark, it is a picturesque area of lakes, streams, and sharply etched, but not tall, mountains. The valley is dominated by one of Norway's larger lakes, Fyresvatn. It is surrounded by rugged mountains and hills. Numerous side valleys send streams rushing down to the large lake on the valley floor. Agriculture and lumbering have always been the main occupations of the people, with hunting and fishing serving as more limited sidelines for the peasants living in this rather remote district. The main area of settlement, the village of Fyresdal, is located at the upper eastern shore of the lake, where the valley widens. Because of the steep and rugged shoreline further south along the lake, for many generations the people in the village led an isolated, provincial existence. Up until recent memory, the only exit from the valley was to the northeast. Not until 1953 was a road built which gave direct access to the more heavily populated districts of lower Telemark.

Vidkun Abraham Lauritz Jonssøn Quisling, the oldest son of Jon Laurits and Anna Caroline Qvisling, emerged from the peasant stock of Fyresdal.[1] His family, however, had for a number of generations held a more privileged status than that of the ordinary peasant family of Telemark. Both his paternal great-grandfather, Rasmus Bakka, and his paternal grandfather, Lars Abraham Qvisling, had been sheriffs (*lendsmenn*). Because of their

more secure economic standing, they had been able to provide their progeny with a good financial start in life. Rasmus Bakka purchased the position of sheriff for his 23-year-old son by paying a sum of 400 *spesiedaler*,
while Lars Abraham in turn was able to give his son, Jon Laurits, the best
education then available in Norway.[2] Quisling's father held an *embede*, the
much coveted life-time tenure bestowed upon the university-educated
members of the civil service hierarchy. As a pastor in the Lutheran State
Church, Jon Laurits both looked after the spiritual needs of the people of
Fyresdal and acted as a state bureaucrat. As was fitting for his social position, Pastor Qvisling's wife, the former Anna Caroline Bang, was the
daughter of a shipowner from Grimstad in southern Norway. She was
15½ years younger than her husband.[3]

The couple's four children, Vidkun, Jørgen, Esther, and Arne, were
brought up in a family that placed great stress on education. All received
the equivalent of a university education: Vidkun became an officer, Jørgen
a physician, Arne an engineer, while Esther died at the tragically young age
of twenty-one after having completed her teacher's education.[4] The rever-
ence for learning which dominated the Qvisling household was due to the
influence of Jon Laurits. He was a local author of some note. As could
naturally be expected from someone in his position, he wrote theological
studies, but in addition he was also very much interested in history, especially the local history of Telemark.[5] Discussions among the Qvisling children and their father were therefore often of an historical and abstract
nature, infused by a strong element of philosophical and mystical speculation.[6] The tendency to theorize abstractly and to bind together uncon-
nected historical facts was a trait which remained lifelong with Vidkun
Quisling, a trait which he derived from his father's influence. It was therefore natural for young Vidkun to lay stress on the fact that his birthdate,
July 18, 1887, fell on the traditional, and incorrect, anniversary of the Battle of Hafrsfjord, which according to the commonly accepted version in
the old Norse sagas brought about the unification of Norway.[7]

No one can depict with exact certainty the nature of the relationship between Quisling's parents while their children were young, nor the degree
of warmth which existed between the parents and children. However, several persons who later became acquainted with them have agreed that the
family was close and harmonious. In Fyresdal the Qvisling family held itself somewhat aloof from their neighbors, and neither Jon Laurits nor his
sons have revealed anything about the atmosphere that existed in the
household. This aloofness was reflected in Vidkun, who never had any
close friends during his early childhood except for his siblings. He preferred to read and to be by himself.[8]

Young Quisling's idyllic life in Fyresdal, where he enjoyed the beauty
of the countryside, the respect which his family received from the local
population, and the reading of history inspired by his father, was changed

abruptly when Jon Laurits Qvisling in 1893 obtained a new position as
pastor in Drammen, a major city located in Buskerud, the province lying
immediately to the east of Telemark. Life in the city was very different for
Vidkun. His family was no longer part of an elite. In the industrial center
of Drammen the family of a simple pastor did not command much respect.[9] Vidkun learned this the hard way when he entered grammar school
for the first time. He naturally spoke the local Telemark dialect of his native Fyresdal, and he therefore immediately became the object of ridicule
for the town boys. But the pastor's son reacted to being scorned by doggedly pursuing his studies. Starting out at the bottom of his class, within a
few short months he was at the top, and here he remained.[10]

His learning abilities won him the admiration of the boys who just a
short while earlier had been his fiercest tormentors. But this did not inspire
him to interact openly and naturally with his classmates. Young Vidkun already possessed the shy and introverted nature which would characterize
him as an adult, and this handicap stayed with him for the rest of his life.[11]

He continued to receive high grades when his father in 1900 moved
back to Telemark, this time to take up his religious duties at Gjerpen, located just outside the industrial city of Skien. In Skien, Vidkun attended
the secondary Latin School, from which he graduated in 1909, receiving
the highest grade possible (*S. tf.*).[12]

At the Latin School, he revealed a special interest and ability in mathematics. His mathematics teacher urged him to continue in this field.[13] Had
he done so, the possibility of a high position as an academician or re-
searcher lay open before him.[14] But the local teacher suffered disappointment. His star pupil graduated from the Latin School at the time of one of
the most important turning points in modern Norwegian history, 1905.
This marked the year in which Norway left the union with Sweden which
had lasted since 1814. The dramatic events of 1905, coupled with the romantic impulses which he had received from his reading of history, inspired Quisling to decide to follow a profession far removed from the
classroom or the laboratory. "I chose to become an officer," he said in
1945, "because of the influence of reading history and because of the influence of the dissolution of the union with Sweden."[15]

Stimulated by nationalistic fervor, young cadet Vidkun Quisling entered the War College (*Krigsskolen*) in the capital, Kristiania, on September
15, 1905. But here he discovered that other bright young minds had
equally been inspired to seek out the military as a profession. In the competition for the top grades, Quisling found himself in the unaccustomed
position of being only fourth highest in his class at the end of his first year
of studies. But this, for him, temporary disgrace merely reinforced his determination to be number one, and he succeeded. When he completed his
studies at the War College in 1908, the pastor's son from Telemark was
once more first in his graduating class.[16]

At this point he briefly interrupted his military education to accept a temporary position at his old school in Skien, the Latin School. He did so no doubt in order to earn money for his future studies, a practice which was common among students. One can only speculate how his country's history might have been different if he had become permanently committed to teaching, for which he was eminently qualified, and had changed careers. But the teacher's call did not have the necessary attraction to lure the young lieutenant away from the military, for in the following year he returned to the capital, enrolling in the Military Academy (*Den Militære Høyskole*). Here the familiar pattern of his educational achievement repeated itself. Not only was he first in his class, but when he graduated in 1911, he could celebrate his greatest triumph. He earned the highest grade ever granted by the Academy, and as a reward he was received in a personal audience by the King.[17]

It was hardly any wonder that everyone in military circles believed that the road for Quisling lay open toward the highest achievements possible within the military. Immediately after his graduation from the Academy he became a junior member (*aspirant*) within the General Staff.[18] Seven years later, in 1918, he was promoted to adjutant (*adjoint*).[19]

He did not spend all of his time at paper work within the General Staff. It was expected that a Staff officer should exercise command, and he served with various field divisions at the same time that he was a member of the General Staff. He had graduated from the War College as a lieutenant in field artillery, and because of his background in this military branch he was transferred to the staff of the General Inspector of Field Artillery in October 1917. In the same year, during his tour of duty as an artillery officer, he was promoted to captain.[20]

It seemed that to all intents and purposes he had settled down to the somewhat tedious life of a career officer, receiving promotions from time to time until he reached the top. He was an exemplary officer, hardworking and devoted to his profession. He carried out the routine of daily activity, showed that his theoretical abilities had not declined by offering ingenious solutions to problems of tactics, and exhibited great stamina during physical exercises, although he never excelled as an athlete. In his relations with subordinates he was firm but never arrogant, assuming a kindly attitude. He was always highly respected.[21]

Yet at the same time he was a most unconventional officer. His silence among his lively fellow-officers was legendary. He could sit for hours without saying a word.[22] He lived ascetically, shunning nicotine and caffeine, and only on occasion taking a glass of wine.[23] Equally unusual was his complete indifference to women, especially among officers who zealously sought to live up to their reputation as dashing gallants. Yet he did not withdraw and sulk, but maintained a friendly attitude.[24]

Another somewhat unusual feature for an officer of his age was that he did not lose his love of learning. In addition to the tactical books which he was required to study as a member of the General Staff, he immersed himself in books on history, mathematics, and philosophy. His fellow officers responded to this uncommon activity with a combination of awe and sarcasm. He became known as "the Professor" because of his encyclopedic knowledge.[25]

The wide range of Quisling's reading was fully illustrated by a special task which he received as a member of the General Staff. All junior members were assigned a particular country which they had to become familiar with. Fate would have it that he received as his special area the vast territory of Imperial Russia. It was expected that he should become thoroughly acquainted with the military capabilities of the empire. As usual, he accepted this new challenge with enthusiasm and thoroughness. He did not stop when he had learned all of the important military features of the country, as did the average junior member, but went on to learn the Russian language and to read its literature.[26]

Because of his close study of Russia, when the post of military attaché became vacant in 1918, there was no one more qualified to fill this position than Captain Quisling, and he was ordered to assume this billet on April 15.[27] His association with Russia would determine the future course of his life.

The young Captain looked forward to his new assignment in Petrograd. The Russian Revolution had just then entered the period of the Civil War, and he anticipated duty that was far more exciting than the routine he was accustomed to within the Norwegian military.[28]

He travelled to Petrograd by railway through Germany in late May 1918. The Treaty of Brest-Litovsk between Lenin's Bolshevik government and imperial Germany had newly been signed, permitting special trains to cross the cease-fire line. Quisling's train ride to Petrograd went over Warnemünde–Berlin–Köningsberg–Kovno–Vilna–Dünaberg–Pskov, and he had the opportunity to send an immediate report back to Norway of the impressions he had received of Germany's and Russia's military fitness.[29]

His first report to the Defense Department does not leave the impression of particularly accurate intelligence gathering. In opposition to the view prevalent in Norway, he declared that Germany seemed to have adequate stocks of food. He noted that soap and leather were in short supply, railway equipment was worn, and the few automobiles that were seen were military vehicles. Nevertheless, he insisted that the situation in Germany was not serious and would not affect the outcome of the war. Conditions in the fall of 1918, he maintained, would favor Germany.[30] Imperial Germany, contrary to his expectations, collapsed in November.

Upon his arrival in Petrograd, he found that he had much to do in keeping the Defense Department informed of the constantly changing military front lines, which bulged forward and backward during the course of the Civil War. In his reports he was straightforward and factual, giving the impression of an objective attitude. Considering conditions in the country, his reports generally gave a correct impression about the military situation. Only on occasion did personal reflections appear, and to cite one example, his assessment of the Russian Revolution proved to be more correct than his evaluation of Imperial Germany:

> Russia's situation at this moment [October 23, 1918] is reminiscent of France's position in the summer of 1793 when the king was executed, the Girondists were crushed, the Jacobins were master, over half of France was in rebellion, and foreign enemies were everywhere on the frontiers. To draw firm conclusions from this similarity must be considered incorrect, but one should not be too sure the Russian Revolution will be easier to crush than the French.[31]

He was not permitted to continue his activity as military attaché for very long. The conditions he reported on, the activities of the White and Red armies, made for such uncertainty in the Russian capital that the Norwegian legation was evacuated in December 1918.[32]

His initial stay in Russia was therefore of short duration. Nevertheless, it proved to be of great importance because it brought him into contact with Frederik Prytz, an individual who would later exercise strong influence over Quisling during many of the crucial periods of his political career.[33] Prytz was serving at the time as the commercial counselor of the Norwegian legation. His first association with Quisling in 1918 did not prove to be permanent. Nevertheless, a tie was established which lasted until Prytz's death in February 1945.

Upon his return to Norway, it took Quisling some time before he was able to finish the work connected with his responsibilities in the legation. Not until the summer of 1919 did he resume his position within the General Staff.

He did not remain long. Once more his military work within the General Staff was interrupted because of his previous connection with Russia. With civil war raging within the country, and with the fate of the young Soviet republic apparently most uncertain, Finland was one of the few countries through which European nations could obtain information about what was taking place within war-torn Russia. Quisling was regarded as the best man suited to gather intelligence, and he was thereupon ordered to assume the position as secretary to the Norwegian legation (*legasjonssekretær*) in Helsinki.[34]

So it was that he began two years of service in the Finnish capital, first as secretary to the legation, a diplomatic post, and later also as military attaché.[35] He assumed his intelligence gathering duties on September 12, 1919.[36]

His reports from Helsinki were of a character similar to that of the earlier dispatches which he sent from Petrograd in 1918. In the fall of 1919 he was primarily occupied with reporting on the Civil War in Russia, in particular General Yudenitch's attack on Petrograd. In the following year he concentrated his attention on the territorial differences in the peace negotiations between the Finns and the Russians. Of special interest was the question of whether or not Finland would obtain the Petsamo district bordering on the Arctic Ocean, which had a direct bearing on Norway's northern boundary. By 1921 the situation had quieted down and he sent home reports on various subjects such as the strength of Russia's armed forces and the condition of the Finnish military. His descriptions of the Kronstadt uprising were particularly noteworthy.[37]

In his reports he did not assume a particularly partisan stance. He was neither pro nor anti Bolshevik. At times his statements seemed to contain an undertone of antagonism towards Lenin's party, but this may merely have been good tone within Norwegian military circles. On the whole, however, he assumed, generally successfully, an objective position. His dispatches were not especially perceptive, nor were they bad reports. They were based on the rapidly changing conditions of the day, and must be evaluated as such. It should be noted, however, that he did not travel into the field to obtain first-hand information. In Petrograd and later in Helsinki he restricted himself to the capitals in which he was posted. If he did travel, the reports fail to show this.[38]

As he had done previously, he carried out his duties in Helsinki with thoroughness and efficiency. His immediate superior, Minister Andreas T. Urbye, was quite impressed with his military attaché and expressed his admiration for Quisling, both then and later. Even in 1945, when Quisling was on trial, Urbye remained a strong admirer of the subordinate who had served under him from the fall of 1919 to June 1921: ". . . an extremely conscientious man, a gentleman, a man who had many interests, and he was extremely knowledgeable."[39] Quisling's accomplishments therefore did not go unacknowledged. Urbye did not hesitate to leave Quisling in charge of the legation as chargé d'affaires when the Minister was absent from Helsinki for considerable periods.[40]

The tour of duty at the legation in Helsinki came to an end in June 1921, when Quisling once more was transferred back to the General Staff. Again his stay at home was brief. As former foreign minister Arnold Ræstad has pointed out, Quisling was well-known within the small group of men who handled Norway's foreign relations, and his reputation was excellent.

During the years 1918 to 1921, Quisling met and became acquainted with, or known to, quite a number of Norwegian officials abroad, and he generally gave . . . the impression of being reliable and efficient. His superiors abroad and at home felt satisfied with the quality and quantity of work put forth by him. So, when asked by a prospective employer about the qualifications of Quisling, they would give him the best recommendations.[41]

In this instance the "prospective employer" happened to be Fridtjof Nansen, famed Arctic explorer, zoologist, diplomat, and Norway's leading humanitarian figure in the twentieth century. Nansen was just at this time at the height of his career, organizing his International Russian Relief Committee under the auspices of the International Red Cross. He was interested in obtaining capable administrators to work under him in Russia. When he visited Urbye while passing through Helsinki on his way to conduct negotiations with the Soviets in the fall of 1921, Quisling was an obvious candidate. Urbye recommended him warmly to Nansen,[42] and the humanitarian was most impressed: "Nansen found that Quisling's knowledge of Russia, and mastery of the Russian and German languages, as well as his General Staff training, made him a promising choice."[43] This was verified by Nansen when he checked with members of the Norwegian diplomatic corps in Kristiania in September. Quisling once again received a high recommendation. This confirmed Nansen's decision to employ Quisling in Russian relief activity.[44] The necessary permission for Quisling to work for Nansen was obtained from the Defense Department, which granted Quisling a leave of absence in January 1922.[45] Once more he returned to Russia.

Nansen's International Russian Relief Committee was already at work by the time Quisling left Norway. The organization's central office was in Geneva, while a sub-office was located in Berlin. The Berlin office was responsible for the transport of food to Russia, and stood in direct contact with the Nansen offices in that country. There were two Russian offices, one in Moscow, the main office, responsible for relief activity in greater Russia and the Volga valley, and a regional office in Kharkov, covering the Ukraine and the Crimea.[46] John Gorvin, an Englishman, was in charge of the Moscow office. Quisling met with him upon his arrival in Russia, and then journeyed on to the Ukraine to assume responsibility for running the Kharkov office.[47]

Considerable controversy has arisen concerning his work in Russia under Nansen, and this of course is due to Quisling's later activity. His supporters have always over-emphasized everything their leader was connected with, while his detractors have tended to downplay his importance. As for Quisling himself, he was always interested in presenting whatever position he occupied in as favorable light as possible. He was responsible for creating many of the myths that surround him. With regard to his relief activity in Russia, he later stated that it was really he, and not Nansen, who was in charge of administering the work that brought food to millions of starving people: "Nansen was a great man, a leader in the arts, a leader in the sciences, but it was I who did the practical work. It was I who carried out the work in Russia, and I state this without any intent to belittle Nansen."[48]

Reality was quite different. Quisling did not have control of the Nansen organization's administration in Russia. He was merely part of an international relief effort whose members were scattered in different offices, some in Russia, some in western Europe.[49] Not only was the Nansen organization concerned with bringing food to the famine stricken areas of southern Russia and the Ukraine, it also carried out humanitarian work to aid the large numbers of refugees who had been made homeless by World War I and by the upheaval which followed in the wake of the war. Nansen had been named League High Commissioner for the repatriation of prisoners of war in the spring of 1920. In the following year he and his assistants accepted the task of aiding Russian refugees, most of whom constituted the remnants of White armies, scattered over an area extending from Central Europe to the Far East. In 1922 the refugee work was extended to include the Greeks, who were being driven out of Turkey by Kemal Attaturk and his followers. In 1923 the Armenians, who also were suffering from Turkish brutality, were added to the burdens of Nansen's organization.[50]

When viewed from this perspective, Quisling's activity in the Ukraine, although important, must be seen as merely a small part of a large international humanitarian effort welded together by Nansen's strong will. Quisling was not even Nansen's right-hand man in the Soviet Union. If anyone deserves to be so described, it was John Gorvin, who had the difficult assignment of dealing with Soviet authorities in Moscow. Above all, however, it was Nansen, through his contacts on the highest international level and his skill at fund-raising, who provided the organization with the impetus and sustenance for its operations. In recognition of his work, he was awarded the Nobel Peace Prize in December 1922.

Quisling's duties as head of the Kharkov office were restricted. He had to implement decisions and to carry out instructions which were made at a higher level. He received the goods earmarked for his area, delivered them to local authorities, and attempted as far as possible to see to it that the aid reached the victims for whom it was intended.[51] This was not an easy job. When he arrived in the Ukraine in January 1922, it was common to see in this area carriages loaded down with the corpses of people who had died from the effects of starvation, typhus, and cholera.[52] He could not help but be affected by the terrible incidents of disease and starvation which he was forced to witness. In a letter to his friends and colleagues in the General Staff he described the desperateness of the situation. The letter contained photographs of such frightful scenes as "corpses which lay in high piles, of a boy who had eaten his brother, etc."[53]

He put his ability to speak Russian and his administrative talents to full work in applying relief. Under most difficult circumstances, he was able to obtain the necessary transportation for the needed goods.[54] No one can deny that he conscientiously carried out humanitarian work of great significance for the people who resided in the region which he administered, but his effort must be seen within the scope of the activities of the Nansen organization as a whole.

His relief work in the Ukraine in 1922 did not extend over a long period. It was concluded at the end of August after a stay of some six months. A new crop had just been harvested, lessening the need for relief. Captain Quisling thereupon once more journeyed home to Norway.[55]

His association with Nansen had not yet concluded, however. He resumed his work in the Ukraine after the New Year holidays, having obtained, through Nansen's intercession, an extension of his leave of absence from the General Staff until the end of June 1923. But the General Staff, somewhat irritated by Quisling's frequent absences since 1918, made it clear that this was the last extension he could expect to receive.[56]

During his second period of activity in the Ukraine he concentrated mainly on completing the work necessary for wrapping up the project, since Nansen's relief activities in Russia were now almost at an end. However, as the deadline for his return to the General Staff approached, he declared that he would not be able to finish his work by the time his leave of absence expired. He once more asked to have the leave extended. The General Staff turned down his request.[57]

Quisling now had to make one of the most critical decisions of his life. The military was insisting that he return to meet the demands of his career as a General Staff officer. During his absences he had been bypassed by a number of officers with lower seniority because he had failed to take the General Staff Examination.[58]

Although he had to decide a question so crucial as whether or not he wished to continue as a professional officer, he temporized. As was true so often during his life, he was unable to make a prompt decision when faced with a difficult personal problem, and he usually permitted someone else to suggest to him what alternative to follow. This time, however, no one was at hand to put forward such a suggestion. He apparently did not believe that the General Staff could consider removing someone with his talents from its ranks.

He refused to accept the routine way in which the military bureaucracy operated. He had not lived up to its requirements; no exceptions could be made. He overstayed his leave of absence, which ended on July 1, 1923. One month later, on August 1, he was dismissed from the General Staff.[59] Yet he retained his rank and pay as a captain in the field artillery and remained on the army's inactive rolls until 1928, when he sought and obtained dismissal as an active officer. However, as a reserve officer he still had the obligation to serve his country in times of national emergency. He now received reduced pay as a captain. In December 1930 he was appointed to the rank of unpaid major in the reserve, but continued to receive his reduced pay as captain.[60]

His removal from the General Staff proved to be one of the most fatal turning points in his life. Had he remained associated with the military, not only would his public career have taken a different course, but Norwegian political history would have developed in a different manner during the 1930s and the first half of the following decade. It proved to be a personal tragedy for him and a national tragedy for his country that he failed to remain within the safe confines of the General Staff. The military, however, no longer had fully the same attraction for him that it had held previously. In the Ukraine he experienced, under the overall leadership of a major international figure, being in charge of a large-scale administrative operation, receiving a salary far higher than that which he was paid as an officer. When he left for his second period of service under Nansen, he still wished to be able to retain his foothold within the General Staff. But with his frequent and long absences from Norway since 1918, that foothold had become tenuous.

Quisling himself always maintained that the real reason why his military career came to an end was that he had a moral obligation to complete his work under Nansen; that he could not leave unfinished the relief activity that he was responsible for: "I could not leave the important work which I was wrapping up in Russia, and I had no alternative but to leave the military when I was denied leave of absence."[61] The question was not so clear-cut, however. Quisling's explanation greatly over-dramatized his importance, a habit which became stronger as the years went by. In fact, his work was nowhere near as important as he later maintained. If it had been so significant, his superiors, Nansen and Gorvin, would no doubt have interceded for him, as Nansen previously had done. It was Gorvin's office in Moscow, not the regional office in the Ukraine, which was responsible for completing the last details of the Nansen organization's work in the Soviet Union.[62]

There appears to have been a more personal reason why he overstayed his leave and thereby terminated his military career. At the very time when he should have made a firm decision on whether or not to return to the General Staff, he was preoccupied with a private matter of considerable delicacy. During his period of service in Russia, for the first time his name was linked with romantic involvement, and not with one woman, but with two. He met both in Kharkov, where they were employed in the relief committee's office. Most extraordinary was the fact that he married both women in due order, *without* obtaining a divorce to terminate the first marriage before proceeding with the second.

He married his first wife, Alexandra Andreevna Voronine, in August 1922, shortly before his first stay in Kharkov was over. The bride had barely turned seventeen, and was nineteen years younger than her husband. She received a Norwegian passport and accompanied her husband to Kristiania. Alexandra received a friendly welcome from Quisling's family, and her name was duly recorded as Quisling's wife in the army's military records when he resumed his employment in the General Staff. She returned with her husband to Kharkov when he again took up his work for Nansen in 1923.[63]

Their marriage began to unravel, however, in the summer of 1923. While his wife was away, Quisling met another woman, a friend of Alexandra's who was five years older. Her last name, Paseshnikova, was too ordinary for the class-conscious Quisling, and it was therefore later changed to the more aristocratic-sounding Pasek. Vidkun secretly married his Maria Basilievna on September 10, 1923.[64]

His marriage to his first wife, however, still remained in effect. Only *after* he had married Maria did he begin to undertake a clumsy and unsuccessful attempt to secure a divorce. When Alexandra returned to Kharkov from the Crimea, where she had been vacationing with her mother, he took her on a trip to Paris, informing her on the way that he wished for a divorce. He left his young wife in France, having provided funds for her stay. In the next year he and Maria came to Paris, where he tried to arrange a divorce from Alexandra through the Norwegian embassy. The indignant chargé d'affaires refused, however, to agree to be party to such a step. Quisling therefore could find no alternative except eventually to move to Kristiania with *both* his wives in the summer of 1924. Alexandra understandably was most unhappy, and after a while found the situation so impossible that she returned to France to live with a relative. Her tie to Quisling eventually disintegrated, but no formal divorce has ever been recorded.[65]

That Quisling could have become involved in such a predicament, and acted in such a manner, revealed a basic flaw in his character. Not merely was he incompetent in managing his personal affairs, but he showed a disregard for societal norms that was extraordinary for someone with his background. In the 1920s this type of behavior was abnormal to say the least for a person with his status and education, and a pastor's son to boot. Not for the last time, he acted as if the ordinary standards of human behavior did not affect him personally. He was lucky that the unfortunate episode involving Alexandra did not become known until after his death.[66] Prior to this time, the few who were aware of his first marriage generally accepted his cover story that his relationship with Alexandra had been a "marriage of convenience" to allow her to escape from Russia.[67]

After the war, the hard core of Quisling's former followers and apologists have strenuously objected to the fact that he had two wives. They have either denied that a first marriage occurred or else have maintained that the marriage was staged simply to rescue a lady in distress.[68] Such opposition is due to the fear that proof of a real marriage with Alexandra would seriously tarnish the image of their former leader that they have worked so hard to construct.

The evidence now available seems to show conclusively, however, that the first marriage was real. Not only was Alexandra's name entered into military records in 1922 as Quisling's wife, but also he himself after the war referred specifically to Maria Quisling as his "*second* wife" during a police inquiry, thereby for once admitting clearly that he had been married before.[69] In addition to this admission and Alexandra's own account, there exist a number of photographs of Alexandra from Kristiania and Fyresdal, including several showing her together with either Maria or Vidkun, or both, as well as with members of the Quisling family.[70] There is therefore little reason to doubt that he was married twice, and that he bigamously married his second wife, Maria, without having obtained a divorce from Alexandra.

With his discharge from the General Staff and his marriage to Maria, by the fall of 1923 he was symbolically and literally wedded to Russia and estranged from Norway. Now that his career as an officer was at an end, he had to seek his future on the basis of his most recent association with the Soviet Union. Of his own volition, or at least as a result of his inactivity, he had chosen to estrange himself from the military: "When I could not be on the General Staff, then I did not want to be in the army either."[71]

His first opportunity for employment following his break with the General Staff grew naturally out of his past work under Nansen. While the Nansen organization was carrying out famine relief in the Soviet Union, it had been equally concerned with the problems of uprooted refugees in the Balkans and the Middle East. Nansen, as the League of Nation's High Commissioner for Refugees, was in search of a capable administrator for this work, and once more he sought to enlist Quisling. The uncertainty of the latter's status in the fall of 1923 was shown by Nansen's letter to Quisling in October: "I have no idea of what your present position is . . ."[72] However, continued Nansen, he had an offer for Quisling if he were available, being convinced that he was the best man for the job.[73] What Nansen had in mind was a mission to relieve the plight of Russian refugees stranded in Bulgaria. Some of these had already been repatriated back to Russia by the end of the spring of 1923,[74] but then the flow of returning refugees came to a halt because of disagreement between the Bulgarian and Russian governments. Diplomatic relations between the two countries were broken off, isolating the refugees. It was Nansen's hope that relations between the Soviet Union and Bulgaria could be renewed so that repatriation could begin once again. Quisling's task was to travel to the Balkans in an effort to facilitate the repatriation.[75]

Not much is known about his work in the Balkans on behalf of refugees, which lasted from late 1923 until the summer of 1925. He was always quite reserved about this period of his life, declaring merely that he had carried out an assignment for the League of Nations in the Balkan and Danubian states concerning the question of the Russian refugees. He never mentioned Nansen in this connection, even though he carried out his assignments as Nansen's subordinate.[76] Since the Nansen organization was busy with the repatriation and resettlement of Russian, Greek and Armenian refugees who had been affected by the turmoil taking place in the Balkans and Asia Minor at this time,[77] it can be assumed that Quisling was engaged in this work during 1923-25, but at present no source has been discovered which can specifically pinpoint his whereabouts in this period.[78] His reluctance to provide information concerning this part of his life is understandable, however, since it was just at this time that he was burdened with the problem of solving the dilemma of having two wives.

The Nansen organization's work in eastern Europe and Turkey was almost at an end when its head received a new challenging assignment from the League of Nations. He was appointed head of a commission to investigate the possibility of resettling Armenian refugees. The Armenians had been subjected to genocide at the hands of the Turks during World War I, and afterwards many of them resided as refugees in a number of countries in eastern Europe and the Middle East. Nansen and the members of his commission received the task of exploring whether it was feasible to transfer these unfortunate people to Soviet Armenia. The commission consisted of five men. In addition to Nansen, the group included a Frenchman, an Englishman, an Italian, and a Norwegian.[79] The Norwegian was Quisling, who performed the dual functions of secretary and interpreter.[80]

The mission to Armenia set out from Trieste on June 4. After a stopover in Constantinople, the group arrived in the Soviet Union on June 14 when their vessel reached Batum. Here they were received by the local officials of the various Soviet republics which would be affected by the resettlement plan.[81]

The commission's main activity was to travel in Soviet Armenia and to report on whether or not the plans for settlement were feasible. By July 2 the commission had completed its work and disbanded.[82] Nansen, accompanied by Quisling, spent some additional time visiting the Caucasus region, and then they proceeded across the Caspian Sea to Astrakhan on July 12. From here the two journeyed by boat up the Volga, going ashore at Saratov to travel back to Norway via Moscow. Altogether, Nansen and Quisling spent some six weeks together in the Soviet Union in 1925.[83]

The Armenian mission accomplished little except to provide Nansen with the opportunity to write a book entitled *Through the Caucasus to the Volga*. Although Quisling accompanied its author during the entire period described in the book, he received scant mention except for an acknowledging sentence in the introduction:

> These introductory words cannot be brought to an end without my hearty thanks to Captain Vidkun Quisling for his untiring kindness as a travelling companion, and for the valuable help he has given the author through his knowledge of Russian and his many-sided attainments.[84]

On an economic level, however, the trip to Armenia proved to be beneficial for Quisling. It provided him with continued employment. The committee set up by the League of Nations to study Nansen's report on his journey came to the conclusion that additional information was necessary. To obtain this, the League committee decided to send a new mission back to Armenia. This time it consisted only of two members, an English engineer by the name of W. McIntosh, and Quisling.[85]

Although McIntosh reported favorably on the scheme to resettle Armenian refugees in Soviet Armenia,[86] the project was never carried out because of the League of Nations' indifference, to Nansen's bitter disappointment.[87] The latter doggedly continued his effort on behalf of the Armenians, however, and Quisling, in Moscow, continued to act as Nansen's representative on the Armenian question. Their work on behalf of the Armenians did not terminate until 1929.[88] Nevertheless, although the two continued to be in touch because of their common interest in the affairs of the Armenians, Quisling's direct involvement in Nansen's humanitarian activity was over following the completion of the second Armenian mission.

Because of Quisling's association with Nansen, dating back to 1922, a considerable amount of controversy later arose in Norway over the nature of the relationship between the two. Quisling's supporters, for purely partisan reasons, have always maintained that the tie between Norway's greatest humanitarian and his assistant had been extremely close. His detractors, for equally partisan reasons, have declared that there was really very little contact between Nansen and Quisling, and that which did occur was of an impersonal nature.

Quisling himself contributed to this dispute because he wanted to identify himself with Nansen both for political and for personal considerations. At his treason trial in 1945 it was therefore not surprising to hear him state: "he [Nansen] was in many ways like a protector and a father to me . . ."[89] As in so many of his pronouncements, however, he was exaggerating in this instance. His general inclination was to take an element of truth and blow it completely out of proportion. There was never any really close friendship between Quisling and Nansen because of differences in age, temperament, and position, and also because the silent, introverted Quisling rarely was able to inspire close friendship.[90] Nansen, for example, never addressed Quisling by the intimate personal pronoun *du*.[91] Nor is there any evidence to show that Nansen ever attempted to use his influence on behalf of his younger assistant. Nansen never recommended Quisling for a position of employment outside of his own organization, nor did he urge that Quisling be given a public honor in recognition of his service in the Soviet Union.[92]

Nevertheless, even though there was no close friendship between them, there is no question but that Nansen was grateful for the work which Quisling carried out. No one can deny that the latter was a thorough and competent administrator, a fact that Nansen appreciated. For example, Nansen wrote the following when seeking to recruit Quisling to participate in the repatriation of Russian refugees from the Balkans: ". . . I am in complete agreement with Major Johnson, Frick and Gorvin [Nansen's associates] that we cannot get a better man than you if it is possible for you to accept the assignment."[93]

Other letters which Nansen wrote to Quisling were of a similar nature. They were cordial, if formal, and expressed gratitude.[94] As late as New Year's Eve 1929, just a few months before his death, Nansen sent Quisling one of his highly-valued original drawings with the wish that 1930 might be a prosperous year.[95] Witnesses such as Nansen's widow, Sigrun Nansen, and Quisling's former chief, Minister Urbye, have also testified that Nansen prized Quisling's work highly. Mrs. Nansen, writing at a time when Quisling was hotly engaged in the election campaign of 1933, presented him with the following accolade on behalf of her late husband:

> Whether in agreement or in disagreement with Mr. Quisling's politics, I believe that many regret the personal and insulting manner that the election campaign has assumed against him.
>   It will certainly be of interest to hear what Fridtjof Nansen felt concerning his helper – he often expressed his pleasure over having such a man for help. An excellent administrator, self-sacrificing and decent, his [Nansen's] face lit up when he mentioned Quisling's name.[96]

Four years later, when Quisling was even more controversial, Mrs. Nansen telegraphed her congratulations to him on the occasion of his fiftieth birthday.[97] Urbye later substantiated Mrs. Nansen's view by similarly taking an opposite stand to those who negated the value that Nansen attached to Quisling: "I have heard it said by a number of sources that Nansen in reality did not prize Quisling very highly, but this does not correspond with my impression."[98] This statement, made in court during Quisling's trial in 1945, repeated the viewpoint that Urbye had often expressed before the war. Another witness to Nansen's admiration for Quisling was provided by a non-Norwegian source, T. F. Johnson, who had been Nansen's personal secretary and head of the office in Geneva. Johnson also interjected rather ironically his own opinion about Quisling's taciturnity: "Quisling was a countryman whom Nansen held in very high esteen. Quisling was always assumed to reciprocate Nansen's sentiments, but I am unaware how that became known, as Quisling seldom spoke." Johnson described him as being as opposite to Gorvin as one could possibly be, yet he managed nevertheless to maintain just as excellent relations with the Soviets and to get things done for the famine relief work under most trying and difficult circumstances.[99]

While unquestionably genuine, Nansen's admiration of Quisling must always, however, be seen within the context of their relationship. Quisling was not Nansen's equal; he was merely one of Nansen's many assistants. It was on this basis that Nansen was grateful for the skill with which Quisling carried out his assigned tasks. Contrary to what the latter wanted popular opinion to think, his work under Nansen was not independent and innovative.

The end of Quisling's association with Nansen not only terminated his direct employment with the various relief organizations that the latter headed, but it also marked the beginning of a change in Quisling's attitude toward the Communist revolutionary movement in the Soviet Union. Although he earlier took special care in his reports from Petrograd not to indicate any particular bias, evidence shows clearly that in his capacity as military attaché in the Russian capital, he was impressed by the new Bolshevik government. His friend, Vilhelm Ullmann, related that Quisling, upon returning from the Soviet Union following his first stay in Russia, "was strongly sympathetic toward the Bolsheviks and their work".[100]

This sympathy toward the Russian experiment did not weaken during the time Quisling worked for Nansen, in particular because Nansen himself always maintained a cordial attitude toward Soviet authorities and often spoke warmly about the Russian people and the significant role which Russia would play in future world history.[101] It was therefore, when viewed from this background, not unnatural to find Nansen's Norwegian assistant writing a pro-Soviet article in the October 2, 1923, edition of a leading Kristiania newspaper, *Tidens Tegn*. In this article he declared his agreement with the Norwegian Labor party, urging Norway to recognize the Soviet Union *de jure*. Not only would such an act benefit Norway materially, he argued (Norway would be the first western country to recognize the Soviet Union, and this would bring favorable trade results), it would also be a humane gesture, helping to re-establish ties among some 140,000,000 people.

It is interesting to note the date when this article appeared. It was published not long after he had been dismissed from the General Staff. He carried with him a life-long feeling of grievance because of the manner in
which he was removed, although he always heatedly denied this.[102] Having
been sidetracked from his original profession, he now hoped to establish a
new career for himself through his contact with the Soviet Union. For the
first time in his life he began to participate actively in political affairs. Although he was away from Norway most of the time since the end of 1923,
he frequently travelled home for brief visits. It was on such occasions that
he attempted to gain a foothold in Norwegian politics.

He naturally turned first to the major socialist party in Norway, the
Labor party. Although it had broken with the Communist International in
1923, the Labor party was still considered a revolutionary organization
which retained favorable sentiments toward the Communist government.
One of the party's leading figures, Alfred Madsen, who later became Minister of Commerce, recalled that Quisling had sought him out in 1924. "I
understood him [Quisling] to mean that he was then very enthusiastic
about the Soviet Union and that he wanted to place himself at the disposal
of the Labor party."[103] Madsen's reaction, as he recalled the incident, was
that Quisling seemed to be an "appealing young man."[104] Apparently encouraged by Madsen's response, Quisling thereupon established contact
with Martin Tranmæl, then the most influential leader of the Labor party.
According to Tranmæl, Quisling called on him in his office in *Arbeiderbladet (The Worker's Paper)*, where he was editor, and brought up a rather
unique proposal. Quisling, maintained Tranmæl, declared that "it was irresponsible for the Norwegian Labor party not to have physical defense organizations". On the basis of his "many years as an officer and after his
stay in and experiences from Russia, he maintained he was especially qualified to be in the forefront of the formation of Red Guards, and he offered
his services".[105]

Both Tranmæl and Madsen later made public their versions of their
meetings with Quisling as part of an attack against him when he was a
member of the Agrarian party government. As such, they had a definite
political purpose – to discredit Quisling – and the charges were therefore
highly subjective. Nevertheless, even when this is taken into consideration,
Quisling at no time was able to provide a satisfactory explanation for his
apparent endeavor to become part of the revolutionary labor movement
during the early 1920s. Both during the parliamentary debate in 1931 and
at his trial after the war, he admitted having met with, among others, Tranmæl and Madsen.[106] His attempt in 1945 to provide a believable explanation for his meeting with Tranmæl was at once pathetic and humorous:

Presiding Judge:	Have you talked with Tranmæl at his office?
Quisling:	Yes.
Presiding Judge:	What did you want from Tranmæl?
Quisling:	To make his acquaintance and to talk about different things.
Presiding Judge:	What kind of things?
Quisling:	It was different things, among others also the situation here in our country. It was moreover while I was here in Norway for a short time before travelling back to Russia. And I have not offered to form any Red Guards, nor has Tranmæl rejected [a proposal] in such a manner. The Labor party formed by itself its Red Guards, the Labor Protective Force (*arbeidervern*), but Tranmæl probably remembers quite well that what I mentioned to him was the question of marching arrangements etc. for the Labor party.
Presiding Judge:	Marching arrangements?
Quisling:	Yes, for example when they had May Day parades and such. Then, I said I felt that this took place in a poor manner, [and] I felt they should correct this.
Presiding Judge:	You were to be sort of an arranger of May Day parades?
Quisling:	No, absolutely not, by no means.
Presiding Judge:	I don't understand what you mean; it seems to me you said that.
Quisling:	It was that which I mentioned to Tranmæl, that they ought to correct this.
Presiding Judge:	And you were to help?
Quisling:	No, I was to travel back to Russia.
Presiding Judge:	But what interest did you have for the manner in which May Day parades were to take place?
Quisling:	It was mentioned in passing during a conversation.[107]

To his disappointment, he received little encouragement from the leaders of the Labor party, who refused to accept his preferred services. But he did not allow this to discourage him in his effort to gain entry into the ranks of Norway's radical left. Giving up on the Labor party, he turned next to the Communists.

His acquaintanceship with leading members of Norway's Communist party was not new. During the time he served in the Norwegian legation in Helsinki he had the opportunity to meet prominent left-wing politicians who travelled through Finland on their way to Moscow. Among these was Jacob Friis, who became a prominent member of the Communist party when it was established in 1923 following a split in the Labor party.

Through Friis, Quisling made the acquaintance of Olav Scheflo, the editor
of the major Communist newspaper in Norway, *Kommunistbladet*.[108] The
two men later provided critical information concerning their relationship
with Quisling. Along with Tranmæl, Scheflo and Friis levelled charges
against Quisling in 1932. Writing separate letters to parliament, they maintained they had held a secret meeting with Quisling in early 1925.[109] They
alleged that Quisling on this occasion had offered to return to the General
Staff "in order to be able to provide the revolutionary labor movement
with important information".[110] In response, Scheflo said he declared that
"we Communists of course would like to be as well informed as possible
on all questions," but that Quisling could not expect to receive any compensation for his services.[111] The matter was thereupon dropped, maintained Scheflo. However, an agreement was reached whereby Quisling
"would support the party by writing an interview with himself about the
Soviet government's language policy – with the intention of showing it was
possible to be a Communist and still be in favor of language reform".[112]

Quisling hotly denied the charges of collaboration Scheflo and Friis
brought against him.[113] He did admit, however, that he had met Friis and
Scheflo on a number of occasions.[114] On the evidence that exists, however,
no definite conclusion can be reached about whether or not he offered to
re-enter the General Staff in order to spy for the Communists. It was his
word against the statements of Friis and Scheflo. On the one hand, the
story seems most unlikely, since Quisling had no means of being readmit-
ted to the General Staff; on the other, he weakened his own case somewhat
when he admitted in court that the subject had been raised, but he insisted
that it was Scheflo and Friis who had brought it up: "These two came to
me and told me that I should enter the General Staff in order to spy for
them."[115] But while the question of whether or not Quisling offered to spy
for the Communists, though plausible, remains undecided, it is clear that
he actively sought contact with the Communists during this time, although
he later tried his best to minimize the fact. The pro-Soviet language interview which he wrote appeared in *Kommunistbladet* on February 21, 1925.

Beyond this one newspaper publication, his contact with the Communists
led to nothing. His efforts to obtain an influential position with the Labor
party or with the Communists thereby achieved no results. During the
summer of 1925 he returned to Russia, serving on the Nansen mission to
Armenia. As previously indicated, his position with the Armenian investigatory commission proved to be the last humanitarian assignment which he
carried out directly. It was at this time that he became reacquainted with
his former colleague from the legation in Petrograd, Frederik Prytz. The
loss of direct contact with Nansen, who would no longer exert an active
influence on his life, and his meeting with Prytz marked an important

transition for Quisling. He was most outspoken in his admiration for the Soviet experiment during the time that he worked for Nansen. Prytz, on the other hand, was much less enthusiastic about the new rulers of Russia.

This man, who would exercise a strong influence over Quisling in the future, had already experienced a remarkable career. There were certain noteworthy parallels between him and Quisling. Both were pastors' sons, both were educated to be career military officers, and both were associated with Russia for many years. Prytz, who was born in Kristiania on February 14, 1878, had been raised in Scotland, where his father served as pastor to Norwegian seamen in Edinburgh. Young Prytz returned to Norway at the age of sixteen to begin his higher education. Trained as a career officer in the Norwegian army, he soon abandoned the rather monotonous routine of the military in order to seek his fortune in Imperial Russia. He obtained a commission as an officer in the Viborg Regiment in 1908, but discovered quickly that there were quicker ways to wealth in Russia than through the military. Departing from the army, he entered the lumber business through the acquisition of large tracts of timber on the White Sea. He established his own lumber company, and became Norwegian vice-consul at Archangel in 1911. Because of his business connections, he was later appointed commercial counselor to the Norwegian legation in Petrograd.[116] Here he met Quisling for the first time.

In the years of upheaval which followed the Russian Revolution, Prytz found many obstacles placed in his way. He had reorganized his firm, Prytz and Company, into a larger joint-stock venture, Russian Forestry Industry, Ltd., in 1917, with himself as managing director. Unfortunately for him, the new enterprise was affected by the vicissitudes of the Russian Civil War, including Allied intervention in the White Sea area. Scarcely was the Civil War over when the Bolsheviks nationalized the firm in the spring of 1920.

When Quisling once more met Prytz in 1925, the latter was in the process of trying to turn his previous losses to gain, which now appeared possible during the somewhat more liberal period of the New Economic Policy (NEP).[117] The meeting proved to be portentous. Prytz's influence and attitudes were to have great impact on Quisling. He was later described by Maria Quisling as her husband's "only confidential friend".[118] Prytz stood behind Quisling as adviser and confidant during a large part of the latter's political career.

Although Prytz and Quisling had discussed the events which they had experienced in Russia earlier, it was now that Prytz's ideas made a permanent impression on his friend. One aspect of Prytz's thought which Quisling found easy to accept – and to expand upon – was the racist idea of "Nordic" superiority. Benjamin Vogt Jr., who worked with both Prytz and Quisling in Russia during the 1920s, has written of how Prytz's racial ideas influenced the younger Quisling. Quisling would later maintain that all of his political ideas dated back to 1918, the year when he first came in contact with Prytz, although Quisling would never admit that Prytz had influenced his thought.[119] It was quite easy for Quisling to embellish Prytz's idea of "Nordic" superiority with the notion that everything of significance in Russian history was due to some alleged contribution made by Nordics, in particular Norwegians:

> Russia is a Nordic land. The word Russian is the same as Norwegian. The original Russians were north Teutons. . . . Russia was founded by Norwegians and has undergone a changing development. It was in my opinion the Nordic motherland, but the Nordic peoples who lived there were not able to control this mighty land, and they succumbed. The majority of the Russian aristocracy was of Norwegian and Nordic Scandinavian blood.[120]

It was more difficult for Quisling to accept Prytz's hostility toward the Bolsheviks. Events and Prytz's influence would, however, turn the former admirer of the accomplishments of the Russian Revolution into a bitter, outspoken foe of "Bolshevism", an attitude that persisted until the day of his execution.

The opportunity for Prytz to have an impact on Quisling occurred when Prytz became his employer. Stationed in Moscow as liaison officer for the Armenian investigation carried out by McIntosh, Quisling once more got in touch with Prytz. Welcoming his former colleague, Prytz placed him in charge of his firm's Moscow office in early 1926.[121]

In the interval since he had last seen his friend, Prytz had been quite active. He had returned to Norway, where he had attempted to exert influence on the government to obtain compensation for his expropriated interests in Russia, but this effort achieved no results.[122] Seeing that nothing could be accomplished by this approach, he now switched tactics and decided to cooperate with Soviet authorities. The time was opportune because Lenin was just in the process of abandoning War Communism in favor of the New Economic Policy, which permitted foreign investments and exploitation of natural resources. Prytz took the lead in representing various Norwegian, Dutch, and English lumber interests in the White Sea – Onega area whose properties had been nationalized.[123] As a result of negotiations with Russian authorities an agreement was reached to establish a mixed company, the Russo-Norwegian Onega Wood Co., Ltd., known in short as Rusnorvegoles, which was founded in 1923. Fifty per cent of the company's shares were held by the Russians, fifty per cent by the foreign interests represented by Prytz. To obtain capital the company mortgaged the accumulated stores of timber in the White Sea – Onega area on the London market.[124]

The firm had been in operation some three years when Quisling was appointed head of its Moscow office. One of his most important functions was to deal with the Russian bureaucracy, and he had no difficulty in carrying out this assignment thanks to his past experience as an administrator in Russia. As previously, he was most effective, but the years had not made him any more talkative. His Norwegian co-worker, Benjamin Vogt Jr. recalled that Quisling "could collapse into a chair in my room at [Hotel] Savoy, and sit there for many hours without saying a word".[125]

He had good reason for remaining silent with regard to at least one of the assignments that he carried out under Prytz. The latter was in a most precarious position for a businessman – he could not make a profit. As it was a mixed company, half of the board of directors of Rusnorvegoles were Russians, and this prevented Prytz from acting freely. His position was made even more difficult by the fact that the ruble, thanks to the manipulation of the Soviets, was officially valued at an inflated rate, two to three times its worth on the black market.[126] Because of the ruble's inflated value, the Russian interests in Rusnorvegoles were able to skim off the company's profits, leaving Prytz and the stockholders whom he represented with no gain at all.[127]

Prytz, who had no love for Soviet authorities because of their past expropriation of his properties, was determined that they would not rob him of a profit. In order to get around their currency restrictions, he proceeded to purchase rubles on the black market, which enabled him to meet the company's obligations in the Soviet Union much less expensively than if he had dealt through the official *Gosbank*. His intermediary in these transactions was Quisling, who exchanged foreign currency, mainly British pounds, in return for black market rubles. The two were able to keep this operation secret for a period of two years.[128]

The opportunity for Quisling to be involved in this type of black market activity without arousing Russian suspicion was in large part due to the excellent cover he gained when he received an appointment to a temporary position as secretary to the Norwegian legation in Moscow. This new post became available because of an international incident on the highest level. On May 26, 1927, Great Britain broke off diplomatic relations with the Soviet Union. The British government alleged that Russian commercial representatives associated with the Soviet trading company Arcos were guilty of espionage. With the end of direct British-Soviet diplomatic contact, it thereupon became necessary for the British to have another country represent their interests in the Soviet Union. As a friendly intermediary with both sides in the dispute, the Norwegian government, using its diplomatic representatives in Russia, volunteered to assume this responsiblity.

The Norwegian legation in Moscow, however, proved to be short of personnel. If it were to be able to handle the increased workload created by the task of taking care of British interests, at least one new secretary would have to be hired. Once this became known, the Norwegian Foreign Ministry received numerous applications from persons seeking the new position.[129] Among the enthusiastic letter-writers was Benjamin Vogt, the Norwegian minister in London, who suggested his son, Benjamin Vogt Jr., as a suitable candidate. He and the other applicants, however, were soon disappointed. Prime Minister Ivar Lykke, who also served as foreign minister, telegraphed the following message to his minister in England: "Since a temporary arrangement has been made with Captain Quisling, there is at present no possibility of appointment for your son".[130]

Quisling's appointment occurred not merely because he was on the scene in Moscow, but more importantly because his former chief in Helsinki, Andreas Tostrup Urbye, was the Norwegian minister in Moscow. Urbye had lost none of his admiration for his former protegé. When the Norwegian mission assumed responsibility for looking after British interests in the Soviet Union on June 2, 1927,[131] Urbye, faced with the need for additional administrative help to cope with the increased workload, felt that the obvious candidate was already present. He strongly recommended that Quisling be given the post, wiring to Oslo on June 9 "with Q as help things will work out".[132] Thanks to this strong support from the minister in Moscow, Quisling was assured of the position. On June 16 a royal resolution was issued which declared that as of June 14, Captain V. A. L. Quisling was appointed as "temporary secretary . . . until further notice", with a salary of 1,350 kr. per month.[133] For that time, this salary was not a mean one. At first his wages were paid by the Norwegian state,[134] but the British government later agreed to cover the expense of Quisling's appointment "for so long as his services are required in looking after British interests in Moscow".[135]

The new secretary fulfilled Minister Urbye's expectations. As he had done so often in the past, he proved most capable in carrying out his administrative responsibilities. His chief, writing from Moscow shortly after Quisling assumed his position, was rapturous in his praise: "Thank you for Quisling. I only regret that you cannot see him at work. I feel twice as secure now".[136] This was not idle talk on the part of Urbye. The new secretary was not treated as a temporary appointee. Instead, Urbye assigned him the work which the legation's second secretary, Sigurd Maseng, had been performing, while Maseng found himself handling the British cases that Quisling had originally been hired to take care of.[137]

This most unusual preference which Urbye accorded Quisling was not simply a reflection of the great admiration which the senior diplomat had for his subordinate. Urbye's favoritism of his protegé was so strong that he actively sought to make Quisling a regular member of the Norwegian diplomatic corps, thereby providing him with the permanent position he had lacked ever since his forced removal from the General Staff. But despite Urbye's influence, this venture did not succeed. The Foreign Ministry, concerned with its prestige, was not willing to open its ranks to an outsider, no matter how skilled he might be. Urbye's support of Quisling led to an acrimonious exchange with the Foreign Ministry, which objected to the fact that Quisling had taken over Maseng's functions. Urbye was forced to back down, declaring that Quisling would concern himself with daily matters of British interest as of May 1, 1928. However, Urbye protested strongly that he as minister had the right to decide how work was to be divided among members of his legation, and he reacted equally negatively to the Foreign Ministry's statement that Quisling's appointment was only temporary.[138] But Urbye's objections were not allowed to stand. He received a strong reprimand from Prime Minister Lykke, who pointed out that while ordinarily the head of a legation decided the apportionment of work among his subordinates, this rule did not apply when the legation has been authorized to appoint temporarily a non-member of the diplomatic corps whose function was to perform a specific task. Lykke then went on to make it crystal clear how the Foreign Ministry regarded Quisling:

> Minister Urbye has understood quite correctly the Foreign Ministry's letter No. 504 when he therein notes an assertion that Captain Quisling will not be able to obtain another position with the Legation when the taking care of British interests comes to an end. Precisely because the Legation, entirely beyond expectations, has entrusted Captain Quisling to carry out the Legation's regular work, and thereby seemingly made him a regular member, the Foreign Ministry has already at the present time desired to declare as clearly as possible, in consideration of the Legation's as well as Captain Quisling's future dispositions, that he cannot under any condition expect continued service in the diplomatic corps.[139]

The possibility of a secure position as a Norwegian diplomat was thereupon definitely ruled out. The uncertainty of his position weighed heavily on Quisling. The situation in the Soviet Union became even more insecure for him in 1928 thanks to his involvement in Prytz's black market financial manipulations. Due to the temporary nature of his employment, the ordinary service regulations which denied diplomats the opportunity to engage in private business activity did not apply in his case.[140] On the other hand, because of his connection with the Norwegian legation, he had an excellent cover for his, in the eyes of Soviet authorities, illegal financial activities. Thanks to the work he carried out on behalf of the Norwegian legation in looking after British affairs, he had permission to reside in the British embassy.[141] For a time this was the perfect location to disguise the exchange of British pounds into black market rubles. However, by the spring of 1928 Soviet authorities had begun to become suspicious of Prytz's activities. Prytz, who was in Moscow at the time, was called in for an interview. The Russians did not, however, have any hard and fast evidence against him, and he therefore was not arrested. Immediately afterwards he fled the country.[142] This left Quisling and the other employees of Rusnor-

vegoles to face the wrath of Soviet officialdom when the necessary evidence
of Prytz's improprieties was at hand. Following a four-hour interrogation
by the Russian secret police, the GPU, Quisling returned "chalk white and
obviously shaken".[143] Beyond this one scare, which had been quite an ordeal, he sustained no further difficulties. The Soviet authorities preferred
to deal directly with Prytz, who now was in Berlin, and in the end an
agreement was made whereby the Russian state took over full control of
the company.[144]

Quisling thereafter continued as before to carry out his functions in the
British embassy. Apparently, the Russians wished to avoid complications
involving the question of diplomatic immunity, although technically it
could be argued that Quisling, who held a temporary position, was not
privileged to receive full diplomatic status. Some doubt remains as to
whether or not he fully understood the illegality of his transactions on
behalf of Prytz. Nordahl Grieg, for example, has indicated that Quisling,
naive and unrealistic, did not realize the implications involved. However,
it is most unlikely that someone who had resided in Russia as long as he
and who had worked closely with Russian officials did not understand the
serious consequences that could result from exchanging black market rubles. But there is no evidence to show that he acted because of pecuniary
motives; he did not enrich himself in any way. It was Prytz alone who pro-
fited from the affair.[145]

The scandal involved in this incident could not, however, fail to have an
effect on Quisling. Although he at first sought to disassociate himself from
Prytz, declaring that he unknowingly had become involved in activity
of whose illegality he was ignorant,[146] he later blamed the Russians, not
Prytz, for what had happened. Not that he ever admitted directly having
participated in black market activity; such an admission would have been
unthinkable for him. Replying at a later date to Labor party accusations
about the incident, he denied that he "in any way had a falling out with the
Russians concerning this case".[147] But he added in response to an interpel-
lation from Alfred Madsen, one of his most unreconcilable opponents in
the Labor party:

> When Mr. Madsen says that it was Norwegians who broke Russian law, I
> can answer that it was the Russians who broke their agreement with the
> Norwegians, an agreement that had been established as compensation for the
> robberies committed earlier against Norwegian property . . .[148]

This incident helped to create a change in his attitude toward the Soviet
Union. Being capable of strong rationalization, it was easy for him with
the passage of time to become increasingly more convinced that it was he
who had been wronged.[149]

The setbacks that he experienced during the first half of 1928 – first the denial of future service in the diplomatic corps, and then the financial scandal concerning black market rubles – apparently caused him to consider resigning his position with the Norwegian legation. He discussed such a possibility with Urbye during the spring of 1928.[150] Matters progressed to the point where his possible replacement had been decided upon. However, Urbye, upon returning from a visit to London in August, found that Quisling was willing, in response to the Minister's request, to continue in his position. Urbye was satisfied with this solution: "Both from what I have seen of his work during many years and from the satisfaction which has been expressed in England with his work, I am extraordinarily grateful to be able to keep him, and I assume that the Ministry is in agreement."[151]

Urbye's influence once again decided Quisling's future. He remained in Moscow, working with matters concerning British interests in the Soviet Union. This phase of his life, like so many others, has been a matter of controversy. The issue has concerned the question of just how important was the work which he carried out on behalf of the British. No one can deny that he actually performed this activity, since the British government paid his salary. However, he later maintained that it was he, and he alone, who had represented British interests in the Soviet Union between 1927 and 1929, and this contention was loyally supported by his followers, who used it as an argument in the attempt to show how important their leader had been internationally.[152]

Such an assertion merely illustrated once more Quisling's proclivity to exaggerate his importance far beyond the boundaries of reality. As Benjamin Vogt Jr., has succinctly pointed out in his criticism of Quisling's point of view, no single individual can represent the interests of one nation vis-à-vis another.[153] It was the Norwegian government, acting through its legation in the Russian capital, which assumed responsibility for taking care of British affairs in the Soviet Union. Ironically, this conclusion was on one occasion presented by none other than Quisling himself. During a parliamentary debate in the spring of 1932, he specifically declared that it was not he, but the Norwegian legation, which had been responsible for looking after British interests in the Soviet Union: "It was not me who took care of British interests in Russia, it was the Norwegian Legation. All correspondence from me went through the Norwegian Legation and the Norwegian Foreign Ministry."[154] Quisling's statement in 1932 therefore directly contradicted his later exaggerated claims about the importance of his role in representing the British government in Russia.

The significance of his contribution was further reduced by the fact that he was not the only member of the Norwegian legation to carry out work in connection with looking after British interests. Minister Urbye himself contacted officials in the Russian Foreign Ministry when weighty matters had to be discussed. The most important documents concerning matters of British interest were handled by Urbye personally. The Norwegian chargé d'affaires, Martin Bolstad, also concerned himself with British affairs. And as shown earlier, when Quisling was first appointed to his position, it was the legation's second secretary, Sigurd Maseng, who assumed the task of dealing with British matters. A spot check by the author failed to reveal a single document of any significance signed by Quisling in connection with the function of looking after British interests. Urbye and Bolstad signed most of the documents, while those of lesser importance simply bore the stamp of the "Norwegian Legation, Moscow".[155] Further proof that Quisling alone did not have responsibility for British affairs is shown by the fact that he was not singled out as the sole recipient of an award by the British government as thanks for looking after British interests during the period when diplomatic relations between Great Britain and the Soviet Union were severed. Both Maseng and Bolstad, as well as Quisling, were made Honorary Commanders of the Civil Division of the Order of the British Empire (C.B.E.), while Urbye, in recognition of the higher position and responsibility he held as minister, was awarded the title of "Honorary Knight of the Grand Cross of the Most Excellent Order of the British Empire (G.B.E.)".[156]

Quisling in reality held a subordinate position. He dealt with daily matters such as the issuance of passports and visas, the extension of aid to British subjects, and the answering of questions of various kinds. In addition, he had responsibility for looking after the property of the British embassy.[157] Although he carried out his work with skill, it definitely was not international in character.

The temporary secretary in the Norwegian legation furthermore did not enjoy the privilege of residing alone in the British embassy. Norwegian personnel were housed in the embassy primarily for the purpose of having it occupied. In 1929 Quisling and his wife shared occupancy of the embassy with a regular member of the legation, Per Prebensen, and his wife.[158]

On the whole, Quisling on a personal level got along quite well with his associates at the legation. They shared Minister Urbye's high respect for his learned background and abilities, and he was not in any way regarded as being unsympathetic. But he lacked a sense of humor to give him balance. Socially, he was completely inept, remaining aloof and silent. "At parties he did not do well; he always stood in a corner by himself".[159]

Once his assignment neared its conclusion, Quisling had to accept the reality that there no longer was a place for him in the Soviet Union. The humanitarian work of the early 1920s had long since ended. There were no positions available for non-Russians in firms backed by western capital; the abolition of the NEP had seen to that. And with the resumption of diplomatic relations between the Soviet Union and Great Britain in December

1929, his temporary position with the Norwegian legation became superfluous. No longer could he hope to achieve what he later declared to have
been his goal in Russia:

> I saw Russia as an area where Norwegian and Nordic influence could be-
> come influential. It was therefore that I wrote my article about recognizing
> Russia *de jure*. I believed that Norwegians should make it [the Soviet Union]
> their area of operation. Even the waterfalls on the Dnieper have Norwegian
> names, our gods come from the Caucasus. I believed that this should occur
> in a peaceful manner, that one should be so farsighted that one understood
> what occurred there [referring to the Bolshevik Revolution], and I sought to
> work in this gigantic land of the future, this greatest of all the world's
> realms.[160]

Now this possibility to work in "this greatest of all the world's realms"
was at an end. He had to return to his native land. But on what basis? As
before, he had to build the future on the past, and once again it had to be
based on his connection with the Soviet Union. But whereas in the past he
had sung its praises, he had now become its enemy, the harbinger of warnings of danger coming from the East.

> When I began to realize that there was no possibility for this [for Norwe-
> gians to work in Russia], but that instead it was possible that exactly the
> opposite would occur, that Bolshevism wanted to take our countries [the
> Scandinavian countries], it was then I had to react in the opposite manner
> also. Then I had to react by seeking to work for the goal of the Nordic
> peoples, in the broadest context, joining together, taking up this Russian
> problem, and meeting the world threat that was approaching.[161]

Much more uncertain of what the future had in store for him than the
above statement indicated, Quisling, accompanied by his Russian wife, departed for Norway in late December 1929, having received an additional
three months salary from the British government as compensation for the
termination of what proved to be his final assignment in the Soviet
Union.[162]

The experiences that he had sustained during his extensive periods
abroad left a permanent impression on him. The man who returned to
Norway at the end of 1929 was very different from the dedicated and idealistic young career officer who had departed to take up his Russian assignment in 1918. His years as a military observer, relief and refugee administrator, and diplomatic associate had exposed him to the ruthless, amoral
nature of international politics. He too became amoral, as the dissolution
of his marriage to Alexandra Voronine and his involvement in Prytz' black
market ruble transactions indicated. However, due to his puritan upbringing, he consistently maintained a moral image, a role which he played most
convincingly. More than most persons, he was capable of rationalization,

being able to convince himself that his actions, no matter how questionable they might appear to others, were always right. This basic part of his character became more apparent at a later date, but it was already evident during the 1920s.

With the destruction of his military career, he also lost the feeling of permanency that the officer corps had provided. His attempt to establish ties with such anti-establishment groups as the Labor party and the Communists was in large part due to his frustration over being dismissed from the General Staff and his desire to revenge himself. In the following years, he became an international vagabond, leading a wandering life which assumed almost a Peer Gynt quality.[163] This contrasted strikingly with the staid, reserved bourgeois manner he observed, which was ingrained from his background and upbringing. Despite his rootlessness, he maintained a firm belief in his destined greatness, which for him was a certainty, having been revealed by his superior educational achievements. Not having gained success abroad, he hoped to find it in Norway upon his return.

CHAPTER II

Political Controversy
1930–1931

He had, to be sure, written some articles of late about the danger that threatened our culture from the East, and of the necessity of finding a strong man who could take the helm, and about fatherland and beating hearts and mother earth and such. But so many wrote like that in this election year.

Sigurd Hoel,
Syndere i sommersol

When Vidkun Quisling returned to Norway from the Soviet Union in late 1929, his prospects for the future did not appear very promising. Save for scattered intervals, he had been away from his native country for a period of almost twelve years. Outside of personal acquaintances within the narrow circle of professional officers and diplomats, he was virtually unknown. He was now 42 years old, without a profession.

In order to escape from this isolated position, one option which he could follow was to enter politics, using as a starting point the experiences he had gained during his stay in the Soviet Union. Inspired by Frederik Prytz, he attempted in this manner to find a place for himself within Norwegian society. But before following Quisling in the many pursuits which he engaged in after his return from Russia, a brief survey of some key developments within Norwegian society during the early decades of the twentieth century will provide a broader perspective for understanding the circumstances in which he sought to create his future.

The political scene which he entered in early 1930 was fragmented by discord which embittered political opinion in Norway. Some of the causes for this disunity were of fairly recent origin, while others were of an earlier date.

Of all the factors contributing to political unrest during the 1920s and 1930s, the most important were the social and economic disturbances created by a long period of depression. Although there were brief periods of revival, the depression as a whole lasted from the winter of 1920–1921 until the end of 1934, and complete recovery had not yet taken place when the country was engulfed by World War II.[1] The depression was in part due to the economic disorder which came in the wake of the First World War, and in part due to governmental financial policies during the 1920s.

One of the most unsettling results of the depression was the large amount of unemployment which resulted. During the first years of economic decline, in 1921–1922, the number of unemployed stood at about 50–60,000. The situation gradually improved for those seeking work, thanks to a period of inflation which came to a head in 1924, but conditions worsened with the introduction of a deflationary monetary policy in 1925, which increased the number of unemployed to a peak of 70,000 in 1927. The next two years saw some improvement, but then came the international depression of 1929–1930. By 1933 the average number of unemployed stood at over 100,000. At this high point of the depression, thirty-two per cent of all workers organized in unions were unemployed. Most of these were in industry or handicrafts, which in 1930 employed a total of some 311,200 persons. With the beginning of improved conditions in 1934 the number of persons out of work gradually declined, but slowly. In 1936 it stood as high as 80,000, and even as late as the last few years before the war between 60,000 and 70,000 persons were seeking employment.[2]

This period of economic decline and mass unemployment was marked by a large number of heated labor conflicts. Between the wars, the largest number of working days lost as the result of strikes occurred in the five-year period between 1920 and 1925. During the next half decade there were fewer conflicts, but in the years from 1930 to the end of 1934 the total percentage of working days lost because of labor disputes once more approached the level of the early 1920s.[3] The hostile atmosphere created by the numerous strikes and lockouts during the depression of the 1920s and 1930s increased class antagonisms and embittered the political conflicts of these years.

Equally exacerbating for many workers and farmers were the financial policies followed during this time. To them it seemed as if they were being exploited by the vested financial interests of the country. A period of inflation inaugurated the monetary crisis. During the early 1920s the value of Norway's monetary unit, the *krone* (crown), declined greatly. In 1917 it had been worth 12.90 in relation to the British pound, by 1924 it had plummeted to 32.60. In response to this galloping inflation, Norway's financial leaders believed that the only way to deal with the problem was to follow a hard-money policy. This view prevailed, and by 1928 the *krone* was firmly based on the pound's gold standard. But while the value of the currency increased, this policy spelled disaster for many debtors. The *krone* was now worth a great deal more than earlier, to the consternation of those who had borrowed money when its value was lower. Farmers and businessmen were hit especially hard. Firms went bankrupt, with resulting increased unemployment, and many farmers were forced to see their farms auctioned off when they were unable to meet their obligations.[4]

The triumph of hard money did not prove long-lasting. The economic dislocation brought about by the international depression affected Norway as it influenced all other countries of Western Europe, although it arrived somewhat later, and its intensity was not as great, mainly because Norway did not have far to drop. But the abandonment of the gold standard in 1931 did not alleviate the situation. A new debt crisis occurred, while unemployment rose beyond previous levels, and labor strife, which had abated somewhat since 1924, once more became widespread. The farmer was not any better off than the unemployed or the striking worker in the city. The economic crisis which followed 1929 was especially severe on the rural segment of the population, whose produce prices dropped drastically.[5]

The frustrations of those affected by the economic and social setbacks of the 1920s and 1930s were increased by the inability of the governments of the period to bring about any lasting improvements. Norway in this respect did not differ from other Western European countries, whose governments were generally ineffective in dealing with postwar economic difficulties, but this was little consolation for the large numbers of Norwegians hard hit by the economic instability of these years. Many held the governments responsible for the depression, and the feeling grew that inadequate governmental action was in large part the reason why recovery did not occur. This seemed to be borne out in the eyes of a large part of popular opinion by the weak position which the cabinets of the 1920s and 1930s occupied.

The governments of this period were minority governments. Lacking a majority in parliament, the *Storting*, and being dependent on constantly shifting coalitions, ministries replaced each other in rapid succession until 1935. It seemed impossible in such a situation for the governments to deal with the economic problems facing the nation. Such political instability tended to produce cynicism toward politics, especially among those who maintained that a government should look after the nation's welfare as a whole and not be swayed by partisan issues.

Governmental instability was, however, merely the reflection of a political trend which became pronounced during the 1920s and 1930s, the fragmentation of political parties. Through the election of 1918 there traditionally had been five political parties participating in the electoral process. Largest and most influential of these was the Liberal party (*Venstre*), which held an absolute majority in the *Storting* for all but three of the years between 1906 and 1918. Next in importance was the Conservative party (*Høyre*), the traditional foe of the Liberals. Lining up next to the Conservatives were the Independent Liberals, a moderate group of liberals which had split from the Liberal party in 1909. The political group, however, which was most dynamic was the Labor party, the major socialist organization which proved to be the party of the future. Finally, there was a small, reform-minded party, non-socialist in character, the Labor Democrats.

The dominant position which the Liberal party had held in politics was weakened in 1918, when it was unable to maintain an absolute majority, thereby inaugurating the period of minority governments. The weakening of governmental authority was enhanced by the enactment of proportional representation in 1919. Not only did proportional representation increase the possibility of minority governments, it also encouraged the formation of new parties. But the introduction of new party groups into the political arena during the 1920s and 1930s was primarily due to questions of economic and political self-interest which divided political opinion into a large number of differing factions, a tendency which in turn was reinforced by the procedure of basing a party's representation in the *Storting* proportionally on the number of votes it had been able to accumulate within each of the country's provinces (*fylker*).

All of the new parties which came into being during these two decades reflected essential unrest within important segments of the population. The Agrarian party (*Bondepartiet*), formed in 1920, was mainly composed of farmers who previously had voted for the Liberal party, but who now felt that the Liberals no longer represented their interests adequately. The Social Democrats and Communists, both established during the 1920s, were offshoots of the Labor party, representing diametrically opposite viewpoints on the question of the Labor party's membership in the Communist International. During the 1930s the Community Party (*Samfundspartiet*) and Quisling's political party, National Union (*Nasjonal Samling*), sought to gain adherents with programs which argued that basic reorganization was needed in Norwegian society.

Of the new political parties mentioned previously, the most important was unquestionably the Agrarian party. Those who cast their ballots for this party did so primarily because of shifts that had occurred, changes in society which they felt were inimical to their interests. Formerly, in the nineteenth and early twentieth centuries, the farmer had held a prominent position in a country which was still basically agricultural. But with the coming of industrialization his status was now eroded by changes in the economy and by the growing class of industrial workers. The feeling of insecurity felt by many farmers was increased greatly by the financial hardships which they experienced as a result of the difficult times of the 1920s and 1930s. In response to the challenge posed by these altered conditions, the Agrarian party declared the farmer to be the real backbone of the country, the moral force capable of joining all of society together in a harmonic unit to meet the problems posed by rising industrialism.[6] This romantic idea of identifying the farmer (*bonde*) with the nation's soul, and maintaining that society needed to be unified rather than divided into factions, gained considerable influence in politics and in society as a whole, even among those who did not follow agricultural pursuits.[7] Because of the farmer's alleged moral superiority, and also because of the economic difficulties he was in, some members of the Agrarian party's *Storting* delegations were so extreme as to borrow from foreign examples, using anti-Semitic slogans.[8] At least to a degree, the racial slogans of Nordic superiority and anti-Semitism later adopted by Quisling were influenced by the tendency of some members of the Agrarian party to use statements with racial overtones when stressing the importance of the farmer in Norwegian society. Quisling was, at least in part, attracted by the racial ideas of the Agrarian party as well as its opposition to the Labor party. It was no coincidence that when he began to take part actively in political work, it was as a speaker for the Agrarians in the election campaign of 1930.[9]

The Agrarian party's resentment against the altered status of the farmer was in particular directed against the political organization representing the majority of workers, the Labor party. The strength of Labor lay, however, not merely in the support it received from the rapidly growing number of urban industrial workers. It also gained many adherents among fishermen, agricultural workers, and small farmers. The role played by the Labor party in organizing lumberjacks irritated in particular those members of the Agrarian party who had large stands of timber, and who were used to dealing with their workers in a patronizing manner.

By the end of the 1920s Labor had emerged as the largest single political party in the country. However, its growth aroused fear and hostility among non-socialists. Opposition to the Labor party was especially pronounced during the early 1920s. At this time the party, inspired by the success of the Russian Bolsheviks, voiced revolutionary slogans and belonged to the Communist International. In reaction, large segments of non-socialist society regarded the Labor party as being treasonable.[10] For many Norwegians, the revolutionary dogma of the Labor party, although it remained only theory and was never put into practice, represented a very real threat, and the strong reaction of non-socialists to this ideology intensified class antagonisms.[11] When therefore Labor became the largest political party in the *Storting* as a result of the 1927 election, although it did not gain an absolute majority, a feeling close to panic occurred in some politically concerned non-socialist circles.

The Laborites, however, because they lacked a majority in parliament, did not control the political situation. Their first government, formed in January 1928, lasted but eighteen days, the shortest government in Norway's history. In the long run this development proved to be reassuring to those who adhered to parliamentary government, since it demonstrated that a Labor government was willing to follow democratic procedure, resigning when it was unable to obtain a majority in the *Storting*. But the immediate effect of this setback was a heightening of tensions. Many members of the Labor party were bitterly disappointed, and this caused it to adopt a more radical party program, which indicated that it might attempt to seize power without the support of the majority of the people. This in turn led to increased opposition to the Labor party, which was effectively exploited by the non-socialist parties.

The fears aroused by Labor's radical statements were shown to be groundless. The party proved unwilling to try to turn its extreme statements into action. But the combination of inflammatory proclamations and lack of resolve to take revolutionary steps on behalf of the working class hurt the Labor party, as was shown in the following election, in 1930. Its *Storting* representation declined from fifty-nine to forty-seven members, brought about by a decrease in the popular vote from 37 to 31 per cent.[12] Thereafter, the Labor party in large part dropped its identification with revolutionary socialism and adopted instead a reformist program. However, this change was not immediately apparent, and fear and strong antagonism to the party continued to be present within non-socialist political opinion. This attitude formed a diminishing, but still fairly important part of political opinion during the decade of the 1930s. It was an attitude which Vidkun Quisling sought to exploit.

Opposition to the Labor party within the *borgerlige*,[13] or non-socialist, circles to which he appealed was of long duration. It reflected not only anti-socialist feeling, but also dissatisfaction with the weak minority governments of the period, ministries which, it was maintained, were unable or unwilling to deal with the alleged revolutionary threat posed by the Labor party and, to a lesser degree, by the Communists. In place of the minority governments, some *borgerlige* desired a strong government of national unity (*nasjonal samlingsregjering*) which would be able to eliminate the division in society created by the Labor party.

This ideal of national union, which Quisling later adopted as the name for his political movement, was personified first and foremost in the figure of Christian Michelsen, who had served as prime minister from 1905 to 1908. Michelsen's term as head of the nation's government had been of great importance in Norway's history because it was at this time, in 1905, that the ties with Sweden were broken, bonds that had held the countries together in a personal union since 1814. As never before, Norwegians had been unified in their common desire to end this union, and although Michelsen had withdrawn from active participation in politics in 1908, he and his supporters kept alive the hope that a national union, similar to that of 1905, might once more come into being. Michelsen assumed the role of the statesman in waiting, ready to take over command if the fatherland required his services. Many believed that his time had come as a remedy to the weak governments which followed the end of World War I. Michelsen himself constantly reiterated during the early 1920s the need for a strong, effective government, in obvious comparison with the ineffectiveness of the governments of the day. Such a government, he maintained, would be the unifying force against the dangers of Russian Communism, which to him were represented at home by the Labor movement.[14]

Michelsen did not live to see if the goal of national union would be realized as he had desired. He died in 1925. But the symbol he represented did not die with him. It was assumed by his friend and political ally, Fridtjof Nansen. With his international reputation, Nansen was the ideal figure to fit the role of the national leader who was above petty partisan politics. Like Michelsen, he was not interested in the infighting of ordinary politics. He aspired to be the head of a government of national union.[15]

The opportunity to launch Nansen as a prime minister candidate came in 1926 with the fall of yet another government, the Liberal ministry led by Johan Ludwig Mowinckel, the first of three governments over which Mowinckel presided. As a solution to the periodic governmental crises, a number of prominent men, led by Olav and Rolf Thommessen, father and son editors of the Independent Liberal newspaper *Tidens Tegn* (*Sign of the Times*), issued a declaration urging that Nansen become head of "a government of national unity".[16]

For the Thommesens, this type of an elitist government, whose legitimacy was based not on a parliamentary majority but on mass popularity, was the apparent solution to the weakening influence they were able to exert in the nation's political life. Their party, the Independent Liberals, was on the decline, and the Thommesens therefore became increasingly opposed to party politics, which they held in contempt. This attitude made itself apparent in the effort to make Nansen prime minister. The supporters of the idea planned to have the proposed government made up of such prominent men that it would be impossible, because of public opinion, for the politicians in parliament to topple it. Although the proposal itself was vague, it was a clear indication of opposition to party politics and to the recurrent governmental crises. It also indicated a certain amount of hostility to the parliamentary system itself.[17]

In order to succeed, however, Nansen's candidacy had to have the approval of the non-socialist party leaders in the *Storting* to whom the appeal was addressed. Although Nansen declared his willingness to form a cabinet, the effort failed because of the refusal of the parliamentary representatives to support it. Nansen, realizing that this was a lost cause, thereupon abandoned the project.[18] The incident was not an isolated one, however. It reflected a distinct element within *borgerlig* political opinion. Later, just a few days after Nansen's death, his former subordinate, the ex-General Staff officer who had served under him in such a hard-working, earnest, and reserved manner, would attempt to assume his mantle.[19]

The endeavor to make Nansen prime minister reflected not only the dissatisfaction which many *borgerlige* felt with the political situation in parliament; it also represented, although tacitly, the widespread desire among the *borgerlige* to have a government which would be able to eliminate the apparent threat posed to society by the Labor party and its affiliated trade union movement, the Norwegian Federation of Trade Unions (*Landsorganisasjonen*), commonly known as the LO. As noted earlier, it was precisely the same aspiration which to a considerable degree had motivated Michelsen and his supporters. Since the *Storting* and the political parties seemed incapable or unwilling to put down the alleged revolutionary menace of the labor movement, several extra-parliamentary organizations had already been established in the 1920s for this purpose.

The first of these was Norway's Community Aid (*Norges Samfundshjelp*), founded in 1920. Arising in response to the fear that the Labor party and the LO might make a concerted effort to take over the country through their control of the labor movement, the Community Aid was organized primarily to serve as a strike-breaker organization in case of a general strike. At its start it had close ties with *borgerlige* governments and vested economic interests. As such, it played an important part in a major labor struggle, the general strike of 1921, when its members assumed many of the tasks of the striking workers.[20] Its importance declined significantly, however, in 1923–24, when its close contact with the government was eliminated. Afterwards it was mainly a paper organization. Led by officers, its ideology was strongly anti-Communist and it exhibited many fascist traits.

The Community Aid helped to foster an even more militant group, the Community Defense (*Samfundsvernet*), which came into being in 1923. Its proclaimed goal was to defend society from the threat of violent revolution, the possibility of which Labor party adherents frequently voiced. To meet this alleged menace, the Community Defense organized itself into cells, with each prospective applicant who wished to join a cell needing to have two sponsors before being admitted. After two years' existence it had approximately 3000 members, most of whom lived in the Oslo area.[21] Among its activities were instruction in the use of firearms and training for street fighting. The Community Defense was a private organization until 1928, when it received semi-official status, with its local divisions being placed under the command of the police.[22] The organization was headed by Major Ragnvald Hvoslef, a friend of Vidkun Quisling's and later one of the founders of National Union.

The fear of possible revolutionary disorder inspired the creation of yet another semi-military force, *Leidangen*.[23] *Leidangen* differed from the Defense of Society, for whereas the latter group received only semi-official backing, *Leidangen* in 1933 was integrated into Norway's military planning. The official responsible for originating this step was none other than Quisling, then serving as Minister of Defense.[24]

These extra-military organizations were first and foremost a *borgerlig*

reaction to the advance of the socialist labor movement. The strong opposition of the Labor party to *Leidangen* and the Defense of Society showed
that the party recognized these groups as being directed primarily against
the labor movement. The two organizations, albeit in a much weaker manner, were a reflection of the same type of mentality as led to the establishment of White Guards in other countries during the interwar period. The
Labor party, upon assuming control of the government in 1935, did not
waste time in eliminating the potential threat posed by the Community
Defense and *Leidangen*. A new police law, passed in February 1936, outlawed the existence of private military forces, thereby sounding the death
knell for the Defense of Society. Later, in July, *Leidangen* was denied state
funds, without which it could not function. Thereupon it too passed out of
existence.[25]

Neither *Leidangen* nor the Defense of Society achieved mass support,
in large part because the use of armed force did not have wide appeal in a
society which had not been at war for over a century, and in which pacifis-
tic idealism was strong. Still, in an extreme form, they manifested the apprehension and distrust toward the Labor party felt by many *borgerlige*.
Somewhat more representative of a wider spectrum of *borgerlig* reaction to
the growth of the Labor party was the Fatherland League (*Fedrelandslaget*), an extra-parliamentary group founded in 1925. Its two most prominent figures were Christian Michelsen and Fridtjof Nansen, and in large
part the League was a reflection of their political ideals. A key purpose of
the organization was to act as force of national union against revolutionary
agitation. In its statements the League always emphasized its consolidating
character. It declared its opposition to political cleavages which split the
country, urging instead solidarity among classes and united action in the
effort to bring about economic resurgence. The Fatherland League proclaimed itself best suited to bring an end to political friction in Norwegian
society.[26]

The League never realized its high-sounding aims. Because its membership included persons from all non-socialist parties, it could never act in a
strictly partisan manner for fear of losing segments of its membership.
Even more debilitating was its failure to win followers within the labor
movement. It remained strictly a *borgerlig* organization, being regarded
with deep suspicion by the working class, which prevented it from being
the agent for attaining the national conciliation which it preached. Furthermore, even among the *borgerlige* it never gained the large following its
founders had hoped for.[27]

Nevertheless, for a time the Fatherland League enjoyed substantial support. In large part this was due to the prestige held by Michelsen and Nansen, and the League always emphasized that it had been founded by these
two famous native sons.[28] At its peak the organization was able to claim a
membership of 100,000, and while this figure is open to question, the

number of adherents to the League at one time was significant. Its growth occurred mainly in the period before 1930. After this year, as the Labor party tended to de-emphasize its revolutionary advocacy, support for the League declined. For a short time, however, in the late 1920s and early 1930s, its influence within *borgerlige* groups was quite strong. Later it fragmented. A considerable number of the leaders and rank and file of National Union, including Vidkun Quisling, were former members of the League.[29]

The Fatherland League, and in a more extreme manner the more militant groups such as the Community Aid, the Community Defense, and *Leidangen*, represented merely one element, although a key element, of reaction to the period of crisis through which Norwegian society was passing, with its economic disorder and class antagonisms. There existed within non-socialist circles a widespread feeling that something had to be done to bring an end to the condition in which the country found itself. Without accepting Marxist ideas, as did the Labor party, at least in theory, many non-socialists felt that the traditional *borgerlige* form of economic politics, with its emphasis on cutting down state expenditures in times of economic adversity, had to be abandoned. There was much disagreement, however, over the question of how change should occur and what form it should take.

> It led not only to lively debate, with contributions in newspapers, journals, brochures, and books, but it also caused a certain amount of disorder within the area of party politics, with splits taking place within the old parties and attempts made to form new parties, partially on the basis of theories concerning the reasons for the crisis and the means to solve them that were more or less the work of charlatans.[30]

Within three relatively prominent *borgerlige* political groups, the Agrarian party, the Independent Liberals, and the Fatherland League, the desire to find a way out of the crisis brought forth at times the expression of attitudes that were clearly anti-parliamentary. The system of parliamentary government, it was felt, failed to deal with the problems of the day. Therefore, a strong government, independent of party politics, was needed to re-establish order and stability. In this context, it was not unusual within these groups to hear expressions of admiration for the dictatorship of Benito Mussolini.[31] When Vidkun Quisling began his career in Norwegian politics, he established ties with all three of these organizations.

He was in particular able to enjoy good relations with the leading newspapers of the Independent Liberals and the Agrarian party, and viewed in perspective, this development was natural. Anti-parliamentary attitudes and expressions of admiration for the fascist dictatorships came especially to the fore in *Tidens Tegn*, in *Nationen* (*The Nation*), the national organ of the Agrarian party, and in *ABC*, the major publication of the Fatherland

League.[32] The press of these groups enjoyed considerable independence, and not infrequently they printed radical views which went quite a distance beyond the official programs of the political organizations for whom they were supposed to speak. *Nationen* often took stands on issues which the Agrarian party did not wish to discuss, and the press of the Independent Liberals, headed by *Tidens Tegn*, on more than one occasion found itself at odds with its own local party organizations.[33]

Nationen gave voice to the feeling of futility that had become widespread within the farm sector. The agricultural crisis, the movement from village to town as the result of industrialization, and the loss of the allegiance of the small farmers and the forestry workers who more and more deserted to the ranks of the Labor party, caused feelings of desperation within the Agrarian party. *Nationen* sought to find in foreign examples the means of ending the declining influence of the farmer, showing marked interest in the fascist tendencies exhibited by the Finnish Lapua movement and in the more specific inspiration provided by the Fascist and National Socialist movements of Italy and Germany. Like some of the Agrarian party's parliamentary representatives, *Nationen* expressed racist attitudes.[34] The editor of this paper, Thorvald Aadahl, was a supporter of Quisling and was influential in promoting his candidacy for the post of Minister of Defense.

Rolf Thommessen, as editor of *Tidens Tegn*, would also later serve as a patron of Quisling. Like Aadahl, Thommessen viewed with disgust the condition the country was in. Through the columns of his newspaper he sought to point the way out of the prevailing dilemma. He belonged to the generation that had just come of age in 1905, the year of separation from Sweden, and throughout his life he continued to judge all things from the perspective of the euphoric national feeling inspired by the events of this year. The inter-war period was an abomination for him, with its governmental crises, class rivalries, strikes, and general antagonisms. Anything new was better than the, to him, deplorable developments which he observed, and all new ideas and theories received a favorable hearing in the pages of *Tidens Tegn*.[35]

What he yearned for was the strong man, a man such as Christian Michelsen who could gather Norwegians behind his banner and correct the evils in society. Such a leader, in an Italian setting, was Benito Mussolini, and Thommessen greeted Fascism with enthusiasm, viewing it as a national movement which should be imitated in Norway.[36]

Thommessen, if in a somewhat exaggerated manner, shared the frustration of his fellow Independent Liberals. Their party had come into being in 1909 as a result of their split from the Liberals, whom they considered as being too radical. They regarded themselves as an elite group, a natural born aristocracy. This feeling was bolstered by the fact that among their founders were Michelsen and Nansen, the two men who would so often be the focus of *borgerlig* attention outside of parliament. For the Independent

Liberals, Michelsen and Nansen served as patrician ideals. Composed in the main of the wealthy farmers of Eastern Norway, proud of their family background, and of the liberal, non-socialist (frequently anti-socialist) intelligentsia of Oslo, this group deplored current political trends.[37] They did not care to take part in the tumult of ordinary political activity, which they felt was beneath them. For them politics was suspect. Adhering to the liberal tradition of the nineteenth century, they maintained that the role of the state should be limited.[38] The nation would have been united under the dominating influence of a strong leader if the Independent Liberals could have had their way. But the *raison d'être* for this commanding figure was to inspire unity, not to expand the power of the state.

In such a party it was a little wonder that the membership participated sporadically and that its organization was poor. The position of party foreman was unimportant and changed hands frequently. For the Independent Liberals, the leading position was instead occupied by "the non-political paternal folk hero, waiting in the wings offstage, who was the chosen one".[39] Christian Michelsen played this role until his death, when he was succeeded, somewhat reluctantly, by Nansen. Later, Vidkun Quisling attempted to follow as the successor to this tradition.[40]

His time did not come until the 1930s. During the 1920s the Independent Liberals, with Thommessen in the lead, searched frantically for something new in politics, something that would lift the party's fortunes to new prominence. In their quest for novelty, they backed the formation of the Fatherland League and sought to have Nansen become prime minister in 1926. Finally, the Independent Liberals' adventurous policy caused them, through the influence exerted by Rolf Thommessen, to give their support to Vidkun Quisling, illustrating once more that every new trend was considered as a possible means to achieve "national union", the declared goal and party slogan of the Independent Liberals.[41]

Vidkun Quisling's political career began within the political circles of the radical conservatives described above. The term "radical conservative" is used to illustrate the ambivalent feelings that existed within frustrated *borgerlige* groups in Norwegian politics in the interwar period. They wished to introduce radical change in order to regain the permanency of a by-gone era. Although such varied groups as the Agrarian party, the Fatherland League, the semi-official self-defense organizations, and the Independent Liberals retained separate identities, their members quite often had close connections, including common membership in quasi-political organizations such as the Fatherland League. And although points of view differed, with not all members sharing common sentiments, the following attitudes made themselves felt in varying degrees of intensity within all of these radical conservative groups: (1) anti-parliamentary feelings, with strongly expressed disrespect for party politics and politicians; (2) admiration for the Italian and German totalitarian movements; (3) a tendency toward racism, including stress on the superiority of the so-called Nordic race, with anti-Semitic undertones; and (4) the general fear of revolutionary Marxism, which was identified with the Labor party.[42]

Such feelings were evident within radical conservative *borgerlige* circles during the 1920s and early 1930s. As such, they were limited in time. But in terms of a broader political tradition, to which these groups appealed, one has to go back to 1905 and to the ideal of "national union". It was the thread of belief in national unity that gave the views expressed by these groups a historic tradition. It was this tradition, inherited through Michelsen and Nansen, that Quisling sought to adopt. "Both the idea and the content of 'national union' grew out of Norwegian historical tradition".[43]

Later, during the dark days of the occupation when Quisling and National Union worked hand in hand with Nazi officials, patriotic Norwegians maintained that he and his movement were merely slavish imitations of more successful right-wing totalitarian movements. As this study later will show, Quisling did incorporate elements of Fascism and National Socialism into his movement. He was not original. But it is a distortion to argue that National Union in its entirety was nothing more than a copy of foreign examples. Its origins, as its name implies, were based on an ideal that preceded it, an ideal that wished to achieve a strong national government that would unite all Norwegians, doing away with various divisive forces which, it was felt, were fragmenting the nation. Quisling, upon his emergence into the arena of Norwegian politics, attempted to build his future on this tradition. It was only when he failed in this endeavor that he increasingly sought to gain success by making use of foreign models.

When he entered politics, he did not begin by taking a pragmatic approach to the problems of the day as would a more ordinary politician. Instead, he always regarded himself as a philosophical statesman who was above the petty details of ordinary politics. His vision was broader; it was international, indeed universal. Such an attitude suited not only his reserved nature, which inhibited him from being able to utilize personal contacts so essential to the regular politician; it also reflected his inclination toward general deduction and mystical speculation, a trait acquired through his father's influence and through his own bookish nature.

He had attempted to establish a reputation in Norway as a thinker already prior to his departure from Russia. At that time he had not yet made the decision to participate in politics. His first publication was therefore not political, but dealt instead with abstract philosophical and religious questions. The title of this work, which was simply a small brochure of no more than nineteen and a quarter pages, was stated in the form of a proposition: "That Inhabited Worlds Are to be Found outside of the Earth, and the Significance Thereof for our View of Life."[44]

In this little pamphlet the author concluded that there were intelligent
beings on other planets in the universe, arguing that since energy and matter are everywhere, the same natural laws prevail throughout the cosmos.
Accordingly, since life and intelligence have developed on our planet, it
was inevitable that the same process must have repeated itself at least in
some instances throughout the vastness of space. But he was not content to
stop here. He went on to formulate more abstract conclusions. He created
the bare outline of nothing less than a new religious view which, he maintained, would provide man with the true realization of the significance of
life. The universe, he said, was "the one living and true God" which had
given birth to the earth, and which would continue to exist long after the
world had disappeared, creating new earths and new stars. It was up to
man to recognize this, and to work for perfection here on earth. This was
the "divine will" as he saw it. This development of the "divine will" would
take place in many areas of organized social behavior: "religion, science,
art, and practical action – *led by an elite*".[45]

He called his new elitist religion "Universism". According to an acquaintance in Russia, Quisling had been gathering notes systematically on
his theory during his stay in the Soviet Union.[46] He corroborated this
when he wrote in the twenty-fifth anniversary yearbook of his graduating
class, *Studenterne fra 1905*: "The question of a unifying explanation of
existence built on scholarship and experience, and which can reconcile religion and science, has engaged my interest more and more during the last
years . . "[47] But he never got much further than gathering notes for his
masterpiece. Except for the small pamphlet, which he published himself in
1929, plus the preface to his major work, which was quoted by his attorney during the treason trial in 1945,[48] no other segment of the religious
theory of "Universism" came to public attention during his lifetime. However, while awaiting execution he wrote a series of brief commentaries,
which were published as part of his wife's diary in 1980.[49] Even today, this
is all that is currently known about what he considered to be his life's mission.

As could be expected, the ideas which he expressed on "Universism"
produced no reaction among the reading public. His pantheistic thoughts
were not really original, nor did these ideas offer any particular religious
appeal to ordinary Norwegians. He made no mention of how this new religion was to be organized, which was in keeping with his character. The
small pamphlet written by the would-be religious philosopher received no
notice.

The significance of this tract was not, however, that it failed to arouse
public attention. Rather, it provided good insight into Quisling's perception of himself. By the time he returned to Norway he had come to consider himself a prophet, someone who was destined for a role of leadership
because of his special intelligence. He was an elitist who regarded himself

as above ordinary Norwegians. Indeed, he felt that the boundaries of Norway were themselves too confining, and that his ideas were those of a world statesman. As a result, in the future he would attempt to assume positions of leadership which were completely unrealistic, in fact at times farcical, reflecting the exaggerated view that he had of his own significance.

What exactly he had hoped to achieve by the publication of his pamphlet cannot be answered definitively. He may have wanted to use it as a means of acquiring an academic post, but while this assumption may be logical, it cannot be stated as a certainty, since he, to the author's knowledge, never made any direct reference to his little publication.

One thing is certain. His pamphlet did not gain any public attention. Were he to succeed in establishing a place for himself, he would have to rely on other means than writing speculative tracts of a philosophical and religious nature.

At the time he came back to Norway, he was encouraged to become involved in politics by his old friend and employer in the Soviet Union, Frederik Prytz.[50] Inspired by Prytz, and also by former acquaintances with whom he came in contact and discussed his past experiences, Quisling quite logically adopted as his starting point in politics his past association with the Soviet Union.[51] But whereas he had earlier interpreted his experiences in Russia in a positive manner when seeking to establish ties with the Labor party and the Communists in the 1920s, he now adopted a negative attitude toward the Soviet Union, seeking to serve as a voice of warning to Norwegians, urging them not to imitate the Russian example.

His former connection with Fridtjof Nansen provided him with his springboard into politics. Nansen did not live to see the political course his former assistant chose to follow. He died on May 13, 1930, not long after Quisling had returned to Norway. Apparently there had not been any contact between the two, although Quisling did receive a thoughtful New Year's greeting from Nansen.[52]

Vidkun Quisling made his definitive entry into the political arena eleven days after Nansen's death. It came in the form of a front-page article in *Tidens Tegn* entitled "Political Thoughts at the Time of Fridtjof Nansen's Death".[53] In this article he clearly revealed the tactics he intended to pursue. Nansen had been one of Norway's most renowned figures during the early twentieth century; one of the few who had gained an international reputation. His sudden and unexpected death therefore inaugurated a period of national mourning. Quisling obviously wished to associate himself with Nansen in the public mind, and, if possible, attempt to appropriate at least part of the mantle of the departed national hero.

As its title indicated, the article concerned itself with political questions. Its author stated that Nansen had not completed his political task at the time of his death, which Quisling described as having been "to liberate the fatherland from class struggle and party politics, and to carry out a national union and reconstruction on the basis of healthy political and economic principles".[54] With Nansen's passing, said Quisling, the Norwegian people were left without a "natural leader", a "*fører*". Although Quisling had never been associated with Nansen politically before, not having been a member of the Fatherland League which numbered Nansen as its most important figure, it was clear that he now, at least by inference, sought to establish himself as Nansen's successor.

Indicating the first public opposition to communism that he had uttered, Quisling declared that there existed in Norway a growing reaction to useless party politics, to labor conflicts, and to "the Bolshevistic and demagogical spirit which is spreading in our villages and towns". To combat this, he argued that what was needed was a "new political orientation", and he modestly declared that he had worked out a ten-point program whose ideas "were in line with those which influenced Fridtjof Nansen".[55]

This program was clearly intended to appeal to those *borgerlige* constituents who feared the permutation that was taking place politically, with the rise of the Labor party, and also to those who felt that change was necessary to overcome the threat from the socialists and to eliminate the effects of the depression. The program emphasized its opposition to the Labor party. Class strife and party politics were declared anathema, to be eliminated in favor of "national politics" which looked after the entire nation's interests. Such politics would be authoritarian, with "a strong and just" government being in power, not dependent upon a "capricious majority" in parliament. Appealing to obvious *borgerlige* sentiments, Quisling's program also called for making government more efficient, limiting the competence of the state, lessening government spending, but making more money available for national defense. His arguments were not restricted just to practical politics, however. Ideological racist viewpoints were also included in the article. He described the Nordic race, to which the Norwegians belonged, as being "the most worthy of all the world's races" and the bearer of civilization. It needed to be maintained and improved. He called for a Nordic union of the Scandinavian states, which he visualized as forming a new world power in northern Europe. This union, and the Nordic race in general, would be the foes of "imported inferior ideas", which he associated with "Bolshevism". The workers were to be made aware of their national consciousness, thereby recognizing the superiority of their race. The imported ideology of Marxism would be crushed by an increase in wealth, creating the basis for a reconciliation of capital and labor, allowing the workers to become capitalists.

Ideas obviously inspired by Mussolini's corporate state were also expressed. Quisling called for the creation of a new governmental organization made up of representatives from various business and labor groups.

This new body was to assume the role of a lower house, while the *Storting* would be relegated to forming an upper house.

In addition to his racist arguments, a reader is especially struck by his emphasis on the need to eliminate "Bolshevism". He applied this polemical term indiscriminately to include the Labor party and the Communists alike. However, because the Labor party in 1930 was a much stronger force than the Communists, who had declined to political insignificance, Quisling in reality used the term "Bolshevism" as a code name for the Labor party, even though it had been seven years since the Laborites had withdrawn from the Communist International.

In order to realize his program, with its attack directed against the Labor party, he maintained it was necessary to abandon the thought of a coalition among the *borgerlige* parties, contrary to the suggestion made by some non-socialist proponents. What was needed, argued Quisling, was a new "party of national union" (*nasjonalt samlingsparti*). Immodestly, he stated the proposition that if only the Fatherland League would change its policy and become an active political party, it could assume the position of a party of national union, since its program and that which he had just propounded were quite similar.[56]

In contrast with his earlier philosophical treatise, he certainly succeeded in calling attention to himself with this article. The Fatherland League was not particularly pleased to have a non-member speak in the name of one of its founders. Joakim Lehmkuhl, its foreman, replied in *Tidens Tegn* on May 29. His response was anything but positive. He commented first that he considered it somewhat strange to find persons outside the League, persons who had not participated actively in its operations, to be so presumptuous as to tell the League in a newspaper article what its policy should be. Quisling, said Lehmkuhl, topped all others because he used Nansen's name as a means of seeking support for his suggestions. Lehmkuhl did not find this particularly attractive. Nor did he have much enthusiasm for Quisling's proposal that the League should form the nucleus of a new political party in 1930: "When a man believes it is possible, six months before an election, on the basis of a superficial article in a newspaper, to form the basis for a completely new political party, that must be his own concern".

Lehmkuhl thereupon dismissed Quisling and went on to state what he believed should be the Fatherland League's primary mission, a mission which he maintained was quite different from that which Quisling had mapped out. The League's basic purpose, argued Lehmkuhl, was to influence public opinion through informational activity. This information should be focused against the Labor party in order to stop its advance by defeating it in the 1930 election. Only then, after the Labor party had been thwarted, would it be possible to go on the offensive. And after the Norwegian people had accepted the League's policy, it would then be possible

to ascertain if the *borgerlige* parties would accept the League's program. At
this time, said Lehmkuhl, if the program were not welcomed by the existing non-socialist parties, the League would make the decision on whether
or not "to go our own way", meaning the formation of a party. Quisling's
proposals were therefore completely repudiated by the chairman, who
closed his article by pointing to the tremendous work which Nansen had
done on the League's behalf, and expressing the hope that it would be possible to further the movement of national reconstruction in Nansen's
spirit.[57]

Quite obviously, Quisling was hardly pleased with Lehmkuhl's response. In turn, he sent a counter-rebuttal to *Tidens Tegn* in which he lam-
basted Lehmkuhl and the Fatherland League, the very organization he had
previously appealed to.[58] In his reply, he exhibited a trait which later
would become all too familiar – a complete lack of moderation when confronted with arguments that contradicted his own views. In fact, as a rule
he was unable to argue rationally at all, as was shown in this instance. He
now declared that the Fatherland League was not the vehicle to carry out
his ideas. Its leadership was weak, its accusations against him were
"shabby", and it was divisive in its activity, alienating the workers rather
than gaining their adherence to the cause of "national reconstruction".
Having, at least to his satisfaction, discarded the League polemically, he
continued to call for a new party which "would make all other parties superfluous". As a parting shot at the League, he declared dramatically that
it had been the need for a new party, based on a program such as he had
authored, which had forced him "as a good Norwegian" to come forward
with his ideas because of his sorrow "that the *fører* and leader [Nansen]
was gone". Once more it is clear that he sought to expropriate Nansen's
halo from the League.

Despite the display of vehement language in this controversy between
Quisling and the Fatherland League, the feud did not prove to be long-
lasting. Indeed, he soon enjoyed the support of the League, becoming one
of its members[59] – thereby completely contradicting by example his previous indictment of the organization. The year 1930 was not one in which
those who opposed the Norwegian Labor party could engage in polemics
against each other. In this election year all of the non-socialist parties were
preoccupied with attempting to halt the advance of the socialists, who in
the previous election of 1927 had gained a very great victory, allowing
them to form their short-lived ministry in 1928. Although the spectre of
socialist rule had initially been brief, the *borgerlige* parties were determined
that this possibility should never repeat itself.

If he were to gain political prominence, Quisling had to participate in
this crusade against the Labor party. With the aid and support of Prytz, he

actively involved himself in electioneering in 1930 as a writer and speaker. He had two main outlets for his activity. He wrote for *Tidens Tegn*, the Independent Liberal newspaper, and he spoke and wrote on behalf of the Agrarian party's election campaign.

The articles in *Tidens Tegn* appeared as a series dealing with conditions in the Soviet Union. He herewith simply continued the anti-Bolshevik effort which he had originated earlier in *Tidens Tegn*, but now in a much broader format. Begun in September, the articles, upon their completion in December, were gathered and published in book form under the title *Russland og vi* (*Russia and We*), thereby enhancing his growing reputation as the embattled foe of Bolshevism in Norway.[60] He accomplished this by declaring that there was no difference between the Russian Bolsheviks and the leaders of the Labor party: "The dominant faction in the Norwegian Labor party is therefore Bolshevistic . . . , they and the actual Communist party [are] just shadows of the same denomination."[61] Therefore, he argued, were the Labor party to succeed, exactly the same type of conditions would result as had occurred in the Soviet Union. He went so far as to project a loss of 300,000 to 400,000 lives as a consequence of revolution in Norway.[62] Quite plainly, one of the basic purposes of the articles was to frighten Norwegians so much by the Russian example that they would not support the Labor party. Although it can be said that some of the criticism which he levied against the Soviet Union was valid – after all, the actions of the Russian Communists during the 1920s were not solely of the kind that necessarily inspired admiration – nevertheless, there was little if any attempt made by the author to be objective. His intent was to paint the Soviet Union as black as possible.

He was not content, however, merely to give a negative description of the Soviet Union. In keeping with his vision of himself as a philosophical prophet, capable of uniting separate pieces of factual information into a universal interpretation which presented a true picture of existence, his articles included nothing less than a political and racial philosophy concerning the Soviet Union's relation to the rest of the world. He set forth the hardly original theory that the Bolsheviks were plotting to carry revolution through the entire world. This theory was not just political, however, but also racial. He maintained that "Bolshevism is an Asiatic-Slavic movement led by Jewish brains".[63] As such, the Bolshevik Revolution, according to him, was an "Asian-Oriental revolt against world civilization" similar to that which Mithridates had carried out against Rome.[64] In order to combat this sinister movement, which he mystically identified with Anti-Christ,[65] and which he also described as "a conspiracy against the Nordic-inspired European civilization",[66] what was necessary was closer cooperation between "Nordic-inspired peoples", first and foremost Scandinavians and Englishmen, and next Germans. He thereupon presented what proved to be the first of innumerable projects for international organizations that he would later submit at various times during his political career. He proposed a "Nordic Federation" made up of Scandinavia and Great Britain, to be joined by Finland and Holland. Eventually he anticipated that Germany, the British dominions, and the United States would affiliate with his proposed federation. Such an international force, he maintained, would "break the thrust of every Bolshevik coalition and secure European civilization and peace in the foreseeable future".[67]

This abstract and unrealistic political philosophy did not receive significant attention in Norway. It tended generally to be ignored. Instead, the right-wing *borgerlige* simply accepted *Russland og vi* as a piece of political propaganda to be used against the Labor party, which was all that they wanted it to be. Quisling's racial interpretation of the Russian Revolution was not commented upon to any great degree, although he was acquiring the reputation of being a thinker in right-wing circles, a reputation which Prytz worked energetically to spread.

More practical was the activity that Quisling and Prytz carried out on behalf of the Agrarian party in the bitter *borgerlig* offensive against the Labor party. Nowhere was this campaign more virulent than in the pages of *Nationen*, the Agrarians' voice in Oslo. Thorvald Aadahl was a bitter antagonist of the Labor party, and his paper continuously heaped vilification upon the socialists. This was especially true at election time, when all of the country's partisan newspapers cut loose against their political opponents. In his editorials and in front-page articles Aadahl propounded the same view of the Labor party as Quisling: that it was synonymous with the Communist party of the Soviet Union. Characteristic of *Nationen*'s strong attack on the Labor party was a cartoon inserted in a front-page article appearing in the October 20th issue which showed an armored car symbolically labelled "the people's will" chasing members of the Labor party across the border into the Soviet Union.

Immediately below this erudite piece of journalism appeared one of a number of articles written by Quisling for *Nationen*. This was no coincidence. He and Prytz had earlier made the decision to campaign actively on behalf of the Agrarian party. Prytz's involvement went so far as to become a candidate, appearing as number twelve on the party's ballot for *Storting* representatives from Oslo.[68] Quisling's participation was not as pronounced as Prytz's, but he too worked energetically for the party's cause. On October 5 he took part in one of its political rallies, where he gave a speech. Once more, in nutshell form, he repeated the same arguments as he concurrently was presenting to the readers of *Tidens Tegn*. The activities of the Russian Communists, or "Bolshevism", were described in the most negative manner possible, and he declared the Labor party to be a carbon copy of the Russian Communists. *Nationen* quoted him as having made the following statement concerning the Labor party: "The Labor party's program in principle means a complete acceptance of the Soviet [Union's] methods. It is an appeal for murder and plunder . . ."[69] He did not neglect his emphasis on race in this speech. He stated that in this time of crisis the world was experiencing, it was necessary for Norwegians to search within themselves for the necessary solutions, and in order to do so, the effort should be made to reach back to "the core in the Norse race's uniqueness".[70] He sought to turn ideology into reality by declaring that the Agrarian party "represents our nation's national core" and was therefore best qualified to "raise our unique Norse banner".[71] Again he appeared as the prophet, not concerned with just the practical realities of the political campaign, but declaring that the Agrarian party, as head of the government, would carry this "banner" externally as well as internally, influencing the affairs of the world. He airily brushed aside Norway's small population and limited influence with the statement that it was not "quantity which counted, but quality".[72]

In an article that appeared in *Nationen* on Saturday the 18th of October, just prior to the election, which was held on the following Monday, he felt obliged to be less philosophical because of the need to make the greatest practical propaganda impact on potential Agrarian party supporters. The article limited itself to the topic of "The farmers and revolution". Once more he held up the Soviet Union as a frightening example. He pointed to the fate of the peasants in Russia as a warning: they had been burdened with heavy taxes, forced expropriation, and loss of their property. He maintained that exactly the same conditions would prevail in Norway if the Labor party were to come to power. It was in the best interests of the farmers, he argued, not to support a social revolution. He hoped they would recognize this, now at election time and also in the future.[73]

To their great satisfaction, the *borgerlige* parties' campaign against Labor achieved success in 1930. As noted earlier, the election was a severe setback for the Labor party, with its *Storting* representation being markedly reduced.[74] This was the most crushing election defeat that the party up to then had endured in its history. To a considerable extent, this rebuff contributed to the elimination of its revolutionary phraseology, with Labor becoming instead a more moderate reform party similar to the socialist parties elsewhere in Scandinavia.

The success of the *borgerlige* did not, however, lead to any significant political change. Labor had been a minority opposition party prior to the election, and its status was not changed, merely being somewhat reduced, while the *borgerlige* parties remained incapable of creating permanent coalitions because of the Liberal party's opposition to such alliances. The pattern of non-socialist minority governments therefore continued. The Liberal cabinet headed by Johan Ludwig Mowinckel maintained its tenuous hold on the government, with the temporary good will of the Conservative and Agrarian parties, who held the balance of power among the divided *borgerlige* factions in the *Storting*.

Because of the unchanged political situation, Quisling and Prytz did not gain any specific rewards for their work on behalf of the Agrarian party in the previous campaign. Nevertheless, the duo were able to obtain certain more intangible benefits. Their contribution to the effort against the Labor party enabled them to make valuable contacts among influential right-wing *borgerlige* political figures and prominent businessmen. Thanks to the polemical articles that he had contributed, Quisling was already familiar to two important Oslo editors, Rolf Thommessen and Thorvald Aadahl. Largely due to his writings, Quisling also caught the attention of wealthy businessmen. Foremost among them was Johan Throne Holst, the owner of Freia, Norway's largest chocolate company. His importance was heightened by his position as head of the influential Norway's Industrial Federation (*Norges Industriforbund*), the association representing the interests of the country's industrial producers. He belonged to the Independent Liberal party, and like Thommessen he was seeking a way out of the economic and political dislocations of the 1930s. Similarly to Thommessen, Throne Holst also came to the conclusion that perhaps Vidkun Quisling might be one means of achieving this end. During the fall of 1930 Throne Holst arranged introductions for Quisling with some of Norway's foremost industrialists and businessmen.[75] Throne Holst did this in his capacity as a leading member of a political pressure group known as Our Country (*Vort Land*). This was a loosely organized group whose purpose was to give financial assistance to anti-socialist *borgerlige* parties.[76] Through the backing made available by Throne Holst and his circle, Quisling was assured one possible means of gaining a stronger entry into politics.

He and Prytz also sought out additional sources of support. Despite the recriminations exchanged previously with Joakim Lehmkuhl because of his article in connection with Nansen's death, Quisling's breach with the Fatherland League was healed after the election. By becoming a member of the League, he could extend the number of his political contacts and potential backers. The League, on the other hand, had noted the attention that Quisling received from his anti-communist writings and speeches. It would be to the League's advantage, it was felt, if he could be at its disposal. The League therefore contacted him in early 1931, asking whether he would be willing to make speeches under its auspices.[77] Despite the strong words he had previously hurled against the League, he agreed to become one of its speakers.[78] In his orations in early 1931 he continued to emphasize the negative aspects of the Soviet regime, declaring that he was merely presenting "the truth about Russia".[79] Similarly, but on a more modest scale, Prytz lent his name to the League by allowing his signature to be attached to a League petition signed by socially prominent individuals gathered in the spring of 1931. It called on the *Storting* and the government to stop "the revolutionary and treasonable activity" of "the revolutionary parties", meaning the Labor party and Communists. The petition urged restrictions against these parties, declaring that this would fulfill the *borgerlige* election promises of 1930.[80]

Quisling's activity in the Fatherland League was not limited to merely being a travelling speaker. He became a member of the executive committee of the League's Oslo chapter. This occurred when one of the members of the chapter, a prominent attorney named Christopher Borchgrevink, wrote to Quisling on January 2, 1931, stating that he had just read *Russland og vi*. The book had made a deep impression on him, declared Borchgrevink, and he had "a burning desire" to nominate Quisling to the executive committee of the Oslo chapter, a feeling which he maintained was mutually "shared by my friends".[81] Quisling allowed himself to be persuaded to accept this position, and before long he was engaged in supervising the propaganda activity of the League's most important chapter in the nation's capital.[82]

Although Quisling and Prytz were able to establish a number of influential contacts as a result of their contribution to such *borgerlige* groups as the Fatherland League, the Agrarian party, and the Independent Liberals, they were not content merely to be participants in organizations led by others. They wished to create political constellations which were entirely their own. As a result, already in the fall of 1930 the first of these linear predecessors of National Union came into being. This initial organization was a rather nebulous group named Economic Defense (*Økonomisk Verneplikt*).

In its program, the organization declared that it did not have confidence in the existing political order, with the non-socialist parties being split into competing factions. What was needed was a firm front against "the revolutionary Labor party", and Economic Defense proposed to establish that front. The creation of such a defense was justified on racial grounds, an argument that Quisling and Prytz had used before. Economic Defense stressed the threat to the Nordic race from the East, "from Slavic and inferior races. We must not be destroyed by the dangerous communist disease." Instead, the program maintained it was necessary to seek protection by forming an organization that would guarantee personal freedom, equality before the law, freedom to own property, and the right to work. As this showed, its economic appeal was directed toward business interests opposed to the Labor movement. This was further indicated by the demand for "safe and peaceful labor relations for our industries". To provide such a safeguard, Economic Defense emphasized the need for it to accumulate capital. It proposed to become the organized economic force for the *borgerlige* in society, the non-socialist equivalent of the Federation of Trade

Unions (LO). As such, Economic Defense maintained that it was non-partisan, seeking assistance from members of all *borgerlige* parties, from the Conservatives, Independent Liberals, Liberals, and Agrarian parties. Finally, Economic Defense declared that it might be necessary, in order to gain defense from the "revolutionaries", to organize an "independent militia" in support of the government.[83]

Despite the emotional nature of its appeal for funds, Quisling and Prytz's brainchild did not achieve any success. The ideas expressed in its program were not new. As we have seen, Quisling and Prytz had earlier declared their racial view and antipathies to the Labor party and the Soviet Union, with little concrete gain except some recognition as being the embattled foes of "Bolshevism" and its supposed Norwegian collaborators. Similarly, the call for a war chest in the battle against the labor movement, and hints of the necessity of establishing some type of volunteer *borgerlig* militia force were imitations of previously existing efforts. Our Country's economic aid to the *borgerlige* opponents of the Labor party and the Community Defense's para-military training to ward off a possible revolutionary uprising from the left unquestionably served as obvious examples which influenced Quisling and Prytz when they decided to launch Economic Defense. Perhaps because of the lack of originality shown in promoting this organization, bringing it into competition with other like-minded groups on the right wing of Norwegian politics, and also because the depression-ridden 1930s were not the most auspicious time in which to solicit economic contributions to fight some alleged future upheaval, Economic Defense proved to be a complete failure. Hardly any money was collected.[84] Never having been more than a paper organization, it simply faded into oblivion.

This did not discourage Quisling and Prytz into abandoning their effort to form a viable organization that they could control. In December 1930 Quisling's petition to the military authorities to be promoted to the rank of major in the reserves was granted. The new title did not bring with it an increase in financial remuneration. He continued to receive a pension based on his years in service, with the rank of captain being the highest he had attained while on active duty. Nevertheless, the higher reserve rank he now possessed had some significance. A noteworthy Norwegian trait of the period was the emphasis that was placed on a person's occupational status. Such social consciousness was a prominent feature of societal culture in the 1930s. Being able to use the title of major enhanced Quisling's status when seeking adherents to causes which he espoused. Emphasis on his higher officer's rank was therefore an important part of his identity when steps began to be made for the formation of a new organization in early January 1931.

The first discussions which led to the founding of this group can be traced back to the fall of 1930. Since this was the approximate time that the vain effort to launch Economic Defense took place, it is likely that Quisling and Prytz intended the two organizations to be parallel endeavors. But whereas Economic Defense quickly proved to be a failure, their attempt to establish Nordic Folk-Rising (*Nordiske Folkereisning*) proved to be a much more serious venture. It was intended to serve as the organization which would, in concrete form, realize the ideals that Quisling up to this time had enunciated only in his writings and speeches.

During the early fall he and Prytz began a loose process of consultation among like-minded sympathizers concerning the projected organization. By mid-November the two had progressed to the point where they had in collaboration drawn up a draft political program, which they circulated among their potential supporters for comment.[85] Work continued in preparation for launching the new organization, and by the middle of January Quisling and Prytz were discussing with their confidants plans for the initial meeting which would mark the formal beginning of Nordic Folk-Rising. The program had now reached the point where it was almost finished, with only a little polishing needed before it was complete.[86] Johan Throne Holst was among the most influential persons whom Quisling and Prytz consulted concerning the program. This leading industrialist, while maintaining his preference for working behind the scenes politically, provided encouragement and support. In a letter to Prytz on January 17, 1931, he declared that Nordic Folk-Rising, as projected in its draft program, provided "the only salvation for our country", and he recommended that Quisling begin his new venture by calling together a limited number of some one hundred persons. He urged Quisling to present his views on the formation of Nordic Folk-Rising at such a meeting, and Throne Holst promised to ask some twenty of his acquaintances to take part.[87]

In preparation for exactly this type of gathering, a letter was sent out to potential supporters, apprising them that Major Quisling had been petitioned by a number of persons to draft a program based on his ideas. In response to this request, he had now drawn up the program for a "Nordic Folk-Rising" in the form of five "logically constructed major points".[88]

In an attempt to avoid arousing the type of jealous suspicion from other *borgerlige* political associations that had met the ill-fated Economic Defense, the letter emphasized that this new organization would not be similar to any existing group, nor would it compete with any such association. Instead, what was planned was a "movement or rising" which would be able to force through certain specific ideas. In this endeavor, it would serve as a coordinating or blanket organization in which "all national organizations" could take part, and in which they would find full scope for their own activity as long as they agreed to carry out the movement's guidelines.[89]

Despite this disclaimer, the projected organization's lack of originality was obvious. The goal of being a political coordinating movement which would force through certain nationalistic ideas was exactly the same task

that the Fatherland League had set for itself. Although his ideology was to
a degree more mystical and racist than the League's, Quisling, because of
his knowledge of and close association with the League, was quite plainly
intent on plagiarizing some of its efforts when he and Prytz planned the
formation of Nordic Folk-Rising.

The readers of the letter were informed that a meeting of "interested
men" would be held "in the immediate future". Here more detailed information would be provided and discussion would take place for the realization of the organization's plans. In reality, however, Quisling, Prytz, and
their small group of consultants had already made the key decisions concerning the new organization, so the possibility of any original contributions by uninitiated participants at the future meeting was precluded. Enclosed with the letter was not only Quisling's program for the organization
and its "temporary bylaws", but also his "explanation" of the program.
Furthermore, there quite obviously could be no discussion about the organization's title. Its name was already printed on the letterhead: "Nordic
Folk-Rising in Norway". This was consistent with Quisling's constant
practice throughout his career of allowing the rank and file of his followers
to have no influence in decision-making. Finally, the conclusion of the letter revealed yet another of his traits: his preference for often surrounding
himself with an element of secrecy. The readers received the impression of
being involved in some kind of intrigue since they were requested to keep
the letter "confidential for the time being".[90]

The long-anticipated initial meeting of Nordic Folk-Rising was held in
the evening of March 17, 1931. As anticipated, the invited persons gave
their approval to the program and bylaws which had previously been
drawn up under Quisling's authority.[91] Some thirty individuals were present, the largest number who would ever attend a meeting of the group.[92]

When writing the program for the new organization, Quisling formulated the most comprehensive and detailed presentation of his political
ideas that he had stated up to that time. This, as will be seen, was the most
significant achievement of Nordic Folk-Rising. The organization's ideological foundation was presented in two small printed pamphlets. One
contained the program and bylaws which were approved at the March 17
meeting.[93] The other provided Quisling's personal commentary on the
program.[94]

Although both pamphlets showed signs of Quisling's authorship, it was
the second, the explanation of Nordic Folk-Rising's program, which reflected most clearly his unique style. It is therefore also the most revealing,
as well as the longer, of the two pamphlets. The first, containing the movement's program and bylaws, gives the impression of being much more the
result of a collaborative effort. It was written down in its final form by
Quisling, acting in concert with Prytz, only after earlier draft versions had
circulated among their close associates.[95]

Quisling repeated many of the themes of his previous writings in his commentary on the Folk-Rising's program, but in this exposition he formulated his views in an all-inclusive manner that brought together in one brief statement the essence of the political ideas that he stood for at this time. Rather than beginning with an explanation of the specific points in the program, he instead devoted more than half of the pamphlet to a political and philosophical discussion in which he sought to provide the ideological justification for Nordic Folk-Rising's existence.

The world, he declared, was in the middle of a critical period due to the rapid transformation of the times. Such sudden change caused great uneasiness in the lives of the people. Adding to this uncertainty, he argued, was the emergence of communism, and he repeated his familiar theme that communism sought to take advantage of international economic dislocation and spread revolution throughout the entire world. Norway too, he maintained, was caught up in this crisis, which was made worse by the inability of incompetent politicians and administrators to deal with contemporary problems. Reflecting the troubled international depression in which Nordic Folk-Rising was born, he deplored the fact that a growing political, economic, and social crisis was ravaging the country: "Our people's wealth and strength are destroyed in unfruitful party politics and meaningless labor conflicts." The present-day parliamentary system, he insisted, was not capable of dealing with "our national tasks". One such major "task" was the problem of Marxism, which he typically identified with the Labor party, declaring that one-third of the population, at least in name, were adherents to Marxism. As he had done in *Russland og vi*, he interpreted such a development in the darkest possible manner. The people's unity was being destroyed, and "the Bolshevistic and demagogic spirit is spreading in our towns and villages, and a bloody social revolution threatens in the background . . ."[96]

He naturally presented Nordic Folk-Rising as the force that would save Norway from such a revolution. A national revival was needed, he insisted, and this could only be carried out by a movement which, like "Bolshevism", was political-religious in nature.[97] Nordic Folk-Rising would therefore compete with Marxism by imitating it, but whereas Marxism looked forward to a classless society, Quisling's ideology for Nordic Folk-Rising was racist: "Such a folk-rising must be based on the fact that Norwegians along with other Scandinavian peoples form the core of the large folk family which represents the most valuable racial contribution to humanity, the great Nordic race."[98]

His emphasis on race was not new. He had used the same general theme in the vague program he had enunciated in the article on the occasion of Nansen's death and also in *Russland og vi*. But in his analysis of the Folk-Rising's program he revealed for the first time the extent to which the racist assumption of Nordic superiority lay at the heart of his political philosophy. He stressed the need for future political development in Norway to be based on consciousness of Nordic racial superiority, and not on what he described as "imported inferior ideas which are definitely unsuited for our uniqueness".[99] Marxism, therefore, was denigrated as being "imported" and "inferior". His racism, of course, was equally "imported", but with his insistence on being recognized as an original thinker, he was scarcely capable of admitting that his racial ideology, or any part of his program, did not originate with him.

Racism did not constitute, however, the sole foundation for Nordic Folk-Rising within his ideological framework. He added a second basis for the movement, which he described as being "a spiritual and conscientious conception of life".[100] In presenting this view, he was enunciating an idea that can be traced back to his pantheistic pamphlet of 1929. The development of world history, he maintained, was the revelation of "the divine will".[101] Within his frame of thought, the maturation of civilization and Nordic racial superiority were closely tied together. He repeated the racial cliché that higher civilizations such as the Indian, Persian, Graeco-Roman, as well as the European and the American, attained their achievements largely due to Nordic contributions. By making his Nordic followers aware of their historical "mission" in the world, he maintained that a feeling of moral strength could be aroused which would match the fervor of the Communists.[102] Declaring that "our political new orientation will be built" on this double foundation of "race and spiritual perception of life", he summed up the philosophy which served as the basis for the founding of Nordic Folk-Rising with the following words:

> By thereby uniting "the Nordic idea" with a religious and moral conception of the world, as well as with consideration to the demand of modern development, there emerges a political doctrine which both builds on realities and is something to live and die for. Only such a movement (religiously determined, national, social, and Nordic or, if one will, social-individualistic) will have the thoroughness and emotional emphasis which is required to conquer the triple obstacle in our society: the laziness of the citizens, uncomprehending liberalism's equivocation and half-heartedness, and the communistic-socialistic quasi-religion.[103]

The five specific points which formed Nordic Folk-Rising's program were also quite revealing in providing an understanding of Quisling's and Prytz's aspirations for the movement, although the program was not as philosophical as Quisling's explanation. The first point made it quite clear that the Folk-Rising was intended to be an anti-Marxist organization, directed against the Labor party in particular: "Clear the way for positive national politics by destroying the imported and pernicious communistic revolutionary movement, which does not agree with Nordic uniqueness and which in itself is fundamentally false and evil".[104] The second point contained his dual philosophical foundation for the movement, based on his postulates of Nordic racial superiority and the "spiritual and conscientious conception of life".[105]

The program's third point stressed the importance of "restoring society's unity and interdependence" by gaining the allegiance of the workers for a policy of "constructive national labor politics" which would further the interests of the workers and of society as a whole.[106] This point provided the clear impression that Quisling and Prytz had been inspired by the success of Hitler's NSDAP in proclaiming itself the party of the German worker. But while Nordic Folk-Rising sought to appeal to labor, its program revealed that economically Quisling and Prytz clearly favored business interests, not the workers. This was obvious, since the majority of those who provided support for the founding of the Folk-Rising had business or professional backgrounds. The workers, said the program, could never gain well-being by following Marxist ideology, but only through "understanding cooperation in a society which provides security for property, for work and its fruits, and which does not hinder free expansion of business and personal initiative".[107] Similarly, the Folk-Rising's program indicated antipathy toward trade union activity, calling for right-to-work laws and for outlawing the closed shop. Quisling's basic opposition to organized labor, led by LO, was further shown by the program's call for the creation of rival "free national labor unions" that would be united in a national organization called Norway's Workers' League (*Norges Arbeiderlag*).[108]

The program's fourth point urged nothing less than a complete transformation of Norwegian society, with the goal of organizing it "as a national and social Nordic people's state on an individualistic basis and with a strong and stable government".[109] Although this segment of the program contained statements calling for decreased government regulations and expenditures, designed to please conservative business interests, it included also a radical proposal for change. Even more explicitly than he had done in his Nansen article, Quisling, in concert with Prytz, favored the establishment of a corporate state. The government would use its funds for a "more systematic regulation and stimulation of business enterprise so that a healthy and uniform economic growth is assured . . ."[110] Such regulation would be carried out by "economic councils" (*næringsråd*) within the different occupations, made up of representatives of workers and management. These councils on the national level would in turn be represented in and subordinate to an institution which Quisling called the "National Assembly" (*Riksting*). Only such an institution, the program maintained, could reconcile the conflicting interests within society and bring about constructive cooperation.[111]

In no other segment were the ambiguities of Quisling's program more apparent than here. On the one hand, he sought to appeal to the traditional

laissez faire values of business interests who felt threatened by the advance
of the labor movement and the depressed economic conditions of the
1930s. On the other hand, these very conditions called for drastic changes,
and Quisling and Prytz clearly received their inspiration from the corporate example of Benito Mussolini's Italy. They did not try to reconcile the
obvious differences between those parts of their program which favored a
reduction of state activity and the corporate elements which would have increased the role of government tremendously. Instead, the program facilely
sought as broad a spectrum of support as possible. But for Quisling, the
goal of establishing a corporate state through the National Assembly remained a basic part of his political aspirations. As will be seen, he tried
constantly to achieve this ideal throughout his life.

He and Prytz favored the creation of the National Assembly not merely
because it would regulate the economy, but also because of the political
change that could be enacted if it came into existence. The two hoped to
eliminate parliamentary government. According to the Folk-Rising's program, the National Assembly would be placed alongside the *Storting*. Although abolition of the *Storting* was not mentioned, they obviously intended to reduce the parliament's importance because of their strong opposition to the existing political system:

> The current parliamentary system with its unfruitful party politics cannot
> solve our national problems. The movement must therefore rally in order to
> organize alongside the *Storting* the previously mentioned *Riksting*, with its
> accompanying institutions, and thereby establish a two-chamber system
> which meets the demands of the times and which in a natural and peaceful
> way can carry forward the new society.[112]

While the country internally would evolve into a corporate state, in external affairs the program called for an ambitious foreign policy, which was
expressed in its fifth and final point, where emphasis was placed on the
need for Norway to assume a prominent position in the world. This could
only be realized by following "a purposeful and positive foreign policy,"
which would result in building up Norway's economic and political
power. Through Nordic Folk-Rising, the country would take the lead in
organizing international cooperation between similar Nordic movements
in other countries. Such cooperation was projected to occur on a grand
scale. Whereas Quisling earlier in *Russland og vi* had called merely for a
"Nordic Federation", this goal had now been expanded to include not only
(1) an international Nordic Federation, but (2) a Nordic League of Nations
(*Nordisk Folkeforbund*), and (3) participation in international cooperation
that would eventually result in unification of the entire world.[113] The program did not reveal how Norway, with its small population and limited international influence, could achieve such an ambitious foreign policy. It
did indicate, however, Quisling's fondness for constructing grandiose

paper plans for world-wide organizations without having any realistic idea of how to achieve such pretentious goals.

With his administrative background and marked tendency to produce ambitious plans on a vast scale, it was not surprising that the program for Quisling's Folk-Rising included the organization's "temporary" bylaws as well. Here it was noted formally that the movement's full name was "Nordic Folk-Rising in Norway" (*Nordisk Folkereisning i Norge*).[114] In this instance, he again indicated his unrealistic, boundless ambition. He viewed the Folk-Rising as but the first of a number of parallel organizations in other countries. Thereby, before his new political organization had even been born, he was already dreaming of being head of an international movement.

The bylaws dealt with more prosaic matters as well, spelled out in specific detail. The movement's initials were "N.F."[115] Its dues for both active members and supporters was the same – two *kroner*.[116] The movement's symbol consisted of a "golden cross on a field of red",[117] the so-called "St. Olav's Cross". This symbol, which originated with Quisling, had considerable significance for the future. Two years later when a new political party by the name of National Union (*Nasjonal Samling*) came into existence with Quisling as its leader, the party emblem was the same St. Olav's Cross that graced the cover of N.F.'s program, and it stood as the symbol for Quisling's politics during his entire career.

The manner in which N.F. was organized revealed yet another of his political traits which remained permanent. N.F. was formed in a rigid, authoritarian manner. The organization's main source of authority, in theory, was a Central Committee (*Sentralkomité*), obviously inspired by the example of the Russian Communist Central Committee. Real power, however, if N.F. had truly become viable, would have been held by a three-man Executive Committee (*Styre*), chosen for three-year terms by the Central Committee. The Executive Committee and the chairmen of various special committees (*arbeidsutvalg*) set up by the Central Committee formed N.F.'s Council (*Råd*), whose function was to serve as the Central Committee's working committee.[118] Had the organization amounted to anything, however, the Council would have been dominated by the Executive Committee, headed by Quisling and Prytz. Such supremacy was certain because the bylaws stated clearly that N.F. was to be led according to the "*Führer*" system (*førersystemet*) with one-man responsibility and authority.[119] This power allowed the leadership to remove any member of N.F. from his position and, if need be, expel him from the organization.[120] The inclusion of such strong authority for the leadership was not merely an idle exercise on the part of Quisling. He insisted that everyone who became affiliated with N.F. had to confirm his agreement with the movement's political ideas in writing, and he was quite willing to use the weapon of exclusion.[121] This rigid conformity to the leader's will was typical of him, as later events would show. Incapable of winning adherents to his side by persuasion and reasonable arguments, he insisted on rigid, undeviating fidelity and submission from his followers.

As will later be seen, his emphasis on exercising strong authority under the *Führer* principle and his readiness to exclude those who differed with him had significant consequences for his future party, National Union. The existence of these features in N.F. foreshadowed later political developments. Similarly, N.F.'s organizational structure was repeated to a considerable degree in National Union. While the party did not have a Central Committee, most likely because Quisling realized the liability of using a term that could be associated with Soviet political organization, it included both an Executive Committee (*Hovedstyre*) and a Council (*Råd*).[122]

When assessing Nordic Folk-Rising's political ideology and organizational structure as a whole – the explanation of the program, the program itself, and the bylaws – one gets the impression that this movement, planned chiefly by Quisling with Prytz's aid and encouragement, had no chance of becoming a force within Norwegian politics. N.F. in large part was simply the artificial creation of these two men. They had the need to establish a vehicle by which Quisling could become more directly involved in politics, and N.F. was the result of their amateurish efforts. It is true that they were supported by a small number of right-wing radical *borgerlige* who had become disenchanted with the political system. But none of these, and this included Quisling and Prytz as well, had any experience in practical politics. This explains why N.F.'s structure and ideology at times seemed quite naive. Perhaps this is best illustrated in the program's point five on foreign policy. Despite his considerable experience in the military and the diplomatic corps, Quisling lacked the ability to assess in a realistic manner the position that Norway occupied in the world. His dream of making his country a power that would occupy a leading place among the Nordic countries, which would dominate the globe because of their alleged racial superiority, belongs to the realm of childhood fantasy, where his romantic view of history and his conception of his own significance had originally been formed.

Although the Folk-Rising's program and bylaws had been approved at the meeting of March 17, 1931, this did not mean that the organization intended to appear publicly, even though its Central Committee had been elected. Instead, the decision was made for the organization to work secretly for a time. As a result, the only real evidence of activity on the part of N.F. after March 17 occurred in the form of meetings of the Central Committee, which were held on a rather irregular basis. At its first conference on March 25 the Committee decided to postpone the selection of an Executive Committee and instead authorized Quisling to act in this capacity for the time being.[123]

At the next meeting, held on April 8, the ambitious decision was made to expand the Central Committee in a carefully planned manner, with the goal of having the Committee eventually evolve into the projected National Assembly.[124] This fanciful decision indicated even more obviously N.F.'s dilettantism. Before the organization had achieved anything beyond its sparsely attended gatherings, it was already making plans for the institution intended to supplant the *Storting*. Such a possibility should have appeared remote, considering the unstable nature of the Central Committee, which from its very beginning was constantly supplementing its membership. From N.F.'s records it appears that only about twenty persons were at one time or another actively involved in the organization.[125]

The most revealing feature of the Folk-Rising, however, which was made clear at the April 8 meeting, indicated how N.F. intended to grow and expand its influence. This was to occur in a clandestine manner through a system of cells and groups.[126] In this fashion, N.F.'s members were to disseminate the organization's ideas and recruit new members and followers. While it was recognized that at some time in the future it would be necessary for N.F. to appear publicly, seeking to gain adherents and to make its influence felt, N.F.'s most important activity would continue to take place secretly through the cells. According to Quisling's drafts, such cells were to be established on all levels of society: in business and industry, professional organizations, local and state administration, labor unions, cooperatives, and the military.[127] Similarly, by having N.F. serve as a blanket organization through which it could gain mastery over affiliated nationalistic organizations, whose members would be regarded as N.F.'s followers, the movement would be able to extend its influence far beyond its own ranks.[128] Quisling never indicated specifically the purpose of the planned cells, but this was plain. When N.F.'s ascendancy had developed to the point where it dominated key segments of society, a coup would take place by which N.F. seized control of government. The Bolshevik overthrow of the Provisional Government in 1917 served as the obvious model. Here again was unmistakable proof of how he and Prytz had been affected by their close contact with Russian affairs during their period of service in Petrograd. But while N.F.'s plans disclosed the extent to which the two men hoped to achieve a repetition of the Bolsheviks' success, there is no evidence to indicate that they sought to realize their ambitions beyond the initial planning stage.

Had such an effort been made, its failure would merely have highlighted the patently unrealistic and amateurish nature of N.F. Quisling's and Prytz's experiences in Russia could not be transferred to Norway. In tsarist Russia, because of the repressive nature of the government, secret societies were necessary in order for opposition political groups to survive. But as soon became apparent, such groups could not exist in Norway, with its small, scattered population and open society.

Quisling's preoccupation with planning the activities of Nordic Folk-

Rising was interrupted in the spring of 1931 by the opportunity for him to engage in more challenging practical concerns. Nevertheless, Nordic Folk-Rising and Economic Defense, although stillborn, were organizationally the linear predecessors of National Union. And ideologically the line of thought expressed in the propaganda of these two organizations can be traced back through Quisling's anti-Bolshevik and racist arguments made in his series of writings in 1930, and in an abstract religious and philosophical sense back to the small pamphlet that he issued in 1929.

CHAPTER III

Minister of Defense

1931–1933

Greatest attention, however, is raised by Quisling's appointment as Minister of Defense. When he was in Russia, he acted almost as a Bolshevik. When he came home, he was a Red Guard. But no one wanted to have any contact with that eager and intrusive gentleman. Then the wind began to blow from a different direction. And the fellow became an adherent of the Fatherland League and of fascism, and began to make "disclosures" of conditions in Russia. And it is one of these, the most loathsome and contemptible political type that is known, who has been placed as head of the Defense Department. A government that begins with such a corpse in its cargo can suffer shipwreck before it knows it.

Arbeiderbladet, May 11, 1931

The practical considerations which ended Quisling's direct involvement with Nordic Folk-Rising resulted from a political crisis which occurred in May 1931. A bitter controversy broke out in the *Storting* over the Liberal government's decision to allow an international trust, Unilever, to take over control of an important industrial firm, A/S Lilleborg Fabrikker. The government suffered a vote of no confidence and was forced to resign. In the maneuvering which followed in parliament, the non-socialists agreed that the Agrarians should be allowed to form a minority government. They in turn decided to have Peder Kolstad, one of their most prominent leaders in the *Storting*, head the incoming government.

The new prime minister-designate was a sturdy, calm, and dependable figure. Coming from a farm background, he had served for many years as principal of an agricultural school before beginning his parliamentary career in 1922. His responsibility for forming a new government proved to be a difficult challenge. The Agrarian party had never headed a government before and therefore lacked qualified candidates to hold cabinet positions. When searching for a competent person to serve as Minister of Defense, Kolstad received the advice to choose Vidkun Quisling. Although other candidates were also considered for this position, Kolstad, after giving the matter some thought, decided to designate Quisling as his choice.[1] Invited to join the Agrarian government, the latter responded without any apparent hesitation, although one of the stipulations for his acceptance was that he had to resign his leadership of Nordic Folk-Rising. Along with the other members of the Kolstad government, he officially assumed his post as Minister of Defense at 2:00 p.m. on Tuesday May 12.[2] On the following day he informed Nordic Folk-Rising's Central Committee that due to his status in the government, it was necessary for him to vacate his position on N.F.'s Executive Committee. The Central Committee thereupon selected Frederik Prytz as his successor.[3] No longer did the Folk-Rising serve as the pre-eminent means of carrying Quisling to political prominence. As a cabinet member, he had gained a solid position within an already well-established party. He no longer had to attempt to rise in politics by beginning from scratch.

Before examining how well he made use of this opportunity, one question remains to be covered. Why did Kolstad ask Quisling, someone who formally was not even a member of the Agrarian party, to join his cabinet? When Kolstad made this decision, there were a number of considerations weighing upon him which caused him to make this fateful choice, propelling a relatively unknown anti-Marxist agitator into the center of Norwegian political life.

The prospective Agrarian party government was not in a strong position when the new prime minister began to chart the course for his administration. It emanated from a party which had been in existence for only eleven years. When called on to provide government leadership, the Agrarian party held only about one-sixth of the seats in the *Storting*. Representing the interests of the rural farm population, it had very few seasoned politicians who were qualified to take over ministerial positions. As a result, only four of the nine members of the cabinet, including Kolstad himself, belonged to the Agrarian parliamentary delegation. The five other ministers, including Quisling, had a much looser association with the party.[4]

Qualified men were therefore hard to come by. When pondering his choice for Minister of Defense, Kolstad concluded that he needed to have someone with a military background. Several officers on active duty were considered, including Otto Ruge, who as commander-in-chief led the army against the German forces in 1940.[5] But Quisling appeared to be as well qualified professionally as the rival candidates. Although technically now a civilian, he was a major in the reserve and received an officer's pension. His past achievements were emphasized by his supporters, who made a point of mentioning their candidate's excellent military school record at every available opportunity. His adherents had another strong argument which they used on his behalf – the administrative experience he had gained while participating in Nansen's humanitarian projects. Furthermore, the fact that he had been associated with such an international figure as Nansen did nothing to lessen his stature in the eyes of Kolstad.[6]

There were political as well as professional considerations which also favored Quisling's appointment. He enjoyed considerable backing from the various radical conservative factions with whom which he had become affiliated. The speeches he had made for the Fatherland League now served to his advantage. Even more important were his ties with the Agrarian party, on whose behalf he had campaigned in 1930. One of his most influential champions within the party was Thorvald Aadahl of *Nationen*. Aadahl was a childhood friend of Prime Minister Kolstad, and served as one of his advisers at the time when Kolstad was in the process of deciding the make-up of his cabinet.[7] The patronage which Quisling received from Aadahl therefore proved to be of major importance for his appointment to the cabinet.

Additional support came from yet another newspaper editor, Rolf Thommessen of *Tidens Tegn*. Already on May 9, before the final decision had been made as to who would fill the post at the Defense Ministry, *Tidens Tegn* could tell its readers: "According to reliable information, Major Quisling has promised to enter the government as Minister of Defense." Thommessen worked to make this possibility a reality, as did another influential Independent Liberal, Johan Throne Holst. Both of these men were personally acquainted with Kolstad, and their influence was considerable.[8] And adding whatever assistance he could muster, Frederik Prytz was always active on behalf of Quisling's cause, working busily behind the scenes.[9]

Kolstad, however, did not make his selection solely because of political and administrative considerations. Although a pragmatic politician who had little in common with Quisling's penchant for unclear theorizing, Kolstad nevertheless shared the antipathy which most *borgerlige* felt toward the Labor party. Quisling's campaign against Labor and its alleged affinity with Soviet "Bolshevism" was therefore not inimical to the Prime Minister, who at the time he announced his decision was said to have declared that his appointee had "written such a good book about Russia".[10] Kolstad's favorable attitude toward Quisling may also have been formed, at least in part, by his earlier nomination to serve on Nordic Folk-Rising's Central Committee. Although Kolstad declined the honor, this incident does not seem to have prejudiced Quisling's later chances of becoming a member of the cabinet; on the contrary, his prospects were probably enhanced.[11]

It did not take the Prime Minister long to discover that he had made a highly controversial appointment. Quisling became the center of dispute, which lasted from the time it became known that he would enter the cabinet until the day the Agrarian government left office. As could be expected, the Labor party continually led the attack against the new minister. Already on the day before the Kolstad government took over, the leading Labor party newspaper, *Arbeiderbladet*, strongly voiced its distaste of Quisling, indicating the line of strategy which Labor intended to follow against someone whom it obviously regarded as a renegade because of his anti-socialist activity since his return from the Soviet Union. The paper called its readers' attention to the fact that Quisling had earlier, in the 1920s, been pro-Bolshevik and had tried to ingratiate himself with the Labor movement. But then, the paper maintained, he had opportunistically changed his political course, becoming an adherent of fascism. Referring to this political type as "loathsome" and "contemptuous", *Arbeiderbladet* warned ominously that a government which contained such a member could easily be defeated.[12]

In part the attacks against him were tactical, intended to make the Minister of Defense an embarrassment for the government. But the extreme bitterness of the charges indicated the intense hatred which Labor felt toward him. He was considered to be a turncoat opportunist, and his previous denunciations of the party, associating it with revolutionary communism, made the Laborites, quite correctly, identify him as one of their major foes.

His first days in the ministry were therefore not very pleasant. *Arbeiderbladet* repeated its charges in an editorial on May 13, adding the information that he had violated Russian laws while in the Soviet Union, referring indirectly to his black market money-changing activity. The editorial concluded righteously that: "It is nothing less than a scandal that a man who has publicly conducted himself as he has shall be called to the King's council table".

Quisling therefore had to respond to a number of embarrassing questions when he took part in his first parliamentary debate on May 19. Specifically, he was asked to explain his earlier enthusiasm for the Russian Revolution and for the Norwegian socialist movement, especially his alleged encouragement of the formation of Red Guards.[13] As indicated earlier, his reply was not totally convincing.[14] He tended to be somewhat evasive, but did reluctantly concede a certain degree of earlier association with and admiration for socialism: "I must admit that I at times held a different view about certain things than I do now."[15] But he maintained that his altered viewpoint had come about because of the changes which had occurred in the Soviet Union under Communist rule: "In contrast to many of the Norwegian labor leaders, I have become wiser and more experienced with the passage of time . . ."[16] Similarly, he denied charges of misconduct in the Soviet Union in connection with Prytz's black market financial manipulations, insisting that he had acted not for "personal gain", but merely "to protect legitimate Norwegian interests".[17]

While the issues raised by the Labor party were embarrassing, they did not seriously undermine his position. The animosity between *borgerlige* and socialist *Storting* representatives was so strong at this time that non-socialists simply did not take Labor party accusations seriously. To the *borgerlige*, Quisling was being attacked for political reasons. Reinforcing this feeling was the fact that the onslaught against him was simply part of a large number of charges brought against the new government by the Labor party, which presented a motion of no confidence already during the first parliamentary debate that the Kolstad cabinet took part in. Quisling therefore did not lack defenders among the *borgerlige*. Prime Minister Kolstad had strong words of praise for his Minister of Defense, citing the humanitarian work which he had conducted for Nansen.[18] A former Conservative prime minister, Ivar Lykke, who had led the government at the time Quisling had been employed by the Norwegian legation in Moscow, also came to his defense, declaring that it was the Russian authorities, rather than Quisling, who should be castigated for their financial manipulations in matters concerning Norwegian lumber interests.[19]

With such assistance, the Minister of Defense emerged from this first stormy *Storting* session without his position being seriously weakened, although even his defenders had to qualify their support somewhat, indicating that they felt there might be some elements of truth in the many charges brought against him.[20] What the debate showed was that the Labor party's hostility against Quisling had become stronger once he entered the government. He was obviously a much more dangerous opponent as a cabinet minister than he had been as a political agitator in the 1930 campaign. The battle between Quisling and Labor continued as long as he was active in politics. As a result, the enmity which he felt toward Labor became a constant element in his political perspective.

It did not take long for the battle to be resumed. As noted earlier, when Quisling joined the Agrarian party government, he agreed, apparently at the suggestion of Kolstad, to sever his ties with Nordic Folk-Rising. To have the Minister of Defense retain his leadership of such a group would have been too much of a political liability. Quisling later accused "the representative of the Jews, [Carl J.] Hambro", the parliamentary leader of the Conservatives, of having forced him to cease his official connection with Nordic Folk-Rising, so it is quite possible that pressure was brought to bear on him, through Kolstad, from *borgerlige* politicians. But Quisling's absence from direct involvement with Nordic Folk-Rising did not mean that a decision had been made to scrap the organization. On the contrary, the Central Committee expressed its determination to expand N.F.'s influence in accordance with its previously established guidelines. Prytz was given responsibility for deciding when N.F. would emerge publicly as a political organization.[21]

It did not prove feasible, however, to avoid associating Quisling's name with the Folk-Rising, nor to allow it to work surreptitiously to gather strength. The existence of the group could not be kept secret. Labor learned about his leadership of the Folk-Rising. On May 28 *Arbeiderbladet* published a front page article accusing the Minister of Defense of having created an organization which it described as exhibiting "a clear fascist tendency". The paper had obtained a copy of N.F.'s program, from which it quoted negatively what it considered to be incriminating material against Quisling. The latter, when contacted by *Arbeiderbladet*, emphasized that he had resigned from the Folk-Rising when he became a member of the government, but he was evasive on the question of whether he had been its leader, and he refused to divulge any information about its present membership.[22] This was merely grist for *Arbeiderbladet*'s mill. Charges against Quisling and the Folk-Rising continued in succeeding issues of the paper, and the group, much against what had originally been intended, was forced to emerge into public view. In order to counter the Labor party's attacks, it made full disclosure of its program to the press on June 5.[23]

This revelation did not especially benefit Quisling or the organization that he had founded. *Arbeiderbladet* immediately labelled the Folk-Rising as being "fascist", no longer content just to describe it as exhibiting fascist tendencies. Most of the *borgerlige* papers in Oslo maintained an embarrassed silence, with only Aadahl in *Nationen* speaking in defense of Quisling, and Aadahl was himself a member of the Folk-Rising. On the other hand, *Dagbladet*, the Liberal party's Oslo newspaper and an outspoken opponent of fascism in Norway and in Europe during the 1930s, did not mince words in its criticism. It described Nordic Folk-Rising's program as being "pure fascism", and declared it "most peculiar that the Agrarian party can choose the leader of such a movement as Minister of Defense". *Dagbladet* asserted Quisling was "completely lacking in balance" and therefore unfit to hold his cabinet position.[24] Such harsh words indicated that he no longer was opposed only by the Labor party and the Communists, but that serious reservations about his competence had cropped up within *borgerlige* parties, most prominently among the Liberals, but with the Conservatives as well.

These disclosures proved to be a most serious handicap for the dilettantish organization founded by Quisling and Prytz. The latter was so strongly affected by the controversy that he no longer wished to have full responsibility for N.F.'s leadership as its "temporary Executive Committee". He therefore requested on June 10 that two other members, Halvor Egeberg and Major Ragnvald Hvoslef, join him in forming a temporary administrative committee (*administrasjonsutvalg*) until a permanent Executive Committee was chosen. N.F.'s Central Committee unanimously gave its approval to this suggestion.[25] Under these altered conditions, an irresolute attempt was made to keep N.F. alive. It did not function, however, as a viable political organization, but merely as a discussion group that was unable to accomplish anything of significance. The political amateurs who made up the Central Committee were only able to produce position papers and abstract discussion.[26] Prytz sought as late as October 1931 to establish ties between Nordic Folk-Rising and other right-wing fringe groups, but nothing resulted from his initiative.[27] By joining the Kolstad government, Quisling escaped the direct onus of failure associated with N.F. This proved fortunate for him because it at best could never have become more than a small sect of true believers.

Quisling was not allowed any freedom from controversy in the period following the disclosures of his involvement in Nordic Folk-Rising. The next dispute concerning the Minister of Defense began only a short time afterwards. In late May and early June an extremely bitter labor dispute broke out at Menstad, located in the Skien district of Telemark, Quisling's native province. It highlighted the last of the major disturbances between labor and capital which accompanied the advance of the labor movement in Norway. The Menstad conflict was an exceptionally violent strike because of the anger generated among the workers by the use of strike-breakers, who carried out loading operations at the docks of Norway's largest industrial concern, Norsk Hydro. The strikers marched in angry protest parades despite a police prohibition against such demonstrations. The height of the unrest occurred on June 8, when a small force of constables became involved in a physical confrontation with the aroused laborers. The police, armed in Norwegian fashion with nothing more threatening than night sticks and firehoses, had no chance. Some fifty of them faced 2000 enraged workers. The fortunate were able to sprint to safety; those less fleet of foot were beaten. Three constables were hospitalized with serious injuries.[28]

The Kolstad government thereupon faced a threat to its authority. It reacted forcefully. Four naval vessels were sent to the area, a company of Royal Guards were dispatched from Oslo, and the unfortunate police constables were allowed to carry pistols and long truncheons.[29] This show of force alone was decisive in bringing an end to the disorder. The military did not have to be employed against the protesters.[30]

Because the armed forces were deployed in restoring order at Menstad, the general assumption by the public was that Quisling had been responsible for sending the military. Depending upon what side of the political fence a partisan observer was on, the Minister of Defense was characterized either as the protector of everything that was good and decent in society, or as the despicable oppressor of the working class.[31]

Neither reaction was deserved. If the general public had been able to peer behind the scenes to observe the government's decision-making, they would have been surprised to see that the controversial Minister of Defense had not made the slightest contribution to the resolve to send troops. During the government's discussion of this question, he behaved in a way that was characteristic of him in almost all of the cabinet meetings he attended – he remained silent. Only when the decision had been made did Quisling quietly leave the room to telephone the necessary orders to the Commander-in-Chief.[32]

While his role in the Menstad affair had been passive, he did not hesitate to take credit for the show of force by the government. To a great degree, the Labor party was responsible for making him appear so prominent. Its press, expressing solidarity with the workers, attacked him sharply as the man responsible for sending troops.[33] *Arbeiderbladet* characterized him as "the half-idiot whom we now have as Minister of Defense", a statement which provides insight into the polemical level of Norwegian journalism during the 1930s.[34] On the other hand, he was the man of the hour for the *borgerlige* who hated and feared the Labor party. To them, he represented a person of stature among *borgerlige* politicians who was finally willing to take stern measures against the apparent threat of revolutionary socialism. The myth of Quisling as the strong, resolute man of action came into being as a result of the Menstad affair.

This disturbance was only the most extreme manifestation of the national dispute between labor and capital during 1931. Beginning in March, a breakdown had occurred in wage negotiations between organized labor, led by LO, and management, organized in the Norwegian Employers' Association (NAF). The result was a combined lockout and general strike at most of the industrial concerns in the country, including Norsk Hydro, although service industries were not greatly affected.[35] Demonstrations occurred throughout the entire country, not just at Menstad. Frequently, striking workers forced their way into places of employment which were still in operation, threatening workers who were on the job, and sometimes compelling them to leave their work. The police in many instances responded in a very weak manner to demands for assistance from employers, which was understandable considering what had happened at Menstad.[36]

So although the Menstad disturbances had been quieted, the situation still appeared to be quite critical during the summer months of 1931. In particular, the atmosphere in Skien remained threatening, and the nervous chief of police in this district called constantly for military assistance to deal with planned demonstrations by the workers, who were angry at the jailing of some of their comrades who had participated in the Menstad hostilities. Seeing the success of the earlier decision to send military units, Quisling suggested at a cabinet meeting on July 7 that troops be mobilized. He was opposed by the Minister of Justice, Asbjørn Lindboe, whose department was in charge of the police. Lindboe followed a policy of using troops only under exceptional circumstances. As a result, Quisling's proposal was voted down by the cabinet.[37]

The strike continued to drag on throughout the summer, which was both long and hot for the striking workers, their union leaders, the government, and the employers. Reports continued to be received by the Ministry of Defense and the Ministry of Justice about the possibility of violence. At the end of August, the usually calm chief of police in Oslo, Kristian Welhaven, cautioned that if the strike were not ended soon, there was a very real chance of disturbances breaking out in the capital. Quite alarmed by this warning, the government met on August 29. It decided that the Prime Minister, the Minister of Justice, and the Minister of Defense were to have authority to make any disposition of the military deemed to be necessary. Following an agreement between the three ministers, a contingency plan was drawn up by the military to protect Oslo in case of outbreaks of violence.[38]

Still, the most explosive area appeared to be Skien, not Oslo, and on August 30 it was decided at a meeting of Kolstad, Lindboe, and Quisling that while troops would not be mobilized, the Menstad prisoners would be transferred as a means of perhaps lessening tension. However, on the very next day the Minister of Justice, Lindboe, was surprised to learn that military units had been mobilized at the military base of Gråtenmoen, just outside of Skien. Lindboe could only assume that the decision to take this rather drastic action had been arrived at by the Prime Minister and Quisling.[39]

It proved, however, that Quisling alone had given the actual order to gather troops at Gråtenmoen. In response later to questions from the press, he declared that he had acted on the request for assistance from the military authorities in the district, who feared that demonstrators might seize weapon arsenals. Whether or not Prime Minister Kolstad had given his approval to Quisling's action remains an unanswered question. Former Minister of Justice Lindboe maintained that Kolstad was quite unhappy with this turn of events.[40] The Labor party's press once more unloaded broadsides against Quisling, who was described as being the chief foe of the working class within the government.

Nothing more came of this event, however. There was no repetition of the Menstad affair. Instead, the strike eventually ran its course, and in September it finally came to an end. The last period of major labor unrest in Norway was over.

Controversial though he may have been, Quisling emerged from this dispute with his position strengthened. His prestige was bolstered by the reputation he had gained within anti-socialist opinion as the Minister of Defense who would brook no nonsense from potential revolutionaries.

Following the end of this period of labor controversy, he for once was left with nothing more to do than supervising the administration of his department. This he did efficiently and conscientiously. As Minister of Defense, he was a good administrator. This was not unexpected inasmuch as he had already demonstrated his ability under Nansen in the Ukraine and while serving with the Norwegian legation in Moscow.

Nevertheless, even the issue of his administrative competency did not remain forever free of controversy. In the emotion-laden atmosphere which existed at the end of World War II, one of the charges levied against him was that he had failed to secure the country's defenses adequately by not demanding larger military budgets during his tenure in the Defense Department. Such a charge lacked objectivity. It was impossible to maintain a strong defense force at a time when anti-militarism, pacifism, and world-wide depression made large defense budgets impossible. Furthermore, the Kolstad government followed a policy of restricting state expenditures, which affected all segments of governmental activity, not merely the Defense Ministry. It was Kolstad, serving also as Finance Minister, who had the final say in the allotment of funds for national defense.[41] The officers with whom Quisling worked were later generally in agreement that he did his best for the armed services, considering the difficult position he was in.[42]

During this period of deceptive calm when he was largely left alone with the concerns of his department, a personal tragedy was taking place which would have a significant bearing on his future in politics. Although Prime Minister Kolstad outwardly appeared to be in perfect health, in reality this was far from true. The heavy responsibility of being prime minister affected him physically. He suffered from migraine headaches, a weak throat, and sleeplessness. Furthermore, he tended to be depressed. As both Prime Minister and Minister of Finance, he was vastly overworked. He was not able to take a vacation during the summer of 1931. To make matters worse, the amount of funds available for governmental administration in Norway at this time was so limited that the Prime Minister, the head of government, did not even have the services of a personal secretary. Nor did he have the private resources to hire a secretary out of his own pocket.[43]

With this excessive workload and lack of free time, it was little wonder that his health deteriorated. By early 1932 the Prime Minister was seriously ill, and his anticipated recovery did not materialize as expected. He attended his last cabinet meeting on January 15, being hospitalized the same afternoon. Faced with this sad fact, it became necessary for the government to make adjustments. Foreign Minister Birger Braadland temporarily assumed the position of acting prime minister, with Church and Education Minister Nils Trædal assuming this post when Braadland was abroad representing Norway at the League of Nations.[44]

While the cabinet was in this leaderless state, a most controversial, unsolved, and possibly simulated criminal attack with political implications took place, which once more brought Quisling back into the spotlight. Foreign Minister Braadland, presiding at a meeting of the cabinet on February 4, 1932, made official a matter about which rumors were beginning to spread. The acting prime minister revealed that two days earlier a Norwegian minister had been assaulted physically for the first time in the nation's history. Quisling was the alleged victim. According to the official police report:

> When the Minister of Defense . . . came to his office in the Defense Department to fetch some documents on the afternoon of Tuesday, the 2nd of this month, at about 5 p.m., he was suddenly assaulted by one or several men when he was about to enter the innermost of the rooms, which lay in darkness. One of the men attempted to stab him in the chest with a knife – an attack that the Minister managed to deflect without serious consequences. However, he was almost simultaneously blinded with pepper and struck over the head so that he collapsed unconscious, and remained unconscious on the floor for some time . . .[45]

The report reflected Quisling's version of what had happened. If it were true, an occurrence of such a nature was bound to have the most serious repercussions. The assault on a cabinet minister, especially one holding the sensitive post of Minister of Defense, was of utmost gravity. Yet the entire incident – soon known as the "Pepper Affair" – proved to have a mysterious, half-shoddy and embarrassing air surrounding it. For the victim, after he supposedly regained consciousness, had acted in a most unusual manner. Instead of immediately sounding the alarm by summoning members of the Royal Guard who were on watch in the building, he left the office, walked downstairs and delivered his keys to the guard on duty, taking care to turn his face as he handed over the keys so that the guard would not notice the marks left from the attack. Once outside, he proceeded to walk to a taxi stand, and, obtaining a cab, travelled home. Not until after Mrs. Quisling, understandably alarmed by her husband's condition, had called Frederik Prytz to the house was the decision finally made to notify the police.[46] It is curious to note that not before Prytz arrived on the scene did anyone have the presence of mind to do the obvious. Either Quisling was unable to act because of the extent of his injuries, or he lacked the ability to decide what should be done in such a situation and left it up to the more forceful Prytz, or he did not wish to have the police involved for personal reasons.

On Wednesday, February 3, the day after the attack, Quisling was back in his office. During the rest of the week he continued to carry out his official duties in the Defense Department and attend cabinet meetings. Not until the end of the week, following office hours on Friday, was he examined by two specialists, both professors of medicine, who recommended that he needed to recuperate in bed for several days.[47]

The Pepper Affair became a *cause célèbre*. As expected because of the mysterious circumstances surrounding the assault, and because of Quisling's controversial character, public opinion divided over the issue on the basis of politics. Whereas the Conservative *Aftenposten* headlined the story as "Attempted Espionage in the Defense Department", *Arbeiderbladet* called it "A Cops-and-Robbers Film in the Defense Department".[48] Quisling's enemies in particular placed great stress on his failure to call attention to the attack immediately after he regained consciousness; and this was a factor that quite a few more neutral observers also found difficult to accept. Even his defenders, while they tried to interpret his inaction in the most positive manner, had difficulty in explaining why their man had behaved in such an unusual fashion.[49] Rumors flew that the affair had not involved espionage, or even politics, but that it resulted from a personal altercation. Such tales circulated widely throughout the corridors of the *Storting*.[50] In the hothouse political atmosphere of Oslo in the 1930s rumor-mongers had little difficulty in concocting various stories,[51] including one to the effect that Quisling allegedly had been having an affair with a woman employed in the Defense Ministry, and that the Pepper Affair was merely the act of vengeance by an injured husband.[52]

This gossip must be doubted because on no other occasion during Quisling's involvement in politics did any other charges of moral misconduct occur. That such stories immediately surfaced is, however, indicative of the antagonisms present in Norwegian politics at the time. Later the Labor party made a far more serious charge, alleging that the whole affair was a deliberate provocation on the part of Quisling; that he had simulated the attack in order to injure Labor.[53]

Once the matter became so emotional, all attempts to reach an unbiased conclusion were impossible. Quisling's detractors seized on the argument that none of the Royal Guards had heard anything unusual at the time of the alleged attack, and that no traces of the pepper supposedly thrown in Quisling's eyes had been found until *after* Prytz and Quisling had been back to the office.[54] Countering such doubts were the findings of the two doctors who examined Quisling on February 5. Both professors of medicine enjoyed a high reputation. Their conclusions indicated that the victim had sustained wounds on his right wrist and on his chest from a sharp instrument, apparently a knife; and that he had received two blows on the head. As a result of being struck, he had apparently suffered a concussion. The two professors furthermore maintained that someone of Quisling's introverted nature who had sustained a concussion could have acted in the manner which he did following the assault.[55] Holes in Quisling's clothing and blood marks from the wounds which were subjected to chemical analysis, added further credence to the fact that an attack had occurred.[56]

But although the findings of the doctors tended to lend support to Quisling's account, no complete and final explanation has ever been presented for the mysterious events in the Defense Ministry. The case was never solved despite the posting of a police reward of 5,000 *kroner*. It remained a mystery, and adding to the suspicion engendered by the case was Quisling's strange and awkward behavior during the police investigation. He refused to allow his wife and housekeeper to submit to police questioning; he was highly critical of police procedures, maintaining that they were conspiring against him politically; but his criticism of the police was weakened by his inability to provide them with any concrete leads.[57] Furthermore, he refused to respond via the courts to the Labor party's open assertion that he had simulated the entire affair as a provocation against the socialists.[58] The mistrust created in many minds by the Pepper Affair was never eliminated, and Quisling as a result was looked upon with increased skepticism not only by the Labor party but by a growing number of non-socialists, who felt that something must be wrong with the controversial Minister of Defense because of all of the dissension which he was arousing. The Pepper Affair therefore became a liability for him.

The dispute created by this incident proved to be the final sensational occurrence of the Kolstad ministry, for the condition of the ailing Prime Minister worsened steadily. He died on March 5, and the government had to seek new leadership. But under Kolstad's replacement the government's existence continued to be tempestuous, and again the Minister of Defense was prominently involved in most of its altercations.

Kolstad was succeeded by Jens Hundseid, the Agrarian party's chairman and parliamentary leader. The new Prime Minister had an entirely different personality from that of his predecessor. Whereas Kolstad had always been calm, careful, slow-moving and thoughtful, wielding his authority over the cabinet with a firmness that yielded respect, Hundseid in many ways was exactly the opposite. He was quick and emotional. His thought was sharp, his tongue caustic, and he was at times prone to take impulsive actions.

An example of Hundseid's defects was shown immediately after the change of prime minister. As the new head of government, he decided to reorganize the cabinet. Three of the ministers, he felt, had to go, including Quisling, who had created far too much sensation under Kolstad to make him palatable to the new Prime Minister. But the cabinet resisted this reorganizational effort, and with the exception of one of those slated to be removed,[59] the ministers Hundseid wanted to dismiss retained their posts. Because of his known antipathy toward the Labor party, and because of the solidarity of the cabinet holdovers against their new chief, Quisling's place in the government was too secure to topple. Hundseid had to give in and accept Quisling's continued membership in the cabinet. The latter, however, never forgave Hundseid for this attempted dismissal.[60]

Although Quisling's strong effort to remain in the cabinet at this time was correct, judged from the perspective of self-interest, the incident revealed a trait which he frequently reverted to. He on all occasions clung strongly to positions that he had gained, resisting strenuously attempts to remove him. He did so emotionally, refusing to look at the realities of the political situation, as a more pragmatic politician might have done. However, when he next sought to maintain himself in office, he was dealing not with the head of the Norwegian government, but with the German occupation authorities.

He did recognize in the spring of 1932 that it was necessary to defend himself against the Labor party's charges resulting from the Pepper Affair. Hundseid's attempt to remove the Minister of Defense was in part inspired by the government's embarrassment over the constant accusations being levied by Labor.[61] On April 5 one of their leaders in the *Storting*, Johan Nygaardsvold, later prime minister in 1935 and head of the government in exile during World War II, requested that Hundseid clear up the matter once and for all. Nygaardsvold asserted that throughout the country, even among members of the Agrarian party, it was generally agreed "that this whole affair was either a private brawl, or else the entire story was fictitious".[62] As for the reward of 5,000 *kroner*, he was bold enough to wager that it would never be collected.[63]

When Quisling rose in parliament to respond to Nygaardsvold's charges

on April 7, he was extremely angry. The content of his reply also indicated
the strategy he intended to follow against the Labor party. What he initiated
was nothing less than an all-out campaign against the socialists, intended to
discredit them completely and, if possible, destroy their political existence.
Upon taking the podium, the Minister of Defense immediately launched an
excited and savage attack.[64] He angrily accused both the Communists and the
Labor party of having received money from "the international revolutionary
leadership" to forment insurrectionary activity in Norway. The Menstad affair, he insisted, had been just one instance of this type of conspiracy. He
maintained that it was not merely a local incident, but that the Communists
had created "a planned insurrection which was to become a rebellion
throughout the entire country".[65] Although he did not go so far in attacking
the Labor party, he argued that it was capable of starting a chain of events
which would lead to revolution. It had not repudiated its revolutionary program of 1930, and it was establishing uniformed organizations that were assuming a para-military posture.[66]

In the conclusion of the speech, he used a tactic employed by fascists elsewhere in Europe – to try to separate the workers from their leaders. He maintained that the problems facing society during a time of economic crisis had to
be solved by cooperation. Introducing what was later to be one of National
Union's familiar slogans, he declared: "Common interest must be placed before self-interest", which meant that "party politics and labor conflicts must
be brought to an end".[67] Here, in an indirect reference, was his call for a corporate state which would end party disputes and labor strife.

His listeners did not pay any attention to his vague ideological utterances.
What interested them were his sensational charges, which caused an uproar in
parliament. The Communists were not represented, but the Labor party,
understandably enough, was highly incensed. On the other hand, the supporters of the Hundseid government were surprised and embarrassed, not
knowing how to respond to Quisling's unexpected statements. They were not
prepared for such serious accusations because, in essence, a member of the cabinet was charging the Communists and Labor with treason. To support such
a contention, Quisling made repeated reference to a pile of documents which
he had with him, alleging these papers contained evidence to substantiate his
accusations. When the speech was over, the Labor representatives, led by
Nygaardsvold, excitedly insisted that these documents should immediately be
submitted to the *Storting*.[68] Making the affair even more difficult for the
Hundseid government was the fact that the leaders of the Liberals and Conservatives, ex-prime minister Johan Ludwig Mowinckel and Carl J. Hambro,
supported the demand that the *Storting* should have access to the allegedly incriminating documents.[69]

The sharp reactions placed Prime Minister Hundseid in a difficult dilemma. He had known that Quisling was going to defend himself in a strong
fashion against the Labor party's accusations, and the Prime Minister had

been disturbed by the potential danger posed by the pending confrontation. This is shown by the fact that the devious Hundseid was carrying *two* written lines of argument in his pocket at the time of the debate, one supporting his Minister of Defense, the other repudiating him.[70] Hundseid undoubtedly was also aware that Quisling intended to use certain classified documents in his defense. However, while the Prime Minister recognized the explosive nature of Quisling's speech, the matter had not been discussed by the government. On April 5, just prior to the start of the parliamentary session, Quisling had asked the cabinet's approval for the use of the documents which he had assembled in his defense. Since there was not time for the ministers to go through the documents, with only a few minutes remaining before the *Storting* bells rang the body into session, he did not receive the government's approval. On the other hand, no one had denied him the right to use the documents to defend himself, but the cabinet was not aware that he intended to bring up such serious charges against the Labor party and the Communists.[71]

When Hundseid faced the *Storting* to respond to the uproar, he awkwardly tried to mollify the protestors. Mowinckel in particular was disturbed by the charges, and Hundseid needed Liberal backing for the continued existence of his government, which of course was his primary responsibility. However, he could not immediately deny the validity of Quisling's accusations and thereby publicly rebuke one of his own ministers. But he was not willing to stand fully behind the charges. Instead, he went so far as to agree to the demand that the alleged incriminating documents be submitted to the *Storting*. The Prime Minister furthermore accorded his Minister of Defense only qualified support, clumsily attempting to distance himself from the views expressed by the angry Quisling:

> I do not wish to disassociate myself in any substantial degree from Minister Quisling's strong words about various conditions in our land. I do not really disassociate myself, but I will say that I feel Minister Quisling used rather strong language. But Minister Quisling should be forgiven for having been tempted to use strong language, perhaps too strong language, after the violent – and I mean violent – persecution and the great stress he has been subjected to as of late.[72]

These words were regarded as a personal affront by Quisling, who would insist that he had been stabbed in the back by his own chief.[73] He later went so far as to maintain that Hundseid, immediately after the dramatic speech of April 7, actually sought to oust him from office, and was only prevented from doing so by the pressure exerted from certain unnamed influential members of the Agrarian party.[74] This assertion may at least in part have been true, although it was denied by Minister of Justice Asbjørn Lindboe, in front of whom the dismissal attempt was supposed to have taken place.[75] One thing is certain with regard to this controversy: Quisling was in a very weak position following his speech, owing to the hostile reaction it provoked. Rumors spread that he would soon be forced to resign, and his sympathizers such as *Tidens Tegn* were plainly worried about such a possibility.[76]

This incident revealed his rather personal and unrealistic approach to politics. He believed that by launching a sudden attack against the Labor party he would be able to strike a damaging blow at his enemies. The reaction of the politicians was exactly the opposite. The speech created an atmosphere in the *Storting* which was antagonistic, causing Hundseid to repudiate partially his own minister. Quisling had not recognized the consequences of his act, and contrary to his claims, he had not made his plans fully known to the government. By his tendency to take direct action without consulting others, he showed a lack of ability and experience as a politician. While denying that he had acted precipitously, he later in the same year indirectly admitted that he had gone off on his own in this matter. Issuing an attack on Hundseid on November 20, he declared that even if a minister had not consulted with the head of the government before committing a certain action,

> nevertheless a chief ought also in politics to value and support a subordinate's initiative in the work for the common declared goal, especially when it is in complete agreement with the party's program and goals [sic], and not to leave him in the lurch at the decisive moment. Even [an] incorrect course of action is better than inactivity and negligence.[77]

The *borgerlige* politicians on whom the Hundseid government was dependent did not agree with such thinking. Their prime concern was to get this embarrassment out of the way as quickly as possible. As a result, the degree of revenge gained by Quisling against his enemies on the left was not very extensive. The following sequence of events resulted from his disclosures. First, the *Storting* received from the Department of Defense, on instruction from Hundseid, the documents upon which Quisling based his incriminating charges. Next, a special parliamentary committee was set up to investigate the entire matter, which quite properly was named "the Quisling Affair". The committee, as could be expected from the composition of the *Storting*, contained a majority of non-socialists, the ratio of *borgerlige* to Labor members being three to one.[78]

After the committee began its deliberations, it turned out that the charges which Quisling had attempted to put to rest by going on the offensive refused to be silenced. Instead, for political reasons, seeking to destroy the credibility of the Minister of Defense and thereby also effectively scuttling the accusations which he had made in the *Storting*, the Labor party renewed its campaign against him in the strongest manner possible. Two prominent former Communists who had rejoined the party, Olav Scheflo and Jacob Friis, wrote letters to the special committee, as did also Martin Tranmæl, editor of *Arbeiderbladet*.[79] Scheflo's letter was dated June 9, while Friis' and Tranmæl's were posted the following day. The two ex-Communists maintained that

Quisling had offered to re-enter the General Staff as a spy for the Communist cause, while Tranmæl repeated the charge that Quisling had indicated his willingness to form Red Guards for the Labor party.[80] This was a serious matter. Quisling was no longer being accused, in more or less general terms, of alleged misconduct in editorial columns and in *Storting* speeches. Instead, three of the country's most prominent left-wing political figures had in writing publicly presented charges to a special investigatory committee of parliament. Even Quisling's backers such as *Tidens Tegn* were seriously disturbed by this development. The paper continued its pro-Quisling view, asserting that he would be able to give an effective rebuttal. But if he were not able to do so, even this bastion of support declared that he then "must immediately resign from the position of Minister of Defense".[81]

In response, Quisling made his usual extensive reply, maintaining that his detractors wanted to divert attention away from their own alleged misdeeds, and that their accusations were simply part of their campaign of villification against him. Replying to specific charges, he treated evasively the question of whether he had offered to organize Red Guards, while denying directly that he had considered spying on the General Staff.[82]

Faced with such conflicting evidence, the *borgerlige* majority on the committee found itself in a rather difficult position when deciding what conclusion it should reach concerning Quisling's accusations. The non-socialist parties supporting the Hundseid government were hesitant to repudiate the contentions of one of the government's ministers. At the same time, they felt that it would be politically unwise to go to extremes and sustain Quisling without reservation when the Labor party definitely was giving every indication of abandoning its revolutionary ideology and becoming instead a parliamentary reform party. The committee majority therefore only gave tentative backing to Quisling's accusations. It agreed that the Labor party and the Communists had received funds from the Soviet Union; that the Communists were revolutionary because of their association with the Comintern, as was the Labor party because it had not formally disavowed its revolutionary program of 1930; and that the tactics displayed at Menstad by certain demonstrators were quite in line with the Comintern's strategy of revolution, although the committee majority hastened to add it could not ascertain to what degree the Comintern was associated with the Menstad disturbances. But on the basis of these findings, the *borgerlige* committee members, partly because the charges could not be substantiated and partly for political expediency, declared there was no need to prosecute individual Labor party and Communist leaders against whom Quisling had made his charges. Nor did the committee majority make any recommendations in favor of having its findings followed up with legal proceedings: "After what has been noted by the Attorney General, the committee's majority recommends that the *Storting* should not express any desire for judicial hearings."[83] As for the Labor party's minority on the committee, it completely dismissed the charges, branding them as lies, and demanded an investigation into the activities of the Minister of Defense and his department.[84]

By advising that no further action be taken, the *borgerlige* politicians, although outwardly providing Quisling with some endorsement, were merely seeking to eliminate this bothersome incident as quickly and painlessly as possible.[85] This was exactly what happened in the *Storting* when the committee submitted its findings on June 30, 1932. The minority report was quickly voted down, with only the Labor party supporting it. In the following debate it was made clear that approval of the majority report simply meant shelving the whole affair, and nothing further would result from it. Once the Labor representatives saw this would be as far as the matter would go, they dropped all opposition to the committee's findings.[86] The majority report was then passed unanimously to the satisfaction of all concerned, following which it was possible to "proceed on to the agenda for the day".[87]

This apparent victory was therefore a reverse for Quisling. His speech had weakened his position in the government, and the committee's findings, adopted by the *Storting*, had not damaged the Labor party at all. At the most, his sensational charges may have increased the anti-Labor feelings of the party's more dogmatic ideological opponents, who already were extremely negative in their attitude toward the socialists. Quisling and his followers would later expediently maintain that the *Storting* had agreed with his accusations. In reality, however, parliament had dismissed the attack: "It could never occur to parliamentarians to draw wide-ranging conclusions from their apparent agreement with him – they had never intended to admit he was right, they had merely found a formula which prevented a political crisis in the matter . . ."[88]

The *Storting* also chose to follow the committee's recommendation that no action be taken regarding the Labor party's accusations against Quisling, since they lay outside of the committee's mandate. The committee's report very carefully avoided this touchy question.[89] In the parliamentary debate on the report, Mowinckel, in his capacity as head of the Liberals, wished to see a legal investigation into the questions raised concerning Quisling's past conduct.[90] But Mowinckel's proposal was effectively opposed by the Prime Minister, who gave careful backing to Quisling.[91] Hundseid had arrived at the conclusion that politically it would have been unwise for him to repudiate his minister when the special committee had arrived at the tactical conclusion that at least some of Quisling's charges were valid. The latter therefore emerged from this critical affair still as Minister of Defense.

He, however, tended to regard the outcome of the affair as a vindication. He declared himself to be content with the committee's majority report. In the parliamentary debate, he repeated his charges, declaring that "not only the Communist party, but also the Labor party aim to paralyze our defense entirely in order to make us defenseless in the critical moment".[92] He quite clearly had no intention of abandoning his campaign against the Labor party

Vidkun on his mother Anna's lap.
Photograph: University of Oslo Library.

Vidkun Abraham Lauritz Jonssøn Qvisling.
Photograph: University of Oslo Library.

Jon Laurits and Anna Qvisling with their children Vidkun (at the back), Esther and Jørgen. Photograph: National Archives of Norway.

The family farm, Lunden in Fyresdal, purchased by Vidkun's grandfather, Abraham Qvisling, in 1843. Photograph: University of Oslo Library.

Quisling (third from the left) and his classmates at the Norwegian Military Academy. Photograph: University of Oslo Library.

Vidkun (on the left) with his parents and brothers, Jørgen (at the back) and Arne (on the right). Photograph: National Archives of Norway.

Quisling relaxing with Maria (on the left) and his sister-in-law Ingerid. Photograph: National Archives of Norway.

Maria (on the left) and Alexandra, Quisling's two wives, on Jørgen Quisling's balcony in Oslo. Photograph: University of Oslo Library.

Vidkun as a young man.
Photograph: University of Oslo Library.

Maria Quisling.
Photograph: National Archives of Norway.

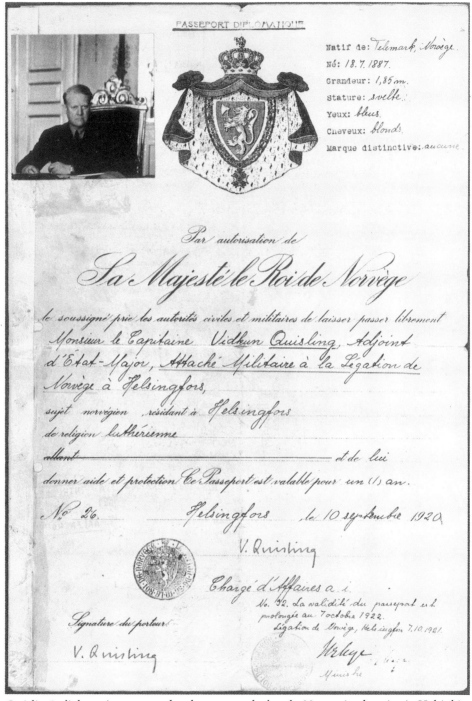

Quisling's diplomatic passport when he was attached to the Norwegian legation in Helsinki. Photograph: National Archives of Norway.

In Russia with Fridtjof Nansen. Quisling on the left, Nansen third from the right. Photograph: National Archives of Norway.

The Armenian Commission of the League of Nations at work. Quisling is standing in the background. Photograph: University of Oslo Library.

Peder Kolstad.
Photograph: University of Oslo Library.

Frederik Prytz.
Photograph: Norwegian News Agency.

Hundseid's government. Back row from the left: Jakob Vik, Minister of Social Affairs, Jon Sundby, Minister of Finance, Ivar Kirkeby-Garstad, Minister of Trade, Asbjørn Lindboe, Minister of Justice. Front row from the left: Vidkun Quisling, Minister of Defence, Birger Braadland, Minister of Foreign Affairs, Jens Hundseid, Prime Minister and Minister of Agriculture, Nils Trædal, Minister of Church, Rasmus Langeland, Minister of Labour.
Photograph: Arbeiderbladet (newspaper).

and the Communists. He continued to press on, believing that he had seized on an issue that would increase his political standing. His speech in parliament on June 30 was therefore not limited to the matter at hand, the Quisling Affair, but was equally a political pronouncement. His words indicated the extent to which he received inspiration from events taking place elsewhere in Europe, in particular in Germany. At the time Hitler's movement was attaining successes which Quisling still only talked about: "Quisling declared that he was not against the workers, only their revolutionary leaders. What he wished to see come into being was a national labor movement, a movement through which labor and capital could be reconciled".[93]

Following the adjournment of parliament, he received personal inspiration to continue on his course during a series of public speeches which he gave in the summer of 1932. Attendance at his presentations was good. The sensational incidents which he had been involved in and the sharp attacks against him by the Labor party had given him a certain notoriety, and people flocked to listen to this controversial minister. His reception was especially enthusiastic in his native Telemark. He also received a positive response elsewhere in eastern Norway, in the farming districts of Trøndelag, and along the west coast district of Møre.[94] Everywhere there were friendly faces to be seen and applause to be garnered. In July he spoke at a meeting of the Fatherland League in southern Norway: "The slandered, abused, and persecuted Minister of Defense spoke, tall and fair like his own race", to cite the words of the League's newspaper.[95] Such a warm reception, when contrasted with the difficult experiences he had just undergone in the *Storting*, persuaded him that his campaign had struck a much more popular vein of goodwill among the people than among the politicians. He was therefore determined to proceed with his strategy of attempting to compromise his enemies on the left.

Stimulated by the events of the summer, when the time came to resume political activity in Oslo during the fall, he seized the opportunity he had been waiting for to launch a new attack against the Labor party. The Minister of Defense utilized the extreme statements made by an officer on active duty within the armed forces over which he exercised administrative control.

As in other western European countries, pacifism was a fairly significant sentiment in Norway during the inter-war period, created by the disillusioned reaction to the slaughter and waste of World War I. The socialists especially favored disarmament, while the *borgerlige* parties more or less were opposed to such a step. Quisling, as Minister of Defense, represented those who attempted to hold the line in preventing drastic cutbacks in the military budget. A strong response could therefore be expected by those who favored maintaining a military posture in Norway when they learned that a naval captain had participated in an anti-war congress held in Amsterdam. Not only had this officer, Captain Olaf Kullman, been present at this pacifist gathering; he had also addressed it, using language that was little pleasing to Norway's current Minister of Defense: "The war has already begun. Even in the small country I come from, an officer who is also a member of the government has inaugurated the campaign of agitation against the Soviet Union."[96] Additional statements made by Kullmann only worsened his difficulties. He believed sincerely but naively that the Soviet Union, which was using the disarmament theme for its own purposes, was the best guarantor of world peace. If the imperialists, said Kullmann, dared to refuse to accept the Russian offer of inaugurating international disarmament, military officers in all of Europe should be prepared to take appropriate action. "Should the criminals dare to start the war, the officers must strike."[97]

Such avowals did not endear the Captain to his military superiors. He was interrogated by them upon his return to Norway, and he repeated his views in even stronger terms. In a public lecture, he went so far as to declare that in the event that Norway took part in a war, he would not hesitate to use weapons against the Norwegian state. Having thereby completely compromised his position, naval authorities were not at all reluctant to relieve him of his command as head of the torpedo battery at Oscarsborg, the fortress guarding the approaches to Oslo harbor.[98] Unknown to all concerned at the time, this very torpedo battery would later perform an act of the utmost importance in Norway's defense against the German invasion in 1940.[99]

With Kullmann's removal, the matter became political. The Labor party, as the champion of anti-war sentiment, did not hesitate to step forward as Kullman's protector. Labor made this issue its own, as the words of Martin Tranmæl demonstrated, spoken at a giant rally on behalf of Kullmann in Oslo on September 30:

> . . . the battle against war is no isolated battle. If we want to strike down war, then we must strike down capitalism and build up a new society based on physical and spiritual labor.
>
> We have a political party which has promoted its demands, which has submitted positive proposals. But we must do more. We must mobilize the working class to take direct action against war. Our strongest weapon is the general strike, first and foremost against the transportation and munitions industries. And when it becomes necessary, it must be supplemented with the military strike.[100]

Observing with great interest the controversy surrounding Kullmann, Quisling quickly drew the conclusion that here was the opportunity for him to continue the campaign begun in his *Storting* speech of April 7. Through Kullmann he could strike directly at the Labor party. If he succeeded in his objective, Labor would be eliminated from the political scene.[101]

The manner in which Quisling launched his move against Kullmann and the Labor party again demonstrated how he often acted when attempting to carry out a political strategy. He sat down and drew up a detailed scheme by himself. Then, without taking any steps to ensure support, he emerged with an extremely controversial proposal. His plan of action in this instance was a 20-page memorandum, drawn up on behalf of the Defense Department, which he submitted to the Justice Department on October 14. It starkly declared that Captain Kullmann should be brought to trial because of his treasonous activity.[102]

Although Quisling was within his area of competence when he used military security arguments to sustain his view that Kullmann should be prosecuted, nevertheless, it was the responsibility of the Justice Department's legal experts to draw up the charges. Quisling insisted, however, that Kullmann be prosecuted as severely as possible on the basis that ". . . the case under consideration is a question of organized treason and preparation for betrayal in time of war".[103] Furthermore, he took the openly political step of broadening the charge of treason to include the leaders of the Labor party. Quisling instructed the Justice Department specifically to indict Tranmæl, as editor of *Arbeiderbladet*, and also "other implicated persons" as soon as possible.[104]

Minister of Justice Lindboe, upon receiving Quisling's missive, was quite astonished. He decided, after recovering, that the only thing to do was to air the matter at a cabinet meeting. However, he reckoned without Quisling, who had no intention of seeing his initiative toned down and perhaps altered entirely. The Minister of Defense therefore employed a tactic that he often resorted to in the future as well: he revealed the contents of his memorandum to the Norwegian News Agency, *Norsk Telegrambyrå*, which in turn made it public knowledge through the press.[105]

The *fait accompli* once more placed the Prime Minister in a most awkward position. When asked by the press about Quisling's move, Hundseid's only response was to say he could not comment on the matter since he had not seen the memorandum.[106] He was far from happy with the predicament that Quisling had created, and it later influenced him to seek once more to get rid of his controversial Minister of Defense.

The latter certainly succeeded in becoming the focus of attention at this time. As previously, the Labor party attacked him vehemently, while the *borgerlige* press agreed that action should be taken against Captain Kullmann and fulminated against the possibility of civil war, and possible treason in time of war. However, not all *borgerlige* newspapers were willing to give Quisling unqualified backing. Among the *borgerlige* there was some reservation about his methods and about his demands that Tranmæl and other Labor leaders be prosecuted. *Aftenposten*, the country's largest newspaper and a chief spokesman for the Conservatives, had serious doubts about Quisling's attempt to involve Labor leaders in the Kullmann Affair by charging them with treasonable activity. In particular, concern was expressed that this could be in violation of freedom of speech. Such arguments irritated Quisling greatly. He took the unusual step of writing an open letter to the paper's political editor, Johannes Nesse. In this letter he forcefully employed the same Red Scare arguments that he had used before, showing conclusively that he hoped the fear of revolution might redound to his advantage:

> A refined system of propaganda and agitation is spreading like a net over the entire country, and a widespread organizational apparatus – all those organizations, groups and individuals who are under the revolutionary labor leadership's influence – is unceasingly in action in order to undermine our present society and prepare the realization of the Communist overthrow.[107]

Kullmann's outspokenness, said Quisling, was a key part of such activity. Revolutionary tacticians, he maintained, were fully conscious that the destruction of the country's military defense was a necessity and a key step for the "armed uprising and seizure of power which they have planned". He alleged such preparation was being carried out by word and by deed, with the support of a foreign power, which, although not mentioned by name, was clearly the Soviet Union. "After this one ought not to come and talk about violation of the right to free speech and about freedom from punishment for traitors who do not cease to conspire and to violate the laws".[108]

His strong assertions did not go unanswered. Editor Nesse, in reply, pointed out one obvious fact: if Quisling's demands were carried out and all persons who wished to alter society and who opposed the use of military force were prosecuted for treason, it would be necessary to arrest "a large number of leading politicians and agitators plus all editors in the country's Labor newspapers".[109] Such men would simply become martyrs for their cause, argued Nesse. An action of this kind would also definitely be an infringement of the right to freedom of speech. He dismissed the possibility of forceful steps against the Labor party unless there was strong support for such a move among all sections of society. Although he expressed himself cautiously, *Aftenposten*'s political editor thereby showed that he considered Quisling's proposal to be completely unattainable.

There were influential persons, however, who did not agree with Nesse's assessment. Factions within both the Agrarian party and the Independent Liberals supported Quisling's campaign against the left. In addition, certain fringe groups on the right-wing edge of conservative *borgerlig* opinion, whose fear of and frustration with the socialists caused them to favor radical measures, also rallied to his side at this time. As a result, a definite trend occurred within part of *borgerlig* opinion to consolidate behind the Minister of Defense in the fall of 1932. Those who joined in backing Quisling were first and foremost concerned with the apparent threat that the Labor party and the labor movement offered to their particular interests and ideologies. Also, while their individual solutions to the problems facing society during economic depression might differ, they tended to agree that the *Storting* was not able to accomplish anything. They therefore favored limiting the legislature's power in national affairs, while the independent authority of the government was to be strengthened. Some were even in favor of eliminating the *Storting* completely.

Such ideas were exchanged at a series of gatherings held in October 1932 at the time the Kullmann Affair was at its height. Quisling naturally was the center of attention. It was Johan Throne Holst, however, who served as the primary instigator for arranging the meetings, thereby once again involving his Our Country group behind Quisling.[110] A number of these events were held, the so-called "gentlemen's dinners" of the fall of 1932. The most important took place on the evening of October 26 at the residence of Carl Løvenskiold.[111] Present were a large number of leading men who belonged to various organizations on the right wing of Norwegian politics. Some were politically significant, while others led fringe groups who wished to improve their position. Among those who did have considerable influence were Throne Holst; Editor Aadahl of *Nationen*; Lehmkuhl of the Fatherland League; Jens K. M. Bratlie, a former Conservative prime minister; and Olav Østby Deglum, the acting foreman of the Agrarian party and leader of its *Storting* delegation now that Hundseid was prime minister. Persons of lesser significance, representing fringe groups, were Major Hvoslef, the head of the Community Defense; his colleague, Colonel C. Fougner, leader of the Community Aid; Dean H. J. Aanstad, chief of a small militant anti-Socialist labor group called the Independent Workers (*De Frie Arbeidere*); and David Seierstad, the chairman of the Rural Crisis Aid (*Bygdefolkets Krisehjelp*), an organization of small farmers which sometimes violently protested against the frequent foreclosures of farms during the depression. Also present and playing a prominent part were two lawyers who were closely associated with Quisling, Johan B. Hjort and Christopher Borchgrevink.[112] Hjort later became Quisling's second in command when National Union was formed.

Under the best of circumstances, such a diverse group would have difficulty in arriving at any concrete agreement. Nevertheless, the general tendency at the meeting was to declare support for Quisling's crusade against the socialists and to condemn the alleged failure of parliamentary government. There was some mention in the numerous speeches that were made of the possibility of carrying out a coup against the *Storting*. The Agrarian government would, according to this scheme, refuse to resign should a vote of no confidence be passed against it. However, this was merely talk, and not everyone agreed.[113] But there was unanimity in the approval uttered for Quisling, with the Minister of Defense being lauded in all of the speeches that were held. Østby Deglum was particularly enthusiastic in his statements, declaring "Norway's farmers unite around Quisling".[114]

Although nothing more than speech-making emerged from this gathering, the discussions indicated that prominent men in politics and business were at least contemplating carrying out some kind of a coup against the parliamentary system of government, and that Quisling appeared to be the figure around whom they might rally. Rumors of such a possibility were already being discussed within political circles in Oslo.[115] Similar speculation circulated concerning the feasibility of creating a new political constellation around Quisling, either within the Agrarian party or else in the form of a brand new party. *Tidens Tegn* broached this question in an editorial on December 2, declaring that while *borgerlige* politicians might concentrate on trying to solve social questions, they were far too equivocal when it came to maintaining law and order against the revolutionary movement. On the other hand, said Rolf Thommessen's paper, echoing arguments used by Throne Holst, the showdown with the revolutionary movement could not be carried out unless social reforms were made at the same time. *Tidens Tegn* insisted that only a new party could carry out both of these goals. There were tens of thousands of voters, maintained the editorial, who were looking for something new: "One of the greatest tasks in Norwegian politics today must be to gather those who are scattered in different parties and groups, but who in reality are in agreement". Minister Quisling, continued Thommessen's mouthpiece, has contributed to just such a development, and this trend would grow as he had a chance to reveal his "positive social attitude". The outcome of this trend, maintained *Tidens Tegn*, would be the formation of a new "middle party", which would be large enough in size to exert influence.[116]

The newspaper in this instance gave evidence of its editor's frustration with being spokesman for the insignificant Independent Liberal party. The atmosphere therefore appeared to be ripe for a push by Quisling. There existed unquestionably in the fall of 1932 a body of opinion in favor of creating some sort of political movement around Quisling, a feeling voiced not merely by *Tidens Tegn*. But unable to carry out concrete new changes by himself, he failed to make any overt move to exploit the situation. He remained at his post in the Ministry of Defense, continuing to launch polemics against Captain Kullmann and the Labor party. But the backing he received as a result of this activity caused politicians to reflect and to speculate.

The nervous and temperamental Prime Minister was among those who were doing a great deal of anxious reflection. Hundseid was, as will be seen, in a very weak political position at this time, and his feeling of insecurity did not lessen when he learned that the acting leader of his party in the *Storting*, Østby Deglum, had been one of Quisling's most outspoken admirers at the October 26 meeting. When informed about what had happened at this gathering, Hundseid's agitated nerves could no longer stand the strain. In a highly distraught state, he threatened to go to the King and submit his resignation. Calmer members of the cabinet prevailed, and as so often, his threat remained but empty talk.[117] But this incident revealed how he feared his Minister of Defense might be preparing a move to oust him. As a result, the Prime Minister obviously was on the lookout for an opportunity to prevent such a possibility by eliminating Quisling from the government.

An apparent justification for Hundseid to accomplish this occurred as the result of a speech that Quisling presented only two days after the famous Wednesday meeting of October 26. On Friday, Quisling addressed a joint gathering of the University of Oslo's Conservative Student Association and the Fatherland League's Student Group. But the speech had repercussions far beyond the limits of the University. There was strong interest in political circles about what the Minister of Defense might have to say to impressionable students, and while the meeting was only open to the members of the two sponsoring associations, outsiders took steps to gain knowledge about the contents of his talk.

The Conservative party in particular was anxious to obtain such information. Its leadership had become quite concerned about Quisling's activity. While some rank and file members might approve of him, the party leaders had never favored his methods, especially those exhibited in the Kullmann case. *Aftenposten*'s careful disassociation from Quisling's call for the prosecution of top members of the Labor party was a reflection of official thinking within the party, shown soon afterwards when the Conservative Central Committee voted unanimously to support editor Nesse's position.[118] In addition to disliking Quisling's politics, even more disturbing for the Conservatives was the possibility that there might be some substance in the rumors about him being the focal point for the creation of a new political party. Such a party, were it to come into being, would draw votes away from the Conservatives, a process they understandably wished to prevent at all costs.

The party leadership therefore made a point of having their representatives present when the Minister of Defense spoke to the students. They took no less than two sets of notes. Unfortunately, these have since been lost, but there is no question as to how the Conservatives chose to interpret the speech. They declared it to have been full of "fascistic" statements, and they immediately brought this to Hundseid's attention.[119] The antagonism which the Conservative leadership by now felt for Quisling came to a head at a central executive meeting on November 5, where the committee, in addition to endorsing editor Nesse's view of the Kullmann Affair, also unanimously agreed that Quisling ought to be removed from the government.[120]

Hundseid responded quickly. Quisling was called up on the carpet and asked to explain just what he had said, both at the Wednesday "gentlemen's dinner" and in his speech to the students. Quisling naturally protested against the accusations, declaring that statements attributed to him from the Wednesday meeting and in his speech were distortions of what had really been said.[121] Hundseid was scarcely mollified by these protestations; indeed, he did not wish to be mollified. He held consultations about ousting the Minister of Defense with other members of the cabinet, and while no decision was reached, Quisling's fate seemed to hang in balance in early November.[122]

The forces for and against the Minister of Defense thereupon indulged in a heated press debate. As could be expected, the pro-Quisling faction found the most outspoken support for their man in the pages of *Nationen*, where editor Aadahl continued to provide unstinting aid.[123] But Quisling's tactics in the Kullman affair, his penchant for acting on his own without consulting fellow cabinet members, and his violent language had seriously disturbed many less partisan members of *borgerlige* parties. The Liberal *Dagbladet* certainly gave utterance to feelings shared by many Conservatives as well as Liberals, although Conservatives might be less willing to state such viewpoints so openly and strongly. The paper portrayed Quisling in a far from flattering manner, pointing out that his "desire to play dictator" made him a danger for the country and for the Agrarian party.[124]

Not unexpectedly, *Arbeiderbladet*'s reaction to *Nationen*'s defense of Quisling was even sharper. The Labor daily accused him of acting in a completely undemocratic manner, carrying out the advice of his circle of friends who had no connection with the government. It declared its sympathy for Hundseid in wanting to get rid of such a troublemaker, but predicted that "Quisling's friends" would make this difficult, in particular since *Nationen* had begun to whip up support for the Minister of Defense.[125]

This description of Hundseid's dilemma was correct, despite Labor's basic animosity toward the government. The Prime Minister desperately wished to eject Quisling from the cabinet, but to oust him was not an easy task. His position with a segment of the Agrarian party, the faction represented by Aadahl, was quite strong. There existed a shared perception that the Agrarian party might split at this time if Quisling were expelled from the government. Wilhelm Dietrichson, the general secretary of the Farmers' Association (*Norges Bondelag*) and a powerful figure within the Agrarian party, feared just such a development.[126]

Persons outside the Agrarian party among the more conservative *borgerlige* also rallied to Quisling's cause at this time. For them he was the farsighted statesman who alone among politicians realized the alleged danger Norway was in, facing the threat of revolutionary disorder. He was hailed as the resolute man who could save the country from such an insurrection. He had been responsible, it was mistakenly believed, for sending troops to put down the disorders at Menstad. He had revealed the machinations of the Labor party by his charges in the *Storting* and now in the Kullmann case. Although more moderate *borgerlige*, such as editor Nesse, may have deplored his methods in the episode concerning Kullmann, there were many others who did not because of their fear of and hostility toward the Labor party. For such persons, the steady barrage of criticism levelled against him in the socialist press merely served as evidence that he was right, thereby increasing their feeling of solidarity with him. From many sources, therefore, both inside and outside the Agrarian party, came warnings against the possibility of Hundseid ridding himself of the Minister of Defense.[127]

Quisling's standing was further strengthened by the fact that the Hundseid government's term of office coincided with the worst period of the depression. Many among the *borgerlige* were frustrated by the apparent inability of the *Storting* and the government to do anything to deal with the crisis and became anti-parliamentarian in their political views. In their opinion, only the Labor party seemed to be acting forcefully at this time, threatening to take over governmental authority, which up to then, with the exception of the brief Hornsrud interlude of 1928, had always been under *borgerlig* control. Only Quisling seemed capable of halting the onward march of the Labor party; he recognized the danger of revolution, which the parliamentary politicians ignored. At least so reasoned many leading business interests. Throne Holst and his Our Country political pressure group illustrated the existence of this tendency in business circles. So too did Knut Domaas, past president of the Norwegian Press Association (*Norsk Presseforening*) and editor of the influential *Handels- og Sjøfartstidende* (*Commercial and Shipping News*), the Norwegian equivalent of the *Wall Street Journal*. He published a pro-Quisling editorial, which *ABC*, the Fatherland League's weekly, enthusiastically reprinted. The editorial hailed Quisling as the figure around whom political consolidation, or union (*"nasjonal samling"*), was beginning to take place. Domaas declared it was too early to judge if Quisling was a great man, but he should be backed because he had "lifted a banner" rallying all "serious patriotism" which wished "to guard this free society against external and internal enemies". Hundreds of thousands were described as moving toward the banner that Quisling held.[128] The business-oriented editor exaggerated the amount of sentiment behind Quisling, which certainly did not number in the hundreds of thousands. Nevertheless, in the fall of 1932 there was a movement afoot among right-wing *borgerlige* who were seeking a rallying point, and for them Quisling was the apparent figure to whom they could lend their support.

The Fatherland League was one right-wing *borgerlig* organization which gave Quisling its full assistance throughout this stormy year. Articles in *ABC* were positive in defense of the actions he was taking, and the League also passed resolutions endorsing his stands.[129] He in turn reciprocated by giving speeches at meetings sponsored by the League.[130] With the strength of the League, which included members from all *borgerlige* parties, behind him, he had one more significant pillar of support in his confrontation with the Prime Minister.

Faced with major opposition to his attempt to remove his refractory Minister of Defense, Hundseid found himself with very weak cards to play. This was due not only to the influence of those backing Quisling, but also because the Prime Minister had just committed a major political blunder, and his position was therefore far from secure. He had burned his hands badly when trying to deal with a difficult issue involving strong feelings of nationalism. Nationalistic sentiments had been intensely aroused in Norway during the movement toward full independence from Sweden, culminating in 1905, and such emotions remained quite intense in the following decades, in particular among right wing *borgerlige*. Although there were considerable nuances within nationalist opinion during this time, there existed a general tendency to glorify Norway's heroic past during the Viking period in the Middle Ages, when a powerful state had emerged. The opposite was true of the long time span extending from the fourteenth to the early nineteenth century, when the Norwegian state first declined, and then ceased to exist, with the country coming under Danish royal authority. Nationalists deplored this "dark" period in Norway's history. Such persons were similarly irritated by the fact that Denmark, without regard for Norwegian sensitivities, had retained the once-Norse islands of Iceland, the Faeroes, and Greenland when Denmark was forced to relinquish Norway to Sweden as a consequence of having remained too long on the losing side during the Napoleonic Wars.

In the 1930s fervent nationalists now demanded that Greenland at least be returned to Norway, and they had gone so far as to send a private expedition to the island's east coast. The expedition proceeded to claim territory on behalf of the Norwegian government, somewhat to the discomfiture of the Kolstad ministry, which was divided on the question of whether officially to recognize the annexation. Among the cabinet members who strongly favored the move was Quisling, while Kolstad at first had serious reservations. Political pressure and the need to submerge differences within the cabinet eventually led to the government's official acceptance of Norway's claim to sovereignty over a part of eastern Greenland in July 1931, later extended to include another piece of territory further to the south in the following year.[131] The issue resulted in inter-Scandinavian discord, however, since the Danes maintained their title to the entire island.

Hundseid, upon taking over as prime minister, attempted to solve the dispute by agreeing to secret negotiations with Denmark, hoping that a compromise could be worked out. News of this effort leaked out, however, and once members of the cabinet learned of the Prime Minister's personal initiative, "all hell broke loose", as Hundseid himself described it.[132] A majority of the ministers firmly continued to endorse the occupation. Forced to explain his actions before the cabinet, Hundseid had to make full disclosure, and his venture was repudiated by his own ministers. Because of the turmoil, which threatened to dissolve the government, the Prime Minister was compelled to break off the negotiations, leaving him with very weak cards against Quisling in the controversy over the Kullmann case.[133] With his cabinet members disgruntled because of the Greenland dispute, and confronted with the amount of support Quisling's defenders were able to generate, Hundseid found it impossible to obtain his colleagues' approval for the dismissal of the Minister of Defense. The ministers were divided over the issue, and Hundseid again had to admit failure in his effort to replace Quisling.[134]

The latter was not one who was inclined to forgive and forget personal injuries sustained in political disputes. The Prime Minister had now twice attempted to remove him, and had been less than enthusiastic in backing his campaign against the alleged revolutionary activity of the Labor party. Obsessed with his determination to carry on with his anti-Communist offensive, and by now completely devoid of any feeling of personal loyalty toward the Prime Minister, Quisling began a vendetta against Hundseid which paralleled his no-holds-barred battle with the Labor party.

The two issues in fact became interrelated. The charges that Quisling had levelled in the memorandum of October 14 against Kullmann and his supporters, as part of his overall strategy against the Labor party, had long been under deliberation in the Justice Department. This difficult question now came to a head. The Attorney General (*riksadvokat*), Haakon Sund, issued his opinion on November 18. Sund agreed that Kullmann could be prosecuted under military law, although not severely, but believed it would be best if only civil law were used in this case, for the sole purpose of removing Kullmann from the navy.[135] It was plain to see that the Attorney General's findings, with which Hundseid concurred, were intended to cashier Kullmann with as little political friction as possible. To prosecute him severely under military law, as Quisling proposed, would stir up a hornet's nest and make the controversial captain a martyr. There was no need to do so, with the Labor party already having resigned itself to Kullmann's dismissal from the service.[136]

The Justice Department forwarded Sund's opinion to the Defense Department.[137] Quisling's response was not long in coming. Believing that Hundseid was acting in collusion with the Attorney General to thwart his campaign against Kullmann and the Labor party, the Minister of Defense launched a bitter attack against the head of the government.

He again resorted to his standard approach, drawing up a long memorandum on November 20 which defended his actions within the government and defined his views. But the purpose of the document was first and foremost to destroy Hundseid's position as prime minister. The Prime Minister stood accused of having had foreknowledge of Quisling's attack against the Labor party and Communists in the previous *Storting* session, and yet having conspired to remove his Minister of Defense by an attack behind his back. Now, in the Kullmann case, maintained Quisling, Hundseid was reverting entirely to form. But Norway must, argued Quisling, once and for all remove the threat posed by "the Communist revolutionary movement". Yet Hundseid, he insisted, did not recognize the danger facing the country and did nothing to rescue the situation. Quisling maintained self-righteously that his method of operations in the Kullmann case had been perfectly correct, and that he had acted out of sincere concern for the country's welfare. Then, pressing against Hundseid's current weakness, he charged the Prime Minister with having acted "behind the back of the government" in the Greenland Affair.[138]

The Minister of Defense concluded that Hundseid was not qualified to lead the ministry at this critical time and should resign. Although the memorandum never stated explicitly who Hundseid's successor should be, it was not necessary to read intently between the lines to discover whom Quisling had in mind – himself. In this remarkable document, he did not restrict himself to defending his actions and levelling blast after blast against the Prime Minister. He also included the outline of a political program, intended to serve as an alternative to Hundseid's policies. Declaring that if Hundseid's intentions in all his previous moves against Quisling had been based on a desire to obtain cooperation between political parties (the only time Quisling recognized that Hundseid's effort to remove him might be based on political considerations and was not merely due to personal spite), this was no solution to the problems facing society. Hundseid stood accused of having abandoned his party's principles in order to receive support from political power brokers, in particular from the Liberal leader, Mowinckel, whom Quisling disliked intensely. What was needed, maintained Quisling, was not compromises, but "clear lines".[139]

The "clear lines" that Quisling called for encompassed a five-point program intended to (1) establish a rational and purposeful monetary policy, (2) bring order in the administration of finances and local affairs, (3) secure inner peace and the opportunity for competition in trade and industry, (4) lessen the crisis for farmers and fishermen, and (5) provide work for the unemployed.[140] The goals he proposed were praiseworthy, indeed no one could object to them, but the main weakness of the program, which was also true of other programs which he later drew up, was that while the goals were described, no means of implementation was provided. He hoped that by calling for such an ideal program in a time of political and economic crisis, he would gain support in his feud with Hundseid and possibly become prime minister. But as one of Quisling's colleagues in the cabinet later pointed out, the Minister of Defense did not show an interest in the critical economic and political problems of the depression during his tenure in the cabinet, and only included his economic program in the memorandum in order to give his attack against the Prime Minister wider scope.[141]

The intended removal of Hundseid occurred at a meeting of the government held on November 21. Here the Minister of Defense read to his assembled colleagues excerpts from his 18-page opus of accusations against Hundseid. But as previously, he had done nothing to prepare the ministers for such a drastic move. True to form, he expected his surprise action to succeed by itself. The cabinet, he anticipated, would be overwhelmed by the suddenness of his move and the cogency of his arguments. Hundseid would be removed and his replacement would be, if all went well, Vidkun Quisling. But nothing of the sort occurred. The other ministers were not prepared to respond and to Quisling's (and Hundseid's) great surprise took no action. The cabinet members simply regarded the incident as a temperamental outburst, part of the then well-known feud between the two men, and they reacted accordingly, hoping that the episode would be restricted to the long document and that remembrance of the event would gradually fade away.[142] The question of Hundseid's possible resignation was never discussed, and not one of the ministers would have been willing to serve in a government headed by Quisling.[143]

The cabinet members' wish that the feud might quiet down proved futile. Neither of the two rivals was willing to abandon his vendetta. On November 24 it was the Prime Minister's turn to return the compliment. At a cabinet meeting he brought up the always touchy subject, for Quisling, of the "Pepper Affair". One of the Labor party leaders, Nygaardsvold, had continued to make repeated allegations that the entire incident had been faked. Hundseid now inquired with seeming innocence if it might not be advantageous to end such speculation once and for all by bringing charges of slander against Nygaardsvold. Quisling, obviously irritated at having this embarrassing question raised, replied testily to the Prime Minister's provocation. The temperamental Hundseid responded by once more insisting that Quisling had to leave the government, but found as before that other members of the cabinet were not willing to acquiesce.[144]

Stimulated by yet another demonstration of Hundseid's wish to be rid of him, Quisling reciprocated. Two days after the bitter exchange in the cabinet meeting, the Minister of Defense made one of his few personal appearances in the office of the Prime Minister during Hundseid's tenure. The purpose of the visit was to deliver a copy of the memorandum of November 20, accompanied by a brief note which repeated the demand that Hundseid resign.[145]

The latter's reaction was characteristic. Once he had time to read the long memorandum and understood its implications, he had a fit of anger during which the product of Quisling's labors was torn to shreds. But this spontaneous act of irritation did not eliminate the offensive document's existence. Although labelled "strictly confidential", Quisling not only sent copies to all the other members of the government, but also had the memorandum stenciled and forwarded to numerous politically prominent persons, some of whom were not even members of the Agrarian party. His commitment to remove Hundseid was total. Almost miraculously, none of those who received the document chose to reveal its contents publicly.[146]

Such an action by a cabinet member, however, was bound to create anxiety within the top echelons of the Agrarian party. It faced a predicament for which there was no clear-cut solution. Neither of the two combatants could be removed without serious political repercussions. Despite the considerable loss of prestige he had suffered because of the Greenland Affair, Hundseid's forced resignation would obviously have resulted in a split, both in the cabinet and in the party, bringing about the fall of the first government which the

Agrarian party had headed. On the other hand, Quisling's position in the fall
and early winter of 1932 was the strongest that he would ever enjoy politically
in Norway. Not only did he have the support of right wing *borgerlige* in the
capital, but he also seemed to enjoy considerable sympathy among the Agrarian party rank and file.[147] His removal was therefore also not possible. Because of this impasse, an attempt was made to arrive at a compromise in order
to paper over the controversy.

At a meeting on November 30, which included Quisling, two other cabinet members, one of whom represented the Prime Minister, and the head of
the Agrarian party's parliamentary delegation, an effort was made to reach
such a solution. Agreement was reached that Kullmann would be tried according to civil law for the purpose of removing him from the navy, while the
question of additional prosecution for violation of military law would be subject to further investigation.[148]

Because of his propensity to interpret everything literally, Quisling did not
fully realize the extent to which he had abandoned his earlier insistence that
Kullmann be prosecuted severely. This was what he in reality had done by
agreeing to have the question of Kullmann's further indictment under military
law postponed pending further investigation. Minister of Justice Lindboe,
whose department was responsible for any additional legal review, intended
to allow the matter to fade away of its own accord, and no one in the cabinet
except Quisling took seriously the Minister of Defense's original demand that
leaders of the Labor party be brought to trial as well.

The cabinet members and the leading administrators of the Agrarian party
hoped now that the dispute had blown over. As part of the agreement arrived
at on November 30, it was stipulated that Quisling's demand that Hundseid
resign should have no significance for any of those involved. There would be
no action taken by the cabinet, with the documents in question simply regarded "as sent and received".[149]

The peacemakers had not reckoned with the temperamental Prime Minister,
however, who sabotaged their efforts by choosing at this point to continue
the battle. The issue in contention continued to be the Kullmann controversy.
Hundseid had now decided to end once and for all Quisling's campaign
against the Labor party through his use of this issue. On December 1 Hundseid insisted at a cabinet meeting that additional prosecution of Kullmann
beyond dismissal from the service be abandoned, and that there was no possibility of bringing leaders of the Labor party to trial for alleged revolutionary
activity.[150] This brought the Prime Minister once more into direct collision
with Quisling, who, when faced with Hundseid's open challenge, refused to
abandon his endeavor to destroy the Labor party.

He reacted by resuming with unabated vigor his attempt to oust Hundseid, while continuing to press on with his crusade against the Labor party in

the Kullmann Affair. In a letter dated December 5 to one of the participants in the compromise meeting on November 30, the Minister of Church and Education, Nils Trædal, with copies made available to the other cabinet members, he insisted on Hundseid's removal. He argued that since the Prime Minister was not willing to abide by the agreement, the basis for an understanding "whereby the Prime Minister and I can continue in the government is eliminated".[151] He repeated his previous charges against the Prime Minister, and he furthermore described Hundseid as following a "compromise policy" toward the revolutionary elements in Norway which was in violation of the Agrarian party's program. Quisling insisted that Hundseid should resign so that it would be possible for the government to continue, under new leadership, its work of carrying out "the national policy" which was in conformity with the party's program.[152]

His interpretation of the Agrarian program was done in such a manner as to bring it into accord with his campaign against the Labor party. He selectively chose parts of the program to demonstrate how he, and not Hundseid, was acting in concurrence with the true wishes of the party.[153] In this letter he showed his ambitions even more explicitly than before. Hundseid was to be removed, after which the government would be united under Quisling's leadership in his attack against the alleged revolutionary movement. The Agrarian party would thereby become an instrument in his hands.[154]

Again there was no response within the cabinet to his dramatic appeal for change. The other ministers were primarily concerned with keeping the government alive in a time of crisis and were too pragmatic to engage one-sidedly in ideological crusades. But, as earlier, Quisling failed to recognize that in a government headed by Hundseid it would be impossible for him to succeed in his campaign against the Labor party. Instead, he doggedly held on to his position in the cabinet at all costs, and at the same time he continued in vain to demand that his view in the Kullmann affair be followed.

This only led to further disagreement between him and Hundseid. At a government conference held on December 6 it was impossible for the cabinet to reach a settlement as to how the Kullmann case should be handled. Once more the only possibility of accommodation was through compromise, and after a good deal of bickering, Foreign Minister Braadland was given the task of drawing up a resolution that both antagonists could agree to. This was done, the draft was submitted, discussed and accepted by the cabinet, and formally issued on December 10.[155]

The Braadland compromise declared that the government, in agreement with the Defense Department's recommendation, had decided that the Kullmann case, for the time being, should be resolved in the following manner: Kullmann's commission was immediately suspended, and he would be brought to trial under civil law in order to secure his permanent dismissal from the service. The question of further prosecution against Kullmann and the others named in the Ministry of Defense's charges would be the subject of additional investigation.[156] Although the government's statement gave the appearance of accepting the Defense Department's view, and thereby satisfied Quisling's penchant for literality, in essence the government resolution had been worked out in such a manner that the disagreement between the point of view expressed by Quisling and that put forward initially by the Attorney General was papered over. Kullmann would be prosecuted according to civil law, not military law as Quisling had originally insisted. While the possibility of further prosecution of Kullmann and the Labor party was left open, subject to further legal review, the probability of this ever occurring was almost nil because any additional inquiry would be carried out by the Attorney General within the Justice Department.

It proved impossible, however, to bring the controversy to an end as long as Quisling remained in the cabinet. Undaunted, he kept on using the Kullmann affair against the Labor party. Thus on December 13 *Tidens Tegn* declared that the government resolution of December 10 did not signify a retreat on Quisling's part, and that the campaign to prosecute Labor leaders such as Tranmæl would continue.[157]

This caused Hundseid to take up the cudgel. He replied on the same day in an interview with the Liberal *Dagbladet*, stating that "the government's resolution was completely in agreement with the Attorney General's recommendation." The Prime Minister went on to declare, in direct contradiction of Quisling, that the issue had not yet been decided, and that the possibility of raising punitive charges against Kullmann would only occur if it were not possible to cashier him in a civil suit. Hundseid thereby once more provided evidence of his intent to prevent Quisling from using the Kullmann case as a political issue.[158]

The latter was most indignant at this latest effort by the Prime Minister to sabotage his campaign.[159] He was as usual supported by *Tidens Tegn*, which described Hundseid's statement as an act of disloyalty against Quisling.[160] During the Christmas holidays Quisling drew up yet another memorandum expressing his viewpoint. He pointed out a number of areas which required, in his opinion, investigation in the Kullmann case, and he also strongly took issue with the Attorney General's viewpoint concerning how the case should be prosecuted.[161] However, when this document was presented to the government, Hundseid reacted strongly, declaring that if the memorandum was officially sent to the Justice Department and was registered, then he would resign. Under pressure from other cabinet members, Quisling agreed that only the first part, containing suggestions for future investigation in the case, would be sent officially from the Defense Department to the Justice Department, while the second portion, which contained his polemic against the Attorney General, would be forwarded as a personal statement to the Attorney General.[162]

Once more Quisling doggedly sought to have his way in the Kullmann case. He expanded his rebuttal of the Attorney General's findings into a verbose message of thirty-one pages. This document was not completed until February 10, 1933.[163] Summarized briefly, it countered Attorney General Sund's conclusion that Kullmann was an idealistic pacifist who should merely be removed from his post, preferably by resorting only to legal procedures based on civil law. Kullman should instead be tried for high treason, insisted Quisling, since the captain's activity was "an integral link" in the conspiracy "intended to paralyze our defense for the benefit of a communist revolution".[164]

In order to ensure that Kullmann would be prosecuted for treason, Quisling sought to circumvent the earlier cabinet agreement – that his rebuttal to the Attorney General would not be protocolled officially, but merely sent as a personal memorandum. On two different occasions, on February 13 and 15, Quisling forwarded the rebuttal along with other official documents to the Justice Department, but in each instance Lindboe intercepted it, returning the offensive missive to the Minister of Defense, and imploring him to abide by the terms of the agreement.[165]

Not until February 28 did Quisling finally respond in the manner which Lindboe desired. The Justice Department received its requested documents minus Quisling's provocative rebuttal. But the latter persevered in his effort to have his way. In what had by now become standard procedure, he made copies of his memorandum to the Attorney General available to those newspapers which backed him, *Nationen* and *Tidens Tegn*.[166] He did this without the knowledge of the other members of the government.

However, by this time his long-protracted attempt to turn the Kullmann case to his political advantage was of no consequence as far as the Hundseid government was concerned. It had already fallen four days before Quisling made public his attack against the Attorney General. The ministry was merely acting on an interim basis until a new government could take over. In the *Storting* the Liberals had abandoned their tacit support of the Agrarian government and had introduced a resolution of no confidence, which received the Labor party's backing. The *Storting* passed this resolution on February 24. On March 3 the caretaker Hundseid government stepped down, and on the following day Mowinckel's Liberals assumed office. After almost two years of controversy as a member of one of the most dissension-ridden governments in Norway's political history, Vidkun Quisling was once more without employment.

His period of service as Minister of Defense revealed many of the traits that were characteristic of him during his entire involvement in Norwegian politics. He could not be faulted for the manner in which he carried out his administrative responsibilities. Among his colleagues in the cabinet, he was respected for his skill in dealing with the day-to-day administrative detail in his department.[167] He could not be held responsible for the locked-in position of defense budgets during his tenure. He was only able to make minor altera-tions to plans that had already been decided before he became a member of the government.[168] The only original step that he succeeded in carrying out within the military during his time in office was the establishment of the state-supported militia, *Leidangen*.[169] Named after the old Viking naval militia, *Leidangen* was part of his anti-Labor party campaign. The *borgerlige* parties in the *Storting* supported its formation in large part because of their fear of possible revolutionary activity by the Labor party, while Labor in turn viewed its creation as a step "to slip fascism in through the back door".[170] *Lei-dangen*, however, never lived up to the expectations of either Quisling or the Labor party. It did not secure approval by the *Storting* until February 1933, shortly before the Hundseid government fell, and it received only 15,000 *kroner* for the purchase of material and military instruction, a pitifully small sum. The organization never amounted to anything of significance. It simply ceased to exist after the Labor government withdrew state support in July 1936. Without government funds, it was impossible for *Leidangen* to provide voluntary military instruction.[171]

From a professional standpoint, Quisling did not leave his mark as an in-novator, or even as a strong caretaker, while in office. He accomplished noth-ing of lasting significance on behalf of the military. Although limited by the strict budgetary requirements of the day, he could have assumed a more active role on behalf of his department within the government. As seen when the Menstad conflict broke out, he was generally extremely passive in the deliber-ations of the cabinet, hardly ever taking part, even when matters of military policy were being discussed.[172] In many respects, he was simply not interested in the ordinary operations of the government. His attention was instead drawn to controversial political questions. The Minister of Justice, Asbjørn Lindboe, later commented that the only issues that really interested Quisling were the battle against the alleged "revolutionary forces" which threatened the existing social order, and the Greenland affair.[173] Both matters, anti-Commu-nism and strong nationalistic support for the claim to Greenland, were issues that he remained deeply committed to in the period after the fall of the minis-try. General Otto Ruge similarly testified that he received the impression that Quisling's mindfulness of the military was not complete, and that he never felt fully at home in his post as Minister of Defense.[174] From Quisling's own perspective, however, his lack of special concern for the military was under-standable. He did not wish to be an ordinary politician. His intent was to use his cabinet position as a springboard for political leadership. Hence he fo-cused his energies on controversial issues not only because he felt strongly about them, but also because he hoped to use them in order to increase his standing and influence in politics.

Viewed as a whole, his tenure as Minister of Defense can be summed up as only a partial success. He had certainly advanced rapidly during the past two years, from being relatively unknown to becoming one of the country's most recognized and notorious political figures. His demagogic denunciation of the alleged revolutionary threat posed by the Labor party and the Communists had gained him a considerable amount of backing. However, he failed to capitalize on this support and turn it into something constructive. Two of his main weaknesses throughout his political career had already become apparent – his tendency to take solo actions without consultation and his inability to interact with other politicians. He never succeeded in mastering the intricacies of lobby politics.

He did not get anywhere in his campaign against Captain Kullmann because of the opposition of the Prime Minister and because of his extreme stand, which tended to isolate him within the government. Faced with this roadblock, he did not resign and attempt to marshall support from the outside, but clung to his cabinet post. This was typical of his general tendency of refusing to surrender any post that he had gained, even though tactically this might be to his advantage. When the Hundseid government eventually suffered shipwreck and was forced to step down, he did not occupy an entrenched position. He was too controversial, and because of his public disagreement with Hundseid, he did not have a clearly defined role to play within the Agrarian party. He once more occupied an indeterminate position, not having a clearly perceived objective beyond his general goal of wanting to achieve leadership of some type of *borgerlig* coalition. He was determined to remain in politics, however, hoping to build a dominant place for himself on the basis of the reputation he had gained within the Agrarian government.

CHAPTER IV

The Formation of National Union and the 1933 Election

There was at that time talk about cooperation between the Conservatives, Independent Liberals, and the Agrarian party, and they wanted me to take part. I discussed the matter with the Agrarian party, and I said: "I will not work with you before hard and fast lines are established . . . I will not participate in such things in our politics as those which have happened, you can do what you will." They squirmed to and fro and attempted by all possible means to persuade me. . . . But they could not bring themselves to do more than make vague statements. . . . They offered that I should become parliamentary representative, a *Storting* candidate certain to be elected, etc. I refused to go along with this, and I had no other course except to seek to create a separate movement and make Nordic Folk-Rising . . . into a political party . . ., and this I did in the spring of 1933.

Vidkun Quisling,
statement in court, September 6, 1945

Despite preoccupation with the Kullman case and his ongoing feud with the Prime Minister, Quisling was aware of other simultaneous developments that would affect his career. Early in 1933 it became apparent that the Hundseid government was on its last legs. The Liberals in particular were discontented with the Agrarian government's pinch-penny approach to the problems of the depression. A change was in order, something new had to be tried. It was only a matter of time until the minority government would lose a vote of confidence in the parliament.

With the fall of the government pending, it therefore became necessary for Quisling to begin preparation of a political base for his future in politics. An indication of what his approach would be was provided by Christopher Borchgrevink, an Oslo attorney who at the time was an uncritical admirer, and who was working hard on Quisling's behalf. *Tidens Tegn* made available most of page one for a lengthy article by Borchgrevink, who did his best to enhance Quisling's standing. He portrayed Quisling as the strong man who could provide Norway with the political leadership that the country allegedly lacked. He was described as a new man in politics not affected by previous divisions in society, and who therefore had a good chance of eliminating class struggle. Furthermore, his strength, said the attorney, lay in his acknowledgement of the central position occupied by the farmers in society. Borchgrevink then introduced his main point: the need to place Quisling at the head of a national coalition government whose core would be formed by the Agrarian party.[1]

Coming a whole month before the fall of the Hundseid government, this article revealed Quisling's hope that his reputation would serve as the basis for the formation of a *borgerlig* coalition, coalescing around the Agrarian party, with himself as its head. However, the difficulty of achieving this goal was great, if not insurmountable, because of the friction between him and Hundseid, which even Borchgrevink was forced to recognize. The conclusion of his article contained an obvious appeal to the Agrarians: "May the party simply not overlook [the fact] that it is leaders and *ideas* that alone are decisive".[2] Personal considerations, in other words, were of no consequence.

In his public statements, Quisling was more cautious and not as direct, but he too sounded the call for a *borgerlig* coalition. During the parliamentary debate of January 31, 1933, he repeated his philosophical viewpoint that the world was in the midst of rapid transition, and only the revolutionaries were taking advantage of the current instability. The greatest task for the *borgerlige*, he maintained, was "to strengthen the foundation of our society and to safeguard future developments".[3] In these indirect terms, he revealed his aspiration of becoming the midpoint of a *borgerlig* coalition. During the time just prior to the fall of the Hundseid government his backers worked on various plans for such an eventuality, which they frequently referred to as a "national block".[4]

This effort became more open once it was absolutely certain that Hundseid's ministry would fall. Minutes before the decisive vote was taken, the Minister of Defense took advantage of his final appearance in the *Storting* to issue a full-scale political program to deal with the existing economic crisis.[5] Acting on his own and not in concert with the cabinet, he intended to show he was capable of providing solutions to the difficulties the country was in. His program repeated the five points he had earlier proposed in his memorandum of November 20, 1932, when he had unsuccessfully sought to oust Hundseid. The most noteworthy aspect of his speech, however, was the extremely harsh and bitter language he used in attacking his political enemies. He declared his relief at being free from governmental responsibility. "Now it is our turn to travel around the country and stir up the people . . . . . . the political drivel in this country must once and for all come to an end . . . .."[6] In its place, he argued that "constructive men" from all political parties should unite to form a "national government of the realm", which would have the authority to carry out "all essential measures necessary for economic and political reconstruction".[7] It was an elitist government that he had in mind, free from the ordinary compromises which were essential under a parliamentary system such as that which then prevailed in Norway, with no one party or distinct coalition enjoying a majority. He maintained that most Norwegians favored such an idea, and he was particularly savage in his attack against Mowinckel, who for Quisling stood as the foremost exponent of party politics:

> Russia's Mowinckel, Kerensky, had his accession in the February Revolution, but he received his October. And I am convinced that we too shall come back. ... I am no party politician, I hold my country above everything. And I maintain that I stand with both feet on Norwegian soil. And there are many who have the same view as I. And I repeat: This is a battle about philosophies of life, and victory is certain, the victory will be ours sooner or later.[8]

He quite obviously was carried away by his own rhetoric, revealing his emotional and single-minded view toward politics. As an elitist, above the usual give and take of partisan maneuvering, he scorned those whom he considered to be ordinary politicians. They, in his opinion, did not comprehend the significance of the world crisis, and were therefore unable to draw up "clear lines", or objectives, to meet the challenge of the times. Assuming the stance of the philosophical statesman, he repeated his oft-stated theme that the depression was not just a financial debacle, but a universal crisis, a turning point in history which ordinary political leadership and superficial measures could not deal with.[9] He believed it was necessary to cut through all political considerations so that distinct policies could be implemented without impediment. The influence of his experiences in Russia was also shown by the parallel he drew between Mowinckel and Kerensky. But if Mowinckel was the Norwegian equivalent of the last head of the Provisional Government, then obviously Quisling still continued to regard Lenin as his model. The ideal of the dynamic intellectual with totalitarian control over society had great appeal to the minister who now was about to relinquish office.

The extreme nature and emotional tone of his speech caused a stir, and Labor's parliamentary leader, Nygaardsvold, rose to ask whether it had been given with the knowledge and approval of the cabinet. The answer was obvious. Quisling had acted on his own. Events would show that he was in the process of divorcing himself from the Agrarian party, though this was not his intent at the time. Hundseid did not even bother to respond to Nygaardsvold's provocative question.[10]

An air of uncertainty had thereby been created concerning Quisling's future even before his tenure in the government had formally come to an

end. Already on the day after his speech, *Aftenposten* headlined a speculative front page article which raised the question of whether Minister Quisling had resigned from the Agrarian party.[11] The paper quoted without
comment *Nationen*, which was anxiously awaiting a clarification from
Quisling. In this fashion, editor Aadahl of *Nationen* kept the public's attention, as well as his party's concentration, focused on Quisling, whom
Aadahl continued to support.

Quisling's answer came in a lengthy commentary in *Nationen*, which
appeared on February 27. In the article, entitled "Clear Lines", he appealed for assistance from agrarian interests, repeating much of what he
had said in the *Storting*. The article, like the previous speech, contained a
curious call for support within the Agrarian party, while at the same time
denouncing party politics. After first flattering the farmer by declaring that
the man who worked the land represented all that was basically good and
sound in the nation, he went on to repeat that he was no ordinary party
politician. Instead, for him there was but one party, which he grandilo-
quently proclaimed included all of the country's inhabitants: "the Norwegian people's great party". Therefore, he insisted that his mission within
the Agrarian party was not restrictive, but had an appeal that extended outside of the party's boundaries.[12]

It was at this point that he bogged down because of lack of clarity, attempting to portray himself as being above petty partisan politics and still
bidding for Agrarian backing. He declared that his program of "national
reconstruction politics" would create "a new society", based on the traditions preserved by the farm population, to be sure, but adapted to meet
"the demands of modern life". He hoped the Agrarian party would be farsighted and flexible enough to take up this work. As long as it did, it
would have his support.[13] He thereby indicated that he expected the party
to conform to his policy, and not vice versa. This statement also provided
evidence of his belief in the strength of his position. He was convinced that
he enjoyed massive backing throughout the country, in particular within
the Agrarian party, for the actions he had taken while a member of the
government, especially for his crusade against so-called revolutionaries in
the Labor party.

Having assumed the posture of being above party politics, he insisted
that his call for "a national government of the realm" did not mean that he
favored a standard type of coalition government. The Agrarian party, he
argued, ought to shun partisan politics and should instead maintain "clear
lines", unbesmirched by petty compromise. However, since the Agrarian
party was a class party, representing therefore by inference only the narrow interests of the farmers, the movement he wished to create needed to
be supplemented by other segments of society that had a "national outlook". According to his logic, this combined movement would then go
forth to form a national government which would have the authority and

expertise to solve the problems Norway faced. As the program for such a government, he again proposed the five points he had made public in his *Storting* speech.[14]

As was so often the case with his programs, his call for a national coalition did not lack broad general ideals, but it failed to specify how its ambitious goals were to be realized. Just how the Agrarian party could have avoided making compromises with the other political groups needed to form a "national" movement, even if it had chosen to follow his advice, was not clear. Nor did he spell out to what extent it would be necessary for the party to abandon its special interests on behalf of the farmer in order to work for the benefit of the entire people. He expected his appeal for "national union" to be enough. And a positive response, to his mind, would take place without any hesitation, and with no bargaining among the various political factions concerned. All would simply rally to the call.

In his article in *Nationen* he had indicated that he would remain associated with the Agrarian party only if it agreed with his point of view. He did not, however, wish to break with the party if this could be avoided because of its obvious strength as an established political organization. Therefore, his article was both a threat to abandon the Agrarians if they did not agree with him and an appeal to party members to sustain his position.

This difficulty was not present when he sought backing from non-agrarian *borgerlige*. To them he could unambiguously stand forth as the leader who was above petty politics, without having to reconcile this stance with allegiance to a specific party. In an article that appeared only three days after his essay in *Nationen*, he paid hardly any attention to the farm population. Writing in his second base of support in Oslo, *Tidens Tegn*, his primary aim was to urge the creation of a national block, to be composed of discontented *borgerlige* who were frustrated by the inability of non-socialist politicians to deal effectively with the problems of the depression.[15] This article was especially noteworthy because it revealed the eclectic nature of his political programs, which became even more apparent a short time later when he founded his own party. Despite his assertions to the contrary, he remained essentially a borrower of ideas. Entitled "Directives", the article contained statements that evoked feelings of nostalgic national romanticism inspired by Norway's past, plus ideas consciously or unconsciously imitative of Italian Fascism and German National Socialism.

He called for the preservation of established values, while at the same time urging progress toward new solutions. He could thereby seek support both from those who desired radical change as the means of solving present-day problems and from those who feared the threat of a revolutionary socialist upheaval. Both traditional party politics and the alleged revolutionary activity of the socialists were rejected because they were destroying the vitality of society. Only determined leadership could get the country out of the difficulties it was in.[16]

Since he wrote this article at the very time Hitler was in the process of
consolidating his dictatorship in Germany, it is interesting to note that his
proposed dynamic leadership would be the guardian of a society which resembled in many ways the ideal community of the Nazi elite: a society
which sought to reach "back to its life-giving foundations", which united
the attributes of individualism and solidarity, which provided security for
life and property, which respected family institutions and the race, which
stood for "blood and earth" (*"blod og jord"* = *Blut und Boden*), which
provided good will to all rather than class struggle, which strengthened the
authority of the state, etc.[17]

In his design for a *borgerlig* block, he expanded his five-point program
to ten, but its tone and essence was the same, and the vagueness concerning
implementation remained. The first point called for law and order, clearly
aimed at the Labor party, indicating his intent to follow his previous crusade. Next came a series of planks dealing with social, economic, legal, and
administrative questions: (2) a just system of law to deal with social and
economic issues; (3) emphasis on lineage and social tradition – implying
Nordic superiority; (4) a sound fiscal policy; (5) modernization of the national administration; (6) more effective local administration and restrictions on local taxation; (7) aid to the farmer – the only time the article
made specific reference to the farm population. Indoctrination was also
provided for, with point (8) declaring the need to change the educational
system so that it stressed national tradition. His call for awakening the
"Nordic spirit" extended into foreign policy and foreign trade. Point (9)
called for a commercial policy designed to further trade and build up the
merchant marine, while foreign policy would be based on cooperation between the "Nordic countries", resulting eventually in a "Nordic union"
with the necessary armed force to protect "our civilization and maintain
peace". In his final point he urged the creation of a strong "national government of the realm", which would have the authority to dissolve parliament and to conduct popular plebiscites. The stimulus he received from
foreign examples is especially reflected in this final point. He had observed
the successful means by which Mussolini and Hitler had subverted representative institutions in their respective countries. In direct imitation of
Mussolini's corporate state, Quisling expressed his intent to establish a
corporate body (*Næringsting*) which would become part of the representative system.

He obviously recognized the unstable economic and political conditions
which had enabled totalitarian dictators to assume power. He witnessed
the same instability in Norway and sought to take advantage of it. What
the country needed, he declared, was "first and foremost *men*". He proposed to set aside parliamentary government, suggesting that a "national
government of the realm", composed of conscientious, national-minded
individuals who were uninfluenced by party politics, be given the opportu-

nity of working unimpeded for a period of three years. According to his argument, parliamentary politics quite obviously were unfit to deal with the situation, since party politicians were too prone to make compromises and were incapable of following coherent plans in a logical manner.[18]

His ambition was readily apparent in these two articles. Having launched political programs in two leading Oslo newspapers, it was obvious that within a short time some initiative could be expected to occur that would involve this controversial figure. For the time being, the Agrarian party stood foremost in his plans, but it did not offer the sole possibility for the future.

He could not be entirely certain of unrestricted backing from *Tidens Tegn*, however. In an editorial appearing in the same issue as "Directives", the paper, while sympathetic toward his general goals, declared that the time was not yet ripe for the formation of a new political movement of the kind that he proposed. With an election approaching in the fall, *Tidens Tegn* had no inclination to disavow its traditional loyalty to the Independent Liberals, who had now adopted the new name of the Independent People's party in an effort to give their party a more populist image. The paper suggested that the Agrarian party cooperate with the Independent People's party in the cities, since the Conservatives could not offer *borgerlige* voters anything new. Thommessen thereby indicated his belief that any independent move by Quisling would be premature at this time. The latter could expect to receive publicity from *Tidens Tegn*, but the paper was not behind him in full force.[19]

His opportunity to use the Agrarian party to his advantage was also hedged with considerable difficulties. His primary obstacle was his obsessive animosity toward Hundseid, whom Quisling was still determined to remove as leader of the Agrarian party. On the very day the Agrarian government left office, Quisling wrote still another memorandum attacking Hundseid. As before, the central question he raised was the Kullmann case. He accused the former prime minister of having deliberately distorted the government's position on the decision of whether or not to prosecute Kullmann under the criminal code.[20] The viewpoint which Quisling propounded in his renewed onslaught was not, on paper, a weak one. The erratic and temperamental manner in which Hundseid had handled the matter did not inspire confidence and left him open to censure. On the other hand, Quisling's actions in the case had not been above reproach, as former members of the cabinet and leading party figures were well aware. However, the decisive issue in the dispute was not who had said or done what on such and such occasions, but rather who enjoyed the highest standing within the top echelons of the party. The question was never in doubt. Hundseid, despite his emotional nature and the poor showing he had made as prime minister, held a solid position. He had been prominent in the Agrarian party from its beginnings, and had been the leader of its

Storting delegation before becoming prime minister. Quisling, on the other hand, had been an unknown quantity to most Agrarians at the time of his appointment to the cabinet. He had not been a member of the party prior to 1931, and during his term of office he was a loner who held himself aloof from its affairs. He was therefore no match for Hundseid, as was shown on March 9 when the former prime minister was again chosen to head the Agrarian *Storting* delegation, thereupon maintaining his position as party leader.

Hundseid's re-election represented a severe setback for Quisling. He did not abandon his attempt to use the Agrarian party, nor did he give up his quest to have Hundseid removed, but he now had to consider other alternatives. As a result, Nordic Folk-Rising, which even as a paper organization had been quiescent during his stay in the cabinet, was revived. On the day following Hundseid's election, a meeting was held of Nordic Folk-Rising's Political Committee. The group's re-emergence was not particularly auspicious. It is doubtful whether it consisted of many more members than Quisling and the three others who signed the minutes, plus a handful of other sympathizers who exerted themselves on his behalf at this time.[21] Nevertheless, the meeting was of interest. It indicated what he and some of his closest collaborators had in mind, namely the creation of a new political party. Significantly, the name proposed for the organization was National Union (*Nasjonal Samling*), which would later be the party associated with Quisling for the remainder of his political career. The group decided that the question whether National Union would act independently or in co-operation "with other *borgerlige* parties" should be decided by subsequent negotiations.[22] The option of Quisling and his adherents joining some kind of a *borgerlig* coalition was therefore not ruled out, and this possibility was explored through discussions with different *borgerlige* political groups. Nevertheless, more than two months before its formal announcement, the party's name had been established as a working title, and during the spring of 1933 Quisling sat at his desk formulating the technical details of its organizational structure.[23] He was also drawing up a party program, receiving advice and suggestions from his collaborators on its contents.[24]

Those who worked with Quisling at this time, including old associates such as Prytz, Hvoslef, and Munthe from Nordic Folk-Rising plus politically ambitious attorneys like Hjort and Borchgrevink, were convinced that he enjoyed widespread approval with the electorate. They strove to gain as much influence for him as possible among various *borgerlige* groups, in an effort to create a broad-based coalition. Uppermost consideration, however, was placed on the need to have *him* assume leadership of any coalition that came into being, a feeling that he shared fully. But for the time being contacts were maintained with various *borgerlige* groups. No ties had yet been broken.

It was necessary, however, for some type of clarification to take place concerning his political future. This was especially imperative in an election year, with preparations needing to be made for the coming campaign struggle with the Labor party. On March 15, Joakim Lehmkuhl wrote to Quisling, urging him to come to a decision concerning previous proposals that he participate in the Fatherland League's election meetings.[25]

Although Quisling maintained his ties with the League, of which he remained a member, his primary preoccupation at this time still concerned the Agrarian party. It was a powerful force, and his prospects would benefit greatly if it could be exploited. But he insisted that the problem concerning Hundseid first had to be settled. Therefore, despite the clear indication of Hundseid's strength, shown by his posts as party foreman and head of its parliamentary delegation, Quisling doggedly strove to remove the Agrarian leader. Instead of being circumspect, he employed his standard direct approach, seeking in practice to achieve the "clear lines" he called for in theory. He chose to write another long memorandum, which he forwarded to the party's *Storting* delegation on March 24.[26] In this missive, he repeated most of the prior arguments he had marshalled against Hundseid. Hundseid, Quisling maintained, was a typical party politician from whom the socialists had nothing to fear. Such politicians, he argued, paralyzed the Agrarian party, preventing it from carrying out its "positive politics". He concluded by insisting that the Agrarian *Storting* delegation immediately take the question up for consideration, issuing the ultimatum that "the whole matter is no longer an object for compromises as far as I am concerned".[27]

His ultimatum did not, however, lead to an immediate breach with the Agrarian party. On the contrary, a serious effort was made to solve the problem, indicating the importance that leading party figures attached to Quisling. Prominent individuals within the parliamentary delegation and party administration, upon receipt of the memorandum, began a hurried attempt to arrange some type of accommodation which would paper over the differences between Quisling and Hundseid.[28] The negotiations, begun in late March 1933, lasted until early May. The Agrarian reaction indicated that the party feared a rupture would have negative results on its voters in an election year. The secretary general of the Farmers' Association, for example, noted on March 27 that he had found strong enthusiasm for Quisling in the district that he was just then visiting.[29] The party's desire to retain its former Minister of Defense was further shown on April 5, when it extended the courtesy of providing him with a confidential copy of its election program for the period 1934–1936.[30] As late as April 27 he participated in one of the party's strategy sessions for the election. Along with the other ex-ministers of Hundseid's government, he attended a meeting of the program committee. As usual when present at group discussions, he sat silent in his chair, giving no indication of any disagreement.[31] He provided no hint that slightly more than two weeks later he would form his own party.

This apparent inconsistency on his part was no inconsistency at all. He and his closest collaborators had all along planned the creation of a movement that would have him at its head. The purpose of the negotiations with the Agrarian party was to attempt to get it to accept his politics as much as possible and to reorganize its leadership in his favor.[32] At the same time, those working on his behalf sought also to create a wide base of support among other *borgerlige* political groups. Hjort, one of the strongest exponents of such a move, urged forcefully that the possibility be explored of bringing together such diverse factions as the Independent People's party, the Agrarian party, and the Fatherland League in a single constellation,[33] and he hoped that it might be possible for the new formation to use *Tidens Tegn* as its major press organ.[34]

The most concrete possibility of reaching an accommodation lay, however, with the Agrarian party. Recognizing the difficulty of having Hundseid and Quisling in the same organization, those who worked for Quisling and those within the Agrarian party who wished to arrange a compromise with him tried to solve the dilemma by seeking to promote an alternative. They proposed the creation of a sister party for the Agrarians. Such a party, under Quisling's leadership, would be a town party, while the regular Agrarian party organization would continue its traditional political activity in the rural districts.[35] Those who sought to heal the split between Hundseid and Quisling had long favored this alternative. Among these was the Fatherland League, which opposed a breach in the *borgerlige* ranks arrayed against the Labor party with an election approaching. Already on March 2, following the appearance of Quisling's "Clear Lines" in *Nationen*, *ABC* sought to paper over the feud. Differences between Quisling and Hundseid were not fundamental, maintained the paper, but merely revealed contrary opinions over which tactics to employ. In reality Hundseid, like Quisling, was the deadly enemy of the Labor party, and *ABC* voiced its approval of Quisling's resolve "to carry the Agrarian party's point of view *into the towns*".[36] The Fatherland League thereby expressed its hope that he would continue to have an active role within the Agrarian ranks. While the possibility of establishing a sister party continued to be explored, the name for the new party organization had already been determined. It would be called the Norwegian People's party (*Det Norske Folkeparti*).[37] The term National Union was thereupon shelved, but, as events would show, only for the time being.

Quisling for a time had high expectations of the Norwegian People's party. He went so far as to draw up formal notification of its founding, to be sent to the Department of Justice,[38] and two of his collaborators sketched out an organizational plan for how the Agrarian party and its sister party would coordinate their activities, with a central Executive Committee composed of representatives from the two parties carrying out this function.[39]

Throughout April 1933 preparations for the new party were continued by Quisling and his lieutenants, while at the same time discussions were conducted with the Agrarian party over the question of clarifying their relationship. At a meeting of Nordic Folk-Rising's Political Committee on April 26, attended by the hard core of Quisling's advisers, which included Prytz, Munthe, Hjort, and Borchgrevink, the laws governing the new Norwegian People's party were drawn up. Quisling also informed his lieutenants of the status of the negotiations with the Agrarian party, maintaining there was a good possibility of cooperation.[40]

On Monday, May 1, the same group reassembled. As before, two of the main questions discussed were how to gain maximum support for the new party now being planned, and the status of the talks with the Agrarian party. Another topic covered the possibility of gaining the adherence of several Conservative parliamentary representatives. The question was also raised whether the Conservative paper, *Morgenbladet*, might be available as a press organ for the party.[41] This indicated that Quisling's collaborators had already ruled out *Tidens Tegn* in this role. Thommessen continued to provide Quisling with considerable publicity in the hope that this might be a catalyst for future *borgerlig* unification, but this was as far as the editor was willing to go.

The talk of bringing elements from the Conservative party into the constellation reflected the ambitions of Quisling's lieutenants, but this was hardly a realistic possibility. What was first and foremost necessary, however, was to resolve the relationship with the Agrarian party. Quisling once again discussed his negotiations with prominent Agrarians. He pointed out that he had stated to the Agrarian parliamentary representatives that the new party was being founded in accordance with the wishes of the Agrarians, and he alleged that the Agrarian party's secretary, Jon Leirfall, had confirmed this.[42] Quisling, however, exaggerated at this point. The Agrarian leaders had knowledge of his plans to form a new party, but they had not given the project their blessing, which was shown by the fact that negotiations were still taking place concerning the extent to which, if any, cooperation between the two parties would occur. The Agrarians continued to be concerned, however, about what effect a split with Quisling would have, as shown in a letter written by Leirfall on April 3.

> With the Agrarian party in the countryside and a sister party in the towns
> . . . in close cooperation, with exchange of political speakers and preferably
> with a joint election declaration just before the election, I believe there is the
> possibility for a new Agrarian party government following the election, and
> with Quisling and Hundseid as leaders for their *separate* divisions, one can
> assume there will be fewer factional aspects. A public dispute at this time
> will destroy us completely and cause a confusion in our ranks which I don't
> even dare to think about.[43]

Despite strong concerns about the repercussions of a break with Quisling, it had not, however, been possible to reach an agreement between the ex-minister and the party in whose government he had served. As a result, he and his lieutenants felt a growing impatience, and it was decided that on May 2, "after the numerous conferences", they would "force a final answer" from the Agrarian party. In addition to Quisling, Prytz and Hjort would take part in the discussion with Agrarian representatives.[44]

The decisive confrontation took place. At first political observers not party to the discussions were uncertain about the outcome. *Arbeiderbladet* speculated on May 4 that a "national party" had been founded the previous evening: "It is Editor Aadahl in *Nationen* and ex-minister Quisling who are in the forefront of the venture. . . . It is now intended that the National party will be a town edition of the Agrarian party with Quisling as chief".[45] The interest that *Arbeiderbladet* displayed indicated a degree of nervousness within the Labor party concerning Quisling's political prospects. The Labor daily proved incorrect in its speculation about the result of the discussions, but it nevertheless was accurate in reporting that formation of just such a party had been under consideration. Not until six days later did Editor Aadahl, in a strongly worded yet evasive editorial, deny that he had participated in the formation of a new party.[46]

The talks had instead reached an impasse. The reason was Quisling's continued insistence that he should have his way and that the Agrarian party should repudiate its chairman. While the Agrarian representatives were willing to seek an accommodation, they refused to consider the demand that Hundseid be forced to resign. To take such a drastic step would have caused serious disarray within the party, much more serious than an eventual break with Quisling, who was informed as early as April 5 that the party's parliamentary delegation had rejected his demand.[47] On May 5 Quisling notified the Agrarian party's Executive Committee that he could not, "under the present circumstances", assume responsibility for the formation of a "parallel party" to the Agrarian party in the towns. As justification, he described Hundseid as a leader whose policy was reprehensible and ruinous for the type of politics which the party should represent. Quisling insisted that for him the primary goal in politics remained the struggle with "the revolutionary movement", namely the Labor party, and he maintained that Hundseid's failure as a leader had been revealed by this critical issue. The reason why he had entered politics, declared Quisling, was not for personal gain, but in order to contribute something toward the solution "of the great national problems" which existed. Since his point of view had coincided with the Agrarian party's program on most important issues, he had worked primarily on behalf of this party. His inability to accept its leadership did not mean that he would abandon his goals, but he would continue "outside of this leadership and on a free foundation".[48]

This letter provided an interesting insight into his association with the Agrarians. Undoubtedly he was correct when he maintained that he had affiliated with the party because its program most nearly coincided with his own political philosophy. During the late 1920s and early 1930s the Agrarians were among the foremost opponents of the Labor party, denouncing the socialists for their ideology and alleged revolutionary threat. But its leadership was also pragmatic, as it had to be, in particular when it assumed responsibility for running a minority government. Quisling, because of his opportunism and theoretical inclination, concentrated almost entirely on ideological considerations in his crusade against the Labor party. Hundseid's attempt to disassociate himself from this endeavor, in part because of the need for support from Mowinckel's Liberals, was regarded as treason by Quisling. The latter considered Hundseid to be morally reprehensible, and dogmatically insisted that he be removed. Since Quisling, even after the fall of the government, refused to drop this ultimatum, in spite of Agrarian attempts to reach an accommodation, no compromise was possible.

His final break with the Agrarian party came at the urging of his advisers, Hjort and Prytz. Realizing that the split was inevitable, Hjort hoped to gain political capital from the division. Writing to Prytz on May 5, he urged that Quisling send the letter announcing his break with the Agrarians as quickly as possible, that confidential copies be made available for political purposes, and that an open letter be sent to the Agrarian party's voters explaining Quisling's position. Furthermore, Hjort recommended that the new party be announced within a short time. Quisling's closest associates were now determined to move rapidly, once it was obvious that the possibility of cooperation with the Agrarian party no longer existed. As he later revealed, Quisling broke reluctantly with the Agrarian party. However, he bore the ultimate responsibility for the split. Prominent politicians within the Agrarian party, the Independent People's party, and the Fatherland League all urged that he remain associated with the Agrarians in order to continue a unified effort against the Labor party. In their minds, as well as in his and his advisers', his political value was significant.[49]

At the time he ceased his affiliation with the Agrarian party, Quisling held the greatest *independent* political strength that he would ever enjoy. Almost all parties, from the Conservatives to Labor, were convinced that he had considerable voter appeal, and were anxious as to how this might affect their fortunes. But he failed to exploit this recognition of his political value. Rather than maintaining his association with the Agrarians, thereby being able to utilize the organization of a solidly established party, he reluctantly broke with them because of his dogmatic ultimatum concerning Hundseid. He thereby had no alternative except to embark on a solo venture, being convinced that he enjoyed great good will among the ill-defined mass of voters.

Hjort, Prytz, and Quisling's other collaborators who stemmed from the circle around Nordic Folk-Rising, followed the strategy of seeking to obtain as broad a base of support as possible for Quisling among mainstream *borgerlige* political groups. There was, however, another element which now attached itself to him at the critical time when he was in the process of clarifying his position. Similar to other West European countries, Norway contained an extreme small right-wing fringe during the interwar period. This group received its inspiration more from foreign sources than from the country's internal situation. Although limited in numbers, persons associated with extreme right-wing politics assumed some importance for the new party being created under Quisling's leadership.

The first attempt to imitate right-wing totalitarian examples had occurred in the late 1920s. As usual, *Tidens Tegn*, constantly the harbinger of various radical conservative ideological programs, provided publicity for the new endeavor, the National Legion, which openly called for an imitation of Mussolini's corporate state.[50] Although the Legion, headed by an Oslo stockbroker, Karl Meyer, failed to gain a following, it did have influence on a small group of extremists who were dissatisfied with parliamentary democracy. Among these was a young journalist, Adolf Egeberg, Jr. He later sought his political salvation in German National Socialism, participating in SS activity in Munich and Berlin while serving as *Nationen*'s correspondent in Germany. Returning to Norway in 1930, Egeberg brought with him his German creed and founded Norway's National Socialist Workers' party. Thanks to the aid of a financial angel, architect Eugen Nielsen, Egeberg was able to publish his own paper, *Fronten (The Front)*. But as had been the case with his predecessor, Meyer, Egeberg's foreign import gained hardly any followers.

These small groups were unable to gain a foothold in politics. Nevertheless, the extreme right wing continued to seek a means of saving the country from the economic crisis of the depression and the threat, as they saw it, of revolutionary socialism. In an attempt to establish a dialogue among the various right-wing factions, with the goal of arriving at a common ideology to counter "Marxism", a new group was formed in 1932, the National Club. Headed by Walter Fürst, an advertising agent, the Club held a number of closed lectures for a select group of ideologues. Fascism and National Socialism were among the topics discussed, the latter being defended by Egeberg. Vidkun Quisling, then Minister of Defense, appeared at one of these meetings and gave an orientation about his political position.[51]

Fürst hoped that the National Club could help to stimulate the formation of a new political party on the far right of the political spectrum. For a while he felt that the Fatherland League might prove to be a catalyst in this direction, and he sought out Quisling on a number of occasions, attempting to persuade the Minister of Defense to make an effort to assume leadership and rejuvenate the League. But the latter was too preoccupied with his political intrigues as a member of the Agrarian government to pay heed to such suggestions.[52]

By early May 1933 the situation had changed, with Quisling's attempt to reach an accommodation with the Agrarian party having stranded. Furthermore, Fürst had stronger cards to play in his push to get Quisling to take resolute action. On May 1 Egeberg had published a National Socialist program in his newspaper. Armed with this program, portions of which Egeberg had read to the National Club, Fürst maintained that if the ex-minister did not act quickly and decisively in forming a party of his own, other politically interested persons such as Egeberg would take matters into their own hands, leaving Quisling behind. As an added inducement, Fürst had at his disposal a suite of offices, readily available to serve as the headquarters for a new party.[53]

In spite of Fürst's inducement, Quisling was most reluctant to commit himself. Although he had used strong words in the letter to the Agrarian party's Executive Committee, he still hoped that the Agrarians would give in and that it might be possible to reach some type of settlement. He therefore appeared uncomfortable and irresolute during the critical period prior to the formation of National Union. He did not have any carefully thought out strategy, despite the fact that he and his close associates had discussed the option of creating a separate party prior to the downfall of the Hundseid government. When the die was cast, when the ties with the Agrarian party were definitely severed, it was Hjort and Prytz among his collaborators who acted forcefully in pushing for the new party, aided in their efforts by the pressure brought to bear from such right wing ideologues as Fürst and Egeberg. Quisling still wistfully and unrealistically hoped the Agrarian party might give in to his demands. At the time when his party was in the process of being born, he acted as a hesitant and uncertain father to the arrival of his new progeny.

His indecision and general lack of assertiveness were shown when National Union came into existence. Not he, but rather Prytz and Fürst made the necessary preparations, gathering together the participants at the organization's initial meetings. Unfortunately for the projected party, the dynamic Hjort was not present, undoubtedly because of an illness, and this in part explains why the whole enterprise assumed such an amateurish air.[54]

National Union's founding occurred in a most disorganized manner during the early days of May. A series of meetings were held at the Grand Hotel, one of Oslo's largest and most prestigious, located on Karl Johans gate, the capital's main boulevard. Present were a small number of persons, at no time numbering more than fifteen. Besides Quisling, none of these were prominent except Johan Throne Holst.[55]

At the initial meeting, held on May 8, those who came discovered to their surprise that the person who they assumed was primarily responsible for the gathering, namely Quisling, was not in attendance. Prytz, however, assured them that Quisling would make an appearance at the next meeting, to be held on the following day, and that there would be an opportunity to ask questions. The first meeting had simply been a trial balloon, intended to see who would come.[56]

True enough, the former Minister of Defense presented himself on the next day, but he did not project a very inspiring image. Obviously uncomfortable, he was most reticent when it came to detailing concrete plans for future action. An interesting aspect of the meeting was that Fürst, not Quisling, was the one who enthusiastically desired resolute action. Fürst pressed energetically to get Quisling to commit himself. The latter, however, confined himself to presenting a speech, couched in his usual philosophical terms. But he presented no program, insisting instead that it should be formed bit by bit as the movement met opposition. "Therefore details cannot be provided for the time being."[57]

His obvious hesitancy occurred in part because of his reluctance to acknowledge that the break with the Agrarians was final. But in addition, his attitude revealed a basic flaw in his political make-up – his inability to make hard and fast decisions at critical times and to have at hand carefully thought out plans. The creation of National Union occurred in an atmosphere of complete improvisation. No one knew with certainty what the new organization portended, and everyone in attendance had his own views of what the movement should be. When the question was raised at the meeting of May 9 of who was backing Quisling and who was providing financial support, there was no answer to this realistic inquiry. Fürst responded: "Isn't it better that we agree that the old parties have done so much wrong that a new party is needed?"[58] And Prytz, replying to the financial aspect of the question, had to admit that no significant progress had been made toward accumulating capital. However, he continued in a more optimistic tone, a financial committee had been established to raise funds. Its goal was a sum of 500,000 *kroner*. Prytz maintained that commitments for 37,000 kr. had already been promised and that there was good hope of collecting "a nice sum in six figures".[59]

Beyond such loose estimates, nothing more concrete emerged from the May 9 meeting. The participants devoted the remainder of their time to vague discussion about what could be included in a program. It was little wonder that criticism of the endeavor's lack of direction was raised at the final meeting of this rather nebulous group, held on May 11.[60] A number of those present, the most prominent being Throne Holst, disassociated themselves and never became members of National Union. As an effort to launch a new party, the meetings were therefore unsuccessful. They provided no significant impetus for the emergence of a political organization. Nevertheless, they served as the inception for Quisling's latest venture in politics.

A clearer definition of National Union's purpose appeared in a fund-raising appeal for the new movement. Although undated, this solicitation gives every indication of having been drawn up at the very time the founding meetings were taking place, and it thereby provides a good understanding of the organization's intent. Its author is not definitely known, but it appears to have been Prytz, no doubt in collaboration with Quisling, since the document's style resembles that of Prytz, and it was he who was in charge of the new movement's financial affairs at the time of its formation.[61] Calling for the raising of 500,000 kr., the same sum Prytz had mentioned at the May 9 meeting, the request provided an ideological explanation why National Union was being created. It maintained that the existing framework of political parties was not capable of carrying out the necessary changes that were required in response to the numerous crises that Norway faced. Instead, a new determined folk-rising was needed, composed of individuals from all political groups and classes who would unite in carrying out reconstruction and reorganization. In an effort to show a line of continuity for such politics, the solicitation declared that the first step had been taken by the Agrarian government in accordance with that party's program, which had been further revised by Quisling in his article, "Directives", in the March 2 edition of *Tidens Tegn*. Now, the appeal continued, a group of politically interested persons, following strong and numerous requests from all sections of the country, had decided to organize an active "national union movement" under Quisling's leadership, and to have the positive viewpoints expressed in "Directives" serve as the basis for the movement's program. Such a program, maintained the request, was in the process of being drawn up. The goal of the national movement was to force through constructive crisis politics that followed healthy and sound economic and political principles. The movement would, in cooperation with all national and social forces in the country, select its own candidates for the coming fall election and attempt to gain a determined nationally conscious majority in the parliament. This majority would protect established society by creating the foundation for a national government, which would truly carry out economic reorganization and a national and social reconstruction in accordance with the national union movement's program.

This flurry of activity in early May did not mean that the party had yet been fully launched. Although National Union's initial meetings had been held and a solicitation for funds had been sent out, nevertheless Quisling had not fully committed himself to the venture. The amateurish nature of the founding meetings and the hesitant and obviously ill-at-ease manner he displayed revealed his basic desire still to use the Agrarian party as the vehicle for his political career. The creation of National Union was therefore not necessarily an end in itself, but rather a means of seeking to apply pressure against the Agrarian party. He undoubtedly hoped that his former party, reacting to National Union as a potential rival, would now make overtures for cooperation by allowing him a prominent place within its ranks.

Evidence of this was provided by the protocol of Nordic Folk-Rising's Political Committee meeting on May 13, 1933, a gathering held *after* the founding meetings of National Union. At this conference, attended by Quisling, Prytz, Hjort, Munthe, and Hvoslef, three important decisions were made. The first was that Quisling would publicize a call for "national union" through the press on Tuesday, May 16. This proclamation would emphasize willingness to cooperate with "the existing *borgerlige* parties". However, the proclamation was not intended to be a public declaration of the founding of a new party. Instead, the Political Committee decided that notification to the Department of Justice of National Union as a separate political party, as required by law, should be postponed "for the time being". Finally, the third and most revealing decision reached at the meeting concerned Quisling's possible future relationship with the Agrarian party: "Quisling will, if asked, declare himself willing to be nominated as a *Storting* candidate for one of the Agrarian party's provincial organizations. However, there is therein . . . no admission that he recognizes the Agrarian party's present leadership".[62] Once more he exhibited his desire to make use of the Agrarian party, while at the same time maintaining his inflexible antagonism toward Hundseid. He still refused to recognize that his wish to play an active role within the Agrarian party could not be reconciled with his insistence that Hundseid be forced to step down. Not until July 28, 1933, was National Union formally registered as a political party, as it had to be if it wished to enter candidates in the coming election.[63] Quisling continued to hope that the Agrarians would yield to his terms, but his hopes were in vain.

The issuance of the call for "national union", contrary to his expectations, proved also to be a liability rather than an asset. In his pronouncement, entitled "National Union", he declared that his movement was not intended to be a party in the same sense as other political parties, but that it would instead form a "movement outside of the parties".[64] The partisan press, however, refused to accept this interpretation. *Aftenposten's* editor declined to publish the proclamation because he insisted that the launching of National Union would have a divisive effect on the *borgerlig* election campaign. Furthermore, Editor Nesse maintained that Quisling's program was permeated by a belief in collectivism which *Aftenposten* found disagreeable.[65] *Nationen* was a bit more courteous, and provided space for small extracts of the announcement. However, wishing to minimize Quisling's break with the Agrarian party, *Nationen* alleged that he had not formed a political party, but was instead continuing to build up Nordic Folk-Rising toward the goal of "national union". The paper declared that there was nothing in his program, which *Nationen* allegedly did not have space to print, that could not be reconciled with the Agrarian party's philosophy. Furthermore, *Nationen* insisted that the Agrarians had on every occasion been ready to take part in the type of "national *borgerlig* government" that Quisling called for.[66]

Only *Tidens Tegn* under Rolf Thommessen was willing to provide full publicity for the venture, which appeared in the May 16 edition. As a political manifesto, "National Union" was both a call for support and a justification. In his effort to explain why a new political organization was needed at this time, Quisling placed stress on the evil times in which Norway found itself, with an alleged catastrophe approaching, and with the old political parties unable to accomplish anything because they were class parties, looking out for the narrow interests of their constituencies rather than the nation as a whole. He argued that the country's crisis could not at present be solved by any *borgerlig* coalition. The Liberals insisted that the Labor party be included in any crisis coalition, which of course was unthinkable, and it was impossible for the Independent People's party, Conservatives, and Agrarians, he maintained, to win a majority by themselves. In addition, he continued, the old parties were not able to reach large numbers of independent voters, who out of disgust with the present system refused to participate in elections. A new movement, he argued optimistically, would be able to capture their allegiance, a movement which at the same time would have the necessary dynamic ideology to match that of "Marxism".

He portrayed political opinion as being tired of party politics, anxious for the future, crushed under high taxes and debt, angry over unnecessary labor conflicts, opposed to "the Bolshevistic and demagogic spirit" which was spreading over the country, and alienated from the Conservatives' lack of will and the Liberals' experiment with the country's fate. He described

National Union as an organization which could allay such discontent. It was not, he said, a political party according to the standard definition, but instead lay outside of party politics; it was a "spiritual movement" in which farmers, workers, and *borgerlige* could reach common understanding. Seeking to provide continuity for such a process, he declared that the foundation for this movement was Nordic Folk-Rising. He described the Folk-Rising as having become quiescent when its foreman entered the Agrarian government. Due to the present situation, he continued, this organization had now decided to come forward as an active political movement under the name National Union.

Having thereby, in his usual fashion, declared the country's established parties incapable of leading the nation out of the present crisis, within the next few lines he called upon some of the very same parties to cooperate with his nascent movement. National Union's task, he maintained, was not to divide, but instead it would cooperate with "all national and social forces in the country". In the approaching fall election it would place candidates in those districts which it considered most suitable, but at the same time it was willing to enter into electoral alliances (*listeforbund*) with the Conservatives, the Agrarian party, the Independent People's party, and the Radical People's party (*Det Radikale Folkeparti*).[67] He thereby declared his intent to cooperate with all *borgerlige* political parties except Mowinckel's Liberals. Acting in concert with these parties, he proclaimed, National Union would seek to gain a "nationally minded" majority in the *Storting* which would maintain the established society. Together this majority would lay the foundation for a government above ordinary politics which would carry out "constructive national politics".

The "constructive national politics" he had in mind were encompassed in a five-point program he delineated for National Union in the final segment of the article. The views expressed in the program did not differ from those which he had stated in previous pronouncements, although they were somewhat more detailed. As a philosophical foundation for the program, he repeated in abbreviated form the same ideas found in Nordic Folk-Rising's program, plus an element copied from Hitler's racial ideas. The twin basis for the program was (1) "blood consciousness and earth, and a spiritual, religious, national and social philosophy of life", which provided understanding for "each individual's worth and possibilities within society's borders", and (2) the changed conditions brought about by scientific developments and modern technology's enormous creativity.

He thereby presented himself as being capable of reconciling Norway's past rural tradition with the demands of a modern industrial society. In the program we again see the dual nature of his proposals. He wanted to act as the innovator who was attuned to the latest advances, but at the same time he did not wish his radical proposals to frighten away persons with conservative convictions from whom he hoped to gain backing. But in attempting to be both innovator and conservator, there were bound to be inconsistencies in his program. Thus in its first point he declared National Union stood for a strong and stable government, but nevertheless a government which did not interfere excessively in areas outside of the state's competence. However, despite the attempt to placate conservatives, his program, if realized, would have meant drastic changes. In imitation of Italian Fascism, it would have set up a corporative chamber (*Næringsting*), lessened parliamentary effectiveness by decreeing shorter *Storting* sessions, established the procedure of popular referendums, and heightened governmental power by permitting the dissolution of parliament. True to the strategy he had followed in the Agrarian government, he also intended to deal with the "revolutionary" labor organizations. They would be denied the right to have a "labor monopoly". Similarly, the Labor party could expect to be outlawed, and the goal he had so rigorously pursued in the Kullmann case would thereupon finally be realized.

Finances were covered in the program's second point. In accordance with his corporate ideals, he favored the strict regulation of the economy through planning. Balanced budgets and a reduction in taxes were promised in an attempt also to appeal to conservative interests, with Quisling for once putting forward a concrete proposal, stating that taxes should not exceed 10 per cent of a person's income. The debt-ridden were also promised an end to the restrictive deflationary economic practices.

In his third point, focusing on economic production, he called for peace and stability within the labor market, which would ensure free and unhindered production. National economic planning was desirable, he maintained, but he then sought to qualify this by declaring that such planning would take place without restricting freedom of industry and free private initiative.

Such a harmonious economic scene would be found within a society enjoying complete solidarity, his fourth point. Class rivalry would disappear. All labor and employer groups would be under the control of the state, indicating once more Mussolini's influence. The state would see to it that all interests and strata of the population received their fair share of wealth. Everything would be done to ensure national solidarity, which would be as harmonious as possible. According to Quisling, an important aspect of maintaining a unified society lay in preserving the purity of the race. Here he revealed once more how he was influenced by the racial ideas of the period. The chronic criminal and the mentally retarded would be denied the right to have children, while "the most valuable" segments of the population would receive encouragement to produce offspring.

In his final point he covered foreign policy. Norway's external relations, he argued, should be based on race. Repeating the point of view he had previously offered in Nordic Folk-Rising's program, although not in detail, he declared that outside of Scandinavia, the Norwegians were most

akin to the people inhabiting the British Isles and Germany. It was therefore natural, he maintained, for Scandinavians, Germans and the British to
join together in a "Nordic League", creating a power bloc and an economic
bloc of great potential. This group, even more than the League of Nations,
could create guarantees for lasting world peace.

He concluded by summing up in a catchy appeal the impression he
hoped his new movement would have: "We will create a unified new Norway with just terms for everyone."

Unfortunately for him and his newly formed organization, the question
was not as simple as this. His program contained a number of contradictions and inferred conclusions which were amply suited to draw criticism.
One of the main charges levied against the program concerned the vagueness of many of its points. While its goals might be exemplary, the program provided few explanations of how they might be achieved.[68] On the
other hand, one of the few concrete proposals that Quisling made, the reduction of taxes to no more than 10 per cent of one's total income, raised
critical comment because of its utopian nature, in particular when compared with the many radical reforms he favored, which would have increased the power of the state, and which would have proportionally increased the state's need for revenue.[69] A further contradiction was his insistence that National Union was not a political party but rather a "movement". It was difficult for outside observers to discern any difference between it and other political parties, despite his denunciation of them, because National Union, like other parties, intended to enter lists of
candidates, and he called for electoral cooperation with all *borgerlige* parties except the Liberals.[70] Uncertainty also surrounded his appeal for an
end to class struggle and the establishment of a unified society unfragmen-
ted by class divisiveness because the program also contained planks favoring the existence of a "strong, free, and independent peasantry", and for
the strengthening of the middle class. If the people were to be truly unified, then special consideration could not be given to any distinct grouping
within society.

In reality, however, his call for an end to class division was not intended
to bring about true equality. He had little sympathy for the industrial
working class, and simply wished to neutralize it through the use of nationalism, following the examples of Hitler and Mussolini. The success
gained by the two fascist dictators also brought into focus a final conclusion which can be drawn concerning his program, namely, the unstated
but obvious fact that if successful, he intended to establish an authoritarian
government with corporative overtones. The many restrictive points in the
program, the insistence on greatly increased power for the state, and the
bitter attacks against party politics and parliamentary political practices, all
provided ample evidence of his aspiration greatly to reduce parliamentary
government in favor of a more authoritarian model. This was not, how-

ever, stated directly in the program. Instead, he declared: "We want a democratic elite government."[71] Once more, here was an example of his proclivity to make contradictory statements. An elite government is by definition non-democratic. He was an elitist who despised parliamentary politics, in part by conviction, in part by his personal failure to succeed because of his personality, which was unsuited for the give and take of practical politics. However, despite his contempt for parliamentary practices, the irony was that if National Union were to succeed, it would first have to engage in electoral politics within a parliamentary framework.

In Quisling's quest for success, National Union had to win or lose on its own merits from the very start. None of the *borgerlige* political organizations welcomed his announcement with open arms. Even *Tidens Tegn* did not ally itself with the newcomer, but continued to serve as the spokesman for the Independent People's party. Its editor did not regard Quisling and his movement as the answer to the political dilemma that Thommessen faced, seeking to find some solution to the twin problems of the advance of the Labor party and the inability of *borgerlige* governments to deal with the economic and social issues of the depression. In an editorial appearing in the same issue as Quisling's proclamation, *Tidens Tegn* pointed out that young people in particular were demanding new politics to deal with the "burning questions" of unemployment, labor union tyranny, and the debt crisis. Such new politics were present, maintained the editorial, in the Independent People's party's new election program, in Hundseid's "sharp and clear speeches", and now in Quisling's call for National Union. The paper expressed the hope that the three groups would cooperate, since they contained the basis for "the new party our people are longing for". But such a party would have to come in the future, and Thommessen thereby indicated indirectly that he did not consider National Union to be the answer.[72]

Another disappointment occurred almost simultaneously. Although National Union's proclamation had been published on May 16, Quisling had chosen a much more auspicious date for the founding of his movement, the 17th of May, Norway's constitution day and national holiday. One of the holiday's highlights at countless celebrations throughout the country was the presentation of patriotic speeches, and it happened to be Quisling's good fortune to be scheduled as the 17th of May speaker at Eidsvoll. It was here in this small village in the eastern part of the country that the founding fathers of modern Norway had drawn up the Constitution of 1814. Surrounded by national symbols, Eidsvoll would therefore serve as the ideal place from which he could announce the start of National Union. However, when representatives of the Labor party in Eidsvoll learned the name of the speaker, they protested vehemently. They applied political pressure through the local municipal council, and the ceremonial committee was forced to remove Quisling from the program.[73] He did not allow this little defeat to deter him. National Union's founding was later proclaimed to have taken place on May 17.

More serious than this minor setback was the inability of NS – the party was soon commonly referred to by its initials – to secure cooperation from *borgerlige* political groups. With the exception of the lukewarm reception provided by Thommessen's *Tidens Tegn*, which represented but a faction within the Independent People's party, none of the *borgerlige* organizations responded with enthusiasm to the announcement of National Union's founding. *Aftenposten*, looking out for the Conservative party, considered NS as a threat, having the potential of being able to steal voters away from the Conservatives. The Liberals had already indicated their distaste for Quisling and his politics when he served in the Agrarian government, and they had no reason to alter their opinion. Due to the breach with the Agrarian party, the Agrarians too viewed NS as the emergence of a rival. While Aadahl continued to sympathize with Quisling and gave him some indirect support in *Nationen*, he dared not openly further National Union's cause. Finally, the organization that embodied the desire for a united effort from all *borgerlige* against the growth of socialism, the Fatherland League, also responded with criticism. Its weekly newspaper, *ABC*, reacted in an interesting manner to the news of NS' founding. Quisling continued to receive praise for his energetic campaign against the alleged marxist revolutionaries, but NS was condemned. *ABC* maintained on May 18 that the only effect which the new party would have in the upcoming election would be to divide *borgerlige* votes and thereby benefit Labor. Quisling was urged to give up his venture and instead return to the Agrarian fold: "Quisling needs the Agrarian party as the Agrarian party needs Quisling." In its next issue, Lehmkuhl expanded the League's argument against NS, pointing out how unrealistic it was for a leading member of the Agrarian party, without an organization and without a press, to step out of the ranks and start his own party five months before an election.[74] The foreman declared that the Agrarian party should still be the party to support in the *borgerlige* anti-socialist campaign. He argued that while the situation might change later, so that it would then be necessary to start a new party, this was not the time.[75] The Fatherland League's leadership revealed thereby that it also regarded NS as a rival, owing to the role the League might later play as an active party. While Quisling continued for a time as a member of the League, he could not expect to receive its aid.

J. B. Hjort, one of the strongest proponents of National Union's formation, responded to the League's charges in an article published in both *ABC* and *Tidens Tegn*. He declared that NS, not the Agrarians, was the party to support for those *borgerlige* voters who truly wished to oppose revolutionary elements. He argued that Quisling deserved credit for the

Agrarian party's anti-revolutionary profile, while Hundseid represented a faction which was incapable of taking a hard and firm stand against the Labor party. There was little if any difference between Hundseid, Hambro, and Mowinckel, maintained Hjort. As for Lehmkuhl's argument that NS should not have been launched so near an election, Hjort meant that it would be of benefit for the League, if it wished to realize its ideals, to support Quisling, because his ideas more than those of the established *borgerlige* parties best represented the goals which the Fatherland League hoped to achieve. Hjort furthermore pointed out that it was unrealistic to expect a political party to emerge fully formed. Only by participating in the political struggle could a movement develop naturally. This was the time for action, as the League should realize, and its activity should not be devoted, said Hjort sarcastically, to evening slide shows as had been the case in the past.[76]

His counter-attack contained a number of telling points, in particular his reference to the fact that Quisling's strong opposition to the socialists was of a variety that was much closer to the League's position than that maintained by the established *borgerlige* parties, who in many instances were not especially enthusiastic about the League. The League, however, could not permit to pass unanswered such an open appeal to its members for backing and sarcastic references to its political effectiveness. It responded by castigating Hjort, while continuing to deal more kindly with Quisling.[77]

The exchange of barbed views with the Fatherland League indicated how one of the chief expectations of Quisling and his advisers had not been realized. They had believed that National Union's emergence would generate excitement and gain followers from the rank and file of various *borgerlige* parties – which in turn would compel the leaders of these groups to cooperate with NS on its own terms. When he founded NS, Quisling believed in the existence of a ground-swell of popular approval for his politics.[78] But there was no all-embracing rush to his banner following his announcement of National Union's formation. Under his lead, NS therefore had to enter the political wilderness and work on its own in anticipation of the rapidly approaching election in the fall.

With National Union having been established at such a late date, and considering the halting manner in which it was founded, it was hardly any wonder that when the party had to build up an organization and conduct a campaign in 1933, the problems it faced were grave to say the least. Everything had to be improvised in a hurry. With no established political leaders except Quisling, who was impractical when it came to innovative planning, and with limited funds available, a negative outcome was hardly unexpected, as Lehmkuhl had prophesied.

The initial organizational plan for the party was provided by its leader, and it was completely ignored. When he first arrived at the offices made available by Walter Fürst, he handed his staff at the Central Office a document which proved to be the translated version of the Russian Communist party's organizational plan. As he had shown previously, his solution to his perceived threat from the Marxists was to fight them through imitation. The staff at the party's headquarters simply put it aside.[79]

National Union's initial organization consisted instead of a number of separate committees, each intended to look after a specialized aspect of party affairs: the Political Committee, Organizational Committee, Foreign Committee, Propaganda Committee, Press Committee, Finance Committee, Planning Office, and Work Organization. Unfortunately for the party, the persons who served on these committees frequently performed their responsibilities in a dilettantish manner, which did not improve NS' fortunes in the short time remaining before the voters were to cast their ballots. Only about half of the committee members actually worked actively on behalf of NS.[80] Coordination between the groups was lacking, and as a result those who did try to exert themselves on NS' behalf were frequently left with the frustrated feeling that they were working in a vacuum, with little to show for their efforts.[81]

The effect of amateurish leadership and lack of coordination had special significance for the party's attempt to secure adequate financial aid. Although regular fundraisers were hired to fill its coffers, and a Finance Committee was set up to supervise this activity, leading NS members, in particular Prytz, kept interfering in financial matters, thereby incapacitating the effectiveness of the fundraisers to a considerable degree. The Finance Committee and its fundraisers were further frustrated by the habit of party officers to make use of funds without leaving an adequate record of receipts and expenditures.[82] In addition, the late start made it difficult to raise money because many organizations and private individuals who might have contributed had already expended the cash they had intended to spend for the election.[83]

With such haphazard practices in finances, it is understandable that adequate bookkeeping was never a virtue with NS. Nevertheless, from the few records that do exist from the 1933 campaign it is readily apparent that the effort to secure campaign funds was not a great success. Altogether, about 33,000 *kroner* were raised by various national and local groups. Party expenditures far exceeded this sum.[84] At the end of October, following the election, NS officials estimated the party deficit to be approximately 23,000 kr., although the final figure was expected to be higher.[85]

With inadequate financing, the party faced great difficulties in reaching the voters, in particular because National Union lacked publications. In an effort to overcome this obstacle, Walter Fürst made a brazen attempt to exploit the country's leading financial newspaper, *Handels- og Sjøfarts-*

tidende. He signed a contract with the paper to publish what appeared to be an advertising supplement for a local transit company. He then proceeded to alter the contract so that *Handels- og Sjøfartstidende* would instead print a newspaper entitled *National Union*. However, when the ruse was discovered, he was informed in no uncertain terms that *Handels- og Sjøfartstidende* would not publish a "fascist newspaper" because of the adverse publicity this would have.[86] Fürst had to accept this setback, and the party remained virtually without a press until after the election.[87]

Inadequate planning occurred not only centrally at party headquarters in Oslo, but throughout the country, resulting in clumsy improvisation. The absence of an established party structure meant that everything had to be built up immediately. This resulted in confusion, since much of the party's campaign work was conducted by persons with little or no experience. There was no lack of enthusiasm, especially among young people, who were attracted to Quisling because he appeared to represent something new and dynamic in politics. However, this youthful enthusiasm not infrequently conflicted with the views of older persons who joined NS because of their conservatism. A Trondheim attorney, for example, complained to Quisling that the local NS organization lacked planning and failed to inspire confidence because it was dominated by young activists.[88] On the other hand, Professor Ragnar Skancke, who succeeded in attracting a number of students to NS at the Technical University in Trondheim, maintained that some party officers in the provinces of North and South Trøndelag held ideological views that were pure conservatism; and that they failed to understand the true purpose of National Union.[89]

In Norway's second largest city, Bergen, youthful optimism predominated. The local NS organization was headed by Hans Hanson, Jr., son of a shipping magnate. He decked his car with NS symbols, which soon became known popularly throughout Bergen as "the Quisling car". Hanson wrote enthusiastically to Quisling about his organization, in particular how the best ladies, the wives and daughters of "the leading men in town" were working on behalf of NS.[90]

Throughout the country the pattern repeated itself. Local NS organizations were created in a rush to meet the demands of the coming election. In some areas youthful enthusiasts predominated, in others older more conservative men held control. NS succeeded in establishing party groups in the majority of the country's provinces, in particular in the towns and larger villages, but in the short time remaining before the election there was bound to be a lack of effective coordination.

The different political viewpoints which appeared within National Union at the time of its founding simply reflected the heterogeneous nature of the party's initial membership. Except for discontent with the prevailing politi-

cal situation, there existed no common denominator to unite the disparate
ideological components which found room in NS after Quisling had proclaimed its start.

Quisling's main strength lay in his reputation as the uncompromising
foe of the Labor party. In addition, his attacks against the "party politicians" in the *Storting* who were unable to meet the problems of the depression won approval from frustrated *borgerlige* who were deeply disappointed by the apparent inability of the existing non-socialist parties to
come up with alternatives that could match the appeal of the Labor party.
Finally, in his call for national unity he voiced an ideal shared by many
borgerlige, who could not understand why the different *borgerlige* parties
retained their separate identities rather than joining against the common
enemy, the Labor party.

His appeal for unity and an end to class divisions had a special impact
because it was couched in nationalistic terms. Nationalists such as Pastor
Martin Tveter were attracted to NS because the party appeared to combine
nationalism with Christianity. Tveter's parish was in the extreme northern
town of Vadsø, where he became a leading spokesman for the party in
northern Norway. He applauded Quisling's choice of the NS symbol because it combined Christian and nationalistic elements – the banner of St.
Olav, a golden cross on a field of red.[91] Quisling similarly adopted a nationalistic motto as the party's slogan, the words attributed to a leading
medieval monarch, Håkon Håkonsson: "Norway was a realm, it shall become a people" ("*Norge var et Rike, det skal bli et Folk*"). Although it
originated with Henrik Ibsen,[92] the slogan, to NS' detriment, not surprisingly became associated with Hitler's similar "*ein Reich, ein Volk*". Another nationalistic element which Quisling inserted into NS' program was
his support of Norway's claim to Greenland. Not only did he personally
feel strongly about this issue, but he also believed it to be of tactical value,
capable of generating voter approval.

The party's stress on nationalism was especially attractive to impressionable young people. NS developed a youthful image to a considerable
extent, with a significant number of party officers being in their twenties
and thirties. This trend was due not only to NS nationalism, but also to the
fact that the party was willing to appoint its younger members to important positions. Other parties were dominated by older men who tended to
keep all aspects of leadership under their control. Not surprisingly, NS influence made itself felt among university students, in particular at the
Technical University in Trondheim and at the University of Oslo. In
Trondheim the NS cause was aided by Professor Skancke, while in Oslo
the NS student organization maintained close ties with related student
groups affiliated with the Independent Liberals, the Conservatives, and the
Fatherland League. Not infrequently these organizations joined to form a
"national front" against radical and socialist groups in the University's Stu-

dent Association.[93] Among the most prominent NS activists was Rolf Jør-gen Fuglesang, president of the NS student organization in Oslo. He be-came the party's General Secretary in 1934, and he remained a life-long Quisling loyalist. Other prominent students who belonged to NS included Bjarne Gran, a history major who wrote on behalf of NS; Herlof Harstad, who became a leading party editor; and the writers Odd-Stein Anderssen and Eiliv Odd Hauge.[94]

Further down the education ladder, National Union gained fervent ap-proval among secondary students in the *gymnasium*, which was out of proportion to the backing the party received from the general population. Swept along by the common tendency to be antagonistic toward party politics, and themselves at an uncritical age, a number of young *gymna-sium* students became strong adherents of NS. The party's success among this group was especially notable in the capital. The extent to which NS in-fluence made itself felt was later indicated in 1935, when the bylaws of the student association at the Oslo Cathedral School, the most prestigious *gymnasium* nationally, were altered so that the association's president was no longer elected, but instead appointed in accordance with National Union's practice according to the *Führer* principle.[95] But while such alle-giance to NS aroused shocked concern among some of their elders, it did not have any significant importance, because the majority of *gymnasium* students were not old enough to vote in the election.

National Union also appeared attractive to persons in certain dissatisfied vocational groups. Professional military officers were highly discontented during the 1930s. The country's poor economy resulted in reduced bud-gets, and at the same time the armed forces were under constant attack from strident pacifists. Military budgets were cut to the point where the officer corps was greatly reduced, with only a small select group being re-tained on active duty. Highly qualified officers sometimes fruitlessly sought positions for years on end. Understandably, the bitterness of these frustrated men was concentrated against the Labor party, which more than any other represented the pacifist, anti-military point of view. At the same time, it was natural for some of the same officers to find the party of their choice in National Union, headed by an ex-General Staff officer and for-mer Minister of Defense. Another aspect of NS which appealed to officers was Quisling's use of the *Führer* principle in decision-making. Orders were to be obeyed, not debated, which was in accord with an officer's own experiences. Similarly, some officers reacted favorably to Quisling's pro-posal to reorganize the state more along corporate lines. The ideal that ex-perts rather than party politicians should be responsible for technical deci-sions was one the hard-pressed career officer could agree to with relish.[96] Among those who were either on active duty or who were of a military background were first and foremost the party chieftain himself, seconded by his trusted friend, Frederik Prytz. Also prominent were Major Hvoslef, leader of the Community Defense who became the party's first General Secretary; Captain A. F. Munthe of the General Staff; Major Eckbo, a prominent financial contributor; Colonel Konrad Sundlo, the army commander at Narvik; Captain Karl Stenersen; and Major Ebbesen, party leader in Møre og Romsdal.[97]

The belief that experts should make technical decisions was also shared by a number of prominent NS members who professionally were educated in the applied sciences. They were convinced that the country's present economic and social difficulties could be solved if only technical experts were given a free hand to apply their solutions. A foremost exponent of this view was Professor Skancke at Norway's leading technical institute. Even more successful was Dr. Gulbrand Lunde, a chemical engineer in Stavanger, who emerged as a key figure in NS activity in the southwest of Norway. He made Stavanger one of the main centers of NS strength, and was later extremely effective in the role of party propaganda leader. Lunde was one of the few able men within National Union who remained loyal to Quisling at all times. Further to the north, in Bergen, Georg Vedeler, an engineer who was employed by a leading shipping line, was also very effective as the regional NS leader, replacing Hanson in this capacity soon after the 1933 election.

Quisling's anti-Labor party stance earned his party some support from business interests that feared the growth of organized labor. Among businessmen in Oslo who played an important part in early NS activity were Ragnar Møllhausen, Otto Sverdrup Engelschiøn, and Jens Rolfsen.[98]

The legal profession was another professional group from which NS recruited a significant number of its prominent members. The most outstanding of these was Johan Bernhard Hjort, who became the number two man in the party. Always intensely interested in politics, Hjort had earlier been frustrated in his quest to develop a political career as a member of the Conservative party. He hoped that NS would now serve as the vehicle for his ambition, and he worked tirelessly on its behalf. Other attorneys of note who joined the party were Albert Wiesener and W. F. Christie of Hamar.

The farmers formed a most important vocational group that provided NS with significant backing. The fears felt by Agrarian leaders had proven correct; part of the farm population did favor the former Minister of Defense. In large part this was due to his vehement denunciation of the Labor party. The extent of agrarian support for NS is indicated by the fact that 25.1 per cent of its candidates in the 1933 election were farmers, the largest percentage coming from any single vocational group.[99] Although the percentage of NS agrarian candidates declined in the 1936 election, the farmers continued to be a segment of the population from which NS received notable support, in particular in eastern Norway. This pattern remained true during the wartime period as well.

To summarize National Union's appeal to different vocations, the party in general obtained backing from most groups who tended to support *borgerlige* political parties. The sustenance NS received from the farmers and from individuals with a technical education was especially striking. In the parliamentary elections of 1933 and 1936 the percentage of NS candidates who were engineers stood at 4.85, which was noteworthy considering the small number of engineers in the population as a whole.[100] On the other hand, NS membership within the working class was quite low, and the same was true among persons with a higher education in the liberal arts.[101] It should be stressed, however, that even within those vocational and age groups from which National Union received most support, such backing represented at all times only a *very small* percentage of the group as a whole. NS never succeeded in gaining significant adherence from any segment of the population, as the election results from 1933 and 1936 make abundantly clear.

Admiration of foreign totalitarian movements, in particular Nazi Germany, was an ideological factor which influenced NS' membership composition. In its broadest form, in terms of having a positive outlook toward Fascist Germany and Italy, this attitude was widespread within NS. However, the same was true for all *borgerlige* parties except the Liberals during the early 1930s. More specifically, a number of those who joined NS and became prominent in its affairs were persons who wished to have Quisling lead NS after Hitler's example. One of the most noteworthy of these was Hans S. Jacobsen, who had studied in Germany and who brought back with him a strong pro-Nazi bias. Similarly, Albert Wiesener had studied in Germany. Walter Fürst, the party's first propaganda leader, had shown his interest in European Fascism as head of the National Club. Adolf Egeberg, Jr. abandoned his leadership of the minuscule Norway's National Socialist party and switched his allegiance to NS. He later served as editor of one of the party's most important publications, *Vestlandets Avis* in the province of Rogaland.

Beyond those who joined NS because of ideological, vocational, or age considerations, one small segment of its membership was characterized by total, uncritical admiration of what they perceived to be Quisling's genius. This group remained steadfastly loyal to him, whereas the majority of those who joined the party for other reasons broke with Quisling during the 1930s. Among the most prominent of these were Harald Franklin Knudsen, who belonged to the noted Knudsen family of Telemark; Orvar Sæther, a teacher; Tormod Hustad, an architect; Haldis Neegaard Østbye, one of the leading female party members; and Ørnulf Lundesgaard, a dentist.[102]

Although it is impossible schematically to cover all varieties of motivation for party membership, in the main this was the composition of the party that Quisling headed in 1933. He assumed the post of Party Leader

(*Partisjef*) because no one else enjoyed the national reputation he possessed. At the time of the party's inception, he held it together. Because of his unclear pronouncements, it was possible for him to gain the adherence of individuals who were primarily concerned with halting the advance of Labor, persons who were traditionally *borgerlig* in outlook, and those who were fully committed admirers of Fascism.[103] Whereas he would later exert a divisive influence on his party, at its beginning he acted as a unifier.

Faced with the prospect of having to proceed alone after National Union's founding, Quisling attempted to compensate for the absence of significant external cooperation by seeking to take over control of a radical farmers' organization, the Rural Crisis Aid (*Bygdefolkets Krisehjelp*). This group had come into being in the fall of 1931 as a direct result of the adverse impact which the depression had on the farmers. While the depression affected all economic groups, the agrarian sector was especially hard hit. More than 6500 foreclosures took place in 1932 alone.[104] The Crisis Aid demanded an end to such auctions and insisted on economic reforms to aid the debt-ridden farmers. It became an organization to be reckoned with in eastern Norway, where the farmers were especially plagued with economic problems. Members of the Crisis Aid gathered in threatening groups when foreclosures and evictions were held, and they at times used coercion to prevent such measures from being carried out.[105]

At its inception the Crisis Aid had been non-political, with its membership open to persons of different political views.[106] However, as the economic crisis deepened and the government and *Storting* appeared unable to offer relief, the Crisis Aid increasingly became more politicized. Party politics and parliamentarianism were castigated for their alleged ineffectiveness, and the Crisis Aid began to adopt a view toward the political system which did not differ much from Quisling's negative attitude.[107] However, while the Crisis Aid in 1932 and early 1933 was harsh in its criticism, it had not yet abandoned the hope that aid to the farmer might come through politics. It simply had not been able to decide whether the Labor party or the Agrarian party, or both, might warrant its support, seeking to gain in return economic relief for its members, who in the main were small farmers. Events, however, conspired to force the Crisis Aid to lend its support to neither of these two established parties, but instead to a newcomer, National Union.

Although several prominent members of the Crisis Aid, including its chairman, David Seierstad, were favorably disposed toward Quisling's politics as Minister of Defense, the most active leader within the organization, Olav Lien, editor of the group's paper, was more skeptical. Lien believed that the Crisis Aid might best gain its ends through the Agrarians and Labor, the parties to which most of Crisis Aid members belonged.[108]

But his plans went awry. Although he belonged to the Labor party, he was excluded from the party because of his commitment to the Crisis Aid. The other possibility of turning to the Agrarians was impeded because of the Crisis Aid's strong hostility toward Jens Hundseid. When Hundseid was re-elected as party chairman in March 1933, it proved impossible for the Crisis Aid to establish any permanent ties with the Agrarian party.[109] The Crisis Aid's poor economic condition compounded its difficulties. It was on the verge of bankruptcy in the spring of 1933, with not enough funds to pay for the cost of publishing its newspaper.[110]

These developments left the organization in a weak condition, considering its intent to use its political influence in the coming election. Despite some reluctance on the part of Lien, its leadership therefore responded eagerly to an invitation from NS to hold discussions concerning the possibility of cooperation. The first meeting took place on May 22, 1933, only six days after Quisling had proclaimed National Union's formation. As had occurred previously, Prytz, not Quisling, was responsible for initiating this contact. The conference was held at Prytz's home, and he acted as NS' spokesman. Quisling, as usual reticent in the presence of men who were not personal acquaintances, sat silent unless addressed directly. His main contribution to the deliberations was to present one of the memos he had written during his feud with Hundseid.[111]

Nothing definite resulted from the May 22 meeting, but the Crisis Aid's Executive Committee did agree to continue discussions. Although Lien, whose voice was decisive, had not yet definitely decided to cooperate with NS, he was left with no alternative. It was essential, he felt, for the Crisis Aid to participate actively in politics not only to exert its influence, but also to prevent eventual disintegration through inaction. The money which Quisling and Prytz held out as an inducement was very tempting, but in addition NS appeared to offer further advantages in a political alliance. As a new party, it did not share the blame for the prevailing economic misery. National Union criticized the same men, the politicians, and to some extent the same conditions that the Crisis Aid denounced. Furthermore, NS had incorporated the terms "national" and "union" in its title, catchwords which many members of the Crisis Aid responded favorably to.[112]

Although Lien personally did not believe NS could solve the problems of the depression any better than the older political parties, he reluctantly made the decision to join the Crisis Aid's fate with that of NS. In an agreement drawn up on July 4, the Crisis Aid leaders literally sold the soul of their organization to NS. The Crisis Aid agreed (1) to denounce publicly the "revolutionary parties", the Labor party and the Communists; (2) to merge its organization gradually with NS and to place its membership lists at the disposal of NS when requested; (3) to support NS in the coming election; and (4) to transfer the organization's newspaper *Bygdefolket* (*The Village People*) to NS when asked to do so. In return, Lien, Seierstad, and

Bygdefolket's publisher were promised 5000 *kroner*, with one to two thousand additional *kroner* being offered to complete the work of liquidating the organization when this became necessary.[113]

National Union could thus look forward to the day when the entire Crisis Aid organization would be its property – lock, stock, and barrel. However, for the time being it was resolved to have the agreement remain secret from the Crisis Aid's membership. Only gradually would the organization be absorbed into NS. The formal announcement of cooperation was therefore presented to the Crisis Aid's members in terms that indicated the adherence of NS to basic Crisis Aid principles, rather than the reverse. The announcement did not occur until August 13, and it stated that NS in its program had pledged itself to a moratorium on debts; the immediate cessation of foreclosures and evictions; a law that would permit the re-evaluation of property, guaranteeing possession of such properties to their owners; and inflation, which would lessen the debt burden that many farmers had outstanding. In order to maintain the fiction of the Crisis Aid's previous non-alignment in politics, a so-called "political organization" was set up as a front, named simply The Village People.[114] This organization joined with NS in presenting joint lists of candidates in the rural districts of five provinces in eastern and southern Norway where the Crisis Aid had its largest membership.[115]

The alliance with and projected takeover of this radical farm organization did little to make up for the absence of nationwide cooperation with any of the *borgerlige* parties. The Crisis Aid was an unproven political quantity, best known for the notoriety it had gained from its strong-arm tactics. It remained to be seen if the organization, in coalition with NS, could generate votes, in particular since the bulk of its membership belonged to parties other than NS. Nonetheless, Quisling hoped that this alliance might make up for his inability to come to terms with the Agrarian party.

The difficulties he faced in the coming campaign remained formidable. NS had no press to overcome the handicap of the negative criticism it received, not only in the Labor party's press, but also in the columns of *borgerlige* newspapers. The only slight compensation for this weakness came in the issuance of a special election publication entitled *NS*, a broadsheet that appeared in six numbers in Oslo during the period August 29 – October 11.[116] Furthermore, NS was hindered by its inadequate organization in the brief period before the election.

Quisling undoubtedly was aware of such practical obstacles when NS came into being, and this in part explains his reluctance to break with the Agrarians. But he also believed in great public enthusiasm for his politics which would serve as compensation. Furthermore, he felt that NS would obtain the votes of many persons who had not voted in previous elections or who were discontented with the existing parties. He based this optimistic opinion on the numerous letters and encouraging inquiries he had received.[117]

This sanguine assessment in the final analysis explains National Union's venture into Norwegian politics. Quisling, his close advisers, and even many politicians outside of NS all shared the assumption that there existed considerable favorable sentiment for his politics, and that NS would be certain to tap this source. Furthermore, he felt that this body of opinion would be so strong that NS would not have to contend with any *borgerlig* opposition, with the exception of the Liberals. Instead, the more conservative *borgerlige* parties were expected to join with National Union. Already in his May 16 article in *Tidens Tegn*, announcing his party's formation, he voiced this strategy, declaring that NS was prepared to establish electoral pacts (*listeforbund*) with all *borgerlige* parties except the Liberals.[118] He hoped that such cooperation would result in a "national minded" majority in the *Storting* which included NS representatives. This majority, he predicted, would organize a "national government" in which NS was expected to play a key role. He thereby delineated clearly NS' goal for 1933. The party could not hope to win a majority in the *Storting* at this early date. Its election program therefore called for cooperation as the best means of gaining power.[119]

What he failed to take into account was that the *borgerlige* parties from the very first regarded National Union not as an ally, but as a rival. Were National Union to gain votes, they felt quite correctly that this would be at their expense. Furthermore, he alienated these parties because while he sought their cooperation, he also described them as being incapable of meeting the challenge of the times, which only NS was ready to respond to.[120]

It was therefore little wonder that the national leadership of both the Conservative and Agrarian parties showed little enthusiasm for National Union. Quisling's party was attacked for being divisive, splitting the *borgerlige* effort against the Labor party. This theme was constantly repeated during the election campaign of 1933, and it proved to be quite effective. From the beginning NS spokesmen were on the defensive when forced to respond, insisting that NS' participation in the election was not divisive because the party was willing to enter into electoral pacts.[121] Such protestations had no impact on the Conservatives and Agrarians, whose leaders continued to regard NS as a rival.

The relationship between NS and Quisling's former party was not improved by the fact that he continued his feud with Hundseid. Charges and counter-charges were hurled by the two party chieftains during the course of the campaign.[122] Quisling's inability to avoid attacking Hundseid, as well as the Agrarian leadership's view that NS was a rival, made any cooperation between the two organizations impossible on the national level.

Aided by the Crisis Aid, which also detested the Agrarian leader, Quisling sought to give the impression that his conflict with Hundseid in the cabinet had resulted from differing views concerning what economic course the government should take. Quisling maintained that he had represented the real interests of the Agrarian party, while Hundseid and his supporters had betrayed the farmers' cause.[123]

Although considerable bitterness was produced by this dispute, there still existed among Agrarians some agreement with Quisling's politics. *Nationen* could not openly support the NS leader, but Aadahl at times provided aid for Quisling's cause.[124] Jon Sundby was another influential member of the Agrarian party who remained favorably disposed. He had served in the government alongside the Minister of Defense, and he had sided with the latter in his dispute with the Prime Minister. Sundby was ranked first on the Agrarian party's list of candidates in Akershus province, and Akershus was one of two provinces in which an electoral pact was entered into between the Agrarian party and NS. Agrarian voters must have been perplexed to note that while in Akershus there existed complete cooperation with NS, in neighboring Oslo the relationship between the two parties was characterized by open hostility.[125] Although the party's leadership was unable to prevent the provincial Agrarian organizations in Akershus and Aust-Agder from joining NS in electoral pacts, the fact that such cooperation was restricted to these two provinces showed that agrarian sympathy for Quisling was limited.

The relationship between Quisling and the Conservative party during the campaign proved to be even more negative. The national leadership of the Conservatives had not changed its opinion of Quisling. After the founding of National Union, the Conservatives regarded him as a foe not merely because his party could deprive them of votes, but also because of ideological considerations. The Conservatives favored, on the whole, a *laissez faire* economic policy, and they disliked the segments of Quisling's programs which called for government control, in imitation of Mussolini's corporate state. They were not reassured by the contradictory segments in his programs which seemed to favor private initiative.

At first the Conservatives responded by attempting to silence NS to death. Little if any mention of Quisling's new party appeared in the Conservative press.[126] The situation changed, however, when the Conservatives announced publicly that they would not under any circumstances enter into electoral alliances which included National Union. As justification, *Aftenposten* referred to NS' cooperation with the Crisis Aid, which the Conservative paper described as a revolutionary movement.[127]

This refusal proved to be a serious defeat for Quisling's politics. Although the Conservatives had earlier indicated their dislike of him as a politician, he had hoped that his strong agitation against Labor would generate such a positive reaction among Conservative voters that the party leadership would be forced to enter a coalition with NS. In his disappointment, his response to this rejection was therefore quite strong. He maintained that the true motive of the Conservatives was jealousy over the fact that NS more than any other party was a popular movement, and that his party was the only force that "the revolutionaries" really feared.[128]

Throughout the campaign he continued to polemicize against the Conservatives for their unwillingness to cooperate. The Conservatives increasingly responded in kind, and the exchange became quite heated.[129] The fray was heightened even more by the Independent People's party entrance into the controversy on the side of NS. Its foreman, Rolf Thommessen, continued to be an exponent of the need for *borgerlig* unity against the Labor party, a theme he repeated constantly in the columns of *Tidens Tegn*. He warmly endorsed the idea of *borgerlig* cooperation with NS, and his newspaper maintained a continuous stream of criticisms of the Conservatives for rejecting Quisling's party.[130]

The public repudiation of National Union by the Conservatives had the effect of isolating Quisling even more. In his campaign speeches, he declared that National Union's enemies were Marxism, which meant the Labor party, "liberalism in its decadent form", which meant the Liberal party, and "conservatism which attempts to turn back development", the Conservative party.[131] The only source of support that he had outside of his own party and the Crisis Aid was provided by the Independent People's party through Rolf Thommessen. The Conservatives were now so provoked by the attacks against them in *Tidens Tegn* that their press began to refer to Quisling's politics as synonymous with dictatorship.[132]

Tidens Tegn, on the other hand, repeated its theme that there existed considerable enthusiasm for the idea of an electoral pact that included National Union, and that the Conservative leadership was not in accord with its members.[133] While the paper exaggerated this point of view in a partisan manner, the contention nevertheless contained a kernel of truth. Some Conservatives disagreed with the party leadership in this dispute. They did so not necessarily because they had accepted Quisling's political point of view, but rather because of their desire to see a united *borgerlig* front against the Labor party. The one city where this opinion most strongly came to the fore was Bergen, where the local party organization disobeyed the national leadership and agreed to enter into an electoral pact with NS and the Independent People's party.[134]

Although *Tidens Tegn* trumpeted this incident as a victory, it had no repercussions for the party as a whole. The Conservative leadership insisted that the Bergen organization withdraw from the electoral pact, and when it refused, it was suspended from the party.[135] In defense of its decision, the party's Executive Committee now referred to NS as a "national socialist dictatorial movement".[136] *Aftenposten* similarly made it absolutely clear to its readers that there was a direct parallel between Quisling and Adolf Hitler: "In Germany there are today conservatives who in bitter regret pass judgement on themselves because they in their time did not do what the Norwegian Conservative party now has done."[137]

As a result of this uncompromising attitude, Quisling's campaign in September and October turned out to be directed as much against the Conservatives as it was against the Labor party. While this was a surprising turn of events, it should not have been unexpected. Not only did the Conservatives fear losing votes and resent negative criticism of their party, but they also had a special reason for comparing Quisling with Hitler. The leaders of the Conservative party were definitely committed to a democratic parliamentary system of government. Hitler's Germany had little appeal for them.

Quisling and other NS campaigners were reduced to making frustrated attacks against the Conservative leadership.[138] He went so far in an election speech as to declare that if they continued their dishonorable campaign against him, he would be forced to make revelations indicating the true character of the Conservative leadership.[139] The disclosures he had in mind quite probably referred to the attempt by the Conservatives to remove him from office by conspiring with Hundseid. His threat had no effect, however. *Aftenposten* responded in a sarcastic editorial by daring him to "sing out", and if he did not, it intended to challenge his manhood.[140] The tone of the editorial illustrated the degree of personal animosity which had developed between Quisling and the Conservative leadership headed by its president Carl J. Hambro.

The most telling attack by the Conservatives was their emphasis on NS divisiveness. Although NS attempted to counter by insisting it was the Conservatives who were breaking rank by refusing to join electoral pacts that included NS, this argument was offset by the fact that Quisling set up lists of candidates in a number of districts in which NS had no chance of electing representatives. NS lists in these constituencies could only draw votes away from the *borgerlige* parties such as the Conservatives, Agrarians, and Independent People's party, who frequently joined in electoral pacts that excluded NS. From a strictly partisan standpoint, NS had to run its own candidates because the new party needed to make itself known as widely as possible. However, this consideration frequently stood in direct opposition to its declared goal of halting the Labor party.

Not only the Conservatives stressed this fact. Although the Fatherland League had, not very enthusiastically, recommended that electoral pacts be established which included NS,[141] the League quickly condemned in strong terms National Union's creation of separate lists.[142]

The decision to establish such lists throughout the country was of special significance because frequently local NS organizations were opposed to such a step. But they were overruled by the party's central headquarters, which in the last instance was Quisling himself. His primary concern was to obtain as much publicity as possible for the party. Appeals for him to change his mind and to withdraw such lists had no effect.[143]

Both the Conservatives and the Fatherland League were particularly upset over the fact that when NS did not have enough qualified candidates in a given district, then the party arbitrarily selected a number of persons who, like it or not, were forced to have their names fill out the vacant spaces on NS lists.[144] *Aftenposten* referred to NS in this connection as a "dictatorial party". Whereas other political parties elected their leaders, Quisling, as NS' "party leader", was self-appointed, and it was he, said the paper sarcastically, who decided by decree where NS would set up its lists.[145]

A second line of attack which the Conservatives used against NS concerned its association with the Rural Crisis Aid. As defenders of the prevailing economic order, the Conservatives had a low regard for the radical agrarian Crisis Aid because of its extra-legal measures to protect the debt-ridden farmers. *Aftenposten* described the organization as revolutionary, and NS was condemned because of its ties to a group of this nature.[146] This placed Quisling on the defensive. Rather than being a benefit for him and NS, as he had originally anticipated, the Crisis Aid controversy became a handicap. At first he tried to minimize the issue, declaring that NS' ties with the organization were basically restricted just to one province in order to consolidate as much strength as possible in a "national direction".[147] Later he shifted ground, declaring that the Crisis Aid, because of the critical condition of the farmers, had been on the verge of being taken over by "revolutionary forces", but National Union had prevented this.[148] *Aftenposten* was not particularly impressed with this line of reasoning. In rebuttal, the Conservative newspaper declared that Quisling had not stopped the Crisis Aid, but was seeking to give it parliamentary representation. In *Aftenposten*'s view, the Crisis Aid had not changed its program at all following its agreement with Quisling.[149] This skepticism toward the Crisis Aid was shared by the Fatherland League. *ABC* maintained that Olav Lien talked the same language as he had three years earlier when he was a member of the Labor party. The Crisis Aid stressed the need for inflation in order to relieve the farmers' debt burden, while the NS said nary a word concerning this issue. *ABC* wondered if this was not similar to the practice of the Labor party, which, in the words of the paper, maintained that it was a democratic party in the countryside, while it assumed a revolutionary posture among the industrial workers in the towns.[150]

These charges quite clearly unsettled Quisling. He had intended to be on the offensive during the campaign, attacking primarily the Labor party for its supposed revolutionary threat to society. Due to the need to defend himself and NS from *borgerlige* assaults, especially from the Conservatives, his crusade against Labor was considerably muted. Nevertheless, he did seek to have NS mount an effective campaign against the socialists. His goal was the same as previously: to have the party outlawed from politics. He continued to equate Labor with the Russian Communist party.[151] The Laborites in turn did not hesitate to describe National Union as Hitler's representative in Norway.[152] For Labor, Quisling's political organization became its most implacable enemy. While the degree of hostility between the socialists and the *borgerlige* parties might vary, and in some instances it could be quite intense, with NS there was not the slightest room for compromise – the battle lines were drawn.

One of the interesting revelations made by Labor in the summer of 1933 was that Quisling, while Minister of Defense, had commissioned his close friend, Captain Adolf Munthe, a member of the General Staff and a political ally in Nordic Folk-Rising, to conduct a secret investigation to discover whether the socialists were stockpiling weapons. Munthe received this assignment immediately after Quisling had hurled his charges against the Labor party and the Communists in his sensational *Storting* speech in April 1932. Although the Captain obtained ample funds for his investigation, no stockpiles were ever found. *Arbeiderbladet* clearly enjoyed publicizing this embarassing fact, in particular since loosely-founded charges of alleged weapon storage for revolutionary purposes were often repeated in *borgerlige* circles during the interwar years.[153]

Political confrontation between NS and the Labor party was not restricted merely to speeches and newspaper polemics. Physical violence also occurred. In imitation of the Nazis, one of Quisling's tactics, intended to appeal to the workers and also to gain publicity, was to schedule rallies in working class neighborhoods. Young Labor party activists responded by disrupting the gatherings. Disorder took place inside the meeting hall, and NS members were beaten up outside.[154] At one such disturbance, the leader of the move to break up the meeting was none other than Einar Gerhardsen, Secretary of the Oslo Labor party and a future prime minister.[155]

Quisling personally suffered his share of difficulty from these conflicts. Following one election rally, he was hit over the head.[156] After another, a window of the car in which he was riding was smashed, and his residence was beleagured by a howling mob.[157] The publicity which resulted from such dramatic clashes did not always produce positive results. Reservations were expressed by, among others, the Conservatives that NS confrontations with leftist opponents were staged for publicity purposes, and many persons were repelled by the disturbances and physical violence which resulted from these conflicts.[158]

When National Union's election campaign concluded in mid-October 1933 after having been conducted for only a few months, the course of events during the campaign had not been very beneficial for the new party. Contrary to the expectations of its leader, no nationwide electoral cooperation had been possible with any of the major *borgerlige* parties. Instead, these parties had been largely effective in isolating NS. Only the Independent People's party, thanks in large part to the effort of its chairman, Thommessen, had cooperated with NS, and the Independent People's party was not a significant force in Norwegian politics. Ties with the Crisis Aid had served only to provide NS' *borgerlige* foes, led by the Conservatives, with an effective weapon. And Quisling's continued crusade against the Labor party had resulted in too much controversial publicity to be especially effective.

In seeking linkage with other organizations in 1933, NS achievements were therefore quite limited, being restricted to election cooperation individually on the province (*fylke*) level. In Norway's twenty provinces, NS formed three electoral pacts that included the Independent People's party, two that involved the Agrarian party, and one that included a rebellious local organization of the Conservative party. In five provinces NS had joint lists of candidates with the Crisis Aid, whose leadership had pawned the organization to NS. In Oslo NS cooperated with the Independent People's party.[159] In the neighboring province of Akershus the two parties were joined by the Agrarian party in the rural districts,[160] and cooperation between NS and the Agrarians occurred also in the rural areas of Aust-Agder.[161] NS' involvement in the farm districts of the latter province, located in southern Norway, took place in the form of a joint list with the Rural Crisis Aid. The Crisis Aid was also NS' sole partner in the rural districts of four other provinces, all located in eastern Norway.[162] With the exception of Oslo and Bergen, which were entirely urban provinces, NS electoral pacts were restricted to farm areas. In the towns the party set up its separate lists of candidates without any agreements with the Agrarian party or the Independent People's party. Furthermore, the cooperation that did take place was confined, with one exception, to the eastern and southeastern parts of the country. The only break in this pattern occurred in Bergen on the west coast. In Norway's second largest city the renegade Conservative organization combined with NS and the Independent People's party in an electoral pact.[163]

After the voters had cast their ballots and the returns were evaluated, it became obvious that the controversy over the emergence of Quisling's new party had been of little importance in determining the outcome of the election. The results revealed that only one party had triumphed, the Labor party. During the campaign Labor had enjoyed having the initiative, while the *borgerlige* parties had represented the status quo. The latter had been in the position of influencing governmental decisions during the crisis of the

1930s, yet they had provided no solutions. Labor, on the other hand, had not been responsible for governmental plans which had proven inadequate to meet the problems posed by the depression. The party also strengthened its position greatly by gradually ceasing its commitment to the Marxist theory of overthrowing capitalist society, to be followed by the introduction of socialism. Whereas in 1930 it had presented the voters with a program which declared popular democracy to be a myth, in 1933 Labor's political manifesto stressed its commitment to majority rule.[164] Because of the negative effects of the depression, Labor, as the foremost opposition party, gained the allegiance of large numbers of voters who abandoned the nonsocialist parties. Were the party to maintain its hold on these newcomers, it had to de-emphasize its adherence to revolutionary theory. Another important consideration in the Labor party's decision to follow a more restrained course was the examples of Italy and Germany, where many of the victims of unemployment and economic chaos had been radicalized into the legions of the Fascist parties.[165]

As a result, Labor's election campaign in 1933 was moderate in its approach, putting forward concrete proposals for dealing with the difficulties of the depression. The party was firmly moving in the direction of becoming a reform party. Because of its less strident tone, the implacable foes of the Labor party such as National Union had difficulty finding credible issues to use against the socialists.

Having conducted an extremely effective campaign under its major slogan, "employment for all" ("*hele folket i arbeid*"), the Labor party enjoyed a stunning success. It increased its votes from 375,000 to more than 500,000, with an accompanying advance in its percentage of the vote from 31.4 per cent to 40.1 per cent. This raised the number of Labor representatives in the *Storting* from forty-seven to sixty-nine, just seven short of an absolute majority.[166] The election victory of 1933 was the final decisive breakthrough for the Labor party in Norwegian politics, creating the basis for its takeover of government control in March 1935.

For all other established parties the election was a disaster. The Conservative *Storting* delegation was reduced from thirty-nine to thirty, the Liberals from thirty-three to twenty-four, the Agrarian party from twenty-five to twenty-three, and the Independent People's party from five to one.[167]

With the Labor party experiencing such a great advance and with the established *borgerlige* parties sustaining an electoral debacle, it was not surprising that National Union's initial venture into the political arena did not meet with particular success. The party's late start, its amateurish organization, its lack of major press support, its quarrel with the Conservative party and, to a lesser extent, the Agrarian party, all contributed to its failure. Most significant, however, was the Labor party's broad appeal to the mass of voters, which neutralized completely National Union's anti-revolutionary theme. The result was that NS failed to elect a single representative. This was doubly disappointing for Quisling. In order to try to ensure his election, he had headed his party's list of candidates in both Oslo and Oppland.

Nationally, NS gained 27,850 votes out of a total of 1,248,686 cast, amounting to 2.23 per cent of the electorate.[168] Of the NS votes, 14,942 came from the rural districts and 12,908 from the towns, which respectively was 1.76 per cent and 3.21 per cent of the total in the rural and urban divisions of the electorate.[169] The party took part in eight of the eighteen rural electoral districts in the provinces and in nine of the eleven urban electoral districts in the towns.[170] If NS' participation in the election is judged strictly by the results it achieved in those districts in which the party entered candidates, it can be said that its performance was somewhat more favorable, but not appreciably. NS gained 3.48 per cent of the vote in the rural districts where it took part and 3.55 per cent in the towns. When combined, NS' national percentage, based on its electoral district participation, was 3.51 per cent of the total.[171]

As for the electoral pacts that NS had been able to enter into on the local level, the outcome of the election was equally disappointing for the party, especially because of the controversy which had surrounded this question. Only in one electoral pact in which NS was involved, in Aust-Agder province, did such an alliance prove instrumental in winning a parliamentary seat. But since it was the Agrarian party that obtained the greatest number of votes within the pact, it was this party's candidate – and not NS' – who secured the *Storting* seat.[172]

Many political observers had expected NS to win at least three seats in parliament, and the outcome of the election was therefore keenly disappointing to those who had joined the newly formed party and who had campaigned energetically on its behalf. Examined more objectively, one cannot say, however, that the result NS obtained in the 1933 election was entirely negligible. Considering the party's brief existence, it managed nevertheless to come in fifth (although a poor fifth) in the results, following the four major parties – Labor, the Conservatives, the Liberals, and the Agrarian party – and outdistancing such established parties as the Communists and the Independent People's party.[173] In assessing National Union's election performance, it should also be noted that the party presented lists of candidates in only seventeen of the country's twenty-nine election districts.[174]

The *borgerlige* political parties, upset by their defeat, were by no means as charitable when evaluating NS' effect on the election. The disastrous result had to be explained away, and NS served as a handy scapegoat, being given at least partial blame for why the *borgerlige* vote had been so greatly reduced. National Union, they maintained, had divided the non-socialist front against the Labor party. This theme was repeated in various versions within a large part of the *borgerlige* press.[175] Not content merely with this, *Aftenposten*'s condemnation was even stronger, declaring that NS, because of the dictatorial threat it represented, had frightened many voters into the arms of the socialists.[176] NS was thereby held responsible both for splitting the *borgerlige* ranks and for increasing the number of votes received by Labor.

These *borgerlige* attacks against NS because of its alleged negative effect on the election were exaggerated. While it was true that the party unquestionably received the bulk of its support from persons who had earlier voted Agrarian, Conservative, or Independent People's party, and that it failed to capture any significant number of voters from the Labor party, its influence on the outcome of the election as a whole was negligible. *Tidens Tegn* pointed out quite correctly after the election that the question of divisiveness – which *Tidens Tegn* continued to maintain occurred because of the Conservatives' refusal to enter electoral pacts which included NS – had not had any noteworthy effect. If the dispute had had an impact on the election, said *Tidens Tegn*, then this would have been obvious in those districts where the controversy was greatest, in Oslo, Akershus, and Bergen. But instead the pattern was the same throughout the country in those districts where the electoral pact issue was not of any importance. The major reason for the Labor party's victory, declared *Tidens Tegn*, was that it had conducted an effective campaign. It presented a moderate and realistic profile, concentrating its attention on the difficulties of the depression and offering solutions which had broad popular appeal. While *Tidens Tegn* was skeptical about whether Labor's promises could be realized, it had to admit resignedly that the socialists' strategy had been highly successful when compared with the campaigns of the *borgerlige* parties.[177]

Quisling was equally unwilling to have NS accept the blame for the *borgerlige* election debacle, but he was much more strident in his response. He too had to explain why his party had failed to achieve its goal, being unable to elect a single candidate. In turn, he blamed the *borgerlige* parties for the poor showing made by NS. "The violent *borgerlige* scare campaign and the fear of division and of wasting one's vote frightened a large number from voting for National Union . . ."[178] The virulence of his reaction to attacks from the *borgerlige* revealed the extent of his frustration at not having been able to gain the cooperation of any of the major *borgerlige* parties. In response to their contention that NS had been judged in the election and was finished, he replied:

> No! We have not been judged. But the borgerlige parties' don't-give-a-damn politics, their weakness in social thought and political goals, their lack of positive effort, their sterile party politics which places party interest and self in-

terest above national consideration; their swindle propaganda, their ambiguous play with the fate of the country and its citizens, all this lack of responsibility and dishonesty has been judged.[179]

The harsh words that he levelled against the *borgerlige* parties could not mask his disappointment over NS' poor election result. His let-down was intense, and it was shared by others within NS. The same feeling was also experienced by NS' partner, the Rural Crisis Aid. The joint lists of candidates with NS in the districts where the Crisis Aid was strongest had not succeeded. Together, the two organizations had obtained their largest number of votes in Quisling's native Telemark, where the combined list of candidates gained some 3,400 votes, which was a fairly impressive nine per cent of the total.[180] But even in Telemark the effort had been in vain.

As a consequence, the negative reaction to the election defeat within the Crisis Aid was quite strong. Many of its members resigned in protest against its decision to participate in politics in alliance with NS, while a large number of those who remained lost their zeal.[181] But although the Crisis Aid was weakened considerably, it managed to gather its remaining members together and continued outwardly as before. Quisling did not attempt to implement the original agreement between NS and the Crisis Aid, which would have meant the assimilation of the Crisis Aid by NS. He was content to allow the Crisis Aid to follow its own course, independent of any direct connection with NS.[182] His disappointment with the election outcome undoubtedly caused him to bide his time, preferring the possibility of a gradual takeover rather than a direct move.[183]

For two years the Crisis Aid continued on an ever-declining path. Not until September 1935 did the organization disintegrate. It was formally dissolved, with its newspaper, *Bygdefolket*, being absorbed into the NS paper in Telemark. At the time, National Union had high expectations that the long-anticipated union would have solid results, with large numbers of Crisis Aid members enrolling in NS.[184] This did not occur. While some of the Crisis Aid's adherents joined NS on an individual basis, the majority did not.[185] Quisling's assumption that if only he remained patient, the Crisis Aid would fall into his hands like a ripe fruit, had not come true. All that NS achieved in its controversial association with the Rural Crisis Aid was the establishment of joint lists of candidates in five provinces, and this proved to be of no consequence for the outcome of the election.

The impact of the 1933 election result also provided the impetus for a break between Quisling and the Fatherland League. The League was firmly convinced that NS divided the *borgerlige* effort to combat the Labor party, but in addition there was another less objective reason why its leaders reacted negatively to NS' emergence as a party. Many members of the League responded positively to NS, being attracted by its activism. In particular, this was true of a considerable segment of young League adherents, who were impatient with the leadership's non-partisan stance in combatting socialism, and who favored direct action instead. When Quisling formed NS, the number of Fatherland League members who joined his party was therefore not inconsiderable. To cite one example: in the west coast city of Stavanger the League's local chairman, vice-chairman, and secretary all joined NS, and the core of NS' local organization in Stavanger consisted of young Fatherland League members.[186]

Following the election, the League's leadership realized that it was necessary to reorganize the organization in a more activistic direction in order to prevent further losses to National Union. Its chairman, Lehmkuhl, carefully attempted to maintain a balance between those who favored the creation of a full-fledged political party and those who wished to have the League continue as a non-partisan *borgerlig* pressure group seeking unity against the Labor party. Lehmkuhl proposed at the League's national convention, held on November 26 and 27, that in the next election, scheduled in three years, the League might enter lists of candidates in those districts where such a move could be advantageous. Although not stated directly, this step was tantamount to beginning the process of changing the League into a political party.[187]

This proposal was adopted by a large majority. But before Lehmkuhl's position could be ratified, it was necessary to defeat a motion that sought to bind the League to National Union. A group of four delegates headed by Hans S. Jacobsen, a leading member of NS, introduced a program which called for political cooperation, preferably leading to unification with other groups that shared a similar "national" viewpoint, such as National Union and the Agrarian party.[188] Jacobsen's endeavor was made with Quisling's full knowledge. The latter and Hjort, who both served on the board of the League's Oslo chapter, were present at the meeting. The motion to have the organization adopt Jacobsen's program was therefore a serious attempt by NS to gain dominant influence within the League. However, the effort suffered a decisive defeat. Jacobsen did not succeed in gaining any backing for his proposal. In the end he was forced to withdraw it, following which the convention endorsed Lehmkuhl's line by a large majority.[189]

In disappointed reaction, Quisling resigned from the Fatherland League, maintaining that he could not belong to two political parties at the same time.[190] On November 30, before the League had even had the opportunity of going public with its revised program, Quisling issued a blast from the columns of *Tidens Tegn* against the organization in which he had served as an officer until just a day earlier, accusing the League, ironically, of dividing "the *borgerlig* front" against the Labor party by forming a party.[191] This led to a bitter personal newspaper polemic between him and Lehmkuhl in *Tidens Tegn*.[192] *ABC*, speaking for the League, joined the fray, sarcastically pointing to Quisling's past record as a splitter in politics.[193]

One of the results of the League's national convention was thus that the division between the organization's leadership and Quisling had widened more than ever, making it difficult for future cooperation between the League and NS. Such cooperation should have been obvious because ideologically the two organizations were quite close. Quisling as a matter of fact accused the League of plagiarizing his program.[194] But despite the closeness of their political views, rivalry took place due to Quisling's insistence on maintaining an independent position at all costs. When he could not have his way in the League, he resigned, just as he had withdrawn from cooperation with the Agrarian party when he could not dictate policy. Due to this dogmatism, the net result of the election of 1933 was that NS was left more alone than ever before. No allies had been gained except for the Independent People's party, thanks to the effort on NS' behalf by Thommessen, and even the Independent People's party had become divided over this issue.[195] Following the setback sustained by the election result of 1933, Quisling's party faced a most uncertain future.

CHAPTER V

The Transition toward Fascism

1934–1936

I have the privilege of sending you National Union's program, from which you will understand that N.S. is a movement similar to National Socialism in Germany.

Vidkun Quisling to Trygve Roseth
March 5, 1934

For members of National Union, prospects seemed bleak indeed following the election defeat. All of their energies had been concentrated on gaining parliamentary representation and thereby being able to influence the country's political course from within the *Storting*.[1] Without a forum in parliament and without a press, disappointed party members could only look to an uncertain future, whose outlines were not made more promising by the considerable debt NS had accumulated during the campaign.[2]

Facing heavy financial obligations and with his hopes smashed, Quisling had no specific strategy in mind for how NS should now proceed. In speeches to his followers on the 26th and 31st of October, 1933, he called upon them to continue the struggle in soldierly fashion. While he castigated his non–socialist critics for their attacks, he declared that he and his adherents would henceforth "occupy ourselves as little as possible with criticism of the *borgerlige* parties".[3] National Union, he declared, should remain aloof from the *borgerlige* parties, concentrating instead on maintaining its integrity. He incorrectly predicted that the *borgerlige* parties, in reaction to Labor's victory, would attempt to unite against the socialists, but he believed this had little chance of success. NS should therefore avoid any involvement in such an effort for the time being. Instead, he urged the party to act independently and to concentrate on what he still considered to be the major political issue, the struggle against Marxism. By placing itself in the forefront of those who fought the socialists, he maintained NS would seize the leadership of this broad movement.[4]

In his goals for the future, he also urged that the party's membership be built up, its organizational structure tightened, and its program taken up for revision. On a more grandiose scale, he reverted to ideas he had held at the time Nordic Folk-Rising came into being. He declared that the influence of the trade unions should be undermined by the creation of NS cells within industry, and that "national" labor unions should be established. Somewhat more pragmatically, he urged NS to prepare for the coming local government elections in the fall.[5]

In seeking to chart a new course for his party, he did not lack goals. But it soon became obvious, as had been true earlier in his career, that he did not have the ability and resolution to plan and put into effect concrete projects in order to realize the goals he aimed at in a general manner. His lack of purpose was in part due to the absence of the person who earlier had been one of his main sources of inspiration, and who to a considerable degree had served as his "grey eminence". Frederik Prytz was no longer always at hand to provide counsel. He had acquired a partnership in a large estate in Sør-Trøndelag in the fall of 1933.[6] He retired to this estate, and although Quisling maintained some contact with him, Prytz's role in NS after the election defeat was largely passive. While he did make a limited contribution to the national block negotiations in 1934,[7] he did not seriously become involved in Quisling's political affairs again until after the German invasion.

Because of his failure to do anything more than make exhortative statements, Quisling's lieutenants began to chide him for his lack of planning. Hjort, on November 4, sent him a typed eight-page critique of his failure to come forward with concrete plans,[8] and Walter Fürst has recorded the frustration that NS members felt over their inability to get Quisling to write a newspaper article for the purpose of bolstering the party's hopes for the future.[9] An even stronger indication of the existence of a widespread feeling among the NS membership that something specific needed to be done was shown by the numerous letters that were sent to Quisling at this time, containing suggestions for various kinds of action by the party leader and/or the party itself.[10] While the degree of pragmatism contained in these proposals ranged from quite good to the absurd, they did indicate dissatisfaction with the status quo.

As a result of his inactivity, he found his subordinates assuming the initiative. Many party members were especially dissatisfied with the party program that Quisling had issued on his own when he announced NS' founding. He had acknowledged in his October 26 speech that the program needed revision, but he did nothing beyond this. The program therefore came under direct criticism in the fall of 1933. J. B. Hjort in particular was pointed in his critique, declaring that the program contained several planks which had weakened the party in the election, and that these mistakes could have been avoided if only Quisling had consulted with his lieutenants. Now, declared Hjort, this disadvantage should be relieved by going over the program, discussing it point by point, and making it so clear and concrete that it would make a positive impression on the voters.[11]

A move in favor of providing the party with a revised program had already begun at the time Hjort delivered his criticism. Hans S. Jacobsen, as always preoccupied with ideological questions, came forward with a proposal for a fourteen-point program on October 27. He modestly described his draft as being a "short and concise, firmly logical program". While he insisted he had no intention of criticizing Quisling personally, he characterized Quisling's previous election program as imprecise and inferior.[12] As a foremost representative of that segment of the NS membership which admired Hitler's Germany, Jacobsen did not hesitate to call openly for a "National Socialistic program".[13]

Quisling was not overly enthusiastic about this challenge to his authority as the party's foremost ideological thinker.[14] Nevertheless, when NS made its move to gain a decisive influence over the Fatherland League at its national convention in late November, a revised version of Jacobsen's program served as the focal point of NS' challenge to the League's leadership.[15] As we have seen, Quisling supported this effort to prevent the League from developing into a political party, and resigned when Jacobsen's proposal was rejected. Nevertheless, there was little chance that the latter's extreme pro-German view could become the official NS ideology at this time. Many members vehemently opposed such a possibility, favoring instead an ideology which laid stress on independent Norwegian nationalism.[16]

Jacobsen's initiative did, however, create action within the party in favor of drawing up a new program. Walter Fürst, its propaganda chief, responded energetically, and, with Jacobsen's proposal as a starting point, sought to rally NS officers throughout the country to come to Oslo so that a program might be formed.[17] As a result of the election defeat, Quisling did not feel confident enough to reject the move. A working committee was thereupon set up to consider the question. It included Jacobsen, and as a consequence its recommendation, presented to Quisling on December 20, was considerably colored by Jacobsen's ideas.[18]

The decision-making process did not stop at this point, however. The committee's proposal created a good deal of dissension among leading NS members. An indication of the extent of the dispute was shown by a proposal from Hjort, Munthe, and Hvoslef to resign from the party's most important committee, the Political Committee, if this would help to create "peace and quiet within NS".[19] As a way out of a potential impasse, it was finally decided to submit the question to the Political Committee, which met on December 27.[20]

In reaction to the proposals from Jacobsen, Quisling drew up a number of drafts of his own.[21] However, in the end neither Jacobsen's concise program nor Quisling's lengthy philosophical treatises were adopted by the party officers. Instead, the more pragmatic representatives on the Political Committee chose to exert their own influence.[22] The results of their labors were discussed and confirmed at a more expanded Party Council (*Råd*), which met on January 28–29. The final step in the ratification process occurred on February 15, when Quisling attached his imprimatur to the new program.[23]

When a comparison is made between Jacobsen's and Quisling's earlier versions and that hammered out in December-January 1933–34, it becomes obvious how much the new program owed to the party officers on the Political Committee and Party Council. It showed clearly that it differed considerably from both Jacobsen's and Quisling's ideals. Rather than being the "short and concise" fourteen-point proposal which Jacobsen had urged, it contained some thirty different planks. Nor did it concern itself with the question of "national socialism", as Jacobsen had hoped. The only reference to socialism was its stress on the Norwegian uniqueness of its philosophy. It favored a "true Norwegian socialism", which guaranteed "order and justice", which united "freedom and individuality with fellowship", and which maintained "values and not forms". Similarly, the program's introduction contained no reference to Quisling's "Universism", with its emphasis on building up a new political-religious movement. It simply repudiated both Marxism and liberal capitalism for being materialistic, stressing instead the need to create a non-materialistic society in which fellowship and the common good would prevail.

To be sure, the program did contain a number of segments which in some respects were similar to what both Jacobsen and Quisling had previously propounded. It echoed Quisling's call for a "national government independent of party politics", and it also included his idea of creating a "National Assembly" which would influence government policy. Similarly, it repeated Jacobsen's proposal favoring a planned economy, which was not foreign to Quisling's thinking either. The program concluded with the same slogan with which Jacobsen had ended his proposal: "We are a realm. We shall become a people". But while it included ideas which, though worded differently, were similar to concepts expressed by Quisling and Jacobsen, nevertheless its major tendency was to exhibit a pragmatism that was foreign to the two ideologists. While its corporate character was obvious, nevertheless its anti-democratic nature was not stressed. It sought to achieve a broad appeal by making general promises to as large a segment of the population as possible: workers were guaranteed the right to work, the farmers' property and family rights would be protected, scientific methods would be utilized more fully in forestry, the fishermen would receive more support from the state, handicrafts and small industries would be protected, the health system would be improved, better educational facilities were promised, Christian ideals would prevail, national defense would be strengthened, the balance of trade would be improved, etc. In this fashion, the party leaders hoped the program would secure wide-based voter approval. Its planks were concisely worded. Gone was the verbosity that had characterized Quisling's former programs.

The program of February 15, 1934, the formal date of its implementation, since it was signed by Quisling at this time, remained National Union's official statement of principles until the party's demise. Although his role in its formulation had been restricted, Quisling later took full credit for it.

While the new party program in many ways was pragmatic, it nevertheless marked a turn in NS' history in the direction of heightening its fascist character. The program, it is true, did not specifically reveal that the party was moving in a more fascist direction. Its goals were stated in general terms, with no indication of how it intended to achieve its aims. However, it was now obvious that NS in general was anti-parliamentary in outlook, thanks to the explicitness with which its goals were enunciated. In point after point the corporate character of the program was clear, while elements of popular democracy, were the program to be implemented, would be diminished or eliminated. Previously, it had been uncertain exactly where NS stood, owing to the lack of clarity in Quisling's pronouncements. One did not even know, for instance, whether he considered NS to be a *borgerlig* party or not, or whether the party was more in favor of capitalist competition or a state-controlled economy. Now his vague pronouncements, allowing him to be interpreted in many ways, were to a considerable degree replaced by a program entitled "We Know What We Want!" Furthermore, this statement of principles had come into being thanks to an initiative originally taken by Jacobsen.

Although his proposal was rejected, and it had only an indirect bearing on the program that was eventually adopted, nonetheless the fact that the initiator of the process was representative of a pro-German outlook within NS could not help but color the atmosphere in the party at this time. Quisling, upon mailing a copy of the program in March 1934, declared that it had received inspiration from German National Socialism.[24] This was the only time prior to World War II that he admitted NS' kinship to European fascism. It is noteworthy that it occurred shortly after the new statement of party principles had been drawn up.

Another indication of the direction in which the party had begun to move was revealed by the Party Council's decision in January 1934 to adopt a uniform. Its choice of a brown shirt was significant. The association with Hitler's *Sturmabteilung* (SA) was obvious even for the politically unschooled. Quisling, however, continued his usual practice of denying that NS imitated foreign movements. In response to criticism that the shirt was a copy of Hitler's brown shirts, Quisling maintained that this was incorrect:

> It is, however, a misunderstanding when you assume that the brown color in our shirt has been copied from Germany. We use standard shirts made of khaki material, which has shown itself to suit our members very well in that they can use the shirt both for work and for sport.[25]

In using a colored shirt as a symbol, NS was not the first in Norway to adopt a practice followed elsewhere in Europe. The Labor party's youth organization already used a blue shirt with a red tie, and in June 1933 the Fatherland League had entered into competition by choosing a grey shirt with a black tie as its challenge to the young socialists. Mowinckel's Liberal government, however, responded immediately and energetically to the possibility of having rival uniformed factions in the streets. The use of uniforms for political purposes was outlawed, first temporarily, and then permanently in 1937 when the Labor party headed the government.[26] Both NS and the Fatherland League protested the government's action to the *Storting*, but to no avail.

National Union's copying of Hitler's successful example revealed itself in another obvious imitative move, the creation of *Specialavdelingen* (The Special Division). This group was usually simply referred to by its initials S.A., which left little doubt as to what it was patterned after. Its most important responsibility was to maintain order at NS meetings.[27] *Specialavdelingen*, however, never became an important part of NS. It was later replaced by another party organization, the *Hird* (NS troopers), which assumed its functions.

In employing symbolism with the intent of increasing its popularity, NS also resorted to using the Nazi salute in 1934. Again it was not the first to do so, inasmuch as the Fatherland League had previously adopted the same practice. Both organizations maintained that this was not an imitation of Hitler (who in turn had merely plagiarized Mussolini's so-called "Roman salute"), but was instead the re-establishment of the old Nordic greeting from the Viking period.[28] However, these denials received little credence among the public at large. Political observers saw this, quite correctly, as a manifestation of the general sympathy with which both organizations viewed Hitler at this time.

National Union's open assumption of a more obvious fascist character was similarly shown by the title its leader adopted. At first when the party was formed, NS members simply referred to Quisling as "the party chief" (*"partichef"*), but many preferred to address him more formally as *"herr Major"*. In 1934, however, his title became *"partifører"* ("the party leader"), and it soon became common practice merely to refer to him as the

Fører ("the leader").[29] The similarity between *Fører* and *Führer* was obvious.

Recognizing that *Fører* bore too close a resemblance to Hitler's Nazi title, and might therefore be damaging, propaganda chief Walter Fürst launched a campaign to have Quisling addressed as *høvding*, the term for a Viking chieftain.[30] For a short time in the summer of 1934 Quisling assumed the "chieftain" title.[31] However, Fürst's effort did not prove long-lasting. It was indignantly rejected as being both ridiculous and anachronistic by those who preferred to refer to Quisling as their *Fører*.[32] From the fall of 1934 until May 1945 he was therefore simply the *Fører* for loyal NS members.

The NS move toward a more direct imitation of European Fascism did not pass unnoticed. Some members voiced concern that NS was copying the Nazi example. The use of the Fascist salute, Quisling's adoption of the *Fører* title, and the choice of the brown shirt as a symbol all received critical comment.[33] Similarly, although it was not yet pronounced, the tendency for NS publications to take on an anti-Semitic tone and to voice approval of Nazi persecution of the Jews was not accepted uncritically by all of Quisling's supporters. One of his most dedicated observers at this time, a former pupil, warned with prophetic accuracy that National Union's admiration for Germany would stop the movement's growth and would turn it into a "political sect" if this trend were not reversed.[34] As the later history of NS would show, the warning was valid.

The inclination for National Union to imitate directly foreign totalitarian examples, although present, had nevertheless not yet become so obvious that it characterized the party. Other political groups were still not averse to entering into discussions with Quisling if this appeared to be to their advantage. Such negotiations occurred during the spring and early summer of 1934, when representatives from the Agrarian party, the Independent People's party, the Fatherland League, and National Union considered the possibility of joining together in a "national block". The fact that National Union was included in these proceedings indicated that it was still regarded as a political force of some potential.

The initiative for the negotiations came from Rolf Thommessen as chairman of the Independent People's party. The election of 1933 had been disastrous for his party, and he subsequently believed that the only option open to it was to enter into a larger coalition. Simultaneously, this could provide a broader base for *Tidens Tegn*.[35] For him the inclusion of National Union was natural, as he had shown in his earlier advocacy of the party's participation in a united *borgerlig* front against the Labor party.

The Agrarian party, however, was the key element in the negotiations. With its twenty-three *Storting* representatives, it was by far the strongest of the four organizations. At a time when the farm population, the Agrarian party's main source of support, was in the midst of the acute economic crisis brought on by the depression, the Agrarians were considering several alternatives as a means of increasing their strength in order to secure favorable legislation for the embattled farmers. Furthermore, the Agrarians, having been ousted from control of the government by the Liberals in the previous year, were by no means averse to returning to power at the expense of the Liberals. Backing from the other participants in the negotiations might therefore prove valuable for the Agrarians in a time of government crisis.

Considering the degree of ill will between Hundseid and Quisling, it seemed strange at first that the Agrarian party entered into talks with three smaller political parties which included NS, but there were a number of ideological considerations which explain the Agrarians' initial willingness to accept NS in the discussions as a potential ally. One common element held by all participants was a feeling of intense nationalism.[36] They also shared a commitment to a strong government and the desire to lessen such a government's dependence on a parliamentary majority. This viewpoint was intensified by the common frustration and resentment with which these parties reacted to the steadily increasing strength of the Labor party's representation in the *Storting*.[37] Additional shared beliefs were also present. For example, Quisling was not the only significant politician calling for the establishment of corporative institutions in the political process. A number of leading Agrarians were in favor of giving the country's economic organizations direct influence in legislative enactment.[38]

Such views were particularly strong within the Farmers' Association (*Norges Bondelag*), Norway's major farm organization, which provided the Agrarian party with a great deal of its political support. Prominent members of the Farmers' Association felt that ideologically the participants in the negotiations were quite compatible with its political outlook, in particular NS.[39] Such an attitude reflected the fact that there still existed a body of opinion within the Agrarian party which retained a certain sympathy for Quisling and what he stood for. Whereas the Agrarian party's representatives in the *Storting* were never very enthusiastic about the national block discussions, the Farmers' Association's leaders were interested in the negotiations and worked actively for their success.[40]

The Fatherland League similarly hoped that the talks would lead to satisfactory results. The League, which only reluctantly had agreed to become a political party the previous fall, always favored the ideal of *borgerlig* unity. Since its relations with the Conservatives and the Liberals were quite strained, it was natural for the League to seek alliance at this time within a coalition which the Agrarian party dominated, the Agrarians being the only major party with which the League felt sympathy.[41] The League also had no objection to cooperation with the Independent People's party or NS, since its ideological outlook did not differ greatly from that of either group. Although the League at times had criticized NS earlier, this had not been due to ideological differences, but because of disagreement over strategy. When NS made public its new program in 1934, *ABC* described it as being "considerably better than previously".[42]

Quisling's participation in the negotiations as head of NS appears to have been motivated primarily by opportunism. He did not seem to have had any concrete goals in mind when the deliberations began, but merely hoped to turn them to NS' advantage. He declared at this time that the Agrarian party's position was steadily deteriorating and that it therefore would be quite doubtful if NS would enter into closer cooperation with it. As for the Fatherland League and the Independent People's party, said Quisling, it was impossible at this time to say what the discussions might lead to. But one thing was certain. He insisted NS would not under any circumstances "give up its independence and its program".[43]

His assessment was open to question on two points. First, although the Agrarian party's strength had declined somewhat, as indicated by its decreased representation in the *Storting*, it was by far the most potent political force among the parties involved in the discussions. Were the national block talks to result in anything at all, the Agrarian party would have to be included. Secondly, Quisling's insistence that NS should unyieldingly maintain its independence and refuse to compromise its program's integrity meant that, as far as NS was concerned, it would be very difficult for the four negotiating parties to agree on any type of permanent union, since the other parties would hardly allow NS to dominate the proceedings.

Although contact between the groups involved in the national block negotiations had existed earlier, the first purposeful move toward initiating discussions occurred when Rolf Thommessen began to work for this goal early in February 1934. At this time he informally brought this idea to the attention of each of the potential participants. Whether or not he would succeed depended on the reaction of the Agrarian party. He was therefore quite pleased when the Agrarian leaders, including Hundseid, responded favorably to exploring the possibility of a national block.[44] The first public indication that the Agrarians were seriously considering this alternative occurred when one of their veteran *Storting* representatives, Nils Nersten, wrote two articles favoring such a move. Thommessen published these in the February 12 and February 23 editions of *Tidens Tegn*. Not surprisingly, the paper warmly endorsed Nersten's viewpoint.[45] By the end of February news that cooperation between the four parties was being considered had become so widespread that Georg Vedeler, the NS leader in Bergen, wrote to Quisling to inquire about this development, in particular with reference to possible cooperation with other parties locally in the coming local elections in the fall.[46]

While the issue was still being tentatively explored, a leading NS member made a determined effort to bring it within a firmer context. Johan B. Hjort, a key Quisling lieutenant, personally invited representatives from the Agrarian party, the Farmers' Association, the Fatherland League, and the Independent People's party to a meeting at his home on the evening of March 9.[47] Whether he took this step with Quisling's approval or did so on his own is difficult to determine, but it is not at all improbable that Hjort acted by himself, since he was known for being strong-willed and energetic, and he may have become impatient with the failure to begin discussions earlier. In any event, he established the initial contact with the participants from the other parties, and only afterwards was Quisling informed and invited to attend.[48] At the meeting, Hjort presented a written proposal for the establishment of a "national joint council" composed of one representative from each of the participating organizations. While the document stressed that each of the groups belonging to the proposed body would maintain its independence, the establishment of such a council would have led to close cooperation between the groups. Of the goals that Hjort suggested, the most important was the creation of a "national block government" and the framing of a new constitution along corporate lines, which would permit the government to be "independent of party politics".[49]

The possibility of common action between the organizations was still at too tentative a stage for the proposal to be acted upon. Similarly, Quisling recorded that an even more ambitious plan by the Fatherland League met a similar fate. The League suggested that the four groups join in forming a new political party.[50] According to Quisling, representatives from the Agrarian party assumed such a vague and uncertain attitude toward the question of cooperation that he believed there was little possibility of any type of joint effort as far as the Agrarian party was concerned.[51]

Had the question of continued contact been left to Quisling, there is every possibility that no further discussions would have taken place. Rolf Thommessen, however, remained undaunted and pushed ahead on behalf of the Independent People's party. He secured the approval of his national executive committee on March 14 for the start of talks between National Union, the Agrarian party, the Fatherland League, and the Independent People's party. The goal of these deliberations, declared Thommessen, was the creation of a national block, and he included the draft of a proposed agreement in the invitation which he sent to the involved parties on behalf of the Independent People's party national executive committee.[52]

Thommessen's action produced results. Both NS and the Fatherland League responded positively. On April 9 the two organizations sent a joint entreaty to the Agrarian party. Their letter stressed the fact that it would be advantageous to establish cooperation on the broadest possible basis and in the firmest possible form, in particular with reference to the coming local government elections in the fall and the national election in 1936. NS and the League asked the Agrarians to appoint a delegation to take part in negotiations on this question.[53]

Although the Agrarian party had earlier been unwilling to commit itself in its response to the premature proposals brought forward at the meeting at Hjort's home, it did not feel it could write off the alternative of creating a national block as a means of increasing its strength. Jens Hundseid, responding on behalf of his party on April 10, did maintain the prevailing attitude of caution, however. He stressed the fact that the Agrarian executive committee did not have a mandate to enter into deliberations whose goal was already pre-determined. Furthermore, the result of any negotiations would have to be approved by the party's national executive committee before a final decision could be made. But with these reservations in mind, he was willing to have the Agrarians take part in discussions on the possibility of "future cooperation", with the understanding that such talks would be non-binding.[54] Six days later, on April 16, the Agrarian party informed the other interested groups that it had appointed a four-man delegation of *Storting* representatives to take part in "confidential, non-binding discussions concerning a possible basis for closer cooperation between National Union, the Independent People's party, the Fatherland League, and the Agrarian party".[55]

With the preliminaries at last completed, the four parties could now begin their deliberations. The Farmers' Association, after its sole entry into the discussions at the meeting of March 9, did not take part. Instead, its interests were represented by its political affiliate, the Agrarian party, through which it was kept informed. The representatives from the four groups held their first formal meeting on May 5.[56] The initial question they faced concerned how the talks were to be organized. They decided that two committees would be established to discuss the specific problems that needed to be resolved before an eventual agreement could be reached. The committees differed in size. The smaller group was a compact working committee which could be called together at short notice should the occasion demand. It was the more important of the two, consisting of the heads of three of the organizations represented, Thommessen for the Independent People's party, Lehmkuhl for the Fatherland League, and Quisling for National Union, while *Storting* representatives Gabriel Moseid and Nils Trædal acted for the Agrarian party. Formally, however, important decisions had to be confirmed by the larger committee, which consisted of the members of the smaller committee plus one or more representatives for each of the participating parties.[57]

Just one month after the delegates from the four parties had held their first formal meeting, a political crisis developed which clearly put to the test the question whether or not the national block negotiations would lead to concrete results. The crisis occurred because of a basic disagreement between Mowinckel's Liberal government and the Agrarian party led by Hundseid. At issue was the dispute over how to solve the economic crisis faced by the farmers. The Agrarians favored direct government intervention, while Mowinckel's cabinet adhered to standard liberal theory, believing that the free play of economic forces offered the best solution. It proved to be impossible for the two parties to reach agreement, and as a result Hundseid announced on June 9 that the Agrarians were withdrawing from their policy of cooperation with the government.[58]

Without the support of the Agrarians, the Liberal government was bound to fall because of the weight of the large Labor party delegation. Hundseid anticipated that the resignation of Mowinckel would lead to the formation of an Agrarian government. He had already established secret contact with the Labor party, seeing the possibility of cooperation with the socialists as one alternative to the dilemma of impasse with the Liberals.[59] But to Hundseid's surprise, events did not develop as he had expected. Once the government crisis broke out, the Labor party unexpectedly declared that it did not intend to support the creation of an Agrarian government, but would itself introduce a motion of no confidence with the intent of felling the Mowinckel government so that Labor might assume office. Mowinckel furthermore stated that if the Labor motion was passed, which was a certainty if the Agrarian party did not back the government, then he would recommend to the King that the Labor party be given responsibility for forming the next ministry. To the surprise of political observers, Norway once more was on the verge of gaining a socialist government.[60]

This set off a flurry of frenzied political activity. On the one hand, the Conservatives worked energetically to restore some semblance of *borgerlig* cooperation, seeking to arrange a compromise on the agricultural question between the Agrarians and the Liberals. On the other, a series of meetings was held by the national block negotiators. In their talks, the main problem was that neither National Union nor the Fatherland League was willing to accept any change in the Agrarian party's politics which might lead to a Labor government. For Quisling and Lehmkuhl, the possibility that the socialists might come to power was anathema. Opposition to the threat of the "revolutionary" Labor party was the predominant political concern of both organizations. The Agrarians had previously been equally dogmatic in their opposition to Labor, but the situation was now changing, with Hundseid having signaled that he was considering cooperation with the socialists as a means of solving the agricultural crisis. Thommessen, the conciliator in attempting to establish a national block, feared that the entire plan might collapse over this question.

The Agrarian party, however, was not yet willing to alter its policy so drastically as to enter into an agreement with the Labor party. The difficulties were resolved when an agreement was reached among the four negotiating parties to unite in support of the formation of an Agrarian government if the Mowinckel government were to fall. Since it was felt that it would be impolitic for the Agrarian party to take part openly in backing such an initiative, representatives from the Farmers' Association now conveniently entered into the negotiations, participating in drawing up a petition in which it was joined by the Independent People's party, National Union, and the Fatherland League.[61]

The four groups completed the document on June 16.[62] It was addressed to the *Storting* representatives of the Conservatives, Liberals, and the Agrarian party. It declared that under the prevailing circumstances, the only alternative to a Labor government was the creation of "a national government of the realm" headed by the Agrarian party "with support from the forces which are close to the agrarian movement". The petition declared that the *Storting* representatives had a national duty to prefer a national government to a government formed by a party whose program and leadership were still revolutionary in character.[63]

This move proved to be the most concrete objective which the parties involved in the national block negotiations actually tried to put into effect. If successful, it would have meant the formation of a government dominated by the Agrarian party, but in which the smaller parties, including NS, could have expected to exercise influence. Although such a government would not have been able to achieve its goals immediately, it would nevertheless have been unique. It would have been above parliament, with the support of forces extraneous to the parliamentary process.

The petition signed by the four groups, with the Agrarian party's covert approval, was never made public. Its drafters planned to issue it when it became obvious that the Mowinckel government would fall. In the meantime, those responsible for the petition set in motion an effort intended to create a body of opinion which would make it impossible for the *borgerlige* parties in the *Storting*, especially the Liberals, to allow the Labor party to take over control of the government. Instead, the Agrarian party would form a government which also included representatives from the other groups who had participated in the national block negotiations.[64] Thommessen ran a series of articles calling for a "national government of the realm" in the June 12, 13, and 14 editions of *Tidens Tegn*, and Lehmkuhl presented a similar view in the pages of *ABC*.[65]

More significant than the traditional attitudes of the Independent People's party and the Fatherland League was a resolution passed at the national meeting of the Farmers' Association. This organization met in conference on June 22–23, when the outcome of the government crisis remained uncertain. It unanimously favored the formation of a government above the political parties as the only means of effectively solving the agricultural crisis.[66] In defense of this stand, the Association's vice-chairman identified his organization directly with the Fatherland League and NS, declaring that all three groups were movements, not political parties, and that he hoped they could combine in a "united front".[67]

Both National Union and *Tidens Tegn* hailed the resolution.[68] NS had especially optimistic expectations at this time, believing that the Farmers' Association's positive expressions might signal the establishment of close ties between NS and the powerful farm organization. Some NS supporters within the Association believed this as well.[69] However, Quisling received a less enthusiastic viewpoint from one NS source within the group, advising him not to take seriously everything the organization's leaders said, since they were renowned for being great "diplomats".[70]

The outcome of the political crisis which had resulted in the passage of the resolution was determined neither by the Farmers' Association, nor NS, nor by any of the other political groups that were following developments from outside of the *Storting*. It was settled in the traditional manner, namely, within the parliament. Thanks in large part to the mediatory efforts of Conservatives, it proved possible for the Liberals and the Agrarians to reach a compromise which called for an increase in agricultural incomes. The Agrarians were not yet willing to seek a solution to the agricultural crisis by entering into an agreement with the Labor party. Nor could they expect success through support emanating from groups outside of the *Storting*. Resolutions such as that issued by the Farmers' Association or the national block negotiators' confidential petition did not have adequate force to ensure the creation of a government headed by the Agrarians and their allies. The compromise between the Agrarians and the Mowinckel government passed the *Storting* just before adjournment at the end of June.[71] However, while the crisis passed, its cause had not been resolved. The Agrarian party remained dissatisfied with the Liberal government's agricultural policy.

Among the participants in the national block negotiations, Rolf Thommessen felt most keenly the disappointment which resulted from the failure to establish a "national government of the realm". When it became obvious that the Mowinckel government would not fall, Thommessen published an editorial in *Tidens Tegn* in which he maintained that a clearing-up process would soon occur in politics which would change the boundaries separating the parties. He now called publicly for a union of the Agrarian party, the Independent People's party, National Union, the Fatherland League and the Farmers' Association.[72]

On the same day as his editorial appeared, he set out once more to realize this over-riding goal. He sent an urgent message to Quisling and to the other delegates involved in the negotiations, requesting a meeting of the large committee on the following day. Thommessen maintained that since agreement existed in favor of the desirability of closer cooperation between the four parties, it was important that this be established now before the *Storting* adjourned. To further this process, he presented a draft proposal of a plan to bring the organizations closer together.[73] In his draft, he repeated his hope that cooperation would eventually lead to the creation of "a large national party". As the first concrete step in this direction, he proposed the creation of a joint council. The purpose of this body would be to coordinate cooperation in elections, and in general to work to increase the feeling of unity among the four.[74]

At the meeting on June 28 the participants were not willing to go as far as Thommessen suggested. A statement was signed which declared that the negotiators had "found it desirable and natural that there be established firm cooperation between the four parties". However, the declaration pointed out that before this could occur it would be necessary for the smaller negotiating committee to come together "as soon as possible" to work out a declaration of principle which could serve as the basis for cooperation between the parties. Only after such an agreement had been reached did the negotiators recommend that a joint council be established.[75]

Although general concurrence had been reached in principle about the desirability of cooperation, nothing concrete resulted from the national block negotiations. To the disappointment of Thommessen, who wished to issue a news release to the press immediately before the *Storting* adjourned for the summer,[76] it was decided that the discussions would continue to be confidential. The future status of the negotiations therefore remained uncertain when the participants disbanded for the summer vacation. Quisling noted that it had been agreed to maintain confidential contact, and that he would recommend to Thommessen that the small committee be called together to organize the groundwork for continued action some time during the summer or early fall.[77]

The Independent People's party tried to maintain momentum during the summer in its attempt to secure permanent cooperation between the four parties. Its general secretary contacted the negotiators in early July and asked them to submit their suggestions and views concerning a joint declaration of principle by August 15.[78] However, none of the parties chose to respond.[79]

By the fall of 1934 it had become obvious that the national block negotiations would not lead to anything permanent as far as NS was concerned. Quisling had agreed to the June 16 appeal for the formation of a government with the Agrarian party as the dominant member and to the June 28 statement calling for future cooperation, because he felt that these steps were in his interest. In both instances he believed that these moves might enhance his standing in politics. Had a "national" government been formed in June, there was good reason to expect that he would have been a member of it. Similarly, he could sign the agreement calling for the desirability of increased cooperation because he expected his party to have a commanding voice in deciding what form this cooperation would take. As before, he was unyielding when it came to making compromises on basic issues. Thommessen indicated in August 1934 that it might prove difficult to get NS to agree with the other parties on the question of democracy. While he did not believe at this time that it would be impossible to reach consensus on this problem, he was ready to consider forming a national block which did not include NS.[80] Thommessen's note of caution was justified. It proved to be impossible to reach ideological agreement with Quisling.[81]

Similarly, interaction between NS and the other parties proved to be most difficult. With local government elections approaching in the fall, political cooperation between the parties discussing a national block became a current issue. The Fatherland League, as usual, championed the ideal of a common *borgerlig* front against the Labor party. NS, however, insisted on having its way, which made joint action difficult if not impossible. The Fatherland League's leaders received a number of reports from the local chapters that NS had reacted negatively to the prospect of cooperation, having declared that it did not consider itself *borgerlig* and therefore did not wish to take part in joint discussions.[82] In response, already in early September leading spokesmen for the League were once more attacking NS for being divisive.[83] At a time when consensus among groups opposed to the Labor party seemed natural, Quisling's insistence on maintaining an independent position could not help but undermine the possibility of a national block, causing the Fatherland League to resume the hostile attitude toward NS which it had maintained previously.

The Agrarian party by the fall of 1934 had similarly ascertained that collaboration with NS resulted in liabilities that were not worth bearing. As could be expected, the former hostility between the two party leaders could not help but diminish the possibility of good relations. While Hundseid's and Quisling's dislike for each other did not prevent the latter from taking part in the national block negotiations, the enmity between the two men was certainly not a positive factor for reaching closer cooperation. Although Thommessen did his best to mediate, contact between Quisling and Hundseid during the national block discussions occurred in anything but a cordial atmosphere.[84] Quisling continued to maintain a completely antagonistic attitude toward his old rival. From a pragmatic point of view, this was certainly not the best way to further a good relationship with the Agrarian party.

Nevertheless, the Agrarians had not yet entirely written off NS by the early autumn. However, an episode occurred at this time which showed clearly that the party's attitude toward NS was at best only luke-warm. In anticipation of the coming election, a fundraising campaign had been organized to collect contributions from business interests on behalf of the *borgerlige* parties. The Agrarian party maintained that NS should be allowed to gain a share of the moneys collected. However, the fundraisers objected vehemently, emphasizing that the Conservatives and Liberals would withdraw from this effort if NS were included. They further pointed out that NS insisted it was not a *borgerlig* party, and it therefore did not deserve to benefit from a united *borgerlig* fundraising effort. Faced with this strong response, Hundseid on September 15 withdrew the condition that NS be included.[85] While this incident did not cause the Agrarian party to adopt the point of view that NS should be excluded from further negotiations, it emphasized the already recognized fact that association with NS could be a political liability. Furthermore, NS intransigence on such questions as whether or not it was a *borgerlig* party certainly did not enhance its potential as a possible ally of the Agrarian party.

From Quisling's self-centered perspective, the political climate in the national block negotiations had worsened to such an extent that NS withdrew from the discussions in the early fall of 1934. He had participated in the deliberations with the hope that NS would obtain dominant influence within an eventual coalition. However, his lack of flexibility seriously weakened the possibility for NS to reach a meaningful agreement with the other parties. While NS was invited to take part in the discussions shortly before they were scheduled to resume on September 19 and 21 for the smaller committee and the larger committee respectively, there is no evidence that Quisling or the other NS representatives attended.[86] Desiring to delineate clearly its separate position from the *borgerlige* parties, and faced with political attacks from the Fatherland League and the absence of support from the Agrarian party, Quisling's party removed itself from the potentially most advantageous contact with other political parties which NS would enjoy in the 1930s.

National Union's departure did not result in the end of the discussions. Contact between the three remaining parties continued, but the only concrete result was a general agreement to work for cooperation in the *Storting* election of 1936.[87] The national block negotiations were bound to fail, since none of the three smaller parties, including NS, had broad enough support to generate significant sympathy for a national block within parliament. Without such parliamentary approval, the Agrarian party, as it turned out, could not hope to achieve any possibility for bringing relief to the crisis-stricken agricultural population. In the end, the only practical choice for the Agrarian party was the one alternative which was anathema for Quisling, namely, to reach an agreement with the Labor party. This occurred in March 1935, when the Agrarian party, in return for significant concessions from the socialists in the area of agricultural policy, joined with the Labor party in voting the Mowinckel government out of office. Afterwards the Labor party formed the first permanent socialist government in Norway's history.

With the absence of representation in the *Storting*, Quisling could not possibly have succeeded in having NS play a dominant role in the national block negotiations. However, his failure during the discussions to maintain favorable contact with potentially friendly parties weakened National Union's position even more. NS emerged from the negotiations isolated to a greater extent than it had been following the *Storting* election of 1933.

Because of his insistence that National Union should maintain an independent profile, Quisling's party had therefore further distanced itself from the non-socialist parties by the time local (*kommune*) elections were scheduled in the middle of October 1934. *Kommune* elections were held every three years in both the rural and urban districts to elect representatives to the local councils. The councils exercised overall governmental authority on the local level. Although traditionally local elections in Norway have not had the same character as national elections, with cleavages frequently taking place because of regional and personal differences created by uniquely local circumstances, partisan politics nevertheless were important. Observers regarded the outcome of the local elections as a barometer reading of a party's standing in the country.

At first its leaders were uncertain to what extent National Union should engage itself in these elections. Doubt existed as to whether it was worthwhile to expend the human and financial resources that would be sorely needed in the more important *Storting* election of 1936. After the issue had been discussed by the party's national executive board (*styre*), Quisling made the decision in April 1934 that the question of whether to enter lists of candidates in the election should be determined by and large on the local level. The party leaders urged NS' local organizations to take part in the election to the widest degree possible under the prevailing circumstances, but that this decision should be determined within each province by the party's regional chairman. Furthermore, in accordance with Quisling's insistence on maintaining NS' independent position on the national level, firm instructions were given to the local party organizations to avoid any form of alliance with the Liberals and Conservatives. Similarly, they were warned not to become involved in bipartisan cooperation where the label *borgerlig* might be used in the presentation of a list of candidates. And while the central leadership had no objection to joint action with the Independent People's party and with non-political groups, special permission had to be obtained before any form of cooperation could be established with the Agrarian party.[88] These stipulations were laid down notwithstanding the fact that Quisling had just recently agreed to take part in the national block negotiations, which included the Agrarian party. The ideological argument that NS was not a *borgerlig* party remained a major concern for him. He considered one of National Union's main tasks to be the goal of capturing nationally minded workers from the Labor party, and he believed that the way to accomplish this was by stressing the argument that NS was different from the *borgerlige* parties in that it wished to unify society rather than to maintain divisions along class lines. This position was similar to the National Socialist claim that Hitler's movement was the party of the German workers.

Some disagreement took place within NS over the wisdom of participating in the election. Those opposed cited in particular the expenses that the party would incur.[89] However, such objections were not sustained. For example, the party leadership in the key regions of Oslo and Akershus, where originally the question of taking part in the election had been in doubt, decided by the end of the summer that NS would field lists of candidates.[90] This decision, which Quisling approved, was undoubtedly correct. After the defeat of 1933, NS quite obviously needed to establish its presence in politics as strongly as possible.

Nevertheless, NS involvement in the election throughout the country as a whole was limited. The party had only been in existence for slightly more than a year, and in many areas it had not yet built up its organizational structure. In the rural electoral districts in the provinces, where the majority of the population resided, NS entered lists of candidates in only five of eighteen provinces (*fylker*).[91] NS participation in the towns was equally limited, with the party restricting its activity to only sixteen of sixty-five urban election districts.[92]

The election campaigns in the various districts in which National Union took part revealed the degree to which Quisling's emphasis on maintaining a separate identity resulted in lack of cooperation with other parties. Such interaction was even more limited than in the previous *Storting* election. Only in one rural election district, in Gran in Oppland province, did NS join with another party, the local organization of the Agrarian party, in presenting a joint list of candidates to the voters.[93] In the towns, National Union's collaboration with other parties was restricted to Oslo and the communities immediately adjacent to the capital. In Oslo, NS joined with the Independent People's party and the Agrarian party in presenting a "National Joint List" of candidates. In the neighboring communities of Asker and Bærum such national joint lists were restricted to just two participants, NS and the Independent People's party.[94]

The degree of election cooperation between the Independent People's party, NS, and the Agrarian party in Oslo was to a considerable extent inspired by Rolf Thommessen, whose *Tidens Tegn* enthusiastically championed the National Joint List in the days before the election. The Agrarian party participated in the List mainly for tactical reasons, shown by the fact that its foremost candidate had feuded bitterly with Quisling just one year earlier in the *Storting* election.[95] As for Quisling, he had no difficulty in working with the two other parties in Oslo, since the program of the National Joint List was clearly influenced by NS. It called for an end to class divisiveness. Its major emphasis was placed on the desire to "hold open the doors" to those within the labor movement who were opposed to "revolutionary politics". This was the only way, declared the program, to prevent the revolutionary Labor party from taking control in the capital and using its position on the city council to its advantage in the decisive struggle for power in Norway.[96]

During the election campaign in Oslo, Quisling similarly argued that it was of the utmost importance to keep the capital out of the hands of Labor. He resorted to historical analogy, drawing a parallel between current conditions in Norway and how control of Paris had been decisive during the French Revolution. He portrayed the election as being a struggle for power in society. The Labor party's promises were described as being deceitful. He compared them with the assurances made by the Bolsheviks before they seized power in Russia, and he urged the voters not to be deceived in a similar fashion. What was needed, he insisted, was not class divisiveness, but rather social justice, solidarity, and a feeling of common interest. He maintained that the coalition between the three parties in Oslo was not *borgerlig* because *borgerlig* politics were based on the party system. He argued that such a system was opposed to national unity, which had to be appealed to if the revolutionary labor movement were to be stopped.[97] While the coalition between NS, the Agrarian party, and the Independent People's party could be depicted ideologically as being above party at least to Quisling's satisfaction, in reality it did not depart significantly from the party system, since alliances of this nature were common among the *borgerlige* parties during this period.

Ideological arguments and historical comparisons did not prove very effective at a time of economic depression and high unemployment. Nor was NS the primary concern for Labor in campaigns throughout various electoral districts in 1934. None of the other anti-socialist parties, however, were any more effective in their propaganda against the socialists. The Labor party broadened its voter appeal by continuing the strategy it had employed so successfully in the previous *Storting* election. It placed stress on the need for reform rather than on the importance of class struggle. The outcome proved therefore to be another Labor triumph. Its percentage of the total vote increased from thirty-three to thirty-nine per cent in the rural districts and from forty to forty-four per cent in the towns.[98] Despite Quisling's warnings, one of Labor's greatest triumphs occurred in Oslo, where the socialists gained an absolute majority of the popular vote and thereby took control of the city council and the office of mayor.[99]

For NS, the election results were at best mixed. The party gained 5,587 votes in the rural districts and 10,543 votes in the towns out of a total of 1,074,050 votes cast. This gave NS 28 representatives from the rural districts and 41 from the towns on the local councils.[100] Of the national vote, NS' percentage at first glance appeared woefully low, amounting to 0.82 per cent in the rural districts and 2.75 per cent in the towns.[101] However, a fairer comparison would be to evaluate NS' performance in only those districts where the party entered candidates. Here NS gained 2.21 per cent of the vote in the rural areas and 4.72 per cent in the towns.[102] These percentages, though higher than the party's national average, were still small when compared with the results of such major parties as the Conservatives, Liberals, Agrarian party, and above all the Labor party.

In the rural districts, NS' best result was obtained in Oppland province in eastern Norway, where thirteen representatives were elected. But of these, seven were from the only joint list that NS and the Agrarian party had agreed to establish. This indicated that NS might have gained more from cooperation with other parties, to the extent that this had been possible, than it accomplished by maintaining its independent posture. In the only additional region where NS cooperated with other parties, in the area around the capital, the National Joint List gained 3.8 per cent of the total vote in Oslo and elected three representatives to the city council.[103] To what extent this result was due to the amount of voter support which the individual parties obtained is difficult to determine, but it appears as if the National Joint List received its strongest backing from adherents of the Independent People's party, since two of the three representatives elected from the List came from this party, while NS gained one representative and the Agrarian party none.[104] In the neighboring district of Bærum in Akershus province, the National Joint List, composed of candidates from NS and the Independent People's party, succeeded in electing three of its candidates to the local council.[105]

The election's outcome showed that NS' major source of support in the rural districts continued to lie in eastern Norway. Almost all of its rural representatives, twenty-seven out of twenty-eight, were elected in four eastern provinces.[106] In the urban districts, NS gained especially favorable results in two locations, the west coast city of Stavanger and the small town of Vadsø, located in the extreme north. In these areas, NS was fortunate to have very capable local leaders, Gulbrand Lunde in Stavanger and Pastor Martin Tveter in Vadsø. Both men effectively used the argument that NS was a champion of the Christian religion against the Marxist atheism of the Labor party. Pietistic Christianity was strong in both towns, and Lunde's and Tveter's efforts proved to be quite successful. NS gained 12.15 per cent of the vote in Stavanger and elected eight representatives, while in Vadsø the party's percentage of the vote was nineteen, with the result that one-fifth of its city council consisted of NS members.[107]

Despite favorable results in a few election districts, the outcome of the local elections of 1934 was not the "breakthrough" in politics that NS later claimed it to be.[108] On the whole, the result was about the same as had been the case in the previous parliamentary election, the only difference being that it took fewer votes to elect representatives to the local councils than to the *Storting*. Subsequently, while the party continued to be visible to the public thanks to its propaganda activity, its influence on practical politics was minimal, even in the local councils on which it was represented. Each council decided who would hold the office of mayor in the district. Of the 747 mayors chosen in 1934, one belonged to NS. The Labor party, by comparison, gained 206 mayors.[109]

Quisling and his co-workers were not quite so sober in their appraisal of the election. They were to some extent buoyed by the fact that NS for the first time had been able to gain representatives. Nevertheless, they recognized that NS was far from a mass movement. With the local government elections completed, the party set in motion a number of activities intended to increase its numbers and to heighten its influence in time for the next major political confrontation at the ballot box, the *Storting* election of 1936.

NS activity during the 1934–1936 period had the dual purpose of strengthening the party internally and broadening its popularity by providing it with an even clearer identity through propaganda efforts. The need to build up the party was obvious, owing to the isolated position which NS occupied. By insisting on maintaining "clear lines" in politics, Quisling had lessened the possibility of significant cooperation with other parties. The prospect for an alliance with the Agrarian party and the Fatherland League had been eliminated by his inability to turn the national block negotiations to NS' advantage. Afterward, the party's mediocre at best performance in the local elections of 1934 did nothing to increase its potential value in any future collaboration with another political group. As a result, even Quisling's most stubborn ally now deserted him. Once the elections were over, the Independent People's party severed the last of its ties with NS. The relationship had largely been based on Rolf Thommessen's championship of cooperation with Quisling, despite the strong criticism which Thommessen at times received from within his own party.[110] In 1934 joint election activity between NS and the Independent People's party had been restricted only to the Oslo area, where Thommessen's direct influence was strongest. In the rest of the country the Independent People's party had either acted independently or had been associated with its traditional ally, the Conservative party.[111] Following the election, Thommessen's interest in Quisling and NS faded. He at last recognized that Quisling was a hindrance to the unified effort against the Labor party which he always sought to achieve. *Tidens Tegn*, previously Quisling's major newspaper outlet in

Oslo, changed its editorial policy. The theme of cooperation with NS no longer appeared in its pages.[112]

The fact that NS now had to act entirely on its own provided an important stimulus for it to build up a strong internal organization. Thanks to its improvised start in 1933, the party at first had been haphazardly organized. Persons holding office both locally and nationally changed frequently. The NS leadership failed to provide effective coordination of party activity. Not until shortly before the local election of 1934 did NS gain a permanent General Secretary. He was a new-baked attorney, Rolf Jørgen Fuglesang, who had just graduated from the University's school of law. He was one of NS' most noteworthy young activists. At the University he had been prominent in student politics as the leader of the NS student organization. Now as General Secretary, he loyally remained at Quisling's side from the fall of 1934 until NS' demise. He worked energetically to establish central control over the party. However, as will be seen, the creation of a centralized bureaucracy which insisted on a dominant role in party affairs led to considerable friction within NS.

Another organizational problem that remained unsettled until the fall of 1934 was the question of establishing a formal structure for the party leadership. When Quisling and his close associates were in the process of forming National Union in the spring of 1933, the highest executive body under Quisling was the Political Committee, which was merely a continuation of Nordic Folk-Rising's Political Committee. However, when NS had been established on a permanent basis, a more representative body was called for. This issue had first been brought up in October 1933 by Hans S. Jacobsen. He proposed the creation of a party council which would serve as the highest NS organ, with the power to appoint and to remove the NS leader. This suggestion was endorsed by the propaganda leader, Walter Fürst. Quisling, in the weak position he was in following the election defeat, was said to have agreed to set up a party council along the lines which Jacobsen had called for. However, the question was postponed during the entire period of the national block discussions.

When it was resolved, it occurred in a manner quite the opposite from what Jacobsen and Fürst had intended. Acting without any formal consultation with leading members, Quisling issued the party's bylaws, which dictatorially decreed that all authority within NS would be under his control. Acting consistently, he set up an organizational structure which was very similar to that which had earlier been drawn up for Nordic Folk-Rising. As the two highest party organs, both dominated by the *Fører*, he established an Executive Committee (*Hovedstyre*) and a Council (*Råd*). The Executive Committee consisted of Quisling, Fuglesang, and four other party members "appointed by the *Fører* in consultation with the Council". There existed, moreover, little possibility that the Council would act independently of Quisling. It was headed by him, and included the members of the

Executive Committee plus the party's regional leaders (*fylkesførere*). The regional leaders could be expected to follow Quisling's lead, since they owed their appointments directly to him.[113] Contrary to Jacobsen's and Fürst's expectations, this arrangement provided little possibility for the party to exercise control over its *Fører*. He had dominant authority over the party officers in positions of leadership. The first Executive Committee consisted of Quisling, Fuglesang, Hjort, architect Tormod Hustad, Christian Jøranli, and Pastor Kjeld Stub. All except Jøranli lived within Oslo or its immediate vicinity, and Jøranli was frequently represented in absentia by his designated deputy (*varamann*), Kjell Gundersen, an Oslo area resident.[114]

An additional guarantee of Quisling's sovereign position lay in the fact that members of the party's central bureaucracy participated in the Executive Committee's deliberations. In addition to Fuglesang, they included National Union's financial director, organizational director, and press chief.[115] The professional experts in these appointive positions could be expected to be loyal to the party leadership. If they were not, they could easily be replaced.

The Executive Committee and the Council never became important organs within National Union. Quisling always jealously guarded his authority. He preferred to work through the NS bureaucracy in the Central Office, headed by Fuglesang. Never very good at discussing problems with persons on an equal basis, Quisling found it to his advantage to have at hand a compliant bureaucracy which carried out his directives. This allowed him to spend a good portion of his time behind his desk, rather than having to be in personal contact with his lieutenants.

As a result, the party's central organization grew in size and increased its authority. This expansion in turn required more office space. From its beginnings, National Union's headquarters had been located in the offices which Fürst had made available in Prinsens gate 7. At the end of 1935, however, headquarters were moved into "large new offices" in Kristian Augusts gate 15. Here Quisling had his office, as did also General Secretary Fuglesang, the party's Press and Propaganda Division, the Organizational Division, the Finance Division, National Union's Youth Organization, and the local party organization in Oslo.[116] Under Quisling's authority, a steady stream of instructions was sent out from the third storey of Kristian Augusts gate 15 to NS officers throughout the country.

Quisling placed special importance on having a number of special organizations within his party, as large and as broad-based as possible. He wished to have NS truly become a mass movement which provided for all of the needs of its members, cultural as well as political. In doing so, he consciously imitated the Labor party, which had successfully established a large number of socialist educational and cultural organizations in order to create a working class culture in opposition to that of the bourgeoisie. He similarly was aware that foreign totalitarian parties, communist as well as fascist, also followed the policy of seeking to provide their members with an all-inclusive cultural environment.

The NS *Fører* therefore placed no restraints on Fuglesang's Central Office when it made an attempt to expand its area of competence to include cultural activity. The Central Office endeavored to establish an NS orchestra, and it similarly encouraged party members to form NS choirs.[117] But unlike the Labor party, which could maintain viable cultural organizations, NS lacked a mass following. Quisling's attempt to imitate the Labor party cultural policy therefore proved barren.

The NS leadership enjoyed greater success in setting up more traditional party groups. Similar to other Norwegian parties, National Union had both a youth organization and a women's organization. From its earliest beginnings the party contained a considerable number of young enthusiasts who became members of National Union's Youth Organization (*Nasjonal Samlings Ungdomsfylking*), popularly known by its initials, NSUF. All persons under the age of twenty who adhered to the party were enrolled in NSUF.[118] National Union's Women's Organization (*Nasjonal Samlings Kvinneorganisasjon*), or NSK, originally emerged from a circle of Maria Quisling's personal acquaintances. The group seems at first to have been troubled by a certain amount of internal strife caused by personal jealousies.[119] Despite this somewhat erratic beginning, it survived to become a permanent part of NS' organizational structure.

The party's strong-arm organization, the *Hird*, was a unique group which evolved in the period 1934–1936. As noted earlier, NS had already organized the *Hird*'s predecessor, the S.A., or Special Division, in early 1934.[120] The S.A., however, never amounted to anything more than a small number of young NS stalwarts who attempted with varying degrees of success to maintain order at turbulent political meetings. Considerable confusion existed as to the S.A.'s area of competence and leadership.[121] For a while it was led by a certain Lieutenant Strand.[122] Later in 1934, when its name had been changed to the *Hird*, no doubt to give it a more Norwegian image and less association with Hitler's SA, the group was headed by Captain Karl Stenersen. The Captain provided the small number of *Hird* members with training as a regular military unit, including weapons instruction and marching drills.[123]

Not until Quisling's second-in-command, Johan B. Hjort, took over control of the *Hird* on March 20, 1935, did the organization became a significant force.[124] Under Hjort, the *Hird* was well-trained and effective, dressed in its distinctive brown shirts and armed with wooden truncheons.[125] It remained small, with the bulk of its activity concentrated in the Oslo area. Hjort succeeded, however, in establishing *Hird* groups in some of the other major population centers as well.[126]

Quisling intended to have the *Hird* play a major role within NS. One indication of this was the fact that someone of Hjort's stature was appointed as its leader. Furthermore, on October 8, 1935, Quisling decreed that the *Hird* would function as a "political school" and fighting machine. It should "unite the movement and activate it". He envisaged the ambitious goal of having the *Hird* act as a unifying force, providing the party with a dynamic element which it previously had lacked. It would carry out an ideological leavening process within NS. Seeking to realize this ambition, he decreed that all male NS members under the age of forty were to undergo *Hird* instruction, and that no one could become an officer in National Union's central organization without having received *Hird* training. While these requirements for the time being were limited to Oslo and Akershus, he declared that in the future he intended to have them apply to the entire NS membership throughout the country.[127]

NS *Hird* units were not, however, restricted just to adult males. Hjort also organized a Women's *Hird* (*Kvinnehird*). Similarly, plans were made for a *Hird* for boys and girls under nineteen, and even for children's *Hird* units for young boys and girls, segregated by sex.[128] By this age division, the *Hird* was intended to be a miniature of society at large, with most age groups represented. The *Hird* units for boys and girls (*Guttehird* and *Jentehird* respectively) remained largely paper organizations during the 1930s, as did also those for young children, but these organizations contained a more active membership during the occupation period. The creation of such children's formations was due in large part to the examples provided by Fascist Italy and National Socialist Germany, where uniformed children's groups were featured prominently in fascist propaganda.[129]

In addition to building up a central party bureaucracy and national groups such as NSK, NSUF, and the Hird, Quisling and the Central Office similarly worked to create a party structure on the local level. With his administrative background, the NS *Fører* believed strongly in the importance of establishing a highly structured party framework throughout the entire country. Responsibility for coordinating this activity rested with the NS Organizational Division (NS *Riksorganisasjonsavdeling*), which worked directly under Quisling and Fuglesang at NS headquarters. The Organizational Division maintained that the party's measure of success could be demonstrated by the extent to which structural expansion took place, an expression which was completely in agreement with Quisling's point of view.[130]

The Organizational Division's goal was to have the NS local organizational structure correspond as much as possible to the administrative divisions in the country.[131] Since Norway at the time was divided into eighteen regional provinces (*fylker*), and with the two major cities of Oslo and Bergen also holding the status of independent regions, this meant that NS' ideal was to create twenty regional party organizations. This, however, proved difficult to attain. While it was simple to draw up such a structure at party headquarters, membership throughout the wide expanse of the country was frequently lacking. Early in 1934, when local party activity in most areas was only beginning, NS headquarters sent out instructions to the regional officers that the party organization in each district should be built up as rapidly as possible. Only when this was accomplished, maintained the central bureaucracy, would it be possible for the party to function as it should.[132] The Organizational Division's directive reflected Quisling's attitude that the creation of a highly structured organization on the local level could not help but lead to an increase in National Union's membership, as opposed to having the growth in membership take place first, thereby allowing a party structure to develop naturally as the total of NS members on the local level increased.

It proved to be next to impossible to meet the ambitious goals which Quisling and the Central Office set for local party organization. In many districts only a skeletal framework came into existence, since there simply were not enough qualified members to fill the many positions which the master plan required. The objective of having twenty regional organizations was indicated by their method of classification, with each receiving a numerical designation ranging of from one to twenty. However, only briefly, just before the 1936 election, did NS succeed in establishing even on paper the desired twenty regional organizations. During most of the party's history, including the wartime period, the number amounted to less than twenty, with more than one region or parts of regions being included in various groupings. Furthermore, the boundaries of these organizations changed from time to time during the twelve years of National Union's existence. In particular, the west coast regions of Hordaland, Sogn og Fjordane, and Møre og Romsdal were always difficult for NS to organize, both during the 1930s and again during the five years of occupation. The regional leadership in these areas changed frequently, and NS membership was low. At times large parts of the west coast had to be administered by the NS organization in Bergen.[133]

Despite these difficulties, in particular in scattered rural districts on the west coast and in northern Norway, Quisling set up an elaborate bureaucratic system throughout the country, analogous to the national party apparatus in Oslo. The NS head in each region was the regional *fører* (*fylkesfører*), who acted as Quisling's counterpart in the region. Serving under him was a staff whose responsibilities coincided with those of the functionaries in the Central Office in Oslo, such as the provincial propaganda leader, organizational leader, financial leader, etc. The regional NS officers in turn presided over a number of districts (*krets*), organized monolithically in the same manner. The district office, headed by a *kretsfører*, was located in the larger towns and villages. Finally, at the lowest level of local organization was the group (*lag*), headed by a *lagfører*. The *lag* was subordinate to the *krets*. If there were enough members, one or more *lag* were set up in the center where the *krets* had its headquarters. However, the largest number of *lag* were located in the small rural townships and villages in the districts.[134]

The creation of such a top-heavy administrative apparatus at a time when the party had only minimal political influence allowed Quisling to have, at least on paper, the type of rigid planning which he always adhered to. In order for NS to function successfully, he believed the party had to be organized immediately from top to bottom. Not only did the local *fylke*, *krets*, and *lag* structure mirror the central party organization, but the special youth and women's groups also had their appointed representatives on the local level, as did also the *Hird* in some instances.

The visionary and unpragmatic sweep of Quisling's ambition, fully seconded by NS planners in the Central Office, was further indicated by attempts to set up a number of special organizations, intended to spread NS influence throughout important sectors of society. In the hope of challenging the workers' allegiance to the Labor party, and seeking to take advantage of the social unrest caused by the depression, NS created a League for the Unemployed (*NS Arbeidsløses Forbund*), whose declared purpose was to fight for a "people's socialism".[135] It became largely a paper organization. The NS Student Group appealed to a more privileged segment of the population, its goal being to win support for NS ideas among university students.[136] An additional grouping within NS' organizational structure revealed that Quisling had not abandoned his predilection for seeking to infiltrate vital areas of society by means of establishing semi-conspiratorial cells, a practice he originally launched in connection with Nordic Folk-Rising. Such cells were now called "supporting points" (*støttepunkter*) in party terminology. They were to be established in the work place. NS members were encouraged to form cells and to spread the party's corporative ideas among fellow employees.[137] NS' meager membership, in particular among the workers, provided no basis for such an endeavor.

NS similarly sought to form front organizations which had special appeal for young people. Such front organizations were intended to include youngsters who were not members of the youth organization (NSUF), and who were to be won over by being inculcated with the "NS spirit". Rules were drawn up governing two such organizations, one intended for young people in rural districts, League of Rural Youth (*Landsungdomslaget NS*), the other for youth in general, NS Youth Guild (*NS Ungdomsgilde*).[138] They too never became more than paper organizations.

With the failure of the above front organizations and the program to establish "supporting points", the conspiratorial side of Quisling's nature remained unfulfilled. The inability of these groups to function reflected basic weakness in party planning. The structure that Quisling and the NS Central Office drew up was far too elaborate. Some of the groups, such as the above, were set up although there was no demand for them. Even those parts of the party apparatus which did operate, frequently functioned badly because persons were appointed to hold positions for which they were unsuited. The detailed structure whose creation Quisling had supervised might have been suitable for a mass party with a large and loyal membership, but not for a small party such as NS, which had been founded only a few years earlier. The structure demonstrated Quisling's passion for administrative detail, believing that this was the key to political success. He did not take into account that a party organization by itself cannot guarantee success – not if the party's ideas did not win support among the public, or if its leaders were lacking in popular appeal.

Another means by which Quisling attempted to broaden his party's influence was through the creation of a party press. Control of publications within the news media had traditionally been an essential ingredient for doing well at the polls, and Quisling shared the prevailing opinion within NS that the absence of regular party publications was a major handicap. Special election issues such as *NS*, appearing just before the previous *Storting* election, could not make up for the lack of regular newspapers.

In seeking to overcome this handicap, no less than twelve NS papers came out during the period 1934–1936.[139] Most parts of the country were covered; the major exception being northern Norway, with no NS paper published north of Trondheim. Although the majority had limited editions, appearing only once a week, and strained economies, the ability of NS to set up so many papers in such a short time was no mean accomplishment, considering the complete absence of a regular party press previously. The first to appear was *Nasjonal Samling* (*National Union*), whose initial number was published in Oslo on March 15, 1934. It came out as a weekly, appearing every Thursday. The subtitle on its mast-head revealed Quisling's ambition of winning members of the working class away from the Labor party, as well as his parroting of Hitler: "Organ for Norway's Working People". The NS leader himself appeared on the masthead as "political editor". He did not, however, possess the necessary journalistic expertise to edit the paper. This was provided by the daily editor, Herlof Harstad, a professional journalist. As an indication of the emphasis that NS placed on having broad press coverage, Harstad also assumed the position of NS Press Director in the fall of 1934, with responsibility for coordinating press activity throughout Norway from party headquarters in Oslo.[140]

The first NS daily newspaper did not appear in Oslo, however, but in Stavanger, in September 1934. The fact that the initial daily publication came out in this location was but another indication of the skillful propaganda activity carried out in the Stavanger area by Gulbrand Lunde. Named *Vestlandets Avis (The West Coast's Newspaper)*, the paper was edited by Arnt Rishovd, who later became the party's most prominent journalist. *Vestlandets Avis* was not as strident in its tone as other NS papers during Rishovd's editorship. It maintained a less partisan profile, which enabled it to work in cooperation with *Rogaland*, the Agrarian party's organ in Stavanger.[141]

Rishovd resigned as editor in early 1935, and in the fall of that year *Vestlandets Avis* was forced to go over to being a weekly. The central party organization was not willing to provide funds for the paper's continued appearance as a daily. Instead, headquarters was planning the creation of a daily in Oslo at this time, intended to replace *Nasjonal Samling* as the party's national newspaper.[142] The first number of this long-awaited daily, named *Fritt Folk (Free People)*, came out on March 26, 1936, with Harstad as editor, Rishovd as editorial secretary, and J. B. Hjort as chairman of the board of directors.[143]

Fritt Folk's appearance received enthusiastic approval from many party members because the publication provided NS with a national newspaper on a daily basis, which was considered essential in the election year of 1936. Compared with the scant newspaper publicity the party had been able to generate during previous campaigns, the situation this year seemed promising. Although three of NS' papers ceased publication prior to balloting, the party still had eight newspapers in operation at the time of the election, plus the youth organization's paper, appearing in the four major cities of Oslo, Bergen, Trondheim, and Stavanger, and in four additional regional centers.[144]

From an organizational point of view, outwardly the party's effort seemed to be a success during the period 1934–36. An organization had been built up in a structured manner, both centrally and locally, and NS had gained an active press. Herlof Harstad claimed that some seventy new *lag* were established throughout the country in 1935, and that NS possessed a membership of 15,000. This boast was considerably exaggerated, with NS' actual membership being 8,369 at the beginning of the following year.[145] Nevertheless, the assertion reflected the optimism which buoyed the party faithful at this time.

While NS acquired a systematic structure during the years 1934–1936, a change occurred in its public image during the same period. To a major degree, this change reflected the point of view which Quisling presented. The political position which he adopted during this period provided National

Union in many respects with an identity which did not change appreciably in the succeeding years.

One of Quisling's noticeable preferences was the attraction that Norway's history had for him, in particular the Viking period. His preoccupation with the past caused him to espouse a unique form of nationalism. He has been described as being possessed "by an almost fanatical nationalism, his world was a national-romantic daydream world . . . ."[146] Daydreams are based on illusion, a fact that the average person is capable of recognizing. Quisling, however, differed in that he attempted to a very great degree to turn his romantic view of history into reality. It must be noted that his use of nationalistic symbolism in part was inspired by a rational recognition that he needed to present his followers with an ideal; a fact that he had indicated previously in his writings, most clearly in his explanation of Nordic Folk-Rising's program. But the major reason for his use of historical imagery lay with the emotional satisfaction this provided him. He gained his sense of mission by identifying himself with heroic figures from the past, in particular with St. Olav.

Because of his stress on the past, National Union made use of historical symbolism more than any other party. Reference has already been made to the NS emblem, the so-called St. Olav's banner of a cross of gold on a field of red, and to the *Hird*, whose name was taken from the personal bodyguard of Viking chieftains. The party salutation was the old Nordic greeting, *heil og sæl*. This choice was not particularly wise, however, because in the popular mind it became easily associated with the similar *Sieg Heil* of the German National Socialists, especially when accompanied by the Nazi salute.

Another Viking term which members of NS frequently used was the word *ting*. Originally this meant a legal assembly of freemen. Now it became a term used in connection with NS meetings. The most important of such gatherings was the national party meeting (*riksmøte*), held annually in the summer. Special care was taken to choose sites that were historically significant. In 1934 the party gathered at Stiklestad, north of Trondheim, where St. Olav died in battle and achieved martyrdom. In the following year the meeting was at Hafrsfjord, on the west coast near Stavanger, where the decisive naval battle was fought which led to Norway's earliest unification under one king.[147]

In his speech at Stiklestad on June 26, 1934, the NS *Fører* declared, as he had previously, how important it was in a time of revolutionary upheaval for a nation to receive sustenance from its historical roots. He drew direct parallels between the time of St. Olav and his own period. If it had then been a question of unifying Norway as a realm, he said, now it was a question of uniting Norwegians as a people. If it had then been characterized by the transition from paganism to Christianity, it was now "a decisive transition period in human history, a new era in world civilization with radical and revolutionary changes in all areas of human life. But that which was new, which now must be carried forward and realized, has to be united with our people's old culture-bearing and ethical values."[148] His direct comparison between what he viewed as his mission as the leader of NS with that of St. Olav was also shown by National Union's expropriation as a party holiday of the traditional date of the patron saint's death at Stiklestad, June 29.[149]

Because of its leader's emphasis on historical imagery, it was natural for National Union to assume the profile of an ultra-nationalist party. In the beginning it adopted the posture, as noted, of Norway's protector against the threat of revolution inspired by the imported ideology of Marxism. However, when the Labor party formed its government in March 1935 and none of Quisling's dire warnings of drastic upheaval proved true, it was difficult for the party to find contemporary issues which allowed it free room for nationalistic agitation. One issue which NS could have emphasized had it wished was the question of the country's poor defense capability. This seemed to be a natural point for Quisling to raise, in particular because of his past association with the military as a General Staff officer and Minister of Defense. The party program did call for strengthening the armed forces, and NS succeeded in attracting some officers. However, the climate of public opinion during the depression was anything but favorable toward increased expenditures for the military. For this reason, Quisling chose not to stress this question.

The one concrete nationalistic issue which Quisling tried to have NS exploit involved the Greenland controversy. He had been emotionally preoccupied with this question since his days in the Hundseid cabinet, when his antipathy toward the Prime Minister had not been allayed by the way the latter had mismanaged Norwegian interests in his aborted attempt to arrange a compromise with the Danes without informing his government. Those who favored occupation of Greenland received an even more severe blow in April 1933, just a month after the Hundseid government had stepped down, when the International Court of Justice at The Hague delivered its verdict in the dispute. The decision was a stinging defeat for Norwegian nationalists. Only one member of the court, not unexpectedly a Norwegian, found in favor of Norway, while the other judges upheld Denmark's sovereignty over the world's largest island.[150]

The Court's decision led to bitter recriminations concerning who was responsible for this national humiliation. In this atmosphere, it was natural for Quisling to involve NS. In his nationalistic fantasy world, he believed Greenland should revert to Norwegian control because the island had been part of the kingdom during the Middle Ages. This point of view became official NS policy. A resolution was passed at the annual party meeting in

1935 which demanded revision of the Treaty of Kiel, dating from 1814, by which Denmark ceded Norway to Sweden without including any of the North Atlantic islands which previously had been Norwegian possessions.[151]

Quisling attempted to capitalize on this issue during NS' election campaign in 1936. As part of a general effort to win publicity for its cause through a number of initiatives, party headquarters, with Quisling's approval, tried to arrange protest meetings concerning Greenland, including opposition to the possible sale of the island to the United States, which was rumored.[152] NS sought to use the meetings as fronts by maintaining that they were non-partisan, but this subterfuge was readily apparent.[153] Undaunted by setbacks, Quisling continued to pursue the issue, which to a considerable degree became an obsession for him. In a radio address just before the election, he repeated his conviction that the controversy would gain support for NS, insisting that Greenland should once more become Norwegian, thereby providing the country's fishermen and hunters with access to the island. He did not allow this rare opportunity before the microphone to pass without levelling an indictment against one of his favorite targets, the "party politicians" whom he held in such contempt. He accused them of having "completely failed their national duty and obligation" in matters of national interest, including Greenland.[154]

While he might attack "party politicians" in general, he could at times be inconsistent when he sought to further NS interests. He failed to mention to his radio listeners, for example, that he belonged to the board of directors of an organization led by the type of party politicians whom he usually denounced. The group was called Danish-Norwegian Settlement (*Dansk-Norsk Ordning*). The NS leader joined it already at the time of its founding in May 1936. Its purpose was identical with part of NS' program: to bring about a revision of the Treaty of Kiel.[155] Quisling became a member of its board first and foremost because its goal was completely in harmony with his nationalistic feelings, but he furthermore quite obviously believed his association with the group would prove beneficial for NS in the upcoming election.

Not everyone in NS agreed with him. Hjort objected to the fact that the *Fører* had affiliated with Danish-Norwegian Settlement without consulting his party colleagues. Hjort opposed Quisling's move in particular because the group was, in his term, a "parliamentary organization", since it included persons prominent in parties represented in the *Storting*. In addition to Quisling, its board contained individuals belonging to the more nationalistic *borgerlige* parties: the Conservatives, the Agrarians, the Fatherland League, the Independent People's party, and the Radical People's party. Among these were former backers of Quisling such as Lehmkuhl, whom Hjort characterized as a "Jew and leader of the false Fatherland League", and Thommessen, about whom there was nothing more to be said. Hjort furthermore disliked the fact that Quisling was merely an ordinary member of the board, one of ten members, while the prestigious positions of chairman and vice-chairman were held respectively by Johan Mellbye of the Agrarian party and Henrik Ameln of the Conservative party. Many of the members of Danish-Norwegian Settlement were political enemies of NS, said Hjort, and he could not resist pointing out, as one of a number of examples, that Ameln had earlier described Quisling as a miscarriage, but that he, Ameln, was not sure whether the abortion had been induced.[156]

Gulbrand Lunde, to whom these objections were addressed, agreed that it was unfortunate that Quisling was merely one of ten board members. Lunde, however, believed that Danish-Norwegian Settlement might nevertheless prove to be a useful tool for the party:

> We can in any event reach quite far into the *borgerlige* press with this organization, and it serves to awaken the people and to arouse hate against the Danes, something which without doubt is of benefit for our movement.[157]

Quisling's endeavor to exploit Danish-Norwegian Settlement did not materialize in the way Lunde hoped. Nationalistic agitation concerning Greenland had little bearing on the outcome of the 1936 election. While the organization continued to exist afterwards, it failed to generate any significant popular response. The only benefit that NS gained from its extreme stand on the Greenland issue was the support of a few ardent nationalists. Most outstanding among these were Gustav Smedal and Adolf Hoel, leading figures in Arctic research and exploration. For the great mass of the people, however, internal economic issues were what mattered. Strident, and at times esoteric, arguments over the question of Norway's claim to Greenland were at best of secondary importance.

For Quisling, his party's identification with the Greenland controversy served a dual purpose of providing him with both an emotional and an intellectual outlet. He genuinely felt that Greenland should revert to Norway. He furthermore believed that this issue served as an excellent means of making the people conscious of their special heritage. This was especially important for him because of the significance he attached to the question of race. As he had shown in his earlier writings, his racist point of view was an essential part of his ideology, providing a rationale for the mission which he maintained the Norwegian people were to carry out. By making them conscious of the heroic accomplishments of their forefathers through use of nationalistic propaganda, he hoped that he would stimulate a feeling of racial superiority in conformity with the racist interpretation of both the past and the present which he preached. NS identification with Norway's history was therefore not merely nationalistic, but also racist.

Norwegians during the Viking period had in Quisling's mind been part of the dominant Nordic race, which he now believed should revive and reassert itself.[158]

Although his racist viewpoint had been included in National Union's ideology from its beginning, not until 1935 did the party's propaganda repeat with increasingly stronger intensity the emphasis that NS placed on the Nordic race's alleged superiority.[159] In its agitation, NS was similar to other European racist parties in that it sought to find a "scientific" basis for its viewpoint. To a major degree, this was provided by Dr. Jon Alfred Mjøen, a foremost expert on eugenics who headed a biological institute in Oslo. Having published his major work on "racial hygiene" in 1915, Mjøen was a well-established figure in Norway's intellectual community in the 1930s. He was a member of the Norwegian Academy of Science and Letters, and he also belonged to several foreign academic societies.[160] While subject to strong criticism, his views were part of the intellectual climate of the times. National Union's enthusiasm for his ideas stemmed first and foremost from the fact that the biologist maintained that the Nordic race was superior to other races, and that it was therefore necessary to protect the Norwegian element within this race from allegedly negative racial groups. Among the different segments who made up the Norwegian population, Mjøen placed the farmers highest because eugenically they were supposedly the purest. It therefore came as no surprise to find racist arguments being enunciated not only by National Union during the 1930s, but also from within other political groups, in particular the Agrarian party.[161] By the time of his death in 1939 at the age of seventy-eight, Mjøen's ideas had gained considerable circulation in Europe.[162] He was hailed by NS as the party's racial expert both before and after his death.

The increased attention that NS gave to the question of race had the corollary effect of turning it into an anti-Semitic party. In adopting this position, NS simply reflected the change that had taken place in Quisling's thought, since the party's ideology at all times reflected the views of its *Fører*. Emphasis on the belief that Norwegians were part of a racial elite, the Nordic race, meant inevitably from an NS viewpoint that there existed inferior races. These were looked down upon because of their supposed negative qualities, and feared because of their potential to defile the blood of the superior Norwegians. The Jews were not the only ethnic group to be singled out for attack. Blacks, Chinese, gypsies, Poles, and Greeks were also among the members of the human species who were branded as being inferior by the NS press. Young women were especially warned against having sexual relations with Jews, blacks, and gypsies. This supposedly would cause the Norwegian *folk* to degenerate into a bastard people, and would inevitably lead to its destruction.[163]

Many so-called inferior races and racial types therefore existed within Quisling's racist perspective. But his party's negative racism was directed first and foremost against the Jews. This was a gradual development. At first National Union's racism was mainly positive, emphasizing Nordic superiority in support of the party's strategy of appearing as nationalistic as possible. The first scattered anti-Semitic references began to appear in NS publications in early 1934. This did not escape public notice. In April a businessman protested on behalf of the Norwegian Jewish community to the NS Executive Committee, pointing to the "malicious" statements made by the NS Press Director, Eyvind Mehle, with the intent to damage the country's Jews.[164] However, not until 1935, especially during the second half of the year, did National Union officially assume a position of open anti-Semitism. Attacks against the Jews occurred in a systematic fashion, with the language in the party press becoming more extreme than ever before.[165]

National Union's heightened virulence against the Jews occurred in a particularly crass form because, as in Germany, anti-Semitism was combined with the party's previous strong condemnation of Marxism. NS maintained that international communism was a world-wide conspiracy, organized and led by Jews.[166] Furthermore, the party strenuously sought to link the Labor party to this alleged conspiracy as part of Quisling's continued drive to discredit and defeat the socialists. Hjort almost invariably referred to the Labor party's ideology as "Jewish Marxism".[167] Haldis Neegaard Østbye, head of the NS Press and Propaganda Office, was equally convinced that the party stood to gain from using anti-Semitism in its agitation against the Labor party. As she indicated in 1935:

> I have noticed so many times in discussions that this [question] concerning Jewish labor leaders is a sore point with Norwegian workers. If we could only convince them that it is the Jews who are behind Marxism, then they soon will be finished with the whole deviltry.[168]

National Union's anti-Semitism was not, however, directed only against the Labor party's leaders, or against socialist or communist movements outside of Norway. The country's small Jewish community also received its share of abuse. This occurred despite the absence of an anti-Semitic tradition. Norway, as opposed to many continental European countries, never had large numbers of Jews within its population. During the 1930s it had one of the smallest numbers of Jews found in any European state, with only approximately 1700 of its citizens being persons of Jewish ancestry.[169] Nevertheless, NS maintained that this minuscule group was a direct threat to the country's security because of its alleged revolutionary convictions, supposedly conspiring to incorporate Norway into a Marxist world state dominated by the Jews. Repeating arguments very similar to those used by the Nazis, NS contended that the Jews were capable of attaining this objective because they possessed most of the world's wealth. Furthermore, they were alleged to control "the world press".[170]

Under the slogan "Norway for Norwegians", Quisling's party sought to whip up popular support by utilizing anti-Semitism.[171] In this endeavor, a considerable part of its attention was directed toward possible Jewish immigration. In 1935 humanitarian interests in Norway suggested that a number of Jewish refugees be allowed to settle in the country. As could be expected, the NS press attacked the proposal vigorously, maintaining that such persons were dangerous Marxists who had fought against Hitler, and they should therefore not be admitted under any circumstances.[172]

NS anti-Semitic propaganda received added stimulus from the Labor government's decision to provide political asylum for Leon Trotsky in 1935. Here was concrete evidence, argued party publications, that the Labor party's pro-Jewish leaders were acting in collusion with one of the chief figures in the international Jewish-Marxist conspiracy.[173] In their agitation against Labor, Quisling and NS also suggested that Trotsky's asylum was a threat to international peace because of the conspiracies Trotsky was said to be involved in.[174]

The NS assault against Trotsky contained many of the propaganda ingredients which Quisling had utilized in attacking "Bolshevism" since his return from the Soviet Union. Thanks to his significant contribution toward securing the Bolshevik victory during the revolution and civil war in Russia, Trotsky was described in *Nasjonal Samling* as "world history's greatest blood-executioner" when he arrived in Norway.[175] Similar epithets with reference to his past were hurled against him, and the theme was repeated constantly in the NS press that he was a threat to Norwegian security. But because of his Jewish ancestry, the agitation that NS voiced came out much more clearly in the party's propaganda than would have been the case had he been non-Jewish.

The tone of the campaign protesting against Trotsky's stay was extremely strident, occurring in an atmosphere of intense emotion. There exist even some indications that NS members may have considered the possibility of assassinating the former Soviet leader.[176] No attempt was made on his life, but six young NS members did break into his residence in August 1936 and stole a quantity of his personal documents. A furor arose over whether or not the purloined material revealed that Trotsky had violated the terms of his asylum by participating in political activity.[177] In large part because of the publicity surrounding this sensational affair and the testimony which came out in subsequent court proceedings, he was interned by the government. The fact that 1936 was an election year did nothing to moderate the political repercussions of the affair. The *borgerlige* parties joined NS in condemning Trotsky's asylum and demanding his deportation.[178] While the affair did not significantly affect the election, Trotsky's continued stay proved to be too great a political liability for the Labor party. At the end of the year he was expelled from the country after Mexico had agreed to provide him with refuge. This was one of the few times during the 1930s when NS enjoyed a propaganda triumph at the expense of the Labor party.[179]

The question why Quisling decided to have NS adopt anti-Semitism as an important part of its ideology is fairly complex. Inspiration for this move did not come from Mjøen, who assumed a neutral position on "the Jewish question".[180] Quisling never discussed his motives. As has been seen, while racism was an important part of the ideology that he presented in his writings during the first years of the 1930s, he did not at this time combine his glorification of the Nordic race with an explicit anti-Jewish stand, nor did his opposition to Marxism include anti-Semitic aspects. The closest he came to identifying Jewish influence with international Communism occurred in *Russland og vi*, in which he declared "Bolshevism is an Asiatic-Slavic movement led by Jewish brains."[181] But his primary concern in this passage was to demonstrate his assertion that "Bolshevism" was an "oriental-Asiatic" movement which stood in contrast to "Nordic-European" principles, and in this context the Jews were not important except insofar as they could be described as being "Asiatic".[182] Similarly, at the time of National Union's founding he showed no interest in making use of anti-Jewish propaganda. His main objective was to present NS as an ultra-nationalist movement in pact with the times, ready to protect Norway from the Labor party, with its foreign ideology.

The change toward adopting an anti-Semitic attitude did not occur until after NS had failed to gain noteworthy success in the elections of 1933 and 1934. It can be assumed that in many ways it was natural for Quisling to agree to such a transition. Not only had his party been unable to obtain a significant percentage of the vote in two successive elections, and thereby the need for change in order to seek to gain a broader base of support seemed obvious, but in addition he could see the example of triumphant National Socialism in Germany. Contrary to his claims of originality, it became increasingly obvious that his party patterned itself after the Nazis to a considerable extent. The NS press also gave full support to Germany's foreign policy as Hitler began to assert himself in 1935–36. Another apparent advantage for NS in adopting its anti-Jewish stance was that it could thereby assume an identity which none of the other political parties had.[183] Whereas such *borgerlige* factions as the Conservatives, Independent People's party, Fatherland League, and Agrarian party were to a lesser or greater degree nationalistic in outlook, and while members of these groups might on an individual basis make statements that could be considered racist in nature, none of these parties were openly anti-Semitic.

Quisling did not, however, adopt anti-Semitism solely as the result of cynical calculation. This kind of tactical move was completely foreign to his character. Instead, anti-Semitism became an ingrained part of his political philosophy. He accepted it completely, and remained a fervent anti-Semite to his death. Even during his postwar treason trial, when he had every reason to downplay his negative feelings toward the Jews, he reasserted his conviction that "the Jews are responsible for a number of the misfortunes which have stricken the world."[184] By 1936, as a result of self-suggestion, he was firmly convinced that international communism was part of the worldwide Jewish conspiracy to control the globe. Just before the 1936 election, the NS *Fører* warned in a front page article in *Fritt Folk* against the possibility of "the entire people (*folk*)" becoming "slaves in a world Soviet republic under Jewish dictatorship".[185] His affirmation of having accepted anti-Semitism as an integral part of National Union's ideology explains why some former NS members who previously had left the party because they felt it did not parallel National Socialism closely enough, now hailed Quisling for having transformed NS into a party that was much more in accord with Hitler's movement.[186]

The change that took place in National Union's ideology, bringing it more into line with National Socialism, corresponded to a remarkable degree with the positions which the party adopted on foreign policy questions. At first NS did not concern itself to any significant degree with external events. It primarily concentrated on internal developments, which was understandable in 1933–34, when Quisling to a major extent focused his attention on the elections, plus the question of the party's relationship with other political groups. On the few occasions when he felt obliged to comment on international affairs, his focus continued to be directed primarily eastward toward what he perceived as the main external threat, the Soviet Union. Thus in September 1934 he warned that the admission of Russia to the League of Nations was a threat to peace because the U.S.S.R. continued to work for the "Marxistic world revolution", on whose behalf the men in the Kremlin were fanatical and inconvertible champions.[187] Should a dispute develop involving the Soviet Union and its allies, on the one hand, and Japan or Germany on the other, he argued from a strictly legalistic interpretation of Norway's responsibilities as a member of the League, then there was a real danger that the country would be obliged to side with the Soviet Union. This, he warned darkly, would have dire consequences, hinting that in a crisis situation the Russians might well take advantage of the opportunity to occupy Norway.[188]

His concern for the Soviet Union as a menacing threat remained a basic part of his political perception of the world. However, Soviet antipathy was placed in a larger perspective as the two fascist totalitarian states of Italy and Germany increasingly expanded the scope of their activity in international affairs. Since Fascism and National Socialism were obviously related to NS, and since the party had not gained the breakthrough he had sought with its anti-Marxism and ultra-nationalism, it was natural for him to engage his party on the side of the fascist dictators in its interpretation of foreign affairs, in particular since fascist successes represented what he himself would like to achieve, namely, unrivaled leadership over his society.

During the time when the first aggressive moves were made by the Fascist states which led eventually to the start of World War II, NS engaged itself in particular in defense of Mussolini's invasion and take-over of Ethiopia. In a speech given at the Colosseum Cinema on October 27, 1935, when the Ethiopian crisis was at its height, Quisling made the same type of appeal to the desire for peace in Norwegian public opinion that he had used earlier in his warning against Russian membership in the League of Nations. At a time when war could mean the destruction of the entire people, he declared, the effort to maintain the nation's neutrality was of paramount importance. However, he contended that the "party politicians" supporting the League against Mussolini were in reality drawing Norway into war. He argued that the League was nothing but an instrument for imperialism and for the forces of the Marxist world revolution. Imperialist powers such as England and the Soviet Union, he maintained, were engaged in this conspiracy, and behind them stood the international Jews. These forces were allegedly interested in exploiting international disputes such as that in Ethiopia in order to destroy Fascism.[189]

This defense of Mussolini came at a time when Fascist aggression in Africa was widely condemned in Norway. Support of Italy was therefore deplored, and even some prominent NS members opposed Quisling's view.[190] They were not originally aware, however, that his commitment on Italy's behalf occurred not merely as a result of his sympathy for Fascism, or because of his ideological conviction that Marxism stood to benefit from the League's sanctions against Italy. He had even more direct reason for his pro-Italian stand. Mussolini's emergence as the first major totalitarian dictator on the extreme right in postwar Europe aroused wide attention. A politically interested individual such as Quisling, who traveled extensively in the 1920s, could not help but be influenced by what occurred in Italy. He followed closely political developments that were taking place throughout Europe, as his extensive file of clippings evidenced, and his name was on the mailing lists of various foreign fascist organizations.[191] As has been seen, his corporate ideas no doubt owed their origins to Mussolini's example.

In late 1934 the head of NS demonstrated even more concretely his interest for Fascism. He attended an international congress in December in Montreux, Switzerland, which established a world-wide Fascist coordinating commission for "national movements". Quisling was elected to the central committee of this organization, whose formal name was *Commis-*

sione de coordinamento per L'intesa del Fascismo Universale, and he later became its propaganda leader.[192] When Mussolini's invasion of Ethiopia occurred, it hardly was surprising that the Fascist coordinating commission came out in strong opposition to the League of Nation's rather weak attempt to support Ethiopia. One of the Fascist commission's moves was an effort to establish an international counterforce to the League. The commission called for the founding of a "permanent organization of European and worldwide character open to all national movements, corporative and social, in all countries" as an alternative to the League.[193] A three-man committee was chosen to write up the statutes for this new international organization. Quisling became a member of this committee. He received the special task of drawing up the organizational plan for the new international,[194] a responsibility he was well qualified for considering the number of similar projects he had been involved with previously.

The fate of the Fascist international resembled that of many other organizations that Vidkun Quisling became affiliated with. It never amounted to anything of significance. News of his personal association with Fascism did, however, have repercussions in Norway. True to his habit of frequently failing to consult his NS officers, Quisling had acted completely on his own when he decided to go to Montreux. The idea that he, who regarded himself as a major political figure of international stature, should be accountable to anyone was completely alien to him. For many NS members, however, the announcement of his participation in a Fascist organization could not have come at a worse time, right when the Norwegian public's attention was riveted on Italian aggression in Ethiopia. Politically, his move was a blunder. It gave his enemies yet another weapon to use in their arsenal of arguments against him and NS. Quisling, they maintained, had sold himself to Fascism; he had become the spokesman for Italy's interests in Norway.[195]

Negative response occurred even within NS. From Bergen the regional *fører*, Georg Vedeler, protested forcibly. News of Quisling's trip to Montreux, said Vedeler, came as a "bomb" to the Bergen NS organization, which had been in the middle of arranging a propaganda campaign entitled "For Peace and National Union". Now, declared the embarrassed local leader, it would be necessary to provide an explanation why Quisling had taken a stand *"for* Italy". Vedeler argued that NS in particular enjoyed a strong position because "we are a Norwegian movement" which had nothing to do with the foreign dictatorial movements. This position, he maintained, had now been destroyed thanks to Quisling's move. Vedeler declared that NS had so much to accomplish in Norway that it was a waste of time to become involved in international conferences, and he decried strongly as a member of the NS Council that Quisling's participation in the Montreux international had not been brought to the attention of the Council beforehand.[196]

Despite its leader's direct involvement, the episode had no lasting effect on the party except for the publicity it provided for NS' enemies. Quisling had acted alone in a rather naive manner, having failed to judge the consequences of his action. His lack of practical ability meant that nothing concrete resulted from his dalliance with Fascism at Montreux. The repercussions from the incident provided added stimulus for him to get the Montreux episode behind him as quickly as possible.

In the future, he sought inspiration and contact not from the Fascists, but from National Socialist Germany. This became progressively more obvious as Hitler's influence on the international scene broadened from 1936 onwards. While NS publications also voiced approval for Mussolini, it was done in recognition of *Il Duce*'s junior role in the Rome-Berlin Axis, and not because of any direct link between NS and Italian Fascism. In the summer of 1936 NS made the announcement that Quisling had resigned his membership in the Montreux international. This piece of news was warmly applauded by pro-German enthusiasts such as Hans S. Jacobsen and Walter Fürst, who had been among the most outspoken detractors of Quisling's involvement at Montreux.[197] Quisling did not, however, commit himself entirely to open imitation of National Socialism at this time. He attempted to maintain a distinction between full support for Germany in foreign affairs while seeking to preserve a separate Norwegian profile for his party at home. But in the public mind, the uncritical backing which NS provided for Hitler's actions meant that Quisling and his party became identified as the Norwegian variety of National Socialism.

The noticeable lack of reservation which National Union provided for the fascist dictators placed the party in an extreme position, which was an important factor in Quisling's political isolation. Internal developments within Norway, and how Quisling's party responded to them, were equally significant for this process of isolation. The Labor party's assumption of governmental authority on March 20, 1935, was one of the most important occurrences in Norway's political history in the twentieth century. This inaugurated the beginning of permanent socialist control of the government, which would last, with only one brief interruption, for the next thirty years.

The Labor government, headed by Johan Nygaardsvold, did not enjoy a majority in the *Storting*. Labor's succession to office was possible only because of the inability of previous *borgerlige* governments to solve the problems of the depression, and by the commitment of the socialists to gradual reform carried out in a democratic manner. Labor came to power thanks to the "crisis compromise" which it entered into with the Agrarian party. This gave the socialists the parliamentary support needed to form a government, while the Agrarians in turn were promised passage of favorable farm legislation. Once in office, Nygaardsvold carried out a pragmatic reform policy, gaining the required majorities for Labor's legislation in the *Storting* by relying on the alternating support provided by the Agrarian party and the Liberals.

For Quisling, this development was a crushing blow. Up to this time his primary mission in politics had been to prevent such an occurrence. National consolidation was supposed to take place behind him and NS, not the Labor party, as was now in the process of happening. Especially bitter for him was the fact that the Agrarian party, which he earlier had been associated with, and which he had been engaged in negotiations with only slightly more than half a year earlier, was responsible for bringing the socialists to office. As could be expected, his response to the agreement between Labor and the Agrarians was anything but mild. This act, he maintained, was "treason which can never be forgiven".[198] From an NS point of view, the idea that the farmers should be the most important group in society had now been destroyed by the Agrarian party's betrayal, resulting in the farmers being handed over to the Marxists.[199]

No matter how shrill his protests, he had no possibility of preventing the socialists from forming their ministry. The Labor party could muster majorities in the *Storting*, a forum in which NS was not represented by as much as a single legislator. Attempts to remove the Nygaardsvold government from office would therefore have to come from outside parliament.

Firmly believing in the rightness of his cause, that the Labor party had to be eradicated, and convinced that there was a body of public opinion opposed to socialist control of government, Quisling tried to make this an issue which could result in increased backing for his party. Typical of NS protests was a resolution passed at the party's annual meeting in late July 1935. It reflected an illusion which Quisling adhered to continuously throughout his involvement in politics. No matter how little backing NS received at the polls or in terms of membership, he always insisted that there supposedly existed a large number of latent supporters for the NS cause within the population. He used this as a pretext for always presenting himself and his party as a significant force in politics. In its statement, the resolution declared that a thousand delegates

> representing 15,000 [*sic*] organized NS members and many times that number of supporters among nationally minded Norwegian men and women, declare a firm and unconditional protest against governmental power in Norway having been turned over to a declared revolutionary and Marxist party leadership. This is a takeover of power which is decidedly in opposition to Norway's constitution and laws . . .[200]

Resolutions such as this were mainly an expression of the frustration which Quisling and other NS members felt against being isolated, while the Labor party enjoyed governmental authority. NS' attempt to make this a public issue met with little response. The *borgerlige* parties, although with varying degrees of reservation, accepted the reality of a Labor party government. Only Quisling's party and a few other diehard anti-Marxist ideologists protested.

In order to benefit from some type of issue that would arouse the public's attention, which NS needed since it did not enjoy the publicity a party gains automatically from being represented in the *Storting*, Quisling engaged NS in a number of activities in 1935–1936. Unfortunately for him, in many instances his actions were so far removed from practical politics and so extreme in nature that the notoriety that NS obtained occurred most often in the form of ridicule against its leader, who more and more came to be regarded as a laughing-stock.

In one such enterprise, Quisling brought charges against the Minister of Justice, Trygve Lie, "in the hope of causing a breach in the compact popular front". Ironically, the accusation of treasonable behavior which he made against the future Secretary General of the United Nations, issued on December 10, 1935, proved to be the very crime that Quisling himself later would symbolize to the world. The NS leader declared that the Minister of Justice was guilty in word and deed of seeking to overthrow the legal order and of attempting to bring Norway under the control of a foreign power, implicitly the Soviet Union. As "evidence" to sustain this serious charge, he declared that "Minister Lie is one of the most extreme leaders of the revolutionary Marxist movement in this country". The Attorney General was not impressed and did not bother to pursue the matter.[201]

In another equally unsuccessful move, Quisling in June 1935 formally submitted a proposed constitutional amendment to the *Storting* on behalf of NS which called for the creation of a corporate body, a so-called Economic and Cultural Assembly (*Kultur- og Næringsting*), alongside the *Storting*.[202] In presenting this resolution, he wished to demonstrate that he was acting in accord with the spirit of the times. His planned amendment reflected his current preoccupation with the Fascist international in Switzerland. It called for the creation of a "corporative, organic organization of society in Norway", replacing "the outlived party system".[203] While his interest in international Fascism cooled, as we have seen, he never gave up his goal of creating corporate assemblies. His disappointment was therefore genuine when the *Storting*, in response to a motion from its president, the Conservative leader Carl J. Hambro, unanimously voted to dismiss the proposal. Reflecting the frustration that NS members in general felt at not having a spokesman in the *Storting*, Quisling could only vent his spleen against the representative body, which he now referred to as an "oligarchy":

The political oligarchy in the *Storting* justified its point-blank rejection of our well-founded proposal by hiding behind alleged precedents, saying that constitutional proposals must be introduced by a member of the oligarchy itself. And there was no member who was willing to assume this task . . .[204]

His inability to gain anything from this endeavor left him feeling more embittered than ever toward the politicians in the *Storting*, and against the political parties on whose behalf they acted. Not only was his pet project dismissed without even a hearing, but the matter also failed to obtain any favorable publicity outside of National Union's limited ranks. No possibility existed for gaining a hearing in the *Storting*, whose representatives, even the *borgerlige*, had no sympathy for NS politics. Many observers by now regarded him with sardonic amusement as an incompetent fool, thanks to the numerous quixotic efforts he had instigated, causing him increasingly to take on the appearance of a political crank. Quisling should have recognized the obvious fact that appealing to the *Storting* offered no opportunity for NS, but he was blind to political reality whenever his personal interests were involved.

Seeking an alternative to the authority of parliament, Quisling made an attempt to enlist the personal influence of the King behind NS politics. In doing so, he exhibited once again his lack of pragmatism. As a constitutional monarch, Haakon VII had reigned largely in a symbolic manner ever since the end of the Union with Sweden. Although the Norwegian Constitution in theory provided the monarch with considerable power, being then the third oldest functioning constitution in the world,[205] in practice the precedent had been firmly established that the king's authority had been superseded by that of the *Storting*. The government owed its existence to the support it received in parliament, and was not dependent on the good will of the king. Haakon VII, whose ascendancy to the throne had been sanctioned by popular plebiscite in 1905, never attempted to exercise any authority beyond the carefully circumscribed limits established during the years parliamentary democracy gained pre-eminence.

Because of his need to have NS escape from the isolation caused by absence of voter support, which denied his party access to the parliament, plus the natural contempt which he felt for the parties in the *Storting* dating from his cabinet experience, Quisling sublimated his craving for political power by assuming a narrow judicial interpretation of the Constitution. In an open letter to the King, published in *Fritt Folk* on August 21, 1936, he publicly urged Haakon VII to employ the political power that was vested in the monarch by the Constitution.[206]

Quisling issued his letter to the King in connection with the Trotsky affair, which was just reaching its climax at this time. The King was requested to call a special session of the *Storting*, which Quisling legalistically pointed out was in accordance with the authority given the monarch in Article 69 of the Constitution. Speaking on behalf of National Union and the "tens of thousands of Norwegians outside of our movement" who supposedly shared NS' view, he maintained that a special session of the *Storting*, once called into being by the King, would be compelled by public opinion to ensure Trotsky's speedy expulsion from the country. Furthermore, Quisling argued that governmental power should no longer be left "in the hands of Trotsky's Norwegian followers, the leaders of the exposed and compromised so-called Norwegian Labor party". He declared that since the government had emerged from "an international revolutionary party", it was in "violation of Norway's Constitution and laws" and should therefore be "removed and replaced by a constitutional national government of the realm in agreement with the Constitution's Article 12 which allows the King himself to choose his Council".[207]

As justification for such an extreme move, he cited one by one all of his major efforts against the Labor party, going back to when he had served in the Agrarian government. As his starting point, he declared dogmatically that the *Storting* had accepted his accusations against the Labor party in the Quisling Affair. Therefore, since the Labor party had been shown to be a revolutionary party, it had no political rights, since it did not respect the laws and the Constitution. But this conclusion, insisted the embittered former minister, had been disregarded by the *borgerlige* parties, and all of NS' subsequent petitions against the socialists had been equally ignored. Hence his appeal to the King in the Trotsky affair was justified by what he considered to be the failure of the majority of the *Storting* to carry out its legal responsibilities.[208]

From a partisan point of view, the letter reflected his true feelings. As a consequence of his subconscious need to be justified in all his actions, he had convinced himself during the course of his long, vain struggle with the Labor party that the socialists truly were a revolutionary threat to society. More pragmatic politicians such as Hundseid and Mowinckel accepted the Labor party for what it was – a reformist party which on occasion might resort to using revolutionary rhetoric left over from the 1920s, although this declined significantly once Labor controlled the government. Furthermore, *borgerlige* politicians might still in the 1930s use anti-Communist arguments against the Labor party with reference to its radical past, but this was merely an electioneering device, not intended to be followed by concrete action. Quisling, however, took such rhetoric seriously. Since the *borgerlige* parties in the *Storting* were guilty of legal obfuscation by their unwillingness to move against the Labor party, then he would have to petition the King to take action. This was his logic.

The public appeal to the constitutional monarch to carry out a royalist *coup d'état* could have had serious consequences if it had been issued by a politician of higher stature. The Ministry of Justice did ask the Attorney

General to examine the letter and to make a recommendation as to whether prosecution might be warranted. However, the Attorney General suggested that no action be taken.[209] Basing his recommendation more on pragmatic interests of state than on a strict interpretation of the legal code, he indicated that any action by the authorities would simply stir up emotions even further, which he believed it was best to avoid. He did not deny that there were possible grounds for prosecution:

> When Mr. Quisling, who after all acts as leader of a recognized political party, time after time – without being stopped by the rejections of responsible authorities – slings forth accusations against another political party, from which the present government is formed, of having committed or prepared acts of high treason and national treason, then this is a serious matter.[210]

But, the practical Attorney General noted, Quisling's serious charges had only succeeded in making him look ridiculous:

> Prosecution is assumed to be unnecessary because the letter and its publication do not appear to have had the harmful effects one might have feared. . . . the letter's publication appears to have aroused conspicuously little attention. The letter was not mentioned in some newspapers, in others it was referred to in a humorous way, and in one leading paper, which is not sympathetic to the government's politics, it was described as "hysterical".[211]

The impression that the letter had exercised no influence on the public at large was borne out by the result of the 1936 election, much to the apparent satisfaction of the Attorney General. Since the effect of the letter had been so insignificant, he chose to consign the case to oblivion:

> Major Quisling, it is true, alleges he speaks for tens of thousands of Norwegians outside of National Union and "even for the overwhelming majority of our people". But this is unclear, and after the outcome of the election it is quite doubtful if he has the authority to act for anyone but his own party.[212]

It was true, as the Attorney General alleged, that the letter was part of National Union's pre-election strategy. Quisling's judicial arguments were not, however, merely drawn up to be used in a tactical manner. The narrow constitutional interpretation which he stated on this occasion represented the firm conviction that he had arrived at. He maintained that the power which the political parties exercised in the *Storting* was not legal, since the Constitution did not specifically provide for political parties. He chose to ignore the precedent that the government was responsible to the *Storting* and not to the King, a practice which had functioned ever since the victory of parliamentary predominance in 1884, more than half a century before he wrote his letter. In his mind, however, parliamentary supremacy was similarly illegal, since it lacked constitutional sanction.[213] The irrelevance of his argument can be shown by the fact that had it been carried to its logical conclusion, then his own appointment as Minister of Defense, for example, would have been illegal, since he had been chosen to serve in the cabinet by Prime Minister Kolstad, who headed the government because of the support he enjoyed in the *Storting*, and not because of royal preference.

Quisling's narrow logic did not apply to every question of legal interpretation, however. Thanks to his unique psychology, he resorted to legalistic arguments only when they supported the positions he maintained. He then contended his point of view should be binding. But when he undertook actions that were contradictory to legal precedent, this was no hindrance for him. On these occasions the law simply did not apply. This was not a conscious act on his part. He assumed automatically that his interests were of paramount importance thanks to the significance he attached to his own person as Norway's destined leader. If the law aided his cause, narrow legal arguments were used. If not, then he ignored the law.

He regarded the democratic political process from the same personal vantage point. Although he had strong reservations concerning "party politics", acquired from his days in the Hundseid ministry, he did not hesitate to involve National Union in election activity, seeking to gain as much voter support as possible in order to elect NS representatives. Only when NS failed to gain the response from the voters that he had anticipated did he attempt to use other means to obtain prominence, employing such unsubtle tactics to limit the *Storting*'s power as his proposed constitutional amendment and his letter to the King. His defeats in these endeavors caused him to look foolish, and in his embitterment his attacks on the parliamentary system became even more extreme. In the first issue of *Fritt Folk*, for example, the NS leader declared that Norway today did not have "a free people's government", but instead a government of brazen deceit.[214] Such vituperation against a government which enjoyed the support of a majority in the popularly elected parliamentary body only served to separate National Union even more from the other political parties in the popular mind.

His position was limited, however, by the fact that he had no alternative to having NS take part in elections. His attempts to circumvent the *Storting* were pathetic. Furthermore, the absence of a mass following precluded the extra-legal street tactics used so successfully by Mussolini and Hitler. Quisling had no option except to direct NS energies toward the voters. This he did confidently in 1936, in the belief that NS' more militant outlook would gain a greater number of votes than those obtained in past elections. It was obvious as the election approached that Quisling's party had undergone a process in the period 1934–1936 which had changed it into becoming much more similar to the continental fascist parties.

The ideological and political changes which NS underwent during 1934–1936 created some negative reactions within the party membership. Although large numbers were not affected, this development nevertheless was of some significance in that it pointed to a lack of clear perception as to what NS stood for. When the party came into being, Quisling in part gained support thanks to the vagueness of his proposals. Some joined largely because of anti-Marxism, others because they believed NS would become a carbon copy of National Socialism, and still others because of the party's strong nationalistic image. With a variegated membership, whose adherence to NS was based on different, and at times opposing, principles, dissatisfaction and defections were bound to occur as the party's political and ideological profile underwent change.

The first faction within the party that became disenchanted with NS' course were persons who were strongly inspired by what was happening in Germany under Hitler. They wished to have NS openly become a National Socialist movement. Most prominent were Hans S. Jacobsen, the regional *fører* in Østfold, and Walter Fürst, the national propaganda leader. Both had played an important part in NS' early history. Fürst had been a driving force in the effort to found National Union, while Jacobsen and Fürst together had pushed strongly for a new party program after the election debacle in 1933, which led to adoption of the changed program in 1934. The two were thwarted, however, in their bid to give it a clear National Socialist outlook. Much to Jacobsen's chagrin, it was "watered down".[215] One segment of the program which he in particular objected to was National Union's endorsement of "Christianity's basic values".[216] He favored instead the pagan element in German National Socialism, which opposed Christianity because of its Jewish origins, and which stressed the pre-Christian Nordic traditions of the *folk*. Norway's conversion to Christianity, made possible by St. Olav's death as a martyr at Stiklestad, was described by Jacobsen as the introduction of "something false and unnatural into our *folk*'s life". It was therefore logical for him to condemn Quisling's adoption of St. Olav's cross as the NS symbol, declaring that the party symbol was non-Nordic.[217]

With such open differences existing, a clear ideological line of division separated Jacobsen from Quisling in 1934–1935. But there were bound to be elements of personal rivalry as well which entered into their relationship. As has been seen, Jacobsen and Fürst tried to restrict Quisling's power when the question of who would have highest authority in NS was in the process of being resolved. They wished to have the head of NS be accountable to a council of leading officers within the party, but failed when Quisling independently solved the issue by establishing the party Executive Committee and NS Council under his control.[218] Jacobsen soon discovered the consequences of having challenged a leader as jealous of his authority as Quisling. Jacobsen received no support from party head-

quarters for his work as regional *fører*. On the contrary, the NS central organization maneuvered against him by aiding a rebellious subordinate.[219]
As a result of the opposition he encountered, Jacobsen ceased to work on
NS' behalf in the spring of 1934, and resigned his position some months
later. He was joined by his close associate, Odin Augdahl, who was the
NS leader in the neighboring district of Follo in Akershus province. Augdahl resigned from the party in November, and Jacobsen took the same
step in January 1935.[220]

Personal differences as well as ideological disagreement were also instrumental in Walter Fürst's departure from the party. He had dedicated himself energetically on behalf of NS since its inception. With his background
in advertising, it was natural for him to assume the post as the NS propaganda chief. In this capacity, he exerted himself to obtain maximum exposure for NS. However, his impulsive nature and artistic imagination caused
him at times to carry out projects that were regarded as beyond the bounds
of propriety by more sober-minded members. Already immediately after
the 1933 *Storting* election, Quisling received a petition signed by forty
prominent NS members requesting Fürst's dismissal because he had, in
their opinion, shown himself to be incompetent, and as a result lacked respect both inside and outside NS.[221] Quisling failed to react, but disapproval of Fürst continued. The propaganda chief's detractors criticized in
particular his enthusiasm for Viking imagery, which he adopted for NS.
Not only did he persuade Quisling to assume the title of "chieftain"
(*høvding*) for a short time, but he also sought unsuccessfully to have the
party use a number of other Viking terms as titles for NS officers.[222] In the
end, Fürst's detractors had their way. On October 1, 1934, he lost control
of propaganda activity within the Oslo region, which he had coordinated
simultaneously with his responsibility for propaganda on the national
level. Fürst protested against not being consulted, but to no avail.[223] In reaction to the intrigue against him, he began to recruit NS members who
were sympathetic to National Socialism into a faction which he headed.
However, this resulted in his expulsion from NS in April 1935.[224]

The departure of persons such as Jacobsen, Fürst, and Augdahl did not
mean, however, that they were followed by a mass defection of persons
who to a greater or lesser degree were sympathetic to German National Socialism. The overwhelming majority of these remained within NS. Jacobsen and Fürst represented an extreme pro-German position in NS, which
did not generate a great deal of support. In addition, their personal opposition to the party leadership further helped to isolate them.

Upon leaving NS, Jacobsen began to publish a pro-National Socialist
journal bearing the prophetic title *Ragnarok*. He was supported by Fürst
and a few other like-minded persons who were disillusioned with Quisling. Jacobsen did not intend, however, to have *Ragnarok* serve as a rallying point for a potential rival movement to NS. He recognized that de-

spite Quisling's lack of open commitment to National Socialism, NS nevertheless represented the best chance for the non-democratic right in Norwegian politics. Jacobsen therefore intended to use *Ragnarok* as a means of pressuring NS to commit itself more fully to his ideals, a goal he believed he could best work for by not being a member of the party. With this in mind, he attempted, despite their former differences, to maintain a cordial relationship with Quisling. In March 1935 he wrote to Quisling, complimenting the NS *Fører* on a recent speech, which Jacobsen described as "outstanding" because its content was "National Socialism through and through, and this is what we need". Jacobsen did not neglect the opportunity to repeat his desire for good cooperation, and he expressed the hope that Quisling would soon write an inspiring article for *Ragnarok*.[225]

NS contained a significant element within its membership that did not share Jacobsen's sentiments. These members stood out clearly because of their strong religious convictions. As Christians, they were decidedly opposed to Jacobsen's pagan National Socialist viewpoint. They therefore were relieved to witness his departure from NS, and they voiced enthusiastic approval when Quisling emphasized that there was no connection between NS and *Ragnarok*.[226]

While the reason for Christian commitment to National Union varied somewhat from individual to individual, there nevertheless existed a common area of agreement. In religious belief they were mainly fundamentalists, and they combined their adherence to the basic tenets of Christianity with a strong feeling of nationalism. They felt that both the position of organized religion and the feeling of national unity were threatened by the advance of the working class, with its Marxist ideology. Equally reprehensible for them was "false liberalism", whose permissive attitude, including a cynical view toward organized religion, had supposedly created an atmosphere for class struggle and moral decay.[227] These Christians supported National Union because it stood for an end to the class struggle, which "creates hate and bitterness between Norwegians and prevents the accomplishment of social justice, which can only be realized in a strong solidaric Norwegian *folk* society".[228] This was how one of their main representatives, Valdemar Hansteen, viewed NS' mission in combating the class struggle. Christianity, they believed, would serve as National Union's spiritual force in the party's effort to create national unity.

Although their number was not large within the party as a whole, the Christian segment had considerable influence in certain geographical areas, and spokesmen for its viewpoint occupied a number of prominent positions. Best known among National Union's Christian advocates during its early history was Pastor Kjeld Stub, who served as garrison pastor at Akershus Castle in Oslo, a position of considerable social prestige. Stub was a personal acquaintance of Quisling, with whom he often appeared on speaking engagements. The garrison pastor contributed also as a leading writer and speaker for the party, stressing the fact that NS would protect Christianity as a basic and creative part of society, and he urged Christian workers to abandon the Labor party because of its "anti-Christian view-point" and to join NS.[229] He enjoyed additional prominence within the party because of his membership on the Executive Committee, and Christian NS members tended to recognize him as their foremost spokesman.[230]

The major region of Christian NS activity was located, however, not in the Oslo area, but on the west coast. It was concentrated in particular in Stavanger and the surrounding district, where Gulbrand Lunde effectively mobilized a significant part of prevailing Christian pietism against what he called the godless atheism of the Marxist Labor party. Thanks to his skillful tactics, NS enjoyed strong political influence in Stavanger through representation on the city council. The party's viewpoint was also spread throughout the district by its daily newspaper, *Vestlandets Avis*. Following Rishovd's resignation, the paper was edited for a large part of 1935 by the architect Valdemar Hansteen, who received considerable assistance in his editorial work from the indefatigable Lunde.[231] Hansteen was known in Christian circles throughout the country as a member of the Norwegian Christian Missionary Society's executive committee. He served also as an NS representative on the city council, where he was a member of the council's executive committee (*formannskap*).[232] His standing within the Christian community could not fail to be an asset in enhancing the party's prestige. It was understandable that *Vestlandets Avis* as a rule contained two sermons in its issues, whereas other NS newspapers restricted themselves to one such sermon.[233] Because of its special character, the NS organization in Stavanger was regarded by many persons, both inside and outside the party, as being basically a religious force.[234]

NS influence among Christians on the west coast moreover was not restricted just to Stavanger. Further to the north, the town of Haugesund had a city council whose composition consisted of one-fifth NS members following the 1934 election.[235] In the neighboring province of Hordaland, Pastor Knut Geelmuyden was a leading NS member. Geelmuyden served for a time as the NS regional *fører* in Hordaland, and he used his position energetically to further the Christian cause within the party.[236]

In addition to the west coast, Christian NS activity was particularly noteworthy in northern Norway. Here, however, its impact was not as widespread. Pastor Martin Tveter was the most outstanding champion of Christian interests within the party in this region. Although widely known, his direct influence was restricted primarily to the extreme north in Finnmark province. Known to his detractors as "the Nazi pastor in Vadsø",[237] he enjoyed considerable respect within his local community. He himself was elected to the city council in 1934 as part of the five-man NS delegation, and due to his prominent position, he became a member of the council's executive committee. Because of Vadsø's location, it was natural for Tveter to be aware of what was taking place in neighboring Finland, where he traveled on a number of occasions. He noted with approval the support that Christian pietists gave to the fascist Lapua movement in Finland, and he expressed the hope that "serious Christianity" united with a serious and intense "love of the fatherland" and conscious opposition to communism and "false" liberalism which he found among the Finns could be transferred to Norway under NS' championship, leading to the unification of the Norwegian people, who were to be "renewed morally, politically, socially, and economically", with respect for "God and fatherland".[238]

Although prominent Christian spokesmen such as Stub, Hansteen, Geelmuyden, and Tveter, plus a number of lesser known Christian clergy and laity, had committed themselves to NS' cause, they never felt entirely comfortable within the party. What disturbed them in particular was the obvious degree of similarity between NS and Hitler's Nazi party, and they were very much alarmed by what was taking place in Germany – by Hitler's strong-arm effort to control the churches and Rosenberg's glorification of the German nation's pagan Nordic past. Tveter voiced his anxiety on this score already in March 1934 in a letter to Quisling.[239] In turn, Quisling sought to reassure the clergyman of NS' pro-Christian character, declaring that he was in full agreement with NS support of Christianity's religious and moral values.[240]

During 1934 Quisling's assurance held true. NS carried out no major ideological changes which could offend its Christian members, and their commitment to the party remained unchanged. The value of their association was shown conclusively in the local election of 1934, when NS enjoyed its few urban successes mainly in those centers where its Christian influence was strongest – in Stavanger, Haugesund, and Vadsø. During the same year the party's Christian members were heartened by the gradual erosion of Jacobsen's influence, and by his eventual resignation from the party.

In the following year, however, the feeling of unease among the Christian membership became stronger. Despite the results of the 1934 election, NS increasingly took stands that tended to alienate its Christian following. This was especially true during the second half of the year, from the fall onward, when the trend to stress racism and anti-Semitism became obvious.[241]

The change in the party's ideology was an extremely risky move, something which even the supporters of anti-Jewish agitation such as Haldis Neegaard Østbye recognized.[242] The pragmatic Gulbrand Lunde, when consulted about Østbye's plan to issue a special propaganda publication stressing alleged Jewish domination of the labor movement's leadership, maintained that NS should concentrate on internal political questions rather than becoming preoccupied with "German anti-Semitic propaganda".[243]

Tveter similarly warned Quisling in early September of the danger of NS assuming an image similar to that of the Nazis. He expressed his concern about the continued influence of Hans S. Jacobsen on some NS members, and Tveter also referred to Quisling's brother, Dr. Jørgen Quisling, who had recently written a brief article in *Tidens Tegn* which was favorable toward Nazi paganism.[244] He realized that Jørgen Quisling's view was not that of his brother, Tveter declared, but he was afraid that it might be regarded as such. It was essential for NS to repudiate the Nazi religious view, he continued, since many Christians were afraid to join because NS in many ways reminded them of Nazism. He pointed in particular to a number of young pastors who were interested in NS, but who would not commit themselves because of what they saw occurring in Germany. He was afraid that they would join a rival Christian political party if NS did not issue a statement in which it confirmed its full commitment to the Church and its opposition to Nordic paganism.[245]

This warning was not an idle one. A new religious party, the Christian People's party (*Kristelig Folkeparti*) had already come into existence. Although still a regional group, restricted to the province of Hordaland, it took part in the 1933 election, and to the surprise of most observers it succeeded in electing its first *Storting* representative. Thus there existed a real possibility that this local faction might evolve into a national party, capturing the Christian adherence that Tveter wanted to gain for NS. This fear proved prophetic. In 1936 the Christian People's party secured an additional *Storting* seat from Hordaland, and it emerged after the war as a permanent force throughout the country.

Soon after the NS pastor in Vadsø had written his letter of advice and warning, the news became public that National Union's *Fører* was directly involved with international Fascism at Montreux. This revelation and the fact that NS was now strongly defending Italy's conquest of Ethiopia, created repercussions both within and outside NS. Not only was support of Mussolini unpopular among the public at large, but Quisling's position was equally condemned by pro-Nazi persons such as Hans S. Jacobsen, who attacked Fascism on ideological grounds. He regarded Rome as the symbol for the centralized state and the Jewish-Christian religion, which in his mind stood in abject contrast to the independent Nordic spirit, best symbolized by Germany.[246] Quisling as a result found himself beset on all sides by his imprudent action. Party leaders protested to him, pointing out that such an uncoordinated move was a tactical mistake which could only hurt NS' cause.[247] But the strongest reaction within the party came from its

Christian membership. A month after Quisling's ties to the Fascist international had become public knowledge, Martin Tveter announced that he could no longer belong to NS. He deplored NS publications which had sarcastically defamed those who tried to defend the interests of "barbarian Negro tribes":

> How can I participate in sending out missionaries to preach the evangelism of salvation and peace, to preach that God does not differentiate between peoples, that Christ gave his life for everyone, and then at the same time defend the Italian imperialistic attack on Ethiopia?[248]

Furthermore, he asked, how could he as a disciple of the Prince of Peace belong to a movement which was affiliated with an international Fascist organization when the leader of Fascism, Mussolini, glorified war?

Tveter's disavowal of NS was not explained solely because of his opposition to Quisling's stand on the side of Fascism. Equally important was the party's increased racism, inspired by the Nazi example. Christianity, said Tveter, was based on universal equality, whereas the teaching of race emphasized the inequality of the different races. Carried to its utmost consequence, he maintained, this would, as in Germany, lead to a Nordic religion which was incompatible with Christianity.[249] In a letter to Gulbrand Lunde, he similarly deplored the anti-Semitism which NS now hailed, beginning in earnest in the fall of 1935. "I cannot now open any [NS] paper without finding an attack against the Jews". He objected in particular to an article in *Vestlandets Avis*, now under the control of its new pro-Nazi editor, Adolf Egeberg, Jr., which had been especially offensive in attacking *Storting* president Hambro, who was of Jewish descent.[250]

Tveter was not the only Christian member who resigned because of NS' changed ideological position. Quisling's Montreux action simply brought this into focus, serving as a catalyst for the release of Christian discontent. It was natural that those parts of the country where Christian influence in the party was greatest felt the disaffection most strongly. In Haugesund the NS chairman left the party in protest against the frequent appearance of racism and anti-Semitism in party literature. And in his stronghold of Stavanger, Gulbrand Lunde witnessed the destruction of a great deal of his work in building up NS. The local organization split when it learned of Montreux, and its number was greatly reduced.[251] Although Lunde remained committed to Quisling, the party's position on the west coast never recovered from this incident.

Quisling responded belatedly with a feeling of concern to the resignations and criticism the NS leadership received during the fall of 1935 and early 1936. Even those party members with Christian commitment who chose to remain, at least for the time being, were strong in their condemnation. The remnant of the local Stavanger organization, for example, repudiated NS' racism, and voiced in particular its opposition to Quisling's connection with the Fascist International.[252] Party headquarters sought to eliminate the discontent by making reassuring statements. In contradiction to what it had previously maintained, NS now adopted the line that the Jewish question was not a problem in Norway. Party newspapers furthermore declared that fanatical anti-Semitism was deplorable. This change in position took place in accordance with a directive sent out by Quisling, calling for a more objective tone in NS publications, after Lunde had warned him against the prominent emphasis which anti-Jewish agitation was receiving in the NS press. An attempt was also made to lessen the importance of Tveter's defection by printing an article authored by Pastor Knut Geelmuyden which re-emphasized the NS program's commitment to basic Christian values.[253]

Christian NS members such as Geelmuyden who remained within the party did so in large part in order to work from within, striving to have it maintain a Christian orientation and, as Valdemar Hansteen put it, preventing it from "sliding into heathendom". Their task was far from easy, as Hansteen resignedly confessed in a pessimistic letter to Tveter: "I only wish we could have stood together and fought for our point of view; often I feel so hopelessly alone".[254] Hansteen and his Christian colleagues had grounds for their pessimism. Despite the reassuring tone which NS adopted toward its Christian membership immediately following Tveter's resignation, there was no possibility of changing the party's course. Racist glorification of Nordic superiority and anti-Semitism had become a fixed part of NS' ideology and continued to receive prominence in its propaganda. Other leading NS members who had protested in the fall of 1935, such as Vedeler who had opposed Quisling's pro-Italian stand, were reconciled with the NS *Fører*.[255] But the foremost Christian spokesmen in the party found it impossible to deny their consciences. Reluctantly they came to the same conclusion as Tveter and gradually severed their ties with NS. Knut Geelmuyden dropped his connection in 1936 after having condemned Nazi persecution of the Jews and deplored NS' pro-German position. Kjeld Stub contributed little after 1935 and became a passive member, although he did not resign until December 1940. Valdemar Hansteen also ceased to work on for NS after he saw that his views were in a hopeless minority, and he withdrew in the late 1930s.[256]

Among the rank and file of the party, it cannot be ascertained specifically how many left because of their Christian convictions in 1935–36. Numerically, their total was not very large, although they were of key importance in specific towns such as Stavanger, Haugesund, and Vadsø, as the negative election results from these towns in 1936 indicated. Morally, how-ever, they held a position which was of far greater importance. They provided NS with a certain element of respectability, which was eliminated by their departure. When National Union faced the test of a *Storting* election in 1936, its image as a party of the radical right was clearer than ever before. An indication of the change that had occurred since 1934 was provided by the contrasting attitudes of Hans S. Jacobsen and Martin Tveter. Whereas Jacobsen had earlier left the party, basically because of his ideological disagreement with NS' leadership, much to the approval of Tveter, by the end of 1935 it was Tveter's turn to depart because it had become clear to him that National Union's ideology coincided with National Socialism and Fascism on points that were in conflict with his "philosophy of life".[257] Jacobsen, on the other hand, had watched with satisfaction the "irreproachable" movement of NS in the "right direction", and he urged the readers of *Ragnarok* to follow his example and vote for Quisling's party in the 1936 election.[258]

Quisling and Hjort were not entirely pleased by this endorsement, and sought to avoid the full embrace of enthusiastic supporters of National Socialism such as Jacobsen and Walter Fürst.[259] But their effort to maintain a semblance of separate identity was lost on the public at large, who in 1936 regarded NS as a right-wing, anti-democratic party patterned after Hitler's and Mussolini's fascist movements. The loss on support from the party's Christian segment had been a major factor in pointing out this development. Other scattered defections had also aided in clarifying NS' position. Among these were the resignations of Bjarne Lie, who had been elected to the Oslo city council as NS' top candidate on the National Joint List, and Knut Hesstvedt, who had been in charge of the party's Central Office before Fuglesang took over as General Secretary. Lie defected to the Labor party, while Hesstvedt joined the Conservatives.[260]

As the election of 1936 approached, NS had already suffered some loss of membership, thanks in large part to the change in Quisling's ideological emphasis. Such defections, although not numerically important, had nevertheless helped to place NS in a clear perspective for the voters. They were also an ominous omen for the unity of a party dedicated to "national union" if the election outcome were to prove unsatisfactory.

CHAPTER VI

The Storting Election of 1936

We have chances in ten to twenty election districts if nothing unexpected
should occur, of which ten are absolutely certain.

Vidkun Quisling,
Samarbeid, October 8, 1936

As the fall election approached, the majority of Quisling's party followers
were anything but pessimistic. In contrast to the previous parliamentary
election in 1933, NS now was a firmly established party after having been
in existence for more than three years. It had a compact membership, a
rigid organization, a clear program, a party press, and a distinct political
profile. Its members were certain that the party would gain representation
in the *Storting*, and some of the more optimistic predicted that NS would
obtain between 70,000 and 100,000 votes.[1]

This confident outlook was in large part based on the considerable activity which the NS organization was able to generate in preparation for
the election. Already by the end of 1935 the Central Office had worked
out a detailed plan covering all aspects of party activity leading up to the
election.[2] The plan came into existence as the result of close consultation
between Quisling, Fuglesang, and Hans L'Orange, the leader of the NS
Organization Division. Characteristic of all three was their common belief
in the importance of detailed planning as a requirement for a successful political campaign. The election plan is therefore especially interesting because it indicated how the central NS bureaucracy under Quisling's overall
supervision hoped the coming campaign would develop.

The plan divided the period leading up to the election into four distinct
phases. The first phase, covering the initial two months of 1936, was intended to activate the party's organization in preparation for the campaign
and to recruit new members under the slogan "The New Norway Needs
You. Enroll in National Union".[3] During March, April, and May, the
plan's second phase, the party would concentrate on "spring propaganda".
This informational period was intended to tell the public "what NS is and

what NS wants". In addition to covering the major planks in the party program, NS agitation would stress three additional points which reflected Quisling's philosophical outlook. These included his national concept of history as being racially determined and spiritual, as opposed to "Jewish Marxism's" international and materialistic interpretation of history; his emphasis on folk solidarity in contrast to class struggle and party politics; and his elitist stress on leadership and responsibility versus what he called the minority dictatorship and party corruption of parliamentary government. Next came the period of "summer propaganda", in June, July, and August, whose goal was to mobilize party members actively through mass meetings, demonstrations, and torchlight processions. Highlighting this process was the annual NS meeting, scheduled to be held in Oslo in June. Now the party members were to be "inspired and fanaticized" to work on behalf of NS, being motivated by a feeling of ever-growing solidarity. Finally, in the last two months before the election, the party would concentrate all its forces on "election propaganda". The goal was to have all agitation by this time reduced to emphasizing certain basic points, which were to be hammered home with "increasing fanaticism, intolerance, and intensity". Much depended, said the plan, on whether or not NS could incite the people so that its program became the issue around which the election campaign would revolve during the "closing battle".[4]

NS strategy for the 1936 election contained no specific reference to the source of its inspiration, but no direct evidence is needed to show that Quisling and his closest subordinates had concluded that the way to success was to use many of the tactics that had provided the Nazis with victories during German elections from 1930 to 1933. Quisling further stressed National Union's distinctly different outlook by deliberately disassociating his party from all other political factions in 1936. On April 22 the NS Executive Committee decided that National Union would enter its own lists of candidates in all election districts, thereby ruling out any voting alliances.[5] All other parties, including those with which NS previously had had some ties, such as the Independent People's party, the Agrarian party, and the Fatherland League, were condemned because of their willingness to accept the parliamentary political process. As the NS daily put it when denouncing a prominent Fatherland League speaker, Anders Lange:

> What good is it to say things which by themselves are excellent and true about the Marxists and their systematic destruction of morals, and to appeal to fight against them, when one in reality participates in a political game *together with* the Marxists?[6]

NS insisted that the entire party structure had to be dismantled. J. B. Hjort wrote that national unity could not be achieved unless the party fences which divided the people were first torn down.[7] NS called for the creation of a unified, organic society, devoid of the internal divisions of a twentieth-century western European democracy. But by assuming such a negative attitude toward other political groups, NS in turn was subjected to no-holds-barred attacks from its declared opponents. Even *Tidens Tegn* now published strong denunciations of NS.[8] Its position in 1936 was especially interesting because of Thommessen's earlier strong championship of Quisling. The paper provided its usual enthusiastic contribution to the election campaign, furthering the combined alliance of the Independent People's party and the Fatherland League in particular, and in a more general manner supporting a broader coalition, which also included the Conservatives and Agrarian party, in a combined effort against the Labor party. But it made no reference at all to NS having any role to play in this *borgerlig* anti-socialist front.[9]

Quisling's isolation was thereby total. This isolation was self-imposed, thanks to his unwillingness to agree to compromises with political groups that had shared some values with NS. Instead, he had progressed to the point where he was completely alienated from the basic principles of the Norwegian political system. He opposed parliamentary government, he opposed the principle of majority rule, he opposed democracy.[10] In this respect, his attitude toward the functioning of the democratic process did not vary from that of Hitler. But conditions in Norway were different from those in the Weimar Republic. Not only did Norway differ in population size, geography, and historical tradition, but the country enjoyed the fortunate experience of having escaped the direct disruptive effects of World War I.

Quisling was a non-democrat forced to exist within a democratic framework. Increasingly he focused his hostility on the enemy that stood in his way – the Norwegian multiparty system. With his conviction that he was the nation's destined leader, he refused to accept the working of this system, based on political compromise rather than direct action, especially during the 1930s when no party enjoyed a majority, and minority governments were required because of the Liberal party's unwillingness to participate in coalition governments. Nor could he understand or accept the influence of such pressure groups in a pluralistic society as the Norwegian Federation of Trade Unions (LO) and the Norwegian Employers' Association (NAF), as well as other interest groups with a mass membership that were able to affect political decision-making thanks to their large numbers and economic power.[11] In his view, such organizations should be under state control as part of his proposed National Assembly (*Riksting*).

Because of his disaffection, he became alienated to a major degree from society as a whole, which he declared to be corrupt, since it followed democratic practices. He despised the working of its political system, since it denied him the authority he believed he deserved, and in his need to rationalize his motives as being for the common good, he developed the belief that the entire political system was an evil that had to be eradicated.

> He hated it [the political system] perhaps deepest and most of all because it destroyed his own political possibilities, but in part also because he was convinced that the entire system was a disaster for the Norwegian people.[12]

He had become an outsider, having steadily been eliminated from having influence within the political process as a consequence of the course he had followed since the fall of the Agrarian government.

As a result of his total opposition to all other political parties, he attempted in 1936 to draw a line of division in politics between NS on one side and what he called the "*borgerlig*-marxist united front" on the other, a plain reference to the popular front movement elsewhere in Europe.[13] Quite obviously, he hoped to divide the political spectrum in this fashion and thereby restrict the voters as much as possible to the alternatives of being either pro or anti NS.

In his denunciation of the *borgerlige* parties, he tended perhaps to be most critical toward his former party because of the "crisis compromise" which the Agrarians had entered into with the Labor party. By this act, he declared, the representatives of the farmers had become what he termed "agrarian-marxists," having gone so far as to join an alliance with those whom he called the sworn enemies of freedom, the agents of world communism.[14]

Writing in the first issue of *Fritt Folk*, J. B. Hjort echoed Quisling's condemnation of the political system. Society, he said, was full of corruption and injustice which had spread to all segments of the population. He specifically pointed to the difficulty that NS experienced in arranging political meetings in what he ironically termed a "free society". He referred to specific instances where NS had been denied access to meeting places, often after what he called "the rabble", meaning left-wing young people, had demonstrated against such meetings.[15] Throughout this entire issue of *Fritt Folk*, the same underlying tone persisted – the implication that NS was undergoing martyrdom for the sake of righteousness; that only it represented the essential interests and moral values of the true Norway. All other parties were described as having sold out for the sake of political expediency or as acting on behalf of the dangerous communist conspiracy.

Despite the strong words that Quisling and other members of his party used against the political process, he had no alternative but to attempt to make use of the system in seeking to obtain political power for himself and his party. In spite of his hostile attitude toward the political order, he did not withdraw NS from participation in elections. If the opportunity for success had been available, as it was for Hitler during the last days of the Weimar Republic, then Quisling would not have had the slightest qualms about climbing to power through parliamentary elections. Only when he and his movement failed to gain the proper backing that was needed in elections did he turn his back on the idea of *Storting* representation. He later admitted as much in one of his major speeches during the occupation. NS, he said, had worked energetically to bring about "organic" change in the system of government "in accord with the Constitution's principles". However, he continued, when the result of the 1936 election showed "that it was hopeless to appeal to people's reason", then

> there was no longer any reason for us in National Union to concern our-selves about the *Storting* and the political parties. We therefore aimed di-rectly toward the goal. We demanded a *vigorous national government of the realm, independent of party politics, and that the Storting be replaced by a council of the realm composed of skilled delegates for the working people, not party politicians.*[16]

Through the election of 1936, notwithstanding his crass attacks against the party system, he sought to find room to maneuver within the existing po-litical framework, trying to establish a broader base for support. While he completely rejected other parties, he did not eliminate the possibility of obtaining backing from economic interest groups that traditionally had supported such parties. NS' best chance lay with the Farmers' Association, which had earlier displayed a certain amount of sympathy for NS and the Fatherland League during the crisis affecting the Mowinckel government in June 1934. Historically, however, the Farmers' Association was a firm backer of the Agrarian party, which it was largely responsible for found-ing. In April 1936 Fuglesang sent a letter to the organization, seeking to use the issue of the Agrarian party's compromise with the Labor party as a means of splitting the Association from its political affiliate. The General Secretary asked the Association to provide NS with financial assistance, emphasizing that his party worked "actively and energetically" on behalf of "national farm politics" in the effort to establish a "free and independent class of farmers" as the foundation for "the Norwegian *folk* society".[17] Furthermore, he argued, if indirectly, that it was now natural for the Far-mers' Association to give its allegiance to NS, since the Agrarian party had deserted its political responsibility and betrayed the basic ideas of the far-mer and the farm movement by entering into compromise and cooperation with "Marxists and the tool of international Bolshevism in our country".[18]

Fuglesang's effort brought no positive response. There did exist, never-theless, some discontent inside the farm organization with the Agrarian party's politics, as was shown when representatives from four local chap-ters of the Farmers' Association later sent an inquiry to Quisling, asking him to issue a statement indicating NS' willingness to support the Farmers'

Association's effort to secure its program's goals.[19] He did not allow such an opportunity to pass, coming out with a three-page statement on August 22. As he had done before, he affirmed that the farmers were the backbone of Norwegian society as the bearers of the people's racial, cultural, and national principles. Therefore, the first goal of national and economic renewal, he declared, was to restore a healthy and strong class of farmers.[20]

This view, he maintained, was fully in accord with the principles of the Farmers' Association. This of course was true, but his main weakness in attempting to solicit support from the Association – in addition to leading a minor party with no *Storting* representation – was that while he declared NS' wholehearted commitment on behalf of the farm population, he could provide no concrete suggestions as to how it intended to better the farmers' position. He held up the promise that the Farmers' Association would represent the interests of the agricultural population in the corporate state that he intended to establish. Such a futuristic plan had little interest for the farmers, who were more concerned with the present than with theories about the future. He also alluded to NS' desire for new legislation concerning the transfer of farm property, and for a reduction in agricultural debts.[21] But once more he could not provide answers as to how this would be accomplished. The basic obstacle that he could never overcome in trying to win over the farm vote was his inability to persuade the farmers that NS could best represent their interests. NS was unable to provide the farmers with concrete prospects for the solution of their problems, and this was recognized even by farmers who belonged to the party.[22] The result of this absence of clarity concerning specific means by which the farm population's position could be improved meant that while NS did gain the votes of individual farmers, they were but a small minority among rural voters. NS had no chance of gaining the allegiance of the Farmers' Association. The majority of the farmers continued as before to cast their ballots for the Agrarian party.

The absence of support from outside of its ranks had no effect, however, on the conduct of NS' political campaign. The party endeavored to follow the strategy outlined in the election plan for 1936. Not all details were carried out on schedule. For example, the appearance of the new daily newspaper in the capital, *Fritt Folk*, intended originally to take place during the first phase of the plan, did not actually occur until the end of March, which was in the second phase. Nevertheless, despite some deviations, NS did its best to follow the central organization's plan. An effort was made to mobilize the party machinery, meetings were held, demonstrations occurred, and marches were carried out, all in an attempt to stir up the voters favorably. One notable step that NS took was to employ a propaganda bus with a loudspeaker system, introduced by J. B. Hjort's Akershus organization.

The use of such a vehicle was a novel practice, and NS proudly hailed its accomplishment, which in the party's opinion provided the public with concrete evidence that NS was in the forefront of technological advance. The party's opposition assumed a less charitable view, maintaining that such "American" practices were alien to Norwegian traditions.[23]

Hjort frequently used the bus at campaign rallies. Members of his *Hird* were also present at such meetings, being deployed to maintain order. Frequently, however, tumult rather than tranquility prevailed at NS election rallies. The pattern of disturbances which had been evident during the 1933 campaign was repeated in 1936. To some extent, NS was responsible for provoking such violence by scheduling meetings at locations where the potential for trouble was great. On the other hand, many young Labor party and Communist party supporters deliberately sought the opportunity to beat up NS adherents. When such brawls occurred, NS members were usually on the losing end as a result of their deficiency in numbers. NS activity in the streets can therefore by no means be compared with the *fascisti* and SA as far as sheer brutality is concerned.

The most sensational single incident of street fighting in 1936 occurred in the inland town of Gjøvik, located in Oppland province in the eastern interior. Hjort and the propaganda bus appeared on the scene for a rally on May 21, accompanied by some fifty *Hird* members armed with rubber truncheons. Large numbers of curious onlookers gathered at the market place, where the meeting was held, including a sizable contingent of young leftists who favored either the Labor party or the Communists. In his speech, Hjort used provocative language, and it was not long before a veritable battle erupted, during which NS members were pelted with rocks. The propaganda bus was battered, its windows were broken, and the driver received a direct hit, resulting in a broken nose, from a stone that smashed through the front window. Upon leaving the market square, the *Hird* members were pursued. They turned to do battle, but were vastly outnumbered and had to retreat under a hail of projectiles which injured an additional number, including one unfortunate individual who literally was partially scalped by a flying block of wood. The beleaguered *Hird* members had to find refuge in an apartment entrance-way, where they were surrounded by the raging mob. They were not able to come out until seven hours later, after units of the state police had been sent to Gjøvik to restore order.[24]

The "battle of Gjøvik" caused a sensation. Although the most dramatic, it was, however, but one of a number of troubled incidents which occurred at NS meetings. While injured NS members received sympathy from those with strong antipathies toward the parties on the left, NS was also deplored for its provocative attitude. The tendency, as in 1933, was that NS received notoriety as a result of these incidents, but the publicity was by no means always positive.

Although Hjort and the *Hird* members involved in the fighting at Gjøvik were hailed as heroes within NS, the incident provided a dramatic illustration of the fact that NS could not expect to maintain the initiative in the campaign, and certainly not in the streets. Nevertheless, the desire to have the party dominate public attention persisted within the NS leadership, which continued to adhere to its strategy. In addition to following the specific points set forth in the election plan, Quisling also instructed the NS regional, district, and league leaders to be ready to take part in "special actions", which the central leadership intended to set in motion at different times during the campaign.[25] It was in this context that NS carried out such individual operations as the attempt to arouse popular indignation over the Greenland issue, the effort to remove the Labor government, and the campaign to expel Trotsky.

Quisling similarly hoped to gain wide publicity from the national NS meeting in Oslo at the end of June. In his foreign policy speech at the party congress, he sought to arouse public interest by calling for the creation of a "Nordic World Union" (*Nordisk Verdenssamband*). This proposal was dutifully accepted in typical fashion by the NS delegates in the form of a "unanimous" resolution. It provided an interesting illustration of the great void between Quisling's vision of the important role he wished to play in world affairs and the reality of the position that he occupied. The notion of establishing some type of union among his loosely defined "Nordic" peoples was not new (the nationalities whom he defined as "Nordic" did not always remain constant). He had done so in almost every political manifesto that he had issued since 1930. Nor did he present novel arguments on behalf of Nordic superiority, and his warnings against the threat posed by a culture-destroying people, i.e., the Jews, were also repetitious. However, the resolution did have some unusual features. It specifically instructed the NS leadership to set up the "Nordic World Union's" headquarters in Oslo. Finally, in its concluding words, he indicated again his lack of originality by directly plagiarizing, of all people, Karl Marx and Friedrich Engels, calling on Nordics of the world to unite.[26]

When bringing up his proposal for this new organization, he let it be known that he had been asked by a very prominent individual to come to London and expound upon the merits of the "Nordic World Union".[27] Nothing more was heard about this alleged influential person. Quite possibly, his contact in England may have been nothing more than a former schoolmate and friend with whom he corresponded regularly.[28] Like his enthusiasm for the Fascist International, which similarly came to naught, this incident provided him with a temporary feeling of greatness, allowing him the illusion of having become the international statesman he wished to be. It had, however, no political consequences, since the "Nordic World Union" was hardly an issue capable of gaining the votes of an electorate more concerned with practical considerations.

Beyond the fact that the "Nordic World Union" was irrelevant as far as politics were concerned, Quisling had no idea of what specific steps needed to be taken in order to create such an organization. As has previously been seen, he could draw up intricately detailed plans for his projected organizations, but beyond issuing general appeals for support, he did nothing to secure their implementation. He expected a mass membership to emerge automatically as the result of his call, and this of course was sheer illusion. The "Nordic World Union" was soon forgotten.

Quisling had to resolve a far more immediate issue when deciding whether he would be a candidate for the *Storting*, and if so, in what district or districts he would head the slate of NS nominees. He was contacted by the NS *fører* in his native Telemark as early as January 1936, asking him to become a candidate. It was not, however, until September 15, only slightly more than one month before the election, that *Fritt Folk* announced Quisling's candidacy.[29] Whereas he three years earlier had been the party's number one candidate in Oppland province and in Oslo, in 1936 he chose to be nominated in Telemark and Oslo.

Exactly why he waited so long before announcing his decision is difficult to say. He may have feared the possibility of yet another defeat. Although his candidacy in two election districts was partly for the purpose of attracting votes, it also indicated uncertainty as to whether he felt he could be elected in a specific district. *Fritt Folk*'s announcement declared that he had not intended originally to be a nominee. While this in part reflected the tradition in Norwegian politics that candidates should never appear eager to run for an elected position, in this instance there was an element of credibility in Quisling's reluctance. Party officials in both Oslo and Telemark urged him to take such a step on a number of occasions before he finally gave his consent. The party's central administration also strongly urged his candidacy.[30]

His appearances on the campaign trail were not necessarily positive for NS. As head of the party, he was of course the best known NS member. He attracted large crowds of curious onlookers wherever he spoke because of the notoriety he had already gained in the course of his political career. His listeners were not particularly impressed by his stage presence or his speaking technique. Although his ability as an orator did improve somewhat, he was never able to appear entirely relaxed. Furthermore, he tended to speak monotonously, interrupting his delivery at times only by brusque gestures and a raising of his voice, which gave him the appearance of being a poor imitator of Hitler. Even his NS loyalists conceded that he was not impressive as a speaker.[31] Despite the large audiences in attendance at NS rallies where he appeared, it is doubtful that many in the crowd were converted to NS' cause as a result of his rhetoric.

During the *Storting* campaign of 1936, National Union labored under a number of handicaps, all of which had some bearing on the party's lack of success. One such factor was that NS spread its election activity too thin. Instead of concentrating its campaign in specific areas where the possibility for obtaining·votes was greatest, as had been done in 1933 when the party restricted its election participation to the southeastern provinces and most towns, in 1936 NS entered slates of candidates in every election district throughout the country.[32] Consequently, the party failed to work effectively in those parts of Norway where its adherence was small and scattered, while the resources used in these areas, both human and economic, quite probably could have been put to better use had they been employed in districts where chances for success were greater. Also, by insisting on running candidates in every district, the party's central organization with Quisling at its head made certain that in a number of instances unsuitable persons were nominated, since the party simply did not have enough qualified members. In one election district, for example, the NS nominees included an individual who was well known locally as a former bootlegger, while another candidate had acquired notoriety throughout the district because his bankruptcy was imminent.[33]

The party furthermore did not have the financial resources to carry out an effective campaign in every district. Expectations were high in the far–flung parts of the country after the Central Office had been able to create a nationwide party framework. Disappointment was therefore substantial when the local organizations were left on their own, at a considerable cost of time and financial resources for their leaders.[34] These NS officers were also frustrated because they did not receive the necessary allocation of speakers that they desired from the central organization.[35] Because their expectations had originally been set too high when the local party groups were established, largely in preparation for the coming election, the tendency for the isolated NS leaders was to hold the central party organization responsible for their inability to work effectively in the conduct of their election activity.

It proved neither practically nor psychologically possible to ignore completely the demands from out-of-the-way NS officials for assistance in the campaign. NS officers in northern Norway were especially preoccupied with their feeling of isolation, insistently and repeatedly requesting financial assistance and speakers.[36] Funds were not forthcoming to any extent, but NS was obliged to send speakers to the north. Gulbrand Lunde carried out a rather successful speaking tour already in the summer of 1935. After repeated urging, Quisling followed suit in late August–early September 1936, seeking to exploit the assurances by party leaders in northern Norway that there existed a good possibility of taking votes away from both the *borgerlige* parties and the Labor party.[37] Lunde, who was one of NS' most effective speakers, in the meantime covered districts on the west coast, which previously had not been visited by major NS figures.[38] While it is by no means certain that NS would have benefited more had Quisling and Lunde refrained from going on these speaking tours, it is nevertheless accurate to say that their visits to outlying areas did not gain the results that were hoped for.

The failure of party organizations to work effectively, locally and nationally, similarly contributed to NS' lack of success in 1936. Although the party had covered the entire country with an organizational network by the time of the election, the local organizations often failed to function adequately. This occurred because there were not enough able persons available to fill the slots that had been created on paper, and frequently the result was that persons who were passive or incompetent came to hold these posts. As Hans S. Jacobsen pointed out: "Quisling drew up an excellent organizational plan for the country, but he could not wait until he had the right men in the right positions."[39] NS officers on the local level therefore changed frequently, a process that had gone on ever since the party was first started. Such instability could not fail to have a destabilizing effect.[40] One NS supporter in Trondheim noted after the election that it was better not to have any NS officers at all, rather than to have officers who did not measure up.[41]

Criticism of the NS organization was not restricted just to the local level. The central party organization also did not function as effectively as could have been desired. The most common complaints from district NS officers were that the Central Office did not respond to correspondence and that the Propaganda Division did not adequately provide the local organizations with needed election material.[42] *Fritt Folk*, the Oslo daily that had been created specifically so that NS would have a major propaganda voice in the election campaign, was similarly subjected to censure from irritated party members. In particular, they were discontented over the paper's failure to answer requests from persons in the districts who wished to subscribe, and also because *Fritt Folk* frequently did not arrive on time.[43]

Despite reproaches directed against lack of organizational effectiveness, this was not the major cause for NS' poor showing in 1936. An overly detailed organizational plan, weak local leaders, inadequate communication, and scattered election campaigning in far-flung regions might weaken NS' efforts in separate districts, resulting in some negative effects. Nevertheless they did not prevent the party from carrying its message to large numbers of voters in 1936. Interest in party speakers was considerable, especially for Quisling, and NS rallies attracted large crowds. Party hopefuls tended to believe that sizable audiences at NS meetings automatically meant that those in attendance would cast their ballots for NS. But this overly optimistic assessment failed to hold true.

The voters were not impressed by the new militant stance NS had assumed in imitation of the fascist parties on the continent. Reports from the districts after the election simply confirmed what election statistics had clearly revealed: that the single most important factor leading to NS' defeat was the public's negative reaction to the content of the party's election campaign. One party official from the southern part of the country noted that NS campaigners had made many speeches, but that these spokesmen had injured NS because of their inopportune and sharp comments. In the town of Lillesand, he continued, NS had organized several outdoor meetings, the last attended by over 150 persons, which by local standards was a sizable crowd. Nevertheless, NS received only a couple of votes in the town.[44] From Trondheim came the same opinion, emphasizing that there was no enthusiasm for copying Germany except among a small group of young people. But adults, especially workers and farmers, were absolutely opposed to such imitation. The correspondent insisted that NS must get away from riding boots, brown shirts, black ties, and bandoleers.[45] A writer from the Bergen area similarly provided the critical comment that the general impression among the public was that NS had obtained its forms of expression from Germany, forms that were foreign to the Norwegian character. In some instances these practices were described as being comical and ludicrous, in other instances directly offensive and irritating.[46]

National Union's increased militancy in imitation of fascism also had a decided influence on how other political groups reacted to Quisling's party. In asserting its separate identity by placing its own lists of candidates in every district, NS maintained that it refused to take part in election cooperation with the *borgerlige* parties because it was not *borgerlig*. Instead, NS demonstratively sought to appeal to the workers in the same fashion as Hitler had done in Germany. The *borgerlige* parties were portrayed as class parties, to which the Norwegian workers would never belong. Only NS, the party asserted, could look after the true interests of the worker, providing him with social and economic justice. Furthermore, NS argued that it alone could gain the allegiance of the nationally minded worker by convincing him that the Labor party was the tool of Jewish Marxism. The party insisted that this international conspiracy, with its headquarters in the Kremlin, was only interested in exploiting the workers, and once Norwegian laborers became aware of this, they would renounce the Labor party and join with NS.[47] As for the *borgerlige* parties, Quisling declared that they were doomed. They had prepared the way for a Marxist takeover by permitting Labor to assume control of the government. Only NS allegedly could prevent a pending national catastrophe.[48]

In its endeavor to present this type of propaganda to the workers, NS published a paper entitled *Oslo Arbeideren* (*The Oslo Worker*) for a period of time in 1936. The party further stressed its attempt to establish a proletarian image by placing the leader of the NS Unemployed Association,

Hilmar Knutsen, as number two on the NS list of candidates in Oslo, immediately behind Quisling.[49] Unfortunately for NS, Knutsen did not necessarily inspire confidence. He had a reputation for being politically unreliable and a confirmed intriguer.[50]

The *borgerlige* parties who were dismissed by NS as being no longer historically viable had every reason to regard NS as an enemy, in particular since NS stated explicitly that it intended to split and destroy all class parties.[51] Having assumed this stance, NS could hardly expect favorable treatment in the *borgerlige* press. *Tidens Tegn* was completely hostile. Any pro-NS contributions it printed were instantly rebutted by negative commentary.[52] The Fatherland League similarly attacked National Union. Lehmkuhl sarcastically dismissed Quisling's party with the following: ". . . no one takes abuse from that quarter very seriously. NS has now once and for all assumed the standpoint that all are corrupt or idiots who do not regard NS as the country's only salvation, and how [NS] will create national union on this basis must be its own affair".[53]

For the *borgerlige*, NS was more than ever a pariah party in 1936. In the 1933 election it had been viewed with skepticism and considerable hostility by many *borgerlige*, but still some limited cooperation had occurred. In the 1934 local elections such collaboration had been greatly reduced. By 1936 NS was completely outside the *borgerlige* pale.

The major concern of the *borgerlige* parties in 1936 was to restrict the Labor party as much as possible from increasing its parliamentary representation and thereby solidifying its hold on the government. Widespread political cooperation took place between the *borgerlige* factions, encompassing the Conservatives, Independent People's party, Fatherland League, Agrarian party, Radical People's party, and Liberals. Although these parties did not form a national alliance, cooperation between them occurred in almost every election district. Within the separate districts, two or more *borgerlige* parties usually combined in setting up joint lists of candidates *(felleslister)* or established looser electoral pacts *(listeforbund)*, or a combination of the two forms of cooperation took place. In a few districts, the whole spectrum of *borgerlige* cooperation was represented, extending from the Fatherland League on the right to the Liberals on the left.[54]

The antagonistic *borgerlige* attitude toward Quisling's party was hardened by the appearance of independent lists of NS candidates in every single election district. Here was specific evidence of Quisling's desire to outcompete and eliminate the *borgerlige* parties, since each vote gained by NS would be a loss to the *borgerlige*'s effort to limit the Labor party mandate. The *borgerlige* therefore continued with increased emphasis the argument they had used before: that NS was a divisive party which weakened *borgerlig* opposition to the Labor party.

This theme was repeated constantly whenever NS was mentioned in the *borgerlig* press, not without effect. Persons who were favorably inclined toward NS because of strong anti-Labor antipathies were nevertheless often reluctant to give the party their votes, since NS was not part of the *borgerlige* cooperative effort, and any votes that NS received would therefore be wasted if the party did not gain enough backing on its own to elect a candidate. The "wasted vote" argument's effectiveness was indicated by Quisling's strong reaction in a pre-election message, in which he called it "swindle agitation". He urged the voters to cast their ballots in accordance with their hearts and convictions. But then he asserted somewhat inconsistently that it was a waste to vote for the *borgerlige* parties, who had already condemned themselves to death by allowing the onward march of Marxism to occur.[55] The attempt by Quisling and other NS spokesmen to negate the effectiveness of this *borgerlig* accusation proved futile. Anti-Labor party emotion was still so strong that even NS members, and in some instances NS officers, failed to vote for their own party, and cast their ballots instead for one of the *borgerlige* parties, in particular for the Conservatives.[56]

In order to attempt to counter *borgerlig* criticism, NS resorted to placing advertisements in the opposition's newspapers. One testimonial it especially wished to publicize as widely as possible was the endorsement that Knut Hamsun gave Quisling.[57] Having won the Nobel Prize for literature already in 1920, Hamsun was internationally as well as nationally recognized as a literary giant. He was without a doubt the most distinguished individual to lend support for Quisling. Included within the author's endorsement was the celebrated passage: "If I had ten votes, he [Quisling] would receive them".[58] However, when NS placed an advertisement quoting Hamsun in the morning edition of *Aftenposten* on October 19, the day of the election, the political editor printed an attack against Quisling immediately alongside it.[59] Fuglesang protested the incident to the Norwegian Press Association after the election, but he received no satisfaction.[60]

When the voters cast their ballots on October 19, there was little doubt in anyone's mind exactly where NS stood, a state of affairs that differed considerably from the previous *Storting* election three years earlier. Quisling, his NS officers, and active members who had worked energetically on behalf of the party had high expectations that NS' firm new image would find favorable response among the electorate. The *Fører* personally contributed to the prevailing feeling of optimism. Just shortly before the campaign's end, he declared that the party should gain between ten and twenty representatives, and he was absolutely certain that a minimum of ten NS members would be elected to the *Storting*.[61]

When the returns came in, NS's disappointment was therefore great. The party received nationally a total of 26,577 votes. This was an absolute decline when compared with the 27,850 votes gained in 1933, and the setback was even more humiliating when the blanket coverage of candidates by NS throughout the country in 1936 was taken into consideration, as contrasted to the limited number of election lists the party presented in 1933. Its total was reduced in both rural provincial areas and in the towns; from 14,942 to 14,151 in the countryside and from 12,908 to 12,426 in the towns. NS' percentage of the total vote also showed a significant reduction, from 2.23 per cent in 1933 to 1.83 per cent in 1936. In the rural districts the decline was from 1.76 per cent to 1.4 per cent, and in the urban districts from 3.21 per cent to 2.74 per cent.[62]

The negative reaction of the voters to NS patterning itself after the continental fascist parties was shown even more concretely when tallies from specific districts in 1936 were compared with what NS had achieved in the same districts previously. One of the most obvious results of the 1936 election was the loss of votes in those centers where NS previously had enjoyed considerable support within the Christian community. Compared with 1934, the NS vote in Stavanger declined from 2559 to 906; in Haugesund it was reduced from 485 to 300; and in Martin Tveter's parish district in Vadsø it fell from 156 to 39.[63]

Another key indication of NS' loss of voter appeal was shown in those provinces in eastern and southeastern Norway where NS had previously presented joint lists of candidates with the Rural Crisis Aid. Quisling had believed it was only a matter of time until NS would be able to capture and absorb the Crisis Aid completely. In November 1935 the NS *fører* in Telemark, where the Crisis Aid had been strongest, reported that the opportune moment was at hand for the Crisis Aid's assimilation into NS. The organization's newspaper had already been taken over by NS' regional paper in Telemark, *Vår Vei (Our Road)*, and NS was in the process of launching a propaganda campaign directed toward the Crisis Aid's membership.[64] However, election statistics showed that this endeavor did not attain its objective. The votes gained by NS and the Crisis Aid jointly in 1933 in the five provinces of Oppland, Buskerud, Vestfold, Telemark, and Aust-Agder, totalling 9,512, were reduced to 4,475 when NS alone entered lists of candidates in these five provinces in 1936, a net loss of over 5,000.[65] The Crisis Aid's association with NS had been of little value, and marked the organization's death knell. Its members in the main rejected NS' bid for their adherence, and chose instead either the Labor party or one of the *borgerlige* parties.

A similar indication of the reduction of NS' voter appeal occurred in the two major towns of Bergen and Trondheim, respectively the second and third largest in the land. NS had gained votes in both towns in 1933 because of its appeal to conservative *borgerlig* opinion. In Bergen, it had joined the electoral pact with the Conservatives and Independent People's party, and in Trondheim the NS organization at first had been controlled by persons with a conservative outlook.[66] In 1936 eyes were open to what NS represented in both districts. The NS vote in Trondheim was reduced by exactly 500, from 1,152 to 652, while in Bergen it declined by over 900, from 2,127 to 1,195.[67] The loss of conservative support was not a phenomenon restricted just to these towns. From other districts, reports were received that persons who had originally joined NS because of Quisling's anti-Marxism and his defense of vested economic interests – persons who by inclination tended to support the Conservatives, but who were attracted to Quisling because of his advocacy of direct action against the Labor party – had now left NS and were undoubtedly back in the Conservative fold.[68]

The pattern of a decline in votes was not entirely consistent. In the three eastern provinces of Østfold, Akershus, and Hedmark, NS increased its total by 1,424.[69] Of this increase, 591 votes were in Hedmark alone, a province where labor conflicts had been strong and intense because of the opposition of farm and timber interests to the Labor party's organization of lumberjacks. The capital, Oslo, was similarly a district in which NS showed a gain in votes, an increase of almost 800, from 5,441 in 1933 to 6,227 in 1936.[70] All in all, however, these relatively meager gains could not make up for what the party had lost elsewhere. Nor could the placement of lists throughout the country balance the losses that NS sustained. The votes gained in the districts where NS entered lists for the first time numbered only in the tens and hundreds.[71] In one town, Molde, the party received but two votes. In another, Holmestrand, the total was five.[72] In no election district did NS even come close to winning a *Storting* seat.[73]

Having sustained such a severe repudiation by the electorate, Quisling was scarcely heartened by the general outcome of the election. The Labor party, which he had continued to depict as the major threat to Norway's independence and security, emerged as the major victor, with its share of the popular vote increasing from 40.09 per cent to 42.51 per cent. However, because of the considerable cooperation that took place between the *borgerlige* parties, the Labor party's *Storting* representation was limited to an advance of only one, from 69 to 70, despite an increase in the popular vote of over 100,000. Nevertheless, the socialists emerged from the election with a reassuring mandate from the people, and with their control of the government on a stronger foundation than ever. Among the *borgerlige* parties, it was the Conservatives who benefited most from election cooperation. They increased their representation in the *Storting* from 30 to 36, although their percentage of the vote only went up from 20 to 21 per cent. The Liberals gained slightly in total votes, but their percentage decreased from 17 to 16 per cent, and the Liberal parliamentary delegation declined by one, from 24 to 23. Of the major *borgerlige* parties, only the Agrarian party suffered an absolute decline in its total votes, although it was slight. Its percentage was reduced from 13.9 per cent to 11.5 per cent, and its *Storting* representation was lowered from 23 to 18.[74]

For Quisling, the results of the election offered no consolation of any kind. The Labor party had been able to strengthen its control of the government, while the *borgerlige* had been able to maintain the status quo in the *Storting*. Neither of the two major political constellations which he had denounced so vigorously had thereby sustained any significant setbacks. In addition to NS, the major losers were other small, and in part, extreme groups. Among the *borgerlige*, the two groups that in the past had been closest to NS' position, the Independent People's party and the Fatherland League, failed in their collaborative attempt to elect representatives to the *Storting*. The Independent People's party lost its single remaining seat in the *Storting*. On the extreme left, the Communist party was beset by internal division. In 1936 it entered candidates only in one district, in Bergen, and failed to elect a representative.[75]

The inability of many of the small extremist parties, NS included, to gain parliamentary representation stemmed not only from defects in their political stragegy, resulting in negative voter response. They were also beginning to be out of touch with the times. An upswing in the economy began in 1935, coinciding almost completely with the Labor party's assumption of governmental authority. Although the problems of the depression were by no means at an end, nevertheless the worst of the economic crisis was over. Considerable progress occurred in the most important sectors of the economy: in industry, agriculture, and the merchant marine.

Radical extremist groups had a difficult time gaining attention in an atmosphere of recovery and renewed confidence. Politically, too, the situation had changed. With the "crisis compromise" agreement, a considerable part of the ideological hostility between the socialists and the *borgerlige* was eliminated. Even the Conservatives declared that the Labor government should be given a fair chance, an attitude that earlier would have been inconceivable. The "crisis compromise" was viewed as an effort to deal effectively with the country's problems in a practical manner, cutting across ideological lines. While antagonism between the *borgerlige* and the socialists remained, in particular at election time, it was not on the high emotional level of a few years earlier, and it was possible for the minority Labor government to gain cooperation from at least part of the opposition in the *Storting*. In 1936 the great majority of the voters showed that they accepted and approved of these conditions by voting for the major parties.

In contrast, this election marked the elimination or the decline of parties on the extreme ends of the political spectrum. The Fatherland League's one venture into direct election participation, although limited, was a total failure, and the League's influence in politics continued to decline. It did not survive the war. Similarly, 1936 was the last time the Independent People's

party presented its own candidates. Its members were absorbed into the
Conservative party. Paramilitary groups such as the Community Defense
were dissolved as a result of being outlawed by the *Storting* in 1936.[76] The
Communist party, even more than earlier, was reduced to operating as a
small sect. National Union did not escape being part of this trend.[77]

In his reaction to the outcome of the election, Quisling could not publicly
recognize that NS' campaign had been a complete failure. As he had done
before, he laid all the blame for his party's poor showing on his political
enemies, in particular the *borgerlige*. He declared that many party sympathizers, and even NS members, had been alarmed by *borgerlig* agitation
concerning the issue of "wasted votes". Similarly, he argued that numerous
voters had been frightened from voting for NS, thanks to *borgerlige* lies
that NS imitated foreign examples and favored dictatorship. He continued
to contend that despite the election's outcome, NS still enjoyed the backing of a large segment of the population, declaring that if those whose
innermost sympathies were with his party had only voted for NS, the outcome of the election would have been quite different.[78]

His refusal to assume any responsibility for NS' resounding defeat was
not shared by all of the party's members. A considerable number who
wrote to him were more critical. One declared bluntly that NS could thank
its failed propaganda for being the one and only reason for the party's
defeat.[79] Another was equally outspoken, insisting that NS needed to
change from misconceived Nazism to Norwegian nationalism.[80]

It was not possible for Quisling, even privately, to admit that NS
should largely blame itself for its defeat. To have done so would have
meant an admission of error on his part, since he as head of the party was
responsible for its political course. But aside from castigating his political
opponents, he could offer no satisfactory explanation, and no concrete
proposals for the future. He maintained that the Norwegian people had
chosen "the way which led to Spanish and Russian conditions, to heightened class struggle".[81] But despite the dangerous position which the country allegedly had been placed in as a result of the election, he declared that
NS still had the responsibility of carrying out with undiminished energy
the task to which it was dedicated: "to unite the best forces within the
people in a national movement in order to preserve Norway's peace and
freedom and to clear the way for constructive national politics".[82] As a slogan for the new and difficult period which the party now entered into, he
chose the resounding motto "forward again".[83]

As the critical voices in the party indicated, not all NS members were
willing to rally unquestionably behind their *Fører*. Disappointed by the
election result, which meant that all their hard work had been in vain, a
significant number of active members insisted that change was necessary.

As part of the feeling of discontent and frustration, Quisling's leadership was also held up to critical examination. But they met a *Fører* who was completely intransigent, unwilling to admit any error. The Norwegian people, he insisted, were at fault; they had been misled. NS, under his leadership, was the only party that perceived reality. In the collision between members who insisted that NS had to change course and the uncompromising, rigid party leader, backed by his faithful loyalists, the result was disunity and division.

CHAPTER VII

National Union's Disintegration
1936–1937

> After four years of activity, National Union is now experiencing complete dissolution.
>
> Walter Fürst,
> *Ragnarok*, May 1937

Johan B. Hjort, the second leading figure in the party, proved to be the most prominent critic who wished to bring about change in NS. To a major degree, the controversy which developed between him and Quisling served as the catalyst for the process of party disintegration which occurred in the period after the 1936 election. Disappointment in the outcome of the election was undoubtedly a major contributing factor to this dispute. It triggered off not only Hjort's demands for change, but also similar sentiments within at least a segment of the NS membership. And once the discord had begun, it increased in intensity as time went on, causing an even larger part of the membership to become discontented with prevailing conditions in the party.

As far as Hjort was concerned, however, the dispute did not originate in the fall of 1936, but went back a considerable period in time. Nor was Quisling at first directly involved in the internal party feud revolving around Hjort. The NS leader did not actively take part in the controversy until after he was provoked by Hjort's desire to bring about fundamental change in the party's structure. Prior to this time, Quisling had in large part sought to stay above this serious quarrel.

In order to understand why Hjort's break with Quisling took the course that it did, and why it had such fateful consequences for the party that the two men had cooperated in founding, it is important to examine the position that Hjort occupied within NS, and why a controversy involving him could have such serious ramifications.

Ever since the beginning of NS there was no question but that Hjort occupied the number two position in the party immediately after Quisling.

Hjort was an outstanding speaker and propagandist, and in addition he was one of Quisling's close associates and advisers. He had been part of the small circle of men who pushed forcefully for the party's founding in the spring of 1933. During NS' early years he contented himself with being a member of the Executive Committee and the NS Council. In addition, he served as regional *fører* in Akershus after this position was created, but took a leave from his post following the local election of 1934.

Although he worked closely with Quisling during the party's first years, this did not mean that the two were always in complete harmony. They were simply too different in their manner of thinking and acting to be entirely compatible, and as a result there was at times an undercurrent of friction in their relationship. Being clear and precise, always ready to take action, Hjort could become irritated by Quisling's vagueness and lack of concrete plans to follow up a general policy decision.[1] Even more frustrating for Hjort was Quisling's tendency to make statements and commitments on his own without having consulted anyone. Hjort disliked being in the position of not being able to influence Quisling's decisions on important matters, as he made plain shortly after the 1933 election:

> To the outside world I appear to be "Quisling's second in command", but internally this is far from the truth. Externally I therefore have responsibility for what occurs, but internally no opportunity to have my opinion represented adequately. This is very unsatisfactory to me.[2]

His discontent at times over Quisling's failure to consult with him did not diminish, and this must be seen in relationship to the bitter dispute that later developed between the two NS leaders. But although Hjort could on occasion voice criticism of the *Fører*, to all outward appearances he seemed to be satisfied with his role until the fall of 1936. No one questioned his standing in the party. Through his numerous speeches and articles, he acted as a major party spokesman. He apparently was content with his party activity, along with his professional work as an attorney qualified to appear before the Supreme Court. However, he appears to have paid a price both professionally and financially because of the time he spent operating on NS' behalf, rather than attending to his legal practice.[3]

Beginning in 1935, the amount of time he expended on party activity became even greater. He assumed a number of new positions at this time, posts that in part had come into being as a result of the new organizational structure which Quisling and the Central Office had created and put into operation. In March 1935 Hjort took over as head of the *Hird*, turning it into a well-coordinated and·effective force. In the summer of the same year he resumed his position as the NS *fører* in Akershus, the province lying immediately adjacent to and surrounding the capital. And in the following year, when the party founded its national daily paper in Oslo, he became the chairman of the board of directors for *NS Presse A/S*, the company which served as *Fritt Folk*'s publisher.

Thanks to his key positions in the party, plus his commanding presence and good looks, Hjort was a well-known figure both within and outside NS. In his late thirties when the party was founded, he had a special attraction for youthful NS members because of his relative young age and his belief in taking dynamic action. He was behind the two most dramatic acts that NS engaged in during the 1936 election campaign: the "battle" in the Gjøvik market square and the burglary of Trotsky's residence. Known as the "Prussian" among party members because of his emphasis on discipline and rapid initiative as well as his mother's German ancestry, he was a subject of admiration, but also of dislike. Any serious dispute involving a person of his stature would therefore be bound to have serious consequences.

It is understandable that such an energetic and dominating personality would tend to create friction within the party, in particular after he took over specific positions of leadership. This occurred in Akershus when he resumed the post of regional *fører* in the summer of 1935. He proceeded immediately to carry out a house-cleaning operation within the Akershus organization, seeking to energize it. A number of local officers disliked his methods intensely, and were either forced out or resigned their positions.[4] Their departure was not peaceful, as was fully demonstrated by the vendetta they began against their former chief.[5]

This development apparently marked the beginning of the party struggle between Hjort and his opponents. Moreover, the quarrel did not remain limited to Akershus. It was an open secret within NS that the ambitious Hjort wished to see the party organizations in Oslo and Akershus unified, preferably under his control.[6] This view did not elicit a very favorable response from the NS officers in Oslo, who regarded it as a direct threat to their authority and positions. Because of their hostility, they were more than willing to provide places within their ranks for discontented former officers and members from Akershus, who thereby gained a strong base from which to continue their attacks against Hjort.[7] He, on the other hand, did not hesitate to respond to the challenge, arranging political meetings in the capital in direct competition with similar gatherings which the Oslo party organization had scheduled.[8]

Unfortunately for the sake of stability, the controversy did not remain restricted to the NS organizations in Oslo and Åkershus. It proved inevitable that the party's Central Office would also be drawn into the rivalry. Not only did it share offices in the same building as both the Oslo and Akershus organizations – a setup that simply invited intrigue – but in addition a number of the officers in the Oslo organization simultaneously held key positions within the Central Office. The close ties between the NS organization in Oslo and the Central Office, plus the instinctive dislike by Fuglesang and other members of the NS bureaucracy for an independent personality such as Hjort, made it natural for the Central Office to engage itself in the dispute.[9] Once it took sides, this meant that party groups under the Central Office's jurisdiction, such as the Youth Organization and the Women's Organization, would also be counted among the anti-Hjort forces.

Both factions appealed to Quisling, each insisting that it acted in his and the party's best interests. Copies of the increasingly acrimonious correspondence between Hjort and the Central Office were sent to Quisling.[10] The NS leader, as was typical when faced with a difficult decision he had to resolve on his own, proved incapable of settling the controversy. On the one hand, Hjort was a longtime associate and a public figure whom it was dangerous to repudiate. On the other hand, the Central Office and the NS Oslo organization were led in large part by younger members who were completely beholden to the *Fører*, and who looked up to him in uncritical admiration. They were part of the bureaucratic apparatus that he had brought into being, and because of his personal attachment to the party officials, they too could not be disavowed. There is no evidence to suggest that he followed the example of Hitler, who was a master at skillfully playing different factions within the NSDAP off against each other. Hitler always maintained control of the situation, reserving for himself the initiative in making decisions affecting the party. Quisling, in contrast, vacillated, and the dispute continued to create dissension.

Since members of the central bureaucracy were involved in the controversy with Hjort almost from the start, this meant that it would be bound to cause complications beyond the simple question of whether or not the party organizations in Akershus and Oslo should be united. Because of Hjort's position as a regional leader, the issue inevitably arose concerning the degree of independence these NS officers should have vis-à-vis the authority of the Central Office. In Hjort's instance, this question reflected not only personal antagonism toward individuals within the Central Office, but also different conceptions between him and the party bureaucracy concerning how the NS national organization should function. Hjort expressed his point of view regarding this matter in a strongly worded letter to Fuglesang, written in early 1936. He complained herein of the tendency for the central bureaucracy to limit local initiative, declaring that the function of the Central Office should be to serve the party and not to give orders. Instead of this occurring, said Hjort, the trend within NS was for paid secretaries to usurp authority from volunteer officers, whose spontaneity and originality were paralyzed by the meddling of the bureaucracy. It was more important, he maintained, to have NS develop "organically", rather than building up a party organization which appeared impressive on paper.[11]

Hjort's organizational philosophy was in agreement with the views of many local NS leaders, including Propaganda Chief Gulbrand Lunde, who resented Fuglesang's attempts to interfere in the Propaganda Chief's area of competence.[12] But Hjort's argumentation in favor of greater independence for regional officials simply exacerbated the breach between him and the central bureaucracy, in addition to making the entire controversy more explosive because in its widened scope it included the possible involvement of other NS officers. Moreover, the difficult question of centralization versus decentralization took on added importance because of Quisling's strong personal preference in favor of a highly structured organization. Furthermore, it was logical to carry this debate one step further, and this would involve the issue concerning what authority the *Fører* should exercise in his relationship with his subordinates in the party. Therefore, when the question came to a head after the election, Quisling was bound to resent all attempts to limit the party's central control.

For the time being, however, he did nothing. Failure to restrict and allay the growing dispute meant that Hjort's other positions in NS were bound to be influenced by the controversy, which thereby spread and increased in intensity. His post as *Hird* leader was of major importance. He had high ambitions for NS' paramilitary force, and these were shared by Quisling. The latter's attitude was undoubtedly influenced by how Hitler and Mussolini had successfully utilized their uniformed formations. Furthermore, the *Hird* served as a practical resource for NS in trying to control the frequent disturbances at political rallies. At the urging of Hjort, Quisling had announced on October 5, 1935, that the *Hird* would serve as National Union's political school and battle formation.[13] He eventually planned to require all male NS members under forty to undergo *Hird* instruction, with no one being allowed to become a party officer in the central organization without such training. For the time being this requirement was restricted to Oslo and Akershus, but Quisling stated his determination to expand obligatory *Hird* service to the rest of the country.[14]

His strong backing for the *Hird* provided Hjort with a potent weapon, as his enemies in the Oslo NS organization were quick to realize. They therefore did everything in their power to sabotage the *Hird* and/or to deprive Hjort of his leadership of the organization. On two occasions his opponents made direct attempts to carry out coups and in this way usurp command of the *Hird*. The first such incident occurred in March 1936 when Orvar Sæther, Hjort's chief of staff, refused to turn over the *Hird* to Hjort on a ceremonial occasion.[15] Shortly thereafter a similar incident took place involving Jens Rolfsen, the regional *fører* in Oslo.[16]

Both of these ventures failed rather ludicrously, but they revealed the extent of hostility directed toward Hjort. Rolfsen had served as Hjort's replacement while the latter was on leave from his position as regional *fører* in Akershus. Rolfsen was unceremoniously removed when Hjort decided to reoccupy his former post. Rolfsen's animosity toward Hjort dated from this time, and as regional leader in Oslo he did his best to oppose his rival in Akershus.[17] Members of the Oslo organization on several occasions thwarted attempts by the *Hird* to hold training courses in Oslo.[18] Similarly, a number of Oslo sympathizers within the *Hird* committed acts of insubordination, with the result that they were excluded or resigned from the organization.[19]

The rivalry degenerated into petty acts of personal insults, in particular after youthful elements on both sides became directly involved. The personal nature of the controversy was well illustrated by Kjell Gundersen, a prominent member of the Oslo faction, who publicly called four *Hird* officers "Nazi riff-raff". Hjort complained indignantly to Quisling about this incident, pointing out that Gundersen's insult was made in the presence of ca. 30 NS members who were called in as *Hird* candidates.[20] Hjort's young followers retaliated in kind, and the relationship between the two factions declined to the level where it was impossible for either side to regard the other rationally.[21]

Quisling did not back his *Hird* chief in this dispute, although Hjort insisted that he was merely attempting to put into effect in Oslo what the *Fører* had previously decreed: that all male NS members in Oslo and Akershus were required to receive *Hird* instruction. Quisling sought to solve the controversy on April 30 by allowing Oslo to establish its own separate *Hird* unit, while reaffirming Hjort's overall command of the *Hird* on the national level.[22] The latter was not at all pleased with this solution, and did his best to prevent Oslo from establishing a *Hird* unit.[23] A definite note of coolness occurred in the correspondence between Quisling and Hjort at this time. Although Quisling did not take sides directly, by his actions he indicated his sympathy for Oslo and the Central Office. Kjell Gundersen, for example, was not censured for his intemperate language against Hjort's *Hird* officers, but received instead an encouraging letter from Quisling,[24] while Hjort's supporters received reprimands for more trivial offenses.[25] It seems clear that Quisling believed Hjort was acting too independently and forcefully against Oslo. Hjort, on the other hand, felt frustrated by Quisling's inability to bring the dissension to a halt, and already on March 25, he gave what proved to be a prophetic warning, that if nothing were done to halt the growing feud, this could lead to NS' division.[26]

Although Quisling had set up guidelines on April 30 for the relationship between the two adjoining NS organizations in Oslo and Akershus, Hjort, because of his irritation over not having received Quisling's backing, disregarded these instructions and acted completely independently of both Oslo and the Central Office in carrying out election activity.[27] Quisling in turn regarded Hjort's assertiveness with some misgiving. He was naturally suspicious, and his concern was heightened by the unsubtle hints he received from Oslo and the Central Office that Hjort was deliberately building up his power in the party.[28] One of Quisling's disciples went so far as to predict an inevitable break between Quisling and Hjort.[29] The former did not, however, take any action against Hjort at this time. What mattered most for Quisling was his position as party leader, which Hjort did not challenge openly. Furthermore, it would have been most unwise for Quisling to disavow Hjort at a critical time just before the decisive election of 1936. The *Hird* leader's standing in NS had been strengthened by the notoriety he and his young followers gained from the "battle" in Gjøvik on May 21. Quisling responded with "an urgent appeal to all NS members, women, men, and young people, to enlist in active *Hird* duty . . ."[30] He went so far as to declare that everyone belonging to NS had an obligation to take a course in *Hird* training.[31] As before, however, he did nothing beyond issuing a general call for NS members to enroll in the paramilitary organization.

The split between the pro and anti Hjort factions thereby remained unresolved, and it created friction during the entire campaign leading up to the election. Hjort's Akershus organization persisted in its practice of scheduling meetings in Oslo as it wished, which irritated and antagonized the Oslo organization.[32] Another source of frustration for Oslo was the close control that Hjort's associate in Akershus, Thomas Neumann, an engineer, exercised over the party's propaganda bus. As could be expected, the bus was not made available very frequently to the Oslo organization, providing it with yet another issue about which to complain to Quisling.[33] Fresh fuel was added to the quarrel by Hjort's open imitation of his opponents in welcoming into his Akershus organization NS members from Oslo who were discontented with the party leadership in the capital.[34] He also supported a faction from the Oslo Women's *Hird* which formed the nucleus for a separate Akershus group. It did not take long before this newly organized unit began to complain to Quisling about indignities suffered at NS rallies, allegedly committed by their former comrades in the Oslo Women's *Hird*.[35]

The result of the ongoing feud was that petty insults, intrigues, complaints, back-biting, and attempts to increase one's authority at the expense of one's rivals were the order of the day in the relationship between important party groups within NS. Even though such a condition cannot be measured quantitatively it could not help but have an adverse effect on the party's effort in the 1936 election.

A vital part of the NS press also became involved in the in-fighting, namely *Fritt Folk*. It published its first issue in March 1936, at the very time the two factions were most embroiled over control of the *Hird*. Because of Hjort's position as chairman of the board of *NS Presse A/S*, which published the paper, *Fritt Folk* was regarded as part of his faction by the Oslo organization, not entirely without justice. The paper did not cooperate very enthusiastically with the Oslo organization, and it would on occasion refuse to print announcements submitted by the Oslo group if it considered these to be in conflict with Hjort's interests.[36]

As it turned out, the major issue of confrontation involving *Fritt Folk* concerned its relationship with the firm *A/S Oslotrykk*. Although this company, which printed *Fritt Folk*, was run by NS members, it was not at first under the direct control of Hjort's *NS Presse A/S*. This proved to be a major handicap for him because the printing firm's chairman of the board, Tormod Hustad, was a prominent member of the Oslo faction and a strong opponent of Hjort's.[37] Although *A/S Oslotrykk* had originally been established for the primary purpose of printing *Fritt Folk*, it expanded its operations to include the printing of party pamphlets, circulars, and propaganda material for Fuglesang's Central Office, plus monthly issues of *NS Ungdommen* (*NS Youth*), the publication of the NS Youth Organization. The leadership of the youth group worked closely with the Central Office and was part of the anti-Hjort coalition.[38] Neither the Central Office nor the Youth Organization were able to pay their printing bills, but *A/S Oslotrykk* simply covered these debts by charging them to *Fritt Folk*, increasing the paper's weekly printing costs from ca. 800 to 1,400 *kroner*.[39]

These added expenses came at a time when the paper was in dire financial straits, having a difficult time maintaining its operations because of lack of capital.[40] Its workers were not receiving full pay, and its quarters were cramped.[41] Hjort's supporters, including Georg Vedeler in Bergen, did not refrain from comparing the difficult conditions under which *Fritt Folk* was forced to operate with the numerous salaried employees and spacious quarters in Fuglesang's Central Office. Vedeler went so far as to recommend a reduction in the Central Office's staff, if necessary, in order to provide *Fritt Folk* with increased working capital.[42]

Convinced that something had to be done to rescue the paper, Hjort was not content to write complaints to Quisling. Acting in his well-known direct manner, he secured the ouster of Hustad and his fellow board member, M. L. Gundersen, with Hjort himself taking over as new head of *A/S Oslotrykk*'s board of directors.[43] This "coup" was not accomplished without protest, however. Gundersen immediately sought the legal counsel of Herman Harris Aall, yet another member of the anti-Hjort forces. This initiated a drawn-out dispute, with Gundersen and Hustad seeking to regain control of the printing company.[44]

Hjort described this effort as being an act of disloyalty to Quisling. The

most important thing, he insisted, was "how one can best protect the operation of the paper".[45] He maintained that this could only be accomplished
by having the paper's leadership also exercise control over its printing
plant.[46] Aall, as could be expected, was of an entirely different opinion, accusing Hjort of having acted in an "illegal" manner, independent of any
party authority. The attorney denounced Hjort as being arrogant and dictatorial toward loyal party members, whose ties with NS could not help
but be weakened by such behavior.[47]

Despite his strong language, Aall was on weak ground when appealing
to Quisling, as the attorney recognized. Quisling *had* approved Hjort's
takeover of *A/S Oslotrykk*.[48] However, the NS *Fører*'s position in this matter was equivocal. Despite his acceptance of Hjort's action, he did nothing
to enforce his decision. His pattern of behavior was very similar to that
which he exhibited earlier concerning the *Hird*. When confronted with a
difficult controversy, he was clearly unable to find a satisfactory solution.
On this occasion, he chose to retire to his cabin in Telemark for his annual
vacation just when the quarrel over *A/S Oslotrykk* was reaching its height.
No end to the dispute was therefore possible, and both sides continued to
disturb his vacation with complaints and accusations.[49]

The quarrel remained unresolved throughout the 1936 election campaign. The election result, which had not been improved by the unsettled controversy within NS, had an immediate effect on *Fritt Folk*.
On October 27 Quisling had to announce that the paper would suspend
publication.[50] He refused to admit, however, that the party's dismal
showing in the election was responsible, maintaining instead that NS
members themselves were primarily at fault because of their failure to
subscribe to the paper or buy its stock. However, he continued in a
more optimistic vein, work was now being done to bring *Fritt Folk* out
again "in good time before Christmas, or at the latest by January 1,
1937".[51] To ensure success in this endeavor, he urged all NS members
to support the paper by buying subscriptions, purchasing its stock, and
placing advertisements.[52]

Other NS officers had a more specific explanation for *Fritt Folk*'s failure. Hjort's enemies charged that the paper's leadership was responsible
because of mismanagement.[53] On the whole, the accusation was exaggerated, since it was primarily the election defeat that caused the paper to fold.
Nevertheless, there was an element of truth in the charge. The paper could
unquestionably have been run more efficiently, in particular when it came
to supplying new subscribers promptly with their copies.[54] Even Gulbrand
Lunde, who was usually in agreement with Hjort, felt it necessary to send
two letters of complaint concerning the failure of subscribers in the Stavanger area to receive issues of *Fritt Folk* as requested.[55]

Hjort defended himself energetically against the charges levelled at him
and *NS Presse A/S*. He did admit that the board of directors might have

made mistakes, but maintained that the paper nevertheless had done quite well, considering the difficult conditions under which it had been forced to operate.[56] At this time he was busily engaged in trying to bring out *Fritt Folk* once more as a daily. In his usual direct manner, he and the board of *NS Presse A/S* were at work clearing up the paper's financial position and seeking new sources of funds. But he complained that the criticism the board was receiving made the situation difficult. In addition, Gundersen, supported by Hustad, was continuing his effort to remove *A/S Oslotrykk* from Hjort's control. Hjort felt his position to be so insecure in his attempt to revive *Fritt Folk* that he was forced to write a letter on October 29 in which he demanded Quisling's backing in ultimatum form: "The board will therefore not accept such criticism, and we are going to resign if the *Fører* does not support us."[57]

Hjort's strong protest did not produce the desired result. The time was past when he could hope to receive backing from Quisling. The specific event that led to an absolute break between the two had occurred three days earlier, on October 26, 1936. At a meeting of the NS Executive Committee, Fuglesang, Hustad, and Rolfsen all attacked Hjort for the alleged failings of *Fritt Folk*'s leadership. Hjort countered by maintaining that his critics had created difficulties for the paper.[58] But despite his strong rebuttals, he recognized that he was in an exposed position. The Executive Committee was dominated by his enemies in the Oslo organization and the Central Office. The latter institution under Fuglesang's steadily expanding influence was an especially dangerous foe. Hjort therefore proposed to Quisling on the 26th a plan calling for complete restructuring of the party.[59]

Quisling's reaction was anything but positive. Hjort, however, felt that the changes which he sought were imperative – because of the election result and because of his weakened position in the struggle with his party foes. He therefore wrote to Quisling on the following day, declaring his dismay that he had been unable to present his viewpoint clearly enough: "I believe that quite thorough-going changes are necessary within the movement . . ."[60] Indicating the seriousness with which he viewed the situation, Hjort tried to regain some of the close ties that he had previously held with the NS *Fører*. He opened the letter with the greeting "Dear Major Quisling," which he had not used in their correspondence since March, and he closed by signing himself "your devoted J. B. Hjort".[61]

The extent of his proposed changes certainly justified his attempt to ingratiate himself. In a carefully formulated memorandum which he enclosed with his letter, he recommended that the Executive Committee be replaced by a small staff which would serve as Quisling's political advisers. In addition, he suggested that the Central Office be reduced to a "personal secretariat" for the *Fører*.[62] Fuglesang, Hjort's strongest rival, would thereby have his power greatly reduced. But Hjort was not content with this. Because of his preference for personal initiative and mindful of his position in the party, he proposed that NS be decentralized so that the regional leaders would enjoy much greater freedom. At the same time, he recommended that the *Hird* be strengthened and that the NS press be guided by standardized instructions issued by a new "propaganda council" headed by the party's Propaganda Chief. This latter change would have doubly strengthened his position, since *Fritt Folk* would have been placed under the overall control of Gulbrand Lunde, who shared Hjort's opposition to Fuglesang.[63]

The most interesting part of Hjort's memorandum, however, was the role he proposed for Quisling. The *Fører* would be given a "freer position" so that he could concentrate on political leadership, writing, and building up the *Hird*.[64] Although not stated, Hjort obviously intended to remove Quisling from day-by-day administrative control of NS, since the *Fører's* emphasis on building up the central party organization had been anything but beneficial for Hjort's position. Instead, the party would be decentralized. Quisling would still be permitted to make general policy, but the party officers, in particular the greatly strengthened regional leaders, would have the power of execution. Furthermore, Hjort's underlying goal was to control the party, using Quisling largely as a front, and thereby eliminating or vastly reducing the influence of his enemies in the Central Office and on the Executive Committee.

Hjort's concern was directed in particular toward Fuglesang and the Central Office, whose growing influence threatened to eclipse the party's number two man entirely. The General Secretary's strength was based not only on his position, but also on his willingness to subordinate himself entirely to Quisling. Fuglesang and the other members of the Central Office served as eager assistants in the move to build up the party organization. In return for such loyalty, Quisling had no objections to Fuglesang's attempts to expand the central organizations' dominance, since the *Fører* himself favored centralized authority.

The NS Battle Organization (*Kamporganisasjon*) serves as a good example of this trend within the party. This new formation came into existence in the spring of 1936. It was created by the Central Office, and its declared purpose was to serve as an elite group, its composition restricted to NS officers and the most active party members.[65] Those who joined were required to sign a seven-point loyalty declaration to the *Fører*.[66] Quisling supported the new venture, since the oath of loyalty definitely bound prominent party members closer to him. Hjort, on the other hand, opposed the group. Not only did he view it as a weapon utilized by the Central Office against him, which it was, but he also objected because the new formation illustrated once more the Central Office's preference for creating party groups on paper and then attempting subsequently to bring them to life. Hjort considered the Battle Organization to be a rival to the *Hird*, and he and his followers did not become members. Other prominent NS members who were opposed to Fuglesang similarly remained aloof. From Stavanger, for example, came the message that Mrs. Gulbrand Lunde and editor Adolf Egeberg, Jr., of *Vestlandets Avis* refused to join the Battle Organization.[67] As of November 3, 1936, it had gained only 428 members, with the largest single segment located in Oslo. In some provinces the new formation did not have any members at all.[68] Hjort commented sarcastically to Quisling that the party's old warriors, those who had truly "battled" on behalf of NS since its inception, refused to join the new group because it was nothing but a paper organization.[69]

Quisling, however, was not impressed by any of Hjort's arguments. The NS *Fører* had no intention of allowing himself to be moved to a front position. He clearly perceived Hjort's proposal as an attempt to oust him from power. Similarly, he regarded Hjort's campaign against Fuglesang as part of this move to take control of NS. News of Quisling's reaction soon became known to NS circles in the Oslo area. Already on October 29 a number of NS officers in the nearby city of Drammen, most of them belonging to the Battle Organization, sent Quisling a declaration of solidarity.[70]

Thoroughly convinced that Hjort was seeking to usurp authority, Quisling took a drastic step on October 30 which set in motion the process leading to his party's disintegration. He announced at a meeting of the NS Council (*Råd*), made up of officers from throughout the country who had gathered to discuss the election defeat, that he had appointed Fuglesang to serve as regional *fører* in Oslo. Quisling thereby openly took sides against Hjort, who on the following day resigned as NS leader in Akershus.[71]

Without a doubt, he hoped that his resignation might have a positive effect, such as Fuglesang's appointment being reconsidered. In the letter announcing his withdrawal, Hjort pointed out to Quisling that there was no possibility of cooperation between himself and Fuglesang, and that he, Hjort, hoped it might be possible to select a regional leader who could unite the two NS organizations.[72]

More significantly, Hjort recognized that his standing as a party leader had declined to the point where he had no choice but to resign and hope that the repercussion would be so severe that it might be possible to change the party in the direction he wished. His breach with Quisling was already a known fact. He had brought forward his proposals for change at the Council meeting on October 30, but he in turn had been castigated by his enemies in Oslo such as Hustad and Rolfsen.[73] To the surprise and dismay of the out-of-town party officers who were not aware of the situation, the meeting degenerated into a series of charges and counter-charges. They left the capital feeling disillusioned and uncertain now that the split between the *Fører* and his second in command was out in the open.[74]

By emotionally aligning himself completely with the Fuglesang faction, Quisling failed to see the consequences this would have. Hjort had a considerable number of followers and sympathizers in NS. Already on November 2, Quisling received a warning from Otto S. Engelschiøn, a party officer in Akershus who also served on the board of directors of *NS Presse A/S*, that "the movement's best forces – not just Hjort" were losing their belief in NS and becoming passive.[75] As an indication that this was not just idle talk, a number of party officers in Akershus left their positions.[76] Hjort himself took the lead in this process of withdrawal, declaring in a letter to Quisling on November 5 that since his criticism of the central bureaucracy had not led to change, "I have assumed that my point of view is not considered correct at the highest level, and I have therefore deemed it proper to make way for other forces whose view is in agreement with the leadership."[77] He, Engelschiøn, and a third member of *NS Presse A/S'* board, M. Knutsen, thereupon resigned their positions on November 12.[78] The disorder concerning Hjort also affected the NS Women's Organization, whose chapter in Akershus complained about attacks against Hjort from the group's national leadership. As a result, these Hjort sympathizers petitioned Quisling to make their group independent so that it could carry out its functions without interference.[79]

In order to try to gain control over the disorder caused by Hjort's moves, in particular in Akershus, Quisling now intervened personally by placing both Oslo and Akershus under his direct control. This, however, was not the type of unification which Hjort desired, and it merely served to provide him and his sympathizers with additional ammunition to use against Quisling.[80]

Quisling initially reacted to Hjort's resignations by maintaining that the latter was not guilty of disloyalty, but that he nevertheless deserved censure for having removed himself from the movement for personal reasons at a critical time.[81] However, the party leader soon learned that his former lieutenant had not withdrawn to the extent that Quisling might have desired. Contrary to his declarations, Hjort had no intention of being passive. When he saw that his resignations brought no immediate result, he next attempted to circumvent Quisling by seeking support among the regional leaders. He did not do so surreptitiously, however, but sent Quisling a letter on November 19, requesting a meeting of the NS Council to discuss internal disagreement in the party. In making this request, he spelled out point by point his position, which he insisted the Council members should be informed of. He declared that the previous Council meeting of October 30 had been so poorly planned and executed that the members travelled home with nothing having been decided. Secondly, although National Union's ideology was correct, he maintained it needed to be formulated more clearly. Quisling should concentrate his attention on this rather than on less important administrative matters. In his third and fourth points he declared that bureaucratic centralization threatened NS' growth, and that persons on the Executive Committee and some party officers were not qualified for their tasks. He furthermore attacked Quisling for having involved himself personally in the administration of the party organizations in Oslo and Akershus. Hjort insisted this was detrimental to NS because the party leader thereby became involved in subordinate administrative work, which brought with it rivalry, gossip, and intrigue. Quisling, maintained Hjort, should be above such petty strife. Finally, in opposition to the Central Office's policy of centralization, Hjort emphasized that decentralization had to occur.[82]

From a strictly legalistic interpretation of NS' bylaws, Hjort was completely within his rights in calling for a meeting of the Council. The party's rules declared that such a gathering could be held whenever a majority felt it was required.[83] For someone as jealous of his authority as Quisling, however, it was unthinkable to call this body into session to discuss what in essence was a challenge to his authority. Hjort was completely ignored, with no response being made.

The latter was not the kind of person who could be shoved aside in this manner. He countered by delivering an ultimatum on November 26. He repeated his demand that the Council be called together and that its members receive copies of his correspondence with Quisling. If this did not occur by 3:00 p.m., Thursday, December 3, then Hjort declared he would personally contact the Council members, sending them copies of the correspondence.[84]

The ultimatum finally forced Quisling to act, but not in the manner Hjort had intended. The *Fører* held a meeting of the Executive Committee, not the Council. As could be expected, Hjort was called on the carpet, at which time Quisling branded him as being rebellious and disloyal. The *Fører* additionally warned Hjort that if he continued to pursue his course, not only he but all who dared to support him would be excluded from the party. Quisling was enthusiastically seconded by Hjort's detractors in the Central Office and the Oslo party group, who maintained he should leave NS because he was damaging the party. Quisling did nothing to discourage such comments.[85]

More than this, however, was necessary to silence the strong-willed Hjort. According to his statement, which appears probable but cannot be verified, he declared at the meeting that he was willing to meet with Quisling in order to discuss their differences face to face. But after having waited three weeks with no response, said Hjort, he carried out his previous ultimatum, writing to the Council members on December 23.[86]

In this significant document, he repeated convincingly much of his earlier criticism. He castigated in particular the bureaucracy within the Central Office, declaring that it stifled independent initiative, especially when led by persons with little imagination. Quisling was held responsible for this because of the backing he gave Fuglesang. Quisling, said Hjort tellingly, was not capable of establishing personal contact with his subordinates based on mutual respect and cooperation. Instead, NS had no independent leaders below Quisling. He led the party by himself, cooperating only with the "functionaries" in the Central Office, and Hjort again emphasized that Fuglesang's central bureaucracy thereby gained a disproportionally strong influence in the party.[87]

This situation, declared Hjort, in what was up to then the strongest language he had used against Quisling, would lead to "pure dictatorship" if nothing were done. But his arguments were obviously inconsistent on this point, indicating the dilemma he faced when challenging Quisling's authority. NS clearly was not a democratic party. Quisling's position was based on the *førerprinsipp*, or leadership principle, the Norwegian equivalent of Hitler's *Führerprinzip*. Hjort, however, chose to interpret the *førerprinsipp* from a decentralized perspective. He maintained that Quisling should restrict his functions to general ideological and political issues, while administrative matters were to be left to elected party officers, who would have full jurisdiction within their districts. What he favored was in reality a form of constitutional authoritarianism, with mutual dependence between the *Fører* and his officers, with the officers in turn being selected by the members on the basis of ability, although Hjort was somewhat vague on this latter point. But it was clear that he opposed an all-powerful "dictator", and that he was not averse to changing the party's bylaws in order to obtain the changes he believed were necessary.[88]

Hjort's arguments were in large part self-serving, being carefully chosen to support his position. However, they did reflect to a degree his political philosophy, in particular his belief in having the party undergo "organic" growth rather than being artificially stimulated by a rigid bureaucracy. His conclusions were well-phrased, worded in such a manner that they would be attractive to regional party officers, many of whom unquestionably were receptive to the idea of increased independence from central control. Quisling was fully aware of this, and a meeting of the Council which might result in the limitation of his authority was the last thing he wanted.

In seeking such a discussion, Hjort followed a strategy which was the exact opposite of Quisling's. He gave the impression that he was acting on principle alone, and that other NS officers, not he, should have the decisive word in bringing about change. He did not attempt to hold onto his remaining strong position in the party, his leadership of the *Hird*. Already on the day after he had posted his letter to the Council, he informed Quisling by mail that he desired to withdraw from his *Hird* post. The latter wasted no time in responding, stating that Hjort's resignation had become effective immediately.[89]

Hjort thereupon retained only one important party position, his membership on the Executive Committee, which also provided him with eligibility to be part of the Council. Quisling, however, moved quickly to deprive Hjort of this post, informing him by mail on December 29 that he had been excluded from the Executive Committee.[90] Quisling thereby indicated his *modus operandi* for dealing with Hjort. The latter would be removed from all of his offices in the party, but not expelled, at least not yet. Quisling obviously hoped that the whole controversy would fade away, in particular since Hjort was no longer a member of the Council.

The attorney stubbornly persevered, however, in his quest to limit the *Fører*'s authority. He protested against his expulsion from the Executive Committee on January 2, 1937, declaring this to be in violation of NS' by-laws, since it occurred without the Council having been consulted.[91] He did not limit his protest to Quisling, but sent copies of both Quisling's letter of expulsion and his own reply to members of the Council.[92]

Contrary to what Quisling had hoped, the matter was of such importance that it could not be eliminated simply by removing Hjort from his posts. The reaction of the regional officers to this stream of correspondence became apparent in late December and January. In their letters to Quisling, many voiced consternation over the turmoil in the party. They declared that it would be a great loss if Hjort withdrew, and they voiced hope that he and Quisling might be reconciled.[93] The influential regional leader in Bergen, Georg Vedeler, deplored the fact that petty quarrels between their subordinates had resulted in strife between the two leaders, and he urged Quisling to meet personally with Hjort to end the dispute so that NS could still make use of Hjort's talents. If a reconciliation was impossible, then Vedeler favored a meeting of the Council in order to clear the air.[94] A significant number of other NS officers shared Vedeler's view. Although not all regional leaders expressed themselves on this issue, of the letters that Quisling received, officers in five provinces came out in support of a Council meeting,[95] while in three provinces they were opposed.[96] Telemark, Aust-Agder, Rogaland, Bergen, and Sogn og Fjordane favored Hjort's proposal, while Oppland, Buskerud, and Møre og Romsdal did not. It must also be noted that since Quisling exercised direct control over Oslo and Akershus, no independent expression of NS sentiment could be made in these two regions. Nevertheless, it is fair to assume that the dominant view in Oslo favored Quisling, while the opposite was true in Akershus.

Despite the limited amount of documentary material available, it is possible to conclude that the majority of the regional leaders tended to favor Hjort's point of view, at least to the extent of wishing to have a meeting of the Council in order to try to settle the dispute. Even one of Quisling's most outspoken backers among the regional leaders reluctantly had to admit this.[97] Quisling, however, reacted angrily to any talk of a conference, declaring that this represented a lack of confidence in his good intentions and competence, and that it was in direct conflict with the party's basic principles and its members' oath of loyalty to him.[98]

In his handling of the dispute, his approach was bound to have negative results. At a time when NS was in great difficulty, having recently sustained a disastrous election defeat, he reacted to internal opposition by assuming a dogmatic stance. Rather than responding in a conciliatory manner, trying to resolve discord, he exacerbated party dissension by insisting upon unquestioned loyalty. His lack of flexibility ruled out any form of compromise. He identified National Union completely with himself, believing that whatever he did was in the party's best interests. From this perspective, he could do anything he desired, being bound neither by consideration for NS officers nor by party rules. With such an outlook, it was natural for him to prefer to dictate, rather than to win support through ability and persuasion. He was also aware, perhaps only subconsciously, that he could not outcompete Hjort in a debate within the Council. Quisling's personality was hardly the type that could have won a majority of the Council over to his side through charismatic appeal. Once more, it is difficult not to draw a comparison between Quisling and Hitler: the *Fører*'s inability to handle dissension contrasted with *der Führer*'s skill in dealing with opposing factions within the NSDAP.

Unable to meet a challenge through direct confrontation, Quisling attempted to use organizational maneuvering as a means of thwarting Hjort's bid for a Council meeting. On the same day that he expelled Hjort from the Executive Committee, Quisling expanded its membership from four to nine. Ostensibly, this was done in order to strengthen contact between NS officers throughout the country.[99] In reality, however, what he sought was to gain the adherence of some of the very persons to whom Hjort was appealing for support. Among these was Georg Vedeler in Bergen.[100] Quisling had no intention, however, of relinquishing any of his power to the Committee. According to his revised plans, the Executive Committee was to meet in Oslo once every month. But in addition, he went on to establish a completely new body which he called the Extended Executive Committee. This included the members of the Executive Committee, heads of sections within the Central Office, leaders of NS organizations subordinate to the Central Office such as the Youth Organization, the Women's Organization, and the editor of the dormant *Fritt Folk*.[101] This body would meet once a week, usually on Monday, to deal with political and organizational matters.

The purpose of this new arrangement was transparent. By including some of the NS officers from whom Hjort was seeking support, Quisling intended to use the Executive Committee as a tool to prevent the Council from considering Hjort's charges. But in addition, Quisling wished to *increase* the concentration of party authority in Oslo. It would be difficult, if not impossible, for members living some distance from the capital to attend meetings every week, and almost as difficult to do so once a month. Furthermore, the Executive Committee included four members from Oslo, and this became an absolute majority once Quisling and Fuglesang were added.[102] However, under the new arrangement, the Extended Executive Committee really became dominant because it met so frequently, and it was largely restricted to the party functionaries and officers in Oslo who were entirely loyal to the *Fører*.

Quisling carried out this change unilaterally, although the party bylaws stated that appointments to the Executive Committee and changes in party rules had to be submitted to the Council.[103] He simply informed members of the Council by letter of his decision, and then declared that there was no opposition to his changes within the group.[104] He ignored completely the objections of several regional leaders, plus requests from a number of others for a meeting of the Council to discuss the changes.[105] He regarded requests for a conference of NS officers as a challenge to his authority. There was therefore no longer any way to alter the party except in the manner he decreed. One was either for the *Fører*, which meant to follow him blindly, or against him. In his mind there could be no middle position.

To some degree, he was correct in his suspicion that attempts to discuss the controversial issues created by Hjort and by Quisling's own organizational change were intended to challenge his authority. Nevertheless, there existed a widespread feeling within the party, shared by many who remained loyal to him as well as by those who sympathized with Hjort, that it was necessary to consider new tactics and methods, as well as ideological change, in response to the election disaster. Even some of Quisling's most devoted loyalists began to have second thoughts, fearing that divisiveness in the party was going too far. One of these, Ørnulf Lundesgaard, who had been one of Hjort's worst critics, now admitted that Fuglesang's faction had not always conducted itself in the most objective and commendable manner, and he recognized that the Central Office had made blunders.[106]

Quisling, however, failed to have any doubts. Party members were responsible to him, and not vice versa. The basic issue which led to the party's division and disintegration proved therefore not to be over centralization or decentralization, which Hjort had originally raised, but rather the question of the *Fører*'s claim to unlimited authority. Despite Quisling's firm conviction concerning where power ought to be concentrated in the party, a person of Hjort's stature could not be eliminated from a leadership position without serious repercussions, a fact that Quisling would not comprehend. With his unwavering belief in his leadership mission, he was simply incapable of taking into account that persons other than himself were of importance in determining National Union's future.

This obvious fact had already become apparent soon after Hjort's resignation as regional leader in Akershus. Mass withdrawal from NS began first in the fall of 1936 among Hjort's young followers in the *Hird* and in the Akershus NS Youth Organization. These young activists were upset by Hjort's resignation, and their initial reaction was to petition Quisling to have Hjort reinstated as regional *fører* of *both* Akershus and Oslo.[107]

Although such a sentiment was unrealistic to say the least, it did represent the admiration many young NS members felt toward Hjort. Quisling, of course, paid no attention to this attitude, thereby displaying his lack of understanding for this emotional issue. On the contrary, he made the matter even more controversial by having the Akershus Youth Organization forcibly joined with the Oslo chapter, with the Oslo youth leader placed in charge of the unified group.[108] This move was highly unpopular in Akershus. It brought a strong protest from Arne Dolven, the NS youth leader in the province and a close ally of Hjort's. Quisling responded by personally excluding Dolven from the party on December 21, 1936.[109]

This expulsion marked a widening in the split between a number of young pro-Hjort supporters and Quisling. Indeed, Hjort included this incident in his memorandum to the Council on December 23, citing it as an example of how the NS bureaucracy was depriving the party of some of its best talent.[110] Many of Dolven's friends began to withdraw from the party following his exclusion. In their disillusionment with the course of events within NS, some of them sought to set up a new youth group which would not be directly affiliated with the party, but which would seek to retain many of its ideals.[111] Symbolic of this, members often referred to their group as an "over-wintering society", indicating that they hoped to survive the internal dissension in NS with their ideals intact until the time when they might once more become actively engaged in party affairs.[112]

The endeavor to launch a semi-independent youth group became imperiled when Hjort was asked to take part. He agreed, but only on the condition that he would be an ordinary member.[113] Quisling, however, reacted with heightened suspicion to anything Hjort was associated with. The NS leader feared that this was the start of an attempt to establish a rival youth group, intended to sabotage his party's Youth Organization. His frame of mind at this time is well illustrated by his reference to the "over-wintering society" as a "*Röhm revolt*".[114] Denials by Hjort and by other members of the group that they were in any way engaged in a conspiracy had no result.[115] Quisling maintained his suspicious attitude, being convinced that every opinion contrary to his own, held by persons who were increasingly disassociating themselves from the party, was direct evidence of a conspiracy.

His vehement denunciation of the "over-wintering society" caused the pro-Hjort group to break entirely with NS. They left the party, but not before exchanging bitter recriminations with their former *Fører*. One of the common charges they hurled against him was that he should resign as party leader because he had violated both the spirit and the laws of National Union.[116] In response, Quisling clearly expressed his conviction that he was indispensable to the party, declaring that it was he who had created the party both as far as ideology and organization was concerned, and that NS for a long time would stand or fall with him.[117] He castigated his detractors, expelling one such "misled youth" from the party for having dared to ask for the *Fører*'s resignation.[118] The latter, however, insisted on having the last word. He pointed out that when many in his age group had joined NS, their political opponents had accused them of youthful immaturity. It was therefore ironic, he contended, that when they protested against Quisling's unfairness and errors, it was the *Fører*'s turn to use this "convincing argument".[119]

Hjort did not immediately follow his young rebels out of the party, but remained for a few weeks more, still attempting to gain a hearing at a meeting of NS officers. He insisted in a letter to Quisling on January 8 that the entire dispute could have been settled if the latter had been more conciliatory. Hjort further pointed out that he had not engaged in any conspiracy against NS, declaring that if he had wished to destroy NS or Quisling's position, he could easily have followed a far more "effective" strategy.[120]

Quisling, however, remained adamant in his refusal to seek any settlement with the party's number two man. Instead, he was provoked by Hjort's letters to the Council, and in retaliation sent off a number of memoranda in which he sought to rebut Hjort's arguments. On January 9 he mailed a five-page statement defending the Central Office, which he maintained was essential for the party's operations.[121] This was followed by two additional mailings on January 20. The first defended his exclusion of Arne Dolven, and Hjort by implication was charged with being behind what Quisling described as Dolven's disloyal behavior.[122] The second concerned Hjort's association with *Fritt Folk*, with Quisling holding Hjort responsible for the paper's poor administration and organization. However, Quisling was somewhat inconsistent in his criticism concerning this matter because he maintained that Hjort and the other members of the board of *NS Presse A/S* had resigned despite the *Fører*'s request that they stay in their positions.[123] If they had carried out their responsibilities so badly, one would have assumed that he would have accepted their resignations without any objection. In the same letter he assured the Council that work was rapidly taking place to have the paper, now under the Central Office's control, come out once more, and he urged everyone to aid in this endeavor.[124] Accompanying Quisling's letter was a report written by Fuglesang and Sigfrid Nylander, the NS Organization Chief, which was even more critical of the way in which *Fritt Folk* had been administered.[125]

Copies of these negative letters and reports were not made available to Hjort, who was subjected to a campaign of criticism behind his back by Quisling and the Central Office. Hjort protested in a letter of January 16, accusing Quisling of having made "false and defamatory" accusations against him on several occasions.[126] He stated his intention of calling together a meeting of party officers and members where Quisling could present his accusations and Hjort could respond, and he asked whether Quisling was willing to agree to such a meeting.[127]

The *Fører* responded evasively to this challenge, a method he had adopted on other occasions when confronted with the charge of having acted in an unethical way. In a reply sent two days later, he insisted on being informed in a clear and unambiguous manner which false accusations Hjort was referring to.[128]

Upon receipt of this reply, Hjort at long last appears to have accepted the fact that he would not be able to obtain his desired confrontation. He resignedly repeated his offer to give Quisling the opportunity to bring up any accusations he might have at a meeting, rather than making them behind Hjort's back. If Quisling refused to do so, said Hjort, then he must bear the responsibility.[129] Hjort received no satisfaction. Similarly, his request for copies of the confidential attacks against him were ignored.[130]

The controversy between the two now rapidly reached its conclusion. Although the breach between them had originated at the end of October 1936, it still had not become public knowledge, with no mention as yet having appeared in the press as late as the end of January 1937.[131] Some leading NS officers such as Georg Vedeler therefore still hoped that the division might be healed. He and a number of NS officers in Bergen petitioned Quisling to reach a solution, emphasizing that if this were not done, NS would receive a catastrophic blow.[132]

Because of Quisling's intransigence, there never had been any possibility for mediation, but in February it was no longer possible even to keep the conflict confined to within the party. It became public knowledge in the February issue of *Nasjonal-Ungdommen* (*National Youth*), the publication of the NS Youth Organization, NSUF. Not only did the issue contain an article by Tormod Hustad entitled "Renegades and Provocateurs", but it also included a notice entitled "Traitors", listing the names of three Hjort supporters who had been excluded from the Youth Organization and the party. Arne Dolven was one of those named.[133] Hustad's article did not go quite so far, in that Hjort was not directly identified by name. Nevertheless, both the title and the content of the article left no doubt that it referred to Hjort and his sympathizers. Hustad furthermore stressed that the first commandment for National Union's members was loyalty to the *Fører*, and those who did not keep this commandment did not deserve any consideration.[134]

The article prompted Otto S. Engelschiøn, who had served as an NS officer in Oslo and Akershus as well as on the board of *NS Presse A/S*, to announce his resignation from NS, declaring that it was an irony that Quisling's little witch hunt was taking place at the same time as the Moscow purge trials, since they were both a manifestation of the same perverse need to throttle all who dared to have independent convictions.[135] Three days later, on February 8, the former number two man in the party announced his departure for similar reasons. In his letter of resignation to Quisling, Hjort declared that he had hoped to remain within the party as an ordinary member, but conditions had deteriorated to the point where this was impossible. He castigated Quisling for the campaign of vilification which had been conducted against him and his associates, in particular since it had gone on behind his back, allowing him no opportunity to respond to what he described as a fantastic gossip campaign. He declared that this type of activity revealed such a lack of honesty and decency among those who now led NS that he no longer wished to be associated with that kind of people. There was no longer, he maintained, any possibility for NS to achieve its goal of creating national unity under the conditions prevailing within the party during the last several months. In a telling description of Quisling's leadership, Hjort depicted him as being afraid to discuss the party's most pressing problems, but instead maintaining himself in power by exclusions, innuendoes, and similar dictatorial methods which encouraged informing and espionage among the party's own officials.[136]

The dispute between Hjort and Quisling, which had now run its course, had demonstrated the obvious differences between these two leading figures in NS' formative years. Quisling was unclear and indecisive in dealing with problems, but dogmatic and unyielding, incapable of compromise, once he had taken a stand. Hjort was quick and decisive, at times arrogant in action. But he acted rationally, and was capable of flexibility and adjustment if he felt that this was desirable. Unlike Quisling, he attempted to deal with a given situation in an objective manner.

When the severe election defeat occurred, Hjort was convinced that NS needed to change. If possible, he hoped to reduce Quisling to a figurehead leader who could be manipulated. Furthermore, he believed that this was an opportune time for him to deal with his party enemies, first and foremost Fuglesang and the Central Office. But he did not prepare his initiative adequately, and he acted too precipitously. He had not consulted beforehand with his fellow regional leaders, and he failed in his bid to obtain Quisling's cooperation. Instead, the latter now sided openly with Hjort's enemies, engaging himself directly in the party struggle. Hjort did not attempt to fight back by holding on to his strong positions in the party. Instead, he hoped by his resignations to force Quisling to reach an accommodation which at least in part would satisfy his original demands for change. In pursuing such a strategy, Hjort acted from the pragmatic viewpoint that the loss of an influential leader such as he was bound to have consequences, and that it was therefore in the best interest of Quisling and the party to reach a settlement. But Hjort failed to anticipate the emotional rigidity of Quisling's nature, which permitted no thought of conciliation. Quisling was convinced that Hjort headed a conspiracy to usurp his authority, a feeling which the Central Office and the Oslo NS organization did its best to encourage.[137]

Faced with this intransigence, Hjort's only recourse was to attempt to secure a meeting of NS officers and in this way try to force through the changes he felt were needed. He was convinced that things could not continue as they had, with the indecisive figure of Quisling holding the position of absolute *Fører*. Once again, however, he was stymied by Quisling's obduracy. After it became obvious that he could not expect to receive a hearing of any kind, there was no alternative except to leave the party, in particular after the campaign of slander against him increased in intensity and began to appear in the party press.

That the departure of Hjort was a disastrous loss for NS was recognized by most intelligent observers within the party. To cite but one example, an NS officer in southern Norway wrote Quisling that Hjort's resignation was a worse blow for NS than even the previous election defeat.[138] The views expressed in this letter were just an obvious reflection of the fact that the resignation of someone who had held such key positions in the party as Hjort had was bound to have serious repercussions. Equally important in assessing his significance was the relationship which he had to the party as a whole. As its second most prominent figure, he had worked indefatigably for NS from 1933 through the election of 1936. One has only to read press coverage of the tremendous activity that he carried out as a writer and speaker to understand his importance for NS. He was irreplaceable to a great degree, and his loss could not be compensated for.[139]

Despite the warnings that he received about the weakening effect Hjort's withdrawal would have, Quisling and his closest associates were at first convinced that this would not have serious consequences.[140] Even as late as April 8, 1937, when it was obvious that opposition to Quisling's leadership was strong as a result of the split, the NS *Fører* could still maintain that his party was able to get along well without those who had left.[141]

Such an assessment was far from realistic. Hjort's departure did not bring the internal unrest to an end, but on the contrary heightened it. During the spring and summer of 1937 NS was wracked by turmoil from which it never recovered in the period prior to the German occupation. Those who had worked directly under Hjort in *Fritt Folk* reacted angrily when they learned of the accusations Quisling and Fuglesang had levelled against the paper's leadership in their confidential memos. Former editor Herlof Harstad denied categorically the accusations of mismanagement made by Fuglesang and Nylander, emphasizing instead the great sacrifices which the staff at *Fritt Folk* had made. They had toiled from ten in the morning until two at night under difficult conditions, receiving inadequate wages, all on behalf of the great cause.[142]

Harstad insisted he would reveal the truth at a general assembly meeting of stockholders in *NS Presse A/S*, scheduled for April 2. He and other opponents of Quisling made full use of the opportunity. They were well represented at the meeting, and not only defended the former leadership and staff of the paper, but levelled serious charges against Quisling as well. One of the most damaging was made by Arne Wiese, *Fritt Folk*'s former business manager. He hinted strongly that Quisling had been financially dishonest, having kept 500 *kroner* of stock purchase funds for his personal use, which he reluctantly repaid in four instalments after Wiese had insisted upon it.[143]

In open debate, Quisling was helpless, and he failed to counter adequately the opposition at the meeting. He was, however, so stung by Wiese's charge of possible attempted embezzlement that he proceeded to publish an open letter of rebuttal in *Fritt Folk*, thereby unwisely revealing the entire incident to the public. He insisted he had kept the money so that he could maintain supervision over *Fritt Folk*'s operations, that he had paid the money back on his own initiative without any prompting, and that it was he who had first informed Wiese concerning receipt of the funds.[144]

This explanation was quite thin, as Wiese made abundantly clear in a letter of rejoinder. He pointed out that he had received far larger sums from Quisling without supervision. The paper used 1,200 *kroner* a day merely to come out, and it grossed 100.00 *kroner* during Wiese's period. He concluded by declaring that the stockholders in *NS Presse A/S* had judged Quisling to be culpable, and he requested that his letter be featured prominently in *Fritt Folk*.[145]

The letter was never published, not only because Quisling consistently denied space for critical commentary, but also because it was probably too close to the truth. Quisling did not even threaten Wiese with legal retribution. The NS *Fører* was financially impoverished. His total income in 1936 had only been 2,000 *kroner*, while the rent that he paid for his flat amounted to 2,100 *kroner*. On the basis of this comparison alone one can well understand his financial position. He had to sell part of his collection of paintings from Russia in order to have enough to get along on.[146] Someone in such straits, who had to maintain a respectable bourgeois status as party leader, could be sorely tempted by a sum of 500 *kroner*. He seems to have been, as Benjamin Vogt has noted, a man "tried to the utmost, who found it too humiliating to admit the bitter truth".[147]

In responding to his critics, Quisling enjoyed the one major advantage of exercising a monopoly over the party press. He hammered away in the pages of *Fritt Folk* against the opposition, who of course had no chance to respond. They were described as being part of a "clique" who had attempted to usurp power after the election. But he went beyond the personal level when attacking his detractors, attempting also to create a clear ideological division between his loyalists and the disaffected elements both inside and outside the party. He described them as having political ideas that favored an extremist form of Nazism which he did not wish to see in his party, emphasizing instead that NS was built on a Norwegian foundation.[148]

At an earlier date his charge that the opposition against him consisted largely of persons who supported National Socialism would have contained considerable truth, in particular since Hans S. Jacobsen and Walter Fürst were once more among his most severe critics in the spring of 1937. But the NS election campaign had shown that Quisling's denial of NS' similarity to Hitler's movement was largely an illusion. Furthermore, the bulk of those who had left the party or who were in opposition, Hjort being the most prominent example, were antagonistic toward Quisling not because of ideological differences, but because of his failings as party leader.

Also, contrary to Quisling's public position, NS was weakened rather than strengthened by the gradual loss of discontented members during the spring of 1937. The party was largely paralyzed by this state of affairs, and its financial condition was critical. Although plans had long been under way to have *Fritt Folk* reappear as a daily, when it finally came out again in February, it was in the form of a small weekly. Even in this reduced state it was unable to make ends meet, with its expenses being more than twice as high as its income.[149] Subscribers refused to pay more for a copy of the weekly than they had for a single issue of the daily, and advertisers insisted on an end to the current disputes within NS before they would pay their bills.[150] Desperately in search of capital, the paper's financial leadership turned to NS contacts in Germany, hoping thereby to secure new capital.[151] But *Fritt Folk* received no life-giving infusion from this quarter. Herman Harris Aall, who frequently acted on Quisling's behalf in Germany during this time, could only advise that the paper should retrench economically.[152]

By early May the party had given up thought of having *Fritt Folk* reconvert to a daily, and the situation was so bleak that Georg Vedeler proposed to Quisling that NS members should instead be encouraged to support an attempt by Walter Fürst to raise capital for a new "national" daily newspaper. Vedeler maintained that NS could in this way infiltrate and take over the paper, but he no doubt had other motives in mind as well, since his primary concern at this time was to try to bring about conciliation between Quisling and his critics.[153] Nothing came either of the proposal or of Fürst's venture.

Vedeler had no reason to be particularly pleased with NS' position at this time. His organization in Bergen was in anything but good shape. The party's major benefactor locally had ceased to pay his 75 *kroner* monthly donation, declaring that he did not wish to support a movement which was on the decline. As a result, NS in Bergen had been forced to dismiss its secretary and to vacate its offices.[154] In Oslo the party's financial position was equally desperate. In early June, NS had to advertise the sale of its proudest attraction from the previous election campaign, the propaganda bus. It was described as being "in good condition and is for sale cheaply".[155]

Responsibility for the party's paralysis rested with Quisling. Because of his uncompromising stand, NS simply could not function until the strife surrounding the question of his leadership had been settled. During early 1937 the turmoil increased in intensity because his reaction to any criticism had been reduced to one crude solution – instant expulsion from the party. It therefore was little wonder that the opposition in turn focused its attention on one demand – that he step down as NS *Fører*.

Involved in the effort to get Quisling to resign his position were not only NS members who became critical of his leadership in 1936–37, but also persons who had broken with him previously. Prominent among the latter were Jacobsen and Fürst. Jacobsen had supported NS in the 1936 election, but he now demanded from the pages of *Ragnarok* that Quisling had to go. If not, said Jacobsen, then the columns would have to march without him.[156] He presented an incisive portrayal of Quisling's failure as a political leader in the May 1937 number of his publication, emphasizing in particular Quisling's inability to make firm decisions in a difficult situation, his failure to establish a personal relationship with co-workers on the basis of mutual confidence and friendship, and his suspicious fear of disloyalty from anyone who presented a point of view contrary to his own.[157] Fürst also described the deteriorating condition of NS in equally clear language. NS, he declared, was now experiencing complete dissolution, with only a few members still working actively for the party, and these were almost all fanatical admirers of Quisling. The majority of members were discontented, waiting for some type of change to take place. Since most of them lived scattered throughout the country, they were passive at the moment, hoping for some miracle to occur which would give them back their confidence in the party. Being far from Oslo, they did not fully understand who was truly at fault. However, said Fürst, more and more members were becoming aware that error lay with the "irremovable dictator", who lacked the ability to lead NS to victory. But out of loyalty considerations they hesitated to express openly the wish that he should step down. In addition, anyone who dared to do so risked expulsion.[158]

Despite the partisan nature of his characterization, Fürst's assessment of what would happen to NS if Quisling remained as leader proved to be prophetic. Fürst pointed out that National Union was Quisling's personal property as long as one member remained in the party. If Quisling therefore did not step down willingly, said Fürst, National Union would degenerate into a small sect which would never amount to anything. The only way out of the impasse, Fürst insisted, was either for Quisling to resign or else to create a new organization outside of NS.[159]

Unlike previously, Fürst and Jacobsen no longer were largely isolated in their opposition to Quisling. A significant segment of the party was similarly skeptical of the leader's ability. Following Hjort's resignation, the foremost figure in the opposition to Quisling was Albert Wiesener, an attorney who had been the party's number one candidate for the towns in Oppland and Hedmark provinces.[160] From March until the end of May 1937, Wiesener served as spokesman for the body of opinion within NS which opposed Quisling's uncontrolled hegemony, insisting instead that it was necessary for the party to exercise control over and demand accountability from its *Fører*.[161]

Wiesener and his closest supporters received the same treatment as those who had previously challenged Quisling, being expelled from the party.[162] On this occasion, however, the opposition refused to withdraw, but instead made an open challenge. It arranged meetings where discontented members within NS could meet with persons who had already left the party.[163] The topic for discussion at these gatherings focused on the party's failings, especially those of its leaders.

The highlight of the clash between Quisling and his loyalists versus the opposition led by Wiesener occurred on Sunday, May 30. Party officers were in Oslo to discuss strategy, and NS had scheduled an open meeting for 8:00 p.m. on this date, at which Quisling intended to speak on the subject of "dictatorship". The opposition took advantage of the occasion by arranging a meeting on the same day and in the same building at 1:00 p.m. It invited the NS officers from throughout the country to attend and discuss the ills affecting the party. Those backing Quisling were most upset by this development, with *Fritt Folk* being forced to declare in the very advertisement announcing Quisling's lecture that the opposition's meeting was not sanctioned by NS.[164] Fuglesang added the warning to loyal NS members not to be fooled by what he described as the mask of objectivity which "these people" attempted to hide behind.[165]

Fuglesang's admonition failed to have the desired effect. Even *Fritt Folk* had to admit that some 200 persons attended the opposition's meeting,[166] and the total was undoubtedly higher, perhaps in the neighborhood of 330.[167] Following a speech by Wiesener in which he presented his analysis of Quisling's failings, the gathering devoted itself to an open discussion of NS' debilitated condition.[168] Among those present were a significant number of NS representatives from local party organizations throughout the country. Party members from Bergen in particular made their presence evident. Their objective was to attempt to salvage what remained of NS by seeking to arrange some form of agreement between Quisling and those who were opposed to his leadership.[169] To accomplish this, the meeting resolved to establish a special committee to consider National Union's future. A number of persons were chosen to participate on the committee, including Quisling and some of his adherents.[170]

This position of attempting to mediate represented the policy of the able NS leader in Bergen, Georg Vedeler, who had sought to bring an end to division in the party going back to the time when the original split between Quisling and Hjort first took place. For Quisling, however, it was unthinkable to consider a compromise, in particular of the type proposed at the May 30 meeting. He would never under any circumstances agree to participate on a committee as only one of a number of equals, especially when the subject for discussion was the future of NS, which in itself was implicit criticism of his leadership. The outcome of the official NS meeting on the evening of May 30 simply made it obvious, as had been the case so many times before, that the leader of NS was incapable of accommodation when his own person was involved in a dispute. The only difference was that on this occasion he demonstrated his intransigence in an open forum, thereby bringing a subject which had only been discussed in party circles and in publication form directly before the startled gaze of many NS members.

The speech he delivered in the evening was anything but conciliatory. In the early part of his presentation the philosophical side of his nature was in evidence. He did indeed discuss the subject of dictatorship, with analogies going as far back in history as Rome. His main theme was that dictatorships occurred in a society whenever conditions made such a development inevitable. Although he distinguished between what he called a "despotic dictatorship", as in Russia, and a dictatorship based on "the people's will", as in Germany, he insisted that NS in principle was opposed to dictatorship. This interpretation was entirely in accordance with NS' official position, which had been adopted mainly as a defensive posture against the telling argument made by the party's opponents that NS was dictatorial. What he favored, said Quisling, was an "organized workers state" where the nation's cultural life and economic interests would be represented in an independent National Assembly (*Riksting*). But as before, he was vague when it came to describing how this system would function, in particular since he warned against irresponsible freedom, symbolized by liberalism, and called for the creation of an elite which would put his ideal system into effect.[171] The political situation in Norway simply made it impossible for him to admit what was obvious – that the corporate system which he championed inevitably required a dictator.

He gave vent, however, to his dictatorial tendencies in that portion of his speech which he devoted to the opposition within NS. He refused to hold a discussion of the party's condition, declaring that NS was not a "student debating society". Furthermore, he attempted to refute one of the strongest criticisms of his leadership by insisting that he had always been willing to meet with his opponents personally to discuss issues in dispute – an argument that J.B. Hjort undoubtedly reacted sardonically to when he heard it. But Quisling maintained that the opposition merely wished to cause a rebellion in the party, and he would not under any circumstances compromise with those who "betray the cause" and were therefore traitors.[172]

In order to document this serious charge, he read the oath of loyalty required from members of the Battle Organization, to which all NS officers, he insisted, were expected to belong.[173] He thereby openly revealed why he had supported Fuglesang's creation of this new organization in the middle of an election year despite Hjort's opposition. He wanted to bind all NS officers to him in an oath of personal allegiance – a primitive way of attempting to secure their loyalty, although it had been successfully employed by Hitler.

The opposition led by Wiesener made repeated attempts during the speech to respond to Quisling's charges, and they continued their vain efforts during supporting speeches made by two of Quisling's loyal regional leaders. But Wiesener, Jacobsen, Fürst, and several others were repeatedly shouted down when they tried to respond to the charges that were hurled against them. When the speechmaking came to an end, the opposition was once more on its feet, demanding a discussion in order to present their views. But they were drowned out by the loudspeaker system, which played the national anthem and other patriotic songs at full blast as the meeting dissolved in confusion.[174]

While the outcome of the meeting of May 30 showed that Quisling's status could not be changed through debate, the two meetings held on this date made it obvious to all political observers just how disruptive the strife within NS really was. Quisling personally condemned the coverage which anti-NS papers gave to the controversy, but his own weekly's commentary did nothing to hide what was taking place. Almost the entire June 3 edition of *Fritt Folk* was devoted to the events of May 30, and while its coverage naturally was partisan, it nevertheless proved revealing. Even the most politically naive NS member, far removed from Oslo, was now aware that the party was torn by dissension over Quisling.

This feeling was heightened by the fact that the opposition did not remain silent in the immediate aftermath of May 30. In an article in *Tidens Tegn*, Wiesener stressed that he had never signed any loyalty declaration to Quisling.[175] He was supported by Jacobsen and Fürst, who pointed out that this had not been NS practice when they were members of the party.[176] But Wiesener contended that even those who had signed the Battle Organization's oath had promised loyalty to NS ideals, the party, and the *Fører*. Wiesener argued that in this instance the oath was no longer binding, since the *Fører* in particular and NS in part had violated the principles which the party really stood for.[177] *Fritt Folk* responded by branding such reasoning as Jesuitical.[178]

Since Quisling remained the unimpeachable *Fører* of NS, the only possible option for erstwhile NS members who had been excluded or who had withdrawn in opposition to him was to seek to create some kind of alternative to their former party. They attempted to establish a "national" movement which they hoped could outcompete NS. Fürst's effort to secure financial backing for a "national" daily was part of this venture. In seeking support for a competitive party, one of those whom Quisling's opponents contacted was Knut Hamsun. But the famous novelist, to his later ruin, remained uncritically committed to Quisling, refusing to have anything to do with what he sarcastically called "the break-away party".[179]

The former NS members enjoyed no greater success with less prominent persons in attempting to establish an alternative to NS. There simply was not enough support in 1937 for two parties on the extreme right in Norwegian politics. A number of ex-NS members found haven around *Ragnarok*, which continued to come out under Jacobsen. J. B. Hjort became one of the contributors to the publication. But *Ragnarok* remained what it had been before 1936 – a minor tract received by a small band of individuals who admired National Socialism and who were discontented with Quisling.

The inability of former members to create a viable alternative did not mean, however, that the May 30 meetings marked the conclusion of the party's internal dissension. While the events of this date served as a highlight in the process of disintegration which NS was undergoing, not all discontented members withdrew. There still remained a significant faction which was determined to resist Quisling's claim to total and unquestioned control over NS affairs. Vedeler headed this group. In letter after letter to Quisling, the Bergen NS chief had attempted to persuade the party leader to reach a satisfactory accommodation with his critics in the hope that NS would sustain the least damage possible.[180] In doing so, Vedeler never challenged Quisling openly, but sought instead to win him over by praising his leadership while still stressing the need for conciliation. But as time went on with Quisling continuing to pay no heed to his advice, Vedeler's patience grew strained. His last attempt at mediation occurred at the May 30 meetings. He had originally been scheduled to appear on the program that evening with Quisling.[181] However, he did not join Quisling at the podium. The events that occurred on that day made it clear that Vedeler stood closer to the opposition led by Wiesener than he did to the *Fører*.

Vedeler's attempt to arrange a settlement marked the beginning of the open split which would eventually separate the NS *Fører* from yet another of his lieutenants. Quisling had previously attempted to secure Vedeler's loyalty by making him a member of the Executive Committee.[182] The latter had reciprocated by publicly remaining loyal while privately working for compromise. As late as the end of May, Mrs. Vedeler's name appeared on a list issued by NS Women's Organization in *Fritt Folk* which affirmed support for Quisling and condemned Wiesener's action.

After May, however, Quisling and the Central Office viewed Vedeler with undisguised suspicion. His independent mediation effort meant that he could no longer be trusted, in particular when his sympathies for Wiesener became openly apparent shortly afterwards. On June 3 the NS paper in Bergen, ironically entitled *Samarbeid (Cooperation)*, prominently printed Wiesener's version of what had occurred at the May 30 meetings.[183]

Vedeler was regarded as a special threat not only because of his position as head of NS in Norway's second city, but also because the party's annual conference had already been scheduled for Bergen that summer. From Quisling's point of view, it would be dangerous to allow such an important gathering to be controlled by someone whom he and the Central Office now regarded as a foe. Their reaction was typical – the potential threat which Vedeler represented would be warded off by organizational maneuvering. As late as May 27 *Fritt Folk* proclaimed the slogan "Forward to the national meeting in Bergen, July 2–4", and the paper contained inspiring pictures of the beautiful landscape through which NS auto caravans would pass on their way from eastern Norway to the west coast. However, the next edition of the paper, which followed the disruptive May 30 meetings, contained no mention of the party gathering. Instead, the only space afforded the conference indicated that the Central Office was making careful preparation to prevent the meeting from getting out of control. Notice was given that the party bylaws stipulated that all matters which NS members wished to discuss at the national meeting had to have been submitted to the leadership at least two months prior to the conference unless special dispensation was granted.[184] Since this announcement came at a time when *less* than two months remained before the meeting, it was obvious that Quisling and the Central Office wished to head off any discussion of internal problems, in particular the *Fører's* leadership.

This notice was followed by another announcement on June 10, just three weeks before the meeting, that the site had been shifted to Hamar, a town north of Oslo. Ostensibly, the reason for this move was that the Bergen NS could not host the gathering because of economic difficulties.[185] Although the Bergen organization did experience financial hardship, the true explanation of course was to remove the national meeting from Vedeler's influence.[186]

With the shift of the conference, Vedeler openly challenged the party leadership. On the same day that the change was announced in *Fritt Folk*, he publicly called on Quisling to show moderation and conciliation. NS needed such men as Wiesener and Engelschiøn, insisted Vedeler, and he urged Quisling to extend an open hand to all those who had previously been excluded.[187]

Such outspoken opposition indicated that the situation in Bergen was out of control as far as the party leadership was concerned. Fuglesang was dispatched to the city in an attempt to bring about a lessening of tension, but he enjoyed little success. The Bergen organization went so far as to set up specific conditions before its members were willing to take part in the conference at Hamar.[188] *Samarbeid* stated categorically that if NS at the annual meeting did not bring about agreement between its program and its form of organization (an implied criticism of Quisling's insistence on unlimited control), change its speakers' propaganda to a more elevated tone, and extend the promise of cooperation to those who had left the party, then so many members would resign that there would not be any more annual meetings.[189]

For once Quisling and the Central Office were forced to yield at least partially because of pressure from within. Describing the conference, *Fritt Folk* afterwards attempted to give the impression that normal conditions had once more returned, headlining the gathering as "the best in the movement's history". In reality, however, the party continued to be plagued by division. The representatives from Bergen were present, having been granted the privilege of presenting their viewpoint. At a conference of NS officers on the morning of Saturday, July 3, Vedeler and his chief lieutenant, Sigurd Stinesen, proposed specific changes in the party's bylaws. The two most important were provisions dealing with the *Fører*'s removal and the requirement that important matters affecting the party be decided by majority vote.[190] The Bergen delegates diplomatically assured the gathering that their proposal concerning the possibility of removing the party leader was not directed against Quisling personally, but contended that such a provision in National Union's bylaws would successfully rebut the charge that the party favored dictatorship. Vedeler and Stinesen did state, however, that the question whether or not Quisling should continue was current and should be discussed.[191]

Although Vedeler did receive a limited amount of approval for his proposals, he had no chance of having his view prevail at an assembly domi-

nated so completely by Quisling loyalists. By the time of the Hamar meeting the overwhelming bulk of discontented NS members had either been
excluded, had resigned, or had simply become indifferent and turned their
backs on the party. The official position taken at Hamar by the majority of
NS officers therefore truly reflected prevailing opinion in what remained of
NS. The question of Quisling's removal was declared to be irrelevant, and
to have party decisions decided by majority vote was described as an attempt to introduce a principle which the movement had always opposed.[192]

Despite Vedeler's failure to receive major backing, Quisling still remained in a defensive frame of mind at the meeting. In his major speech,
his tone was clearly influenced by the opposition he had encountered during the last nine months. He insisted that there was no need to change the
party's bylaws since he always considered the advice of the Executive
Committee and the Council. Charges of dictatorship, he argued, were
therefore false. His fortress mentality made itself apparent when he declared that NS was surrounded by enemies on all sides, and that his movement therefore needed to have rules which protected it from intrigues and
attacks. He furthermore rejected the concept of decision-making by popular vote, since this had a demoralizing effect and opened up the possibility
for intrigues. NS' system, he continued, was based on responsibility
whereby leaders made decisions after having listened to the advice of subordinates. This principle, he declared, was in accord with the societal system which NS wished to establish.[193]

In his concluding remarks, he once again returned to the question of
disunity, issuing an appeal to have NS put behind it the split which had
lasted for three-quarters of a year.[194] *Fritt Folk*, when summing up the results of the conference, similarly tried to bring an end to the issue of party
division, declaring that NS was through with being concerned about former members who had turned against the party following the election. NS
intended instead to move forward in a positive manner.[195]

One NS member, however, Vedeler, was by no means in a positive
mood as a result of the Hamar gathering. He was just the last in a line of
prominent NS figures who had taken the public position that the party's
internal difficulties were caused by Quisling's person. He returned in a
frustrated mood to Bergen, and his discontent with Quisling continued to
be expressed openly in the columns of *Samarbeid*. The effect of this criticism was not inconsiderable, since copies of the paper were sent to a number of NS members throughout the country, including some in Oslo.[196]

Vedeler served as chairman of the board of *Samarbeid*, and he further
indicated his opposition toward Quisling by changing the paper's statutes
so that it no longer served as an NS publication, thereby eliminating the
possibility of the Central Office being able to take over control of its
operation.[197] Those who backed Quisling in both Bergen and Oslo were
shocked and angered by this turn of events, but as one of Quisling's loyal-

ists in Bergen put it, "catastrophic results" would follow if Vedeler left the party.[198] He was one of the few remaining NS officers who enjoyed respect outside the party because of his ability. NS was in such a debilitated state that it sought to retain him despite his outspokenness. Vedeler, however, remained adamant, demanding major concessions from Quisling, threatening to resign if these were not made.[199] In a final ultimatum, made at the end of August, he declared that only positive action from Quisling could save NS.[200]

The latter felt that his party was so reduced that he accorded Vedeler something that would have been unthinkable a few months earlier, a personal meeting to discuss their differences. He attempted to persuade Vedeler to remain in the party. But the *Fører* remained unwilling to grant the demands that Vedeler insisted upon. Quisling could no more make adjustments affecting the leadership of the party at this time than had been true earlier in response to any of his previous critics. Having received no satisfactory answer, Vedeler and Stinesen jointly announced on September 9 that they were resigning their positions within the Bergen NS.[201] With them departed the driving spirit which had made the NS organization in Bergen one of the most effective within the party.

Vedeler's resignation marked the end of the long-lasting effort by dissatisfied members to bring about change in the party, going back to Hjort's attempt in the fall of 1936. Quisling emerged from this series of confrontations with his control over NS more secure than ever. But as a result of his fixation to remain dominant, he completely ruined his party. It was but a shadow of the confident movement which in the previous year had looked forward to the upcoming *Storting* election. With but few exceptions, only the diehard, uncritical admirers of the *Fører* remained.

The 1936–1937 period provided Quisling with a number of setbacks, not solely political but also personal. Following the party meeting at Hamar, he went off for a much needed vacation with his immediate family in Fyresdal. Even in this isolated spot, however, the effects of the still ongoing party schism continued to reach him. In his honor, the Central Office had organized a campaign to collect funds from NS members for an appropriate gift when the *Fører* celebrated his fiftieth birthday on July 18.[202] However, the raising of money did not take place unhindered. In Bergen, Vedeler's organization retaliated for the outcome of the Hamar meeting by sabotaging the collection campaign. *Samarbeid*, for example, refused to publicize the effort because of alleged "space shortage".[203]

Quisling's financial position also remained far from problem-free. The sale of paintings in order to supplement his limited income did not occur without difficulties. At least one such painting was sold in the United States, with Quisling's younger brother, Arne, acting as intermediary. The outcome of the transaction was anything but satisfactory. Quarrels occurred with art dealers concerning sale price and commission, and the dispute ended in expensive litigation.[204]

This was not the last time Quisling became involved in legal proceedings over disputed sale of his paintings. In August 1939 he once more revealed his lack of experience in choosing art dealers on whom he could rely. He charged that between January 1936 and the summer of 1938 he had delivered some fifty paintings to a dealer in Oslo for sale on a commission basis. But the dealer, according to Quisling, had sold the paintings for far less than true value and had pocketed most of the sales sum. The outcome of the trial came as a blow for Quisling. The art dealer was jailed, but Quisling was unable to collect any compensation.[205]

As he opened his congratulatory letters and telegrams on his fiftieth birthday, he had reason to be concerned about both his political and financial position. But to all outward appearances, he did not appear to be downhearted, despite whatever moments of dark contemplation he may have had privately. Photographs from the summer of 1937 show him smiling and in good physical condition for a man of his age. The influence of his former military training and the lean years in Russia was still apparent. None of the morose corpulence that marked his features during the occupation was yet in evidence.

It by no means seems as if he viewed his position at this time from the same bleak perspective of historians who would later analyze his political career. Although he had been highly disturbed and to a considerable degree frustrated by opposition within NS after the election, his uppermost concern at all times was to retain his leadership, and he had succeeded in this single-minded effort. Because of his compulsive self-preoccupation, he lacked the ability to recognize the objective fact that the loss of persons such as Hjort, Wiesener, Vedeler, and a host of other officers and influential members was bound to damage NS irrevocably. Quisling identified National Union entirely with himself. Whatever actions he undertook were therefore beneficial for the party. All other members were isolated individuals who were of no consequence when compared to him. The fact that he remained as unchallenged party leader was therefore proof for him of NS' continued viable existence.

Only such an optimistic attitude could have prompted the national meeting at Hamar to resolve to have National Union take part in local elections in the fall.[206] Blind faith and an unwillingness to face reality lay behind this decision. The NS organization lay largely in ruins. Only one party newspaper survived outside of Oslo, and this, ironically, was Vedeler's hostile *Samarbeid*.[207] Even worse, shortly after the annual meeting, *Fritt Folk* went under once more, not having the resources to survive even as a weekly. The paper announced on July 8 that it would take a one month "summer vacation".[208] The vacation proved to be more protracted than hoped for, with *Fritt Folk* not being published again until October 9. This meant that for most of the period before the local elections NS was without a single press organ.

Fritt Folk's temporary demise was but the most dramatic omen of impending disaster in the local elections. Only in a very few election districts was it possible for local NS organizations to put up candidates. When the results of the balloting of October 18 were announced, National Union received 1,164 votes in rural districts and 258 votes in the towns.[209] Respectively, this amounted to 0.15 per cent and 0.06 per cent of the total.[210] NS participated only in six provinces and in three towns. When compared with the previous local elections in 1934, the party's number of elected representatives declined from sixty-nine to seven. In rural constituencies, it elected representatives to county councils in but two provinces, Hedmark and Oppland, three and two respectively.[211] The party's total town representation consisted of two, one in Hamar and one in Gjøvik.[212] In Oslo, NS chose not to run candidates under its own name. Instead, they were designated as "The Vocational City Council List". Of the 189,425 votes cast in the capital, the NS candidates received 792, far short of what was needed to elect even one representative.[213] This contrasted greatly with the 1934 election, when the "National Joint List" in which NS took part received more than 5,000 votes. NS total representation on the local level in 1937 was thereby reduced to insignificance, with its seven isolated representatives being confined to two eastern interior provinces, including two of the larger towns in this region.

Quisling's humiliation was only deepened by the voters' continued preference for the Labor party's reform socialism. Despite his claims to the contrary, the Nygaardsvold government was not regarded as revolutionary Marxists by the majority of the electorate. Labor's percentage of the popular vote increased from thirty-nine per cent to forty-two per cent in the rural districts and from forty-four to forty-five per cent in the towns.[214] No other single party could challenge the socialists' broad base of voter approval. In comparison, National Union, which Quisling had described as the only party capable of rescuing Norway from the "revolutionary" Labor party, had received so little support that it was reduced to being largely a nullity.

The election statistics of 1937 provided eloquent testimony concerning National Union's reduced status. It was no longer a party, but rather a political sect. Almost all able persons had left NS because of their disgust with Quisling's leadership. Gulbrand Lunde served as a major exception. His strong dedication to NS ideology bound him to Quisling, although he too had certain reservations about the party leadership, in particular the expansive role of the Central Office. At NS headquarters, the shrewd and personable Rolf Jørgen Fuglesang continued to hold sway as Quisling's obedient subordinate. But beyond drawing up memoranda and organizational charts, Fuglesang revealed little original talent. Like Quisling, he could not claim credit for any significant innovations that proved successful. Of the remaining members of the sect, the overwhelming majority were uncritical admirers of the *Fører*. He found reflected in their adulation the same image which he believed in: the strong, unyielding political prophet who alone perceived historical truth, and who was destined to lead his country because of his special talents.

This ideal corresponded badly with reality. In the fall of 1937 NS lay in ruin. Primary responsibility for this outcome rested with Quisling. National Union had in large part been formed because of the existence of a body of opinion on the right wing of the political spectrum that was discontented with prevailing conditions during the early 1930s. Because he was the sole member of NS with a national reputation, thanks to the renown he had gained as Minister of Defense, he was the only figure capable of serving as a rallying point for those who wished to form a new party.

As NS leader, however, he had many failings. He could inspire a certain amount of respect with his book learning and abstract political-philosophical theories, but he lacked the ability to carry out practical politics in a steadily changing situation. He attempted to compensate for this by imitating the successful examples of the fascist dictators on the continent, which only resulted in creating a negative reaction among most voters, including some NS members. In addition, he was neither a good speaker nor a realistic organizer. Most of his projects were never realized. He also failed to control internal disputes within his party. He tended at first to ignore them, which caused them to become exacerbated, with continued disruptions being the result, in particular when he became involved in a partisan manner.

His major fault during the time NS played an active role in politics during the 1930s was his lack of flexibility. He could not compromise, insisting always on "clear lines". This trait proved fatal following the election defeat in 1936. All viewpoints contrary to his own were regarded as signs of disloyalty and treason. In the discord which resulted from Hjort's proposals for change and Quisling's heavy-handed response, it should be emphasized that Hjort was ambitious. He recognized Quisling's failings, and wished himself to play a more dominant role in NS. On the other hand, he was unquestionably one of the party's most able men, and was recognized as such. The way in which he was handled by Quisling and the Central Office was bound to be detrimental.

After the party split had run its course, the *Fører* was left with his small band of adherents, in the main as uncritical and stubborn in their convictions as he. But as an active force in politics, he was finished. In the long run, only by actively seeking support from outside his country's borders could he hope to reach the position of prominence which he believed his special talents demanded and required.

CHAPTER VIII

The Political Sect

1937–1939

I saw clearer than others, I saw with prophetic vision what would happen. This is something which cannot be denied, I saw plainly what would happen.

> Vidkun Quisling,
> statement in court, September 6, 1945

. . . when the apostle Paul defended himself before the governor, the governor said in a loud voice: "You are mad, Paul, your great learning is driving you insane." Then answered Paul: "I am not mad, O mightiest governor, I speak true and sober words."

> Vidkun Quisling,
> statement in court, September 7, 1945

For almost three long years following his party's disintegration, Quisling and his small devoted sect strove fruitlessly to rebuild NS and to reassert its influence in politics, but to no avail. Internally, the party never recovered from the shocks it sustained in 1936–1937. Almost all able persons had abandoned NS and there was no one left capable of energizing it. Quisling as always could issue broad appeals for support, but he lacked the practical ability needed for rebuilding and reactivation. In most parts of the country, NS ceased to operate. At best, it functioned sporadically in some limited areas. Throughout Norway's widely scattered districts there remained isolated members who, although disillusioned by the bitter factional strife which had torn the party apart, still hoped it would re-emerge some day.[1] But NS lacked the means and ability to reassert itself. The remnants of the party were largely restricted to the Oslo area, where it revolved around Quisling.[2] Because of his inability to act successfully as a pragmatic leader, he concentrated most of his attention on foreign affairs. Except for its annual meetings, all held at Hamar in the remaining pre-war years, NS in large part failed to display any significant activity.[3] In late

1938 the public perception of NS as having been virtually eliminated was so pervasive that *Dagbladet* carried an epitaph for Quisling's party, declaring that there was no reason to believe that this "Nazi movement" would reassert itself in Norway.[4] The paper's author would have been clairvoyant had it not been for the German invasion.

Foreign observers shared the view that NS was finished politically. The German minister to Norway, Heinrich Sahm, bluntly offered this conclusion in his annual reports for 1937 and 1938 to the Foreign Ministry in Berlin.[5] The Minister's critical assessment did little to aid the efforts that Quisling and his sympathizers were making to establish permanent contacts in Germany during this period.

The NS *Fører's* lot during most of these three years was therefore to be largely isolated both at home and abroad. His major solace was the uncritical admiration he received from his little band of followers within what remained of NS. Some of his female admirers in particular could reach almost ecstatic heights in their adulation.[6]

He needed the consolation which such enthusiasm provided. It was nowhere to be found outside of NS' small numbers. Even persons who previously had been warm admirers now avoided contact and identification with him. Editor Aadahl in *Nationen* courteously but firmly declined to accept Quisling's articles because this would be damaging politically.[7] His political insignificance was brought home in full force when he learned that Victor Mogens, who had succeeded Lehmkuhl as foreman of the Fatherland League, had been invited to Germany to take part in Hitler's fiftieth birthday celebration in April 1939.[8] The NS leader, on the other hand, was ignored, and he had to content himself with sending a congratulatory telegram.[9]

Despite such humiliations, he remained undaunted in his conviction that sooner or later he would triumph. It was this belief, shared by his small number of uncritical loyalists, which sustained him during this bleak period.[10]

In his first public statement about the disaster his party experienced in the local elections of 1937, he admitted that NS had been weakened by the defection of former members who had continued to agitate against him from outside the party. But he insisted that the party had undergone consolidation in the months just prior to the election, and he hoped that the election results would not have an adverse effect on this process. He furthermore declared that NS had not really made a full effort in the elections, having entered candidates in only a limited number of districts.[11] But he could not disguise the fact that his party had sustained serious losses. By his own account, the most severe setback occurred in Oslo, where it could have been expected that the party would do its best, since its remaining strength was

primarily concentrated here. He simply had to admit that previous supporters had deserted, either because they feared wasting their votes on NS
or, as he put it, because they had been made victims of his opponents' un-
savory agitation and false accusations.[12] He denied, however, that there
was any truth in his opponents' claim that NS was finished.

In his general reaction to the defeats which NS suffered during 1936–
1937, it is difficult to avoid drawing a parallel between Quisling and the example provided by Lenin in the years just before the 1917 revolution.
These were the most difficult in Lenin's life. Because of Quisling's detailed
knowledge of Russian society, he was fully aware of the history of the Bolsheviks. His words therefore appear in particular to echo Lenin when he
declared in 1937 that defeat simply served the purpose of creating more
clarity and had the effect of welding together a truly battle-ready and experienced party core. Such a development, he maintained, did not signify
defeat, but preparation for victory.[13]

Writing privately, General Secretary Fuglesang provided a more candid
assessment of the local election results, admitting that it would possibly
have been wiser if NS had not taken part.[14] Like Quisling, he conceded
that the worst setback had been in Oslo, where the voters had displayed no
confidence in NS. He attributed this first and foremost to the incidents involving Hjort and Wiesener.[15] However, the General Secretary was not
willing to acknowledge that NS' humiliation had been due merely to internal disunity. He alleged that analogous developments had occurred elsewhere in Europe, where other "national movements" had sustained election defeats.[16]

In presenting this interpretation, he merely repeated Quisling's viewpoint, which asserted darkly that certain "mighty forces" were at work,
against which NS could not hope to compete.[17] Because of his fascination
with alleged plots and conspiracies, Quisling hinted rather broadly that
prevailing political and economic developments in Europe were being manipulated by an international Jewish capitalist conspiracy.

Not unexpectedly, considering his position, Fuglesang, while admitting
that conditions were definitely not in NS' favor, insisted that the party's
main effort should be devoted toward building up its organization so that
it would be ready to take advantage of any change in the political situation.
At the same time, NS should strive as much as possible to present the public with what he called impartial information concerning events both
abroad and at home.[18] On paper his goals seemed pragmatic, but like his
leader, he provided no clue as to how they could be achieved. Because of
NS' shrunken condition, there was no chance for their realization.

By the end of the year even the most optimistic within NS could no
longer avoid recognizing the decline which the party had experienced. In
his combined Christmas and New Year's greeting to the faithful, Quisling's mood was bleak, but still as dogged and unyielding as always, if in a

fatalistic manner. He declared 1937 to have been the most difficult year in the movement's history. NS had sustained election defeat, desertions in the ranks, and economic difficulties. But none of this mattered, he insisted. What counted was the party's shining and steely determination to gain victory or go under.[19]

His sense of mission remained intact. He continued to apply himself toward the distant objective of gaining political prominence with the same stubborn determination that he had revealed as a youth in quest of academic achievement. But whereas the educational system had provided him with clear guidelines, in politics the situation was without precedent. Lacking instinct and insight, he could only continue on his isolated course.

As the basis for his ongoing quest, he had no other alternative within Norway than to try to make use of what remained of his party. The condition of NS hardly served as a source of inspiration. Economically it was in a state of bankruptcy. Its financial manager in 1937 was John Thronsen, a 24-year-old who had previously been dismissed from the NS office in Akershus by Hjort because of alleged incompetence.[20] Thronsen owed his position to his unquestioned loyalty to Quisling and his close ties with Fuglesang. After the war, Thronsen described NS' fiscal condition in 1937 with one word: "bad."[21] The party obtained its limited income almost entirely from contributions. Hardly any dues were collected.[22] Its poor financial state was made even more precarious because of the large debt which it had accumulated, in particular because of expenses incurred during the 1936 election campaign.

In order to deal with these difficulties, a special finance committee was established. In particular, it was directed to concentrate on finding ways to reduce the party's debts. Its task was formidable. One approach it took was to solicit funds through contributions, but many NS members who were asked to meet with the committee in the summer of 1937 simply refused to show up.[23] This was but one indication of the effect of the strife which was still taking place within the party at this time. Even the usually optimistic Fuglesang had to admit that the work of raising money was going a little slowly.[24] The finance committee was able to secure pledges totalling only ca. 200 *kroner* a month.[25] Considering the fact that Fuglesang's monthly salary alone cost the party 600 *kroner*, the amount raised could hardly be described as a success. After the local government elections, Fuglesang announced that he hoped to rid NS of its debt by offering the party's general creditors only ten per cent of their outstanding claims, while NS creditors were asked to grant their party a two year moratorium for the payment of debts.[26]

Fuglesang was no more successful in reducing the debt in this manner than the party had previously been in raising funds. The finance committee as a result took drastic steps, deciding that the only way out of the economic morass was to economize. The party's fortunes actually could be measured by the luxuriousness of its central headquarters. It was now time for the Central Office to move again, this time to smaller and more Spartan quarters on the fourth floor of Klingenberggaten 5. Simultaneously, the Central Office's budget was cut drastically. Thronsen and Fuglesang were thereupon forced to find additional sources of income. The two succeeded in latching on to jobs for a time as traveling salesmen for a candy company. This at least allowed them to contact local NS groups while on the road, and in this manner they made their contribution toward trying to keep the party alive at the grassroots level.[27]

A dispute soon arose, however, over whether Fuglesang was entitled to travel expenses, plus his regular salary as NS General Secretary, while he was on the road as a candy agent. Dora Bull, a major force on the finance committee, who believed in maintaining the lowest expenditures possible, and who was a confidante of Herman Harris Aall, came out in open opposition to Fuglesang. She criticized the Central Office in particular for its financial transactions, maintaining that they were not entirely aboveboard. Quisling decided that Fuglesang should have his travel money, but the latter was forced to accept the finance committee's budget changes, which implicitly meant that Dora Bull's criticism was valid. Revenue collected for the party's national meeting was removed from the Central Office's budget, money intended for payment of the party's debt similarly could not be included in the Office's budget, and Fuglesang's previous practice of collecting funds for a stated goal and then using the money for another purpose was no longer permitted.[28] Furthermore, although he resisted fiercely, the General Secretary had his salary reduced.[29]

By the end of 1938 National Union operated on a bare bones budget, a budget which Thronsen was able to manage to Dora Bull's satisfaction.[30] This allowed the party headquarters to continue to function, but at an absolute minimum. There was only enough cash on hand to pay for the small number of staff members who aided Quisling. The local organizations received no money and had to fend for themselves.[31] With such an absence of funding, it was hardly surprising that most local NS groups ceased to operate.

The reduced state of the NS organization permitted Quisling little opportunity to exert any political influence through the party. The same was true of the NS press in most of the period before the coming of the Germans. *Fritt Folk*, the only paper to survive the schism, suffered a major reduction in its subscribers. When it ceased to come out as a daily in October 1936, it had a total of some 2500 regular subscribers, not a particularly large number, since *Fritt Folk* was officially National Union's national spokesman.[32] This relatively low number was offset in part, however, by the regional NS newspapers in 1936, which allowed the party a better potential for spreading its message. But as a result of the internal strife during 1937, the number of subscribers declined drastically during the interval before *Fritt Folk* came out again as a weekly, beginning in mid February. Its difficulties were not improved by a threat from the Labor party to boycott all businesses which advertised in *Fritt Folk*.[33] By the time it once more went under, in July 1937, its subscribers had declined to 890.[34]

This proved to be the last time that the paper had to suspend publication until the end of World War II. But when it re-emerged in October 1937, *Fritt Folk* was reduced to the absolute minimum. Appearing once a week, on Saturday, it contained but four pages.[35] No attempt was made to maintain a separate editorial staff. Its operation was controlled by Fuglesang's Central Office. All costs were kept at the lowest level possible. Haldis Neegaard Østbye, who headed the NS Propaganda Office at party headquarters, served also as unpaid editor for the next three years. Having married into a leading family in the skiing industry, she was independently wealthy and could offer her services without compensation. The only expenses that *Fritt Folk* incurred were for the cost of printing the paper and postage for mailing issues to subscribers.[36] NS claimed that some 6000 copies were printed in each issue.[37] This number appears to have been exaggerated, even though *Fritt Folk* was NS' sole paper during this time. Evidence seems to show that a considerable portion of each edition did not go to paid subscribers, but was simply handed out as political propaganda by party members or distributed free of charge to what remained of the local organizations.[38]

With *Fritt Folk* being the only press organ that NS still retained, Quisling naturally was quite preoccupied with the paper.[39] It now served as the sole publication in which he could be guaranteed access to the public. As a result, each edition usually included an article by the *Fører*. The paper's importance for him was augmented by the fact that with the party organization largely in a shambles, *Fritt Folk* was the sole means by which he could maintain contact with scattered members and sympathizers. He explicitly recognized this, stating that with conditions being what they were, *Fritt Folk* was the most important, the cheapest, and the most suitable propaganda means that NS controlled.[40]

The value he attached to the paper revealed itself in another interesting fashion. Hjort's challenge to his authority remained a fixation in Quisling's mind. That Hjort at one time had controlled *Fritt Folk* was a fact that Quisling recalled vividly. Although Hjort had not attempted to use the paper in his quarrel with Quisling, the latter remembered the opposition he had encountered from Hjort's sympathizers at the last general assembly meeting of *NS Presse A/S* in the spring of 1937. He was therefore determined that no potential rival or opposition group should gain control of the paper. This prompted him to draw up a secret contract with John Thronsen, who as NS financial manager within the Central Office also served as publisher of *Fritt Folk*.[41] According to the terms of the agreement, Quisling could make any changes in the paper that he might want to carry out. Furthermore, after having received a three months' notice, Thronsen was obligated to resign as publisher and to leave operation of the paper in Quisling's hands. Only two copies of the contract were made, one for each of the signatories.[42]

Although *Fritt Folk* escaped the trauma of folding up for a third time, it was a constant struggle simply to keep the paper functioning. It was sustained by its limited number of subscribers, the contributions NS was able to scrape up from its small membership, plus a few secret payments made by sympathizers outside the party. Funds for operating the paper were hard to come by, and Quisling complained publicly about the lack of support which *Fritt Folk* received. With reference to the Labor party's daily, *Arbeiderbladet*, he declared that future school children would read with surprise that the agents of the Comintern had an extravagant newspaper in Oslo in 1937, while the "Norwegian national forces" struggled with a four-page news sheet which sometimes came out and sometimes did not.[43] He criticized in particular business interests who advertised in *Arbeiderbladet*, while *Fritt Folk* was practically boycotted. To place advertisements in the Labor daily for business reasons, he maintained, was shortsighted because the Labor party would soon eliminate all freedom. In contrast, he alleged it was not only good business but also "insurance" to advertise in a "national" newspaper such as *Fritt Folk*.[44]

Appeals for advertisers and new subscribers brought little response. The NS paper continued to limp along with its small format, volunteer staff, and limited readership. Only by tapping financial sources outside of the country could it hope to grow in size. In the end, this proved to be the solution to its difficulties.

During the desperate period from 1937 to early 1940, the most serious problem that Quisling faced was the almost total absence of a party structure which could lend support to what he advocated. On paper the NS organization that he had constructed continued to exist, but to an overwhelming degree it no longer functioned.

This was true in particular on the local level. In large part, only in the major towns did NS demonstrate any activity, and even here it was sporadic. This was true even in such former strongholds as Bergen and Stavanger. In late 1937 Quisling received a critical letter from Bergen. The new regional *fører* on the west coast who had succeeded Vedeler, maintained the writer, had demonstrated remarkably little activity. No one knew who had been appointed to fill party positions in Bergen, since no conference of party officers had been called. In addition, there had not been any general meeting of party members since early May. The writer complained that it was now late November, making it impossible to schedule a meeting until after the New Year.[45] Gulbrand Lunde reported from Stavanger in the following year that the NS organization in the city was still alive, but that it carried out little activity. A few membership meetings had been held, but that was all.[46]

On the national level, the party's central organization did not engage in a great deal more activity. Most of what did occur took place in connection with *Fritt Folk*. Ever since Hjort's resignation, the *Hird* had lacked central leadership, and it consisted solely of scattered units in some towns.[47] Worse was the fate of the NS Unemployed Association, which had been renamed the NS Workers' Association. The change of name did not provide it with any greater success. Its leader, Hilmar Knutsen, resigned early in 1938.[48] By this time the group had ceased operation. Other NS formations such as the Youth Organization and the Women's Organization retained their old leaders, but they were largely paper organizations, with only sporadic activity being registered.[49]

Continuing true to form, Quisling was unable to come up with any plans to energize the moribund organization. He could only make appeals. At an NS Council meeting in February 1939 he stated the obvious fact that the party organization was not functioning as it should. It was necessary, he declared, to get more persons involved in NS activity. As he put it, the main task now was to activate the movement and to instill more fanaticism, resolve, and sacrifice into its work. Once this had been accomplished, then the party would soon obtain the financial resources it needed.[50] But he failed to point out the means to accomplish this most needed objective.

Rather than presenting specific proposals as to how NS could be strengthened, Quisling's organizational effort was largely restricted to shifting about the meager personnel resources that he still retained, plus indulging in theoretical speculation as to how society would be restructured once NS came to power. Two party institutions that continued to exist were the Executive Committee and the NS Council. Both met fairly regularly during the period from 1937 to 1940, but accomplished nothing of significance. Since they were composed entirely of Quisling loyalists, and since he completely dominated the selection process by which members were chosen, it was inevitable that all initiative was concentrated in his hands concerning what these two bodies could propose. Since he had no plans himself for bringing NS to life, it was little wonder that the Executive Committee and the Council could not on their own come up with any novel approaches regarding tactics and strategy. All that Quisling was capable of doing was to decide who would serve on the two bodies, and this did not signify anything new, since those whom he appointed were bound to be uncritical admirers.

Johan Throne Holst.
Photograph: Norwegian News Agency.

Rolf Thommessen.
Photograph: Norwegian News Agency.

Walter Fürst.
Photograph: University of Oslo Library.

Johan B. Hjort.
Photograph: National Archives of Norway.

Quisling speaking at National Union's second national rally, held at Stiklestad on St. Olaf's day (29 July) 1934. Photograph: National Archives of Norway.

Members of National Union marching to the national rally at Stiklestad.
Photograph: National Archives of Norway.

From the national rally at Stiklestad. Kjeld Stub standing between Vidkun and Maria.
Photograph: National Archives of Norway.

On a propaganda tour with the National Union bus, here at Klepp south of Stavanger in 1935. Quisling is standing at the rostrum. Photograph: National Archives of Norway.

Vidkun and Maria on an excursion to Fyresdal, accompanied by members of the Hird *in Telemark, 1936. Photograph: National Archives of Norway.*

At Gulbrand Lunde's home in Stavanger. From the left Maria, Petter Østbye, Marie Lunde, Halldis Neegård Østbye, Gulbrand Lunde and Quisling. Photograph: National Archives of Norway.

Quisling and his wife at the national rally at Hamar in 1938. Photograph: University of Oslo Library.

Victor Mogens. Photograph: University of Oslo Library.

Hans Wilhelm Scheidt. Photograph: Dagbladet *(newspaper).*

Herman Harris Aall. Photograph: Norwegian News Agency.

Albert Viljam Hagelin. Photograph: Norwegian News Agency.

The changes he instituted at a meeting of the Council on February 5, 1939, were therefore largely cosmetic in nature, although the composition of the Executive Committee and the Council was changed notably in character. Whereas the Council previously had been mainly restricted to the regional leaders, plus the membership of the smaller Executive Committee, Quisling now expanded the Council to include twenty-six additional party members. The newcomers were persons whom he described as having shown their worth in the work they carried out for NS.[51] In other words, they were devoted admirers who had continued to exert themselves for him. In addition, the Executive Committee received four new members, being expanded to a total of fourteen. Included among these for the first time were two female members. Quisling had long been under pressure by some of the more active women within NS to provide them with representation.[52] To their annoyance, he procrastinated considerably.[53] He was no more enthusiastic in favor of women's emancipation than most right-wing ideologues, but in the end he had to surrender, in particular because he recognized that NS would be worse off without the services of Mrs. Østbye, Dora Bull, and others.

By carrying out this expansion, he did provide recognition for the most active of his small band of loyalists. He no doubt hoped that by taking such a step, they might be energized even more. But in the type of party which he dominated as the possessor of all authority, it was necessary for the *Fører* to lead the way. He, however, had shown himself incapable of devising strategy for internal politics, and his suspicious nature prevented able subordinates who could act independently from being members of NS. At the time he expanded the Executive Committee, one of the new appointees, Birger Meidell, assumed the place of Pastor Kjeld Stub. Stub resigned his post ostensibly because of health reasons.[54] His departure marked the breaking of one of Quisling's few remaining links to political respectability, going back to the early years of NS' existence.

The leader's inability to revitalize his party was further emphasized by his frequent tendency to escape the unpleasant reality of NS' reduced circumstances by engaging in abstract planning about the future. From the time of his first years in politics, he had consistently emphasized his corporate ideas. Even in the late 1930s, when NS should have been concentrating on immediate plans, a considerable amount of time was devoted to his ideal corporate state. When arrangements were made for the annual party meeting in 1938, held in July, the main topic for discussion which the organizers concerned themselves with was the new form of government which NS intended to introduce. To no one's surprise, this proved to be the *Fører's* old plan for a National Assembly (*Riksting*), composed of two chambers, a Cultural Council (*Kulturting*) and an Economic Council (*Næringsting*).[55]

Another example of his concern with form rather than substance also came to light in July 1938. In his abstract fantasy world, where he saw NS playing a leading role not only in Norway but in Europe as a whole, he identified his party directly with fascist groups elsewhere on the continent. According to the terminology he employed, NS was part of these related "national movements". In order to institutionalize this identity, he added a subtitle to the party name. As of July 28, its official title became National Union (NS): The National Farm and Labor party.[56] As the name change made clear, he wished not only to show that NS was a "national" party in an international context, but that it directed its appeal to the masses, to the workers and farmers. He believed that the change would strengthen NS' position. But beyond the small amount of personal satisfaction that he received from having thought up this move, it had no significance. The subtitle was never referred to in ordinary usage.

From the fall of 1937 onwards, Quisling was not bothered by the problem that had previously given him the greatest difficulty, namely opposition to his leadership which divided the party and brought about loss in membership. Some internal quarrels did occur, but they were minor in character and could in no way be compared with the dissension of 1936–37.

A certain difference of opinion developed in 1938 between the NS leader and his regional *fører* in Buskerud province, Trygve Tellefsen, who at the time of Hjort's break had been one of Quisling's most outspoken defenders. Quisling and the Central Office did not particularly care for the way in which Tellefsen independently handled a personal dispute within his regional organization without paying heed to party headquarters. Furthermore, he made certain innovative proposals for NS's future organization after the local elections in 1937. Specifically, he suggested that a propaganda council be established to coordinate all informational activity nationally. Such a proposal immediately brings to mind one of the changes Hjort had brought up in 1936. Quisling's reaction to Tellefsen's advice was not enthusiastic.[57] The *Fører* remained suspicious of any ideas that did not originate with him or his trusted underlings in Fuglesang's office. Tellefsen's party career certainly was not strengthened by this incident. He retained his post as regional *fører* for the time being, but during the war he had to be content with a much less prestigious office on the *krets* level.[58]

Another controversy which was much more open and direct involved Quisling and S. L. Lilleide, the former regional *fører* in Oppland province. He too had supported Quisling in the dispute with Hjort, but by late 1938 he had reached a different conclusion: that it was the *Fører* who prevented NS from having any possibility of success in politics.[59] Not very subtly, Lilleide insisted that Quisling should come to terms with his foes who had left NS. Harsh words were exchanged between the two at NS headquarters in Klingenberggaten 5. Lilleide later offered reconciliation, but only if Quisling agreed to call on all former members to resume their old posts in the party. Furthermore, Lilleide recommended the need to change the party bylaws so that the leader's appointment and removal were in the hands of a new party council.[60] Even the most diplomatic individual would not have succeeded in persuading the *Fører* to abandon his supreme authority over NS, and Lilleide was far from diplomatic. His frustration with Quisling appears to have been heightened by his aversion to Fuglesang and the Central Office.[61]

His break had no serious repercussions. By the time Lilleide left, those who felt the same as he were already outside of NS. Some internal quarrels continued to take place, but they involved personal antagonisms and did not include any challenge to Quisling's control. Those who became involved in such quarrels invariably insisted that their sole motivation was to protect NS' interests, while their enemies were described as being injurious to the party.[62] In reality, however, these incidents generally reflected efforts by persons in Quisling's small band to gain greater influence with the leadership at the expense of their rivals. In such disputes, Fuglesang was frequently involved. There existed a certain amount of jealousy within the reduced party concerning his influence with the *Fører*, thanks to the General Secretary's close proximity to Quisling.[63] The latter, however, maintained his protective influence over Fuglesang, who continued to serve as his protégé.[64]

Within the small sect of true believers, there was no possibility of any real challenge being made to the *Fører*'s position. However, even among these individuals a certain amount of resignation set in as the years went by and as NS' insignificance continued to deepen, indicating awareness that there was little chance for recovery, at least not in the immediate future. An indication of this was provided by a tendency among some loyalists to look upon the *Fører*'s past enemies in right-wing politics with a certain amount of tolerance, even approval. For example, Konrad Sundlo, the army commandant at Narvik and the NS regional *fører* in Nordland, who addressed Quisling in almost idolatrous terms, nevertheless admitted that he allowed persons who had previously been Quisling's bitter foes to have access to his home. Furthermore, Sundlo advised Quisling not to quarrel with the Fatherland League, Hjort, Wiesener, and Jacobsen. Instead, Sundlo urged that they be encouraged to work actively in spreading "national" information. As justification for this rather heretical viewpoint, he predicted that the leadership of right-wing "national" forces in Norway would sooner or later be assumed by National Union and its brilliant leader.[65]

Similarly, Chr. Jøranli in Oppland continued to maintain ties with Lilleide even following the latter's quarrel with Quisling and resignation from NS. Jøranli emotionally and angrily rebutted allegations by his rivals in

Oppland, who used his association with Lilleide as a means of seeking his removal as regional *fører*. Despite his exposed position, Jøranli insisted that Lilleide was an asset who could be won back to NS.[66] By assuming such a diehard stance in defense of someone who had openly squabbled with Quisling, Jøranli certainly did not find favor with the *Fører*. Instead, one of Jøranli's main opponents, Willy Klevenberg, gained the leadership's approval. Klevenberg, a young businessman from Gjøvik, was appointed to the NS Council by Quisling in February 1939. During the war, Klevenberg advanced to the position of being head of the party's Press and Propaganda Division under General Secretary Fuglesang.[67]

Although he had to pay attention to the concerns of party members from time to time, in the main Quisling preoccupied himself with other questions which interested him more. In his role as a political prophet, he regularly issued policy statements of an international character. Although the size of his readership was hardly encouraging, he made full use of *Fritt Folk*'s columns. The themes he dealt with were serious enough, however, at a time when increasing tensions and conflicts steadily brought Europe closer to the holocaust of World War II.

To a considerable extent, his preoccupation with foreign affairs can also be considered a form of escapism, allowing him to concern himself with weightier matters than the daily problems and trivia involving his little sect, whose very existence was in question. However, this was not entirely an escape from reality. He always exhibited a strong tendency toward constructing grandiose international programs, a characteristic which was simply heightened at a time when he could no longer exert any influence on internal political developments.

When his party was nearing the height of its divisive split in early 1937, he again produced another of his broad schemes calling for Nordic cooperation. Despite the fact that his efforts in this direction time after time had resulted in nothing, he continued undauntedly to present his prophetic visions of an ideal world order. But there may have been a slight element of sought-after pragmatism in his timing in 1937, since his proposal could have been made for the purpose of distracting NS members from the ever-accelerating division within their ranks. If this was part of his reasoning, it failed completely to realize its intended goal.

Although his earlier call for the creation of a Nordic World Union in June 1936 had amounted to nothing more than a few perfunctory notices in *Fritt Folk*, he did not change his approach. In the first part of March he announced the formation of a similar organization, which he called the Greater Nordic Peace Union (*Stornordisk Fredssamband*). While he declared that this association had been created as early as January 14, there is no record of its existence prior to its formal announcement in the March 11 issue of *Fritt Folk*. As before, the goal of this new group was to bring about union and cooperation among the "Nordic" countries. Its program called for cultural, economic, and political cooperation among Nordic peoples the world over. It would also work to secure the future of the Nordic race. In his most concrete proposal, Quisling declared that the Peace Union would create a greater Nordic political union consisting of the Scandinavian states, Great Britain, and Germany. Eventually this would be expanded into a universal peace system, first in Europe and then the world over, which would secure righteous peace in the world and work for the positive advance of world civilization. This was fully in accord with his constant visionary ideal of a heaven on earth. He also had a poetic slogan on hand for his new peace organization: "From the north, peace on earth!", which rhymed slightly better in Norwegian, "*I fra Norden, fred på Jorden!*"[68]

On a more practical level, he did provide arguments intended to show Norwegians why it was to their advantage to promote peace, in particular between Britain and Germany. If a war should break out, he declared, Norway would inevitably become a battlefield because of the collision of British, German, and Russian interests. The country's peace could only be secured on the basis of cooperation between kindred countries around the North Sea who were also Norway's greatest trading partners. His recurrent anti-Communism was also evident. A greater Nordic association would, he said, serve as a means of preventing the planned Soviet advance toward the Atlantic.[69]

The ideas that he expressed when seeking to launch the Greater Nordic Peace Union did reflect his thinking at the time, and were not primarily tactical in nature, although his emphasis on peace was certainly intended to create a favorable impression on popular opinion. His main fear remained the Soviet Union. He definitely opposed the possibility of a war between Germany and England, which might give the Russians their opportunity to expand unhindered. But although he strove to present the appearance of serving as an objective mediator between the Germans and British, there was no question whom he would side with in the eventuality of war, as upcoming events in 1939 would evince clearly.

In seeking to promote the Greater Nordic Peace Union, he tried to set it up as a front organization, much in the same way that NS had attempted to exploit the Greenland issue before the 1936 election. He argued that peace and cooperation between Scandinavians, Germans, Englishmen, and the Dutch was an obvious goal for all Norwegians, and this overall objective should therefore not be divisive. He declared that the Peace Union was completely independent of National Union, being open to everyone. In order to make the organization even more attractive, considering the hard economic climate of the 1930s, membership was free. All that a person had to do was to sign up.[70]

Despite repeated advertisements in *Fritt Folk*, very few chose to join. Although he had no aversion to greatly inflating statistics to his advantage, Quisling at this time did not even hint that he was enjoying success in enrolling members in the Peace Union. Despite the failure, he persevered. With his party falling apart over the controversy surrounding his leadership, he continued his effort to place himself at the head of an international organization of right-wing movements that were sympathetic to Nazi Germany. In this endeavor, he actively sought to propagate his views abroad. His earlier call for a Nordic World Union was now translated into both German and English in the form of an article. In Germany the Nazis did not consider him important enough to give his views broad coverage, and only printed excerpts.[71] In England he experienced slightly better success. His article, minus a considerable amount of nationalistic Norwegian material, was published early in 1937 by a small journal with National Socialist sympathies, the *British Union Quarterly*.[72] However, the nationalistic outlook of small pro-fascist groups in northern Europe frequently hindered the possibility of any real cooperation taking place between them, as Quisling had earlier experienced with Fritz Clausen in Denmark. The editor of the *British Union Quarterly* did not endorse Quisling's view completely, adding the reservation: "National Socialist policy differs according to national needs and character . . ."[73]

The article not only repeated his call for cooperation between the "Nordic" countries and warning against conflict between Germany and England, but also contained the essence of his political philosophy in compact form. His belief in Nordic racism, with its accompanying anti-Semitism, remained undiminished. The "Nordic Principle", he said, rested on Nordic traditions, thought, and cooperation, which stood in contrast to the hatred, envy, and class warfare of "Jewish liberalism and Marxism". He identified his "Nordic Principle" with the "Divine", while Jewish controlled liberalism and Marxism were "diabolical".[74] If only the Nordic racial principle were recognized and followed, he insisted, then it would be possible to advance to a higher stage of civilization: "As in times past, it must be the mission of our great family of peoples to do away with an obsolete world and create a new world which can place the whole human family on the upward grade".[75]

Except for the publication of this article, the political prophet's attempt to create Nordic cooperation received no response from abroad. There was no reason why people outside of Norway should react seriously to political manifestos issued by an unknown figure, the head of an insignificant party, in one of the small Scandinavian states. But Quisling was never realistic about his status and never considered giving up his mission to play a key role in uniting the "national" forces in "Nordic" Europe. The ongoing strife within NS during the spring and summer of 1937, plus preoccupation with the local elections in the fall, prevented him from making any additional effort during this year. However, by early 1938 yet another venture was planned on behalf of Nordic unity.

This involved the issuance of a new publication that Quisling apparently intended to utilize as the organ for his international movement. Entitled *Greater Nordic Union (Stornordisk Samband)*, it appeared in the form of a small journal. Originally it had been projected to appear in February, but it did not see the light of day until July.[76] Quisling discreetly stayed in the background, perhaps in order to give the impression that his attempt to form an international movement was not merely a solo venture. Officially, *Greater Nordic Union*'s co-editors were two of his young protégés, Fuglesang and Thronsen. But it was Quisling's ideas that served as editorial policy. As the journal's official program, Fuglesang and Thronsen merely reprinted the Norwegian version of Quisling's Nordic World Union proclamation from June 1936. Its rather ambitious goal, however, was to provide up-to-date commentary on the key issues of the times within culture, politics, society, and economics.[77]

With the meager resources and lack of support which NS had at its disposal, the publication had no hope of realizing its exaggerated goal. Although it declared itself open to contributions by persons outside of NS, the articles which appeared in its pages were invariably written by the most prominent among Quisling's coterie of followers. Herman Harris Aall, Konrad Sundlo, Jens Rolfsen, Fuglesang, Haldis Neegaard Østbye, Tormod Hustad, and Christian Knudsen all placed their pens at the disposal of the journal in the attempt to keep it going. Only in one issue, devoted almost entirely to the Spanish Civil War, did *Greater Nordic Union* succeed in publishing an article written by an important foreign source. The author was General J. F. C. Fuller, the noted British military historian. His article was pro-Nationalist and anti-Republican, containing warm praise for Franco's successes.[78] Exactly how *Greater Nordic Union* managed to solicit this article is unclear. Quisling was seeking to establish contact with Fuller at this time, apparently through a female friend from his school days who resided in England.[79] But if the article was the result of this endeavor, there is no evidence to suggest that it led to anything more.

The issue containing Fuller's article proved to be the final number of *Greater Nordic Union*. As but another indication of the completely impractical planning that occurred under Quisling, the journal had originally been scheduled to issue ten numbers a year. It appeared only four times, three issues in 1938 and one in 1939. It served merely as another addition to the number of unsuccessful ventures associated with Quisling's politics.

With his broadly conceived but improbable schemes for creating large multi-national organizations leading nowhere, the only forum in which he could express himself remained confined almost exclusively to the limited space available in *Fritt Folk*. In commenting on Norwegian foreign policy, he continued to pay special attention to the country's membership in the League of Nations. With Germany's withdrawal from the League in 1933 and the Soviet Union's admission in the following year, it is not difficult to understand the attitude he maintained toward the League. He persevered in declaring that the League was an instrument of the international conspiracy against Germany, with communism being a driving force. Norway, he warned, had become part of this international coalition, and the country was in danger of being drawn into war as a result of its commitment.

In an attempt to camouflage this obvious pro-German bias, he tried to use the ideal of neutrality in his favor, knowing that it enjoyed the approval of the overwhelming majority of the people. For once gaining access to the columns of *Tidens Tegn*, he argued that Norway could only be truly neutral if it withdrew from the League.[80] Although Norway by 1937, when he wrote these words, was in the process of repudiating the League's failed policy of trying to employ sanctions against aggressors, adopting instead a policy of strict neutrality, he insisted stubbornly that neutrality was impossible as long as Norway continued to belong to the international body. The only conditions under which he could accept Norwegian membership in the League were if Germany decided to re-enter, with the Soviet Union at the same time being expelled.[81]

In addition to seeking to use neutrality in his favor, he similarly tried to present himself as the exponent of peace. The key to preventing war in Europe, he maintained, lay in bringing about reconciliation between England and Germany. But such appeasement meant, not unexpectedly, that it should occur entirely on Germany's terms. He voiced approval for the *Anschluss* between Germany and Austria. He further declared that the treaties of Versailles and St. Germain had to be abrogated and that Germany be granted colonies. Such a standpoint was simply an echo of Hitler's policy.[82]

In the move to bring about better relations between Germany and England, he naturally emphasized the part that the Scandinavian countries would play in this effort, first and foremost Norway. Exactly why Norway should be the most prominent among the Scandinavian countries, he failed to explain, but the place that he imagined for himself in this activity needs hardly be mentioned. The Scandinavian countries, he insisted, were ideally suited because of their geographical location and historical tradition to serve as intermediaries between their British and German "cousins".[83]

This plan, which he announced immediately following the German seizure of Austria, was not new. The emphasis on peace and reconciliation between Germany and England, the two great "Nordic" military powers, was merely the continuation of his scheme for a Greater Nordic Peace Union. But in urging the creation of an international Nordic association, a certain note of caution crept into his calculations, reflecting his nationalism. He insisted that his peace union would only operate within a framework which allowed each nation freedom of choice, thereby guaranteeing little Norway full equality with its Nordic partners, in particular with the Germans and British.[84]

In his constant emphasis on the position that Norway should occupy in international affairs, which was completely out of proportion to its real status, he was in reality elevating the Norwegians to being a twentieth-century chosen people. But they were special only because he was destined to be their leader. The Norwegians, he warned, should now carry out their country's historical mission. In referring to this sense of mission, he again revealed the messianic vision for the future which he had first propounded in his 1930 pamphlet – a vision of a heaven on earth, with him serving as its harbinger. While he did not state this in detail in his newspaper articles, nevertheless the underlying theme was there. He proclaimed that if the Norwegian people were to remain free and independent in the ongoing world struggle, and if they were to develop a Norwegian and Nordic, and possibly universal, principle as their mission in the cause of world solidarity, then they had to join together in carrying out such a unified national effort. Their hour of fate was at hand. They needed to carry out their mission on behalf of peace and "our Nordic-inspired European civilization". In the meantime, he warned of the overhanging risk of being drawn into war for the sake of Czechoslovakia, international finance capitalism, Marxism, and the Jews.[85]

Only someone who regarded himself as a political prophet could write in such terms. He made no attempt to disguise the call that he felt, being convinced that only he could save the country. He maintained that the only way Norway could carry out the mission which he had drawn up for its people would be if they rid themselves of the party politicians who were guilty of deception and betrayal, and who through their popular front politics and support for the League were leading the country into war and disaster.[86]

In presenting himself as the one leader capable of rescuing the country, he insisted that the people had but two choices: either communism or National Union.[87] But National Union, in his interpretation, was not simply an unimportant little sect. Instead, he identified it as but a part of the seemingly victorious forces of fascism which were sweeping over Europe. Writing in the spring of 1938, he declared that "nationalist" movements were on the offensive everywhere in the world. He especially received inspiration from Spain, where the Nationalists were gaining the upper hand in the Civil War. Ignoring the insignificance of his party, it was much easier for the visionary to identify with Franco's legions and to infer that just as the Nationalists were gaining victory in Spain, so too "nationalism" (read NS) would eventually triumph in Norway. The parallel which he drew was obvious, pointing out that the Nationalists had not elected a single representative to parliament in 1936, while now they were the victorious party in Spain with between two and three million members. The bourgeois parties, on the other hand, had disappeared, and the popular front government was in its death throes.[88]

It is easy to see how he could persuade himself that the parallel applied to Norway as well. Elsewhere too, he pointed out, nationalism was advancing while the capitalist and Marxist states were either undergoing disintegration or being taken over by "nationalist movements". Such an inevitable process, he argued, could not be stopped at the borders of Scandinavia. In Norway the "party politicians" had already sealed their fate by their foreign policy toward Spain, having "bet on the wrong horse" in the Civil War.[89]

His view was vastly exaggerated. The Labor government in reality had maintained a policy of official neutrality. Popular opinion on the whole tended to be sympathetic to the Republicans, although Franco's forces enjoyed some support among the *borgerlige*. But Quisling did not view the Spanish Civil War as a specific incident. Only he had known that the events in Spain were merely part of a global political process in which he and National Union were destined to play a prominent part. Nationalism, he declared, "is the twentieth century's dominant political idea, and it is bound to gain victory".[90]

Through his foreign policy statements it was transparently easy to discern that more than ever Quisling sided with the non-democratic, nationalistic totalitarian forces in Europe, first and foremost Nazi Germany. Nevertheless, because he had to function within a democratic society, he attempted to camouflage this commitment to some extent by combining his profascist position with popular goals such as the maintenance of peace and neutrality. But in doing so, he consistently tried to manipulate these ideals in a pro-German manner. For example, *Fritt Folk* in the fall of 1938 deplored the anti-German viewpoint expressed in *borgerlige* and socialist newspapers alike at the height of the Czechoslovak crisis. This condemnation of Germany, the NS paper declared, took place because the world press was owned and dominated by the Jews. With few exceptions, the paper maintained that the same was true in Norway. This allegedly had the effect of leading popular opinion astray and increasing the risk of war "for our disarmed and defenseless country".[91] Similarly, in a later article *Fritt Folk* quoted a warning from the Nazi *Völkische Beobachter*, which threatened neutral states that permitted anti-German propaganda with being regarded as enemies. *Fritt Folk* concluded that the Norwegian people would pay the price for "the Marxist government's senseless foreign policy and the party politicians' irresponsible gamble with the country's interests".[92] But the demand he issued through *Fritt Folk* that no anti-German sentiment should be allowed to appear in the press simply provided renewed confirmation of his anti-democratic convictions. The idea of restricting journalistic commentary was anathema to the overwhelming majority of Norwegians of all political persuasions.

On issue after issue leading up to the Second World War, he continued to provide support for Germany, while at the same time maintaining that he favored peace and neutrality. When the Czechoslovak crisis appeared to bring Europe to the brink of war, he insisted that the only solution to the so-called Czech problem was to dismember the country, with Bohemia and Moravia coming under Germany, while Slovakia should go to either Hungary or Germany. As for Ruthenia, he declared it should become part of an independent Ukraine, to be created along with additional territory drawn from Poland, Rumania, and the U.S.S.R.[93] How an independent Ukraine could come into being without a major war in eastern Europe involving the U.S.S.R. was a problem which he failed to take note of.

He was not at a loss, however, when it came to finding someone to blame for Norway's increasingly exposed position as events in Europe led toward war. At every opportunity, he and his adherents attempted to blacken the reputation of all leading politicians in the country. He felt passionately that they were to blame for blocking him from the position of leadership that he deserved. One of the strongest accusations which he levelled against them was that they were responsible for bringing the country to the verge of war. Not only Foreign Minister Halvdan Koht, Prime Minister Nygaardsvold, Mowinckel, and Hambro, but the entire political system as well, were held responsible for this development. On the other hand, maintained Quisling, NS time after time had warned against the impending catastrophe. The only solution possible, he insisted, was for the Norwegian people in this "twelfth hour" to rid themselves of the "war politicians" and thereby free the nation from a government which was part of the international conspiracy for war. Mowinckel, Koht, Hambro, and Nygaardsvold were to be held accountable for their crimes against the fatherland and against peace and freedom.[94] It required little imagination to determine whom he would like to see succeed the "war politicians".

The manner in which he raged against those who in his mind deceived the people and prevented him from gaining leadership provided a telling explanation why *Fritt Folk* on its own could never amount to more than a four-page news sheet. The *Fører's* biased and agitated commentary had no chance of gaining a hearing beyond the limited readership that subscribed to the paper. Although it was not infrequently absent from the polemics of the 1930s, the majority of Norwegians respect restraint and objective reasoning, a quality that Quisling demonstrably lacked. His highly emotional attacks and dire warnings revealed the rage of a frustrated individual who had convinced himself that what he said was true, in particular because he felt thwarted in not being able to achieve the success he needed in politics.

One of the main charges which he levied against his enemies, the party politicians, was that they had failed to maintain the armed forces adequately. This issue served as but one more example of his critical attitude in general toward politics in a democratic parliamentary framework. During most of the 1930s the country was primarily preoccupied with its severe economic problems. Any political party which advocated increased defense expenditures at a time of low wages, high unemployment, and numerous bankruptcies and foreclosures would have committed political suicide. Military expenditures were cut back as much as possible, with the bottom being reached, ironically enough, at the very time Quisling served as Minister of Defense. Neither he nor any other politician could have prevented this.

Toward the end of the 1930s, however, after economic recovery had begun, the Labor government took steps toward increasing the allocation of funds for the military, although slowly at first. This resulted in political disagreement. Some *borgerlige* politicians (minus Mowinckel's Liberals), in particular the Conservatives, favored higher defense spending and criticized the government.

Quisling's attacks on the poor state of the military reached their height at just this time. Superficially, it therefore seemed that he was not alone in his disparagement of the country's defenses. Furthermore, from a strictly theoretical viewpoint, some of his criticism was valid. In view of the demands that World War II would make, Norway was not properly prepared. In particular, his warning that the air defense system was inadequate proved to be perceptive.[95]

A realistic appraisal of the situation in Norway prior to the German invasion, however, would hold public opinion as a whole, influenced by still poor economic times and idealistic considerations, as being largely responsible for the country's reduced military capability, and not any particular political party. There was no strong public demand favoring greater support for the military. Even after the war began, the great majority of the people believed that Norway would be able to escape direct involvement, as had been true in World War I. Very few had the foresight to see that the Second World War would be quite different.[96]

Quisling's denunciation differed, however, in that he regarded the issue of national defense strictly from an ideological perspective, as he did all issues. Not only were his political enemies held responsible for the poorly prepared armed forces, but he remained equally critical when special appropriations *were* made for the armed forces. Any increased armaments, he insisted, were directed one-sidedly against Germany and were therefore in violation of the people's wish for neutrality. In his total repudiation of the political system, he furthermore maintained that the real issue concerning national defense was not how many millions of *kroner* were expended, but who was in charge of the armed forces. At present it was the hated party politicians, whom he lumped together under the description "judaic-marxistic-democratic". As with all other critical matters that he raised, the only solution possible from his point of view was for him to take over, declaring that the defense forces had to come under a national and professional leadership so that the country's confidence in the armed forces could be restored.[97]

In his attacks on figures whom he hated within the political establishment, he raised yet another issue, an old obsession, that of Greenland. Although some fervent nationalists still smarted under the feeling of injustice created by the International Court decision of 1933, most Norwegians considered the dispute to be settled, as shown in the 1936 election, when NS' attempt to revive the controversy met with no response.

For Quisling, however, the subject remained very much alive. It had become part of his nationalistic make-up, and could never be abandoned. Furthermore, he believed that this question provided him with yet another argument to prove his assertion that the "party politicians" had neglected Norway's real interests by not pursuing the claim to Greenland more effectively.[98] While there was some truth to this accusation, since both Mowinckel and Hambro had regarded the Greenland controversy as nationalistic folly, and the Labor party had been equally negative, the International Court's decision was not based on who had said and done what in Norway during the 1920s and early 1930s, but rather on which country had exercised sovereignty over the island for the longest period in recent history.

Quisling, however, continued to serve on the board of Danish-Norwegian Settlement, which doggedly maintained that Norway's claims to Greenland had to be accepted by the Danes. Hardly anyone except like-minded nationalists paid much attention to the organization. The fact that Quisling was re-elected to its board in September 1938 indicated its peripheral position. He was joined on the board by a rather variegated group which included a number of his detractors such as Rolf Thommessen and Victor Mogens, while Hans S. Jacobsen served as an alternate. As for the ordinary membership of the organization, in addition to NS adherents, it also included nationalistic individuals who belonged to groups such as the Conservatives, the Fatherland League, and the Agrarian party.[99]

Quisling was closely associated on the Greenland question with another member of the board of Danish-Norwegian Settlement, Dr. Gustav Smedal, who in his writings continued to press the argument that Norway was justified in not giving up its claim.[100] As could be expected, his viewpoint did not receive a particularly positive response in Denmark. Included among Danish publications which commented critically on Smedal's writings was *National-Socialisten* (*The National Socialist*), the paper for the Danish National Socialist Workers' party headed by Fritz Clausen. He held a position in Denmark similar to that which Quisling occupied in Norwegian politics, and the two corresponded. But on the question of Greenland they could reach no agreement. Quisling protested against the attacks on Smedal in Clausen's paper. Indicating the importance that he attached to Greenland, Quisling maintained there could be no possibility of cooperation between the two countries as long as the issue remained unresolved. Furthermore, he predicted that the controversy would not die down, but would grow sharper as nationalism in Norway increased in strength.[101] He of course visualized being in the forefront of the growing nationalistic indignation over Greenland that he predicted.

Although the Greenland question never assumed any importance beyond the abstract ideals of nationalistic romantics, it revealed the impreciseness of Quisling's thought. As the great exponent of Nordic unity, he could not even find room for compromise with another Scandinavian country over a relatively unimportant issue such as this. He never clearly thought out what Norway's relationship would be in a union with other "Nordic" countries, including major powers such as England and Germany. Airily, he identified himself as Norway's preordained leader, and he simplistically assumed that whatever he willed would be accomplished.

Anti-Semitism was an even more pronounced component in his political outlook in the period prior to the outbreak of the war. He emphasized his negation of the Jews in an increasingly virulent manner. While anti-Semitism had become a significant part of National Union's ideology as early as the second half of 1935, and had been of some importance in the 1936 election, it became far more pronounced after NS declined to insignificance. There was a direct link between Quisling's increased emphasis on anti-Semitism and the growing severity of anti-Jewish persecution in Nazi Germany.

Not only did Quisling absorb an anti-Semitic viewpoint, but it became one of the cornerstones of his ideological perspective. As with Nazi racial fanatics, he now discovered evidence of the international Jewish conspiracy everywhere. In his mind, the Jews were always in control of the forces in opposition to the various "nationalist" movements that he identified with. They supposedly dominated the political leadership within the large western democracies and the Soviet Union.[102] This provided him with the basis for explaining why England increasingly adopted a stronger stand against Hitler's expansion in 1938–39. The Jews had allegedly found a bastion for speculation in England and in that country's "offspring", the United

States. He nevertheless reconciled his heightened hostility toward England with his program for the Greater Nordic Peace Union by pointing out that England still belonged to the Nordic race and had a Nordic outlook. Therefore, he declared that there were strong national movements in both England and the U.S. battling the growing power of the Jews.[103]

By the time he had dogmatically and unalterably assumed his anti-Semitic stance, there no longer existed any opposition in NS to such a viewpoint. His followers were as anti-Semitic as their *Fører*. As early as October 1937, immediately following NS' defeat in the local elections, *Fritt Folk* printed a full defense of the alleged authenticity of *The Protocols of the Wise Men of Zion*.[104] Almost every issue of the paper included direct or indirect attacks on the Jews. A favorite method of revealing the alleged international conspiracy was by indicating how persons with non-Jewish names in reality were Jews and part of the plot.[105]

The degree to which Quisling had become a fervent anti-Semite was revealed in the special interest he took in gathering lists of names of leading Norwegians who were of Jewish heritage. Most prominent was Carl J. Hambro, the Conservative party's foreman and president of the *Storting*. Quisling wanted in particular to obtain a copy of Hambro's geneology. The informant in Bergen who provided this information also came to the conclusion that there might well be more than 5000 persons with Jewish blood in the city.[106] Since the total number of persons of Jewish heritage numbered less than 1800 in all of Norway when they were deported to death camps in Germany, the reliability of these statistics can be questioned. Quisling, however, took his source seriously, asking for additional information about persons of Jewish background in Bergen. In return he received a newspaper in which an X had been marked next to the names of persons who, the informant maintained, had "Semitic blood".[107]

Quisling's public identification with anti-Semitism became total when he presented a number of anti-Semitic lectures in late 1938 and early 1939. In these speeches he gave free reign to his negative interpretation of the Jews.[108] A leading columnist for *Dagbladet*, Anton Beinset, provided an interesting analysis of Quisling when reporting on one of these lectures. Although hardly impartial, Beinset's portrayal rang true to life. He pointed out that Quisling's Nazi vulgarity was so disjointed, illogical, and full of contradictions that the lecture would have been a fiasco if presented by a member of a school debating society. Beinset contrasted Quisling's anti-Semitic irrationality with the clear and logical manner which the then Minister of Defense had earlier presented his arguments in his celebrated attack on the Labor party during the Quisling Affair. The journalist declared that it was difficult to believe that this was the same man who now stood and drivelled, without any inner zeal or strength, his anti-Semitic phrases which had no real meaning.[109] This description illustrated strikingly how the extent of Quisling's decline had influenced his outlook. His rationality was largely gone. Only the rage and frustration remained, causing him to seek any means, no matter how imitative, in his quest to regain the prominence which he felt should be his.

As Beinset's description illustrated, Quisling's anti-Semitic viewpoint could hardly win support beyond the small number of dedicated anti-Semites already in existence who needed no convincing. Because of his extremism, Quisling had become so controversial that many persons were automatically repelled by his very connection with any particular cause. In his attacks against the Jews, for example, he advocated reinstatement of the constitutional provision which had previously barred Jews from Norway.[110] The repeal of this restriction, which occurred in 1851, was regarded by many as one of the most progressive pieces of social legislation in the nineteenth century, and it was closely identified with the outstanding nationalist poet of the period, Henrik Wergeland. Such an extreme stand, which sought to turn back the clock, could only injure Quisling. Similarly, resolutions drawn up at his anti-Semitic rallies protesting against Jewish refugees from Germany being admitted to the country failed to gain any significant response.[111]

The reaction by the public against anti-Semitism was overwhelmingly negative. This sentiment, however, was formed first and foremost not by Quisling's agitation, which received but passing comment, but rather by the news media's coverage of Nazi persecution of the Jews in Germany. As an indication of the extent to which he was isolated in his support of anti-Semitism, former NS members such as Hjort and Wiesener now deplored the brutal excesses of the Nazis. While they still maintained a generally sympathetic outlook toward Germany, they outspokenly declared their opposition to the uncivilized savagery under which the German Jews suffered.[112]

Even Quisling was compelled to repudiate the violence which occurred during the Crystal Night pogrom in 1938.[113] But he continued to voice his anti-Semitic convictions, and he therefore remained directly associated with support for the German persecutions. As a result, he and NS received their share of criticism for what was going on in Germany. He retaliated by bringing charges against the Labor party newspaper in Drammen for slander, even though he was warned by his friend, Konrad Sundlo, that he had little chance of success in attempting to have the editor prosecuted.[114] Sundlo's advice proved correct. In addition to having a weak case at best, the political climate was hardly encouraging for such a step.

Convinced as always that in the end he would either triumph or go under, Quisling continued on his course with little heed for public opinion. Having made anti-Semitism a cornerstone of his ideology, it was natural for him also to adopt the Nazi party's strong opposition to the Freemasons.

NS did not, however, emphasize its hostility to the Masons to the extent that it manifested its anti-Semitism. This was in part because the Masons did not fit so nicely into Quisling's racial concept, since they were of Christian Norwegian heritage, and also because some NS members had ties with the group. For example, Frederik Prytz was a high-ranking member of the Masonic order.

Nevertheless, NS did not evade or downplay its opposition to the organization. Here again the imitative side of Quisling's strategy became obvious. Although there was no particularly strong sentiment against the Masons in Norway, he adopted this position because it was part of Hitler's program. In attacking the Masons, Quisling resorted to a tactic that he had used previously. He established a front organization, fittingly entitled Norwegian Front (*Norsk Front*). It came into existence in May 1938, with the declared intent of fighting the Masonic movement. Although supposedly independent, it was controlled by a board composed entirely of NS members, who regularly kept Quisling informed of what it carried out.[115]

Norwegian Front's activity was largely restricted to sensational lectures, accompanied by slide shows, which purportedly "unmasked" the Freemasons and their ritual. These lectures did succeed in drawing fairly large audiences of curious spectators. Quisling chose to grace one such meeting with his presence, accompanied by members of the *Hird*, who provided protection. But beyond the admission fees collected at the lectures, plus the sale of small amounts of anti-Semitic literature at the meetings, Norwegian Front did not make any significant contribution toward increasing National Union's strength. The organization was restricted to a total of approximately forty members at the end of May 1939.[116]

Due to the meagerness of his restricted resources, Quisling primarily concerned himself with issue-oriented commentaries during the late 1930s. He did not, however, entirely refrain from taking part in specific political controversies. One matter that aroused his attention, causing him to become highly agitated, was a *Storting* decision in the spring of 1938 to amend the Constitution in order to hold future national elections once every four years, as opposed to the previous practice of having triennial elections.

In order to enact this change, two amendments were passed by large majorities on the afternoon of April 5. The first amendment, to Article 54 of the Constitution, stated that elections would be held every fourth year. Only this change met with any noteworthy opposition, but it passed by a majority of 123 to 24, far more than the two-thirds needed for passage of a Constitutional amendment.[117] The second amendment, to Article 71, simply declared in accordance with the previously passed amendment that the *Storting* representatives served terms of four years. It received near unanimous approval, with only one diehard voting against passage.[118]

The enactment of these electoral changes occurred fully in accordance with the requirements for the passage of amendments to the country's Constitution. Article 112 of the Constitution required namely that a proposed amendment must be introduced in the *Storting*, but its passage could not occur until a subsequent election had been held. This was to allow the voters an opportunity to make their views known in the campaign preceding the election. In this instance, the two proposed amendments had been introduced in the *Storting* prior to the 1936 election.[119] Therefore, the representatives chosen as a result of this election acted in conformity with the Constitution in passing the two amendments.[120]

Despite the legality of the amendments, a certain amount of controversy erupted over the way that the *Storting* chose to interpret the significance of their action. The majority of *Storting* members, those who favored the amendment to Article 54, maintained that their term therefore did not expire in 1939, as would have been the case if the amendments had not been passed, but would instead continue until the end of 1940, with the next election scheduled for the fall of 1940. Some political observers disagreed, pointing out that it would have been much more appropriate for the amendments not to go into effect until *after* another election had been held, in 1939, since the present representatives originally had been elected for a three-year period. It therefore appeared unseemly to the critics for the *Storting* unilaterally to extend its own term for an additional year.[121]

Although such criticism did occur, it did not lead to any political division. On the contrary, all of the major parties, *borgerlige* and socialist alike, agreed to the passage of the amendments. The Conservatives and Liberals voted unanimously in favor of passage. With one exception, the representative of the minor Community Party, 23 of the 24 members who voted against came from the Labor party and the Agrarian party. But they were minorities within their own delegations. Only 18 of the 70 man Labor party delegation voted no, while 5 of the 18 Agrarian party representatives held the same view.[122] Consequently, there existed bipartisan support for passage. Among the public at large, the question failed to arouse significant interest, and it soon ceased to be a political issue.

For Quisling, however, this change was of major importance. He gave it his immediate attention, and the legal position that he and NS assumed toward the government and the *Storting* in the future would be based on his interpretation of the four-year mandate question.

His reaction came in the first issue of *Fritt Folk* which was published after the *Storting*'s action. He did not deny that from a formal legal point of view, the passage of the amendment which changed elections to every fourth year was acceptable. He maintained, however, that the people had been fooled, not being given an opportunity to discuss the change. Furthermore, he presented arguments, ironically enough from a democratic perspective, declaring that the reform had not gone far enough because it did not permit dissolution of the parliament and popular referendums. However, he consoled himself with the belief that the extension of the period between elections would not save the political system from certain destruction.[123]

However, on the question of the *Storting* extending its mandate from three to four years, there was no inconsistency in his argumentation. From the first he insisted in strident language that such a step was entirely illegal. Dramatically he declared that it was necessary to go back in history to the period of the French Revolution, to the Convention of 1795, in order to find a similar example of parliamentary disregard for prevailing opinion and for the law. He described the *Storting*'s action as having the character of a *coup d'état*.[124]

His view was colored by his hatred for the parliamentary system. At best, questions could be raised about the propriety of the *Storting* of extending its own term, but not about the legality of the move. But Quisling's irrational hate for the *Storting* was so great that he became convinced of the correctness of his logic. Here was the weapon which he believed could be used to destroy the parliament's reputation with the public. He insisted that the representatives who had voted to extend their terms should be prosecuted according to Article 98 of the Constitution, which called for at least five years' imprisonment for anyone who attempted to change the Constitution illegally.[125] In addition, he maintained that the present *Storting*, because of its unlawful action, was not entitled to sit beyond the end of 1939. Thereafter it would be an illegal body, and so too would be the government, whose authority was based on the *Storting*.[126]

Except for his small number of dedicated followers, hardly anyone paid attention to Quisling's protestations, as by now was the case concerning all questions which he raised. Yet the desperateness of his condition, as well as his determined insistence that he was correct in his interpretation, caused him to believe that this issue could be used successfully in future political campaigns. He emphasized to members of the NS Council when they met on February 5, 1939, that the *Storting* which came into session in 1940 would be illegal, and that NS must not let go of this fact.[127]

In accordance with this view, NS tried as best it could to exploit the issue. In February 1939 Quisling deplored the refusal of the *Storting* by a large majority to submit the question to the Supreme Court.[128] In presenting this argument, from an objective point of view he ignored the fact that in Norway the *Storting* by precedent held the highest political authority, and it therefore was not customary for parliament to allow its decisions to be tested in the courts. The *Storting* always guarded its power jealously, with the Supreme Court's position being secondary to that of parliament.

NS also attempted to launch a campaign over the issue. The agitation was intended to last from the beginning of November 1939 until the time when the *Storting* met "illegally" in the following year.[129] The party drew up a standard speech on "the *Storting*'s fourth year", to be used by its speakers on their lecture tours.[130] A brochure entitled "The Illegal *Storting*" also made its appearance, which Quisling hailed as the basis for NS' campaign against the *Storting*'s "*coup d'état*".[131] The campaign never amounted to anything.

As a last resort, Quisling sought to draw the person of the King into the controversy. Employing the same type of legalistic argument that he had previously used when NS tried to use the monarch to prevent Labor from assuming control of government, Quisling pontificated that the King was the highest guardian of the Constitution. Therefore, since the current *Storting* allegedly had no mandate to continue after January 1, 1940, he maintained that the King should refuse to open the parliament after the beginning of the new year. He concluded by issuing a thinly veiled threat, maintaining that the attitude which a large segment of the population would adopt toward the future of the monarchy would be determined by whether royal authority was on the side of the politicians or on the side of the "people" in this issue.[132]

As previously, the monarch ignored this abortive bid to have him become involved in a partisan matter. The question had already been settled in the appropriate political forum. The possibility that Haakon VII might take sides in a political dispute of this type was unthinkable, as was indeed obvious to almost everyone except political cranks.

While the question of extending the *Storting*'s mandate by one year proved to be of passing interest, for Quisling it remained a matter of permanent concern. He convinced himself that not only had the party politicians again revealed their inclination to act according to their own selfish interests, but that in this instance they had done so specifically in order to thwart him. He would later go so far as to argue that the main reason why the *Storting* extended its term was because it feared to hold an election in 1939 due to National Union's increased popularity. He declared that the people had become aware of the extent to which the political system was bankrupt, and the politicians allegedly feared the risk of being ousted by the voters if the election were held as originally scheduled.[133]

By eventually drawing such a conclusion, he showed again his great need to build up his feeling of importance. Had an election been held in 1939, there is no reason to believe that the result would have been any more auspicious for NS than the outcome of the local election of 1937. But for Quisling, such an objective evaluation of his sect's insignificance was impossible. Therefore, any argument, no matter how tenuous, was employed in his effort to increase National Union's standing, and thereby also his own stature.

The lack of consistency in his logic was especially apparent in matters concerning the *Storting*. It was at best contradictory for one of the most bitter opponents of parliamentary democracy to make use of democratic arguments in opposing a decision made by a representative body which he intended to abolish. He was not very convincing as the defender of popular sovereignty.[134] His opposition to the *Storting* was well known, dating back to his difficult relationship with it when he held governmental office. NS' failed attempt to introduce an amendment to the Constitution in 1935 which would have established a corporate body alongside the *Storting* was simply the formal beginning of the party adopting a position which eventually called for the complete abolition of parliament. In February 1939 Quisling declared that in addition to demanding a "national government of the realm independent of party politics", he similarly wished to see the complete reorganization of society into his corporate model. The nation's cultural and economic activity would be organized in his two-chambered National Assembly, with its cultural council and economic council. For public consumption, he maintained that his ideal representative system would see the two corporate assemblies gradually supersede the *Storting*.[135] No longer was there any talk of a corporate body serving alongside the *Storting*. Furthermore, he did not specify how long the transition would last. In internal party correspondence, however, the transition period was not mentioned at all. It was simply assumed that the *Storting* would be replaced by the corporate assemblies. Since the crushing election defeats in 1936 and 1937, he and his followers had determined that since his party could not win within a democratic framework, then the solution was to replace it with the new governmental system which he advocated.[136]

Symptomatic of this attitude within NS was the amount of time spent during its annual meetings discussing the abstract theme of how the new form of government would be organized.[137] This tendency simply mirrored that of the party leader. As NS continued to be of little importance in practical politics, it could freely indulge in speculation and theorizing, which was one of the few channels of activity that it had available.

At no time, however, did Quisling specify how his new governmental system would come into being, and what form it would take. His reluctance to go into detail was understandable. Had he done so truthfully, he would have had to admit that his proposed system could come into being only through revolutionary means, and the form of government which it would adopt would have to be dictatorial. He always insisted NS was not dictatorial, but this denial was strictly tactical, and it was not very convincing. Even within NS itself, members recognized that the plan to impose Quisling's ideal system on society was a drastic break with the past. One oldtime party member, who declined to accept Quisling's appointment to the NS Council in 1939, pointed out specifically that abolition of the *Storting* could only be achieved through revolution. This critic furthermore directed attention to NS' major weakness in advocating changes which in reality would result in dictatorship. She showed how this placed the party in a most awkward position. People were constantly asking NS members how it was possible to introduce the new changes which the party proposed without dictatorship. In particular, Quisling's correspondent stressed how inadequate and conscience-stricken she felt when asked if she really favored a dictatorship.[138] For those still within the party who raised such serious reservations about NS' position, no satisfactory reply was possible.

In its search for an issue, any issue, which might bring the party the attention it so desperately needed, the NS leadership resorted to resurrecting an accusation which had previously failed to win any particular notice. In May 1939 Fuglesang wrote to Herman Harris Aall, commenting that NS had again launched an attack against the Minister of Justice, Trygve Lie. NS repeated the charges it had made as part of its political agitation prior to the 1936 election. Lie, NS maintained, was guilty of treasonable connections with the Soviet Union, having allegedly made a political agreement with Russian sports officials when he headed the Labor party's athletic organization. This accusation was made in *Fritt Folk*, but when the *Storting* asked the authorities to investigate, Thronsen and Fuglesang refused to provide any details. They expected Lie to sue for slander, resulting in full publicity for NS in court. If the Minister of Justice failed to respond, then they believed that this would be a victory in itself, which could be followed up at a later date.[139]

As before, the hope of raising a major controversy over this question proved fallacious. It was regarded as but another example of NS irresponsibility, issuing charges which on face value were ridiculous. The renewed accusations received even less credence than earlier. Lie completely ignored the matter, and his reputation suffered no decline. The day when NS accusations were taken seriously had disappeared.

On the other hand, for Quisling and the true believers who still followed him, the charges which they levelled against their political enemies were made in earnest. Because of their intense emotional commitment to their cause, they were certain that the Labor party as well as the *borgerlige* "party politicians" who opposed NS were capable of the most sinister activity.

Above all, Quisling himself best represented this behavioral pattern. One particular incident provides a good illustration. In early 1940, shortly after the start of the year, he met two good friends whom he had not seen for a long time. He insisted that they should go to a restaurant together, which they did, spending the next couple of hours in conversation. As long as their discussion concerned neutral subjects, such as talk about their boyhood, student days, and mutual acquaintances, Quisling acted pleasantly and congenially, as he always did among old friends.[140] However, when the conversation turned to politics, he made such extreme statements that one of his friends, Vilhelm Ullmann, began to feel uncomfortable: "He [Quisling] explained how there were armed Communists and Bolsheviks throughout the country; he explained to me how they were supplied with weapons for communist uprisings throughout the land."[141] In particular, Ullmann was made uneasy by the "violent accusations" which Quisling made against persons in the Nygaardsvold government, first and foremost Trygve Lie. Ullmann knew personally a number of the ministers, and he was particularly well acquainted with Lie. But Quisling refused even to listen to the objections which Ullmann raised. Ullmann later explained: "It was when he began with these political, I may well call them ravings, that I . . . became seriously alarmed about his mental condition because I received the impression that he actually believed all that he raved about."[142] Quisling's boyhood friend interpreted this painful episode as primarily the result of "the crushing defeats which he suffered due to his political activity in National Union. I knew that he in many ways was proud, and . . . that he lived to a considerable extent in a world of fantasy."[143]

There was an additional psychological element which entered into Quisling's violent outburst against members of the Labor government that Ullmann had not been aware of. Quisling had just returned from Germany, having met with leaders of the Nazi party and the German military in December 1939. In accusing Trygve Lie and other prominent socialist politicians of being agents of the Russian Communists, he sought to rationalize his own conspiratorial activity with the Germans. In his mind, he firmly believed that while the socialists were engaged in a plot to seize control of Norway and bring it under Soviet domination, his actions in contrast were always in the country's best interests.

The episode concerning NS' renewed charges against Trygve Lie marked but one additional defeat in Quisling's dismal record of failure during the bleak period 1937–1939. Try though he might, NS had no chance of re-emerging as a party of any significance. With its incapable leadership and its extreme stands, which alienated most Norwegians, NS could not anticipate any success. Improvement in the economy made it even more difficult for an extremist party to stir up discontent. Under the prevailing conditions, it could only expect to continue as an insignificant sect, headed by a political prophet whose frequent irrational warnings and comments made him appear as a figure of both tragic and comic dimensions.

There appeared to be but one way of improving the party's condition if National Union were to become the important political movement that its leader and small number of remaining members believed it should be. Since there seemed to be little possibility for Quisling to be able to achieve anything on his own, NS would have to gain outside assistance and support. The idea of seeking such external aid was not foreign to the membership at large. To many of them, this seemed to be a realistic alternative to the party's present condition. As early as April 1938, a suggestion along these lines emerged from a meeting of the NS provincial organization in Oppland. NS officers at this gathering agreed that they had no interest in trying to regain the allegiance of former members who had left in "rebellion". Regional *fører* Jøranli reported that, on the other hand, the party officers had concluded that NS should establish connections with Berlin. As to how such contact should be made, Jøranli declared that this was best for the *Fører* to decide.[144]

Quisling did not need any prompting. He had earlier come to the same conclusion, although the existence of a body of opinion within NS which agreed with the general method that he was attempting to employ made his decision even easier.

CHAPTER IX

The Turn to Germany
1937–1939

we . . . will probably first see each other again when the action has succeeded and Norway's Minister President is Quisling.

Alfred Rosenberg,
diary entry, December 20, 1939

The first sporadic contacts which Quisling established with representatives
of the Nazi party extended as far back as 1930. His claim of being an original thinker to the contrary, he followed with intense interest the sequence
of events that were taking place in Germany, and received inspiration from
them. Dating back to the period *before* he joined the Kolstad ministry,
Quisling busily clipped out newspaper articles dealing not only with the
Nazis, but with fascist movements throughout Europe.[1] His name
appeared also on the mailing lists of various fascist groups, both German
and non-German.[2] Quite clearly, right-wing totalitarianism definitely represented the wave of the future for the former army officer and administrator, who was just then beginning his push to find a place for himself within
politics.

He demonstrated his changed political outlook when he made his initial
contact with a well-known Nazi, Max Pferdekämper, one of the first to
join Hitler's movement and a personal crony of a number of its leaders.
When Pferdekämper visited Oslo in December 1930, Quisling came calling
at his hotel. According to Pferdekämper, Quisling first presented a recita-
tion of his previous accomplishments, including his assertion that he had
represented British interests in the Soviet Union from 1927 to 1929. On the
basis of this vita, he asked to be placed in contact with leaders of the Nazi
movement.[3]

Pferdekämper's account of this meeting is particularly interesting because of its similarity to the way in which Quisling had earlier, in the
1920s, endeavored to establish connections with Labor party and Communist leaders. As with Pferdekämper, Quisling had come direct, expecting to

have his credentials and his personal presentation immediately admit him to a privileged position in the political group with which he was seeking to establish ties.

Upon his return to Germany, Pferdekämper did mention Quisling's name to a number of prominent party officials, including Himmler.[4] However, except for being placed on Nazi mailing lists, there was no follow-up to Quisling's request.[5] Therefore, when Pferdekämper next visited Norway in November 1932, he found to his chagrin that no firm ties had been established with Quisling. The latter had now become Minister of Defense, and when Pferdekämper paid a call at his office, Quisling made no effort to conceal his displeasure over the lack of attention he had received from the Germans.[6] Pferdekämper wrote once more to Himmler, recommending that the Nazi leadership establish permanent contact with Quisling.[7] However, soon afterwards the Nazi representative changed his view, now advising Himmler not to seek ties with Quisling because of the position he occupied.[8] It is not possible to ascertain directly whether it was Quisling or Pferdekämper who concluded that it could be damaging for the Minister of Defense if it became known that he had connections with the Nazis. On the surface, however, it seems clear that Quisling had the most to lose from such a revelation, considering in particular the controversy which surrounded him during his period in office.

It is possible that the previous failure of the Germans to provide Quisling with the attention he felt he deserved may have contributed to his brief association with fascism in 1935. The post of propaganda leader for the Fascist International was in keeping with his elevated image of himself. In any event, there was not a great deal of contact between NS and Nazi representatives during 1933–36, when NS aspired to become a major force in politics. Quisling did receive an invitation to take part in a congress sponsored by a Nazi front organization, the Nationalist International, in the summer of 1935, but he declined, citing his work on behalf of NS as a reason for not attending.[9] Later in the summer he received, thanks to a recommendation by Pferdekämper, an invitation from *Der Stürmer* to attend the party's annual congress in Nuremberg.[10] Once again, Quisling chose not to respond to such a general overture.

While he did not display noticeable enthusiasm for wanting to establish close ties with Germany during the years when NS seemed to have a chance of becoming a significant force in Norwegian politics, on the German side there similarly existed no strong sentiment in favor of creating a firm relationship with Quisling and NS. The Nazi party's Office of Foreign Affairs (*Aussenpolitisches Amt*) under Alfred Rosenberg was the organization most concerned with seeking contact with ideologically related groups outside of Germany. In 1934 the head of the Scandinavian section of Rosenberg's office, Thilo von Trotha, came to Norway to attend NS' annual meeting at Stiklestad. He held conversations with Quisling and other NS officers. Although Trotha personally sympathized with NS aspirations, he was realistic in his assessment of the movement, recognizing that it did not play a major role in Norwegian politics.[11] At a later date, probably in 1936, Trotha introduced Quisling to Rosenberg when the NS leader visited Berlin.[12] However, no permanent association resulted between Quisling and Rosenberg at this time. The Germans did not attach any special importance to NS. They regarded the party as but one of a number of groups in Norway that had pro-German sympathies, and with which ties were maintained in a rather loose fashion.[13]

While contacts were tenuous during the period when Quisling and his NS associates believed they might prevail through their own efforts, the situation became very different after the party underwent its process of disintegration. It was now explicitly recognized that aid from abroad – and this meant Germany – would have to be secured if NS were to have any chance of once more becoming a force to be reckoned with in politics. Therefore, with an ever-increasing and sustained effort, Quisling sought to arouse favorable attention from the Nazi party and the German administration.

Herman Harris Aall acted as one of the earliest and most enthusiastic exponents of gaining assistance from Germany. He was one of the older NS members. His pro-German viewpoint stemmed in large part from an intense Anglophobia, which he had developed during World War I, caused in particular by what he regarded as Great Britain's flagrant violation of freedom of the seas. He had an academic background. Although he had obtained two doctorates, in jurisprudence and philosophy, an unusual accomplishment, he failed to gain a permanent appointment at the University, which naturally estranged him from the academic establishment.[14]

He and other leading NS members were at first primarily interested in tapping German sources for funds. As early as 1935, Aall called Quisling's attention to a proposed scheme whereby NS might be able to gain funding from abroad. Aall suggested that NS publish an "inter-Germanic and Nordic" daily newspaper, which would be sustained by advertisements and subscriptions from business interests wishing to promote trade between Germany and Scandinavia. What he in particular had in mind was German advertisements in the proposed newspaper.[15]

This plan was far too grandiose and had no chance of being realized. The projected paper was to be multilingual, written not only in Norwegian, but in German, Finnish, and Dutch as well.[16] Not even the largest and most solidly established Norwegian publication could have succeeded in carrying out such a scheme, in particular during a period of depression. The incident illustrates Aall's inability to reason realistically when considering political alternatives, although he always liked to think of himself as a pragmatic activist. However, while he often was impractical, he had a knack for making contacts, although not always particularly important ones. In this instance, he discussed the newspaper project with Ernst Züchner, the Scandinavian expert within the foreign division of Goebbels' Propaganda Ministry.[17]

Aall had ample opportunity to widen his circle of German acquaintances. Although he lived in Sweden, he spent long intervals in Germany from 1936 onwards. He discovered a kindred spirit in Berlin, a Norwegian-American professor, Charles Stangeland, who taught in the German capital. While in Germany, Aall frequently stayed with Stangeland. He used the professor's residence as his base of operations for forays into the maze of party and governmental bureaucracy, trying at all times to further Quisling's and National Union's interests.[18] In this endeavor, Aall used arguments that were very similar to those which Quisling would expound at a later date when he personally came to Germany in search of Nazi backing. Writing to Dr. Hans Dräger, head of the Nordic Liaison Department (*Nordische Verbindungsstelle*), which served as Goebbels' contact with the Scandinavian countries, Aall emphasized Norway's strategic importance and how Germany's potential enemies, Russia and England, allegedly were interested in the country and might even divide it among themselves. He also stressed what he described as the danger of Norway being controlled by the "revolutionary" Labor party. As justification for why NS deserved German support, he repeated an incorrect claim which had become an article of faith among Quisling's little band: that only NS had prevented Labor from gaining an absolute majority in the *Storting*.[19] This alone had supposedly kept Norway from coming under Marxist rule.

When acting as Quisling's agent, Aall did not work alone. Already on the scene was another faithful NS member, Olaf Fermann, who resided permanently in Germany as a businessman. He became a member of NS as early as 1933, when he paid a call on Quisling in Oslo. It was typical of Quisling that, although he had never met the man before, he appointed Fermann on the spur of the moment to serve as National Union's representative in Germany. Acting in this capacity, Fermann tried whenever possible to alert German officials to Quisling's pro-German views.[20] When Aall came to Germany, he and Fermann got along well together, the two cooperating without any rivalry in their effort to further Quisling's interests.[21]

In their work, Aall and Fermann succeeded in gaining a number of contacts within the German administration. However, the officials whom they became acquainted with were almost always on the lower level within the state and party bureaucracy. Furthermore, the reaction of the Germans who knew the two NS agents was not always positive. Such departments as the Foreign Ministry and the Propaganda Ministry were fully informed through their sources about National Union's relatively insignificant standing. The effect of this information was reflected in the polite but unresponsive attitude they adopted toward the NS representatives in Germany.[22] The Propaganda Ministry regarded Fermann with considerable mistrust.[23] As for Aall, he came to be considered by many as an intellectual crank, although his academic credentials did provide him with some status. Because of his pro-German sympathies, he was among the Norwegians invited to attend the festivities in honor of *der Führer*'s fiftieth birthday. In an inept and rather inappropriate manner, Aall tried to take advantage of the occasion. At a reception hosted by Foreign Minister Ribbentrop, Aall circulated among the guests, seeking to persuade the Norwegians present to sign a petition of recommendation on behalf of Quisling.[24] Such behavior did not merit the Foreign Ministry's approval, which consistently maintained a realistic, critical assessment of Quisling and NS' position.

Other efforts made by NS to secure German backing were equally amateurish, almost farcical in their method of execution and the level at which they operated. In a most awkward attempt to gain the attention of the German leadership, Quisling had previously, in the early fall of 1938, sent the duo of Fuglesang and Thronsen to attend the Nazi congress in Nuremberg. The two NS officers arrived without an invitation. They had been instructed by Quisling to hand over to the Nazi leadership a resolution passed at National Union's annual conference. The transparent intent of this move was the expectation that the resolution would result in a favorable response toward NS by the Nazi hierarchy.[25]

The venture did not result in the outcome that Quisling had hoped for. Arriving in Nuremberg with no plan as to how they would accomplish their mission, Fuglesang and Thronsen were taken in tow by a functionary of the German Labor Front. Their guide was not very impressed by the credentials which the two young Norwegians presented. He assumed an air of superiority, declaring that it was not possible for foreign parties to enter into an organizational relationship with the NSDAP. The NS party resolution was conveniently "deposited" without ever reaching its intended destination.[26]

Following their stay in Nuremberg, Fuglesang and Thronsen travelled on to Berlin, where they contacted Fermann. They were able to discuss more substantial matters with him than what they had accomplished at the Nazi congress. Specifically, they brought up the possibility of establishing a means by which Norwegians in Germany could provide *Fritt Folk* with the financial backing which the paper sorely needed. Fermann fully agreed with the necessity to make such an effort and promised to work on its behalf.[27] Fuglesang next met with Ernst Züchner in the Propaganda Ministry to discuss obtaining an import license for *Fritt Folk* and questions concerning future currency transactions involving the paper. While Fuglesang preoccupied himself with this matter, Thronsen travelled to Dresden to consult with Viljam Hagelin, another of Quisling's contacts in Germany, who later would serve as the NS leader's key source of access to leading German figures.[28]

The attempt to solicit funds for *Fritt Folk* from the Norwegian colony in Germany met with but limited progress. By the end of 1938 Fermann could report back to NS headquarters that he had established account number 3966 on behalf of National Union with the Dresdner Bank branch on Potsdamer Strasse III in Berlin. Furthermore, he had secured two patrons who would regularly contribute fifty *Reichsmark* each month, while Fermann promised he would pay double that amount. He had also made the necessary arrangements so that subscribers to *Fritt Folk* in Germany could obtain the paper through their local post offices. In order to enable him to work more effectively toward obtaining subscribers and contributors, he urged NS to provide him with a letter of solicitation which he could utilize when working on *Fritt Folk*'s behalf.[29]

Quisling wasted little time in responding. He sent a two page "Appeal" to Fermann on January 5, 1939, in which he marshalled arguments for why pro-German Norwegians in the Third Reich should provide *Fritt Folk* with financial aid. He pointed out that almost all newspapers in Norway had adopted a negative attitude toward Germany. Only National Union's publications, first and foremost *Fritt Folk*, presented a fair and understanding attitude concerning Norway's relationship with the Third Reich. In making this assertion, he could be accused of hyperbole, since *Fritt Folk* was NS' *only* regular publication. However, the need to present as favorable an image as possible in Germany led him to exaggerate tremendously. He declared that National Union's informational work alone prevented a general deterioration in public opinion toward the adoption of an open anti-German sentiment. There existed, he continued, tendencies in this direction, such as unwillingness to purchase German goods. Appealing to the commercial interests of Norwegian businessmen in Germany, he declared that great damage could result if conditions continued to decline, and under certain circumstances this could even be directly dangerous for peaceful relations between the two countries. It was therefore in the interest of every Norwegian in Germany to support *Fritt Folk* through subscriptions, advertisements, or direct contributions.[30]

He was not loath in the same solicitation to overstate vastly the role NS played in opposition to the Labor party, alleging that even NS' enemies had acknowledged that his party alone had prevented the Marxists from gaining a majority in 1936. Rather illogically, he declared that the *borgerlige* parties were the ones who had benefited from this NS effort, but that this in no way detracted from the party's importance. He proclaimed that the decisive battle with communism in Norway had yet to be fought. Although the other parties were fooled by Labor's "popular front" tactics, NS remained vigilant with its "clear and firm lines", being the only "national" political movement of any importance in Norway.[31]

In his effort to obtain favorable attention from abroad, another tactic he resorted to was his practice of sending congratulatory telegrams. He was particularly active during the first half of 1939. On January 28 he congratulated the *Fichtebund* on its twenty-fifth anniversary, declaring that Germany under Hitler had become the great power that Fichte had maintained it should be.[32] One month later the Spanish dictator, Francisco Franco, received a Quisling telegram on the occasion of the Nationalist victory. In what became the standard form in such messages, Quisling heaped superlatives on Franco, with whom the NS leader identified. The Nationalist triumph was described as a victory for Christian civilization and for order and justice over the threat of Bolshevism, a force, said Quisling, which also menaced his country. He signed himself as head of the National Union movement and former Minister of National Defense.[33]

He reserved his most complimentary praise for the luminary from whom he above all wished to gain notice, Adolf Hitler. In his telegram to Hitler on his fiftieth birthday, Quisling hailed the effort *der Führer* was making for the good and greatness of his people, "our Germanic and Nordic *Brüdervolk*". Quisling furthermore hailed Hitler as the "hero" who had saved Europe from "Bolshevism" and Jewish hegemony, and who had renewed the principle of "blood and spirit" without which European civilization could not exist. Not only did the NS leader associate Hitler's successes with his own mission, but he also hoped to interest *der Führer* in the creation of the Greater Nordic Peace Union, expressing the hope that all "Germanic and Nordic" peoples would join such a union in order to protect their "sacred qualities" and to provide Europe and the world with order, justice, and peace.[34]

In writing this message, he obviously intended to ingratiate himself with the Nazi leadership. Even if the telegram did not reach as high as Hitler, Quisling still believed that it might be put to use in Germany. Writing two days after the telegram had been sent, he forwarded a copy to Aall, pointing out that in a sense it contained a program which Aall might find useful in his work.[35] Since the latter's "work" largely involved the promotion of NS, the purpose of the telegram was clear.

The act of sending such messages was not solely politically motivated, however, but also fulfilled a psychological need, permitting him to satisfy his urge to play the role of a prominent nationalist leader. It served as an escape mechanism from the harsh reality of being the head of an insignificant and ridiculed little sect, made up in large part of political eccentrics and fanatics. He also used his telegrams as a means of bolstering his standing among his own followers within NS. He confided, for example, to Aall that he had received an extremely gracious reply in response to his telegram to Franco, an assertion which the *Fører* repeated at a meeting of the NS Executive Committee on March 20, 1939.[36] He failed to point out, however, that the acknowledgement came not from Franco, but from a Spanish consular representative in Oslo, who sent a one sentence note of thanks on behalf of the Generalissimo.[37]

There is no evidence to indicate that Quisling received any response to his telegram to Hitler, which must have been humiliating. Such cavalier treatment reflected the prevalent attitude toward Quisling in all circles of the Nazi party and the administration until June 1939, when events began to turn more in his favor.

Of the various German departments, the Foreign Ministry consistently maintained the most realistic assessment of NS' true position in Norwegian politics. This was because the Foreign Ministry had diplomatic representatives in Oslo, persons who as a rule were professional diplomats of the old school, and who accordingly were not significantly affected by ideological considerations.[38] In his annual report for 1937, Dr. Heinrich Sahm declared that NS had not been able to rebound from its election defeat, and neither had the Fatherland League.[39] Later reports from the German legation in Oslo to the Foreign Ministry were in exactly the same vein – Quisling and National Union were no longer of any significance in Norwegian political life.[40]

It took considerable time before the NS agents in Germany became fully aware of the low regard which important agencies had for Quisling and NS. Not until the very end of 1938 did Fermann receive a tip from a young commercial representative, who sympathized with NS ideologically, revealing the extent of the negative assessment. Fermann passed the information on to Aall, pointing out that Quisling, NS, and *Fritt Folk* were not mentioned favorably in the Foreign Ministry, the German legation in Oslo, and the Foreign Division of the Propaganda Ministry. He complained bitterly that all the work he had been doing during the year had been of no value because bureaucrats had secretly been regarding him with contempt, not daring to state their views openly. He declared his relief, however, over now being informed. If not, then he and Aall could have worked for years without any possibility of success.[41]

Such knowledge did indeed prove useful, but it brought no immediate results. In March 1939 Fermann maintained he had succeeded in reaching an agreement, at a publicity meeting for commercial interests held just before the Leipzig Fair, whereby German firms in Norway would purchase the same number of advertisements in *Fritt Folk* as they placed in other newspapers. Fermann requested that *Fritt Folk* notify him of whether this commitment was being honored.[42] The expected advertisements were not made, and John Thronsen had the unhappy chore of sending clippings to Fermann of advertisements by German firms in *Aftenposten* and other papers which did not find their way into *Fritt Folk*.[43] German businesses operating in Norway recognized that if they advertised in the NS paper, they stood a good chance of having their sales adversely affected. Quisling and his party were much too compromised because of their admiration for Hitler. In one incident, Quisling personally experienced the coolness which German business interests felt toward NS. He complained indignantly to Aall that his old friend, Major Ragnvald Hvoslef, had been rejected as a potential manager of a German outlet in Norway because he was a "Nazi".[44]

As for Quisling, such rebuffs left him feeling baffled, frustrated, and angry. He had believed that the approaches which he and his representatives made to the Germans would be met with an instant and positive response. He had expected that German money would be made available to finance NS activities, first and foremost its pro-German propaganda, in the same way that the Soviet Union allegedly had earlier supported the Labor party, and supposedly still provided financial aid for the Communists. He was quite preoccupied with the fact that the Communists were able to publish two daily newspapers in Norway, while NS barely succeeded in bringing out a weekly. He stressed this strongly in his attempt to secure funds for *Fritt Folk* in Germany.[45] Other NS members, including Fuglesang, were equally obsessed in their belief that the Communists allegedly were receiving money from Moscow.[46]

When he learned the reason why German support was not forthcoming, Quisling became vexed, and he expressed his displeasure to Aall in direct terms. He declared that only fools judged circumstances according to surface phenomena, and that NS was not approaching the Germans as supplicants. He warned that if the Germans continued to act as they did, they risked alienating "the national movement" and thereby losing an important base of support.[47]

These words of bravado were based on his need to maintain the illusion that he was dealing with the Germans from a position of equality. Contrary to what he asserted, he *was* a supplicant. His small sect needed German money in order to survive, as he himself demonstrated by his actions if not by his words. He continued to seek Nazi backing, but with no more success than before, complaining to Aall in March 1939 that he had not heard anything "from our Germanic brothers".[48]

The problem he faced, reduced to its simplest element, was to get the Germans to take him seriously. In order to do so, he increasingly stressed the strategic importance of Scandinavia for Germany in the event of a war, in particular Norway. Perhaps this could be the key to arousing the attention of the Nazis. When he learned that Aall would be making yet another trip to Germany, Quisling pointed out that the Germans would be wise to listen to what Aall had to say. The NS leader insisted that just as the Germans had allowed victory to slip out of their hands in World War I because of their inept eastern policy, there existed the same possibility at the present time because of their policy in Scandinavia, which could be fatal to them.[49] In other words, the longer the Germans waited in aiding Quisling and NS, the more difficult it would be for him to secure a pro-German attitude in Norway and in the rest of Scandinavia.

Aall did his best for Quisling during his stay in Germany, as demonstrated by his activity during Hitler's birthday celebration. But no satisfaction was received. The Germans maintained their attitude of not attaching very great importance to the NS leader, whose mood failed to improve by not having been invited to Berlin to take part in the festivities. Writing to Aall afterwards, he complained that everything was being done to place Scandinavia in "the anti-German league", but German diplomats had no understanding of what was taking place. He continued to argue that Scandinavia's position could be crucial in the event of a conflict, and its outlook would be decided to a very great degree by developments in Norway. Completely distorting NS' true condition, he maintained that his party served as a breakwater against anti–German propaganda, and should NS give up, this propaganda would irresistably overflood everything. In a burst of candor to his confidant, he openly displayed his anger and irritation with the Germans for failing to comprehend the alleged value of NS. He warned that he would soon be fed up with the Germans' lack of understanding, whereby they supported NS' enemies and traitors against the movement, while NS in turn was undervalued and insultingly disregarded.[50] Because of his feeling of being slighted, he went so far as to hint to the Anglophobe Aall that he might change positions and adopt a pro–British attitude. The British, Quisling alleged untruthfully, were beginning to show an interest in his movement, supposedly having made several recent inquiries.[51]

Despite his open display of anger and his warning that he might turn against the Germans, there was no chance that he could make good his threat. He had no contacts of any importance in England. The NS leader was in a locked-in position. Were he to gain foreign support, it would have to come from Germany. He had openly and for far too long identified himself with the Nazis. But as he indicated in his letter to Aall, National Union did not enjoy a monopoly in holding a pro-German position in Norway. On the contrary, NS was but one of a number of small political groups which maintained a favorable attitude toward the Third Reich, and which with greater or lesser degrees of success had opened channels of communication with Germany.

As the incident involving invitations to Hitler's birthday revealed, during the first half of 1939 the head of the Fatherland League, Victor Mogens, was valued higher than Quisling. Even such a loyal NS member as Aall recognized the potential benefit of reaching an understanding with Mogens and strongly urged Quisling to make such an accommodation.[52] Furthermore, the *Fører*'s reference to German support for enemies and traitors against NS was due not just to his anger, but was based on fact.

The German legation in Oslo considered many of Quisling's "renegades" to be far more valuable friends of Germany than the NS leader.[53] Persons such as Jacobsen, Fürst, and Hjort had contacts in Germany, and they had no reason for providing their acquaintances with a flattering picture of Quisling and his standing in Norwegian politics.[54]

Because of the controversy that he would later arouse during negotiations in the early period of the German occupation, Ellef Ringnes in particular served as a noteworthy example of someone who provided the Germans with a negative impression of Quisling. Ringnes was a prominent businessman. He was the former Austrian consul general in Norway, and because of his background he had good contacts with the Third Reich, which after March 1938 included Austria. He was also a leading member of the Norwegian-German Association (*Norsk-Tysk Forening*), a pro-German business and cultural group which maintained a distinctly cool attitude toward Quisling and NS. Ringnes had at one time, from 1936 to 1938, actually belonged to NS, having provided the party with a certain amount of financial backing.[55] He had in this capacity also worked with Aall and Fermann in seeking to provide NS with favorable contacts in Germany.[56] However, although he had originally sided with Quisling during the spring of 1937 when NS was torn with dissension,[57] by the end of 1938 Ringnes had become convinced that the head of NS had no future prospects in politics.[58] He also warned Aall at the time that influential Germans viewed Fermann rather coolly. Aall, however, chose to stand firm in his association with Fermann. While Ringnes and Aall had been friendly acquaintances for some time, their cooperation on Quisling's behalf now ceased.[59] Ringnes in particular enjoyed good relations with the Propaganda Ministry, and his newly-formed critical attitude toward Quisling was but one additional negative source affecting the way in which members of Goebbels' ministry regarded the NS leader.[60]

Because of their inability to establish channels of communication to the highest levels of the Nazi administration, Aall and Fermann were fated to play subordinate roles in Quisling's quest to form substantive ties with the NSDAP. This was not the case, however, with the third Norwegian agent who undertook to work for the NS *Fører's* cause in Germany. Actually, Albert Viljam Hagelin was in many respects more German than Norwegian. He was born in Bergen in 1882,[61] but moved to Germany prior to World War I. Here he studied architecture, after which he worked for an architectural firm in Oslo during the 1920s. But he later decided to devote himself to being a businessman. He returned to Germany, and by the mid-1930s he was a prosperous resident of Dresden, where he engaged in the wholesale coffee trade. Thanks to his commercial activity, he had a number of contacts in business and political circles.[62]

He began to act on behalf of Quisling at a considerably later date than Fermann and Aall. The businessman from Dresden met Quisling for the first time in 1936. He later explained that he had contact with the NS *Fører* both before and after the election, and this appears reasonable. Quite probably he also became an NS member at this time, although he was always deliberately evasive on the question of his party affiliation.[63] Quisling had thereby acquired what proved to be an extremely valuable source of support in Germany. Hagelin sent a congratulatory telegram from Dresden on the occasion of Quisling's fiftieth birthday in 1937.[64] Not until the following year, however, did he begin to play a key part in Quisling's German strategy, establishing ties with NS members in the country, including Aall.[65] By the start of 1939, Hagelin was fully engaged in work on behalf of the NS cause, a commitment Quisling valued greatly. The NS leader wrote to Hagelin in April, expressing his heartfelt thanks for the work that the businessman was carrying out.[66]

With his background as a man who had been forced to make his way in the world strictly on the basis of his own ability, and who had succeeded in gaining wealth despite the harsh economic conditions of the period, Hagelin combined an outward show of joviality and good manners with immediate, decisive action and a total commitment to having his own way. He quickly eclipsed both Aall and Fermann. Before long it was plain to see that in Hagelin, Quisling had regained the type of supportive figure that he needed, someone he had lacked ever since Prytz abandoned his direct interest in politics.

Initially, Hagelin could offer something which neither Aall nor Fermann had succeeded in obtaining – the possibility of extensive financial support. Exactly what type of backing Hagelin first discussed with Fermann and Aall cannot be ascertained, but it is clear that he held out the promise of providing NS with a solid economic base, either personally or through his political and business connections.[67]

Prior to the time Hagelin came into the picture in full focus, NS activity in Germany had largely concentrated on attempting to raise funds for National Union's propaganda activity in Norway, first and foremost *Fritt Folk*. This endeavor had invariably stranded. During the first half of 1939, however, the campaign on behalf of Quisling took a turn in a more positive direction, although he at first was not aware of this.

Having obtained information through Fermann that there was no chance of gaining a favorable response from the Foreign Ministry or the Propaganda Ministry, the NS agents stopped cultivating officials in these ministries by the end of 1938, turning their attention to other parts of the Nazi administration which appeared to be more promising. Hagelin played a key part in this move when he succeeded in establishing the first really significant link with the Germans.

Quisling's breakthrough came about as the result of a favorable response from Rosenberg's Office of Foreign Affairs. This recognition was long in coming. Rosenberg's office had been established already in 1933 in conjunction with Hitler's takeover. As a representative of the Nazi party, the Office of Foreign Affairs aspired to have a strong influence in determining German foreign policy. Competition with the Foreign Ministry was therefore inevitable.[68] Rosenberg delegated responsibility for the Scandinavian countries to the Northern Section (*Abteilung Norden*) within his office. Although Thilo von Trotha, its first head, had been sympathetic toward Quisling and NS from an ideological perspective, he had recognized NS' lack of importance and therefore did not recommend that the Office of Foreign Affairs should serve as Quisling's patron. Since Rosenberg was notoriously dependent on the advice of his subordinates, Trotha's influence prevailed.[69]

When Trotha made arrangements for Quisling to visit Rosenberg in 1936, this was apparently only a courtesy call which involved no commitment on the part of the *Reichsleiter*. Another factor explaining the absence of any firm connection between Quisling and the Office of Foreign Affairs prior to 1939 was the fact that the Northern Section to a great degree allowed its contacts with Scandinavia to be maintained by the Nordic Association (*Nordische Gesellschaft*) in Lübeck, which on the surface was a business and cultural association devoted to fostering ties with Scandinavia, but which had become a front organization under Rosenberg's and Trotha's control.[70]

Norwegians who had ties with the Nordic Association tended to maintain the aloof attitude toward Quisling and NS which was typical in business circles. For Fermann and Aall it had therefore been natural to seek connections with influential persons within the Foreign and Propaganda ministries in 1937–1938, rather than with Rosenberg's organizations, since these ministries also maintained channels of communication with Scandinavia. Aall's and Fermann's lack of interest in the Office of Foreign Affairs and the Nordic Association was further strengthened by the rivalry which existed between Rosenberg and the two ministries to which the NS representatives were appealing. Both the Foreign Ministry and the Propaganda Ministry resented Rosenberg's involvement in foreign policy and relations with pro-Nazi organizations abroad, and the two ministries therefore did their best to lessen the influence of the Office of Foreign Affairs.[71]

The situation took on a new outlook due to the lack of enthusiasm for Quisling by the Foreign and Propaganda ministries. Even more significant, however, was a personnel change which occurred within Rosenberg's office. Hans Wilhelm Scheidt assumed leadership of the Northern Section at the end of 1938.[72] He was a self-confident, brash young National Socialist, only thirty–one at the time he took over his new assignment. He already had a rather turbulent history professionally speaking. Scheidt was born of German parents in Moscow in 1907, but he moved to Germany with his family as a young boy. His educational achievements were not particularly auspicious. He failed to graduate from the *gymnasium*, and after a period of trying various educational and vocational alternatives, like so many other rootless young Germans, he enrolled in the ranks of the SA in 1929. He advanced rapidly within the party, thanks in particular to his speaking talents. By 1931 he was already a *"Reich* speaker" for the NSDAP, travelling throughout Germany during the ceaseless agitation which the National Socialists carried out prior to Hitler's triumph. He first began to work for Rosenberg's organization in 1935, when he became the "commandant" of the Foreign Office's educational training center (*Schulungshaus*). He was simultaneously engaged in work on behalf of the leadership of the Nazi youth movement.[73]

His assumption of control over the Northern Section marked the emergence of the second key individual who along with Hagelin would exercise a profound influence on Quisling's activities in 1939–1940. One of Scheidt's first ventures after he took office was to deliver a lecture in Oslo. On this visit, in January 1939, he met the NS leader for the first time. It appears that Hagelin had been responsible for setting up the meeting. He was a personal friend of Scheidt's cousin in Dresden, through whom he had met Scheidt at a tennis tournament.[74] Since tennis was not a normal outdoor mid-winter activity in pre-war Germany, it is assumed that Hagelin had become acquainted with Scheidt before the latter left for Norway and his talk with Quisling. By early 1939 the relationship between the trio Quisling, Scheidt, and Hagelin was well established.

Unlike the first head of the Northern Section, Trotha, Scheidt, young, impulsive, and ambitious, completely lacked political judgement. Although he had no direct knowledge of Norwegian affairs, he immediately became the champion of Quisling's cause. He went so far as to proclaim himself as *the* German "expert" on Norway, and he determinedly fought to prevent all other Germans from intruding into his monopoly over Quisling. In this endeavor, he was given virtually a free hand by Rosenberg, thanks to the *Reichsleiter*'s inability to exercise proper control over his subordinates. On the contrary, because of Rosenberg's weakness, once Scheidt had adopted Quisling's position as his own, he would prepare the way for Quisling's access to Rosenberg, and thereby into the higher echelons of the Nazi party.[75]

Hagelin and Scheidt turned their attention to the immediate question of concern for Quisling's backers in Germany: how to obtain adequate funding for National Union's pro-German activity in Norway. In this effort, they were joined by Quisling's old confidant, Aall. One of the main claims Hagelin had made when boasting to Aall and Fermann about his influential contacts in Germany was his acquaintanceship with Herbert Göring, a cousin of the powerful Hermann Göring.[76] Hagelin now had occasion to prove his worth by seeking to employ his channel of communication to the Reich Minister and head of the *Luftwaffe*. Hagelin, Scheidt, and Aall busily employed their time in the spring of 1939, seeking to find the means whereby Göring's various offices could be tapped for funds. Hagelin decided to write direct to the Reich Minister and have the letter delivered personally by Göring's cousin, Herbert.[77] To make the letter as impressive as possible, Hagelin included Quisling's personal biography, which the NS leader had sent in response to a request from Aall.[78]

In the letter, written on May 18 and delivered on the following day by the willing Herbert,[79] Hagelin repeated a number of the arguments which Quisling had employed on many previous occasions when seeking aid. Hagelin emphasized the alleged treasonable ties between the Labor party and Moscow, the pro-English outlook of the *borgerlige* parties, and how Norway's strategic position was of importance for Germany. Quisling's new spokesman insisted that the NS leader was capable of decisively altering the anti-German atmosphere in Norway, but that funds were required for this effort. Specifically, Hagelin declared that Quisling intended to establish a large daily newspaper with an edition of 25,000 copies, appearing with twelve pages on weekdays and sixteen on Sunday.[80] In making this claim, Hagelin demonstrated not only that he had a good imagination, but also that he had been away from Norway for a considerable time, since Sunday papers were not published. To realize the ambitious undertaking, he suggested that Göring should provide Quisling with a "loan" of six and a half million marks.[81]

Hagelin informed Aall on May 25 that the letter had been sent to the Reich Minister.[82] The situation in Germany involving Quisling and his representatives now began to assume the characteristics of a web of intrigue, thanks to a unique incident concerning Aall. The aging scholar, then sixty-seven years old, became enmeshed in the schemes of the *Abwehr*, the German intelligence service. When he attended Hitler's fiftieth birthday celebration in April, Aall renewed ties with an old acquaintance, Dr. Walther de Laporte, whom Aall knew from past meetings in Germany, going back to at least 1934.[83] A captain supposedly attached to the High Command, de Laporte in reality was an *Abwehr* agent. He in turn introduced Aall a few days later to his superior, another captain, Dr. Theodor Gottlieb von Hippel. Using the rather transparent code names La Roche and von Hohenstein, the two operated under the cover of a false travel and import and export agency located in Sybelstrasse 40, just off the Kurfürstendamm.[84] No one suspected that this office was part of *Abwehr's Abteilung* II, the intelligence service's espionage section.[85]

As a result of the discussions that Aall conducted with Hippel and de Laporte, he agreed to become part of the operation which the two agents controlled. On June 8 the three signed a contract. Aall too had received a code name, Dr. Alwaz. By the terms of the agreement, he agreed to become the head of an office, or "*center*", to be set up in the Swedish city of Malmö. His assignment was to lead an ostensibly independent political movement whose ideology was labelled as "controlled individualism" or "social individualism".[86] This was Hippel's brainwave, he being something of a political ideologue. He had, in the period prior to Hitler's takeover, been engaged in theoretical speculation as to how to reconcile freedom for the individual with the restraints required for the collective benefit of society as a whole.[87] It was natural for someone such as him to find refuge within Admiral Canaris' intelligence service, later renowned for its opposition to Hitler.

Aall enthusiastically accepted Hippel's political principles, declaring that they were in accord with his own ideas. Having received the necessary financial support enabling him to set himself up in Sweden, by the third week of June Aall had rented quarters in Drotningstorget 1 in Malmö. He thereupon was ready to begin his work to spread "social individualism" in various countries throughout the world. In this fashion, Quisling's representative had been recruited as an *Abwehr* agent. Aall later maintained that he had no idea at the time of Hippel's and de Laporte's real activity, and that it was not until during the war that he learned that de Laporte was a member of the *Abwehr*.[88] The records of the activity of the Malmö "center" establish beyond a doubt, however, that the representatives of "social individualism" in various countries were *Abwehr* agents, and that Aall definitely knew that they were acting on Germany's behalf in a concealed manner. His "center" functioned as a clearing house for making payments to German agents abroad.[89] Aall was aware of these payments, although it cannot be ascertained exactly how much information he received from Hippel and de Laporte. His major purpose in Sweden, however, was to spread pro-German propaganda through various cultural channels, and he wrote prolifically in this context. Among his contacts was his old friend in Berlin, Charles Stangeland, whom he visited frequently.[90]

Aall was staying with Stangeland at Motzrstrasse 5 when he conducted his discussions with Hippel and de Laporte concerning the establishment of the Malmö "center". During the course of their conversations, Aall naturally mentioned Quisling and the activity of NS in Norway. Hippel, who had little knowledge of Norwegian conditions, expressed an interest in Quisling. It was in this context that Aall invited Quisling to come to Berlin.[91] Aall paid for the visit, probably using funds provided by the *Abwehr*.[92]

Aall's association with the *Abwehr* therefore provided the impetus for
Quisling's journey to Germany in June 1939, a trip that would have fateful
consequences. Quisling later explained that he decided to go to Berlin because of Aall's "new theory of society . . . social individualism".[93] The NS
leader, however, had no knowledge of what "social individualism" entailed
at the time he departed from Norway. His primary concern for going to
Berlin was the one that had been uppermost in his mind for so long,
namely the need to acquire German backing.

Aall rather naively made no attempt to monopolize Quisling during the
latter's stay in Germany. When Aall learned that Quisling had accepted the
invitation, he informed Hagelin, asking whether the businessman would
come to Berlin to meet with Quisling. The energetic Hagelin did not have
to be asked twice. Writing to Aall on June 5, he replied that he would, of
course, come to Berlin to talk with "our friend", and he asked Aall to reserve a room for him at the hotel where "Q." would be staying.[94] Hagelin
requested that Aall telegraph him as soon as it became known when Quisling would arrive. Hagelin did not have to wait long. On the very next day
Aall received a telegram from Quisling, declaring that he would be arriving
on Thursday, June 8, at 6:13 p.m., Stettiner Bahnhof. He announced he
would remain five to six days.[95] Aall immediately sent the information on
to Hagelin.[96]

The NS leader arrived as planned on June 8, the very day when Aall formally signed his agreement with Hippel and de Laporte. After having been
briefed by Aall, Quisling and Hagelin on the following day quite probably
met Hippel in his disguised quarters on Sybelstrasse. According to the latter's postwar account of the meeting, Quisling and Hagelin enthusiastically
accepted the basic ideas of "social individualism" and agreed to use NS on its
behalf, receiving in return "a considerable sum".[97] Whether Hippel's statement is completely accurate is uncertain, in particular because he had a reputation as an adventurer with an overactive imagination.[98] There is no question, however, but that Quisling did at least in part commit himself to becoming an advocate for "social individualism". This is revealed in the correspondence he subsequently carried on with Aall after the latter had moved to
Malmö.[99] During the summer and fall of 1939 Aall provided Quisling with a
regular monthly payment of 250 *kroner*, which undoubtedly came from the
Abwehr.[100] An additional source of documentary evidence relating to the NS
leader's involvement with the *Abwehr*'s "social individualism" is found in
Aall's postwar statements, which were made prior to, and therefore independent of, Hippel's account. Aall, however, described the meeting between
Quisling and Hippel as occurring at the time of a later visit by Quisling to
Germany, in December 1939. Aall may have confused the two trips, or he
may have been attempting to mislead his police interrogators. He stated that
he, Quisling, Hagelin, de Laporte, and Hippel had been present, at which
time Quisling declared that he was willing to work on behalf of "social indi-

vidualism" in Scandinavia. In return, said Aall, Quisling received on the spot a check for 15,000 *kroner*.[101]

Although the meeting with Hippel showed that Quisling had no qualms about becoming a paid propagandist for the Germans, his involvement with the *Abwehr* proved to be of peripheral significance. In addition to Aall's contacts, another German source was highly interested in meeting the NS leader. Hans Wilhelm Scheidt became directly involved in Quisling's visit, and his stay, which had originally been expected to last some five to six days, proved to be of considerably longer duration. Scheidt cleared the way for Quisling, providing him with direct access to Rosenberg at a meeting held on June 13.[102] The NS representative in Germany, Fermann, drove Quisling and Hagelin to the conference, but was forced to wait outside.[103] Fermann thereby received a very firm indication that Hagelin had become Quisling's foremost adviser and agent in Germany.

The NS leader took full advantage of his opportunity to talk with Rosenberg for a protracted period of time. The visionary *Reichsleiter* was a receptive listener, since he and Quisling both liked to consider grand international schemes. The latter discussed in detail his favorite themes. He brought up his idea of a union of Germanic states which could serve as a bulwark against the Soviet Union. He also stressed Scandinavia's strategic value in the event of war, and NS' importance in Scandinavia as a propagandist for Germany. In this connection, Quisling made his standard request for funds.[104]

Rosenberg was favorably inclined, but the Office of Foreign Affairs could not possibly provide the desired funding. Rosenberg's office was kept on a tight budget, being unable to gain the support it wanted.[105] In order to find a potential source of financial backing, it therefore became necessary for Rosenberg to fall back on the scheme which Hagelin and Scheidt had worked on before – to try to get Göring's organization to open its coffers. With Rosenberg's approval, Scheidt thereupon accompanied Quisling to a meeting on June 16 with undersecretary Paul Körner, Göring's deputy in the four-year plan program. Once more, Quisling marshalled his arguments. He concentrated on emphasizing Scandinavia's strategic and economic significance, and on NS' alleged importance in contributing to a pro-German viewpoint.[106] Scheidt was pleased with the result of the conference, declaring that Körner had been understanding and had been willing to meet with him later about the matter.[107]

What counted most for Scheidt, however, was that he had been able to create a strong activist position for himself through his ability to monopolize Quisling. Quisling's cause had become Scheidt's cause, and he was prepared to pursue it relentlessly, thereby binding Quisling to the Office of Foreign Affairs. He reported back to Rosenberg on June 16 that he had given Quisling a great deal of attention during the last two days, and that he had gained the impression that the NS leader had full confidence in him.[108]

While in Berlin, Quisling also visited the Minister of Agriculture, Rudolf Darre, with Fermann once more loyally providing transportation.[109] Exactly what they discussed at this meeting remains unresolved. Quisling maintained after the war that it was merely a social call, made on behalf of a school friend who was personally acquainted with the Darre family.[110]

Following his stay in Berlin, Quisling travelled north to Lübeck to attend the annual "Nordic week" celebration of the Nordic Association, Rosenberg's front organization.[111] During the course of his stopover, Quisling had the opportunity to establish a truly close personal relationship with Rosenberg. One evening following the end of the formal proceedings for the day, the NS *Fører* took part in the conversation of a small group which included Rosenberg. Although usually taciturn in the company of others, Quisling obviously was inspired by the cordial atmosphere and launched into a discourse, talking about the great powers and international politics, and about the possibility of greater Nordic and Germanic cooperation. He inspired Rosenberg, who believed that in Quisling he had discovered a kindred spirit.[112]

Quisling returned home in late June, heartened by the knowledge that he had the sympathy and backing of Rosenberg and his organization. The Office of Foreign Affairs was now fully committed to the NS leader, as its coordinator, Arno Schickedanz, revealed on June 24. He wrote directly to Hans-Heinrich Lammers, the head of Hitler's Chancellery, interceding for Quisling. In the letter, Schickedanz indicated how Rosenberg's office had accepted without reservation Quisling's slanted interpretation of political conditions in Norway. The Norwegian public was described as being completely manipulated by "the Anglo-Saxon and Moscow propaganda". Quisling, it was asserted, did not on his own have the resources to beat back this propaganda. Schickedanz thereupon raised the question whether it would be possible for Quisling to receive funds so that he could begin a successful counteraction. Schickedanz declared that Quisling estimated that he "only" needed a loan of approximately six million *Reichsmark* to undertake this task.[113]

Upon departing for Norway, the prospective recipient of these millions had obviously been stimulated by the atmosphere in which he conducted his discussions in Germany. He therefore could not help but feel a letdown when he contrasted the excitement he had experienced in the Third Reich with the regular routine of Oslo. He did not relish his return to Norway, where he again had to face the reality of his insignificance. Writing to Aall, he complained that conditions remained the same as before, with the majority of people not having any understanding of what was happening in the world. His disgust with the public for failing to heed his admonitions was revealed in the sarcastic comment: "Ibsen knew his people".[114] Tired after his hectic stay in Germany, he felt the need for a rest. He informed Aall that he would spend a long week in Telemark, and would be back in Oslo on about July 10.[115]

During the summer of 1939 he paid a considerable amount of attention to Aall's project in Malmö, indicating that he was involved at least to some extent with the operations of the *Abwehr* agents Hippel and de Laporte. However, from the evidence available it appears as if he devoted himself entirely to ideological questions, and it cannot be ascertained to what degree, if any, he was aware of the espionage activities associated with the "center". He served as a critic for Aall, with the latter submitting drafts of "social individualism"'s ideology to Quisling for comment.[116] The NS *Fører*, as usual inspired when dealing with abstract ideological considerations, went so far as to incorporate the term "social individualism" into National Union's ideology at the annual meeting of the party in August.[117] While he had no difficulty in reconciling "social individualism on a national foundation" with NS' principles, his motivation in large part was monetary. He received his 250 *kroner* a month from Aall in the form of bank drafts.[118]

While Quisling was preoccupied with Aall's ideological planning and with preparations for the NS annual meeting in August, his two strong backers in Germany, Hagelin and Scheidt, concerned themselves with more important matters. Following Quisling's discussions in Germany, Scheidt left soon afterwards for Norway, ostensibly for the purpose of ascertaining whether Quisling's account of the political situation in the country was really correct.[119] In truth, however, Scheidt had already made up his mind. His stay in Norway merely served the purpose of strengthening the apparent "expertise" that he commanded, thereby giving his "reports" the color of authenticity which they needed, in particular since they were forwarded by Rosenberg and Schickedanz to other German officials. For *Reichsleiter* Rosenberg, support for Quisling was equally important. His Office of Foreign Affairs was under fire from a number of critics within the administration, most notably the Foreign Ministry, which questioned whether it should continue to exist. His link with Quisling was therefore important for Rosenberg, providing him with a justification for his office's worth.[120]

Once back in Berlin, Scheidt proceeded to draw up his report to Rosenberg on July 15. Not surprisingly, Scheidt declared that he had found Quisling's description of Norway to be entirely accurate.[121] It was important for him to stress that *Storting* president Carl J. Hambro was a "full blooded Jew" and that the Labor party had a secret agreement with

Moscow.[122] Scheidt went on to declare that in the event of a war between Germany and Russia, "the Norwegian communists" (i.e. the Labor party) would carry out a revolution in order to hand northern Norway over to Russia, while southern Norway would become a Soviet republic under Russian domination.[123] Similarly, he insisted that England in the event of war intended to use bases in southern Norway and Sweden for attacks against the Third Reich.[124]

The political novice had no inhibitions against attacking German diplomats in Norway for failing to draw the same conclusions as he. Interestingly, not only did he recommend that the threat to Germany be averted through support of Quisling, but also that similar aid be provided for *Nationen*. In Norway, Scheidt had met, among others, Quisling's former champion, editor Aadahl.[125] Scheidt's superficiality was amply illustrated by the fact that he could make such a suggestion on the basis of this brief meeting.

In reality, the arguments that he used in his report to Rosenberg were largely not his at all, the reference to *Nationen* being an exception. Three days before Scheidt wrote it, Hagelin had posted a letter to Scheidt from Dresden. In his letter, Hagelin used almost word for word many of the arguments which Scheidt incorporated into his "report".[126]

This incident provided good insight into the political strategy which Rosenberg's office employed. It was not interested in following a policy based on a realistic assessment of the situation in Norway, as a professional diplomat would have been. Instead, conditions were altered and interpreted in a manner consistent with the position which the Office of Foreign Affairs had already adopted. Had it not been for the tragic consequences of their actions, the cooperation between Scheidt and Hagelin could have been reduced in significance to comic antics, carried out by two political adventurers who gave free rein to their imagination in their common effort to bolster the interests of their front man, Quisling. In many ways, the politics which he later became identified with stemmed from the creation of these two hard-driving, imaginative schemers. Through Scheidt, Hagelin could make his influence felt on Scheidt's immediate superior, Schickedanz, and on Rosenberg himself. As for Scheidt, he assumed responsibility for all correspondence having to do with raising money for Quisling in Germany. Scheidt did so in his official capacity as head of the Northern Section.[127]

Because he also headed the Office of Foreign Affairs' educational center, Scheidt was responsible for hosting a group of young NS members who attended a fourteen-day seminar. During his previous stay, Quisling had asked that a number of dependable NS members, whom he personally would pick out, be given the opportunity of attending a course in Germany. The *Reichsleiter* gave his consent.[128] As a result, some twenty-five young NS adherents, including Fuglesang, arrived in Berlin in early August to attend a series of lectures devoted to explanations of various aspects of the Third Reich.[129] Although suspicion later developed that the trip might have been part of the conspiratorial activity that Quisling engaged in, in particular since he chose the participants, there is no evidence to support this view. The incident did reveal, however, one additional indication of Quisling's ties with Rosenberg's organization. Furthermore, the appearance of Norwegians at Scheidt's educational center did nothing to lessen his pretensions of being a Scandinavia expert.

During the summer and fall of 1939, however, he did not achieve any noteworthy success in furthering the claim that Quisling's assessment of the situation in Norway was correct, and that the NS leader therefore deserved full German backing. Scheidt's embroidered report of July 15 had been forwarded by Schickedanz to Dr. Lammers in the Reich Chancellery on July 29.[130] But like the previous letter which Schickedanz had sent to Lammers on June 24, Scheidt's "report" did not elicit any response. The attempts by Hagelin and Scheidt to solicit financial assistance through Göring's organization similarly led to no result. Scheidt made repeated entreaties, and even Rosenberg personally attempted to intercede at a meeting with Göring, but with no success.[131] Both Quisling and Hagelin, who hoped to have the matter expedited advantageously, were chagrined.[132] Despite the firm backing from Rosenberg's office, no major economic assistance materialized. The only payments that Quisling received were the small sums forwarded by Aall, but Hippel and de Laporte could not hope to come up with the large-scale financing which Quisling insisted he needed.

When World War II began, Quisling quite plainly was confused by the rapid developments which led to the outbreak of the conflict. From the time of his initial entry into politics he had constantly proclaimed his opposition to communism at home and abroad. National Union's increasingly close identification with Hitler's National Socialism, in particular from 1935 onwards, had been justified in large part by Hitler's stance as the champion against communist expansion. Now, however, the German dictator and his Soviet counterpart had to all intents resolved their differences in the Nazi-Soviet Pact. As a result, Hitler had a free hand in attacking Poland, following which Stalin joined in the partition of that unfortunate country.

For Quisling, who less than three months earlier had been preaching to his German contacts about the alleged danger which Russia posed to Norway and to Germany's strategic interests in Scandinavia, this turn of events was plainly unsettling. He had only the official German propaganda explanation to go by, which heaped blame on Poland and on the Western powers of Britain and France, and this justification left him unresolved. He wrote to Aall on September 18 that the most recent events had created a number of important questions in his mind, questions that had to be settled. He was therefore glad that Aall would be coming to Oslo shortly so that they could have a chance to discuss the situation.[133]

With regard to internal politics, however, it was much easier for Quisling to adopt a firm position following the start of the war. As before, he and NS remained alienated from all other parties. The tendency in Norway, as in the other Scandinavian countries, was for partisan activity to be diminished in favor of a common effort to deal with the problems of this difficult period. Quisling, however, continued to criticize all aspects of government. In his letter to Aall, he maintained it was "scandalous" how the government had neglected the country's defense and supplies, but he emphasized most strongly his fear that cooperation between Hambro and the "Marxist government" was an indication that Norway was being "betrayed". The fact that it was possible for a "blood Jew" (Hambro) to work together with "spiritual Jews" (the Nygaardsvold government) left him feeling highly suspicious.[134] This illustrated once more his intense emotional need to identify himself completely with Norway. Subconsciously too, he ascribed motives to his political enemies that were similar to his own. Just as he conspired with the Germans, his opponents were, no doubt, in contact with the Western allies, in particular the British.

After he had a chance to consult with Aall, Quisling committed an act that later aroused some attention and puzzlement, but which merely re-emphasized the amateurish and theoretical approach he had to politics when left to his own judgement. He dispatched another telegram, this time to Neville Chamberlain. Having first discussed its contents with the equally theoretical Aall, Quisling sent the telegram on October 11.[135] Pointing out that he had been charged with "the care of British interest in Russia" from 1927 to 1929, he declared that he was speaking on behalf of almost everyone in Scandinavia in deploring the "fratricidal war" that had broken out between Germany and Great Britain. Seeking to appeal to Chamberlain personally, the NS leader declared that he had been impressed by the Prime Minister's declaration of September 30 concerning Anglo-German relations. Today, said Quisling, the question was one of saving Europe and civilization by creating peace with Germany in the spirit of Chamberlain's declaration. Such a peace, Quisling maintained, could only come about through the "fusion of British, French, and German interests" in a European federation. In order to accomplish this, he permitted himself to suggest that the British "should in accordance with the tested method of the federalization of America, South Africa, and Australia" invite each European country to choose ten representatives as delegates to a convention which would draw up the constitution for a "commonwealth of European nations", in turn to be submitted for plebiscitorial approval in each of the countries involved. In closing, he praised Chamberlain as being the only statesman who could bring Europe back to peace and reason under the present circumstances. The NS leader signed himself as "Former Minister of Defense", and he did not fail to mention that he was a Commander of the British Empire.[136]

The telegram was Quisling's solution to the European conflict after six weeks of war, and after Poland had been crushed and conquered. In sending it, his motivation was clear. He regarded himself as a statesman whose views merited the attention of the British prime minister. Furthermore, the telegram's contents did represent its author's true convictions. He had consistently emphasized the need for cooperation among "Nordic" countries and the danger of war between Germany and England which might be to Russia's advantage. He was therefore disturbed by a war which allowed Russia to stay on the sidelines in a favorable position. But his advocacy for peace did not in any way detract from his pro-German position. There was no mention of Germany having to restore any of its gains. On the contrary, the bid for peace would have to come from Chamberlain, not from Hitler.

The British response indicated a realistic perception of the NS leader's standing and the value of his proposals. It came in the form of a brief, polite, and non-commital one sentence reply from the British legation in Oslo.[137]

The legation's circumspect acknowledgement was fully justified by the unaltered, unequivocal pro-German position which Quisling adhered to after the war began. His total commitment to the Nazi cause was demonstrated again following the outbreak of the Russo-Finnish War in November 1939. Considering how he had always warned against Soviet aggression in his anti-communist crusade, one might logically have assumed that he would immediately have come out in support of the Finns as the victims of communist aggression. But he did nothing of the sort, and NS instead went so far as to issue strict orders to its members not to join up with the Norwegian volunteers who fought on the Finnish side during the Winter War.[138] Quisling's reason for assuming this stand was transparently obvious. Germany remained neutral in the conflict, in accordance with the terms of the Nazi-Soviet Pact, and he had no intention of adopting a policy that was in opposition to Germany's position. He had no wish to risk estranging the Germans, whose patronage he needed. Privately, however, he had serious reservations about Hitler's agreement with Stalin, and his anti-communism remained as strong as ever. But while he might voice his objections in private conversation and correspondence, publicly no such doubts about Germany were apparent.[139] He defended the pact as a necessity, but he did not go so far as to abandon publicly his opposition to communism and the Soviet Union, which he continued to reaffirm in his articles.[140]

In his defense of Germany's conduct during the Russo-Finnish War, Quisling and NS were in the same position that all sectarian parties find themselves in when they, for ideological reasons, completely identify their cause with a foreign power. The rapid changes in policy which great powers make from time to time leave their foreign affiliates looking ridiculous as they desperately scramble to bring their ideological outlook into conformity with the temporary interests of their patron and ideal. In doing just this during the Winter War, Quisling disappointed a few of his remaining sympathizers, who up to then had still retained a certain degree of admiration for him because of his adament anti-communism. One such individual, an old officer, wrote to Quisling in January 1940, declaring his displeasure. He had expected that Quisling, in view of his many years of struggle against "Bolshevism", would have been the first to volunteer to fight in Finland. Instead, the officer commented acidly, Quisling had allowed himself to be taken captive by what the officer described as the most idiotic movement that had ever existed – Nazism. Previously, said the writer, Quisling had fought for Norway and against Russia. Now he was fighting for Germany and against England.[141]

Because he had not received the funding that he had anticipated, and because of his desire to orient himself first-hand about the political situation in the Third Reich, Quisling by early winter 1939 was once more interested in journeying to Berlin in order to reach a satisfactory accommodation. As had been the case for his previous visit in June, Dr. Aall prepared the way for the Fører's journey. Aall had travelled to Berlin already in early November. As on previous occasions, he stayed with his friend Professor Stangeland in Motzrstrasse 5. On November 27 Aall sent an invitation to Quisling to come to Berlin.[142]

On the day that Aall forwarded his invitation, Quisling became involved with another person who also played a part in the NS leader's all-important visit to Germany in December 1939. He attended a book exhibition at the German legation in Oslo, where he happened to meet a German historian.[143] Dr. Ulrich Noack, whose wife was Norwegian, had arrived in Oslo in the fall of 1939, ostensibly in order to write a history of Scandinavia. In addition, however, he had a secret mission: to report about political conditions in Norway to the Information Division in the Foreign Ministry. The German legation in Oslo was ordered to give him all possible assistance in carrying out this task.

Despite backing from the Foreign Ministry, Noack did not prove to be a very competent agent. He wanted to play an active political role, and he therefore interfered in matters about which he had neither knowledge nor competence. As a consequence, he was soon disliked both by members of the legation and by the Norwegians with whom he became acquainted. Many Norwegians regarded him simply as a spy.[144]

Quisling, however, had no reservations about Noack. The two held long discussions at the NS leader's home during the first week of December. At this time, Quisling made certain that Noack received a complete résumé of his past accomplishments, including his outstanding military examination. Noack was impressed enough to include all this in his report to the Foreign Ministry.[145] In their conversations, Quisling insisted that the Nazi-Soviet Pact could not last, and that Germany should attack Russia already in the following spring. He argued that the Red Army would disintegrate in the same way that the Polish army had collapsed. Once Russia was conquered, then England would be faced with the difficulty of fighting a two-front war in Europe and the Middle East. Illustrating his concept dramatically on a world map, he pointed to the area which he maintained lay within Germany's "natural continental sphere of influence", which should be joined in a "federal system" under German leadership. Not surprisingly, he included Scandinavia solidly within this sphere. According to Noack, Quisling declared that the Norwegians, as part of such a system, could aid in the economic exploitation of Russian territory by being assigned the vast lumber territory along the Dvina, an idea that he certainly had acquired from his association with Prytz.[146]

Noack responded enthusiastically to Quisling's ideas. When he learned that Quisling was planning a trip to Germany, he sat down and wrote letters of introduction for Quisling to his contacts in the Foreign Ministry. When the NS leader left for Berlin by train on December 9, the historian was at the station to see him off and to give him the introductory letters.[147] It was further agreed that Noack himself would leave on the following day to join Quisling in Berlin.[148]

Not until after he had held the first of two long discussions with Noack did Quisling respond positively to Aall's invitation.[149] He telegraphed on December 5 to inform Aall that he had just received his letter. Quisling did not waste time, declaring that he would be in Berlin already on the evening of Friday, December 8. Indicating his dependence on Hagelin, Quisling asked that the Dresden businessman be contacted.[150]

The trip did not go as smoothly as Quisling had anticipated. He encountered difficulty in obtaining a visa, indicating that the German legation in Oslo may have sought to obstruct his departure. On December 7 he was forced to contact Aall, asking the latter to intercede on his behalf.[151] Aall apparently solved the problem by going directly to State Secretary Ernst von Weizsäcker in the Foreign Ministry, who made it possible for Quisling to secure the needed visa.[152]

Having received the green light to depart, Quisling telegraphed ahead to Aall that he would arrive tomorrow, Sunday, 7:55 p.m., Stettiner Bahnhof. This time too, however, the helpful scholar received little pleasure from Quisling's company in Berlin. Hagelin was on the scene when Quisling arrived on the 10th, and much to Aall's annoyance, the resourceful businessman took over complete control of Quisling's itinerary. Whereas Aall appears to have been mainly interested in having Quisling meet with his *Abwehr* superiors, Hippel and de Laporte,[153] Hagelin held out much better prospects than discussions with second-level intelligence officers. Acting in cooperation with Rosenberg's office, Hagelin had come up with an alternative to Göring's organization which could provide Quisling with the resources he needed. They had secured contacts within the navy. The way was clear for the NS leader to meet with the commander-in-chief, Grand Admiral Erich Raeder.

The German naval commander had ample reason for desiring contact with the visitor from Oslo. Raeder had since September 1939 considered the possibility of gaining control of the Norwegian coastline. The outbreak of hostilities in 1939 had been an unwelcome occurrence for the head of the *Kriegsmarine*. His long-range planning was based on building up the battle fleet to the point where it could match the British fleet. The attack on Poland and the declaration of war on Germany by Britain and France completely altered the situation. The German navy could not hope to challenge the Royal Navy on the high seas. Its warfare had to concentrate primarily on the strategy of destroying Allied merchant shipping. In this context, it was necessary for the navy to have a wide area of access into the North Atlantic for its U-boats, destroyers and MTBs. The coast of Norway was therefore of great strategic interest for Raeder, also because its possession would permit Germany to avoid the damaging effects of a naval blockade such as that which the Royal Navy had employed against Imperial Germany in World War I.[154] On the other hand, were Norway to come under British control, the situation would become even more critical. This would enable the British to tighten the blockade, and Norwegian territory could serve as useful bases for attacks against German targets.

The Grand Admiral's concern about Norway revealed itself clearly when the post for a new naval representative was created in Germany's Oslo legation. *Korvettenkapitän* Richard Schreiber received this appointment on October 1, just at the time when Raeder first began to pay particular attention to Norway. Schreiber at first was subordinate to the naval attaché in Stockholm, but from December he served independently as naval attaché in Norway.[155]

Already prior to coming to Oslo, Schreiber had met Scheidt at a restaurant in Berlin. Their meeting was hardly coincidental, in particular since Scheidt carried a message from Rosenberg, inviting the newly appointed naval representative to meet with the *Reichsleiter*.[156] Schreiber accepted the invitation, visiting Rosenberg before going on to his assignment. He later claimed that their meeting was short, consisting largely of a discourse by Rosenberg on his "Germanic" ideas, but it hardly seems likely that Rosenberg would take the time to seek out Schreiber merely to lecture him on Germanic ideology.[157] The subject of Quisling and NS undoubtedly came up in the conversations between Schreiber, Rosenberg, and Scheidt. Schreiber in the future cooperated closely with Scheidt in abetting Rosenberg's pro-Quisling policy, thereby coming into conflict with members of the diplomatic corps in the German legation and the Foreign Ministry.[158] It appears that Schreiber initiated his cooperation with Rosenberg's organization already at the time he began his Norwegian assignment, and that he had a hand in making the arrangements which brought Quisling to Raeder. Raeder later wrote that he had received support from Schreiber and Captain Schulte-Mönting, who cooperated with Rosenberg's organization, allowing contact to be made with Quisling and Hagelin, who came to Berlin in early December, and were introduced to Hitler by Raeder with the approval of Rosenberg.[159]

The resolute and adventurous Hagelin, undaunted by his failure to obtain financial aid from Göring's organization, also played a part in the scheme to combine Quisling's and Rosenberg's interests with those of the navy. During the winter of 1939–1940, Hagelin established ties with Captain Erich Schulte-Mönting, who served as Raeder's personal adviser. There is reason to believe that Hagelin may also have had personal contact with Raeder during this period.[160] Admiral Hermann Boehm, who served under Raeder as commanding admiral in Norway, stated in his postwar memoirs that Hagelin became acquainted with the Grand Admiral and arranged the connection between Raeder and Quisling.[161]

So while Quisling on his train ride to Berlin on December 9 and 10 still remained uncertain as to which approach he should follow to secure total commitment from the Germans, as indicated by his dealings with Aall and Noack, Hagelin and Rosenberg, waiting for his arrival, had no doubts at all. For them there was only one option to consider. It led directly to Raeder and the navy. And through Raeder, the highest goal might be reached: an audience with Hitler himself.

Upon his arrival in Berlin, Quisling almost immediately found himself under the guidance of Hagelin and Rosenberg. The *Reichsleiter* arranged to have the NS leader quartered in the Office of Foreign Affairs educational center.[162] Already on the next day, on the morning of December 11, Rosenberg took the initiative to report to Hitler about Quisling's visit.[163] For the time being, however, the situation was not conducive for Hitler to receive Quisling. Nevertheless, Rosenberg noted his determination to pursue the possibility.[164]

Before Quisling could hope to meet with Hitler, it was necessary for him to brief his sponsors. In conversation with Rosenberg on the 11th, Quisling painted as dark a picture as possible about conditions in Scandinavia. He used all possible arguments, the great majority being based on speculation and fantasy, to alarm the Germans, whose nerves were naturally high-strung by the uncertainties of war. Quisling may possibly have believed his arguments, no matter how fanciful, thanks to his subconscious ability of self-suggestion. In Rosenberg he had a responsive listener. Quisling maintained that public opinion in Scandinavia was steadily more anti-German because of the Russo-Finnish War. In Norway the so-called "English party" was becoming increasingly stronger, and "the Jew Hambro continues to work against us". In Sweden, Quisling alleged, discussions had already been held about providing bases for the British fleet. In reaction to this threatening situation in the north, Rosenberg noted that Quisling presented a drastic remedy: "He advanced once again the concrete proposal to prepare the way for a German landing at the request of a new government which would fight its way forward".[165] Although Rosenberg stated that Quisling had made such a suggestion previously, this is the first specific evidence of his plan to carry out a pro-German coup in Norway, enabling the Third Reich's forces to occupy the country. However, both Hagelin and Scheidt had earlier in the year raised such a possibility in their correspondence, so the idea was not foreign to Quisling's most immediate advisers and henchmen.[166]

During his stay in December, Quisling repeated this plan to all prominent Germans who received him. He had thereby crossed the boundary separating activity which was questionable to that which was directly treasonable. Previously he had sought German financial backing in order to strengthen NS politically. Now he offered to act as the instrument by which the Germans gained military control of his country.

Aware of the interest which the navy had in Norway, Rosenberg sent Quisling directly on to Raeder.[167] Accompanied by Hagelin, the NS leader arrived at naval headquarters at noon on December 11. Like Rosenberg, the Grand Admiral proved to be an attentive listener to what Quisling had to say about alleged conditions in Norway. In his meetings with Raeder and with other German leaders, it must be kept in mind that Quisling was introduced as having a much higher status than that which he really possessed, due to the build-up which he received from Rosenberg's organization. He was presented not merely as the leader of a political party that was friendly to Germany, but as an experienced military expert, a former Minister of Defense and General Staff officer. To Germans who had little or no knowledge about Norway, these credentials seemed impressive. He could therefore state his viewpoint with authority, in particular to someone who already was favorably predisposed such as Raeder.

The NS *Fører* repeated many of the same opinions that he had supplied to Rosenberg, but he understandably placed more stress on matters of military interest when talking to Raeder. He maintained that the Norwegian government had concluded a secret agreement with England whereby the British had permission to enter Norway if the country became engaged in war with a third power. He went so far as to specify that the British had plans to land near Stavanger, and that they intended to use Kristiansand as a base of operations. In order to make the situation appear especially sinister, he insisted that the Norwegian government, the *Storting* and the press were all controlled by one individual, "the well known Jew Hambrow [*sic*], who is a special friend of Hoare Belisha [*sic*]".[168] Since Leslie Hore Belisha, a Jew, served as British Minister of War, Quisling's attempt to link Hambro with this key Allied official took on special significance. In making this assertion, he used exactly the same argument that Hagelin had advanced earlier, in November, when he wrote to Schickedanz. Hagelin declared that the two were "both Jews and high-ranking Freemasons" who cooperated closely together.[169] It is not possible to say whether the argument originated with Quisling or Hagelin, but there is no doubt that the NS leader was influenced in a major way by the more assertive Hagelin during his stay in Germany. Hagelin was especially imaginative, weaving together a string of loose facts, distortions, and direct falsehoods into a whole fabric which appeared plausible to unknowledgeable Germans. Hagelin and Quisling influenced each other, each making use of arguments derived from the other.

In his conversation with Raeder, Quisling went on to assert that the entire press was in English hands. The evil genius, Hambro, furthermore misused his position, allegedly conspiring with "countless British agents" to bring the country completely under British control. Quisling then pointed to the danger for Germany if Norway were to be occupied by the British. The mouths of the Elbe and Rhine would be outflanked by the Western powers, and the Baltic would become a war zone, with German commerce being hindered. At the present time, he maintained, the Norwegian public was anxious because of the Russo-Finnish War. He declared his understanding for why Germany at the moment could do nothing to hinder the Russian advance, but he stressed the broad desire in Scandinavia to prevent the Russians from gaining greater influence. Hambro and his supporters, said Quisling, wished to restrict Russian expansion by seeking England's aid, a rather interesting assertion considering how contrary it was to Quisling's earlier claims that the Jews and the communists were part of the same all-encompassing conspiracy to gain world domination.[170]

He now came to the critical point in his conversation with the Admiral. His "national party", said Quisling, wished to prevent any fighting with Germany caused by a British attempt to gain bases in Norway. NS therefore wanted to anticipate such a move by "placing appropriate bases at the German forces' disposal". In preparation for such an eventuality, he claimed that NS already had agents in key positions within the railroad, postal, and intelligence services all along the Norwegian coast. However, he argued, it was now absolutely necessary for Germany to change its policy toward Norway, by which he really meant toward NS. Because of the incompetence of German diplomats, he asserted, his connection with Rosenberg's organization had not "led to the desired result". But it was now necessary during this visit, insisted both Quisling and Hagelin, to establish clarity in Germany's policy for the future. Quisling presented the argument that after January 10 the existing government and *Storting* would be illegal. He would repeat this legal argument constantly in attempting to justify any future coup on his part. He was referring to his strong, emotional, and incorrect claim that the *Storting* had illegally extended its term from three to four years. According to his line of reasoning, its mandate would expire at the end of 1939, and therefore when it met again in January 1940, it would be acting illegally, as would also the government, since its authority was based on the parliament. In this situation, he hinted rather broadly, a "political revolution" was possible, during which his "national party might not remain passive". He therefore declared that he wished to hold military discussions, and he asked to have the willing Scheidt assigned as his German representative.[171]

Raeder was demonstrably impressed by Quisling's argumentation. It fitted in perfectly with his desire to obtain strategic bases in Norway. He therefore promised to discuss the matter with Hitler, assuring Quisling and Hagelin that they would be informed of the outcome of his meeting with *der Führer*.[172] The head of the navy expressed himself even more optimistically to Rosenberg later in the day, declaring that Quisling's arrival had been "a stroke of fate". The Grand Admiral had grounds for his anticipation that events were in his favor. On the very next day he was scheduled to confer with Hitler.[173]

Exactly twenty-four hours after he had held his discussions with Quisling, Raeder met with the head of the Third Reich. Present were also General Keitel, head of the German High Command (*Oberkommando der Wehrmacht*), General Jodl, chief of the *Wehrmacht-Führungs-Amt*, and Captain Karl von Puttkammer, Hitler's naval aide. In his briefing, Raeder described his conversation with Quisling and Hagelin. The naval commander emphasized Quisling's position as "former minister of war [and] leader of the national party". He further added that Quisling gave a reliable impression, and then went on to recount the latter's analysis of the situation in Norway. The Grand Admiral pointed to Quisling's portrayal of the anti-German atmosphere in Norway, the alleged pro-British sentiment in the country through the supposed influence of Hambro ("Jew and friend of Hore-Belisha"). Raeder also emphasized "Quisling's conviction" that there existed a pact between England and Norway concerning a possible English occupation of Norway. In this event, he continued, Sweden would also assume a hostile position toward Germany. The likelihood of an English in-

vasion of Norway was very threatening, said the Grand Admiral, para-
phrasing Quisling, and such an invasion could occur within a short time.
He went on to repeat Quisling's unsound assertion that the *Storting* would
be illegal in January, allowing the possibility for a political revolution.
Raeder similarly cited Quisling's claim that he had good connections
within the officer corps and that his followers held key positions, for example within the railroad system. Raeder declared that Quisling was prepared to take over the government and to request German military support. The NS leader, said Raeder, was now ready to discuss military preparations with the *Wehrmacht*.[174]

Speaking now for himself, the Grand Admiral introduced a note of caution and show of objectivity which could serve as a cover should Quisling's
visit not have the desired results. He declared it was not possible to know
to what extent persons such as Quisling were acting for their own advantage, and how far they really had Germany's interests at heart. However,
having made this reservation, Raeder proceeded to use military arguments
similar to those that Quisling had given to him. The British, he insisted,
must be prevented at all costs from gaining control of Norway; this could
be decisive for the outcome of the war. Sweden would thereupon be completely under British influence, and the war could spill over into the Baltic.
The German navy would thereby be prevented from carrying out operations on the oceans and in the North Sea.[175]

Much to Raeder's pleasure, Hitler, who until this time had been unresponsive to his naval commander's arguments concerning Norway, now
appeared to be moved by the line of reasoning which Quisling, through Raeder, was making. *Der Führer* expressed his agreement, characterizing a British occupation of Norway as intolerable. Raeder could therefore afford to
mention possible negative repercussions resulting from German action
against Norway. A German occupation of bases along the coast, he said,
would naturally bring about a strong British response to block the transport
of iron ore from Narvik to Germany, resulting in surface warfare which the
German navy in the long run would not be capable of sustaining.[176]

Hitler, however, was clearly interested in pursuing the Norwegian
question. He considered the possibility of meeting Quisling personally so
that he might get an impression of the Norwegian, but decided that he
would first talk with *Reichsleiter* Rosenberg, "since he [Rosenberg] has
known Quisling for a long time".[177]

Raeder thereupon pressed on to recommend that if *der Führer*'s reaction
to Quisling were favorable, the *Oberkommando der Wehrmacht* should be
allowed to come to an agreement with Quisling concerning plans for the
preparation and the carrying out of an occupation of Norway, based on
two possibilities: "(a) peacefully, that is to say, the German *Wehrmacht* is
called to Norway, or (b) by use of force". Hitler agreed with the
suggestion.[178]

It now remained for Hitler to be briefed by an additional source concerning the former Norwegian Minister of Defense who had made such a good impression on the head of his navy. As he had said he would, the *Führer* later in the day called Rosenberg to the Reich Chancellery to discuss Quisling and his plans. Hitler stated that he was inclined to receive Quisling. However, he wanted to know how Quisling had planned to carry out his takeover of the government. Furthermore, *der Führer* also wished to have concrete information concerning Quisling's relationship with the Norwegian army in the event of an action in Norway.[179]

Rosenberg, of course, did not have such specific details at his disposal. The *Reichsleiter* therefore had to have a long discussion with Quisling on the evening of the 12th in order to obtain the information which Hitler requested.[180] As could be expected, the NS leader did not have any carefully thought out plans. He had come to Berlin without any clear goals except the need to obtain German support, and in order to achieve this he had painted as bleak a picture as possible about conditions in Norway. He had concocted his tale along with Hagelin. In a wartime situation, Quisling hoped he might, through German military backing, be able to achieve the position of leadership which he had been unable to obtain through politics in peacetime. But while specific plans were lacking, he had at his disposal his imagination, so capable of reasoning abstractly. He put it to full use in the company of the sympathetic and inspiring *Reichsleiter*, who like Quisling gained great satisfaction from allowing his imagination to dwell on plots for the future.

In response to Hitler's demand for information, Rosenberg conscientiously drew up a detailed memorandum about Quisling and the NS leader's proposed action. The latter's career was described in glowing terms. Quisling, maintained the *Reichsleiter*, had a reputation as "one of the best-known Scandinavian general staff officers". He had served as military attaché in Finland, represented British interests in Russia during 1927–1930, and had been the Norwegian Minister of War from 1931 to 1933. In the latter year he had founded National Union, a party which "stood and stands for an anti-Semitic point of view and goes in for the most intimate cooperation with Germany."[181] Quisling's ability to combine fact and fiction was demonstrated by Rosenberg's assertion that NS had 15,000 members and two to three hundred thousand sympathizers. NS had ca. 8,500 members at its prewar height, but following its disintegration it had been reduced to practically a nullity, and the contention that the party had sympathizers numbering in the hundreds of thousands was but another illustration of Quisling's propensity to exaggerate. No doubt in order to explain why NS with this alleged large following did not have representation in parliament, the memo stated falsely, quite possibly on Quisling's insistence, that NS had not participated in *Storting* elections.[182]

As legal justification for a seizure of power, Rosenberg repeated the NS leader's claim that the *Storting*'s mandate would be illegal in January. Quisling had further maintained that as "an old officer and former minister of war" he had "the most intimate connections with the Norwegian army". As evidence of this, he produced a letter from his follower in Narvik, Colonel Sundlo. Quisling also mentioned the names of Hvoslef and the commandant of the war college at Halden to give weight to the pretense that he enjoyed support within the army. This claim was largely fictitious, and the same was true concerning the assertion that the King was favorably disposed. Haakon VII was described as being well acquainted with Quisling from the time the latter had served in the government, and he maintained that he believed that the King regarded him highly, although the monarch was reputed to be pro-British. The report also reasserted Quisling's anti-Semitic viewpoint, which he knew the Germans would react favorably to, with "the Jew Hambro" being held responsible for all anti-German sentiment in Norway.[183]

In describing the specifics of Quisling's alleged plan of action, Rosenberg cited the NS leader as having suggested the following: a number of carefully selected Norwegians would be sent to Germany as soon as possible for special instruction by "experienced National Socialist fighters who have training in such actions". After having completed their course, these intended coup makers would return to Norway and immediately proceed to carry out their coup:

> The occupation of important centers in Oslo must follow quickly, and at the same time the German fleet, together with proportional contingents from the German army, must be moved into a previously determined inlet in front of the approach to Oslo, following a special appeal from the new Norwegian [Quisling] government. Quisling does not doubt that such an action – if it succeeds instantly – will immediately bring him support from those parts of the army which he now has connections with.[184]

Rosenberg added that Quisling of course had never discussed such a possibility with his contacts in the army. This statement provided clear indication of Quisling's authorship of the "plan" which Rosenberg described. In Quisling's mind, all he had to do was act, and the army would immediately rally to his side. This was exactly the same type of procedure which he had followed in politics. The failure of past actions because of his lack of preparation to bring about a proper response had by no means daunted his belief in pursuing such a course. As for the King, Quisling was equally optimistic, believing that the monarch would "respect such an accomplished fact".[185]

Rosenberg had intended to discuss the information he received from Quisling with Raeder before proceeding further. However, the *Reichsleiter* had the misfortune of re-injuring a bad leg when he collided with a door on the night of December 12, and he was therefore forced to send the plan that he had obtained from Quisling in the form of a written memorandum, appended to a letter which he addressed to Raeder on the following day. In this letter, Rosenberg declared that it remained to be decided "whether or not we shall recommend a reception [with Hitler] for *Herr* Minister Quisling". Rosenberg clearly acknowledged herein Raeder's superiority on this question, declaring that only the Grand Admiral had the competence to judge the technical features in Quisling's plan, and whether or not a quick military operation was possible. However, Rosenberg was of the opinion that "one must act when one *can* act". He requested Raeder, if he endorsed giving Quisling an audience with Hitler, personally to introduce the Norwegian visitor to *der Führer*, since Rosenberg was still immobilized. He also asked Raeder to phone him at home after having read the memorandum.[186]

The Grand Admiral remained eager as ever to utilize Quisling's visit as a means of realizing his goals. He phoned Rosenberg on the evening of the thirteenth and agreed that the two should meet, because of the *Reichsleiter's* incapacitation, at Rosenberg's home on the following morning. In their conversation the next day, both agreed that Quisling's proposed course of action was fraught with danger. Nevertheless, they were prepared to push on: "We were in agreement on the riskiness as well as on the necessity of this action." They further agreed that because of Rosenberg's bad leg it would be necessary for Raeder alone to "take Q[uisling] to *der Führer* so that he can gain a first-hand impression of his [Quisling's] personality".[187] The way was thereby open for the politically insignificant leader of a small pro-German sect, completely isolated from the mainstream of political opinion in his own country, to meet with the most powerful and feared man in the world, the dictator of the Third Reich.

Quisling did not reach Hitler because of his own efforts. The determining factor which decided whether or not he might gain the vital assistance that he had sought after for so long was the degree to which prominent German officials believed they could bolster their own positions by supporting him. In this Rosenberg and Raeder were in agreement: they both could use Quisling for their own purposes. Rosenberg backed Quisling in order to assert the interests of his Office of Foreign Affairs in his rivalry with the Foreign Ministry, while Raeder utilized Quisling's arguments in order to gain Hitler's attention for the navy's plans concerning the Norwegian coast. And Quisling willingly allowed himself to be used, not only by Raeder and Rosenberg, but to a degree also by persons in subordinate positions such as Scheidt and Hagelin, who promoted Quisling as a means of increasing their influence. This provided once more a striking illustration of a major aspect of the NS leader's political behavior. He could act as a front for more assertive individuals as long as they served his interests, and as long as his position as leader remained unquestioned. He exercised predominance in questions of theory, but allowed himself to be guided by others when it came to dealing with specific details and when deciding which action to take in a given situation.

Once Raeder and Rosenberg had agreed to move ahead, events proceeded quickly. Already by the afternoon of December 14, Quisling was ushered into Hitler's presence by the Grand Admiral.[188] The NS leader was accompanied by his two creative advisers, Hagelin and Scheidt. The latter came as the representative of Rosenberg's office. Scheidt's attendance also indicated that Quisling's request to have the impetuous young member of Rosenberg's organization serve as his liaison man had been acceded to. Scheidt had been serving with his army unit, but was specifically recalled to Berlin so that he could escort Quisling when the latter met with Hitler.[189] For the next several months Scheidt remained closely associated with Quisling. The importance of this connection proved to be considerable.

Hitler began the meeting in standard fashion by delivering a monologue which lasted for twenty minutes. He insisted that he preferred to have Scandinavia remain neutral in the war, but that he would never permit England to gain a foothold in the region, for example at Narvik. Next *der Führer* became acquainted with Quisling's political thought. The latter had brought along one of his memoranda, entitled "The Necessity of a Greater Germanic Union", which Hitler read through. As later developments would show, the general ideas which Quisling expressed in his treatises did not displease *der Führer* as a rule. The NS *Fører* had occasion to impress Hitler even more by describing the political situation in Norway, a subject which the latter, like most Germans, knew nothing about. The NS leader depicted the "illegal condition" his country's government would be in after January 10, when the *Storting* reassembled. Norway, he maintained, would then be in the hands of the "Marxists and the Jewish democrats". He of course also stressed the strategic importance it would have for Germany to save Norway from a British takeover.[190]

That evening the trio of Quisling, Hagelin, and Scheidt visited Rosenberg to report on their conversation with Hitler. All three were very pleased, as well they might be.[191] *Der Führer*'s reaction had been positive. As a result of his discussion with Quisling, Hitler ordered the *Oberkommando der Wehrmacht* to set up a small staff to begin to investigate "how one can carry out the occupation of Norway".[192] In this manner, through Raeder's and Rosenberg's use of Quisling, the German military machinery first began to make concrete plans for the possibility of an operation against Norway. Quisling alone cannot be given sole responsibility for this development. Had there not been interests in Germany, most notably the navy, that favored such a course because of the war, there would have been little chance for Quisling to gain a hearing. On the other hand, the NS leader's importance must not be underestimated. Had he not added a note of authenticity to Raeder's warning regarding the danger of the British gaining control of Norway, Hitler's interest in Scandinavia would no doubt have been aroused more slowly, and perhaps not with the same intensity, in particular during the winter of 1939–40 when his attention had originally been concentrated on planning for the campaign in the west against France and the Low Countries.

The discussions leading to Quisling's audience with Hitler took place without recourse to the German experts who had best knowledge of Norwegian affairs, the Foreign Ministry's officials in the Wilhelmstrasse who regularly received reports from the legation in Oslo. Rosenberg understandably wished to keep the Foreign Ministry completely isolated. Thanks to the realistic evaluations which came from Norway, the Foreign Ministry as before refused to attribute any importance to Quisling. Curt Bräuer, the Minister in Oslo, maintained pressure and encouragement on the Norwegian government to follow a policy of strict neutrality in the war, while at the same time assuring his superiors in Berlin that Norway was capable of adhering to such a neutral position, which was in accord with German interests.[193] When Bräuer learned of the NS *Fører*'s trip to Berlin through a conversation with Noack on December 10, just before the historian was about to follow after Quisling, the Minister did everything he could to sabotage the venture. Unaware of the possibility of Quisling meeting with Rosenberg and Raeder, Bräuer assumed that the sole purpose of the journey was for the NS leader to gain access to the Foreign Ministry by bringing up the plan for a German attack on the Soviet Union which he had discussed so enthusiastically with Noack. The Minister therefore telegraphed his superiors in the Foreign Ministry, warning them of Quisling's and Noack's scheme. In addition, Bräuer sent a report to Berlin which stressed Noack's unpopularity in Norwegian circles. In his account, the Minister described Noack's and Quisling's ideas as completely unrealistic, being based on fantasy.[194]

When Noack came to Berlin on the evening of December 11, he immediately phoned his contacts in the Foreign Ministry, but when he arrived at the Wilhelmstrasse on the following morning, he received a chilly reception. The Foreign Ministry had no interest in the idea of a campaign against the Soviet Union at this time, and Noack was given strict orders to concern himself only with his academic pursuits in Norway and not to meddle in politics.[195]

He received an additional setback when he later attempted to renew his ties with Quisling by phoning the latter at Rosenberg's residence, possibly on the evening of the 14th. Quisling no longer had any need to seek the assistance of the Foreign Ministry, whose representatives in Oslo had such a low regard for him. Now he enjoyed access to the head of the Third Reich himself. Quisling therefore maintained a detached and cool tone in his telephone conversation with Noack, who was plainly informed that the NS leader had no desire to follow up on their discussions concerning a possible German offensive against Russia.[196] Noack's humiliation was thereby total.

During the following days the NS leader had far more important matters to concern himself with. He saw at firsthand how the German military and political apparatus began to concentrate on the issues that he had brought up at his meeting with Hitler. On December 16, accompanied by Hagelin and Scheidt, Quisling attended a conference arranged by Hitler's military adviser, General Jodl. They discussed strategy with Hitler's naval aide, Captain Karl von Puttkamer, and Ambassador Walter Hewel of the Foreign Ministry. Quisling and his two co-conspirators attended a similar meeting two days later, at which Hewel and Colonel Rudolf Schmundt, Hitler's personal *Wehrmacht* adjutant, were present.[197]

Quite likely because of Ambassador Hewel's attendance at the December 16 conference, the Foreign Ministry now for the first time became aware of the real significance of Quisling's presence in Berlin.[198] State Secretary Weizsäcker telegraphed Bräuer personally on the 16th, requesting specific information on Quisling, NS, and Hagelin. Bräuer responded quickly on the next day, but his counsel did not prove particularly helpful. He could do nothing except to provide a realistic analysis of Quisling's status in Norway. The NS leader, said Bräuer, viewed Bolshevism as the great danger for Europe, and was concerned about the effect of the Nazi-Soviet Pact. Quisling was described as being obsessed with the idea of Germanic cooperation, and wished to include England in such activity, but was decidedly more sympathetic toward Germany than England. His political importance, however, was insignificant, and his prospects for the future not very good. *Fritt Folk* was able to publish editions of not more than 1000 copies. As for Hagelin, the German legation had no information about him.[199]

While this evaluation was true as far as Quisling's standing in Norway was concerned, in Germany the situation was quite different. What mattered in Berlin was that Quisling enjoyed Hitler's favor, and Ribbentrop had to take this into account. Again accompanied by Hagelin and Scheidt, Quisling was called to another meeting with *der Führer* on December 18.[200] Hitler repeated his wish that Norway should remain neutral. His belief in this possibility, however, had definitely been altered as a result of Quisling's influence. Hitler asked the latter whether he was aware of the repercussions that would result from German support for a Quisling government: "*Herr* Minister Quisling, if you request aid from me, do you realize that England will declare war on you?" Quisling did not hesitate, replying: "Yes, I realize this, and I anticipate that Norway's trade is going to be laid low for a time." Hitler's favorable impression of Quisling remained undiminished at this meeting, despite the presentation of yet another written memorandum containing the latter's geo-political reasoning. On this occasion it was a *Denkschrift* on the strategic value of the Faeroes, Iceland, and Greenland, the old Norwegian colonies from the Middle Ages. Hitler allowed this sample of Quisling's romantic nationalism to pass, reading the memo without comment. Finally, Quisling asked the burning question which had obsessed him so long: *"Herr* Reich Chancellor, have I understood correctly that you will help us?" *Der Führer* replied unequivocally: "Yes, I will."[201]

Quisling left the conference in a state of bliss. Riding in the car that took him back to Rosenberg after the meeting, "quiet and happy", he suddenly said to Scheidt: "I have noticed that there is something such as fate. I have presented my ideas to different persons, but have not enjoyed ... progress. And now suddenly, at the decisive moment, we receive help."[202]

His euphoria was shared by the Rosenberg organization. Their championship of Quisling's cause had prevailed. The Foreign Ministry's Norwegian policy had been ignored, with the Wilhelmstrasse being frozen out. Together with Scheidt and Schickedanz, Quisling and Hagelin enthusiastically considered how the coup in Oslo should be executed. Already on the 19th of December, Schickedanz discussed with Dr. Lammers of the Reich Chancellery the results of the meetings which Quisling had held with representatives of the military on the 16th and 18th. Lammers had been instructed to keep Hitler à jour concerning the Office of Foreign Affairs' co-operation with Quisling.[203]

The summary of Schickedanz's talk with Lammers showed that planning up to that point had concentrated on certain specific questions associated with the coup, but not with its actual implementation. Adequate preparation, said Schickedanz, had to be made to assure Quisling's permanence in office and to prevent a reaction against him by the military. Consideration also had to be given to the "country's 95 per cent hostile opinion" and to the uncertainty caused by the King's position. Necessary funds had to be made available for carrying out the operation: "the delivery of coal, transport of ships, etc." Schickedanz insisted that the planning for the coup be prepared by a centralized political leadership acting in close cooperation with the Reich Chancellery. This would exclude the Foreign Ministry. Schickedanz felt bold enough to suggest that this be done "in order not to overburden the Ministry", with only Ribbentrop being kept informed about developments.[204]

At the time Quisling left Berlin, he had every reason to believe that the situation in Germany was completely under control, with Rosenberg's office in charge of the necessary preparation for the coup which would place National Union's *Fører* in charge of the Norwegian government. Hagelin and Scheidt were ready to accompany Quisling to Oslo in order to make certain that there were adequate channels of communication back to Rosenberg in Berlin.[205] When Quisling, as usual accompanied by Hagelin and Scheidt, came to say farewell to Rosenberg on December 20, their talk concentrated once more on the proposed seizure of power. Specifically, the conversation focused on such details as the need for absolute secrecy, the way in which carefully selected NS members would travel to Germany in order to receive training for the coup, the question of what response could be expected from the King, and the manner in which key centers of administration would be occupied.[206]

Quisling warmly thanked his host for his aid and for the understanding which the *Reichsleiter* had shown. Both men were obviously in high spirits. Rosenberg anticipated finally having the opportunity of visiting Scandinavia, which up to then had not been possible because of the democratic governments which were in office. On parting, he and Quisling shook hands, and Rosenberg looked forward to the time when the coup had succeeded and Norway had a Minister President by the name of Quisling.[207]

On his way back to Oslo, the latter was equally satisfied with the outcome of his visit. Its results had been beyond his anticipation. Instead of petitioning various administrative departments for aid, he had been received by the *Führer* himself, who had promised direct aid for the takeover of government. As was his custom, the NS leader interpreted this literally. Events during the next months would show that his expectations were too optimistic. German support was forthcoming, but plans change rapidly during fluid wartime conditions. The shifting course of events and the conflicting interests which collided during this period of uncertainty would in the end lead to a climax in Norway which catapulted Quisling headlong onto the stage of world attention.

CHAPTER X

Quisling Becomes a Synonym for Treason
January 1940 – April 15, 1940

> The Nygaardsvold government has resigned. The national government has taken over governmental power, with Vidkun Quisling as prime minister and foreign minister . . .
>
> Vidkun Quisling,
> radio proclamation, April 9, 1940

When Scheidt, accompanied by Hagelin, followed after Quisling to Norway on December 22, 1939, he carried a pass which stated that he was on a "special mission" for *der Führer*. Rosenberg had obtained this valuable document for Scheidt by writing personally to Dr. Lammers in the Reich Chancellery.[1] The purpose of the trip was for Scheidt to inform himself as thoroughly as possible about the situation in the country.[2] His stay in Oslo lasted from December 24 to January 2.[3] Once back in Berlin, the energetic and abrasive young *Amtsleiter* proceeded to write yet another report for Rosenberg. The news he brought from Norway contained the standard black interpretation that he, Hagelin, and Quisling commonly used. For example, the new Minister of Defense, a professional officer named Colonel Birger Ljungberg, was described as being definitely "anglophile".[4]

While Scheidt continued to portray the Nygaardsvold government as being anti-German, he optimistically announced that Quisling was acting in full accordance with the plans that had been discussed in Berlin. The NS leader, said Scheidt, was preparing a propaganda campaign, and he had begun to raise funds for this purpose in order to have a cover story to account for the money which NS received from Germany. Scheidt further recorded that Quisling was in the process of selecting the required number of "dependable men" who were to spearhead the projected coup. According to Scheidt, Colonel Sundlo had already made all necessary preparations for taking over the strategic port of Narvik, and Quisling allegedly had to calm down the impatient commandant, restraining him from acting too precipitously.[5]

In his usual abrupt fashion, Scheidt favored pushing ahead with the coup. So too did Hagelin. Writing to Rosenberg on January 13, Quisling's major adviser repeated Scheidt's negative appraisal of conditions in Norway. Hagelin's purpose was clear: he hoped to inspire the Germans to move quickly by describing the situation as being critical for the Third Reich. He contended that the government had no intention of remaining neutral. Future developments in Norway were extremely threatening for Germany, he argued, and they could only be altered if a "national government" came to power. In order to spur the Germans into action on behalf of such a government under Quisling, Hagelin insisted on the need for immediate action. Already in a few weeks it might be too late, with Germany supposedly being in danger of losing the war if she did not initiate a move against Norway before England did.[6]

In Germany, however, the possibility for direct intervention was not as clear-cut as Hagelin desired. Ribbentrop's ministry had no intention of allowing Rosenberg's Office of Foreign Affairs to decide German policy toward Norway. Immediately after Quisling's visit, the Foreign Ministry attempted to bring the entire enterprise involving Quisling under its authority. Ambassador Hewel met with Rosenberg on December 21 and pointed out that Ribbentrop had delegated the Norwegian question to Werner von Grundherr, head of the Scandinavian Section in the Foreign Ministry. Rosenberg, however, was strong enough to reject the move entirely. Similarly, when Grundherr phoned Schickedanz on the following day, insisting on having a discussion with Scheidt before the latter left for Norway, Rosenberg's organization could shrug off this belated attempt by the Foreign Ministry to exert its influence. Schickedanz with satisfaction informed Grundherr that Scheidt had already departed. Furthermore, Schickedanz brushed off Grundherr's statement that the Foreign Ministry viewed the matter to be of utmost importance by pointing out that Rosenberg had promised Hewel to keep Wilhelmstrasse informed.[7]

The Foreign Ministry was by no means willing to drop the matter at this juncture. Weizsäcker sent a personal message to Bräuer, informing the Minister of Scheidt's expected arrival. Bräuer received orders to follow Scheidt's activity in a discreet manner. The Minister was instructed to discuss the question only with Ribbentrop, Weizsäcker, or Grundherr, indicating the importance which the Foreign Ministry attached to the issue.[8]

Upon leaving for Norway, Scheidt had been told to contact the German legation in Oslo, but not to reveal the purpose of his mission. However, in a conversation with Bräuer, he received the impression that the Minister fully understood why he had come to Norway. This irritated Rosenberg's young subordinate, and he complained strongly in his report that the Foreign Ministry should not be involved. Only he and Rosenberg, insisted Scheidt, should deal with Quisling.[9]

The clash of interests between the Foreign Ministry and the Office of Foreign Affairs focused increasingly on Scheidt, the most active proponent of Rosenberg's involvement in Norway. When the Foreign Ministry learned that Scheidt had travelled to Norway on a special pass issued by the Reich Chancellery, it protested strongly. All such visits, it insisted, had to have the approval of the Foreign Ministry.[10] When Scheidt came back to Berlin, he clashed frequently with officials in the Foreign Ministry over what was the true state of affairs in Norway. Ribbentrop confirmed this after the war, stating: "Scheidt was repeatedly in my office. He caused us a number of difficulties."[11] In a conversation between Scheidt and Grundherr on January 9, the two strongly disputed whether or not the former should receive a permanent cover for his activity by being granted a position in the Oslo legation. Grundherr refused to accede to this request. He and Scheidt also had entirely different opinions about the political situation. Scheidt repeated the standard view of the Rosenberg organization, as provided by Quisling and Hagelin, that the Norwegian government was a tool of British interests. To this the head of the Scandinavian Section replied curtly that he had the impression the government did its best to defend its neutrality.[12]

The Foreign Ministry saw no reason to change its policy toward Norway. In his annual report for the previous year, dated January 18, 1940, Bräuer did not lessen his negative assessment of Quisling's status, despite the favorable reception Hitler had recently given the NS *Fører*. Bräuer insisted that "National Union is of no importance and will as far as one can judge also in the future be of little importance ... in that country." The Minister, no doubt to soften his criticism, declared that Quisling had personal integrity. However, said Bräuer, the NS leader lacked clear political perception, critical judgement, and the firmness needed to follow a single policy consistently.[13]

A few days later Bräuer followed this up by sending an additional message which disputed the contention that Quisling enjoyed considerable sympathy within the officer corps. The Minister correctly pointed out that while the Labor party had previously been anti-military, the Nygaardsvold government now had the backing of the military as it became more nationalistic, being in the process of building up the armed forces. Quisling, the report stated, had few sympathizers among the officers, and scarcely any among the younger officers. According to Bräuer, the general antipathy toward Quisling in the officer corps stemmed from two major reasons. The first was his reputation for formerly having been pro-Bolshevik. The second came from the common belief that his party was nothing but an "imitation" of the Nazis.[14]

Despite its vigorous opposition to Rosenberg's policy, the Foreign Ministry failed to prevent Scheidt from returning to Norway on January 20, where he continued his advocacy on Quisling's behalf. However, during the second half of January the Ministry began to lose interest in the NS leader. This was but one piece of evidence pointing clearly to a single conclusion. The policy which Rosenberg's office stood for – the sponsorship of a German-backed coup in favor of Quisling – was no longer being given serious consideration in Berlin. Instead, planning for Norway was proceeding along quite different lines. Becoming aware of this, the Foreign Ministry no longer had reason to regard the Office of Foreign Affairs as a serious rival as far as Norway was concerned.[15] However, while the conflict between the organizations thereby died down, the antagonisms between the two rival offices continued to exist in latent form. As will be seen, they revived strongly in the confused situation that resulted from the German invasion in April.

An alternative to Quisling's proposed plan had existed already from the time before he gave his views to Hitler. On December 12, at the very meeting where Raeder presented his favorable impression of Quisling to *der Führer*, the commander-in-chief of the navy mentioned two possible approaches which could be followed in gaining control of Norway. The first involved the type of operation that Quisling urged: a coup followed by immediate German assistance. The second was entirely military in nature, with a forcible invasion taking place. Although Raeder had used Quisling as a means of turning Hitler's attention toward Norway, the Grand Admiral, because of professional considerations, favored a military operation, rather than the political plan which Quisling, Rosenberg, Scheidt, and Hagelin all strongly advocated.[16]

After Quisling returned to Norway, a relatively brief period of uncertainty existed in Germany as to which of the two alternatives would be chosen. However, because of Rosenberg's inclination to be passive in the implementation of plans, much the same as Quisling, the issue was never very seriously in doubt. Rosenberg apparently did not seek to raise the question directly with Hitler. Instead, discussions occurred at a lower level between Schickedanz and Lammers. The latter had been informed of the Foreign Ministry's objections to Scheidt's visit to Norway, and Lammers brought the matter to Hitler's attention on December 29.[17] Already at this juncture *der Führer* had reservations about a possible combined political-military plan along the lines previously discussed with Quisling, and Lammers passed this on to Schickedanz on January 4. Hitler had expressed skepticism about the ability of the Norwegians to maintain secrecy. Lammers added the rather ominous warning that it would be good if the operation succeeded, but if it failed, it would "cost the heads of those responsible". Rosenberg noted the danger and immediately became cautious. He was not known for taking stands which might bring Hitler's wrath down upon his head. The *Reichsleiter* now assumed the view that "the Norwegian matter must be slept on".[18]

As a result, he did nothing concrete to further the continuation of Quisling's coup project. The *Reichsleiter*, however, did not inform Scheidt or Quisling of the changed situation. He undoubtedly hoped that altered conditions in the future might once more make the plan feasible. Scheidt believed as late as the beginning of February that the operation was still on, and that he had responsibility for nursing it along.[19]

The dramatic incident involving the *Altmark* in mid-February eliminated, however, any remaining doubts about whether the scheme in support of Quisling was feasible.[20] Rosenberg discussed with Hitler on February 19 the Norwegian situation in the aftermath of the *Altmark* affair. The *Reichsleiter* confided to his diary that as a result of his talk with Hitler, "the *political* plan of the Norwegians" had been abandoned because of his recommendation. It is obvious that Rosenberg sought to save face by stating he was responsible for discontinuing the political plan. In reality it had long been abandoned, although the *Reichsleiter* had not been specifically told this. He now had to accept the fact that his Norwegian protégé, Quisling, had been relegated to the sidelines. As he noted in his diary, Quisling and Hagelin would eventually be placed "at our disposal if we are forced to protect ourselves from an English attempt to cut off our connections with Norway".[21]

It is in a sense ironic that the "political plan" proposed by Quisling and sponsored by Rosenberg was shelved in favor of a strictly military operation whose origin was largely inspired by Quisling's first meeting with Hitler on December 14, 1939. The small staff that Hitler ordered set up to plan a possible occupation of Norway, which came into being on the same afternoon as his talk with Quisling, worked diligently. As part of the *Oberkommando der Wehrmacht* (OKW), it carried out its task entirely independently of the stratagems of the Rosenberg organization. By the middle of January the staff had completed its initial study, known as *Studie Nord*, which it forwarded to the separate service staffs for their comments.[22] The plan was soon withdrawn, however. Hitler's increased interest in and concern for Scandinavia caused him to direct General Wilhelm Keitel, the head of the OKW, to keep all further planning involving a Norwegian operation entirely under the OKW's control. According to the order Keitel issued on Hitler's behalf on January 27, *der Führer* wished *Studie Nord* to be further refined under his personal supervision and coordinated directly as an integral part of Germany's total military planning. Keitel maintained leadership over the operation's ongoing preparation, which was strengthened in terms of manpower, and which received a new code name, *Weserübung* (Weser Exercise).[23]

German planning for an invasion of Norway thereupon entered a much more immediate stage. While Hitler's motives for embarking upon *Weserübung* remain not entirely clear, it appears that his original interest in Norway, first aroused by Quisling's visit in December, was increased even more by evidence of possible Allied operations in Scandinavia as a consequence of the Russo-Finnish Winter War, which was nearing its completion at the time *Weserübung* was instituted. For Hitler, Norway had become an area to which he attached considerable strategic importance.

Der Führer's decision to elevate the project from a theoretical study to concrete planning for action was of utmost importance, in particular since he deliberately avoided using the regular service staffs, and instead kept it under his control within the OKW. As he was the possessor of both political and military power in the Third Reich, no division existed between military strategy and political decision-making under Hitler. The fact that he gave high priority to *Weserübung* meant that he seriously considered its implementation.[24]

On the Allied side in the war, the First Lord of the Admiralty, Winston Churchill, had been concerned with Scandinavia's strategic importance since the beginning of hostilities. He was especially eager to block the transport of Swedish iron ore to Germany, part of which was sent by rail to Norway and shipped from the ice-free port of Narvik. He initially received little support for his viewpoint, but the situation changed following the Soviet invasion of Finland at the end of November 1939. Because of the Nazi-Soviet Pact, the British and French regarded Russia at this time as virtually an ally of Germany. Beginning in December, under the pretext of providing aid to the Finns, the Allied governments and military staffs gave serious consideration to operations in Scandinavia. This included not only Churchill's original plan of mining Norwegian waters to halt iron ore transport, but also the possibility of landing a combined British-French force that would seize Narvik and the Swedish iron ore fields as well as going on to aid the Finns. In addition, the strategically important Norwegian towns of Stavanger, Bergen, and Trondheim would be occupied in anticipation of a German countermove. By February 5 the plan had been approved by the Allied Supreme War Council.[25]

Not only Allied and German military planners, but world opinion in general, briefly turned its attention to Norway in mid-February as a result of the dramatic incident involving the *Altmark*. This tanker was a supply ship for the raider *Graf Spee*, a pocket battleship. Although British forces had been on the alert for the *Altmark*, it managed to elude the Royal Navy on its way back to Germany from the South Atlantic, and found refuge in

Norwegian waters. Disguised as a non-combatant, but carrying British prisoners from ships sunk by the *Graf Spee*, the *Altmark* received escort from Norwegian patrol boats as she moved south along the coast toward Germany. However, on the night of February 16, on direct orders from Churchill, a British naval force brushed the patrol boats aside. The *Altmark* was boarded and, following a brief exchange of gunfire in which seven Germans were killed, the prisoners were freed and carried triumphantly to England.

The Nygaardsvold government strongly protested against this violation of Norway's territorial waters, and Minister Bräuer assured Berlin that the Norwegians were determined to maintain their neutrality.[26] Hitler, however, was enraged. For him the incident provided evidence of the government's inability to prevent the British from carrying out anti-German military operations in Norwegian territory. The *Altmark* episode prompted *der Führer* to speed up urgently operation *Weserübung*. Its scope was expanded to include Denmark as well as Norway. From this time onwards there was no hesitancy on the part of Hitler to press the operation to its inevitable conclusion, a German invasion. On February 21 General Nikolaus von Falkenhorst was received personally by Hitler and placed in overall charge of *Weserübung*'s planning, having been designated as commander of the army units that would land in Norway.

In the meantime, however, the Allies had progressed the furthest. By the end of February the force intended to occupy Stavanger, Bergen, and Trondheim was in the process of carrying out its preparations. In early March the Norwegian and Swedish governments were informed that they would soon be requested to allow the passage of forces intended for the relief of Finland. Both governments protested, with the Norwegians emphasizing that they did not wish to have their country become a battlefield.[27] However, they did not intend to apply armed neutrality in case of an Allied invasion. At the cabinet meeting which discussed the Norwegian response, Foreign Minister Koht informed his colleagues that if the Allies nevertheless landed troops, the government must not resist, but limit itself to protests. If Norway were dragged into the war, said Koht, steps must be taken to avoid becoming involved "on the wrong side".[28]

Despite the protests, the British decided on March 12 to press on, but with a landing restricted only to Narvik. However, on the same day the Finns resolved to accept Russian terms for a peace settlement. Shortly thereafter the British government cancelled the operation. The Allied troops that had been gathered were now dispersed.[29] From a military point of view, the abandonment of the Scandinavian incursion in March meant that the Allies, unknowingly, lost the edge that they had maintained over the Germans. Events in early April 1940 would show that the Allies never regained the advantage.

In Germany the planning for *Weserübung* continued unabated. Hitler signed the directive for execution of the operation already on March 1. The motives given were military in nature, in accord with Hitler's ideas and the advice he had received from his military consultants: (1) the need to prevent British military action in Scandinavia and the Baltic, (2) to ensure Germany's continued supply of Swedish iron ore, and (3) to secure strategic bases for Germany's air and naval forces, to be used against England.[30]

Four days later, on March 5, the specific operational orders for *Weserübung* were ready. Almost the entire navy would be involved in the invasion, making it extremely risky. Landings were planned for seven different points along the coast, from Oslo to Narvik. To compensate for the superiority of the British fleet, the *Luftwaffe* would be heavily committed in the operation.[31]

When these plans were nearing their completion, the Germans for the first time received direct evidence that the Allies were considering a landing in Scandinavia. On March 6 the army commander, General Franz Halder, noted that England and France had requested the right of passage through Norway and Sweden.[32] By March 10, however, the Germans became aware of the changed conditions brought about by news of peace negotiations between the Finns and Russians. Two days later, when the Winter War was over, General Jodl noted in his diary: "The peace Finland-Russia deprives England, but us as well, of the political basis for action in Norway."[33] Unlike the case with the Allies, however, the end of the Winter War did not cause Hitler to cease his plans for an invasion. Although the Germans assumed there was no immediate danger of an Allied landing in Norway, they had no reason to believe that the British and French had abandoned their strategic goals in Scandinavia. Hitler fully committed himself to an invasion on March 26. At a meeting on April 2 with the top military commanders involved in the operation, *der Führer* set the date, ordering the occupation of Norway and Denmark to take place on the morning of April 9, 1940. On the next day the first supply ships left for their destinations. Operation *Weserübung* had begun.[34]

Unknown to Hitler at the time he made the decisions which set *Weserübung* in motion, the Allies had again resumed planning for a move against Norway. Churchill never ceased for a moment advocating a military operation against the coastal approach to Narvik. Similarly, in France top officials favored Churchill's viewpoint, believing not only in the military value of such a venture, but also being concerned with the desire to stimulate French morale. At the meeting of the Supreme War Council on March 28, attended by Premier Paul Reynaud and Prime Minister Chamberlain, the decision was made to present the Norwegian and Swedish governments with diplomatic notes, warning them of unilateral Allied actions. Mines would then be laid along the Norwegian coast. Following this conference, the Allied military commanders voiced concern about a possible German counteraction. The British and French therefore decided that if the Ger-

mans reacted, the Allies intended (1) to seize Narvik and the railroad leading to the Swedish iron fields, and (2) send forces to Stavanger, Bergen,
and Trondheim to secure these key sites.[35] The Allies were not resolute,
however, in executing their plan. It was delayed, and the British cabinet resolved that if the Norwegians were hostile, the operation would be restricted to action by air and sea.[36] The diplomatic notes were not delivered
until April 5, while the mining was postponed until April 8.[37] By this time
Weserübung had been in operation for five days.

The British action against Narvik was not deemed critical to the Allied war
effort, as shown in the halfhearted manner in which it came into being.
The operation succeeded only in creating confusion for the Norwegian
government, significantly blinding it to the danger of the German invasion,
which occurred almost simultaneously. Foreign Minister Koht declared
later that the receipt of joint notes from the British and French ambassa-
dors "filled my mind so entirely that they could even set aside any thought
about the possible German attack".[38]

The Germans, on the other hand, carried out *Weserübung* resolutely,
being determined to execute the invasion quickly and thoroughly. The
OKW realized from the start that *Weserübung* had to be completed rapidly, with the Allies, Denmark, and Norway being taken entirely by surprise. Total secrecy was therefore maintained. This meant that even the
question of the political future of the two victim countries was kept entirely outside the sphere of the Foreign Ministry, which under ordinary
circumstances could have been expected to have a significant influence over
matters affecting Germany's relations with other nations. Not until April
2, just the day before *Weserübung* began, were the civilian authorities informed of the pending action.[39] At such a late date it was impossible for
any changes to be made.

For the same security reasons, it proved impossible to make use of the
political plan involving Quisling. The OKW excluded any foreign involvement in *Weserübung*. A number of military planners, having met Quisling
in December, were aware that he was a pro-German sympathizer who
could supply them with information, but they did not accord him any
place in the political scheme of things following the invasion. Instead, they
intended that Germany would make use of the existing Norwegian government. They expected that the Norwegians would be completely surprised
by the suddenness of the attack and would be unable to offer any effective
defense. The Germans assumed that the Nygaardsvold government would
thereupon bow to the inevitable and attempt to reach some kind of working relationship with the successful invader.[40] In pursuing this strategy, the
political plan for Norway was identical with that for Denmark, where a socialist government also held office. In Denmark the German operation

worked entirely as anticipated. Had the Germans also been able to execute their original plan for Norway, Quisling would have occupied a far different role from that which he assumed in such a sensational manner in April.

The NS *Fører* had no specific knowledge that the direction of German planning had changed, and that his "political plan" was no longer under consideration. His main source of support in Germany, Rosenberg, always adapted his views to Hitler's thought. As the *Reichsleiter* later admitted, the political plan contained numerous dangers which could have resulted in failure. For this reason, he said, it was deliberately delayed, but its abandonment was never made known to the Norwegians.[41]

While Quisling failed to receive specific information about military plans for the invasion, this did not mean he had been abandoned. Hitler did not repudiate his promise of support. Rosenberg's organization continued to act as an enthusiastic promoter of Quisling's cause. The *Reichsleiter* refrained from any criticism of the military and political planning for the operation against Norway, but he used every available opportunity to call Hitler's attention to the reports that he received from his sources in Norway, Scheidt and Hagelin.[42] Rosenberg and his office provided Quisling with advice and financial backing, ready to extend more active assistance should the situation permit.

The same was true of the navy, thanks to its commander-in-chief. Although the Grand Admiral in December 1939 had preferred a military to a political operation against Norway, he did not repudiate the favorable attitude he had toward Quisling. On the contrary, it seems that Raeder became more positively inclined toward the NS leader when the he learned of the Allied intent to land forces in Scandinavia under cover of the Russo-Finnish War. This apparently confirmed his belief that Quisling had been right all along when he warned of a pending British move against Norway. Raeder's favoritism extended to the point that he declared prior to the invasion that he supported making use of Quisling by installing him as head of the government.[43] Another indication of the navy's active assistance was provided by its attaché in Oslo, Captain Schreiber, who had been personally appointed to his post by Raeder. Schreiber worked closely with Scheidt, the two being in complete agreement in their negative attitude toward Norwegian foreign policy. In opposition to the diplomatic representatives in the German legation, they had no belief in the government's policy of neutrality, assuming instead that the cabinet acted in deliberate collusion with the British.[44]

Because of the role which Rosenberg's organization served, acting as a base of contact with Quisling through Scheidt and Hagelin, a channel of information existed in Germany about alleged conditions in Norway which lay outside the control of the traditional source of intelligence from foreign countries, the Foreign Ministry. Scheidt and Hagelin remained energetic as always in fabricating reports, which Rosenberg then passed on to Hitler.[45] Had it not been for the fact that such material reached the highest level of power in the Third Reich, and was apparently believed to some degree by the ever vigilant *Führer*, the contents of the reports made for amusing reading. Scheidt and Hagelin, on their numerous trips back and forth between Berlin and Oslo in the period between December 22, 1939, and April 9, 1940, concocted as much hard and loose information as possible in their single-minded effort to present "evidence" that the Norwegian government was a tool of the British, and that Quisling therefore should receive more German aid.[46]

Such assistance was forthcoming. In the late winter and early spring of 1940, Quisling no longer had to face the problem of lack of funds. In accordance with Hitler's instruction, the Foreign Ministry made available 200,000 *Reichsmark*.[47] This money, in the form of British pounds, was transferred to Norway in two equal installments. Scheidt took the first with him on January 19,[48] while Hagelin carried the remainder to Oslo in early March.[49]

With this significant amount of capital at his disposal, Quisling could expand National Union's operations. But while the volume of party activity increased, money alone could not produce a political following. Scheidt wrote in his reports that Quisling was in the process of setting up a net of NS agents along the coast to gather intelligence on Germany's behalf,[50] but this alleged spy network was merely the product of Scheidt's fertile imagination. NS simply did not have the necessary manpower to carry out such an undertaking. The German funds were used primarily for an expansion of *Fritt Folk* and an enlargement of the party's administration.

Already in January 1940 the result of the first German instalment was apparent. *Fritt Folk's* second issue, appearing on January 13, revealed that the paper had doubled in size, from four to eight pages.[51] In addition, shortly thereafter the total number of copies printed was increased to 25,000. Quisling bragged to Aall that he considered this number to be quite good, in particular since *Aftenposten's* weekly news magazine, published by the country's largest newspaper, only had an edition of 20,000 copies.[52] *Fritt Folk's* edition of 25,000 copies appeared for the first time on January 20, at which time the NS organ brazenly challenged the other Oslo papers to produce publication figures that could equal those of Quisling's paper.[53]

Most of these copies, of course, had to be given away in the form of free propaganda, since there was no major demand for *Fritt Folk*. Moreover, the quality of the paper could not be changed overnight despite the infusion of funds. For the time being it remained a propaganda sheet, making no effort to serve as a source for up-to-date news. But in order to meet the requirements posed by *Fritt Folk*'s expanded operations, Quisling could now afford to employ a professional NS editor. Arnt Rishovd replaced the loyal and unpaid Haldis Neegaard Østbye, who continued to serve the paper in the reduced capacity of an assistant. Rishovd's name appeared on *Fritt Folk*'s masthead on January 20, in the same edition announcing its greatly expanded number of copies.

The paper's huge increase in size and aggregate copies was only the first step toward Quisling's primary goal for *Fritt Folk* – to have it come out again as a daily. Scheidt reported already in February that the 200,000 *Reichsmark* set aside for Quisling were not enough if he were to convert his weekly, as he had previously planned. Quisling would need, insisted Scheidt, 45,000 *kroner* a month to meet the costs for printing, mailing, and the expenses of a growing staff. As always, Scheidt did not spare himself when arguing for increased assistance.[54]

In response to Scheidt's request, more funds were made available. According to Rosenberg, he reached an agreement with Ribbentrop whereby Quisling would be paid £ 10,000 through Scheidt, beginning on March 15 and continuing for the next three months.[55]

While Rosenberg's statement cannot be controlled, it is certain that the Germans provided Quisling with subsidies beyond the original 200,000 *Reichsmark*. This allowed him to proceed with converting *Fritt Folk* to a daily. On March 14 John Thronsen signed an agreement with a major Oslo printing firm whereby *Fritt Folk* would be printed on a daily basis with a total of eight pages.[56] Thronsen testified after the war, and Quisling corroborated this, that he had received four payments from Quisling totaling 70,000 *kroner* for *Fritt Folk*'s operations. Quisling explained that the money allegedly came in part from an "election fund", and in part from a "personal loan" from Hagelin.[57]

On Monday, April 1, slightly more than two weeks after Thronsen had signed the contract, Quisling's newspaper could once more be obtained on a daily basis from newsstands in Oslo.[58] Its initial appearance as a daily revealed that the German funds had not been spent entirely in vain. As far as journalistic competence was concerned, *Fritt Folk* now exhibited an image which was striking when compared with its predecessor, the amateurish weekly. The hiring of Rishovd and other full-time staff members had clearly achieved results. While *Fritt Folk*'s partisanship had not diminished, it was now a true newspaper, reporting on contemporary events, rather than merely printing propaganda articles.

The availability of German money also meant that Quisling could now afford to provide the NS administration with increased personnel and expanded quarters. *Fritt Folk* announced on February 17 that the Central Office and the paper's editorial office had both moved from the fourth floor of Klingenberggaten 5 to the third storey of Rådhusgaten 17. The increased annual rent which the party had to pay was considerable, from ca. 4,000 to 16,000 *kroner*.[59] Moreover, NS continued to occupy its old headquarters in Klingenberggaten 5, which were now taken over by the NS organization in the greater Oslo area and its youth organization.[60] Exactly how many new positions were created as a result of NS' expanded operations it is not possible to determine, but a conservative estimate, provided by Thronsen, is that the staff at Rådhusgaten 17 was doubled in number.[61]

While NS could increase *Fritt Folk*'s issues and hire more personnel, there is no indication that the party expanded its activity to any extent in early 1940, contrary to what Scheidt had maintained and Quisling had hoped. There was no growth in membership. The party's condition remained the same as it had been since its disintegration in 1936–1937. At the time of the German invasion, no more than a few hundred persons at the most worked actively for NS. In addition, there were a number of isolated former members scattered throughout the country who still retained their sympathy for Quisling despite being cut off from party activity. A significant portion of this group was later drawn back into the party during the first two years of the occupation.[62] But at the time of the invasion the Germans could hardly count on the support of more than a limited number of active NS members that Quisling could rally at a given moment.

For what it was worth, the Germans could expect to receive Quisling's backing at the time of invasion. Having held discussions on how the Third Reich, in collusion with him, might secure Norway as a base of operations, and after having obtained financial aid from the Nazis, it was impossible for him to operate other than as a German agent. But because of his need to rationalize and intellectualize his behavior, he now identified Germany's actions in World War II as being identical with his philosophical aspirations. In his New Year's message to his followers he declared that the war between Germany and England was above all else a struggle between two different philosophies of life. He described Germany as representing a force which sought after the highest ideals, while England was depicted as the exponent of liberal materialism. The struggle between these two ways of life, he said, was a death struggle in which the Norwegian nation would inevitably be involved.[63]

Writing later in the year in *Fritt Folk*, exactly one month before the German attack, he presented his personal assessment of the country's condition. His tone remained that of an Old Testament prophet, excoriating his people because of their lack of faith. His political viewpoint, as represented by National Union, had always been correct, he insisted, but the people had not listened. The key to peace, he maintained, had been reconciliation between England and Germany, and he had therefore worked so energetically for the union of all "Nordic peoples" in a Greater Nordic Peace Union. If only a significant number of influential persons had supported him in this effort, he maintained, then the country's interests would have been secured, with NS on behalf of Norway leading the other Scandinavian states in mediating peace between England and Germany. However, the Norwegian people had failed their would-be savior, choosing "Barabbas" instead. He even put the blame on the Norwegian people for the fact that NS had deteriorated and was in such bad shape.[64]

His condemnation of the hated party politicians in the *Storting* continued to be as fierce as ever. He declared that members of this "democratic-marxist clique assembly" had no hope of retaining their position if Germany won the war. They were therefore committed to what he sarcastically called "the victory of the 'democracies'", and Norway had to be maneuvered into the conflict on England's side. He indicated no recognition of the government's interest in wanting to maintain neutrality for as long as possible.[65]

While he condemned the alleged intrigue to secure Norway's participation on the side of the Allies, he expressed no reluctance to have the country join in alliance with Germany. He admitted that this was a highly serious matter, but that the country nevertheless had a good chance of coming safely through the holocaust. On the other hand, he declared that Norway had no possibility of sustaining a war with the Third Reich. Hitler's Germany also had his public support because of his latent anti-communism. Despite the Nazi-Soviet Pact, he still described Germany as "Europe's bulwark against Bolshevism". If Norway did not heed his warning and drive the politicians who held power illegally from office, then he predicted that the country's fate was sealed. It would be forced into the abyss because of the politicians' alleged conspiracy.[66]

As his newspaper articles revealed, the NS *Fører* did not hesitate to declare openly in early 1940 that he preferred to have Norway come into the war on the side of Germany. It was therefore entirely consistent for him to place himself at the disposal of German intelligence officers who were seeking information concerning Norway's ability to resist an invasion. While Quisling had not been informed about the plans for *Weserübung*, as a former officer and Minister of Defense he certainly was aware that something was being planned within the German military. He based this not only on his discussions in December, but also on later contacts that he had during the spring. On March 22 Herman Harris Aall arrived in Oslo, escorting his *Abwehr* contact, Captain de Laporte. The latter's mission, among other things, was to determine the extent to which aid could be expected from NS in the event of a German invasion. He held a number of meetings with Quisling, first at the residence where de Laporte and Aall were staying, later at National Union's new headquarters in Rådhusgaten 17. Aall was present only at the initial meetings, while Quisling and de Laporte preferred to meet alone during their subsequent talks.[67]

According to Aall, de Laporte raised the question whether German volunteers would be accepted in Norway in case of a British attack. Quisling and Aall supposedly said that they favored such a move, but only if the volunteers were placed under Norwegian command.[68] It need hardly be said that the Norwegian command Quisling had in mind was a government headed by him, and not the Labor government of Johan Nygaardsvold.[69]

His conversations with de Laporte could not help but give Quisling the general impression that events were in the making. Their talks were entirely in line with what he had previously discussed in Berlin. However, he did not know that the *Abwehr* agent was acting outside officially approved channels and in no way represented actual German planning. When Scheidt learned that Quisling had held political and military discussions with de Laporte, he grew incensed at the thought of potential rivals establishing themselves within a domain that he considered exclusively his own. Scheidt travelled immediately to Berlin at the end of March and submitted a scathing denunciation of de Laporte. The report eventually reached Hitler himself, and de Laporte received a severe reprimand for having acted outside his area of competence.[70] Having delivered his broadside against the *Abwehr* agent, Scheidt immediately hurried back to Oslo, where he continued his close cooperation with naval attaché Schreiber.[71]

Soon after de Laporte and Aall had departed back to Berlin, Quisling once more came in contact with another representative of the German intelligence service. But this time the meeting was entirely official, coming from the highest level. Schreiber and Scheidt received orders through military channels in Berlin to arrange for Quisling to travel to Copenhagen to hold talks with an intelligence officer.[72] The order originated with Hitler himself, indicating his continued interest in the head of NS.[73] Colonel Hans Piekenbrock, chief of the *Abwehr*'s espionage division, *Abwehr* I, received the assignment of meeting with Quisling. By the time the two conferred at Hotel d'Angleterre on April 3, *Weserübung* had already been set in motion. The information that Quisling provided therefore had no bearing on the implementation of the operation. Specifically, what the Germans wanted were details that would make it easier for them to complete the invasion, allowing them to carry it out more speedily. Quisling readily complied. He provided general intelligence about the army and air force, about troop strength, about the location of air bases, and the state of readiness of the defense forces. One question in particular proved to have major significance later – the preparedness of coastal defenses. Quisling informed Piekenbrock that the coastal batteries would not fire without first having received cabinet approval. Since the German political plans were based on the surprise and capture of the Norwegian government, the German military would later hold Quisling responsible for the failure of these plans because of resistance from naval batteries.[74]

Although he provided the information that he had available, he failed to give precise answers to specific questions that Piekenbrock brought up, indicating that he was by no means knowledgeable about current military dispositions.[75] Despite this deficiency, however, the German military appeared to be pleased with the outcome of the secret meeting. General Jodl noted in his diary on April 4 that Piekenbrock had just returned from Copenhagen with good results from his conversation with Quisling.[76]

In return for supplying the *Abwehr* Colonel with intelligence, Quisling apparently expected to receive a briefing about the most recent German plans toward Norway, but the Germans continued to keep this information to themselves.[77] Nevertheless, even more than the earlier discussions with de Laporte, the meeting with Piekenbrock must have given Quisling the clear impression that Germany was committed to carrying out an operation against Norway. But he still remained in the dark as to the actual date of the invasion and the planned disposition of forces, not to mention the political plans which the Germans intended to execute.

After the war, the NS leader refused to admit that the meeting with Piekenbrock had ever occurred. Instead, he insisted that his trip to Copenhagen had been solely for the purpose of meeting with his counterpart, the Danish Nazi leader, Fritz Clausen.[78] Quisling did indeed confer with Clausen during his stay, but he quite probably used the meeting as a cover.[79] His denial of ever having met Piekenbrock, considering the circumstances under which it was made, is entirely understandable. On trial for his life, he could hardly admit that as a retired officer on half pay, with an obligation to return to active duty in times of national emergency, and as a former Minister of Defense, he had been willing to divulge military intelligence which could be useful in an attack against his country, an attack which more than likely would take place, as Quisling knew full well. Despite the disavowal, the weight of evidence indicating that the meeting took place is overwhelming. Keitel, Jodl, Rosenberg, and Piekenbrock himself have all provided testimony which fully supports such a conclusion.[80]

Quisling returned from Copenhagen still without specific confirmation of where and when the expected invasion would occur. On April 7 he held a regularly scheduled meeting of the NS Council, attended by most of the hard core of his small group of adherents. The Council discussed routine matters of a general nature.[81] Although the invasion came less than forty-eight hours afterwards, there is no evidence to support the assumption sometimes inferred that Quisling had foreknowledge of the coming attack and therefore called the Council together to discuss the coming critical situation for NS. On the contrary, the ordinary manner in which the meeting was conducted provided additional substantiation of the conclusion that he still remained uninformed of German plans.

On the following day, April 8, the first rapid series of military movements took place which plunged Norway into war. With little warning, the government was forced to improvise as best it could in an entirely new and difficult situation, while the people as a whole were stunned. Norway had not been at war since 1814, and the generations that had grown up since the Napoleonic Wars assumed peace to be the normal state of affairs. The outbreak of World War II and the subsequent violent events affecting the country, such as the *Altmark* incident and the sinking of Norwegian merchant ships by German submarines, had caused some unease. Still, not until April 8, when the news became known that British warships had laid mines in Norwegian territorial waters outside of Narvik, did the people begin to recognize the very real possibility that their country might not be able to avoid direct involvement in the war.

Attention naturally enough was focused first on the British. Koht had determined that Norway should demonstrate its intention of maintaining strict neutrality. The naval command was told by Koht on the morning of the 8th, in concurrence with Nygaardsvold, that the naval forces at Narvik should resist if the British attempted to enter the harbor and capture German ore carriers. Later in the day the government protested against the mine-laying to the British, giving them forty-eight hours in which to sweep up the mines.[82]

As for the Germans, the Norwegian Foreign Ministry and armed forces had been receiving reports about a possible move against Norway during early April, as late as the night of April 8.[83] These reports were vague, however, and they were not the first of this nature. Koht believed up until April 8 that the German naval force was directed against the British fleet, not against the Norwegian coast. On the late afternoon of April 8, when he received information that the German ships might be moving toward Narvik, he countermanded the previous order to the commanding admiral, indicating that the forces at Narvik should "shoot at the Germans, not the English".[84] Only by the late evening of April 8 did the government become convinced that apparently the main danger came not from the British, but from the Germans.[85] By then the invasion was but a few hours away.

For Quisling, news of the British mine-laying served as inspiration for immediate action. He had, without any direct evidence, warned of a British move against Norway for so long that he regarded the mine-laying as simply confirmation of his prophesies. He therefore resorted to the underlying goal of the plan that he had discussed in Berlin – National Union's takeover of the government. During the morning hours of April 8 he sat down and wrote out a proclamation, which was posted on the same day.[86] In this address to his "countrymen", he asserted that the evidence was now at hand which showed that the "party politicians" had led Norway into the world crisis. They must not be allowed, he insisted, to deliver Norway to England and France in order to save their own skin. Such a move would only cause Norway to share "Poland's fate". It was imperative, said Quisling, to remove the Nygaardsvold cabinet and the other party politicians, headed by Mowinckel and Hambro, so that they could no longer influence the country's government. Since National Union, he asserted, had been the only organization that had analyzed the situation correctly, it was the only force that could save Norway's "freedom and independence" during the coming crisis. It was therefore, he insisted, National Union's "duty and right" to demand power. He asked Norwegians to act responsibly and report for service on behalf of the "national movement".[87]

Hardly any notice was given to this proclamation during the trying hours of April 8. His statements were disregarded as but another insignificant utterance from a person generally regarded as a political fanatic. Furthermore, there was no force behind his strong words, providing but another example of his practice of calling for action, yet failing to have any means of realizing the desired objective. But whereas his announcement had no effect on April 8, when the country's attention was focused primarily on the British mine-laying venture, on the next day, when the German onslaught came, he found the necessary confederates who possessed the initiative and audacity to turn his general goal into reality.

Weserübung was carried out in the early morning of April 9. The operation's emphasis on secrecy and rapid execution resulted in a striking success. With one major exception, the defenders along the coast were taken by surprise and overmanned. Despite some scattered resistance, the German vessels gained entrance to their destinations and were able to set troops ashore, thereby securing vital harbors. Arendal, Kristiansand, Egersund, Stavanger with its strategic airfield at Sola, Bergen, Trondheim, and Narvik were all occupied by German forces.

The British, who had kept troops in readiness for landings in Norway in anticipation of a German reaction to the mining action, were similarly surprised. When the Admiralty received information that a strong German naval force was emerging from the Baltic, it drew the erroneous conclusion that the Germans were not on their way to Norway. Instead, the British assumed that this was a direct challenge to their control of the Atlantic sea lanes. Anticipating a major encounter with the German navy, the Admiralty disposed its ships in such a manner that only chance encounters took place with the German force on its way to Norway. As a consequence of this decision, the British troops that were intended for landings in Norway, consisting of two brigades and one battalion, were ordered back on shore from the vessels that had originally been provided to carry them across the North Sea. As a result, these troops, which could have been of valuable help for the Norwegians, were not available during the critical first phase of the invasion when the *Wehrmacht* units came ashore and began their gradual conquest of the country.

The one critical part of *Weserübung* which did not go according to plan proved to be of vital significance not only for the manner in which the German takeover of Norway was carried out and for the fate of the Norwegian government during the war, but it also had an impact on Quisling's position and the subsequent reputation which he received. If *Weserübung* were to be completely successful, a key requirement was the need to capture quickly the responsible Norwegian constitutional authorities. If the King and the cabinet came under German control, the country's ability to resist would be paralyzed, and the government would be forced to accept a German occupation. The success of the naval unit sent to capture Oslo was therefore of great importance.

The squadron that moved up the Oslo fjord on the early morning of April 9 was spearheaded by the new 12,000 ton heavy cruiser, the *Blücher*. It carried the military personnel charged with the responsibility of setting up the German occupation administration. The naval force, which included two other cruisers and a number of lesser vessels, had no difficulty in forcing its way past defenses in the outer Oslo fjord. However, when the squadron reached the narrow straits in the inner fjord at Drøbak slightly after 4:00 a.m., the naval batteries were manned and ready at the old fortress of Oscarsborg, located on an island in the fjord. Moving forward at reduced speed, the *Blücher* presented a looming target. The old Krupp cannons at Oscarsborg opened fire at 4:21 a.m., and the *Blücher* received direct hits both from the fortress and from batteries on the mainland. As a result, the cruiser was soon aflame, with its steering mechanism destroyed. At slow speed it continued further up the fjord, where it received a *coup de grace* from torpedoes fired from a battery which was part of Oscarsborg's fortifications. Completely ablaze, the dying vessel drifted on, then anchored up and slowly sank. Of the approximately 2400 men aboard, some 1000 perished in the cold water and burning oil. The other ships in the flotilla turned back down the fjord, with several having received hits from the Norwegian batteries, resulting in one additional sinking.[88] The plan to take Oslo by surprise had thereby failed, giving the government time to react to the pending danger of being captured.

In the capital, the first reports came at midnight of foreign vessels forcing their entry into the outer Oslo fjord. By 1:30 a.m. the cabinet had gathered at the Foreign Ministry. The government resolved to order mobilization of the army brigades in the southern part of the country, the brigade in northern Norway having already been placed on active duty. Despite some confusion as to the form in which the order should be issued, it was carried out by the military, supplemented by a communiqué from Koht, which was broadcast on the radio in the morning.[89]

At 4:15 a.m., just shortly before the *Blücher* was reduced to a blazing, sinking wreck, Minister Bräuer arrived at the Foreign Ministry to issue his ultimatum.[90] He was received by Koht in a room lit only by two candles, Oslo having blacked out as a precaution against an air attack.[91] Until the evening of April 8, Bräuer had received no official confirmation about the coming invasion. At this time, he was handed his instructions by a special courier from Berlin. It had been anticipated that the ultimatum would be delivered *after* the Germans had seized the most important locations in Oslo, with the government and the King having been brought under German control. As a result of the elevated status that he could expect to hold as the official representative of the Third Reich in occupied Norway, Bräuer had been promoted to Plenipotentiary of the Reich in Norway (*Bevollmächtigter des Reichs in Norwegen*).[92]

The ultimatum maintained that the Germans intended to occupy strategically important sites in order to protect the kingdom from an anticipated attack by the British and French. The Third Reich, it was asserted, had no intention of violating Norway's territorial integrity or political independence. Any resistance, however, would be crushed. Specifically, the ultimatum contained a list of thirteen points which ennumerated how the Norwegians were expected to cooperate in allowing Germany to assume occupation of the country.[93]

Koht consulted with his colleagues, and returned to inform Bräuer that Norway would resist.[94] Since the naval squadron intended for Oslo had been turned back by the batteries at Oscarsborg, the newly promoted Reich Plenipotentiary had no means of preventing the cabinet from putting its decision into effect. Recognizing its exposed position, the government resolved on the early morning of April 9 to leave the capital. As a result, the ministers, the royal family, and almost the entire *Storting* left Oslo. For many, this began a period of moving from place to place which did not end until the royal family, the government, and some members of the administration landed in exile in England in June.

The fleeing authorities stopped first north of Oslo at Hamar, and then moved eastward to Elverum in fear of possible German capture. On the evening of April 9 the *Storting* agreed to delegate its constitutional authority to the cabinet until normal conditions could be restored. This "Elverum mandate" provided the government with its legitimate sovereignty during the war, which proved to be of great value during the next five years until regular peacetime procedures could be reinstated.

The escape of all possessors of popular legitimacy was a severe blow to German expectations. Having assumed all along that there would be no resistance, they had anticipated that Norwegian authorities would surrender to superior power.[95] The Third Reich planners in particular had placed great emphasis on capturing the King. According to the letter of the Constitution, he held the highest government authority. He also served as the living symbol of the nation. With him in their power, the Germans could look forward to making political and administrative changes built on a quasi-legal foundation.[96]

When they could not carry out *Weserübung's* political plans, considerable confusion resulted among the German officials in Oslo on April 9–10. Because of the strict secrecy under which the operation had been planned, the Foreign Ministry had been unable to work out any possible alternatives or changes. Bräuer was truly in a spot. He had responsibility for carrying out a policy about which he had not been informed until the last minute, and which completely contradicted the encouragement of Norwegian neutrality that he had pursued almost to the day of the invasion.

On one question, however, the issue was clear. Bräuer had received no orders, either written or oral, which indicated any official German intent to encourage formation of a Quisling government. No mention was made of Quisling in the sealed instructions which Bräuer opened on the evening of April 8.[97] With the Minister's past record of repeatedly emphasizing the NS leader's insignificance, and with all political authority, according to his instructions, in his hands as Reich Plenipotentiary, there was hardly any possibility that Bräuer would turn to Quisling.

While the official German plan omitted the NS *Fører* entirely, the confused situation in Oslo resulting from the government's withdrawal permitted representatives of those institutions within the German hierarchy which favored the NS leader to make a move on his behalf. These were Rosenberg's Office of Foreign Affairs, represented by Scheidt, and the navy, whose interests were looked after by naval attaché Schreiber.

Ever since he had come to Norway, Schreiber had opposed the proneutrality view of the German diplomatic corps, and he had not hesitated to present his standpoint personally at the Foreign Ministry in Berlin. Although he did not maintain direct contact with Quisling, Schreiber was sympathetic to his cause, and he kept himself fully informed of Quisling's activity through Scheidt.[98] In his positive attitude toward Quisling, Schreiber acted fully in accord with his superior, Grand Admiral Raeder.[99]

Unlike Bräuer, Schreiber had secured knowledge quite early about German planning for an attack against Norway. He learned of this personally from Raeder in February. In the middle of March the naval attaché visited the offices where Falkenhorst's staff was at work, and he received a report of the date of the invasion immediately after it had been decided.[100]

Unlike the regular diplomats in the Foreign Ministry, Rosenberg's Office of Foreign Affairs, even more so than the navy, was intent on supporting Quisling should the opportunity arise. While the foreign policy officials adopted the view that the German takeover should occur as smoothly as possible, with governmental and administrative machinery remaining as intact as circumstances permitted, Rosenberg and his subordinates were concerned with politics from an ideological perspective rather than from a bureaucratic one. They wished not only that Germany should succeed in occupying Norway, but that its people should be converted to Nazi ideology.[101] As political missionaries, they warmly regarded Quisling as one of their own.

In Scheidt, Rosenberg's organization had the most ambitious and single-minded exponent of this policy conceivable. For him, Quisling and NS had to be supported, no matter what happened. Unlike Schreiber, Rosenberg's agent had not been informed of *Weserübung*'s specific details, but he expected something to occur shortly, and he was determined to exploit the situation as fully as possible when the time came.[102]

Informed by Schreiber, Scheidt received news of the pending invasion at about the same time as Bräuer was opening his special instructions from Berlin.[103] Scheidt stayed overnight at Schreiber's residence, and early in the morning on April 9 the two drove down to the harbor to meet the expected arrival of the naval force, with the *Blücher* at its head. Schreiber, who wore his naval uniform under a civilian overcoat, had orders to report to the flagship. With no sign of the squadron, they went on board a German merchant ship already in the harbor, which was loaded with equipment for the invasion force. Here they learned that plans had not gone as expected in the Drøbak Sound. They returned ashore and drove away from the harbor. A few minutes later, Schreiber stopped to let Scheidt off at Hotel Continental.[104] Inside, both Quisling and Hagelin had rooms. Lying in the very center of Oslo, just a few minutes away from the *Storting* building and the Royal Palace, and close to the harbor, Hotel Continental became the site of the cabal which led to the fateful actions by Quisling later in the day.

The NS leader had late the previous evening occupied a room at the hotel. A party member who accompanied him, Harald Franklin Knudsen, was responsible for the move, allegedly in order to protect the *Fører* from possible danger at his home in the uncertain political situation that existed in Oslo.[105] It may have been a coincidence that Quisling moved into a room at the very hotel where Hagelin happened to be staying, but this appears unlikely, since Quisling no doubt knew where Hagelin was living.[106]

After he left Schreiber's car, Scheidt first went into the hotel to meet with Hagelin. The two quickly agreed it was necessary to contact Quisling.[107] While Knudsen later maintained he had never seen Scheidt or Hagelin before April 9, Scheidt immediately came to the room where Quisling was staying, although it was checked in Knudsen's name. When the latter answered the door, Scheidt asked to see Quisling. This occurred early in the morning, some time between seven and eight. The only record of the initial contact on April 9 between Quisling and the two men who

would exercise such great influence over him on this day, Scheidt and
Hagelin, comes from the postwar recollections of Knudsen, which are not
entirely trustworthy.[108] He maintains that he first told Scheidt and then
Hagelin that he had no knowledge of Quisling's whereabouts. Nevertheless, the two later in the morning succeeded in making arrangements, with
Quisling's approval, for a meeting.[109] After this had been decided, Scheidt
immediately went to the German legation in order to discuss the situation
with Schreiber. Already at this early hour, around 9:00 a.m., the two apparently considered the possibility of Quisling, with Hagelin's assistance,
assuming control of the government.[110] The energetic duo now drove to
Hotel Continental. Schreiber had shed his overcoat, and in full uniform insisted to the hotel porter that he wished to speak with Quisling or
Hagelin.[111] The naval attaché conferred briefly with Hagelin on the phone,
and then he and Scheidt went upstairs to talk with Quisling and his adviser.

The discussions that followed appear to have been critical for Quisling's
decision to agree to stage a coup as head of a pro-German "government".
As always when faced with a difficult decision, at first he was uncertain.
The situation was not what he had expected. According to the discussions
he had held in Berlin, a Quisling government was supposed to come into
being first, and then it would call for German backing. The proclamation
which he had issued on the previous day in reaction to the British mine-
laying was fully in accord with this original plan. But now, confusingly for
someone not capable of making rapid decisions in a changing situation, the
Germans had suddenly appeared as invaders without any call from a Quisling government. While he remained as committed as ever to Germany,
nevertheless he hesitated to act.

Scheidt and Hagelin, however, proved to be very persuasive. According
to Knudsen, Scheidt assured Quisling that Hitler would favor the formation of a government by the NS leader after the Nygaardsvold cabinet had
placed itself on England's side in the war.[112] On the basis of his own contact with Hitler, there was no reason for Quisling to doubt this assurance.
Scheidt and Hagelin were more than capable of providing him with the
resolution and will to act that he lacked when left to himself.[113] According
to Scheidt, only after long persuasion did Quisling agree to form a government. Scheidt, in reporting this to Bräuer, may have been exaggerating, as
he was prone to do, but there is no question that Quisling needed to be
convinced before he was ready to take such a drastic step, the most fateful
step in his life.[114]

Schreiber's presence as a representative of the navy also acted persua-
sively in favor of the coup idea. As a military man, his primary goal was
to halt Norwegian resistance, allowing the *Wehrmacht* units to occupy the
country as quickly as possible. He believed this could best be accomplished by having Quisling lead a pro-German government. As Schreiber

declared in a report which he wrote on April 9: "Quisling was the self-evident man because his predictions and warnings had been fulfilled; he had also had the correct political vision with his pro-German politics."[115]

Thus it was on the basis of the assurances he received from Rosenberg's energetic subordinate and a naval attaché, plus the advice of Hagelin, that Quisling, without any contact with the official German representative in Norway, Bräuer, and with no assurance of support from Berlin except the general promise he had received from Hitler in December, based his decision to step forward as the head of a government under German protection. Although he initially was unsure about proceeding with this venture, the lure of gaining the position of authority that had so long eluded him was strong. As he testified after the war, he had considered forming a "government" already on the morning of April 9.[116]

Following his meeting with the trio of Scheidt, Hagelin, and Schreiber, Quisling took a trip out into the streets alone. Apparently, he wanted to see for himself what the situation was like in Oslo.[117] He discovered what everyone in the capital experienced on that confused day. The population was paralyzed by what had happened, being completely unprepared for the invasion. While the naval squadron moving against Oslo had been turned back, it landed troops to the south of Oscarsborg on both sides of the fjord. These soldiers began to march toward the city. Much closer, the defenders of Fornebu, the major airfield just outside of Oslo, lacked the necessary strength and armament to protect the field from air attack. The Germans gained control over the airport on the morning of April 9, and immediately began to land troops. These forces marched on Oslo, which fell without resistance by late morning. The residents could only gather at the curbside along Karl Johans gate to watch silently as the invaders marched over the cobblestones on their way to take control of strategic positions throughout the city.

While the onlookers responded in shocked sorrow to this sight, for Quisling it was reassuring. In his mind, the successful German capture of the capital merely showed that his predictions had proven correct – that the Germans were militarily superior and that the Norwegian government had ignored the need to provide adequate military defense. The last hesitancy that he may have had about proclaiming himself the head of a pro-German government disappeared with his assessment of the disorganized situation in Oslo, his knowledge that the Germans were in the process of securing control of the capital, and that the Nygaardsvold government had fled.

He made his first public appearance in his self-proclaimed role some time after 1:00 p.m. Accompanied by Scheidt, he went to his former headquarters, where he had served as an officer and as a cabinet member, the Ministry of Defense.[118] He declared to the astonished officers and staff members who remained at their posts that the Nygaardsvold government had been set aside, and that he had formed a new government. Consequently, he insisted that his orders be obeyed.[119] During his initial stay in the Defense Ministry, his main effort was directed toward contacting various fortifications guarding the approaches to Oslo and Trondheim which were still in Norwegian possession, thereby posing a threat to German transport and supply lines. With Schreiber's and Scheidt's assistance, he sought to reach these forts in order to persuade them to surrender, but he failed to make telephone contact.[120]

Later in the day, probably between 5:00 and 6:00 p.m., he returned to the Defense Ministry. This time he succeeded in reaching Colonel Hans S. Hiorth, the commanding officer of the army regiment at Elverum. Quisling told Hiorth that "the Marxist government" was on its way from Hamar to Elverum. Having been introduced as "head of the government", Quisling ordered the Colonel to arrest the Nygaardsvold cabinet.[121]

The general public had not yet been informed of Quisling's unilateral action. However, the Minister of Defense, Colonel Ljungberg, told members of the *Storting* at a meeting which began at Hamar at 6:30 p.m. that "Quisling had taken over command" in Oslo. Ljungberg had earlier received reports from the Ministry of Defense concerning Quisling's activities in the building.[122]

In between his two appearances in the Ministry of Defense, Quisling was at Hotel Continental, holding consultations with Scheidt, Hagelin, and a number of NS loyalists who gradually assembled at the hotel, which had become Quisling's headquarters. He was making preparations for the time when he would publicly announce his takeover. The text of his proclamation, which he intended to make over the radio at the first available opportunity, was drawn up during the course of an hour-long conference with Hagelin and Scheidt, held some time between 4:00 and 6:30 p.m.[123]

Harald Franklin Knudsen initially received the assignment to work out the arrangements at radio headquarters for Quisling's address, but he failed miserably. The German guard at the entrance refused him admittance.[124] Scheidt therefore had to intervene personally. After neatly talking his way past the guard, he proceeded to fool the Norwegian radio officials into assuming that he had the authority to arrange for Quisling to speak. Scheidt pulled out an impressive identification document, and he also arranged a telephone authorization from the German legation, giving approval for Quisling to use the facilities. The latter arrived at the studio shortly thereafter.[125]

In reality, Scheidt bluffed when he succeeded in gaining access to the microphone for Quisling. Scheidt had no permission from Bräuer, as the official German representative in Norway, allowing the establishment of a Quisling government. When Bräuer later learned of Quisling's radio announcement, he was flabbergasted. This move in no way complied with his instructions.[126] When Hagelin earlier in the day had attempted to persuade Bräuer to allow Quisling to form a government, the diplomat had politely but firmly dismissed Hagelin.[127] In order to circumvent the Minister, Scheidt apparently had arranged to have a confederate at the legation make the phone call which authorized Quisling's radio address. This definitely occurred without Bräuer's knowledge.[128]

Thanks to Scheidt's clever tactics, Quisling went on the air at 7:32 p.m. His listeners reacted with astonishment to his announcement. Already at a loss because of the German invasion, the Norwegian people naturally identified his proclamation as being a direct part of the German takeover, as did the world at large.

In his radio proclamation, Quisling felt the need not only to announce the establishment of a new government, but also to justify his coup in order to provide it with some sanction:

> After England had violated Norway's neutrality by placing mine fields in Norwegian territorial waters without meeting any resistance except the usual insignificant protests from the Nygaardsvold government, the German government has offered the Norwegian government its peaceful assistance, prefaced by a solemn assurance to respect our national independence and Norwegian life and property. In response . . . the Nygaardsvold government has declared general mobilization and has given the pointless order to the Norwegian forces to resist the German aid with armed might.

Not only this, said Quisling, the government had thereafter "fled" after having irresponsibly gambled with the country's fate. He declared that under these circumstances it was National Union's right and duty to take over control of the government "in order to protect the Norwegian people's vital interests" and the country's "security and independence". He further maintained that only NS could save Norway from the "desperate situation" which the "party politicians have led our people into". He thereupon announced that the Nygaardsvold government had "resigned", being replaced by a "national government . . . with Vidkun Quisling as head . . . and foreign minister . . ." He also included eight other ministers in his government, with but one possible exception all NS members. He closed by urging everyone to remain calm and sensible, declaring that by a common effort it would be possible to "rescue Norway freely and safely through this enormous crisis".[129]

The self-appointed new head of state obviously did not feel secure in his hope that the people would unite behind him because later in the evening, at 10:00 p.m., he repeated his previous message, but at this time he felt the need to add a passage threatening public officials who might not accept orders from his government. He declared that any resistance to the Germans was not only "fruitless", but constituted "criminal destruction of life and property". He ordered all civil servants, and "especially all of our country's officers in the army, navy, coastal artillery, and air force . . . to obey orders from the new national government". Anyone who did not, he warned, would be held personally accountable, being faced with the most "serious" repercussions.[130]

Despite his explanations, the actions which Quisling took on April 9, 1940 constituted a revolutionary *coup d'état*, intended to aid the invading power. The legally elected government still functioned. It had resolved to offer resistance to the invader. For anyone who believed in the normal democratic rules which determined the process by which the country was governed, Quisling's action constituted a fundamental breach of established values. It was treason.

Such considerations had little if any meaning for him. His contempt for "party politics", in particular for the "Marxist" Nygaardsvold government, was well documented. Furthermore, he was convinced that military developments had occurred as he had predicted. Because of his belief in his infallibility, he had no qualms once he had made up his mind to "take power". Such an attitude, which gave no heed to the insignificance of his following, and which rejected the normal requirements for gaining governmental authority, was fully in accord with the justification which he provided after the war. He maintained he had not originally made any preparations on April 9 for taking action, but that he had decided during the day that something had to be done: "I was *fører* for the political movement whose opinion had proven to be right . . ." He insisted he could not simply sit by and watch Norway being conquered without doing something.[131]

Contrary to what he asserted, his action was not needed in order to prevent collapse and chaos in the capital. Responsible civil servants remained at their posts, and they paid no attention to his claims. Furthermore, Bräuer, the official German representative, regarded Quisling as a usurper and did his best to remove the NS leader from his self-appointed position.

In his defense of his act, Quisling on the whole was correct when he declared he had not made any preparations before he proclaimed himself head of state. He had proceeded in an improvised manner, in collaboration with Scheidt and Hagelin. Only a few of the "ministers" whose names he announced had been consulted before he appointed them. The absence of careful planning needed for the success of an endeavor of the magnitude which he sought to realize would have caused more realistic political figures to hold back. But not Quisling. He remained convinced that action on his part was the only thing that mattered.

It did not take long before it became clear that he would not achieve the success that he anticipated. His initiative only caused complications. Not even among those from whom he had expected automatic support, the individuals whom he had designated as ministers, was there any unanimous acceptance of his government. In addition to Hagelin, who was appointed Minister of Commerce and Supplies, only two others were in Oslo, Tormod Hustad, named Minister of Agriculture, and Professor Birger Meidell, designated Minister of Church and Education. Quisling had conferred only with these three before making the list public. The inclusion of Hagelin, who had spent most of his life in Germany and who possessed hardly any expertise about Norwegian conditions, was but one indication of the personal manner in which Quisling made his appointments. Of the remaining five persons on the list, all reacted negatively. Two of these, Jonas Lie, a high police official, and Major Ragnvald Hvoslef, Quisling's old associate, completely ignored the NS *Fører* and reported for duty with the army.[132] Two others who were in Trondheim, Frederik Prytz, Quisling's long time friend, and Professor Ragnar Skancke, expressed their negative reactions to the news of their appointment, both in the press and to German authorities.[133] In Stavanger, which was also in the hands of the Germans, Dr. Gulbrand Lunde attempted to send a telegram to Quisling in which he declared he could not "without knowledge of the present situation and circumstances accept any appointment as minister in your government". When he could not send the telegram, Lunde took the precaution of depositing it at the provincial administrative office in Stavanger.[134]

The completely unexpected manner in which Quisling had acted resulted therefore only in confusion for everyone concerned. Not only did it cause surprise and discomfiture among his followers who had not been consulted, but it also served as an additional element of uncertainty for the Norwegian government, which was still seeking to establish a clear policy in the disruptive atmosphere caused by the German attack. But perhaps Minister Bräuer was the person most directly affected by the radio announcement. Quisling's proclamation created a completely new situation for which the surprised diplomat had no orders whatsoever.[135]

When the Norwegian government succeeded in avoiding capture and ordered resistance, Bräuer continued to adhere to his original instructions. He hoped that the government would soon recognize that armed combat against superior forces was fruitless. He therefore sent a message to Hamar at 12:40 p.m. on April 9 in which he declared that resistance was "meaningless" and would only complicate the situation. He also repeated the previous assurance that Germany would respect Norwegian territorial integrity and political independence, pointing to the example of Denmark. Only token hostilities had occurred in Denmark, with the government, despite formal protests, being forced to accept German occupation.[136]

At Hamar the mood was anything but positive. During the day reports had been coming in about continuous German successes. The possibility of conducting negotiations could therefore not be rejected out of hand. The Foreign Ministry in Oslo was informed that the government would place the question of negotiations before the *Storting* when it met at 6:30 p.m. The message was relayed on to Bräuer, who received it at 8:20 p.m.[137]

The tone of the *Storting* meeting was quite pessimistic because of the bleak military information which its members were receiving. Narvik and Trondheim had fallen; after capturing Bergen, the Germans were advancing along the railroad into the interior; German warships were steaming up the Hardanger fjord; the vital airfield at Sola outside of Stavanger was under German control; Oslo had fallen, etc.[138] The British promised aid, but it could not be expected immediately.[139] In a somber address, Prime Minister Nygaardsvold pointed to all the negative factors which the government had to face: the Germans occupying the most vital points along the coast, the recent example of Germany's brutal crushing of Polish resistance, the weak military position of Norwegian forces, and the danger that the government and *Storting* might be forced further and further eastward into Sweden. He wondered how the people would react if the result of resistance to the Germans was "a king and a government and a *Storting* without an army, without a country, and without a people". He therefore recommended negotiations.[140] Illustrating the precariousness of the situation, the meeting had to be suddenly adjourned before a decision could be made because a German force was advancing on Hamar, threatening to capture the entire base of Norwegian political legitimacy – the *Storting*, the government, and the royal family.[141]

When the parliament reassembled at Elverum at 9:40 p.m., it immediately approved without debate the decision to appoint a delegation to negotiate with the Germans. At 12:10 a.m. Koht sent a message to the Foreign Ministry, to be passed on to Bräuer, which declared that the delegation was ready "to negotiate and reach an agreement about a peaceful settlement of the military invasion".[142] Quite clearly, the government and *Storting* at this point believed that resistance offered little hope, and that a negotiated settlement appeared to be a better alternative.

In Oslo, Bräuer on the evening of April 9 was pleased by the fact that he had been able to re-establish contact with Koht. But he was disturbed by Quisling's radio proclamation. Scheidt, announcing this *fait accompli* to the astonished German Minister, had pulled out a letter of authorization signed by Rosenberg.[143] This caused Bräuer to wonder if the Nazi party, through Rosenberg's office, was directly intervening in the Foreign Ministry's area of competence. Faced with Scheidt's challenge, Bräuer did not feel strong enough on his own to repudiate Quisling's move. He therefore decided to phone Berlin to seek renewed instructions.

After some difficulty, Bräuer managed to reach Ribbentrop at the Reich Chancellery. The Minister summarized the events of the day, and then gave a negative assessment of Quisling's action. The proclamation, insisted

Bräuer, was damaging to what he had been able to achieve – the possibility of renewed negotiations with the Norwegian government.[144]

Ribbentrop, however, refused to provide Bräuer with specific guidelines on how to proceed. The matter had to be submitted to *der Führer*. After a long pause, Bräuer suddenly heard Hitler himself at the other end of the line. As usual, the head of the Third Reich came not to listen, but to give orders. He insisted that the invasion had gone well, and there was no reason to reject Quisling. Hitler repudiated completely the idea of making use of the Nygaardsvold government. It had angered him by daring to offer resistance. He ordered Bräuer to seek an audience with the King and to attempt to persuade him to return to Oslo. In his discussions with the monarch, said Hitler, Bräuer could yield on other issues involving the conduct of government in Norway, but not on Quisling. *Der Führer* emphasized that the King would have to accept Quisling as prime minister.[145]

Bräuer attempted to interject as best he could that Quisling was of little value for German interests. Hitler, however, remained adamant. If the King wished to save his dynasty, then he would have to recognize Quisling. In order to secure this goal, Hitler ordered Bräuer to speak with the King alone, with no member of the government present.[146]

Hitler's insistence that Quisling be recognized as head of government proved to have decisive consequences. Yet when he made his decision, Hitler did not appear to be following a carefully thought out plan, but instead acted on the spur of the moment. As Rosenberg's diary revealed, the atmosphere surrounding Hitler was one of jubilation and triumph on April 9 as reports came in on the success of *Weserübung*. Some resistance had occurred in Oslo, but it did not appear serious. Nor did the escape of the Nygaardsvold government seem to be a problem. Rosenberg, when complimenting Hitler on his success, congratulated an elated warlord: "He laughed all over his face: Now Quisling can form his government. . . . We expressed the hope that the fleeing Norwegian government had not dragged Quisling with it."[147]

Hitler, believing the military situation to be under control, and being favorably inclined toward Quisling because of the warning that the NS leader had delivered about the danger which England posed to German military interests in Norway, decided to make good his previous promise of support that he had made in December. The King would have to bow to the inevitable and accept Quisling, the military situation being what it was. When insisting on royal recognition, Hitler followed the legalistic approach of imposing a settlement which had been characteristic of German planning for the political side of the invasion and occupation. The consent of, in theory, the highest authority under the Constitution would be in the best interest of the Germans, who believed this would cause the least disruption. Hitler was already looking forward to the coming *Wehrmacht* of-

fensive in the west against France and the Low Countries, and he wished
to have the Norwegian question settled as soon as possible.

Bräuer, on the scene in Norway, had a much better understanding of the
political situation. He knew it would be difficult if not impossible to secure
the King's recognition of Quisling because of the complete absence of any
significant support for the NS leader. His person was anathema to all responsible political leaders, and the general public regarded him as a pro-
German fanatic, that is, when any attention was given to him. Yet the
Minister had no choice but to attempt as best he could to carry out Hitler's
orders. When Bräuer received the news at 1:30 a.m. on April 10 that the
Norwegian delegation, consisting of Koht and one representative from
each of the three major *borgerlige* parties, was ready to come to Oslo to
conduct negotiations, he phoned Elverum and declared that he would instead travel to meet the Norwegians. Specifically, he requested to be allowed to talk personally with the King.[148]

Bräuer held his meeting with the Norwegians at Elverum in the afternoon of April 10 at 2:45 p.m. After some protests, he had his way and
spoke alone with King Haakon for some ten minutes. The two were then
joined by Foreign Minister Koht, who remained present for the duration
of the meeting. As he had been instructed by Hitler, Bräuer insisted that
Quisling's government be recognized by the King since the Germans refused to deal with the Nygaardsvold government. Later in the discussions,
the German Minister conceded that the main issue involved in the composition of a government acceptable to Germany was Quisling's position as
prime minister. Appointments to other cabinet posts were open for
discussion.[149]

Despite this hint at possible accommodations, Quisling served as a
stumbling block that ruled out any agreement. Contrary to Hitler's desire
to divide the King from the Nygaardsvold government, Haakon VII declared that he could not appoint a government which did not enjoy public
support. In addition, as a constitutional monarch, he had to submit the
question to his legal advisers, the cabinet.[150]

Bräuer did not wish to wait in order to learn the result of the cabinet's
deliberations. It was therefore agreed that he would be informed of the decision during the course of his journey back to Oslo. The King submitted
the German ultimatum at a meeting of the government, which had moved
eastward to the village of Nybergsund in order to be safer from the threat
of being taken captive. On the night of April 9–10 a German force, specially assembled to capture the Norwegian authorities, had reached within
five kilometers of Elverum before being driven back by a hastily gathered
group of Norwegian soldiers.

In the deliberations at Nybergsund, Haakon VII's influence was of major importance. The King declared he could "not appoint as prime minister Quisling who, I know, enjoys no confidence either among our people as a whole or in its representative assembly, the *Storting*." While King Haakon insisted that the government should make its decision independently of his view, he stressed that he would abdicate if the cabinet accepted the German demand. By taking this dramatic stand, he eliminated any doubt and indecision within the cabinet, which unanimously resolved to advise the King to follow the course of action that he had enunciated so forthrightly.[151]

Hitler's ultimatum that Haakon VII had to accept Quisling thereby ruled out any possibility of the Germans gaining control of Norway as the result of a negotiated settlement. It cannot be stated categorically that an accommodation similar to that which occurred in Denmark could have been worked out if Hitler's demand had not been made. However, the possibility for such a settlement was very real on April 10. The Germans held the most important strategic points in the country, there was no chance of immediate Allied assistance, Norwegian resistance had not been mobilized effectively, and the governmental authorities were in danger of either being captured or being driven across the frontier into Sweden. On the very day the government refused Hitler's ultimatum, the commanding general declared there was no chance to resist the Germans unless Allied aid arrived within the next three days.[152] Although the general was immediately removed from his command, the incident did nothing to brighten the gloom at Nybergsund. Yet no matter how pessimistic the outlook, no one was willing to accept the alternative and recognize Quisling. This information was phoned to Bräuer, who stopped on his return trip to take Koht's message: "Resistance will continue as long as possible."[153]

While Bräuer carried out his day-long mission on the 10th, Quisling and his confederates had been busy in the capital. They became aware of the Minister's journey to confer with the King already in the morning.[154] However, they were not informed of Hitler's insistence on recognition of Quisling, a secret that Bräuer deliberately withheld from them.[155] In reaction to the news that the German representative had instructions to negotiate with the King, Quisling, along with Scheidt and Hagelin, realized that his government could not exist merely on the basis of his personal proclamation. If it were to become permanent, it would have to have the King's sanction, since this appeared to be the requirement under which the Germans operated. The decision was therefore made to send a special emissary from Quisling to the King. Captain Kjeld Stub Irgens, the master of the flagship of the Norwegian-America Line, was chosen to carry out this mission. He received the assignment because: (1) he was personally acquainted with the King, and (2) he happened to be Hagelin's brother-in-law.[156] Irgens, who had never met Quisling before, obtained his instructions from the head of the "national government" slightly after 2:00 p.m. However, he did not reach Elverum until that night, and he was not received by the King until 7:00 a.m. on the following morning.[157] According to Irgens, Quisling's message requested the King and the royal family to return to Oslo, with Quisling's assurance of loyalty and expression of desiring to establish an agreement in Norway similar to the one which had come into existence in Denmark "so that war can be avoided".[158]

By the time Irgens reached the King, however, both the monarch and the government had made their decision in response to Hitler's ultimatum. The King informed his acquaintance Irgens that he would only come to Oslo if the *Storting* and the cabinet accompanied him, and any new government would have to be formed in accordance with constitutional practice. He would not accept a Quisling government.[159]

Irgens returned to Oslo, where he reported on the failure of his mission to Quisling at about 3:00 p.m. Thursday, April 11. The goal of reaching some type of accommodation with the King still remained a matter of high priority, however, and Hagelin prevailed on his brother-in-law to make yet another trip. Irgens met with Quisling and Hagelin in the evening, and at this time the two both stressed that neither Quisling nor his government would stand in the way of a settlement if this were in the country's best interest.[160] Obviously, what mattered most for them now was to get the person of the King back to Oslo so that they would have him under their control. On the following day, however, Hagelin informed Irgens that the mission was cancelled because of increased Norwegian military resistance.[161] Nevertheless, until the intensity of combat eliminated the possibility of further contact, Quisling continued in vain to seek to persuade the King to come to Oslo. On the morning of the 12th another Quisling emissary, an army colonel, made a venture to reach the King, but he was unable to get through the lines.[162]

In addition to seeking a royal accommodation, Quisling's awareness that his government had no sanction caused him to send a telegram to Hitler on April 10, informing *der Führer* of his action, hoping thereby to secure Hitler's approval. In the telegram, Quisling expressed his thanks to Hitler "in the name of the Norwegian people" for the "grandiose help" which the Germans had provided "for the protection of Norway's neutrality and integrity". He further assured Hitler of future friendship and cooperation between the two "Germanic brother folk".[163]

To demonstrate his assurance of cooperation, Quisling indicated by direct example his intent to sabotage continued Norwegian resistance. Furthermore, it was in his interest to bring about a cessation of hostilities. With the country completely pacified, and with the King and the Nygaardsvold government either captured or in exile, he expected to have full control of society in alliance with the Germans. On the morning of April

10 he twice attempted to send messages over the radio which called upon Norwegian forces to lay down their arms. This time, however, Scheidt was not on hand to bluff Quisling forward to the microphone. The *Wehrmacht* control officer in charge of the studio, considering such behavior to be an insult to an officer's code of honor, point blank refused to allow the messages to be sent, sarcastically commenting that "Quisling is not a major in the German army".[164]

Quisling therefore was restricted to communicating his proclamations via the press. On April 10 he called on all officers and everyone liable for active duty to disregard the Nygaardsvold government's general mobilization. Instead, those in the armed forces should return home.[165] On the following day he went even further, characterizing the government's attempt to continue mobilization as being "criminal" and a "completely meaningless gamble with human lives". He warned that if this did not stop, those who were responsible for mobilization and those who took part in it could be brought to trial for murder.[166] He issued a similar order to the navy on April 12, and this time it was broadcast over the radio. He encouraged naval officers not to sacrifice lives in vain, but urged them instead to bring their ships to ports under German control "since a continued struggle is hopeless".[167]

The disturbed situation which existed in the capital at the time of its capture and during the next few days did provide Quisling with some initial advantage. Rumors swept Oslo on April 10 that British and French planes would bomb the city in a counter-strike against the Germans. This caused a considerable percentage of the population to flee into the countryside. In another of his announcements, Quisling sought to reassure the people that there was no danger associated with remaining in the city.[168] In such a stunned atmosphere, at first there were some scattered indications of acceptance of his government. Members of the King's Royal Guard served as sentries at his headquarters at Hotel Continental, with one of the Guard officers being assigned as the NS leader's adjutant for a few days.[169] The Oslo newspapers during the same period provided Quisling with coverage, making reference to him as "prime minister".[170]

German authorities in Norway, both civilian and military, did not at this time create any formal hindrances for the Quisling government. However, their attitude toward Quisling during the period April 11-13 can best be described as benevolent neutrality, while underneath the surface there existed considerable misgivings and even direct hostility. Despite Hitler's ultimatum that Quisling should receive royal sanction as prime minister, this did not result in recognition of the NS leader's government once the King refused. Instead, Bräuer received orders from the Foreign Ministry to maintain contact with the King. He was instructed to arrange a meeting with the monarch, and then to inform General Falkenhorst of where and when it was scheduled to take place. Obviously, the transparent intent of this move was to secure the capture or death of the King.[171] Although there are no specific sources revealing the originator of this plot, it is unlikely that Ribbentrop would have dared to institute such an audacious action on his own. Quite probably, the idea was approved by Hitler himself.[172]

Bräuer sent a message to the King on the morning of the 11th in which he declared his willingness to discuss new proposals. However, the King responded by stating that any new offers should be communicated to Foreign Minister Koht.[173] The possibility of luring the King into a trap was thereby eliminated. This marked the final defeat of the German effort to arrange in one way or another a takeover of Norway without having to resort to a protracted military campaign. Now there was no alternative except to subdue the country by force. Already on the afternoon of April 11 the *Luftwaffe* unleashed air attacks against the headquarters of Norwegian governmental activity, Elverum and Nybergsund. Both centers were largely reduced to ruins, with considerable loss of life. However, the primary German objective – the annihilation of the King and the members of the government – was not achieved either on this occasion or later, despite repeated air raids.

For the time being there existed no alternative for the Germans except Quisling's government. At noon on April 10 its leader had ensconced himself in the *Storting* building, which thereafter served as his headquarters. He was accompanied by his two ministers in the Oslo area, Hustad and Meidell, plus all active NS members whom they could scrape together, who were not many.[174]

During the five days that this so-called government existed, it did not succeed in accomplishing anything substantive. Everything which it attempted to carry out had to be improvised. None of Quisling's ministers except for himself had ever administered a department. Even worse, the majority of the offices which Quisling had established were never manned due to the absence of most of the ministers whom he had appointed on April 9. In a makeshift effort to try to compensate for this, Quisling, in addition to having declared himself "prime minister" and "foreign minister", also sought to issue orders as "minister of defense" and "acting minister of justice".[175] However, the few changes that he and his ministers tried to initiate were largely stymied by the systematic obstruction of regular civil servants, who ignored the instructions and orders which they received.[176] Quisling's inability to shut down the Communist party's Oslo newspaper, *Arbeideren (The Worker)*, served as but one example of how his will was thwarted. In his "Governmental Decree No. 1", issued on April 13, he gave rein to his underlying antagonism toward the Communists, declaring that the publication, printing, and distribution of *Arbeideren* was forbidden. However, this "decree" was conveniently deposited in a drawer within the Justice Department and forgotten.[177]

Of the civil servants, Kristian Welhaven, Oslo's chief of police, acted as an especially irritating thorn in Quisling's flesh. Welhaven had been ordered by his superior, Minister of Justice Terje Wold, to remain in Oslo and to assist the German authorities in securing an orderly takeover of the capital. The police chief carried out his duties effectively, gaining the respect of his German contacts. He also played an important part on April 9 as an intermediary between the Norwegian government, with which he remained in telephone communication, and Minister Bräuer.

When Quisling learned of this, he immediately wished to bring the police chief under his authority in order to sabotage Bräuer's attempt to reach an accommodation with the Nygaardsvold government. Welhaven received an "order" to report to Quisling on the evening of April 9, which the police chief completely ignored. Quisling next tried to use the German military to bring Welhaven under his control, but the Germans rejected this move. Quisling persevered, attempting to persuade the chief of police in a neighboring district to take over in place of Welhaven. The replacement candidate refused, and his discussion with Quisling degenerated into a quarrel during which the stubborn police chief was requested to "step down".[178] On the following morning, April 10, Quisling phoned Welhaven personally, but he was told that if he wished to meet with Welhaven, he would have to come to police headquarters.[179]

Two days later Quisling responded by sending a letter in which he, as "acting head of the Department of Justice and Police", notified the police chief that he was suspended from his position, being replaced by a faithful NS member.[180] Welhaven received news of his "suspension" while in conference with a German military police officer. Bräuer was immediately informed, and the chief of police shortly thereafter was told to take no notice of the letter from Quisling, which was described as being based on a misunderstanding. To ensure that Welhaven would encounter no further difficulties, the Germans provided him with a personal bodyguard consisting of a non-commissioned officer and four soldiers.[181] As this episode dramatically demonstrated, the Germans in Oslo paid no attention to Quisling's attempts to assert himself if such moves conflicted with their interests.

With no significant active support forthcoming from German officials in Oslo, Quisling and his entourage tried as best they could to solicit some sanction from leaders of key organizations. Of major importance were the representatives of industry and labor. Quisling recognized that if he succeeded in obtaining a degree of backing from these sources, his government would gain a considerable amount of the authority which it lacked. Already on the morning of April 10 he called a conference with representatives of the major business and industrial organizations. Only two responded, but one was the managing director of the influential Norway's

Industrial Federation (*Norges Industriforbund*).[182] On the following day
the "prime minister" succeeded in holding a meeting with the managing director of the Bankers' Association, plus another prominent banking
official.[183] Finally, on April 13 he met with a three-man delegation from
the Federation of Trade Unions, LO.

He failed, however, to derive any advantage from these limited contacts
because he did not concentrate adequately on exploiting the present situation. He was more preoccupied with the future, conducting long monologues as to how he would organize society in accordance with his corporate ideal. His listeners were in no position to argue with him, and politely
followed his discourse. They were primarily concerned with keeping industry in operation and maintaining tranquility among the workers. But
they did not specifically declare their loyalty to the Quisling
government.[184] On the contrary, a number of leading industrialists were especially interested in eliminating the self-proclaimed administration. One
of these, Lorentz Vogt, director of Norway's Industrial Federation, who
had met with Quisling on April 10, played an active part in plotting against
the NS *Fører*. The latter, however, was in no way disappointed with the
outcome of his discussions. Since he had not met direct dissent, he believed
that his coup regime enjoyed the backing of the groups involved in the
talks. In particular, he was pleased by what he considered to be the favorable attitude of the Federation of Labor, whose leaders called on the workers to maintain order.[185] As later developments would indicate, he was entirely unrealistic in making such an optimistic assessment. At best, his talks
with the representatives from economic organizations indicated that they
would not publicly oppose his government.

In the vacuum that existed, he nevertheless for a short time could at
least superficially play the role of "prime minister". At noon on April 12
he held a news conference in the *Storting* building. A large part of the session was restricted to a monologue by the "prime minister", in which he
sought to justify his position. In doing so, it was equally necessary for him
to defend the German invasion and to condemn the Nygaardsvold government for ordering military resistance. As before, he accused Norwegian
authorities of having wanted to maneuver the country into the war "on the
so-called democratic side". A peaceful solution could have been achieved,
he insisted, if only the German terms had been accepted in a settlement
similar to that which had been made in Denmark.[186] He failed to add the
obvious that the Danes were forced to accept the German occupation because Denmark's geographical position, so very different from Norway's,
made defense impossible.

When he addressed the major purpose of the news conference, the need
to justify his government's existence, he began rather defensively by insisting: "We are no Kuusinen government". This was hardly an auspicious
statement. His reference to the puppet government which the Russians had

established at the time they invaded Finland, only a few months previously, indicated his awareness of the widespread feeling that he was a German pawn. He maintained, however, that this was not true, declaring that he had never wanted to become a dictator. Nor was NS a copy of the Germans. His party's program, he argued, had been written already in 1918, before National Socialism had come into existence. In making this assertion, he conveniently failed to remember that National Union's present program had been formed in 1934 after considerable internal unrest in the party.[187]

He went on to discuss in detail the political system which he intended to set up. This was his corporate model, with its economic and cultural chambers. Again he resorted to the awkward ploy of arguing that his system was not dictatorial, while declaring that "party politics shall never be restored". His system, he maintained, was "a true people's government".[188]

The news conference provided the press corps with a clear indication of Quisling's prophetic inclination, which he had similarly revealed in his talks with the representatives of business and labor. This attitude of course was quixotic, coming at a time when his government could hardly be said to exist. For Quisling, however, it was his prophetic vision for the future which represented reality, a reality that he was intent on achieving. It therefore was natural for him to comment on world affairs as well, since he as usual perceived himself as playing the role of an international statesman. In assessing the wartime situation, he predicted that events were moving in the direction of closer cooperation between nations. He was deliberately vague on this point, since Norwegians were hardly enthusiastic about their country being joined with Germany, but it was obvious that he was referring to his previous emphasis on cooperation between "Nordic" states: "Norway and Scandinavia cannot defend themselves alone in the battle between the great powers. Another system must come into being." He decried the fact that his attempt to create friendship between England and Germany had failed. Hitler, he declared, had been willing to live in peace, but "the power brokers in England" were responsible for following a policy which led to war.[189]

The journalists were interested in asking more concrete questions. In response to one query, Quisling asserted that the Western Allies had no chance of altering the military situation in Norway. The newsmen also wished to learn the "prime minister's" attitude toward the royal dynasty. His reply, made just shortly after he had tried to establish contact with the King, showed his awareness of the benefits which his government would gain if it had the monarch's recognition, especially because of the stress which the Germans placed on the King's constitutional authority. Quisling therefore declared that he had never intended to oppose the dynasty, and that he was interested in coming to an agreement with the King because it was advantageous to maintain a monarchy.[190] This was a change in position. In his radio address on April 9 Quisling had not even mentioned the King.

His belated wish to reach an accommodation with the monarch was obviously determined by tactics. Furthermore, the "prime minister" was rather condescending, implying it was more in the interest of the King than it was for him to reach a settlement. Nevertheless, had such an agreement been possible, Quisling would have welcomed royal recognition. It would have provided him with an aura of constitutional legitimacy, a mantle he always sought to assume. However, he failed to recognize that he personally made this impossible by the radical revolutionary program which he insisted on implementing. If accomplished, this would have completely transformed the political system. He was blind to the fact that his regime either had to be revolutionary or constitutional.[191] His attempts to claim sanction in the Constitution for acts that were clearly unconstitutional simply resulted in making it obvious that his entire program was based on subterfuge.

On the very day he insisted to the press that he desired to reach an accommodation with the King, Quisling issued the following proclamation:

> In accordance with Article 41 of the Constitution, the national government has for the present taken over the country's administration.
> Oslo, April 12, 1940.
>
> Vidkun Quisling
> head of government[192]

When those who desired to verify the validity of this claim referred to the Constitution, they discovered that Article 41 in no way provided sanction for Quisling's takeover of administration. As he had shown in his pre-war assertion that the *Storting* was illegal, he was capable of interpreting legal provisions in the most inconsistent manner if this could provide him with a veneer of legality. Article 41 stated that if the King were outside of the realm without being in command of the armed forces, or if he were sick and could not carry out his responsibilities, then the eldest prince, as long as he had reached his majority, would temporarily assume the King's authority. If the prince could not meet these obligations, then the prime minister would assume control of the kingdom's administration.[193] At the time Quisling issued his proclamation, Haakon VII was not only within the kingdom, but he was carrying out his responsibilities as commander in chief. Furthermore, Crown Prince Olav, aged thirty-six, was also on active duty in the field. Finally, the legally elected prime minister continued to exercise his constitutional duties.

Quisling's claim that he had assumed administrative control over the country was not based entirely on constitutional fiction, however. When he issued his proclamation on April 12, his government appeared outwardly to have acquired a certain degree of permanence. In a ceremony conducted that afternoon, the NS *Fører*, accompanied by a German escort, marched into the government's administration building. Symbolically, the purpose of this demonstration was to show that Quisling exercised firm control over the state bureaucracy. To the onlookers watching him proceed into the building along with the accompanying Germans, this seemed to mark formal recognition of the "prime minister's" authority.[194] This view proved to be unfounded, however. As far as responsible German officials in Norway were concerned, Quisling was allowed to retain his self-proclaimed position only in lieu of no better alternative, in particular since he enjoyed *der Führer*'s favor. But they did not feel that he was of any value for German interests. This attitude, which was shared by Minister Bräuer and army authorities, was not, however, apparent to the public.

In the end, the question of whether or not Quisling would retain his position would be based on the German perception of his value to them. The attempts made by Quisling and his close advisers to secure support for his regime were exerted mainly in the vain endeavor to demonstrate that he enjoyed popular appeal in the country, and that he therefore was worth retaining in office. But from the beginning he and his closest associates, Scheidt and Hagelin, recognized the obvious fact that the *sine qua non* for the Quisling government's future existence depended on gaining recognition and backing from Berlin. On April 11 Quisling therefore attempted to telephone Hitler personally. *Der Führer*, however, was in a military conference and refused to take the phone. Quisling was told to phone back at 5:00 p.m. By the time he could place his second call, his position in Norway had become even more uncertain than earlier. German recognition, which he had assumed would be forthcoming automatically, had not materialized. Instead, Bräuer was attempting to reach a settlement with the King. In the afternoon, Irgens had returned bearing news of the King's rejection of Quisling's proposals. It was therefore decided even before Quisling made another effort to contact Hitler that the situation had become so serious that Hagelin should go on a mission to Berlin.[195]

Quisling gained scarcely more satisfaction from his second telephone conversation than he had from his first. Since the call went over Sweden, allowing Swedish intelligence officers to monitor the dialogue, Hitler again refused to take the phone, instructing Ribbentrop instead to talk with Quisling.[196] The Foreign Minister in turn avoided direct contact with Quisling by delegating the chore to Ambassador Hewel, who was in Hamburg, not in Berlin.[197] Because of his lower rank, Hewel could not make policy decisions. He was restricted to receiving information, which he passed on to higher authorities. He did state that the Germans had not expected such strong resistance in Norway, which was why the initial invading force had

been so small. He asked Quisling about the political situation in the country, but the latter could only provide an account of conditions in Oslo,
which he described as currently being calm. In response to Hewel's question whether Quisling had formed his government, the NS leader, indicating the uncertainty he now felt, evasively answered that the government
was ready, but supplied no details. Hewell declared he would pass the contents of their talk on to Hitler, whereupon Quisling interjected that he was
sending his colleague, "Minister" Hagelin, to Germany. The ambassador
did not encourage the visit, stating merely that Quisling would receive instructions through the German legation in Oslo.[198]

When he replaced the telephone in its cradle, Quisling remained uncertain, having received no assurance of German support. His lack of success
simply provided good indication of the indecision which existed in Berlin
by the 11th concerning Quisling's value. Originally, when the invasion
seemed to be progressing without major difficulties, Hitler had been prepared to back a Quisling government. But by the 11th a number of disqui-
eting reports had reached Berlin, indicating that the NS leader was a liability. Through Bräuer, the Foreign Ministry emphasized the great distaste
for Quisling within the population, and Hitler now was receptive to the
Ministry's point of view. Rosenberg weakly interjected the argument that
Quisling had shown his value in providing military information and by his
warnings of the Nygaardsvold government's alleged collusion with
England.[199] The head of the Office of Foreign Affairs was in no position,
however, to exert any influence on Germany's policy toward Norway at
this time. He had to act quite circumspectly, having recently received a
sharp reprimand from Hitler for his amateurish involvement in foreign
affairs.[200]

Quisling's standing in Berlin was further weakened by critical reports
from the *Wehrmacht*. The military noticed with alarm the effect of Quisling's proclamation on April 9. Rather than weakening the will to resist, it
caused exactly the opposite to occur. Lieutenant Colonel Hartwig
Pohlmann, who had presented Bräuer with his instructions on April 9,
noted the next day that Quisling's action had created "bad blood", causing
many young men to stream through Oslo in order to join Norwegian
units. German officers in Trondheim were even stronger in their condemnation. This was particularly important at this time because the *Wehrmacht*
forces in Trondheim were isolated, appearing to be particularly vulnerable
to a British attack. Berlin therefore monitored the situation with considerable anxiety. In a report on the 11th, which Hitler read, the *Wehrmacht*
declared that the city's population, which previously had been passive, had
become aroused in favor of resistance because of Quisling.[201] In a telephone conversation with the German legation in Stockholm, officials in
Trondheim used even franker language. Everyone in the city, they said, repudiated the Quisling government, preferring instead a completely Ger-

man administration. The German consul in Trondheim went so far as to refer to Quisling's ministry as a "gangster government", and to Quisling himself as a "criminal".[202] This critical, even hostile attitude, did not remain restricted just to the military and diplomatic officials. In Oslo, long-time German residents similarly voiced their objections to Quisling.[203] Even Scheidt, not noted for his critical opinion of the NS leader, now had to admit that Quisling lacked support: "The atmosphere here is against Quisling. He is not popular at the moment. He enjoys no success. One doubts if he has any response among the people."[204]

The *Wehrmacht*'s opposition stemmed not only from the increased resistance which the military encountered, but also from its contention that Quisling was directly responsible for the two major military setbacks which the Germans encountered when carrying out the invasion. In addition to the failure of the squadron headed by the *Blücher* to capture Oslo, the second major defeat occurred at Narvik. The town was captured from its Norwegian defenders without difficulty, but the British navy launched two attacks on April 10 and 13 which resulted in the loss of all ten German destroyers which had spearheaded Narvik's capture. As a result, the troops in the town were cut off from outside aid and subjected to Norwegian and Allied attacks. The *Wehrmacht* made Quisling the scapegoat for these setbacks. They accused him of having given incorrect information concerning the strength of Norwegian defenses at Oscarsborg. As for Narvik, he supposedly had assured the Germans that they could expect to make use of an artillery battery guarding the approaches to the town. The battery proved to be non-existent, and the Germans therefore had no means of preventing superior British naval forces from gaining entry and sinking the destroyers.[205]

Quisling's standing with the military was worsened even more because of personal antagonisms which developed between him and several leading officers in Norway. General Erwin Engelbrecht, in command of the forces that captured Oslo, discovered to his surprise that he was living under the same roof at Hotel Continental as the man who claimed to be prime minister. Engelbrecht's instructions contained no mention that Quisling should take over as head of government. After a heated argument between the two at about midnight, April 9–10, Engelbrecht sought permission from the German legation to *arrest* Quisling.[206] Because of Hitler's intervention on the latter's behalf earlier in the evening, the General was denied the pleasure of incarcerating the NS *Fører*. The incident did provide a striking illustration of the attitude which many professional army officers displayed toward Quisling. Falkenhorst, Engelbrecht's immediate superior, shared his subordinate's dislike, if not so outspokenly.[207] Only within the navy, thanks to Raeder's influence, did Quisling enjoy support during the occupation.

The combined effect of the negative reports coming from Norway, plus the uncertainty of the military situation, caused Hitler to have doubts about Quisling. Never one to admit mistakes, *der Führer* now changed his mind. His earlier enthusiasm had changed to negative, critical questioning by the 11th.[208]

Hagelin, on his journey of intercession, did his best on Quisling's behalf. He met first with Rosenberg on the morning of the 13th, and later in the day with Hitler and Ribbentrop.[209] Even Rosenberg, reflecting the spirit of skepticism in Berlin, was restrained in his discussion with Hagelin. But the latter, as before, had no scruples against lying if need be in order to try to enhance Quisling's position. Hagelin insisted in his talk with Rosenberg that the German legation had been responsible for the failure to reach an agreement with the King. He similarly argued it was untrue that Quisling lacked backing. On the contrary, the emissary maintained that Quisling enjoyed the confidence of businessmen and shipowners, who supposedly were happy to be rid of the "Marxist government".[210] In his later conversation with Hitler, Hagelin told the *Führer* with a straight face that Quisling enjoyed the support of fifteen per cent of the population, and that it was a lie that Major Hvoslef had refused to serve in Quisling's government.[211]

Hitler, however, remained unconvinced. At this time, on April 13, he was extremely irresolute as to how to settle the political dilemma in Norway. If possible, he would have preferred a "Danish solution", but he himself had made this impossible, thanks to his ultimatum that King Haakon had to recognize Quisling as prime minister. The fact that the *Wehrmacht's* position at Narvik was becoming critical did nothing to calm the *Führer's* agitation. In the end he approved the decision to have Undersecretary Theodor Habicht from the Foreign Ministry accompany Hagelin back to Oslo in order to report on the situation. The choice to carry out this delicate mission was not a good omen for Quisling's patrons. Habicht was an outspoken personal enemy of Rosenberg, having earlier had a strong disagreement with the *Reichsleiter* over German policy toward Afghanistan.[212]

Habicht and Hagelin arrived in Oslo on the 14th. The latter unhappily reported to Quisling that Hitler's recognition of the "national government" would not be forthcoming.[213] This weakened Quisling more than ever before. While Hagelin had been on his mission to Berlin, certain developments had occurred in Norway which set in motion a strong movement leading to Quisling's removal as "head of government".

Already soon after Quisling had announced the formation of his government, a number of influential persons were at work, determined to eliminate him from his self-proclaimed position. When Bräuer returned from his unsuccessful effort to persuade the King to accept Quisling, the German Minister was besieged by people with different backgrounds and interests, but who were all united in insisting that Quisling had to be removed. The individual who originally initiated the means by which Quisling would be ousted was Johannes Rivertz Jr., a prominent Oslo attorney with good connections. His father, Johannes Rivertz Sr., served on the Supreme Court. The Court, as the one major governmental institution which remained in the capital, became the legitimizing agent through which a successor to Quisling's government could be appointed.[214]

Rivertz Jr., conceived of the idea of establishing some type of administration in the occupied parts of Norway in order to avoid economic chaos. He broached this idea to Wolfgang Geldmacher, a German domiciled in Norway, and learned from him that Berlin had not yet recognized Quisling. Geldmacher responded enthusiastically, as did another German, Dr. Ulrich Noack, Quisling's former acquaintance from the previous winter, who now was a bitter enemy, thanks to the snub he had received. Rivertz Jr., raised the issue with his father on the morning of April 12, who in turn brought it before his colleagues on the Supreme Court when they assembled early in the afternoon. As a result of its deliberations, the Court urged young Rivertz to contact the German legation in order to persuade it to postpone any recognition of Quisling. Rivertz Jr., was instructed to tell Bräuer that "the Supreme Court had discussed the matter and will possibly be able to find a solution".[215]

Accompanied by Geldmacher and Noack, Rivertz Jr., thereupon drove to the German legation, where they met with the Minister. Bräuer expressed interest in the Supreme Court's initiative, promising that no decision would be made for at least the next twenty-four hours, thereby eliminating any possibility for Quisling to gain German recognition during this period.[216]

The Minister's preference at this time was to try to reach an accommodation that approximated the goal that had been spelled out in his original instructions. This involved some type of arrangement with the King. By April 12 Bräuer was seriously pursuing the possibility of finding a method of getting rid of Quisling. Shortly after Rivertz Jr. and the two Germans had left, Bräuer held a conversation with two leading Norwegian industrialists. He declared that he wished to re-establish contact with the King, even if indirectly, through prominent Norwegians. He also indicated German willingness to abandon Quisling after a short interval.[217]

For Bräuer, there was little reason to equivocate over the benefits of removing Quisling. Having always had a negative opinion of him, the Minister had this view amply reinforced by persons whom he came in contact with on April 11 and 12. Not only important industrialists, legal representatives, and members of the German community in Oslo, but other influential people strongly declared their opposition to the NS leader. The highest political and administrative officials in both the city and region of Oslo, along with Police Chief Welhaven, let Bräuer know that they were not willing to work with Quisling.[218] The Bishop of Oslo, Eivind Berg-grav, also met with Bräuer on the 12th and told him that Quisling had to be replaced. According to the Bishop, Bräuer categorically informed him that the Germans had not installed Quisling, nor had they recognized his government.[219] Such assurance could only be taken as a sign of encouragement for those who were anxiously attempting to circumvent the possibility that the Quisling government might become permanent.

In addition to establishment figures who worked against Quisling, a number of persons who were ideologically sympathetic toward Germany also did their best at this time to sabotage Quisling's position. Among these were Victor Mogens of the Fatherland League and J. B. Hjort. Both enjoyed the confidence of the German legation, and their influence was not negligible.[220]

In the end, however, the movement to eliminate Quisling coalesced around one person, Paal Berg, Chief Justice of the Supreme Court. Berg at first had been predisposed to try to discuss the situation with the King. With Bräuer's permission, arrangements were made for him to travel through the German lines in an attempt to reach the King.[221] Bräuer assured Berg on the morning of April 13, when the latter was preparing to leave, that the Quisling government no longer stood in the way of a new solution. The Minister did add that Quisling's removal would have to take place in a decorous manner, since the Germans had maintained contact with him.[222] Berg's trip never materialized, however. The German military command refused to allow the Chief Justice to proceed, an indication that the fighting was becoming more intense. Nor was it possible for Berg to talk with the King by telephone, which he sought to do via the Norwegian legation in Stockholm.[223]

With this attempt having failed, Berg and his Supreme Court colleagues, in consultation with leading business, administrative, and religious representatives, were left to their own resources. By the morning of the 14th their consensus was to have the Court, with Bräuer's permission, eliminate Quisling's government by approving the creation of an administrative body in those areas of the country that were under German occupation. With this in mind, Berg scheduled a meeting of the Supreme Court for 10:00 a.m. Prior to the meeting, he sent two prominent industrialists as emissaries to Bräuer. They carried the message that the Court might "be willing to appoint an Administrative Council as a replacement of Quisling's administration". Bräuer gave his sanction, and the emissaries hurried back to Berg with this information. The preliminaries for the removal of Quisling had thereupon been completed.[224]

As these developments were unfolding, Quisling knew that a movement was afoot to secure his ouster. Desperately he sought to find some means of preventing this from occurring. With this in mind, he phoned the managing director of the powerful Industrial Federation, Lorentz Vogt, who played an important part in the discussions intended to get rid of Quisling. When Quisling now insisted on another meeting with Vogt, the latter consulted with Berg. The Chief Justice recommended that Vogt attend the meeting, but that he should avoid making any commitment.[225]

Vogt met with Quisling at Hotel Continental. In attendance were also the ever-present Scheidt, plus Quisling's "aide", Harald Franklin Knudsen. From the way he began the discussion, Quisling plainly hoped to use tactical maneuvers to head off the formation of a successor to his government. He proposed that a type of governmental council be established, consisting of his original government and a number of other persons appointed by it, plus an additional number of prominent individuals, including Chief Justice Berg, Bishop Berggrav, and the rector of the University. This "official group", totaling twenty-one persons, would make up the government. Furthermore, an additional nineteen persons would be included in the governmental process (exactly how is unclear), representing business, industry, and labor.[226] From this description, not only did Quisling seek to pre-empt the move spearheaded by Berg to replace him, but his proposed alternative included many of the elements of his corporate system, the National Assembly, which had become a fixed idea with him.

Such a grandiose scheme, concocted in a time of stress and change, had no possibility of being realized. Asked to have the Industrial Federation approve the idea, Vogt tried to be evasive by saying that he would have to present it to the Federation's president and board of directors. Faced with this rebuff, Quisling gave vent to his frustration. He became threatening, indicating the desperateness of his situation. He informed Vogt that he knew a sabotage effort was being made against his "national government", and warned that such activity was dangerous. Vogt responded that he did not engage in sabotage, but was only concerned with maintaining industrial production. The discussion rapidly deteriorated into a quarrel. Quisling finally demanded a declaration of loyalty, declaring that if it was not forthcoming, Vogt would be removed from his position. "This is my ultimatum," said Quisling, upon leaving the room. According to Vogt, who was quite upset, he told Scheidt, who remained behind, that he would under no circumstances cooperate "with an insane person such as Mr. Quisling". Although the president of the Industrial Federation held a conference with Quisling later in the afternoon in order to calm him down, the attempt to pressure the Federation enjoyed no success.[227]

The Quisling government's tenuous existence was weakened even further on Sunday, April 14, by an act of sabotage which occurred the previous night. Young saboteurs attempted to blow up a strategic bridge located directly on Oslo's southern border, seeking thereby to cut off an important transportation artery to the capital. Highly disturbed by the incident, fearing it could be the beginning of partisan warfare, General Falkenhorst reacted by planning to take drastic steps to prevent such actions from being repeated. He intended to execute several leading Norwegians in retaliation, including Chief Justice Berg, Bishop Berggrav, and a number of shipping magnates. Fortunately for the intended victims, Minister Bräuer calmed the agitated general by persuading him that more peaceful means could obtain the same objective. Bräuer had little difficulty in convincing Falkenhorst that the antagonism toward Quisling was the main reason for disorder in the country.[228] The high command in Norway was already firmly convinced that militarily it would be advantageous if Quisling were removed.[229] With both the military and the diplomatic authorities in Norway in agreement, and with the Supreme Court having emerged as the instrument by which Quisling's ouster might be carried out, the prospect for such a move was therefore already extremely favorable by the morning of April 14.[230]

Having obtained Bräuer's endorsement, Chief Justice Berg met with the assembled justices at 10:30 a.m. While all were in agreement that Quisling should be forced out, at first some favored the appointment of an administrative body by local authorities, rather than by the Court. While these alternatives were being discussed, Berg left for a conference at Minister Bräuer's residence. This meeting, which began at about 1:00 p.m., proved to be quite significant. For the first time, Bräuer and Berg negotiated face to face, having previously used go-betweens. In addition, Bräuer had with him someone whose support was of utmost importance, Undersecretary Habicht, who had arrived by plane from Berlin that morning.[231]

Berg indicated in the discussion that while the country was in a crisis situation not anticipated by the Constitution, he personally was willing to propose to the Supreme Court that it appoint an administrative body, responsible for providing civil administration in those districts that were under German occupation. The diplomats countered by insisting at first that a real government be set up in the occupied areas, which they referred to as a "governmental commission" (*Regierungsausschuss*). Berg, however, opposed this, favoring instead that the body be called simply something such as "administrative council". In the end, the Germans gave way, but they stated that the term *Regierungsausschuss* would be used in the German translation of the proclamation establishing the body. Berg responded that the Norwegian name had to be official, but that he had no objection to the term which the Germans wished to use in their translation. The two diplomats also at first wanted to include Quisling as a member of the planned Administrative Council, but Berg rejected the suggestion as impossible, "and they gave in". However, they did insist that Quisling be provided with an honorable withdrawal.[232]

The fact that Bräuer and Habicht were willing to go as far as they did in compromising their original goal of seeking to establish a true government indicated the extent to which German officials on the scene wished to get rid of Quisling. For Bräuer, the opportunity of having an Administrative Council established by the Supreme Court meant that it would be possible to cooperate with persons who, in contrast to Quisling's government, enjoyed approval within the population. The Minister hoped that this would pave the way for an eventual settlement with the King and the government once Quisling's ouster had been carried out.[233] But Bräuer and Habicht, in giving in to Berg's insistence that the new organ simply be referred to as an administrative body rather than a governmental commission, made a decision that would later have dire consequences for them both.

Once the meeting was concluded, two steps had to be taken. The Norwegians had to carry out consultations and arrangements in preparation for the appointment of the new civilian administration. The Germans had to employ the necessary pressure to get Quisling to resign.

Just as he was leaving the conference, Berg met Bishop Berggrav, who had been called to the Minister's residence. Berggrav had been requested to meet with the Minister for another reason. Bräuer wished to have him hold a radio address, using his authority to appeal for calm within the disturbed population. With Bräuer's permission, Berggrav therefore had the opportunity to indicate over the radio that there might soon be established "a legal arrangement" for Norwegian administration in areas under German occupation, "in understanding with the German Minister".[234] For the first time the general public thereby received a hint that Quisling's government might soon be stepping down.

Berg in the meantime had returned to the Supreme Court, where he made his viewpoint clear. He urged the Court to take responsibility for appointing an Administrative Council, consisting of seven members. A number of justices felt that the King's approval was needed, but Berg insisted that the Germans would not accept such a reservation, and he had his way. However, in its proclamation the Supreme Court declared its confidence that the King would approve the Court's action in view of the extraordinary situation the country was in.[235]

On the German side, a considerable number of meetings were required before the issue was settled, although action took place rapidly on April 14 and 15. Bräuer not only had to deal with Quisling, but he also had to secure approval from his superiors in Berlin. Furthermore, with Habicht present as a special emissary from Ribbentrop, Bräuer had to share responsibility.

Fortunately for him, it did not take long for Habicht to become convinced that the Minister's course of action was correct. Following his arrival by plane on the morning of the 14th, the Under Secretary immediately began to orient himself. After a preliminary meeting with Bräuer, he next had a conference with the highest army commanders, Generals Falkenhorst and Engelbrecht. The two made no attempt to disguise their objections to Quisling. They insisted that he was a hindrance for the military.[236]

When sent to Norway, Habicht had no preconceived ideas concerning Quisling. But he needed no more time than his session with the generals before becoming convinced that their opinion was valid. To Bräuer's satisfaction, Habicht immediately accepted the option of appointing a new civilian administration. By the time he and Bräuer met with Berg in the afternoon, the Under Secretary had fully committed himself to this alternative.[237] Bräuer could thereupon report to the Foreign Ministry late in the afternoon that Berg was "ready to form a governmental commission" which would "take charge of administration until normal conditions are restored". As for Quisling, the Minister declared that the NS leader would be allowed to withdraw in an honorable fashion, and that he would be given responsibility for carrying out duties in connection with the cessation of hostilities.[238]

At about 5:30 p.m. Bräuer and Habicht drove to Hotel Continental, where they attempted to persuade Quisling to resign voluntarily. Hagelin and Scheidt were also present. Although the minutes of the meeting may not be trustworthy because their tone seems to suggest that they were drawn up by someone sympathetic to Quisling, perhaps Quisling himself, there is no doubt but that Bräuer and Habicht pressured him to step down, while Quisling, seconded by Hagelin, argued in favor of maintaining his position.[239] The meeting apparently ended without a conclusion, but in reality the issue had been decided.[240] Quisling and his backers simply refused to accept the fact that, without official German approval, their cause had no hope.

Soon afterwards Paal Berg informed Bräuer that the Supreme Court had agreed to issue a proclamation establishing the new civilian administration.[241] Still, before Bräuer and Habicht could act, they had to have final approval from Berlin. Up to this time, despite the Minister's strong requests, he had not received permission from the Foreign Ministry to proceed.[242] However, after Berg had confirmed the Supreme Court's willingness to cooperate, Bräuer and Habicht were able to gain a commitment from Ribbentrop. The Reich Foreign Minister was now willing to accept the replacement of the "Quisling government" with a "governmental commission". What mattered most in Berlin at this time was the need to arrive at a political solution in Norway as soon as possible because of the uncertain military situation. This was shown by Ribbentrop's expressed desire to have the King return to Oslo and recognize the "governmental commission".[243] His use of this term also indicated that Bräuer and Habicht had failed to make it clear to the Foreign Minister that the coming Administrative Council would not be a true government.[244]

Even at this time, however, reflecting the personal commitment that Hitler still felt toward Quisling, Ribbentrop emphasized that "*der Führer* wished by all means that we hold Quisling in reserve" so that it was possible "to go back to him in case the coming government does not act according to our wishes". Habicht and Bräuer assured their chief that Quisling would be provided a worthy retreat. Habicht, however, bluntly stated his negative assessment of Quisling to Ribbentrop, describing the NS leader as being "uncertain and weak", and having "no support".[245]

Having at last to their satisfaction received clear directives from Berlin, Bräuer and Habicht late in the evening arranged yet another meeting with Quisling. This time the discussion was held at Bräuer's residence, not at Hotel Continental. The Minister no longer conducted negotiations, but instead informed Quisling and Hagelin what the German position was. They were told that Hitler had made a definitive decision concerning the imminent change in Norwegian political leadership. Quisling, however, still refused to give in. Seeking more time, he insisted that he would have to think about the matter overnight.[246] Ribbentrop, waiting to receive confirmation of Quisling's acceptance, was advised after the meeting by Bräuer that the issue had not been fully settled. Quisling, said Bräuer, had been told about the proposed solution. Bräuer indicated that further details would be worked out in the morning, at which time the Foreign Minister would receive additional information.[247]

The following day proved to be truly a "blue Monday" for Quisling. Frantically, although all hope was gone, he endeavored to prevent the Administrative Council from supplanting his "national government". At about 8:30 a.m. he phoned Paal Berg, asking the Chief Justice to meet with him in order to discuss the possibility of arranging a "coordinated effort". Berg had actually intended to have a talk with Quisling that day in order to persuade him to step down voluntarily. However, Bräuer, whom Berg consulted, informed the Chief Justice that he should not have any discussion with Quisling before the Minister had had an opportunity of meeting with the NS leader.[248]

While Quisling was seeking an alternative, any alternative, that would allow him to remain in a position of apparent authority, Bräuer had total command of events on April 15. Having stymied Quisling's effort to establish contact with Berg, the Minister called Quisling to a meeting at the German legation at about 10:00 a.m. The head of the "national government" arrived alone, with neither Hagelin nor Scheidt apparently being allowed to attend. Quisling was received by Bräuer and Habicht. He began by declaring his reservations about the proposed political arrangement, insisting that he wanted to present his objections to Hitler. Bräuer, however, replied that *der Führer* had already made his decision, and if Quisling continued to refuse to cooperate, he would simply be bypassed. From this point onwards, he had no hope of being able to exercise any influence on the German authorities. He was told to prepare a declaration, to be used in connection with his demission.[249]

While Quisling was being submitted to this humiliation, Paal Berg arrived. He and Bräuer conferred briefly afterwards about the make-up of the Administrative Council. The Minister declared that Quisling would be stepping down, but that this should occur in a manner satisfactory to the NS leader, who should also be given a new position as compensation.[250] Bräuer then left it to Berg and Quisling to work out by themselves how the transfer of authority should occur. Quisling, however, refused to consider the question at hand, preferring instead to talk politics. He insisted that the Supreme Court had assumed a grave responsibility in its decision to appoint an Administrative Council. Attempting to show that he remained a force to be reckoned with, he told Berg that "I have not yet made my decision", indicating he might still continue as "head of government".[251]

The value of his empty threat was soon exposed when Berg and Quisling again talked with Bräuer. The Minister handled Quisling with authority, cutting off any discussion of politics. In a final desperate move, the latter insisted he enjoyed the support of the business community and labor, a contention that Berg immediately contradicted. Soon afterwards a mortified Quisling left the legation.[252]

His claim that he had business and labor support rested on the most transparent illusion – his earlier discussions with leaders of the economic organizations. But as part of his last-ditch effort to remain in office, on the previous day he had sent out an invitation to the major business organizations and the Federation of Trade Unions to have their delegates meet with him at 12:00 noon in the *Storting* building. The business organizations consulted with Ingolf E. Christensen, the regional governor (*fylkesmann*) of Oslo who was designated as head of the Administrative Council. He advised them not to attend. The trade unions similarly refused to come unless they received a written order from Police Chief Welhaven, whom they considered to be the highest authority in German occupied territory.[253] Such an order was hardly forthcoming.

Bräuer, however, made certain that he knew exactly what the position of such powerful economic interests was. At about noon he called together a number of prominent leaders from business, industry, and labor. Without exception, all pledged that they would back the Administrative Council.[254] Not unexpectedly, there was no expression of support for Quisling.

The final matter that Bräuer needed to resolve on the 15th was the manner in which Quisling would step down and the position he would occupy once the Administrative Council had been set up. Since Quisling had earlier refused to discuss this matter with Berg, he no longer had any say in determining his own future status. Berg and Christensen negotiated the issue with Bräuer at the German legation. The Minister at first insisted that Quisling should be allowed to take part in the meetings of the Administrative Council, but Berg and Christensen successfully rejected this possibility. In the end an agreement was reached whereby Quisling would formally hold the title of Commissioner for Demobilization (*Beauftragter für Demobilisierung*) under the Administrative Council. To this Christensen, as leader of the projected Council, had no objection, since the title was an empty one. The German military in reality would be responsible for any demobilization of Norwegian troops.[255]

The formalities involving Quisling's demission proved to be more difficult to reach agreement on. In particular, the wording of speeches had to be worked out. Bräuer gave Berg an oral summation of what he intended to have Quisling say, to which the Chief Justice had no particular objections. But the two disagreed about what Berg should say on behalf of Quisling. Bräuer initially desired that Berg, speaking for the Supreme Court, should absolve Quisling of any unlawful behavior. When Berg refused, the Minister next tried to persuade the Chief Justice to acquit Quisling on his own. Again Berg refused. Negotiations over this difficult issue became protracted. Berg worked until mid-afternoon, drawing up several drafts before he finally succeeded in writing a statement that was acceptable to the Germans.[256]

As the recipient of this unknown attention, Quisling was not yet ready to accept a graceful exit. On the contrary, having left the legation in a distraught mood, he did not abandon his doomed effort to prevent the Administrative Council from coming into existence. In a highly agitated state, he phoned Bishop Berggrav shortly before 11:00 a.m. The Bishop was one of the least likely persons Quisling could hope to persuade to act on his behalf. Nevertheless, he ordered Berggrav to go to the German legation and put an end to "this craziness" concerning the creation of an Administrative Council. Obviously unaware of the irony of what he was saying, Quisling warned the Bishop that he and others who were behind the formation of the Administrative Council were guilty of treason. Asked to explain exactly what he meant by this statement, Quisling responded: "Yes, you are delivering the country's administration to the Germans". Somehow, this line of reasoning made no impression despite a repeat call from Quisling five minutes later.[257]

In the same disturbed emotional state, Quisling shortly thereafter phoned yet another key official involved in setting up the Administrative Council, Ingolf Christensen. Quisling urged the latter to meet with him at noon in the *Storting*. When Christensen demurred, the NS leader became threatening. He warned that force would be used to prevent the Administrative Council from coming into being. The designated members of the Council were scheduled to meet at Christensen's office at noon for preliminary discussions. Quisling menacingly told Christensen that he would put a stop to the meeting, and that he would prevent Paal Berg from attending.[258]

Alarmed by this threat, Christensen contacted the police, informing them that Quisling was in such a frame of mind that he was capable of doing anything.[259] Police Chief Welhaven responded by mobilizing his men, including his German bodyguards, to take up strategic positions protecting Christensen's office.[260] Welhaven declared after the war that he had been informed that Quisling actually sent out spies to reconnoiter the situation at the regional administrative building, but that he had found it hopeless.[261]

This proved to be Quisling's final attempt to prevent his ouster. His highly distraught attitude and his willingness to go to extremes indicated that Christensen and Welhaven were not acting irrationally in taking strong precautions. Had Quisling had the opportunity to employ force at this time, it is not at all unlikely that he would have made use of it because of his obsession with maintaining himself as the nominal head of government.

At 5:00 p.m. the formal ceremony took place which marked the end of his "national government." Held in the Norwegian Academy of Science and Letters, the gathering included both Germans and Norwegians – administrators, business representatives, diplomats, military officers, and the press. Quisling did not attend. The glum faces of the newly appointed members of the Administrative Council, as shown in press photographs, revealed clearly that they did not relish having to cooperate with the Germans, but that they did so out of a feeling of responsiblity. Bräuer gave a brief speech, after which Berg and Christensen read proclamations by which the Administrative Council came into being. Berg's statement, made on behalf of the Supreme Court, said specifically that the Council was temporary, that it would be in charge of civil administration only in those parts of the country occupied by the Germans, and that the Supreme Court, in appointing the Council, did so under the assumption that the King would approve this "emergency action".[262]

After the brief half hour ceremony, Berg and Christensen drove to the radio station in order to make public announcements that Quisling's "national government" had been replaced by the Administrative Council. As prearranged, Quisling was also present, ready to give his version of why the change was taking place. He began by again justifying his takeover, maintaining that he had assumed governmental authority "to save the country and the people from chaos". However, he declared that the Nygaardsvold government's mobilization order and its defiant attitude toward the Germans were creating danger of continued bloodshed, something which he and his colleagues were not prepared to assume responsibility for. On the other hand, he alleged, the Administrative Council was ready to do so, and he thereby transferred his authority to the Council. He called for a return to peaceful conditions as soon as possible in order to rebuild the country, and he closed with a resounding "Long live Norway".[263]

For Berg, Quisling's speech came as a total surprise. It did not correspond at all with the oral summation that the Chief Justice had earlier received from Bräuer.[264] Berg found himself in the unfortunate position of having to give thanks to a man who had carried out a treasonable coup against the legal government, and who openly continued to voice opposition to the government's policy. By thanking Quisling, Berg therefore risked compromising the Administrative Council not only with the general public, but more specifically with the legitimate authorities headed by the King. Berg, however, had no choice. Were he to back down at this critical moment, he would jeopardize the results of the last hectic days of negotiations which had resulted in Quisling's removal. In an almost unrecognizable voice, Berg therefore made a short statement of thanks over the radio.[265] He declared that Quisling, at a time when there was no executive power in Oslo, had placed himself at the country's disposal in order to avoid bloodshed and to maintain calm in the occupied districts. Quisling, said Berg, had once again "shown his feeling of responsibility and his patriotism" by stepping down. The Chief Justice therefore thanked "Mr. Quisling" for his previous declaration, which had made possible the settlement arranged by the Supreme Court.[266]

Considering the true background for Quisling's ouster, the difficulty that Berg had in expressing these sentiments is understandable. Quisling's "national government" had thus been eliminated. It had never in any sense been a true government. It enjoyed no authority, and it accomplished nothing except to cause confusion. Quisling's coup occurred in a political vacuum, and had it not been for Hitler's hasty and imprudent endorsement, the move would have been squashed already on April 9 by German diplomatic and military officials. However, the sensational and unexpected manner in which Quisling announced his government, appearing to outside observers to be directly linked with the brilliantly executed German invasion, made the name Quisling thereafter synonymous with someone who worked hand in hand with the enemy in the betrayal of his country.

CHAPTER XI

The Fører *versus the* Reichskommissar
April 1940 – September 1940

I was summoned to *Reichskommissar* Terboven on June 25. He recommended I should resign from the leadership of the movement because I supposedly stood in the way of an alleged agreement with the Norwegians. . . . *Reichskommissar* Terboven informed me that he intended to establish a new government in Norway. The *Reichskommissar* would choose those persons whom he deemed acceptable to represent National Union in the government. . . . if I were to oppose this, he intended within two months to create a new movement. If this occurred, National Union would of course be denied any support. . . . My party and its supporters would thereby be reduced to a sect and treated accordingly. If I accepted his offer and temporarily gave up the party leadership to a substitute, he would maintain support of the NS movement, but I was to accept an invitation from the German Reich government to conduct studies in Germany about the constitutional basis for cooperation with Scandinavia.

Vidkun Quisling to Adolf Hitler, July 20, 1940

Curt Bräuer bore primary responsibility for Quisling's ouster. In pushing for the creation of the Administrative Council, the Minister believed that Quisling's removal had eliminated the main obstacle to reaching a peaceful accommodation with the Norwegians. As a first step, he hoped for the King's recognition of the Administrative Council, to be followed by a permanent agreement.[1]

Bräuer did not remain in Norway long enough to learn the result of his policy. Already on April 16, the day following the Council's creation, he received an order from Foreign Minister Ribbentrop to report to Berlin.[2] Although he did not know it, his diplomatic career was over. Bräuer never returned to Norway.

In Berlin, Hitler was in a rage, brought on by the military situation in Norway, which at the moment did not appear promising. Bräuer and Habicht, who had returned earlier, became the objects against whom Hitler vented his spleen. Hitler was furious when he learned that Bräuer had helped to create a strictly administrative body instead of establishing a regular government with which a settlement could be made. Even worse from the *Führer*'s perspective, the Council looked to the King for its legitimacy. Hitler ranted against Haakon VII, who dared to go against his will. *Der Führer*'s sympathy for Quisling also came into play, with Bräuer being condemned because he had removed the NS leader entirely. The Minister's rational arguments, justifying his course of action, had no effect. He was dismissed from the diplomatic corps and dispatched to active duty in the army. Habicht suffered a similar fate.[3]

Hitler's explosive outburst was due to German recognition by the 17th of April that Norway would not be captured as easily as anticipated. Not only had the King and the government escaped, but the Allies were landing troops to reinforce the Norwegians within a week after the invasion. In the southern part of the country the situation was still very uncertain, with the British in the process of linking up with Norwegian units. In the north at Narvik, where Raeder's loss of ten vessels had reduced by one half the number of destroyers in the German navy, General Dietl's isolated position was becoming increasingly more difficult.

This situation obviously also had a positive effect on the Norwegian government's attitude. The arrival of British troops seemed to open up the prospect of a successful campaign against the Germans, with most of the country still unoccupied. *Storting* president Hambro phoned Bishop Berggrav from Stockholm with the encouraging news that the Bishop could expect "great things" to happen after five days.[4] In Oslo the atmosphere became optimistic when the news arrived that British forces had joined with the Norwegian units fighting to halt the German advance north of the capital. Enthusiastic patriots already looked forward to the entry of victorious Norwegian and British forces into Oslo in time to celebrate the national holiday on May 17.[5]

In its response to the creation of the Administrative Council, the Nygaardsvold government's position clearly was colored by this deceptively optimistic outlook. It did not grant the recognition which such backers of the Council as Berg, Christensen, and Berggrav had hoped for. Although the cabinet expressed its pleasure at the failure of Quisling's "so-called government", it specifically emphasized that the Administrative Council was an emergency body which in no way could be considered as a substitute for the legal government. It stressed that the Council did not represent the people's will, nor did it have any basis in Norwegian law, being dependent on the good will of "the power which has forced its way into the country by use of brutal violence". Grudgingly, the cabinet admitted that the Council might be of value in protecting Norwegian rights in enemy-controlled areas. But it insisted that the Council would cease to exert any influence as the legitimate government proceeded to regain its territory.[6]

The statement indicated the Nygaardsvold government's determination to re-establish its control by military means. Bräuer's policy of encouraging negotiation once Quisling had been ousted thereby ended in failure, thanks in large part to the momentary confidence inspired by the arrival of Allied forces.

When news of the Norwegian position reached Berlin, at the latest by the early morning of April 19, the German reaction showed that the final tenuous alternative in favor of a negotiated settlement had been eliminated as far as the Third Reich was concerned. Ribbentrop proceeded to summon the Norwegian minister, who had remained in Berlin as long as there existed a possibility of reaching an accommodation. The Minister was curtly informed that the personnel in the Norwegian legation would have to leave the country, which they did already on the same afternoon.[7]

By April 17–18 it was at last clear to the Germans that they would have to obtain control of Norway solely by military means. Until this became obvious, German policy had shifted constantly since the beginning of the invasion. In under a week no less than four political alternatives had been attempted without success: cooperation with the Nygaardsvold government, a coup regime under Quisling, the attempt to gain royal sanction for Quisling as prime minister, and the Administrative Council as a "government".[8] Now, with only a military solution possible, Hitler decided to impose his will directly by appointing a Nazi administrator as the highest civilian authority, with the title of *Reichskommissar* (Reich Commissary). On April 19, Josef Terboven, a leading party official in the Rhine province, was summoned to the Reich Chancellery and informed by Hitler that he was *der Führer*'s choice to become the chief German administrator in Norway.

The man who would exercise the strongest direct influence over the country until the end of the war had thereby secured his office. An interval took place, however, before Terboven could fully assume his new responsibilities. His appointment had been sudden and unexpected, brought about by the immediate needs of the existing situation. He needed time to familiarize himself with Norwegian conditions, and also to wrap up his duties in Essen. Therefore, General Falkenhorst, as the chief military commander in Norway, also assumed supreme civilian authority in the areas under German occupation from April 19 to April 24. But this step in large part was a formality, with the General exercising authority in name only until Terboven was ready to come to Norway on a full-time basis.[9]

While these significant developments were taking place within the chambers of the Reich Chancellery, no one in a leading position in Norway was informed of the changes that were being made. Members of the Administrative Council were told by the acting head of the German legation, its counselor, Hans Joachim von Neuhaus, that Minister Bräuer was only expected to be in Berlin for one or two days before returning.[10] Prominent German and Norwegian figures in the capital acted on this assumption.

As had been previously decided, Quisling now held the official position of being in charge of the demobilization of Norwegian troops who had surrendered. It remained to be seen to what extent he could turn this function to his advantage. Already at the first meeting of the Administrative Council, on the morning of April 16, the matter of Quisling's relationship with the Council became a central issue. The overriding question was whether he would be independent of the Council's authority, or subordinate to it. But its first confrontation with Quisling did not involve his role of being in charge of demobilization. Had this been the case, he would have held strong cards, since the Germans had formally guaranteed him this post at the time the Council came into existence. Instead, the controversy that developed on April 16 concerned the fact that during the time he headed the "national government", a number of his NS followers had obtained Norwegian army uniforms from depots in Oslo. They marched about the capital, indicating their allegiance to Quisling by attaching an armband with the NS symbol to their uniforms.[11]

Upon taking over, the Council immediately challenged this practice, citing the 1937 law which specifically forbade political parties from making use of uniforms. Christensen, as head of the Council, telephoned Quisling about this matter. The NS *Fører* at first refused to recognize that he was under the Council's jurisdiction. However, even by telephone, when faced with an authoritative figure such as Christensen, he eventually gave in, promising that the uniforms would be returned to their depots during the day. He further promised that he would cooperate with Christensen, although he made the reservation that he would obtain the German legation's view concerning the degree to which he was obliged to obey the Council's orders.[12]

Later in the day, however, he attempted to renegue his promise to have the uniforms returned. Scheidt had advised the vacillating Quisling to take a firmer stand. The NS leader thereupon phoned Christensen, letting him know that he had secured Scheidt's permission for continued use of the disputed uniforms. Scheidt made this authorization in his capacity as "Liaison Leader" (*Verbindungsführer*) with NS. Christensen, however, remained firm, informing Quisling that the Council would not accept the practice of NS members wearing uniforms, a view that he repeated to Scheidt. Christensen told Scheidt that the Council would not guarantee order in the occupied areas if the practice continued. Scheidt tried to evade the issue by declaring that he would discuss it with the German legation.[13]

The Council, however, had no intention of being sidetracked. It sent a three-man delegation headed by Christensen to meet with Neuhaus. In addition to discussing the uniform controversy, they also wished to obtain clarification as to Quisling's degree of subordination to the Council. Neuhaus understandably expressed himself cautiously, since he was only acting head of the legation, but he did indicate his approval of the Council's viewpoint. In doing so, he was merely adhering to Bräuer's policy of backing the Council.

Christensen could therefore report to his colleagues on the next day that the German legation had indicated that Quisling was under the Administrative Council's jurisdiction, and that he was obliged to receive orders concerning his duties from it. Furthermore, Quisling's sphere of operation in carrying out demobilization had been narrowly circumscribed. He had to restrict his actions entirely to specific tasks involving military demobilization, not being allowed to deal with broader questions which had economic implications.

The delegation that had met with Neuhaus and other members of the legation's staff similarly interpreted the diplomatic representative as having approved of the Council's view opposing NS members wearing army uniforms. Finally, a minor matter of a different nature was also settled, which added another insult to Quisling's reduced status. Neuhaus agreed that the Council could remove three NS members whom Quisling had appointed to key positions with the Norwegian News Agency when he had headed the "national government".[14]

The uniform issue had not been definitely settled, however. Captain Schreiber intervened on NS' behalf within the legation. But he was nicely circumvented when the matter was referred to the military high command for a final decision. Falkenhorst bore Quisling nothing but ill will. Not unexpectedly, the high command declared that according to international law the Administrative Council, having authority in occupied Norway, had the right to settle the matter. The Council, basing its decision on the law of May 13, 1937, thereupon outlawed the wearing of uniforms on April 18.[15]

His defeat on the uniform question came as a severe blow to Quisling. He always placed great importance on the outward symbols of authority. Furthermore, the question of NS members wearing army uniforms tied in directly with his position of being in charge of demobilization. If NS members dressed in uniforms had been given the opportunity to take part in the demobilization process, this would have provided them with an aura of state authority that Quisling felt would have increased his stature and freedom of action.

This possibility had been deftly circumscribed by the Council. As a result, his position of being in charge of demobilization was reduced to a hollow façade. He had originally requested on April 17 that he should be provided with an office in the Defense Department. He was supported by the German legation, and Christensen felt that he had no alternative but to agree. The head of the Council personally met Quisling at 10:30 a.m. on April 18 in order to arrange for him to occupy his office. Upon returning to the Council, which was in session, Christensen informed his colleagues that four members of the armed forces, two from the army and two from the navy, had agreed to work under Quisling. But Christensen had spelled out clearly to Quisling and his subordinates that their task was solely restricted to demobilization within occupied territory: "arrangements of the transition from military to civilian, the gathering of material that belongs to the state, and the care of this material." Christensen also told Quisling to maintain close contact with the Administrative Council.[16]

On the next day Christensen made absolutely certain that Quisling, in his capacity of being in charge of demobilization, was under the jurisdiction of the Council. Christensen received clarification from the German legation that the army supplies which Quisling had obtained control of came under the overall administrative responsibility of the Council's Supplies Department.[17]

From this locked-in position, and with his followers denied the opportunity of wearing uniforms, Quisling showed no interest in the practical aspects of carrying out demobilization. He made no attempt to exploit his position. The actual task of carrying out the process was therefore performed by persons who were fully loyal to the Administrative Council.[18]

Unable to make effective use of his formal post, Quisling was reduced to issuing political proclamations in the immediate aftermath of the Council's formation. Again he was an outsider, attempting to improve his political status. His decline was indicated immediately after he officially stepped down as head of the "national government". He and his followers were informed rather brusquely that they would have to vacate Hotel Continental. The German military, who requisitioned the entire hotel, had no desire to share quarters with the NS leader. He and his entourage, including Scheidt, were thereupon forced to move to Grand Hotel on Karl Johans gate.[19]

With the advice of his closest collaborators, Hagelin, Schreiber, and Scheidt, with the Naval Attaché in particular taking an active part, Quisling's new political course was mapped out. It appeared in the form of an appeal, dated April 18, which was printed in *Fritt Folk* the following day. Entitled "Let the Country Have Peace", the article sought to convey the impression that Quisling was a man of peace. It stressed how he had attempted to establish contact with the King in order to arrive at a non-violent accommodation. Quisling insisted that his motives had been completely selfless: "I clearly expressed that my goal was not dictatorship and not a copy of Germany, but a free national Norway headed by the royal house". Similarly, he maintained that his government had left office solely because of the desire to establish peace. But now, when hostilities had not ended, he called on Norwegians to cease their resistance: "Let England carry out its war alone. Our Norwegian boys' blood is far too valuable to be sacrificed in British mercenary service". He declared that the best course to follow was to reach a settlement with the Germans similar to that which had been made in Denmark, thereby moving the war to outside of Norway's boundaries.[20]

The article mirrored the attitude of Quisling and his backers in the days immediately before Terboven took over as head of the new German administration, the *Reichskommissariat*. Quisling's advisers were still unaware of Bräuer's fall and therefore believed that the ex-Minister's policy was still being followed. Consequently, great emphasis was placed on Quisling's attempts to reach an understanding with the King. However, since it had become clear that no compromise was possible with the monarch after the arrival of Allied troops, any future agreement which the Germans might be able to arrange would most likely to be made with a pro-German faction. It was therefore important for Quisling's backers to maneuver their man forward so that he would be the obvious candidate to take part in such an arrangement.[21]

Recognizing the need to give Quisling as much publicity as possible, his call for peace was written in both Norwegian and German for the purpose of dispersing it widely through the press and radio. But it only appeared in *Fritt Folk*. All other papers refused to print it.[22] And when Scheidt sought to have the proclamation broadcast over the radio, the German military censor sabotaged the attempt by referring it to the Administrative Council, which calmly tabled the request on April 19.[23]

Blocked by the Council, Quisling and his advisers were in such a locked-in, isolated position that their only recourse was to write a letter of complaint against the Administrative Council to the absent Bräuer. Quisling accused the Council of having sabotaged his important activities. He furthermore charged it with doing nothing to prevent anti-Quisling propaganda from being spread. He therefore insisted that German authorities should clearly delineate the role his movement should play in Norwegian affairs, and he demanded German support.[24]

He similarly sought German backing by sending a birthday greeting to *der Führer* in which he stressed his movement's common cause with Germany: "We are still hoping for the national rebirth of our Fatherland in a free and lasting league of Germanic peoples, and are fighting on for this idea".[25]

His expressions were intended to influence a political situation which no longer existed. He dated his letter to Bräuer as late as April 21, at which time the *Reichskommissariat* had already been established. On the very day Quisling finished his letter, Josef Terboven landed for the first time on Norwegian soil.[26]

Hitler's decision to appoint a party man as the Third Reich's highest political representative in Norway marked a clear departure from the policy he
had followed up to Bräuer's dismissal. In one way or another, Hitler had
hoped to maintain a certain continuity with the Norwegian constitutional
system by seeking to exploit the King. But with Terboven's appointment,
Norway received a National Socialist chief administrator, responsible directly to Hitler. This marked the beginning of the nazification process in
Norway.[27]

The new *Reichskommissar* was ideally suited for his new assignment.
Tough and ruthless, he was an old-time party member who had joined the
NSDAP in 1923. He became the Nazi leader in his home town, Essen,
where his street fighters made him one of the most notorious party chieftains in the Ruhr region. Following the Nazi takeover, he received a number of additional positions, the most important being that of *Oberpräsident*
of the Rhine province.

As Nazi *Gauleiter* and provincial *Oberpräsident*, Terboven had a reputation for jealously insisting on independence in the areas under his jurisdiction. He did not get along well with several of his colleagues on the
local level in the party. On the other hand, he enjoyed good connections
with members of the top Nazi hierarchy and with powerful economic interests. In particular, he was recognized as Göring's man. The support of
the powerful Reich Marshal, who also had overall leadership of the
economy, added concrete evidence of Terboven's prominence as one of the
leading party figures on the district level. His name was well known in the
Reich Chancellery. He was at the height of his career when appointed to
his post in Norway at the age of forty-one.[28] He was chosen personally by
Hitler, who was advised by Terboven's patron, Göring.[29]

Because of the manner in which his selection was made, Terboven became a subject of controversy from the moment he was designated *Reichskommissar*. All who had a vested interest in Norway were bound to be dis-
trustful. The *Wehrmacht* received no notice of his appointment, although
Norway was still an area of military operations. Similarly, despite its interest in the country and championship of Quisling, Rosenberg's office had
been ignored. Nor was Grand Admiral Raeder happy, since Norway was
so important for his navy, and since he personally supported Quisling.[30]

As shown by his past record, Terboven did not avoid controversy, but
rather thrived on it. Intelligent and tough-minded, he was despotic in his
determination to have total supremacy over his area of competence. In
Norway, he insisted on being responsible only to *der Führer*, and that
there should be no independent authority that lay outside the *Reichskommissar*'s control.[31]

He received his initial order to meet with Hitler in the evening of April
19 to discuss the new assignment. They spoke alone, and there is no record
of their conversation.[32] However, it seems likely that Quisling's name was

mentioned in the course of their talk, and that Hitler told Terboven he should cooperate with the NS leader. Hitler informed Raeder three days later that he had given Terboven such instructions.[33]

Before he could effectively occupy his post, the necessary preparations had to be made to assemble the subordinates who would serve under Terboven in the new occupation administration.[34] Similarly, he needed to gain some firsthand acquaintance with his new assignment before he formally assumed his position. He therefore made a quick visit to Oslo by plane on April 21–23, returning to Berlin to receive the formal appointment to his position from Hitler on the 24th.[35] It came in the form of a special *Führer* decree which spelled out specifically the powers which the *Reichskommissar* had been entrusted with.

Hitler's decree of April 24 revealed quite clearly his resolve to handle personally the political situation in Norway. It began paradoxically by stating that the Nygaardsvold government was responsible for the state of war with Germany because of its proclamations, behavior, and encouragement of military resistance. Therefore, in order to maintain order in the occupied parts of the country, Hitler proclaimed these to be under the jurisdiction of the *Reichskommissar*. He had the responsibility for protecting the Third Reich's interests and of exercising the highest governmental authority in civilian matters. In carrying out his duties, he could make use of the Administrative Council. Previously existing law would remain in effect "as long as it is compatible with the occupation". However, the *Reichskommissar* could enact new laws through the use of decrees. Under Hitler's proclamation, military control in Norway continued to be held by the commander-in-chief of the armed forces. However, Terboven was placed in a strong position vis-à-vis Falkenhorst, since all military decrees affecting the civilian population were to be enforced by the *Reichskommissar*. Furthermore, Terboven at the time of his appointment reached an agreement with Himmler whereby the SS chief gained a certain degree of influence in Norwegian occupation politics. But the *Reichskommissar* in turn had a say in the choice of SS police appointees in Norway. The arrangement worked very well for Terboven. There were no controversies between his administration and SS police officials, as occurred in other occupied territories. Through his personal contact with loyal SS officials, Terboven maintained control over the German police, who could be placed at the disposal of the military only with his approval.[36]

The large amount of autonomy which Terboven received was due to *der Führer's* frame of mind at the time he drew up the decree. He was highly irritated by the situation in Norway. The military was not in his good books because of its failure to capture the country by surprise, plus the uncertainty created by the presence of Allied forces. The Foreign Ministry was in disgrace because of Bräuer's discredited policy. As a result, Hitler chose a trusted party officer who was made personally responsible to *der Führer* himself. Article 6 of the decree stated: "The *Reichskommissar* stands directly under me and receives guidelines and instructions from me."[37]

Such a principle was naturally in accord with Terboven's own preference. Even before Hitler's decree had been formally announced, Terboven set out to create unchallenged authority for himself in Norway. During his initial introductory visit, he took the opportunity of visiting the man who potentially could be his greatest rival, General Falkenhorst. But he discovered already at their first meeting that the commander-in-chief would pose no threat. The latter adhered to the traditional viewpoint of maintaining a clear line of division between civilian and military affairs, with the military's duties sharply delineated. He revealed no desire to challenge the headstrong and ambitious Terboven.[38]

Similarly, the *Reichskommissar* designate did not have to worry about poor relations with the *Luftwaffe* commanders in Norway, under Göring's leadership. But Terboven failed to recognize at the time that the navy was an entirely different force to be reckoned with, thanks to Raeder's support of Quisling. This remained an unknown, dangerous factor for Terboven.

Much more obvious was the role that the Foreign Ministry wanted to play. Although his ministry was in disgrace with Hitler, Ribbentrop hoped it would be possible for the personnel in the legation in Oslo to remain as the Foreign Ministry's representatives in the *Reichskommissariat*. Terboven, however, soon shattered Ribbentrop's illusion. The *Reichskommissar* allowed the Foreign Ministry only a short period to close down its legation. Neuhaus was recalled to Germany on May 8, and on May 21 Hitler decreed that all diplomatic personnel should return to Germany. This decision was carried out within a short time, with those members of the legation who remained in Norway being absorbed into the *Reichskommissariat*.[39] The Foreign Ministry's influence, which until April 19 had been predominant in civilian affairs, was thereby entirely eliminated.

Little did Terboven realize when he first came to Norway that he would encounter his greatest difficulties within the German sphere of influence from a Norwegian, Vidkun Quisling. The hindrance which the NS leader provided came not so much from himself, however, as it did from his backers. Because Hitler apparently had encouraged Terboven to work with Quisling, the *Reichskommissar* designate made a point of meeting the NS *Fører* already during his fact-finding tour, on April 23. Used to making quick judgements, Terboven was not overwhelmed by what he saw. According to one of his close associates and confidants in the *Reichskommissariat*, Hans Dellbrügge, Quisling gave the impression of being completely inadequate when asked to provide the practical Terboven with information. Quisling maintained NS had some 30,000–50,000 members, perhaps as many as 100,000, with an additional 150,000 sympathizers. Yet he could produce no up-to-date membership list, nor could he furnish the names of NS party officers outside the Oslo area. The reason for his inability to supply Terboven with this information was, of course, that NS generally lacked an organization outside the capital.

Terboven was also shocked by NS' poor financial condition. Despite the previous generous cash grants from Germany, the party was in economic chaos. It did not have a balance sheet, and its income was limited. Everything was up in the air, including *Fritt Folk*, which once more faced the familiar possibility of collapse. Quisling could not even account for how much money had been spent previously. On the other hand, Terboven noted that the NS *Fører* could express himself in detail on ideological questions. He talked about how Norway, as an independent state, would become a member of a greater Germanic union. He also expressed his conviction that his countrymen in time were bound to accept him as their leader.[40] Quite perceptively, Terboven noted that Quisling's method of seeking to become Norway's leader was through imitation of Hitler: "In general . . . T[erboven] had the impression that Q[uisling] to a high degree attempted to copy Hitler". In accomplishing this, the most important matter for Quisling was the appearance of his party's uniform. Terboven observed how Quisling constantly reverted to this question, which appeared to be uppermost in his mind.[41]

Terboven received the overall impression that NS needed a great deal of reorganization before it could hope to assume any responsibility for forming a government. The party's membership had to be brought up to date, and it had to be placed on a firm financial footing.[42] As for its leader, he was convinced that Quisling "was not the appropriate personality to lead such a party".[43]

The *Reichskommissar* would have no reason to change his first impression of Quisling. Indeed, it became a permanent conviction and formed a basic part of Terboven's politics in Norway. This did not mean, however, that he ideologically felt estranged from Quisling. On the contrary, the *Reichskommissar* recognized that Quisling and NS stood closest to Nazi Germany among the different groups within the Norwegian political spectrum. But as a hard-headed realist, he perceived immediately that NS was not an asset, despite its affinity to the German cause.[44] If the party were to be of benefit for the German authorities, it would have to be strengthened. For the time being, it had little if any usefulness.

Terboven made his viewpoint abundantly clear to Quisling after the *Reichskommissar* had assumed office. On Sunday, April 28, the NS leader and Scheidt were invited to meet with Terboven, who had set up temporary headquarters at Hotel Bristol, yet another major hotel in central Oslo.

The *Reichskommissar* informed Quisling that he sympathized with NS, and that the party would receive German aid. However, he indicated that he did not intend to use National Union as a political instrument. As justification, he argued that if he openly favored NS, Norwegians would regard the party as traitorous. In addition, he maintained that he planned to impose a number of stringent measures in the immediate future, and he did not wish to have NS share the burden of unpopularity which would result.[45] His true reason for not being willing to rely on NS was because the party, as presently constituted, was more a hindrance than a help.

Not all high-ranking Germans agreed with the *Reichskommissar*. Forces in both Berlin and Norway were at work to provide Quisling with a more significant role than the one Terboven had assigned. With Bräuer's policy having been terminated in disgrace, Alfred Rosenberg saw his opportunity to secure an influential position for his office in Norway. In seeking to realize this goal, he followed his usual policy of supporting his protégé, Quisling. Already on April 19, the day when Hitler first discussed the establishment of the *Reichskommissariat* with Terboven, Rosenberg sent his *Führer* a report from Scheidt in Norway which complained about how "our friends", meaning Quisling and NS, had been treated badly by German officials.[46]

Rosenberg failed to exert any influence at the time Hitler proceeded to establish the new institution. Shortly afterwards, however, the military situation in Norway, which previously had resulted in a severe setback for Rosenberg's pro-Quisling policy, now shifted in Germany's favor. The landing of British troops had not resulted in the benefits which the Norwegian government had expected. The first units that linked up with the Norwegian army were poorly trained and inadequately equipped Territorials. The Germans, encountering these forces for the first time in the period April 21–23, had no difficulty in driving them into retreat.

The outcome of the campaign in central Norway, however, was decided in the end by Germany's air superiority. The British landing bases on the west coast were under constant air attacks, which disrupted the possibility of providing British and Norwegian forces fighting in the interior with needed supplies and reinforcements. By April 26 the British decided to cease operations in central Norway. Thereafter, only in the north, at Narvik, could Allied and Norwegian units continue their advance against General Dietl and his men, who were being put under increased pressure.

The mercurial *Führer*, who had received direct information about these military developments, was in an ecstatic frame of mind when Rosenberg came to dinner on April 25. Hitler drew him aside and gave a joyous account of the British defeat. Furthermore, Hitler had received captured British documents from Norway which indicated, at least to his satisfaction, that not only had the British been planning an invasion of Norway, but that the Norwegian government had made a confidential agreement which sanctioned such an action. Rosenberg saw his chance to interject quickly that this showed that Quisling had been right all along when he pointed to collusion between the Nygaardsvold cabinet and London. Hitler agreed completely.[47]

This provided Rosenberg with the opportunity to put in a good word on the NS leader's behalf: "I now told *der Führer* that I considered it necessary that Q[uisling] and his colleagues also should be treated properly." Quisling, he continued, should be allowed to carry out his political activity without hindrance. More concretely, Rosenberg made attempts to have his office secure influence in Norwegian politics. He insisted that only the Nordic Association, controlled by his organization, had any real understanding of Norway. Terboven, said Rosenberg, had not yet been able to acquire firsthand knowledge about the situation. The *Reichsleiter* used this argument in order to provide his people with key positions. Scheidt, Rosenberg pointed out, was ideally suited to serve under Terboven, in particular since Quisling had requested that Scheidt be allowed to remain in Norway. According to Rosenberg, Hitler gave his consent to Scheidt's continued stay.[48]

Rosenberg, however, had the even more ambitious goal of being able to control Norwegian affairs from Berlin. He therefore proposed that his subordinate Schickedanz should be given an office in the Reich Chancellery as a special deputy in charge of coordinating all messages to and from Norway. Hitler, in the euphoria caused by the changed military situation in Norway, was in such a mood that he literally could not say no to Rosenberg. Schickedanz secured the coveted position.[49]

Already on the same day, April 25, Schickedanz conferred with Dr. Lammers, making the necessary arrangements for Rosenberg's lieutenant to take over his new post. Rosenberg felt truly triumphant about this rapid development, believing he had already outmaneuvered Terboven at the very beginning of the *Reichskommissariat*. He confided to his diary that Terboven's face had fallen, but that he had to accept the arrangement.[50]

Rosenberg's apparent success was aided by Raeder. As before, the Grand Admiral acted in tandem with the Office of Foreign Affairs on Quisling's behalf. Rosenberg went so far as to refer on May 8 to Schreiber, Raeder's representative in Oslo, as "our co-conspirator".[51] At the time the *Reichskommissariat* was in the process of being formed, Raeder took the opportunity during a conference with Hitler to speak in Quisling's favor. The Grand Admiral praised Quisling's and Hagelin's effort on Germany's behalf, while Falkenhorst and Bräuer were criticized for not having given Quisling the assistance he needed. Raeder declared that only time would tell whether Bräuer's recall and Terboven's appointment would create a more favorable situation. The Grand Admiral, who unlike Falkenhorst had no reticence about involving himself in political affairs, recommended to Hitler that Terboven needed to cooperate with Quisling.[52]

In response, Hitler stated that Terboven had been instructed to consult with the NS leader. Raeder thereupon could do nothing except wait and see how events in Norway materialized – whether Terboven would indeed respond positively toward Quisling. But the Grand Admiral already felt hostility toward Terboven. The *Reichskommissar* was Göring's man, and the heads of the navy and the *Luftwaffe* were not friendly. They had clashed repeatedly over the execution of *Weserübung*. Therefore, from the beginning of the *Reichskommissariat* the navy followed a policy in Norway which not only favored Quisling, but which also was antagonistic toward Terboven.[53]

While Raeder had to wait for the outcome of future developments, Rosenberg could act far more quickly, thanks to the favorable response he had received from Hitler. Schickedanz left for Oslo already on the morning of April 27. The purpose of his visit was three-fold: (1) to orient himself about conditions in Norway, (2) to reassure Quisling of support and, (3) if feasible, to install Scheidt in a position under Terboven.[54] The fact that Rosenberg was uncertain about the possibility of gaining a permanent post for Scheidt seems to indicate that Hitler's approval was not firm, and that it might have been subject to negotiations with Terboven.

It is not possible to ascertain Schickedanz's time of arrival, but it appears to have been on the 28th. This was the very day when Quisling and Scheidt had their conference with the *Reichskommissar*, at which time he poured cold water on the idea that NS could expect to assume a predominant position. But while they were crushed by Terboven's negative attitude, the two received renewed inspiration from Schickedanz's arrival. Rosenberg recorded that Schickedanz's unexpected appearance came as that of a *"deus ex machina"* for Quisling and his followers.[55] Rosenberg's lieutenant assured Quisling that sentiment in Berlin differed greatly from the viewpoint Terboven had expressed. Schickedanz declared that *der Führer* intended to reward Quisling, and that Terboven did not have the final say in determining what would take place in Norway.[56]

Encouraged and assisted by Schickedanz, Quisling and his close advisers planned a counter-strategy against the *Reichskommissar* during the next two days. Their intent was to thwart Terboven by having NS assume a leading role in Norwegian affairs. To accomplish this, they decided to appeal over Terboven's head to the one person who could overrule him – Adolf Hitler. Two letters were drawn up and signed by Quisling. Although written in German, indicating that Quisling made use of Scheidt's and Schickedanz's assistance in their formulation, the ideas expressed in the letters were typical of Quisling's reasoning, and he must therefore be considered their main author.[57]

The first, dated May 1, was addressed directly to Hitler. In order to avoid the charge that Quisling was going behind Terboven's back, it was forwarded via the *Reichskommissar*, who received a brief appended note. The second, however, did not pass through official channels, being addressed to Schickedanz. Its major purpose was to allow him to carry it personally back to Berlin, where it could be circulated for the purpose of giving added weight in support of Quisling's attempt to make a comeback.

In his brief note to Terboven, Quisling indicated, as he would later repeat all too frequently in his relationship with the *Reichskommissar*, that he had had second thoughts after their discussion of April 28. Having thoroughly considered the situation, said Quisling, he had concluded that immediate steps needed to be taken in order to prepare for future Norwegian-German relations. In an attempt to reassure Terboven that this move was not a violation of the *Reichskommissar*'s decision concerning NS, Quisling added that his party's current activity was in accord with what had been discussed at the meeting of April 28.[58]

Terboven needed only to read through the letter to Hitler to recognize the transparency of Quisling's reassurance. His course of action directly contradicted Terboven's stated policy toward NS. Ever since his forced resignation, Quisling had sought by every means to discredit the Administrative Council. It not only stymied NS operations, but acted as a roadblock to his constant goal of heading a government. His resentment and hostility toward the institution was therefore very great, an attitude that he freely expressed to Hitler.[59]

Quisling described the Council as being composed of individuals who were pro-English, and who cooperated with German authorities only for opportunistic reasons. He castigated its head, Christensen, as "a known Freemason ... who publicly assumed an anti-German position only three weeks before the arrival of your troops". Quisling further complained that the Council failed to honor Hitler's expressed wish that the NS leader and his party should be respected. Instead, said Quisling, "my followers ... are reviled as traitors and punished in various ways, and ... my person and political viewpoint are hotly attacked in the press". He went on to insist that only NS, and not the Council, could achieve "real internal peace in Norway".[60]

He did recognize, however, that he could not hope to eliminate the Administrative Council immediately, in particular because Hitler had just recently stated in his decree establishing the *Reichskommissariat* that Terboven should make use of the Council in administering Norway. Quisling therefore made three proposals to Hitler, intended to allow NS to take over the government gradually. First, Quisling planned to "build up my movement intensively". In this connection, he stated rather defensively – which was understandable in the light of the greatly overinflated claims he had made of having strong popular backing – that he had never alleged having majority support in Norway. "Behind me stands a small but resolute minority which represents the people's true interests." Secondly, he asked to be allowed to appoint two of his lieutenants to the Administrative Council. One would take over the Department of Justice and the Police, while the second would head a completely new Press and Propaganda Department. Such a move, said Quisling, would permit "reliable persons from the national movement" to carry out a "gradual permeation of the executive apparatus". Finally, he reverted to a theme that he had followed before and which he would attempt to realize all too frequently again, namely, the desire to establish a corporate state under his control. Representatives from Norway's economic and cultural life, said Quisling, must be systematically organized in preparation for "the creation of a national government under my leadership". He insisted that public opinion, which now was hostile to Germany, could be transformed by making full use of the "propaganda apparatus" so that it adopted "an understanding and friendly attitude", thereby preparing the way for "a firm constitutional bond between all Germanic states".[61]

While his letter to Hitler was formal, containing specific recommendations, the second letter, which Schickedanz took with him to Berlin, was much more personal in nature. It basically sought to generate sympathy for Quisling's position, thereby creating a positive emotional response which would allow the implementation of the proposals he made to Hitler. He insisted that his political goal had always been to establish "a free Germanic league under German leadership". This had prompted him to form his government on April 9, and he argued that there had been a good possibility for success. He complained that he had been forced to step down by Habicht and Bräuer, who stood accused not only of having conducted negotiations behind his back with "anti-German cliques", but also of having forced him to conduct "the last decisive negotiations" on April 15 without his "confidential colleague and translator, Hagelin", even though Quisling did not have "adequate command of the German language". He further complained that he had not been allowed to talk with *der Führer* at the time, being convinced that Hitler would have acted on his behalf. Quisling went on to denounce the existing situation in Norway, thereby attacking Terboven for the first time, although not by name. While he and his followers were now completely isolated, "German authorities in Norway" were described as working with "exactly the same circles who already once before have betrayed Germany". He insisted that the basis for his complaint was not personal, but rather involved the great goal of the Germanic League. This body, he claimed, could only come into existence if Norway took the lead, and this could only be accomplished by the removal of the old politicians in favor of a "national government".[62]

Quisling couched his statements in the letter to Schickedanz in terms that had great appeal for Rosenberg. The ideological concept of a "greater Germanic federation" was exactly the type of program which the *Reichsleiter* favored. The same idea had been expressed by Quisling in his December meetings with Hitler, and not without success. *Der Führer*, with his strong belief in racial stereotypes, could very well respond positively to such a concept. For him the Scandinavians were fellow Aryans, and this explains why the German occupations of Denmark and Norway, harsh though they were, differed considerably from the far more brutal, and in some instances genocidal, practices followed in other areas of the European continent.

In his letters, however, Quisling touched upon the one factor that made it impossible for him to gain the adherence of the majority of Norwegians. He had been stamped with the brand of treason from the first day of the invasion. Whereas previously he had been reduced to being regarded as a pro-fascist nonentity, now he assumed a much more sinister image, that of being a threat to the nation's moral integrity and to the possibility of Norway surviving as a political unit. Public consensus agreed overwhelmingly in the spring of 1940 that Quisling was guilty of treason. One anonymous writer summed this up succinctly in a letter to Quisling, declaring that 99 per cent of the people, or more, regarded him as a traitor to his country and its people.[63] Even those who were pro-German in 1940, and whose influence was not insignificant, viewed Quisling in the same light, believing his politics to be without value because of his reputation. Appeals for an end to Norwegian resistance, which continued to appear in *Fritt Folk*, simply heightened popular resentment.[64] By openly currying favor with the Germans, publicly as well as behind the scenes, he eliminated forever the possibility of gaining widespread popular support. The stigma of being a traitor remained attached to him permanently.

He could therefore never hope to secure control of government through popular sanction. Nor did he possess the ability of gaining the cooperation of German authorities on the scene in Norway. First Bräuer and then Terboven found him to be a minus quantity, serving as a hindrance to the successful execution of their policy. His sole hope rested therefore in Berlin. Here, the will of Adolf Hitler ultimately prevailed in determining whether Quisling would obtain the position which he fervently believed should be his.

The letter that Schickedanz brought with him to Berlin, plus other reports that Rosenberg's man had also collected, therefore assumed great importance in the furtherance of the NS leader's cause. But Schickedanz returned on a Saturday, May 4. Not until the following Tuesday, May 7, did Dr. Lammers of the Reich Chancellery read the correspondence which Schickedanz had arrived with.[65]

By this time it was too late for Quisling's letters to have their desired effect. Terboven had intervened. He resented most strongly the attempt which Rosenberg's office made through Schickedanz and Scheidt to influence Norwegian affairs. Once alerted, he therefore moved quickly to thwart the strategy which Quisling had adopted with the assistance of Rosenberg's subordinates. Whether this was the sole reason for Terboven's decision to travel to Germany cannot be determined, but it certainly was an important factor. Having arrived by plane, he talked with Hitler on May 8, before Lammers had a chance to inform *der Führer* of Schickedanz's correspondence.[66] The *Reichskommissar* therefore enjoyed the advantage of discussing the political situation in Norway with Hitler on his own terms.

Exactly how Hitler responded to Terboven's views is not known, since only the latter's version, as reported by Scheidt, is available, which is not the most objective source one could wish.[67] Nevertheless, one thing is certain: Terboven did not feel that any significant restraints had been imposed upon him as a result of his conversation with Hitler. He came back to Norway more determined than ever to strike down the challenge raised by the backing which Quisling received from Rosenberg's organization.

Immediately following his return, Terboven held a conference with Quisling and Scheidt on May 9. According to Scheidt, Terboven declared that Hitler had simply smiled when he read Quisling's letter. There was no possibility for NS to receive the two departments in the Administrative Council which Quisling had requested. Furthermore, Terboven made use of the opportunity that the failure of the attack against him had opened up by moving to eliminate Scheidt and to gain closer control over National Union. The *Reichskommissar* informed Scheidt that he would have to leave the country by the middle of the following week, since his position as liaison man with NS had been eliminated. Terboven had arranged to have German advisers for NS come to the country, rendering Scheidt's assignment superfluous.[68]

Scheidt protested against the decision, but to no avail. During the following days Rosenberg's man did everything in his power to try to find some means of remaining in the country. Quisling, who had depended on Scheidt for advice and support ever since the latter had committed himself to the NS leader's cause, tried to help. He wrote to Rosenberg on May 12, praising Scheidt for his "great understanding of the Norwegian mentality", and suggesting that he be made head of an office for the Nordic Association in Oslo.[69] Scheidt also sought backing from members of the *Reichskommissariat*, and an attempt was made to find a post for him through the navy. But all of these endeavors to evade Terboven's will were crushed. On May 16 Scheidt was called in by the German police and told in no uncertain terms to leave the country within two days.[70] He had no choice but to comply. The usually optimistic Scheidt was in a low humor when he departed, telling his friends that he had literally been deported by the *Reichskommissar*.[71] For Scheidt, it appeared at the time that his effort in

Norway had only culminated in defeat at the hands of Terboven. By May 20 Rosenberg's representative was back in Berlin.[72]

Having eliminated Scheidt, Terboven planned to bring NS closely under his supervision. It was for this purpose that he had arranged to have Nazi political advisers come to Norway in order to oversee NS' affairs. By the middle of May two such specialists had arrived. In addition to using them to gain insight into the true condition of NS, Terboven hoped, at least for the time being, to increase the party's strength. He recognized that NS would have to improve considerably before it really amounted to anything.[73] But because of the interest that Hitler had indicated in Quisling's cause, Terboven felt obliged to make such an endeavor.

He remained determined, however, to prevent any outside intrusion into Norwegian affairs. To implement this policy fully, he had one remaining obstacle to overcome – Schickedanz's post in the Reich Chancellery, charged with transmitting communication between Germany and Norway. This arrangement was completely unsatisfactory for Terboven, and he never utilized it. Instead, he sent his messages to Germany via Göring's Air Ministry.[74] As a result, Schickedanz's position became superfluous. Terboven moved to terminate it completely when he next travelled to Germany, arriving on May 21. He brought with him one of his subordinates, Otto Marrenbach, who had been assigned to set up a permanent liaison office in Berlin for Terboven's *Reichskommissariat*. Marrenbach completed his task by June 4, at which time Terboven informed the Chancellery that his new liaison office with Norway was now functioning, thereby ending the need for Schickedanz' services. The latter was duly informed on June 8.[75]

Rosenberg's office had thereby been completely outmaneuvered. It was the *Reichsleiter*, and not the strong-willed Terboven, who was left with a "fallen face". The former had no intention, however, of ending the struggle. This simply marked the end of one phase in the ongoing battle between the two. If Rosenberg were to succeed, he had to go to the top, to Hitler. He and his co-workers would follow this course in the future.

In pursuing his objective, Rosenberg continued to receive Raeder's assistance, with the navy staying committed to Quisling's cause. This meant that the navy and the *Reichskommissariat* remained on collision course. The collision came, figuratively speaking, when the Grand Admiral paid a personal visit to Norway. His arrival coincided with Terboven's maneuvers against Rosenberg, the *Reichskommissar* having just ordered the expulsion of Scheidt.[76] Ostensibly, Raeder made the journey in order to inspect naval installations, but his primary reason was political. It was therefore natural for him to meet Terboven, but the outcome of their discussion proved satisfactory for neither. The two could not agree at all, and the

Grand Admiral became highly agitated by the domineering manner in which Terboven rejected his viewpoint.[77]

If there had ever been doubt whether the navy's politics in Norway conflicted with *Reichskommissariat*'s, the dispute became clear at this meeting. In the aftermath, Admiral Hermann Boehm, the commander of naval forces in Norway and Raeder's personal friend, who shared his chief's pro-Quisling attitude, kept the Grand Admiral fully informed of political developments.[78] From now on both sides knew that battle lines had been drawn. The navy's direct involvement in opposition to Terboven's politics proved important for Quisling not only because he enjoyed the navy's backing, but also because he gained a channel of communication to Berlin which lay outside of Terboven's control. This proved to be invaluable following Scheidt's forced departure, which had ended the direct line of communicaton with Rosenberg's office.

Upon his return to Germany, Raeder immediately swung into action on Quisling's behalf. He sent Hitler the final report that Schreiber had written as naval attaché. The unfortunate Schreiber had seen his position with the German legation, like all such posts, eliminated by Terboven. Under the circumstances, it was hardly unexpected that the report was strongly supportive of Quisling.[79] Raeder followed up this initiative when he met personally with Hitler on May 21. In his comments, the commander of the navy was highly critical of the Administrative Council, echoing Quisling's line that it was hostile to Germany's interests and needed to be replaced by a government that was pro-German.[80]

By the last third of May a concerted offensive was being carried out by the navy and Rosenberg's office against Terboven's policy. The latter soon felt its impact. When he met with Hitler on May 22, the day after Raeder had presented his viewpoint, it became clear that Rosenberg and the Grand Admiral had made an impression on Hitler. Terboven received explicit instruction that he was expected to take into account Rosenberg's interests in Norway. This meant that any political arrangement which the *Reichskommissar* made would have to include Quisling.[81]

Considering Hitler's generally positive view of Quisling, this turn of events was not surprising, especially when consideration is given to Raeder's and Rosenberg's effective lobbying. But for Terboven, this development was completely unacceptable. He based his policy on being the sole holder of political power in Norway, responsible only to Hitler. Psychologically it was impossible for him to change his course and adopt Rosenberg's pro-Quisling viewpoint. Despite Hitler's clear instructions, Terboven refused even to make a partial change in favor of Quisling.

By the end of May the *Reichskommissar* had gone so far as to discount NS almost entirely as a political factor, at least for the immediate future. As evidence of this, the advisers whom he had appointed to oversee NS were removed from their positions at the end of the month or in early June. This indicated that he had ruled out the idea of working with NS. He instead followed a policy of orienting himself toward other forces who seemed to offer better opportunities for Germany's political course.[82]

This included a number of persons who assumed a friendly posture, favoring conciliation and accepting the occupation as a reality which could not be avoided. This pro-German faction tended to coalesce around Victor Mogens, the head of the Fatherland League. He had declared his understanding for the justness of the occupation already during the first days of the invasion.[83] At the same time, however, he was anything but sympathetic toward Quisling and the "national government". The foreman of the Fatherland League regarded the NS leader as a stumbling block to the possibility of permanent cooperation between the Norwegians and the German occupation authorities. Mogens hoped instead that his organization would assume a major role in any arrangement that was worked out.

In pursuing this endeavor, he received the backing of a number of individuals who had previously been important members of NS before the party's disintegration. These included Hjort, Thomas Neumann, Albert Wiesener, and Otto Engelschiøn.[84] With the bitter memory of the feuds that led to his party's decline, Quisling became especially concerned when he learned that these former antagonists were now cooperating with Mogens against him. Quite naturally, he regarded them as his most dangerous Norwegian competitors.[85]

His concern was justified to a considerable degree. Mogens, Hjort, and others in their circle had good connections with German authorities in Berlin as well as in Oslo, both civilian and military.[86] Their well-placed ties consequently permitted them to enjoy some influence with the Administrative Council. On April 20 it designated Hjort to head a special committee charged with looking after the welfare of Norwegian prisoners of war.[87] When making its selection, the Council was fully aware of Hjort's pro-German position. Just three days earlier he had submitted a memorandum in which he declared that under the circumstances Norwegians had to accept the occupation, whose final form would require further negotiations.[88]

Although his appointment did not take place without some feeling of disquiet, Hjort, as always, performed his duties with great efficiency. Knowledgeable political observers were quick to note the irony of Quisling's former chief rival now carrying out many of the functions that had originally been intended for the NS leader after he had been forced to step down as head of the "national government".[89]

Hjort's standing was improved by his relationship with the *Reichskommissar*. Terboven preferred to be briefed about Norwegian conditions by his German subordinates, and only rarely did he consult directly with Norwegians. Hjort was one of a small number of persons associated with the Administrative Council with whom the *Reichskommissar* talked personally.[90] When the ever-ambitious Hjort therefore at the end of May attempted to solicit Paal Berg's support for the establishment of a new party whose alleged purpose was to neutralize Quisling, the move took on special significance. Whether this was an independent initiative, or whether it was done with the tacit understanding of Terboven, is impossible to say. Berg, however, aware of Hjort's pro-German inclination, refused to have anything to do with the venture, which never materialized.[91]

Ellef Ringnes was another disillusioned former Quisling supporter who now maintained close ties with the *Reichskommissariat*, and who worked against Quisling's interests. Ringnes' connection with Terboven's organization was so strong that the Administrative Council appointed him to serve as a special "liaison link" between it and the *Reichskommissariat* in a number of cases where such a contact was deemed necessary.[92] Despite the cautiousness of the Council's language when choosing Ringnes for this assignment, it was obvious that he would be given the task of handling questions that were especially delicate in nature.

The *Reichskommissariat* similarly furthered the interests of Walter Fürst, yet another previous NS member who had broken with Quisling. As the leader of a voluntary Labor Service, Fürst proposed to the Council early in May that it set up a committee to consider establishing an officially sanctioned public labor organization. He enjoyed the backing of Mogens, who openly favored the idea.[93] More significantly, the *Reichskommissariat* exerted pressure on the Council to approve the plan. Thanks to the *Reichskommissariat*'s influence, Fürst overcame all opposition. By June 13 he headed a Labor Service (*Arbeidstjeneste*) which enjoyed the Administrative Council's sanction.[94] Its grudging acceptance of Fürst as chief of the Labor Service was also to some degree influenced by Quisling. The latter was attempting to establish a rival NS labor service, a development that both the Council and Terboven wished to prevent. Quisling was outmaneuvered. Once the Administrative Council's Labor Service had been approved under Fürst's leadership, Terboven urged Quisling to place his fledgling labor service under Fürst's command.[95]

During the spring and early summer of 1940, Quisling had to contend with yet another antagonist with whom he had formerly cooperated, this time on the German side. Dr. Ulrich Noack, through whom Quisling had briefly attempted to curry favor with Ribbentrop's Foreign Ministry, but who had been dropped thanks to the more promising possibilities offered by Rosenberg and Raeder, continued to revenge himself. The personal resentment which Noack felt because of having been abandoned in such a cavalier fashion undoubtedly influenced his attitude. Having worked actively against Quisling during the "national government" interlude, he openly assumed a hostile position at the end of May. He wrote a memorandum, dated May 20, which he delivered to the *Reichskommissariat*, allowing copies to circulate within political circles in Oslo. He attacked Quisling in the strongest possible terms, stating in writing what more discreet persons preferred to say privately in oral form. Quisling, said Noack, was the most hated man in Norway. Because of the resistance that he had inspired, Noack maintained that Quisling had the blood of thousands of German soldiers on his hands. Any attempt to increase the political standing of Quisling and his small band of followers, argued Noack, would lead to "bloody disturbances".[96]

As an alternative to Quisling, Noack strongly championed Mogens and the Fatherland League, pointing out specifically that many of Quisling's "earlier followers" had joined with the League. Together with persons from all parties and classes, said Noack, the League wished to achieve an inner renewal of Norway's political life. To clear the way for this possibility, the historian literally urged that Quisling and his closest associates should be sent into exile on the continent.[97] Thereafter, with the aid of Mogens, it would be possible to begin to change the political system. Noack argued that the best way to accomplish this would be to call the *Storting* back into session. The parliament could be used either to approve a new government or to recognize the Administrative Council as an interim body until a permanent government could be created.[98]

This memorandum proved to be revealing not only because of the information it provided concerning the aspirations of Mogens and his associates, but also because much of the strategy outlined by Noack was to be followed by Terboven in his attempt to rearrange the governmental structure in the summer of 1940.

The *Reichskommissar* returned to Norway just when the Noack memorandum was being discussed. It was obvious to observers that some kind of change was imminent. Rumors abounded during May about various possibilities and combinations for governmental alteration that were being speculated about.[99]

Terboven made it clear that the Germans, when the change occurred, would not permit it to take place through the regular practice of popular elections. On May 27 he suddenly proscribed political parties from holding public meetings.[100] Four days later, on June 1, he gave a speech in which he hinted clearly what general direction he wished political developments to take. He sought first to divide the people from the King and the Nygaardsvold government by describing these as having acted as lackeys of the British, while the majority of Norwegians, he maintained, had wished to be neutral and had not wanted war with Germany. But the main thrust of his address was to encourage prominent persons in politics and business to grasp the hand that Germany extended "honestly, sincerely, and without reservation" in "comradely cooperation".[101]

From the tone of his speech it was obvious that Terboven urged the replacement of the Administrative Council without stating, at least in public, what he preferred in its place. Because of the favorable military situation for Germany at the time, he believed he was in a strong position vis-à-vis the Norwegians with whom the *Reichskommissariat* would eventually negotiate, and he felt it to be to his advantage to maintain several options.

One course that he did not intend to pursue was to give Quisling and NS any assistance as participants in a future settlement, despite Hitler's transparent recommendation that he do so. Terboven stated explicitly on June 4 that he would never accept a Quisling government, and that NS was not mature enough to play any political role.[102]

His negative assessment of NS was not obvious to political observers, however. Because of Hitler, Terboven could not repudiate the party entirely, even if he had wanted to. He left NS' existence as an open alternative. But it appeared to outsiders that he was favoring the party. The May 27 prohibition against political meetings did not apply to NS. Two days later it announced a meeting to be held on June 5 with Quisling as speaker.[103] But Terboven, in permitting NS to enjoy such special status, did so grudgingly. It was a concession which he felt obligated to make because of Rosenberg's influence in Berlin.[104]

During early June 1940 the uncertainty about future political development was broken by the decisive results which Germany obtained on the battlefield. The campaign for southern and central Norway had already been won by the end of April. The British, unable to overcome German superiority, in particular in the air, were forced to evacuate. Their last forces were evacuated by sea during the first days of May. At this time Norwegian army units in the southern half of the country had no alternative but to capitulate. The King and the government, however, moved to Tromsø in the north, which served as the capital of independent Norway for over a month. The government hoped that in northern Norway, where Germany appeared to face considerable military difficulty, it might be possible, with Allied aid, to retain at least a part of the country as a haven, free from German control. For a brief period this seemed not unlikely. Enjoying numerical superiority, Norwegian and Allied units recaptured Narvik on May 28, driving Dietl's troops from the town and forcing them into a precarious position, pinned up against the Swedish frontier.

This Allied victory, giving the Germans their first land defeat in World War II, proved to have only psychological significance. At best, Norwegian and Allied forces only had an outside chance of holding on to northern Norway. German spearheads were already advancing rapidly northward along the coast. But the fate of northern Norway was decided elsewhere in Europe – beginning with the German offensive against the Low Countries on May 10. Within a short time British, French, and Belgian forces were trapped at Dunkirk, with their backs to the English Channel.

Because of this severe crisis, the Allies had decided to evacuate northern Norway already several days before the capture of Narvik.

Without Allied backing, the Nygaardsvold government could not sustain military operations by itself. But the government's resolution to resist, which had first become categorical in response to Hitler's favoritism of Quisling, remained determined despite the apparent hopelessness of the situation. The King and government made the decision to continue the war effort overseas with the means at their disposal. There was no serious sentiment in favor of making a separate peace with Germany.[105]

In a final proclamation before leaving for England, Haakon VII declared that he and the government would act as spokesmen for the people's independent national existence so that none of the rights of a free state might be lost. They would protect Norway's political sovereignty so that when victory was eventually achieved, the country could resoundingly resume its national freedom.[106] Five years later, despite the determined efforts of NS under Quisling's leadership, with the active backing of the German occupation authorities, it did indeed prove possible for the Norwegian people to resume their democratic traditions.

The departure of the King and government on June 7 meant, however, that the governmental structure in the country, now entirely under German control, had to be rearranged. The Administrative Council had been established on an interim basis, and, from the Norwegian perspective, on the assumption that it was acting in accord with the legal government's expectations. With the government and royal family having gone into exile, both Germans and Norwegians recognized that political change was at hand.

Any move toward governmental reorganization had to originate with the *Reichskommissar*. Groups such as NS and the Fatherland League might propagandize, either directly or indirectly, in favor of their particular cause. Only Terboven, however, as the possessor of highest political authority, could institute change, subject to the approval of Hitler. Determined as ever to dominate politically, Terboven took the initiative in mid June, delegating his subordinate, Dr. Hans Dellbrügge, to begin negotiations with leading Norwegian political figures. The *Reichskommissar* made this move without having secured Hitler's initial approval, being convinced that *der Führer* would react positively once he, Terboven, had successfully reached an agreement.[107] But the *Reichskommissar* continued to make the mistake of failing to take fully into account outside German interests wishing to influence development in Norway, such as the Rosenberg organization and Raeder's naval command.

Although a ruthless National Socialist, Terboven was a realist, as his political plan clearly indicated. Despite his short period of residence in

Norway, frequently interrupted by trips to Germany, he had already in less than two months gained good insight into the power relationship between various political constellations in the country. Furthermore, he possessed the proper combination of skill and unscrupulousness to take advantage of the prevailing situation. He planned to establish a State Council (*Riksråd*) as a new government in place of the Administrative Council. The State Council would serve as a pro-German collaborationist government, acting in accord with the interests of the *Reichskommissariat*.[108]

Unlike the unfortunate example of Quisling's "national government", however, Terboven planned to have the State Council made up of persons with much greater political strength. This would have included individuals who were either pro-German, but non-NS, or who were realists, believing, as was natural in the summer of 1940, that Germany had won the war and that it was therefore necessary, however painful, to cooperate to some extent with the Nazis in order to protect Norwegian interests. As time went on, Terboven believed it would be possible to change the State Council into a collaborationist body, in part by political pressure and in part by coopting its membership.[109]

Whether or not NS would have a future role in politics was something which Terboven left open for the time being, in spite of his certainty that the party needed a much broader base of support than the small but faithful clique that surrounded Quisling. In principle, the *Reichskommissar* was not entirely unsympathetic toward NS. The party was the political formation in Norway which was closest to National Socialism.[110] But Terboven considered Quisling to be incapable as its leader, and he was also difficult to deal with.[111] Terboven therefore intended to have NS play a minor part during the period when he strove to establish the State Council. But he was careful not to disown the party. It continued to carry out political activity, receiving financial support from the *Reichskommissariat*. Terboven had other motives concerning NS as well, however. This apparent favoritism of NS created doubt about his true intentions, allowing him to exert pressure on Norwegian negotiators during the State Council discussions. For Quisling's opponents, it was impossible to determine whether or not he enjoyed the *Reichskommissar*'s favor.[112]

In Terboven's own mind, there was no doubt concerning his attitude toward Quisling. Not only did the *Reichskommissar* consider him to be of little value, but the NS *Fører* also represented a threat to Terboven's power because of his connections in Germany. Terboven preferred to have someone more beholden to him as the leader of NS. He therefore deliberately promoted the political fortunes of Jonas Lie, yet another foe of Quisling's, during the State Council negotiations.

Terboven's choice of Lie was once again evidence of the *Reichskommissar*'s realism. From a German perspective, Lie in many ways appeared to be an ideal figure to patronize. Ruggedly handsome, he was gregarious, outspoken, and shrewd. He projected the image of a man's man, a perception that had been enhanced considerably by his exploits on the Norwegian side during the campaign against the Germans in April. But although he, as opposed to Quisling, had fought the *Wehrmacht*, his pro-German sympathies remained strong. Furthermore, as a high police official, he knew how to take orders.

Rather ironically, Quisling had at one time considered Lie to be his man, as shown by his attempt to appoint Lie as "Minister of Justice" in the "national government". Previously, Lie, if not actually a secret member of NS, had definitely sympathized with Quisling's party. While his refusal to join the "national government" conformed to the norm rather than the exception among those who had been nominated for this ill-fated endeavor, his very strong categoric statements, rejecting any connection with Quisling, made him stand out. His repudiation of the NS leader and his service as an army officer in the campaign against the *Wehrmacht* did not, however, cause Lie to fall into disfavor with German military and police officials, with whom he had enjoyed good ties since before the war. Only three days after his capture, he was allowed to return to Oslo, escaping the internment that was the lot of ordinary prisoners without favorable connections. Arriving in the capital on May 4, he had not moderated in any way his opinion of Quisling's attempted takeover in April. He stated to the press that he had been "completely horrified" when he learned he had been appointed by Quisling to take part in the government of usurpation.[113]

It did not take long for Terboven to learn of Lie. He was called to the *Reichskommissar*'s attention by a German police official. Thanks to Terboven's subsequent support, Lie was appointed police inspector in the Justice Department by the Administrative Council. When negotiations began concerning the make-up of the proposed State Council, Terboven was firmly committed to Lie's appointment as Minister of Police.[114]

In reaction to his disavowal, Quisling and his NS loyalists regarded Lie not only as a renegade, but also as a threat.[115] In order to weaken his standing, *Fritt Folk* published an article on June 8 which accused him of having persecuted an officer who had pro-German sympathies at the time Lie was serving in the Norwegian army. The article clearly reflected National Union's suspicion of the police official, declaring that he ought not to be entrusted with any position having to do with legal and political matters, and that he should be watched closely in the future.[116] The *Reichskommissariat* was not at all pleased by this attack. It responded by having the German advisers assigned to instruct the party intervene, giving NS a reprimand for the article's publication.[117]

During the summer months of June and July, Terboven's intended use of NS became clearly apparent. The party would continue to operate under

German patronage and protection, not as an independent entity. It would be a tool of the Germans, to be used in securing their interests. With Nazi instructors having been assigned, an attempt was made, beginning in June, to recruit new members and to revitalize the party. Speakers were sent out to different parts of the country to try to arouse enthusiasm for the NS cause. Simultaneously, letters were mailed to former members, seeking to reawaken their devotion to the party. All this activity, however, achieved meager results. Little support for NS could be stirred up at this time. At the end of August it still remained a small sect, having far fewer adherents than it had possessed in 1936.[118]

Financially, the party continued to be completely dependent on the *Reichskommissariat*, a reliance Terboven exploited fully. In order to keep NS under his control, he only made available enough money to keep it functioning at an existence level. This was particularly true at the time when he was promoting Lie for leadership of the party, seeking to displace Quisling. The amount of money doled out to NS declined from 40,143 *Reichsmark* in June to 18,300 in July.[119]

In an effort to reduce its dependence on German funds, Quisling and his backers conducted a separate collection campaign during the summer. The results were scanty.[120] The party had no choice but to continue to operate within the limits prescribed by the *Reichskommissariat*, with no chance of making any gains without German assistance. This was shown in July, when two of Quisling's loyalists attempted to have the Administrative Council establish a special department for Arctic and Antarctic Affairs, an area of interest which had special appeal for a segment of the NS members. But the *Reichskommissariat* showed no interest in backing the venture, and the Administrative Council quickly rejected it.[121]

Quisling was similarly kept under strict control. On June 24, when the State Council negotiations were reaching their midpoint during the early summer, he was permitted to give a speech over the radio. This was simply part of Terboven's strategy during the negotiations, exerting pressure by using the threat of holding Quisling in reserve. In his address, the NS *Fører* presented his views in his usual blunt manner, making no attempt to disguise his desire to head a government. He repeated his standard argument that Norway needed a "national government of the realm" and corporate control of the economy. This viewpoint was completely contrary to the line Terboven followed during the State Council negotiations. *Deutsche Zeitung in Norwegen*, the official German newspaper in Norway, omitted all reference to Quisling's statement.[122]

For the time being at least, Terboven was free to pursue his strategy without fear of meeting any strong challenge. Quisling appeared to be firmly under his thumb. Furthermore, the Germans clearly enjoyed a psychological advantage when carrying out the negotiations with responsible Norwegian political representatives. The military situation was never as bleak as in the summer months of 1940 for those favoring the Third Reich's defeat. The flight of the Norwegian government was followed by the capitulation of France. It appeared as if Britain would soon either be defeated or forced to make peace on Germany's terms. Feelings of hopelessness and disillusionment were strong in Norway. Informed opinion generally believed the Allies had lost the war.[123] Not infrequently, the tendency during this period of pessimism was to hold the Nygaardsvold government responsible for the tragedy that had befallen the country. This defeatist attitude was especially pronounced in the Oslo area, and it definitely affected the State Council negotiations.[124]

These discussions took place just at the time when France collapsed in defeat. Terboven expertly turned the Reich's military supremacy to his advantage, pressuring the Norwegian negotiators to make one concession after the other. The latter felt that with the apparent German victory in the war, it was necessary to gain the best possible terms under extremely difficult circumstances.[125] They hoped at all costs to be able to maintain as much Norwegian control as possible over administration. There existed strong apprehension that the governmental departments would either be placed directly under German commissaries, or they would be administered by a new Quisling government. Of the two feared alternatives, the possibility that Quisling might be allowed to make a comeback aroused the strongest negative feelings.[126]

The discussions originated with an informal initiative by Terboven through Dr. Dellbrügge on June 12. The demands that Terboven insisted upon were made brutally clear when presented formally at a meeting of the Administrative Council on the following day. The *Reichskommissar* wished to have the Nygaardsvold government declared invalid, while King Haakon should be deposed. To take their place, the *Storting* would be called into session in order to recognize a new government, the State Council. In return for complying with these terms, Terboven, through Dellbrügge, promised that the position of *Reichskommissar* would be abolished, with Hitler appointing a special representative to look after German interests in Norway.[127] Terboven's approach was quasi-legal, intending to use the parliament as an instrument through which a collaborationist government would be granted a semblance of legitimacy.

In response to the demands forwarded through Dellbrügge, a number of difficult meetings were held among the most politically prominent figures in Oslo. Present were members of the Administrative Council and the Supreme Court, including Christensen and Berg, representatives from the major parties in the *Storting*, business and labor delegates, and Bishop Berggrav.[128] The removal of the King was the most severe demand for the Norwegians to accept.[129] During the course of the discussions, leadership of the negotiations with Dellbrügge was assumed by the *Storting*'s Presidency (*Presidentskap*) since the parliament would bear the burden of ratifying any agreement that was made.

On June 18, strongly affected by the news of France's pending capitulation, the members of the Presidency gave in to the German demands. In a letter addressed to Hitler, formulated under the watchful eyes of Dellbrügge, they declared their willingness to sanction a State Council that would be approved by the *Storting*. The presidential board also agreed that the authority granted to the Nygaardsvold government by the *Storting* for the duration of the war would be null and void, with the government no longer recognized as legal. Furthermore, the letter stated that since the King was outside Norway's borders, he could no longer exercise his constitutional responsibilities. It therefore requested the King to surrender his authority.[130] Pressured by the Germans, the Presidency threatened that if the King did not respond to their request within fourteen days, then they would be obligated to work for passage of a *Storting* resolution deposing the royal dynasty.[131]

Having forced the *Storting*'s Presidency into making these concessions, Terboven believed that the situation was well in hand. It now remained for him to gain *der Führer*'s approval. With this goal in mind, he left Oslo on June 18. He met Hitler two days later at *der Führer*'s headquarters.[132] There is no firsthand account of the discussion at the meeting, but it appears that Hitler, at least in principle, approved Terboven's plan.[133] The latter flew back to Oslo on Saturday, June 22. On the following Monday the *Reichskommissariat*, acting as before through Dellbrügge, began the final stage of the negotiations, which concerned the composition of the State Council.[134]

If the Norwegian negotiators had been under the impression that they would have the final say in the make-up of the Council, their delusion was soon dispelled. Whereas they favored a body that was relatively limited in size, the Germans insisted on a much larger Council, with a total of fifteen to sixteen departments. More significantly, strong disagreement took place over who would serve on the body. The only candidate whom the Norwegians and Germans could agree on was Christensen, who was nominated as the Council's president. The Norwegians preferred to have representatives from the major political parties, while the Germans insisted on persons who were not politically prominent.[135]

Because of the weak Norwegian position, the Germans had their way. The number on the Council was set at sixteen. Only four members of the Administrative Council were scheduled to serve. The *Reichskommissar*'s influence was plainly apparent by the inclusion of persons closely identified with the policy of cooperating with the Germans. The Fatherland

League group was represented by Mogens as head of the Information Department, J. B. Hjort in charge of the Reconstruction Department, and Ellef Ringnes as Foreign Minister. In addition, Jonas Lie was selected to head the Police Department, while Captain Irgens had been designated as the candidate for the Interior Department. Although Irgens had previously had ties with Quisling, he denied, as did Lie, that he was a member of NS. Irgens at least at this moment appeared to be more closely associated with Terboven than with Quisling. The only clearly identifiable member of NS chosen to be part of the Council was Axel Stang, the projected leader of the Department of Sports and the Labor Service.[136] Even he, however, was reputed to be cooperating with Terboven at this juncture.[137]

By having persons who were suspected of being connected with NS, such as Lie and Irgens, and an outright member of the party such as Stang, beholden to him, Terboven had relegated Quisling to the sidelines. This was not apparent, however, to the Norwegian negotiators. They regarded Lie and Irgens with suspicion, believing them to be secret members of NS.[138] Stang's candidacy created even more difficulty. Christensen and the *Storting*'s Presidency refused to accept an NS member on the Council. It appeared as if the negotiations would collapse over his inclusion. However, on June 29 Dellbrügge provided Christensen with a sensational piece of news. Terboven's representative showed Christensen a letter signed by Quisling in which the NS *Fører* declared he had accepted an invitation to go to Germany in order to work for establishing closer cooperation between the Scandinavian countries and Germany. The letter further stated that while he was in Germany, he would be replaced by a person who enjoyed considerable goodwill in Norway.[139]

This apparent concession broke the deadlock. Stang's membership on the Council was now accepted. The incident provided telling evidence of the extent to which politically prominent individuals feared and opposed the establishment of a government influenced by Quisling. In return for the opportunity to remove him from active participation in politics, responsible politicians were willing to agree to a settlement that possibly had far-reaching consequences.

With Quisling due to leave for Germany, the NS threat no longer seemed strong. The Norwegian negotiators and Dellbrügge could therefore celebrate the apparently successful outcome of their discussions on June 29. They agreed that the *Storting* would be called into session on July 15 to ratify the creation of the State Council. The two sides exchanged polite speeches to mark the ostensible conclusion of their negotiations.[140]

Terboven's apparent concession to send Quisling to Germany was in reality no compromise. The *Reichskommissar* had earlier made up his mind that Quisling had to be removed. Already on June 25, four days before the agreement, Terboven called Quisling to a conference. This was on the day immediately after the NS *Fører*'s radio address, whose content Terboven exploited. He made it abundantly clear that Quisling was not his choice to head a government. Even worse, he announced categorically that Quisling would have to give up serving as leader of NS. Were he to remain NS *Fører*, said Terboven, division would be created among Norwegians. Terboven gave the assurance that NS would be represented in the government that he was in the process of setting up, but he would decide which NS members would take part. He threatened that if Quisling refused to comply with his demands, he would create a new political movement that would eliminate NS within two months. NS would also be denied German financial backing. But if Quisling agreed, Terboven guaranteed continued funds for the party. As for Quisling, when he stepped down from his leadership position, he would become the guest of the government in Germany. No doubt the irony was intended when Terboven informed Quisling that he would study the legal basis for German-Scandinavian cooperation while in the Third Reich.[141]

The NS leader attempted to protest against his banishment. He insisted that Hitler would not approve of such a step. Terboven, however, lying calmly, countered by saying that *der Führer* had already given his consent. This rejoinder completely deflated Quisling. Having no authority to refer to, he could come up with no effective counterarguments to those of the forceful *Reichskommissar*. As was common when he confronted Terboven alone, Quisling could not avoid being dominated by the more assertive *Reichskommissar*.[142]

When Quisling revealed what had transpired at the meeting, his close advisers had to try to rescue the situation, if not in whole, then in part. This followed an all too familiar pattern in the relationship between Quisling and Terboven. It became necessary for Quisling's lieutenants to stiffen his resolve vis-à-vis the *Reichskommissar*. In this instance, Hagelin in particular was very active. The *Fører*'s defenders spread the news that their leader had only gone along with Terboven because he did not have full command of German.[143] In meetings with representatives from the *Reichskommissariat*, Quisling's backers made every effort to get him out of his quandary. However, Terboven acted decisively to put an end to Quisling's procrastination when he once more held a face to face meeting with the NS *Fører* on June 29. The latter was pressured into signing a declaration of intent, promising to step down for the time being as leader of NS, accepting instead an "invitation" to go to Germany.[144] Furthermore, the *Reichskommissar*, without any consultation, informed Quisling that he had chosen Jonas Lie to be the acting head of NS.[145]

Terboven's promotion of Lie to take over as NS leader, supposedly only for the duration of Quisling's absence but in reality on a permanent basis, tied directly in with the *Reichskommissar*'s strategy for the creation of the State Council. Lie had already been accepted as a member of the body. Through him, Terboven planned to create a mass political movement that would gradually assume domination of the Council. Those members who were not beholden to the Germans would eventually be eased out. In carrying out this project, Terboven intended to make use of his protégés from the Fatherland League, who would join Lie's movement, as would also Fürst and Axel Stang, who would be in control of the Labor Service. With persons dependent on German good will in charge of the government, with Lie's political movement being the only one allowed to exist, and with the manpower and economic resources of the Labor Service at German disposal, Terboven believed that the situation in Norway would be fully in hand. In the heady atmosphere of triumph in the summer of 1940, he undoubtedly looked forward to the time when Norway would be completely absorbed into the Thousand Year Reich.[146]

Because there was no room for Quisling in Terboven's scheme of things, those who backed the NS leader or whose interests were linked with him fought energetically to defeat the *Reichskommissar*'s attempted takeover of NS on behalf of Lie. Not the least of these was Hagelin, who saw his entire position threatened if Lie managed to supplant Quisling. Hagelin therefore busied himself with sending off a stream of reports to Rosenberg's office at this time, warning of what Terboven was attempting to do.[147] Hagelin and Quisling, who remained in Norway for the time being, were especially concerned with preventing Lie, whom they regarded as a traitor, from taking over leadership. Backed energetically by Hagelin, Quisling never accepted Lie as his replacement. He insisted in correspondence with the *Reichskommissariat* that he alone would determine who would succeed him while he was in Germany. Terboven, however, continued to stress that Lie, upon Quisling's departure, would assume "temporary leadership".[148] The stalemate between the two remained unresolved, its outcome being decided by the broader question of whether or not Terboven's political strategy enjoyed success.

Despite their opposition to the *Reichskommissar*'s plans, Quisling and Hagelin acted on the assumption that the State Council would become a reality. They therefore tried to secure as much NS influence on the Council as possible, although their prospects, considering Terboven's attitude toward Quisling, did not appear particularly good to say the least.[149] Nevertheless, the two persevered, in particular the indefatigable Hagelin. He went so far as to promote his own candidacy for foreign minister, while seeking at the same time to prevent foes of NS such as Mogens, Ringnes, and others from being represented on the Council.[150]

Quisling and Hagelin clearly did not prefer the alternative of trying to exert NS influence through the State Council. They regarded its establishment in the same manner as they had previously viewed the Administrative Council. They would accept only it if the preferred option of having Quis-

ling head a government could not be realized. But at the same time they
were seeking the *Reichskommissariat*'s consent for NS membership on the
Council, they were doing everything in their power to sabotage Terboven's policy. They continued to be sustained in this effort by their allies
in Germany, Rosenberg's office and Raeder's naval command.

Rosenberg, despite the defeat he had suffered at the hands of Terboven,
had no intention of relinquishing his plans to have his organization play a
major role in Norway through support of Quisling. He therefore began a
counteroffensive against the *Reichskommissar* after the latter had succeeded
in expelling Scheidt from Norway and eliminating Schickedanz from the
Reich Chancellery. Typically, Rosenberg conducted this offensive largely
on paper. He and his staff drew up a voluminous series of reports justifying why Quisling should be assisted, and showing why Terboven's policy
was in error.[151] Much of the information they utilized was provided by
Hagelin, who kept Rosenberg's organization well supplied with a continuous stream of highly colored reports. He succeeded in sending his attacks
against Terboven out of the country thanks to the conduit which the navy
made accessible to him. Schreiber, who unlike Scheidt had managed to stay
in Norway as Admiral Boehm's adjutant, forwarded Hagelin's reports to
Raeder's chief of staff in Berlin, who in turn relayed them on to
Schickedanz.[152] On the basis of these accounts, plus information supplied
by the always eager Scheidt, Rosenberg's office presented a large memorandum, complete with thirty appendices, to the Reich Chancellery on
June 20.[153]

   This material arrived too late to influence Hitler's discussions with Terboven, when the *Reichskommissar* gained approval for going ahead with
his plan for setting up the State Council.[154] However, during the time that
Dellbrügge was conducting his negotiations concerning the make-up of the
Council, and Terboven simultaneously was making his move to oust Quisling as head of NS in favor of Lie, in Berlin the barrage of reports emanating from Rosenberg's office increasingly made themselves felt.

   Simultaneously, the navy continued to exert itself on Quisling's behalf.
This occurred not solely because of Raeder's personal positive attitude
toward the NS *Fører*. More significantly, the navy wished to occupy a
dominant economic and military position in Norway in order to satisfy its
interests. In particular, it desired to use Norway's metallurgical resources
for its construction needs. Raeder therefore remained closely associated
with Rosenberg's organization in seeking to secure a government led by
Quisling, a government that would be tied to the *Kriegsmarine* as well as
to the NSDAP's Office of Foreign Affairs. The navy already regarded Terboven with suspicion because of his connections with Göring, Raeder's
bitter enemy within the military command. Therefore, when the *Reichs-*

kommissar attempted to sidetrack Quisling, the navy inevitably moved to thwart Terboven's plans.

The latter did not appear to be fully informed at the time concerning the extent to which the navy had committed itself in the struggle on Quisling's behalf. Had Terboven been aware of this, he would have been far more guarded in his discussions with the naval command in Norway. On June 30, after Dellbrügge had completed the State Council negotiations, Terboven held a breakfast for the commanders of the three branches of the German military in Norway. They met at Terboven's new residence, Skaugum, whose previous occupants had been the Crown Prince and his family. Falkenhorst and the air force commander, Hans Jürgen Stumpf, had no objections as they listened to the *Reichskommissar*'s optimistic plans for the State Council and for Jonas Lie's replacement of Quisling. Admiral Boehm's reaction, however, differed considerably. He both raised questions and stated objections. But Terboven, in a confident mood after the apparently successful conclusion of his move to reorganize the governmental structure, took little notice and talked with far too much candor for his own good.

He bluntly stated his assessment of Quisling. He maintained that he had repeatedly sought to cooperate with Quisling by holding a number of discussions with him. But Terboven declared that while Quisling was a respectable person, he was extremely stupid. He lacked ideas and sought to gain success almost entirely by imitating *der Führer*. Terboven further stressed that Quisling had been overwhelmingly rejected by the Norwegians and was totally lacking in support. The *Reichskommissar* argued that it was therefore impossible to work with Quisling, since he stood in the way of allowing the Germans to reach a settlement with the Norwegians. This was why, said Terboven, he had decided to replace Quisling with Lie. He bragged how he had called the NS leader to a meeting, and how he had induced Quisling to accept his fate with the use of "drinks and a club". According to Terboven, Quisling had first rejected the idea of stepping down, but gave in when the *Reichskommissar* drew the comparison with Hitler, who had also withdrawn from politics for a year following the failure of the Munich coup in 1923.[155] Terboven no doubt neglected to mention that the reason for der *Führer*'s absence was that he languished in jail during this period.

Boehm immediately forwarded this information to Raeder.[156] Although the exact time of their meeting is not known, Raeder soon afterwards discussed these developments with Hitler, rejecting completely Terboven's course of action in Norway.[157]

The strong opposition emanating from Raeder and Rosenberg began to have results by the early part of July. Their constant resistance to Terboven's Norwegian policy affected Hitler, as the *Reichskommissar* discovered when he flew to Germany on July 1. He expected to receive *der*

Führer's final approval for the establishment of the State Council. But when he met with Hitler on the following day,[158] he discovered to his shock that his entire plan was in serious jeopardy. Although no specific account of the meeting exists, it is clear that *der Führer* rejected Terboven's approach, insisting instead that Quisling should not be abandoned.[159] Hitler did not, however, provide a specific formula for how Norway should be administered. He had other more important matters which preoccupied him at this time, shortly after the fall of France. Nevertheless, he showed clearly that he was angry with Terboven because of the latter's treatment of Quisling. For the time being, however, the Norwegian question had to be postponed until Hitler had the opportunity to give it his full consideration.

Terboven rather unwisely did not allow even this rebuff to prevent him from attempting to carry out a course of action that he was determined to pursue. The strong-willed *Reichskommissar* proceeded instead to move forcefully against his opposition in Norway. On July 3, after he had held his meeting with Hitler, Terboven was no doubt responsible for having Hagelin called in and questioned by the secret police. During this rather disagreeable interview, Quisling's lieutenant was strongly encouraged to accept Jonas Lie's designation as the new leader of NS. Terboven followed this up when he returned to Oslo on July 5. He was clearly interested in getting his hands on any incriminating material that he could use against Quisling. The Gestapo carried out a thorough inquiry concerning Quisling's past, including the Pepper Affair and his sympathy for Communism in the 1920's.[160]

These moves were simply a prelude to Terboven's most ambitious undertaking – to secure Quisling's ouster from Norway. The *Reichskommissar* proceeded to carry out the deportation immediately under cover of an invitation to visit Germany, signed by Goebbels, which Terboven had brought with him. To his shock, Quisling found himself dispatched out of the country on July 5 under the escort of one of Terboven's close subordinates, Georg Wilhelm Müller, head of the *Reichskommissariat*'s Propaganda Department.

This decisive effort by Terboven to rid himself of Quisling did not turn out as expected, however. Hagelin, jealously guarding the *Fører*'s interests, telegraphed immediately in code to Schickedanz that Quisling had been sent to Berlin.[161] Rosenberg's organization thereby had the opportunity to move to secure control of Quisling. When the latter arrived in Germany, it proved impossible for Terboven's man, Müller, to keep Quisling under his authority. Within a short time the NS leader had found refuge with Rosenberg.[162] Terboven's hope of freeing himself from Quisling's influence had thereby suffered a severe setback.

With Quisling at their side, Terboven's enemies now had a firsthand source of information which they could effectively make use of against the highhanded *Reichskommissar*. Rosenberg immediately drew up a critical memorandum, based on a personal conversation with Quisling. The document did not restrict itself just to the *Reichskommissar*. Through Rosenberg, Quisling made full use of the opportunity to attack his most dangerous rivals in Norway, the Fatherland League group centered around Victor Mogens. Using the most telling arguments that he believed would influence Hitler, Quisling insinuated that leading members of the League either were Jews or had close ties with Jews. For example, the memorandum emphasized Mogens' marriage to a "Jewess".[163]

With the aid of Schickedanz, Quisling also drew up a personal letter addressed to Hitler. He issued a blanket complaint against the treatment he had received from German officials, going back to the time of Dr. Bräuer. He maintained that not one of the assurances of support which he had received from these officials had actually been carried out. Instead, he alleged that the Germans in Norway had been hoodwinked by anti-German plutocrats, while he had unfairly been pilloried as a traitor. This discriminatory treatment, said Quisling, had continued under Terboven. He revealed how the *Reichskommissar* had worked to oust him as head of his party by threatening to withhold funds for its use and by seeking to have the "renegade", Jonas Lie, assume leadership. Quisling appealed to Hitler to intervene and to change the decisions that were being made in Norway. As he had done before, he insisted that he would already have secured the support of the majority of the people if only he had received full German backing from the very beginning. He furthermore argued that he understood the Norwegian mentality, something which the German officials on the scene had been incapable of doing. In asking for Hitler's personal support, Quisling, as previously, presented himself as the completely loyal vassal, declaring that he placed himself at *der Führer*'s disposal to work for "my fatherland's and Greater Germany's joint goal", which he described as "a greater Germanic union with Norway's free adherence to the Greater Germanic Reich".[164]

This letter, dated July 10 but quite probably written earlier, was forwarded to Hitler along with Rosenberg's memorandum.[165] With the *Reichsleiter* pursuing Quisling's interests in such a strong manner, ably seconded by Raeder, direct intervention by *der Führer* became a certainty. Hitler, who still retained personal sympathy for Quisling, could not ignore the constant attacks against Terboven, in particular when the NS *Fører* was in Germany complaining of severe mistreatment at the hands of the *Reichskommissar*. Through his personal involvement in the question of Norway's political future, Hitler thereby eliminated the possibility that Terboven by himself would be able to shape developments in Norway. Although the exact date cannot be determined, Hitler met personally with Quisling some time soon after the latter had arrived in Germany, quite probably some time on or about July 10.[166]

The Nazi warlord could not on the spur of the moment make concrete decisions concerning Norway, but he did assure Quisling of his full confidence. Furthermore, Hitler moved to place the independent-minded *Reichskommissar* completely at his disposal. Terboven came to Germany on July 11, no doubt upon orders from Berlin. He remained away from Norway for no less than ten days.[167] He had lost control of the course of events. Immediately after he arrived in Germany, instructions were sent to the *Reichskommissariat* in Oslo which ordered that all political preparations should come to a halt pending future decisions.[168] Terboven's plans for a State Council had thereupon been placed on ice. No significant political movement occurred in Norway for the duration of July and August. Not until September, following key decisions by Hitler, did political activity resume.

This rather protracted delay was caused by Hitler's preoccupation with England during the summer months. He did, however, meet with Terboven and gave the *Reichskommissar* a clear indication of his attitude toward Norway. Hitler had determined that any political settlement would have to include a place for Quisling. Terboven did his best to persuade his *Führer* that Quisling was a liability, but he failed to win approval for his point of view. Hitler totally rejected Terboven's arguments, and to complete the latter's humiliation, he received instruction from Hitler to consult with Rosenberg about the political situation in Norway.[169] Terboven, who had all along sought to have a free hand, found it especially bitter to have to take into account Rosenberg's interests, in particular since he previously believed he had successfully thwarted Rosenberg's attempt to exercise influence in Norway.

As ordered by Hitler, the two rivals met on July 20. Rosenberg persevered in his effort to influence Norwegian affairs through Quisling. But Terboven, despite the reprimands that had seriously undermined his authority, still sought to create a political solution as close as possible to his original plan. Because of Hitler's strong backing for Quisling, the *Reichskommissar* reluctantly had to concede that Quisling would continue as NS *Fører* and that he would play a future role in politics. Terboven took special care, however, not to specify the exact position which Quisling could expect to hold. The *Reichskommissar* furthermore refused to commit himself to allowing NS to have greater representation on the State Council, despite Rosenberg's urgings. He similarly did not respond to Rosenberg's endeavor to secure more direct influence in Norway by having a number of his subordinates stationed in the country.[170]

Rosenberg derived little satisfaction from the meeting, having received no concrete concessions. This caused him to write yet another letter to

Hitler on the next day, urging the direct establishment of an NS regime. Rosenberg also continued to attack Terboven not only for having mistreated Quisling, but also for his opposition to Scheidt and Hagelin, and for his attempt to remove Quisling in favor of Jonas Lie.[171]

The failure of the meeting between the Nazi ideologue and the assertive *Reichskommissar* meant that Hitler would still have to make a decision. Terboven came back to Norway on July 21 with the bitter knowledge that he no longer had control over future events. He could at best hope to add his restricted opinion as but one of a number of participants in a decision-making process whose final conclusion would be determined by *der Führer*. Terboven tried to keep his defeat to himself, informing his co-workers in the *Reichskommissariat* as little as possible of what had occurred.[172] He went so far as to maintain that Hitler had accepted his recommendations. But he could not avoid, even if indirectly, touching upon the setback his plans had received. He had to make known to his immediate subordinates that Quisling would continue as NS leader rather than languish in exile.[173]

This was an especially unpleasant pill for Terboven to swallow because while he was in Germany his subordinates, acting on his previous orders, had made an attempt to take over leadership of Quisling's party on behalf of Lie. However, when they sought to execute this move, they ran into intransigent opposition from Quisling's loyalists. The ever-resourceful Hagelin stood in the forefront of NS' defense. When informed by officials of the *Reichskommissariat* that Quisling had been removed and that Lie had succeeded him, Hagelin on the spot improvised a delaying tactics, telling the surprised Germans that Quisling, before departing for Berlin, had appointed him as acting head of NS.[174]

The *Reichskommissariat*, of course, refused to accept Hagelin's brazen claim. It attempted to coerce NS into accepting Lie by applying economic pressure. The Germans drastically reduced the amount of funds which they made available. NS received less money from the *Reichskommissariat* during July 1940, when Quisling's fate hung in the balance, than in any month following the invasion.[175] As a result, NS was hard-pressed, forced to take out loans in order to make up for the loss of German financing.[176]

Hagelin's resourceful action proved to be of some importance. Although Quisling's ultimate fate rested with Hitler, if Terboven had been successful in temporarily replacing Quisling with Lie, this could have exerted a weakening influence on Quisling. In order to restore him, Hitler would have had to repudiate his *Reichskommissar*, which he might have been reluctant to do. Thanks to Hagelin's bluff, this eventuality never materialized.

Quisling therefore did not have to be directly concerned about his party's leadership during his absence, although the threat of Lie, supported by Terboven, always lingered in the background. In July and the first half of August, while Hitler was absorbed in the Battle of Britain, Quisling spent a great deal of time travelling in Germany, becoming acquainted with the Nazi party's apparatus and learning about the economy. Formally, he did so as Goebbels' guest, but in reality Rosenberg acted as his host. In his travels, the NS leader often had Scheidt along as guide, the latter making a limited comeback following his previous dramatic ouster at the hands of Terboven.[177]

While Quisling enjoyed his summer excursions, in Norway considerable uncertainty existed about the delay in arriving at a permanent political settlement. Hagelin informed Schickedanz on August 5 of the worry which NS members felt about not having received any news concerning their leader in Germany.[178] But as time elapsed, those who were informed, which included many who were not pleased by developments, increasingly gained the impression that Quisling's comeback was assured.[179] It only remained for Hitler to set aside time to make a definite decision.

Terboven did take advantage of Hitler's preoccupation with other matters to try to neutralize the effects of Quisling's return. The determined *Reichskommissar* had not yet given up his endeavor to further the interests of the Fatherland League group. The *Reichskommissariat* permitted individuals such as Mogens, Albert Wiesener, Hjort, and Jacobsen to engage in propaganda activity which went so far as to include attacks on NS. On the other hand, Quisling's party was held in check, not being allowed to retaliate against Mogens. Furthermore, NS continued to be denied financial support, which it desperately needed, in particular in order to keep *Fritt Folk* in operation.[180]

If Terboven could no longer discredit Quisling entirely, then he hoped at the least to be able to infiltrate NS with persons whom he trusted, and who might be useful in future attempts to outmaneuver Quisling. Terboven indicated his intentions when he briefly visited Germany for consultations in early August. At this time, one of his close associates, Hans-Hendrik Neumann, who bore responsibility for providing NS with guidance, made a revealing proposition to Schickedanz and Scheidt. Neumann futilely attempted to persuade the two members of Rosenberg's staff to use their influence with Quisling in order to permit Lie, Mogens, and Jacobsen to become members of NS.[181] While the incident had no future ramifications, it did reveal that while the *Reichskommissariat* could exercise daily control over NS in Norway, in Berlin Terboven's representative had to appear before Quisling's backers as a supplicant.

This hiatus ended on August 16, when Hitler made a preliminary move to eliminate the uncertainty of the political situation in Norway. *Der Führer* received Quisling, who was accompanied by the ever-present

Scheidt. Dr. Lammers and Martin Bormann were also in attendance, indicating the importance that Hitler attached to the discussions. Quite uniquely, Hitler complimented Quisling by allowing him to begin the meeting. The NS leader responded by repeating past complaints about the mistreatment he and his party had received at the hands of German administrators, from Bräuer to Terboven. Hitler, becoming impatient after a while, interrupted to raise the more concrete question of what Quisling had to suggest as a solution. As always, the NS *Fører* responded by stating his preference for an NS-controlled government, although he professed that at this point it did not matter whether or not he assumed leadership. He did insist, however, that the *Storting* should be dissolved, and that the new government should have the goal of working toward the time when Norway would be directly united with Germany.[182]

In response, Hitler did not make any commitment concerning Quisling's proposed NS government. *Der Führer* was primarily interested in smoothing over the friction between Quisling and Terboven. He maintained that Bräuer and Habicht had assumed a negative attitude toward NS because they had been fooled by Norwegian jurists, and that Terboven in reality only wished to do what was best for Quisling and NS. Unfortunately, said Hitler, German representatives at times had difficulty in gaining a true understanding of conditions in foreign countries. He declared agreement with Quisling's practice of going directly at one's goals in politics, and he promised to call Terboven to Berlin in the next few days in order to have a discussion about Norway. At the end of the meeting, Hitler applied his famous charm, thanking Quisling for having provided warning of the danger that England posed for Norway, and assuring him of Hitler's conviction that Quisling was always motivated by the highest ideals which would lead toward the creation of a greater Germanic union. *Der Führer* further declared that a new, rejuvenated Norway would soon learn that membership in such a union was in its interest, and that it would take its place in this union under Quisling's leadership. Hitler gave full assurance that Quisling could place his trust in him.[183]

Quisling was jubilant over the result of this meeting, drawing the conclusion that he had received *der Führer*'s promise to give him future control of Norway's government. His optimistic outlook soon spread to his followers in Norway. Konrad Sundlo sent out a bulletin to the party faithful on August 18 in which he indicated that reports from Berlin revealed with certainty that "Quisling has received leadership of the future development in Norway". He did concede that details had not yet been clearly worked out as to whether Quisling would head solely an NS government, a government dominated by NS, or something else. However, Quisling's leadership, said Sundlo, was certain. The colonel reported he had personally talked with an NS member who had been with Quisling in Berlin, and that "Quisling was in sparkling humor over this turn of events". NS members, said Sundlo, could expect their *Fører* back home "any day now".[184]

The prognosis of Quisling's imminent return proved accurate. He came back to Norway just two days later. *Fritt Folk*, which printed an enthusiastic welcome, also admitted for the first time that he had been absent in Germany. The NS paper could not avoid confessing that prospects had been bleak for a time during the summer. But it now confidently asserted that the future would be bright as a result of the *Fører*'s comeback: "Quisling has now returned, and we now know that victory is ours".[185]

As he had done earlier, and would later repeat, Quisling made the mistake of assuming that Hitler's general statements of support meant he had promised the NS leader dominant control over Norwegian affairs. This interpretation proved to be far too optimistic. When Hitler met with Quisling on August 16, his thoughts were inevitably colored by wartime considerations. Just previously, at the end of July, he had made the fateful decision to launch an attack against the Soviet Union. Such an invasion would invariably involve Norway's northernmost provinces, Finnmark and Troms. Already in early August the Germans began to stage a strong build-up of troops in this region.[186]

These military requirements precluded any possibility that the Germans might lessen their sway in Norway. This state of affairs differed entirely from the conditions that had been in effect less than two months earlier, following the fall of France. At that time general opinion within the *Reichskommissariat* had expectantly assumed that most of the German administration in Norway would soon be abolished. When making plans for the establishment of the State Council in June, Terboven had acted on this assumption. He looked forward to being replaced by a special emissary once the Council had begun to function. He anticipated receiving Hitler's permission to return to his old post as *Gauleiter* in Essen, which since the fall of the Low Countries had the potential through expansion of becoming one of the greatest industrial centers in the world.[187]

During the second half of July, however, the possibility of abolishing the *Reichskommissariat*, which the Germans had promised the Norwegians during the State Council negotiations, disappeared forever. Instead, the trend from this time onward was to build up the *Reichskommissar*'s administrative apparatus, enabling it to extend its control over Norwegian administration.[188] Hitler revealed no inclination of lessening German domination in August. On the contrary, he already looked forward to the time when Norway would be absorbed into the Greater German Reich, discussing enthusiastically with Albert Speer his plans for converting Trondheim into the Reich's northernmost cultural center.[189]

Hitler called Terboven to a meeting on August 21 in order to provide his *Reichskommissar* with orders concerning the political situation in Norway. This corresponded fully with what Hitler had told Quisling he would do.[190] But the NS leader did not receive a free hand in Hitler's instructions to Terboven. Typically, *der Führer* did not commit himself to details. He indicated that the composition and type of future government in Norway would have to result from negotiations between Quisling and Terboven, with Hitler reserving ultimate power for himself by having the final say.

Terboven thereby sustained the setback of having to remain in Norway for the duration of the occupation as the head of the *Reichskommissariat.* He also suffered the fate of having to maintain, at least outwardly, a semblance of cooperation and comradeship with a man whom he disliked intensely. Terboven objected to Quisling not merely because he regarded the NS leader as a political liability, but more importantly because he thwarted the *Reichskommissar*'s ambitions. But the latter could no longer openly oppose Quisling when he returned to Norway, as he had done previously. Because of Hitler's good will, the NS *Fører* enjoyed a strong bargaining position. Terboven, on the other hand, was in disfavor, a fact that Hitler had made quite plain to him in their discussions.[191]

The bitter rivals, now forced to try to seek a settlement, held two meetings in late August, the first on August 23, the second on August 27 or 28.[192] The only item that they agreed upon was the necessity of replacing the Administrative Council with a more pro-German form of government. But beyond this obvious conclusion, they failed to reach a satisfactory arrangement. Terboven proposed setting up a purely German administration. He argued that this would function on an interim basis only until NS was in an advantageous position to take over the government.[193] His obvious ploy was to buy time while exercising full control over the country's administration.[194] But Quisling, dealing from strength and acting on the advice of Hagelin, rejected this attempt to thwart NS from gaining direct representation in the new government. As always, he responded directly, insisting on the creation of a "Norwegian government" in which NS would enjoy an absolute majority. In support of this proposal, he presented arguments that were general in nature and which he did not substantiate. He went so far as to declare that the public was ready to accept his type of government. Were a German administration to be established instead, not only would this please Germany's and NS' opponents, he maintained, but it would cause great disappointment in wide circles, also outside NS.[195]

Not merely should his party hold a majority in the government that he envisaged, but he further insisted that NS members should be given the most important positions in the new body and exercise actual leadership. As a concession to Terboven's earlier politics, Quisling declared that if his terms were agreed upon, he personally would not join the government.

However, the officially designated head of government, whom he referred to as "the Minister President", had to receive his sanction, even if this person did not formally belong to NS.[196]

When presenting arguments in favor of such a government, Quisling's reasoning was not particularly well substantiated. He acknowledged indirectly that NS was held in contempt by the majority of the people when he declared that if the head of the government did not belong to NS, opposition to this new body would essentially be broken. Similarly, he admitted that his small group of followers did not include experts needed to run certain departments. Those placed in charge of social affairs, agriculture, labor, and finance, he agreed, could come from outside of NS. This, he alleged, would give the government a broader base, but he insisted on maintaining control by exercising his approval of those who were to hold these positions.[197]

No matter how inadequately reasoned or supported his views might be, Terboven could not ignore the NS leader and his party. Because of Hitler's support for Quisling, the amount of financial backing which NS received from the *Reichskommissariat* increased tremendously, beginning on August 22, just two days after Quisling's triumphant return. On August 26 Terboven paid off all of the party's outstanding debts. From this time onwards NS received large and regular financial payments. In September the party obtained 234,850 *Reichsmark*, no less than almost thirteen times the amount it had been given in July when Terboven was trying to rid himself of Quisling.[198]

So great was the NS leader's influence at this time that it is not an exaggeration to say that he exercised veto power over the *Reichskommissar*. When Terboven indicated he might go ahead with the implementation of his plan for a German administration without Quisling's approval, the latter, acting on the advice of Scheidt,[199] insisted that his views be presented to Hitler.[200] Terboven had no means at this time, either formally or informally, of preventing Quisling from going over his head and appealing directly to Berlin. Quisling's partisans maintained their direct line of communication to Germany thanks to the navy's independent position. At the time Terboven received Quisling's objections in written form, with the message that they be forwarded to Hitler, they had already been sent unofficially to Rosenberg's office, and then on to the Reich Chancellery.[201]

With the two antagonists unable to reach agreement, Hitler again had to become directly engaged. *Der Führer* called both Terboven and Quisling to Berlin, whereupon he focused his attention on the Norwegian question in talks held on September 4 and 5.[202] Contrary to what he and his backers had anticipated, Quisling did not succeed in gaining the type of government he desired. Instead, Hitler decided to give Terboven approval to resume the long-stalled State Council negotiations. However, *der Führer* carefully balanced his decision in such a manner that neither Terboven nor Quisling had the upper hand. Quisling was not frozen out. His representatives were guaranteed posts in the government which would result from the negotiations.[203]

Despite this assurance, the outcome of the discussions with Hitler was disappointing for the NS leader. His party would not immediately be permitted to form a government, and the *Storting* had not been disavowed. By again being able to renew negotiations with the parliament's leadership, Terboven had the opportunity of seeking to achieve his old goal of reaching a quasi-legal agreement which the German administration could turn to its advantage. Quisling received a further setback at this time when he failed to persuade Hitler, through Lammers, to abolish the title of *Reichskommissar* in favor of a less authoritarian-sounding term.[204]

Upon returning to Oslo, Terboven did not, however, enjoy a free hand when representatives from the *Reichskommissariat* resumed the State Council negotiations. The *Reichskommissar* occupied an entirely different position from the one he had held in June. He now had to take into account Quisling's interests. NS had to be represented in the government, and the party leader had to be consulted concerning its make-up. These requirements greatly restrained Terboven's freedom of action, adding a severe liability to his task of reaching a settlement.

Nevertheless, he moved quickly to try to make the best of the situation. He met with Quisling already on September 7, the day the negotiations were resumed. The conference between the two took place with no one else present, a situation that Terboven usually turned to his advantage, since he could dominate Quisling with his more forceful presence and his ability to benefit from the NS leader's somewhat restricted command of German. The *Reichskommissar* came prepared to the meeting, having at hand a complete list of candidates for the new State Council. He proposed that the body be made up of fifteen department heads. Of these, he suggested that four be from NS, while an additional four members would be obligated to NS in one way or another, although they might not formally belong to the party. In this manner, Terboven maintained that Quisling's party would enjoy a "majority" on the Council.[205]

Although this arrangement on paper appeared to give NS predominance on the Council, thereby creating the possibility for NS later to take complete control of government, a closer examination of Terboven's proposal revealed that it was fashioned in such a way as to give him considerable influence, if not ascendancy, over the body. No specific details were provided as to how the four members designated as "sympathizers" would be obligated to NS. Furthermore, this possibility did not appear very likely, since none had previously been favorable toward Quisling.[206] In addition, only one of the four NS members whom Terboven recommended was fully committed to Quisling, namely Gulbrand Lunde, who was nominated to head the Department of Information. Jonas Lie, the proposed Minister of Police, was hardly a reassuring prospect for Quisling. Axel Stang, scheduled to head the Labor Service Department, also had direct ties with the *Reichskommissariat* dating back to the earlier State Council negotiations. The last NS candidate happened to be Quisling's old friend, Frederik Prytz.[207] But the latter was not in Quisling's good books at this time. Not only had he earlier refused to accept appointment in Quisling's abortive April government, but he also strongly opposed Hagelin's influence. Prytz had become a bitter enemy of Hagelin within NS, having established ties with the *Reichskommissariat*.[208] His loyalty to Quisling, especially when the latter was advised by Hagelin, could hardly be depended upon.

The only really significant indication that Quisling did enjoy greater strength than previously was the reduction of the Fatherland League faction's representation, which Terboven had favored in June. Only Ringnes remained designated for the Foreign Ministry, while such strong foes of Quisling as Victor Mogens and J. B. Hjort were omitted entirely.

Quisling naturally objected to Lie becoming a member of the State Council as an NS representative, considering the threat Lie had previously been to his leadership. But Terboven acted insistently on Lie's behalf, declaring that he would guarantee that Lie would apologize for his past actions, and that he would henceforth be loyal to Quisling and NS.[209] Some time during the next few days Lie humbled himself before Quisling.[210] The former "renegade", if still under suspicion, thereupon was received back into the fold.

The State Council negotiations resumed later in the day after Quisling had held his meeting with Terboven. The Norwegian participants were alarmed to discover that the basis for the talks had changed greatly from what had been their understanding when they had last met in June. Not only was NS much more strongly represented on the list of prospective members, but the two main German concessions had been withdrawn. Quisling remained in the country and the *Reichskommissariat* would not be abolished. Moreover, while the Germans now withdrew these previous promises, they continued to demand that parliament should declare the throne vacant and that the State Council's members could be co-opted without the *Storting*'s approval.[211]

Despite these revised conditions, the Norwegian negotiators felt the need to proceed with the discussions. In addition to the strong leverage which the Germans exerted because of their military predominance, the Norwegians were intimidated by Dellbrügge's threat that if a State Council failed to come into existence, then Hitler would decide on either a commissarial type of government or a Quisling administration.[212] The possibility of having a system in which no major Norwegian interests were represented to mitigate the effects of the occupation clearly affected the Norwegian decision to accept the altered circumstances under which the negotiations took place.

Terboven, however, could not manipulate the proceedings as he wished. He was under extreme pressure to reach an agreement as soon as possible. Hitler expected a rapid settlement, with Terboven being scheduled to meet his *Führer* already on September 11.

The Council deliberations entered into a new phase on September 10, when for the first time the regular *Storting* representatives met in their respective party groups to vote on the results of the negotiations, which had been conducted by the parliament's Presidency up to that point. Despite strong pressure exerted by the board, the representatives refused to force the King to abdicate. A simple majority of 75 to 55 did agree to suspend him until a peace settlement could be made. This did not prove to be a binding vote, however, because (1) it was strictly advisory, (2) numerically it could not have been implemented since a two-thirds majority was needed for a change in the Constitution, and (3) some twenty representatives from northern Norway were not present to cast their votes.[213]

The vote did serve as a guideline for the *Storting*'s Presidency, whose members persevered in continuing the negotiations. In his need to reach a quick accommodation, Terboven now gave in on his previous demand that the King be removed, declaring himself willing to accept the King's suspension.[214] But while the Presidency tentatively acceded to this point, no agreement could be reached concerning future appointments to the State Council. The *Storting* insisted that it, through its leaders on the Presidency, should have the final say in approving the Council's composition. This claim by democratically elected representatives conflicted with the basic principles of Nazi Germany. It also served as a roadblock to a future NS takeover of the government, which Hitler currently favored. In addition, Terboven hardly approved of having members on the State Council outside of his direct influence. For these reasons, the *Reichskommissar*'s representatives only gave meaningless assurances on this question. The *Storting* representatives, on the other hand, refused to leave the issue unsettled, insisting that the Presidency should have the final say.

The objections had not been overcome by the time Terboven departed for Berlin on the afternoon of September 11.[215] The deadlock could only be resolved following his return from Germany, where once more everything depended on *der Führer*'s attitude.

On the eve of his visit to Germany, Terboven faced difficulty not merely because of the *Storting*'s objections to having its influence virtually eliminated, but also due to continued obstruction from Quisling, ably seconded by Hagelin. The latter again reacted with consternation when he learned how Quisling had been dominated by Terboven at the September 7 meeting. Hagelin responded by exerting himself strenuously to bolster the NS leader's position. As a result, a second meeting was arranged between Quisling and Terboven on September 9, resulting in the removal of Prytz, Hagelin's rival within NS, from the State Council list in favor of a much more compliant and anonymous NS member, Thorleif Dahl.[216] In order to avoid any possible attempt by Terboven to circumvent Quisling's claims, a letter was also drawn up and sent to the *Reichskommissar*, spelling out specifically Quisling's viewpoint in the discussions that he had held with Terboven. This clear delineation of the NS *Fører*'s stand was done in accordance with instructions received from Rosenberg's office. Quisling was especially concerned with having direct command of the NS members on the Council in order to prevent any type of insubordination. His need to secure such control was obvious because of Terboven's previous attempt to remove him, and also because of the memory of challenges to his authority that had weakened NS in past years. The four NS members on the State Council were therefore required to adhere to "absolute discipline" and to give full "loyalty" to NS and its leader. If they resigned from the party, they would automatically be removed from the government, to be replaced by NS members approved by Quisling.[217]

In addition, Quisling insisted that the four members of the Council designated as NS sympathizers should also be under specific obligations to him. He wished to have them sign a declaration promising to further NS' program and the party's interests, and to "cleanse their departments and areas of administration of persons hostile to NS and the Germans", replacing such individuals with NS members. If anyone violated his declaration, then Terboven would be obliged to replace him with an NS member. But what mattered most for Quisling was that all non-NS members of the State Council, both those obligated to sign the NS loyalty declaration and those who were not, should only administer their offices on a temporary basis. They were to be replaced by NS members as soon as possible "so that the complete takeover of power by NS shall occur at the latest in the spring of 1941". Hagelin's influence on Quisling was revealed especially by the NS *Fører* declaring his preference that his chief adviser be allowed to assume a ministerial post as soon as possible, ideally by initially joining the State Council at its inception as Minister without Portfolio.[218]

This insistence that NS should exert strong dominance over the State Council from the beginning came as a most unwelcome demand for Terboven, whose negotiators were having enough difficulty in attempting to secure the *Storting*'s approval. In particular, the requirement that non-NS members should be obligated to sign loyalty declarations posed a severe problem. Terboven attempted to avoid this touchy matter by seeking to

postpone its implementation until all necessary preparations for the State
Council had first been made. He undoubtedly intended to pressure Quisling to forego the declarations or to accept rather innocuous statements,
something which the *Fører* might be forced to approve rather than be held
responsible for the failure of the entire State Council plan. Hagelin feared
this possibility, and his fears were not groundless.[219]

Any attempt to secure loyalty declarations from persons outside of NS
was an extremely difficult enterprise, as an incident involving Ellef Ringnes
so amply demonstrated. He was nominated as Foreign Minister on the
Council. However, because of his connection with the Mogens faction, he
was definitely not in Quisling's good books. The latter therefore insisted
that Ringnes be forced to apologize for having acted against NS, much in
the manner that Lie had been compelled to make his peace with Quisling.
Terboven agreed to the demand, and Ringnes, accompanied by a representative from the *Reichskommissariat*, arrived to present his apology to
Quisling on September 10. Hagelin also was present.[220] The meeting turned
out to be anything but harmonious. Quisling and Hagelin did not find
Ringnes' apology satisfactory.[221] On the other hand, Ringnes reacted with
astonishment when Quisling suddenly demanded that he sign an affirmation of loyalty. He indignantly refused. Ringnes had no knowledge that
such a declaration would be a prerequisite for service on the State Council,
since Terboven had kept it secret from even his representatives who were
engaged in the negotiations.[222]

This clash showed just how hard it would have been to obtain the required loyalty statements from non-NS members on the proposed Council. To their satisfaction, however, Quisling and Hagelin used the incident
as justification to demand that Ringnes be dropped as Foreign Minister. In
his place they proposed Captain Kjeld Stub Irgens.[223] The latter served as
an acceptable compromise candidate. While he had established a cordial relationship with the *Reichskommissariat*, he had previously acted on Quisling's behalf, and he was after all Hagelin's brother-in-law.

When Terboven, accompanied by Quisling, departed for Berlin on the
11th, he understandably did not leave in a happy frame of mind. His
Führer, who was already exasperated with him, would certainly fail to ap-
preciate the fact that the political situation in Norway remained unsettled.
Not only had the *Storting* representatives proved to be reluctant in acced-
ing to Terboven's terms, but Quisling, encouraged by Hagelin, was insisting on concrete assurance that NS would control the Council, illustrated
most recently by their demand for loyalty declarations and the elimination
of Ringnes.

Terboven, however, was not the only major participant in determining
Norway's political future who had anxiety about the coming meeting.

Hagelin had been left behind, and he feared that without his presence to back up the less forceful Quisling, the NS leader might just compromise away the strong advantage he possessed. In a letter to Schickedanz on the day of Quisling's departure, Hagelin voiced his fears, providing a revealing indication of his opinion of Quisling as a negotiator:

> You must without reservation make it clear to Victor [Quisling's code name] ... that he *never* negotiates by himself ... Similarly, you must make it clear to him that he in the future abides by agreements that he has made with you in each instance and *under all circumstances*, and that he on no account allows himself to abandon [the agreements].[224]

But while he expressed himself bluntly, Hagelin realized how touchy Quisling was on matters concerning his status as leader of NS. Hagelin therefore emphasized the need for Schickedanz to give his advice "very diplomatically" so that "Victor" would not be offended or feel that he had been talked about.[225]

Hagelin's worries proved unwarranted. The meeting with Hitler went clearly in Quisling's favor. Already on the evening of September 11 he met with *der Führer* for a two and a half hour conference. Schickedanz reported optimistically on the outcome to Rosenberg on the following day: "All in all, things are going well and Terboven must follow a line that he has steadily opposed".[226] In a subsequent meeting attended by both Quisling and Terboven, Hitler confirmed that the *Reichskommissar* would have to accept the inevitability of Quisling's takeover of the government in the not too distant future. Hitler charged Terboven with responsibility for concluding the State Council negotiations in a satisfactory manner, which meant that an NS majority had to be ensured. Hitler even involved himself in the make-up of the Council, declaring that he approved of Quisling's candidate, Irgens, as a replacement for Ringnes.[227]

Moreover, the meeting made clear that the State Council would merely serve as a temporary institution, soon to be supplanted by a pure NS government headed by Quisling. The NS *Fører* thereby had his expectation realized, being convinced that his government was scheduled to come into existence at the latest in the spring of 1941. He received further direct affirmation that he could expect to head a government even if Terboven did not succeed in inducing the *Storting* through threats and persuasion to sanction the State Council. If the goal of establishing a State Council failed to materialize, then Hitler ordered Terboven to appoint a commissarial form of government in consultation with Quisling.[228] And in the eventuality that a commissarial government were established, it would not, like the State Council, be permanent, but would serve merely as a caretaker body for an eventual Quisling government.

Having received these assurances from Hitler, Quisling was truly in a happy mood when he visited his patron, Rosenberg, on the morning of the 13th. The *Reichsleiter* was equally pleased, magnanimously praising his Norwegian protégé for having placed his honor in the hands of *der Führer* in the service of the ideal of the greater German Reich. Rosenberg sarcastically made reference to the fact that inferior "diplomats" had sought to commit acts that dishonored the Reich, an obvious reference to officials who had opposed Quisling, such as Bräuer, Habicht, and Terboven. However, Rosenberg stressed how he had worked with all his might to overcome such "dishonor", and he could now proudly boast that he had received the supreme accolade: *der Führer* himself had perceived that he had been right.[229]

Both he and Quisling savored their victory. The NS leader could therefore travel back to Norway, pleased with the outcome of yet another in his series of visits to Berlin, being convinced that he now would soon have governmental authority within his grasp. He carried with him Rosenberg's wish for everything good for the future. But the *Reichsleiter* also noted in his diary, prophetically as it turned out, that Quisling now had to assume full responsibility for looking out for himself.[230]

After returning to Oslo, Quisling's rival at first still hoped he might be able to obtain a State Council, despite the fact that he had almost no room to maneuver. He had been specifically instructed in Berlin that except for the question of the King being "suspended" rather than removed, no additional concessions would be allowed.[231] In spite of this severe limitation Terboven, through his representatives, almost managed to bring off this difficult task. Tentative agreement was reached with the Norwegian negotiators on September 16 on almost all points, except for their insistence that the Germans should specifically indicate the exact nature of the relationship between the *Reichskommissariat* and the State Council. Although this issue still remained unclear, there was a very good likelihood that the discussions could have been brought to a successful conclusion, in particular since both the *Storting*'s Presidency and Christensen exerted themselves in realizing this goal, believing it to be in the country's best interests.[232]

This possibility ended abruptly when yet another concession was demanded from the German side. On the evening of September 17 Müller, who had just succeeded Dellbrügge as Terboven's chief representative in the negotiations, insisted that NS should be given yet another office on the Council. This involved shifting out Ole F. Harbek as head of the Justice Department with either Sverre Riisnæs or Herman Harris Aall, both NS members. This demand brought the talks to an end. Neither the Presidency nor Christensen were willing to make further concessions.[233] Christensen summed up the unwillingness of the Norwegian side to proceed further:

I have been driven from position to position, now it has got to end. I do not believe that it is Harbek's person [that is at stake], but that they want an NS man in the Justice Department. . . . for me there is something known as self-respect, and if one has to give it up when accepting a position such as this, then it is best instead to avoid it.[234]

This development, which so dramatically and abruptly terminated the negotiations, did not originate with Terboven, but rather with Quisling and Hagelin.[235] The latter in particular played the dominant role in making this demand, since he continued to be the driving force behind Quisling. Earlier, in his letter to Terboven of September 10, Quisling had designated Harbek as the first member of the State Council to be replaced by an NS representative. But Quisling and Hagelin had now speeded up the timetable, insisting on Harbek's removal even before the State Council had come into being. As a result, they undermined the very creation of the State Council.[236]

For them, this turn of events was not unwelcome. Quisling had from the beginning been suspicious of the Council, afraid that its founding might prevent him from heading a government. Not only did the concept of the Council originate with Terboven, but Quisling also feared that the "plutocrats", with Christensen at their head, would dominate the body and outmaneuver him and his NS representatives, much the same as occurred with the Administrative Council. His clear intent to create difficulties revealed itself when Irgens was asked by Christensen to try to persuade Quisling to agree to a compromise at the time the discussions were at an impasse over the question of Harbek's removal. Christensen alluded to the possibility of NS being compensated by the post of Minister of Church Affairs in return for permitting Harbek to remain on the Council. But, said Irgens, Quisling was not interested in any compromise.[237] Nor was Hagelin, who bluntly declared that he hoped the entire enterprise would fail.[238]

He and Quisling succeeded. Terboven was in no position to reject their wishes. The NS *Fører* enjoyed the *Führer*'s personal approval, something which the *Reichskommissar* so decidedly lacked at the time. The latter had furthermore learned through sad experience that Quisling and Hagelin possessed excellent channels of communication with Berlin. If Terboven were to try to thwart a step in the direction of Quisling's takeover of the government, an eventual goal which had Hitler's sanction, it would not be long before this became known in Germany. And Terboven fully recognized that he could expect no mercy from his rivals in Berlin. Therefore, rather than risk the small amount of good will that he still retained with his *Führer*, the *Reichskommissar* allowed the break to occur, doing little to try to salvage the negotiations after he had been compelled to accept the request for Harbek's replacement.[239]

Failure to create a State Council through a quasi-legal acknowledgement by the *Storting* meant that another system of government had to be established. Faced with this responsibility, Terboven naturally resorted to carrying out the alternative plan that he had at hand: a commissarial form of government. Already on September 20 he had made the decision to proceed with setting it up.[240] Once this had been determined, the actual implementation took place rapidly. No reluctant Norwegian negotiators had to be overcome. The *Reichskommissar* simply journeyed to Berlin one final time in order to secure Hitler's approval, which he obtained on September 24. On the next day, Wednesday September 25, he announced the formation of the Commissarial Council (*Kommissariske Statsråd*).[241]

This outcome was in many ways a compromise between Quisling and Terboven. The former, advised and encouraged by Hagelin, could look forward to having a majority of NS members in the new administration. The Commissarial Council would not be a German administrative unit, as Terboven initially had maintained it would be. Furthermore, Hagelin, whom Terboven had successfully excluded from previous lists of candidates for office, was now scheduled to occupy the important post of Minister of the Interior. In one sense, therefore, Quisling was pleased with the coming of the Commissarial Council. His representatives enjoyed much stronger representation than they would have had on the State Council. Most important for him, however, was his assumption that the Commissarial Council would serve only as an interim body, to be followed in the immediate future by his own takeover as head of government.

The arrangement was not, however, entirely one-sided in his favor. Members of the Commissarial Council were formally appointed by the *Reichskommissar* who, contrary to Quisling's expectation, remained in the country. Indeed, his organization had increased greatly in size and influence during the course of the summer, with all important administrative decisions needing to have its sanction. Quisling could not expect to receive a free hand under the German auspices, as he had hoped for. He would not even be a member of the Commissarial Council, and could only exert his influence indirectly through its NS officeholders. But since the Council would not act as a true government, with each member responsible only for his own department, ultimate authority rested with the supervisory power exercised by Terboven's *Reichskommissariat*.

Final responsibility for the decision to establish the Commissarial Council rested, as always, with Adolf Hitler. Like the other participants in the Norwegian drama, *der Führer* was not entirely pleased with this outcome. He would have preferred a State Council, established on a foundation of quasi-legal recognition by the *Storting*. For this reason, he continued to order Terboven to keep on with the negotiations almost to the very end. But Hitler, flushed with the victories that he had achieved in 1940 and disdainful of democratic politicians, had no inclination to allow any concessions that permitted even a rudimentary vestige of representative government. This explains the German unwillingness to make any meaningful compromises and the support that Quisling received at the time the State Council talks reached their climax. But in backing the NS *Fører*, Hitler succeeded only in ruining the possibility of establishing the State Council. Sustained insistence on greater NS representation eventually destroyed the negotiations.

In agreeing to the Commissarial Council, Hitler adhered to his policy of maintaining a strong *Reichskommissariat*. The wartime importance of Norway made it imperative for Germany to exercise direct military, political, and economic control over the country. Strategically, it occupied a much more vital geographical location than its sister Scandinavian state, Denmark. Because of this difference, and also the manner in which the Germans gained domination over their country, the Danes experienced greater freedom during the early period of their occupation. The personal sympathy he felt for Quisling, as well as his desire to check the ambitions of his out-of-favor *Reichskommissar*, caused Hitler to decide that only NS should enjoy German patronage in Norway, but always under the supervision of his authorities. While Hitler might have been displeased with Terboven for attempting to act too independently, he had no intention of weakening the power of the German system of administration. The strong-willed *Reichskommissar*, in reaction to the disappointment he felt when he failed to establish the State Council owing to Quisling's and Hagelin's effective guerilla tactics, had wished to leave Norway as soon as possible once it became clear that NS would enjoy a majority on the Commissarial Council. However, when he raised this possibility in Berlin, indicating a preference for a new assignment in Belgium, Hitler blocked any such move. Terboven had to remain in Norway, with Quisling at his side.[242]

The decision by Hitler had long-term repercussions. He destroyed completely the possibility of making a political arrangement that might have succeeded in gaining a degree of popular support. Despite his cynical and ruthless nature, Terboven had proposed a political plan of action that was more realistic. It would have allowed the Germans to compromise established political groups, drawing them into partial or full collaboration, thereby preparing the way for future nazification of society. When this approach was abandoned in favor of almost total backing for NS alone, any possibility for obtaining societal approval of a German-sponsored administration was eliminated. Hitler, influenced to a considerable degree by the pro-Quisling reports he received through Rosenberg's and Raeder's organizations, failed to realize the extent to which Quisling was anathema to the overwhelming majority of the public. Equally important, he had not yet gained full insight into the NS *Fører*'s failings as a political leader.

CHAPTER XII

National Union in the Commissarial Council

1940–1941

> *There is civil war in Norway now*, caused by a party that wanted to elimi-
> nate all parties and that calls itself National Union. . . . What is it they really
> want from us, these assailants: Yes, first and foremost they wish to use force
> against us. They want to impose upon us a societal system that we have not
> been willing to accept.
>
> Trygve Wyller, *Norsk Front* (underground newspaper)
> April 1941

Reichskommissar Terboven proclaimed the establishment of the Commissarial Council in a radio speech delivered at 8:00 p.m., September 25,
1940.[1] Those who listened were left with few illusions about the future.
From what he said it was plain that the occupation had now assumed a different character. Reflecting Nazi Germany's optimistic world view in the
autumn of 1940, he emphasized that decisions were taking place which
would change Europe's face entirely, with new developments emerging
which would continue to expand for centuries to come.[2]

Considering his past efforts to oust Quisling, however, Terboven had
to swallow a bitter pill when he stated that in Norway only Quisling's
party had been in harmony with the world-shaking events of 1940, having
perceived the significance of the National Socialist revolution. Only NS,
said Terboven, had been willing to disavow the nihilistic policy of the Nygaardsvold government. It had repudiated Norway's dependency on the
British by turning resolutely toward Germany, being prepared to cooperate fully with the "brother folk".[3]

Through a rather biased comparison with NS, Terboven also used his
speech as a means of seeking to compromise and denigrate the major political parties, with whose representatives the *Reichskommissariat* had been
conducting negotiations up to just a few days previously. These parties, he

alleged, had not been in touch with reality because they were pro-British and had supported the "criminal politics" of the Nygaardsvold government. But once it had fled, the *Storting*'s leaders, he declared, had been willing to abandon their ideals, being ready to disavow the King, the Nygaardsvold cabinet, and previous parliamentary resolutions in order to permit the establishment of a State Council. All this, said Terboven sarcastically, they were willing to concede in return for the *Storting* being allowed to continue to exist.[4] He could not of course admit that he was forced to halt negotiations with those whom he was now attempting to besmirch because of Quisling and his backers' successful machinations. Instead, the *Reichskommissar* insisted that he personally broke off the discussions when the *Storting* representatives, "through judicial tricks", sought to gain decisive influence over the State Council on behalf of the "old parties".[5]

Considerable popular resentment toward the *Storting* did exist because of the concessions its leaders had made during the State Council discussions, in particular over the suspension or removal of the King. But Terboven's attempt to exploit this irritation on behalf of NS was too barefaced to enjoy any hope of success. Nevertheless, by turning his back on the representatives of the "old parties", he definitively broke all connections with politicians whom Hitler regarded with deep distrust. Also acting in conformity with *der Führer*'s will, Terboven concluded by emphasizing that the only way Norway could win back its "freedom and independence" would have to be through National Union.[6]

True to this principle, he proclaimed that the King and the royal family would not return to Norway,[7] that the same was true for the Nygaardsvold government, that the Administrative Council's term in office was over, and that no political activity would be tolerated except that of the officially sanctioned party, NS.[8] But he was careful to point out that those serving on the Commissarial Council received their appointments directly from him, whose authority stemmed from the *Führer*.[9] Terboven clearly wanted it to be understood that while the Commissarial Council at its inception included nine of thirteen NS department heads, nevertheless its mandate came from him, not from Quisling.

The NS *Fører* therefore found himself somewhat on the political periphery when the Commissarial Council came into being. Although Terboven's standing had been diminished by his inability to achieve the State Council, he nevertheless remained the executor of German political power. He only mentioned Quisling in passing on two occasions in his speech on September 25. The *Reichskommissar*, acting true to his disdain for Quisling, placed stress on NS as a political organization, rather than on the person of its leader.[10] Officially the latter had no direct affiliation with the Commissarial Council, since he was not a member. The only real influence that he could exercise was through the majority of its department heads, who belonged to his party.

This influence, however, was not insignificant. By using the declarations of loyalty from all NS members on the Council, potential troublesome elements, Jonas Lie in particular, could be kept in line. Furthermore, after the Council had begun to function, Quisling provided overall coordination among the NS department heads. He met with them weekly. At these conferences, decrees being considered by the administrators were presented to Quisling, giving him the opportunity to insist on changes that he felt were required.[11] On the other hand, he had no direct means of bringing pressure to bear on the non-NS members of the Council. Terboven had assured him that they would be loyal to NS' program, but this pledge proved to have no practical significance.[12]

Although four of the thirteen Council members initially did not belong to NS, only three remained outside the party. The fourth, Thorstein Fretheim, who led the Agriculture Department, was an NS sympathizer. At the time of his appointment he was considered by Hagelin to be already as good as a party member.[13] Fretheim officially joined NS in May 1941. The three remaining department heads were all experts who administered vital segments of the economy. These were Erling Sandberg, head of the Finance Department, Øystein Ravner, in charge of the Supply Department, and Sigurd Johannessen, who led an integrated department which included trade, handicrafts, industry, and fisheries.

These important offices were held by persons outside of Quisling's control because the Germans were unwilling to place NS ideologues in charge of key departments, so important to the war effort, for fear of the disruption that would ensue. Carlo Otte, leader of the *Reichskommissariat*'s economic division, attended a meeting with Terboven and Quisling in September 1940, where he learned for the first time of the pending creation of the Commissarial Council. Otte, who enjoyed a good working relationship with the specialists in the Administrative Council, was appalled when he discovered that Quisling had no firm nominees for the economic departments in the Council. The NS *Fører* was more interested in the other positions. He gave Otte the distinct impression that he regarded economic matters as being of secondary importance.[14]

In making this assessment, Otte correctly perceived Quisling's priorities. Above all, he wanted NS to control those departments that were most visible and which would permit the party to exert direct influence on the population. Economic administration, in his view, was not as significant. Furthermore, Quisling did not yet have qualified NS experts to fill the three departments in question.[15] He therefore had to resign himself to the fact that they were led by department heads who to a major degree represented the same viewpoints as those found previously within the Administrative Council. Terboven, because of his antipathy toward Quisling, had no objection. In addition, it was in the *Reichskommissar*'s interest to maintain as harmonious as possible a relationship with the business community, which could be conducted much better through Sandberg, Ravner, and Johannessen, who belonged to this stratum, rather than through NS representatives.

As a result, during the Commissarial Council's existence the three non-NS members occupied a special position. Not unexpectedly, they were regarded with strong distrust by Quisling.[16] From his perspective, this negative attitude was fully justified. Sandberg, Ravner, and Johannessen worked energetically to prevent NS from gaining influence over economic matters. Their main concern was to protect Norwegian interests as fully as possible, and the degree of success they achieved in this endeavor was recognized after the occupation. They did receive criticism for having agreed to serve in a collaborationist administration, but in the end they were vindicated in the courts.[17] The three maintained close contact with their predecessors in the Administrative Council, who continued to hold important economic positions.[18] When subjected to NS opposition, it was also natural for them to seek help from Otte. The latter, who professionally remained convinced that NS could not administer economic affairs, was quite amenable to providing the non-party department heads with needed protection.[19]

Although NS propaganda frequently referred to the Commissarial Council as the "national government", this was largely an empty phrase because it was far from being a true government. Its members were not only appointees of the *Reichskommissar*, but in carrying out their duties, the commissarial department heads were directly responsible to German supervisors. Each department was subordinate to a section of the *Reichskommissariat*, which provided counsel and directives dealing with specific issues.[20] The Council members were free to state their views and make recommendations, but decrees issued by their departments had to have the approval of the *Reichskommissariat*. Various attempts to avoid such restrictions met with repeated failure.[21] In addition, the Commissarial Council did not function as a unified government. Its members were simply a group of individual administrators who were responsible for the functioning of their respective departments. There was no true collegiality. In addition to the NS members' conferences with Quisling, all department heads met once a week to keep each other informed about the current matters within their areas and to discuss matters of common interest. Yet no binding decisions could be made. No one acted as the formal head of the Council at these sessions. Irgens presided, but this was simply out of respect for his seniority as the oldest member. He had no specific authority over his colleagues.[22]

In addition to trying to present the Council as a viable political institution, some NS propagandists at first went so far as to state that it protected society from the horrors of immediate German administration. They described Poland and Czechoslovakia as frightful examples of what could happen under direct German control. However, such a critical view of Quisling's patron, even if used to try to enhance the party's public position, could not be tolerated. Gulbrand Lunde, who as NS propaganda chief was seeking to establish a positive attitude toward the Third Reich, ordered an end to such an anti-German viewpoint.[23]

Quisling and his followers were by no means pleased to accept the fact that members of the Commissarial Council owed their appointment to the *Reichskommissar*. Furthermore, as noted, Quisling viewed the institution only as a temporary expedient, soon to be replaced by a permanent government under his leadership. Therefore, from its very inception NS publications adopted the practice of referring to the department heads as "acting" (*"konstituerte"*) cabinet members.[24] This was done in order to disguise the unpleasant reality of the Council's subservience to Terboven. At the same time, the term "acting" was intended to give the impression that the Council served as but a predecessor to the full and complete return to normal government.[25] This usage was entirely at variance with that of the *Reichskommissariat*, which consistently used the correct title "commissarial" (*"kommissariske"*) cabinet members when referring to the department heads on the Council.[26]

Since the great majority of its members belonged to his party, Quisling had a special interest in portraying the Council as dynamic, leading a process that would inevitably culminate with his takeover. However, its domination by the Germans could not be hidden. As for Terboven, the creation of the Commissarial Council was a disappointment. Having originally favored either a State Council or a purely German administration, for him the body was a weak compromise solution, containing so many vulnerable points that it required constant supervision. To provide this, the *Reichskommissariat*'s dual system of administration was strengthened, with an increased number of German bureaucrats supervising the Norwegians.

This arrangement, which had begun even before the formal proclamation of the Council, proved to be permanent for the duration of the war.[27] Although outward symbolic changes occurred within the Norwegian collaborationist administration, the power and authority of the *Reichskommissariat* remained unchanged. It was responsible to no one in Norway, its freedom of action limited only by orders and instructions from Berlin.

Quisling did not believe that the *Reichskommissariat* would become a permanent institution under Terboven. Instead, he regarded the coming of the Commissarial Council as his victory over the representatives of the traditional political order, who had been thwarted in their negotiations with the Germans. Similarly, he viewed the Commissarial Council as a partial defeat for the *Reichskommissar*, who also had seen his goal of creating a State Council disintegrate. Furthermore, Quisling looked forward to new triumphs over Terboven. He already anticipated the time when the *Reichskommissar* and his administration would be out of the picture entirely, while a "national government" headed by the NS *Fører* himself controlled the Norwegian scene. It was in this sense that Quisling regarded the Commissarial Council as a *Zwischenlösung*, a temporary solution.[28]

He was not the only one who held this outlook during the early fall of 1940. His allies in the navy were equally confident, even jubilant, in their belief that they had triumphed over Terboven and felt optimistic about the future. Grand Admiral Raeder, writing to his subordinate in Norway, Admiral Boehm, declared: "We can be quite proud of the result we have gained with reference to the internal political solution of affairs in Norway. We have won out everywhere along the line . . . ."[29] Raeder thanked Boehm for his "understanding cooperation" in contributing to Terboven's defeat, and he conveyed a similar expression of appreciation to Captain Schreiber. The Grand Admiral wrote that he was pleased with his decision to allow Schreiber to remain in Norway because "his judgement has proven to be very accurate".[30] Quisling was equally satisfied, knowing he could continue to rely upon the navy, with Boehm and Schreiber on the scene to send direct reports to Germany, a line of communication which the vigilant and jealous *Reichskommissar* had no control over.

With his sanguine view of the future, the political goals which Quisling had in mind as the basis for his relationship with the Third Reich were extremely ambitious. They included the following: (1) removal of German control of administration; (2) creation of an independent national government; (3) elimination or reduction of the *Reichskommissariat* to an embassy or a legation; (4) establishment of diplomatic representation in those countries where this was possible; and (5) laying the foundation for a new military defense force.[31]

To reach these broad-ranging objectives, Quisling intended to sign a formal peace settlement with Germany. In his mind, this did not appear to be a serious obstacle. Already within eight days after Terboven had announced the founding of the Commissarial Council, Quisling had formulated a completely new system of government. According to his plan, he would succeed the King, serving as head of state, while his major adviser, Hagelin, would be promoted to the office of prime minister. Their good friend in Rosenberg's office, Schickedanz, would become German ambassador to Oslo. Terboven, of course, would already have been recalled.[32]

As was his wont, Quisling drew up this rosy concept on paper. It soon became obvious, however, that this ambitious design would be difficult to achieve. Yet he never lost sight of these objectives, and from the start of the Commissarial Council he and his close advisers strove to attain their re-alization. In this effort, he was urged on by Hagelin, who continued to be the main force behind the NS *Fører*'s move to fulfill his ambitions. To ac-complish this, Hagelin worked to undermine the *Reichskommissar* by sending a steady stream of negative reports to Berlin. As previously, Hage-lin could conduct this activity thanks to his helpful accomplices in Berlin – Rosenberg's office and the commander-in-chief of the navy. Schickedanz and Scheidt were in continuous contact with their friends in Oslo, aided and abetted by the ubiquitous Schreiber, who remained attached to Boehm's staff.[33]

In his dispatches, Hagelin endeavored to discredit those German authorities who blocked the way for Quisling's takeover. But he faced major obstacles. Criticism of Quisling emanated not only from Terboven, but also from the army command. Hagelin, as always, remained un-daunted by difficulties. He attacked Falkenhorst's command along with the *Reichskommissariat*, maintaining that the army, through its policy of requisitioning wartime luxuries such as coffee, wine, and liquor, acted not as a protector but as an occupying force that treated Norway as conquered territory.[34] Terboven received added condemnation from the suddenly cost-conscious Hagelin, who decried the *Reichskommissar*'s alleged expen-ditures of 100,000 *kroner* for a private railroad car and 40,000 *kroner* for personal hunting trips.[35]

While such complaints were specifically intended to get the *Wehrmacht* high command in Norway and the *Reichskommissar* into hot water for al-leged mismanagement of funds, the overall purpose was to try to weaken these institutions. Quisling and Hagelin immediately wanted to gain more freedom for the Commissarial Council. Hagelin complained bitterly that it was impossible for NS to work for an understanding between Norway and Germany when its activity was continuously thwarted by the *Reichskom-missariat* and the military. He went so far as to threaten that the Council might feel compelled to step down because of the steadily worsening situa-tion, leaving the *Wehrmacht* responsible for controlling the country.[36]

Such a warning was sheer bluff. Quisling had shown time after time that he never willingly abandoned any position. Hagelin merely used this as a tactic to exert pressure in Berlin to provide Quisling and his department heads with more independence. This was further revealed by Hagelin's proposal that a special office for Norwegian affairs be established in the Reich Chancellery, which would have direct contact with Norway through Hagelin's Interior Department. This would have allowed him to create a special section for foreign affairs within his department.[37] If such an arran-gement had been realized, Terboven of course would have been nicely cir-cumvented. In a similar vein, Quisling's number two man called for a peace settlement between Norway and Germany as soon as possible, thereby clearing the way for a Quisling government.[38]

It was hardly a coincidence that Schreiber, who maintained communication with Rosenberg's office at the same time as Hagelin, repeated many of the same themes as Quisling's chief lieutenant. Schreiber stated that NS, as a nationalistic movement, favored a free and independent Norway, associated with Germany in a union based on protection and understanding, bound together by "Germanic blood" and similar political processes. Like Hagelin, he warned that NS might withdraw from politics if Norway were forced to accept terms that were impossible "for a freedom-loving people".[39]

Hagelin's and Schreiber's correspondence was forwarded to the Reich Chancellery by Rosenberg, who remained adamant in his determination to increase his organization's influence in Norway through Quisling.[40] With this in mind, Rosenberg's office urged Quisling and Hagelin to come to Berlin as soon as possible to discuss future "constitutional development" in Norway.[41] Schickedanz, who forwarded this proposal, had a personal motive as well in favoring this recommendation. As Quisling's designate as German ambassador in Oslo, he had a great deal to gain if Terboven were forced to depart.[42]

In reply, Quisling declared that he and Hagelin would gladly travel to Berlin "to discuss the matter more fully", but he suggested the need to ascertain prior to such a meeting what the official attitude toward a possible political change in Norway might be. In his assessment of the current situation, he was not as negative as Hagelin, declaring that developments were not "unfavorable". He did, however, decry the fact that "NS and I are burdened with the full responsibility for governmental leadership" without being able to exercise "the necessary independence", and without NS involvement in the Commissarial Council really "constituting a government".[43]

He enclosed a memorandum, dated October 25, in his reply to Schickedanz in which he spelled out in some detail the program that he advocated in the fall of 1940. As he had done before in discussions with leading Nazi officials in Berlin, he maintained that the goal for the future relationship between Germany and Norway should be the creation of a greater Nordic or greater Germanic association (he used the two terms interchangeably). He therefore stressed the importance of establishing peace and normal relations between the two countries as soon as possible in order to lay the foundation for such an association.[44]

To accomplish this, he asserted, it would be necessary to make a transitional arrangement that enjoyed the full support not only of the Norwegian people, but of all Scandinavians. This would greatly aid in preparing the way for the greater Germanic association. The five steps which he delineated reflected his ambition to be as independent as possible: (1) creation of an "independent Norwegian NS government" headed by Quisling as "regent"; (2) abolition of the position of *Reichskommissar* in favor of a "special plenipotentiary" or "special representative" of the Reich; (3) establishment of Norwegian neutrality, to be recognized by Germany; (4) the right for Germany to exercise military hegemony in Norway for the duration of the war; and (5) the immediate start of secret negotiations to reach a peace settlement and the realization of the greater Germanic association so that agreement could be prearranged before official talks began.

Not content with this blueprint for the immediate future, he went on to present a fifteen-point outline of the visionary "greater Germanic association". Among the items noted here was that Norway would remain "free, inseparable, and independent", united with the Reich in a "greater Nordic association"; there would be a joint foreign policy, joint air and naval forces, but a separate Norwegian army; the association would have a common flag, but the Norwegian national and merchant flags would continue to exist; Norway would be governed by a "regent" and an independent national assembly; the national assembly would be corporate, based on the country's "economic and cultural life"; close collaboration would take place between "the German and Norwegian national movements"; economic cooperation would occur; joint travel, living, and employment rights would be guaranteed for citizens of both countries, although Germans could not acquire property in Norway "without concession from the Norwegian government".[45]

Quite plainly, Quisling wished to have the best of both worlds – to be united politically and economically with the mighty Third Reich while enjoying independent authority as unrivaled master of Norway. As regent (*riksforstander*) he would also be able to realize one of his historical fantasies, since several prominent figures in Norway's past history had held this title.

Quisling received word from Berlin at the end of October reaffirming the navy's commitment to him. Raeder remained convinced that his service would enjoy greater benefits in Norway with a Quisling government in office. The Grand Admiral informed Admiral Boehm that he would welcome a change in political leadership, meaning the elimination of Terboven. Raeder asked Boehm to pass this news on to "the gentlemen with whom you are acquainted", namely Quisling and Hagelin.[46]

Encouraged by the assurances he had received from Berlin, Quisling arrived in the German capital on December 4 in pursuit of greater freedom and the creation of his own government.[47] During his stay in Germany, he had contact with both Dr. Lammers in Hitler's Chancellery and Grand Admiral Raeder.[48] In the meantime Admiral Boehm continued the navy's offensive in Norway, calling for all-out backing for Quisling and his party. In a long memorandum to Raeder, which he forwarded on December 12, Boehm delivered a detailed complaint against members of the *Reichskom-*

missariat and other German officials, who in his opinion had failed to provide Quisling with the aid that he needed for NS to enjoy success. Of particular interest in this memorandum is Boehm's almost identical repetition
of earlier proposals made by Quisling in his memorandum of October 25.
In addition to insisting that NS receive full assistance, Boehm recommended that secret peace negotiations be concluded no later than April 1,
1941, at which time Quisling would become head of state as regent. The
Reichskommissar, of course, would unlamentedly be sent on his way, replaced by a special German representative.[49]

In working to secure these results, Boehm loyally followed Raeder's orders. But it became obvious for all concerned by the year's end that the
moment definitely was not favorable for major political change. For one
thing, Terboven had gained full knowledge of the navy's complicity in the
machinations that were being directed against him.[50] Never slow to react
when challenged, he immediately took up the gauntlet. He began to make
life uncomfortable for Boehm, submitting the thin-skinned Admiral to a
number of personal indignities involving questions of protocol on formal
occasions in Oslo.[51]

The situation in Berlin at this time also did not offer encouragement for
the embattled Admiral's support of Quisling. Raeder sent warning on December 30 that Terboven was "laying mines" against Boehm, and with
success.[52] The highest political echelons in Berlin had been alerted to the
navy's involvement in Norwegian politics. Quisling had been indiscreet
enough to state during his visit that he preferred to work with the navy
rather than with the other branches of the armed services, and that he
would like to see Boehm assume overall military command in Norway.[53]
He had also quoted Boehm as sharing the same view as himself on the
question of future Norwegian armed forces. Because of Terboven's
"mines", Hitler had this matter called to his attention. He also received the
complaint that Boehm had been unfriendly toward Goebbels when the latter had paid a visit to Oslo.[54] The Grand Admiral was hard pressed to defend his subordinate. He could only deny the allegations, declaring rather
fulsomely that Boehm was not engaged in political activity, and that the
statements attributed to Quisling were based on a misunderstanding.[55]
Raeder disliked the uncomfortable position he was in. He regarded conditions as being anything but favorable, and he admonished Boehm to be
circumspect.[56]

The adverse political atmosphere for Quisling and his mentors stemmed
not merely from the effect of Terboven's "mines" exploding, but even
more importantly from military concerns. Hitler was preoccupied with
plans for his attack against the Soviet Union. The directive for the implementation of this hazardous undertaking had just been issued in December. Since he feared a British counterstroke against Norway, *der Führer*
was especially concerned that no action should be carried out in the coun-

try that might cause instability.[57] His concentration on military matters therefore doomed all efforts by Quisling and his patrons to change the political status quo in late 1940 – early 1941. In his discussions in Berlin, Quisling had proposed that he be allowed to form a new government on January 30 1941, which happened to be the anniversary of Hitler's takeover of power.[58] Prevailing German wartime priorities, however, made this an idle wish. He returned to Norway in mid-December with his expectations unfulfilled.[59]

While his perpetual goal of exercising complete governmental control still eluded him, Quisling did have the opportunity after September 25 1940 of using the NS members on the Commissarial Council to try to reshape the Norwegian people into the ideal society that he desired. He at least had the satisfaction of having regained prominent status due to Hitler's direct intervention on his behalf. He therefore had German authority behind him when he began this major endeavor. But at the same time, he was being tested. The degree of success he attained would definitely have a bearing on the extent to which he might hope to lead a government.

As a result, while the effort on his behalf continued externally, within Norway Quisling set in motion a campaign to nazify society after September 25. In order to achieve this ambitious change, a build-up of National Union was an obvious first requirement for him and his lieutenants. The reconstruction of NS into a strong, dynamic party appeared to offer the prospect of helping the *Fører* far toward acquiring the government leadership which he longed for.

Even though the party had been aided by the *Reichskommissariat*, the earlier NS drive to increase its rolls in the summer of 1940 had resulted in very little. Quisling's unpopularity proved to be a great hindrance. In some districts NS only succeeded in gaining a fraction of the number of adherents the party had previously had.[60] The first statistics from the summer of 1940 which appear to be reliable date from August 27, when membership stood at 4202. Most who joined the party at this time were persons who had previously belonged to NS, and who now took the opportunity to reaffirm their commitment. Very few were new recruits.[61]

Conditions improved greatly following Terboven's speech of September 25, proclaiming the formation of the Commissarial Council. A significant number of Norwegians reacted to the announcement that NS was the only political organization permitted to exist. Between October 9 and October 26 membership grew by no less than 7,096, the largest single increase NS experienced during the entire occupation. Thereafter a less spectacular but nevertheless steady growth occurred, so that by the end of 1940 total enrollment stood at 23,755, almost six times the number NS had held a scant half year earlier.[62]

Although motives for joining the party varied from person to person, with many undoubtedly being influenced by a variety of reasons, nevertheless it is obvious that this sudden influx, coming at a time when Germany appeared to be winning the war, was in large part stimulated by opportunistic considerations. Even *Fritt Folk* admitted, if indirectly, that many of the new recruits joined because of self-interest, not because of ideological conviction, and that party veterans often did not welcome the opportunists.[63]

This reaction, however, was far from the minds of Quisling and his top lieutenants. They viewed the new growth as evidence that momentum was now clearly in NS' favor. Herman Harris Aall, in a radio speech on October 18, went so far as to declare that the people would shortly be allowed to participate in a plebiscite in order to legitimize the government change that had recently taken place.[64] Optimistic party members and their German advisers believed at this time that NS would be able to obtain full power over society by following the same pattern that Hitler's NSDAP had used in Germany.[65]

National Union's recruiting campaign was therefore intensified during the fall of 1940. The party was encouraged and aided by its Nazi advisers. A permanent staff had been set up within the German administration for the purpose of overseeing political matters, in particular to advise and guide NS. Its head was Paul Wegener, one of Terboven's top officials, who served as acting *Reichskommissar* when Terboven was absent on his frequent journeys. Indicating the degree to which the *Reichskommissariat* aided NS recruitment, no less a person than Joseph Goebbels was invited to Norway to lend his prestige to the NS drive.[66]

Although the membership campaign did produce results in the fall of 1940, it was by no means an unqualified success. While organized resistance to NS had not yet materialized, spontaneous acts of popular opposition to NS recruitment did take place. When party speakers appeared in the towns, large crowds frequently gathered and openly expressed their antagonism by shouting, whistling in derision, and singing the royal anthem.[67] On one occasion when Quisling came to the small industrial center of Askim to hold a speech, someone hostile to the *Fører* set off the fire alarm at the rubber factory. Everyone, both those within the meeting hall and those gathered outside, immediately departed, leaving Quisling facing an empty auditorium.[68]

On the whole the growth of NS membership not unexpectedly tended to follow the pattern of Germany's military success, again providing evidence that those who joined the party did so largely for opportunistic reasons.[69] During the early months of 1941 the rapid increase of the previous half year levelled off. Thereafter growth continued, but not as quickly as earlier. From the beginning of May until the end of the year NS averaged slightly less than 900 new members per month.[70] At the start of 1942 party membership stood at 34,434, showing an increase of 10,000 during the past year.[71]

By the late summer of 1941 the German advisers declared themselves satisfied with NS' rate of growth and recommended that it should cease recruitment for the time being. Instead, they urged NS to consolidate its position by building up its administrative apparatus.[72] But what counted for Quisling was the need to gain as many members as soon as possible to bolster his chances of being allowed to head a government. Therefore, in the fall of 1941 NS set the ambitious goal of gaining no less than a total of approximately 100,000 members.[73] Each region was given a specific quota of new members to recruit, based on the census of 1930. This target would have given NS some 3.3 per cent of the population.[74] However, it could not be reached. For the country as a whole less than forty per cent of the quota had been filled by the spring of 1942.[75]

Although growth continued, it slowed down noticeably in conformity with German military setbacks in 1942. The party reached its peak in the fall of 1943, with a membership of some 43,000.[76] Thereafter the total declined absolutely, with some one thousand members leaving the party on the average during the next twelve months.[77] For the final period of the war, it is impossible to say exactly how many sought to resign during the winter of 1944–1945. The number was considerable. However, such persons were faced with punitive actions when they attempted to withdraw. Many therefore simply ceased to be affiliated with NS without formally resigning.[78]

Altogether it is estimated that a total of approximately 60,000 Norwegians belonged to NS, including its youth organizations, at one time or another during the course of the occupation.[79] This number was far from what Quisling had hoped to reach. Despite German aid and backing, and despite being the only organization with access to the media, NS, with a maximum membership of less than two per cent of the population, never succeeded in becoming a mass organization. Its inability to generate popular support proved to be a fundamental weakness which Quisling was unable to overcome. During the winter of 1941–1942, when he continuously made demands for greater power, German rejection was justified time after time by reference to NS' small membership.[80]

Quisling's failure to attract a mass membership was largely due, in the final analysis, to the obvious fact that he was perceived as a collaborator. He was directly associated with the power that had deprived Norway of its sovereignty. His insistence that he was carrying out a campaign to win back independence within a greater Germanic federation was disregarded as inconsequential propaganda by the overwhelming majority.

The public's view of him as a traitorous conspirator became even stronger as the occupation progressed because of his acts. To prove to the Germans that he deserved to be trusted as the head of a government, he assisted their war effort by taking part in the formation of Norwegian military units, recruited to fight on Germany's behalf.

He justified this by declaring that these troops would allow him to uphold Norway's position within Hitler's new order. By taking part in the conflict, he claimed, Norway would be able to exercise some influence when the war ended. His volunteers, he argued, would serve as the means of getting the country out of the impasse which the despised party politicians and other intriguers had driven it into, and which the enemies of National Union were trying to perpetuate. He further maintained that the creation of volunteer units was the first step toward building up a new national defense force.[81]

He engaged in such recruitment also because he sincerely favored a Nazi victory, and because he recognized that he had no political future in the event of a German defeat. But by promoting military units that fought on Germany's behalf, he simply reinforced his image as a collaborator among the majority of the people, whose distaste for him increased proportionally with whatever action he undertook. This personal dilemma remained unchanged during the entire occupation.

In 1941 he promoted the creation of three military units, Regiment Northland, the Norwegian SS, and the Norwegian Legion.[82] Regiment Northland was formed in January, and the Norwegian SS later in May; on both occasions Heinrich Himmler came to Norway and took part in the inaugural ceremonies.[83] Quisling's joint appearances with the feared head of the SS and the German police provided added proof to the public of the close ties that the NS *Fører* had with Germany's war of conquest.

The propaganda that NS used in its attempt to secure greater support similarly took on the stigma of being identified with the Germans. This could not be avoided because time after time it merely consisted of direct translations from German. To cite but one of numerous examples, the *Hird* worked to recruit new members in the autumn of 1940 under the motto "Norway wake up", the Norwegian rendition of the Nazi slogan "*Deutschland erwache*".[84] Forgotten were Quisling's insistent denials from before the war that his ideology was original, not an imitation of foreign movements.

Instead, he now doggedly stressed NS' common identity with the German cause. Not only did this reflect his natural empathy for the Third Reich, but it demonstrated the ideological conformity that was part of his campaign to gain greater authority from the Germans. One constraint which had previously burdened him, the Nazi-Soviet Pact of 1939, was removed by Hitler's attack against Russia in June 1941. This major change in the war allowed Quisling to resume with full force the anti-communist theme which had been a fundamental part of his ideology. No longer did

National Union's propaganda have to be directed primarily toward Great Britain as the main wartime enemy.

NS propaganda once more portrayed Germany as the defender of European civilization against the alleged Jewish Communist conspiracy. Similarly, Quisling maintained that in Norway he and his party were the sole guarantors of the country's freedom and independence against the menace of a Russian takeover. Newspapers, magazines, posters, and radio broadcasts all carried horror stories about the alleged communist monster which threatened from the east.[85]

His close identification with Germany made it equally natural for him to stress more than ever his adherence to National Socialist anti-Semitism. His tirades against the Jews as the supposed masterminds behind the international conspiracy against superior Germanic culture took on an even more crass tone. In March 1941 he participated in an anti-Semitic congress which Rosenberg sponsored at Frankfurt-on-Main. In a speech at this gathering, Quisling proposed the creation of a joint European law as a means of finding a solution to the "Jewish question". His appearance at this conference received considerable publicity in Norway.[86]

As he showed in countless speeches during this period, including his address at Frankfurt-on-Main, Quisling remained true to his prophetic vision of being the international statesman and philosopher who interpreted the unfolding of world history to lesser mortals. He persevered in his prewar practice of describing the course of events in messianic terms, with the very existence of civilization at stake. At the same time, as the philosophical prophet whose insight allegedly revealed a man of genius, he continued to look forward to a utopian future where mankind had advanced to a higher stage of civilization on earth which approximated the old ideal of a Christian paradise.

These elements of his world view were repeated frequently, as shown in one of his major propaganda speeches to NS members, which he held in Oslo in September 1941. Here he raised the question of whether the evil forces in the war would succeed in destroying the Germanic peoples and the fundamental Nordic principles on which their civilization rested, creating thereafter a Jewish world order in the form of a world Soviet republic and Comintern, and a new League of Nations. As the evil forces engaged in this conspiracy, he lumped together materialism and Judaized religion, the Freemasons, capitalism, Marxism, democracy, Bolshevism, England, the United States, the Soviet Union, Churchill, Roosevelt, Stalin, Wall Street, and the London Stock Exchange. The Nordic people's own blindness, declared the would-be messiah, also contributed to this danger. Or, he continued, would it be possible for the new Germany to succeed in protecting Nordic principles by winning this war, which he described by the Viking term *Ragnarok*, and thereby creating a new order which would protect the Germanic world in Europe, lying between the Jewish controlled Anglo-Saxon power in the west and the Jewish controlled Russian-Asian world power in the east. If the Germanic world prevailed, said Quisling, then it would be possible to set aside the old and create a new world that would lift human development up to a higher level.[87]

His world view at this time did not fail to include elements of his earlier romantic nationalism. As part of the new order that he visualized after Germany had won the war, he expected Norway to recover all territories that had ever been part of the kingdom. Not unexpectedly, the Swedish government took umbrage at this and protested. Its Foreign Ministry sarcastically rejected the German contention that the Swedes should not concern themselves about Norwegian affairs, responding that it certainly was of concern for Sweden when the party in office in Norway called for the return of the provinces of Jämtland, Härjedalen, and Bohuslän.[88]

When Quisling presented his dogmas in public, knowledgeable observers quickly detected a trait that provided another piece of evidence of the inspiration he received from the Third Reich. Having attended a number of Hitler's speeches, Quisling, like so many others, was impressed by the Nazi dictator's emotional speaking style. Never a particularly good orator himself, he sought more than ever during the war to imitate Hitler's manner of speaking. Like Hitler, he would begin a speech by talking in a calm manner, thereafter becoming increasingly more agitated and emotional as he progressed.[89] But while he made every effort to gain the hypnotic effect on his audience that Hitler so often achieved, Quisling's speeches remained unconvincing except to the limited number who were already believers.

In his push to increase his power over society in 1940–1941, one complaint that Quisling could not levy against the Germans, not even those in Norway who opposed him personally, was that NS lacked adequate financial resources. Once Terboven had been blocked from setting up a State Council, NS received a free hand to expropriate the property of all other parties which had been outlawed by the Germans. It made the most of the opportunity. It took over the Conservative party's headquarters, turning the building into offices to meet the increased needs of the NS bureaucracy.[90] Similarly, *Fritt Folk* expanded greatly in size after September 25. This was made possible not only through increased German funding, but also because NS' national newspaper took over the printing plant and press offices of *Arbeiderbladet*.[91]

In addition to giving NS political spoils, Terboven similarly granted it the resources of a number of organizations whose holdings the Germans had confiscated. In October 1941 Quisling received the property of the Freemasons, valued at approximately ten million *kroner*.[92] Similarly, when the Boy Scouts were disbanded, their assets went to NS.[93]

Its greatly improved financial condition allowed NS at first considerable economic independence. Initially no sharp line of division existed between state and party expenditures. This permitted NS to charge part of its expenses against the state budget.[94] However, Quisling, encouraged by Hagelin, went too far in attempting to exploit this advantage. As part of his ongoing effort to bolster his party's authority, Quisling and his NS department heads launched a move in the spring of 1941 against the Finance Department headed by Erling Sandberg, one of the Council's non-NS members.[95] Sandberg resisted, however, refusing to approve uncritically all of NS' financial claims. In this confrontation, he received the full backing of the *Reichskommissariat's* economic division under Carlo Otte, which now established a strict rule separating party expenses from state expenditures.[96] In a direct slap at Quisling, the *Reichskommissariat* no longer permitted him to charge the costs he incurred on trips to Germany against the state budget.[97]

In protest, Quisling went so far as to hint that he might consider retiring if the decision were not reversed.[98] But this and other attempts by NS to obtain greater control over state finances during the period of the Commissarial Council proved fruitless. Because of his expertise, Sandberg enjoyed the confidence of the *Reichskommissariat*, and proposals to replace him with an NS member were rejected.[99]

Despite the limitations which Terboven and his officials could impose, with adequate funds and a considerable growth in party membership during 1940–1941, Quisling built up NS organizationally to a greater degree than had previously been possible. As he had always done, he believed that having a detailed party structure was of the utmost importance. Form was what counted. He remained rigidly convinced, despite past experience, that once the framework of the party had been created in detail, then the membership would fill in naturally. He emphasized strengthening the party organization because he always regarded NS as his instrument, which he would use to transform Norwegian society into his corporate ideal. He revealed this intent clearly in one of his key mottoes for NS: "The party is above the state and uses the state to build society".[100] Although his employment of NS in the attempt to bring about social change was greatest after he had formed his all NS government in February 1942, from the beginning of the Commissarial Council he energetically utilized the party in this endeavor, consciously seeking to blur the line between state and party activity.

National Union's organizational structure was quite similar to that which had existed before the party underwent disintegration in the 1930s. The main difference was that German backing during World War II permitted Quisling to build up NS to a far greater degree than earlier. It was divided into two distinct levels. On the national level the party functioned under the "National Leadership" (*Riksledelsen*), while on the local level the various "regional organizations" (*fylkesorganisasjonene*) were responsible for implementing the decisions of the National Leadership.

On the national level the leadership provided coordination of the party's administrative and propaganda activity. It included Quisling's Chancellery, Fuglesang's General Secretariat, the Organizational Division, the Press and Propaganda Division, the Economic Division, the party court, which settled internal NS disputes, *Fritt Folk*, the NS printing plant, and the party's national supply depot.[101] In addition, a number of "special organizations" were also part of the National Leadership. These were quite important because they often served as the chief agents through which Quisling attempted to exert NS influence on the public. Each had a distinct function through which the party sought to extend its control. The special organizations included the *Hird* and its subdivisions, the NS Youth Organization, the NS Women's Organization, the NS Labor Organization, the NS Student Organization, the NS Farm Groups, the NS Aid Organization, the NS Foreign Organization for party members residing abroad, and the various military formations that NS sponsored.[102]

The activity of the NS Aid Organization provided a good example of how the special organizations were intended to serve as spearheads spreading party influence into society. When Quisling created the Aid Organization by special directive in the summer of 1941, he declared that its immediate purpose was to provide relief for needy NS members. However, he intended it to expand in the future to the point where it would serve as "a general national relief organization, to function in all social areas".[103] But while it did seek to realize his goal, because it was clearly identified as a branch of NS, it proved to be no more successful than the other "special organizations".

At the apex of the National Leadership stood the *Fører* himself. His experiences through the years had reinforced his determination that no one should ever again be able to challenge him as party leader. He therefore demanded total loyalty from everyone admitted into the party. All new initiates were required to "promise loyalty to my *fører*, Vidkun Quisling", and to swear "to honor and obey him" at all times.[104]

Serving in clearly subordinate positions were a number of "national leaders" (*riksledere*). These included the heads of the four major divisions of the party on the national level, plus the leaders of the four most important "special organizations".[105] While they occupied leadership positions, they could make no independent decisions, but had to refer all major questions to the *Fører*. They could only implement policy through the guidelines Quisling provided, both on the national and local levels.[106] Ultimate authority for all NS activity during the war rested with Quisling, as was natural for a party adhering to the *Führer* principle. That is not to say that the original ideas for all measures that the party attempted to carry out were initiated by him, but they had to have his approval before being put into effect.

Throughout the country the local party organizations were constructed to be miniature versions of the leadership on the national level. In each major subdivision the regional *fører* held sway, although his administrative area geographically did not always conform to regional boundaries. Under him were offices that were the exact duplicates of those on the national level. The same pattern repeated itself on the lower district (*krets*) and group (*lag*) levels throughout the regional *fører*'s administrative domain.[107] NS was therefore, in conformity with its *Fører*'s emphasis on uniformity, organized in a symmetrical manner from top to bottom.

As had previously proven true in the 1930s, Quisling's emphasis on a highly structured party organization did not necessarily ensure success. Even with full German backing, National Union's restricted and unevenly distributed membership frequently did not have the capacity to fill all of the numerous positions in the party's detailed organizational plan. Even as late as the end of 1942 many local NS posts remained vacant.[108] Furthermore, the quality of persons appointed to fill slots in the party structure not infrequently proved to be insufficient.

Another limitation which Quisling had to work under was that of the restrictions imposed upon NS by its staff of German advisers in *Einsatzstab Wegener*. Led by Wegener, Terboven's second-in-command, this group consisted almost entirely of persons who had experience within the National Socialist party. The *Einsatzstab* had responsibility for giving Quisling aid and advice on how to build up his party, and also to provide guidance on NS' conduct of political activity and use of propaganda. Wegener's officials exerted influence even on the local level, with one member being assigned to each of the party's regional leaders.[109]

While the *Reichskommissariat* might disagree with Quisling on the question of how much freedom he and his party should have politically, it needs to be emphasized that at no time after the start of the Commissarial Council was there any disagreement between him and the Germans over the desire to nazify society as much as possible by bringing it under NS control. Any difference of opinion that did occur was over means, not ends. Therefore, Quisling had full German approval when he began a concerted NS offensive on a number of different fronts in the fall of 1940 to introduce "the new order" that he hoped to achieve.

If "the new order" were to be established, one of the first targets that NS had to secure was effective control of the governmental apparatus. With this in mind, the most energetic NS department heads, led by Hagelin, began a coordinated drive to replace elected officeholders and state and local administrators with NS adherents. In support, Terboven issued a decree on October 4 which gave members of the Commissarial Council the right to transfer or to remove all civil servants who did not back the new order one hundred per cent.[110]

As the force behind this effort, Hagelin maintained the record for activism that he had demonstrated amply so many times before. His influence was at its greatest height in 1940–1941. He was undoubtedly the key figure in the NS hierarchy after Quisling. He was second-in-command within the party, serving as acting head in the *Fører*'s absence. The Interior Department had been created specifically for him. The most essential administrative offices were under its jurisdiction. This, coupled with Hagelin's preference for bold action, explains why his department exhibited the greatest amount of activity in seeking victory for Quisling during the early years of the occupation.[111]

In order to gain control of all administrative assignments on the national level, the Interior Department established a special NS Personnel Office for Public Service (*Nasjonal Samlings Personalkontor for Offentlig Tjeneste*), known by its acronym NSPOT, to monitor state appointments. NS attempted thereby to make certain that its members received as many positions as possible. Acting on the instruction of Hagelin, NSPOT issued a special notice in February 1941 which declared that it exercised approval not only over appointments to administrative offices, but also over all promotions and transfers.[112]

Despite Hagelin's strenuous efforts, the expectation which he and Quisling shared of turning the central state administration into a pliant tool proved to be unachievable. The party's inability to gain significant numerical support again was the general reason for this failure. There simply were not enough qualified NS members capable of filling specialized positions in the bureaucracy. As late as the end of the war only 17.3 per cent of all posts within the government departments were held by NS members.[113]

In the various departments, NS gained the highest percentage of positions within Jonas Lie's Police Department. This was due to a combination of factors. The police were used to obeying orders, a trait that Lie skillfully exploited to the utmost. In addition, he applied pressure at a very early date, when no effective resistance had yet been formed. As a result, more than 60 per cent of the higher police officials and 40 per cent of the rank and file joined NS during the fall and winter of 1940.[114]

While this at first seemed to be a noteworthy triumph, in the long run it did not prove as significant as had been initially assumed. Although large numbers of policemen belonged to NS, as resistance stiffened during the occupation, Quisling discovered that he could not rely on the police, who not infrequently directly or indirectly refused to obey orders.[115] Because of this lack of dependability, Lie felt compelled to establish a special force, the State Police (*Statspolitiet*), in the summer 1941. Patterned after the Ge-

Proklamasjon

Til det norske folk.

Efter at England hadde brutt Norges nøitralitet ved å utlegge minefelter i norsk territorialfarvann uten å møte annen motstand enn de vanlige intetsigende protester fra regjeringen Nygaardsvold, tilbød den tyske regjering den norske regjering sin fredelige hjelp ledsaget av en høitidelig forsikring om å respektere vår nasjonale selvstendighet og norsk liv og eiendom. Som svar på dette tilbud om løsning av en for vårt land helt uholdbar situasjon, har regjeringen Nygaardsvold iverksatt almindelig mobilisering og gitt den hensiktsløse ordre til de norske stridskrefter å motsette sig den tyske hjelp med væbnet makt. Selv har regjeringen flyktet efter således lettsindig å ha satt landets og dets innbyggeres skjebne på spill.

Under disse omstendigheter er det den nasjonale samlingsbevegelses plikt og rett å overta regjeringsmakten for å verne om det norske folks livsinteresser og Norges sikkerhet og selvstendighet. Vi er de eneste som i kraft av forholdene og vår bevegelses nasjonale mål kan gjøre dette og derved redde landet ut av den desperate situasjon som partipolitikerne har ført vårt folk op i.

Regjeringen Nygaardsvold er trådt tilbake. Den nasjonale regjering har overtatt regjeringsmakten med Vidkun Quisling som regjeringschef og utenriksminister og med følgende andre medlemmer: professor Birger Meidell, kirke og undervisningsminister; politichef Jonas Lie, justisminister; dr. Gulbrand Lunde, socialminister; direktør Albert V. Hagelin, handels og forsyningsminister; arkitekt Tormod Hustad, landbruksminister; professor R. Skancke, arbeidsminister; godseier Frederik Prytz, finansminister; major R. Hvoslef, forsvarsminister.

Alle nordmenn opfordres til å vise ro og besindighet i denne for vårt land så vanskelige situasjon.

Ved felles anstrengelser og alles godvilje skal vi berge Norge fritt og frelst gjennem denne svære krise.

Oslo, 9.–4. 1940.

VIDKUN QUISLING

Quisling's proclamation to his fellow countrymen on 9 April 1940.
Photograph: Norwegian News Agency.

The new head of government holding a press conference in the Storting on 12 April 1940.
Photograph: Norwegian News Agency.

Curt Bräuer, the German plenipotentiary,
emerging from a meeting with the King
and Koht at Elverum.
Photograph: Norwegian News Agency.

Paal Berg.
Photograph: Norwegian News Agency.

Ingolf Christensen negotiating with Hans Dellbrügge.
Photograph: Norwegian News Agency.

Quisling in uniform at his desk in November 1940.
Photograph: Norwegian News Agency.

Quisling's meeting with Alfred Rosenberg in Berlin, 1942.
Photograph: National Archives of Norway.

Admiral Erich Raeder (on the left) and Admiral Hermann Boehm (on the right) at Fornebu Airport, August 1940. Photograph: Norwegian News Agency.

The members of the Commissarial Council holding their first meeting on 26 September 1940. From the left and clockwise round the table: Rolf Jørgen Fuglesang, Axel Stang, Ragnar Skancke, Sverre Riisnæs, Thorstein Fretheim, Sigurd Johannessen, Tormod Hustad, Kjeld Stub Irgens, Albert Viljam Hagelin, Birger Meidell, Jonas Lie, Erling Sandberg, Øystein Ravner and Gulbrand Lunde. Photograph: Norwegian News Agency.

Terboven receiving Hagelin at his office in the Storting. Quisling is standing in the background. Photograph: National Archives of Norway.

The Christian Joint council. From the left: Director General Kristian Hansson, Professor Ole Hallesby, H.E. Wisløff, perpetual curate, Bishop Eivind Berggrav, the Rev. Ingvald B. Carlsen, Ludwig Hope, general secretary, and the Rev. Ragnvald Indrebø. Photograph: Norwegian Home Front Museum.

Christmas party in the mission house in Calmeyer Street, December 1941. From the left: Johan Andreas Lippestad, Quisling, Gulbrand Lunde, Jonas Lie and Sverre Riisnæs. Photograph: National Archives of Norway.

Vidkun and Maria on a visit to Jørgen Quisling's in Middelthun Street, Oslo.
Photograph: University of Oslo Library.

Rolf Jørgen Fuglesang takes over the Ministry of Cultural Affairs on 27 November 1942.
Photograph: National Archives of Norway.

stapo, it was made up entirely of loyal NS members, and it therefore served as a reliable tool for carrying out Quisling's will.[116]

Hagelin and his subordinates in the Interior Department were equally concerned with dominating government on the local level as well as the central administration. In order to accomplish this, a great deal depended on how well they would be able to manipulate the regional governors (*fylkesmenn*) in each of the nineteen provinces. If successful, Hagelin could use the regional governors to aid in the elimination of democratic self-government throughout the country. Once this process had been implemented, the Interior Department intended to co-opt the regional governors, replacing them with NS members. This conformed fully with NS' program, which called for strengthening the office of the regional governor as an agent of the central government.[117]

In following this strategy, the Interior Department enjoyed considerable success, despite the fact that only one of the original regional governors joined NS. Ironically, this single exception proved to be none other than Quisling's most bitter opponent from his days in the Agrarian government, Jens Hundseid. The former prime minister appears to have become a member in part because of genuine fear that Quisling might exact vengeance if he did not join the party, in part because of his desire to retain his prestigious position.[118] While the other regional governors did not follow his example, they did not resign their offices. They thereby became unwilling accomplices in the process whereby NS assumed control of regional administration. During the next two years they were gradually ousted in favor of NS members.[119]

Before they were dismissed, however, they served the purpose that Hagelin intended. The degree of success which NS obtained in extending its influence over local government was largely due to the quick action he took. His department issued decrees already in early October by which appointive civil servants on the municipality (*kommune*) level within the regions came under the direct control of the Interior Department, which now arrogated to itself the power to appoint, dismiss, and suspend persons in these positions.[120] Later in October the Department followed this up by decreeing that all previously elective positions in local government would henceforth be appointive, with the Department naturally reserving for itself the right to make such designations.[121]

The absence of any form of coordinated resistance during the first year of occupation permitted Hagelin to move rapidly in exerting effective control over local administration. This was attained by yet another decree, dated December 21, which introduced the NS *fører* principle on all levels of local government. Beginning on January 1, 1941, decisions on the provincial and municipal levels were made respectively by appointive regional

governors and mayors. Local elections were abolished. All offices throughout the land were thereby made appointive, controlled by Hagelin's Interior Department.[122]

This change from democratically elected local governments to the totalitarian *fører* system which Quisling desired was made possible by the regional governors, who aided, however reluctantly, in the introduction of
the new order. In many instances they sought to use their influence to have
persons outside of NS appointed as mayors. But even when they succeeded, their small triumphs in reality damaged their primary intent of
keeping local government as free of NS influence as possible. By persuading reputable persons to serve alongside NS members, they created an aura
of legality for the system that Hagelin had imposed. Thereafter it proved
impossible to maintain a strict line of division between NS and the opposition. Although the number of NS mayors appointed in 1941 varied from
province to province, once the process had been set in motion, non-NS
mayors were replaced by party adherents as the occupation progressed. By
the end of the war all mayors were NS supporters, although a few were
still not formally enrolled in the party.[123]

Hagelin's successful takeover of local government proved to be the most
decisive triumph which the party attained. The resistance leadership later
declared that the failure of the regional governors to resign constituted
"one of the greatest mistakes that has occurred during the occupation".[124]
This did not mean, however, that NS was able to dominate completely the
administrative apparatus locally. On this level as well, NS did not have an
adequate membership base which could supply recruits for all positions,
with the result that opponents of the party frequently were able to keep
their posts.[125] Nonetheless, Hagelin's Interior Department did enjoy control of the key positions within local administration, and while at present
there have been no studies that have measured the extent to which NS had
penetrated the local bureaucracy by the end of the war, the party continued to carry out this process until the occupation's conclusion.[126]

Quisling experienced quite a different outcome when yet another of his
subordinates made a parallel move to assume control of the judiciary.
Sverre Riisnæs, in charge of the Justice Department, decreed in November
1940 that all laymen who served on judicial tribunals would come directly
under his authority as of January 1, 1941. He thereby arrogated to his department the right to appoint and dismiss such lay judges (*lagrettemenn,
domsmenn,* and *skjønnsmenn*).[127]

Unlike Hagelin, however, Riisnæs immediately encountered direct resistance. The Supreme Court quickly issued an opinion that he had acted
in violation of both the Constitution and the Hague Convention. Not
unexpectedly, he in turn rejected the Court's protest.[128] This dispute

caused Terboven, ever jealous of his power, to intervene, since any display of independence, if permitted to stand, was a threat to his authority. He informed the Court that it had no right to challenge decrees approved by his *Reichskommissariat*.[129]

Riisnæs thereupon moved to turn the Supreme Court, like other parts of government, into an obedient tool of NS. On December 6 the Justice Department issued a decree which lowered the mandatory retirement age for civil servants from seventy to sixty-five. This change was aimed directly at the Court. Riisnæs' strategy was to eliminate the older justices and to replace them with NS members, while allowing the younger justices to remain for a time, only to be gradually removed later. Quisling personally discussed this approach, similar to that which Hagelin had followed, in a telephone conversation with Riisnæs. But the Supreme Court, thanks to an informant in the Justice Department, learned of what was afoot.[130] The Court declared that the new mandatory retirement rule was unconstitutional because it impinged upon the independence of the judiciary. Similarly, it rejected Terboven's view by insisting that according to international law the Court did have the right to present opinions concerning the legality of decrees issued by the occupying power. The justices therefore announced their intent to resign because they could not carry out their lawful functions. They officially left their positions on December 21, with Riisnæs not yet having had the opportunity of replacing them with NS judges.[131]

This was a disappointment for Quisling because it prevented a gradual NS takeover of the Court. Instead, by standing directly on principle, the justices drew a clear line of demarcation between the old legal order and the new usurped authority exercised by the Germans through NS. A new NS-controlled Supreme Court was soon appointed, and Riisnæs' Justice Department retained authority over the courts. But by their resignations the members of the Supreme Court made it evident that henceforth the system of justice was under Nazi control, a distinction that was appreciated and approved of by those opposed to Quisling and the occupying power.[132]

Quisling's move to secure control over the different branches of government was but one part of his campaign to gain domination over the Norwegian people which he set in motion through the NS-controlled departments and party organizations in the fall of 1940. His initiative was carried out on a wide front.

As a result, eventually almost all Norwegians, to a greater or lesser degree, were forced to take a stand for or against NS. The *Fører* could not, of course, hope to be able to bring pressure to bear on every person on an individual basis. But it would nevertheless be possible for him to exert direct influence on the general public through NS if the party, in addition to controlling the administrative and judicial systems, also succeeded in bringing the great majority of professional and private organizations immediately under its supervision. Therefore, Quisling's fall offensive involved a number of the most important organizations within society.[133]

In his push to have NS take over these groups, he once more revealed his imitative bent to emulate Hitler. Just as Hitler had used the process of *Gleichschaltung* to bring German society into line, so Quisling intended to carry out the process of *nyordning*, the new order, whereby Norwegian society would similarly be under the thumb of the *Fører*.

The attempted takeover of the organizations furthermore was natural, almost inevitable, because such a move was completely in accord with his ideological outlook. Ever intent on establishing his version of the corporate state, he had short-range and long-range goals in mind. The short-range goal was the introduction of the new order, with NS gaining control of the organizations. Once this had been accomplished, he planned to go on to setting up the new corporate body, the National Assembly (*Riksting*), which would serve as the cornerstone of his totalitarian state. The creation of the Assembly was of utmost importance for him. It would mark his final victory over the hated parliamentary system, symbolizing the inauguration of the new era under his leadership.[134]

Again it was his department heads on the Commissarial Council who led the drive, each within his designated area of competence, but Quisling approved all moves against the organizations. His freedom to act was circumscribed only by the obvious need for German approval, first and foremost that of the *Reichskommissar*. But while they remained hostile rivals for power, Terboven did not object to a successful Quisling move to introduce the new order, since it was in Germany's interest to increase its domination over Norway through a surrogate.[135]

With one major exception, in the fall of 1940 NS initially followed a strategy toward the organizations of restricting its offensive largely to discussions, attempting through pressure exerted in negotiations to secure leadership of certain select groups.[136]

The exception to this pattern occurred when the Department of Sports and Labor Service under Axel Stang forcibly attempted to take over Norwegian athletics. This was intended to give NS the opportunity of influencing the approximately 300,000 persons who belonged to sports clubs. Had this succeeded, it would have enabled NS to bring within its sphere a vital part of the population, a large percentage of the country's young people.

Prior to World War II the athletic organizations were divided along ideological lines. Norway's National Association of Athletics (*Norges Landsforbund for Idrett*) was officially non-partisan, while the smaller

Workers' Athletic Association (*Arbeidernes Idrettsforbund*) was affiliated with the Labor party. However, the German invasion speeded up a move already afoot to unite these previous competitors into one national organization. They reached agreement just prior to September 25, with an interim board of directors being appointed.[137]

Stang reacted by seeking to stop this drive toward amalgamation, since it was beyond his jurisdiction. His department decreed on November 10 that it had assumed authority over all national and international athletic contests in Norway. The athletic organizations' interim board protested, and when it continued to oppose the NS effort to dominate sports, it was removed on November 22. Stang appointed in its place an "athletics *fører*", who took charge of all organized sport activity.[138] Furthermore, the athletic clubs were required to belong to a new NS-controlled Norwegian Athletic Association.[139]

The response from the athletic clubs proved to be completely the opposite of Quisling's expectations. They gave full support to their ousted leaders by instituting a boycott of all sporting events sponsored by the NS Athletic Association, which lasted for the duration of the war. The boycott was effective, with the overwhelming majority of athletes forming a nationwide front against NS.[140] *Fritt Folk* was forced to fill its sports pages with coverage of competitions held elsewhere in the world. The few contests that Stang's department eventually was able to arrange, usually consisting of a mixture of NS and German participants, were completely ignored by the general public.[141]

When Quisling, through NS, tried the more indirect approach of using negotiations to secure control of important organizations, the Farmers' Association was selected as the first target. Of the various economic interest groups, it had previously been closest to Quisling ideologically. While it had never officially endorsed NS, he enjoyed a certain amount of sympathy within its ranks dating back to his earlier affiliation with the Agrarian party. For this reason, it appears quite likely that he chose to start with the Farmers' Association because he believed it to be the easiest potential quarry. But in addition, other considerations were taken into account. The farmers formed a major segment of the population. A successful takeover of their most important interest group would have provided NS with considerable impetus in its effort to secure control of other organizations.[142]

At first it appeared as if NS prospects were quite favorable. Among the farmers who belonged to the Association, especially those from the eastern provinces, there existed a considerable residue of bitterness left over from the labor conflicts with agricultural and forestry workers affiliated with the Labor party.[143] NS, with its past record of hostility toward the socialists, benefited from this feeling.

Discussions between representatives of NS and the Farmers' Association began already on September 27, only two days after the establishment of the Commissarial Council. Initially the negotiations went as Quisling had hoped.[144] However, when the political situation became clearer after the confusion from the summer gradually disappeared, sentiment toward NS began to change. Those who belonged to the Association or who worked closely with it became increasingly alarmed that it might be fully absorbed by NS. This feeling was heightened by the fact that an effort was afoot within NS to establish a "Norwegian Farmers' Corporation" (*Norges Bondesamband*) that would include within its membership all persons associated with agriculture.

In reaction to the threat of an NS takeover, individuals both inside and outside the Farmers' Association exerted strong pressure on its leaders to remain firm and to break off the negotiations.[145] The decisive showdown came at a national conference held on November 15–17. The outcome was in doubt until the conclusive vote. However, the group's venerable and highly respected chairman, Johan Mellbye, personally influenced the final decision when he dramatically declared that no basis existed for cooperation with NS. He cited a recent severe attack against the Farmers' Association by the leader of the new NS Norwegian Farmers' Corporation as justification for his argument. Backed by the Association's two vice-chairmen, Mellbye threatened to resign unless the assembled representatives supported his viewpoint. By a vote of 108 to 39 the delegates backed their chairman, deciding not to conclude any agreement with NS, thereby breaking off the negotiations.[146]

To some degree, Quisling unwittingly was responsible for this setback. He failed to push forcibly for a rapid decision by the Farmers' Association, which most likely would have gone in NS' favor.[147] Also, he did not exercise effective control over his subordinates, most notably Steinar Klevar, head of the NS Norwegian Farmers' Corporation. Whereas Quisling intended to use the Farmers' Association as the base for creating the new, all-encompassing NS farm organization, Klevar wished to have his group fulfill this function. As noted, it was his sharp attack that provided Mellbye with the needed reason for opposing direct cooperation with NS.[148]

Having failed to secure control of the Farmers' Association through persuasion, more direct measures had to be employed. Its two vice-foremen were coerced into resigning. Mellbye received similar pressure. Dr. Gustav Richert, the *Reichskommissariat*'s agricultural leader, attempted first to persuade Mellbye to cooperate with NS. When Mellbye refused, he was urged to resign. The old patriarch, however, stubbornly persevered. Richert in the end had to obtain a writ from Terboven which removed Mellbye as chairman. Thereafter he was kept interned on his farm.[149]

His ouster, which occurred on March 3, 1941, failed to have its desired effect. Although his departure allowed NS sympathizers within the Farmers' Association to take over, this proved to be a Pyrrhic victory. The forced expulsion and internment of a respected figure such as Mellbye caused considerable resentment, which was well exploited by organizers of the growing resistance to NS which had materialized by the spring of 1941.[150] When it became plain that the Association had simply turned into an NS front, it ceased to be a viable force. It became largely a paper organization, with little support except from the small number of farmers who were NS members or sympathizers.[151]

Even more significant than the Farmers' Association in terms of numbers and political influence was LO, the National Federation of Trade Unions. With its some 300,000 members, it formed the most important single organized pressure group in the country. Because of its influence, LO had long been the subject of Quisling's interest, dating back to the 1930s. The question of how to secure NS control of the large mass of workers who belonged to the federation was a matter of considerable importance for him.[152]

Because of LO's vital role in maintaining wartime production, the authorities in the *Reichskommissariat* were equally concerned with its fate. The Germans decided immediately after the inception of the Commissarial Council to replace the LO leaders. In part this was because of an earlier refusal by the top labor officials to cooperate with NS in any way. Such open opposition could not be tolerated at a time when Hitler had decided to give NS a monopoly over political activity. Furthermore, Quisling had a personal grudge against the old LO leaders, Elias Volan and Nic. Næss, because of their unwillingness to back him in April 1940, having instead thrown their weight behind the Administrative Council.[153] Of uppermost concern for the *Reichskommissariat*, however, was the need to maintain order within the economy. The Germans therefore unilaterally appointed the LO leaders, without NS being able to exercise any influence in determining its make-up.[154]

The new union leaders, consisting of Jens Tangen as chairman, Ludvik Buland as vice-chairman, and Erling Olsen as secretary, were therefore in a relatively free position in relation to NS. The *Reichskommissariat*'s officials responsible for labor relations, led by Dr. Rudolph Kasper, who headed the *Abteilung für Arbeit und Sozialwesen*, recognized that disruption would be sure to occur if NS were given permission to carry out its corporate objectives on the labor front.[155] Although Tangen and Olsen had previously been part of a union faction that had gone quite far in urging collaboration with NS, the situation had changed by the time they assumed office. The regular staff within the LO administration successfully persuaded the new leaders that they did not have to work with NS in any meaningful way. Under Tangen, LO followed a policy of cooperating when necessary with officials in the *Reichskommissariat*, while ignoring NS administrators in the Commissarial Council as prudently as possible. At the same time, many LO officers took an active part in the developing resistance movement.[156]

Confronted with this common interest between LO and the *Reichskommissariat*, the NS officials responsible for seeking to extend party control over the union movement, and thereby realizing Quisling's corporate goals, found themselves in a weak, exposed position. Chief among them was Birger Meidell, the head of the Social Department. He made a strong effort to set up formal ties between his department and leading trade union representatives. But LO, with Dr. Kasper's backing, thwarted all of Meidell's moves.[157]

Quisling protested against LO being able to remain free from NS influence. He warned that its officials, whom he described as being leaders of "marxistic-communistic" trade unions, were cooperating with other anti-NS groups while seeking to maintain cordial ties with the *Reichskommissariat* so that they could play the Germans off against NS.[158]

While he frustratedly denounced the trade union leaders, he did nothing more. Most noteworthy was his unwillingness to back up Meidell. This was because the latter's attempt to secure influence over LO aroused strong opposition from the *Reichskommissariat*. He also provoked additional annoyance because he was one of the few NS department heads who tried to follow an independent policy, which frequently conflicted with the wishes of Terboven's administrators. Quisling, however, remained aloof from disagreements between Meidell and the *Reichskommissariat*. As was his wont, which he would demonstrate time after time during the occupation, the *Fører* in the final analysis was content to maintain a façade of NS authority.[159] As long as his party outwardly dominated the Commissarial Council, he was unwilling to take any concrete steps that might jeopardize the illusion of NS control, even though this meant that his department heads were placed in a position where they had little if any room to maneuver against the *Reichskommissariat*.

The controversies surrounding Meidell also included an important question of political strategy. Some division of opinion existed within NS in 1940–1941 concerning the best means for the party to gain its ends. Both sides agreed on the common goal of creating a Norwegian version of a National Socialist state under Quisling's leadership. But they were divided over how this could be achieved. Should the party seek to establish its system directly and forcefully, or should it follow a more cautious approach?

Meidell and his colleague in the Shipping Department, Irgens, wished to adopt what they considered to be a constructive strategy. They wanted to avoid divisive conflicts, stressing instead the need for NS officials to demonstrate that they were capable of fulfilling their responsibilities, including the protection of Norwegian interests.

Those who favored the opposite method wanted to accomplish as much as possible within the shortest period of time. In their opinion, Norwegian society should be transformed from top to bottom. NS needed to take over all important institutions and organizations, with its members installed in every key position. Those advocating this view would not refrain from using force if need be.

Quisling obviously adhered to the latter point of view. For him there was hardly any question at all as to how to proceed. With his emphasis on the *Führer* principle, he believed it was merely a matter of discipline and obedience. The Norwegian people, he repeated often to the Germans, were law-abiding and would obey the proper authorities.

Terboven and his subordinates were not impressed by these assurances. He had deliberately restricted NS personnel from taking charge of finance, trade, and industry because he did not believe the party was competent to administer these important economic sectors. When Meidell and Irgens therefore attempted to follow an independent course and extend their departments' control over vital segments of the economy, they encountered difficulty from the *Reichskommissariat*.

Meidell in particular became highly frustrated because of the restrictions which the Germans placed on him. He furthermore did not enjoy Quisling's favor because he opposed pressure from the *Fører* and the Germans to oust civil servants in his department and to replace them with NS members. Finding his position intolerable, Meidell attempted to resign in March 1941. Quisling, however, refused to accept his resignation, insisting that he should obey party discipline and remain at his post.[160]

Irgens experienced similar difficulties. In February 1941 the *Reichskommissariat* demanded that all Norwegian shipping in territorial waters should be considered military booty, to be placed before a prize court in Hamburg. Irgens doggedly resisted this attempt at expropriation, carrying on correspondence with the Germans for approximately three months.[161] Terboven finally became impatient with Irgens' delaying tactics, informing the latter on May 13 that he would proceed unilaterally, with German naval authorities in Oslo taking charge of the ships.[162]

Irgens responded by tendering his resignation directly to Terboven.[163] By taking such a strong stand, even though he received no backing from Quisling, the independent-minded department head succeeded in protecting the vessels in question. The Germans feared that Irgens' departure, coupled with seizure of the ships as war prizes, would arouse so much resentment that the move would be harmful. Irgens was therefore told that the matter would not be settled until after the end of the war. He was asked to withdraw his resignation, which he agreed to do, since he had gained his ends.[164]

Irgens was so exhausted, however, by this confrontation that he took a three-month leave of absence. But in accordance with his long-term policy, he did not allow his department to be run in his absence by an NS activist who might try to nazify it rapidly. Instead, he made arrangements to have two non-NS department heads, Johannessen and Sandberg, act in his place.[165]

Because the *Reichskommissariat* did not always apply full force behind his department heads' attempts to gain control of various economic organizations, Quisling witnessed the failure of every effort which he directed NS to launch. Rather than strengthening his position as he had hoped, on each occasion when NS authorities began discussions with various organizations after September 25, 1940, they were invariably rebuffed.

In yet another endeavor, Meidell sought to exert pressure on the leaders of the fishermen to have their organization, Norway's Fishermen's Association, join a proposed corporate group. This move was effectively blocked thanks to unified opposition from the fishermen and Sigurd Johannessen. As head of the Trade Department, Johannessen wished to prevent NS from extending its authority over the fishing industry, and he worked to keep its influence to a bare minimum.[166] Thanks to this joint obstruction, plus Meidell's low standing with the *Reichskommissariat*, the Fishermen's Association remained largely free of NS intrusion for the rest of the war.[167]

Similarly, various organizations within the medical profession, including separate associations of doctors, nurses, dentists, pharmacists, and midwives, rejected a move sponsored by Hagelin's Interior Department to set up a corporate body that would have included all health service personnel.[168] Gulbrand Lunde's Propaganda Department was no more successful when it tried to establish a corporate organization for members of the press. The board of directors of the Press Association unanimously voted this down in January 1941.[169] This failure was particularly noteworthy because German censorship had controlled the press ever since the beginning of the occupation.

Although German reluctance to give NS a free hand did not extend to the public sector, here too Quisling learned by the end of 1940 that time was running out. The initial public confusion and discouragement from the spring and summer were increasingly replaced by a determination to resist NS encroachments. Even within public administration, where Hagelin earlier had enjoyed great success, opposition had stiffened by the end of the year. He learned this when he sent out a strongly worded ultimatum to all state and local civil servants on December 16, demanding loyalty to the new regime. They were ordered to support NS in every way by aiding the party to reach its goals "quickly and effectively" in the "best interest" of the country and its people. Strict reprisals were threatened against anyone who failed to cooperate. Such a refusal, said Hagelin, constituted a hostile act, and he warned ominously that drastic punishment would "hereafter strike every enemy of the state".[170]

The leaders of the organizations of civil servants were not intimidated. They responded rapidly, drawing up a negative reply. They duplicated this rejection and sent it to their members, with the result that the overwhelming majority of civil servants sent in protests to Hagelin. In some municipalities (*kommuner*) up to 98 per cent of those employed in administration took part in defying the Interior Department.[171]

The school teachers formed yet another key group that Quisling and his officials specifically singled out. If they could be made to obey the party, then Quisling could expect to impose his credo on future generations within the classroom. Ragnar Skancke, Quisling's longtime loyalist, had the direct responsibility for seeking to achieve this important goal.

Skancke drew up a declaration of loyalty, dated November 20, 1940, in which the teachers were to promise that they would "positively and actively" work to gain understanding for NS' program and ideas among their pupils. Like Hagelin, he applied coercion, warning that the teachers risked being fired if they did not sign the declaration. He pointed specifically to Terboven's decree, which authorized dismissal of persons hostile to NS.[172]

However, before this declaration could be sent out, one of the leaders of the budding resistance movement, which was just beginning to form, obtained a copy of Skancke's letter. Thereupon the element of surprise was lost. Acting in close consultation with the leaders of the teachers' organization, the resistance responded by drawing up a counter-declaration, which was sent to teachers throughout the country. As a result, when Skancke's Department of Church and Education began to mail out the NS loyalty declaration to teachers in certain districts, the response consisted overwhelmingly of copies of the counter-declaration. This statement declared that the teachers would remain true to their responsibilities and consciences, and that they would, as previously, obey all "lawful" decisions by their superiors. By stressing that they were required to obey only lawful orders from the Department of Church and Education, the teachers effectively circumvented Skancke's claim that they owed full allegiance to NS.[173] Skancke had no choice but to admit failure by halting the distribution of any more loyalty declarations.

While the outcome of this confrontation was but another in the long series of setbacks that Quisling received in National Union's attempt to dominate or take over various organizations and professional groups, on the other side of the battleground this episode had the effect of causing local and national leaders of the various teachers' organizations to establish closer contact. A common feeling of unity bound the teachers together, making them even more determined to defeat future moves by Quisling and the Department of Church and Education to gain control of the minds of school children.[174]

As in the case of primary and secondary education, Terboven had no objections to NS attempting to secure dominance over instruction on the university level. It therefore did not take long for NS to move against the University.[175] Here too it was Skancke, as head of the Church and Education Department, who spearheaded the offensive. He acted not only with Quisling's direct encouragement, but also in full understanding with the *Reichskommissariat.*[176]

Already on the day after Skancke took office, the president of the Students' Association was arrested, and the group's funds were placed at the disposal of the small NS student organization.[177] Skancke followed this up by issuing a unilateral decree on October 15 whereby he usurped the authority to make appointments to the ranks of associate and full professor from the academic departments. He did not waste any time in using his increased power. On the next day two appointments were made, in geography and history. The new professors were naturally both NS members. A week later Quisling's old associate, Herman Harris Aall, realized a long held, cherished ambition when he was named professor of jurisprudence.[178] The University's faculty leaders in the Senate of the University protested against these politically motivated appointments, but to no avail. More effective action was taken by the students, however, who boycotted the lectures of the new "professors". As a result, the NS appointees, while continuing to draw their salaries, soon requested, on various grounds, to be relieved of their lecture responsibilities.[179]

No further moves were made by Skancke for the time being. Under the circumstances, the situation at the University remained fairly normal. The one major difference was the existence of a far greater feeling of solidarity among students and faculty than in ordinary times – a feeling of common antipathy toward NS and the Germans which was shared by all except the small NS element.

The next NS attack did not come until 1941, when on February 7 Skancke removed some thirteen examiners who were scheduled to take part in evaluating candidates for graduation in the school of law. He replaced them with persons most of whom were NS members. Skancke was prompted to take this action by his colleague, Sverre Riisnæs, and not without reason. Included prominently among the ousted examiners were a number of the former Supreme Court justices who had resigned in protest against Riisnæs' effort to nazify the judiciary. In response to the ousters, the University, both faculty and students, declared solidarity with the embattled law faculty. Faculty members threatened with mass resignations, while the law students refused to be examined by the NS appointees. The impasse was finally solved thanks to considerable effort on the part of the University's rector and the dean of the law faculty, resulting in a compromise with Skancke. They agreed that none of the NS examiners would be used, but neither would former justices of the Supreme Court. However, all of the other regularly appointed examiners would test the law candidates, and their future designation would be made on the recommendation of the law faculty and the Senate. With the restoration of the past practice of faculty control over the appointment of examiners, the outcome of the incident was viewed as a victory for the University over Quisling and his representative, Skancke.[180] Once more NS had experienced defeat when seeking to gain effective control of an important institution. Except for a few additional NS appointments, which had no significant effect, the University continued to function largely unaffected by NS influence until September 1941.

The *Hird* was the most controversial party group that Quisling utilized in striving to establish his ascendancy over society through the many-sided offensive which he launched in the fall of 1940. The actions that he ordered his paramilitary force to carry out did not differ greatly from what he had conceived as its main function in the 1930s. He planned to use the *Hird* in the streets, following the example of its source of inspiration, the Nazi SA. But in contrast with the small force that he had at his disposal in the 1930s, usually greatly outnumbered by its rivals, during the occupation he had the opportunity of employing the *Hird* on an entirely different level. Not only was it larger, but at first it faced no organized opposition.

It did, however, initially experience some difficulty from the Germans. In the summer of 1940, before Terboven had been forced by Hitler to give Quisling's party political predominance, the *Reichskommissariat* had effectively put the brakes on the *Hird*, going so far as to threaten to dissolve the still small party formation if it became involved in disorders. But after September 25, with NS as the only permitted party in the country, Quisling could use the *Hird* as he wished.[181] The prominent role he assigned it at this time simply served to show how he continued to follow blindly his assumption that if only he adhered to the same tactics as Hitler had employed, then he could expect to gain similar triumphs in Norway.

He used the *Hird* as his personal force. It had responsibility for carrying out any political activity that he might decide on. Upon joining, *Hird* initiates took an oath of personal loyalty in which they promised "obedience" to Quisling "until death".[182] In order to increase its membership "because of the great demands required of the *Hird* also from a numerical point of view", Quisling signed a decree on January 23, 1941, which required all physically able male NS members aged eighteen to thirty to belong to the *Hird*.[183]

He had need for numbers. Beginning already during the fall of 1940, he systematically put his unit into action. By showing that he controlled the streets, he believed that he could instill fear and respect. Not merely would this, in his opinion, result in increased NS membership, but it would also prepare the way for further advances as the NS moved toward gaining overall domination of the people.

The exact opposite occurred from what Quisling and his *Hird* leaders expected. Rather than stimulate respect for NS power, *Hird* brutality strengthened and consolidated public resistance. In the period after the beginning of the Commissarial Council, people began to show their antagonism to NS and the Germans in various ways. Symbols of different types were worn by the opponents of NS, not merely to indicate that they were against the party, but also to encourage and spread resistance. Among the most prominent methods of showing opposition were the display of Norwegian national colors – red, white, and blue – on jackets, the wearing of flowers in buttonholes to celebrate the King's birthday, the display of paper clips in buttonholes to symbolize the need for solidarity, and the use of brightly colored red, white, and blue ski caps, which were especially popular among young people.[184]

Quisling let the *Hird* loose to remove such symbols, with the wearers often being assaulted. Nationally minded Norwegians, in particular the young, frequently fought back. During the winter of 1940–41 these confrontations became numerous, especially when young *Hird* members carried their campaign into the schools. They deliberately used force to intimidate their opponents. The *Hird*'s main publication declared at this time that the unit's "patience has come to an end. The national revolution *shall* be carried out, and we will make certain that this occurs. The intellectuals and plutocrats who sabotage and resist will be marched down and swept aside".[185] Members of the *Hird* frequently beat up their victims, not only on the streets but also in the classroom. At times teachers and school administrators were similarly subjected to physical abuse.[186]

These acts of lawlessness were not interfered with. The regular police were generally opposed to such acts, and on occasion individual policemen went so far as to show sympathy for the *Hird*'s opponents. However, the police were under strict orders from their NS superiors not to interfere.[187] The organization furthermore was supported by officials in Riisnæs' Justice Department, who refused to bring charges against *Hird* members accused of inflicting injuries, no matter how serious.[188]

Such uncontrolled use of force created a very strong negative reaction. Used to having authorities who maintained order, the people increasingly felt fearful of living under conditions that many felt approached a reign of terror. Later during the occupation such a state of mind became commonplace, especially after the Gestapo began to act with greater force, but during the fall and winter months of 1940–41 this kind of activity was relatively new. A general feeling of revulsion arose, directed not only against Quisling's street fighters but against the entire NS organization.[189]

As a consequence, spontaneous protests broke out against *Hird* brutality. Violent street tumults occurred in Oslo on December 14 which involved thousands of people. Members of the *Hird* were literally besieged in their headquarters, outside of which fighting with the public took place throughout the day.[190] Other demonstrations broke out in various parts of the country, protesting not only against the *Hird* but against NS authorities in general.[191]

Unrest within the schools reached new heights in February 1941 when NS authorities ordered the pupils to attend a Hitler Youth exhibit. This resulted in demonstration marches and protest meetings. Simultaneously, school children in Bergen went on strike in disapproval of *Hird* violence. This in turn inspired the teachers to take a clear stand against NS. Teachers in Oslo refused categorically to allow their pupils to visit the Hitler Youth exhibition. It was also at this time that the first organized illegal resistance group was formed among the secondary school teachers in Oslo.[192]

Quisling had no intention of repudiating this disorder and unrest, in particular since he had instigated the *Hird* campaign. In an interview in *Fritt Folk* published later in the year he voiced the official view toward the *Hird* and its controversial activity. Arguing that his street fighters had behaved with more decency and restraint than anticipated, he further maintained that they had been subjected to provocations. The *Hird*, he insisted, worked unselfishly for Norway's cause, serving as an example for the nation's young people. He declared that it would be nice to have the *Hird* popular, as it deserved to be, but if it were not, then he hoped to have it strike fear in the hearts of those who were working against the people's vital interests.[193]

He did not realize his expectations that the schools would be forced to comply with the *Hird*'s demands. Instead, the teachers and pupils emerged victorious, with NS being compelled to abandon its offensive on the school front for the time being.[194] Use of the *Hird* only resulted in heightening the tendency of the great mass of the people to resist NS moves to strengthen its authority. Furthermore, the *Reichskommissariat* watched with interest the outcome of the *Hird* action. Terboven was kept fully informed as to how the *Hird*'s brutality increased the people's alienation from NS.[195]

Because of the negative response to violence, Quisling was forced to abandon gradually his use of the *Hird* as street fighters. Instead, the force tended to fade into the background. It became largely a recruiting ground for the various military formations which Quisling helped to form. *Hird* members made up by far the largest number among those who served in different military units that were organized in Norway during the war.[196]

Quisling's failed *Hird* campaign proved to have consequences not only due to the increased opposition which it inspired within the population as

a whole, but also because it helped to bring into being organized resistance
to oppose the efforts that NS was making. This was especially unfortunate
for Quisling. The atmosphere of lawlessness and officially approved injustice served as the catalyst which created greater cooperation and consolidation among vital groups within Norwegian society. These formed the basis
for organized resistance to Quisling and the Germans during the war.
They included first and foremost the various voluntary associations, the
economic and professional organizations, and the Lutheran State
Church.[197]

Because the overwhelming majority of the people officially belonged to the
Church, its involvement on the side of the resistance that began to consolidate against NS in the fall and winter of 1940–1941 proved to be of special
significance. With its moral authority and its potential broad base of support, the Church was an opponent that Quisling would have preferred to
avoid. This was the initial approach which he adopted toward the Church
in the fall of 1940. Its religious authority was not challenged in any way.
On the contrary, Skancke's Church and Education Department assumed
an outwardly favorable attitude, going so far as to make available an extra
appropriation of funds.[198] This did not mean, however, that Skancke intended to allow the Church to remain free of NS influence. He sought to
extend its sway over religious matters as prudently as possible. He indicated this already at the end of September when NS, through his department, attempted to take over radio transmission of Sunday services. To
have sermons delivered over the air by pro-NS pastors would have been a
significant propaganda advantage for Quisling's party. The move, however, was effectively blocked by Church officials. Bishop Berggrav of
Oslo, who earlier had taken part in the move to secure Quisling's forced
resignation in April, was especially effective in preventing NS from securing control of religious broadcasts.[199]

Although NS followed a cautious approach at this time, pulling back
when meeting resistance, leading Church figures were already determined
to take active measures that were bound to lead to confrontations with
Quisling's party, rather than accept the status quo and remain quiescent as
long as NS did not directly threaten the Church's position. The religious
leaders assumed this stand largely because of their beliefs, being convinced
that Quisling's ideology was anti-Christian in the same way that German
National Socialism was opposed to Christian values. Bishop Berggrav in
particular pointed to the ties between Quisling and Rosenberg as evidence
that NS' *Fører* shared Nazi pagan convictions.[200]

Out of the common belief that the Church needed to be united in order
to present a solid front against NS in the future, a meeting was held at
Berggrav's episcopal residence on October 25, resulting in the unification

of leading factions within the Church. In peacetime such a step would have been unthinkable. The various low church, pietistic, high church, and liberal elements within the state church were ordinarily in constant opposition to each other. Now, however, a shared concern for Christian values brought these previously feuding groups together in a Christian Joint Council (*Kristent Samråd*) in which three persons predominated. These were Berggrav, Ole Hallesby, the leading conservative theologian, and Ludvig Hope, the lay head of the China Mission. Under the direction of this trio of imposing figures, the Council served as the general staff for coordinating the Church's moves against NS authorities from this time onwards, with the key decisions being made at its meetings.[201]

The first open public breach between the Christian Joint Council and NS authorities occurred when the religious leaders took a strong stand against NS' campaign to make inroads into society. In particular, the Church carefully and deliberately chose to voice its opposition to the lawless activities of the *Hird*. Berggrav, after consultation with Hallesby and Hope, led the bishops in drawing up a letter of protest which was sent to Skancke. The latter attempted to ignore the bishops' address, but unsuccessfully. The denunciation, along with an addendum plus copies of correspondence which the bishops had exchanged with Skancke, was printed in a total of 50,000 copies and sent throughout the country in the form of a pastoral letter to all congregations. It was thereafter read from most pulpits on Sunday, February 9, 1941. Although the Gestapo and the police managed to confiscate ca. 20,000 copies, the remainder reached their intended recipients, and were in many cases reproduced in large numbers. The bishops' pastoral letter also gained a wider audience, since it was smuggled out of the country. As intended, it quickly reached England, with its message being broadcast back to Norway by London Radio.[202]

In addition to stressing their specific opposition to the use of force and the other acts of illegality permitted by NS authorities, with specific reference to the *Hird*, the bishops made the blanket indictment that injustice was endemic in Norway. As evidence, they pointed to the resignation of the Supreme Court. Finally, the bishops strongly rejected a decree by Jonas Lie's Police Department which sought to void a pastor's pledge of confidentiality to all who might confide in him.[203]

Thanks to the publicity which the letter received, within an eight-day period scarcely a person was unaware of the bishops' repudiation.[204] From this point onwards the Church was clearly identified as being in the forefront of resistance to Quisling and NS. In adopting this position, the Church succeeded in its effort at unity, preventing Christians from being influenced by Quisling's ideology. During the occupation the Christian groups in the population, especially the low church pietists, were the most implacable opponents of NS.

After the bishops' protest, active hostility existed between the Church

and Quisling's party. The Department of Church and Education now took
over supervision of the radio's religious programs. Hereafter, only a small
number of NS clergymen and laymen as a rule participated in religious
broadcasts.[205]

With the great moral force of the Church also antagonistic to his effort to
have NS influence permeate society, Quisling discovered once more the
bitter fact that having an NS majority on the Commissarial Council did not
automatically mean that his expectations would be fulfilled. His optimistic
anticipation that the Council would simply be a brief interim arrangement,
allowing him to begin the process whereby he made society subject to his
power, had proven false. Not only did the Council remain in place much
longer than he expected, but he did not obtain the benefits that he anticipated from having placed NS members in charge of most government offices. NS did enjoy some limited gains in such areas as securing command of
the police and supervising the appointive process for government service.
Quisling managed to build up his party's organizational structure to his
satisfaction. He also witnessed a considerable increase in NS membership
in comparison to the party's prewar strength, but the growth was not as
great as he had hoped. Most disappointing of all, NS did not gain the supreme position which he desired. Neither through negotiations, intimidation, or the *Hird*'s use of organized violence did he succeed in establishing
effective control over the people as a whole. The great majority of NS endeavors in this direction ended with being rebuffed. The offensive which
he launched so enthusiastically in the fall of 1940 on the whole succeeded
only in creating a resolve to resist. At first this feeling was unorganized,
being experienced on an individual basis, or at the most within groups of
like-minded persons. But by the second year of the occupation the determination to oppose NS inroads began to take on a more organized character that eventually encompassed the nation as a whole.

CHAPTER XIII

The Development of Organized Resistance and the Quest for Governmental Authority

1941 – January 1942

I have without success placed myself at the beck and call of the Norwegians. I will now force them to their knees.

Josef Terboven, quoted by Hermann Boehm,
September 9, 1941

. . . if Norwegians see that their country has regained its freedom through an independent government, then they will begin to have faith in Germany, and Norway will become an active link in the Germanic-European New Order . . .

On the basis of these considerations, I can only urgently recommend the establishment of an independent government in Norway.

Vidkun Quisling to Adolf Hitler
September 17, 1941

By the early spring of 1941 it was obvious that the gap which separated Quisling and his followers from the great mass of Norwegians could not be bridged. Instead, this breach would grow ever greater, with the number of persons who attempted to bridge the gap by maintaining various degrees of benevolent contact with NS members, the so-called "striped ones" (*de stripete*), declining as the occupation progressed.

Quisling's inability to secure a larger following was due to several factors. However, the public's repudiation occurred first and foremost because the overwhelming majority of the people regarded their opposition to NS as a fight against evil. As a people, Norwegians have a moralistic outlook, a character trait which the Lutheran tradition has helped to foster. They are therefore quick to react to specific instances of injustice. In his various attempts to subvert established institutions and organizations through stealth and coercion, Quisling violated societal norms.

The homogeneous nature of Norwegian society similarly was in Quisling's disfavor. The people collectively maintain a strong feeling of unity, regarding themselves as an extended family. This conscious attitude of national cohesiveness proved to be extremely important in sustaining a unified front against Quisling's NS, who were identified as collaborators with a foreign oppressor. This united stand, which isolated NS members as social pariahs, was especially crucial because it exercised direct pressure on individuals who under different circumstances might have wavered, being tempted by considerations of personal gain into possibly affiliating with Quisling's movement.

NS was further weakened by its inability to attract influential persons into its ranks. Almost without exception, those who enjoyed a high standing in society were in opposition to the party. Those few prominent individuals who did join were not numerous enough to exert any influence. Instead, they ruined their reputations by becoming associated with the party.

This negative reaction toward Quisling's party resulted from the specific actions he had initiated, going back to the very beginning of the occupation. Societal solidarity against NS generally increased in direct proportion to the various offensive actions which Quisling launched. His party, it is true, had experienced some outward successes in 1940, including takeover of governmental administration on the national and local levels, rapid growth in membership, and penetration of the police. Still, Quisling had been stymied by popular opposition in his overall drive to nazify society. He was further hampered because even though he generally was backed by the Germans, nevertheless the *Reichskommissariat* would not give needed assistance if an NS move was perceived to be contrary to German interests. This was shown most fully in the *Reichskommissariat*'s refusal to allow NS to have a free hand within the economic sector.

With resistance increasingly coalescing, in particular after the Church and the Supreme Court added their great moral authority to the struggle, the situation in early 1941 was characterized not merely by defense against NS initiatives. Instead, the organizations threatened by an NS takeover went on the offensive, carrying out a deliberately coordinated counteraction. Such a move was of the utmost importance for the opposition. Along with the Church, the various professional and economic organizations were the only independent associations that were free of NS and German influence. Therefore, any effort they undertook, in particular if it was coordinated, represented one of the few ways in which a large segment of the population could express itself politically. With all parties except NS outlawed, and with the popular media, the press and the radio, under German censorship, only the organizations and the Church could give public expression of hostility toward NS. The independent existence of these groups served therefore as an open challenge to Quisling's attempt, through the NS-dominated Commissarial Council, to expand his party's influence.

The process by which the organizations eventually united in a common action occurred over a period of time. The first meetings between leaders of several associations, held to discuss the possibility of planning some countermove to NS' offensive against various sectors of society, took place as early as November 1940. Not until after the beginning of 1941, however, did these consultations develop to the point that they included representatives from a relatively large number of groups.[1]

When these talks had reached a fairly advanced stage, a move by the National Union Personnel Office for Public Service, aiming to control the appointive process for persons employed in the public sector, caused the first protests from a number of organizations. Although NSPOT had come into being in October 1940, when Hagelin created the office as part of the NS takeover of government administration, the issuance of its decree of February 15, 1941, marked the first time its existence became generally known. The office's ruling aroused tremendous concern among opponents of NS because it politicized public appointments. Specifically, applicants for public positions were required to state whether or not they were NS members, if they were in agreement with the "new order", and to prove whether they were reliable from a NS standpoint.[2]

After considering this matter, the leaders of a number of organizations sent a protest letter to Terboven on April 3. It stressed in particular the harm that would occur if appointments were decided on the basis of the applicant's political affiliation, and requested that Terboven revise NSPOT's February 15 ruling. Twenty-two leaders of national organizations signed the protest. The majority represented public employees, but a number were from the private sector. Among these were heads of the national associations of doctors, lawyers, dentists, engineers, and architects. Most influential of all, however, was the Norwegian Federation of Trade Unions, LO.[3]

Those who signed the letter did not forward it to Terboven in order to gain redress of a specific grievance. They intended it to be an act of public protest. The *Reichskommissar* fully understood this, since the letter's contents were broadcast over London Radio before he had even received his copy.[4]

Despite this rather blatant act of defiance, he decided not to respond.[5] In choosing to avoid a confrontation, he did so in large part because of the locked-in position he was in during this phase of the occupation. He could not repudiate NSPOT because he had no alternative except to support NS publicly, thanks to the assurance that Quisling had received from Hitler at the time of the Commissarial Council's formation. However, Terboven, as those behind the scenes knew, not only had a low opinion of Quisling's leadership, but also wished to maintain tranquility within the economy. His best course was therefore to ignore the letter.

He could also afford to overlook the protest because it was not all-inclusive. With the exception of the private organizations noted above, the demonstration was mainly restricted to the public employee groups that were directly affected by NSPOT's rule. Despite its limited participation, however, the protest took on the character of being an expression of popular opinion. This was shown by the enthusiastic reaction which the letter provoked. It served to indicate that organizations still existed, along with the Christian Joint Council, that could serve as spokesmen for the popular will.[6]

Encouraged by the response that the protest received, and further stimulated by Terboven's failure to take punitive action, the leaders of various organizations resolved to take another initiative.[7] But this move was considerably greater in scope. The heads of forty-three organizations put their signatures to another letter of complaint, addressed once more to Terboven. Its broader intent was also shown by the fact that it protested against all NS actions since September 25, 1940, rather than against a single provocation. The new remonstrance declared that NS, through its department heads on the Commissarial Council, through the use of violence by the *Hird*, and through various attempts to increase the party's power and privileges, was acting in an illegal manner which created unrest within the population. In their conclusion, the heads of the organizations requested a response from Terboven as soon as possible, not only to this letter but also to the previously unanswered protest of April 3.[8]

This statement, even more than the earlier protest, was intended to be a political demonstration. As previously, the text was forwarded to London before Terboven had the opportunity to read its contents. Dated May 15, it did not arrive on his desk until May 19.[9] Its purpose was not to persuade him to change German policy by restricting NS. Instead, its primary intent was to stiffen resistance against NS. As one of the originaters of the letter later declared, what was needed at that time was an action "to manifest the Norwegian people's attitude" and "to weld together the front [against NS]".[10] Such a broadbased initiative served as an indicator to show the general public's hostility to NS, but more importantly, it provided the people with concrete evidence of their common agreement and unity, and that they still possessed organizations that could give voice to commonly shared views.[11] The letter fulfilled its intended purpose. Thousands of copies were spread throughout the country, serving to stimulate the solidifying resistance to Quisling's party.[12]

Not all important groups, however, joined in the May protest. In particular, two key employer organizations, Norway's Industrial Federation and the Norwegian Employers' Association, did not.[13] Nevertheless, the challenge was as clear a manifestation of popular opinion as possible under the circumstances. Some 700,000 people belonged to the organizations that participated. Largest were LO with its 300,000 members and the Norwegian Women's National Council with some 200,000 members. And while perhaps some thousand persons who belonged to the protest groups might not have agreed, either because of NS membership or because they wished to be neutral, there were many thousands more outside these organizations who wholeheartedly favored the viewpoint expressed in the letter.[14]

When Terboven received the May 15 letter, he was already under considerable pressure from NS to move against the very groups that had joined in the protest. It is interesting to note that NS' strategy toward the organizations changed at approximately the same time these groups first began to make plans for their challenge to the party. By January 1941 it had become obvious to NS that its attempt to extend party influence over key organizations through pressure exerted during negotiations had been a failure.[15] In NS' view, a new, more forceful, approach was needed. As was natural at this time, the Interior Department spearheaded this action. Hagelin enthusiastically grasped the opportunity to try to bring the organizations under the control of his department.[16] But while the implementation was left to him, it could not have taken place without Quisling's full approval. The latter's long-range goal remained his corporate ideal, the establishment of a National Assembly (*Riksting*). This over-riding ambition could not be achieved unless the organizations were completely under NS dominance.[17]

The Interior Department began a two-pronged initiative as the party's new strategy toward the organizations. First, it sought to obtain detailed information concerning the organizations by seeking to draw up a national register, to include all organized groups. However, the department was flooded by an avalanche of reports during February and March from various groups ranging from national associations to small social circles. The entire registration drive ended in chaos, with the party unable to make use of this massive amount of material. The fiasco did not result from any deliberate attempt to sabotage the effort, but rather from the Interior Department's incompetence.[18]

Hagelin's second approach did not require extensive expertise, and it therefore had the possibility of achieving more significant results. The Interior Department drew up an ordinance regulating all organizations, which Hagelin forwarded to Terboven on March 13. The goal of this decree was obvious: to have the "new order" exercise its authority directly over the organizations, which would be controlled by a special office within the Interior Department. Hagelin did take into consideration one specific German interest, however, in that his proposed ordinance did not include economic organizations, which Terboven unquestionably would have objected to.[19]

The *Reichskommissar* did not respond immediately to Hagelin's proposal. Nor, as we have seen, did he take any steps after the initial letter from the organizations on April 3. But while he was still reviewing the situation, the protest from the forty-three organizations arrived on his desk. This challenge was too important for him to ignore, in particular since NS, through Hagelin, was urging takeover of the organizations. If the *Reichskommissar* had done nothing, it would have provided Quisling with a potent argument, since he could have alleged that Terboven was failing to control anti-Nazi elements in Norway. The next initiative would therefore have to come from him.[20]

In his reaction, the *Reichskommissar*'s options were limited. He had to mete out some form of punishment, since accommodation was impossible. The letter from the forty-three organizations contained general criticism of Quisling's entire policy, a policy that enjoyed direct German endorsement since September 25, 1940. To disavow Quisling and NS was out of the question.[21]

The careful consideration that Terboven gave before he disclosed his response showed the seriousness with which he regarded the matter. For a considerable time NS was uncertain of his decision.[22] Then in mid-June certain indicators revealed that the signatories to the May protest letter could expect a forceful German reaction. On June 12 three of these were arrested by the Gestapo, while the remainder were ordered to appear before the *Reichskommissar* on the 14th, later postponed to the 18th.[23] Shortly thereafter NS received the first sign of Terboven's intentions. The *Reichskommissar* gave general approval to Hagelin's proposal to establish NS control over the organizations by enactment of an Associations Ordinance. It was Terboven, however, who had the final say concerning which organizations would be brought under direct NS leadership through the appointment of special NS commissioners, and which groups would be excluded from such supervision.[24]

He made careful arrangements to give his showdown with the leaders of the organizations symbolic significance. He planned to have the June 18 meeting mark NS' formal takeover of a large part of the country's organizational structure. Quisling too attached great importance to this event, which he showed by personally instructing the new NS commissioners about their responsibilities. They received a briefing from their *Fører* just two hours before Terboven met with the unfortunate representatives of the organizations.[25]

When the latter arrived for their confrontation with the *Reichskommissar* at his headquarters in the *Storting* building, they were intimidated by the large number of armed German police and NS members who were present, plus the fact that the hall was decorated for a special occasion.[26]

After keeping them waiting for an hour, Terboven deigned to appear. He began by ordering the arrest of five of those present, while a sixth, who was not in attendance, was taken into custody later in the day.[27] Having demonstrated his power in this frightening fashion, he went on to make a harsh and contemptuous speech. The only point that he and the targets of his sarcasm could agree on was that their protest had been a political demonstration.[28]

Having delivered his tirade, Terboven left as abruptly as he had arrived. His place was taken by Hagelin, who made public the Associations Ordinance. Quisling's lieutenant thereafter announced what the fate of the various groups would be. Some were immediately dissolved. These included the professional associations of teachers and academicians. Twenty-seven other organizations were placed directly under the leadership of NS commissioners.[29] Only one major group that had taken part in the protest remained largely unaffected, LO. This resulted from Terboven's continued desire to avoid labor disturbances. To Quisling's disappointment, the *Reichskommissar* therefore kept LO free of NS control.[30] The Federation of Labor did not, however, escape entirely unscathed. Its vice-foreman, Ludvik Buland, who had signed the protest on LO's behalf, was one of the six persons arrested on June 18. He later died in a concentration camp.

The outcome of the confrontation was that NS secured control of a significant number of organizations, the major exception being some vital groups within the economic sector. Through Hagelin's Interior Department, Quisling could henceforth use the Associations Ordinance to NS' advantage when asserting the party's dominance over the country's organizations. This included groups that had not signed the protest, and that originally were not immediately affected by the action taken on June 18. Hagelin created a special office in his department for the specific purpose of supervising the extension of NS control over the organizations.[31]

Quisling therefore had no reason to be displeased with the manner in which the organizations had apparently been cowed. True Terboven, not the NS *Fører*, had made the vital decisions as to when and how the takeover would occur. Furthermore, LO remained outside NS' domain. Nevertheless, from Quisling's viewpoint the results were advantageous. The Interior Department's original proposal had been largely implemented. NS therefore appeared to have increased its power significantly. He expected that his party would now have the opportunity of exercising authority over associations that enjoyed a considerable membership. This seemed to be a far superior position compared with NS' previous inability to gain influence through negotiations.

The instigators of the protest action, the leaders of organizations that now were either under NS leadership or had been dissolved, did not, however, necessarily consider the outcome as a victory for Quisling. Their political demonstration, intended to serve as a symbol of opposition to Quisling and the Germans, had succeeded both internally and externally. The protest and Terboven's stringent counteraction were heralded widely in Allied propaganda as evidence that the overwhelming majority of Norwegians remained uncowed.[32]

The events culminating with Terboven's move against the organizations marked a change in the character of the occupation. Until this time acts of resistance had largely been public, with those protesting making direct reference to established laws and international rights. After June 18, 1941, however, this type of public protest, planned by groups that acted independently of NS control, was not possible, with one important exception – the Church. Opposition to NS and the Germans continued to manifest itself publicly, as we shall see, but this opposition hereafter generally had to be organized in secret through underground activity.

Following enactment of the Associations Ordinance, Quisling still had to have NS deal with one important problem concerning the various organizations that had been placed under his party's control. It remained to be seen whether NS would make effective use of its power by being able to manipulate the large mass membership at its disposal. For Quisling, his immediate objective was therefore to secure NS control through the party commissioners heading the organizations so that the rank and file could be influenced by their new leaders in fact as well as in theory.[33]

This meant that the struggle between Quisling's party and the organizations was not over. It simply continued under altered circumstances during the summer of 1941. While NS endeavored to regulate the members in the organizations, their old leaders strove to prevent the party from gaining its objective. Resistance took place in a variety of ways within different groups, but the goal was the same – to turn the organization into an empty shell so that the newly appointed NS commissioner headed nothing of substance. This was achieved by having the officers of the organizations resign their positions, while the rank and file withdrew their membership, either actively or passively. Although the speed with which the resignations took place varied, the outcome was always the same. The NS commissioners became heads of paper organizations.[34]

This development did not mean that all organized activity free of NS domination ceased to take place for the duration of the occupation. On the contrary, the associations as a rule continued to function, but henceforth in a clandestine manner, with a mix of old and new leaders. A whole web of illegal organizations came into being, each unit by and large representing the same membership that had existed at the time the group had been independent. The great majority of those who had previously belonged to the organizations before they were taken over by NS obeyed the orders issued by the illegal leadership. In this way the illegal organizations formed a major part of the growing resistance movement that was being formed in opposition to Quisling's effort, backed by German authorities, to nazify society.[35]

Failure to control the officers and members of the organizations came as a complete surprise to Quisling and his subordinates, as indicated by the absence of any prohibitions in the Associations Ordinance against officers leaving their positions or members resigning from their organizations.[36] As he had done previously, Quisling continued to believe that the key to assuming power was simply to take over at the top, and then all problems that stood in his way would be solved. But NS' inability to manipulate the organizations again demonstrated the fallacy of this assumption. He did not, however, abandon his fixed idea. Indeed, he could not, since he found it impossible to secure a mass following through persuasion. His lack of charisma and the repugnance which he aroused meant that coercion, when the Germans allowed it, was the only recourse he could resort to.

In reaction to the large number of resignations which made NS authority over the organizations worthless, the party responded by wishing to introduce compulsory membership. This practice, moreover, was quite in accordance with NS ideology, since the system that Quisling hoped to achieve left no room for anyone outside of his corporate structure. However, it was the party commissioners in charge of the organizations, whose membership was rapidly disappearing, who specifically insisted on this solution in the summer of 1941.[37]

Various draft decrees were drawn up within Hagelin's Interior Department during the summer and early fall, intended to deal with the problem of defections. But these proposals failed to secure Terboven's approval.[38] His refusal therefore had the effect of bringing NS' offensive against the organizations to an end for the time being. This question faded into the background during the fall months. Not until February 1942, when Quisling had secured his goal of heading a government, would the issue of involuntary membership in a corporate structure once more become current.[39]

Quisling's position had therefore not been strengthened a great deal as a result of the confrontation with the forty-three organizations. Although the Associations Ordinance formally gave the Interior Department considerable leeway to move against all organizations, this authority could not be used without the sanction of the *Reichskommissar*. Such approval, as the refusal to utilize compulsory membership demonstrated, would not necessarily be forthcoming. Terboven maintained his determined insistence of keeping maximum power in his hands. The forty-three organizations had challenged his predominance by questioning his favoritism of NS. They had been duly punished, but retaliatory action was largely limited to those who had protested. His policy of keeping order within the economy continued to take precedence, as shown by his unwillingness to allow a takeover of LO. Quisling's party therefore remained at the disposal of the *Reichskommissar*. It would not be allowed to commit acts that might result in economic disruption.

During the summer months of 1941, while NS was engaged in its fruitless attempt to consolidate control over the organizations, events led to a climax in Norway. The resulting repercussions colored the nature of the occupation for the duration of the war. The *Reichskommissar* played the dominant role in this development. But while Quisling and his officials occupied supporting positions, it appeared at first as if the NS *Fører* and his movement had made significant gains.

On August 2 Terboven made public a decree, dated July 31, which would have long-lasting consequences. It gave him authority to invoke a state of emergency. Included within it were provisions for the Gestapo to take all steps to maintain "public order", the establishment of special courts-martial, and the meting out of death sentences or long-term imprisonment.[40]

The *Reichskommissariat* also issued another decree, which stood in close relationship with the first, providing added evidence that the character of the occupation was changing. Norwegians living in strategically important parts of the country were ordered to turn in their radios. This affected those districts and towns that faced west toward England.[41]

NS in particular welcomed this second decree. One of the many frustrations experienced by Quisling and his officials after September 25, 1940, most notably Gulbrand Lunde, was the party's inability to make effective use of propaganda. Listeners increasingly ignored the NS-controlled radio, preferring instead to obtain information from Norwegian language broadcasts beamed from London. NS therefore not only applauded the *Reichskommissar*'s action, but urged that all radios be impounded. *Fritt Folk* demanded that protection of the people's "spiritual welfare" required an end to "poisonous injections from London".[42] This presupposed tacit recognition by NS, however, that it could not compete effectively in influencing public opinion.

Terboven issued these decrees not solely because of internal considerations. The shadow from the battle zones extended across all areas of occupied Europe. With the invasion of Russia in June, the war took on a new dimension for the Third Reich. At this critical time, with all effort directed toward the annihilation of Soviet defensive capability before winter, the Germans would permit no possible unrest in occupied areas that could detract from their offensive operations across the Russian plains. Similar harsh decrees, soon accompanied by acts of repression, were put into effect throughout the continent.[43] It was hardly a coincidence that Reinhard Heydrich, Himmler's second–in–command, arrived in Norway for consultations with Terboven and German police officials on September 3, just one week before the *Reichskommissar* declared a state of emergency in Oslo.[44]

When he took action on September 10, Terboven had a ready justification at hand. Although the state of emergency affected a considerable number of organizations, institutions, and individuals, it first and foremost was directed against LO. Terboven deliberately targeted the trade union leadership. Although LO officers had previously been quite compliant toward the German authorities, in particular in the fall of 1940 when Jens Tangen became foreman as a result of German pressure, by the spring of 1941 the attitude of the organization had changed considerably. Its leadership had been influenced by persons both within and outside the Federation of Labor who favored stronger resistance to the Germans.[45] LO's participation in both protest letters to Terboven pointed to the leadership's changing attitude. In addition, LO increasingly tended to be on a collision course with the *Reichskommissariat* by insisting on higher pay for its members in the summer of 1941. On June 30 the LO secretariat sent a letter to Terboven which he could not help but react negatively to. It insisted that the union officials arrested because of participation in the protest actions be released, and also that negotiations take place concerning a cost of living increase. Although couched in polite terms, the letter revealed a threat by the secretariat to resign if its terms were not met.[46] The *Reichskommissar* responded by blustering, warning of dire reprisals. However, he did nothing for the time being, indicating that he had not yet decided on a specific course of action. He even went so far as to release some of the imprisoned union leaders.[47]

The *Reichskommissar* had no intention, however, of giving way. The critical war situation that followed in the wake of the attack against the Soviet Union made him more determined than ever to maintain order. Conditions being what they were, he did not have the slightest hesitation in September against taking the strongest measures against any form of opposition.

The event that prompted Terboven to declare a state of emergency took place in a number of factories in Oslo, beginning on September 8. The workers reporting for work on Monday morning learned that their milk rations had been abolished. They reacted immediately, setting in motion a spontaneous strike at several of the largest places of employment. On the following day the "milk strike" became city-wide, spreading throughout Oslo.[48]

This gave Terboven the excuse he needed to move against LO. He proclaimed a state of emergency. Although the strike was spontaneous, and the trade union leaders – who realized how precarious the situation was – begged the workers to return to work, their fate was sealed. The LO secretariat and many local union leaders were arrested. Two were immediately executed, while a large number of others received prison terms. At the same time, in order to make effective use of terror, Terboven took action against persons and organizations who either were suspected of being instigators of resistance, or who might become so in the future. Important economic organizations such as the Employers' Association and the Craftsmen's Federation (*Norges Håndverkerforbund*) were taken over, receiving NS leadership. Prominent journalists were removed from their positions and in some instances imprisoned. Charitable societies were dissolved, as were also the scout organizations. The University's rector was removed, being replaced by a professor who belonged to NS.[49]

This was the first time the Germans employed systematic terror on a large scale. The Gestapo and SS units swarmed throughout Oslo, arresting more than 300 persons. The use of torture, first begun in the spring, became more severe and more widespread during the state of emergency. The workers who had unleashed the repression, but who were already in the process of returning to their jobs when the state of emergency was declared, were not forgotten. They were threatened with trial by courts-martial if they attempted to resign from their unions, which were now in the process of being placed under NS leadership.[50] Members of the Employers' Association and Craftsmen's Federation similarly were forbidden to withdraw.

While the state of emergency was strictly a German operation, Quisling and his officials had reason to believe that NS would gain considerably. The *Reichskommissariat* used the state of emergency to dictate a number of changes that appeared to go in NS' favor. To Quisling's great satisfaction, all radios were now confiscated. This, he believed, would greatly reduce the influence of the government in exile in London.[51] But while the public in general were required to surrender their radios, NS tried to use this as a new ploy in its campaign to recruit members. Persons belonging to NS could petition to keep their radios. This privilege, the party hoped, might serve as an inducement for NS membership. It gained few recruits, however, for the party's slim ranks.[52] Instead, while the majority of Norwegians, fearing severe punishment if they did not comply, did hand their radios over to the Germans, nevertheless a significant number were carefully hidden away.

Following the forced expropriation of radios, the resistance movement and the government in London exerted themselves to an even greater degree in spreading information to the public. In addition to broadcasts from London, news printed in underground newspapers became more important than ever before. The first illegal papers had begun to appear regularly during the fall and winter of 1940. With the seizure of the radios, the underground press assumed responsibility for disseminating radio reports from London throughout the country, thereby making such news available to a mass readership. The total number of people engaged in illegal newspaper distribution during the war was considerable. It has been estimated that some 20,000 persons took part in this risky activity, with between three to four thousand falling into the hands of the German police.[53]

Dissolution of the scout organizations was another apparent benefit that NS gained from the state of emergency. A major competitor of the NS youth organizations was thereby removed.[54] From Quisling's point of view, however, the most significant gain his party secured was the takeover of LO and its affiliated trade unions. This move was carefully coordinated between Quisling and Hagelin, on the one hand, and the *Reichskommissariat's* supervisor of NS affairs, Wegener, on the other.

The NS officer whom Quisling selected to become LO president was Odd Jarmann Fossum, who up to then had been the leader of the insignificant NS Labor Organization (*NS Faggruppeorganisasjon*). On the morning of September 10, at the start of the state of emergency, Fossum received a message to attend a meeting with Quisling, Hagelin, Wegener, and three other German officials. Having given him no prior notice, Quisling simply ordered Fossum to take command of LO. The NS *Fører* also handed him a list of NS members who would head the different trade unions which belonged to LO, plus the party members who would lead union chapters on the local level.[55]

LO thereby received its NS leadership in exactly the same manner as the protesting organizations had experienced in June – from above. Quisling was determined that this vital organization, with the largest mass membership in the country, should be firmly under party control. To make absolutely certain that this occurred, he shortly afterwards set up a joint committee to discuss all questions of common interest between the party and LO. It was made up of representatives from both NS and the NS-controlled Federation of Labor. But Quisling was concerned that NS should have dominant influence on the committee, thereby eliminating the possibility that LO, even under NS leadership, might seek to establish an independent base that could challenge his authority. He therefore decreed that the party would have four representatives on the committee, while LO was restricted to a minority of three.[56]

He had thereby attained one of his most desired goals. His party was now in charge of what had been the main bastion of support for his bitterest political enemy during the prewar years, the Labor party. NS made a full effort to exploit its advantage. This was vital, since LO was the key organization in Norwegian society, not only because of its mass membership but also because of the economic importance of organized labor. However, Quisling had to watch in frustration as this apparent prize also failed to become the tool for NS that he had anticipated. Opponents of NS established a secret illegal leadership within the trade union movement known as the

Trade Union Committee (*Det faglige utvalg*). It was made up of persons who had carried out illegal resistance activity among the workers even prior to the state of emergency.[57]

As the Trade Union Committee became organized, being integrated as part of the national resistance movement, it increasingly assumed the lead among the workers by issuing special instructions (*paroler*) that were spread from workplace to workplace throughout the country. It also published its own illegal paper, *Fri Fagbevegelse* (*Free Union Movement*). Consequently the official NS leadership of LO discovered that its position had been largely supplanted by the Trade Union Committee. Fossum and his subordinates were further effectively stymied because union members simply boycotted all activities that their NS leaders sought to organize. Even such major union issues as wages and working conditions tended to be kept outside the control of the NS leadership, being settled instead through informal agreements between the workers and their employers.[58]

It was impossible, however, for Quisling to stand idly by and watch such an important prize as LO escape effective NS domination. As will be seen, control of the workers continued to be a vital part of his future plans to transform Norway into the corporate state that he envisioned.

Even after LO had formally come under NS leadership, one key sector in society still remained largely outside the scope of Quisling's influence. This included vital areas of the economy in finance, trade, and supply, which continued under the supervision of the non-NS department heads in the Commissarial Council. This state of affairs had become an ongoing source of irritation for Quisling and his immediate circle of NS officials. They therefore seized upon using the state of emergency as a means of attempting to take over the economic departments. As always in the forefront of initiatives to expand Quisling's authority, Hagelin appears to have been the driving force behind this move. In a letter to Quisling on the first day of the state of emergency, he directly accused the three non-NS Commissarial Council members and the Price Director, Wilhelm Thagaard, of deliberately sabotaging the availability of food supplies and encouraging unrest. Hagelin thereby attempted to link these prominent officials with the discontent that had led to the state of emergency. He furthermore maintained that Thagaard's aims were anti-German. He clearly intended to influence the *Reichskommissariat*, since he wrote his letter in German.[59]

Five days later Hagelin followed this up by writing directly to Wegener, complaining on behalf of Quisling against Price Director Thagaard, whom he specifically charged with being hostile to the Germans and their economic interests.[60] Quisling joined in on September 17 by sending one of his long memoranda, which went directly to Terboven. He repeated Hagelin's arguments, but he placed them in a much broader context, providing justification for why he should be permitted to form an independent NS government. He decried the fact that business and financial circles had scarcely been touched by the "new order" up to this point. He conveniently overlooked the fact that NS had just been allowed to take over the Employers' Association and Craftsmen's Federation as a result of the state of emergency. He adamantly insisted that hostile financial interests shielded themselves behind the non-NS department heads. They and members of their departments were described as being 100 per cent hostile, serving as a cover for those who were resisting the Germans.[61]

Terboven was not swayed by Quisling's and Hagelin's views. He felt that it was not in his interest to allow NS to take over the remaining departments in the Commissarial Council. His economic officials in the *Reichskommissariat* worked well with the Norwegian professionals in the three departments, and for the moment this was what counted the most.

In a related matter, Terboven had no objection, however, to NS securing administrative control of the University. He despised intellectuals and academics in general, and he therefore had no personal interest in protecting the University. Nevertheless, it was NS, not the Germans, who pushed most forcefully for the party to take over its top position. This was but part of Quisling's general policy of asserting dominance over all important organizations and institutions from above.[62]

In addition, however, both he and the Germans had a more concrete reason for having NS assume leadership at the University. Its rector, Didrik Arup Seip, had been a constant thorn in the flesh of Quisling since the beginning of the occupation. Seip worked as openly as possible to sabotage all NS moves to gain strength within the University. Thanks to support from the great majority of faculty members and students, he had largely succeeded. It was therefore not particularly surprising that he was dismissed during the state of emergency. A special meeting was held at the University for this purpose, with armed soldiers conspicuously present.[63] Seip was arrested afterwards, as were also three professors who were especially well-known for their anti-German attitude. Skancke, using his power as Minister of Church and Education, appointed himself as rector. However, within a short time Adolf Hoel was delegated to serve as acting rector under Skancke. The introduction of the "new order" at the University was accompanied by the *fører* principle. Faculty influence over University affairs was thereby eliminated, with Hoel assuming the privileges previously vested in the Senate.[64]

For the time being, this was as far as NS went in exercising direct authority over the University. This was a surprisingly restrained approach for NS, characterized by a professor who experienced it as being one of "wise moderation".[65] Except for the arrest of Seip and his three colleagues, no one else was deprived of personal freedom. In addition, although Hoel belonged to NS, he was a regular faculty member. As such, he benefited from a certain amount of good will, in particular since he did not appear to enjoy his new status.[66]

While the takeover of the top position at the University went smoothly, NS influence remained quite limited. Having bided his time, Skancke moved to deal with this problem by calling a student meeting some two months following Seip's removal. On this occasion Skancke proceeded to oust the elected student representatives from their posts. As could be expected, they were replaced by hand-picked party members, who had been selected from the small pool of NS students that was available. The general student body reacted strongly to this usurpation. Two days later, on November 14, a spontaneous protest strike broke out, with the students boycotting all instruction. Although the majority returned to their studies soon afterwards, some simply abandoned their university education for the remainder of the occupation.[67]

Quisling hoped that these steps would result in both faculty members and students being brought under NS control, with the party being able to use its top positions to manipulate the academic community. But again it was shown that it was one thing to have formal authority, and quite another to establish moral ascendancy. NS failed to secure anything but opposition. It had too few students and faculty members. The party did not have the human resources to replace recalcitrant faculty members, and its representation among the students amounted only to a small minority.[68]

Precisely because the party lacked moral authority and legitimacy, the University community at best paid only grudging attention to the NS officeholders, administrative and student, appointed by Skancke. Instead, a secret leadership came into being at the University as elsewhere in society. But here there were two sets of leaders, one for the students and one for the faculty. Although compelled to operate incognito, these unofficial directors tended to dominate University affairs. In particular, they coordinated the vital function of endeavoring to halt further NS inroads.[69]

When Terboven lifted the state of emergency in Oslo on September 17, after it had been in effect for seven days, the German occupation had assumed a different character. His use of systematic terror during the state of emergency had been applied for the purpose of ending organized resistance to his power. He wished to demonstrate not only that he was capable of employing terror against the workers in particular, but that he would use similar force in the future if need be.[70] For the workers, the students and faculty at the University, and the members of organizations that were either placed under NS leadership or dissolved, it meant that one more part of their free existence had been eliminated.

Quisling viewed the state of emergency from a completely different perspective. It appeared to have strengthened his party because of the added number of organizations and institutions that were formally placed under NS leadership. Nevertheless, he was by no means fully satisfied. Terboven remained an impediment, preventing Quisling from achieving what he wanted most of all – a government under his direct control.

The use of terror by the German police, who carried out Terboven's commands, increased in intensity as the occupation progressed. But the endeavor to crush resistance through intimidation did not have the desired result. On the contrary, the shock caused by the severity of repression during the state of emergency created an even greater feeling of repugnance within the population toward the Germans and NS. The two trade union leaders who were executed, Viggo Hansteen and Rolf Wickstrøm, became martyrs, since they had done nothing to encourage the "milk strike", but instead had striven to persuade union members to return to work. The public quite correctly perceived that they had been murdered in order to serve as a warning. But their execution and similar acts of terror created stronger opposition. Especially noteworthy is the fact that organized resistance on a national scale, involving not just separate, often individual, acts of defiance, but coordinated activity by the underground leadership that was being formed in Oslo, began to consolidate during the fall of 1941 following the state of emergency.

Organized resistance, quite obviously, could not be carried out effectively unless there already existed strong opposition among the people to the goals which NS and its German sponsor attempted to realize. A negative public attitude toward Quisling had been formed over many years, as we have seen, extending back to the period before the occupation. This feeling had been greatly heightened by his attempt to usurp leadership during the invasion. But not until after September 25, 1940, when the political situation became clear with the founding of the Commissarial Council, did it become possible for the general discontent within the population to focus on specific targets. As Trygve Lie wrote in his autobiography: "With the administration entirely in the hands of the Germans and the quislings, the battle lines were clear, and the Norwegian resistance movement grew".[71]

Despite Quisling's claims, echoed by his department heads, that NS was working for Norway's independence, the general attitude among the public, as recognized in an internal NS report, was that the members of the Commissarial Council had no real influence, being simply "*Werkzeug der Deutschen* – tools of the Germans".[72] But anti-NS feeling did not reach the great height that it eventually rose to during the occupation merely because party officials followed German orders. It was Quisling's attempt to nazify society that hardened the public's resolve to resist.

We have already noted the individual acts of protest and opposition to

NS' various offensive strategies after September 25, 1940. Such defiance, occurring in particular when NS was backed by the German police, made it obvious even to the most optimistic in Quisling's party that they were generally regarded as pariahs by the overwhelming majority of society. The *Fører* was forced to recognize the existence of such strong hostility. The refusal of the people to accede to his leadership served as a constant frustration for him. He gave vent to this feeling in a speech in Trondheim in the fall of 1941, when his anger expressed itself in threatening language. Warning those who were skeptical or in opposition to NS, he maintained that they had but one choice: "Either you will follow us, or else sooner or later you will be destroyed".[73]

His words were not an idle threat. Under him NS set in motion a purposeful campaign to identify and isolate its strongest opponents. In order to try to stigmatize such outspoken foes, NS propaganda in early 1941 coined the term *jøssing* as an epithet for those who were antagonistic toward Quisling's cause. The word was derived from *Jøssingfjord*, where the British had boarded the *Altmark* in February 1940. Quite obviously, Quisling wished to depict the party's enemies as being pro-English and thereby treasonous.

He asserted that the *jøssings* were the cause of all problems. The *jøssings*, he declared in August 1941, were seeking to terrorize the population. By working against NS, they allegedly were working against the country's interests. In declaring opposition to these "terrorists", he argued that Norway's position could become strong only if the country were unified, which meant being united under him.[74]

Despite NS' propaganda effort, *jøssing* never gained the negative connotation that Quisling intended it to have. Instead, those who received this label considered it an honor, indicating that they were patriots. They were the ones who most clearly stood in opposition to the "quislings", and who maintained an icy distance from "the striped ones" (*de stripete*), who were held in contempt because they attempted to keep a foot in each camp.[75]

Quisling had occasion to experience personally the hatred of the *jøssings*. On September 19, 1941, just two days after the state of emergency had been lifted, *Fritt Folk* plaintively informed its readers about an act of vandalism in the cemetery at Gjerpen, the site of the Quisling family's burial plot. The paper displayed a large picture of a placard set up by persons unknown, who harshly and crudely made known their opinion of the NS *Fører*. The sign read: "Garbage to be deposited here".[76]

It was not surreptitious acts of contempt such as this, however, which made it obvious to all NS members, from Quisling on down, that the *jøssings* influenced the public's perception of the party. The way that people in general behaved toward NS members provided the best indication of society's attitude toward the party. In the countryside reaction was, on the whole, definitely negative, although it might vary somewhat from district to district. In the towns, however, an "ice front" was maintained toward Quisling's followers, who were literally frozen out. No one except other party members or sympathizers would have anything to do with them socially. As but one illustration of this, *Fritt Folk* announced on November 29, 1941, the opening of a special restaurant bearing the symbolic name Viktoria. The stated purpose of the new establishment was noteworthy. It had been created to give NS members "a place where they could feel at home", as opposed to other restaurants where, the paper complained, not everyone had been treated hospitably, especially NS members.

Quisling took direct measures to try to deal with *jøssing* hostility. In May 1941 he established a special intelligence division within the *Hird*. Its reports were to go directly to him. The new intelligence group was ordered to keep the NS leaders informed "about the activity of political opponents", as well as to report on the general state of public opinion.[77]

Intelligence gathered concerning prominent *jøssings* was not intended merely for general information. NS engaged in drawing up what it called "*jøssing* lists" during the winter of 1941–1942. Persons whose names appeared on these lists would, if the situation warranted, be subject to arrest.[78] Indicating the thoroughness with which the party leadership wished to pursue this course of action, General Secretary Fuglesang sent out a directive to all regional leaders on January 16, 1942, ordering that these lists be drawn up in every town and district throughout the country.[79]

National Union's intensified effort to destroy *jøssing* influence occurred at a time when those on the other side were in the process of organizing themselves in order to offer more effective counteraction. Prior to the punitive measures against the forty-three organizations in June 1941, opposition had largely been open. The most noteworthy exceptions were secret newspaper work and covert activity by persons within the trade unions who favored a tougher stand than that taken by the LO leadership. Conditions simply did not favor underground activity on a large scale prior to the summer of 1941. An early attempt, begun in 1940, to establish a national resistance network had failed owing to a combination of inability to maintain security on the part of those involved and to the fact that popular opinion had not yet crystalized to the point where an illegal resistance organization could generate adequate support.[80]

With the takeover of many organizations by NS commissioners in the summer of 1941, the situation changed drastically. The illegal groups that came into being immediately after June 18 to repulse NS did not remain isolated, but sought from the start to establish contact with each other.[81]

As a result of cooperation between the various secret committees, a fully developed structure had developed by January 1942. Known as the Coordinating Committee (*Koordinasjonskomiteen*), or KK for short, this group, as its name implied, served as a central planning organization which coordinated the countermoves by the different secret committees of economic and professional groups against NS' attempts to control their members.[82]

At the same time as this organizing effort was taking place, another important civilian resistance group, the Circle (*Kretsen*), emerged. It developed over a considerable period of time, from 1940 to 1943. Prominent within the Circle were a number of leading figures who had earlier worked against Quisling in the spring and summer of 1940, the most noteworthy being former Chief Justice Paal Berg.[83] One of the most important early meetings of this group occurred on June 20, 1941, only two days after Terboven's and National Union's move against the forty-three organizations. The main function of the Circle was to maintain contact between the resistance movement, which became popularly known as the Home Front, and the Nygaardsvold government in England.[84]

Although they formed two separate groups, close cooperation always took place between the Coordinating Committee and the Circle. This was possible because certain key members belonged to both. It was critically important to have such interaction because careful coordination of illegal activity had to be maintained. The Coordinating Committee's chief function was to draw up special instructions (*paroler*) that were sent throughout the country, serving as guidelines for the type of actions that were to be taken to resist NS moves. The use of such orders proved to be the commonest and most effective weapon employed by the Home Front against Quisling's efforts to carry out nazification. The first of these special instructions had already been issued by early December 1941.[85]

In addition to the two civilian underground groups, a military resistance organization also took form, eventually becoming an integral part of the Home Front. However, it took time before this military group became adequately consolidated to the point where it could establish permanent cooperation with the civilian resistance. Known as Milorg, the acronym for Military Organization, it gained official recognition from the exile government in November 1941. But it was not until the fall of 1943 that the process leading to close coordination with the civilian resistance groups was completed. Nevertheless, Milorg grew in strength from 1940 onwards, gradually emerging as a vital source of opposition to Quisling's various campaigns to secure greater power over society.[86]

The growth of an illegal resistance network during the second half of 1941 had a significant impact on future strategies that Quisling chose to employ. All of his future offensives were met by countermoves, usually in the form of instructions that were sent out following consultation among the civilian resistance leaders. However, after the September state of emergency, neither side challenged the other. The remainder of 1941 was characterized by relative quiet. But beginning in early 1942 the major confrontation took place between Quisling and the newly organized civilian resistance. Its outcome settled once and for all whether he, through NS, would succeed in his endeavor to establish successful leadership for himself by creating the type of corporate society that had always been his goal. But before examining this conflict, we need to ascertain the degree of success which he realized in his quest to head an NS government.

The proclamation of the Commissarial Council did not mean that Terboven for one minute agreed with the generally accepted viewpoint, held both in Berlin and by Quisling, that the Council was a temporary body, to be followed by a Quisling government after a limited interlude. Therefore, whereas the *Fører* and his close associates impatiently sought to realize his aspirations, Terboven embarked on a deliberate campaign of obstruction. He refused to allow himself to be pinned down to an exact date when Quisling might expect to form a government.[87] In addition, he looked for the opportunity to weaken Quisling's standing. As part of their responsibilities, he instructed his subordinates to accumulate incriminating material, which he intended to use against Quisling at the appropriate moment.[88]

The ongoing friction between *Fører* and *Reichskommissar* did not mean that they disagreed over major objectives. Both naturally favored all measures that would enable Germany to win the war as rapidly as possibly. They were equally in agreement over the basic need to nazify Norwegian society.[89] But Terboven continued to hold a low opinion of Quisling's value, and he never willingly would relinquish paramount power in Norway. On the other hand, while Quisling was dedicated to German victory and the creation of a Germanic federation based on race, his commitment was motivated first and foremost by the realization that only through German support could he expect to lead a government. He always anticipated becoming an *independent* head of state, acting in cooperation with the Third Reich.

These conflicting expectations led, as we have seen earlier, to his allies maintaining their undercover campaign against Terboven during the fall of 1940, while the *Reichskommissar* retaliated by taking countermeasures. These were directed first and foremost against Admiral Boehm and the navy. The dispute continued into the next year as well. Terboven greatly resented the navy's sponsorship of Quisling, which he regarded as being an infringement into his area of competence. He expressed his pique personally to the Admiral in February 1941, declaring that he, the *Reichskommissar*, was far more politically astute than Quisling. He also stated his annoyance with the navy for backing Quisling, insisting that he would have no

difficulty in persuading the NS *Fører* to accept German political goals –
meaning Terboven's total control – were it not for the assistance which the
navy gave to Quisling.[90]

Naval officers in Norway reciprocated Terboven's hostility. In the same
manner as the *Reichskommissariat* collected material which it hoped to use
against Quisling, navy officials were busily engaged in gathering incriminating evidence against Terboven. Captain Schreiber, working closely
under Admiral Boehm, cooperated with Scheidt and Schickedanz in this
effort.[91] Neither side indicated any inclination to seek a compromise, resulting in continuous friction between the two factions during 1941. Instead, Boehm and Terboven reached an informal agreement during their
talk in February whereby they would continue to fight internally ("to bash
each other's head in" was the expressive phrase used by the *Reichskommissar*), but externally they would present a façade of unity.[92]

Quisling personally felt Terboven's annoyance on several occasions.
Officials in the *Reichskommissariat*, reflecting their superior's low estimate
of him, were not above inflicting indignities on Quisling. While these incidents had no lasting significance, they nevertheless were humiliating. Early
in 1941 he was informed that his radio speeches would be subjected to censorship by the *Reichskommissariat*'s press division, which summarily ex-
cised certain political references. But he found this to be intolerable because the press division allowed its censorship of his speeches to become
public knowledge through a broad directive sent to all newspapers.[93] The
*jøssing*s thereby gained yet another propaganda issue that they used with
telling effect against the NS *Fører*. An internal NS report in March 1941
pointed to the fact that the general public enjoyed the irony of Quisling
having to submit his speeches for German approval. In the public mind,
this was but one more piece of evidence disproving his claim of leading an
independent Norwegian movement.[94]

He sustained an even greater insult on January 30, 1941, when the press
division decreed that the media should no longer refer to him as National
Union's *Fører*, but merely as the party "leader".[95] The pretext for taking this
step was clear: Quisling should not be confused with the one and only
Führer. Not unexpectedly, he protested strongly against this high-handed
action, pointing out that his title had long been used in Norway and in no
way could be confused with Hitler's. He further complained indignantly
that the press division had issued its order publicly without any consultation. This, said Quisling, meant that the matter would without a doubt be
used against him. He directed his irritation in particular against Müller, the
head of the press division, who had written the directive. The latter shared
Terboven's dislike of the NS *Fører*, going back to the time when he had been
active in the negotiations concerning establishment of a State Council. Quisling was well aware of Müller's attitude, pointing out that this was not the
first time that he and his division had displayed their anti-NS tendencies.[96]

Quisling's strong protests paid off. Müller had gone too far in subjecting the NS *Fører* to this type of treatment, and the press division shortly thereafter had to issue another directive, which laconically declared: "The previous announcement concerning Quisling's title is herewith withdrawn. The former term shall be used: National Union's *Fører*".[97] But while Quisling avoided the humiliation of losing his title, the incident was illustrative of Terboven's hostility. Müller would not have dared to act in this manner without the *Reichskommissar*'s tacit approval.

Quisling fully reciprocated this ill feeling. Externally he attempted to maintain the façade of solidarity with Terboven, but he and his backers continued their behind the scenes campaign against this impediment which blocked him from forming a government. He remained convinced that the Commissarial Council would be of short duration, lasting no longer than six months.

He had adopted unilaterally the belief that he would form his own government at the latest on March 1, 1941.[98] In his rigid mind, the date was fixed – it was destined to mark his takeover. Terboven moreover might actually have gone so far in the fall of 1940 as to pay lip service to this view in order to put off Quisling for the time being.[99]

But the NS *Fører* had received no concrete commitment as to when he would be permitted to take office. German officials, headed by *der Führer* himself, had declared in September 1940 that Quisling would soon lead a government. But unlike him, they had set no specific date, leaving the matter as only a general principle, to be acted upon when and if conditions permitted. This gave Terboven ample room for his machinations.

The uppermost consideration for the Germans was always the state of the war. The time was therefore hardly auspicious for Quisling to pursue his plan for becoming head of government in early 1941. He had already been told during his Berlin visit in December that conditions did not permit the formation of a government at the end of 1940. There was therefore no indication that the situation had changed so greatly that the possibility might materialize by March 1.

Hitler continued to be fully absorbed with preparations for *Operation Barbarossa,* and he was overly fearful of any unexpected development that might hinder his long-awaited opportunity to smash the Russians. He remained convinced of Norway's vital strategic importance for the Reich's domination of the continent. He was therefore obsessively concerned about a possible British invasion of Norway, aided by an internal uprising, when Germany's all-out drive against the U.S.S.R. had been launched.[100] Orders were sent in mid-February to the *Wehrmacht* in Norway, instructing the military concerning what steps to take to hinder such a possibility.[101]

With this being the main consideration of the German leaders, information they received at this time regarding the lack of success NS was experiencing in gaining popular support did nothing to heighten Quisling's chances. Heinrich Himmler spent more than half a month in Norway in late January and February 1941. His main source of information was Terboven, with whom the *Reichsführer SS* travelled widely. It goes without saying that the briefing Himmler received was anything but flattering for Quisling.[102] Such an assessment could not fail to have negative consequences when Himmler and other Nazi authorities considered measures to be taken in order to make certain that Norway remained quiet while *Operation Barbarossa* ran its course.[103] To increase Quisling's scope of activity, and thereby risk heightened unrest, was clearly not in Germany's interest.

Shortly afterwards an incident occurred which dimmed the NS *Fører*'s chances even further. On March 4 a force of British and Norwegian commandos landed in the Lofoten Islands in northern Norway. The primary purpose of the raid was to disrupt German shipping and to destroy fish oil storage tanks, while at the same time giving a needed morale boost to the Allied war effort and serving as a means of disconcerting the Germans. Carried out on a limited scale, the raid was successful. In addition to destroying fish oil plants and storage tanks and sinking 19,000 tons of shipping, the commandos captured 213 Germans and twelve NS members. They were carried off to England, accompanied by some 314 Norwegians who chose to spend the rest of the war on the other side of the North Sea.[104]

Although this operation had only limited military significance, its impact on Hitler proved to be important. He viewed it as but the first move in a British attempt to establish a beachhead on the continent.[105] He therefore ordered naval defenses along the northern coast to be strengthened, plus an increase in the air force units stationed in the area. Because of their concern about the possibility of civilian resistance in occupied Europe when *Barbarossa* went into effect, the Germans noted with alarm the escape of Norwegians to England. The incident provided them with an unsettling indication of general sentiment toward the occupying power. In order to prevent the raid from serving as a source of inspiration for future resistance, Terboven personally went north and took charge of the punitive measures that were carried out for the purpose of intimidating the population as a whole. This included the burning of property of those who had gone to England, and the arrest, deportation, and imprisonment of a number of persons who had aided the commandos.[106] In general, the spring of 1941 witnessed the introduction of a number of new decrees prescribing increased punishment for anti-German activity.[107]

The Lofoten raid had the further effect of heightening the bitter feud between Terboven and Admiral Boehm. This resulted from the sinking of the *Hamburg*, a modern refrigerator fish-processing vessel which the Germans considered extremely important in their attempt to increase the Reich's food supply. Terboven had exercised control over the ship while it was in Norway, and he had ignored several warnings from Boehm against allowing it to be based in the dangerously exposed harbor at Svolvær.[108] Nevertheless, the *Reichskommissar*, true to form, complained to Hitler that the navy had failed to provide the *Hamburg* with adequate protection.[109] Boehm reciprocated by sending off reports that maintained Terboven was culpable. Neither, however, succeeded in avoiding some stigma associated with the sinking of this important vessel. The incident served only to poison the relationship between the two, with constant reference being made to it in the war of reports that they continued to fight for another two years.[110] Because of the added acrimony generated by this episode, Quisling's close ties with the navy did nothing to improve Terboven's attitude toward him.

Circumstances were therefore hardly propitious for Quisling to expect that he might be allowed to attain his goal. Because of the opposition that NS had engendered, internal conditions in Norway were definitely not in his favor, while in Berlin total preoccupation with the war effort overshadowed everything else. Consequently, the hopeful expectations that Quisling had held the previous fall of assuming office after a six-month interval now seemed almost a hollow mockery. Instead, rumors were rife in Oslo that the NS-dominated Commissarial Council was considered a failure in the eyes of the Germans, who intended to introduce another type of administration.[111]

Yet just at this time, less than a week after the Allied landing in the Lofoten Islands, he sent another long letter to Dr. Lammers. It was the deterioration of his fortunes more than anything else that caused his close advisers to urge him to write to Berlin, rather than simply allow the field to be dominated entirely by his enemies. Although they were fully aware of Hitler's concentration on military matters, Rosenberg's office had earlier strongly encouraged Quisling to make a written appeal. Scheidt went so far as to forward a suggested draft on February 27.[112] Quisling's German allies were simultaneously doing their best on his behalf to secure a favorable hearing. Rosenberg sent a memorandum to Hitler on March 4 in which he insisted that it was Terboven's negative actions in Norway, not Quisling's limitations, that were responsible for the unwillingness of the public to look with favor on Germany.[113] Rosenberg's subordinate, Schickedanz, similarly continued to forward anti-Terboven reports from Norway to Dr. Lammers in the Reich Chancellery. One such message, containing comments from Hagelin and Schreiber, was sent on March 5.[114] The opportunity to have direct access to Lammers was of special importance at this time. As chief of the Reich Chancellery, he gained increased influence on

German internal politics as the war progressed, along with his ally, Martin Bormann. After 1943, however, Lammers was shunted aside by Bormann.[115]

Responding to the prompting from Berlin, Quisling dutifully sent off his letter to Lammers on March 10. He did not bring up a great deal that was new. As previously, he voiced complaints against the *Reichskommissar* for not giving full support to NS. He specifically mentioned instances when Terboven, and also Falkenhorst, had acted in a manner that gave the public the impression that German authorities lacked respect for his movement. The *Fører* quite clearly wished to give Terboven the blame for NS' inability to gain popular approval. If only Hitler would give him permission to form an independent NS government, Quisling insisted, then conditions would change. If this administration were allowed to come into being at the same time as a preliminary peace settlement was signed which enrolled Norway in a union of independent states associated with the Third Reich, then the population, he argued, would definitely alter its attitude in favor of Germany.[116]

He furthermore pointed to the understanding that had been reached in September 1940, whereby he had anticipated he would be allowed to form a government within a six-month period, no later than March 1, 1941. Since his entreaty to Hitler in December to be permitted to take office on January 30 had not been realized, he now requested Lammers to pass on to *der Führer* the wish that the NS government be proclaimed on May 17. In Quisling's mind, the national holiday was a most appropriate date for his takeover. To add to the historical symbolism, he further hoped that Hitler would announce his approval of this step on April 9, the anniversary of the German invasion.[117]

Lammers' response provided a good indication of Quisling's standing in Berlin. The *Reichsminister* delayed his reply until April 7, in a letter that was as short as Quisling's had been verbose. He declared that the matter had been presented to Hitler, who had decided that the current wartime situation did not allow him to implement Quisling's suggested changes. Hitler further stated bluntly that Quisling's difficulties with Terboven and Falkenhorst were simply due to "misunderstandings", and that these should be cleared up through the "good will" of the parties concerned.[118]

This reply was a grave disappointment. Quisling's status, if anything, had been weakened by Hitler's refusal. Not only had he been denied his aspiration of leading a government, but unlike the position in the previous fall, he did not even have the consolation of being assured the likelihood of this possibility at some near date. Moreover, his political fate remained uncertain, with rumors continuing to crop up periodically that some new arrangement was in the pipeline that would exclude him completely.

He therefore had little to offer his followers when he gave a radio address on the eve of the anniversary of April 9, the date which had witnessed his dramatic coup the year before. The only reassurance he could make was his assertion that the "coming peace settlement will find Norway neither as a German protectorate nor as a part of the greater German Reich".[119] To the disappointment of his NS listeners, he had to refrain from mentioning the formation of an all-NS government. Nor could he indicate any favorable prospect of a preliminary peace with Germany. Furthermore, his bombastic assurance of April 8, when examined closely, said nothing specific about Norway's future political status.

He insisted in his speech that he made his declaration with Terboven's full approval, which the latter afterwards readily confirmed. This placed Quisling's assurance in its true perspective. It was merely propaganda, calculated by Terboven to placate NS and public opinion. The *Reichskommissar* later made similar vague pronouncements, intended to give the false impression that Norway could expect to be at least quasi-independent in the future. Such declarations were equally propagandistic in nature.[120] No one subsequently harbored the illusion that Germany would have permitted any independence in its occupied territory had Hitler gained mastery of the European continent.

The reports which Quisling's allies in the navy, Schreiber and Boehm, sent to Berlin at this time revealed that the public had no false hopes about Germany. Schreiber wrote that the "Germanic idea" was recognized as simply reflecting the fact that Norway would become an integral part of the Third Reich, merely another *Gau*.[121] Since Quisling stood as the foremost Norwegian exponent of the "Germanic idea", his collaboration had proven to be catastrophic as far as the public's attitude toward him and NS was concerned. Admiral Boehm reported that NS members were regarded as "revealed traitors" by the great mass of the people. He was equally negative in his assessment of the population's feelings toward the occupying power. After one year of German control, he said, the entire people was united in its opposition to, hatred for, and active resistance against the Germans.[122]

Quisling's naval friends continued to maintain, however, that the uncongenial atmosphere in Norway was largely due to the policies of the *Reichskommissariat* because of its failure to assist NS fully. Boehm and Schreiber adhered to the line that the best solution would be a Quisling administration. This, they argued, would provide the people with the assurance that the country's future would be in the hands of a Norwegian government.[123]

The likelihood that this type of regime would come into existence became more remote than ever in the spring and summer 1941. Not only did Hitler display no interest whatsoever, but relations between Terboven and top NS officials deteriorated even further. Despite the common assurances by Quisling and Terboven that they were in agreement concerning Norway's status after a peace settlement, there continued to be a complete lack of harmony in their behind the scenes relationship. Among Quisling's lieutenants, Hagelin in particular remained outspoken in his effort to assert NS interests. As the most aggressive proponent of NS independence within the party leadership, he decried the fact that Terboven's subordinates created difficulties for the appointment of NS members to public positions.[124] Hagelin singled out in particular three German officials who had long been known for not being especially friendly toward NS, namely Müller, Otte, and Hans Clausen Korff, the leading financial expert.[125] In a letter to Lammers, forwarded to the Reich Chancellery by Schickedanz, Hagelin denounced the overbearing attitude of the German administrators toward the NS department heads, plus the lack of independence which the Commissarial Council suffered under. He also decried the *Reichskommissariat*'s greatly expanded size. In order to establish a more harmonious relationship between NS and German officials, Quisling's lieutenant suggested that the NS *Fører* and he be allowed to meet with Hitler to discuss the situation.[126]

If Hagelin had succeeded in arranging such a meeting, which he did not, its true purpose would not have been that of simply trying to arrange greater freedom for NS department heads. The poor relationship between party officials and the *Reichskommissariat* was simply a ploy, intended to allow Quisling to bring up the matter that was of primary concern. The NS *Fører* revealed this in a conversation with Paul Wegener on May 29. Now, Quisling insisted, was the opportune time for him to form a government.[127]

His repeated requests had by then assumed a nuisance quality, but he doggedly felt he could not let up. This attitude was shared in Berlin, where Rosenberg's office encouraged him to press his case in the hope that the wartime situation might change.[128] Moreover, Quisling felt pressured by the apparent re-emergence of a rival who might threaten his standing. This potential challenger was not a newcomer. It was Jonas Lie, Terboven's earlier candidate to supplant Quisling as leader of NS. Lie emerged as the head of an SS faction within NS in 1941. This development was made possible by the heightened influence which Heinrich Himmler exerted in Norway during this period. The volunteers recruited by NS for Regiment Northland became part of the *Waffen SS*, with Himmler personally presiding when they took their oath of allegiance.[129] The *Reichsführer SS*, because of his racist belief in Aryan supremacy, always exhibited a special interest in Scandinavia, a trait that he displayed to the full during his visit to Norway early in 1941. At this time he developed his cordial relationship with Terboven. Himmler returned once again later in the year, accepting the oath of allegiance in Oslo from yet another new formation, the Norwegian SS (*Norges SS*), on May 21. Its newly appointed head was Lie, Terboven's and Himmler's man.[130]

Immediately after the ceremony, the *Reichsführer* returned to Germany, accompanied by Quisling, who spent two days inspecting the Norwegian volunteers in Regiment Northland.[131] According to a report drawn up at this time by Scheidt, which he sent to Rosenberg, Quisling was in a dejected frame of mind during his stay, being concerned with the growing influence of the SS in Norway. Scheidt also strongly criticized Lie, repeating earlier NS accusations against him of being a renegade. According to Scheidt, Quisling had been opposed to Lie being appointed as head of the Police Department, but he had been forced to accept Lie as a result of pressure from Terboven and Himmler.[132] Rosenberg's office was not the only Quisling supporter to recognize the threat that Lie apparently posed. Admiral Boehm, in the draft of a letter to Raeder in June, expressed his fear that Quisling was in danger of losing his NS leadership, with Lie as the most likely replacement, thanks to Terboven's sponsorship.[133]

Hitler's commitment to Quisling proved to be too great to allow these fears to be realized, but this was not clearly apparent at the time. The serious prospects for Quisling's future produced a feeling close to desperation among his chief advisers during the early summer. Hagelin, as always convinced that bold action was the only solution, insisted that Quisling had to become more active and resolute.[134] Stimulated by Hagelin's prodding, Quisling drew up a letter addressed directly to Hitler. More than at any time previously, his bitterness revealed itself through use of language that bluntly stated his feelings. He decried the lack of German backing in Norway for himself and his movement, both in the past and at present. But despite the difficulties that this had caused, he insisted that progress had been made. He remained convinced, however, that conditions would have been much better if NS had been allowed to assume power directly in September 1940.[135]

Hitler never received this strong expression of Quisling's sentiment. The letter was stopped by Rosenberg's office. Quisling's confederates were alarmed that *der Führer* might react in a most negative fashion if he read the NS leader's candid opinions. Scheidt therefore wrote to Hagelin, advising that all future correspondence on Quisling's behalf should be worded "in the old official manner".[136]

The aggressive assertiveness expressed in this letter, thanks to Hagelin's inspiration, was similarly evident in the ongoing hostile relationship between Quisling's subordinates and their German supervisors. Led by Hagelin, the NS department heads went on the offensive during the summer of 1941, criticizing their lack of independence and decrying the cavalier attitude of the experts in the *Reichskommissariat*. In particular, these complaints were directed against two officials who had earlier been targets for NS, Otte and Korff. Hagelin went so far as to declare that he no longer found it possible to cooperate with them, and that the other NS department heads supported his position.[137] NS at the same time endeavored to expand its influence within the Commissarial Council by again turning against a non-NS member, Sandberg, bitterly attacking him because his Finance Department had refused to give in to the party's fiscal demands.[138]

This NS thrust, emerging from the Commissarial Council, was not intended to make narrow gains. It was directed toward an audience outside of Norway, hoping to have an impact on officials in Berlin. No one really anticipated that Terboven would freely make any concessions. Not unexpectedly, the *Reichskommissar* reacted sharply to this NS challenge of his administration's authority. Hagelin's complaints were repudiated in a strongly worded letter in which Terboven reasserted the *Reichskommissariat*'s responsibilities, defended his subordinates, and pointed out that fiscal matters were being handled in a proper manner.[139] He thereby put Hagelin in his place. But the latter remained as pugnacious as ever, showing no intention of abandoning the campaign of undermining the *Reichskommissar* and his administration with the assistance of NS' German contacts.

The effort by Quisling and his backers to assert themselves remained completely overshadowed during the summer by Hitler's massive gamble to invade the Soviet Union. The onslaught against Russia had repercussions in Norway as well. Quisling at this time involved NS in the formation of yet another military unit, the Norwegian Legion, which was sent to the eastern front.[140] Similarly, Gulbrand Lunde, Quisling's equivalent of Joseph Goebbels, quickly used the invasion as cause for reviving National Union's anti-Bolshevik propaganda agitation.[141] But the argument that Norwegians should join the Third Reich in the crusade to protect European civilization from the Asiatic threat of Bolshevism had little positive appeal for a people who each day witnessed what it meant to be part of a "European civilization" dominated by Nazi Germany. Lunde's propaganda therefore soon began to concentrate on another theme as well: that Finland, which was participating in the war against the Soviet Union, deserved to receive Norwegian assistance. Because of overwhelming favorable sentiment for Finland during its earlier Winter War with Russia in 1939–1940, this argument proved to be a clever one, which Lunde sought to exploit to the utmost. In a speech made in Oslo on June 27 he declared: "Today you have the opportunity again to make a sacrifice for Finland, and thereby also for your own people's freedom and future. . . . Your place is in National Union's columns".[142] But despite the skill with which Lunde attempted to propagandize Finland's victorious advance as an ally of Germany, NS publicity failed to dent the icy disdain of the great mass of the population. Although a few individuals were inspired to join NS units that later were formed to fight in Finland, the people as a whole remained impervious to appeals on behalf of their eastern neighbor.

Quisling witnessed the attack on the U.S.S.R. with mixed emotions. He definitely reacted positively to the opportunity of having his party resume its strong anti-Bolshevik ideological perspective. However, the German leadership's preoccupation with the Russian campaign meant that his bid for government ascendancy remained unfulfilled. Scheidt wrote from Berlin on June 24 that Rosenberg was of the opinion that six to eight weeks would have to elapse before it would be opportune to bring the matter to Hitler's attention again.[143]

Patience was never one of Quisling's strong points. Already on August 2 he once more marshalled his arguments in another letter to Lammers. Writing prior to Terboven's use of repressive measures during the state of emergency in September, Quisling emphasized the need to act more forcefully than the *Reichskommissar* had done. The NS *Fører* insisted that "Norwegians must be converted" to the new order with "a certain amount of harshness. This force, however, must be carried out by a Norwegian government and not by foreigners". He maintained that he could have broken the "English-Bolshevik" inspired opposition much earlier if only NS had been given full power. Not only did he maintain he could halt this resistance, but he asserted he could turn public opinion 180 degrees, making it pro German: "With an independent government, Germany's position in Norway becomes simply more secure. If Norwegians see that their country has regained its freedom, England's best propaganda instrument is finished, and they [the Norwegians] will begin to gain confidence in Germany". He also used his party's military contribution to the German war effort as an argument in favor of the creation of a government led by him: "It is of course obvious that we Norwegians must feel it as a humiliation that while we send our best sons in the *Waffen SS*, in the Norwegian SS, and in the Norwegian Legion in the common war on Germany's side, on the other hand we are a captive country because of Germany".[144]

He therefore proposed that the *Reichskommissariat* be instructed to make the necessary preparations for the takeover of government by NS, which should occur on September 25, 1941, the anniversary of the founding of the Commissarial Council, which he continued to refer to as "the temporary solution". Rather than existing for only six months, as he had originally anticipated, he now hoped that one year would be the length of time that the Council would hold office. He similarly expressed the desire to have a preliminary peace agreement completed with Germany by the time he assumed power, and that negotiations concerning Norway's ties with Germany would similarly have been carried out.[145]

Once again the prevailing wartime situation was used to justify why a decision concerning the governmental situation in Norway could not be made at this time. Lammers responded on August 17, informing Quisling that he had discussed the latter's letter with Hitler. The *Reichsminister* declared that Hitler was of the conviction that the questions raised by Quisling needed to be given thorough consideration and should be resolved personally by *der Führer*. However, Hitler had said that he needed to concentrate all of his energies on directing the war, and he asked Quisling to postpone the matter until conditions allowed him to turn his attention to it.[146]

Hitler's response, although disappointing, was not unexpected. Raeder had written earlier to Boehm that operations in Russia had to be completed before the political issue in Norway could be settled, a point he repeated on August 28.[147] Similarly, Scheidt wrote to Hagelin on behalf of Rosenberg on the 19th, instructing that for the time being no new initiative should be made from Oslo. In particular, no letter should be sent direct to Hitler.[148]

Correspondence between Hagelin and Rosenberg's office during this period continued to reveal just how carefully the effort on Quisling's behalf was coordinated between Berlin and Oslo. Scheidt assured Hagelin on August 19 that Rosenberg, in conversation with Hitler, would make use of the opportunity to bring up complaints from Hagelin and Quisling concerning the situation in Norway. Scheidt also pointed out that Raeder could be expected to put in a good word for Quisling. And while no letter should be sent to Hitler immediately, Scheidt had drafted just such a missive for future use, which he forwarded to Hagelin. Here again was proof that much of the material included in Quisling's correspondence with the Reich Chancellery first originated in Rosenberg's office under the facile pen of Hans-Wilhelm Scheidt.

Although his petitions did not gain immediate results, the fact that Quisling and his most important protagonists in Norway, Hagelin, Boehm, and Schreiber, had access to Hitler through the Reich Chancellery continued to upset Terboven. It was obvious to everyone concerned that this channel was used to undermine the power of the *Reichskommissariat* and, if possible, eliminate it altogether. When Terboven therefore learned that Quisling had been in communication with Hitler through Lammers, he was anything but pleased. He immediately dispatched Paul Wegener, who supervised NS activity, to secure an explanation for why the NS *Fører* had gone behind the *Reichskommissar's* back.

The showdown came at a meeting on August 28, which lasted for two and a quarter hours. Wegener made it clear to Quisling that his superior was highly upset over this occurrence, which he regarded as a "disloyal action". Terboven was especially annoyed, said Wegener, because he had repeatedly emphasized in his many conversations with Quisling the importance of maintaining an open exchange of opinions. Wegener further stressed that the *Reichskommissar* was the sole official who had been delegated responsibility by Hitler to oversee the political situation in Norway.[149]

Not forced to deal with Terboven in person, Quisling parried Wegener's charges quite well. He diplomatically maintained he had no intention of causing any disagreement between himself and the *Reichskommissar*. As for the views that he had expressed in his letter to Lammers, he asserted that they were identical to those which he had stated not only to Terboven, but to the *Reichskommissar*'s co-workers as well. Quisling played his trump card when he pointed out that Hitler had specifically told him in their previous meetings that he could address the *Führer* directly concerning important matters. Quisling similarly maintained that Lammers had also allowed him to contact the Reich Chancellery about the question of the formation of an NS government. According to Quisling, both Lammers and Raeder had informed him when he was in Berlin in March, after he had taken part in the anti-Jewish congress at Frankfurt, that a decision concerning the creation of a solid NS government should be ready by August. Quisling therefore insisted that his correspondence with Lammers in no way could be considered improper.[150]

Having deftly defended himself against Wegener's charges, he in turn used the occasion to raise a number of complaints of his own. First and foremost, he expressed his concern about Terboven's unwillingness to make a commitment as to when he could expect to head a government. Terboven, said Quisling, was always evasive when this important subject came up. He went on to repeat a criticism that he had made to Lammers, insisting that Terboven was not acting forcefully enough to control Norwegian society. Quisling alleged that he had always favored beginning with a "hard, really clear decision", whereas the *Reichskommissar* had made "dangerous compromises" in his quest to maintain order. To support this contention, Quisling pointed out that he had favored the confiscation of radios since the beginning of the year, whereas the *Reichskommissar* only now had taken the first steps to remove radios from the population "after the damage ... had become greater". Another issue raised by Quisling was his contention that he had often warned of "the great danger in the trade unions". Here too he was quite specific, denouncing the failure to remove LO's legal counsel, Viggo Hansteen, whom Quisling described as a "Red Army colonel and Communist". In raising this charge, he incurred the liability of being considered partially responsible for Hansteen's execution during the state of emergency.[151] At the time he brought up this matter, however, Quisling simply revealed his frustration with Terboven for not having earlier backed NS in its bid to assume control of the Federation of Trade Unions. Quisling similarly and even more forthrightly decried the fact that he allegedly had been prevented from employing more direct action against the Farmers' Association, with the result that the takeover of the organization had dragged out and led to considerable unrest.[152]

Neither Quisling nor Terboven really gained anything from this exchange, since the opinions expressed were not new. However, the assurance with which Quisling presented his arguments seemed to indicate that he now felt the campaign on his behalf appeared to be making headway. Terboven, on the other hand, had real reason to be concerned. The fact that Quisling's views had reached Hitler showed that criticism of the *Reichskommissar* had received a hearing on the highest level of the Third Reich.

During September there is evidence to suggest that developments had begun to take a turn in Quisling's favor, reversing the negative situation which had prevailed up to this point in 1941. On September 6 Scheidt sent a highly optimistic letter to Hagelin from Berlin. Rosenberg's aide claimed that conditions were now better for Quisling than at any time during the last year and a half. Hitler's attitude toward Quisling, reported Scheidt, was positive. He therefore emphasized how important it was for Quisling to pursue his objectives openly and forcefully. Scheidt furthermore indicated that Terboven's stock did not stand very high in Berlin. Hitler alone, said Scheidt, would determine the proper time for discussions concerning the questions associated with forming a government. The proper attitude toward Terboven, advised Scheidt, should be one of cool reserve.[153]

Although no additional documentation is at hand to corroborate Scheidt's confident assessment, subsequent events do indicate that Hitler in the fall of 1941 did adopt a view toward Quisling quite similar to that which he had held in the late summer of the previous year. The successes of the German divisions on the plains of western Russia in the weeks immediately after the start of the campaign produced a feeling of ebullient optimism in Hitler. He was therefore in a positive mood when Quisling's advocates, Rosenberg and Raeder, reminded him of his earlier commitment to have the Commissarial Council serve as a transitional body. Satisfied with the course of the war, *der Führer* once more viewed Quisling from a rosy perspective – as the comrade who had earlier warned him of the danger of a British invasion of Norway.

When the same men who pleaded Quisling's cause with Hitler were critical in their appraisal of Terboven's performance, the latter's cause did not prosper. In particular, one aspect of Terboven's appointment as *Reichskommissar* now came back to haunt him in the fall of 1941. At the time of his departure for Norway, he had received an express command from Hitler to turn the Norwegians into *der Führer's* "friends".[154] Terboven's enemies in Berlin were quick to emphasize that the Norwegians were not becoming friends; rather under Terboven anti-German feeling was constantly increasing. The negative reports emanating from Quisling's circle of supporters held the *Reichskommissar* personally responsible.

The fact that conditions in Berlin appeared to be changing in his favor was reflected by Quisling in his next letter to Dr. Lammers, dated September 11. It was worded as diplomatically as possible in "the old official manner". Quisling expressed his appreciation to Lammers for having presented Hitler with his previous letter of August 2. He fully understood *der Führer*'s decision to postpone discussions for some weeks, and he assured Lammers that he remained committed "to the Germanic policy" enunciated by Hitler in September 1940. He could well express his adherence to this line, since it had held out the possibility of the creation of an all NS government under his direction in the future. He now eagerly declared he was ready to discuss this question at the earliest possible moment. Indicative of his dependence on his chief adviser, he requested that Hagelin be invited to attend the prospective talks.[155]

Quisling wrote this letter just when Terboven unleashed the police during the state of emergency in Oslo, an event that had significant consequences for the future careers of both Quisling and Terboven. Until this time, despite some individual acts of harsh repression against specific incidents of anti-German resistance, Terboven's conduct on the whole had been guided by moderation. But as has been seen, his policy changed with the outbreak of the "milk strike". As one of his subordinates in the *Reichskommissariat* who disagreed with this reversal put it: "If he had in the beginning been inclined to treat the Norwegians well because Hitler wished to 'win' them, then he changed his methods from the time of the state of emergency and began a reign of terror".[156] The adoption of this coercive line was not antithetical to his true feelings, however. On the contrary, moderation was never his strong point, and he appears to have leaped at the opportunity of making use of methods that were more to his liking. Admiral Boehm reported that Terboven, reacting to the "milk strike", declared on the day before he made use of the state of emergency that the situation was not unwelcome. He had to no avail placed himself at the beck and call of the Norwegians. Now he intended to force them to their knees.[157]

When he adopted these repressive measures, however, Terboven left himself open to charges by his enemies that he had gone too far – that the use of executions, arrests, and imprisonment was much too strong a response. He had sought to avert such criticism by attempting to have the *Wehrmacht* agree that a state of emergency needed to be proclaimed. In this way the military would have a share of responsiblity for what followed. But at a meeting with the *Wehrmacht* representatives on September 9, he received a sharp setback. Admiral Boehm, not noted for being charitable toward the *Reichskommissar*, declared that he was unaware of any internal disorder which required such a drastic step.[158] Boehm instead reported to Raeder that the "milk strike" had already come to an end *before* Terboven declared the state of emergency, which was therefore hardly required.[159]

By being forced to take full responsiblity, Terboven thus had to bear the brunt of any negative consequences that might result. Such repercussions were felt almost immediately. In Berlin the highest levels of the military reacted with consternation to the apparently serious situation in Norway, a response brought about by egoistic reports from Terboven justifying the need for repression. The concern which his action aroused was shown by the following communiqué from the OKW on September 13, issued when the state of emergency was at its midpoint: "Concerning the situation in Norway: According to the reports at hand, the hostile attitude toward Germany within the Norwegian population has reached intolerable dimensions. Should this condition continue or even intensify, the German forces and the defense of Norway are exposed to immediate danger".[160]

Because of his special interest in Norway, reflected not only by his firm conviction that it was of utmost importance militarily for Germany, but also by his racially inspired feeling of affinity with its people, Hitler inevitably became personally alarmed over the disarray caused by Terboven. His aroused interest did not bode well for the *Reichskommissar*. The German warlord demanded a full account concerning the situation in Norway.[161] Furthermore, Terboven was not in a position to control, and thereby manipulate, the information forwarded to Hitler. Quisling too was asked to present his views, including his perception of the state of emergency.[162]

Quite pleased with the opportunity, the NS *Fører* responded with another of his long memoranda, which he drew up on September 17, the same day the state of emergency was lifted. As he had done so many times before, he marshalled all arguments that could be persuasive in convincing Hitler that he should be allowed to lead a government. He began by exhibiting his philosophical bent, declaring that his assessment of the political situation in Norway had always been based on the necessity of establishing "the new order" as quickly and effectively as possible, thereby creating the groundwork for a fundamental regulation of the relationship between Germany and Norway. This was of "decisive importance", he insisted, (1) because of Norway's military and political significance for the outcome of the war; (2) because Norway allegedly was the key to the political future of all of Scandinavia, with the other Nordic countries being compelled to follow Norway in setting up a "new order"; and (3) because Norway could serve as an international example for the ongoing "construction of the Germanic-European new world order".

Becoming more specific, he provided his explanation for why it had not been possible to establish the new order up to this time. While NS, he argued, had not been given full power to carry out his program, his party nevertheless had been held responsible for all unpopular developments. When the Commissarial Council was created, he continued, NS' enemies at first were completely "paralyzed" because they assumed that his party really had assumed power. However, once it became obvious that this was not true, "resistance became deeper and organized itself once again, also because London radio's unhindered propaganda of agitation and lies created a very fertile soil". Groups that he described as plutocratic and Marxist-Communist had thereby joined forces, and these relatively small cliques had been able "to terrorize" wide population groups and create the impression that "the majority of the people were against Germany and our NS movement." This development, he argued, had occurred not only because NS lacked authority, but also because resistance circles were able to exert a certain degree of influence with German officials in Norway. Here he struck a direct blow against Terboven, pointing out that NS' opponents in business and financial circles, among clerical and intellectual representatives, and not least within "the marxistic-communistic trade unions" had all been able to play the *Reichskommissariat* off against NS. Specifically, he declared he had "many times called attention to the dangerous activity of the now shot attorney Hansteen", a statement Quisling lived to regret.

He launched yet another attack against the *Reichskommissar* by criticizing his subordinates, mentioning Otte and Korff by name. Many of Terboven's officials, he insisted, had no understanding of what was required. They therefore delayed and even hindered necessary actions. Furthermore, he accused them of behaving in such an insulting manner toward his department heads on the Commissarial Council that he repeatedly had been forced to intercede in order to prevent them from resigning.[163]

Having made these major complaints, it is interesting to note that in his prescribed solution, Quisling did not seek to disassociate himself from the repressive moves that Terboven had made during the state of emergency. On the contrary, because of his blind belief in direct action, Quisling repeated his earlier assertion that Norwegians needed to be converted to the "new order" with a certain degree of harshness. He did, however, deny the effectiveness of *German* use of force by repeating another of his claims – that any compulsion should be carried out by Norwegians because repression by foreigners only inspired hatred. Nevertheless, with his logic somewhat in disarray, he used the events of the state of emergency to argue that it provided proof of his contention that "clear lines" were needed, which could only be attained by his long-desired NS government:

> Developments during the state of emergency have again shown in practice what I have always maintained. It has been shown that every calculated attempt at a general strike can very easily be strangled at birth by arresting the mob leaders. It has been shown that one can without any kind of disorder confiscate the radio sets and carry out extremely far-reaching actions without complications, such as the takeover of trade unions, the Employers' Association, and the dissolution of large resistance organizations.[164]

Terboven was fully aware of Quisling's arguments, since the *Reichskommissariat* had been specifically instructed to forward the NS *Fører*'s assessment to Berlin. Placed on the defensive by the controversy over the state of emergency, Terboven soon afterwards felt compelled to make a gesture toward Quisling. Since the latter had earlier petitioned Berlin to be allowed to take office no later than on the first anniversary of the Commissarial Council, September 25, Terboven sought to placate him by holding a ceremony on this date. At this time the *Reichskommissar* announced that the department heads in the Commissarial Council would no longer be referred to as cabinet members (*statsråder*), but instead would hold a more imposing title as "ministers".[165] In the speech he gave on this solemn occasion, with Quisling listening, Terboven furthermore felt obliged to take public notice of a question that he had long evaded. He declared that he "knew of National Union's desire to take over full power and thereby also full responsibility".[166] Considering the opposition that he had encountered for more than a year from Terboven on this matter, Quisling heard with irony the *Reichskommissar* say that he too had always worked toward this goal. However, true to form, he once more avoided being pinned down as to when the assumption of "full power" would occur, pointing out that only Hitler could determine the proper moment.[167]

Despite his recognition of Quisling's aspirations, Terboven's little ceremony on September 25 was largely cosmetic. The title "minister" did not in any way alter the status of the department heads. They continued to be closely regulated by their German supervisors.[168] The only additional change that occurred at this time involved two personnel changes on the Commissarial Council. Quisling's longtime loyal follower, General Secretary Fuglesang, who had earlier served as the Council's secretary, had his status elevated to minister.[169] The other change involved Meidell, who now was allowed to resign. His position had become impossible by his attempt to maintain some degree of independence from German control.[170] His relationship with the party leadership was also poor because of his insistence on following a slower, more cautious approach when making NS appointments in his department, which aroused Quisling's ire. Meidell was replaced by a more pliable figure, Johan Andreas Lippestad, an ambitious NS bureaucrat who headed the party's national organization.[171]

These rather insignificant alterations in the standing and composition of the Council did not mean, however, that the status quo had been restored in the adversary relationship between Quisling and Terboven. The latter had been weakened considerably because of his precipitous action in declaring the state of emergency. With Terboven in disfavor, Quisling's cause could prosper. The latter arrived in Berlin on October 6 in order to be present when the latest NS-sponsored unit, the Norwegian Legion, gave its oath of allegiance to the German cause.[172] His journey worked to his advantage. He appears to have received some kind of pledge during his stay that he would be allowed to reach his goal of forming a government in the immediate future. This was reflected in the large number of optimistic statements that he and leading NS members made in speeches and press releases after his return to Norway.[173] As but one example, he announced in a speech on November 16: "It is but a matter of time before NS takes over full power here in this country".[174]

While he and his lieutenants were in a positive mood during the last quarter of 1941, the *Reichskommissar* was anything but satisfied. He was discouraged by the setback his career had received, and in October he sought once more to use his contacts in Germany to obtain a new assignment. He would have preferred to go either to Belgium or to return to his old *Gau* in Essen. His hopes of getting away from the scene of his apparent failure, however, were dashed. In the eyes of the leadership in Berlin, he had already forfeited his chances for a career outside of his present post.[175]

But while Terboven's fortunes were on the decline, no hard and fast decision had yet been made in Quisling's favor. While the NS *Fører* had been given general assurances, these appear to have been made on the condition that he and the *Reichskommissar* should reach an agreement on the terms whereby he took office. Only after this consensus had been worked out would it be forwarded to Hitler for final approval.

Quisling therefore needed to muster arguments to strengthen his case vis-à-vis the *Reichskommissar*. As could be expected, the NS *Fører* used any new development that might bolster his position. He wrote to Wegener on November 8, criticizing the fact that several Norwegian merchant vessels sailing for the Allies had been captured by the Germans and confiscated as war booty by a prize court in Hamburg. The court had justified its decision on the grounds that a state of war continued to exist between the Third Reich and Norway. Quisling declared that this legal interpretation created an intolerable situation for National Union, in particular for his ministers on the Commissarial Council. The people, he maintained, found it incomprehensible to see, on the one hand, a Norwegian administration which cooperated with Germany, with Norwegian volunteers fighting and falling "shoulder to shoulder with German soldiers", while Germany, on the other hand, expropriated Norwegian property with the justification that the two countries were at war. To solve this dilemma, he proposed his standard solution: the formation of "an independent Norwegian government" and the signing of a "peace settlement" as soon as possible.[176]

Negotiations between Quisling and Terboven concerning an NS government did take place. Although the exact date cannot be ascertained, the two probably held their meeting some time during the second half of November.[177] On this occasion Quisling discovered to his considerable surprise that the *Reichskommissar* was willing to accept an all NS government. But his elation soon changed to chagrin when Terboven proposed that Hagelin should head the government. This astounding suggestion was certainly cause for surprise because of Hagelin's pugnacious opposition to Terboven ever since the *Reichskommissar* took office. Quite obviously, he simply hoped to cause mischief, seeking to divide Quisling and Hagelin and thereby create friction within NS that would be to his advantage. In making this dramatic proposal, he was not, however, at a loss for arguments. He insisted that it would be best to have an NS government that did not include Quisling in the period before a peace settlement had been signed in order to avoid compromising the NS *Fører*. It was also in Quisling's interest, said Terboven, to stay outside the government until the *Reichskommissariat* had been disbanded so that he could avoid the onus of working under a German administration.[178]

Quisling refused point blank to agree to this proposal. With his penchant for formalities, and by this time justifiably unwilling to accept any reasoning from his rival that reflected the slightest degree of deviousness, he exhibited no interest in Terboven's plan. The NS *Fører* insisted that only he should lead an administration that made peace with Germany.[179]

Terboven's weakness at this time was clearly apparent. He could not dictate terms as to how an NS government should be constituted. He could only make suggestions, while Quisling could veto any conditions he did not like. For the time being, Terboven therefore remained a passive figure, with the initiative remaining with his opponent. The latter's opportunity to travel to Germany worked to his advantage once more. He journeyed to Berlin in early December, arriving on a truly historic occasion. He witnessed the euphoria that swept the German capital at the time of Japan's dramatic entry into the war, with daily reports of the crushing victories which Germany's ally inflicted against American and British forces in the Pacific. He was a guest of honor in the *Reichstag* on December 11 when Hitler, arousing the type of mass emotionalism that he was capable of, dramatically issued his declaration of war against the United States.[180]

In this highly charged setting, with the Germans convinced that the war had taken a decisive turn in their favor, Quisling secured even more direct assurances than those he had received during his previous visit in October. This time he was told unequivocally that he would be permitted to form his government. Only the specific details regarding the time and actual conditions of his takeover remained to be worked out.[181] Stimulated by these pledges, he returned to Norway on the 13th in a highly elated mood. As *Fritt Folk* put it: "the *Fører* was in radiant humor. We sought to gain an interview with him, but for the time being he would only say that it had been an extremely interesting trip." His infectious optimism spread to his lieutenants, causing Hagelin to declare: "When we know for certain that the future is ours, then it does not matter as to the exact time of the takeover".[182]

The high degree of optimism within leading NS circles was most understandable. Quisling, as always overconfident in his expectations for the future, believed he was on the threshold of realizing his long sought after goal. He anticipated he would assume real power, with the *Reichskommissariat* either eliminated or greatly reduced in authority. Furthermore, he believed that the peace settlement that he had constantly asked for would be achieved. He therefore looked forward to serving at the head of an independent country in alliance with the Third Reich and under German military protection.[183]

Quisling had yet to learn that one's fortunes can change rapidly in the uncertain conditions that prevail during wartime. The jubilant atmosphere in Berlin did not last long. Reality soon reasserted itself, with the recognition that no quick victory was in sight. As far as Norway's place in German strategic planning was concerned, this point was brought home by two military operations that occurred at the end of December. Quisling could not have received worse Christmas presents than those which arrived in the period December 26–28. Allied commandos, consisting of combined British and Norwegian units, landed at two different points along the coast. The first incursion was in the Lofoten Islands, the scene of the previous raid of March 1941, which had also had an impact on Quisling's political future. The second attack occurred further south, on the west coast in the Vågsøy-Måløy area.[184]

As had been true of the earlier Lofoten incursion in the spring, these operations produced no significant military results. However, their impact on Hitler's military planning, and also on his view of the political situation in Norway, proved to be of major importance. *Der Führer*'s already quite high perception of the country's strategic value was magnified greatly by the December raids. He remained convinced that the Allies might strike against the continent via Norway, and that these attacks were precursors of the anticipated invasion. He expected that it would include not only British forces, supported by the U.S., coming in from the west, but also a coordinated move by the Russians from the east, possibly aided by Sweden's entry into the war on the Allied side.[185] In a *Führer* conference with his military advisers on January 22, 1942, he went so far as to declare that Norway had become the "fateful area" ("*das Schicksalsgebiet*") that would decide the outcome of the war.[186]

His preoccupation with the country's strategic importance caused Hitler to concentrate vital parts of the Third Reich's armed forces in Norway in order to repel the expected invasion. During January and February the major capital ships of the navy were moved to Norwegian waters, while submarine strength was also increased.[187] At the same time, the total number of army troops rose greatly. German forces increased from 100,000 at the beginning of the year to 250,000 by the summer, and the number did not stop at this point. In 1943, thanks to Hitler's concern, more than 400,000 members of the German military were stationed in Norway.[188]

As will be seen, there were, of course, other factors as well which influenced the form and standing of the office that Quisling would hold. First and foremost, it was naive for him to believe that he would be allowed to head a government that was largely independent of German control. Hitler at no time would have permitted this, no matter how positive wartime developments might have been for the Reich. Nevertheless, the two raids in December greatly reduced the amount of leeway he was willing to grant Quisling. *Der Führer* could hardly have dared to risk political innovations, accompanied by the threat of internal unrest, in an area he considered to be of primary importance for the outcome of the war. Furthermore, specific problems were bound to occur that would affect Germany's military position in Norway if Quisling's desire to secure a peace settlement and recognition of independence were realized, even as mere formalities.[189]

The individual whose political future was most directly affected by these considerations had no real appreciation of how the situation had changed. Up to just a few days prior to the actual ceremony which inaugurated his administration, Quisling continued to believe that his expectations would largely be fulfilled. His assumption was based on the fact that concrete preparations were being carried out for his apparent takeover of authority. What made this progress all the more noteworthy was that it had been initiated by none other than the one person who previously had exerted himself to the utmost to hinder him from forming a government, Josef Terboven.[190] Some time prior to January 22, most probably after the 15th, the *Reichskommissar* proposed to Quisling that they should discuss the implementation of a Quisling government.[191] Terboven's decision to take this step was most likely motivated by his realistic conclusion that this was inevitable, and that it was in his interest to play an active part in the process leading to its inception, rather than being forced to accept passively developments that he could not influence.

The two worked out an agreement setting up a calendar of events which specifically indicated what would transpire in the period immediately prior to the proclamation of Quisling's government. According to its terms, a declaration would be issued on January 28 in which Hitler and Quisling announced the establishment of a preliminary peace between Norway and Germany. Quisling insisted that the German government should, in recognition of the preliminary peace, invalidate the judgements of the Hamburg prize court that approved the seizure of Norwegian vessels as war booty. Then after a two day interval, the moment that Quisling had long awaited would finally be realized. He would be sworn in as the head of a Norwegian government. Germany would recognize the new government *de jure* on January 30, while the provisions for a permanent peace settlement would be worked out during the course of further negotiations.[192]

These were the terms that Terboven's immediate subordinate, Wegener, carried with him to Berlin on a mission to secure Hitler's approval. Wegener expected to be back in Oslo on January 24.[193] Up to the time of his return, the discussions between Quisling and Terboven had been surprisingly smooth, apparently in the former's favor. But danger lurked underneath the seemingly placid surface of agreement between the two old antagonists. For one thing, Terboven had carefully made certain that he negotiated with Quisling alone, keeping the more forceful Hagelin in isolation.[194] This did not bode well for the NS leader, whose record in previous bargaining with the dominating Terboven was marred by repeated setbacks. This proved to be especially important because one area of significant disagreement did develop during their talks. Quisling had always worked to free himself of the *Reichskommissariat*'s control, and he quite naturally favored the elimination of Terboven's position once he assumed office. Terboven resisted, insisting that if a critical military situation should occur in Norway, the *Wehrmacht* would be forced to declare the country a war zone and take over full authority, thereby destroying the basis for existence of an independent government.[195] Faced with this forceful argument, Quisling reluctantly gave in. But as he was prone to do, he optimistically declared that this was a "last temporary solution" on the road to full freedom. He confidently expected Terboven to leave once a final peace settlement had been worked out, at the latest in May or June.[196]

Some disillusionment already began to creep in at the time of Wegener's return, carrying with him Hitler's conditions. This became apparent at the airport upon Wegener's arrival, where he promptly got into a violent altercation with Hagelin. Quisling's adviser, irritated by the fact that he had been excluded from the confidential negotiations with Terboven, exploded when he learned of Hitler's decision. *Der Führer* first of all had not agreed to any declaration of preliminary peace. His refusal to give Quisling this key concession was based not only on military considerations, but also on policy issues at stake elsewhere in Europe. Hitler at this time strongly rejected granting a peace settlement to Vichy France, and he therefore had no desire to establish a precedent for such an agreement by accommodating Quisling.[197]

The NS *Fører* also discovered to his dissatisfaction that January 30 would not mark the date of his takeover. With his usual concern for historical symbolism, he had continued to insist on having the anniversary of Hitler's inauguration as chancellor as the day on which he too, he believed, would assume power. But *der Führer* refused to share anniversaries with anyone. Quisling's day of glory was shunted forward to February 1.

He found these changes to be deeply disappointing, eroding significantly the importance he had attached to gaining governmental leadership. In response, egged on by the ever offensive-minded Hagelin, he sought to shore up his position in a letter to Terboven on the 26th. He expressed his concern over how it would be a burden for him to be in charge of an administration that acted in juxtaposition with the *Reichskommissariat*. He could therefore accept this only as a transitional arrangement, lasting no longer than three months. He further requested that Terboven, in the speech which the *Reichskommissar* would deliver on February 1, should specifically declare "that the establishment of the national government in its present form means the final step toward full independence". In the last segment of the letter Hagelin's influence made itself transparently obvious, with Quisling asking that his Minister of Interior be allowed to accompany him on the visit to Hitler that was planned after the "national government" had taken office.[198]

This attempt to maintain a strong front vis-à-vis the *Reichskommissar* resulted only in humiliating retreat. Bolstered by the signals he was receiving from Berlin, the quick-acting, decisive Terboven showed no inclination to permit Quisling to hold an advantage. On the contrary, he proceeded to give Quisling a severe reprimand. Terboven refused to accept any restraints on the continued existence of his office, declaring that only *der Führer* could determine when a Quisling government could receive "full independence". Furthermore, he rejected a point that Quisling had made in his letter – that Wegener had allegedly informed Hagelin of a three-month time limit, at whose expiration the *Reichskommissariat* would begin to disband. Wegener, Terboven declared curtly, had done no such thing. Furthermore, he stated bluntly that he wished to hear no more complaints about difficulties that Quisling might sustain from having to work in cooperation with him.[199]

Confronted with such a strong rebuff, Quisling felt he could not risk antagonizing Terboven further. On January 29 he forwarded another letter, which, in contrast to that sent three days earlier, was noteworthy for its conciliatory tone. He declared at this time that he was convinced "without a doubt" that the establishment of the coming "reorganization" ("*Neuregelung*") scheduled for February 1 marked "a great step forward", and he thanked Terboven profusely for making it possible. Furthermore, he backed down on the question of a time limit for the departure of the *Reichskommissar*, declaring that such a decision of course rested with "*der Führer*". Finally, and humiliatingly, he had to admit, if indirectly, that he had been misled by Hagelin – that Wegener indeed had not indicated any specific time for the establishment of a completely independent NS government.[200]

Quisling's quick capitulation reflected his constant concern with outward formalities. What mattered most of all for him was the symbol of office. While he strove to make the office important, in the last instance this was not his ultimate concern. Now that the opportunity once more was at hand for him to head a government, he did not dare risk losing his chance by being firm with the *Reichskommissar*.

Despite this apparent reassertion of Terboven's dominance, however, the situation in reality was not yet so clear-cut. Terboven did not obtain specific confirmation as to what his status would be in relationship to Quisling until the morning of January 29. Then, in a telephone conversation with the *Reichskommissariat*'s leading legal authority, Rudolf Schiedermair, who was in Berlin, the anxious *Reichskommissar* received the news he had been waiting for. To his relief, Schiedermair relayed the message that Quisling would be completely under Terboven's authority.[201]

The lines of command were thereby clearly drawn. When the curtain went up for the next act in Quisling's career, it meant that one character had not changed roles. Terboven continued to remain the dominant political figure in Norway, still possessing the authority Hitler had vested in him by the decree of April 24, 1940.[202] This was clearly the way the Nazi leadership in Berlin perceived the situation. Goebbels noted already on January 24 that the "Norwegian political structure" and "the position of the *Reichskommissar*" would not be changed. Quisling, wrote Goebbels, would serve largely as a good example for other countries.[203] As the Propaganda Minister indicated, Quisling would still continue to receive second billing in the exercise of power. He would only be allowed to go as far as the Germans deigned to permit.

CHAPTER XIV

The Attempt to Dominate Society
February – September 1942

Today National Union has conquered Norway. All that remains is to clear the battlefield. There has never existed a political movement in Norway as strong as NS. And there is no opposition that we cannot defeat.

Vidkun Quisling, speech at Hamar,
June 24, 1942

February 1, finally designated as the historical date for Vidkun Quisling's "takeover of power" ("*maktovertagelse*"), differed little from other winter days of early 1942. It was grey and icy cold, providing but added reinforcement to the bitter feeling of resignation which the people of Oslo felt from the deprivations of war and occupation. No signs were evident until the last minute that this date would mark the occurrence of something special.

Private instructions had earlier been sent out via National Union's internal communication channels that a party rally would be held on January 30. As a result, members of the *Hird* had begun to gather in Oslo by the end of January. But Hitler's unwillingness to allow anyone to share his anniversary forced NS to announce a two-day postponement of the "rally". Not until Friday the 30th did the press reveal that an important event would take place two days later on Sunday, February 1.

Only at this late date did some coordinated activity begin to take place in order to provide the proper setting for the coming occasion. During the evening hours of Saturday large portraits of Quisling were posted prominently, bearing in bold letters the simple inscription "*Norge*" – "Norway". No additional information was provided, with the result that rumors ran wild throughout the capital.[1]

This was hardly an auspicious build-up for the takeover which Quisling had yearned for for so long. Nevertheless, it marked the beginning of a new phase of the occupation, during which he would be committed as never before in his quest to gain domination of the country in order to remodel it into the corporate ideal that he had always sought to attain. The eight-month period between the beginning of February and the end of September marked the highpoint of his effort, with Quisling leading his party in the strongest offensive that NS generated during the entire war. The outcome proved to be extremely significant for him. It determined his position once and for all for the remainder of the occupation.

The uncertainty and improvisation which prevailed when he was appointed as head of government resulted from the fact that up until just a few days prior to the actual ceremonies, specific orders had not yet arrived from Berlin defining the degree of power he would exercise. As we have seen, Terboven did not receive confirmation until the 29th that Quisling would be fully responsible to him. Therefore, when the decision was finally made to proceed with the inauguration on February 1, all preparations had to be carried out in great haste.

The first issue that needed to be settled concerned the question of the source from which Quisling derived his authority to lead a government. For propaganda purposes, he and the Germans shared a common interest in trying to disguise as much as possible the fact that he owed his position wholly to the occupying power. However, the Germans were in charge, with all decisions concerning the "takeover of power" emanating from the *Reichskommissariat*, whose legal expert, Schiedermair, in a telephone conversation with Terboven on the 29th actually proposed the course that was later followed. He recommended that Quisling's designation as head of state receive sanction from two separate institutions: from the Supreme Court, now composed entirely of NS judges, and from the commissarial ministers.[2]

The necessary steps were taken in great haste on the 29th and 30th.[3] Two Supreme Court justices were called to conference with Minister Riisnæs on the 29th. They met at NS headquarters, where Riisnæs informed them that the ministers of the Commissarial Council had decided to resign and to urge Quisling to succeed them as head of "a new national government". The Supreme Court, said Riisnæs, needed to confirm that there were no constitutional hindrances for such a step. Although NS members, the two judges were also legal experts, and they showed considerable reluctance to proceed as Riisnæs suggested. In the end, however, they gave in, and on the following day the required resolution was duly issued.[4] Although drawn up by an NS body, the document was noteworthy for the negative manner in which its conclusion was phrased: "The Supreme Court finds under the prevailing constitutional and political situation no conclusive constitutional reservation against National Union's *Fører*, Vidkun Quisling, forming a Norwegian national government at the request of the ministers . . ."[5]

The NS ministers were somewhat more positive in their "request", whose final version was completed on the 31st. As one of their main points, they declared that consideration of the country's "independence and welfare" demanded a "Norwegian national government" to protect the country's interests, and they therefore had resolved to resign their posts and appeal to Quisling to form such a government.[6]

With these preliminaries out of the way, the major events of February 1 could be carried out. The effort to give the occasion a semblance of legality went according to plan, beginning early in the afternoon. At 12:15 p.m. the "retiring" ministers assembled at Terboven's office in the *Storting* building. Also in attendance were Quisling, along with Terboven's chief subordinates in the *Reichskommissariat*, Wegener, Schiedermair, and the feared head of police, Friedrich W. Rediess. A few Norwegian and German journalists were also on hand to immortalize the event. For those in the know, the irony of the observance could not have been more apparent when Hagelin, as spokesman for the ministers, stepped forward to inform Terboven of their decision to step down and to thank the *Reichskommissar* for their past mutual cooperation. In response, Terboven went through the formality of accepting the resignations, declaring that under the Commissarial Council the foundation had been established for the time when the Norwegian and German peoples would be joined in an "inseparable comradely union".[7]

The highlight of the day came one hour later within the walls of the medieval fortress overlooking Oslo harbor, Akershus Castle. These looming walls, built to protect the capital from the types of invasion that were customary in bygone centuries, were closely identified with key periods of Quisling's life. Here he had served at military headquarters, just behind the Castle, and he had taken part in ceremonies on the parade ground – as a cadet, as a young and promising General Staff officer, and as Minister of Defense in attendance on the King. Now he returned under the paternalistic control of the Germans to proclaim himself head of a "Norwegian national government".

As he trudged across the snow-covered cobblestones of the fortress at the side of his official benefactor, and behind-the-scenes contemptuous rival, the *Reichskommissar*, receiving the Nazi salute from *Wehrmacht* soldiers and his *Hird* followers, Quisling's visage was severe. The time that had elapsed since the beginning of the occupation did not rest easily on his shoulders. In less than half a year he would turn fifty-five. Nothing remained of the athletic frame, acquired from military training and from a sportsman's long hikes in the Telemark countryside, which he had still possessed as late as his fiftieth birthday. Now lack of exercise and too many good dinners had added numerous pounds to his frame, giving his body a dumpy appearance, with the impression that it was about to explode into considerable corpulence. In public his face was stern and dour, the corners of the mouth downturned. He attempted to present an aura of seriousness and responsibility, to give the impression that being the Norwegian people's *Fører* was a most solemn undertaking, capable of being filled only by someone with an outstanding mental capacity. His faith in himself as the great visionary political leader remained undimmed, and he wished to project this image to the world.

Despite its improvised character, arrangements had been made to try to make his inauguration as impressive as possible. Within NS mythology it became known as "the Act of State at Akershus" ("*Statsakten på Akershus*"). When Quisling and Terboven, with their accompanying entourage of German officers, entered the hall built by Haakon V (1299–1319), the spectacle that greeted them seemed appropriate enough. The hall had been decorated with German and Norwegian banners, with the swastika and Quisling's orange and gold "St. Olav's banner" especially prominent.[8]

Terboven spoke first. His words were hardly auspicious for Quisling. As was his wont, the *Reichskommissar* had no desire to enhance Quisling's prominence and thereby outwardly reduce, even symbolically, his own importance. Therefore, rather than addressing his remarks primarily to his rival's new role as head of a government, Terboven used a major part of his speech to level a blistering attack against Bishop Berggrav. Why the primate of Oslo deserved to be the target of his wrath remains somewhat unclear. It may have been due to the prelate's adroit leadership in the Church's opposition to NS. But by taking this approach, the *Reichskommissar* certainly negated the significance of the Act of State, which his listeners immediately recognized.[9] Even more important was what he left unsaid. He completely ignored Quisling's wish to include a statement indicating that the new government represented the last step prior to full independence. Nor did he make any mention of a possible future peace settlement with Quisling's government.[10]

When Quisling in turn rose to speak in his new capacity, he faced the challenge of undoing the impression that Terboven had made and to turn the occasion into a truly memorable event. But much as he would have liked to, he could not avoid having to recognize that whatever authority he derived was dependent upon German consent. Whereas Terboven had in his preceding speech accorded him only perfunctory notice, Quisling opened by making repeated mention of the *Reichskommissar*'s alleged good will toward NS. Even more revealing, the first words that he uttered as leader of a supposedly true government were not in his native tongue, directed to his countrymen, but in the language of the occupying power. Only after he had addressed the Germans in his audience did he feel free to turn his attention to the Norwegians.[11]

In this portion of his speech he also indicated the degree of dependence which he felt toward Germany. Speaking in his hurried and staccato delivery, he insisted that the war was not merely Germany's war. It was a war of freedom for Norway, the Germanic peoples, and Europe against England, the United States, and the Soviet Union. But above all it was a war of independence against "international Jewry", which allegedly controlled these three parts of the world. Therefore, he argued: "Germany's victory is Norway's victory. Germany's defeat is also Norway's defeat; yes, as far as human eyes can see, Norway's destruction".[12] Since he always identified Norway's fate with his own, it is clear that he recognized, even if only subconsciously, that if Germany were vanquished, it would also mean his defeat, and perhaps his destruction.

In order to have his government appear as independent as possible, he had to deal with the difficult question of by what right his National Government had come into being. As indicated previously, unlike the Commissarial Council, he could not admit that his administration owed its existence to the grace of the occupying power. He therefore resorted to his standard solution of making general reference to a number of legal and factual arguments of doubtful validity. Legally, he declared NS to be the only "legitimate" political authority in the country, meaning that it alone received German sanction to exist. He further pointed to the party's *de facto* exercise of sole political activity. He gave added importance to NS by maintaining it was the strongest political organization that had ever existed in Norway; a spurious allegation to say the least. He went on to argue that the Labor party's "marxist government" had committed treason by resisting the Germans and then fleeing the country, while the *Storting* and the royal family were equally guilty of treason because of their support of such a government. But above all, he insisted, beyond all legal argument and the actual holding of power, NS possessed "a special and higher legitimacy" because his movement alone represented what he called "the nation's will to live". He depicted NS as a "revolutionary national movement" which received its legitimacy by being in step with historical development, represented by the "national revolution", i.e., fascist expansion throughout Europe. This was, he maintained, the absolute value which gave his party the prerogative to lead a government. Thanks to his ability to perceive what was right, NS alone had correctly pointed to what would occur in the future. And because he and his party were prescient, "we represent, whether we are a majority or a minority, the true will of the people".[13]

With the formation of this government, which allegedly represented the people's will (whether or not they realized it), Quisling emphasized that a major goal had been reached. Norway again, he stressed, had a "national government". Only one more step now needed to be taken before the country had gained its "full national freedom and independence".[14] What he alluded to, but obviously could not mention, was his inability to realize all of his aspirations. No peace settlement had been made, the *Reichskommissariat* still remained in place, and Germany had not recognized his regime as independent.

As he was inclined to do, he brushed aside these reverses by declaring ambitiously that his government would always be able to solve any remaining problems in the future. The thing that mattered, he concluded, was that the foundation had been established for the creation of "a new, a free and great nationally conscious Norway". Carried away by his need to draw historical parallels, he pontificated that this day was the greatest in Norway's history – greater than May 17, 1814 (the anniversary of the Constitution), greater than June 7, 1905 (which marked the end of the union with Sweden).[15] His flight of fancy showed just how far his illusionary claims transcended reality. The day that he proclaimed as the greatest in his country's history had been made possible only by careful German orchestration. At best, his views found acceptance only among his small minority of followers, even though he referred to his party as the strongest that had ever existed in Norway.

Hereafter National Union's ideology always referred to the Act of State as the foundation on which its government's legitimacy rested. "Today we have a Norwegian government which has not been appointed by German authorities" was how *Fritt Folk* later in the year referred to current conditions.[16] Not merely did Quisling assert that his government did not owe its existence to the Germans, he also claimed the greatest authority ever held by any governmental leader in modern Norwegian history. He insisted that he had assumed the powers that had previously been divided on a tripartite basis between the King, the cabinet, and the *Storting*. Using historical analogy, he declared these powers were now concentrated in his hands in the same way that King Sverre, one of Norway's strongest medieval kings, had seized full authority by force of arms.[17] But his assertion of power did not stop here; it was in theory unlimited. Even the Constitution, the second oldest functioning in Europe, had to give way if its clauses served to impede his aims.[18]

A consideration to which he attached major significance was that he should outwardly enjoy trappings that corresponded to his claims of power. He assumed the title of Minister President in his capacity as head of the National Government. In triumphant procession, his cortège of automobiles left Akershus Castle after the Act of State. The motorcade drove up Karl Johans gate, where at the end of the boulevard the Minister President established his new headquarters in the Royal Palace. Only a small number of NS adherents were on hand to hail their leader, in contrast to the large crowds who turned out when King Haakon received acclaim.[19] But as opposed to the exiled King, Quisling planned to have it both ways – he would exercise true domination over the people as well as enjoying the symbols of royalty. As if to demonstrate this, elite members of his street fighters, known as the *Førerhird*, were installed as guards at the palace, occupying the posts previously patrolled by the Royal Guard.[20]

As another part of the festivities held on February 1 to celebrate the Act of State, that evening a gala performance took place at the National Theater. In planning this event, the most important persons expected in attendance were of course the Minister President and his wife, whose plush chairs were located in an elevated central position. The gala went on as scheduled, with leading NS dignitaries and their wives in attendance, headed by the ministers in the new National Government. But the reality of how most Norwegians felt toward the NS leader imposed a dampening effect, shredding the fog of illusion that he had created. The chairs reserved for Vidkun and Maria Quisling remained empty that evening. Rumors of an assassination plot forced the Minister President to stay away from the performance arranged to honor his takeover.[21]

As Quisling showed by his statements and actions during the Act of State, the Germans were willing to go quite far in giving the impression that his National Government actually enjoyed independent authority. The occupying power attempted to create this perception not only in Norway, but also externally to the rest of the world. As evidence of this, Quisling had declared in his inaugural speech that one of his priorities was to bring an end to what he viewed as an intolerable situation whereby Swedish diplomatic representatives in Berlin looked after the interests of Norwegian citizens on behalf of the Nygaardsvold government. His indignation was perfectly understandable. This situation reflected the unpleasant reality that a state of war existed between Norway and Germany, a state he hoped to abolish as quickly as possible through his projected peace settlement.

The Germans believed it would be advantageous to give foreign observers the impression that Quisling's government really amounted to something in international affairs. On the day following the Act of State, the Swedish government was notified that its diplomats should cease taking care of Norwegian interests in Germany, since this function had been assumed by the new National Government.[22]

Official government spokesmen in Berlin would not, however, take any more concrete steps to add to the illusion that Quisling's ministry truly had freedom of action. In the immediate aftermath of the Act of State, Berlin did go so far as to say that his desire for a peace settlement could expect to receive a "favorable echo" in Germany.[23] But the Reich's position very quickly became more reserved. The Germans now declared that while the possibility for a peace settlement did exist, no final decision would be made concerning this question for the time being. Furthermore, in response to the interest which the creation of the Quisling government aroused, in particular with the international press, Reich spokesmen stressed mainly the importance of "the psychological atmosphere" in which the Act of State took place.[24]

This official German position obviously paralleled the personal viewpoint of Propaganda Minister Goebbels. As he expressed in his diary on February 3:

> Quisling's appointment as premier has created a sensation in the countries at war with us and has drawn in its wake great waves of angry commentary. Quisling is hated violently in the entire enemy world and is now the target for vile calumniation. He has actually succeeded in becoming a symbol, although he doesn't really deserve it. But the more he is attacked abroad, the more it becomes our duty to support him. I therefore gave the German press instructions to give his appointment a good build-up . . .[25]

But while Goebbels was alert for the opportunity to promote Quisling abroad, he had his own personal views about the NS leader's pretensions:

> Quisling . . . makes the somewhat grotesque claim that in his hands . . . is concentrated all the power formerly held by the King, the Parliament, and the Prime Minister. That's laying it on a bit thick . . . Nevertheless we release this version, since naturally we are highly interested in letting the Norwegian Government appear as big and independent as possible.[26]

Goebbels, however, had no intention of allowing the illusory show of independence to assume an element of reality. In particular, he made it clear that Quisling should not appear to have been elevated to Hitler's rank:

> On the other hand I forbid using the word *"Führer"* in the German press when applied to Quisling. Even if he calls himself *Fører* in Norway, and even if the word *Fører* can easily be translated as *Führer*, I nevertheless don't consider it right that the term *Führer* be applied to any other person than the *Führer* himself.[27]

As Goebbels' attitude showed, in reality nothing had changed as far as Germany's command in Norway was concerned. He commented sardonically about Quisling: ". . . after all there is a *Reichskommissar* standing beside him!"[28] Terboven's continued stay nullified completely all of Quisling's assertions of holding power. This was specifically recognized by the military. Falkenhorst, in his capacity as *Wehrmacht* commander, issued a directive on February 11 which declared categorically: "Executive power remains in the hands of the *Reichskommissar*".[29] The General never harbored any doubts as to the real significance of Quisling's takeover. He did not even bother to attend the Act of State, being content merely to send Quisling a one-sentence congratulatory note.[30]

The *Reichskommissariat* exercised the same control over the National Government that it had maintained over the Commissarial Council. Quisling, it is true, had obtained an official position from which he could pursue his program, rather than formally having to operate outside the administration. But the reality of the situation soon showed his phrasemaking during the Act of State to be hollow. In his treason trial he had to admit, after repeated prodding, that every decree enacted by his government needed Terboven's approval before it could be made public.[31]

The extent to which Quisling was limited by German restrictions revealed itself even in the title which he assumed as technical head of state. Minister President was not a Norwegian term. The common designation for the head of government is Prime Minister (*statsminister*). Minister President was strictly German, referring to the office of the Prussian prime minister. It had never been used before in Norway.

Quisling personally would have preferred the choice of another title. With his inclination to draw historical parallels whenever possible, he had indicated as early as the fall of 1940 that he would like to be called Regent (*riksforstander*). This title had previously been used throughout Scandinavia and therefore had historical meaning for Norwegians. In yet another of his visionary plans, in 1942 he actually anticipated becoming Regent in the future, with his use of Minister President being restricted to a brief period. Once peace with Germany had been established, thereby making the *Reichskommissar* superfluous, he intended to call into session his long-awaited National Assembly, which would approve him as Regent.[32] The course of history, however, did not follow the path he had anticipated. The limitations imposed by future developments forced him to retain his German title for the duration of the occupation.

When he assumed office, Quisling remained remarkably optimistic, believing that the constraints under which he served were only temporary and that he would soon be free of Terboven's influence. He placed special faith in an assurance he had earlier received when he learned he would become Minister President. He had been told he would be permitted to pay a "state visit" to Germany once he had been installed in office. What pleased him most was the knowledge that this included an official reception by *der Führer* himself. His stay in Berlin, he hoped, would give him an opportunity to secure new commitments from the Germans. He wished in particular to obtain a specific time frame in which he could expect to receive full recognition as head of an independent government.

He therefore departed on his state visit with high expectations in early February. His previously expressed wish to have his strong man, Hagelin, accompany him had been granted. In addition, his entourage included NS General Secretary Fuglesang and Thorvald Thronsen, a high-ranking *Hird* officer. But another member of the group accompanying the Minister President cast a grey shadow over the visit. Quisling did not have the opportunity to pursue his goals in Berlin free from the encumbering influence of the *Reichskommissar*, who went along as a personal escort for the Minister President on his first official journey.[33]

Upon his arrival on February 12, Quisling was received with all of the pomp due a visiting head of state. *Reichsminister* Lammers, in his capacity as chief of the Reich Chancellery, was on hand to meet the Minister President, along with an honor company of *Waffen-SS* troops, which was duly inspected. That evening Quisling and his group dined with Lammers.[34]

The next day, Friday the 13th, marked the highlight of the visit. Quisling was granted the opportunity to hold lengthy conversations with Hitler. In the course of their talks, the Minister President brought up arguments that he had prepared thoroughly. As usual, he had committed his viewpoints to paper in a detailed manner prior to leaving Norway. He brought with him a lengthy memorandum "concerning the new order in Norway", plus a draft version of a preliminary peace treaty. He presented orally the contents of both of these to Hitler.[35] Of primary concern was the preliminary peace settlement. Recognizing that military considerations were uppermost in Hitler's mind, Quisling stressed the argument that a peace settlement would have the effect of strengthening the German military. According to him, a peace settlement, accompanied by recognition of Norwegian independence, would eliminate entirely the basis for organized opposition to Germany in Norway. He maintained that those who were now engaged in illegal resistance activity, carrying out sabotage and serving as Allied spies on behalf of the cause of national independence, would no longer have any legitimate ground for their acts once Germany had recognized the country as free and independent. They would no longer, he alleged, receive any assistance from the general population. The Reich's military position, he continued, would also be enhanced by the National Government, which would support Germany with all of its forces.[36]

Quisling also raised the point that his government would be able to establish diplomatic relations with foreign countries once a peace settlement had been secured. This would be to Germany's advantage, he maintained, because many legations controlled by the Nygaardsvold government would thereby be eliminated, reducing its "dangerous influence" against Germany. To illustrate this, he pointed out that if his government could establish a "national Norwegian legation" in Stockholm, Germany would immediately benefit because the large amount of Norwegian tonnage in Swedish harbors would come under his jurisdiction.[37]

As befitted someone concerned not only with the present, but who also looked prophetically toward the future, he had no hesitation in spelling out for Hitler his personal vision of the type of joint defense that would exist after the war, when Norway was part of the "Germanic federation". Germany, he declared, would enjoy disposition over needed airfields and harbors in Norway, with a unified "Germanic" air force and navy exercising responsibility for providing protection in the air and at sea. However, the Minister President insisted that his government should have control of the country's coastal defense and the maintenance of a separate "Norwegian national army". He further urged that planning for the creation of a unified defense force should begin immediately. As part of this process, he suggested that new clauses be inserted in the Norwegian Constitution to permit conscription, allowing him to organize an army corps of three divisions. This would allow added participation in the war on Germany's side. As part of this contribution, he declared that once a peace settlement had been concluded and his National Government had been strengthened enough, Norway would sign the Anti-Comintern Pact and join the Axis Powers, assuming all of the obligations which members of the Axis were required to share.[38]

He expressed these views to Hitler in an atmosphere of conviviality that was fully in keeping with a "state visit". *Der Führer* carefully refrained, however, from committing himself to any of his visitor's arguments. Quisling failed to perceive that his goals hardly corresponded either with Germany's present military needs or with the plans which Hitler had for occupied Europe after the war had reached a victorious conclusion. Goebbels, the calculating cynic, attended the luncheon that Hitler gave in Quisling's honor on the 13th. The Nazi Propaganda Minister came away with an impression that was far from flattering, and that did not bode well for the Minister President's quest for special consideration. Goebbels confided to his diary: "As for myself, I have the impression that Quisling is in fact nothing but a quisling. I can't feel any sympathy for him. He is a dogmatist and theoretician in whom one can evidently not expect to develop great statesmanlike qualities." This frank characterization took on special importance because it reflected to some extent the reaction that Hitler himself had in his talks with Quisling that day, a response that Hitler passed on to his Propaganda Minister: "As for Quisling, he developed very naïve ideas in his talk with the *Führer*, as the latter confided to me. He thinks he will be permitted to build up a new Norwegian Army, protect the Norwegian harbors himself, and finally create an entirely free Norway." To this, Goebbels added in his diary the coldly realistic observation: "*Das ist natürlich naiv . . ..*" Hitler, Goebbels continued, "replied evasively to these claims".[39]

While Quisling's endeavor to gain concessions met with no noteworthy response, German propaganda presented his visit as a success. On the day after his meeting with Hitler, he held a press conference. This was followed by a short address over the German radio. In the afternoon, accompanied by Terboven, he was the guest of honor at yet another reception, hosted by Göring.[40] But while outwardly all respect continued to be shown the Minister President, his hosts carefully stage-managed and kept his official visit under control. Terboven appeared constantly at Quisling's side, being present not only at Göring's reception but also during the discussions with Hitler, along with Lammers and Bormann. The German media were under orders to report only the official communiqués concerning the visit. The press chief in the *Reichskommissariat*, responsible for all news appearing in the Norwegian press, received strict instructions from Berlin not to allow newspapers to make any reference to Quisling's trip which had to do with "foreign diplomacy questions, peace negotiations, peace possibilities, etc." Rather melodramatically, Berlin ordered that the discussion of such matters was prohibited under penalty of death.[41] Naturally, no mention appeared in the Norwegian press.

The official visit came to an end on February 15, with Lammers once more on hand to see the Norwegian delegation off.[42] But Quisling did not immediately return home. He stayed on in Germany for a few days longer. Freed at last from Terboven's shadow, he had the opportunity of meeting alone with his leading German backers, Rosenberg and Raeder. He was Rosenberg's house guest for several days, and on Monday the 16th he met with the Grand Admiral.[43] It came as a relief for him to be able to exchange views and information with Germans who were personally sympathetic to his cause. His two confidants did not, however, receive a very realistic assessment from their protégé. Quisling's credulous nature caused him to view his prospects in much too favorable a light. Impressed by Hitler's general professions of good will and by the pomp surrounding his state visit, he came away with the belief that he could expect to improve his position in the future. In a letter to Admiral Boehm, written soon after he had spoken with Quisling, Raeder reflected the attitude that the NS *Fører* had conveyed: "Quisling's state visit has now taken place, and in my opinion came off quite well. Even though the current arrangement . . . is not at all satisfactory, I do believe one can say that *der Führer* has assured Quisling the possibility of favorable development in the future".[44] The Grand Admiral's letter did not, however, indicate any lessening in the tension between Terboven and those who challenged him by interfering in Norwegian affairs on behalf of Quisling: "I have not exchanged a single word with R.K., although I have met him several times at parties, since his entire behavior was completely unsympathetic . . ."[45]

Terboven's conduct should have told Raeder that the situation in Norway had not changed in any way as a result of Quisling's visit. As he had done previously, Hitler kept all future options for himself. He did contemplate the possibility of perhaps making a new move in Norway some time during the spring, but everything depended on military considerations. The potential step that he had in mind was some kind of a peace settlement. But it would have been a peace drawn up in Berlin and presented to Quisling, not a negotiated treaty. As for the form of government that would have followed a peace agreement – whether it would have been similar to that in the Protectorate of Bohemia and Moravia or in the puppet state of Croatia – Hitler chose to leave open for the time being. Similarly, he had not determined whether or not the *Reichskommissar* would be replaced by a special emissary (*Reichsbevollmächtigter*) in the event of a governmental change.[46] But the alternatives that he considered would only have been symbolic. Quisling's formal status might have been changed, but real power would have continued in German hands.

When Quisling returned to Oslo on February 18, he remained convinced that his journey had been a success and that he could expect a favorable outcome in the immediate future. But the visit had not achieved any specific results beyond general expressions of understanding and allusions to possible change at some unspecified time. His standing continued to depend on the good will of *der Führer*, on the fate of the German armed forces fighting on far-flung battle lines, and on what he would be able to achieve as Minister President.

Although German overall control of government administration remained unchanged after February 1, 1942, National Union's *Fører* had obtained some advantages by the Act of State. Not only did he secure the external trappings of office, but more significantly, he gained a freer hand to pursue his objectives. Terboven, aware of the residual good will that Quisling still possessed with Hitler, was willing to allow the Minister President considerable latitude in seeking to realize his ambitions.

The latter did not waste any time in launching a political offensive immediately after the Act of State. Even before he left on his state visit, he had set in motion National Union's most concerted effort to break down opposition and to establish supremacy over society. This offensive and the conflict it engendered made 1942 the most critical year of the entire occupation. The lines became more tightly drawn than ever between Quisling and his minority of NS loyalists versus the broad mass of the population, whose heightened feeling of moral outrage and hostility was increasingly organized more effectively by the Home Front. Both sides were aware of the importance of this struggle and used all of the resources at their disposal.[47]

While the major part of National Union's activity during 1942 was concentrated on this internal offensive, it should not be considered an isolated move which had no bearing on Quisling's attempt to win greater authority from the Germans. The two went hand in hand. He believed that a successful effort which netted his party more control over the population would in turn bring him greater freedom of action, since any increase in his mastery of the people would correspondingly heighten his value to the Germans.[48]

He always defined this dual endeavor in the most idealistic manner. For him and his followers, the ultimate achievement which NS strove to realize was "the re-establishment of Norway's freedom and independence".[49] To achieve this, he aimed at two major complementary objectives. Internally, the culmination of the NS offensive would result in the creation of his long-awaited corporate National Assembly, the *Riksting*. He believed that the realization of the Assembly would change the relationship between his National Government and the Germans. The coming of the Assembly would also mark the conclusion of peace with Germany, his second objective. He envisioned thereby full recognition by the Germans of his government's independence.[50]

While these objectives formed the key part of his aspirations for 1942, they did not stand alone. They were part of a series of projected steps that he had logically worked out at the time he initiated National Union's political offensive in early February. Each goal, if realized, would have led inexorably to the next. The two immediate steps which the NS offensive had targeted were (1) gaining control of the nation's youth through nazification of the school system and compulsory membership in National Union's Youth Organization, and (2) forced membership of all wage earners in a series of corporate groups. Once the second goal had been achieved, the foundation would have been established for the creation of the National Assembly, and the accompanying peace settlement with Germany.

With Quisling already assuming that he would gain the independence that he always craved, his future plans were exactly those that he had revealed to Hitler during his state visit. He looked forward to the time when, as head of a sovereign government allied with the Third Reich, he would sign the Anti-Comintern Pact, bringing Norway into the Axis Powers as a full-fledged member. As such, Norway would thereupon take part in World War II as an active belligerent. This would allow him to carry out the final step, symbolizing that he had truly reached his aspiration of being the complete master of an independent country: the mobilization of troops to fight under his banner.[51]

He followed his usual practice of drawing up his vision for the future in detailed memoranda. In the detached calm of his study, the achievement of his ambitious undertakings seemed logical as he systematically spelled them out on paper. Ever committed to his belief in taking strong, direct action, he was determined to secure their implementation.

Fanciful as his aspirations may have been, the resistance movement realized from the start that he would do everything in his power to carry them out. Although the Home Front did not have detailed knowledge of his plans, the underground newspapers, in their commentaries on the Act of State, recognized clearly that his installation as Minister President would undoubtedly be followed by a forceful attempt to break society's opposition to nazification. One such illegal publication, *Eidsvoll*, voiced the fear of the underground movement as to what might occur if Quisling enjoyed success. The paper assumed that he would conclude a "peace" with Germany, followed by Norway's entry into the Axis Pact, with war being declared by the Minister President's government against the Allied Powers.[52] As *Eidsvoll*'s article illustrated, the Home Front had a clear perception of what was at stake in the struggle.

Quisling plunged ahead with his planned drive to reorganize society in the shortest period possible. He initiated this move already at his first meeting with his ministers at the Royal Palace on February 5. The cabinet proclaimed three laws on this occasion. Two in particular had wide-ranging implications. One decreed that all young people between the ages of ten and eighteen were required to perform "national youth service" through compulsory membership in NS' Youth Organization.[53] A second law disclosed the establishment of a new NS-controlled teachers organization, Norway's Teachers Corporation (*Norges Lærersamband*). According to this decree, all educators except those at the university level were obligated to belong to this corporate body.[54]

The third law issued on February 5 also was compulsory in nature. It required all publishers to join the Norwegian Publishers' Association, yet another NS-led organization. In the period immediately following, a large number of similar laws were issued whose intent was to organize forcibly the members of different occupations and interest groups.[55] Such compulsory membership was part of Quisling's move toward organizing a corporate society. However, the critical struggle during the spring of 1942 resulted from his attempt to obtain effective control over the minds and hearts of the nation's youth and their teachers.

He involved himself wholeheartedly in this endeavor, which was exactly the kind of enterprise that he had looked forward to. In his self-created role as the nation's high-minded but strict leader, he intended to impose the proper "spirit" of "the new age" that he represented on his errant countrymen. What better way to accomplish this than through indoctrination of children? In his speech at Akershus Castle he had declared that NS had established the foundation for "strong and healthy national-socialist Norwegian politics" which held out the promise of a rich future for the people if they would only make a unified effort. In order to accomplish this, he insisted that what the people needed was "a strong schoolmaster, one of their own who understands them deeply, and who can teach them national discipline".[56] As the nation's "schoolmaster", he intended to apply the proper instruction, not being willing to tolerate any rebelliousness from his pupils. He expected everyone to obey the *Fører*.

He appointed a leader whom he could depend on as head of the new Teachers' Corporation. Orvar Sæther belonged to the small group of party faithful from the 1930s whose admiration for the *Fører* had remained undeviatingly worshipful. Such loyalty mattered a great deal to Quisling, who had previously assigned Sæther to a wide number of party positions. Although he had experience as an elementary school teacher, Sæther was hardly a good choice for the difficult task at hand. He was described by his German colleagues in the *Reichskommissariat* as being "to a high degree unsuited for his position".[57]

In his methods, Sæther closely imitated his *Fører*, being a convinced practitioner of seeking to reach his objectives by direct onslaught. The Teachers' Corporation, he declared, had been created in accordance with "National Socialism's basic principles" to carry out certain specific requirements. It intended "to educate and lead the teachers onto the roads that they must follow if they are to fulfill their essential societal responsibility in the new Norway . . ."[58] One of their tasks would be to work closely with the NS Youth Organization to enroll all youngsters between the ages of ten and eighteen in its ranks.

Obviously modelled after the compulsory participation in the *Hitlerjugend* that was required of German children, the law establishing forced membership in the NS Youth Organization declared that its basic purpose was to provide each boy and girl with a "national upbringing" and to allow them to serve "their people and fatherland".[59] Quisling's real intent, however, was to give his party the opportunity to indoctrinate young people at an impressionable age. Axel Stang, whose Department for Labor Service and Athletics had overall responsibility for "youth service" within NS, alluded to the real reason for this type of compulsory activity: "Norwegian youth is now assured a planned and correctly prepared upbringing during the years that are decisive for the creation of their character . . . The importance of this can scarcely be overestimated".[60]

In choosing children and teachers as prime targets, Quisling and his cohorts once again exhibited a complete absence of tactical insight. Hardly anything was bound to arouse greater antagonism within the population than NS' endeavors to dominate the upbringing and education of children. Sæther's deliberate linkage of mandatory membership in the NS Youth Organization with the demands made upon educators compelled to belong to the Teachers' Corporation made the situation even more explosive. The teachers, upon pain of dismissal, were required to indoctrinate their pupils with party beliefs. As a result, the Home Front gained a golden opportunity to exploit the strong emotional response among the people to what they perceived to be flagrant violations of basic moral principles.[61] In addition, Quisling could hardly have chosen a group more solidly unified in its opposition to NS than the teachers. They had resisted earlier attempts to secure their loyalty and cooperation since the fall of 1940. When NS forcibly assumed leadership of their organizations in 1941, the teachers' protest in the form of resignations was higher in percentage than that of any other similarly affected group.[62] Despite the dismissal and imprisonment of a number of their most prominent colleagues, the teachers maintained a united front against NS, a show of solidarity made even stronger by contributions to an "illegal" strike chest for the benefit of the families of those who had been ousted or arrested.[63] The educators had thereby indicated that they were willing to make great sacrifices out of a commonly shared conviction that their stand was morally right. Quisling clearly had not understood this forewarning.

From the time the law establishing the Teachers' Corporation came into existence, there never was any inclination from the teachers, spearheaded by their illegal leaders in Oslo, to accept Quisling's decree passively. Hectic consultation to determine the best countermove occurred immediately. The underground leadership was well organized, maintaining regular contact with teachers throughout the country. It also consulted closely with the two major Home Front groups, the Coordinating Committee, to which it belonged as a subordinate unit, and the Circle.[64]

The teachers' protest therefore took place as a result of carefully coordinated planning. There was never any doubt as to what was at stake in the battle over obligatory membership in the Teachers' Corporation. The resistance recognized that this unit was intended to be a key part in Quisling's projected National Assembly. In one of the instructions (*paroler*) sent to the teachers, drawn up by former Supreme Court Justice Ferdinand Schjelderup, the Home Front made clear how it regarded the situation:

> They *cannot*, in fact, do without us today, the quislings. The fact is that the battle that has now begun will be decisive for their own position of power.
>
> . . .
>
> It is clear that the establishment of the corporations (*sambandene*) as the basis for Quisling's *Riksting* is his decisive and perhaps also his last attempt to document "that he has the people with him". If he can in this instance show results to the outside world, the planned assault against young people from ten to eighteen . . . will be easier to achieve. Above all, he will create possibilities for a "peace settlement", with ensuing mobilization either on or behind the German military front.[65]

The teachers' underground leaders demonstrated good tactical skill and psychological insight by placing greatest stress on the educators' aversion to taking part in NS' indoctrination program. Forced membership in the Teachers' Corporation, while an important part of the protest, received less emphasis.[66] The protest, succinct and to the point, was mailed from Oslo on February 14. Each recipient was asked to declare: "I am unable to take part in the education of Norwegian youth according to the principles established for NS' youth service because this is in conflict with my conscience". Furthermore, since membership in the Corporation required active participation in NS indoctrination, plus other demands which were in violation of the teachers' contracts, those signing the protest concluded: "I cannot regard myself as a member of Norway's Teachers' Corporation".[67]

The result was not long in coming. Beginning on February 20 and continuing during the following days, the protest letters poured into Skancke's Church and Education Department. The overwhelming majority of teachers signed the protest.[68]

The unrealistic nature of Quisling's basic assumption that he could have his way without engendering any opposition as long as his National Government issued laws which the "law-abiding" public would be bound to respect, was revealed when the extent of the teachers' protest became clear. He had naively failed to instruct his officials to take steps to meet a possible countermove. Faced now with a giant protest on its hands, NS desperately sought to improvise. All other measures were abandoned in order to try to break the teachers' opposition.[69]

Quisling as usual could come up with no alternative except the use of force. The protesting teachers were to be coerced into abandoning their resistance. They were informed that they would be considered dismissed from their positions unless they withdrew their resignations from the Teachers' Corporation by March 1. If they failed to heed this warning, they would also be denied their pensions, and they could expect to be drafted for forced labor "in northern Norway or other places".[70] To demonstrate that this was no idle threat, teachers' salaries for February were withheld in a number of areas.[71]

This blunt attempt at intimidation had scarcely any effect. Very few allowed themselves to be frightened. Instead, the protest statements continued to stream in.[72] This placed Skancke and Sæther, the two NS officials in the forefront of the confrontation, in a difficult position. In repeated assurances to the press they had belittled the action, insisting that only a small number of misguided teachers were taking part. With his bluff called, Skancke had to consider enforcing the ultimatum. But were this to occur, the NS claim that only a small minority had taken part in the protest would be revealed as a lie to the entire world, with Skancke facing the unwelcome prospect of firing the great majority of the country's teachers. Such a possibility was intolerable. To save face, Skancke's department decreed on February 26 that all instruction would cease for one month, beginning on the following day. Lack of fuel for heating the schools in midwinter served as the lame excuse for this unprecedented action.[73] This pretext fooled no one, least of all the teachers. But their enforced vacation did not mean that Quisling had admitted defeat. On the contrary, he and his advisers began to lay plans to take even more coercive measures against the recalcitrant educators who stood in the way of his goals.

The initiative remained, however, not with NS but with its opponents. By linking their protest against being forced to join the Teachers' Corporation with their opposition to the NS Youth Organization's indoctrination program, the teachers had placed themselves in the forefront of a massive resistance campaign. Many persons who previously during the occupation had been but passive onlookers to protest activity now became actively involved. This included in particular parents whose children might be forced to join the Youth Organization against their will. A parents' protest action resulted. The initiators of this operation were a number of women teachers in Oslo who were concerned in particular about the consequences of having school children subjected to NS proselytism. Their protest took the form of sending a commonly worded letter to Skancke's and Stang's departments. In it the parents declared that they did not wish to have their children take part in compulsory NS youth service because this would be in violation of their consciences.[74]

The parents' opposition received tremendous support. Copies of the declaration were duplicated and spread in large numbers. Friends, relatives, and neighbors of those affected were also mobilized to take part. Consequently, beginning on March 6 another avalanche of mail descended on the NS departments in Oslo. Somewhere between 200,000 to 300,000 letters were received. While many sent in duplicate protests, including ones bearing fictitious signatures, the strong outpouring of opposition indicated the depth of feeling that had been aroused by Quisling's attempt to control the minds of children.[75]

This protest proved to be especially effective because, unlike the teachers, parents could not be dismissed. Nevertheless, despite the strong resistance, NS doggedly went ahead in certain parts of the country in trying to enforce compulsory service in the Youth Organization. As much as anything, however, this was a face-saving gesture. Beginning in March, children in some locations were ordered to attend NS youth meetings. When they did not comply, their parents were threatened and even arrested on occasion. But opposition remained bitter and determined. In the end NS had to give up. This effort only added to the festering hatred for Quisling and his party within the population at large.[76]

The possibility that he might succeed in inculcating young people with National Union's ideology was made even more uncertain by the direct entry of the Church into the conflict when it was at its height. The very fact that this NS campaign was of such a nature that the Church could easily become engaged illustrated once more Quisling's failure to take tactical considerations into account when he and his underlings began this poorly conceived venture. For the Church carried with it great moral authority, as it had already demonstrated when it used its prestige against the rampages of the *Hird* in 1941.

On February 14, 1942, the same date the teachers' resistance leaders sent out their protest declaration, the bishops of the Church issued their own letter attacking mandatory membership in the NS Youth Organization. It was hardly a coincidence that this statement appeared at the very time that the teachers' opposition took shape. Bishop Berggrav in particular maintained close contact with the persons within the Home Front who were responsible for drawing up the teachers' protest.[77] The bishops' letter was not intended to be read by Skancke alone. Copies were made and distributed throughout the country, being received "with joy in wide circles".[78]

Such a reaction was understandable because the bishops could take their stand strictly on theological grounds. They denounced Quisling's plan, declaring categorically that it would create division between parents and their children. Therefore, the bishops maintained it was a direct breach of the Fourth Commandment.[79] Thanks to the unquestioned religious probity which the bishops assumed over a question of moral significance such as this, their criticism could rally not only members of the State Church, but persons of different religious persuasions as well. All other denominations gave their full support, including the Catholic bishop.[80]

Further adding to the difficulties which Quisling now had on his hands was the fact that the Church's protest, bringing it directly into the mainstream of the opposition to NS in the campaign involving the nation's youth, was not an isolated incident. At this very time a crisis was coming to a head in the long simmering dispute between the Church and NS authorities which dated back to the founding of the Christian Joint Council.

A showdown proved to be unavoidable. Since the Christian Joint Council's first appearance, the intransigent attitude of the religious leadership, personified perhaps above all by the uncompromising stance of Bishop Berggrav, indicated that sooner or later a decisive clash would occur. It proved doubly unfortunate for Quisling that he lacked the ability to avoid such a confrontation at this critical juncture. Indeed, there is no indication that he even recognized the disadvantage of engaging in a dispute with the Church at the very time the struggle with the teachers and parents was reaching a climax.

He was not alone, however, in desiring to deal forcefully with the Church's opposition. Indeed, his options may have been narrowed by the fact that none other than Terboven wished to move against Berggrav in order to eliminate the Bishop's recalcitrant opposition. Exactly what motivated the *Reichskommissar* remains unclear, but there is no doubt that he had developed an intense personal dislike of the Bishop by early 1942.[81] Perhaps the key to understanding Terboven's strong antagonism lay with Berggrav's open but skillful exercise of leadership during 1940–1941 in resistance to Quisling and NS, and thereby indirectly also to the German cause.

The *Reichskommissar* for once was therefore more a colleague than a skeptical observer when Quisling began his dramatic showdown with the Church in February. Fittingly enough, the incident that triggered the confrontation was the Act of State whereby he proclaimed himself Minister President. In celebration of this event of "historic consequence", Skancke ordered that an NS pastor be allowed to hold a religious observance in the National Cathedral at Trondheim, complete with uniformed *Hird* mem-

bers and NS banners. Such a ceremony was especially offensive to the opponents of NS, since Norwegian monarchs traditionally were crowned in
the Cathedral. In protest, the Cathedral Dean, Arne Fjellbu, refused to
cancel his originally scheduled service, but held it later the same day. As
opposed to the sparsely attended NS observance, the Dean's service attracted several thousand people who demonstrated their solidarity against
Quisling. Despite attempts by the police to lock them out and to disperse
them, plus the bitter cold of sub-zero temperature, the people held their
ground, singing hymns and patriotic songs.[82]

This incident created the divisive issue which separated the Church
from NS authorities for the duration of the war. The Church protested
against what had occurred, but the only result was the ouster of Dean
Fjellbu on February 19. Five days later the bishops took a definitive step.
Critical of what had taken place at the Cathedral, they announced their
joint resignations from their official state positions, but not their *church*
functions. In effect, the bishops broke off all relations with the state, as
represented by Skancke's Department of Church and Education, but retained their religious duties as heads of their bishoprics.[83]

The immediate reaction of Skancke's department was to suspend the
bishops and to order the deans (*domprostene*) to assume control of the
bishoprics. But once again Quisling and his officials discovered that while
it was easy to give commands, compliance was not at all assured. The
deans refused categorically to obey, joining instead the bishops by giving
up their state functions.[84]

This effective clerical disobedience brought Quisling personally into the
fray. With his pretensions of having assumed power previously divided between the King, the *Storting*, and the government as a consequence of the
Act of State, he had arrogated the position of being the supreme head of
the Church, previously exercised by the King in Council. The bishops' action was therefore directed against him. Immediately after the bishops announced their resignations, he could only rant against them in a critical letter sent to all members of the clergy. He accused the bishops of using
Christianity as a shield in order to carry out "anti-national politics in service of anti-Christian capitalism and communism". The enraged *Fører* in
particular singled out Bishop Berggrav, who stood accused of nothing less
than having "destroyed Norway's freedom and independence". This indicated that Quisling, quite correctly, regarded Berggrav as a major obstacle,
standing in the way of the Minister President being able to establish his will
over the people and thereby lay the foundation for what he hoped would
be an independent government.[85]

Berggrav was immediately removed from his post. He and his fellow
bishops were placed under police guard. In early March the remainder of
the bishops were also expelled from office.[86] But this use of force brought
no positive results for Quisling. The bishops were regarded as martyrs.

When the clergy read the bishops' protest from their pulpits, the churches were crowded as never before. The pastors and members of congregations sent declarations of full support for the suspended bishops.[87] Quisling's action against the Church's highest religious authorities merely made resistance to him and NS so much more a matter of moral conviction. The people who filled the churches to overflowing, which in peacetime would have been unusual, were moved by the bishops' stance. Many wept openly.[88] The Church's ability to arouse such a deep emotional response showed the extent to which popular resistance to Quisling's offensive had been strengthened.

The Church as an institution benefited by being solidly unified, enabling the clergy to make carefully coordinated moves. In the face of such rapid execution, Quisling and his ministers were unable to respond effectively. The climax of the Church's challenge to Quisling came on Easter Sunday, April 5, when the majority of the clergy read a declaration entitled "The Church's Foundation" (*"Kirkens Grunn"*) to their congregations. The statement had been drawn up by the Christian Joint Council and quickly distributed throughout the country. "The Church's Foundation" directly repudiated Quisling by strongly affirming the independence of the Church from the state in spiritual matters. It further proclaimed the word of God to be sovereign over all ideologies.[89]

As a consequence of giving their adherence to this document, the great majority of pastors followed the lead of the bishops, resigning their civil functions while declaring their intention to continue to carry out their religious responsibilities on behalf of their congregations. Of 699 clergymen who headed congregations, 645 announced their resignations. An additional 151 out of 155 ordained ministers who were engaged in other religious activity similarly declared their written adherence to "The Church's Foundation", divorcing themselves from state authority.[90]

By severing their relationship with the administration, led by Quisling's officials, the pastors naturally forfeited their salaries. But the congregations now assumed responsibility for providing direct economic support for their pastors. An illegal office was established in Oslo for the purpose of coordinating this effort. As a result, the clergy and their families did not suffer major hardship.[91] Unless they were part of the minority who were ordered to leave their parishes, they continued to carry out most of their religious duties, strengthened by the knowledge that they enjoyed the full backing of their congregations.

Quisling on this occasion responded rapidly to the pastors' defiance. As head of the Church, he issued a number of laws on April 7, only two days after "The Church's Foundation" had been read from the pulpit. These laws permitted him to follow new procedures in the appointment of bishops. They also allowed the ordination of "qualified laymen" without the required theological degree. In accordance with his laws, Quisling appointed new bishops and a number of new pastors during the next few weeks. All were either NS members or sympathizers. Many "lacked not only theological or any academic education, but also the most elementary moral requirements for pastoral service".[92] Similarly, the authors of "The Church's Foundation" within the Christian Joint Council were dealt with swiftly. They were placed under arrest. With one exception, they were later released, but not permitted to resume their religious positions. Bishop Berggrav, however, continued to be interned for the duration of the war. In this way, Quisling's most dangerous religious opponent remained isolated.[93]

Quisling did not believe that his NS forces had been defeated at the time the pastors resigned their state affiliation. In the same way that he was determined to pursue the confrontation with the teachers after their successful protest, he simultaneously kept attacking the clergy in no uncertain terms. On April 8 the NS-controlled press published one of his articles in which he accused them of being "swindlers and traitors".[94] His intemperate language indicated the increasingly emotional manner in which he reacted to opposition during the trying period in the spring of 1942. He regarded all those who stood in his way as traitors because, in his view, working against him was tantamount to working against Norway.

To overcome the clergy's resistance, he resorted to his standard procedure of applying coercion, despite the many previous instances when this alleged panacea had failed to produce satisfactory results. He simply lacked the flexibility and subtlety to conceive of any alternate approach. On April 8 he sent a special telegram to all protesting clergymen, informing them that their resignations were an "act of rebellion directed against Norway's freedom and independence".[95] He threatened the most dire penalties if they did not resume their ties with the state, with an ultimatum to do so by 2:00 p.m., April 11.[96] If they did not respond by this time, he warned them to be ready to move from their parishes within one week. The clergy's reaction was not what he had hoped for. In contrast to previous occasions when the Church and Education Department had been literally engulfed by letters of protest, when the ultimatum expired, the Department's mail was singularly empty of any response. Only two pastors were frightened by Quisling's threats into resuming their state affiliation.[97]

The Minister President's warning was not, however, an idle bluff. A number of pastors were subsequently expelled from their parsonages, a practice that NS authorities adhered to for the duration of the war.[98] But it simply proved unfeasible for Skancke's department to remove all protesting pastors. Furthermore, many of those who were compelled to move nevertheless continued to carry out their religious functions. As a result, after the great majority of clergy broke with Quisling's government, there existed two Lutheran churches in Norway. One consisted of the small number of pastors who sympathized with or belonged to NS and who retained their official status, augmented by the "qualified laymen" whom Quisling appointed to fill clerical positions. Within this church the Minister President received acclaim as the country's religious head. The Department of Church and Education issued a new catechism in 1943, which provided school children with the following explanation of the Fourth Commandment: "Above all we owe obedience to the *Fører* and the state administration. To rebel against the authorities and against the state is to resist God's order and results in punishment".[99] Such a bold statement represented Quisling's attitude perfectly. The catechism's final sentence similarly reflected a view which only the small number of adherents who belonged to the "official" church could accept: "Now the old sun cross symbol shall again unify the Norwegian people around Norway and around God".[100] For "God" read Quisling.

The second church existed side by side with the Minister President's church, but completely overshadowed the latter. This church was the continuation of the old State Church, whose clergy had supported their bishops and broken with the National Government. Their services enjoyed high attendance, while the NS pastors delivered sermons that were generally received only by empty pews.[101] Perhaps in the clearest possible way, the division made obvious by the confrontation between Quisling and the Church demonstrated how he had polarized the great majority of the people against him and his party.

He sustained further damage in the spring of 1942 because news of the setbacks he received in his conflict with the Church, the teachers, and the parents could not be kept secret from the outside world. This resulted in greater notoriety for him, which in turn reflected badly on the Germans. Goebbels noted caustically that "events in Norway are having considerable effect upon Swedish sentiment. The Church fight started by Terboven and Quisling seems to me completely superfluous".[102] If anyone, Goebbels was fully aware of the damage that could be caused by negative publicity. On the Allied side, the Norwegian government in London expertly exploited the defeats that Quisling sustained. Throughout Allied countries in the spring of 1942, Norway served as an example of the "strength that can live in a democratic people who are anchored in a national and Christian culture".[103]

Externally as well as internally Quisling had thus been weakened by the offensive he set in motion during his first three months as Minister President. Rather than achieving the quick breakthrough that he had constantly predicted would occur when he headed a government, making him and his party the masters of society, he had succeeded in creating an all-powerful alliance against him, combining the Church, the schools, and the home. All his efforts were stymied as a result of this invincible coalition, whose moral fortifications could not be breached.

German authorities in Norway, civilian and military, reacted with mixed emotions to the tremendous conflict that Quisling had generated through his ill-considered assault. On the one hand, many of them, with Terboven in their lead, had earlier warned against Quisling's failings as a political leader, but Hitler had ignored such counsel. Falkenhorst, never an admirer of Quisling's, noted in an official report that the *Fører*'s government had created difficulties for itself as a result of its "hasty measures against the teachers and pastors". The general pointed out that this had resulted in growing resistance and "greater unity among Quisling's enemies".[104] On the other hand, the Germans could not simply sit by complacently and watch the Minister President go down in humiliating defeat. This would also mean a setback for the occupying power, since Quisling enjoyed its public endorsement. Furthermore, Terboven had fully learned his lesson from the difficulties he had encountered because of Quisling's past favor with Hitler. The *Reichskommissar* realized that he could well be held accountable if he made no effort to aid the NS *Fører* in trying to overcome the difficult situation he had created for himself.

Despite Terboven's direct personal involvement against Berggrav when the campaign against the Church was instituted, the Germans were determined to take no severe action against the clergy as a whole. This decision was in large part based on the experience the Nazis had gained from religious opposition in Germany. No such restraints held them back, however, in the policy they chose to apply against the teachers. Their successful resistance was damaging not only to NS, but represented also a threat to German authority.[105] By March 1942 it was obvious that the teachers' opposition could never be overcome merely by NS bluster. The Germans resorted to harsher measures in actively backing their weak ally.[106]

Direct intervention became a certainty after Terboven conferred with Quisling in mid-March. They reached agreement that "for the time being" 1,000 of the protesting teachers would be deported to perform forced labor in northern Norway.[107] This was not, however, a unilateral German action. Terboven simply gave his approval to punitive steps which NS, under Quisling's supervision, had been preparing to execute since early March. Quisling therefore bore responsibility for the harsh treatment which the arrested teachers received at least as much as the *Reichskommissar*. In early March, Sæther's Teachers' Corporation sent out telegrams to NS regional leaders and district heads of the Corporation, requesting them to compile lists of teachers opposed to NS. Those whose names were recorded would be considered for forced labor. The lists were duly drawn up and sent to the Teachers' Corporation before March 17.[108]

Among those who were reported to NS authorities in this manner, some 1,300 male teachers were arrested on March 20.[109] They were taken into custody by Norwegian police, but handed over for ill-treatment by German guards in concentration camps. Here the teachers were subjected to gruelling physical degradation in an attempt not only to coerce them into joining the Teachers' Corporation, but also to have them serve as an example to frighten the majority of protesting teachers who remained free. The arrestees were forced to undergo living in freezing cold and unsanitary barracks, deprivation of adequate food, and physical punishment, which included crawling over parade grounds covered with slushy snow and mud. A small number gave in and joined the Teachers' Union, the great majority did not.[110]

The stubborn resistance of the imprisoned teachers resulted in greater maltreatment. Some 500 were placed on board a small coastal steamer, the *Skjerstad*, and shipped to the extreme northern part of Arctic Norway, to Kirkenes close to the Russian border. The voyage, which lasted from April 15 to April 28, took place under frightful conditions. The small ship, of some 700 tons, was certified to carry 150 passengers. The 500 prisoners, accompanied by fifty German guards, were so crowded together that it was difficult to sleep. They were cold, received little food, and were often denied adequate medical treatment.[111] The torment experienced by the *Skjerstad* teachers was not merely intended, as earlier, to induce educators to join the Teachers' Corporation. Instead, NS authorities and the Germans were now intent on using the incident as a warning to everyone who resisted NS. For this reason, the journey received great publicity in the NS-controlled press as the *Skjerstad* proceeded slowly along the coast with its unfortunate human cargo.[112]

Evidence is clear that while the Germans were in charge of the actual deportation, Quisling provided his full support. Time after time he had warned that opposition to NS would result in harsh punishment. His threats were now being fulfilled, and he strongly endorsed the treatment accorded the teachers. His stand aroused consternation and repugnance. Many members of the clergy in Trøndelag, led by the deposed bishop and Cathedral dean, pleaded with him on behalf of the teachers.[113] Even NS members reacted against the maltreatment. An NS doctor who examined conditions aboard the *Skjerstad* before it left Trondheim telegraphed a protest to Quisling.[114] One of Quisling's ministers, Irgens, also tried to intervene, offering to use his authority as head of the Shipping Department to halt the voyage.[115] But Quisling remained obdurate, refusing to consider any steps to end the journey or to improve conditions on board the vessel.

As the steamer moved north, exposed to all of the threats facing shipping in those dangerous waters, its journey became a symbol for both sides engaged in the most bitter confrontation of the occupation. For Quisling and his party, it represented their determination to take strong measures to reach their goals. For those in opposition to NS, the majority of the population, the teachers' plight was a symbolic act of encouragement not to give in. The teachers on board the *Skjerstad* were themselves fully aware of what they stood for. As one of them wrote in an account that he was able to smuggle out: "If things give way here, then everything can give way. If things hold here, then everything will hold. And there is reason to believe that things are holding now".[116]

The *Skjerstad* incident proved to be important not only within the country, but it had international repercussions as well. Because of the publicity it received, its symbolic importance was used effectively in enemy propaganda. Allied newspapers carried accounts of the teachers' plight on their front pages.[117] The incident therefore served as yet another propaganda defeat for Quisling, blackening his reputation even more in world opinion. "The scenes with the 500 teachers aboard the slave ship unified with dramatic sharpness the conflict between the human being and state power".[118]

The use of terror failed to frighten the teachers into compliance, and it served to increase opposition within the population in general.[119] Quisling, however, remained convinced that increased use of force was the only solution. The Teachers' Corporation at the end of April sent out requests for additional lists of teachers to be dismissed or deported. The Germans, however, put a stop to this plan to expand the campaign against the teachers.[120] Having ultimate responsibility for maintaining stability in the country, Terboven could not allow the conflict to go on indefinitely. Therefore even though he continued to threaten the teachers with harsh punishment in the event their protest turned into a strike, he in reality signaled a retreat.[121]

In the vain hope that at least some additional teachers would give in, the so-called "fuel vacation" actually lasted longer than the one month Skancke had originally announced. But there was no sign of compliance. In many parts of the country the teachers continued to provide instruction, but in private homes. Eventually normal education had to be resumed. Some schools reopened again as early as April 9, and on the 25th Skancke's Department of Church and Education officially revealed Quisling's defeat, attempting of course to camouflage this from the public. The Department maintained that the law establishing the Teachers' Corporation had been misunderstood. The teachers allegedly had not been required to cooperate with the NS Youth Organization. This represented a direct disavowal of Sæther, who had demanded exactly the opposite. Furthermore, as far as compulsory membership in the Teachers' Corporation was concerned, the educators were informed that their protest was of no consequence, since everyone who taught in the schools automatically became members of the organization. Such an interpretation, however, made the entire NS campaign to force the teachers to withdraw their resignations entirely meaningless.[122]

The teachers, however, and not Quisling's officials, had the final say in this conflict. Before resuming their duties, those who had backed the protest read a joint statement to their pupils in which they reaffirmed their determination never to teach anything that was "in conflict with their conscience".[123] The teachers furthermore expressed their disagreement with the NS view that all who taught in the schools automatically belonged to the Teachers' Corporation.[124]

To allow the teachers to return to work unchallenged under the terms of such a declaration was a stinging humiliation for Quisling. But he could not resort to closing the schools once more and making mass arrests, since Terboven would not permit such a move. He therefore had no alternative but to accept this as the final outcome of the teachers' conflict, if with ill grace.[125]

The frustration that he felt was indicated by a specific incident in which he personally took part. Escorted by Skancke, Jonas Lie, and a large contingent of police, the Minister President on May 22 descended on Stabekk School, located at the west end of the capital. Its teachers and pupils had long enjoyed a reputation for being among the most dedicated anti-NS protagonists in the Oslo area. Since Quisling could no longer punish the teachers as a group on a nation-wide basis, he intended to make an example of this school, which he regarded as a center for what he later described as "terror activity that took place during the teachers' conflict".[126]

Upon his arrival, the teachers were ordered to attend a meeting with their visitors. Here Quisling made a speech in which his bitterness over being stymied by the teachers' nation-wide opposition found expression. He accused them of being personally responsible for his failure to obtain a National Assembly that spring. In this way, he maintained, the teachers had contributed to preventing Norway from becoming "a free and independent realm".[127]

Each teacher was thereafter obliged to submit to an interrogation by Skancke in which the Minister President frequently took part. One of the questions which in particular interested Quisling was whether the teachers had been coerced into joining the protest. With his steadfast belief in his sacred mission to lead his country, he had convinced himself that anyone who opposed him must be deluded or misled. Since the teachers were among the best educated and most informed, he therefore assumed that their opposition to him could only have occurred as a result of a terror conspiracy.[128]

When none of the teachers, not even in his presence, agreed to admit that they had been in error, Quisling became enraged. He ordered them to be arrested.[129] They were imprisoned for a considerable period of time, but experienced no additional ill treatment. Upon their release, they were not allowed to resume their teaching careers for the duration of the occupation.[130]

The vehement expression of personal dissatisfaction that he displayed at Stabekk indicated the extent of his disappointment for having failed to secure the defeat of the teachers. They had been singled out for tactical reasons, with NS and the Germans believing them to be an easier target than the Church and the parents, but they did not prove to be the weak link – on the contrary. In his offensive against the teachers, the Church and the parents, Quisling had viewed it as the campaign which would lay the foundation for his corporative national socialist society. Since their expectations had been so high when the offensive began, the ensuing failure, as demonstrated by inability to break the teachers' opposition, was therefore especially heavy to bear for the Minister President and his increasingly disillusioned followers.[131]

On the other side of the front line, those who stood in opposition to Quisling were particularly inspired by the teachers. When NS similarly attempted to take over a number of organizations in the spring, the most prominent being Norway's Youth League (Noregs ungdomslag), the newspaper publishers, and the attorneys, members of these groups reacted with mass protests and resignations that were completely in character with the successful example of the teachers.[132] This opposition was skillfully coordinated by a Home Front leadership that functioned increasingly in a more assured and experienced manner to draw a clear-cut line to obstruct all of Quisling's initiatives.[133]

Exactly what would have occurred if the opposite had taken place – if he had succeeded in achieving his goals – cannot be answered with certainty, but without a doubt the occupation of Norway would have taken on a completely different character if he had been even partially successful in the nazification of society. This would have had serious repercussions for the postwar future. As for the wartime period, in the final analysis everything depended on the Germans and how they assessed the situation. But it can be concluded that Quisling would have been in a strong position to insist he be granted at least some token of increased sovereignty, although effective control over Norway would have remained in Hitler's hands. In view of the assurances that he had received in Berlin in February, plus continued backing from Rosenberg and Raeder, Quisling could not have been ignored. It is not inconceivable that he might have managed to eliminate at least the person of the Reichskommissar, although some type of German administration would undoubtedly have remained.

While the question of what the result would have been if Quisling had enjoyed success remains a matter of conjecture, there is no doubt as to what the actual outcome of his defeat in National Union's effort to take control of the country's young people really meant. The successful resistance spearheaded by the teachers, accompanied by moral support from the Church and indignation from the parents, had far-reaching repercussions. It encouraged other groups to emulate the same kind of obstruction. Furthermore, it placed in jeopardy the hopes that Quisling had for establishing a corporate assembly and concluding peace with the Germans.[134]

This outcome was particularly significant because while the battle with the teachers and the Church raged at its most intense level, Quisling had simultaneously set in motion planning within the upper echelons of his NS administration toward reaching his ambitious goal of creating a corporate body, the National Assembly (*Riksting*). Quisling set the early date of May 1 for the time when he would proclaim its founding. He had looked forward to this ever since the Act of State, being convinced that it would be a vital advance in his quest for greater freedom, since he believed it would bring him close to his sought after peace with Germany.[135]

In endeavoring to realize this major ambition, he faced great opposition, however, in particular because he had shown his hand. The Home Front leaders were fully aware of the significance he attached to obtaining the National Assembly.[136] With the Home Front being determined to block this move at all costs, the NS struggle with the teachers was especially bitter, since the Teachers' Corporation was but one of the corporations which Quisling planned to include in the Assembly.

The planning which he began was much broader in scope than the single thrust to set up a Teachers' Corporation. It involved no less an effort than to find the means by which all segments of the economy would be included within his corporate structure. To accomplish this, two extremely ambitious projects were launched. Each was led by leading NS economic experts who worked on their designs directly under Quisling's overall supervision.

The Minister President seized the opportunity to embark on this activity because the elimination of the Commissarial Council had also ended the time when the economic departments were administered by experts who did not belong to NS. He could thereby engage his party with full force in the economic sector, being limited, however, by the restraints that Terboven could impose at any time. But as was true with Quisling's offensive against the schools, he at first received considerable leeway from the *Reichskommissar* in making plans for corporate control of the economy. This created the chance of advancement for the figure who steadily rose to become Quisling's leading economic expert, Alf L. Whist. The latter held the post of NS Ombudsman for Trade and Industry in early 1942. Serving directly under Quisling, Whist received responsibility for coordinating all NS economic planning. Although not yet a member of the National Government, he nevertheless enjoyed a stronger mandate than many of the ministers because of the broad range of authority that he had been granted.[137]

When Whist had assumed office, Quisling immediately gave him the task of drawing up a plan for bringing the trade and industrial associations under direct party control as part of his corporate structure.[138] Acting in accordance with these instructions, Whist presented a plan to his *Fører* on March 12 in which he proposed that all areas of economic production be organized into ten business groups (*riksnæringsgrupper*), which in turn would make up a corporate umbrella organization, a National Chamber of Trade and Industry (*Riksnæringskammer*). But Whist assumed a somewhat cautious attitude toward trying to form such an ambitious enterprise, advising Quisling to postpone decreeing a law establishing the business groups and National Chamber until some time after May 1. He suggested this delay because Quisling intended to announce yet another corporate body on this date. Whist believed that it would be to Quisling's advantage to keep the two new formations separate in the public mind, in particular since they both involved the economic sector.[139]

This second major undertaking that Quisling hoped to realize was the creation of an even more important corporate body, Norway's Labor Corporation (*Norges Arbeidssamband*). He had begun NS designs for the formation of this body already in September 1941, when the party was allowed to take over LO during the state of emergency.[140] The initial planning, however, appears to have been mainly theoretical, which was understandable since Terboven would not sanction any additional changes in the economic sector at this time. Not until after the new year, when he stood much stronger, did Quisling appear to commit himself fully to implementing the Labor Corporation.[141] On the late date of March 16, 1942, he formally appointed J. A. Lippestad, who served as Social Minister in the National Government, to be in charge of the founding of the body.[142] Lippestad, however, had actually been involved in this work for a considerable period of time.[143]

The ambitious nature of the Labor Corporation was shown by the great number of people who would be forced to belong. This encompassed all employers and employees. Such long-established organizations as LO, the Employers' Association, and the Craftsmen's Association were scheduled to be absorbed into the new corporate structure. With its founding, one of Quisling's basic goals would have been attained. Its authoritarian, corporate nature was obvious. The Labor Corporation was intended to maintain social stability within the economic sector. The basic weapons for workers to strike and for employers to conduct lockouts were prohibited. Instead, the Corporation would assume responsibility for controlling all wage settlements and regulations governing working conditions. It would also take charge of apprentice and job training, leisure time activity, and welfare payments. In essence, the Labor Corporation was intended to function as the country's greatest single unifying body, through which Quisling would be able to implement his social and economic policies.[144]

As one of the concessions that he had received upon becoming Minister President, Quisling had been assured by the Germans that the Labor Corporation would be created on May 1. This fitted in nicely with his emphasis on historical symbolism. By proclaiming the Corporation on this date, which would, he hoped, also be the day on which his National Assembly came into being, he intended to usurp the international holiday for organized labor.

His NS subordinates, led by Lippestad, did not enjoy a free hand in the planning, however. They had to work closely with the *Reichskommissariat's Sozialabteilung*, which provided overall supervision. The Germans were interested in having the Labor Corporation conform as much as possible to its Third Reich counterpart, the German Labor Front, after which it was patterned to a considerable degree.[145] Lippestad and his co-workers did not wish to have the Corporation become merely a slavish imitation of the Labor Front, however, and some friction developed.[146]

When completed, the plans for the Labor Corporation were essentially a compromise. The Germans dropped their demand that the body should become an integral part of NS, with the NS planners for once employing the argument that such a step was completely unrealistic because it would cause great unrest. Similarly, unlike the Labor Front, whose membership was voluntary, the Labor Corporation had no hope of success without compulsory membership. From Quisling's point of view, however, the major difference between the Labor Corporation and its German counterpart was the role that he intended his corporate body to play. Although not a great deal was mentioned about this to the Germans, he planned to have the Labor Corporation serve as one of the cornerstones in his National Assembly, quite probably its most important part.[147]

Initially it seemed as if the Minister President would succeed in establishing the Labor Corporation. Under Lippestad's direction, careful planning for its launching took place in March.[148] As part of this preparatory groundwork, NS proceeded to issue a propaganda publication entitled *Norwegian Labor Life (Norsk Arbeidsliv)*. Lippestad intended to have it eventually serve as the official publication of the Labor Corporation.[149] Despite the severe wartime shortage of paper, no restrictions were imposed on *Norwegian Labor Life*, which was printed and mailed free of charge to no less than 200,000 households.[150]

Lippestad's group of NS planners appears to have completed its work by the first half of April.[151] Because of the importance Quisling attached to the Labor Corporation, special stress had been placed on making the ceremonies marking its founding as elaborate as possible. The festivities on May 1 were arranged to end with a mass meeting at the University Hall in the evening. Here Quisling would appear in triumph as the main speaker. As a symbolic background for such an important event, it was intended that the Minister President would be surrounded by the banners of all of the trade unions in the Oslo area. But in seeking to realize this part of the project, the NS planners ran into the same type of obstinate intransigence toward Quisling that organized labor had demonstrated before. Despite nominal NS leadership of the trade unions, none of those who were invited to send representatives to take part in the ceremony agreed to come. Furthermore, only one union consented to deliver its banner to NS within the deadline that was set. This act of defiance indicated that the workers appeared ready to resist, following in the footsteps of the teachers.[152]

The anticipated showdown never materialized on May 1, however. The uproar that Quisling had aroused in his conflict with the teachers and the Church had already made it impossible for him to set up his corporate body, the National Assembly, on this date.[153] The Labor Corporation experienced a similar fate. Terboven concluded during the second half of April that too many risks were involved in trying to establish this organization, and he definitely indicated on April 21 that the plan had been dropped.[154] All that Quisling succeeded in gaining at this juncture was another empty symbol. May Day was officially proclaimed an NS holiday, being given the prosaic name of "the day of labor" (*"arbeidets dag"*). *Fritt Folk*, in its coverage of May 1, pathetically tried to be positive in its commentary in order to disguise just how badly Quisling's plans had turned out, in grim contrast to the great expectations that he had looked forward to achieving on this date: "The streets were filled with people who were outside enjoying the day of labor".[155]

Terboven's dramatic turnabout was for once not motivated by a desire to embarrass Quisling. The abandonment of the Labor Corporation was yet another result of the effective opposition mounted by the teachers and the Church, with the support of the great mass of the people, especially the parents. Terboven became convinced that even larger disturbances would follow if Quisling simultaneously was allowed to proceed with his experiment to reorganize the economic sector.[156] As the *Reichskommissar* put it quite aptly: "If . . . the workers also begin to strike, I will have the whole country in an uproar." He could scarcely risk this at a time when Hitler was obsessed with Norway's military importance because of his fear of an Allied invasion. Referring to Norwegian society as being stuck in the mud, Terboven declared the need to get it "unstuck" again.[157] The Home Front further exploited Terboven's dilemma by its resistance to Quisling, knowing that the Germans could not risk a decline in productivity at such a critical period in the war.[158]

Quisling followed the example of *Fritt Folk*, trying outwardly to put on as positive a face as possible after the demise of his Labor Corporation project. NS propaganda spread the story that he had simply resolved for the time being not to set a fixed date for its founding.[159] He kept on insisting that its future existence was very definitely assured.[160] Acting in accordance with this attitude, NS planners continued to formulate new ideas for the creation of the Labor Corporation after May 1. The party similarly maintained a propaganda campaign which called for the establishment of such a body. But there is nothing to indicate that this amounted to anything more than wishful thinking on the part of Quisling and his NS officials.[161]

The failure of the Labor Corporation to come into being also had a negative impact on Alf Whist's parallel effort to organize all trade and industrial activity into business groups under NS control. His original plan had been predicated on the assumption that the business groups would come into being after the law creating the Labor Corporation had been proclaimed on May 1. But since this failed to materialize, his projected groups for trade and industry were similarly placed in limbo.[162]

As Quisling watched his NS offensive unfold during the late winter and early spring, he did not neglect external considerations. He maintained his optimistic outlook concerning his future relationship with the Germans. The ceremonial pomp and solicitous attention that he had received during his February visit with Hitler, plus the apparent leeway he had obtained in being allowed to proceed with his plans to change society, initially caused him to view the coming months expectantly. Boehm reported to Raeder in early April that Quisling, after having recovered from his first disappointment over not having been given complete freedom of action in February, was quite satisfied with the Act of State, or at least gave every impression of being so.[163] Quisling clearly believed that the conditions imposed by the Act of State were only a preliminary stage that would be followed by full recognition of his government's independent status later in the spring.

Since he had not, however, secured specific confirmation from Hitler that his wishes would be acceded to, he continued his campaign to convince *der Führer* of the advantages that would accrue for Germany if he were granted a peace settlement. In March he once more directed his arguments toward Hitler's obvious preoccupation with military considerations, presenting *der Führer* with a memorandum that focused on Germany's naval interests in Norway. Quisling listed a number of arguments alleging how the Reich's naval position in Norway would be strengthened by a peace settlement. Accordingly, he suggested that a peace treaty would bring the following benefits: (1) persons committing acts of espionage and sabotage on behalf of the Allies would no longer have any justification for doing so, (2) Norwegian sailors could serve in the German navy, (3) Norwegians could assume responsibility for manning the coastal defenses, and (4) formal recognition of Quisling's government would bring an end to the "emigrant government's" legation in Stockholm, thereby eliminating its strong anti-German influence in Sweden.[164]

Whether Hitler ever read this memorandum is not known, but if he did, he did not bother to reply.[165] Quisling's viewpoint was too transparently self-serving to have any attraction for *der Führer*. His main concern for the navy was for it to retain full control of the Norwegian coastline, whose valuable bases provided security for the bulk of the German fleet.

Much to Quisling's surprise, however, another ranking German official soon afterwards inaugurated discussions with the NS *Fører* concerning a possible peace agreement. But since it was Terboven who took this step in April, suspicion immediately comes to mind concerning his true motives. His timing could not have been more disadvantageous for Quisling than at this time, with the teachers' struggle and the Church conflict both at their peak. It appears that Terboven fully intended to exploit Quisling's difficulties.[166]

The *Reichskommissar* initiated the subject of peace negotiations in a discussion with Quisling, only to declare later that he did not believe conditions were favorable for such talks to continue because of the problems that had arisen in connection with the Church and the teachers, plus his obligation to take into account the needs of the armed services. Despite his all-consuming desire to conclude an agreement, Quisling at this juncture was in no position to do anything but accede to Terboven's line of reasoning. The Minister President felt compelled to agree to what he termed "this temporary postponement" of the peace negotiations.[167]

His battle with the teachers and the Church had thereby again resulted in another severe setback, one affecting the formal status of his government. But he remained as obdurate as ever in his desire to secure a permanent peace with Germany, and planned to resume his agitation at the first possible moment. With this in mind, he requested at a meeting with his ministers on May 28 that they submit reasons from their respective departments why it was necessary to reach a speedy peace settlement with Germany. At least two of the ministers responded, and there is reason to believe that he obtained similar replies from most of the others.[168]

Reinforced by his cabinet's dutiful backing, the Minister President again made another direct appeal to Hitler in a memorandum dated June 9. This time the thrust of the message was to assure Hitler that Quisling was in such a strong position in Norway that a settlement should no longer be postponed. In making this assessment, he had to gloss over as best he could the fact that his offensive to gain control over society had been brought to a standstill because of broad popular resistance. He asserted on the contrary that the conflict with the teachers and the Church had come to a satisfactory conclusion, with his government and his party both emerging strengthened from the confrontation. The increased power of his party, he continued, was shown by NS now being able to head all departments in the government. In addition, he pointed out that all regional governors were NS members, as were all Supreme Court justices, and the bishops of the State Church were either party members or sympathizers. NS membership, he maintained, had never been higher, numbering some 45,000, while the party's strength was further revealed by its control over all important organizations. Having described the situation in this favorable light, he argued that he and his government were unable to ascertain any reason why a peace settlement should not be made.[169]

In an accompanying letter to Hitler, bearing the same date, Quisling as usual spelled out in exact detail how he proposed the agreement with Germany should be carried out. He first looked forward to the establishment of a preliminary peace, which he asserted had already been anticipated in May. It should now, he suggested, take place in July. In accordance with his propensity for wanting to make use of historically significant dates, he proposed that the preliminary peace be proclaimed on July 18, the traditional date for Norway's unification as a result of the battle of Hafrsfjord in 872, which figured so prominently in his historical frame of reference. Continuing to be mindful of the symbolic importance of anniversaries, he further proposed that Norway join the Anti-Comintern Pact and declare its adherence to the Axis Powers in solemn ceremonies on September 25, 1942, the second anniversary of "NS' takeover of power". Finally, he urged that negotiations aimed at establishing a final peace settlement with Germany begin as soon as possible.[170]

Exactly twenty days after he had penned his memorandum and letter, he received Hitler's response in the form of a letter from Lammers.[171] Its contents could not have been more disappointing for the Minister President. It curtly informed him that wartime conditions made it impossible to change the relationship between the Greater German Reich and Norway in the form of either a peace settlement or a preliminary peace settlement.[172] Indicating that the Reich leadership recognized the extent to which Quisling depended on Hagelin's advice in his dealings with the Germans, Lammers also sent a copy of this letter to Hagelin in order to reinforce Hitler's decision.[173]

Hitler's brusque refusal was to a great degree dictated by military demands. With his critical June offensive in the Soviet Union still in its initial stage, he could hardly afford time to consider the political situation in Norway. But in addition, the disorder caused by Quisling's ill-fated offensive did not give Hitler cause to favor any change at just this time. Reports of the unrest aroused by Quisling's measures had created an unfavorable impression within the Nazi hierarchy.

Although he personally had contributed to this negative attitude through his involvement in the attack against Berggrav, Terboven was not one who could refrain from trying to take advantage of the difficulty Quisling was in. There is evidence to indicate that the *Reichskommissar*, working through his subordinates, gathered as much incriminating information as possible documenting Quisling's failure during the spring of 1942. He did this for the purpose of trying to persuade Hitler to abandon his support for the Minister President. While Hitler had so committed himself to Quisling that he showed no inclination to allow the Minister President to fall from his nominal position as head of state, Terboven's critical reports certainly did nothing to improve the German leadership's view of Quisling's abilities.[174]

Hitler's curt rejection of Quisling's proposals did not cause the latter to abandon his bid to acquire as much independence as possible. On the contrary, his dogged determination to improve his position was heightened. While he had to accept the fact that a peace settlement could not be obtained in the immediate future, he tried to recover ground by proceeding once again in a much more vigorous manner to establish the National Assembly. His earlier assumption that he would have the Assembly in place by May 1 had proven to be wishful thinking. He and his advisers now recognized that the function of such a quasi-representative body would be severely circumscribed because of the absence of a peace settlement. Nevertheless, if he succeeded in bringing it into existence, he believed this would give added weight to a future demand for peace.[175] And since Hitler in his June decision had not specifically prohibited Quisling from seeking to create a National Assembly, the latter did not in any way feel inhibited from attempting to proceed with this ambitious undertaking. On the contrary, during the summer of 1942 he and his NS officials were motivated more than ever toward working for its achievement.

As he had frequently shown, the concept of creating a National Assembly had been a fundamental aspect of Quisling's political philosophy since the 1930s. He intended it to serve as one of the chief instruments by which he converted society to his political ideal. In his speech during the Act of State he had repeated this resolution, declaring that his government would call together a "national assembly" as soon as conditions permitted.[176]

Although he could not state the obvious, German authorities of course were the power brokers who determined whether the time was ripe for a National Assembly. As long as conditions were unsettled during the spring, when the teachers and the Church offered effective, bitter resistance, Quisling could make no concrete plans for setting up the Assembly, since the Germans would not sanction such a move at this time. Furthermore, he and his subordinates became far too preoccupied with the immediate problems resulting from the NS offensive to give serious attention to matters of broader concern. While specific plans were made for the creation of entities that were intended to be key components of his corporate structure, such as the Teachers' Corporation, the Labor Corporation, and Whist's business groups, Quisling made no serious effort to have comprehensive plans drawn up for the Assembly. His original date of May 1 had proven to be but another of the unfulfilled aspirations he generally enunciated when first embarking on a venture. It fell victim to the bitter resistance his campaign aroused in the spring. As late as May, NS planning consisted of only vague preliminary drafts.[177]

In June, however, specific plans for setting up the body began to take form. Although kept secret within a small group of top NS officers, the decision of going ahead with the Assembly was apparently discussed at a national meeting of party officials in mid-June. This came at a time when Quisling still hoped to realize his peace plans, not yet having received Hitler's veto. When *der Führer*'s rejection arrived on the 29th, Quisling simply resolved to press on. But for the time being the matter continued to be treated in strictest confidence, with planning and discussions restricted to a limited number of NS administrators.[178]

News of Quisling's intention to go ahead with the National Assembly did not meet with full approval within the party. Several key officials, including Whist and Minister of Agriculture Fretheim, voiced reservations, believing that the time was not opportune for such an ambitious endeavor.[179] But their objections simply served to illustrate that opinions contrary to the party leader's had no effect in a system where the *Führer* principle prevailed. Once he had made his decision, Quisling was determined to proceed in the most direct manner possible.

What mattered most for him was the creation of a façade that would give the impression that Norway, under his leadership, once more had a representative assembly on the national level. With form, not function, being his primary concern, he did not spell out clearly how this body would operate. Therefore, fundamental questions concerning the Assembly were never answered, such as what would be the relationship between it and the government, how its members were to be selected, and what matters it would deal with.[180]

There can nevertheless be little doubt as to Quisling's true purpose. With his intense dislike of representative democracy, there was not the slightest chance that he would have allowed the Assembly to act as an independent body. He planned to have it play a subordinate and largely symbolic role, always controlled by the party, which in turn was completely under his personal domination. With his ever vigilant determination to preserve final authority in his hands, he would never consider any delegation of power. He pointedly emphasized this concern when he called for the creation of the Assembly during the Act of State, declaring that the *Führer* principle would always be "our basic principle in governing the state and society".[181]

This determination to deny the projected body any real authority was never stated categorically, however. The party bureaucrats involved in planning the National Assembly were therefore concerned about making it appear to be as impressive as possible, and some even deluded themselves into believing that it would be truly representative of society, at least to a certain degree.[182] The first public hint that something major was in the process of being formulated occurred on August 5, when *Fritt Folk* announced that National Union would hold its eighth national conference in Oslo on September 26. The paper made no mention of a National Assembly, but soon afterwards Hagelin's Interior Department issued an internal memo which declared that it would be founded on September 25 in connection with the party congress.[183] With his fondness for chronological symbolism, Quisling intended in this way to mark the second anniversary of his party's "takeover of power". This put the party planners under great time pressure. From early August onwards they therefore worked hectically to try to have all preparations completed by September 25.

Because of the secretive manner in which arrangements were carried out and the short time span in which plans had to be completed, the effort never achieved careful coordination. As a result, the whole operation became "a chaos of plans and drafts and future guidelines".[184] In large part this was because Quisling, who with his propensity for wanting to achieve his ends within the shortest possible time, had failed to take into consideration the amount of detailed planning and preparation that was required before a wide-ranging institutional change of this nature could have any chance of success. The fact that a number of the more capable and realistic NS administrators recognized this shortcoming and expressed their concern only made the enterprise that much more difficult to achieve.[185] Even the Interior Department's initial memorandum about establishing the Assembly reflected this feeling of restraint, declaring that the body would be called into existence on September 25 "if this is possible".[186]

Another major weakness in planning the National Assembly was Quisling's lack of consistency in defining exactly what he wished to create. He had never divulged in detail how his corporate body would be organized. At times he gave the impression that it would only consist of economic representatives. On other occasions he included a cultural component, but he was not consistent in indicating whether the cultural representatives would have their own chamber, thereby forming a bicameral assembly, or whether they would be joined with the economic representatives in a unicameral body.

The *Fører's* inability to give his planners firm guidelines plus the absence of consensus within NS were reflected in the improvised nature in which the planning was carried out. Initially it was assumed that the Assembly would be made up entirely of economic representatives.[187] Not until considerably later, well into September, were the plans altered to include cultural representatives.[188] In its final form, the projected *Riksting* emerged as a bicameral body, with 120 representatives forming the Economic Chamber (*Næringsting*), while 80 members made up the smaller Cultural Chamber (*Kulturting*).[189] The great change that Quisling wished to indicate with the creation of the Assembly was further revealed by the fact that party planners were simultaneously writing drafts of a new Constitution containing his totalitarian principles.[190] But this work, whose results proved barren, only served to dilute even more the rather confused manner in which plans for the National Assembly were carried out.

While prospects for a new Quisling Constitution remained indeterminate, its possible enactment having to wait until after a National Assembly had been created, a more concrete step was being prepared to make certain that the corporate body's creation would take place. Although Quisling had striven since September 1940 to have his party secure effective control over the country's organizational structure, he had witnessed time after time how NS had failed in its attempts to exercise effective leadership over organizations that nominally were under its jurisdiction. He hoped to remedy this by enactment of a new organizational law (*fullmaktslov*) which would require *compulsory* membership, with no possibility of resignation, either direct or indirect.

In addition to this long-sought after objective, in the spring of 1942 it became imperative for him to have NS expand its operations to include the business sector. Its organizations had largely been unaffected by previous moves in 1940 and 1941 against educational, professional, and labor associations. But now, with Quisling pushing for creation of a National Assembly, the business organizations obviously needed to be brought under National Union's authority, since representatives in the Assembly's Economic Chamber would come largely from these groups. The party administrators who had responsibility for dealing with the organizations were therefore engaged in formulating the new organizational law at the same time as plans for the National Assembly were drawn up.[191]

While the law was being drafted, a disagreement that would have future ramifications developed between two of Quisling's leading advisers. Alf Whist, the NS Ombudsman for Business and Trade, and Hagelin, in his capacity as head of the Interior Department, were at odds. Their dispute included both a clash over personal interests and basic policy differences. Each wanted to exercise effective control over the business organizations. On the question of policy, Whist favored a law that would specifically allow the forced merger of these organizations into larger units. Hagelin opposed this, for once favoring a less radical line whereby NS would exercise control of the business organizations largely in the form in which they already existed.[192]

In this struggle, Hagelin's view generally prevailed, indicating that he still retained his standing with Quisling as the party's number two man. The Interior Department, which under Hagelin's leadership had spearheaded earlier NS moves to control organizations, continued to be the administrative agency which coordinated this type of activity, although at times it was required to consult with other departments under whose jurisdictions some organizations might naturally belong.[193] But while Hagelin emerged as the apparent winner in this encounter, Whist had not sustained a damaging blow to his influence with Quisling. On the contrary, his party career remained on the rise.

The new Law Concerning Organizations and Associations came into being on August 20, 1942, more than a month before the planned unveiling of the National Assembly. However, the law was kept under the wraps of strictest secrecy. This move was dictated by both offensive and defensive considerations. Quisling and his strategists did not intend to give the Home Front the opportunity to take any counteraction against the law. It was intended to be applied as a weapon, to be used by making it public and employing its provisions if opposition developed to Quisling's main effort of establishing the National Assembly.[194]

The organizational law of August 20 was significant in its own right, however, since it marked Quisling's final attempt to have his party exert direct influence on Norwegian society through the authority which NS held over the organizational structure. It served as the conclusion of the drive to dominate the organizations. The new law supplanted the previous Organizations Ordinance of June 18, 1941.[195] On paper it now appeared that Hagelin had obtained much of the power that he had previously failed to receive from Terboven during the period of the Commissarial Council. Through the new authority which the law granted the Interior Department, Quisling could now bring NS influence to bear directly on the business organizations. Most important of all, however, the law specifically required compulsory membership in all organizations that were under NS leadership.[196] No longer, if the law's provisions were sustained, could NS control be sabotaged by leaders of organizations who abandoned their posts and by the mass resignations of the regular members.

The wisdom of keeping the Law Concerning Organizations and Associations secret soon became clear, indicating that Quisling had at least attempted to draw upon experience gained from previous encounters that his party had lost. At the end of August the Home Front leadership learned that he remained determined to establish the National Assembly.[197] Until this time the resistance movement had been largely focusing its attention on the possibility of NS renewing its effort to create the Labor Corporation. Now the Home Front immediately changed its direction, carrying out a quickly organized campaign to thwart Quisling from setting up the National Assembly.[198]

Under the overall guidance of the Coordinating Committee, which now included their representatives, the business organizations began a massive protest in early September against being forced to take part in the National Assembly. One of the key purposes for this action was for business interests to demonstrate to world opinion that NS was deceitful in maintaining that the party enjoyed the support of the business community.[199] The protest was spearheaded by three influential groups, the Industrial Association, the Norwegian Bank Organization, and the Norwegian Insurance Companies' Association. These all threatened that their leaders would leave their positions and their members would resign if attempts were made to coerce them into being represented in the National Assembly.[200]

Before these ultimatums could be issued to the members, however, NS had gained knowledge of what the protest would entail. In response, Quisling's party proceeded to play what it considered to be its trump card. The Law Concerning Organizations and Associations was made official on September 9. Since it specifically prohibited exactly the kind of activity that the business organizations threatened to carry out, Quisling and his administrators believed they had effectively nipped the protest in the bud. But for them to pin their hopes solely on a law proved to be illusory. By this time there was scarcely any respect left in any quarter for the NS government's laws. All that the public proclamation of the organizational law accomplished was that the business organizations revised the notices they sent to their members so that the new law could be included in the joint protest.[201]

Rather than halt opposition against the establishment of the National Assembly, the NS announcement of the organizational law was followed by an act of massive disobedience. This development was particularly significant because NS officials now faced the direct opposition of the business organizations for the first time during the war. The confrontation resulted not only in mass protests by members of these groups, but it created widespread unrest within the business community in general. A wide spectrum of organizations from industry, banking, insurance, and retail trade took part, with threats of resignations being made unless the National Assembly plan was rescinded. The protest action was broadly based, with the business organizations presenting a solid front against NS.[202]

For the leadership of the Coordinating Committee, the involvement of the business community in organized disobedience to the Quisling administration marked an important advance. It was equally important, however, for the Home Front to have the labor movement take part in the opposition to the National Assembly.[203] Because Terboven had imposed the death penalty during the state of emergency in 1941, persons belonging to the trade unions, in contrast to members of many of the professional organizations, had been forced to remain in LO after the federation received its new NS leadership in September. Quisling had experienced, however, that such coerced membership was largely nominal. The workers increasingly gave their loyalty not to the NS appointees, but to the Trade Union Committee, whose underground leadership maintained close ties with the Coordinating Committee.

The Trade Union Committee resolved to join with the business organizations in the effort to sabotage the National Assembly. The Committee also decided to use this episode as an opportunity to have the workers officially withdraw their membership in LO. The labor movement's protest was therefore not merely against the Assembly, but also directed toward LO's NS leadership. These officials were criticized for their inability to provide the workers with tangible gains. Working class families suffered from rising prices and increased difficulty in obtaining food. This failure of the NS trade union officials, plus the workers' protest against planned LO representation in the National Assembly, served as the Trade Union Committee's justification for launching a mass resignation drive from LO.[204]

Although the number of resignations was not as extensive as the Home Front leaders had hoped because of the quickly improvised nature of the protest, nevertheless the workers' action, when combined with the business organizations' opposition, proved to be highly effective. By mid-September 1942 complete confusion prevailed within the economic sector. Tens of thousands of people within business and labor were actively demonstrating their hostility to Quisling's corporate assembly.[205] This state of affairs was but another indication of the massive hostility that existed within all segments of the population against his intent to transform Norway into the totalitarian corporate state that he wished to create.

Again Quisling and his chief officials were unable to deal with this type of demonstration. Except for the enactment of the Law Concerning Organizations and Associations, no measures had been taken to defeat organized disobedience. Therefore, when the mass resignations poured into Oslo, NS was powerless to do anything to halt this steady stream. Social Minister Lippestad urgently called together a series of meetings with labor leaders in a frantic effort to try to get the workers to cease their resignations.[206]

When Lippestad failed to have any measurable success, Terboven and his officials, who up until this time had remained largely in the background, felt compelled to intervene directly on September 21. Once they had made this decision, they did not hesitate to take appropriate strong measures. Representatives from the workers and employers were called in by the Gestapo and threatened with the death penalty if the resignations were not withdrawn. A number of prominent persons were arrested, and the threat of imposition of martial law like that of the previous September lay in the air. Everyone perceived that the Germans were not bluffing.[207]

Faced with the possibility that many of their leading figures would be executed and that martial law would be declared, there was little that could be gained by the protesting organizations except to give in and to call upon their members to withdraw their threatened resignations. However, the massive action had not been in vain. Already by the time the Germans resorted to coercion, it was becoming clear that Quisling would not reach his goal.[208]

With this being the outcome, the business organizations felt that they had secured their objective. The threatened resignations of their leaders and members had been contingent on Quisling establishing the National Assembly and including business representatives within his corporate body. With the Assembly eliminated, the basis for the protest had been removed as far as the business groups were concerned. They resumed their everyday functions, with the bulk of these organizations remaining outside of NS control.[209]

For the LO members who had been forced back into their NS-led Federation of Trade Unions, the situation was somewhat different. While their underground leaders were pleased to see that the National Assembly would not come into existence, the rank and file were still compelled to belong to an organization headed by members of Quisling's party. In reality, however, this meant little. Although LO remained under NS domination, the last remnants of NS influence over the workers largely disappeared after September 1942. Under its NS leadership, LO became a dead organization, serving as a hollow mockery of what had once been the most viable force within the economic sector.[210]

On the other side of the battle line, the events that culminated in September 1942 marked yet another advance for the Home Front in its increasingly more effective organized opposition to Quisling's efforts to change society. One branch of the resistance, the Coordinating Committee, in particular emerged from this critical conflict with greater authority. Thanks to its success in organizing first the protest against the National Assembly, and then its skill in coordinating an orderly retreat when the Germans threatened to apply terror, its status had changed. It had now emerged as a strong organization that was capable of issuing orders that were obeyed, rather than merely serving as a general body that coordinated the separate protest actions made by individual groups such as the teachers, the clergy, the labor unions, and various professional groups.[211] When Quisling in the future again sought to realize new goals, he would in the long run be confronted with a better organized and more effective resistance effort.

For Quisling, his vain attempt to secure the National Assembly marked the final and most disastrous defeat that he sustained in 1942, the year that marked the turning point for his politics during the war. For the German refusal to sanction the Assembly was not just another setback, such as his inability to create the Labor Corporation earlier in the year. Instead, the cancellation of the National Assembly proved to be the effective end to his quest for greater independence, although he continued to strive for this until the very end of the occupation.

This decisive reverse came as an especially severe blow because the year had begun so auspiciously for him. He had gained office as Minister President, and he received more freedom than ever before to carry out his plans. It is true that he had generally suffered setbacks in the various NS campaigns that he had set in motion earlier, but this had not prevented him from advancing the status that he and his party enjoyed. However, as Minister President he and his National Government were directly responsible for the growing turmoil that occurred in the ensuing months, resulting only in failure after failure for him to realize his goals, culminating with the cancellation of the National Assembly. To understand why the inability to establish the Assembly represented such a drastic turning point for him, the attitude of the dictator of the Third Reich toward the NS *Fører* during the summer and early fall was of critical importance. Because as always it was Adolf Hitler's decision that determined exactly what Quisling's status would be.

In spite of Hitler's direct refusal in June to consider his petition for a peace settlement, not even a preliminary peace, the Minister President had bullheadedly persevered in trying to secure this objective. In early August he even took the audacious step of making a secret journey to Germany, armed with yet another memorandum for Hitler and another draft peace settlement. He attempted to place the blame for the disturbances in Norway on the fact that no permanent agreement had been made concerning the country's position. Not unexpectedly, his recommendations to Hitler were identical with those that he had previously proposed: Germany should recognize Norway's independence and unity; Quisling's government should be allowed to have diplomatic representation abroad; and Terboven's *Reichskommissariat* should be gradually phased out.[212]

In seeking to realize what by now were clearly unrealistic objectives, Quisling continued to heed the advice of Hagelin, who pulled no punches in his ongoing campaign to weaken and discredit Terboven. Via Lammers, the Minister of the Interior sent Hitler a long memorandum in August listing instances of the *Reichskommissar*'s highhanded actions. Its implications were plain. Terboven, not Quisling, should be held responsible for the anti-German sentiment in Norway.[213] Hagelin also tried to gain greater independence for Quisling's administration by designating certain individuals living abroad to act as semiofficial consular representatives for the National Government. This step clearly intended to reduce the *Reichskommissariat*'s control over Norwegian affairs, and Terboven responded wrathfully when he learned of this.[214]

Hitler's reaction to Quisling's proposals came almost immediately. At a conference on August 11, attended by Lammers, Bormann, Ribbentrop, and Terboven, Hitler denied the requests in no uncertain terms. No peace negotiations, he reiterated, would be possible for the duration of the war, not even concerning a preliminary peace. The relationship between Norway and the Reich would only be determined after the war's conclusion, and then strictly as a unilateral German decision. Similarly, *der Führer* declared categorically that the National Government would not be permitted to establish diplomatic ties abroad. Hitler gave Terboven the enjoyable assignment of personally communicating this decision to Quisling "with all clarity and sharpness". Lammers thereafter would confirm the decision in writing.[215]

This put an end to Quisling's peace plans. Hitler's sharp refusal indicated the extent to which he was tired of Quisling's repeated suggestions. The critical importance of the German offensives in the summer of 1942 meant that he had little time or interest in Quisling's ambitious plans, nor any liking for them. The negative reports that *der Führer* was receiving about internal conditions in Norway also did nothing to improve the Minister President's standing.

Terboven did not notify Quisling of Hitler's command until August 26. But while this killed the last hope for achieving a peace settlement at this time, it made Quisling more determined than ever to set up the National Assembly. As yet, Hitler had not established any specific prohibition against this effort. However, when the National Assembly appeared to be almost within his grasp, Quisling in mid-September received Hitler's crushing veto of his project. The exact date of when he was informed cannot be ascertained, but it appears to have been on about September 14, just eleven days before the Assembly's anticipated formal opening. By September 17 the news of this disappointing outcome began to filter down through the NS administration.[216]

Whether Quisling obtained the message concerning Hitler's decision from Terboven or from Lammers also remains unresolved. However, Lammers, on behalf of Hitler, sent Quisling a letter on September 17 which served as formal confirmation of *der Führer*'s resolve. The letter not only stated that the National Assembly was prohibited, but it specified in no uncertain terms the position that Quisling henceforth should adhere to in his relationship with the Germans. In addition to repeating previous denials of any peace talks, *der Führer*, said Lammers, would be especially thankful if Quisling would see to it that all discussions within NS aimed at changing Norway's present political and constitutional status were brought to an end. This broadside obviously was aimed at Hagelin in particular. Furthermore, it was Hitler's wish that no Norwegian representatives be established abroad, not even commercial envoys. Norwegian interests in foreign countries, Hitler declared, would be represented by the appropriate Reich authorities. Hagelin's attempt to bypass Terboven by appointing special agents abroad had thereby been thwarted.

For Quisling, however, the most humiliating aspect of this letter was contained in the segment which spelled out his future relationship with the *Reichskommissar*. Hitler specifically demanded that Quisling discuss all political questions only with Terboven, who was expressly described as being *"der Führer*'s sole responsible representative" for civilian affairs in

Norway. Quisling's chagrin was even greater when he learned that in the future all messages that he wished to send Hitler could only be forwarded through Terboven.[217] Not only was he thereby formally cut off from consulting with his valuable patrons in Germany, Raeder, Rosenberg, and their subordinates, but he could no longer use them as friendly intermediaries on his behalf with Hitler. Hereafter he would be completely subordinate to the German official who had consistently opposed him ever since assuming the post of *Reichskommissar*, and against whom Quisling in turn had schemed relentlessly with the aid of his advisers. Thanks to Quisling's mismanagement, compounded by the uncertainties of the war, Terboven gained this added authority. To his satisfaction, his power over civilian affairs in Norway had never been greater than by the end of September 1942.

Terboven's opponents, Quisling's friends in Germany, immediately recognized the severity of the defeat their protégé had sustained. Raeder wrote to Boehm in October, declaring helplessly that there was nothing more he could do on Quisling's behalf: "In the new situation, which is in accordance with Hitler's will, we must exercise the greatest caution. When an opportunity occurs, I will at the most be able to ask Hitler to permit Quisling to contact him personally concerning politically important matters."[218] As but an indication of the navy's reduced influence due to Raeder's previous support for Quisling, the Grand Admiral asked Boehm to warn Schreiber to remain inconspicuously in the background.[219]

To what extent the wave of protest against the National Assembly brought about Hitler's determination to veto Quisling's plan cannot be determined exactly. There is no question, however, but that the unrest influenced Hitler's resolution of the dispute to some extent. The threatened mass resignations occurred prior to his decision, but they had not yet reached their height when Quisling was informed that he would have to cancel his undertaking. *Der Führer* undoubtedly resolved to act at least in part because of reports coming from Norway, in particular those originating with Terboven and Falkenhorst.[220] But the total frustration of Quisling's plans in September was not due merely to the opposition that his projected National Assembly generated. Instead, this was but the final outcome of the process of popular protest and resistance that he had created immediately after he had assumed office and began his drive to transform society. The widespread antagonism to his moves, effectively coordinated by the increasingly experienced Home Front leadership, created so much unrest that the Germans had ample reason for deciding to rein him in.

With Hitler having turned down his plan for the National Assembly, it now became necessary for Quisling to camouflage this defeat in the best way possible. The planned celebration scheduled for September 25 had to be altered in the light of the new situation. This event could not be cancelled outright – the party had already committed itself too much. After apparent top level consultations had been carried out within the NS administration, by September 21 the changed plans were at hand. Instead of the National Assembly, it was decided that Quisling would hold a *Fører* Council (*Førerting*), a meeting of party officers, on the 25th.[221]

When it met, the Minister President tried to make the best of the new situation. He announced the creation of a Cultural Assembly (*Kulturting*) to the assembled NS leaders. He further declared that he intended to bring an Economic Assembly (*Næringsting*) into existence as soon as possible. One could therefore have concluded that his National Assembly ideal was still alive, since he had always planned to include these two chambers in his corporate body. However, he indicated at this time that this was not the case – that he instead had completely altered his long-standing design for a National Assembly. Publicly he continued to insist that it would be created as soon as conditions permitted. However, whereas he had earlier stressed its corporate character, to be made up of representatives from the economic and cultural sectors, he now insisted that the Assembly would be entirely *political* in its functions. He declared that it would serve as "the political representative of the people", and as such would have no direct contact with the two other bodies.[222]

Although he gave no explanation for this radical departure from his earlier plans, it was unquestionably due to his desire to cover up his defeat over the National Assembly.[223] But his detailed exposition on projected assemblies really amounted only to empty verbiage. Hitler had dictated that no political change would be permitted for the duration of the war, and nothing Quisling said could alter this basic fact. He could not, of course, reveal this to his listeners. In other segments of his speech, however, he did indicate, if indirectly, how his standing had been altered by his final defeat in 1942. He resorted to using ideological terms that projected an image very different from that which he had presented just a few months earlier. Rather than emphasizing the term "national", which he had done immediately after he took office as Minister President, he now more than ever talked about Norway as a "national socialist" society.[224]

He imparted an even clearer message to his followers when he addressed them at the national conference the following day. His words provided direct evidence of the German repudiation of his policies, and that he had taken this criticism to heart. No longer did he stress the importance of regaining freedom and independence. Instead, he talked about the "new Europe" that was being formed under Germany's leadership, and how Norway needed to contribute to this coming union. Paying specific heed to Hitler's warning in the September 17 letter from Lammers, Quisling now declared that the future relationship between Germany and Norway could not be determined until after the war. He categorically ordered NS members not to discuss this question, and urged them instead to work toward the common goal of securing a German victory.[225]

He had thereby been reduced to being largely a sounding board for German policy, which he was responsible for imparting to his NS followers. Perhaps the most ironic incident that occurred in connection with his humiliation was the decision by the NS-controlled Postal Service to go ahead and issue a stamp in honor of the National Assembly. The stamp appeared with a portrait of Quisling in profile and a caption which read "the National Assembly 1942". But despite all attempts that he and his party officials made, no amount of effort could disguise the magnitude of the defeat he had sustained. His opponents were fully aware of his weakened condition. A Home Front report written at this time contained a cryptic epitaph for his plan to establish a corporate body: "The National Assembly aborted with a Cultural Assembly and a postage stamp".[226]

By mid-September 1942 Quisling had lost all of the freedom of action that he had been granted when he took over as Minister President. Germany's future policy toward him and the position he would hold in Norway was succinctly summed up at this time by Dr. Wilhelm Stuckart, who headed an investigatory commission to Norway for the Reich Ministry of the Interior. He submitted his report to Martin Bormann on September 26. Stuckart declared categorically that Quisling's policies in 1942 had been entirely unsuccessful, resulting only in increased resistance, with 95 per cent of the population being hostile to NS.[227]

Despite this low assessment, it was not possible, however, for the Germans to repudiate Quisling and his party because no other pro-German factions existed any longer. Stuckart therefore recommended continued cooperation with National Union. But he pointed out that it had been a mistake to allow Quisling to act on his own, and that this could only be corrected by bringing the NS *Fører's* party and government again under strong German control. This meant that Terboven, as the sole representative of the Reich in civilian matters, would be responsible for internal developments. Quisling, Hagelin, and other prominent NS officials, Stuckart declared, should not be allowed to bypass the *Reichskommissar*.[228]

The Interior Ministry's representative, whose views bore the clear influence of Terboven, in particular criticized Hagelin sharply, repudiating the independent policy that Quisling, acting at Hagelin's urging, had attempted to carry out. During his stay in Norway, Stuckart held a meeting with Quisling, where he made it plain to the NS leader that he and his party would have to change the focus of its propaganda. Stuckart specifically told Quisling that he should no longer stress the need for a peace settlement and greater independence for Norway. Instead, "the idea of the new Europe", with acceptance of the common Germanic leadership, should be emphasized. Ever servile in defeat, and preoccupied with keeping his office at all costs, Quisling promised that he would highlight these new themes in his speech to the *Fører* Council on September 25, a promise which, as has been seen, he kept.[229]

The period during which Quisling had been given the greatest amount of freedom to try to carry out his program of restructuring Norwegian society had proven to be short, restricted to slightly more than seven months. Following this interval, he came under greater German control than at any other time previously during the occupation because of the depth of his failures. The extent of his setback was shown also by the total absence of protest on his part. He did not give the slightest hint that he might consider resignation. Besides his characteristic inclination to cling to whatever symbols of authority he had gained, his reverse had been so absolute that he could not mention resignation even as a threat. As leader of a collaborationist government and party, he therefore had to acquiesce to being fully subservient to the *Reichskommissar* and his officials. Only by complete cooperation with German authorities in Norway could Quisling hope to be granted a renewed chance to assert himself. As one Norwegian historian has written with only some degree of exaggeration, Quisling was "reduced to being Terboven's errand boy".[230]

CHAPTER XV

The Quest for Greater Authority Through Closer Collaboration

September 1942 – December 1943

> Our *Fører* has emphasized repeatedly the importance of a voluntary Norwegian war effort. Norway's position in a new Europe depends upon our effort at the front lines.
>
> Jonas Lie to Eyvind Mehle,
> March 31, 1943

Quisling's reduced standing revealed itself most clearly in his inability after September 1942 to make any important changes without initial German approval. Instead of seeking to implement independent goals, he now had to operate within a far more restrictive environment. He sought, however, to make the best of the new situation. Through total subservience to German interests, he wished to demonstrate his value and that of his party. He hoped in turn that the Germans would reward their ally with greater authority. But his increased submissiveness, which happened to coincide with "the turn of the tide" against Germany and its allies in World War II, created a certain degree of conflict and dissension among his own followers in NS. He felt, however, that he had no choice if he wished to continue as Minister President. His interests were tied to the will of the Germans more completely than ever before, as he personally continued to demonstrate by his repeated reference to his government as "Norway's national socialist government".[1]

The necessity for him to accommodate German authorities in Norway was heightened by his greater isolation from his Third Reich supporters. Not only were they unable to do anything for him, but worse, several lost the positions that earlier had provided them the opportunity to exert their influence on his behalf. Grand Admiral Raeder, because of disagreements with Hitler over naval strategy, was ousted in January 1943. Soon afterwards, in March, Raeder's good friend, Admiral Boehm, was removed from his command. With his protective patrons having been eliminated, Schreiber also had to leave Norway.[2] As a result of this abrupt transition, Quisling could no longer count on what had formerly been one of his strongest pillars of support – the naval high command.

Similarly, if not as dramatically, the pressure that Rosenberg could bring to bear in Norway was eliminated by his continued loss of Hitler's good will, occasioned by the failure of Rosenberg's policies as Reich Minister for the occupied eastern territories. The extent to which his power in Norway had been virtually destroyed was shown in the summer of 1944, when he had to petition Terboven to ask that Quisling be allowed to attend an anti-Jewish congress in Germany which he, Rosenberg, had arranged.[3] Although Terboven gave his consent, his total control over Quisling made itself apparent when he, not Rosenberg or the Minister President, decided which NS minister would be permitted to accompany his *Fører* on the trip.[4]

Quisling's determination to collaborate fully in the execution of German policies during this period revealed itself starkly in the degree of cooperation that he exhibited in the tragic arrest and deportation of Norwegian Jews in the fall of 1942. While ultimate responsibility for this action rested with the Germans, who in Norway as elsewhere in Europe carried out Hitler's genocidal racial policy, there is no question but that Quisling favored arrest and deportation as the solution to "the Jewish question" in Norway, and participated fully in its implementation. And while the evidence is not entirely clear, it may be true that in 1942 he actually went so far as to recommend to the Germans a speedy expulsion of the Jews.[5] Such a recommendation would have been completely in accord with his total commitment to Nazi anti-Semitism, as revealed in his public speeches and private statements both during and after the war.[6] The extent to which NS authorities, under Quisling's leadership, acted jointly with the Germans in rounding up the country's Jews, stands in direct contrast with the attitude of administrators in occupied Denmark when faced with the same situation. Not only did the German effort, thanks in large part to Danish opposition, occur almost a year later than in Norway, but the entire enterprise, when it did take place, was actively resisted by Danish (and some German) officials, as well as by the general population.

In Norway, on the other hand, NS ministers consistently followed an anti-Semitic policy from the time of the Commissarial Council. Jewish physicians and attorneys were not allowed to engage in their professions, attempts were made to prevent marriages between Jews and non-Jews, and from January 1942 onwards Jews were required to have the letter J stamped in their identification papers.[7] In March 1942 Quisling altered the

Constitution by restoring an obsolete article, previously abolished in 1851, which denied Jews admission to the kingdom.[8]

When the Germans set in motion their direct attack against the Jews in the following fall, Quisling and his NS subordinates were involved from the beginning. Quisling's personal contribution came in the form of signing two discriminatory laws against the Jews. The first of these, dated October 26, allowed the state to expropriate the property of all Jews. NS authorities duly carried out such expropriations, beginning on November 6, when Hagelin authorized the takeover of the property of 125 Jews in Oslo.[9] Here again the actions of Quisling and his lieutenants stands in stark contrast with the situation in Denmark. The property of Danish Jews, including those arrested by the Germans as well as those who fled to Sweden, remained untouched for the duration of the war.[10] The second law dated from November 17. It required the registration of all Jews within two weeks.[11] As subsequent police actions showed, its purpose was obvious: to assist the police in making arrests.

In the meantime, even before these laws were issued, the jailings had already commenced. Scattered arrests occurred during the entire occupation, but the following sequence affected the overwhelming majority of the Jewish community. In northern Norway most male Jews were incarcerated already during the spring and early summer of 1941. In Trøndelag imprisonment of male Jews took place when the Germans declared a special state of emergency in the first part of October 1942. The remainder of adult male Jews were subjected to arrest beginning on October 26, 1942, as a result of a law which Quisling had signed two days earlier. The process was completed on the night of November 25–26, 1942, when orders were given to the police to round up *all* Jews.[12] The seizures were made under the auspices of the NS, being organized by members of the NS led and dominated State Police, who acted in close cooperation with their German counterparts.[13] Furthermore, the *Hird* played an active part as well, serving as guards in the prison camps where the Jews were gathered before being shipped to Germany.[14]

In seeking to counteract the arrests, the resistance movement, taking considerable risks, did everything in its power to assist as many as possible to flee across the border to Sweden.[15] Thanks to this effort, during the course of the war some 925 Jews were able to escape the gas chambers. But not all were as fortunate. Of the approximately 100 who remained in Norway, the majority imprisoned in concentration camps, 23 died. Altogether, 759 Jews were deported. Most of them died at Auschwitz. Only 25 survived the war.[16]

Quisling made no effort to alleviate the distress of the men, women, and children who were brutally herded on board the transit ships. He received an appeal from the opposition Church leadership on November 10, before the deportations had begun, admonishing him to: "Halt the persecution of the Jews and stop the racial hatred which the press is spreading in our land". He did not respond.[17]

Once more, the plight of the Jews in Norway is brought into sharper focus when comparison is made with the other Scandinavian country that experienced German occupation during World War II. In Denmark the overwhelming number of Jews, some 7,900, managed to find refuge in Sweden, thanks to concerted assistance by all segments of the population.[18] Of the small number whom the Germans did manage to apprehend, only 52 died in captivity, mainly old people, while 420 survived, primarily because of the active support they received from the Danish administration and public.[19]

The fact that so many more Norwegian than Danish Jews perished must be directly attributed to the fact that in Norway there existed a collaborationist administration and political party whose officials, from the Minister President on down, were strongly anti-Semitic. In this situation, NS participation in the arrest and deportation of the Jews was self-evident. The fact that almost half of Norway's Jewish residents died in concentration camps is therefore directly attributable to the cooperation that Quisling's administration provided in bringing about the seizure and expulsion of these unfortunate human beings.

Whether Quisling at the time personally knew of the fate awaiting the deported Jews in Auschwitz's gas chambers is a matter of interpretation. He, of course, denied it in his postwar trial, and there is no absolute proof to contradict his disclaimer. However, there is no question but that he knew that their lives were in danger when they were deported. Furthermore, ample circumstantial evidence exists, in the author's opinion, to indicate that Quisling probably was aware of the "final solution" at the time of the deportations. If ordinary crew members on board the transport ships knew that their human cargo was doomed, then it is unlikely that the Minister President, with direct access to high-ranking German contacts, intelligence from his own police officials, and the observations which he made personally during his travels in Germany and Poland in 1942, was unaware of what was in store for the Jews.[20]

Despite the severe defeat which he had sustained in September 1942, when resistance from the economic organizations had contributed to the rejection of his plans for the National Assembly, Quisling remained preoccupied with bringing these groups completely under NS domination. Since he no longer represented a threat, Terboven had no objections to efforts in this direction, provided that they occurred under overall German supervision, and that economic productivity was not adversely affected.

With the *Reichskommissariat*'s approval, the National Government issued a law on February 22, 1943, which provided for a "general national work effort". This law had significance for a wide variety of different areas, a number of which will be examined later. In this context, however, of special importance was the fact that it specifically opened the way for NS to attempt once more to reorganize the economic organizations after the corporate model that Quisling always sought to achieve.

In accord with his usual penchant for symbolism, May 1 was again chosen as the date for the official promulgation of a new body, intended to control all economic activity in Norway. Named Norway's Business Corporation (*Norges Næringssamband*), the new corporate body was formally established by Minister Eivind Blehr, head of the Business Department.[21] But while it was nominally part of his administrative sphere, Blehr exercised little direct authority. Its president, Alf Whist, served immediately under Quisling as the party's economic expert, having primary responsibility for the renewed effort to bring all business activity within Quisling's corporate framework.

The Business Corporation's all-encompassing nature was revealed in its structure. It consisted of ten "business groups" (*næringsgrupper*), which included banking, farming, fishing, insurance, retail trade, hotel and restaurant enterprise, industry, shipping, and transportation. All individuals or companies engaged in any type of business activity had to belong to one of these groups, while they in turn were under the overall supervision of the Business Corporation headed by Whist.[22]

With the establishment of the Corporation, Quisling appeared at last to have realized one of his chief ambitions in creating a corporate society. On paper, the country's economy had at last been placed under his authority. But this realization proved to be yet another empty victory. While NS from May 1943 onward formally regulated all economic organizations, and thereby all economic activity, with NS members being appointed as leaders of the various "business groups", in reality this meant very little as far as its ability to exercise actual control was concerned. The Corporation proved to be largely an empty shell, with business people seeking to have as little to do with it as possible. Instead, many prominent business leaders became part of the resistance movement after organizations which they had headed became nazified under the Business Corporation.[23]

Whereas Quisling at least had the satisfaction of formally bringing all economic activity under NS supervision, he faced continuous disappointment in his ongoing effort to establish a parallel Labor Corporation (*Norges Arbeidssamband*), intended to give NS total supervision over both the workers and their employers. The *Reichskommissar*, recalling the labor unrest which resulted in 1942 when this concept originally was launched, continued to block approval of a plan which most certainly would have created new disturbances, thereby resulting in the loss of labor productivity. Quisling, however, had so committed himself to this enterprise that he could not abandon it without loss of prestige. From time to time he therefore appealed to the workers to organize such a Corporation, and NS propagandists obediently echoed the *Fører*'s call.[24]

Odd Jarmann Fossum, the NS head of LO, was among the leading officials who agitated in favor of the Labor Corporation so that Quisling could maintain a façade of alleged labor support for the venture.[25] But the propaganda effort exerted by Fossum and other so-called spokesmen for organized labor failed to hide the awkward truth that the Germans would not permit Quisling to take any further steps to reorganize the labor force into a corporate structure. NS did have formal leadership of LO, but this failed to provide Quisling with the effective NS dominance over the workers that he had originally hoped to achieve. Widespread opposition stymied NS officials from controlling the rank and file of the Federation of Trade Unions. Many workers ceased to pay union dues, while others refused to become LO members when they accepted new employment.[26]

As the occupation lengthened and as the news from the battle fronts became more bleak for those favoring the German cause, Quisling and his loyalists continued to be faced with the frustrating fact that while NS now controlled all formal centers of power, this did not provide the party with real authority, because whenever possible most Norwegians avoided direct contact with NS officials, while non-NS members in important positions often did their best to sabotage Quisling's initiatives. This proved to be true not only, as we have seen, in religion, education, professional and business organizations, and organized labor, but also in public administration. NS' inability to control the administrative apparatus effectively was especially noteworthy because it was in this sector that the party had experienced its most significant early success, thanks to Hagelin. But during the course of the occupation only about six per cent of the regular civil servants outside of the police became NS members.[27] As could be expected, those administrators who refused to join were frequently a source of annoyance for NS leaders. Fuglesang in 1944 complained not only about the "negative attitude" of anti-NS civil servants in the various departments, but also concerning the tendency for *NS members* in the administration to be influenced by the prevailing anti-party viewpoint found within the state bureaucracy.[28]

The need to work more closely with German officials during the latter period of the occupation, resulting not only from his more restricted position but also from his belief that he could best promote his interests through such cooperation, caused Quisling increasingly to place greater emphasis on economic policy. This corresponded with the German need to exploit Norway's resources ever more efficiently as the wartime situation worsened. Quisling's growing concern with economic questions was evidenced by the rise of Alf Whist within the party hierarchy.

The latter was a newcomer to NS. His background lay within the field of insurance, where he had achieved considerable success in organizing and leading a number of companies. His NS membership did not predate the occupation. However, already in 1940 he secured the backing of some of NS' most prominent figures within the business community, resulting in his appointment as head of the State Wine Monopoly, which controlled the sale of wine and liquor.[29] Within a year Quisling promoted him to serve as the party's leading economic expert (*NS ombudsmann for næringslivet*). As we have seen, he acted as one of the leading strategists in the effort to create the National Assembly and, while this failed, he did subsequently realize the establishment of the Business Corporation. To augment Whist's authority even more, Quisling next made him, on November 2 1943, a member of the National Government with the accompanying title of minister. Although he at first served without portfolio, he received considerable authority from Quisling, with broad power to control economic policy. He could dictate and enforce economic directives to all state and local institutions, including government departments.[30] This made him more powerful than some of the ministers who headed specialist departments.

His predominant influence over economic policy continued to increase after his appointment as minister. Because of the importance he attached to economic matters in his relationship with the Germans, Quisling steadily became more dependent on Whist. The former insurance executive therefore became one of the major figures in the constellation of NS advisers who surrounded Quisling during the final period of the war.[31]

In addition to his economic expertise, Whist possessed another quality which Quisling prized highly. Unlike Hagelin and several other ministers in the National Government, Whist did not attempt to follow independent policy initiatives which could conflict with German interests. Instead, he got along well with officials in the *Reichskommissariat*, which from his viewpoint was essential since he was often in contact with them.[32]

His ascendancy caused resentment among the other ministers, in particular those whose authority was lessened as a result of the broad powers which Quisling granted Whist. One minister, Hustad, went so far as to declare that Whist acted almost as an attorney for German interests, and he even hinted at the possibility that Whist might be in German pay.[33] But when he became engaged in conflicts with other ministers, Whist could depend upon the backing of Quisling. This allowed him to maintain his powerful position.[34]

While Whist's influence increased, the standing of another cabinet official who formerly had been the Minister President's main source of strength was on the decline. After 1942 the relationship between Quisling and Hagelin, increasingly became more strained.³⁵ The Minister of the Interior at first had not been popular with many of the NS old guard, who resented the prominent position which this newcomer had gained immediately next to Quisling.³⁶ However, as long as Quisling felt that Hagelin's counsel was invaluable, the *Fører's* confidence meant that Hagelin's position was un-challengeable.

After the setbacks of 1942, however, Quisling, felt that he could no longer follow the assertive policy which Hagelin still favored. With his heightened emphasis on cooperation with the *Reichskommissariat*, Quis-ling began to shy away from Hagelin's ongoing efforts to challenge Ter-boven directly. The Minister of the Interior, however, refused to abandon his bellicose attitude. He followed the same course that he and Quisling had formerly adhered to, going back to the time of Terboven's appoint-ment, which was to secure as much independence as possible for the NS *Fører* within the broad general framework of alliance with the Germans. Unlike Quisling, Hagelin remained undaunted by what had occurred in 1942. He worked with unabated energy to break the tight restrictions which the *Reichskommissariat* maintained over the National Government. He urged Quisling to attempt to take advantage of Germany's worsening military position in order to secure real authority for his government. Had such a move been possible, it would naturally have resulted in a decline in the power of Hagelin's archrival, Terboven. To accomplish this, Hagelin urged Quisling to seek a meeting with Hitler in order to voice discontent with the manner in which the *Reichskommissariat* exercised authority in Norway, and he hinted not too subtly that he should be allowed to partici-pate in any upcoming discussion with *der Führer*.³⁷

Although Quisling was granted audiences with Hitler in April 1943 and again in January 1944, Hagelin was frustrated by being denied the oppor-tunity to present in person his criticism of the *Reichskommissar*. Terboven made certain that Hagelin remained in Norway, while the *Reichskommis-sar* accompanied the Minister President during his meetings with Hitler.³⁸ Because of his irresolute manner, Quisling was hardly the one to argue forcefully against Terboven during these conferences, and any reservations concerning the *Reichskommissariat* that he was able to bring to Hitler's at-tention were diplomatically ignored.³⁹ As a result, Quisling more than ever felt that it was fruitless to pursue Hagelin's policy of confrontation.

The growing estrangement between the two inevitably resulted in a de-cline for Hagelin within the National Government and NS. Quisling ceased to support his former number two man in inter-governmental feud-ing, with the result that Hagelin no longer enjoyed the prestige he had pre-viously held during the first period of the occupation. This reduction in Hagelin's standing revealed itself most dramatically in a dispute with Fi-nance Minister Prytz during the spring and summer of 1943. Prytz, following his elevation to cabinet level by Quisling, had emerged from the relative obscurity that he had been in during the first two years of the occupation. He increasingly regained the strong influence that he previously had enjoyed with Quisling. In direct contrast to Hagelin, Prytz enjoyed cordial relations with the Germans. His contacts with the occupation authorities provided him with added power. However, as was true with Whist, this aroused resentment and suspicion among many of the other ministers.

When Prytz went so far as to discuss with officials in the *Reichskommissariat* the possibility of replacing certain members of the National Government with persons who would be more amenable to the Germans, the resentment felt by other cabinet members boiled over, causing a number to react strongly. Hagelin led this coalition, moving forcefully against Prytz in the cabinet in April 1943. He received the support of a large majority of his colleagues, who naturally disliked Prytz's discussions with the Germans, which might cost them their positions. Of the ministers, only Whist, Fuglesang, and Axel Stang failed to join Hagelin in condemning Prytz for his alleged uncollegiality.[40]

The fact that Hagelin was able to lead a majority consisting of nine of twelve cabinet members against Prytz indicated the extent of opposition to the latter. In part, this reflected Prytz's status as a newcomer to the cabinet, as were Whist and Fuglesang, while those who had served in the Commissarial Council backed Hagelin, Stang being the only exception. Because of the criticism that he received in the cabinet, it therefore appeared as if Prytz was in serious jeopardy, but this was hardly the case. In a system where the *Führer* principle applied, the *Fører* had the final say. While Quisling typically showed indecision at first when Hagelin, seconded by his allies, attacked Prytz,[41] the Minister President in the end left no doubt that he backed his Finance Minister. Prytz remained in the cabinet, and he had Quisling's full support when he took his revenge against Hagelin by reducing the latter's authority through bureaucratic infighting.[42]

This confrontation showed conclusively that Hagelin no longer enjoyed Quisling's confidence, and his position in the government was thereby weakened. But he was hardly the type who would cease to try to assert himself. As he steadily lost influence, he used ever more emphatic language when advocating his policy. Whereas ministers such as Prytz, Whist, and Fuglesang, with Quisling's approval, followed the line of close cooperation, Hagelin urged his fellow ministers to join him in taking a defiant stand against the *Reichskommissariat*. In his arguments, he now stridently voiced a nationalistic viewpoint, insisting that NS naturally had to be in opposition to the German officials, since their institution threatened to destroy all Norwegian independence:

> We who are the exponents for Norway's national movement, who are work-
> ing for Norway's freedom and independence, can no longer defend [the ar-
> gument] before the Norwegian people, whose interests we are pledged to
> protect, to cooperate with the *Reichskommissariat* when it . . . declares that
> its political goal is to eliminate Norway's freedom and independence.[43]

If this policy of total German domination over Norway were also the official policy of the Reich government in Berlin, said Hagelin, then he urged
his fellow ministers to consider the possibility of resigning in protest. This
question, he insisted, had to be answered unequivocally.[44]

The *Reichskommissariat*, which had long regarded Hagelin as a thorn in
its flesh, could hardly be expected to accept his criticism passively. It
moved to take advantage of his weakened status. Dr. Schiedermair, Terboven's legal adviser, confidentially told two leading NS members that
Norway's international position would be quite different if only Hagelin
could be removed from the government. Since the two who listened to this
assertion were among Hagelin's most bitter enemies, Prytz and Ørnulf
Lundesgaard, the head of Quisling's Chancellery, Schiedermair's allegation
received the friendly response that he desired.[45]

With his authority eliminated since he no longer enjoyed Quisling's approval, and on the defensive owing to attacks from both the *Reichskommissariat* and his opponents within NS, Hagelin by the spring of 1944
reached the conclusion that his sole remaining option was resignation from
the government. He rather self-righteously maintained, however, that it
would appear cowardly to do so at a time when militarily conditions were
becoming graver than ever for Germany, and he would therefore wait for
a more appropriate occasion.[46]

By the time he came to this resolution, in early June 1944, Hagelin to
all intents and purposes no longer enjoyed any prominence within Quisling's NS hierarchy. Through his stubborn adherence to the policy which
he had maintained from the beginning, he was finally reduced to insignificance once Quisling abandoned this approach. The latter revealed again
that he did not dare risk losing his position by following a course of action
that was politically dangerous, but which was the only one that could gain
him any semblance of real power. It was more important for him to retain
the outward façade as the alleged head of state, the Minister President. In
a sense, it was realistic for him to adopt the policy of conciliation with the
Reichskommissariat that Prytz and Whist favored. Quisling's government
had no chance for freedom of action after the fiascos of 1942. But in abandoning his former chief adviser, Quisling also in fact gave up the possibility of securing true independence. Henceforth, no matter how hard he
strove to obtain some degree of real authority, he could only act under the
supervision of the *Reichskommissariat*. He had become the German puppet
that he was always characterized as in Allied wartime propaganda.

One important area of collaboration that he engaged in involved encouragement of volunteers to enlist in various military units that fought on the eastern front. In promoting their formation, he indicated two motives, both intended to increase his influence. First, he wished to show his willingness to contribute to Germany's war effort, hoping thereby that he would be rewarded by being granted more freedom. Secondly, the effort to create military units had as its ultimate goal the establishment of a separate Norwegian army. The existence of such a force, he believed, would be of major advantage for his long-range projection of gaining the greatest independence possible under overall German hegemony.[47]

He therefore took active part in the recruitment of young Norwegians. He carried this out both in public solicitation through the media and via directives to NS officials.[48] Because of his underlying goals, his appeals urging participation in the war on Germany's behalf were ones of total commitment. In January 1941, for example, he used the slogan "Germany's battle is Norway's battle! Germany's victory is Norway's victory!" when calling on "nationally conscious Norwegians to fight under our German brothers' victorious banners".[49] Various inducements were offered by NS officials to encourage such enlistments. Volunteers who were minors did not need parental permission. Those who had families were offered financial support for their dependents by the government; not, it was maintained, as "public assistance", but as payment against "the Norwegian state's . . . debt of gratitude to those who risk their lives for the new Norway's future".[50] Additional material incentives included promises that the volunteers, upon completion of their service, could look forward to such rewards as civil service positions, farmland, and dual German-Norwegian citizenship.[51]

German officials favored obtaining as many recruits as possible. This coincided with Henrich Himmler's pan-Germanic policy of having suitable "Nordic" volunteers from throughout Europe serve in *Waffen SS* units. The bulk of the Norwegians who fought on the German side were enrolled in such SS formations.[52] This was not, however, primarily a German enterprise. The recruiting campaigns took place with Quisling's full encouragement and cooperation. Already during the early fall of 1940 he had proposed to Dr. Lammers that Norwegians be permitted to volunteer for service in the German military.[53] He also had discussions at this time with his confederates in the navy concerning how the Norwegian army that he planned to establish would be positioned within the framework of the European new order that Hitler would form once Germany had won the war.[54] Nothing significant resulted from these early consultations, but beginning in 1941 Quisling took part in promoting a series of military units, an activity he continued for the duration of the war.

Considering the relatively small total of young men who joined these formations, a large number of different units were set up. These included

Regiment Northland (*Regiment Nordland*) in January 1941; the Norwegian SS (*Norges SS*) in May 1941; The Norwegian Legion (*Den Norske Legion*) in June 1941; the Germanic SS Norway (*Germanske SS Norge*) in July 1942; the SS Ski Battalion Norway (*SS Skijegerbataljon Norge*) in August 1942; three SS police companies organized respectively in October 1942, March 1943, and April 1944; and SS Armored Grenadier Regiment Norway (*SS Panser-Grenadierregiment Norge*) in March 1943. Altogether, approximately six thousand men served as Quisling's "front fighters" (*frontkjempere*) during World War II.[55] The great majority of these belonged to the above-mentioned units, which Quisling and his NS subordinates propagandized in favor of. Only some 400–500 Norwegian volunteers went into the German navy, and some seventy-five served in the *Luftwaffe*.[56] The latter, however, were also in large part recruited through NS.[57]

The Norwegian Legion was undoubtedly the most ambitious of the various units that Quisling helped to recruit. His motive for promoting this force was nothing less than to have it serve as the start of his new Norwegian army. The timing seemed propitious, since announcement of the Legion occurred at the time Hitler launched his offensive against the Soviet Union. Through the NS-controlled media, Quisling could therefore call for a crusade against his arch-enemy, "Bolshevism". Furthermore, in the propaganda campaign to enlist volunteers, special emphasis was placed on the promise that the Legion would fight in support of Finland against the Russians. This was done in order to appeal to Norwegian sympaties for Finland that had been aroused by the Soviet Union's aggression during the Winter War of 1939–1940. Such feelings were still strong in 1941, and NS solicitation for aid to Finland through the Legion proved to be effective to a certain degree.[58]

Quisling, however, was entirely unrealistic in his estimate of the Legion's potential. Carried away by the heady enthusiasm resulting from the onslaught against the seemingly weak and defeatist Russian armies in 1941, he presented the Germans with a plan to have the Legion become a force of 30,000 men, divided into seven battalions. Looking forward to when it would serve as the core of the resurrected Norwegian army that he would command, he set up a sizable general staff in Oslo, made up of officers who were NS members or sympathizers.[59] Giving added weight to the independent character of the Legion was the emphasis on making it appear to be as Norwegian as possible. At first it was commanded solely by Norwegian officers, it dressed in distinctive Norwegian uniforms, and it carried Norwegian weapons.[60]

Quisling's unrealistically high expectations did not materialize. Although some 1,900 men were initially attracted to the Legion by NS propaganda, a considerable number had second thoughts and withdrew, while others did not qualify physically. The result was that only 1,000 men made up the first contingent that was sent to Germany for specialized training.[61] Approximately 2,000 front fighters served in the Legion during the course of its existence.[62] It never came close to fulfilling Quisling's projected seven battalions, nor did it ever meet several of his other expectations. It did not become the nucleus of the new Norwegian army. In Germany it lost its separate command, being placed under German leadership and integrated into the *Waffen SS*. Equally unsuccessful was the ambitious venture with the general staff in Norway. It was disbanded by the Germans in December 1941 under the pretext that its leadership had proven to be incompetent.[63]

An additional setback for the Legion and its recruitment drive resulted from failure to send it to Finland as originally anticipated. Its deployment on the siege line against beleaguered Leningrad did not have the same propaganda value as would have been true had it been sent in support of the Finns. As a result, NS experienced difficulty in gaining additional recruits once the Legion had been dispatched to the Leningrad front. Adding to its problems, the original volunteers only enlisted for unreasonably short terms of six months service, but the Germans refused to honor these unless replacements were found. The outcome was that the bulk of the Legionaries served for a two-year period, while Quisling was forced to order a recruitment campaign within NS during the summer of 1942 in an effort to gain the needed replacements.[64]

The Legion was formally disbanded in May 1943, with the bulk of its 700 remaining front fighters joining yet another new unit that Quisling, despite his earlier disappointments, helped promote, the SS Armored-Grenadier Regiment Norway.[65] As had been planned with the Legion, the Regiment was intended to be solely Norwegian in composition and leadership, with a projected total of some 3,000 men. Instead, when formed it amounted to only 700 volunteers who became part of an SS division composed of various nationalities, and led by German officers.[66]

Perhaps in many ways the SS Ski Battalion Norway proved to be the most successful of all the different units that Quisling and NS established. Organized in August 1942, it remained intact until the end of the war. Although part of the *Waffen SS*, it was distinguished by being under separate Norwegian command. This and the fact that it served on the Finnish front accounted for its relative popularity, despite its comparatively late start. As late as just before the end of the war the Ski Battalion counted 1,200 men.[67]

Although failure to take full advantage of the propaganda value of aiding the Finns at an early date diminished the effectiveness of Quisling's recruitment drive to some extent, this was not the most significant factor explaining the relatively small number of front fighters. Much more important was his inability to appeal effectively to a broad base of support in NS' recruitment effort. The front fighters were drawn overwhelmingly from NS families.[68] Such a narrow base was incapable of producing large numbers of volunteers, no matter how hard Quisling pursued this endeavor. *Hird* members were especially exposed to recruitment into the different units that were formed, and they contributed a high percentage of those who enlisted.[69] At times recruiting campaigns that Quisling initiated resulted in *Hird* members virtually being pressed into military service.[70] This explains in part why he in 1943 once again sought to make *Hird* membership obligatory for the great majority of adult male NS members.[71] In this endeavor too, however, he suffered disappointment. A preponderance of party members found various pretexts to avoid *Hird* service.[72]

Quisling's inability to raise significant numbers of front fighters had the effect of lessening even more the value that the Germans placed on his collaboration. The difference between what he optimistically estimated and the small total actually recruited could not help but cause responsible German authorities in Norway to view with skepticism future projects that he proposed. But he did not allow the comparatively limited number of volunteers to cause him to abandon his objective. If Norwegians would not willingly offer to fight, then they would have to be coerced into doing so.

Quisling's effort to force Norwegians into military units fighting on behalf of Germany culminated during the spring of 1944. This attempt did not, however, build upon the open recruitment of military units. Instead, it was based on yet another venture that Quisling and Terboven had inaugurated jointly in February 1943. At this time they proclaimed the beginning of a drive to obtain forced labor for German war production, which was named the "National Work Effort" ("*den nasjonale arbeidsinnsats*").

The use of compulsory registration and administratively directed employment of the unemployed was not a new practice. It had begun as early as October 1940, and subsequently regulations were passed which extended administrative authority to direct the labor force. The *Reichskommissariat* began the practice, acting in coordination with the Social Department under Lippestad. Until 1943, however, it occurred only on the local level, and included not only compulsory employment at German installations, but also work that was essential for the population as a whole.[73]

The law governing the National Work Effort was different in that it had nationwide application. It came into existence as a direct result of the devastating German defeat at Stalingrad. This resulted in a general mobilization of the labor force in Germany at the end of January. The law of February 22, 1943, which established the Work Effort in Norway, was but a copy of the German plan, with certain modifications.[74]

Terboven's *Reichskommissariat* therefore initiated the Work Effort, acting in concert with planning throughout occupied Europe. This was hardly surprising since Terboven maintained overall supervision of the economy during his entire tenure in office. However, the actual implementation of the Work Effort was carried out by the NS-led Social Department, acting under close German guidance.[75] Quisling as Minister President signed the law on February 22, thereby maintaining the façade that his National Government had sole responsibility for its enforcement.[76]

Although it originated with the Germans, Quisling personally worked with full energy on behalf of the Work Effort, totally committing NS to making it a success. In addition to his general desire to help the Germans win the war, he was obviously motivated by recognition of how his interests would be served if the program proved to be successful. Not only would this demonstrate the value of his collaboration, but he could also expect to gain increased power and prestige. If his administration obtained effective control over a significant part of the labor force, to be mobilized on behalf of Germany's wartime needs, this would enable him not merely to extend NS' authority over the people, but such an achievement would strengthen his ongoing campaign to obtain concessions for his government. In addition, the Work Effort could be utilized as the first step in an eventual NS effort to draft entire age groups into labor battalions that would be compelled to aid the Germans.[77]

He was therefore directly associated with the Work Effort from the start. On the day it was announced, he co-signed with Terboven a telegram to Hitler which declared their joint support of the "total effort" of Norway's labor force in "the Germanic peoples' ... struggle against Bolshevism".[78] He and Terboven also appeared together at a mass NS propaganda rally on the 22nd, where the law establishing the Work Effort was officially announced. In his speech, the Minister President indicated that the defeats of the previous year had not caused him to abandon his determination to bring society under his control. His hope to attain this overriding ambition now rested with the Work Effort, which he described as a means of "strengthening the new order which alone can save Norway".[79]

In his propaganda, however, he no longer stressed how he, through NS, would preserve Norway's "freedom and independence". Accepting his almost total dependency on the good will of the *Reichskommissariat*, he declared that "we as good and nationally conscious Norwegians must become one with Germanic and European joint interests". To obtain as much unity as possible behind the Work Effort, he concentrated almost entirely on presenting a dark and foreboding description of how Norway, after Stalingrad, was threatened by the Russians. The people had no other alternatives, he argued, except National Union or "Bolshevism". He concluded by calling on his NS followers to rally the people behind the Work Effort in order to have Norway become self-sufficient, and to protect the country against "the Red Peril"![80]

The law of February 22 gave the Social Department authority to organize all labor that was not "fully utilized or which is used in work that is no longer necessary". It applied to all men between the ages of eighteen and fifty-five and to all women between twenty-one and forty.[81] The first step that Lippestad's department took was to seek to register everyone deemed eligible to participate in forced labor projects. This included not only the unemployed, but also all persons whose work was judged to be inconsequential for the conduct of the war.[82] The Directorate for Employment and Unemployment Insurance was placed in charge of coordinating the registration. This time the party took precautions in advance, with NS officials on the local level placed in charge of supervising the registration to make sure that civil servants did not attempt to sabotage the effort.[83]

At first it seemed as if the Work Effort would be successful and that Quisling for once could notch up a victory in his quest to extend National Union's influence over the population. NS employed skillful use of propaganda, appealing to the people's feeling of solidarity by declaring that the Work Effort was intended to benefit society as a whole by increasing production in such vital areas as farming and lumbering.[84] Lippestad, for example, insisted that the government had a responsibility to provide an adequate food supply, and he promised that the Work Effort would be carried out only within Norway's borders.[85]

Confronted with such clever tactics, the Home Front leaders at first were unable to agree on a forceful response. They realized that they might encounter serious difficulty through lack of support if they attempted to organize a total boycott.[86] The Home Front therefore restricted itself at first to trying to create as much chaos and confusion as possible by recommending that false registration forms be sent in, and also urging everyone who might be drafted into the program to avoid whenever possible work on behalf of the Germans.[87]

Such advice was too vague and general to be effective. Consequently, registration proceeded largely without difficulty, as did also the first actual call-up of persons assigned to labor projects.[88] Quisling's officials who were in charge of organizing the Work Effort thereby gained a considerable headstart over the resistance movement. Not until the middle of April did the Home Front obtain specific confirmation that persons compelled to take part in the Work Effort were being assigned to German military installations in Norway, and in a few instances actually sent out of the country. In reaction, the Coordinating Committee sent out an instruction on the 17th which called on the public to boycott the Work Effort fully. No one was to register or report to work if ordered to do so.[89] This call for opposition remained permanent and uncompromising.[90]

From this time onward the resistance movement's effort to destroy the Work Effort became far more active. In response to NS authorities attempting to compel registration by withholding ration cards for males born between 1888 and 1925, a sabotage operation was conducted on April 20 against the office in Oslo which housed the archive containing names of persons registered for the Work Effort in the immediate vicinity of the capital. Explosives were thrown through the windows, demolishing the archive. This marked the first successful underground venture against offices holding records of persons who might be called up for forced mobilization.[91] Not until considerably later, in the spring of the following year, were similar sabotage operations carried out against locations outside of Oslo.

The Home Front's opposition was strengthened by support from the Church. Ole Hallesby and Ludvig Hope, two leaders of the Christian Joint Council who up to then had escaped internment, wrote an open protest letter to Quisling on May 8, with copies sent to all pastors. Hallesby and Hope declared that forced labor which compelled individuals to assist the German war effort was a breach of the Hague Convention. They requested Quisling not to force Norwegians to take part in work that violated their consciences and feelings of legality.[92] As they had already anticipated, Hallesby and Hope were arrested soon afterwards and interned in Grini Concentration Camp outside of Oslo. As a result of their incarceration, the last remnant of the Church's independent *public* leadership was eliminated. Thereafter the religious leadership was reorganized secretly, and it functioned in coordination with the other illegal underground groups that were organized in the Home Front.[93] The Church's opposition to the Work Effort therefore had the effect of removing the last vestige of independent public opposition to Quisling's regime.

The conflict concerning the Work Effort was by no means settled, however. In spite of the Home Front's attempt to cause chaos and to arouse public resistance, its success was limited, in particular at first because of its initial hesitation. Although in some areas, especially in the Oslo region, the use of false registration forms and organized sabotage caused disorder, throughout the country as a whole registration proceeded relatively smoothly, with some 300,000 persons being registered.[94]

Of those who were actually forced to participate in labor projects, the greatest number by far were enrolled in the months immediately after the program began. During April, May, and June 1943, 34,411 persons were put to work. Thereafter the general tendency was for the number to decline.[95] If the initial planning for the Work Effort had been coordinated more smoothly, it could have achieved better results during the spring and summer of 1943. Unfortunately for Quisling, the German organizations that stood to benefit from the call-up did not cooperate effectively. When several thousand people arrived as ordered to their reporting places in Oslo in April, the necessary accommodation, supply, and transport facilities had not yet been made ready for them. They were therefore sent home for a few days, only to experience the same situation when they dutifully returned. They once again had no alternative except to go back to their home communities, whereupon pressure from the Home Front and from personal acquaintances began to take effect. A large percentage of these individuals ended up refusing to take part in the Work Effort.[96]

As a result of this pattern, the number of persons who reported for service in the Work Effort dropped during 1943. The most effective boycott took place in the Oslo area, whose relatively compact population could best respond to the resistance movement's instructions, in particular since its leadership had its headquarters here. In the rest of the country, especially in rural districts where the sparse population could more easily be kept track of, it was much more difficult to avoid being called up.[97]

For the Home Front leadership and the Nygaardsvold government, the reaction to the Work Effort in 1943 constituted at least a partial disappointment.[98] Popular opposition to NS had not been as united as in 1942, in part because the Work Effort affected the entire population, not merely certain specific groups in society. For Quisling and his patrons, however, the outcome similarly did not meet their expectations. It produced far fewer forced laborers than originally anticipated.[99] Nor did his political standing improve to any degree. But since the Work Effort had not been a complete failure in 1943, it proved to be natural for him to use it as the basis for an even more ambitious venture in the following year – to enlist involuntarily entire age groups of young men on behalf of the German military.

When Quisling's NS officials encountered stiffening resistance against the Work Effort as 1943 progressed, this proved to have a number of consequences. It affected not only the nature of the occupation and the role of his government, but it had a direct personal impact, since several of the charges brought against him after the war stemmed from this period. As part of its attempt to sabotage the Work Effort, the Coordinating Committee issued a special directive encouraging the police not to participate in rounding up persons who were required to serve as forced laborers. In the Oslo area in particular the police responded positively. By early June the internal memos of Jonas Lie's department revealed that the regular police force could not be depended upon when ordered to seize persons who refused to report for the Work Effort.[100]

Terboven, always determined to crush opposition to measures that his administration had approved, reacted forcefully when he learned of the police's reluctance to enforce compliance. He decided to apply terror tactics, using Quisling's government as his agent. He resolved to put to death

Gunnar Eilifsen, a policeman who on August 9 had disobeyed a direct order to arrest two girls who refused to participate in the Work Effort.[101] At a meeting on August 13 attended by Quisling, Lie, and Justice Minister Riisnæs, Terboven demanded Eilifsen's execution within forty-eight hours. He stated flatly that if his ultimatum was not heeded, he personally would take charge and enact drastic measures against the police force as a whole. Such a move, he pointed out, would place the NS government's claim to independence in a most awkward light.[102]

Confronted with Terboven's assertiveness, Quisling, as usual, complied. He declared that there was nothing that could be done, and on the following day the Justice Department issued a special law under which the execution could be carried out. Acting according to this law, Lie appointed a special tribunal of high NS police officials who, as expected, found Eilifsen guilty. Because of Terboven's insistence, the penalty was death. The sentence was brought before Quisling, who refused to exercise his power of clemency, contending that this was impossible because of Terboven.[103] At 5:00 a.m. on Monday, August 16, Eilifsen was shot. At the conclusion of the war, Quisling was charged with his murder.[104]

The law by which Eilifsen was condemned had to be applied retroactively in order to be used. While it was enacted primarily because of Terboven's demand, Quisling's administration also favored such a law.[105] Entitled "Temporary Law Concerning Actions to Maintain Calm and Order during Wartime", it had extremely wide-ranging implications. As justification for its enactment, it maintained that a state of war existed in Norway because of the "Soviet Union's and its allies' offensive actions against Norwegian territory and Norwegian citizens". Specifically, the law therefore declared that certain formations belonged to "the nation's armed forces"; namely, the police, members of Quisling's *Fører* Guard, members of the Germanic SS Norway, and the *Hird*.[106] Under its provisions, not merely could military law be applied against the police, but it also established a legal foundation for Quisling to attempt to build an armed force. In its broadest application, however, his administration sought to use the law as a club over society as a whole, threatening anyone who opposed the NS government with the death penalty. As *Fritt Folk* declared: "It [the law] is a serious warning to the entire Norwegian people, and it is a deadly threat against those who act against the country's most solemn interests".[107]

To emphasize that the law was not intended merely to apply against Eilifsen, on the morning of his execution NS officials and the Germans moved concertedly against the entire police force in the Oslo area, and also against officers of the Norwegian army. In action taken against the police, Terboven again indicated his determination to use terror in order to obtain a force that could be depended upon. He was seconded in this effort by Jonas Lie and the NS leadership within the Police Department. Only an hour after Eilifsen had been shot, some 600 to 700 members of the police reported as ordered by their superiors on Monday morning, having turned in their sidearms the previous week. Upon their arrival, they discovered that a number of their fellow policemen had already been arrested. Lie, in ultimatum form, informed them of Eilifsen's fate, and he insisted that everyone present sign a declaration of loyalty to carry out their duties and to obey orders. To emphasize the seriousness of the situation, German troops with their weapons in firing position surrounded the meeting place. Nevertheless, a considerable number refused to sign. Lie thereupon threatened to charge the resisters with mutiny, declaring that they would be tried according to military law in the same manner as Eilifsen. Under the prospect of possibly being shot, all but fourteen eventually signed. Those who held out were arrested and driven away by the Germans.[108]

This show of force had scarcely the desired result. Already in 1942 an illegal police leadership group had been formed within the resistance movement. Following the events of August 16, it now considered the possibility of ordering its followers within the police to go underground, but upon consultation with the civilian leadership of the Home Front it was decided that the police could aid the resistance movement better by remaining in their positions.[109] On the German side, Terboven continued to be suspicious of the police, declaring that he doubted their reliability and that therefore many would have to be arrested. The NS head of the State Police, the Norwegian equivalent of the Gestapo, cooperated with the Germans in drawing up a list of policemen from throughout the country whose loyalty to NS and the Germans was in doubt. Some 470 were arrested later in August 1943, and by the end of the year several hundred of these had been sent to a concentration camp in Germany.[110] Nevertheless, in spite of these harsh actions, both NS authorities and the Germans remained convinced, quite correctly, that the majority of the men in the regular police corps were unreliable to the Nazi cause.[111]

In the early hours of August 16 a similar operation was carried out against officers of the Norwegian army. Because the police force could not be trusted, the Germans themselves made the arrests.[112] This move was a reversal of German policy, indicating their concern about the growing resistance movement. Following the end of hostilities in Norway in 1940, officers in the military had received an amnesty from Hitler, being released from captivity in return for taking an oath to refrain from any future service against the Third Reich. However, because of Germany's violations of international law in its occupation of Norway, a significant number of the officers considered their oaths no longer to be in effect. They either began to take part in resistance work or else fled to Sweden in order to make their way to England to join the Norwegian armed forces in exile.[113]

Both Terboven and Falkenhorst were aware that a growing number of officers were engaged in underground activity. Terboven believed that by imprisoning them it would be possible to strike a serious blow against the military branch of the resistance movement, Milorg. Having secured Hitler's approval, the arrests were carried out. Some 1,100 officers were rounded up, to join several hundred who had already been arrested. Approximately 1,300 were sent to a concentration camp in Poland, remaining under *Wehrmacht* protection until the end of the war.[114]

The incarceration of the officers did not, however, have the effect that Terboven had desired. Although some Milorg leaders were caught in the net, the military resistance did not suffer any lasting setback. The positions previously held by those arrested were filled by civilian members of Milorg.[115]

Although the move against the officers originated solely with the Germans, nevertheless it had an impact on Quisling and his government, not least because the arrest of the officers occurred at the same time as the action against the police.[116] This meant that announcement of the arrest of the officers coincided with the official proclamation of the law of August 14, 1943. Because of the common date which these two occurrences shared, it became all the more obvious that the legal justifications for their enactment were in direct conflict. In the official announcement of the arrest of the officers, Falkenhorst declared that on order of *der Führer* the Norwegian officers would be transferred to Germany as prisoners of war.[117] Yet on the very same page of *Fritt Folk* on which this announcement was printed appeared also the proclamation of the law of August 14, 1943. It stated that Norway was in a state of war with the Soviet Union and its allies, not with Germany. The Third Reich was described as Norway's ally.[118] The arrest of the officers thereby severely compromised Quisling's assertion that Norway should be regarded as being in a state of war with the Allied powers and as an ally of the Third Reich.

Such an obvious conflict in fact could not escape the attention of the public. The Home Front proceeded immediately to point this out in an unsigned letter to Falkenhorst, published in the underground press. Emphasizing agreement with Hitler's and Falkenhorst's view that Norway was in a state of war with Germany, the letter declared that Quisling's law and the resulting action against the police were but the most serious of a series of violations of international law that had occurred during the occupation. The Home Front warned that the use of terror against the police had aroused great unrest in the population, and that if the law were applied against other groups in society, this would lead to "desperate resistance and force us to employ means we have hitherto rejected".[119]

More than ever before, the events of August 1943 placed Quisling and his relationship with the Germans in the most questionable light. It revealed the dubiousness of his assertion that Norway, under his leadership, should be considered in alliance with Germany and at war with the Soviet

Union and its allies, and that as a consequence NS authorities could take strict measures against opposition elements in society. On the contrary, these incidents showed as before that the Germans would use whatever legal arguments they wished as justification for their actions. Underlying this opportunism was the fact, however, to Quisling's constant discomfiture, that the Third Reich never at any time officially declared an end to the state of war against Norway which had existed since April 1940.

Quisling's unilateral act in proclaiming the law of August 14, 1943, left him in an even more awkward position because of the reaction this caused within his own government. Several of his ministers were disturbed by the implications of this move, and the fact that the cabinet had not been consulted.[120] News of general discontent within the ranks of the Quisling administration even reached as far as Berlin, where Goebbels commented on this in his diary.[121]

Despite the undercurrent of unrest, the only minister to make an open response was Irgens, who had previously been the senior member of the Commissarial Council. He wrote a letter of protest to Quisling, dated August 31, 1943, in which he insisted that important decisions such as the enactment of the law of August 14 should have been submitted to a cabinet meeting, rather than being decreed by the Minister President alone.[122]

Irgens' objections contained deeper implications because he not only disagreed with the manner in which it was issued, but with the law itself. In a memorandum which he drew up simultaneously with his protest to Quisling, he denied the Minister President's allegation that Norway was at war with the Allies and an ally of the Third Reich. The official German position, Irgens pointed out, remained Hitler's decree of April 24, 1940, which declared that a state of war existed between the two countries. He insisted that this condition was unchanged, as shown by the decisions of German prize courts and the recent imprisonment of Norwegian officers. Norway's official relationship with Germany, he commented, could not be altered by statements made in the preamble to a law. Only a formal agreement between the two countries could change Norway's status. While such a step should have occurred at the time of the formation of Quisling's government on February 1, 1942, Irgens noted with unintended irony that the matter was still very much up in the air. His conclusion was therefore that there existed no state of war with the Allies and no alliance with Germany. Because of this, it was incorrect, he contended, for the Quisling government to make use of military laws against the country's citizens. In a veiled attack against the execution of Eilifsen, he declared that it was the responsibility of the occupying power to carry out punishment against Norwegian citizens for alleged infractions of military law.[123]

Irgens intended to read the memorandum, with reference to his protest letter to Quisling, at a meeting of the cabinet. The Gestapo, however, learned of the offensive document and confiscated it in a raid on Irgens' office.[124] Such action by the German secret police against a member of Quisling's government indicated quite clearly the cavalier attitude of the occupation authorities toward members of the National Government during this phase of the occupation.

Although the disagreeable memorandum was removed in this manner, Quisling at the next meeting of his ministers referred to Irgens' protest letter, although without reading its contents. Because of his poor ability to argue resolutely in a group, he chose to rid himself of the controversial missive by passing it on to the Minister of Justice for his opinion. Riisnæs in turn procrastinated in the period after the meeting, despite Irgens' repeated requests for an opinion. However, a month later the Minister of Justice, refusing to provide Irgens with a written copy, read a statement to the cabinet vindicating Quisling's procedure. The latter thereupon proceeded to lecture his ministers, insisting that he alone would make important political decisions, while they were restricted to matters relating solely to their limited areas of responsibility within their departments.[125]

This incident provided good insight into how the National Government functioned. The *Führer* principle was in operation at all times. While Quisling might ask for comments from his ministers when cabinet meetings were held, he paid little attention to them. He would already have made his decision in consultation with the single minister under whose jurisdiction a particular matter might rest. Never at any time did he allow his cabinet members to vote on an issue.[126]

Through his rigid adherence to the *Führer* principle, he successfully squashed Irgens' challenge. The Shipping Minister failed to receive support from any of his colleagues.[127] Nevertheless, the incident was significant. Despite Irgens' setback, the fact that he chose to confront his Minister President indicated the weakness of Quisling's position. Not only among the population at large, but within National Union's ranks as well, some party members were convinced that their country legally remained at war with Germany. This undermined Quisling's attempt to ignore reality by maintaining that such a condition did not exist, and that he could act independently as the head of a sovereign state. Not only the actions of the Germans, but also a realistic perception of the National Government's legal position by a critic such as Irgens, showed clearly the untenable nature of the pose that Quisling attempted to maintain.

Quisling's declining stature was weakened still more as a result of yet another conflict in 1942–1943. The University continued to serve as a symbol in the struggle against his authorities' attempt to extend their control over society.

During the early period of the occupation the policy which the Department of Church and Education had followed toward the University had generally been moderate. While the rector and a few professors had been removed from their positions, and while NS had forced the faculty, with little permanent success, to accept a small number of party members as professors, until the fall of 1942 the NS administration made no effort to establish policy which affected instruction.[128]

The situation changed just prior to the start of the fall semester of 1942, when Ragnar Skancke demanded that a number of NS members be given special preference for admission to study medicine and pharmacy without having to meet academic requirements. At a conference with the deans whose schools were affected, held on September 4, Skancke alleged that this was a German demand, and that the University might be shut down if agreement were not reached.[129] It did not take long, however, for leading faculty members to discover through personal contacts that the Germans were not directly involved, and that the initiative came from Skancke.[130] Encouraged by this information, the separate faculties passed a resolution on September 11 reaffirming their commitment to academic achievement as the sole criterion for admission.[131]

Faced with this forceful countermove, Skancke decided that greater pressure would have to be applied and reported the matter to Quisling. After hearing Skancke's account, the Minister President decided to intervene personally.[132] The deans of the schools of medicine and natural science were ordered to attend a meeting at his official headquarters in the Royal Palace on September 11. At this conference he made a number of violent threats against the deans, faculties, and students if the admission rules were not changed. If opposition to NS demands continued, he stated menacingly, some 4,000 students and younger faculty members would be deported and made to take part in forced labor at a place where there was little food and clothing, and inadequate housing. Older faculty members would be arrested and their property confiscated, insisted the enraged Quisling, while the deans were personally warned that they would be put to death. In his highly agitated state, he maintained also that he had received full authorization from Terboven when making these threats.[133]

Having already received assurance that Skancke's attempted change did not have the *Reichskommissariat*'s sanction, the deans were aware of the emptiness of Quisling's bluster, which undermined his threatening attitude completely. It appears that he did not fully understand the situation owing to Skancke's failure to keep him thoroughly informed.[134] When the deans replied that they had in no way violated directives from Skancke's office when voicing opposition to the new admission policy, they received support from the NS head of the University, Adolf Hoel. Quisling's menacing attitude thereupon completely evaporated. He was unable to present a solution to end the impasse.[135]

The incident revealed as so many times before that when faced with strong opposition, NS initiatives had no chance of succeeding unless they received backing from German authorities. The deadlock was settled by a compromise, which in reality amounted to a reversal for Quisling's administration. Shortly after the meeting on September 11 an agreement was worked out whereby none of the NS students whom Skancke had attempted to force on the University would be admitted. On the other hand, the regularly enrolled students in medicine and pharmacy were placed at a disadvantage, since they were not allowed to take all of their required courses during their first year of study. This was done to placate NS, whose candidates could not formally conduct any studies at all. As a further sop to NS, it was agreed that persons not regularly admitted to the University nevertheless could attend lectures. Such permission, however, had no practical significance.[136]

Following this settlement, the University experienced no new initiatives from NS authorities for the time being. The principle of basing admission solely on academic qualifications had been upheld, and the fall semester of 1942 proved to be quiet.[137] This did not mean, however, that NS had abandoned its policy of seeking to give preference to its students. Skancke simply needed time to recover from his defeat.

The main weakness that NS revealed in its attempts to gain dominance over the University was the failure to coordinate its moves, as witnessed by the disagreement between Skancke and Hoel. As leader of the party, Quisling bore ultimate responsibility for this defect. It revealed itself once more following the start of the National Work Effort in February 1943. Although persons studying at the University were exempt from forced labor according to the program's guidelines, NS student leaders decided to use it as a means of getting rid of some of their most bitter foes among the undergraduates.[138] With the cooperation of Lippestad, under whose Social Department the Work Effort was administered, twenty-one students received notice in April that they were being drafted to take part in labor projects.[139]

NS administrators at the University had not, however, been informed of this action, and they reacted strongly. In particular, acting rector Hoel took decisive countermeasures to prevent students from being forced into the Work Effort. His primary concern was to keep the University functioning without disruption.[140]

With NS administrators and faculty members pitted against the NS student leaders, and with the German officials in the *Reichskommissariat* once again deploring a step that did not have their approval, the issue was referred to Quisling. Although the NS student leaders insisted at the time they carried out their initiative that they had the Minister President's full backing, he denied this when he discussed the problem at a meeting with Hoel and Skancke. Instead, he insisted that Rector Hoel should have the final say over all matters affecting the University. With Quisling's backing, Hoel could thereby rescind the call-up of students for the Work Effort, and he furthermore proceeded to weaken the influence of NS student leaders who were responsible for this interference with his authority.[141] But while the incident ended to his satisfaction, as well as to that of the great mass of non-NS students and faculty, from an NS point of view it was but another setback, revealing internal disarray and lack of a coordinated policy.

When NS next resumed its ongoing campaign against the University, in the fall of 1943, party officials had learned from past experience and did not repeat previous errors. On August 21 Skancke's department issued a set of rules for the admission of students. The new policy had German approval, having been drawn up in consultation with the *Reichskommissariat*'s officials in charge of educational policy.[142]

The revised rules completely changed the process by which students entered the University. Rather than the individual faculties determining the number admitted and what their qualifications should be, according to Skancke's directive his department would decide how many students should be admitted, while the NS rector would specifically determine who would gain entrance. The fact that under this new policy NS members would be given preference was made obvious by Skancke's insistence that "other things" besides academic grades would be taken into consideration when determining admission.[143]

The altered policy aroused a strong reaction. In coordination with the Home Front, a protest was drawn up which gained the approval of all faculty members except the minuscule number of NS professors. Emphasizing its support of the University's obligation to maintain its traditional values for student admission, the protest indicated the possibility that the faculty would resign if the new rules were implemented.[144]

In response to this overwhelming opposition from all segments of the faculty, Skancke and Hoel appeared to retreat, indicating a willingness to negotiate concerning the wording of a new admissions policy. With their approval, a number of faculty committees were established to study the question.[145]

In the following period the committees made considerable progress, and it appeared that a compromise solution might be at hand. However, Quisling learned on October 14 that members of the faculty had stated in writing that they considered Skancke's admission rules of August 21 to be null and void. Quisling at once ordered a halt to the negotiations, decreeing that Skancke's rules should immediately go into effect. To emphasize the

Minister President's determination to impose his will, on the following day the State Police imprisoned ten professors and more than fifty students.[146] Quisling personally gave the order to carry out these arrests to the head of the State Police.[147]

It is difficult to pinpoint exactly who bore the responsibility for initiating the jailings. Some sources indicate that it was the Minister President.[148] This explanation is plausible because he was more than capable, as previous events have shown, of acting precipitously when faced with an apparent affront to his authority. On the other hand, NS officials, most prominently Skancke, have insisted that Quisling acted only after having received threats from Terboven.[149] In providing this explanation, however, Skancke appears to have been motivated by a desire to avoid having Quisling assume culpability for an unpopular act, attempting instead to have the Germans serve as villains. Nevertheless, even if Quisling did instigate the process which led to the arrests, as is most likely, he could not have acted without Terboven's approval. He was in direct contact with the *Reichskommissar* concerning the situation at the University immediately before the jailings began.[150] Furthermore, there is no reason to assume that Terboven, with his Nazi contempt for intellectuals, had any personal sympathy for the outspoken foes of NS who were rounded up on October 15. It was Quisling, however, who launched the action against the University in October, with Terboven remaining discreetly in the background.[151]

Despite Quisling's personal involvement, the jailings did not result in any change toward the University by NS authorities because, beyond ordering the arrests to be made, the Minister President did not have any policy to implement. As a result, the situation remained highly uncertain. Negotiations continued between the representatives from Skancke's department and faculty leaders over the contents of the disputed new set of admission regulations.[152]

This state of irresolution came to an end not because Quisling decided on a course to follow, but rather by an act of arson. A resistance group set fire to the University's Hall, the Aula, in the early morning hours of November 28.[153] The operation was largely symbolic, intended to call attention to the plight of the University, and little damage resulted.[154] The incident, however, produced severe retribution. Terboven was incensed and acted immediately. His natural antipathy toward intellectuals was heightened by his conviction that most of the students were active in the resistance movement. He therefore resolved to arrest them and close the University.[155]

The *Reichskommissar* was astute enough to implicate others in such a venturesome move, especially as he proceeded without prior approval from Berlin. He discussed his plan with Quisling on November 29. The latter offered no objections, and he thereby had been maneuvered into becoming an accomplice to the *Reichskommissar*'s effort to eliminate the University as a source of opposition with one stroke. Similarly, because of the scope of the planned action, Terboven consulted with Falkenhorst as well.[156]

When German soldiers began to round up students and faculty members throughout Oslo on the morning of Tuesday, November 30, the arrests therefore occurred with Quisling's tacit approval, although Terboven had sole responsibility for instigating the move. As a result of his unilateral action, the University remained closed for the duration of the war. Of those arrested, most faculty members were eventually released, as were a considerable number of students. However, some 700 students were sent to concentration camps in Germany.[157]

When he chose at least tacitly to associate himself with Terboven's draconian measure, Quisling failed to foresee the widespread uproar which would result. The arrests and the closing of the University aroused international attention, first and foremost in the other Scandinavian countries, but also within the wider scope of world opinion. The issue lent itself readily to Allied propaganda, which effectively exploited the incident.[158] In neutral Sweden, reaction was especially strong. Critical statements were made in the press, at the universities, and within parliament. Reflecting public opinion, the Swedish government chose to involve itself directly, sending a protest note to Berlin in which the Third Reich was asked to alter its policy toward the University and to treat the students leniently.[159]

Since Terboven had not forewarned Berlin of his intent, the controversy caught Hitler by surprise. He was anything but pleased. Germany at the moment was engaged in delicate trade negotiations with Sweden, and Terboven's untimely move appeared to threaten their outcome.[160] Hitler was further incensed by Terboven's lack of finesse, and he expressed himself forcefully concerning the *Reichskommissar*'s incompetence. Goebbels and Himmler joined their *Führer* in condemning Terboven. Himmler held the *Reichskommissar* responsible for the failure of the SS to recruit more Norwegian volunteers, while Goebbels more generally decried the unfortunate propaganda effects of the affair.[161]

The outcome of the University crisis therefore proved to be anything but pleasant for Terboven. He received a severe reprimand from Hitler for the manner in which he had handled the situation.[162] But for reasons of prestige, *der Führer* could not publicly disavow his representative in Norway. Ribbentrop was therefore instructed to reject sharply the Swedish protest.[163]

As a result of the clumsy and brutal manner in which he tackled the crisis, Terboven emerged from the incident in greater disgrace with Hitler than ever before. The *Reichskommissar* shared a common destiny with Quisling. Hitler allowed them both to retain their positions largely for reasons of prestige. It would have been an admission of failure for his policy in Norway to remove either of the two.

When contrasted with the great expectations that he had had for his future career earlier in the war, Terboven found it frustrating to witness how his standing with the Nazi leadership had deteriorated. Long before the University crisis, Hitler had written him off as a candidate for higher position within the Third Reich. As Goebbels noted in his diary on May 9, 1943: "Terboven is out of the question. Terboven didn't measure up to expectations in Norway. He considered the Norwegian problem so to speak an SA man's job. Instead it demanded tremendous political cleverness. This Terboven did not possess".[164] Goebbels similarly commented several times later in the year on Terboven's inability to be flexible, instead always acting in a heavy-handed way.[165] Because of his continued harsh behavior, Goebbels concluded, not flatteringly, that the *Reichskommissar* had become "the most hated man in all Scandinavia".[166] It was little wonder therefore that Goebbels, reflecting Hitler's attitude, referred to the handling of the University fire as "Terboven's stupid action. . . . Here you can see again what dire consequences result if everybody does as he pleases. It was Terboven's duty to seek the *Führer's* advice in this matter; the *Führer* would surely have absolutely forbidden the coup . . ."[167]

In his exposed position, Terboven had to accept full responsibility for the outcome of the University crisis. It proved impossible to shove the blame on anyone else, which he certainly would have done if the opportunity had been at hand. Considering the severe reprimand he received, it was not surprising that rumors abounded that he might be ousted.[168]

Unlike what happened earlier during the occupation, Terboven's loss of favor with Hitler did not benefit Quisling. Because of previous failures, Quisling's own standing with *der Führer* was anything but high. Furthermore, he never attempted to disassociate himself from any of Terboven's severe actions in 1943 by assuming an independent posture. The Minister President could therefore hardly try to exploit an embarrassment such as the University crisis against the *Reichskommissar*, since he had personally indicated his approval. In addition, the worsening wartime conditions that Nazi Germany experienced during 1943 hardly made Hitler prone to allow collaborationist leaders the opportunity to enjoy greater freedom as the new and fateful year of 1944 approached.

CHAPTER XVI

The Failure of Mobilization

January 1944 – December 1944

> ... No Norwegian will allow himself to be fooled into fighting for our op-
> pressors against our allies. We know that, NS knows that, and the Germans
> know that. Therefore, it is likely that a mobilization will be camouflaged. It
> can most easily be carried out through the Labor Service, which we now for
> several years have become used to regarding as a relatively harmless group.
> ...
> It is therefore time to eliminate the Labor Service. ...
> The directive is: Strike against the Labor Service. ...
> For the country's and your own sake: Follow the directive.
> Home Front directive,
> February 26, 1944

During much of 1944 the Minister President's chief priority concerned a
plan to mobilize Norwegians to take part in the war. His goal was not
new. As far back as early 1942 he had looked forward to full military involvement on Germany's side. He had hoped that this would be the next
step following the signing of a formal peace treaty. However, when the
longed-for peace settlement could not be attained in 1942, he did not drop
the idea of mobilization. On the contrary, he sought to put into effect a
project to call up entire age groups for service on the eastern front.

In seeking this objective, his underlying motive remained unchanged.
Successful implementation of forced mobilization, he believed, could not
help but strengthen his standing with Norwegian society and with the Germans, in particular at a time when the Third Reich was experiencing severe
military setbacks. But his increased emphasis on this ambition also gave
evidence of his tacit recognition that *voluntary* enlistment in the military
units that he had helped organize had proven to be inadequate.

During the fall of 1943 he received encouraging information about the
existence of similar sentiments in favor of mobilization within the SS hierarchy. Lieutenant General Gottlob Berger, responsible for securing non-

German recruits for *Waffen SS* regiments, held opinions that coincided remarkably with those of the NS *Fører*. Desiring additional Norwegian soldiers, Berger recommended to Himmler that peace be made with Norway in order to permit a subsequent mobilization. He further insisted that a peace treaty would be advantageous because it would severely hamper opposition to the occupation. Quisling's government, he maintained, would be able to deal effectively with the resistance movement, whose members could be charged with treason for having acted unlawfully against Norway's sovereign government on behalf of an illegal exile group in England.[1]

Through Berger's subordinates in Norway and from other sources as well, Quisling learned of the general's views.[2] The Minister President responded by launching his own initiative in a conversation with Hans-Hendrik Neumann, Wegener's successor as head of the *Reichskommissariat*'s special staff in charge of coordinating activity with NS. Quisling suggested that no less than 50,000 men be mobilized for service in Russia, arguing that this would be an effective means of harnessing unused strength for the war effort. He further insisted that mobilization would contribute to a feeling of European solidarity and trust.[3]

He did not meet a particularly positive response. Terboven's and his immediate subordinates' skepticism about Quisling's ability to carry out planned projects had been vindicated many times before. They therefore assumed that the mobilization proposal had no chance of success.[4] Neumann did nothing to encourage the scheme. When asked to express his objections in writing, he sent Quisling a letter on December 18 in which he quite effectively raised a number of arguments against mobilization.[5]

With devastating irony, he pointed out the deficiencies in Quisling's proposal. While the scheme to mobilize a contingent to serve against the enemy might be desirable, said Neumann, he did not believe it was feasible. Many men would flee to Sweden as soon as they learned that they were liable for mobilization. Meanwhile, a huge apparatus would be needed to apprehend those who remained. A force of "reliable men" would have to deliver the mobilization orders personally and to bring in each one of those who were drafted. Such a body could not be raised. The police, he pointed out, could not be relied on. In addition, a mobilization of this magnitude would create internal disorder that could only be quelled by German might. But this in turn would lead to a lessening of the Quisling administration's authority, since outside intervention would make it obvious that the government could not master the situation. The use of duress would also cause the Germans to lose even more of the sympathy that they allegedly still retained within the population. Neumann also raised the argument that the removal of 50,000 men engaged in essential work could not be compensated for. He further maintained that a mobilization would also seriously weaken NS. For public relations reasons, NS members would have to take part in any mobilization. But this would result in the loss of party officials who held important positions. They could not be re-placed by reliable individuals, he asserted, which meant that if the project were carried out, persons hostile to the party would supplant Quisling's followers who had been called up.[6]

Despite this biting critique, so representative of the *Reichskommissariat*, Quisling did not abandon his effort. Since Terboven had no interest in the proposal and could not be counted on to forward it to Hitler, Quisling's only alternative was to call it to *der Führer*'s attention personally. Fortu-nately for him, this opportunity was at hand. He received a letter from Lammers in mid-January 1944, containing the message that the Nazi dicta-tor wished to have a personal meeting with the Minister President.[7] They talked for almost three hours in Hitler's field headquarters at Rastenburg on January 21.

Quisling used the opportunity to submit his proposal to mobilize three divisions in the name of European unity against the Bolshevik onslaught.[8] But he could not escape Terboven's negative influence. The *Reichskommis-sar*, accompanied by Neumann and Senator Otte, had also come to Rasten-burg. He argued against mobilization, voicing his doubts that Quisling could effectively carry it out.[9]

Hitler, ever master of the situation, diplomatically did not commit him-self. But by refusing to take a stand, he in reality turned down the project. It was dead – at least as far as the German authorities were concerned.[10]

This was made quite apparent on the following day, when Quisling and his entourage of NS ministers had a long meeting with Himmler. Here too, however, they were escorted by two of their supervisors from the *Reichs-kommissariat*, Neumann and Otte. One of those present, Jonas Lie, noted that the gathering discussed "re-establishment of a Norwegian defense force and questions related to this". Quisling indicated quite unrealistically his desire to establish schools for officers and NCOs in preparation for "a later call-up of several age groups". He visualized an international Euro-pean defense system headed by *der Führer*. It would have a common air force and navy, but the "national armies" would be under control of the individual countries. He promised that "Norway's contribution" would be three divisions.[11]

Although he had long been familiar with Berger's advocacy of the very view that Quisling urged, the *Reichsführer SS* failed to provide any encour-agement. Even someone as sympathetic to the idea of common military co-operation among Nordic Aryans as Himmler could do nothing without Hitler's sanction, a hard fact that he made clear at the meeting.[12] Quisling had to return to Oslo on the 24th with the sole consolation that he at least had been able to submit his ideas to Hitler in person. *Fritt Folk* in its coverage of the trip could inform its loyal readers of nothing more concrete than the vague commentary that "a number of important questions concerning the continent and the Germanic peoples future" had been discussed.[13]

While the Germans did not take the prospect of Norwegian mobilization seriously following this visit, it continued to be important and to create wide-ranging repercussions both for Quisling and the Home Front. The Minister President had by no means completely given up hope that he might seize a chance to carry out the venture. During the early months of 1944 there were many indications that the idea of mobilization was still alive.[14] Quisling personally heightened this impression by appointing a special committee to study the creation of a National Conscription Service (*Riksutskrivningsverk*) that would be responsible for registering and calling up all men who might be mobilized. Alf Whist, asked by Quisling to comment on the committee's recommendation, further provided evidence that mobilization was contemplated when he emphasized that the *military* nature of the law establishing the Service had to be disguised.[15]

It was, however, a memorandum written by Minister of Justice Riisnæs that more than anything created the impression in the spring of 1944 that NS intended to carry out conscription. Dated January 17, it was addressed to General Berger. It must be viewed in connection with Quisling's later attempt to gain approval for mobilization during his trip to Rastenburg. The document was drafted to coincide with the Minister President's arrival, and Berger not only enjoyed close contact with Himmler, but it was known that he favored some of the same objectives as Quisling.[16]

Riisnæs, like Quisling, called for mobilization against the Russians. There were, however, several differences between his proposal and that of Quisling. Riisnæs favored a larger draft of 75,000 men between the ages of 18 and 23 in five age groups, rather than the three age groups of 50,000 that Quisling visualized. Furthermore, whereas the latter planned to have the mobilized troops serve in distinct Norwegian units, Riisnæs suggested that they be incorporated into *Waffen SS* divisions. However, they were to be indoctrinated with the view that they were "not German, but Germanic soldiers".[17] The variations between Quisling's and Riisnæs' plans may merely have been due to a desire on the part of the latter to make his scheme as attractive as possible to Berger, which it certainly was from a *Waffen SS* perspective. The contrast, however, may also have been a reflection of Riisnæs' personal outlook. He was noted for being among the most pro-German of Quisling's ministers.[18]

His plan did not have the effect its author desired. It became public knowledge in an amazingly short time. A secretary in the office of the Minister of Justice made a copy and quickly passed it on to the resistance movement.[19] Already on January 21, the day Quisling was recommending mobilization to Hitler, key members of the Home Front were assembled to evaluate the significance of Riisnæs' proposal.[20] Within a few days many more had learned of the scheme. A leading resistance figure noted in his diary on January 28: "The entire town [Oslo] now knows about Riisnæs' letter."[21] Two days later it was published in *Bulletinen*, a major underground paper.[22] The document enjoyed the dubious distinction of becoming known to more people in a shorter period of time than probably any other item that Quisling's administration tried to keep secret during the occupation.

The significance of Riisnæs' memorandum was that the resistance movement regarded it as being connected with Quisling's visit to Germany.[23] The Home Front had thereby been warned of the possibility of mobilization long before any overt move had been made. By mid-February the Home Front had formed what it considered to be a clear picture of Quisling's intentions:

> There exist reliable reports that Quisling, during his meeting with Hitler in January 1944, offered Hitler three divisions of Norwegian troops. At the same time there was made public in this country Riisnæs' infamous recommendation to mobilize five age groups of Norwegian youth who were to be used as support troops on the eastern front. Furthermore, Quisling has recently ordered the organization of a "National Conscription Service".[24]

The resistance movement immediately resolved to oppose any attempt at mobilization. Already on February 4 the Council (*Rådet*), the leadership group within Milorg, telegraphed London that the Home Front was considering several alternatives, including a general strike.[25]

Although the Home Front had organized and led opposition to Quisling's initiatives on numerous earlier occasions, its move in this instance took on a different character. Thanks to the early information which they had gained, the civilian leaders of the Home Front were determined to go on the offensive, rather than wait for Quisling to launch a mobilization campaign before taking countermeasures. In making its plans, the Home Front concluded that the NS-controlled Labor Service (*Arbeidstjenesten*) was the most likely tool that Quisling would use when seeking to carry out forced mobilization. The Coordinating Committee issued a directive against the Labor Service through its network of agents on February 26. It was read over London Radio on March 15. The message was clear: no one should report to the Labor Service if ordered.[26]

The origins of the Labor Service, known by its A-T initials, went back to the depths of the depression. Originally named the Labor Battalion (*Arbeids-Fylkingen*), its foundation was largely due to the initiative of Walter Fürst. Like the Weimar Republic's Labor Service (*Arbeitsdienst*) and Roosevelt's Civilian Conservation Corps, it provided unemployed young men with work, such as clearing forests and creating productive farmland. It was not affiliated with NS, although thanks to Fürst's influence, many of those who first joined belonged to the party. He continued to work actively with the organization after he broke with Quisling. During the 1930s the group led a vicarious existence, changing names frequently. At first it received state funds, but later it had to rely on private donations. While he usually, but not always, served as leader of A-T, Fürst was always its driving force during these years.[27]

As noted earlier, A-T received the Administrative Council's endorsement after the beginning of the occupation. The Council's head, Ingolf Christensen, urged enrollment in the group, asserting that here was an area where Norwegians and the occupation authorities could cooperate. Many persons outside of NS became part of A-T during the summer of 1940, in particular army officers who had been released from captivity. Among them were a number who later would play leading roles in Milorg. A-T at this time received advisers from the *Arbeitsdienst*, which Hitler had nazified after he came to power. German influence thereafter became steadily more pronounced.[28]

Although A-T remained voluntary under the Administrative Council, it was organized along *military* lines and could therefore easily be transformed. Quisling, however, at first made no overt move to take over the organization during the ensuing period of the Commissarial Council. Although nominally under Axel Stang's Department for Labor Service and Athletics, it retained its independent character. Fürst was replaced by a non-NS head on October 1, 1940, who received Quisling's assurance that A-T would not be involved in politics.[29]

The character of the organization nevertheless changed considerably. The German advisers increased pressure to remake it into a true copy of the *Arbeitsdienst*. It ceased to be voluntary when Stang issued a number of decrees in the following spring which allowed the conscription of young males into the Labor Service.[30] NS influence grew ever greater, with the party having gained control over appointments by the close of 1941.[31] When the Nazi salute was introduced in April 1941, the head of A-T and a number of prominent non-NS officers resigned in protest, only to be succeeded by a new leader, General Carl Frølich-Hanssen, who belonged to NS.[32] By the end of the occupation NS members held the majority of higher positions within the force.[33]

Although the Labor Service became NS-dominated, it was not considered to be a typical party organization by the average Norwegian. Those who were conscripted annually to serve in its ranks generally were not members of NS. The organization enjoyed considerable sympathy because of its work, especially in rural districts.[34]

Despite his NS membership, Frølich-Hanssen resolutely wished to keep

A-T out of politics, devoted to its primary function of manning public work projects, and in this he received support from his German advisers. As a result, recruiters seeking volunteers for service in NS-sponsored military units were not allowed within A-T camps, even though this policy was bitterly attacked by outspoken critics among the NS ministers such as Riisnæs and Lie.[35]

A-T had therefore been politicized only to a restricted degree prior to 1944. Nevertheless, the Home Front's leaders, alarmed over rumors of mobilization, regarded it as a potential threat. A-T had registers containing the names and addresses of tens of thousands of prime candidates for military service. This was of special concern for the Coordinating Committee, with its responsibility for consolidating internal resistance. Already in mid-January 1944, before the Riisnæs memorandum became known and prior to Quisling's visit to Germany, the Committee discussed the possibility that many more men might be called up for A-T service than the usual annual contingent of 5,000.[36] Such conjecture proved to be realistic.[37]

When the Home Front learned of Quisling's and Riisnæs' proposals for mobilization, it concluded that its fears were entirely justified. It immediately began its drive against the Labor Service. The resistance recognized, however, that it faced considerable difficulties. It expected that at least two to three months would be needed before its directives would begin to take effect. Nevertheless, the Coordinating Committee worked under intense pressure throughout the spring, issuing a large number of directives, articles, and appeals against the threat of forced mobilization through A-T.[38] Time was of the essence, since conscripts scheduled for service in 1944 had orders to report for duty in May. London Radio, as always, assisted in the effort to persuade the draftees not to report. The Home Front also attempted to break down A-T from within by urging those of its officers who were considered reliable patriots to leave their posts.[39]

Quisling worked to counteract this campaign through statements in the press and radio. He insisted that false rumors were being circulated which alleged that the call-up for A-T service was in reality war mobilization. He promised that the A-T contingent for 1944, consisting of 8,000 men, would be engaged solely in traditional public work projects.[40] His denials were not without effect. The operative group within the civilian resistance, consisting of members from both the Coordinating Committee and the Circle who were responsible for day-by-day resistance activity, received numerous requests to reconsider the Home Front's decision. But the group refused to accept Quisling's protestations at face value and instead moved more vigorously than ever against A-T.[41]

The struggle between Quisling, seconded by his NS administrators, and the Home Front over A-T in 1944 was not restricted merely to whether or not the force would gain its annual quota of conscripts. The operative group was equally concerned with the need to destroy A-T's records. These contained the names and addresses of men who had previously been liable for call-up, some eighty to ninety thousand persons. Such records would obviously serve as a key resource for any possible mobilization. Activists within the Home Front, including younger members of the operative group, further reasoned that demolition of A-T archives would boost the morale of men who were liable for A-T conscription. They would know that an active resistance organization stood behind the campaign to disrupt the Labor Service.[42]

In order to carry out this exploit, the civilian resistance required cooperation from Milorg. This was the first occasion that the military branch of the resistance actively took part in sabotage operations in a significant way. It therefore took time for preparations to be made, and also to receive permission from the Norwegian military command in England.[43] Because of its inexperience, Milorg's initial attempts at sabotage were not impressive. Planned for execution on the evening of May 5, none of the operations in Oslo were successful. Outside the capital only four were carried out, with varied results.[44]

In part because of these failures, but to a more important extent because of the Labor Service's entrenched position and the Home Front's late start, the first results of the attack against A-T did not prove particularly troublesome for Quisling. The great majority of A-T conscripts ignored the Home Front's directives. Only in some limited districts did strong opposition against A-T materialize. It is estimated that less than 30 per cent of those who were called up failed to report.[45]

Despite this initial setback, the Home Front's campaign nonetheless marked yet another turning point during the occupation, with repercussions for everyone affected – Quisling and his party, the Home Front, German authorities, and the population at large. Not only did the resistance movement seize the initiative, but in doing so it issued directives in the name of the Home Front Leadership (*Hjemmefrontens Ledelse*). This was the first time this term was used during the occupation. It gave the impression that a unified resistance leadership stood in opposition to NS and the Germans. This had an immensely stimulating effect on members of the general public who were expected to obey the Home Front's instructions. For Quisling the consequences were negative because it meant that all undertakings that he attempted to carry out would be met by a resistance leadership whose influence over the general population, already considerable, would grow even stronger during the final phase of the occupation. From this time onwards all directives sent out by the resistance were proclaimed on behalf of the Home Front Leadership. Furthermore, its instructions against the Labor Service were now distributed parallel to those in opposition to the Work Effort (*Arbeidsinnsatsen*), which continued to be in effect.[46]

In reality, however, there did not yet formally exist a Home Front Leadership, although contact and cooperation was close and overlapping between the three main Home Front groups: the Coordinating Committee, the Circle, and Milorg. As one Norwegian historian has noted, these divisions within the resistance movement existed for a "remarkably long period of time".[47] A truly unified Home Front Leadership was not set up until the late fall-winter of 1944–45. Until this time, the different parts of the Home Front continued to carry out their functions as separate but interrelated groups which worked closely together, in particular from the fall of 1943 onwards.[48] Nevertheless, the *illusion* had been established that a Home Front Leadership existed. Therefore, the offensive against A-T marked an important step in the process that eventually led to a firmly united single Home Front Leadership.

Although the first sabotage actions against A-T did not prove particularly discouraging for Quisling, the resistance movement's use of this weapon also marked a significant change in the conditions under which he operated. Prior to the spring of 1944, the Home Front had not engaged in sabotage activity to any significant degree.[49] Its most influential leaders within the Coordinating Committee and the Circle had been opposed to such operations. They adhered to the policy that sabotage should be restricted to the final period of the occupation, the liberation phase. Consequently, almost all officially sanctioned sabotage before 1944 was carried out by specially trained agents who came from and returned to England.[50] The major exception to this pattern involved a number of spectacular acts by Communist partisans, who were not under the control of the "official" resistance movement, the Home Front, which enjoyed recognition by the exile government in London.[51]

The Home Front's policy of relative inaction in the use of sabotage changed, as we have seen, with Milorg's attacks against A-T offices. A number of factors accounted for this change. In part it was motivated by the need to meet the challenge from the communists, who were arousing considerable attention by their sensational operations. A further inducement resulted from the Home Front's desire to inspire the general population, which suffered from war-weariness after four long years of occupation. An added stimulus for change was provided by younger members of the Home Front, who wanted to pursue a more aggressive form of resistance than the older leaders.[52] Both the initiative to ask Milorg to sabotage A-T offices and the decision to issue directives in the name of the Home Front Leadership originated with the younger, active members of the operative group.[53] Above all, however, it needs to be emphasized that the issue which served as the catalyst for the Home Front's decisions to initiate these changes was the ongoing campaign against A-T. From the spring of 1944

onwards, both Quisling and the German authorities were opposed by a resistance movement that was far more offensive-minded than earlier. This
trend for the Home Front to take more overt physical action continued to
accelerate for the remainder of the occupation.

Quisling made his move in May 1944. But while the Home Front, through
its campaign against A-T, had long anticipated his attempt to carry out
forced mobilization, it discovered to its surprise that the call-up would *not*
be through A-T, but rather through the Work Effort.

A demand from the occupation authorities had set this development in
motion. The *Reichskommissariat* insisted that the Germans would need
some 20,000 men and 3,000 women for various projects during 1944.
However, it was impossible to obtain this many laborers by following the
regular procedure of ordering persons registered with employment offices
to report for service in the Work Effort. Quisling was fully aware of this,
and he sought to turn it to his advantage. He believed that the possibility
might now be at hand for the mobilization of entire age groups which he
favored. He therefore proposed to call up all young men born in 1921,
1922, and 1923 for service in the Work Effort.[54] This plan originated solely
with him. There was no German pressure to take this approach.[55]

Considerable doubt existed, however, both within NS and among the
Germans as to whether his proposal was feasible. Johan A. Lippestad,
whose Social Department would have overall responsibility for the plan's
execution, had serious reservations. By the spring of 1944 the Social Department was already experiencing considerable difficulty in administering
the regular Work Effort. The Home Front's directives, initially ineffective,
were now bearing fruit. Large numbers of those who were ordered to take
part in the Work Effort refused to respond. This was especially true in the
Oslo area, where it was easier to maintain anonymity than in the smaller
towns and rural districts.[56]

Members of the *Reichskommissariat*, including its head, were equally
reluctant to endorse Quisling's recommendation. The latter, however,
raised a point in favor of his plan which he knew would be especially attractive to the Germans. He specified that if the men who were to be conscripted into the Work Effort were not sent out of the country, then they
could be used in Norway to relieve German troops for frontline duty. It is
difficult to determine whether Quisling, when raising this possibility, intended to use the draftees as a labor group or as a trained armed force. It is
fair to assume, however, that he preferred the latter alternative if it could
be achieved, because of the importance he attached to having an independent military force. On this occasion he did not meet an absolute rejection
because Terboven, despite his earlier opposition to Quisling's schemes for
creating an armed force, had no objections to the possibility of obtaining

more Norwegian labor for military construction projects. Quisling therefore, albeit somewhat reluctantly, received approval to go ahead with his
attempted mobilization.[57]

Having secured this essential permission, he ordered his NS subordinates to begin planning. The reluctant Lippestad received responsibility for
coordinating strategy, both with the *Reichskommissariat* and within NS.
Final approval for the plan's execution rested with the Minister President.[58]

Quisling personally sought to prepare the way for successful mobilization through a propaganda campaign which NS instituted in May. Not
unexpectedly, it was directed against the Soviet Union. As he had done so
frequently, he tried to exploit fears of "Bolshevism", but on this occasion
he could direct attention to an agreement made by the government in exile
which permitted Allied, including Russian, occupation of Norwegian territory which might be liberated from the Germans. In his major speech at
this time, headlined by *Fritt Folk*, he accused the King and the exile government of having committed what he so often stood accused of – treason.
No responsible person, he asserted, wished to have Russian Bolshevik
troops on Norwegian soil. The people, he argued, should therefore be
grateful because they were under Reich protection, and should support the
German defense force with all possible assistance.[59]

The aid he referred to was not specified. He had no intention of allowing the mobilization plans to slip out. Having learned from past failures, he
wished to have the start of the project proclaimed at the last minute in
order to prevent Home Front countermeasures.[60] The actual announcement of the beginning of the mobilization campaign therefore was made
without warning on May 19. NS authorities declared suddenly that those
belonging to the three age groups should report within the next few days
for registration with the local employment offices of the Labor Directorate
(*Arbeidsdirektoratet*), which were under the administration of Lippestad's
Social Department.[61] All young men in the affected age groups were required to register, except those who had earlier served in A-T.[62] Very little
time was given for them to respond. In the Oslo area they had only a two-
day period of grace before registration was required.[63]

As had been done previously in propaganda on behalf of both the Work
Effort and A-T, NS sought to stimulate feelings of national solidarity at
the time of the call-up. The announcement stressed the need for additional
labor in such areas as farming, lumbering, and construction. Those who
were registered, said *Fritt Folk*, could expect to serve in one of these labor-
intensive sectors for a period of only six months.[64]

The ensuing struggle "was perhaps the greatest during the entire
occupation".[65] It certainly included the *direct* participation of the greatest
number of people who actively took part in opposition to one of Quis-

ling's endeavors. This was due to the many individuals who were immediately affected. The three age groups born in 1921, 1922, and 1923, when added to the two age groups who earlier in the spring of 1944 had become liable for A-T service, totalled five age groups numbering in excess of 75,000 men. This was exactly the number that Riisnæs had proposed to be mobilized. The Home Front could not avoid drawing a direct connection between this massive effort by Quisling to conscript labor and Riisnæs' earlier memorandum to Berger.[66]

Quisling's attempt to restrict knowledge of the operation to its planners proved impossible. His strategy simply could not be kept secret owing to the need to have so many persons from outside the party in important administrative positions because of NS' lack of adequate manpower. As could be expected at a time when Germany's inevitable defeat was becoming ever more apparent, leakage of Quisling's plans became even greater during the final period of the occupation. The Coordinating Committee learned of the project by May 12. It immediately responded by sending out a directive.[67] The resistance movement warned that the call-up of entire age groups for the Work Effort was not an ordinary measure to increase production, but instead was a disguised attempt to carry out a *military* mobilization on behalf of Germany. No one, the directive stated, should be fooled by NS denials and assurances. The Home Front effectively made the point that Quisling's word could not be trusted:

> Frightened by the Home Front Leadership's directive calling for a strike against A-T because of the mobilization danger, Quisling sent out his denial: only the usual force, 8,000 men, would be called up. Now everyone can judge the value of his denial. Three age groups, 80,000–90,000 men, will be sent to serve the enemy.
> Remember Riisnæs' letter: five age groups were offered to the enemy.
> Remember Quisling's repeated offers to *der Führer*: three divisions.
> The Germans have found that now is the time to accept the offers.[68]

The directive emphasized in particular that Norway was at war, and all aid should be denied the enemy. No one should allow himself to be registered, and all members of society were encouraged to aid those who resisted.[69]

The impact of the directive was heightened by the Home Front's advanced knowledge of the mobilization plan. It was sent out already on May 14, five days before NS made the official announcement. The Home Front thereby gained a headstart, which it never gave up. It was aided by having resources which allowed widespread dissemination of information. London Radio again contributed significantly by beaming the message to those listening illegally to its broadcasts. The order was also spread in large quantities throughout the country in printed form. In the Oslo area alone 100,000 copies were distributed.[70]

Early awareness also permitted the Home Front to employ a weapon that had now become a permanent part of its arsenal – sabotage. Milorg was determined to make amends for its general lack of success against A-T offices earlier in the month. Furthermore, the Home Front's assault against A-T and Quisling's labor mobilization overlapped. The renewed acts of sabotage that Milorg now conducted therefore proved to be simply a continuation of its previous operations. This was in particular true because A-T records and machines were to be used in carrying out registration for labor mobilization. In the early morning of May 19, just hours before NS-controlled newspapers announced the call-up, explosives ripped through an office in Oslo which housed a vital punchcard machine intended for registration use. And in the late afternoon a daring daylight raid was carried out against the main employment office in the capital where registration was scheduled to begin on the 21st. Other successful sabotage operations were executed in Oslo and throughout the country, both at this time and later in May and June.[71]

Although the physical destruction was considerable, of even greater importance was the psychological impact which these acts created. They provided clear evidence to the general population that the Home Front possessed both the will and the ability to use force when conditions warranted. Sabotage operations therefore contributed to the success which the Home Front gained over Quisling.[72]

No one knew at the time, however, what the outcome of the struggle might be for the minds of the Work Effort conscripts. Both sides therefore awaited the results with great suspense. They were not long in coming. Already by the evening of May 21, the first day of registration, the outcome was obvious. Only a very small minority had registered as ordered. For NS the disappointment was intense. Even the most loyal of Quisling's followers recognized the magnitude of the defeat he had sustained. Rolf Holm, the NS regional leader in Oslo, reported: "The action against the Work Effort must be considered 100 per cent successful for our opponents."[73]

For the adversaries whom Holm referred to, the resistance movement, the outcome created a feeling of tremendous joy and satisfaction. It was a great victory, brought about by many months of effort going back to early in the year when the Home Front, fearing a possible mobilization, had issued its first directive against A-T. And whereas the effort against the Labor Service had not been particularly successful, now the tide had turned. The affected age groups followed the Home Front's instructions in overwhelming numbers.[74] This indicated that Quisling's administrators enjoyed little if any authority. In the days that followed, *Fritt Folk* announced in vain on behalf of the Labor Directorate that all men born in 1921, 1922, and 1923 who had not registered for the Work Effort must do so as soon as possible, and no later than May 30.[75]

In response to this open defiance, the NS-controlled police launched sudden raids throughout the towns, arresting on sight males who appeared to be in the age groups that should have registered. In turn, this caused a mass exodus from the towns, especially in southeastern Norway, including Oslo. Young men by the thousands took to the countryside. Here they found refuge with family and friends, or they banded together to form hidden encampments in the forests. Because of their direct challenge to the NS authorities, they assumed a heroic quality in the public mind. Soon they were popularly known as "the boys in the forest" ("*gutta på skauen*"). Full of youthful optimism, they were confident and determined to hold out.[76]

For the more coolheaded of the Home Front's operative group, this development, while marking yet another tremendous propaganda defeat for Quisling, also created a significant problem. The thousands spread throughout the forests lacked food and supplies. At first their needs were met haphazardly by friends, relatives, and volunteers, but the Home Front soon took over effective control, supplying the camps in an organized manner, thereby also bringing them under the command of the resistance movement.[77] Recognizing that the boys could not remain indefinitely in the hastily improvised camps because of the danger of encounters with German patrols and the approach of harsher weather in the fall, the Home Front worked to disperse them as quickly as possible. For practical reasons, only a small number could be absorbed into Milorg's system of underground cells. Many more were spread throughout farms in the countryside, while some 1,500 were guided across the border to join the Norwegian "police troops" being organized in Sweden. The remainder stayed in the camps for the time being.[78]

Quisling and his subordinates were completely at a loss to prevent this exodus. Except for the first police arrests, NS officials almost entirely gave up any attempts to capture those who escaped. Nor did the Germans offer any support. They allowed Quisling to take full responsibility for this fiasco. A report drawn up by the Home Front in June 14, 1944, provided a good assessment of the situation:

> Except for some scattered *Hird* raids of small size and importance, the authorities have not made any effort to capture the boys who have avoided registration. The Germans are still astutely staying in the background and show no signs of wanting to take over the failure.[79]

NS authorities were reluctant to act in large part because of the Home Front's increased power. In mid-summer the operative group sent a strongly worded message to all sheriffs (*lensmenn*), warning them against taking any steps. Asserting that it was acting on behalf of the legal government, the Home Front emphasized that the struggle was in its final phase and that it would "use the strongest means", meaning liquidation, against any sheriff who arrested a young man who was acting on behalf of the fatherland. When the Home Front demonstrated that this was no idle threat, not only were the sheriffs frightened, but it also assured the "boys in the forest" that the resistance movement was providing them with full protection.[80]

Quisling bore full responsibility for failing to prevent this development. Terboven had given him a free hand to carry out labor mobilization, and the result was that almost all those who were to be called up had taken to the countryside. At a meeting held soon after the magnitude of the debacle was apparent, the *Reichskommissar* could not refrain from asking the humiliated Minister President a sarcastic question. What might have been the result, queried Terboven, if the three age groups had really been called up for *military service*, as Quisling had originally proposed, rather than merely for the Work Effort? The implication was readily apparent: the fiasco would have been even greater.[81]

Although he had no answer to this devastating question, Quisling was never one to admit failure if he could avoid doing so. He either rationalized defeat by finding some ready explanation, or when this proved impossible, as now, then he tried to shift the blame over to others. In this instance he sought to hold his ministers accountable, singling out in particular the hapless Lippestad. Quisling in effect demoted his Social Minister by creating a new position, a special National Director (*Riksfullmektig*) for the Work Effort. Although the latter nominally held a subordinate post within Lippestad's department, in reality he assumed independent control over the Work Effort. Quisling's appointee, Christian Astrup, previously the NS regional *fører* in Bergen, assumed his post on June 15. Henceforth it was he who acted on Quisling's behalf in trying to rescue the Work Effort's labor mobilization, which up to that time had provided the NS *Fører* with nothing but humiliation.[82]

The Minister President was not yet ready to acknowledge the full and complete collapse of his mobilization effort. He still had one last card to play in attempting to turn this campaign into a triumph. The NS officials who had planned the tactics for carrying out labor mobilization had assumed all along that an enforcement mechanism would be needed to compel registration. Quite shrewdly they decided to use the threat of hunger to gain their ends. Ration cards, which were issued periodically throughout the year, would be withheld from males within the three age groups unless they could produce evidence of registration.[83] But in attempting to implement this requirement, the administrators had to depart from previous practice. Heads of households had earlier been able to receive ration cards for food and clothing on behalf of their family members. Under the new rule each individual would have to pick up his card personally at the ration office.[84]

It proved difficult, however, for Quisling's government to institute the new procedure. Non-NS administrators within the Business Department (*Næringsdepartementet*), which had responsibility for issuing the cards, were in close contact with the Home Front. They were able to delay immediate implementation, arguing that there was not enough time to make the necessary changes before the next distribution was scheduled. But Lippestad, who desperately needed to find some method for remedying the situation, was determined to proceed with the imposed restrictions when the cards were subsequently scheduled to be issued, in August.[85] To try to make the NS clampdown even more effective, Astrup and Karl Marthinsen, chief of the State Police, worked out an agreement on July 18 whereby the NS police unit would use its power to arrest those not complying with registration.[86]

When seeking to put this method into operation, NS authorities again discovered that it had been impossible to keep their tactics secret. Not only did the Home Front have informants within the Business Department, but it also learned of Astrup's and Marthinsen's arrangement. It could therefore plan its countermeasures. Nevertheless, the problem facing the Home Front was difficult. To stymie the NS move, it needed to obtain ration cards for everyone in the three age groups, some seventy to eighty thousand men. After unsuccessful efforts had been made to secure counterfeit copies, the operative group decided that its only remaining option was to steal the needed cards. On August 9 an armed resistance group highjacked a truck loaded with some 75,000 ration cards in broad daylight on the streets of Oslo.[87] Quisling's final card had been trumped.

In frustration, with the Home Front safely out of reach, the only retaliation NS authorities could take was to punish the population as a whole. When reacting in this manner, party officials felt, not without reason, that the dramatic highjacking could not have succeeded without support from the general population. Many persons witnessed the event, but no one called the police. As *Fritt Folk* fumed: "When revolver bandits become so brazen that they dare to steal an entire truckload of ration cards in the middle of Oslo . . ., then this must be because, among other things, the gangsters count on a certain amount of sympathy from the public."[88] Rations for the population as a whole were reduced by four to six per cent, while the entire liquor and tobacco quotas were abolished for three months.[89]

This measure showed that NS authorities knew they could expect little if any public support, and it also revealed their general irritation. But by the summer of 1944 the effectiveness of Quisling's administration had deteriorated to the point that even this weak gesture could not be enforced. The Home Front's successful theft caused confusion and uncertainty among NS administrators in the Business Department. It served as a distinct warning, indicating the danger of trying to change the rules governing the issuance of ration cards because the Home Front was strong enough to thwart any steps they might take. As a result, the Business Department sent out instructions to its offices in August, specifying that ration cards should be distributed as previously without any restrictions.[90]

This was but one manifestation indicating that the Home Front had become so strong that it could dictate terms to NS officials. Immediately following the highjacking, the resistance had telephoned Alf Whist, who recently had taken over as Business Minister. He was told that if he rescinded the requirement to have all persons personally pick up their ration cards, then the stolen cards would be returned. Quisling's chief economic adviser capitulated at once. Consequently, beginning in mid-September the Home Front gradually returned most of the stolen cards, 10,000 at a time, while the NS authorities proportionally rescinded the ration restrictions. In the end only the withdrawal of tobacco and liquor quotas remained in effect, a sacrifice which at least the majority of the public was willing to bear.[91]

The attempt to use control of ration cards as a means of securing compliance for Quisling's labor mobilization ended with the Minister President being forced to sustain yet another set-back. His defeat was total. NS authorities made no further attempts to use administration of food supplies as a weapon for the rest of the war.[92]

With the Home Front's successful disruption of this means of securing forced registration for labor mobilization, Quisling was completely at a loss as to how to proceed. Therefore, when he at last had to admit that his administration lacked the power to carry out the project by itself, he humiliatingly had no alternative except to turn to the Germans. He found this especially disagreeable because of his earlier assurances to Terboven that if only he were given approval, he would secure the call-up of the three age groups. But the *Reichskommissar* would not proffer any assistance. He refused to become involved for military reasons. During this critical period of the war the Germans could hardly afford the internal unrest that compulsory labor mobilization undoubtedly would have created.[93]

The failure of the project proved therefore to be a devastating blow to Quisling's prestige, so embarrassing that Terboven ordered the press to cease any mention of the effort whatsoever.[94] Of the approximately 70,000 young men who belonged to the three affected age groups, NS administrators were able to put to work only about 300.[95] But the setback that Quisling sustained at this time was so severe that it was not restricted just to the attempted labor mobilization. The defiance of NS authorities by the "boys in the forest" influenced other administrative functions as well. Both the regular Work Effort and the Labor Service increasingly were in a state of collapse. The Home Front continued its offensives against both programs without letup. Its members were satisfied with the results. A-T officers as well as conscripts now escaped in ever-increasing numbers from the labor camps. The organization in the end became a hollow façade, while the Work Effort similarly ceased to be of any significance.[96]

When it became obvious that the NS officials were stymied and that no new efforts would be made to revive labor mobilization, the Home Front gradually closed the camps housing the "boys in the forest" during the fall. The dispersal process continued, with some choosing to go to Sweden and others to remain in the countryside, working in the forests and on the farms. The majority, however, decided to risk returning home on the assumption that they no longer needed to fear any type of retaliation.[97] The Home Front warned them to be careful because of the danger of arrest.[98] In reality, however, they had little to fear – the feasibility of renewed labor mobilization was dead and buried. This was confirmed by Whist in a newspaper release in which he appealed to them to come home. He assured them that both Quisling and Terboven had promised that no reprisals would be made.[99] Whist's overture had little relevance except that it officially acknowledged the demise of labor mobilization. Most of the "boys in the forest" had already long departed from their encampments when he made this announcement in mid-November.

The continuous offensive which the Home Front had waged and the willingness of young men to respond to its directives were the key reasons why Quisling suffered such a decisive defeat. But in addition there were other factors that influenced this outcome – considerations which Quisling and his planners failed to take into account. The males selected to be called up for labor mobilization were between twenty-one and twenty-three years old. They were of an age that was ideally suited for military service, a fact that they and the population at large were fully aware of. Therefore, when the attempt was made to conscript just these age groups, both those directly affected and the general public reacted strongly, believing the Home Front's warnings to be correct – that this really involved *military* mobilization. Furthermore, the "boys in the forest" belonged to the segment of the population best suited to oppose a call-up. They were of an age when they were not particularly hindered by family and career considerations, and they could therefore resist without being burdened by outside obligations. They were also aided by the season in which Quisling sought to put his mobilization project into effect. The late spring and summer was the ideal time for young men to escape into the countryside, not having to concern themselves about the inclement weather of other, harsher seasons. And while they were scattered on farms and in forest encampments, they received a morale booster which gave them added encouragement to hold out. Soon after their exodus came news of the Allied invasion of Normandy.[100] Norwegians who opposed Quisling and his administration were now more certain than ever before of Germany's pending defeat.

For Quisling, the thwarting of his plan was equally the beginning of the end. He had, as we have seen, encountered numerous earlier failures of a serious nature. But the setback involving labor mobilization was especially damaging because it marked a new breakthrough for the Home Front, the group that had more and more stood out as his most significant source of opposition as the occupation progressed. For the first time it had succeeded in mobilizing a mass movement within the *general* population, thereby greatly augmenting its authority. Consequently, its instructions could no longer be considered mere exhortations, asking the public for support. Instead, they took on the character of authoritative decrees that all patriotic citizens were expected to obey. From this time the Home Front enjoyed a position of command among the great mass of the people. They recognized the existence of a Home Front leadership that could take effective countermeasures to frustrate Quisling and his officials.[101]

The Home Front's ability to engage in future opposition was heightened by its awareness of the increased authority and respect it had gained. The Norwegian legation in Stockholm commented on this attitude within the population in a memorandum to the government in London: "A new spirit has been formed and a will to contribute prevails, such as one has hardly seen the equal of earlier".[102] The note was based on reports from Norway, including an exuberant letter from one of the more cautious and realistic resistance leaders, written at the end of May when it was clear that Quisling's initial attempt to carry out registration for labor mobilization had failed:

> This in my opinion is the greatest victory we have won here at home. Spirits are very high, we are today one people and one soul. The divergences and disagreements that we have had from time to time have disappeared, and everyone is united in one common struggle.[103]

On the opposite end of the spectrum stood the Minister President and his NS adherents, more discouraged than ever by this latest setback. It marked yet another decline in his standing. Not only did he and his administration continue to lose what little influence they had with the public, but he had also managed to reduce his prestige with the Germans even more. Terboven had already anticipated this development. If Quisling's venture, contrary to what the *Reichskommissar* expected, had enjoyed success, the Germans would still have been the major beneficiaries, since they would have gained an added source of labor from the mobilized age groups. But when the venture turned into a fiasco, Terboven had shrewdly stayed in the background. He is alleged to have told his associates that he was willing to accept this result, even though it somewhat adversely affected his own prestige, because it meant the definitive end to Quisling's old demands for a peace settlement, increased sovereignty for the National Gov ernment, an independent armed force, and military mobilization. As will be seen, Quisling had not yet abandoned these goals, but Terboven believed that the Minister President was now so compromised that he had forfeited the last remnants of his ability to act independently. Already before the losing venture had run its course, the *Reichskommissar* was looking forward to the moment when he could report to Hitler on the abysmal results of Quisling's attempt to carry out labor mobilization.[104]

By the fall of 1944 the Minister President's position was weakened even further by the Third Reich's declining military fortunes. Without German backing, he could not survive in office for a minute, a state of affairs that NS members, whose fates were tied to his, were quite aware of. When therefore even German propaganda could not disguise the obvious fact that the *Wehrmacht* was being driven back on all fronts, defeatism became a serious problem within NS ranks.

Aware of this growing despondency, Quisling sought to inspire his followers to continue to believe in victory. In a speech on September 4 he argued that no battle was won without some difficulties and reverses. As was his wont, he resorted to historical analogies, pointing out how the Romans, the Prussians, and even the Bolsheviks – whose goals he reproached while admiring their determination – had in the end gone on to victory after having suffered serious defeats.[105] Germany and its supporters would similarly be victorious, and he demanded that all NS members must carry on the struggle and do their duty. Any wavering, he insisted, was unworthy.[106]

The day on which he made this speech was hardly suited to arouse confidence. Appearing on the same front page with his speech was the news that Finland had withdrawn from its alliance with the Third Reich. The armistice with the Russians had gone into effect on September 4. By its terms the Finns were obliged to secure the removal of German forces from their soil no later than the 15th.

With distressing events such as this being repeated constantly during the final phase of World War II, it was little wonder that some NS members, in particular the opportunists who had joined when German victory had seemed assured, were now wavering in spite of Quisling's exhortations.

The growing strength of the Home Front, with its ability to command obedience from the general public, was a second factor which contributed to growing pessimism within NS. The majority of Quisling's adherents were fully aware that should Germany be defeated, they would be punished once the war was over. The Coordinating Committee in late September 1943 had issued a "Warning to the Enemy's Helpers", which was printed by the thousands, and which was also published in many of the underground newspapers. Here the Home Front emphasized that NS as an organization provided aid to the enemy, and its members were therefore *collectively* guilty of treason. In addition, since the party was based on the "*Führer* principle", all those who had sworn that they would follow the *Fører* shared responsibility for his actions. For each day that passed, warned the Home Front, the guilt of NS members increased. Only by resolute acts in support of the Norwegian people's struggle, and not merely resignation from the party, could former NS members hope to receive some leniency.[107]

This notice that a day of reckoning would come caused considerable consternation already in 1943. As a result, the NS leadership felt the need to try to reassure its members through a series of articles written for the press by a NS legal expert, who not unexpectedly interpreted NS activity as being in accordance with international law.[108] There was every indication, however, that many of Quisling's followers remained apprehensive, and that a significant number were already attempting to withdraw. On September 16, 1943, before the Home Front had issued its warning, Lippestad felt compelled to send a message to NS bureaucrats, reminding them that party members in the administration were *required* to wear the party insignia "as visual proof that they belong to Vidkun Quisling's fighters".[109] The fact that such a memo had to be sent showed that at least some of the "fighters" were losing their zeal.

Even more significant, Quisling was witnessing the actual loss of NS members through resignation. Especially frustrating was the defection of those who held public positions. In reaction to this growing trend, he again resorted to his standard recourse, using coercion to intimidate NS bureaucrats who might be considering withdrawal. Against them a special type of pressure could be applied – the threat of being dismissed. As early as October 1942 the *Fører* issued a directive which decreed that all officials who resigned from the party should be dismissed.[110] However, the lack of qualified NS personnel to fill posts that became vacant in this manner made it impossible for him to have his subordinates apply the rule consistently.[111]

The reluctance of some members to wear NS insignia in public and the attempts by others to disassociate themselves completely from the party were not caused solely by Germany's military defeats. These behavior patterns also reflected a reaction to the deep-seated hatred that existed within the general population. Internal NS documents indicate that by the spring of 1944, if not earlier, many members lived in constant fear of physical violence.[112] Those who held public positions were especially exposed. The editor of *Fritt Folk*, for example, spoke of difficulties in obtaining adequate protection for the newspaper, and he deplored the fact that it had been necessary to provide guards for its employees.[113]

To a considerable extent, the decline in party morale occurred as a result of external developments over which the *Fører* had no direct influence. However, as the occupation progressed, a controversy arose within the party which he could have handled decisively had he so desired. With so many of NS' new recruits having joined in part if not fully because of opportunistic motives, corruption became a matter of concern, especially for many older members from the prewar period who belonged because of their convictions.[114]

The degree to which this issue became a topic within the party was fairly extensive, in particular with reference to a number of those who held high positions in the NS hierarchy. Even Quisling was reluctantly forced to recognize this subject publicly. In a speech at the end of July 1944 he insisted that the best elements within the people belonged to NS. If a few "black sheep" should crop up within the NS flock, intoned the shepherd, "then we know that we also have the will to clean this up . . ."[115]

Contrary to his assurance, "black sheep" were present in far larger numbers than he cared to admit. Not unexpectedly considering his past reputation, Hagelin's name figured prominently as a target of accusations and rumors.[116] But while innuendos about graft flourished, both among NS members and within the public at large, there was no means by which devoted party members could officially deal with this problem, which they felt was a cancer on the body of NS. Blatant incidents of corruption it is true could result in the arrest of those involved.[117] But the party leadership, from Quisling on down, preferred to disguise such misconduct as much as possible, maintaining that exposure would only result in bad publicity, which NS' opponents were sure to exploit.[118]

This was what Herman Harris Aall experienced when he, as one of the party's oldest members, attempted to bring the subject up for discussion in an article which he had drafted. He pointed out that misconduct occurred in all organizations, but the important thing, he insisted, was how the *leadership* reacted to such irregularities. He argued that it should permit open criticism of misconduct within NS if it wished to gain the people's trust. But Quisling did not share Aall's view, perhaps in part because he himself had used his position to acquire material gain.[119] Aall's article was therefore denied publication. Fuglesang reinforced this act of censorship by issuing a directive as Minister of Culture and Public Information which prohibited internal party matters from being discussed publicly in the press and in periodical literature.[120]

However much Quisling and Fuglesang wished to cut short consideration of this divisive and embarrassing question, an order from the leadership was not sufficient to halt it, not even within a party based on the *Führer* principle. While Aall was disgusted with the decision, he abided by it, but others did not. Young idealistic members in particular reacted strongly against the corruption they witnessed, irregularities that stood in sharp contrast to the ideal of self-sacrifice on behalf of Norway which the party stressed ideologically. An article appearing in the NS Youth Organization's paper, *Nasjonal Ungdommen*, in May 1944 bore the blunt title, stated as a question: "Are there Rats in the House?" The article's contents left no doubts that "rats" had indeed infested the "house" (read NS), and Quisling, alluded to as the house's "watchman", was criticized for not having acted against the rodents. But the young people who lived in the "house" insisted that the "rats" be smoked out, even if the interior for a time retained a smoky odor. If this were not done, declared the article, the entire "house" would eventually collapse because of the "rats'" depredations.[121] Similar accusations that individuals had joined the party for personal profit, bringing greed and corruption into NS ranks, were published in the NS periodical *Germaneren (The Teuton)*.[122]

Although those who expressed such forthright views were censured and removed from their positions by the zealous Fuglesang, acting as defender of the party's virtue on behalf of Quisling, the issue of corruption refused to disappear.[123] The critical views stated in *Germaneren*, for example, appeared at the very end of the occupation. For the more idealistic among Quisling's followers, the existence of recognized corruption within the party continued to have a demoralizing impact, especially as their *Fører* refused to deal with the problem effectively.

The ministers whom Quisling chose to serve in his National Government during the final years of the occupation provide additional understanding of his status during this period. When changes were required, the Minister President made the final decision to remove a minister, and he similarly determined the successor to the post. However, the first who had to be replaced did not leave office because he had fallen in disfavor. On the contrary, the loss of Gulbrand Lunde was a severe blow for Quisling. As head of the Culture and Public Opinion Department, Lunde acted as the Norwegian equivalent of Josef Goebbels, to whom he bore a striking resemblance. In charge of NS propaganda, he was one of the few ministers serving under Quisling who combined ability with initiative and imagination. Because of his aggressiveness, NS influence had penetrated a number of vital cultural sectors to a significant degree, including publishing, radio, the theater, and the arts.[124] As a consequence, his sudden death on October 25, 1942, meant that Quisling had been deprived of one of his most able subordinates, someone who had also been true to the *Fører* since the very beginning of National Union.

Reaction to the news indicated the feeling of loss that occurred within NS. The first shock was followed by widespread misgivings that the propaganda chief's death was due to foul play. This suspicion arose from the manner in which the fatal mishap occurred. Lunde and his wife, also a leading party member, both drowned when their car plunged into deep water as a result of the chauffeur's miscalculation when boarding a ferry. An extensive investigation followed, but it failed to find any evidence of wilful wrongdoing.[125]

Faced with having to find a suitable replacement, Quisling chose Fuglesang. The latter thereupon gained a department of his own in addition to continuing to hold his traditional post as NS General Secretary. This appointment did not, however, prove to be particularly advantageous, judged from what was in Quisling's best interests. Although Fuglesang adhered to the policy of attempted infiltration and domination of culture that Lunde had begun, he lacked Lunde's innovative outlook. Furthermore, he continued to be primarily interested in his responsibilities as head of the party apparatus, and thus he tended to neglect the Culture and Public Opinion Department. As a consequence, his work as propaganda chief could quite correctly be summed up as not being "especially energetic".[126]

Whereas the succession of Lunde was brought about by an act of fate, with Quisling cautiously appointing an old trusted follower in his place, the later changes that he made in his cabinet were due to calculation. He wished to have new ministers who were in tune with the changed policy that he adopted toward the Germans. With emphasis on cooperation, he was compelled to eliminate a number of his old guard who were not flexible enough and who refused to accommodate themselves to the altered conditions. Not surprisingly, this involved acting in accord with not only the German authorities, but also the NS official who under Quisling most prominently emphasized economic collaboration, Alf Whist.

Architect Tormod Hustad, one of Quisling's earliest loyalists who headed the Labor Department, was the first to be removed because of the changed situation. His downfall began when he strongly opposed the terms of certain hydro-electric concessions that Whist had negotiated with the Germans. Hustad's irritation was pronounced because, while the question of waterfall concessions should have come under his jurisdiction, he had been denied the opportunity to lead the negotiations. Quisling had ignored Hustad's protests and backed Whist, with the result that the Germans received the terms they desired, which were extremely favorable. Subsequent relations between Hustad and Whist remained highly strained. When Hustad therefore was indiscreet enough to suggest that Whist benefited personally from his close ties with the Germans, the latter called this to Quisling's attention. The *Fører* used these injurious comments as a pretext to remove Hustad. He was suspended from his position on January 13, 1944, followed by dismissal on February 1.[127]

His ouster was not a serious loss for Quisling, despite the devotion that Hustad had always shown. He had received his post primarily because of his loyalty, as had been consistently true of all the appointments that he had obtained from Quisling, including membership in the ill-fated April

1940 "government". But as Labor Minister he was not very energetic, playing largely a passive role. Now, when he proved unwilling to recognize the reality of the changed situation and failed to make peace with Whist, he had to go.[128]

Upon his removal, the department's name was changed to the Traffic Department, but it carried out the same functions as before. Hustad's successor, Hans Skarphagen, possessed different qualities. He had been a professor at the Technical University in Trondheim since 1936, where Skancke served as rector, and he had been an early member of NS. He had previously held a number of posts within the administration, eventually becoming the second-ranking official in the Labor Department under Hustad. Skarphagen, however, had wisely sided with Whist in the dispute with Hustad.[129] As Traffic Minister, he was considerably more thorough and professional than his predecessor.[130] He was also someone who, as Quisling and Whist knew, would not raise objections to projects involving cooperation with the Germans.

Eivind Blehr was another minister who had to be dismissed because of conflict with Whist and German interests. As head of the Business Department, on paper he appeared to hold a powerful position. When the National Government was formed, two previous departments, the Supply Department and the Department for Trade, Industry, Handicraft and Fisheries, had been combined into the Business Department under his leadership. Outwardly this made him the minister who had responsibility for the bulk of the country's economic activity. But his authority was weakened greatly by Whist's rise to prominence, first as head of the Business Corporation and then in November 1943 as minister without portfolio in the Quisling government.

Because of the value the Minister President attached to him, Whist, and not Blehr, assumed primacy as the major NS economic expert. As Whist supplanted him, Blehr increasingly tended to be on a collision course with his rival. In the hydro-electric concession dispute, Blehr backed Hustad.[131] He similarly sought in other ways to restrict Whist's area of competence, and he appealed to Quisling for support.[132] But the Minister President offered him little comfort. Not only would Quisling hardly disavow his chief economic adviser, on whom he depended, but in addition Blehr had further weakened himself by his opposition to the Germans. On a number of occasions he had sought to protect Norwegian interests, assuming "a firm and fearless position toward the Germans".[133] On top of this, the unfortunate Business Minister was affected by the fiasco of the labor mobilization, since his department was in charge of issuing ration cards. Quisling, in search of scapegoats, sought to shift part of the blame over to Blehr's shoulders.[134] The latter's fate was thereupon sealed. On Friday, June 9, 1944, Quisling appointed Blehr's rival, Whist, as head of the Business Department, beginning on the following Monday.[135]

The latter thereupon enjoyed unrivaled authority as the dominant figure on economic matters within NS. In addition to heading the Business Department, he retained his party post as NS ombudsman for economic activity, and he continued to preside over the Business Corporation. His power was increased even further because, upon his takeover, the Business Department absorbed most of the functions of yet another ministry, the Shipping Department. Along with Blehr, Kjeld Stub Irgens was also dismissed from his post.[136]

Of the changes which Quisling made among his ministers, it seems paradoxical that Irgens remained in office as long as he did. In part this was due to his national reputation as a captain in the prestigious Norwegian-America Line and, at least during the early part of the occupation, his family ties with Hagelin. Quisling also owed Irgens a debt of gratitude because of the attempt he had made to persuade King Haakon to return to Oslo in April 1940. However, as head of the Shipping Department, Irgens was hardly the compliant subordinate that Quisling desired. He appears to have accepted this position largely because he believed in 1940 that Germany would win the war. With his long career as a mariner, his primary concern was to protect Norwegian shipping interests, not only from the Germans, but also from NS.[137]

In pursuing this policy in a determined manner, he enjoyed considerable success. His threatened resignation in May 1941, followed by the conduct of successful negotiations, prevented the Germans from seizing the portion of the merchant fleet that was in home waters as a war prize.[138] He also worked energetically to prevent NS from politicizing his department. He refused to appoint party members, and he loyally protected his subordinates, even warning them of pending NS raids in search of incriminating evidence. This was consistent with his practice of ignoring the fact that many of his employees were actively opposed to NS. Other actions on his part provided further indication that he was hardly a dedicated party man. He refused to take part in NS propaganda activity; he frequently appealed to the German police on behalf of prisoners who had been subjected to maltreatment, including torture; he sought to aid the Jews to avoid arrest; and, as we have seen earlier, he protested against Quisling's law of August 14, 1943, which resulted in Gunnar Eilifsen's execution.[139]

When Quisling sought to bring Irgens under control by ordering him to appoint NS members to top positions in the Shipping Department, the command was simply ignored. The specific event, however, which cost him his job occurred in May 1944, when he refused Quisling's request that all NS ministers join in the propaganda campaign against the Nygaardsvold government for having signed an agreement that would permit Soviet occupation of Norwegian territory. By the time he made this dissent, Irgens had lost all remaining influence and prestige with the Minister President. To prevent him from taking any last minute obstructionist actions, Quisling abruptly fired him at 5:00 p.m., Friday, June 9, with Whist scheduled to absorb the operations of the Shipping Department on the following Monday.[140]

These ministerial changes cannot be interpreted as having weakened Quisling's management of the National Government. It definitely was in his interest to remove Hustad because of ineffectiveness and Irgens for lack of dedication. The firing of Blehr can also be described as beneficial because it resulted in the elimination of his rivalry with Whist, and all doubts were thereby removed concerning the latter's full authority to deal with economic matters on Quisling's behalf. Only Fuglesang's appointment proved to be somewhat disadvantageous for Quisling.

Nevertheless, while he benefited administratively from most of these changes, they also served to illustrate his weakened standing, more than ever dependent on German good will. He had been deprived almost entirely of any opportunity to pursue an independent policy vis-à-vis Terboven of the type that he had followed prior to the fall of 1942. Only toward the very end of the occupation would he seek to revert to this approach. The removal of three ministers, moreover, was in part a reflection of his subservience to the *Reichskommissariat*. Hustad and Blehr had sought at least to a degree to protect Norwegian economic interests from the Germans, interests that Quisling willingly compromised in attempting to curry favor. Irgens even more forcefully had worked to safeguard Norwegian shipping. In the end, therefore, his removal became an obvious requirement. But with the departure of Hustad, Irgens, and Blehr, the Minister President signalled clearly his abandonment of those NS ministers who within a broad framework of cooperation with the Germans still attempted to maintain a national point of view.

His policy toward the Germans did not bring him any major benefits in 1943–1944. He remained completely dependent on the *Reichskommissariat*. His NS administration continued to need its approval before any laws could be enacted.[141] Only Hitler's protective hand prevented Terboven from seeking Quisling's ouster. But the *Reichskommissar*'s disdain for his defeated rival was widely known among those with good political connections. In December 1942, at a meeting where Terboven was present, his subordinates let their Norwegian guests, a number of prominent businessmen, know that the Germans had made a serious error in allowing NS to assume administrative control in September 1940. Quisling's party was described as a complete fiasco.[142]

In contrast to the situation earlier during the occupation, Quisling could no longer make effective use of the one option that could neutralize the dominating *Reichskommissar* – a direct appeal to Adolf Hitler. With the elimination of his former allies, Rosenberg and Raeder, the NS leader learned through experience that his conversations with *der Führer* no longer brought satisfactory results. On his visits in April 1943 and again in January 1944 the *Fører* met with Hitler, but on each occasion he had been closely shepherded by Terboven and his subordinates. Quisling was allowed to voice his views, but Hitler carefully avoided making any positive responses. He had committed himself so strongly in Quisling's favor that he could not drop him, but with each debacle that followed after the Minister President's assumption of office, his status with Hitler declined. By 1944 the significance of his visits to Germany had deteriorated to the point that they were largely symbolic, intended to convey the propaganda message that regular consultations occurred between the Minister President and the German dictator. In this way they also served to flatter him, since he gained a certain illusion of power by being permitted to meet with *der Führer*. Hitler was quite aware of the importance of satisfying not only Quisling, but the vanities of other pro-German collaborators as well.[143]

Except for these occasional meetings with his puppet, Hitler had no intention of altering the status quo in Norway. Germany's increasingly desperate military position hardly persuaded him to consider making political changes in Quisling's favor, even if the latter's ineptitude had not been a hindrance. Within Hitler's conceptual framework, Norway continued to be of vital importance. Because of the strategic significance which he attached to the country, he remained fearful of an Allied invasion of the continent coming through Norway, both in 1943 and in 1944.[144] As a result, the number of troops sent north to strengthen the *Wehrmacht* garrison increased dramatically, from seven to thirteen divisions during May to October 1943. By December the build-up had reached the point that Jodl reported the presence of 430,000 German troops in Norway.[145]

Under the existing circumstances, with little prospect for any changes that would allow him greater freedom, Quisling remained in his locked-in position. Not only he and his NS subordinates, but also his enemies, recognized the frustrating dilemma he was in. In April 1944 the Home Front issued a communiqué which trenchantly referred to his predicament. It pointed out that the Germans had never officially declared an end to the state of war between Germany and Norway. As long as this condition remained, no number of interpretive tricks could "explain away [the fact] that aid to the Germans is treason". As a result, the communiqué continued, Quisling "is feeling quite uncomfortable". He therefore at all times had sought "to create a different situation, first peace and later military cooperation with Germany. Then his treason would no longer be so clear and evident".[146]

Reflecting frustration over being deprived of the opportunity to conduct independent activity that might improve his status, Quisling could at times express himself quite emotionally against the Germans in *private* conversations, including discussions with members of the *Reichskommis-*

sariat. On such occasions he could be outspoken, pointing out for example how the Germans were exploiting Norway's natural resources without compensation.[147] In addition to venting his feelings, he no doubt hoped that he might obtain greater understanding for his viewpoint through voicing his discontent. But such diatribes failed to bring any results, at least in part because he did not threaten to follow any alternative strategy. Never at any time did he even mention the possibility of resigning in protest.

In his public statements there was never any hesitation or any lessening of enthusiasm in his emphasis on NS' allegiance to the German cause. Ever since it had been installed as the official collaborationist party, beginning with the Commissarial Council, one of his main themes had been that only NS, because of its special relationship with the Germans, was capable of regaining freedom and independence for Norway within a Germanic federation.

This assertion had been repeated once again, though in a more muted manner, on the occasion of National Union's tenth anniversary, celebrated on May 17, 1943. Everything had been done to make the day as joyous as possible. The self-proclaimed "climax" was the *Fører*'s speech in one of Oslo's larger cinemas. Members of the *Hird*'s children's groups were lined up on both sides of the street in front of the theater when he arrived, greeting him with flower bouquets. Once inside, the first object that those in attendance noticed was a large bronze bust of the *Fører* in the foyer, while the stage from which he spoke was decorated with NS' symbols, the sun cross and an eagle in gold, which stood out against a pretty background of young leafy birch trees and a mass of spring flowers.[148]

The object of this adulation assured his followers that NS' goal was "a free, great and happy Norway whose national existence is truly secured". His historical mission was to lead Norway into a "Germanic federation". This alone would give the Norwegian people an assurance for tomorrow, which he declared had been guaranteed by none other than *der Führer* himself: "We have Adolf Hitler's word that Norway has a great future and a special task to fill in the new Europe".[149]

Despite this appeal to chauvinism, even Quisling recognized the need to add the pledge that Norway, with its small population, would not lose its identity within the anticipated federation. He therefore again made reference to Hitler's word as an alleged guarantee. *Der Führer* had promised, Quisling declared, that nothing more would be demanded from Norway within "the coming Germanic and European new order" than that which was "absolutely essential for our two Germanic people's joint interest and for European security . . ." Furthermore, the coming new order, he maintained, would be built upon the individual people's "uniqueness and free development".[150]

This insistence that only support for NS and its *Fører* would allow Norway to maintain its freedom within a Germanic federation received a shocking reversal some four months later from none other than Quisling's most dangerous detractor, the *Reichskommissar*. The timing for this episode could not have been less auspicious for the Minister President. It came when NS was celebrating the third anniversary of its "assumption of power" with the establishment of the Commissarial Council. Now Terboven gained his revenge for having been forced to abandon the State Council in 1940 in order to take Quisling's interests into consideration. In clear undiplomatic terms he informed Quisling's assembled NS lieutenants, who were gathered at a "leader meeting" on September 26, exactly what Norway could expect under a National Socialist hegemony after the war. It corresponded in no way with the illusory future that Quisling consistently had promised.

Terboven deliberately downgraded many of Quisling's long-standing goals. The *Reichskommissar* insisted that in this period of the European new order the ideals from the earlier democratic era had to be abandoned. As an example for his criticism, he declared that wide circles within NS emphasized in their propaganda that their highest goal was to have Norway emerge free and independent after the war, and that NS alone could guarantee such an outcome. This view, said Terboven bluntly, was outdated, part of "the old democratic jargon".[151]

Continuing in this vein, he sarcastically described Quisling's emphasis on obtaining greater freedom and independence for Norway – which meant greater independence for himself – as being of "secondary" importance. What mattered, insisted Terboven, was that one could already see the new historical period emerging out of this gruesome total war – the "Germanic era" based on National Socialism in which the Germanic peoples would grow together to form "one single large and mighty realm". Norway, in other words, could expect to be absorbed into this new Europe that was dominated by Germany. The one consolation that he could offer was that this process would be gradual, and that *der Führer* would allow the Norwegians to retain their "national uniqueness".[152]

Equally derisively, Terboven made a direct attack on Quisling's attempts to reach some type of settlement that would give his government formal status in its relationship with the Third Reich. The *Reichskommissar's* words left no doubt about whom they were directed against:

> One requests urgently conclusion of a peace, the establishment of a federation, announcement of a kind of Europe Charter (Europe Declaration) etc. – demands that bypass this period's decisive problems and which *der Führer* therefore is not able to fulfill because of well-considered reasons which he clarified for the Minister President during his last visit [August 1943].[153]

Having made these pronouncements, which all too clearly informed the listening NS officials of Germany's intentions, he then proceeded to read a declaration from Hitler containing a pledge for the future. Hitler's statement took on a completely different meaning in the light of what his *Reichskommissar* had just said than it would have done if its text had been allowed to stand alone:

> It is *der Führer's* unalterable will to allow a national and socialist Norway to come into existence in freedom and independence when this fateful struggle is carried to a victorious conclusion – a Norway which only yields to a European community's higher level those functions which at all times are absolutely necessary for Europe's security . . .[154]

In view of what Terboven had declared, Quisling had no guarantee whatsoever as to what form the "national and socialist" Norway would assume. Hitler alone would decide this, and his intentions in reality corresponded exactly with Terboven's brutally frank statements. Norway could expect merely to be a part of a "European community" that was completely under German dominion. In the meantime, the Minister President and his followers could continue to adhere to their assigned role – to aid the German war effort as much as possible. They could expect to serve as tools, nothing more. In his speech, Terboven had again bluntly and directly revealed the basic motive underlying German policy in Norway: "Everything which immediately serves our war effort is important, everything else is unimportant".[155]

The NS "comrades" to whom these words were addressed reacted with understandable alarm. The *Reichskommissar* had repudiated a number of the essential principles which their party stood for, including some of Quisling's most cherished ambitions. If Terboven's pronouncements became public knowledge, NS would stand revealed as a party whose sole reason for existence was to aid in securing a victory that in turn would result in the elimination of Norway as an independent entity. His forceful language was therefore anathema for NS, and his speech was censored. The party administration sent out a secret order to its officers, informing them that: "The speech must be treated in strict secrecy and its contents must not under any circumstances be reported to others".[156]

The order was carried out, but Terboven's bombshell still left the Minister President in a difficult predicament. He could not publicly disavow the *Reichskommissar* – he was in no position to do so. He could only attempt to suppress the speech and to ignore it. On the other hand, Hitler's message required a response – formalities had to be maintained. In his reply, Quisling chose to place special emphasis on his old theme of securing Norwegian independence through NS. *Der Führer's* assurance that a free and independent National Socialist Norway would emerge after the war, answered Quisling, had been "received with the greatest satisfaction".[157] But while he continued to stress this point, this was not an act of defiance on his part. In his telegram to Hitler, he agreed with what *der Führer* expected implicitly and what Terboven had stated explicitly: greater emphasis on Germanic solidarity and more concerted backing for Germany's war effort. Perceiving this signal clearly, Quisling inevitably chose to comply. He pledged to Hitler:

> I recognize that the Norwegian people's fate in this new European order is dependent on an unwavering national and socialistic social order in Norway and a special effort on behalf of the joint victory.
>   I assure you, *Führer*, that Norway to a constantly increasing degree will become conscious of its Germanic and European responsibility, and is willing to make a total commitment to this.[158]

At least to a degree, therefore, Terboven's speech had served its purpose. In his public statements, Quisling thereafter increasingly emphasized Germanic cooperation in defense of "Europe" during the war, and allegiance to the coming Germanic federation once the war had ended in victory. In his propaganda speech of May 15, 1944, attacking the Nygaardsvold government for its agreement with the Allies, especially the U.S.S.R., he strongly emphasized the need for such cooperation, declaring that Norway's fate was tied to Germany's and Europe's fate. But in order to enable Europe to gain victory, he declared, it was necessary for all material resources within the individual parts of the continent to be coordinated militarily, economically, and politically. He pledged that Norway in close cooperation with Germany would work actively toward this goal, insisting that if all of the continent's strength were organized, victory for the "new Europe" would be assured. This, he argued, was the only solution for Norway – the only way to establish a secure foundation for its people's freedom and future.[159]

In his argumentation in favor of greater support for a German victory, he implicitly indicated his recognition that the only way *his* future could possibly be assured lay with a triumphant Third Reich. He remained obsessed with his most basic underlying conviction, which identified *his* fate with Norway's fate. But now that Germany so obviously was losing the war, a strained note of urgency made itself felt in his appeal. It became even more pronounced following the news of the Allied landing in Normandy. In his reaction, he repeated the argument that Norway's destiny was tied to a victorious outcome in favor of Germany. However, during the spring and summer of 1944 a noteworthy change appeared in his emphasis. He no longer stressed the belief that the future would be in the hands of a *Germanic* federation. More and more the emphasis was on the "new Europe", a far more general term than the Germanic racial union that he previously had looked forward to. He now tried to give his arguments more idealism by portraying the war as a struggle between Europe and its culture, defended by Germany, on the one hand, and the alleged evil forces on the other who were seeking to destroy the continent's superior tradition. And whereas he had earlier attempted to rally support from the public through propaganda directed toward Norwegian nationalism, under the new conditions that existed during the final phase of the war he changed his approach by seeking to arouse a feeling of identity with a common European ideal. Norway's fate was now linked to Europe's fate, and a unified Europe had to be created if the continent were to survive and maintain its identity. England and the United States, with their capitalistic and imperialistic interests, and "Bolshevism", with its "red world imperialism", were described as being engaged in a conspiracy to prevent a European union from taking place.[160]

With this change in emphasis, Quisling maintained that the war was not between states or even ideologies. This was a radical departure for someone who for so long had preached against the dangers of "Bolshevik" ideology and who had championed so strongly the ideal of Nordic racial superiority. Now he insisted that historical development had led to a war between *continents*. But in this struggle, only Germany's victorious emergence could guarantee Europe's future because, as *Fritt Folk* put it:

> Germany's National Socialist viewpoint provides also the people of Europe [with] the guarantee that a victorious Germany will not misuse the power which the victory provides, but will honestly and sincerely work to accomplish its historical task to unite Europe on a modern foundation which can satisfy also the individual peoples' need for national development and independent national life within the great union.[161]

While he continued almost to the very end of the war to declare in public his faith in an inevitable victory on behalf of "Europe", a close reading of his speeches in 1943–1944 shows that he felt compelled to take into consideration, at least in part, not merely that Germany had suffered military reverses, but also that internal developments in Norway were not going according to plan and that NS was faced with determined opposition. At a *Hird* rally in October 1943 a note of pessimism became apparent when he commented upon the number of his followers. He admitted that NS simply had too few members to carry out the ambitious goals he had committed his movement to perform. The party, he confirmed, needed to be twice as large, while the *Hird* ideally should have been three to four times its present size. Publicly, however, he continued to maintain an optimistic tone, declaring that it was not impossible to reach the size that he preferred.[162]

By the summer of the next year, however, with the *Wehrmacht* being driven back on all fronts, even he had resigned himself to the fact that there was little chance of increasing National Union's membership. At the end of July he was reduced to declaring his frequently used cliché that quality was what counted, not numbers:

> We know that we in National Union are in agreement with the best in our people (*folk*), and that we express the people's will to live. To what extent the majority is with us or not is not the question today, and is of no decisive importance.[163]

The deteriorating situation within Norway forced him to address other difficult issues as well. He had to admit the existence of active resistance to him and his movement. In his October 1943 address to the *Hird* he referred to "our opponents here at home" who to a greater or lesser degree were active in what he called a "criminal front" that was treasonable to the fatherland. This opposition, he declared, was not just spontaneous; it was encouraged and aided by the exile authorities in England. He focused his attention on them, declaring that King Haakon and his allies were extending the total war's front lines into civilian society by helping to set up illegal organizations and "terror groups". They were also depicted as being guilty of encouraging "boycotts, sabotage, and [use of] explosives" through the spreading of "lies and poison". He maintained nevertheless that this evil influence from abroad could be counteracted, and he assigned the *Hird* its old mission of taking care of internal enemies. Those who aided the exile government, he threatened, would be dealt with forcefully. They would be "rendered completely harmless, if not through persuasion, then through the law of the most powerful".[164]

The fact that the public indicated its support for the exiled King and government was a matter of special concern and irritation for him. In attempting to counteract their influence, he repeatedly showed that he had no remedy other than the usual threat of force. In his speech attacking the Nygaardsvold government on May 15, 1944, for example, he warned that those who obeyed orders or instructions from "the previous king and crown prince or from the emigrant government" were "guilty of treason against the fatherland" and could be punished severely in time of war.[165]

The irony contained herein was not lost on those who were informed about the speech. Here was the man who throughout the world had become the symbol for treason denouncing those who opposed him – persons who considered themselves patriots for being loyal to the legal King and government and who obeyed the directives of the Home Front – of having committed the very crime that he stood accused of.

In 1944 Quisling's attempts at intimidation were less frightening than ever before. His failure to carry out labor mobilization had demonstrated in particular not merely the futility of National Union's endeavor to use force, but also the degree of unity that prevailed against the party and its *Fører*. In turn, NS members' feeling of despondency grew even deeper because of the critical atmosphere in which they lived. Germany was losing the war, the *Fører* was unable to accomplish his objectives, and the overwhelming majority of the people regarded them as pariahs. They were a class of outcasts, against whom the "ice front" was maintained by former friends, acquaintances, and even family members.

Faced with this ever worsening situation, uncertainty and dejection spread within party ranks. Tension grew, and with conditions as bleak as they were by mid-1944, internal dissension was unavoidable. Not merely did there exist discontent within the party because of corruption. In addition, there was some exasperation with the party leadership due to the long series of failures that Quisling had recorded. As an indication of this feeling, Roald Dysthe, who was prominent within NS broadcasting circles, went so far as to write a secret memorandum in the fall of 1944 in which he accused Quisling of being responsible for all existing problems. Dysthe drew the conclusion that the Minister President ought to be replaced by some kind of state council.[166]

Unfortunately for him, the memorandum was discovered by none other than Quisling himself. Predictably, he became highly agitated, convinced that this provided evidence of some kind of a conspiracy against him. As a result, the ever suspicious *Fører* had Dysthe arrested and excluded from NS in November 1944.[167] Quisling's pattern of behavior in this instance was strikingly reminiscent of how he had earlier dealt with internal dissent, although fortunately for his party foes, he did not have the power of arrest at his disposal before the war.

Another indication of opposition to the leadership was provided by Dr. Klaus Hansen, who as professor of medicine had been prominent in NS attempts to take over the University. He also served as head of the Norwegian-German Society (*Norsk-Tysk Selskab*), a society for friendship with Germany. In this capacity, he refused to obey orders from NS officials, and by the spring of 1944 he had gone so far as to attempt to undermine the party administration. Ever vigilant on Quisling's behalf, General Secretary Fuglesang, who had developed a personal animosity toward Hansen, waited for the opportune moment to have the doctor excluded from the party and removed as leader of the Norwegian-German Society.[168]

One thing which Hansen and Dysthe had in common was that they sought support from outside NS. Because of Quisling's total control of the party, opponents of the leadership had no effective alternative during the war except to seek the *Reichskommissariat*'s backing. Dysthe and Hansen were both able to establish close personal contact with members of the German administration. In these two instances, however, such ties did not prove helpful enough. The *Reichskommissariat* did not wish to involve itself in infighting within NS that would have been disruptive, especially as both Dysthe and Hansen committed serious and embarrassing indiscretions.[169] Their exclusion from the party caused no significant repercussions.

Thus, to the very end of his political career, Quisling proved to be irremovable as NS *Fører*. No changes were possible within the party without his agreement. Notwithstanding the many setbacks and defeats that he had experienced, his position remained secure. Because of the absolute authority that he had established over NS already before the war, regardless of the high cost he had sustained due to loss of membership, there was no possibility of removing the *Fører* from within. The *Führer* principle that served as the bedrock for his power prevented any change from taking place. The failure of Dysthe's and Hansen's rather insignificant and certainly ineffectual opposition merely provided added evidence to sustain this fact. National Union continued to be bound by his will to the end. The ultimate control that he maintained over the party served as a microscopic example of the kind of authority he wished to hold over society as a whole.

In addition to the power that he exercised over NS, another advantage which he benefited from as nominal head of government was the material benefits that came with his position. The perquisites that he enjoyed as Minister President help to explain, at least in part, the stubborn manner in which he clung to his post – a characteristic by no means unique to him. His life style had changed considerably from when he had lived on a shoestring before German funds became available, forced to sell his paintings in order to supplement his meager income. He now resided with Maria in a magnificent mansion on the Bygdøy Peninsula, one of the most exclusive suburbs of Oslo. Originally called Villa Grande by the wealthy shipping magnate who constructed the building, but who went bankrupt before it was fully completed, it was renamed Gimle by Quisling. The name did not prove auspicious, but it was highly representative of his historical romanticism. In the mansion named after the saga tradition's home of the gods, where they lived in their new world after the *Ragnarok* which had destroyed the old, he could withdraw into surroundings which he felt were appropriate for his high position. Here he gave free play to his idealization of the Viking period. Gimle's furnishings bore witness to this, often being in a massive neo-Viking style. The entire cellar, for example, was refurbished in this manner, being converted into a large room named the *Hird* hall.[170]

At Gimle the Minister President could at last play the role of the national leader that he had hoped to become. He held lavish receptions and parties for NS members and for distinguished German visitors. The expense was considerable, but that did not cause him any personal concern since the bills were paid by the state. Gimle's wine bill for the first months of 1945, abruptly terminated by Quisling's arrest in May, alone was estimated at more than 50,000 *kroner*. A cursory postwar inventory showed that the wine cellar contained a cache of between six and eight thousand bottles.[171] Quisling insisted that he personally had not contributed to the liquor bill, having maintained his habit as a teetotaler.[172] There is evidence to the contrary, however, which seems to indicate that during the war he relaxed his inhibitions against consuming alcoholic beverages. He was photographed on a number of occasions indulging in what almost certainly appears to be an after-dinner drink with his coffee.[173] There cannot be the slightest doubt, however, concerning his enjoyment of other delights of the table. He grew more and more massive. His many NS uniforms, no matter how carefully tailored, could not disguise the increased number of pounds he had gained. His added weight, combined with his usual dour image, gave him an even more phlegmatic appearance than before.

The life style that caused such visible changes in his appearance was made possible by a tremendous improvement in his financial position. From being almost a bourgeois pauper before the war, he had received an income of 100,000 *kr.* a year during the period of the Commissarial Council when he, technically speaking, held no official position. His salary jumped to 240,000 *kr.* when he became Minister President, and by 1944 it had reached 400,000 *kr.* a year.[174] Especially advantageous for him was the decision by his old friend, Frederik Prytz, in his capacity as Finance Minister, which decreed that the Minister President did not have to pay taxes.[175]

In addition to his tax-free income, Quisling also used state funds for improvements on his personal properties. More than 5,300,000 *kr.* were spent on Gimle. An additional 1,433,000 *kr.* were disbursed for work on his "cabin", located outside of Oslo in Asker. Appropriately enough, considering his standard imitation of Hitler, he named it the Eagle's Nest (*Ørneredet*).[176]

The *Fører* also benefited substantially from his leadership of NS. When he celebrated a birthday or an important party anniversary, he delighted in receiving gifts from various party organizations. In consideration of his taste, these were often replicas of Viking antiquities, frequently in silver. To cite but one example, on his fifty-seventh birthday in 1944 he received a set of elaborate silver knives from the Second Police Company, then performing military service on the Finnish front in Russia.[177]

The gifts he obtained could also be in money. The most noteworthy occurred when Prytz presented him with 300,000 *kr.* which the Finance Minister had collected from various "friends" of the Minister President who wished to remain anonymous. Perhaps because he was all too familiar with Prytz' business practices, Quisling made no effort to inquire closely into who the "friends" were who had contributed this rather munificent sum. The funds were spent for improvements on the Eagle's Nest and on the Quisling farm in Fyresdal.[178]

Beyond the use of such gratuities and his state income, he employed other means of enhancing his surroundings. The saying "to the victor belong the spoils" was certainly applicable to him. At the elaborate parties at Gimle, as well as in the Eagle's Nest and at his properties in Fyresdal, were silverware, china, furniture, and paintings that he had expropriated and taken into personal use. These had belonged to individuals or institutions that were considered to be enemies of NS, politically or ideologically. Most prominent were valuables that had been owned by members of the royal family, the Masonic Lodge in Oslo, and the Norwegian Society (*Det Norske Selskab*), an exclusive club for Oslo's establishment which was regarded as a *jøssing* stronghold.[179] In order not to give their users a clue as to the original owner's identity, the monograms on the silverware were frequently removed. Similarly, the name plates on the paintings were replaced with Quisling's initials.[180]

He also took advantage of his position in order to increase his property holdings significantly. His acquisition of Gimle through use of state funds occurred already before he took office as Minister President. The Eagle's Nest not only benefited from a considerable expansion of the "cabin" itself, but additional land was also acquired for the property. He accomplished this by taking over an adjoining parcel, owned by a fund for needy persons suffering from tuberculosis.[181] The fact that he virtually expropriated land from a charitable organization aroused considerable comment, but at least he paid for the property, some 12,500 *kr.* [182] The same was not true concerning the manner in which he took title to the parsonage in Fyresdal. He had been born and spent his early boyhood here, but it belonged to the state, like most parsonages in Norway. This proved no longer to be a hindrance, however, now that he, at least formally, was head of state. Skancke, as Minister of Church and Education, simply deeded the property free of charge to the Minister President.[183] As justification for his takeover, Quisling later argued that the parsonage had earlier been part of his family's holdings in Fyresdal, and that he wished to prevent it from falling into decay.[184]

Feelings of family responsibility could be exhibited in other ways. He used his office for the benefit of relatives, providing them with presents and exercising his influence on their behalf.[185] In every fashion the master of Gimle had therefore acquired what he wanted as far as the *outward* trappings of power were concerned – wealth, property, luxury, and influence. But on a comparative scale, this study has shown that after 1942, as his personal wealth increased, so his political status declined.

He never accepted his reduced standing with resignation. Until the very end of the occupation he strove to escape from the impasse he was in. He and his immediate advisers remained convinced that only one solution could bring him and his movement out of their impotent condition. An agreement would have to be worked out with the Germans which would provide the National Government with clearly defined political legitimacy. This alone, they felt, could convince the hostile public that the government had authority and was capable of protecting Norwegian interests.

Before this could be accomplished, however, Quisling and his closest confidants were preoccupied with the major prerequisite that had to be concluded – the signing of the long-desired peace treaty with Germany. Only after it had been secured could his sovereign position as head of government be truly confirmed. But such a possibility to all intents and purposes remained an impossibility. As previously shown, Hitler in increasingly less diplomatic language had indicated his opposition to any agreement, culminating with his unambiguous message in August 1942 that no such settlement could be made until after the war.[186] But despite the clarity of his edict, the Minister President could find no alternative except to try to discover some means by which he might be able to change *der Führer*'s attitude.

Such a likelihood might materialize, Quisling's advisers felt, if wartime conditions worsened to such an extent that it could appear to be in Hitler's interest to agree to a peace treaty. Quisling and his counselors therefore constantly sought to turn Germany's deteriorating military fortunes in 1943–1944 to their advantage, using arguments based on current conditions to justify the alleged need for an agreement. Finn Støren, who became Quisling's closest adviser on foreign policy from 1943 onwards, was blessed with a fertile imagination, which he put to use on the Minister President's behalf. An ex-consul for Costa Rica, Støren did not possess especially imposing credentials, but he had the ability to marshal convincing foreign policy arguments on behalf of the National Government in spite of its feeble condition. He noted in August 1943 how Mussolini's overthrow and arrest had resulted in great loss of prestige for Germany. Støren submitted the opinion that Germany's repute could be restored and strengthened if the Third Reich now concluded formal peace settlements with those countries that were under its occupation. This would lead to a lessening of tension with the occupied peoples, he maintained, allowing political factions that cooperated with Germany, such as NS, to take part in the war effort with renewed strength.[187]

He presented this and similar arguments to German officials whenever a convenient occasion arose.[188] But standing in the way of the settlement that Quisling and Støren so urgently desired was the state of war that had existed since April 1940, plus the added hindrance that Germany had taken advantage of the rights which an occupying power enjoyed whenever this was judged opportune. While opinions within NS were divided over the question of whether or not Germany was at war with Norway, Støren declared categorically that such a condition existed. He quite realistically pointed out that a large part of the public therefore considered it to be their duty to give their allegiance to the government in exile and to obey its instructions as long as conditions remained unchanged.[189]

Not everyone in NS, however, shared Støren's opinion. Quisling at least publicly always asserted that a state of war no longer was in effect. Aware of this attitude, Frederik Prytz expressed his views carefully when he sent a memorandum on this subject to Quisling at a later date, in September 1944. Prytz maintained that he personally felt that a state of war did not exist. But he had to admit that certain German actions, including the arrest of Norwegian officers and the seizure of Norwegian ships as war prizes, certainly provided persuasive evidence for those who believed the contrary. Most Norwegians, he conceded, agreed with the exile government that a condition of war still prevailed.[190]

This perception, leading NS members would argue, in turn shaped the people's negative attitude toward Germany. Støren in particular was quite critical of the Reich's occupation policy, declaring as early as August 1943 that Norwegians generally felt that they had been subjugated not only militarily and politically, but also economically. Many were therefore of the opinion, he asserted, that Norway was on its way toward becoming a German economic colony.[191] In the fall of the following year he wrote even more bluntly that the Third Reich's policies had not succeeded in gaining friends for Germany in Europe. On the contrary, its politics had everywhere – except possibly in Finland – created strong enmity.[192] A number of prominent NS figures agreed with Støren that this anti-German attitude was also directed against those who cooperated with German authorities for idealistic reasons. He candidly observed that the people were of the belief that Quisling's administration acted on behalf of the occupying power without consideration of its own country's interests.[193]

Such critical arguments did not bring any noticeable results. The Minister President, Støren, and other leading NS dignitaries presented these opinions privately to German officials, both to functionaries in the *Reichskommissariat* and to visitors from Berlin, in an effort to gain sympathy and win support for Quisling's standpoint.[194] They received a polite, at times even friendly, reception, but nothing more. Frequently the listeners could not have provided direct aid even if they had been so inclined because they were lower ranking officials who could do nothing more than write reports to their superiors on what had been discussed.

In an attempt to maneuver the National Government into a more independent position through using a somewhat different approach, Støren in March 1944 discussed with members of the *Ostministerium* in Berlin the possibility that Quisling's government might be given responsibility for administering a German occupied area in Russia. In a confidential memorandum, he reported to Quisling that this in part was intended to demonstrate to world opinion the possibility of cooperation between free sovereign states within Germany's Europe. More importantly, however, with

Quisling's government assuming such jurisdiction, Støren hoped to set up an office in Germany which would eventually evolve into an embassy. If successful, Quisling would thereby have gained a potential means of eliminating the *Reichskommissariat*'s dominating control. Støren openly informed the officials with whom he dealt that the NS government's goal was to reduce the *Reichskommissariat* either to an embassy or to the office of a Reich plenipotentiary.[195]

Writing somewhat more circumspectly in June to Werner von Grundherr in the Foreign Ministry, who had earlier been on a visit to Oslo, Støren insisted that a Norwegian office in Berlin was intended to act as a means of coordinating operations with various German administrative departments. For the time being, it was therefore not intended to serve as an independent diplomatic agency.[196]

The Red Army's steady offensive against retreating German forces brought the unlikely possibility of a Norwegian protectorate in the east to a conclusive end. Even more improbable was the prospect of obtaining improvement in the Quisling government's status through the *Reichskommissariat*. Støren had forwarded his critical comments concerning the relationship between Germany and Norway to the *Reichskommissariat*, including a proposed peace agreement. In response, Terboven invited Støren to coffee on September 20. Their discussion took place in a cordial atmosphere, but no one was surprised when Støren failed to win acceptance for his views. Instead, Terboven as usual dominated the conversation, harping in particular on why *Quisling* and *Hagelin* were responsible for the absence of a settlement between Germany and Norway because of their sabotage of his attempt to establish a State Council in 1940.[197]

Considering Terboven's attitude toward Quisling, plus the fact that he had long known that one of Quisling's primary goals was to eliminate the *Reichskommissariat*, this outcome was hardly unexpected. Even before Støren's meeting with Terboven it was clear that the only chance which the Quisling government had for a change in status rested as always with the head of the Third Reich. Through his German contacts, Støren had emphasized in August the need for a meeting between Quisling and Hitler. The time for such a conference, he insisted, was running out.[198]

Terboven was not particularly forthcoming about this matter either. In his conversation with Støren he condescendingly declared that he would have no objections if Quisling wished to send some written comments to *der Führer*, but he did not foresee the possibility of a conference in the immediate future because Hitler was too busy.[199] Despite these dampening words, at this time or shortly thereafter Quisling received assurance that he *would* be granted his desired interview with *der Führer*.[200] This prospect set off a period of rather feverish activity within the Quisling administration in preparation for the coming meeting, which the ministers, along with their chief, hoped would lead to a decisive change in his favor.

When he marshalled the arguments that he intended to present to Hitler, Quisling wished to give the impression that his views did not represent his opinion alone, but instead had broad backing among the people. Because of the importance which he attached to the upcoming meeting, various drafts concerning the National Government's need for a peace settlement were circulated among the ministers and other high NS officials within the administration.[201] Prytz in particular took an active part in drawing up position papers. It was one of his proposals, dated September 25, 1944, which Quisling adopted. After having been submitted to the Minister President for his approval, it was endorsed unanimously by the ministers on September 28.[202] Because the document represented Quisling's official position, it deserves specific attention.

As Quisling and his chief spokesmen had earlier endeavored, but now with greater plausibility, Prytz sought to use the worsening war situation as a means of gaining concessions. With Finland's recent capitulation, he foresaw, quite correctly, the possibility that the *Wehrmacht*, for strategic reasons, would be forced to retreat from a part of northern Norway. Russian or other Allied troops, he argued, would thereupon certainly occupy the vacated territory. Once this had been carried out, the exiled government would undoubtedly establish its presence in the north. This would enable it to demand support from the general population with increased strength, being able to declare, said Prytz, that it alone was the legitimate government which fought to regain Norwegian freedom and independence.[203]

This argument would be especially effective, he declared, because of the existing governmental situation in Norway. Presenting a view that the Minister President had always adhered to, Prytz maintained that contrary to what NS "and the great majority of the Norwegian people" had expected when the National Government was formed, the *Reichskommissar* had retained his power and used his office to limit the NS administration's functions. This, said Prytz, had had a "humiliating and irritating effect", going on to declare that with a certain amount of justification it could be stated that "the National Government cannot be said to represent an independent Norwegian administration, but is only a form of administration under German leadership".[204]

Only an immediate change in the NS government's standing *before* representatives of the exiled government had arrived in northern Norway, he insisted, could rescue the situation. What was needed was "clear lines in Norway's relationship with the Greater German Reich" in order to give the National Government a solid foundation of authority. He thereupon recommended that the Minister President should seek to have Hitler agree to four specific principles: (1) that a condition of peace existed and had always existed between the Third Reich and Norway, represented by the National Government; (2) that the Minister President as "regent" assumed full governmental authority; (3) that Germany would respect Norway's "freedom, independence, indivisible character, and inalienability"; (4) that the *Reichskommissariat* be withdrawn and that Germany be represented in Norway by an embassy, while Norway in turn would establish an embassy in Berlin.[205]

These four points in essence represented the basic goals that Quisling had always sought to obtain from the Germans: a peace settlement, full governmental power for his administration, elimination of the *Reichskommissariat*, and diplomatic representation abroad. If these concessions were not made, Prytz predicted a gloomy prospect for the Germans. The great majority of Norwegians, he stated mendaciously, still maintained a neutral attitude toward the National Government, being willing to work "loyally" as long as they perceived that Quisling's administration was acting in the country's best interests. But if they saw that the NS government had little chance of securing freedom and independence for Norway, Prytz feared that the people would more and more give their support to the exiled government and follow its directives to a greater degree than before. "The National Government's position will thereby become impossible, and the situation could lead to chaos which in the last instance could become a serious threat for the German occupation of Norway".[206]

While Prytz had regained his position as Quisling's key internal political adviser, the Minister President possessed in Finn Støren a capable counselor in the area of external relations. In recognition of his ability, and also as an indication of his lingering hope of gaining concessions from Germany, Quisling in September appointed Støren as the National Government's special envoy for foreign policy matters. But because the Quisling government never obtained diplomatic status, Støren was popularly known simply as the Minister President's "unofficial foreign minister".[207]

When seeking arguments that might prove useful for Quisling, Støren laid special weight on the situation in Scandinavia. Germany, he declared caustically, was now paying the price for having followed a policy of isolating the Nordic countries from each other. By not permitting NS authorities to establish contact with the other Scandinavian states, he argued, an important opportunity had been lost. And now as a result of this imposed isolation, Sweden was increasingly assuming the position of leading a front against Germany in Scandinavia. This trend had been strengthened by Finland's capitulation, followed by its recognition of the Norwegian and Danish exile governments. If this development continued, he contended, then there was a real possibility of fratricidal civil war within Scandinavia, with Sweden entering the war in opposition to Germany and to those within Scandinavia who still remained loyal to the Third Reich. He therefore urged recognition of the alleged fact that the policy of dividing the Nordic countries not only had weakened Germany, but also had been detrimental to all groups that had committed themselves to the German cause. Because of its current isolation, he continued, there was no possibility for the Quisling government to contribute toward altering this situation.[208]

Only a change in German policy, he maintained, could reverse the deteriorating situation in northern Europe. The key to this possibility was Finland's difficulties. Støren argued that the Soviet Union's severe treatment of Finland was arousing concern in Sweden. This issue, he insisted, should be exploited for the purpose of creating a Scandinavian union against the danger from the east. The Quisling government, he proclaimed, could serve as the instrument which carried out the ambitious scheme of changing Sweden's position from anti-German to anti-Soviet. The possibility of a civil war in the north would thereby be eliminated.[209]

Støren insisted that this goal could be attained only if the following preconditions were met: (1) Quisling's long sought-after peace settlement and the elimination of the *Reichskommissariat*; (2) the creation of an independent Danish government composed of representatives from agriculture, industry, and labor; (3) permission for the Norwegian and Danish governments to enjoy diplomatic representation and to pursue independent foreign policies; (4) cooperation among German, Norwegian, and Danish authorities toward setting up a Finnish government in exile, preferably in Norway; (5) the three pro-German "governments" – Norwegian, Danish, and Finnish – would immediately establish contact with Sweden in order to secure its cooperation in a united Nordic front against the Soviet Union.[210]

While Støren certainly perceived Germany's increasingly desperate condition clearly, his suggestion for change in Scandinavia was utopian to say the least. Like Prytz' proposals, Støren's arguments were intended to rescue Quisling from his locked-in position by allowing him greater independence within the bounds of political and military cooperation. With this in mind, he and his advisers were not content merely with the general terms of a peace agreement. They proceeded in the fall of 1944 to draw up a document which was complete down to the most minute details. It was forwarded to Germany upon completion. All it needed was Hitler's and Quisling's signatures.[211]

This procedure hardly created surprise in Berlin. By this time German authorities, from Hitler on down, were well acquainted with Quisling's penchant for drafting ambitious projects on paper. But neither the peace proposal nor the arguments that the critical situation in Scandinavia required immediate attention brought the results that he and his confidants had hoped for. During the second half of 1944 Hitler was far too concerned with the Allied advance in the west and the Russian drive from the east to turn his attention to political considerations in Scandinavia. Terboven proved indeed to have been correct when he insisted in September that *der Führer* was too busy to meet the Minister President in the immediate future. Quisling did not receive his promised audience until January 1945. By this time the situation in Scandinavia, as elsewhere in Europe, had become much worse for the Third Reich and its collaborators.

The course of events showed that Prytz and Støren were correct when they predicted that German forces would have to evacuate parts of northern Norway. They were not, however, uniquely prophetic. Already at the end of August or in early September this possibility had been discussed between Quisling, Terboven, and *Wehrmacht* officers.[212] It was quite probably on the basis of information derived from such talks that Prytz and Støren wrote their commentaries.

With Finland forced to sign an armistice with the Soviet Union in September, followed by a Finnish declaration of war against the Third Reich on October 1, the possibility of withdrawal in the north became a certainty now that the German forces retreating from Finnish territory into Norway were in an exposed position, inviting a Russian attack. In early October the OKW decided to evacuate all of Finnmark province and the northern part of Troms province. Russian attacks speeded up this process. The Germans were driven back, and on October 18 Soviet forces crossed the Norwegian border. The *Wehrmacht* rapidly retreated from eastern Finnmark, but the Russians refrained from launching a vigorous pursuit. Stalin gave higher priority to winning the war on other fronts. The last engagement occurred on November 6. Thereafter the Russians halted, being content to occupy the South Varanger region in eastern Finnmark.[213]

In carrying out its strategic retreat, the *Wehrmacht* pursued a devastatingly destructive scorched earth policy. Anything that could be of value for the Russians was demolished or removed. This included the Norwegian population in the north, who were deported in order to prevent them from providing aid to the Russians. But before taking action, German authorities first discussed this question with Quisling.[214] He voiced no objections, especially as the Germans intended to allow his NS administration to assume responsibility for the evacuation. He was quick to perceive an opportunity to improve the status of the National Government, which had been so devastated by the failure of labor mobilization.

He was not alone in recognizing the advantages his regime might gain if it succeeded in carrying out such a major operation. The Norwegian government in England, through Foreign Minister Trygve Lie, advised the Swedish government not to aid refugees from northern Norway who wished to travel through Sweden, declaring that an evacuation would be "exploited by the Quisling authorities for political propaganda against Russia".[215] Similarly, the Home Front's first directive concerning the removal of the population declared that the deportees should not be given assistance because this would benefit the Germans militarily.[216]

In spite of the fact that a successful evacuation might bring luster to his government, Quisling had considerable difficulty in obtaining help from his NS subordinates in carrying out the project. They recognized that no personal benefits would be gained from being associated with such an unpopular venture. Quisling first asked Hagelin to head the operation in his capacity as Minister of the Interior. The latter declined, citing poor health. He supported this with a medical statement, and avoided any involvement by immediately taking leave of absence.[217] Similarly, General Frølich-Hanssen refused to comply when Quisling attempted to have the Labor Service play a leading part in the evacuation. The general maintained that it was impossible to build up and strengthen A-T to the point that it could participate.[218] In the end Quisling was reduced to having to pressure two of his ministers, Lie and Lippestad, into leading the evacuation for the National Government.[219] Lie was placed in overall charge of the project with the title "Coordinator (*Styresmann*) for Finnmark", while Lippestad was appointed second-in-command.[220]

The two flew north on October 11, with Lippestad returning to Oslo the very next day in order to brief Quisling and the ministers on conditions in Finnmark. After several days of consultations, Lippestad again went back to northern Norway to aid in trying to put the NS evacuation into effect.[221]

The plan that Quisling's ministers attempted to implement was hastily improvised and poorly formulated. It was based on voluntary compliance. At first NS officials did not even issue a formal announcement concerning evacuation, but attempted to frighten people into leaving their homes through a "whispering propaganda" campaign. This approach proved unproductive and was soon abandoned.[222] Instead, Lie announced publicly on October 17 that voluntary evacuation had gone into effect. He sought to panic the population into departing by describing the alleged horrors that would await them under the Russians if they did not leave. He warned ominously that a "superior people" such as the Norwegians could expect a dire fate, including "murder and plunder, terror and despotism, rape, ungodliness and moral decay".[223]

To Lie's considerable surprise, his scare tactics had no effect. He later admitted that he had miscalculated the population's lack of fear of "Bolshevism" and its willingness to accept the danger of being caught in a battle zone.[224] Not only in northern Norway but throughout the entire country the Russians were generally regarded as liberators, not as the depraved *Untermenschen* depicted in Quisling's NS propaganda. National Union's anti-Russian publicity appears indeed to have had the opposite result from what he desired – it tended to legitimize the Russians in the popular mind. This was borne out by the fact that the Communist party enjoyed the highest electoral support it has ever received in the first postwar election.

When it was obvious that the Quisling administration's voluntary evacuation had no chance of succeeding, the Germans intervened. Terboven recommended total destruction in the north and forcible removal of the population. Hitler agreed, sending the *Reichskommissar* a *Führer* decree on the night of October 28 which imposed a scorched earth policy, with no consideration being given to the wishes of the people.[225]

Beginning on October 30, the inhabitants of Finnmark and northern Troms were systematically driven from their homes by German troops. Some 50,000 people were evacuated, most by small fishing boats. The *Wehrmacht* insisted on having sole use of the coastal road. Not everyone, however, complied with the deportation. In particular in eastern Finnmark, where the Russian advance occurred rapidly, and in the interior plateau area, some 23,000–25,000 people avoided the roundup. On a number of coastal islands groups of people also escaped from Nazi deportation by overwintering in caves and other primitive shelters.[226]

When carrying out their withdrawal, the Germans burnt and destroyed everything that could possibly be of any use to the Red Army. The result was that hardly a structure remained standing between the Lyngenfjord in northern Troms and those areas in eastern Finnmark that the Russians had liberated quickly. A whole section of the country had to be rebuilt after the war, and the inhabitants had to reorganize their lives completely.

German force alone was responsible for the deportation and destruction. NS officials, from Lie and Lippestad on down, simply assisted as best they could when their aid was needed, but Quisling's administrators played no independent role. They merely served their German superiors. Consequently, Quisling gained nothing from the part which NS played in the forced deportation – not even the hatred of those who saw their homes go up in flames and who faced an uncertain future when packed on board the teeming fishing boats. This hatred was reserved for the Germans, and justly so. Their responsibility for the deportation was obvious, while National Union's role was insignificant.

This feeble activity on the part of the Minister President's administration proved to be the last project of any significance which it attempted to perform. The almost total manner in which NS officials were overshadowed by the Germans in carrying out the evacuation provided a good illustration of how Quisling's movement had declined. Although the deportation was largely a military effort in which even the *Reichskommissariat* played a subordinate role, it indicated how, in 1944, the Germans regarded NS administrators as menial helpers, nothing more. This impotence stood in considerable contrast to the ambitious determination of the newly appointed Minister President in 1942, when he had been given an opportunity to try to carry out some of his most fundamental goals.

CHAPTER XVII

Collapse

January 1945 – May 9, 1945

Who do you think will be ranked highest in Norwegian history: Haakon the last and his men who betrayed Norway to Bolshevism, or we in National Union who at a decisive turning point maintained the Norwegian people's national independence and led them into a new historical epoch?

Vidkun Quisling, radio address,
January 1, 1945

In some things we have perhaps failed, and in many things we have not, under the war's pressure, gained what we aspired. But no one can rightfully deny our honest will, nor that we also have carried out a great effort for [our] country and [its] people.

Vidkun Quisling, radio address,
May 5, 1945

When Vidkun Quisling gave his last New Year's address in the evening of Monday, January 1, 1945, his small number of listeners, mostly NS members who still retained their radios, had little reason to feel encouraged. The war in Europe was nearing its end. In the west German forces were once more retreating before superior American and British armies following Hitler's last desperate offensive, the Battle of the Bulge. In the east the Russians were poised to strike against the weakened *Wehrmacht* defenders, whose forces had been depleted by the removal of divisions to the west, to take part in the ill-fated offensive in the Ardennes. Within three months, units of the Western Allies would make contact with the Red Army in the midst of the ruins of the "Thousand Year Reich".

In spite of Germany's impending collapse, many NS members continued to hope that somehow the situation might be saved, perhaps by the sudden introduction of new miracle weapons that would rescue the Reich.[1] Quisling shared this feeling almost to the very end of the war. But in his radio address he had little specific encouragement for the party faithful. All he could do was to admonish them to be strong and to maintain their zeal on National Union's behalf. Only if the Norwegian people joined the party's crusade could the country be saved, and prophetically he used a biblical analogy to propagandize against his number one obsession: the threat of a communist takeover. The Norwegian people, he warned, had but two roads to choose: either National Union's "narrow way" to national rebirth or "Bolshevism's broad road to perdition".[2]

In spite of his recurrent anti-Communist theme, which he never abandoned, and the guarded optimism he expressed concerning an eventual German victory, the tone of the speech as a whole was defensive, even pessimistic. Indirectly, the *Fører* showed that he recognized the possibility of the enemy being victorious. He defended the manner in which NS had "governed" during the previous years, while admitting the fact that many Norwegians disagreed because they believed in the "royal *jøssing* propaganda" against NS. He was especially critical of the symbol in whom the majority of Norwegians placed their faith, King Haakon. The King stood accused of making war against his own people and of preparing the way for a Bolshevik takeover of the country. The bitterness of his attack against the King, and also against the government in exile, indicated the chagrin he felt that they, not he, were on the winning side in the war. Precisely because of this unspoken recognition, he voiced on the other hand a fanciful desire to reach some type of reconciliation with those who opposed him. He wished all his countrymen at home and abroad a happy new year, declaring that everyone wished "to save and not destroy our fatherland". He expressed the hope that since concurrence could be reached about this goal, then perhaps it might be possible to agree on the means to attain it.[3]

The process he referred to was his leadership. Even at this late date he could conceive of no other alternative than himself and his party. It therefore continued to be a great disappointment for him that he remained in a supportive, subordinate role in his relationship with the Germans. As before, only through their good will would it be possible for him to realize any of his ambitions. Consequently, he assured Hitler of his cooperation in the coming year, and less sincerely also promised the *Reichskommissar*, whom he still hoped to remove, his continued collaboration: "I am convinced that all problems that affect Norway also in the future will be solved in friendly cooperation with you, *herr Reichskommissar*. To make this cooperation more and more intimate is my wish and that of my colleagues".[4]

Contrary to what he wrote to Terboven, Quisling no longer placed his faith in acting in accord with the Germans as the sole means by which he might be able to attain his desire for greater independence. As we have seen, he and his major foreign policy adviser, Støren, had hoped since 1943 that the worsening military situation might force Hitler to make a peace settlement as a concession to Norwegian national feeling. But the meeting with Hitler at which Quisling intended to bring up this subject had been repeatedly postponed during the fall and winter of 1944–45.[5] It was subsequently alleged that the delay resulted from Terboven's demand that Hagelin be removed as Minister of the Interior. Not until this price had been paid would Quisling be allowed to confer with Hitler.[6] But Hagelin's resignation became effective on November 8, 1944, and still there was not the slightest indication that the desired meeting could now proceed.[7] As late as January 17, 1945, Støren continued to complain that the time for discussion of Norway's sovereignty had been postponed indefinitely.[8]

Considering Hitler's preoccupation with military planning during this period, the repeated delays in the meeting with *der Führer* were understandable. When the Minister President was finally allowed to come to Berlin, his visit was arranged at very short notice. Already on January 20, Quisling, accompanied by Støren, arrived in the battered capital, here to begin what the two considered to be *the* decisive discussions – resulting in what they hoped would be Hitler's grant of greater freedom for Quisling to act as the leader of a sovereign country.[9]

The importance which Quisling and Støren attached to this visit was further underlined by the fact that they remained for more than a week in Berlin. During this time the Minister President met with Hitler on several occasions. These sessions were relatively brief, however, since *der Führer*'s attention was riveted on the *Wehrmacht*'s shrinking front lines. In the intervals between his talks with Hitler, Quisling and his Norwegian subordinates concentrated on attempting to gain support for their cause from influential persons within the Nazi hierarchy. Discussions were held with Goebbels' and Himmler's representatives, and with Quisling's old ally, Rosenberg.[10] Expressions of sympathy by Goebbels and Himmler were interpreted much too positively by Støren as an indication of backing for Quisling.[11]

While the Minister President and his associates were working to secure his interests, another high-ranking visitor from Norway was doing his utmost, as always, to frustrate Quisling's objectives. The *Reichskommissar* never failed to be present in Berlin whenever top-level discussions concerning Norway occurred. He was not disappointed by their outcome on this occasion. Hitler concluded his final meeting with Quisling by continuing to adhere to exactly the same point of view that Terboven had always advocated. Quisling's request for a peace settlement was rejected once more, which meant that the *Reichskommissariat* remained in Norway. Prominent NS officers, Støren among them, tended therefore to conclude that Quisling's mission had stranded largely because of Terboven's influence.[12] This view rather naively failed to recognize that Hitler had never intended to weaken German control. Such a possibility was more remote than ever in January 1945 because of the *Führer*'s mania against making concessions that could be interpreted as a sign of weakness. The Germans had scheduled Quisling's visit, as earlier, largely for propaganda purposes, intended to give the impression that Hitler consulted with his declining number of European vassals.[13]

Following a farewell session between *Führer* and *Fører*, the last time they would ever see each other, a communiqué was issued containing the usual polite diplomatic phrases. The discussions were described as having been "trustful and cordial", with "complete agreement and candid understanding" having been reached concerning all questions of joint interest. But on the vital issue of a peace settlement, the communiqué stated exactly the opposite of what Quisling wished to hear. *Der Führer* reconfirmed precisely the same view that he had authorized Terboven to state on his behalf in September 1943: that "Norway's full freedom and independence" would be re-established only after the victorious conclusion of the war, with Norway at that time assuming the responsibilities that were in accord with the security of the European community.[14] Hitler's unwillingness to use more precise language provided but additional proof of his unaltered determination to retain Norway under the domination of the Greater German Reich.

Quisling understandably was despondent following this decisive rebuff, complaining strongly that Hitler too had now gone back on his word. But he did not for a minute consider a break with Germany. Instead, he asked his low-level representatives in Berlin to continue to work on his behalf.[15]

Støren, upon his return to Norway, issued a report to the NS ministers in which he was equally dejected, complaining how highly disheartening it was that this should be the result of nearly five years of struggle and loyalty.[16] He did affirm, much too optimistically, that the National Government had obtained assurance that Norway would regain its sovereignty if Germany won the war. On the other hand, he bemoaned how deeply discouraging it was to have the country continue to lack such sovereignty. The present situation, he maintained, placed the National Government in great difficulties because there was no way to disguise the fact that Germany had been unwilling to agree to grant a peace agreement.[17]

The only conclusion that the ministers could draw was that the situation remained frozen. The *Reichskommissar* and his administrative apparatus continued to be dominant, while the Minister President and his administration stayed in their dependent positions. After his last meeting with Hitler, Quisling could no longer even hope for a change in status as long as the war lasted. This was explicitly confirmed at a "*fører* meeting" of the most prominent NS officers, held on February 17–19, 1945. Both Terboven and Quisling spoke at the gathering. Here again emphasis was placed on the necessity to postpone the question of restoration of Norwegian sovereignty until after the war was over.[18]

With his supremacy over Quisling reconfirmed, Terboven could even afford to be somewhat magnanimous. On the occasion of the third anniversary of the formation of the National Government, the *Reichskommissariat*
announced that the *Storting* building, which German administrators had
occupied since April 1940, would be "returned to Norwegian authorities".
Fritt Folk printed a photograph of the building with the caption: "The
Norwegian flag flies again over the *Storting*". But while the NS paper pathetically tried to give the impression that this was a historic occasion, it
signified no change whatsoever. Neither Terboven nor Quisling bothered
to attend the ceremony marking the event. The *Reichskommissar* was represented by one of his subordinates, Dr. Koch, while the newly appointed
Minister of the Interior, Arnvid Vassbotten, did the honors for the National Government.[19]

Quisling's inability to gain concessions at the January meetings with
Hitler did cause his government to try to modify its dealings with German
authorities to a certain degree. Støren at the first ministerial conference
held after Quisling's return, pointed out in his report of February 1 that
the Minister President's government had but two alternatives. The first option was to resign, but even Støren, who preferred to have Quisling follow
as independent a policy as possible, did not recommend this course. Resignation, he warned, would allegedly lead to chaos. In his opinion, the National Government therefore was required to continue in office because of
the heavy obligation it had assumed. Nevertheless, he urged that it should
now recognize explicitly that a state of war existed *de jure* between Germany and Norway, and should act accordingly. While it should seek to
oppose all so-called destructive tendencies and work to maintain law and
order, it should also look well after the Norwegian people's interests vis-à-
vis what he now termed the foreign civilian administration. In this fashion,
Støren proposed that Quisling's ministers should adopt a less compliant,
even somewhat antagonistic, attitude toward the *Reichskommissariat*.[20]

Quisling was unwilling to go so far as to recognize the existence of a *de
jure* state of war, but in the months after the January meeting it became apparent that there was less inclination on the part of NS ministers to be as
deferential as earlier in carrying out projects which economically were
solely of benefit for Germany. Støren had earlier, before the ill-fated conference with Hitler, urged linkage between the National Government's
economic cooperation and German recognition of Norwegian
sovereignty.[21] When such recognition was not forthcoming, Støren's advice was implemented, although very cautiously. Even Alf Whist, previously noted for his close ties with the *Reichskommissariat*, now displayed
a different outlook. When Senator Otte, in his capacity as leader of the
Reichskommissariat's *Abteilung Arbeit und Sozialwesen*, sought in February and March 1945 to carry out the drafting of "antisocial and work-shy
elements" into the Work Effort, Whist was not forthcoming. His car on

one occasion inexplicably broke down, preventing him from attending a key meeting. He procrastinated in other ways as well, offering objections to the scheme, which included the old suggestion to withhold ration cards from those who refused to take part. His obstructionist tactics were successful. Otte, who had previously benefited from a good working relationship with the NS minister, was now reduced to writing critical letters in which he tried to force the reluctant Whist to commit himself.[22]

A number of additional developments occurred within the National Government as well as in the wake of Quisling's January 1945 meeting with Hitler. During the previous fall, when preparations for the anticipated discussions were at their height, some of Quisling's close associates, already looking beyond the expected peace settlement, were making plans for policy and personnel changes within the NS administration. Ørnulf Lundesgaard, as head of Quisling's chancellery, wrote a memorandum at the end of October 1944 in which he proposed that once Norway's constitutional position had been clarified, the National Government should concentrate on carrying out an active social policy on behalf of the public. Moreover, he suggested that those policies which during the past years had been "most irritating for a large part of our people" should be abandoned and transferred to the German administration. NS, he argued, should now concentrate on attempting to realize the "socialistic" planks within its program. To accomplish this radical change, he further suggested a wholesale alteration in personnel within the government. Quisling should be elevated to the position of regent, with a prime minister serving under him. In addition, Lundesgaard recommended that no less than six of the current ministers should be replaced: Hagelin, Stang, Riisnæs, Prytz, Lippestad, and Lie. Most interesting of the points raised in the proposal was Lundesgaard's suggestion that Lie's unpopular Police Department should be eliminated entirely.[23]

The extreme nature of these recommendations was but one of many indications of the realization within NS that the situation was so desperate that something drastic had to be done in a last-ditch effort to gain popular acceptance. Lundesgaard was not alone in considering such internal political changes. Among leading NS figures, at least Støren and Sverre Riisnæs were similarly in accord with Lundesgaard's desire for a radical new policy, and others appear to have been involved as well. Some time in early 1945 the trio provided Quisling with a proposed wholesale reorganization of the departments within the government.[24]

Not all NS officials were enthusiastic about this recommendation. Alf Whist in particular was horrified when he learned of the proposal these three *"Dummköpfe"*, as he described them, had come up with, and he immediately passed this information on to the *Reichskommissariat*. Whist's reaction was understandable. His economic outlook was regarded as much too "liberal capitalistic" by party officers such as Lundesgaard who now favored the pursuit of a more socialistic economic policy.[25] Because of this divergent view, the proposal which Lundesgaard, Støren, and Riisnæs presented included a provision that called for a draconian reorganization of the Business Department. This included the dismissal of more than one hundred administrators and the arrest of a number of Whist's closest subordinates.[26]

Upon being informed by Whist, the *Reichskommissariat* refused to stand idly by. It inquired into the matter. Quisling in response attempted to downplay and to minimize the issue, declaring that its consideration occurred in full understanding with the ministers. He further assured the *Reichskommissariat* that he would personally discuss the matter with Whist. The latter, however, remained unalterably intransigent in his opposition to the scheme. He declared his full support for his subordinates, and threatened to resign if the changes were put into effect.[27]

His obstruction, with the *Reichskommissariat*'s backing, made it impossible for Quisling to respond positively to the proposed changes. Whist remained in his post, his subordinates were not arrested or dismissed, and nothing was done to carry out the new social policy recommended by Lundesgaard, Støren, and Riisnæs. The failure of this idea was but one example of how the Minister President and members of his old guard almost frantically considered various alternatives to escape from the hopeless state he was in as the war neared its conclusion, but how in the end he remained powerless to take any initiatives of his own. The personnel changes made by Quisling during the final period of the occupation therefore took place not as a result of a drastic modification in policy, but as a natural result of earlier developments, and always with the full understanding of the Germans.

Of the ministers to be affected by the changes, Hagelin was the most obvious candidate. He had to all intents and purposes distanced himself completely from the Quisling administration by the time of his resignation. Already as early as the fall of 1942 he had begun to alter course, no longer working as actively as earlier in seeking to carry out Quisling's programs. In part this was because, as noted previously, Quisling no longer followed his advice to the degree that the NS leader had done previously. But in addition, Hagelin moved in this direction more and more as the certainty of Germany's eventual defeat became clearer.[28] By the fall of 1944 it was obvious that his usefulness in the National Government had entirely come to an end. Since the conclusion of September he had been absent on the sick leave which he took to justify his refusal to follow Quisling's order to assume leadership of the ill-fated attempt to evacuate Finnmark. In his absence the Interior Department was nominally headed on an interim basis by Lippestad, but since the latter was in Finnmark as Lie's second-in-command, in reality the post stood vacant.[29]

As Hagelin had become completely superfluous, his departure was inevitable. It was this fact which explains why he left the NS government, and not Lippestad's later assertion that Hagelin's resignation was the price Quisling had to pay in order to be allowed to see Hitler.[30] Hagelin himself confirmed in letters to Quisling that he was not able to carry out his work in a manner that Quisling considered satisfactory, and that he left his office in agreement with the Minister President. His final request was the self-serving wish that his resignation be announced in such a manner that it did not give the impression of having been motivated by Germany's declining military position.[31] Contrary to this assertion, however, the devious Hagelin thereby showed clearly that one of his main motives for abandoning the Quisling government was his recognition of Germany's pending defeat.

With Hagelin's resignation, effective on November 8, 1944, the last formal ties were broken between Quisling and the man who before the war had been instrumental in providing the powerless NS leader with significant contacts within the Nazi hierarchy. Ever the realist, but still the adventurer, Hagelin had realized that his strong effort to assure Quisling political power had come to nought, and he now endeavored to remove himself as far from the sinking NS administration as possible. He sought instead to establish ties with the winning side. As he himself put it, by the end of the war he was the best *jøssing* of them all.[32] But his opportunism was to no avail. Having earlier committed himself so strongly on Quisling's behalf, he also shared the *Fører*'s fate.

As Hagelin's successor, Quisling gained an effective minister in Arnvid Vassbotten. Previously a member of the NS Supreme Court, he was noted for his ability, although he never became a leading figure within the party. He was also, as the new head of the Interior Department, a cautious and pragmatic administrator. Recognizing that this was not the time to follow an aggressive policy, he carried out his responsibilities in an impartial manner.[33]

Even before the process of replacing Hagelin had been carried out, well-informed NS members knew that it was only a matter of time before another of Quisling's ministers would be forced to leave office. In this instance, however, the Minister President had no wish to retire his subordinate, but a fatal illness decreed otherwise. His old friend, Frederik Prytz, had developed cancer. Already by October 1944 speculation had begun concerning who would be Prytz's successor in the Finance Department.[34]

Of those under consideration, Whist was an obvious candidate. But the very qualities that had previously been his major strength – his business background and his close ties with the Germans – were now to his disadvantage. Those who urged a change in social and economic policy such as

Lundesgaard were fiercely opposed to Whist.[35] Perhaps even more importantly, Prytz took an active part in the deliberations concerning the choice of his successor. He too was strongly against Whist, whose *laissez faire* economic views he considered dangerous.[36]

With such opposition against him, Whist was eliminated from consideration. Prytz instead favored his immediate subordinate in the Finance Department, Per Einarson von Hirsch. Prytz voiced this preference to both Quisling and Terboven. Von Hirsch, Prytz felt, would be certain to continue his policies.[37] Although leading NS members were of the opinion that von Hirsch did not have the stature to serve as minister, the deadlocked situation in the National Government allowed no alternative. Von Hirsch was constituted Finance Minister upon Prytz's death on February 21, 1945. Aware at the time of his appointment that the war would soon be over, he simply continued to run the department in the same manner as Prytz had done previously, being primarily concerned with maintaining tranquility.[38] Although he served until the end of the occupation, he never received a permanent appointment, and he therefore was not regarded as a full member of the government. He did not participate in ministerial conferences, and can be said to have functioned as a caretaker rather than as a policy maker.[39]

Quisling was especially hard-hit by Prytz's death. He had lost the man whom he regarded as his oldest friend. Despite previous estrangements between them, Quisling's feeling of loss was both genuine and rational. Prytz had been his mentor in critical periods of his life, going back to the time they first met while serving in the Norwegian legation in Petrograd. With his death, Fuglesang and Skancke were the only remaining ministers who had been close to Quisling from the period prior to the war, but neither were as near to him personally as Prytz had been.

The final substitution within the Quisling government came almost as an anticlimax. Thorstein Fretheim, the Minister of Agriculture, had occupied a somewhat unique position during the entire period of NS administration. Originally he was one of four department heads in the Commissarial Council who did not belong to NS when the Council was formed. Unlike his non-NS colleagues, however, he chose to join the party in May 1941, and he continued in his position when the National Government came into being. As a member of the party, he aided NS in its attempt to gain control of the farm organizations. However, he was never among the ministers who aggressively sought to nazify society. He restricted himself almost entirely to promoting farming and forestry. His lack of enthusiasm for NS and German attempts to exploit Norwegian agriculture resulted in considerable criticism from those within the party who were more ideologically committed. In the end this resulted in his ouster on April 21, 1945, hardly more than two weeks before the end of the occupation.[40]

At this late date, his dismissal had no significance whatsoever. With so short a period remaining before Germany's total defeat, there was no time or reason for Quisling to consider a replacement. The Agriculture Department continued to function without a leader. In essence, this was exactly what the Interior and Finance departments had experienced as well, even though formally they had received new heads. During this last period of the occupation the department heads, like the Minister President himself, were simply caught in a situation over which they had no control. But unlike Quisling, who desperately sought various means to escape from his predicament, the more realistic administrators passively awaited the outcome of the war.

This final period of the Second World War was marked by heightened tension for Quisling resulting from the Home Front's expanded acts of sabotage and violence. Although such resistance activity never reached the level of that in neighboring Denmark, it nevertheless showed a considerable increase over what had taken place earlier during the occupation.

As a result of the changed sabotage policy which Milorg put into effect in the spring of 1944, groups of operatives now began to live permanently in forest and mountain hideouts. Sabotage activity increased markedly, especially from the fall, against such targets as German shipping, fuel depots, and industrial plants. Furthermore, Allied difficulty during the Battle of the Bulge created the added need for more sabotage in Norway. On December 5 Milorg received an order from the Allied High Command to include the railroad network in its attacks in order to hinder the withdrawal of German troops to the western front.[41]

Parallel with this heightened use of sabotage, Milorg also greatly expanded its practice of liquidating persons considered dangerous for the Home Front. In 1944 this included not only agents and informers employed by the Gestapo and the NS-controlled State Police, who had earlier been targeted for execution, but also other individuals who were perceived to be a threat to the resistance, first and foremost members of the police.[42]

This expanded use of force created added respect, even fear, for the Home Front's authority among the public at large, thereby restricting even more the limited degree of control Quisling's officials could hope to exercise.[43] The NS authorities, again in a defensive posture, reacted to Milorg's operations with a propaganda campaign against what was termed "bandit activity". Quisling personally made repeated attacks in his speeches against this type of opposition, referring to it as "criminal plots against Norwegian life and property".[44] Acting in cooperation with the Gestapo, the NS police increased their raids and surveillance activity in an attempt to limit and, if possible, to destroy the resistance. Summary executions were carried out against saboteurs who were captured. Another method employed to try to limit sabotage involved greater forcible use of ordinary civilians to serve in a "citizen guard" system, keeping watch over sites that were especially vulnerable to possible sabotage. Always opposed to this system, the Home Front sent out a new, sharply worded directive against the "citizen guard", calling on the public not to report if ordered to do so. Many persons, especially in the Oslo area, responded to the appeal despite being threatened with punishment. The police frequently had to force people from their homes at night in order to compel them to take part.[45]

The Home Front did not go unpunished for the increased operations which Milorg carried out. In particular during the final three months of 1944 the Gestapo greatly expanded its effort to defeat the resistance by arresting as many of its major figures as possible, both in Oslo, where the central leadership was located, and the district leaders throughout the country.[46] This had a considerable impact. The Home Front's civilian leadership was seriously depleted by the Gestapo raids, with a number of key members being arrested or forced to flee to Sweden. The loss of these vital individuals was one of the factors which led to the final consolidation of the Home Front Leadership into one cohesive unit. Such unity, it was felt, was needed at this time in order to maintain effective coordination over the resistance movement's varied activities. An added factor contributing to this process was the fact that an agreement was reached in late 1944 between representatives of the Home Front and the government in exile concerning how Norway would be administered in the immediate postwar period. As a consequence, in the months when the war neared its conclusion the civilian Home Front leaders concentrated their attention more on planning for the period after the end of the occupation, when the resistance movement was delegated to assume authority on an interim basis on behalf of the government, and less on the waning struggle against the Germans and their NS supporters in the Quisling administration. Therefore, with these tasks at hand, it was felt that a clearly defined Home Front Leadership was needed at this stage of the occupation. This came into existence around New Year 1945 under the overall command of a dominant adversary of Quisling within the Circle, former Chief Justice Paal Berg. Along with him, representatives from the Circle, the Coordinating Committee, Milorg, the underground police organization, the underground economic and legal groups, and the farmers formed a unified Home Front Leadership. Thereupon the process of consolidating the Home Front, begun in the spring of 1944, was completed. The twelve-man committee which made up the Leadership, with its operative group in charge of day-to-day affairs, remained basically intact for the duration of the war.[47]

As a result of this development, at the beginning of 1945 Quisling's main organized opposition was more tightly structured than ever before. Although its primary focus was now directed toward planning for after the war, the Home Front, through Milorg, continued with increased vigor to carry out the policy of sabotage and liquidation. The Gestapo's counter-measures did not succeed in forcing a decline in its offensive operations.

The Home Front's extended use of violence caused serious concern among the Germans, both in the *Wehrmacht* and within the *Reichskommissariat*. From the very beginning of this trend, Terboven, as always, had wished to take harsh reprisals. But Berlin, remembering all too well how the *Reichskommissar*'s severity had earlier resulted in unwelcome repercussions, gave him orders not to take drastic measures. However, following his visit to Germany in January, where Quisling had unsuccessfully made his last attempt to obtain *der Führer*'s approval for his plans, Terboven did secure permission to react more forcefully. Still, he was not allowed to go as far as he desired.[48]

Such retaliation included the shooting of hostages. Before this practice began on a systematic basis, intimidation was used to try to halt the Home Front's violent opposition. Quisling personally notified seven prominent industrialists to meet with him on February 3, 1945. Five responded and attended the conference. Here Quisling warned that neither NS nor the Germans would tolerate continued acts of sabotage and liquidation. If these actions did not cease, he threatened, prominent Norwegians, such as those with whom he now spoke, could expect to be shot in retaliation.[49] Through indirect contacts, the Gestapo sent a similar message to the Home Front Leadership, giving notice that they would execute a large number of hostages unless the sabotage operations came to a halt. The Home Front Leadership, however, paid no heed, emphasizing instead in a report to England that it had no intention of changing its tactics "because of German threats".[50]

The Home Front's determination not to give in to Quisling and the Germans was dramatically emphasized in the most sensational liquidation of the occupation, the shooting of Major General Karl Marthinsen. A dedicated NS member, he had headed the State Police since the spring of 1941. He gained the added position of leader of the Security Police in the summer of 1943, becoming thereby one of two chief police officials immediately subordinate to Jonas Lie. Marthinsen's power was strengthened even more when he succeeded Oliver Møystad as *Hird* Chief in June 1944. He was justifiably regarded as one of the most ruthless and dangerous tools of the Germans.[51] This was due in particular to the role which the State Police played during the occupation. It gained a reputation of being virtually indistinguishable from the German police when it came to ruthlessness in combatting the resistance. The force was entirely Norwegian in composition, but it stood in close and continuous contact with the *Sicherheitspolizei*, frequently receiving its orders and assignments directly from the Germans.[52]

Marthinsen's fate was sealed when the Home Front's operative group received reports at the end of January which indicated that he planned to take total control of National Union's various paramilitary formations in order to use them against the resistance movement during the last phase of the war. Highly ambitious as well as ruthless, he intended also to replace Lie as leader of the Police Department. The Home Front already regarded Marthinsen as a most dangerous opponent, and feared what might happen if he, known for taking quick and decisive action, were able to put his plans into effect. Not willing to risk such a possibility, the Home Front Leadership decided to act pre-emptively and approved a proposal that he be eliminated, although it was aware that this would probably cost many lives. On the morning of Thursday, February 8, Marthinsen was gunned down in his car while on his way to his office in Oslo.[53]

The reaction from both the *Reichskommissariat* and Quisling's administration was immediate and violent. Within the next two days more than thirty prisoners and hostages were shot in retaliation.[54] Those executed did not receive a regular trial. They merely appeared briefly before special German or NS tribunals, and then were summarily shot. Quisling refused to grant clemency to those tried by NS courts.[55] He thereby created grounds for one of the charges that he would face after the war.

This action in part reflected Terboven's preference for taking harsh measures, but Quisling fully shared the *Reichskommissar*'s strong feelings against Marthinsen's liquidation, and against the killing of NS members in general. After the war he continued to refer to such Home Front killings as "sneak murders".[56] He therefore agreed that Marthinsen's death required strict retaliation. NS officials shared his view and voiced no objections to the executions.[57] Following consultation with Terboven, Quisling issued a special decree giving the Police Department authority to take all necessary steps to maintain "calm, order, and security". The Police Department in turn offered rewards up to 10,000 *kr.* for information leading to the arrest of "saboteurs or murderers and their helpers . . ."[58] A special police staff was also established under Lie's leadership for the purpose of combating terror and sabotage more effectively.[59]

These steps illustrated how damaging this incident had been to the prestige and authority of both Quisling's administration and the Germans. On the other side of the battleline, the execution of so many in retaliation for Marthinsen's liquidation proved to be a stronger countermeasure than many in the Home Front Leadership had anticipated. It found the reprisals to be so shocking that for a brief time it considered the possibility of calling a general strike, similar to that which the Danes had carried out in Copenhagen in the summer of 1944. However, the resistance leadership soon concluded that the public would not support this type of protest. Psychologically, the people in general were not willing to make such a serious commitment in response to reprisals that had been triggered by a Milorg killing.[60] Therefore, for tactical reasons the Home Front decided to halt the liquidation of leading NS figures for the time being.[61]

The resistance leadership did not, however, abandon its emphasis on increased sabotage. Indeed, in the period immediately following Marthinsen's liquidation the Home Front reaffirmed its commitment to pursuing offensive-minded operations.[62] This was possible because in the fall of the previous year, and even more during the following winter, the resistance for the first time received large amounts of military supplies from the Allies. Strengthened by weapons and munitions delivered via parachute, Milorg increased its numbers considerably during the last months of the occupation in the winter and spring of 1944–1945.[63]

Milorg's growth and its expanded operations illustrated the waning strength of Quisling and his German allies. Although the Germans were numerically far superior, they were generally powerless to halt Milorg's increased activity. Milorg continued to concentrate much of its attention on attacking the railroad network during the final months of the war. The highlight of this campaign occurred on the night of March 14–15, when underground forces cut the major north-south railroad lines in more than 1,000 places.[64] Although the Germans were able to repair these breaks soon after they occurred, nevertheless such destruction was an irritant that was noticed at the highest levels of the Nazi hierarchy. This was shown in Goebbels' diary entry of March 17, commenting on the situation in Norway:

> A series of major acts of sabotage and assassinations has started in Norway. The Norwegians apparently cannot wait for the time when they come under Soviet control. We are dealing with this wave of sabotage and assassinations with the utmost severity. Terboven has a proper job on his hands here.[65]

The "job" was duly carried out. Fourteen young Norwegians who had earlier been arrested as saboteurs were executed in retaliation. Provoked again by this practice of shooting prisoners, the Home Front sent the Germans a sharply worded warning which declared that continued use of terror against prisoners would result in new forms of resistance, including the threat of a popular general strike. The warning was heeded, with this wave of shootings being the final execution of hostages carried out by the Germans. This indicated their recognition that the war was lost and that the day of reckoning would soon be at hand.[66] The Home Front did not reciprocate. Acts of sabotage continued unabated until the end of April. At this time, however, the resistance halted its operations, not wishing to risk antagonizing the enemy during the critical period just prior to their capitulation.[67] An uneasy atmosphere of calm ensued during the early days of May. But considerable activity and planning took place behind the scenes on both sides.

Of particular concern for Quisling in the spring of 1945 was the continuing spread of defeatism among his followers, a fact that he reluctantly had to recognize, even if indirectly.[68] Within NS there existed substantial unrest among ordinary party members following Marthinsen's liquidation. Confidential German reports from Norway showed this to be true. They indicated not only how feelings of insecurity had increased by the killing of the State Police chief, but also by a number of armed raids against A-T camps.[69] Heightening their uncertainty was the fact that with Germany's defeat becoming ever more imminent, NS members' estrangement from the rest of the population was greater than at any time before. In recognition of this, the new commander-in-chief of German forces in Norway, General Franz Böhme, commented on NS' unpopularity in a directive dated April 16. He pointed out how those Norwegians who had worked actively on behalf of the German effort to create a new Europe were being treated as "traitors and deserters" by the anti-German segment of the population. In seeking to bolster the flagging spirits of NS members, Böhme ordered his *Wehrmacht* units to cooperate as fully as possible with NS in an attempt to give these pro-German Norwegians the feeling that they did not stand alone.[70]

On the opposite side, the Home Front Leadership was equally aware that doubts and uncertainty existed among Quisling's followers. Having stopped its killing of dangerous opponents, the Home Front countered by making greater use of psychological warfare. It intensified a propaganda campaign which it had maintained against NS for a long period during the war. The purpose of the campaign at this stage of the occupation was to frighten NS members so as to prevent them from taking part in last-ditch actions against resistance forces. Warnings were issued in writing which declared that all punitive acts carried out by NS against the resistance movement would be registered.[71] Such warnings were not just idle. Both those in NS and their enemies were fully aware that Quisling's adherents would stand accountable for their actions following a German defeat. The coming judicial process against NS members had been announced in the underground press and over London Radio long before the end of the occupation.[72]

While NS regarded the future gloomily, the resistance leadership on the other hand was so confident of its heightened power that it issued a proclamation on March 20, announcing the Home Front's purpose and program for the immediate postwar period after the end of the occupation. The Home Front leaders emphasized that their organization had become a popular mass movement, with men and women from all levels of society taking part, fighting side by side. Only a small minority, maintained the proclamation, did not support the Home Front – those who had "entered Nazism's service" or who were weak or fearful. The Leadership further stressed its organization's legitimacy, pointing out that it represented the

entire resistance in close cooperation with Norway's constitutional authorities. The Home Front's primary goal was to have the country revert to
normal conditions as soon as possible once the war was over. The proclamation had special significance for Quisling's followers, since among the
tasks that had to be carried out was the just trial and sentencing of all "war
criminals and traitors" as quickly as possible.[73] The proclamation had extra
meaning, since it enjoyed the exiled government's full backing. Its contents
were widely disseminated, being broadcast over London Radio, with
printed copies being distributed throughout Norway.[74]

Perceptive party members were therefore fully aware of what they
could expect should Germany go down in defeat. In anticipation of such a
likelihood, there existed some sentiment within NS in favor of adopting a
more conciliatory position toward the party's opposition. Quisling's foreign policy adviser, Støren, was among those who voiced this view. In
early March, commenting on the situation that had arisen in the wake of
Marthinsen's killing, he declared that he did not oppose the battle being
carried out against "murderers and saboteurs". More critical than ever of
the Germans, he maintained, however, that the practice of having parallel
German and NS courts issue death sentences had been established by the
Germans to give NS co-responsibility for the executions. He further argued that the many death sentences merely had the effect of lessening respect for life, adding to the atmosphere in which "political murders"
thrived. In opposition to this situation, he stressed the need for a change in
German judicial policy. He favored the release of all prisoners who had
been arrested as hostages, and he further urged the complete elimination of
the practice of taking hostages. In general, he insisted that the German policy of handing out severe sentences over which NS authorities had no influence should be altered and made more lenient. The NS administration
should try, urged Støren, to gain the concessions which he recommended
through negotiations.[75]

By now he was completely disillusioned, making no effort to disguise
this from Quisling. Influenced by the failure of his diplomatic efforts to
gain concessions from the Third Reich, and affected equally by the disastrous defeats that the *Wehrmacht* was sustaining, he bitterly informed
Quisling of his conviction that the Germans were merely interested in exploiting Norway. He admitted that he finally recognized he had been deceived, and bluntly pointed out that Quisling similarly had been wilfully
misled: "As the situation now stands, I have the feeling that the German
authorities are deliberately making a fool of you, *herr* Minister President,
as well as of National Union and the Norwegian people". Norway, he declared, remained in a *de jure* state of war with Germany, a situation which
affected not only the exiled government in London, but also the National
Government. All efforts to change this state of affairs had failed, and he
stated his conviction that as difficulties increased toward the end of the

war, German war levies would more and more assume the character of the "plundering of a war-torn people".[76]

While Støren was more trenchant in his observations than the average NS member and also more outspoken, he was not alone when he pointed out to Quisling, albeit as diplomatically as he could, the possibility of a German collapse in 1945.[77] General Secretary Fuglesang similarly admitted the existence of defeatism in a speech to dedicated members of the party's youth organization: "There are many NS members who today are indulging in speculation about what will happen in Norway in the future".[78] He declared, however, such speculation to be "reprehensible". Fuglesang personified an opposite extreme within NS: the dedicated members who followed their *Fører* to the end, continuing to believe in a possible German victory despite the dismal reports streaming in from the retreating front lines, which even *Fritt Folk* could not disguise. While fears and uncertainty for the future caused a significant number of members to become passive, the core of the party continued to function until almost the very end of the occupation. The party apparatus and the various NS organizations remained active, if on a reduced level. So too did NS propaganda, with its special emphasis on the need to save Europe from "the danger from the east", and with its ongoing attacks against the "emigrant government" and the Home Front's sabotage activity.[79]

In his public statements, the *Fører* persisted in attempting to inspire his followers to believe that despite the bleakness of the present situation, in the end they would be on the winning side. As late as April 23 he maintained that he was not at all concerned with what occurred on the front lines. Instead, he declared that victory would be gained in the long-run.[80] This stubborn assertiveness was not merely for public consumption. Not until just days before the capitulation did he finally concede that he could no longer depend on German armed might as a means of retaining his office.

His hope for salvaging his position was not based solely on wishful thinking. Indicating the strategic value which Hitler always attached to the country, at the very end of the war the Germans still retained a formidable force in Norway, approximately 364,000 men, including a number of elite units.[81] The potential power of these troops was heightened by the fact that the Allies had committed all of their forces in Europe toward the invasion of Germany, and hence had no reserves available should it prove necessary to fight a Scandinavian campaign. If the German divisions in Norway therefore defiantly chose to hold out even after a surrender on the continent, they would prove to be a difficult foe to deal with. They were well equipped and supplied, and in addition they were fully ready to take countermeasures against any attack from the outside. The *Wehrmacht* had with thorough precision made preparations for destruction on a vast scale in the event of an invasion.[82]

The potential for continued resistance in Norway was not regarded as just an idle possibility. The government in England considered the threat to be quite real. On April 12 Foreign Minister Lie, indicating that the German divisions in Norway might decide to fight on, requested the Swedish government to make preparations for possible intervention into Norway.[83] The Swedes wisely did not accede, in the belief that such a step might merely serve to provoke the *Wehrmacht*, but for a time the Norwegian government, showing how seriously it viewed the situation, persisted in its attempt to pressure the Swedes into considering intervention.[84]

Not unexpectedly, the *Reichskommissar* was the foremost official in Norway who strove to realize the worst fears of the government in exile. He shared completely his *Führer's* view that as a true National Socialist, he should resist until death, and he sought actively to have this viewpoint prevail within all of the occupation forces in Norway. But his influence was limited by the fact that he did not enjoy any direct authority over the *Wehrmacht*. He disliked this intensely, not least because he feared that the military commanders failed to share his determination to fight to the end. During the final months of the war he therefore made a bid through his contacts in Berlin to gain control over the military, or, as a second best alternative, at least to have an SS general appointed as commander-in-chief in Norway.[85] The possibility for the out-of–favor *Reichskommissar* to be granted such power was highly unlikely, as Goebbels noted in his diary on March 10:

> Terboven has submitted a memorandum to the *Führer* about the system of command in Norway in an emergency. He proposes that he should become deputy Commander-in-Chief to Böhme to ensure that political affairs would be handled correctly in an emergency. I do not think that the *Führer* can accept this proposal.[86]

While Terboven failed to obtain the influence he desired over the military, he doggedly continued almost to the very end to try to induce the *Wehrmacht* command to follow a policy of resistance. On March 15 he held a meeting with General Böhme, Admiral Otto Ciliax, the naval commander, and other prominent officers. He proposed the grandiose scheme that Hitler, Himmler, Goebbels, and the other Nazi satraps should take refuge in "Fortress Norway" (*Festung Norwegen*). In this connection, he asked the *Wehrmacht* commanders whether they could guarantee the loyalty of their troops in the event of a military collapse on the continent. Neither Böhme nor Ciliax was willing to give such an assurance, and the admiral instead quite negatively urged Terboven to aid in an orderly evacuation of Norway in the event of a German capitulation. Undaunted by the lack of enthusiasm which he received from the military commanders, the *Reichskommissar* informed them that he intended to follow Hitler's order to fight to the last man. He further warned that he had considerable forces at his disposal that would follow such a policy, including elements of the *Wehrmacht*, the SS, police troops, and *Organisation Todt*.[87] Indicating that this was not just idle talk on the part of the *Reichskommissar*, a Nazi party meeting in Oslo sent a greeting to Hitler on the occasion of the *Führer*'s last birthday, April 20, with the promise that "Norway will be held!" Terboven and his counterpart in Denmark, Dr. Werner Best, were present at the gathering.[88]

The possibility that Norway might be the Third Reich's final bastion was not regarded as a fanciful illusion held by Terboven alone. This frightful prospect was considered to be quite possible by the government in London. King Haakon later admitted that he had feared just this eventuality in early May:

> I thought: Now come Goebbels and Göring and Himmler and the whole bunch flying to Norway and seeking protection with the German army up there. We shall have a fight to the finish, war between desperate German forces and Allied armies on Norwegian soil.[89]

Quisling fully shared Terboven's desire to have the German forces in Norway ready to offer resistance, but from a different perspective. The Minister President wished to have the *Wehrmacht*'s continued presence serve as the power basis for maintaining him in office. Unlike Terboven, whose world would come to an end with the fall of the National Socialist social order, Quisling vaguely and unclearly hoped to construct a new foundation for himself and his NS regime in the future. Recognizing the obvious fact that he had no chance of survival if he had to rely on the Norwegian population, his only alternative source of support lay with the German military.

In his attempt to find a means to have these units at his disposal, he presented a number of quite fanciful plans, which indicated how he more and more distanced himself from reality in his desperate effort to find some way of escaping from the defeat that was inexorably approaching. His plans took on the character of wishful thinking where he focused his attention in considerable detail on his ideal solution, but gave no thought to the hard reality of how these utopian goals were to be realized.

One plan that he proposed called for the creation of some type of international organization which would have continued the war in Norway even if Germany had been forced to capitulate. Referred to as "the European Liberation Committee (in Scandinavia)", it was intended to be part of a general "European Liberation Movement". His terminology gives the impression that he envisioned this organization would carry on a continuation of the struggle against Russia and the Western powers in defense of the "Europe" and its culture which he depicted in NS propaganda. The plan's unreal quality was shown in particular by his detailed design for how this organization would be structured, with its large number of commissions, offices, congresses etc.[90]

Indicating even more directly his dependence on German military might, in another scheme he broached the fantastic idea of having the *Wehrmacht* forces in Norway naturalized as Norwegian citizens. When asked after the war how he had intended to carry out this rather unique process, he provided evidence of the formalistic, yet illogical, manner in which he regarded his position as Minister President. He replied that he "as head of state had authority by law to give anyone Norwegian citizenship".[91] Then, as Norwegian citizens, he intended to have his newly acquired soldiers "fight in the Norwegian army against Bolshevism" from their bastion in *Festung Norwegen*.[92] In his mind, the war would now continue only against the Soviets. As for the U.S. and Great Britain, he told Dr. Best on April 20 that he hoped to arrange an armistice with them, with Sweden serving as an intermediary. He maintained that a cease-fire could be achieved because the Western Powers would prefer to make an agreement with him rather than face the possibility of having the Russians advance further into Norway.[93] To motivate the ex-Germans to whom he had assigned the task of protecting Norway from the onrushing "Bolshevik" hordes, he privately came up with the even more fanciful proposal to have the soldiers' families emigrate from Germany up to Norway: "wives and children and sweethearts". Thereupon, having completely burnt the bridges to their former fatherland, and with their loved ones sharing their fate, they would be committed to a new life in Norway, first as soldiers and later as laborers and farmers. This was Quisling's ideal future for the warriors whom he hoped to acquire. The Allies, he insisted, would choose not to fight a determined force of many hundreds of thousands of dedicated soldiers, holding a country that was easily defended. They would instead accept the proffered armistice, which would result in his having available nearly half a million troops in defense against the Russians.[94]

The impractical aspects of this proposal were so obvious and so numerous as to make the entire plan not merely faulty, but completely based on free fantasy. The German command would never under any circumstances willingly have surrendered control of its forces, and the soldiers would not have wished to remain in Norway as opposed to returning to Germany – even to a Germany in ruins. With Germany's transport system in disruption and with no supplies available, it would furthermore have been impossible to bring the families to Norway. Finally, the Soviets, with their major armies in Germany, posed no threat to Norway. Nor was there any possibility that the Allies would turn against the Russians in 1945. To believe in such a prospect was not merely wishful thinking, but it also showed how little understanding Quisling had of conditions within the enemy countries. Propaganda stressing Allied solidarity had so permeated American and British societies that any sudden switch in 1945 against the Russians would have been impossible. Yet Quisling was not alone in hoping that fear of a "Bolshevik" takeover of Europe might convince the U.S. and Great Britain into changing sides in the war now that the menace of Nazi Germany had been eliminated. His foreign policy adviser, Støren, had conceived of this eventuality. He had similarly suggested to Quisling that the German forces in Norway should form a foreign legion under what he referred to as a free and independent Norwegian flag, and thereby serve as the basis for a Scandinavian bulwark which would prevent the Russians from gaining control of the North, including Finland.[95] Such desperate solutions were by no means confined to Quisling and his advisers. Ideas of a similar nature occurred to leading Nazi officials during the dark days of the Third Reich's *Götterdämmerung*.

Despite its nonsensical features, the scheme did illustrate how the Minister President sought as long as possible to operate from a position of strength. With regard to gaining control of German troops, he could only make a hopeless effort. But the situation was different with another, smaller, potential force that he expected to use during the final period of the war. He had always exercised ultimate authority over the *Hird* as its highest leader.[96]

Throughout the occupation he had regarded this paramilitary group as part of his "armed forces". But one of the main difficulties he encountered with the *Hird* was German unwillingness to issue it arms unless it came under direct German command, a move it had always resisted.[97] Not until January 1945 did he succeed in obtaining the necessary weapons. At this time a force of some 3,000 men in the *Hird*'s Alarm Units (*Alarmenheter*) received arms. Members of these units were to cooperate with the German police in operations against Milorg's sabotage efforts.[98]

As the possibility increased that Norway might become a theater of military operations, Quisling wished to go further and to mobilize the entire *Hird*, which consisted, at least on paper, of some 8,000 men.[99] On February 20 a tentative mobilization plan was issued which stressed that only Quisling, in consultation with the head of the German police, Rediess, could mobilize or demobilize the *Hird*. If Norway were attacked, he ordered all *Hird* units to report to the nearest German military force and to act in concert with the Germans, under their command.[100]

This plan was soon superseded by a far more ambitious venture, whose planning began already at the end of February. It called for the creation of no less than twenty-three *Hird* battalions, each numbering 550 men. If realized, this would have given Quisling a force of some 12,000–13,000 men. Considering the fact that the *Hird* at the most only numbered 8,000, with only 3,000 actively taking part in its operations, this venture appeared to be but another example of how his ambition was out of proportion to what could really be achieved.[101]

Nevertheless, although it was unlikely that this numerical goal could be realized, his intention to have the *Hird* ready for use in the spring of 1945 was a serious venture. It received full cooperation from the Germans on the assumption that if an Allied invasion occurred, the *Hird* battalions would come under German leadership. During the next several months preparations were made for setting up the battalions. Serving under Quisling as leader of the *Hird* was Henrik Rogstad, a fanatic who was just as aggressive as his predecessor, Marthinsen. Under Rogstad's command, *Hird* units carried out regular weapons training. They also took part in actual operations against resistance groups. In the spring of 1945 armed *Hird* units participated alongside German police and military forces in carrying out systematic searches in areas where Milorg groups were believed to be operating.[102]

The Home Front reacted with alarm to these developments, assuming quite correctly that Quisling planned to use the projected *Hird* battalions as a means of defending his National Government even following a German collapse. The seriousness of his intentions revealed itself graphically at the end of April when he indeed *did* attempt to carry out a total call-up, issuing a secret mobilization order for all *Hird* members between the ages of eighteen and fifty-five.[103] If it had succeeded, this would have given him a considerable force, and in addition he had other armed units that he planned to use. The State Police had earlier received a full supply of weapons and were therefore armed as a regular military unit. Beyond this, the last Ski Battalion of front fighters to participate in combat in Finland had returned home and were at the disposal of the German police, but Quisling now made strenuous efforts to bring the force under his command. From the Home Front's perspective, all of these moves presented the distinct impression that he was preparing for civil war.[104]

Although this interpretation was by no means farfetched, it needs to be modified somewhat. Quisling had not made a decision to fight when he tried to mobilize the *Hird*. He was simply seeking to build up as strong a power base as possible so that he might be able to influence the course of events. The preparations he made for organizing the potential for armed resistance showed, however, that if there had been a likelihood of retaining his position by the use of force, he would have been quite willing to have the issue decided by weapons.

Fearful of the prospect that a considerable number of the *Hird* might respond to Quisling's attempted mobilization, the Home Front reacted strongly. Warnings were sent to *Hird* members and their families with the ominous notice that death could be the fate of those who took up arms against their countrymen. Impressed by this threat, and also convinced that the approaching defeat could not be avoided, many of National Union's more realistic members opposed the possible use of weapons at this late date. The number who responded to Quisling's order was therefore quite small. At the most, in some places about ten per cent obeyed. Many of those who should have reported simply went into hiding.[105]

Terboven's determined attempts to follow a diehard policy of resistance were equally frustrated at this time. His strongest opposition, unlike that experienced by Quisling, came not from the Home Front, however, but from his fellow Germans. At Easter time the *Reichskommissar* sought to carry out a massive sweep in search of Milorg encampments throughout Nordmarka, the expanse of hills and forests immediately north of Oslo. This plan was foiled by none other than the head of the Security Police, Heinrich Fehlis, who successfully appealed to Berlin to have the operation postponed. Unlike the *Reichskommissar*, Himmler's police officials in Norway pragmatically opposed meaningless acts of force at this late date.[106]

Effective decision making over what would occur at the conclusion of the war rested, however, neither with the police nor with the *Reichskommissar*. Because of its control of almost 400,000 men, decisive authority lay now in the hands of the *Wehrmacht* command in Norway, with its headquarters strategically located at Lillehammer, some three hours by car north of Oslo. By mid-April the Home Front was aware that a growing sentiment was developing within the command in favor of a peaceful settlement. The more fanatical higher officers, however, concerned in particular with questions of professional honor, still remained unreconcilably opposed to surrender.[107]

As the final days of the occupation began in early May, Quisling's future, as it had during the entire wartime period, continued to rest in German hands. But whereas he had previously been bound by the political decisions of Nazi authorities, now his options were restricted by what the *Wehrmacht* command chose to do in the last days of the Thousand Year Reich, as Germany collapsed.

At the end of April the Minister President still maintained a slight degree of hope that an independent German military force might remain in Norway, serving as a power base that would allow him to stay in office.[108] With Hitler's suicide on April 30 it therefore became necessary for him, and even more so for the *Reichskommissar*, to ascertain the attitude of the military command in view of the changed situation. Having earlier supported Terboven in his determination to fight to the end, Quisling accompanied him to a meeting at Lillehammer on May 1. But the small hope that Quisling retained for the *Wehrmacht* to choose to hold out disappeared entirely at this conference.[109] Although the high command under Böhme remained divided over the question of capitulation, it had never taken seriously Quisling's scheme to have the German forces remain in order to serve as an independent buffer against the Russians. Böhme adhered to the rigid code of the Prussian officer, acting in strict accord with the orders he received from the OKW in Germany.[110] Now that Hitler was dead, Böhme loyally followed instructions from *der Führer*'s successor, Grand Admiral Karl Dönitz.

Even prior to the Lillehammer meeting, however, the Minister President in large part had been forced to abandon his hope for a miracle that would rescue the Third Reich. Other actions that he took at the end of April provided proof that he had recognized at last that there was hardly any possibility for the Germans to avoid the consequences of a defeat. The incident which in particular appears to have forced him to deal with this, for him, unfortunate fact was the information that one of the Nazi party's main pillars, SS chief Himmler, had offered on April 23 to negotiate a separate peace with the Western Allies behind Hitler's back. News of this specific evidence of impending Nazi defeat reached Norway and spread like wildfire throughout Oslo and other larger towns, causing spontaneous demonstrations of joy to break out.[111] Bitter and disillusioned with the Germans, Quisling now sought to find an alternative course that he could follow, which would allow him to continue to head some kind of administration during the transition period from war to peace. As an indication of the changed attitude that existed at the top of the party, the NS editor of *Aftenposten* now wrote that Norway really had been neutral during the entire war.[112]

A further reflection of Quisling's attempt to change course was shown at a meeting which he held with his ministers at the Royal Palace on April 29, shortly after Himmler's proposal had become public knowledge. The outcome of this meeting, at least symbolically, was quite dramatic. It constituted nothing less than an attempt on Quisling's part to divorce his administration completely from its past. The National Government confirmed the need for Quisling to be as free as possible politically "so that all responsible national forces can unite in order to bring our country through the critical period before us". All other considerations, it was declared, must give way to the effort "to prevent chaos, civil war, and military activity on Norwegian soil".[113] His ministers therefore placed their posts at his disposal, but with the understanding that they would continue to serve for the time being.[114]

One of the alternatives that he proposed to pursue as a result of this move was a completely impractical project to establish contact with the Home Front, to be followed by the formation of a coalition government between the resistance movement and NS! The fact that he could even consider such a concept again illustrated his inability to assess his position critically. He perceived the obvious fact that it would be to his advantage to establish a tie with the winning side in the war, represented first and fore-most within Norway by the Home Front, but he lacked the sense of real-ism to recognize that this was impossible because he was anathema to the resistance as well as to the general population. The Home Front, of course, did not even consider the idea – it was too absurd.[115]

Another possibility which appeared on paper at this time was a plan to revise the NS government radically. Quisling, according to this proposal, would assume the title of regent; NS as an organization would be dis-banded in favor of a new coalition between NS and LO; and a government consisting of almost entirely new members would be formed, led by a prime minister who would head a new party known either as the "Norwe-gian Socialist Party" or the "National Labor Party".[116]

This scheme too merely reflected the frantic search for any possible al-ternative that Quisling and his close associates engaged in at this time. Nothing came of any of these efforts. The most serious, the endeavor to sever all ties with the past by seeking to assume a position of neutrality, which had been decided upon at the Palace meeting of April 29, ended in pathetic failure. As before, the Germans retained a final veto over any ac-tion that Quisling tried to carry out. The proclamation that the ministers had placed their posts at his disposal so that a new government could be formed with a broader basis of support was simply blocked by Terboven, who refused to allow it to be made public.[117]

This left Quisling more than ever in a state of limbo. He could not en-deavor to change his political course and try to reach some accommodation with his opponents in the Home Front. Not only was this impractical, but Terboven also would not permit any deviation to take place. Even at this late date, when Nazi power throughout Europe had been virtually elimi-nated, the Minister President had no control over the role he would play – the Germans made the decisions.

With Hitler's suicide, ultimate authority over Quisling and over Norway passed into the hands of Admiral Dönitz, who faced the unenviable re-sponsibility of trying to find some orderly method of exercising his man-date over what remained of the Thousand Year Reich. Having established his headquarters at Flensburg, close to the border with Denmark, the Ad-miral assumed his post as Germany's new *Führer* on May 1. He immedi-ately ordered the German leaders in the occupied countries to attend a meeting with him in Flensburg. In Norway this directive included both Terboven and General Böhme.[118]

No thought was given to Quisling during this critical period. Conse-quently, he was limited to sending a telegram to Dönitz on May 2. In this message the *"Norwegischer Ministerpräsident"* expressed his "personal heartfelt sympathy" and condolences on behalf of the Norwegian people for Hitler's "hero's death", and he sent Dönitz his "sincere wish" as the Admiral assumed the "difficult and responsible task" of serving as the German people's new leader.[119]

Quisling could do nothing but remain on the sidelines and await the outcome of the meeting that Dönitz held on May 3. Realizing that surrender was inevitable, the Admiral on this occasion declared his intention of ending the war, but he hoped to negotiate as favorable terms as possible. As far as Norway was concerned, for him the only thing that counted was the large, undefeated force that he still had at his disposal. He recognized the importance of the *Wehrmacht* units in Denmark and, especially, in Norway because they at least gave the Germans a sorely needed bargaining chip that could be used to try to obtain concessions. Böhme was told to keep his troops at full readiness, but not to take any independent action. Insistent on maintaining full and final control, Dönitz emphasized the need to obey orders from Flensburg.[120] To strengthen the commanding general's authority even more, he appointed Böhme as supreme commander of all forces in Norway, which now for the first time brought naval and *Luftwaffe* units directly under his command. Upon his return on May 4, Böhme therefore possessed heightened prestige. He ordered his forces to remain on the alert, ready to repel any attack.[121] But neither he nor anyone else yet knew how the war would end for him and his men. Events on the continent, as they had throughout the war, would determine how the occupation would conclude.

Because of the lack of a clear policy from Quisling at this time, considerable disarray existed within NS. This was especially heightened by the *Fører*'s attempted mobilization of the *Hird* at the end of April. Consequently, uncertainty prevailed during the first days of May over whether the party would resist or capitulate. A Home Front report written on May 3 provided a very good assessment of the confused situation in Oslo. On the one hand, the report stated, there were certain elements within NS who favored a policy of full resistance. The most prominent were Jonas Lie and Henrik Rogstad, the recently appointed *Hird* chief. The latter's influence appeared to grow when he also succeeded to Marthinsen's old post as head of the State Police on May 3.[122] Furthermore, these diehards enjoyed Terboven's full support. The *Reichskommissar* was responsible for Rogstad's takeover as leader of the State Police, despite Quisling's opposition to the appointment.[123] The Home Front report further showed that armed *Hird* groups, including members of the Youth *Hird* as young as thirteen and fourteen, were roaming about the city, adding to the tension which prevailed.

Those favoring resistance, however, were not at all representative of NS opinion, but constituted only a minute minority within the party. Most members were paralyzed with panic. The last thing they wanted was to risk exposure to violence at a time when they knew their cause was doomed.[124] Many sought, but with no success, to try to change sides and to establish ties with their *jøssing* enemies. The second-in-command of the State Police, to cite but one example, attempted to offer his services to the Home Front for the purpose, as he explained, of maintaining order.[125]

The possibility of NS resistance was lessened even further by the failure of Quisling's secret *Hird* mobilization. Reaction was so negative within the party as a whole that a number of leaders in the districts took the unprecedented step of publicly denouncing the venture, which they considered to be a move toward civil war.[126]

With the obvious collapse of his effort to mobilize the *Hird*, and with the progressive decline of Nazi control in Germany, Quisling during the first days of May at last abandoned any lingering thoughts of using force to try to stay in office. Although Terboven succeeded in compelling him to accept Rogstad as State Police Chief, the Minister President resisted pressure to lead a last-ditch armed resistance by NS.

Finally recognizing that he could not in any way directly influence the course of events, he resigned himself to calling on his NS followers to remain calm. He had not, however, relinquished the belief that he still had a role to play in politics, as shown by his belated attempt to appeal to former enemies. He now adopted a conciliatory manner to the hostile majority, far different from that which he had used toward the *jøssings* earlier in the occupation. This accommodating, even apologetic, tone became apparent immediately after the April 29 Palace meeting of the NS ministers. *Fritt Folk*, in a May Day editorial, clearly reflected this changed attitude, expressing regret that National Union had not been able to reach its goal of social justice. The NS organ further declared its patriotic concern for what might happen to the country at the war's end. It appealed for cooperation among all Norwegians, weakly using the cliché that "blood is thicker than water". The paper quite obviously reflected Quisling's newly established position against the use of force, declaring its horror at the thought that "Norwegians should carry weapons against Norwegians". What was needed instead of conflict, it proclaimed patriotically, was "order, discipline, unity, and love for the fatherland". Quite revealingly, *Fritt Folk* admitted directly that the NS government did not exercise control over developments in Norway, resignedly confessing that this lay outside "our National Government's hand".[127]

With Norway's future dependent on decisions made at Flensburg, and with no possibility of exerting sway over the mass of the people at this time, the only practical thing Quisling and his loyalists could do during these uncertain days was at least to try to keep the bulk of NS members in line behind the *Fører*. For this purpose, Fuglesang issued an appeal on May 4 which emphasized that National Union's prime task was to maintain order and thereby prevent a possible deterioration into "civil war, anarchy, and chaos". NS members were to keep calm and to show their discipline during this difficult period. They were urged to maintain their faith in the *Fører*, who would make the correct decisions needed to bring the country and its people through the dangers ahead. Fuglesang above all emphasized how important it was to "Stand fast and immovable behind Vidkun Quisling!"[128]

Fuglesang's insistence on the need to maintain unity and to avoid the possibility of civil war was addressed directly to those within NS such as Lie and Rogstad, who wanted to use force in order to maintain the party's position. A *Fritt Folk* editorial two days later used even more blunt language, condemning those few who attempted to carry out "private catastrophe politics". Such individuals had to recognize clearly, demanded the editorial, that it was "the *Fører* who has responsibility and who determines policy".[129]

The *Fører*, however, was not determining policy, but merely waiting to learn the result of the Flensburg meeting. He received this news from Terboven in a conference on May 5. As he had previously told his officials in the *Reichskommissariat*, the latter informed the attentive Minister President in a non-committal manner of Dönitz's decision: the Admiral intended to end hostilities, but the forces in Norway, because of their bargaining value, would remain in a state of readiness. Contrary to his earlier viewpoint, the *Reichskommissar* did not mention one word about continuing resistance.[130] He too had finally recognized that such a course was impossible. There was no support for such a suicide effort – certainly not at Dönitz's headquarters. Similarly in Norway, sentiment in favor of holding out alone had been eliminated from consideration among German authorities in the military, in the police, and even in Terboven's own *Reichskommissariat*.[131] He was therefore left with no choice but to abandon, at least overtly, the policy he had earlier pursued so relentlessly while Hitler was still alive. He too could but wait for whatever final decision Dönitz would make.

At last informed of German strategy, Quisling now knew definitively of the Admiral's commitment to concluding the war under the best possible terms, and that even the *Reichskommissar* would no longer seek to fight to the last man. Still, on May 5 the Minister President was in the same position as Terboven and Böhme in not yet enjoying the certainty of knowing exactly how the war would end in Norway. He remained groping in the dark, trying to find the right course of action to follow. He continued to be isolated, however, because of his inability to comprehend realistically the true position he was in. Events simply passed him by, without his being able to exert any influence at all.

His failure to stake out an independent strategy revealed itself in the final radio address that he would ever make, delivered in the evening of the same day that he had met with Terboven. The speech was greeted with considerable interest by the people, who were curious to know what course of action he intended to follow at the war's close. When the news therefore leaked out that he would hold a radio address, the public awaited the speech with nervous anticipation in the belief that he might present some significant announcements. In Oslo large numbers gathered in front of loudspeakers in the streets to receive his message. But the listeners were disappointed, as were those who read the text of the speech in the press the following Monday.[132] This was only natural because the Minister President could give no concrete assurances. The Germans alone had the power to make decisions. A secret Home Front report from May 6 included a very penetrating analysis of the speech's content and tone, and of the position which the NS *Fører* held:

> We are of the opinion that it [the speech] was very weak, markedly defensive, and clearly bore witness that Quisling is completely outside the course of events and unable to exercise any influence . . . NS has been pawns of the Germans during the entire war, but never has this been more obvious than at present.[133]

But while it is true that the address clearly indicated Quisling's weak standing, its contents proved nevertheless to be of some interest because it provided insight into his political outlook at this time.

In spite of his repeated attempts to find some new course to follow, his speech showed that he still, even in public, dogmatically remained true to his fascist ideals. From a tactical point of view, this was hardly the time to eulogize Hitler, yet this was how the Minister President began his address. If the war did not end with Europe being swallowed by "Bolshevism", he declared, Hitler would be recognized by future history as the savior of European culture and civilization because he had succeeded, through National Socialism, in making Germany a bulwark which halted the force of the Red deluge. As this praise of the late dictator showed, Quisling had not abandoned his penchant for political philosophizing. Consistent with what he had practiced throughout his career, he tried to find a meaning for his politics through vague historical analogies of rather doubtful veracity. According to his interpretation, Europe in 1945 faced its greatest crisis since the creation of European civilization on the ruins of the Roman Empire 1,500 years earlier. As he had maintained since the 1930s, the threat to Europe came from "Bolshevism, which now controlled 300 of the continent's 500 million people, having gained not only all of the territory previously held by the Tsar, Finland and Poland inclusive, but also the Balkans, the Danube basin, and half of Germany". Furthermore, he depicted this evil force as threatening to capture control of Italy and France. In Scandinavia, he described Finland and northern Norway as having already been taken, while Sweden stood ready to fall.[134]

Recognizing that he probably would soon have to answer for his actions during the occupation, the bulk of his address, however, concentrated on his role in Norway. He presented a highly personal account of his political activity in which he sought to justify his conduct. Many of the arguments that he now presented were the same that he would later repeat when on trial after the war. He had always, he insisted, idealistically worked on behalf of his country throughout his career in politics. He had "unwaveringly followed a clear, unbroken policy, namely, to attempt to rescue the Norwegian people from war, chaos, and communism". In a world of change and turmoil, he had endeavored to obtain a secure place for Norway's continued existence, despite the upheavals and the creation of new political units that were taking place. In seeking sanction for his actions during the war, he quoted a so-called Danish legal expert, who had written: "The chief of state, the government, in particular those civil servants who place themselves at the occupying power's disposal", do not deserve to be called "deserters, etc.", but instead carry out a service on behalf of their country that is "considerably greater" than that of those who "with weapon in hand resist an occupation . . ." In support of this viewpoint, Quisling maintained that his government had always sought to protect the country's interests. He further continued to insist that he had obtained Hitler's promise that Norway's independence would be restored once the war was over. Another piece of fiction which he attempted to uphold was the assertion that his National Government had *not* been installed by the occupying power, but had legally assumed office.[135]

Considering the situation he was in, the tone of his address was understandably conciliatory, to a degree unthinkable when contrasted with the threatening manner he had used when there still remained the possibility that Germany might win the war. He even went so far as to make, for him, the most unusual concession that NS had not been entirely successful. He used this admission as the basis for appealing to all Norwegians for cooperation. Any effort to remove his government by "illegal means", he warned would result in chaos, and he called upon all "responsible" Norwegians to join with NS in a united effort: "We on our side are willing to cooperate with all loyal and positive forces who honestly work on behalf of the people's well-being and [for] Norway's benefit". Showing how futile this appeal really was, however, he was forced to address persons within NS who now were actively seeking to distance themselves by repudiating what the party had previously stood for. He rejected all tendencies "within our ranks" to compromise "our national and social principles". To the end, he insisted that he as NS *Fører* alone was the guardian of the party's eternal principles.[136]

The only really firm commitment he could make on this occasion was to repeat a point which by now had been established as NS policy at the very end of the war – that the party would refrain from using force, and would seek a peaceful transition. He therefore did not emphasize the role of those NS units that were under arms, declaring that their only duty was to maintain order and to protect life and property. They would only act in support of the police, and he disclaimed that they had any *military* significance.[137]

This address was to all intents and purposes his capitulation speech. He knew now that no hope remained for the *Wehrmacht* to continue as a power factor. German troops had already surrendered on several fronts – in Italy on May 2, and in the Netherlands and Denmark on May 4. The only question that remained unsettled was when and how the occupation would terminate in Norway, but that the end was near was quite certain. His speech was the last to be printed in the NS press. The very date on which it was published, May 7, was the final day in which NS-controlled newspapers appeared.

In its last editorial, *Fritt Folk* further illustrated the plight Quisling was in, pointing out to its NS readers that the *Fører* could not provide any specific information about the future because he had no control over what was happening. The paper presented this awkward message more indirectly, however, pointing out that rapidly changing conditions made it impossible for "the responsible head of state" to give the people a concrete picture of the situation, and what was being done by the "Norwegian government" to solve the crisis. Furthermore, said *Fritt Folk*, the people undoubtedly understood "that there has not occurred any change in the circumstances that Norway is an occupied country, where of course the occupying power in the last instance still has the decisive word".[138] It is noteworthy that on the last day of the occupation the paper finally indicated publicly the true nature of the relationship which had always existed between Quisling and the Germans during the war.

His followers could therefore only abjectly await whatever fate was in store for them. Their party would have no influence in determining the final outcome of the occupation. This their foes had already perceived. In the Home Front report of May 3, which came at a time when the resistance movement still was not certain whether the assurances that NS would seek to avert civil war were true, the conclusion was "that the party's role in a possible final struggle here in this country will be of little significance. Everything depends on the German reaction".[139]

As late as May 5–6, however, this realization had not yet fully sunk in for Quisling and his ministers, who never became reconciled to their defeat. On both days the Minister President held *fører* conferences, which included members of the National Government and the most important party leaders.[140] With the knowledge that he now had of Dönitz's plans, his immediate concern continued to be to try to have NS play as prominent a role as possible in the transition period from war to peace. He still unrealistically hoped it might be possible for NS to reach some type of accommodation with the Home Front. Therefore, the participants at the two-day conference spent most of their time discussing the formation of a new police force, to be made up of members of the *Hird* and the Home Forces (*Hjemmestyrkene*), the term by which the Milorg units now were popularly known. Typical of the hothouse atmosphere which surrounded Quisling and his loyalists, they did not even consider the obvious question of whether such a force was feasible. Instead, he and his lieutenants limited themselves to the subject of how the new police uniforms were to be decorated.[141] When Olaf Fermann brought up the more realistic suggestion that the situation was so critical that it called for the dissolution of NS, he was told to "shut up".[142]

Nothing that NS could have attempted during the final days of the occupation would have resulted in anything of significance. Like previous endeavors to establish a link with the Home Front, the scheme to set up a new police force amounted to nothing more than wishful thinking. But Quisling and his immediate advisers could conceive of no other alternative than to continue to try to establish a connection, however tenuous, with the opposition. This resulted in one additional farfetched venture, the last of its kind. Quisling agreed to have three of his ministers, Fuglesang, Lippestad, and Vassbotten, make a trip to the Swedish border in order to attempt to reach some kind of a settlement with Norwegian exile leaders in Sweden. The trio proceeded east to the frontier on May 7, the final day of the occupation. They failed to establish contact with anyone.[143]

These desperate efforts simply served to illustrate how prominent NS leaders, from the *Fører* on down, were frantically grasping at any possible straw as their world was collapsing around them. The fact that Quisling resorted to such futile schemes did not mean that he necessarily believed they would succeed, merely that they were worth trying in the vain hope that there was a *chance* of success. At the same time more practical measures were taken for the worst alternative – that the war would end with him and his party leaders being taken prisoner. With this in mind, during the last hectic days of the occupation, NS officials worked systematically to destroy as much incriminating evidence as possible. At Quisling's headquarters in the Royal Palace the NS archives went up in smoke, with the destruction of documents taking place continuously from the afternoon of Friday, May 4, until the afternoon of Monday, May 7.[144] Similar burning occurred in the various offices of government and party officials. Sometimes there was not enough time to cram the incriminating documents into the stove, so they were simply incinerated on the office floor.[145] Not all

The Leader greets the Hird.
Photograph: National Archives of Norway.

'Dishonour and contempt Quisling's conduct on himself has brought.' An anonymous contribution to the Norwegian postage stamp competition in 1941. Photograph: University of Oslo Library.

Quisling, surrounded by members of the Hird, speaking at a midsummer rally in 1941. Photograph: National Archives of Norway.

The Act of State at Akershus on 1 February 1942. Quisling and Terboven shaking hands. Photograph: National Archives of Norway.

Terboven making a speech at the Act of State. Photograph: National Archives of Norway.

From the balcony of the Grand Hotel, Oslo, Quisling acknowledges the cheers of a torchlight procession on the night of 1 February 1942.
Photograph: National Archives of Norway.

Quisling holding his first Council of State at the royal palace, sitting in the King's place. To his right and in order round the table: Kjeld Stub Irgens, Tormod Hunstad, Sverre Riisnæs, Gulbrand Lunde, Axes Stang, Eivind Blehr, Rolf Jørgen Fuglesang, Frederik Prytz, Johan Andreas Lippestad, Jonas Lie, Ragnar Skancke, Thorstein Fretheim and Albert Viljam Hagelin. Photograph: Norwegian News Agency.

Alf Whist.
Photograph: University of Oslo Library.

Seeking audience with Hitler:
– I'm (a) Quisling!
– And what's your name?
Caricature by Stig Höök, alias Ragnvald Blix.
Göteborgs Handels- och Sjöfarts Tidning *(newspaper) January 1944.*

Quisling's residence, Gimle on Bygdøy.
Photograph: Norwegian News Agency.

At the mass graves in Trandum Forest, where nearly 200 members of the resistance movement were executed and buried by the Germans. Photograph: Norwegian News Agency.

In the exercise yard at Akershus. Photograph: University of Oslo Library.

Before the court of inquiry, May 1945. Photograph: Norwegian News Agency.

Erik Solem.
Photograph: Norwegian News Agency.

Henrik Bergh.
Photograph: Norwegian News Agency.

Annæus Schjødt.
Photograph: Norwegian News Agency.

such damning material, however, went up in flames. In a daring action on May 2, the Home Forces raided the Police and Justice departments, seizing archives containing two and one-half tons of documents. Included in this haul were papers that later proved to be of value for the prosecution in the postwar trials of prominent NS members.[146]

As Quisling awaited the approaching end of the war that would lead to *his* treason trial, he distanced himself even more from reality. As has been seen, the collapse of the German hegemony, which he had assumed would always prevail, caused him to fantasize about a number of unrealistic alternatives, which would somehow rescue him from the dilemma of going down to total defeat. Such a mental reaction was neither unique to him, nor particularly abnormal, as shown by the similar behavior of a number of leading German officials in 1945. Escapism in time of stress is not at all an unusual behavior pattern. In addition to the attempts to establish ties with the Home Front so that he could continue to play an important role during the transition phase, an even more bizarre idea which he considered was to retire from politics altogether in order to enter the ranks of the clergy. Specifically, what he had in mind was to become the pastor (*sogneprest*) of his father's old parish in Fyresdal. He actually went so far as to write an initial draft announcement of his appointment. Except for mentioning fleetingly that his desire to become a clergyman was "perhaps unusual", he did not consider the obvious fact that his lack of theological training made him unfit for the post. Instead, oblivious to such a pragmatic consideration, he simply declared: "Minister President Vidkun Quisling, as a result of the power he exercises in his authority under the constitution as head of the Norwegian Church, wishes to be appointed as parish pastor in Fyresdal, whose office is vacant, and where eight of his ancestors . . . have been pastors".[147] As additional grounds for his wish, he argued that "the current great world crisis" had a "religious core", and he now wished to offer all his energy to work on behalf of Norwegian society in the promotion of a "reformed Christianity" that was in accordance with modern development.[148] He saw himself, in other words, in the role of a religious prophet, seeking in religion to realize the same ultimate goals that he had failed to achieve as a political prophet.

He did not, however, actually attempt to carry out this unique prospect, although he stated that he had discussed the question with Skancke in the latter's capacity as head of the Church and Education Department.[149] It therefore never amounted to more than another example of his predilection to produce unrealistic plans. He did not, however, at any time deny that he had considered this unlikely possibility. Instead, the defense produced it during his postwar trial in the attempt to weaken the prosecution's argument that he always sought to keep his office. He maintained that he had originally written this proposal two years earlier, but when questioned closely by the presiding judge, who pointed out that its contents precluded this possibility, he countered by insisting that it had been "rewritten" in the spring of 1945.[150]

Although its exact date cannot be determined, there is good reason to believe that he authored this draft shortly before the end of the war, after he had become aware of the certainty that he could not hope to play an active political role any longer. Skancke later recalled that he had discussed this matter with Quisling as late as the morning of May 8, which was *after* the German capitulation had been announced and less than twenty-four hours before the Minister President surrendered.[151] But for him, as for most German and NS officials in Norway, military and civilian alike, the war came to a conclusion with an abruptness that left him paralyzed, unable to respond. Already on May 7, before he made the futile effort through his ministers to establish contact with opposition representatives in Sweden, Germany surrendered unconditionally at 2:41 a.m. The capitulation was total, affecting German forces on all front lines, including the troops in Norway. According to its terms, all hostilities were to end at midnight on May 8.[152]

News of the signing of the capitulation did not reach Norway, however, until the mid-afternoon of May 7.[153] But there was evidence at hand before this time to indicate unmistakably to the Minister President that the war could be over at any minute. On the previous day his Belgian counterpart, Leon Degrelle, had arrived from Copenhagen, trying to find a refuge in Norway now that the *Wehrmacht* units in Denmark had surrendered. He apparently was present when Quisling met with Terboven on the morning of May 7. With the situation being what it was, one can well understand why both collaborators "expressed their dissatisfaction with German politics" to Terboven.[154]

In the evening, after the news of the capitulation had been announced over the German radio, the Minister President again had a discussion with Terboven at Skaugum. This was the final meeting between the two antagonists who had rivaled each other for power ever since the *Reichskommissar* had set foot on Norwegian soil in April 1940. As concerned as always with practical matters, Terboven, for once generous, offered to place a plane at Quisling's and Degrelle's disposal so that the two could attempt to escape together. The *Fører* rejected, however, this last opportunity to get away by joining Degrelle on his flight to Spain. Quisling chose instead to await further developments with a number of his ministers.[155] In an obvious negative thrust at the Nygaardsvold government, he later assumed a heroic stance during his trial, maintaining he had always been of the conviction that he should never flee from his people.[156]

The overwhelming majority of his "people" were offering but scant thought to the Minister President when he turned down Terboven's offer.

While Quisling retired into isolation at Gimle, a delirious celebration began in the streets of Oslo that continued almost without interruption well into the summer. The unrestrained joy that possessed Norwegians when they learned that the period of Nazi oppression was over is indescribable. Only those who experienced a similar liberation from the Germans in other European societies fully know the depth of emotion that was aroused during those exhilarating days in the spring of 1945. Pictures of tens of thousands of people coming together on May 7 and May 8 to join in spontaneous celebration provide a clue, however, to the exaltation with which Quisling's countrymen greeted the news that the war was over.[157]

While Norwegians had already begun their celebration of the end of World War II, the most powerful man in Norway, at least for the moment, still refused to recognize that the conflict had resulted in defeat. Ever the obedient officer, General Böhme continued to keep his troops on alert, never considering altering his posture of readiness to take military action until he had received a direct order from his superiors in Flensburg. Not until 9:10 p.m. on May 7, when he obtained personal confirmation from Dönitz that the final capitulation had been signed at Rheims that morning, did Böhme at last feel satisfied that he had received the instructions which he believed were necessary to begin the process by which his troops would lay down their arms.[158] Later in the evening the General received an additional message from Flensburg. Dönitz informed him that he was now not only the highest German military authority in Norway, but also the number one civilian official as well. The *Reichskommissar* was thereby deposed.[159] Dönitz removed him because Terboven's presence would merely have served as a hindrance in the arrangements that Böhme needed to make in order to carry out the terms of the capitulation.

These major events served as but the framework for Norway's transition from an occupied state to a nation that was in the process of regaining its independence and sovereignty. Already during the evening of May 7 the Home Front's Home Forces began to take control of the police stations and prisons in Oslo. Some members of the German police, the *Sicherheitspolizei*, knowing that the game was up as soon as the announcement of the capitulation became known, had already begun to try to hide themselves among the regular *Wehrmacht* troops. The Germans also gave up internal control of Grini, the large concentration camp just outside Oslo. Under tremendous jubilation the prisoners received the news that they were free.[160] In a pattern similar to the actions of the German and NS police, the NS editors abandoned their control of the press. The Home Front's representatives thereupon stepped in on the night of May 7–8 and began making preparations for the issuance of their own newspaper in Oslo. Following successful completion of an improvised agreement with the German press authorities, the Home Front published a single newspaper, *Oslo-Pressen*, numbering 450,000 copies, the largest edition ever published in Norwegian press history. Appearing in the streets on the morning of May 8 under the banner headline "Our struggle is crowned with victory", it was snatched up by news-hungry Osloites, who received their first uncensored newspaper in more than five years.[161]

As these events showed, the Home Front Leadership, acting according to the terms of the agreement with the government in London, in a gradual manner simply filled the vacuum left by the disappearance of German and NS officials. To maintain order during this transition period, the Home Front mobilized its Home Forces on May 7. A dangerous situation was thereby created for the possibility of an armed confrontation because the surrender did not officially go into effect until midnight on May 8. Ever a stickler when it came to correct military behavior, General Böhme insisted on maintaining formal control according to the letter of his instructions. However, the Home Front via telephone worked out an informal agreement with Lillehammer by which the Germans indirectly agreed not to hinder the Home Forces overtly from maintaining order, while the latter in turn gingerly treated the Germans with respect, being under strict instruction not to try to disarm members of the *Wehrmacht*.[162]

With the Germans already beginning the process of gradually withdrawing into special reserves where they were completely demobilized, the celebration was even greater in Oslo on May 8 than it had been the previous evening. The capital was still not fully under Home Front control, but the Home Forces were in the process of taking over the city, while German police authority was disintegrating fast.[163] There were not many Germans in the streets, and those who appeared were ignored.[164] Considering the experiences of the past five years, the population reacted in a remarkably restrained manner at the time of liberation. Very few private acts of violence were carried out against Germans and against individual NS members. The Home Front did its best to ensure a peaceful change, issuing its last directive, which called for "Solidarity – discipline – moderation". It was obeyed in all respects. The lack of excess provided good evidence of the people's continued solidarity in obeying the Home Front's final instructions.[165]

Aware of German sensibilities, the Home Front waited until the capitulation formally went into effect at 12:01 a.m., May 9, before having its administrators assume office. But in the course of two days, the country had made the transition from war to peace in a joyous but remarkably peaceful fashion. Just months earlier very few persons in the Home Front and in the government in London had believed such an "ideal alternative" was possible.[166]

For the man who had done everything in his power *not* to have a peaceful changeover occur, this development was especially bitter; one which he was unwilling to experience personally. When he received the final setback of being ousted from office, Josef Terboven retired to his luxurious mansion, Skaugum, where Crown Prince Olav and his family would soon reestablish their residence. Here the ex-*Reichskommissar* ensconced himself with his longtime ally, Friedrich Rediess, the head of the German police. As always cool and realistic, Terboven knew that he would have no chance of avoiding the death penalty if taken prisoner. And as the dedicated National Socialist that he was, he preferred to follow his *Führer*'s example rather than to risk the unlikely prospect of finding haven in such parts of the world as South America or Spain. Rediess, who had overall responsibility for the acts of torture and murder committed by his police during the occupation, fully shared Terboven's outlook. Soldiers were ordered to make ready explosive charges in preparation for their imminent act of self-destruction. The two Nazis drank for hours to steel their courage. Suddenly the police general seized a pistol and shot himself. Dragging the body out into his personal bunker in the garden, Terboven thereafter lit the fuse of a waiting explosive charge. A few minutes later his guards carried away a concrete fragment covered with bits of bloody flesh, all that remained of the man who had been, under Hitler, the most powerful official in Norway.[167]

Terboven's suicide on May 8 occurred in a remarkably parallel manner to the deaths of two members of that small faction within NS that had shared the *Reichskommissar*'s commitment to fight to the end. Jonas Lie similarly recognized that as leader of the NS-controlled police, he could expect no clemency after the war. He therefore worked out of self-interest until the last days of the occupation to have NS follow a policy of resistance. Upon learning of the capitulation, he retreated to a farm in a suburb of Oslo on the night of May 7, accompanied by two other diehards, Henrik Rogstad, the *Hird* chief and head of the State Police, and Sverre Riisnæs, the Minister of Justice. Lie was determined not to give up without a struggle. When informed that the Home Forces had taken control of police headquarters at Møllergaten 19, he sent a force of front fighters that he had gathered into Oslo to recapture the station. But the German police were in no mood to permit final reckless measures by NS desperados. Having committed themselves to a peaceful capitulation, they refused to tolerate an act that could jeopardize the agreement. The head of the *Sicherheitspolizei*, Fehlis, therefore provided the Home Forces at police headquarters with a goodly supply of arms. Learning that their opponents had weapons, the front fighters lost their courage and abandoned the venture, dispersing instead.[168]

When he realized he no longer had an armed force at his disposal, Lie barricaded himself in a bunker along with Rogstad and Riisnæs. The trio had a large amount of arms and munitions, plus cases of liquor to strengthen their fortitude. Upon being surrounded by members of the

Home Forces, they tried at first to negotiate a surrender under which they would be interned as "officers", thereby gaining military status. The Home Forces instead demanded unconditional surrender, whereupon Lie and Rogstad chose to die in the bunker. Only Riisnæs, waving a white flag, eventually emerged to face what lay in store for him.[169]

Unlike Terboven and Lie, National Union's *Fører* did not seriously consider suicide at the war's conclusion. Once it became obvious that the Germans would shortly begin to abandon their control of Oslo, he too withdrew to the outskirts of the city, to Gimle, but here the parallel with Terboven and Lie ends. Following his final conference with the *Reichskommissar*, he returned home to have dinner with Maria early in the evening of May 7, at about 6:00 p.m. While they were dining, he broke the news to his wife that they probably would soon have to leave Gimle, and she should therefore begin to pack. After their meal, she immediately set to work, aided by her servants. The packing of personal belongings continued until midnight, with Quisling stopping in from time to time to check on their progress.[170]

He had no intention, however, of seeking to flee. His goal was to try to reach a negotiated settlement by which he would surrender under the most favorable terms. In an attempt to bargain from a position of power, he surrounded Gimle with what he could gather of his armed followers from the *Hird*, the Ski Battalion, and other NS formations. Most of NS' combat groups had already dispersed during the last two days, but still he was able to have at his disposal a force of approximately two hundred men.[171]

With the majority of his ministers having joined him at Gimle, on Tuesday, May 8, he appeared at least initially to project a position of outward strength. The Milorg leadership had not yet been able to mobilize fully its Home Forces in Oslo. The Home Front therefore was indecisive at first in determining what approach it should take when dealing with Quisling, not knowing for certain whether he intended to fight.[172] Consequently, the local Milorg chief in Oslo sent an envoy to Gimle in the early afternoon of May 8 with an offer to Quisling. He was told that if he surrendered, he and Maria would be interned under the Home Forces' protection in a villa in the exclusive Holmenkollen suburb of Oslo. According to the Milorg go-between, Dr. Bjørn Foss, Quisling rejected the proposal since it failed to include his ministers.[173]

He assumed, however, that this was but the beginning of the negotiations that he had anticipated. At the conclusion of his discussions with Dr. Foss, they agreed that Gimle would remain in contact with the Milorg envoy by phoning police headquarters at Møllergaten 19. Quisling tried to give the impression to Foss that he still had the potential to fight, declaring that in the Oslo area alone he had 30,000 men ready to defend him. But he maintained that he would not use force to protect himself because in the end the Home Forces would inevitably prove to be superior because of the Allied support that they could draw upon.[174]

This attempted show of bravado fooled no one, and did nothing to improve the atmosphere at Gimle. Maria Quisling recalled that dinner with the ministers that afternoon was silent and sad. She had already completed her packing in the morning.[175] Now she along with everyone else could only await the outcome of what they hoped would be successful negotiations.

The atmosphere became even more depressing later that evening. By revealing that he did not plan to resort to arms, Quisling had unwittingly given the Home Front exactly the information it desired. Thereafter all thought of possible internment disappeared from consideration. When Gimle later tried to re-establish contact with Dr. Foss, he was no longer available.[176] Instead, the ministers, seeking to resume negotiations on their *Fører*'s behalf, found themselves dealing with the Home Front's leading police officials, who had just assumed command at Møllergaten 19. As a result of the discussions that followed, Lippestad received a safe conduct pass to come to the police station in the late evening of May 8 to talk with the new head of the criminal division, Lars L'Abée-Lund.[177] For those at police headquarters, all doubts now disappeared concerning the prevailing attitude at Gimle. The police interpreted Lippestad's willingness to negotiate as a sign that the NS hierarchy had accepted defeat and would not resist.[178] Furthermore, by Tuesday evening Milorg's mobilization of its Home Forces units was in the process of being fully carried out, its members being well-armed with British-supplied weapons. Some 1,000 Home Forces irregulars were now in position, ready to attack Gimle if need be.[179]

Oslo was not yet, however, completely under the Home Front's control. As an indication of the air of uncertainty that still prevailed, just before the automobile carrying Lippestad arrived at Møllergaten 19, a group of drunken German sailors, despondent in defeat, began to shoot wildly about them with automatic weapons and rifles in the district immediately adjacent to the police station. The noise of gunfire reverberated, muzzle flashes lit the darkness, and bullets ricocheted down the streets. The police spent a number of anxious minutes wondering whether the NS minister would be able to reach the station unscathed. To their relief, his car pulled up safely just shortly after the shooting stopped. He began discussions with police officials at 11:47 p.m. The talks continued into the early minutes of May 9, to 00:25 a.m.[180]

Lippestad tried to resume bargaining along the same lines as earlier in the day in the meeting between Quisling and Dr. Foss. He insisted that Quisling must not be jailed as an ordinary criminal, but indicated that the former Minister President would surrender if he obtained a guarantee that he would be interned in a villa. Lippestad made reference to Foss' earlier visit, but indicated the commonly shared view at Gimle that Foss' offer could not have been legitimate, since it had been impossible to contact him at the telephone number where he said he could be reached.[181] Although he met several of the police leaders, Lippestad got nowhere. The arguments he presented carried no weight, and he received a disheartening response to take back with him through the Home Forces' lines. The police maintained they had no knowledge of Dr. Foss' previous contact with Gimle. Moreover, they refused to make any concessions. Instead, they made it clear to Lippestad that the order for Quisling's arrest had been issued, and the former Minister President would be seized, if need be by force, if he did not surrender willingly.[182]

Before he left, Lippestad resignedly indicated that he anticipated an unpleasant reception when he returned to Gimle with the police's terms.[183] His presumption was correct. The ministers had assumed that negotiations would continue on Wednesday.[184] News of the police's harsh conditions therefore came as a shock. As Fuglesang later confirmed, everyone at Gimle was now glumly aware that incarceration would occur under the strictest conditions.[185] Frantically during the early morning hours of May 9 the ministers tried, either through intermediaries or in direct conversation with Møllergaten 19, to persuade the police to postpone the deadline for surrender, set for 6:00 a.m., and to alter their terms and permit internment for Quisling.[186]

The latter was highly distraught. Having experienced so many disappointments during the occupation, followed by the surrender of Nazi Germany, which ended any possibility for him to be active in politics, he now faced the ultimate disgrace of being arrested as a criminal. The possibility of being imprisoned and tried as a traitor was what he had always dreaded the most. To avoid this prospect, he began even before the German surrender to prepare the line of defense that he would follow after the war. Not only was this a conscious effort on his part to try to convince others of the rightness of his actions during the occupation, but with his strong predisposition toward self–suggestive rationalization, he was equally engaged in persuading himself that everything he had done had been motivated solely by his concern for Norway. He sought to use every available opportunity to convince his listeners of his sincere intentions. During his discussions with Dr. Foss in the afternoon, when the two could clearly hear the sound of cheering from Oslo in celebration of the liberation, he had spent more than an hour in a defensive monologue justifying his past deeds.[187]

His first reaction, upon learning the police's terms, was therefore one of irrational anger whereby he rejected the ultimatum completely. Instead, he indicated through his intermediaries that he intended to telegraph Crown Prince Olav, relating how well he had governed the country during the past five years as head of state. He insisted that he would not allow himself to be treated as a common prisoner, and demanded a written guarantee from the head of the police that he would be interned and treated correctly. If these conditions were not met, he threatened that the NS members at Gimle would defend themselves until negotiations were resumed. Allowing his distraught fantasy full play, he maintained that if the Home Forces dared to use coercion against him, 200,000–300,000 armed men would rise as one throughout the country and sweep the Home Forces aside.[188]

When all efforts by intermediaries had failed, he personally took the phone at 5:44 a.m. on Wednesday morning to talk directly with the acting national police chief, Sven Arntzen. The latter had personally taken charge of the arrangements for Quisling's arrest. The prospective prisoner complained in the strongest terms concerning the possibility that he who had governed Norway in such an outstanding manner now faced being treated as an ordinary felon. He further emphasized that negotiations had previously taken place at Gimle, indicating his desire to keep such discussions alive in the hope of reaching a favorable arrangement. If the police continued to maintain their rigid demands, he threatened, then they would be responsible for all ensuing bloodshed. Arntzen, however, remained unyielding. No negotiations had taken place, he maintained, and he repeated his uncompromising ultimatum that Quisling's capitulation must be unconditional. The only concession that he earlier had been willing to make was that the deadline for surrender would be extended by half an hour to 6:30 a.m.[189]

Quisling was furious when he concluded this fruitless conversation. His threats had proven useless, and in his heart he knew that any attempted armed resistance would be futile. In one last desperate effort to rescue the situation, a call went out from Gimle at about 6:00 a.m., requesting that Quisling be allowed to send a telegram to the Crown Prince indicating his willingness to surrender his authority to the heir to the throne. The police curtly refused to permit the telegram to be sent.[190] Having discovered every avenue of escape blocked, Quisling finally saw that he had no choice but to comply, since he excluded a last-ditch armed defense or suicide. Shortly after six he indicated to a go-between that he and his ministers were ready to report to police headquarters.[191] He embraced Maria one last time, and for a moment considered a double suicide, but just as quickly rejected this way out.[192]

A final call from Gimle came to Møllergaten 19 at 6:15 a.m. Lippestad was on the line, requesting instructions on how to pass through the perimeter around Gimle. When asked, he indicated that he would not be reporting alone. At 6:22 a police control point notified Møllergaten that a cortège of automobiles had left Gimle, bound for Oslo.[193]

There was little traffic on the road to impair their progress so early in the morning, especially since gasoline was strictly rationed. At 6:45 the small procession of three automobiles pulled up in front of police headquarters. In the lead was Quisling's personal *"fører-car"*. He had received this monster of an automobile from Hitler as a personal gift. It served as an ideal vehicle for an unpopular leader. The car was a specially constructed Mercedes weighing four and one-half tons, with armored plating and inch-thick, bulletproof windows. As further protection, it also had specially built gun slots.[194]

As a security precaution, the police had deliberately set the deadline for his surrender as early as possible in the morning. Only a small group of onlookers therefore gathered outside when the most notorious figure in Norway entered the police station. They were attracted more by the unique presence of the *"fører-car"* than anything else. Following him into the building were the majority of his ministers – Fuglesang, Stang, Lippestad, Skancke, Vassbotten, and von Hirsch. Of those not present, Whist and Skarphagen were arrested separately, while Lie and Riisnæs remained in their beleaguered bunker, surrounded by Home Forces troops.[195]

Inside police headquarters, the former Minister President was received by the acting chief of police in Oslo, Henrik Meyer, who informed him and his officials that they were under arrest. Quisling protested, terming this an outrageous action. He repeated his standard defense in which he insisted that as head of state he had performed great services for his country and that he did not deserve the treatment he was receiving.[196] Indicating that he may have deluded himself into believing he might still be interned, he brought with him no less than four suitcases loaded with clothing, food, and drink. He obviously had intended to maintain the same life style that he was accustomed to at Gimle, since his luggage contained chocolate, cigarettes, cigars, and liquor, items not available for ordinary Norwegians. His ministers were similarly provisioned.[197] The manner in which they had outfitted themselves showed that at the time their bags were packed they too had hope of internment. But only cells awaited them at Møllergaten 19, although Quisling insisted that he had expected to be housed at Holmenkollen.[198]

Instead, he who had once maintained that as Minister President he possessed the authority of the *Storting*, the government, and the King combined, was now booked in the same manner as any ordinary suspected felon. He demanded that a formal protest be registered, indicating that he had expected better treatment. He regarded the entire procedure as a humiliating, degrading experience, in particular having to submit to a body search by the prison doctor like any other prisoner. The complaint was duly registered.[199] He and his ministers were received in a correct, impersonal manner at the time of their arrest. Police Chief Meyer emphasized to his guards that the newly arrived prisoners were to be treated in the same way as all other inmates awaiting trial.[200]

The booking was accomplished rapidly. By shortly after 7:00 a.m. Quisling had been placed in his cell.[201] His active period in Norwegian politics had thereby come to a sudden end. In the same building where so many of his foes who opposed NS and the Germans had been jailed during the war, awaiting torture, imprisonment, and often death, he now began the last and briefest chapter in his life.

CHAPTER XVIII

Imprisonment, Trial, Execution
May 9 – October 24, 1945

If my activity has been treason, . . . then I wish to God for Norway's sake that a good many of Norway's sons should become traitors like me, only that they be not thrown into jail.

> Vidkun Quisling, defense statement,
> September 7, 1945

His criminal activity has been so extensive and has caused so great harm that it must be subject to the law's most severe penalty.

> From the judgement against Quisling,
> September 10, 1945

Except for the limited time each day when he could pace about within the narrow confines of the prison's yard, Norway's most notorious prisoner was kept strictly confined to his cell in Oslo Kretsfengsel, the jail located immediately adjacent to police headquarters at Møllergaten 19. Out of concern that he might injure himself, and to prevent unauthorized individuals from gaining access to him, he was kept under constant surveillance.[1]

Prison officials had special reason for providing him with full protection. Immediately after the war's conclusion there was some sentiment in favor of bringing him before a court martial to receive a summary sentence, followed by execution at the hands of a firing squad. Responsible authorities insisted, however, that he should be tried according to standard legal practice.[2] The public would thereby have full knowledge of the evidence which served as the basis for the sentence that he would receive. This decision proved to be correct not only from a legal standpoint, but it was equally wise when viewed from a political perspective. As shown by later developments, had Quisling been executed summarily, his apologists would have used this as proof to sustain the myth that he had suffered a martyr's death.

In the immediate postwar period, however, it was impossible to follow strict legal rules that had previously been in effect. Under regular Norwegian judicial procedure, a suspect was entitled to appear before a judge within twenty-four hours after arrest in order to allow the pretrial court (*forhørsrett*) to determine whether there were grounds for prosecution, and whether or not the suspect should remain in custody. However, because of the large number of NS members and others who were jailed after the war under suspicion of different forms of collaboration, the interval between arrest and pretrial court appearance was extended considerably, up to four months.[3]

By comparison, the number of days Quisling spent in prison before his first court appearance was relatively brief. Seventeen days after his jailing, he travelled a few hundred yards from the prison to Oslo Courthouse. Despite the short distance, all security precautions were taken. The streets were cordoned off by armed police and soldiers, and the prisoner was driven in a black police van, accompanied by an armed military escort. The crowd that had been allowed to gather at some distance from the entrance caught only a glimpse of the former Minister President as he hurried out of the rear of the van into the gateway of the building, dressed in hat and raincoat despite the warm May sunshine.[4]

In the large courtroom on the first floor where the pretrial proceedings were held, full security measures continued to be in effect. Armed soldiers were positioned throughout the room, with one on either side of Quisling after he took his place in the witness box. At his first public appearance since his arrest, his face revealed nervousness and anxiety, and he had to struggle to maintain his composure. The surroundings added to his discomfort. Many death sentences had been pronounced by German judges in this dark room. Now the legal process had begun that could result in the same outcome for him.

The occasion certainly aroused publicity. Places were reserved for no fewer than fifty journalists, most of them foreigners. American and British interest was especially high in securing firsthand reports concerning the man who had become the symbol for treason during World War II. From the moment he appeared in the doorway, he was constantly bombarded by the flashing lights of press photographers as he made his way to the witness box.[5]

In the courtroom he came face to face with two men who for the next several months would exert a dominant influence on his life. Annæus Schjødt acted as prosecutor in the case, while Henrik Bergh served as the court-appointed defense counsel. Both were highly qualified experts in jurisprudence, but in having Bergh as his defender, one of Quisling's handicaps during the proceedings became apparent. Since all NS lawyers were automatically debarred from practicing law following the end of the occupation, the former *Fører* could not receive legal services from any of his followers. Bergh, however, was a skillful defender, with a long and varied legal background. Quisling later expressed admiration for and confidence in his attorney.[6]

Although the outcome was obvious, officially the purpose of the pretrial appearance was for the court to determine whether there were sufficient grounds for the police request that Quisling should remain imprisoned. For this purpose, a preliminary indictment was made public by the prosecution. Both the presiding judge and the prosecutor, Schjødt, emphasized that further investigation would undoubtedly result in more extensive charges at the time of the trial, and that the preliminary indictment was merely presented in order to permit the court to decide whether or not the accused should remain in confinement.[7] This proved to be a correct assumption. The prosecution's charges had been expanded considerably when Quisling later went on trial in August. Nevertheless, the preliminary indictment of May 26 contained much of the core of the charges that Schjødt introduced later during the trial. Quisling learned that initially he stood accused of treason; illegally seeking to bring Norway under foreign domination; aiding the enemy during wartime, including encouraging Norwegians to bear arms on behalf of the enemy; changing the Constitution illegally; and murder.[8]

He was questioned by the judge on each of the counts, and given full opportunity to explain himself. His replies were verbose and frequently emotional. While generally allowing him the privilege of giving as copious an answer as he wished, the judge did point out several times that the inquiry was not a trial, that he later would be given full opportunity to provide a detailed defense, and that he only needed to provide a short reply to the questions raised at the preliminary hearing. His defense attorney, Bergh, similarly urged him to give concise answers. But this type of response went against his nature. Before long he again replied with long monologues wherein he both attempted to present a favorable image of himself and to avoid giving concrete answers. Repeatedly he insisted, often in a tear-choked voice, that he had worked night and day to save Norway during the past five years. When questioned about specific actions that he had committed during the occupation, he sought to justify them in the most favorable manner, frequently trying to place blame for negative developments either on the Nygaardsvold government, which he described as having inadequately protected Norwegian interests, or on the Germans who, he maintained, had often pressured him and his NS administration.

The charge, however, which most visibly affected him was that of murder, concerning his complicity in the execution of Gunnar Eilifsen.[9] Since he had both signed the law of August 14, 1943, by which the policeman received the death sentence, and since he had refused to grant Eilifsen clemency, Quisling quite obviously was fully aware that this precise charge, while it did not involve the broad political and legal principles found in other parts of the indictment, was extremely serious and difficult to avoid

responsibility for. In this instance, he took considerable time before answering the judge's questions. When he did reply, he tried to escape accountability by seeking to blame Jonas Lie and the Germans for the law's
enactment. When examined closely concerning why he had not granted
clemency, he faulted the Germans for pressuring him, insisting that if he
had pardoned the policeman, the Germans would have gone ahead and
shot not only Eilifsen, but many more Norwegians as well.[10]

It hardly came as a surprise that Quisling's explanations, however
wordy and expressive, failed to impress either the judge or the spectators.
His assertion, for example, that he had governed Norway well during his
three years as Minister President provoked suppressed merriment. Under
the circumstances, the judge's decision was inevitable. He drew the obvious conclusion that because of the seriousness of the charges, Quisling
might attempt to avoid prosecution if allowed to go free until his trial came
up, or he might actively seek to suppress evidence. The court therefore
agreed with the request that he should remain in custody.[11]

Quisling appealed the decision on the spot. He complained that while
the court record contained a correct account of his answers, it nevertheless
did not present an accurate picture of his case because he had not been allowed to explain himself fully. His objection was duly noted in the court
record. Thereafter the courtroom was cleared, while the prisoner, accompanied by his armed escort, was driven back to his cell.[12] Four days later
the High Court (*lagmannsretten*) rejected his appeal.[13] He remained behind
bars until his trial began.

Quisling's objection that he had not been allowed to give a full account at
the inquiry was not merely a handy argument to justify his appeal against
continued incarceration. As happened so often when he faced a skeptical
questioner who demanded a logical explanation, and when forced to deal
with specifics rather than broad generalities, he had not been convincing.
Later, with no one present to ask probing questions, he proceeded to draw
up a detailed twenty-five page statement in which he replied to each of the
five charges in the preliminary indictment, and in addition he made a number of opening and closing comments.[14] While not required legally to make
such a response, he presented it in the endeavor to shed "full light" – the
phrase he had used in the pretrial inquiry – on the initial charges. He also
wanted to establish a documentary record for future defense of his actions.
In his cell he had ample time, as this commentary indicated, to pursue his
favorite habit of writing position papers.

It is noteworthy that in his response he seldom referred to legal arguments that could be used in his favor. On the few occasions when he did
resort to such reasoning, his views most often were pedantic, narrowly formalistic, and completely unrealistic. Generally, however, he used almost

solely political, historical, and moral arguments when discussing the charges in the indictment. This, of course, was a matter of necessity, since his legal position was weak to say the least. Indeed, he attempted to remove his case completely from the legal sphere by maintaining that his activity during the war was a political matter, not an issue for criminal proceedings. He insisted therefore that his past actions should either be investigated by a special commission or brought before a Court of Impeachment (*riksrett*).[15]

On the whole, the presentation that he made in his rebuttal, considering his weak position, was quite good. It generally gave the appearance of being both rational and logical. To someone not acquainted with the specific deeds he and his party had committed during the war, his argumentation could be accepted as being rather reasonable.

He did not, however, restrict himself to the war years. Instead, he gave a favorable review of his entire public career, going back to when he had been active in Russia.[16] He insisted that his sole consideration at all times had been to serve his country. When he did deal with critical issues, he continued the pattern observable at his preliminary inquiry. He sought whenever possible to avoid accountability for incriminating acts by seeking to shift the blame on to others. He denied any responsibility for the events of April 1940. The Nygaardsvold government, he insisted, should be held liable for bringing on the German invasion due to its alleged inadequate defense policy and its inability to defend the country's neutrality.[17] As for *his* actions during the first two days of the invasion, he spuriously maintained that a state of war had not begun until *April 11*, which he claimed had been the first day of mobilization. He had simply assumed governmental authority on April 9, he professed, out of a feeling of obligation to protect Norway's interests, since the government, parliament, and royal family had all fled.[18]

As for the acts he had initiated during the occupation, he argued in a general manner that everything his NS administrations had done was entirely legal. A country's citizens, he insisted, were not required to be loyal to a government in exile or obligated to obey its orders.[19] Despite all appearances to the contrary, he doggedly maintained he had not sought to alter the Constitution.[20] Nor had he intended to place Norwegian troops at the disposal of the Germans. He described the men who had fought for him on the eastern front as strictly "volunteers", declaring that his goal had always been to have them become the core of a future Norwegian armed force.[21] He once more tried to avoid being held accountable for Eilifsen's execution by placing responsibility for the enactment of the law of August 14, 1943, on the shoulders of Sverre Riisnæs and Jonas Lie. As for the killing itself, Terboven was described as having demanded it be carried out, which Quisling stated he reluctantly agreed to only because he wished to prevent additional executions.[22]

Perhaps the only really effective legal argument that he put forward was his contention that laws and ordinances passed by a government in exile did not have application unless they were later enacted in a proper manner. And even when properly approved, he argued, they could not be applied retroactively.[23] In this fashion, he attempted to avoid those parts of the indictment which were based on laws and ordinances issued by the Nygaardsvold government in England. As will be seen, this line of reasoning was followed by Quisling's defense throughout the entire legal process.

Only in the introduction and conclusion did he reveal his tendency at times to escape from reality, allowing his imagination free play to indulge in wishful speculation in which the world became what *he* wanted. In his opening statement he grandiosely proclaimed that he and NS had governed Norway as long as Olav Tryggvason – one of the most heroic kings of the Viking period – "and [we] have governed it well". The treatment that he and his NS followers were receiving after the war was therefore described as shameful and he demanded full "redress and compensation" for the "injury and insult" that he had sustained.[24]

This claim can at least be seen as an attempt, however farfetched, to maintain his complete innocence by going on the offensive. But in his conclusion he placed no limits on his propensity for vague historical philosophizing. In his most excessive glorification of himself, he had always been the great, all-seeing, superior being, far above the petty concerns of ordinary mortals. This attitude originated with his feeling of not coping in his daily struggle with concrete persons and events. His inferiority complex at times became so strong that it produced an extreme opposite in his prophetic manifestation. He had only infrequently revealed this characteristic earlier, but in prison, as he worked on his defense, he fully indulged in self-idealization. He analogously compared himself with St. Olav and Cromwell who, like him, had been misunderstood by their contemporaries, but who later were vindicated by history. Not merely did he portray himself as a great man, but also as the prophet who clearly perceived the future. He specifically referred to himself as a misunderstood prophet: "No prophet is accepted at home". In this capacity, he maintained that he had always unselfishly worked toward one goal: to make Norway "a model state in the new world order" which was developing everywhere with "irresistible power". In his most philosophical manner, he insisted that his involvement in politics had never been motivated by party interests, a means of earning a living, or a personal quest to satisfy vanity or a craving for power. For him, politics had been "public pragmatic action in the service of historical development for the benefit of one's own people and to further God's Realm on Earth which Christ came to found". Never had he openly shown his messianic complex more completely than in this description of himself as the Norwegian people's savior.[25]

On June 19, just two days before he completed his detailed exposition, he experienced an unsettling incident, which disturbed his usual prison routine. Without prior notice, he was suddenly removed from his cell. Accompanied by his armed guard, he was driven to Trandumskogen, a forest area located north of Oslo. During the war it had been part of a large German military complex. A grisly discovery had just been made here. The Germans had used Trandumskogen as an execution site for the killing of almost two hundred members of the resistance, whose bodies had been dumped in mass graves.[26]

The public was shocked by this revelation. Quisling was brought to Trandumskogen for the specific purpose of having him view in person the type of atrocities his German allies had committed. The incident had no further consequences, but it served as but one indicator of the bitter hostility that existed toward him and his party in 1945.

Not having been oriented beforehand, he was noticeably nervous when driven to the forest. The trip was fairly long, then taking about one and a half to two hours. Upon being shown the mass graves and the remains of those shot by the Germans, he naturally found the sight unpleasant, and at first made no comment. As time went on, however, his inquisitive nature revealed itself, and he began to ask for information beyond that which he first received when told why he had been brought to the site. He noticed NS prisoners had been put to work digging up the corpses, which he reacted to with distaste. When queried by a journalist, he declared he had no idea that such mass killings had occurred.[27] The veracity of the statement is unlikely. While he may not have been informed in detail about the shootings in Trandumskogen and at other German military camps, he undoubtedly knew about such executions through information supplied by his police officials and from other NS contacts with the Germans.

He was happy to depart from this tragic location, where bound and blindfolded men had been shot down and toppled into a waiting ditch.[28] His departure did not go unnoticed, however. News that he was present had spread rapidly among the appalled spectators. A crowd began to gather, and while it was kept at a distance, disparaging remarks accompanied the former Minister President as he drove off in the police car, back to prison.[29]

The assumption made at the pretrial inquiry that the charges against the accused would be considerably expanded proved to be amply justified. Annæus Schjødt completed the bulk of his indictment on July 11. The five original counts remained unchanged, but the prosecution had increased considerably the number of grounds on which they were based. In addition, four new charges had been added, which meant that Quisling, when brought to trial, would face a total of nine counts. Furthermore, at the time the trial began, the prosecution would insert several more specific grounds in the indictment as added justification for the charges against him.[30]

With the presentation of the indictment, Quisling and Henrik Bergh now had the opportunity to examine the charges in preparing the defense's case. As he had done earlier, Quisling chose to answer with a detailed reply, completed on August 7, thirteen days before his trial began.[31]

His response totalled twenty-five printed pages. It revealed that the accused was obviously shaken by the "numerous and severe charges" brought against him. He complained about the fact that he faced not only accusations concerning his political behavior, but that the indictment went so far as to seek to deprive him of his "good name and reputation".[32] In attempting to negate the indictment's thoroughness, he described it as being so detailed that one could not see the forest for the trees. By being so concrete and itemized, he argued, it failed to provide a complete account of why he had acted as he had. He maintained that the individual sections of the criminal law cited against him were not important. What should be considered instead, he insisted, was (1) under what conditions had he acted, (2) what had been his motives, and (3) what had he accomplished.[33]

His arguments, especially when trying to find legal justification for his actions, continued often to be narrowly formalistic and unrealistic in application. Nevertheless, on the whole his rebuttal to the July 11 indictment was presented as effectively as possible. There was no indication that his mental faculties were impaired in any way, a conclusion that would later be verified in the course of his trial.

He did not attempt to ignore any of the charges, but provided a defense against each specific point raised by the prosecution. Since these will be covered in the account of the trial, only a general reference will be made here to the contents of his August 7 response to the indictment.

As before, he diligently sought to present the best justification for his actions. Not content to be on the defensive, he repeatedly attacked the Nygaardsvold government, which he described as being responsible for the calamities that befell Norway prior to, during, and after the invasion.[34] On the other hand, he continued to insist that the sole motive for everything he had done was "to serve my country and people in the best manner".[35] As proof of this contention, he referred several times to Paal Berg's words of thanks on April 15, 1940, for Quisling's alleged patriotism and responsibility at the time of the German invasion.[36]

He especially emphasized how he, as a good patriot, had striven to protect and to maintain Norway's independence from the Germans. In this regard, however, he was not so naive as to assume he could completely wash his hands of all involvement with the Third Reich. While critical of many German actions in Norway, not surprisingly especially those of Terboven, he continued to praise Hitler for his alleged dedication in defending Europe from a Communist takeover. Above all, however, Quisling insisted that his policy toward the Third Reich had been based on the fundamental assumption that Germany would win the war, a presumption that he maintained had been justified at the time. And acting in accord with this belief, he maintained he had sought to establish as independent a position for Norway as possible.[37]

Having authored this formal written response, which was included in the documentation used in his trial,[38] he had done what he could to prepare for his defense. In his two pretrial statements he had shown clearly his determination to defend his conduct as strongly as possible. He indicated no regret, and no intention of asking for clemency. It now remained to be seen how well he could present a credible defense when facing a skeptical tribunal and confronted by an aggressive prosecutor.

As the date of the trial approached, interest in the Quisling case remained great because of his notoriety, not only in Norway but internationally as well. His pending court appearance even overshadowed an earlier dramatic case which Quisling had attempted to exploit, Leon Trotsky's trial and subsequent expulsion. In the late summer of 1945 many foreign journalists and legal observers, anticipating a sensation, arrived in Norway to observe Quisling's trial. As a result, the courtroom in the Oslo Courthouse was much too small. The proceedings were therefore moved to the largest hall available. Ironically, this proved to be the Oslo Masonic Lodge, whose property Quisling stood accused of stealing in one of the counts which he faced. Because so many wished to be spectators, special tickets had to be issued for the proceedings. The number of Norwegians in attendance was therefore limited considerably owing to the large foreign contingent.[39]

The start of the trial also resulted in a change in the defendant's place of incarceration. For security reasons, he was moved from Oslo Kretsfengsel to the familiar confines of Akershus Castle, which served also as a prison after the war. From here it was easy to transport him the short distance to the Masonic Lodge, which lay immediately adjacent to the military installation.

With the necessary preparations having been duly carried out, the attention of the entire world was directed toward Oslo when Quisling went on trial for his life in the High Court, *Eidsivating lagmannsrett*. He appeared before a judicial tribunal of nine members. Four were professional judges, while the remainder were laymen who had been chosen by lot: two barbers, a plumber, a chemical worker, and a bookkeeper.[40] Ordinarily, the number serving on such a panel was restricted to seven, but two additional persons were included in this important case as a precaution against a possible loss of a panel member due to illness or other reasons. If all were still present at the end of the trial, which proved to be the case, two would be removed by lot, one judge and one layman.[41]

A highly respected judge, Erik Solem, served as the president of the court (*lagmann*). As such, it was he who was responsible for conducting the proceedings. Previously, he had been a member of the Supreme Court, having belonged to the group of justices who resigned in protest against NS Nazification of the courts. After the war, he had been specially assigned to preside over major treason trials, that of Quisling unquestionably being the most important.

Despite Solem's legal experience, his participation in the Quisling case created considerable controversy. This was because he had been a leading member of the Home Front, and he furthermore had been one of the authors of a special law (*landssvikanordningen*) which served as the basis for the indictments of many persons accused of treason. Henrik Bergh therefore quickly raised an objection before the trial began, insisting that Solem lacked objectivity and should be disqualified. The question was brought before an appellate panel of the Supreme Court, which refused to sustain the challenge. It pointed out that the legislation which Solem had authored had no direct application in Quisling's case. As for the defense's contention that Solem should be removed because he earlier had expressed opposition to Quisling's policies during the war, the panel insisted that if this objection were applied broadly, there would hardly be a person in Norway qualified to sit in judgement at the trial.[42]

Serving therefore with the Supreme Court's sanction, Solem performed ably as an effective court administrator during the trial. It was a major accomplishment on his part to complete such a complex and wide ranging hearing within a relatively short period, while at the same time giving both the prosecution and the defense, including the defendant personally, all the time they required to conduct their case. Only one fault could be found with Solem's conduct. He did not always conduct the proceedings in a completely unbiased manner. His strong temperament, heightened by his deep personal involvement in the resistance movement, caused him at times to voice impatience or irony during the trial, especially when Quisling attempted, not infrequently, to avoid giving a direct answer to a difficult question.[43]

At 10:00 Monday morning, August 20, 1945, Solem opened the proceedings by declaring the court in session and introducing the members of the tribunal. The large hall was filled to capacity. The first rows were set aside for the some two hundred foreign journalists who had come to cover the trial, representing press bureaus, newspapers, and magazines from many countries. When the trial began, anxious photographers, to Quisling's open annoyance, rushed through the cordon of guards to snap his picture.[44] Such occurrences, however, were rare. On the whole, the trial took place under the strictest protocol. During its entire length there occurred no unexpected outbursts from the spectators, and not the slightest hint of any type of demonstration.[45] An American journalist, having perhaps expected a more emotional atmosphere, reported that the proceedings were conducted in a manner reminiscent of "the quiet decorum of a Lutheran Church service".[46]

After opening the trial, Solem proceeded to read verbatim the detailed indictment. It provided proof of the extensive preparation made by the prosecution since the issuance of its preliminary indictment of May 26. Schjødt and his staff had worked extremely hard in gathering evidence, with some documents being submitted for use in the trial just a few days before it began.[47] As a result, a large number of grounds for the charges were given in the indictment – especially in the major counts which Quisling faced.[48]

The initial count charged him with treason as defined under the military penal code. In addition to referring to his radio speech of April 9, 1940, in which he usurped governmental authority, and his attempt to recall mobilization on April 10 (grounds A and B), four additional grounds had been added to substantiate this charge: C – on April 11 the press had publicized yet another of his demands that mobilization be halted; D – on either April 9 or 10 he had attempted to induce the naval batteries on Bolærne in the outer Oslo fjord to cease fire, and, furthermore, as a reserve officer, he should have responded to mobilization in April 1940; and E – on April 12 he issued an appeal to Norwegian naval officers to surrender.[49]

The second count referred to the section in the civilian criminal code of May 22, 1902, which imposed penalties against those who sought to bring Norway under foreign jurisdiction. Of the charges, this was the most extensive. Not only did it include all the grounds in the first count of the indictment (ground A), but it encompassed a number of additional detailed grounds: B – his prewar conspiracy with Nazi leaders concerning a German occupation of Norway, and his receipt of secret funds for this purpose; C – his formation of the April 9 "government," his order to Colonel Hiorth at Elverum on April 9 to arrest the Nygaardsvold government, and his aid to the Germans on April 9 in seizing control of the Defense Department; D – his efforts during the period April 15 – September 25, 1940, to eliminate the legally recognized Administrative Council so that he might come to power and be able to work for Norway's inclusion in a Germanic federation under German leadership; E – his service to the occupying power during the Commissarial Council and as Minister President; F – his aid to the Germans in suppressing Norwegian resistance activity and his attacks against the legal government, his work to raise volunteers for the German military, and his attempt to persuade Nazi authorities to carry out mobilization of Norwegians on behalf of Germany.[50]

The third major count referred to the section in the civilian criminal code dealing with those who illegally bear arms against Norway. As grounds for this count, the indictment referred to all those cited under the first two counts, plus the grounds found in count V.[51]

In count IV the defendant stood accused of having sought to change the Constitution illegally. Reference was made not only to his efforts in April 1940 and as Minister President (grounds A and B), which had earlier been parts of the pretrial indictment, but also, in ground C, to the fact that he had sought during the entire occupation to establish and expand a Nazi form of government, while in ground D reference was made to all of the grounds cited in count II.[52]

Following consultation with the defense attorney, Schjødt agreed to eliminate one of the grounds for count V, ground C, which had charged Quisling with being an accomplice in the deaths of front fighters who had served on his behalf against the Russians.[53] This accusation quite obviously was based on rather tenuous legal reasoning, which explains why the prosecution dropped it. The remaining four grounds were serious enough for the defendant, however, since they were used to substantiate the charge of murder – either for having directly caused the death of another or for having contributed thereto. The count was no longer restricted merely to the execution of Gunnar Eilifsen (ground D), but had been expanded to include A – charging Quisling with being an accessory to the murder of Viggo Hansteen by the Germans; B – the Minister President's encouragement of the deportation of Jews to German death camps; and E – his refusal to grant clemency to fourteen condemned Home Front members, twelve of whom were shot in retaliation for Marthinsen's liquidation.[54]

The remaining four counts all involved accusations of economic malfeasance. As such, they assumed secondary importance in the trial. Schjødt specifically commented in his opening statement that he did not feel it was necessary to use these charges as a basis for the verdict which he intended to request. Nevertheless, these counts were included for a very specific purpose. The prosecution wished to present the public with as complete a picture as possible of Quisling's character, thereby preventing any misconceptions and the creation of possible future myths that could arise over whether or not he had used his position illegally for his own enrichment.[55]

Of these economic charges, count VI was by far the most detailed. It was based on the section in the criminal code concerning theft of another's property. Quisling stood accused of personally having benefited from the theft of belongings from A – the Royal Palace; B – the Norwegian Society; and C – the Masonic Lodge. In addition, as NS *Fører* or as Minister President, he was charged with the confiscation of goods owned by D, the political parties in September 1940; E – persons declared guilty of "hostile activity toward the people and the state" by a law of March 19, 1942; F – Norwegian Jews, whose property was seized on October 26, 1942; and

G – persons defined as having fled the country illegally by the law of May 20, 1943.[56]

Count VII referred to the section of the criminal code concerning persons who illegally obtain property belonging to another. As grounds for this accusation, it was charged that Quisling allowed payment of state funds for himself and his ministers to which they were not entitled, including his personal salary, funds for Gimle and the Eagle's Nest, payments to NS, funds to the *Hird* for weapons training, and payments to volunteer front fighters in various military formations.[57]

The two final counts concerning economic misdeeds were relatively simple. Count VIII referred to the sections of the criminal code concerning receipt of stolen property. Two grounds were cited for this charge: A – Quisling's receipt of the present of 300,000 *kr.* from Prytz, and B – a gift to Quisling from Dietrich Hildisch, a prominent businessman, in the amount of 400,000 *kr.* in 1944. The last count, IX, concerned the section of the civilian criminal code which referred to persons who obtain illegal gains through the neglect of another's affairs that is under the accused's jurisdiction. As basis for this charge, reference was made A – to count VII, and B – Quisling's takeover of the Fyresdal parsonage in 1944.[58]

Following the listing of these numerous charges, the indictment contained three brief paragraphs which became the focus of one of the most contested parts of the case. The prosecution made use of provisional decrees enacted in exile by the Nygaardsvold government which allowed extended application of the death penalty. Two decrees dating from October 3, 1941, separately affected the military penal code and the civilian criminal code, while a second decree of January 22, 1942, referred to the civilian criminal code alone.[59] When linked with the serious crimes that Quisling stood accused of having committed, it was obvious from the very beginning that the prosecution intended to demand the death penalty.[60]

Considering the fact that the indictment's reference to the provisional decrees stressed the fact that the accused's life was at stake, the final paragraph seemed anticlimactic, even banal. It stated briefly that the prosecution intended, under the provisions of the criminal code, to seek economic compensation in an amount proportionate to what the defendant had gained from his illegal actions.[61]

Having heard the indictment read, the defendant, when asked, declared he was not guilty of any of the charges.[62] The prosecutor thereupon made a preliminary address in which he documented his charges.[63] In the course of his statement, he contradicted a number of Quisling's written explanations. Essentially, however, Schjødt was simply providing the court with an outline of what he intended to prove, and the prosecution's charges were discussed in far greater detail later in the trial during Quisling's testimony and the examination of witnesses. However, in his introductory remarks Schjødt raised two fundamental points which served as the bedrock of the government's case. In refuting the defendant's contentions that his actions in April 1940 were justified because of the Nygaardsvold government's alleged incompetence in looking after Norwegian interests, the prosecutor emphasized that such a viewpoint was groundless in a representative democracy: "Discontent with a country's politics and its results does not give any citizen the right to actions of the kind that Quisling has taken, and does not in any way excuse his actions."[64] In a second basic statement of principle, he similarly demolished another main point made by Quisling: that his activity during the occupation was legal because he had served as head of state, or, during the Commissarial Council period, as leader of the only legally recognized party. Schjødt instead stressed that:

> This case shall be judged according to Norwegian law and jurisprudence, and according to Norwegian law and jurisprudence the accused has never been head of state in Norway. That he has attempted to set himself up as such, that he has entered German service against his country, does not exempt him from any Norwegian criminal law, but is in itself to a high degree a punishable offense.[65]

Despite the great number of divergent facts, contradictory explanations, and differing interpretations brought into play during the course of the trial, these two vital principles provided the major basis for why Quisling was on trial for his life in a liberated Norway.

Following the conclusion of the prosecution's address, Solem asked whether the defendant wished to present an explanation to each of the charges against him. Quisling answered without hestitation in the affirmative.[66] During the court's detailed examination of the defendant which followed, the trial entered its most critical phase. In keeping with Norwegian court procedure, the questioning was led by Solem as the tribunal's presiding judge. The prosecutor at this point was largely restricted to reading the documentary material on which the questioning was based. As a rule, only after the presiding judge had finished with a point did the prosecuting and defense attorneys raise questions.

Solem carried out his interrogation basically in chronological sequence, beginning with Quisling's activity in the period before the German invasion. With reference to that part of the indictment charging him with having sought to bring Norway under foreign jurisdiction (count II, ground B), much of the questioning concerned his dealings with leading figures in the Third Reich during 1939–1940, in particular Rosenberg, Raeder, and Hitler. In reply to the judge's pointed questions, Quisling found it extremely difficult to offer a plausible defense because the prosecution had been able to accumulate a large number of incriminating documents, in particular from Rosenberg's office and from Raeder's naval command. Time after time he had to insist that their contents gave a false picture of his viewpoint and goals. He denied being involved in conspiratorial planning with Rosenberg's office.[67] He declared that the German accounts of his meetings with Raeder and Hitler were inaccurate.[68] He had not, he maintained, received any funds from Rosenberg's office via Scheidt.[69] As for Scheidt's reports from Norway concerning his dealings with Quisling in early 1940, the latter denied having had any contact with Rosenberg's representative before April 9, 1940. The defendant tried to destroy the credibility of this evidence by testifying that Scheidt often had written a great deal of "nonsense".[70]

Quisling's repeated denials and attempts to explain away such incriminating evidence were not especially convincing, in particular since there was no doubt as to the authenticity of the documents. Rosenberg had vouched for this in an interrogation at Nuremberg, and his testimony was read into the court record.[71] It was significant that Quisling, despite his protestations, did admit he had planned to seize power under certain conditions. Placing the best possible light on this revelation, he declared that if the British and French had landed troops in Norway in 1940, he would then have proceeded to take action against the Nygaardsvold government, since it would not have offered resistance. Having assumed control, his "national party" would then have appealed to the Germans for assistance. His motive, he argued, would have been to establish a good relationship with the Germans, who would thereby have come to Norway as "helpers", and not as "conquerors". He emphasized how important the need to be in favor with the Germans had been because they would inevitably have succeeded in taking over the country.[72] But contrary to the material in the documents, he steadfastly denied that he had ever taken part in any discussions involving plans for a preventive action on the Third Reich's behalf, coming before an Allied move against Norway.

He also had considerable difficulty in providing a convincing explanation in response to another accusation against him, that of treason under the military penal code (count I, ground D). This charge in part grew out of his failure to report for mobilization in 1940, as all reserve officers were obliged to do. The prosecution provided documentation to show that Quisling had received a written order to report to the General Staff in the event of mobilization.[73] In reply, the defendant maintained that he had obtained special dispensation from the army so that he would not have to serve under the Nygaardsvold government "either in peace or in war".[74] He rigidly adhered to this lame explanation, even after the former commanding general who supposedly had given this dispensation appeared as a witness and completely rejected the assertion.[75] The head of the General Staff in 1940 similarly testified that he had no knowledge of any special arrangement with Quisling in the event of a mobilization.[76]

Of the offenses which the defendant was charged with, the most wide ranging concerned his activity in April 1940, when he usurped governmental authority and attempted to establish himself as head of state. These were also among the easiest for the prosecution to prove because the majority had occurred publicly before the entire nation, either over the radio or in the press. No less than four of the five main counts at least in part stemmed from his effort to seize power in April 1940: treason under the military penal code (count I, grounds A, B, C, D, and E); provisions in the civilian criminal code against seeking to bring Norway under foreign jurisdiction (count II, grounds A and C); provisions in the civilian criminal code against those who illegally bear arms against Norway (count III); and the civilian criminal code's prescribed punishment for those who seek to change the Constitution illegally (count IV, ground A).

When asked to comment on the factual substance on which these counts were based, he had no alternative but to admit having carried out such actions as the radio speech of April 9, in which he proclaimed himself prime minister and declared the Nygaardsvold government dismissed (count I, ground A; count II, ground A); his attempt to halt mobilization on April 10 (count I, ground B; count II, ground A); and a further effort on April 11 to halt mobilization through the press (count I, ground C; count II, ground A).[77] He did deny, however, the less easily verifiable treason charges of having sought to convince the fortress at Bolærne to cease fire (count I, ground D), and that he had broadcast an appeal to Norwegian naval officers to surrender on April 12 (count I, ground E).[78] When confronted with the accusation that he had ordered Colonel Hiorth at Elverum to arrest the Nygaardsvold government on April 9 (count II, ground C), Quisling could not disavow the fact that he had telephoned Hiorth, since he knew that the Colonel would be called as a witness. But he attempted to deny that he had commanded the Colonel to make an arrest, maintaining instead that he had merely advised Hiorth to do so. Quisling's explanation on this point, however, was very implausible. His testimony frequently contradicted what he had just said previously, and he never tried to hide the fact that he believed the Nygaardsvold government should have been arrested.[79]

On the whole, he was deliberately quite vague when Solem and Schjødt asked him specific questions about the background and motives for the formation of his April 1940 government (count II, ground C). He could not recall, for example, whether Scheidt had been present when deliberations took place at Hotel Continental about whether he should proclaim a government. He finally admitted that Scheidt had been in attendance, but he then said he could not remember when his German contact had arrived.[80] He was equally vague in providing details about the incident where he had assisted the Germans in seizing control of the Defense Department (count II, ground C), all the while insisting that his motive in accompanying the Germans to the Defense Department had been to *prevent* them from taking over the building. He refused to be pinned down concerning the exact time when this event occurred on April 9 because it would have been especially incriminating for him to admit that it took place *before* he had declared himself head of the government, and that he therefore had no authority whatsoever, not even self-proclaimed, to act as he did.[81]

In short, the testimony he gave concerning his activity in April 1940 was hardly convincing, despite his best efforts to provide a justifiable explanation. His main contention was that he had acted as a patriot in an emergency situation, improvising desperately in order to save his country after the government had abdicated its responsibility.[82] But when he had to respond to questions concerning specific details, he quite often directly contradicted himself, or else he tried to avoid the question by giving a vague general answer or by dodging it completely through seeking to change the subject.

The prosecutor had equally good documentation at hand to support his charges when the court moved on to examine Quisling's role in the period after April 1940. Time after time the defendant was confronted with the incriminating pro-German viewpoints he had expressed in his correspondence during the war. In responding to questions concerning the accusation that he had worked to undermine the Administrative Council in the period April 15 – September 25, 1940 (count II, ground D), he tried to provide an explanation for his expressed sympathy for the German cause by resorting to an argument that he employed frequently throughout his trial. He insisted that his pro-German statements were motivated tactically – that he had presented the NS case "from their [the German] point of view" in order to influence the German reader to act on his behalf.[83] He, of course, was only concerned with protecting Norwegian interests.

When dealing with the charge that he had contributed to bringing Norway under foreign jurisdiction by his formation of the National Government in February 1942 (count II, ground E), he sought to employ a legal argument to justify his takeover as Minister President. He maintained that legally there existed no hindrance to his forming a government. He cited the fact that the *Storting*'s Presidency had asked the King to abdicate in the summer of 1940, and the King could not reign from outside the country without the *Storting*'s approval. At the most, insisted Quisling, Haakon VII's reign had expired six months after he had left Norway.[84] However, not merely legally, but politically as well, Quisling's argumentation had little basis in reality. The King had not abdicated, nor had the *Storting* ever taken any formal step to remove him. The entire question became moot with the German termination of the State Council negotiations and the forced imposition of the Commissarial Council.

The formation of the National Government was also included in the indictment's count IV, ground B – illegally seeking to change the Constitution. Quisling denied that he had acted in such a manner, maintaining instead that as Minister President he had conducted himself in accordance with the King's prerogatives as prescribed in the Constitution.[85] Again he attempted to use a narrow legal interpretation as justification, ignoring completely the fact that the King's authority over the course of years had been restricted by the development of democratic practices. Quisling could find no sliver of legal backing, however, to explain the basis for his self-proclaimed takeover of the power previously held *collectively* by the *Storting* and the sovereign. He could only maintain that this had been a "transitional arrangement" which was not intended to be permanent.[86] His defense against this charge was extremely thin, a fact that Solem pointed out. The presiding judge declared that realistically it might be possible to carry out political change through the exercise of raw power, either one's own or through that resting on the "bayonets" of a foreign invader. But *legally*, insisted Solem, there was but one way to change "Norway's Constitution and laws, and that is . . . through the *Storting*". All other means were illegal.[87]

Not unexpectedly, Quisling found it equally difficult to explain the help he had provided to the Germans during the occupation, this coming under the charge of seeking to bring Norway under foreign jurisdiction (count II, ground F). Such assistance was especially hard to defend in the light of the barbarous methods employed by the Nazis during the war. When questioned, he again resorted to evasion. He maintained that he had no more knowledge about the existence of concentration camps than the average Norwegian, and he denied being aware of the use of torture during the war.[88] As for his encouragement of the recruitment of volunteers to join the various military formations that fought on Germany's side, he declared that his primary motive had been to use this as a means of trying to regain full sovereignty through the restoration of an armed force.[89] Quite obviously, however, it was impossible for him to come up with a plausible explanation for why he had urged the Germans to permit him to carry out a *forced mobilization* of Norwegians. He therefore denied point blank ever having done so, even though the prosecution provided ample documentation to the contrary.[90]

He continued his pattern of denying involvement whenever possible when confronted with count V, charging him with direct contribution to another's death or being an accessory thereto. Accused of having personal responsibility for the execution of Viggo Hansteen by the Germans (ground A), he testified that he had only wished to have Hansteen removed from his position with LO, not put to death.[91] In general, the defendant tried to distance himself as much as possible from the state of emergency in September 1941 under which Hansteen was executed.[92]

In response to the accusation that he had contributed to the murder of Norwegian Jews (ground B), Quisling again resorted to evasion. He denied he had ever encouraged hatred against the Jews. As for their arrest and deportation, he insisted that the Germans were the guilty ones. He had personally, he professed, had very little knowledge of what befell the Jews. He allegedly had no prior knowledge of the fact that they would be arrested, nor was he aware of their fate when sent to Poland.[93] He was willing to acknowledge only one element of the anti-Semitism that he had voiced so consistently during the war – his ideological commitment to belief in an international Jewish conspiracy. Asked by Solem whether he had ever in his speeches presented the view that the Jews were guilty of having committed many calamities in the world, he replied: "Yes, that is my absolute conviction".[94] Still, he continued to maintain that he in no way approved of the German treatment of the Jews. Schjødt in turn felt that Quisling's anti-Semitic agitation had been so obvious during the war that it was not even necessary to document the defendant's own statements to this effect.[95]

So much attention had earlier been given to the accusation that Quisling was responsible for the execution of Gunnar Eilifsen (ground D) that the trial shed relatively little light on this question. The accused continued to hold the Germans responsible, insisting that if he had granted clemency, the Germans would have shot the policeman anyhow, and a number of other Norwegians as well.[96]

His line of defense remained similar in response to the final accusation under this count, concerning his complicity in the execution of fourteen persons, the first two in May 1944 and the remainder following the Home Front's liquidation of Marthinsen in February 1945 (ground F). He argued that he could not have granted clemency to those initially put to death because of the special nature of the situation under which they were convicted.[97] As for those shot in February 1945, he again alleged that he had been compelled to accept the executions because the Germans would have killed many more Norwegians if he had not.[98]

Because of the lesser importance which the prosecution attached to the economic charges against the defendant, the court did not spend a great deal of time examining him on each of the specific grounds in these counts, especially as witnesses were later scheduled to testify on these matters. In response to the points under the indictment's count VI accusing him of theft, Quisling for once did not have to face a number of difficult questions. Instead, he was in large part allowed to read from his previously prepared written response of August 7. In answer to grounds A, B, and C, wherein he stood accused of having stolen items from the Royal Palace, the Norwegian Society, and the Oslo Masonic Lodge, he declared that he had simply taken charge of the belongings of persons or organizations out-lawed by German authorities. His motive, he maintained, was not personal gain, but merely to keep such property under Norwegian control.[99] He did not, however, entirely avoid having to answer the court's inquiry concerning this count. Solem in particular wished to have an explanation for why the engraved initials in the Norwegian Society's silverware had been removed. The defendant was quite obviously nettled by this question. He could only try to maintain that he had nothing whatsoever to do with the removal of the initials, but he could provide no plausible answer for why it had been done. He was reduced to insisting that everything which the Society had previously owned had become his personal property after the organization had been dissolved by the *Reichskommissariat*.[100] As for the charges involving the confiscation of property belonging to the political parties, to persons hostile to the NS administration, to Jews, and to persons who had fled the country (grounds D, E, F, and G), he maintained that the takeover of such property had been forced upon the NS administration by the Germans. Furthermore, he pointed out that in two instances such possessions were not retained by NS, but became state property (grounds E and G).[101]

With regard to the charge that he had illegally used state funds as payment for himself and his ministers, for National Union and the *Hird*, and for volunteers in the various military units that NS had organized (count VII), he argued that he had been justified in using public revenue to carry out his official obligations as head of state. He further contended that such moneys had not been used for personal purposes.[102]

The eighth count in the indictment concerned large sums of money that he had received from prominent NS members. He testified that the 300,000 *kr.* which he had obtained from his finance minister, Prytz (ground A), was a personal gift that Prytz had collected from friends who wished to be anonymous, and did not involve any public funds. The prosecution believed otherwise.[103] Quisling also explained that another large sum in the amount of 400,000 *kr.* which he had accepted from Dietrich Hildisch (ground B) had been intended to be used for humanitarian purposes. But when a question arose over whether Hildisch owed outstanding tax payments on this money, Quisling declared he had paid back the amount which Hildisch appeared to owe in taxes, some 300,000 *kr.*[104]

Of the charges involving economic malfeasance, count VIII was definitely the weakest. The prosecution suspected that Quisling had received the funds illegally, either as a result of theft from the state or through tax evasion, but for once the arguments which the defendant presented could not be breached. Recognizing its weak position, the prosecution eventually dropped this count.[105]

In contrast, the explanation which he gave to the main point raised in the indictment's final count (count IX, ground B) was extremely feeble. He stood accused of having illegally taken possession of the Fyresdal parsonage, which was state property. As justification, he explained first that the parsonage had been in his family "for 400 years", which was untrue. He further said that he had not really wanted the property, but he had felt obliged to take it over since it was falling into decay. He insisted that he had not intended to use the parsonage personally, but had planned to turn it into a humanitarian institution, an orphanage. As for the arrangement by which he secured title to the property, he tried to avoid any involvement whatsoever, maintaining that Skancke, as Minister of Church and Education, alone had been responsible for the transfer.[106]

On this point as well as on the countless others throughout his trial, Quisling attempted to escape responsibility by shifting blame onto others. His entire testimony in essence amounted to a complete repudiation of the *Führer* principle that he previously had championed so strenuously. This evasiveness struck one of the observers at the trial, a young legal expert who later became one of Norway's leading constitutional authorities, Professor Johannes Andenæs, as being the main characteristic which Quisling displayed during the entire courtroom proceedings:

> The strongest impression that I retained was a deep disappointment over the lack of stature in this *fører*. This was not the man who came forward and said: "I did it, I believed it was right, and I take responsibility for what I have done." Instead one saw a man who on every point tried to escape responsibility.[107]

This endeavor to avoid accountability was a deliberate strategy which Quisling consistently followed. His attempts to dodge the accusations levied against him were carried out in a rational, calculated manner. All of his mental resources were directed toward achieving this aim, another fact that Andenæs observed:

> Quisling demonstrated a clearly defined ability to detect what was dangerous for him. He always had excuses, circumlocutions, [and] evasions at hand when he scented danger. When no other escape was possible, he denied point blank, even when faced with irrefutable evidence, while at the same time showing great inventiveness when it came to bringing up points which could in any way weaken the evidence.[108]

Almost all of his attempts to evade the charges were fruitless. The evidence presented by the prosecution was too overwhelming for even the slickest prevaricator, a league to which Quisling, despite his best efforts, did not belong. Furthermore, the damaging material which came up during the court's questioning of the defendant was reinforced in many instances by the testimony of witnesses. No less than fifty-five persons were called to testify. Of these, the overwhelming majority, forty-eight, served as witnesses for the prosecution.

The quality of the testimony by the prosecution's witnesses was at times uneven. Although much was quite telling, in a minority of instances it was not particularly effective. Included within the latter category were accounts based on secondhand information, those which were repetitive, or which dealt with peripheral or insignificant points.[109] Viewed as a whole, however, the testimony of the witnesses served to sustain the prosecution's case on a number of points.

Two leading officers from the General Staff substantiated the fact that the defendant's attempt to terminate the mobilization order on April 9 had caused considerable confusion, greatly increasing the difficulty which the military had in carrying out mobilization.[110] This testimony strongly sustained the charge that Quisling was guilty of treason (count I, ground B).

From an emotional point of view, the description of the inhuman manner in which the deported Jews met their deaths at Auschwitz was even more damning, especially as it was presented as firsthand evidence by two of the small number of twenty-five who had survived the death camp.[111] Brought face to face with these men, who graphically but objectively described the crime that he had encouraged and contributed to, Quisling had no recourse except again to try to deny direct involvement. He went so far as to maintain that he had no knowledge of the deportation of the Jews until after their forced departure, even though it was obvious to everyone in the courtroom that he was fabricating.[112]

The spectators observed an even greater use of fantasy and evasion when Quisling's former number two man, Hagelin, was brought in to testify. He had been preceded on the witness stand by several persons who had personal knowledge of the large sums of money that he had carried with him during the months prior to the invasion.[113] The prosecution therefore quite obviously intended to use his testimony to corroborate the charge that Quisling had conspired with the Nazi leadership in 1939–1940 to bring Norway under German control, and that he had received funds for this purpose (count II, ground B).

The courtroom was filled with dramatic tension when Hagelin appeared, with the two former leading NS figures confronting each other. They studiously avoided direct eye contact. Each knew that the other had so much incriminating information that any defense which they individually were capable of establishing would crumble if either testified openly. As a witness, Hagelin therefore proved to be a great disappointment for the prosecution. He insisted that he could remember nothing because he allegedly had been receiving medical treatment for loss of memory since

November 1944. Because of this fictitious disability, he consistently denied any knowledge of the incriminating subjects raised by Schjødt: he did not recall having discussed politics with Rosenberg and Scheidt, or of having met Raeder and Hitler prior to April 1940. His memory was clear enough, however, to deny having received any financial support for NS from the Germans. All the money he had exchanged in 1940, he insisted, had been his personal funds. With the sudden pleading of loss of memory whenever any incriminating point was raised, combined with startling clarity of mind whenever he could offer a plausible explanation, his appearances provided a comic touch to the proceedings, despite the seriousness of the charges under consideration. At one point he went so far as to declare he had never been an NS member. Although he appeared in the courtroom on no less than three different occasions, more than any other witness, he consistently made his testimony valueless by pleading loss of memory whenever questioned about events that could be incriminating for him.[114]

The prosecution nevertheless was able to obtain testimony which confirmed that *Fritt Folk* had suddenly received large sums of money in 1940. John Thronsen confirmed he had been given 70,000 *kr.* by Quisling for the paper in the period before April 9.[115] Confronted with this testimony, Quisling maintained he had secured about 50,000 *kr.* as a personal loan from Hagelin.[116] Brought back as a witness concerning this detail, Hagelin's memory again suddenly failed him, and he refused either to confirm or deny having made such a loan.[117]

Despite Quisling's and Hagelin's best efforts, each in his own way and independent of the other, to try to evade their conspiracy with Nazi officials before the invasion, the prosecution's evidence was so solid that no amount of disingenuousness could succeed in persuading the court that they were not culpable. Schjødt was equally successful in presenting credible witnesses who corroborated Quisling's radio address of April 9 and his failure to report for service as a reserve officer in response to the mobilization of Norwegian forces (count I, grounds B and D).[118] The same applied to the defendant's order to Colonel Hiorth to arrest the Nygaardsvold government, and the aid that Quisling had provided to the Germans when they assumed control of the Defense Department (count II, ground C).[119] The prosecution encountered difficulty, however, when it came to obtaining support for the charge that the accused had attempted to induce the batteries at Bolærne to cease fire, and that he had broadcast an appeal to naval officers to surrender (count I, grounds D and E). While it appeared that Quisling had tried to gain access to the radio in order to transmit an order to Bolærne, no message had actually been sent. There was even less direct evidence from witnesses connecting him with the appeal to the naval officers on April 12.[120]

When the economic charges against the defendant were substantiated by witnesses, the prosecution effectively strengthened its case. Testimony from the witness stand provided strong proof that Quisling had used his position for personal gain, not in the selfless manner that he always maintained. Despite the lesser importance of the economic charges, the prosecution effectively achieved its goal of revealing weaknesses in Quisling's moral character, thereby establishing concrete evidence which would serve to contradict any later attempts at myth making. The prosecution's witnesses testified to how Quisling had appropriated property from the Royal Palace, the Masonic Lodge, and the Norwegian Society for his own personal use (count VI, grounds A, B, and C). Especially damaging was the testimony of how the initials on the Norwegian Society's silverware had been removed with his full knowledge, and how the original owners' nameplates on valuable paintings by some of Norway's major artists had been replaced with the Minister President's initials. Evidence was also given of how a number of buildings on Quisling's various properties had literally served as warehouses for fine furniture which had been acquired illegally.[121]

One of the witnesses who testified concerning theft of state property, the Royal Palace's caretaker, in a side reference provided information which contained a small but revealing insight into Quisling's activity just prior to the German capitulation. The defendant had earlier in the trial emphasized strongly that he had not burned any incriminating papers whatsoever in the days just before his surrender.[122] The caretaker testified, however, that papers were burned continuously at the Palace from Friday, May 4, through Monday, May 7, and that Quisling had been present on all of these days when the archives in his chancellery went up in flames.[123] The defendant, in response, could only lamely, and incorrectly, declare that he had last left the Palace at noon on Saturday, May 5.[124]

Witnesses were also called to provide evidence concerning the prosecution's contention that the defendant as Minister President had illegally made use of state funds (count VII). Those who testified, including NS members, provided detailed information showing payment of state funds to provide for Quisling's salary, for NS military formations, for the party, for needy party members, and for improvements on Quisling's properties.[125]

In addition to persons who had direct knowledge about events that were covered in the indictment's charges, both the prosecution and the defense called witnesses who provided information concerning periods in Quisling's life that fell outside the framework of the indictment, but which were referred to in order to shed light on his character. In support of his conclusion that Quisling had always craved power no matter from what source, Schjødt produced Friis and Tranmæl, who told of the defendant's attempts to establish ties with the Communists and the Labor party in the 1920s.[126]

In an attempt to discredit Quisling's assertion that he had always warned against weakening Norway militarily during the 1930s, Schjødt called to the stand Alfred Zimmer, a retired officer who had served as a key economic administrator within the Defense Department. Zimmer made the point that Quisling's budgets were the lowest of any Minister of Defense in the period 1925–1937. This conclusion, however, was not allowed to stand unchallenged. The defense attorney, under skillful cross-examination, countered with questions which revealed that figures alone did not prove anything. Bergh showed that Mowinckel, the most pacifist of all prime ministers during this period, also had the highest military budgets. The defense attorney further indicated that Quisling, as Minister of Defense, had been able to exercise little control over cabinet budgets that had already been predetermined by others.[127]

While Quisling's defense attorney could on occasion score points concerning minor issues such as these, small victories of this nature took place relatively seldom during the trial. Bergh had a very weak hand to play when it came to providing a credible defense. Almost all of the persons whom he called for the defense were character witnesses, and *all* of these testified concerning Quisling in the years before the war. Of these, perhaps the most surprising appearances were made by two generals who were hardly sympathetic to NS. Otto Ruge, commander-in-chief during the campaign in 1940, expressed his admiration for Quisling's ability when they both had served on the General Staff. Halvor Hansson was equally positive in his estimation of what Quisling had accomplished as Minister of Defense.[128] Appearing also as a defense witness, Andreas Urbye continued to praise the work that his former subordinate had performed for the Norwegian legation in Russia.[129] The positive testimony which affected the defendant the most, however, came from his boyhood friend, Vilhelm Ullmann. Quisling was deeply touched, having recourse to using his handkerchief,[130] when he heard Ullmann's description of how his classmates had looked up to Quisling:

> I am certain that I speak on behalf of all [our] friends when I describe him as a very trustworthy, kind, and good friend. In our opinion, he was extraordinarily learned; we looked up to him, we admired him, yes I dare say that we placed him on a pedestal . . .[131]

The praise he received from the defense witnesses allowed Quisling to be viewed from a broader perspective, providing a more varied image of him as a person. But the positive testimony from such witnesses had no impact whatsoever on the major charges against him. Except for a few peripheral points, the defense had no means of attacking the essential parts of the indictment.

After the witnesses had given their testimony, it was necessary for the court, before the trial could continue, to come to a clear conclusion concerning a major issue. The defendant's mental faculties needed to be ascertained. Solem therefore closed the court proceedings on Saturday, August 25, postponing the trial while Quisling submitted to a brain examination.[132]

Because of the defendant's unique personality, in particular his exaggerated view of his own ability as a political prophet, the question of his mental faculties was bound to arise. Even the possibility of insanity could not be ruled out entirely. To deal with this question, the court had appointed two psychiatrists as expert witnesses, Dr. Jon Leikvam and Dr. Johan Lofthus. They examined Quisling extensively in the period preceding the trial, issuing a report on June 18 in which they concluded there were no symptoms of insanity, nor any evidence that Quisling suffered from inadequately developed or permanently impaired mental faculties. Leikvam and Lofthus therefore expressed the opinion that there were no grounds for the defendant to submit to further judicial psychiatric observation. They adhered to this conclusion when called as expert witnesses during the trial.[133]

In the course of the proceedings, however, the question arose whether Quisling could be suffering from an organic brain disorder that might not be detectable as a result of an ordinary psychiatric examination. The only way this could be answered would be for him to undergo extensive physical tests. Quisling gave his full consent to submit to this type of examination.[134]

It was both long and painstaking, with a large number of different tests being performed. It took place over a three-day period, Saturday, August 25 – Monday, August 27, at the national medical center, *Rikshospitalet*, under the leadership of Professor G. H. Monrad-Krohn. He was assisted by a team of two other professors of medicine and three doctors. Not only was the examination extensive, but at times also extremely painful. At one point during the tests one of the guards allegedly found the proceedings to be so gruesome that he fainted.[135] Quisling, however, stoically endured the ordeal with admirable fortitude.

The examination came to the result that he had all along anticipated and desired. There was no evidence of any organic brain disorder. The only physical maladies which the tests revealed was that he had a somewhat reduced, but not abnormal, angle of vision, and that he suffered from polyneuritis, a nerve inflammation which resulted in some numbness in his legs. The latter affliction did not appear to have been of recent origin, brought about by the effects of his imprisonment. More than fifteen years earlier, members of Quisling's family had expressed their concern about the discomfort that he was experiencing from sciatica, a closely related disorder.[136]

Quisling's physical examination therefore corroborated the previous psychiatric conclusion that there were no mental grounds to prevent him from being held fully accountable for his actions. In later testimony before the Supreme Court, one of the psychiatrists, Dr. Leikvam, provided additional information concerning his findings. He related that he had met with Quisling some eight to ten times before June 18 and had discussed a variety of different questions with him. He had found the accused to have a "surprisingly sharp logical ability", often accompanied by "deep insight and broad knowledge". Leikvam thereby simply confirmed the widely held opinion that Quisling was intelligent and well read. The psychiatrist did note, however, that while Quisling's mental faculties were not impaired, and while he did not have paranoid ideas, his entire attitude nevertheless exhibited a "paranoid coloration". This, said Leikvam, had been present since childhood: "an embarrassed, shy, and self–conscious character with a strong desire to assert himself".[137] Leikvam further declared that Quisling had a "marked ability to repress and forget those actions which he now can defend [but with] difficulty".[138]

The conclusion that Quisling, despite his "paranoid coloration", had normal mental faculties, seconded by Leikvam's colleague, Dr. Lofthus, did not remain unchallenged permanently. A leading Norwegian psychiatrist, Professor Gabriel Langfeldt, in a book published considerably later, in 1969, argued that Quisling had suffered from a "paranoid mental illness".[139] Langfeldt contended that if Quisling had been subject to judicial psychiatric observation before his trial, he would have been found to have "inadequately developed and/or permanently impaired mental faculties". From a legal viewpoint, this did not mean that he would have been regarded as insane. He would still have gone on trial, considered to be responsible for his actions. Even so, stated Langfeldt, with such a diagnosis it was quite probable that the court would not have pronounced the death sentence.[140]

In support of this interpretation, Langfeldt marshalled a considerable amount of data concerning Quisling. His opinion was weakened, however, by the selective nature of his evidence, which as a result was not always convincing.[141] In addition, his viewpoint was made more difficult to sustain by the impreciseness of his terminology.

Langfeldt personally had good reason to admit that the psychiatric legal diagnosis "inadequately developed and/or permanently impaired mental faculties" was too vague, lacking precision.[142] In another famous postwar treason case, he had applied this very same diagnosis, following a period of judicial psychiatric observation, which he led personally, of Knut Hamsun. On the basis of his diagnosis, Langfeldt had determined that the famous author was not responsible enough to stand trial for his NS membership during the war. Acting on this opinion, the authorities had concluded that Hamsun was not mentally competent to be prosecuted. The outcome of this case, however, was that the novelist at the age of ninety mustered his "permanently impaired mental faculties" to write his final masterpiece, part fiction and part autobiography, in which he attacked Dr. Langfeldt.[143]

With a unique personality such as Quisling, who combined a shy, introverted nature with an unbalanced assessment of his greatness, and who frequently exaggerated his accomplishments and sometimes even directly fantasized, it is difficult to determine definitively what side of the boundary he was on – that vague and unclear boundary separating supposedly "normal" human beings from those who to one degree or another are mentally disordered. If his actions are evaluated as a whole, however, and not just selectively, there is valid reason to support the conclusion that his behavioral pattern was not irrational enough to be considered psychotic.

While Quisling's philosophical and religious ideas were unusual, mystical speculation was by no means entirely unique to someone of his generation and educational background. Moreover, in his daily routine there was no evidence of unusual behavior. Throughout his public career he as a rule consistently acted in a rational manner. Not infrequently, his actions could be criticized for being impractical, but they were always understandable in terms of what he hoped to accomplish. Not one among his close associates, including his most bitter detractors in both the prewar and occupation periods, indicated any doubts about his reason. Even Professor Langfeldt, despite the objections he raised concerning the psychiatric procedure and conclusions of Leikvam and Lofthus, agreed that Quisling most probably could not have been considered insane.[144] This consensus that he was not deranged is important to note. Because of the pressure of public opinion, only clear proof that he was insane could have prevented him from receiving the supreme penalty in 1945.

When the trial resumed on Wednesday, August 29, considerable speculation was aroused by the fact that the defendant did not appear in court.[145] The explanation for his absence, however, was quite simple. He was so exhausted by the difficult tests he had just undergone that he needed several days to recuperate. The court therefore only met for less than an hour in order to enter into evidence the results of Monrad-Krohn's brain examination and the findings of the two court-appointed psychiatrists. In consideration of the defendant's need to rest, the court recessed until Friday, August 31.[146]

On Friday Quisling had returned to the courtroom, but another major participant was missing. The failure of Henrik Bergh to appear showed that trial pressure was beginning to affect Quisling's defense attorney. He was bedridden, suffering from an acute case of kidney colic. Indicating how much he had come to rely on Bergh, Quisling objected to the trial continuing without his attorney being present. Solem responded by pointing out that the assistant defense attorney, Eilif Fougner, who had been present all during the trial, could act on the defendant's behalf. Furthermore, the court that day would be occupied with the prosecutor's summation, during which the defense would not have occasion to interrupt, and Bergh would have available for consultation a full stenographic record of what had been said in court during his absence. Quisling, however, refused to be persuaded by Solem's assurances, and he continued to argue against resuming without Bergh. He made a formal objection, which the court overruled after it had recessed to discuss the matter.[147]

Having been turned down on this point, the accused immediately provided proof that the recently completed brain examination had in no way diminished his ability to present a defense. Through Fougner, he entered into the court record a detailed written objection to the provisional decrees which the prosecution had included in its indictment. In doing so, he revealed a shrewd tactical sense. He attempted to pre-empt the prosecutor, knowing fully well that Schjødt intended to request the death penalty. Quisling therefore tried to demolish the legal validity of the provisional decrees on which application of the death penalty rested. Again, however, he was overruled. Solem informed him that the Supreme Court had already handed down a decision in another treason case which had upheld the legal validity of the provisional decrees.[148]

Undaunted by the court having twice rejected his arguments, the defendant remained combative. Knowing that the trial would reach a critical point with the prosecutor's first summation, he sought instead to focus attention on his physical condition. He now objected to the treatment he had received as a prisoner. He denounced the fact that his property and private papers had been confiscated without his permission. He further maintained that he had been subjected to "mental torture" during his imprisonment at Oslo Kretsfengsel (though not at Akershus Castle). Not merely the soul, but also the flesh had suffered according to his account, since he declared he had lost forty pounds during his first month in jail.[149]

A decline in weight of almost forty pounds in one month was quite probably an exaggerated claim. It is clear, however, that Quisling lost weight during his imprisonment. But he was not singled out for special treatment. At a time when the food supply for the general population continued to be rationed, the diet of persons incarcerated in prison was bound to be more restricted than that which he previously had enjoyed at Gimle. During the first hectic period immediately after the liberation, when large numbers of suspected collaborators were imprisoned, conditions in the prison camps were not good. The amount of food available was at times inadequate. However, this problem was alleviated in the course of two months, and by July standards in the prisons were much improved. Moreover, at no time did the detainees suffer health deterioration or significant exposure to epidemic diseases.[150] With Quisling receiving the same food ration as an ordinary prisoner, it was understandable that he lost much of the weight he had accumulated during the occupation. His clothing hung loosely on him during his court appearances.

Obviously nettled by this series of unexpected objections, Solem responded with the observation that there were many who had lost considerably more weight during the occupation, but if Quisling wished to make a formal objection, he could do so later during his defense address to the court. When the latter persisted in voicing his complaints, Solem, quite irritated, interrupted to say that many prisoners of NS had lost weight during the war "and suffered in jail many times more than you have suffered these days, when you have received decent, correct treatment as any detention prisoner receives here in Norway". Insisting, however, on having the last word in this matter, the defendant declared his belief that "history" would make the final judgement about how he had been treated.[151]

Not until this string of protests had been dealt with could the prosecution begin its statement. Schjødt summed up his case in a direct, effective manner. He had the advantage of being able to refer to the considerable body of material which the prosecution had been able to present as evidence. This allowed him to make the damning observation that this data had provided "a clear and sufficiently complete picture of the most extensive and the most malicious treason that our country at any time has seen".[152]

Looking ahead to the defense attorney's summation, which would follow, Schjødt recognized not merely the need to emphasize how the evidence had patently indicated the extent of Quisling's treason, but also the obvious requirement for the prosecutor to deal with the question of the defendant's motives. Having hardly any documentation to sustain his case, it was plain that Bergh would have to emphasize the less tangible considerations of the mind in his presentation. In discussing the question of motives, Schjødt therefore had to give careful heed to this issue. He had a twofold task: (1) to destroy the legal foundation for the possibility that the defendant's motives might be a mitigating factor for his treason, and having done this, (2) to show nevertheless that Quisling's motivation was not idealistic.

In carrying out the first part of this double objective, Schjødt emphasized strongly that no motive, not even the most idealistic, could excuse the defendant from standing accountable for his actions before the law: "No one has the right to follow his view concerning what the country's interests are without consideration of the law and without consideration of what the country's real authorities have decided."[153]

Having hammered this point home, the prosecutor then turned his attention to whether the defendant's motivation *had been* idealistic. In dealing with this issue, Schjødt first made the telling deduction that 99 per cent of all traitors, if held accountable, would maintain that their motives had been unselfish. He emphasized, however, that he was not willing to believe for a moment that Quisling's motives had been idealistic. Instead, Schjødt

presented a consistent portrayal he adhered to without deviation throughout the trial. The former NS *Fører*, said Schøjdt, had been "greedy for
power", having unswervingly sought to achieve positions of prominence
throughout his adult life.[154] In support of this interpretation, the prosecutor made the effective observation that the defendant both before the war
and during the occupation had never freely surrendered any position that
he had attained: "He can never go, has never gone willingly from any position of power."[155]

As everyone expected, Schjødt demanded the death penalty. This was
the only logical conclusion to the strong case which the prosecution had
presented. Furthermore, the call for the death penalty corresponded completely with the mood of the public. As the legal basis for this demand,
Schjødt cited section 80 of the military penal code concerning treason
(count I). He further referred to sections 83 and 86 of the civilian criminal
code, applicable respectively to those who seek to bring Norway under
foreign jurisdiction and to those who illegally bear arms against Norway
(counts II and III), with the death penalty being permitted under the provisional decree of October 3, 1941. In addition, he also invoked the death
penalty for murder, with reference to section 233 of the civilian criminal
code under the provisional decree of January 22, 1942 (count V). With the
exception of the few minor grounds that he had previously dropped,
Schjødt also asked the court to find the defendant guilty of the other
counts in the indictment, which fell outside the prosecution's demand for
the death penalty.[156]

The postwar use of the death sentence in the most serious cases of treason and war crimes marked a considerable departure from previous Norwegian practice. Before the war, no execution had been carried out for a
long time, extending as far back as 1876, eleven years prior to Quisling's
birth. Reflecting the public's opposition to the death penalty, it had been
removed from the civilian criminal code in 1902. However, the ultimate
sanction had still remained on the books as part of the military penal code.
Under provisional decrees enacted on October 3, 1941, it had been extended to have application in peacetime as well as during war.[157] In the
course of World War II, the possibility of using the death penalty had been
further broadened by its reintroduction into the civilian criminal code
through the Nygaardsvold government's provisional decrees, enacted in
England. On the other side of the battle line, as we have seen, neither the
Reichskommissariat nor Quisling's administration had shrunk from using
the death sentence.

As justification for requesting this severe penalty, Schjødt argued that
Quisling's offenses involved "flagrant and many-sided treason" carried out
consistently for at least a six-year period, if not longer. During most of this
time, said the prosecutor, this treason took place in a situation "where our
country's fate was in jeopardy and where the enemy treated us with a hard

hand". Such treason, he continued, was regarded as "the most detestable of all crimes" because it had such wide ranging and fatal consequences, and because it rejected and attacked a nation's feeling of solidarity.[158] Quisling had carried out his treasonable activity, insisted Schjødt, in a deliberate, calculated, and unprincipled manner:

> The accused has led this treason, and he has enticed and threatened country-men of all ages to follow him. He has not shown any consideration for any-one, he has committed his crimes at a mature age, and he has benefited well from an education which should have taught him to feel responsibility for his country.[159]

Upon completion of the prosecution's statement, Solem adjourned the court until the following Wednesday, September 5. The court had agreed to this adjournment in response to a request from the defense counsel. Bergh needed all the time available to allow him to prepare thoroughly the material which he intended to introduce on behalf of his client's most diffi-cult defense.[160]

When the defense attorney presented his major address to the court, it was obvious that he had made effective use of his allotted time. His summary was thorough and well organized, lasting over a two-day period. In par-ticular, Bergh provided striking proof that he not only had a keen legal mind, but that he also possessed good psychological insight. He employed his imagination to construct a very skillful defense.

Considering the predicament he faced in trying to build up a credible case, he succeeded admirably in presenting the least incriminating explana-tion possible for Quisling's treasonable acts. Lacking concrete factual evi-dence to sustain his arguments, Bergh's main line of defense always rested on his favorable interpretation of Quisling's alleged motivation. In pursu-ing this approach, he succeeded in establishing a permanent myth concern-ing his famous client, the so-called "Quisling puzzle" ("*gåten Quisling*").

In doing so, it needs to be noted that the defense attorney was not nec-essarily attempting to ascertain objective truth. He merely sought, as any good lawyer would, to fulfill his main responsibility of providing his client with the best defense possible. Yet despite the fact that he was presenting a legal defense, and very definitely not establishing historical proofs, Bergh's analysis has assumed a lasting quality. For many who are familiar only with isolated portions of Quisling's career, or who know his life merely as a general outline, his personality has indeed assumed the character of a "puzzle".

The fact that this concept has remained tied to Quisling is unfortunate because Bergh's analysis, from a historical viewpoint, is incomplete. De-spite the considerable familiarity and insight that he had gained from contact with his client, the attorney himself fell into the category of those who only had fragmentary knowledge of Quisling. He admitted this in court. Although he researched his case conscientiously and presented it well, he felt personally that the three-month period which he had had available for preparation had not been adequate. During his defense summary he pointed out to the court that he had been forced to pluck out scattered facts from archives, newspapers, and literature in an attempt to shed light on the defendant's personality and activity. But such material, he declared, "of course can never be as enlightening and encompassing as it ought to be".[161]

In raising this issue, he was describing an abstract ideal which could never be realized. From a legal standpoint, the documentation which he and Schjødt had available was quite adequate for the purpose of conducting a trial. But in view of the fact that much more documentary material has come to light after its conclusion, the evidence presented during the course of the trial was not satisfactory for the purpose of providing a full *historical* understanding of Quisling's life. Considering, however, the restricted time available from the end of the occupation until the beginning of the trial, a rather remarkable body of material had been compiled.

When conducting his case, the defense attorney, in contrast to the prosecutor's appeal to legal provisions and reason, recognized that he could establish a successful defense only through an indirect appeal to the court's emotions. He opened his defense address in this manner by seeking to establish an element of sympathy for the accused, pointing out that Quisling was being tried in a courtroom in which he was completely isolated. None of his former followers could be present to follow the proceedings. All those who would decide his fate, including his defense attorney, had been on "the other side" during the war. In such a situation, insisted Bergh, it was important to allow the defendant the right to be understood in terms of *his* ideas and feelings. It was also necessary in a case such as this, counsel argued, to try to understand the accused's personality as far as possible.[162]

In support of this contention that the defendant's personality had to be understood, Bergh promptly introduced his concept of "the Quisling puzzle", which epitomized the defense's effort. How was it possible, he asked, for someone such as Quisling, who had participated "with honor ... in Nansen's great humanitarian effort", and who had always been regarded morally and intellectually as a "first-class person", now to be seated in the courtroom, accused of the serious charges that he faced.[163]

Bergh never provided a full answer, nor was this his intent. He merely sought to *raise* as many questions as possible in the court's collective mentality. In addition to calling attention to the defendant's unique personality and ideas, Bergh also pointed to the fateful influence which Quisling's experiences in Russia had on him. The defense further emphasized the importance of Quisling's alleged disillusionment with parliamentary government during the 1930s, in particular in the area of military defense policy.[164] With such a background, Bergh argued, it was possible for Quisling to view events from a completely different perspective to that of the majority of Norwegians during World War II.

The defense attorney thereupon turned his attention to the specific charges raised in the indictment, doing his best to disprove them or at least to lessen their seriousness. In this endeavor, his emphasis continued to be on the defendant's motivation. Quisling's main fear in 1940, insisted Bergh, had always been that Norway would share Poland's fate, becoming a battlefield and partitioned between the major powers. His actions in April 1940, said Bergh, must be considered in the light of his distrust of the *Storting* and the government, especially the government's alleged unwillingness to defend the country.[165] The attorney stressed that it had never been Quisling's "intention" to aid the enemy or to damage Norway's capacity to resist, and therefore the treason provisions in the military penal code ought not to be applied against him.[166]

In seeking to defuse the significance of incriminating German documents which implicated Quisling, the defense attorney tried to cast doubt on their truthfulness.[167] In an interesting analogy, he compared Quisling's behavior with the actions of *Storting* members, parliamentary leaders, and prominent individuals in business and labor during the summer of 1940, pointing out how they too had compromised themselves in unconstitutional negotiations with the Germans.[168] He attempted to make light of the economic charges, maintaining that they should not have been included in the indictment, considering the seriousness of the other counts.[169] He similarly sought to restrict, if not eliminate, the possibility that the death sentence might be imposed on his client.[170]

In his conclusion Bergh again returned to his main concept of the "Quisling puzzle". This time he attempted to persuade the court to judge the defendant less severely in the light of his mental condition. Because of the expert testimony of the psychiatrists, defense counsel was restricted in the degree to which he could make use of psychological arguments. In view of their findings, he declared that he was not arguing that Quisling was either insane or had permanently impaired mental faculties.[171] But he did go so far as to state the opinion that there was something unique about Quisling, "either physical or mental which none of us, not even the doctors, understand".[172]

Bergh concluded by pointing out that his client had both orally and in written form declared to the court that he was not guilty. The defense attorney therefore requested the court to reach a verdict which was in accord with Quisling's plea or, as a subsidiary request, that the defendant be treated as leniently as possible if found guilty.[173]

Because of the effective manner in which he defended his client, Bergh was subjected to some hostile commentary in the press during the course of the trial. Many persons failed to heed the fact that the defense attorney was simply fulfilling his duty. When Bergh had completed his address to the court, Solem therefore found this to be an appropriate time to deal with this misconception. The president of the court stated that in view of the defendant's plea, the defense attorney's request for a judgement of not guilty was the only logical one he could make. Bergh, said Solem, had thereby fulfilled his responsibility.[174]

The completion of the defense attorney's summation was followed by a relatively brief period of rebuttal by the prosecution and the defense. Both Schjødt and Bergh concentrated largely during this exchange on the question of Quisling's motives. In contrast to the presentation of the factual evidence, where the two attorneys could differ only over minor details, on this occasion they had the opportunity to make clearly opposing interpretations.

Schjødt had no hesitation in repeating his main theme when assessing the defendant's motivation. Upon examining the different phases of Quisling's life, said the prosecutor, it became clearly apparent that Quisling had reacted to every situation either with an argument for seizing power, or for retaining power if he already possessed it.[175] The prosecutor furthermore proceeded to add another dimension to his assessment of the defendant's character. While Quisling was greedy for power, insisted Schjødt, he lacked resolution and was weak. He always needed to have someone over him in order to feel secure – a Nansen, a Kolstad, or a Hitler. And among his subordinates he required obedient underlings who could provide him with the flattery which he needed, not persons who could present independent views.[176]

In addition to emphasizing once more this critical, negative assessment of the defendant's motivation and character, Schjødt recognized the obvious need to destroy, not merely during the trial but also for posterity, Bergh's skillful creation of the "Quisling puzzle". The defense attorney's main strategy, said Schjødt, had been to broaden this concept, and on this basis to seek to convince the court "that Quisling is not entirely sane", although he avoided stating this directly. Schjødt scornfully rejected the concept of such a puzzle:

> The "Quisling puzzle" – yes, that is the remnant of the *fører* myth, but also the foundation for the construction of a possible new myth, and at the same time a slogan which scarcely has the right to exist. Quisling only becomes a puzzle if one does not keep to the conclusive evidence, both with regard to his person and [his] actions during the last six years, which we have in front of us, but instead blindly concentrates only on the quite worthless comments about how he supposedly was as a child and youth.[177]

The prosecutor also took time to refute a number of other defense arguments. The actions of the *Storting* leaders and other prominent Norwegians during the negotiations with the Germans in the summer of 1940, he maintained, were not analogous with Quisling's behavior. They were of a completely different character both when it came to the right to act on the country's behalf, and with consideration to "motives, goals, and means".[178]

With reference to the most serious aspect of the trial, the potential application of the death penalty, Schjødt refused to be drawn into a philosophical discussion on the issue. The death penalty's existence as part of the Norwegian legal code, he said, was a fact whether one liked it or not. And if the death penalty were at any time to be employed, "then it must be against him who has had the leadership of this disgusting and widespread treason".[179]

In his brief response, the defense attorney concentrated primarily on emphasizing strongly his belief that the prosecutor was blind to the subjective element in the case, and therefore had failed to understand Quisling's personality adequately. As a key part of the "Quisling puzzle", Bergh reiterated his contention that Quisling had acted in what he believed to be good faith, and that he did not have treasonable motives. Only such an interpretation, Bergh emphasized, could explain how it was possible for Quisling to repeat at the trial what he had said to the *Storting* in 1932 – that the Norwegian Communists were guilty of treason because of their ties to Moscow – while insisting that *his* actions, in comparison, were in no way treasonable.[180]

With the completion of the case for the prosecution and the defense, the trial reached one of its high points. The defendant now had the opportunity to make an uninterrupted final statement in his defense before the court recessed to reach a verdict. His address could be as extensive as he wished to make it. All eyes were on Quisling as he rose to speak. The spectators witnessed a completely different figure from the one who earlier had to resort to evasions, denials, and lies when confronted with the court's and the prosecutor's constant succession of difficult questions. He now had the chance to build up *his* version of reality, which he did with considerable force and skill. Many in the courtroom were strongly impressed by his effort, in particular foreigners who did not have the background to judge the accuracy of his statements.[181]

Vidkun Quisling on this occasion once more provided evidence in support of those who had testified to his superior mental ability. For two days he addressed the court, speaking without notes. He generally spoke in a calm, firm voice. Only once, when discussing the Labor party's attacks against him in 1932, did he lose his composure. At this point he slung accusations and attacks with vehemence, almost anger, against his Labor party detractors in a manner reminiscent of his previous style of political agitation. He regained his composure quickly, however, after Solem suggested that he moderate his language.[182]

His endeavor to maintain a calm, objective, yet forceful image was sustained only as a result of considerable exertion. The spectators noted how he at times had to make a special effort to maintain his control.[183] This was due not only to his emotional state, but also to physical impairment. He had to force himself to keep speaking, as he suffered considerable distress from polyneuritis. In the afternoon of the first day of Quisling's address, Bergh called the court's attention to the fact that his client was not feeling well. Asked if he preferred to have the trial adjourn until the next day, Quisling replied that he had difficulty in standing. The court thereupon recessed at 2:50 p.m. on September 6, an hour and ten minutes early. When the trial resumed on the following morning, Quisling was informed that he could sit if he wished while addressing the court. He preferred to stand, he responded, since it was "so uncomfortable to speak while sitting".[184]

He experienced no difficulty, however, in finding the proper tone in his address. Free from Solem's and Schjødt's probing questions about concrete details and issues, he could give his ideal version of himself. To the courtroom he therefore described himself in the most idealistic manner, as the unselfish leader whose only motive at all times had been to act on behalf of his society. During the last fifteen years, he maintained, he had not enjoyed any personal life at all. His sole preoccupation had been to fight for "my people". Having to his satisfaction established this claim as a fact, he proceeded to reverse the concept of the "Quisling puzzle". He declared that it was the Norwegian people who were a "puzzle", not he, since they could allow a person of his caliber to be tried for treason.[185]

In the very detailed personal account of his life that followed, he continued to give a flattering, at times an exaggerated, and not infrequently a completely imaginary depiction of his accomplishments. A close reading of his defense statement reveals clearly that he presented as actual reality certain achievements and possible options which quite obviously only reflected his imaginary ideals, and which were completely outside the limits of objective, even subjective, truth. Often the achievements he described were exaggerated or had never taken place, and the options he maintained were at his disposal could never have been carried out. To cite but one example of the latter, he declared that he often had asked himself if he, as Minister of Defense, should not have destroyed the parliamentary system of government, since it supposedly, from his viewpoint, was not adequately serving the country's interests: "Did you fulfill your duty to the Norwegian people when you didn't crush this filth?"[186] He had indeed wished to crush parliamentary democracy, but in his court address he presented an ideal situation as a reality which could have been achieved.

His speech was broader, more rambling, and more biographical than his two earlier written defense statements. Essentially, however, he repeated in a more general fashion the same arguments that he had previously used as justification for what he had done, both prior to and during the occupation. Before the German invasion, he insisted, his goal had been to keep Norway truly neutral through maintaining a strong defense, but this had been foiled by the allegedly incompetent Nygaardsvold government, which he declared had secretly conspired to hand Norway over to the English.[187] And once Norway had come under German control, he argued, he had prevented the country from enduring a worse fate through his assumption of authority. Had he not acted as he did, he maintained, the country would have been exploited in a far more "ruthless" manner, and the unrest caused by such exploitation would have been suppressed by the "sharpest reprisals".[188] Thanks to his struggle, he insisted that if the outcome of the war had been different, "the people would have given me the recognition that I deserve for my effort, and National Union would quickly have gained a large majority of the people".[189] Because the war had not concluded as he expected, he could only proclaim himself to be a misunderstood prophet. But he was convinced that history would eventually judge that he had been correct.[190]

As evidence of the fact that he had spent considerable time preparing for his defense address, he repeated almost verbatim in his conclusion many of the statements he had made in his first written declaration of June 24 in response to the preliminary indictment. And he completed his address to the court with the identical dramatic words that he had written in June: If his activity truly had been treasonable, then he would ask before God that a good many sons of Norway should also become traitors like him, only that they be not thrown into prison.[191]

The court thereupon withdrew to reach its verdict. Following two days of deliberations, Solem again declared the court to be in session at 2:00 p.m., Monday, September 10. The courtroom was hushed, its occupants awed by their knowledge that Quisling's fate had been determined and that the judgement would now be rendered. Before the verdict was read, Solem placed special weight on maintaining the decorum which had prevailed during the trial. The reading of the court's judgement, he warned, would be long, and he insisted on having absolute calm. Anyone who could not remain for the entire session would have to depart now, he announced, for no one would be permitted to leave once the reading of the judgement had begun. He thereby prevented a rush of reporters from the hall as soon as the defendant's sentence became known.[192]

In the hour and a half that followed the court presented a detailed judgement, providing the legal basis for the conclusions which the tribunal had reached for each of the grounds included in the indictment's nine counts. As anticipated, the verdict overwhelmingly confirmed Quisling's guilt. The defendant was found guilty of all counts except count VIII, which the prosecutor in large part had previously dropped. Only in a few of the more minor peripheral grounds enumerated in the other counts did the tribunal find that the prosecution had provided insufficient evidence: count I, ground D – that he had sought on April 10, 1940, to send a message to Bolærne urging surrender; count I, ground E – that he had sent a similar message to Norwegian naval commanders on April 12, 1940; and count VI, ground E – that his administration had carried out illegal confiscation of property belonging to persons declared guilty of hostile activity against the state.[193]

In reaching its judgement, the court was almost entirely unanimous in its conclusions. Only on two questions in count V concerning the charge of murder did the tribunal indicate a divergence of opinion. The majority found Quisling guilty of premeditated murder for his part in the execution of Viggo Hansteen (ground A), while one professional judge voted in favor of manslaughter.[194] In its conclusion concerning the defendant's responsibility for the deaths of the deported Jews (ground B), two members of the court, including Solem, believed Quisling to be guilty of murder. However, the majority found him guilty only of manslaughter.[195]

The ensuing sentence delivered by the court was what everyone expected, including the defense attorney and most probably even the defendant himself.[196] Quisling received the death sentence under the military penal code and the civilian penal code, as amended by the wartime provisional decrees. He was further sentenced to pay a fine of 1,040,000 *kr.*, plus 1,500 *kr.* in legal costs.[197]

According to Norwegian judicial procedure, the question of guilt determined by a High Court (*lagmannsrett*) cannot be appealed. Solem, however, informed Quisling that he had the option of appealing to the Supreme Court on procedural grounds if he (a) found the penalty too strict, (b) believed the trial procedure had been carried out in an illegal manner, or (c) felt that the law had been applied incorrectly. Quisling at once replied that he would appeal to the Supreme Court, and that his defense attorney would in due course provide the necessary legal justification.[198]

Under ordinary circumstances, the day on which he received his death sentence should have been a happier one for Quisling. It was his twenty-second wedding anniversary.[199] According to *Dagbladet*, Maria Quisling sent him a postwar luxury to mark the occasion – several pounds of fruit. The paper went on to report that the condemned man did not appear to be downcast by the thought of his pending execution. He had, upon returning to his cell, again declared that history would judge him differently. On the following morning he slept quite late.[200]

At least from outward appearances, he seemed to be in better condition than his defense attorney. The latter had not been present in the courtroom when the sentence was announced. Assistant defense counsel Fougner had acted in Bergh's place. The latter once again had been forced to take to his bed because of illness.[201] But he was soon well enough to draw up the appeal, which he submitted to the Supreme Court on September 28, 1945.[202]

He presented Norway's highest court with what was basically a pro forma procedural appeal, whose contents revealed no surprises. It challenged in a general way the court of appeals' main conclusions in reaching its verdict. The defense attorney quite obviously knew that the Quisling case, because of its significance, would automatically be reviewed by the Supreme Court. Using wise tactics, he therefore contented himself with drawing up a broad framework for the appeal, recognizing that the essential arguments would be those that he made in person before the justices.

In a written plea on Quisling's behalf, Bergh questioned both the High Court's application of the law and its sentence. He raised a total of six objections to the manner in which the lower court had applied the law. The appeal maintained under point A that Quisling had not sought to bring Norway under foreign jurisdiction, and that he had not contributed to Norway becoming involved in hostilities. Under point B the defense basically argued that Quisling's actions in April 1940 fell outside the law because Norway was not officially at war. As for Quisling's administrative responsibility for illegalities committed during the war, which came under point C, Bergh declared that his client's decisions were temporary, and were not intended to alter the Constitution illegally. On point D the defense appealed against the finding that Quisling was guilty of the murders of Hansteen, Eilifsen, and fourteen other persons, while under point E a similar objection was raised with regard to Quisling's involvement in the extermination of the deported Jews. Finally, in point F the appeal challenged the validity of the economic charges under which the defendant had been found guilty.[203]

The appeal maintained that the death penalty ought not under any circumstances to be applied in this case. As justification for this protest, Bergh argued that (a) inadequate consideration had been given to the defendant's sense of purpose and patriotism in April 1940, (b) too much weight had incorrectly been applied to his encouragement of Norwegians to fight on the eastern front, and (c) insufficient heed had been paid to his motives concerning the question of his involvement in the deaths of the persons whose murder he stood accused of. Finally, the appeal challenged use of the provisional decree of October 3, 1941, which extended application of the death penalty under the military penal code to peacetime, thereby allowing its use against Quisling.[204]

When the appeal came before the Supreme Court, the legal proceedings once again were back in the Oslo Court House, where Quisling had made his first court appearance in May. The hearing was opened by Chief Justice Paal Berg on Tuesday, October 9. Presiding over a panel of five justices, Berg, from his restored position as head of the Supreme Court, faced Quisling from quite a different perspective than he had just some months earlier as leader of the Home Front.[205] The appellant specifically asked to be allowed to be present at the hearing, a request to which the court acceded.[206] The appeal proceedings took two days to complete.

In his major statement in support of the appeal, Henrik Bergh repeated, though in a more specific manner, the points of contention which he had raised in his written argument against the High Court's application of the law. He stated under point A that Quisling had not intended to surrender Norwegian sovereignty if Norway had become a member of the projected greater Germanic federation. Nor had the appellant, declared Bergh, deliberately worked to bring Norway into the war. On the contrary, said the defense, Quisling's motive had been to spare Norway from war and its destruction through securing a peaceful occupation by the Germans.[207] With reference to point B in the appeal, Bergh maintained that Norway formally was not at war until April 19, 1940, when the last diplomatic ties with Germany were broken, and Quisling could therefore not be judged guilty of military treason for actions which he committed in the period April 9–11.[208] In reply to the judgement that the defendant illegally had sought to alter the Constitution, point C, the defense attorney declared that this was incorrect. All administrative changes during the occupation were temporary, he maintained, and could not be viewed as permanent changes.[209] In discussing point D, Bergh sharply attacked the court of appeals' finding that his client was guilty of premeditated murder in regard to the death of Viggo Hansteen. There was no causal relationship, he argued, between Quisling's negative statements about Hansteen and the German execution of the LO attorney. With regard to Quisling's failure to grant clemency to persons executed during the war, Bergh asserted that it was inconsistent to maintain that the former Minister President had lacked legitimacy to act as he had during the war, and then to attack him for having failed to exercise his authority in a certain manner.[210] Responding to the High Court's conclusion that Quisling was guilty of manslaughter because of his involvement in the deportation of the Jews, the defense countered that Quisling had no more knowledge of their fate than the average Norwegian.[211] As for the economic crimes which the defendant had been found guilty of, Bergh dismissed these as being unimportant. He further pointed out that he had been instructed by Quisling to ignore them in order not to lose sight of the major issues involved in the case.[212]

While Bergh stressed each of these points except the latter, it was obvious that the brunt of his appeal was directed primarily against the sentence of the lower court. He specifically stated at the opening of his address that the most important question in the appeal concerned the sentence which his client had received.[213] His main obligation at this stage in the legal process quite obviously was to fulfill his responsibility to Quisling by seeking to avoid the death penalty. As he had done so masterfully earlier in the lower court, Bergh again placed his major emphasis on understanding Quisling not on the basis of his actions, but subjectively, viewed from his own perspective. As Bergh put it, it was necessary to take into consideration the thoughts and feelings which had dictated the appellant's actions.[214] Bergh thereupon proceeded to give a skillful defense version of Quisling's entire life.[215] In this most subjective interpretation, his actions were made quite understandable, as judged from his own point of view. Special emphasis was placed on how he had reacted to the alleged failure of the politicians to provide an adequate military defense during the 1930s, and on the pressures he had been subjected to from the Germans during the war.

In seeking to avoid the death penalty, Bergh also raised a significant legal objection. He argued that Quisling could not be sentenced to death under the military penal code because the provisional decree of October 3, 1941, which had extended the imposition of the death penalty under the military penal code to apply also after the conclusion of hostilities, would assume a retroactive character if used against Quisling. The latter, insisted Bergh, had committed the acts under which he stood convicted in April 1940, a year and a half prior to the enactment of the provisional decree. He therefore maintained that Quisling could not be executed under the military penal code, but could instead only receive a maximum sentence of life imprisonment.[216]

Although he never specifically made use of his concept of the "Quisling puzzle", Bergh indirectly also brought before the justices the question of Quisling's mental faculties in a clear attempt to get the sentence reduced. Citing the testimony of previous witnesses, he subtly tried to raise as much doubt as possible concerning this key issue. He concluded with the personal observation that he had had some thirty to forty conversations with his client, who steadfastly had maintained he had a clear conscience. Bergh consequently insisted that Quisling must have acted in good faith. On this basis, he argued that it would serve no useful purpose to take Quisling's life. The defense therefore requested the Supreme Court justices (1) to declare the sentence void because of incorrect application of the law or, alternatively, to annul the sentence on insufficient judgmental grounds; or (2) to reduce the sentence.[217]

In his refutation of the defense attorney's appeal, the prosecutor enjoyed having a far easier task of simply sustaining the High Court's judgement. Going through the specific points raised by Bergh concerning how the law had been applied in reaching the sentence, Schjødt time after time referred to previous court decisions and legal commentaries which sustained the High Court's sentence.[218]

Schjødt recognized as well as Bergh, however, that the most important issue in the appeal to the Supreme Court concerned the subjective evaluation of Quisling's motives. Since the defense had made this the main basis for its appeal, the prosecution too had to give this question considerable attention. Schjødt consequently spent a substantial amount of time refuting Bergh's interpretation.[219] In doing so, the prosecutor maintained the same view of Quisling that he had presented at the trial: that the NS leader had "acted out of ambition and lust for power".[220] To satisfy the craving that arose from such scarcely ideal motives, said Schjødt, Quisling had already very early in his political career "shown an opportunism" that was "quite revealing".[221] The prosecutor, contrary to Bergh, refused to believe that Quisling had acted in good faith. There were too many facts to the contrary, said Schjødt, which provided evidence that the appellant had not had ideal motives at the time he committed his actions.[222] The prosecutor did not rule out, however, the possibility that Quisling eventually, as a defense mechanism against his obvious treason, might have been able to rationalize idealistic motives in defense of what he did. But such subjective considerations, insisted the prosecutor, could in no way decide the outcome of a criminal case.[223]

The lower court's death sentence, argued Schjødt, should be allowed to stand. He insisted that it was based on correct application of the law, and stood in clear relation to the crimes for which the appellant had been convicted. There were therefore, he maintained, no grounds for reducing the sentence.[224]

In sustaining this viewpoint, Schjødt had to deal with Bergh's objection that application of the death penalty under the military penal code in peacetime, as permitted by the provisional decree of October 3, 1941, was retroactive. In his counterargument, the prosecutor pointed out that the provisional decree had not introduced *new* punishment for a crime, but merely removed a restriction that stood in the way of a previously established legal provision for capital punishment. Therefore, he insisted, the application of the death penalty in peacetime under the military penal code did not assume a retroactive character which was in conflict with the constitution.[225]

Responding to the prosecutor's rebuttal, Bergh continued to press the issue of Quisling's mental faculties. This tactic was quite clearly the best that the defense could pursue at this time. Bergh therefore requested that the two court-appointed psychiatrists, Leikvam and Lofthus, should be called before the panel to explain the basis for their conclusions about Quisling's state of mind. The defense attorney justified his motion with the observation that he considered the psychiatric testimony to be "very meager, . . . almost a conclusion without motives".[226] After recessing briefly to consider the request, the justices gave their consent to this motion.[227]

Bergh failed, however, to bring out anything new in the additional testimony of the two psychiatrists. Dr. Jon Leikvam, the more loquacious of the two, again declared there was no evidence to indicate that Quisling, despite the unique nature of his ideas, could in any way be considered insane. Leikvam based this conclusion on the many conversations that he had held with Quisling during the latter's imprisonment, and on his observation of the defendant during the trial.[228] In a very brief appearance, the other psychiatrist, Dr. Lofthus, tersely maintained his previous position: that there were no grounds for further psychiatric observation in view of the absence of (1) insanity, (2) inadequately developed mental faculties, or (3) permanently impaired mental faculties.[229]

The prosecution did not allow the opportunity to pass without trying to take advantage of the testimony of the psychiatrists. Schjødt brought up one of his main theories concerning Quisling's mental faculties, asking Dr. Leikvam if the appellant could have felt that he was motivated by high ethical ideals. The psychiatrist replied that it was difficult to respond to this question since so much time had elapsed. He had, however, the impression that Quisling "on the whole had been in good faith". But, continued Leikvam to Schjødt's satisfaction, it was obvious that Quisling, like everyone else, "explains away" unpleasant facts, and that he "rationalizes and embellishes".[230]

In their final exchange the two attorneys continued in large part to disagree over the subjective issue of Quisling's motives. Bergh persisted in maintaining his contention that the prosecutor had failed to understand the appellant, and hence his portrayal of Quisling was incorrect.[231] Schjødt, however, had the last word, and he used the occasion to hammer home a telling comment concerning the question of motive in understanding Quisling. Any psychological investigation, said Schjødt, if it is to be exact and scientific, must rest on a secure factual foundation: "Words are easy and cheap". Nothing revealed more, he continued, about motives and intentions than the actions which a person carries out. How often, asked Schjødt rhetorically, had anyone ever admitted that his motives "were . . . not the best".[232]

When questioned if he wished to add anything to what his attorney had previously said, Quisling arose to present once more a viewpoint that stood in complete contrast to the one the prosecutor had just presented. In this, his final public statement, he steadfastly refused to indicate any sign of remorse. He continued in general terms to depict himself as the misunderstood idealist as he had done so many times before. He maintained that the defendant described in his trial was not him, he was an "unknown man". The High Court, he continued, had failed to give a true account of his person. He declared that the lower court had committed many errors, but the "capital error" which it made was to condemn as a traitor someone "who has always loved his fatherland above everything else".[233] He and his followers, he insisted, were the ones who had truly "borne the burdens" of the occupation, and who had felt its effects stronger than anyone else.[234] He predicted in messianic terms that the Norwegian people would assume "blood guilt" if he were executed.[235]

He spoke, however, of his pending death in terms which showed that he now had scant hope of avoiding execution. He presented his viewpoint in a calm, controlled manner, but it was obvious to the listeners in the courtroom that he had resigned himself to the fate from which he could not escape.[236] His conscience was clear, he maintained, and he deserved neither death nor prison. He did not fear death, but he regretted its imposition in consideration of those who were near to him, and he stated that he feared the consequences it would have for the Norwegian people.[237] In his concluding words he returned to one of his major themes – that the party politicians were responsible for the catastrophe which befell Norway in 1940. It was not he who was guilty in this case, he insisted, but rather the "old power brokers" whose "neglect" had obliged him to fulfill his "duty" to his fatherland by assuming the heavy responsibility that he had carried during the occupation. He asked the justices to take into consideration the views that he had expressed, and, with a last pointed reference to Schjødt, that he be not judged on the basis of the "superficial psychological analyses" that had been made of him.[238]

The Supreme Court justices issued their decision two days later, on Saturday, October 13. Justice Sigurd Fougner, designated as the first member of the panel to vote on the appeal, had drawn up the opinion.[239] He upheld the High Court's findings on each of the points concerning the application of the law which the appeal had questioned.[240]

In discussing the lower court's imposition of the death penalty, Fougner fully shared the High Court's opinion that the serious crimes committed by the appellant warranted the severe sentence that he had received. Fougner added the further observation that Quisling's alleged ideal motives could not be given any significance in determining the appellant's penalty. His treason was obvious, and its effect had been especially damaging in April 1940. "Chaos must not be allowed to reign during a country's hour of fate." Fougner emphasized the need to make it clear, both for the present and the future, that there was no place in society for "one who at a time that is critical for his country follows his will rather than the constitutional authorities, and thereby betrays his country."[241]

The justice similarly denied the defense claim that the application of the death sentence was retroactive in Quisling's case. Fougner found that the provisional decree of October 1941 had been enacted in wartime. As such, it therefore fell within the framework of the previously established statute permitting the death penalty, and it could therefore not be considered to be retroactive in character.[242]

The other four justices, without dissent, unanimously agreed with this opinion.[243] Having failed to give support for even a single objection in the appeal, the Supreme Court decision put a definitive end to the possibility of finding a legal means for avoiding the death penalty. The process against Quisling had thereby run its course, having been carried out in full accordance with the aims of Norwegian authorities. They had wished for him to have a fair, open, and speedy trial. This he received. In a legal process as broad and as detailed as this, questions can inevitably be raised concerning specific points in the case. But viewed as a whole, the legal treatment which Quisling experienced was as fair as it could possibly have been. The trial and appeal were conducted in strict accordance with prevailing Norwegian legal practice. The evidence presented in court against the defendant was overwhelming. As the Swedish legal expert present at the trial, Hemming-Sjöberg, observed: had Quisling been Swedish and tried before a Swedish court of law, the outcome inevitably would have been the same – he would have been condemned to death.[244]

In the aftermath of the Supreme Court's rejection of his appeal, there now existed but one possibility for the doomed prisoner, again back in the jail next to Møllergaten 19, to avoid the ultimate sentence. King Haakon VII, as head of state, was the only authority who had the power to issue a grant of clemency and thereby reduce the sentence – the type of clemency that the Minister President had been unwilling to extend during the war.

A single person worked actively to obtain mercy for Quisling, and not unexpectedly this was the woman closest to him. His devoted wife, encumbered though she was by her ties to the most hated man in the country, her Russian background, and the sheltered life she had previously led, tried to carry out a one-person campaign on behalf of her husband. In her quest she considered the ultimate step of seeking an audience with the King, whom she had met socially as wife of the Minister of Defense during the now distant time of the early 1930s. Quisling's defense attorney, Bergh, advised her, however, that such an attempt could only have negative consequences.[245]

She therefore instead sent a personal letter to the King, pleading for mercy. She wrote it already on October 9, before the Supreme Court panel had rendered its decision, but she assumed, correctly, that the court probably would sustain the sentence. In her letter she insisted that all of Quisling's actions had been idealistic and unselfish, motivated only by his love for his people. She assured the King that her husband had always had the highest respect for the royal family, and she hoped the King would forgive the "strong words" Quisling had expressed "under the pressure of the occupation and in the heat of the struggle". Emotionally, she concluded with a personal plea: "I, his wife, am so desperate, and I pray to God night and day that he may be saved. And now I cry out to Your Majesty: be merciful!"[246]

Maria Quisling wrote similar appeals, though not quite so personal and emotional, to prominent Norwegians, asking them to use their influence on her husband's behalf. Already on October 1 she had written to the commander-in-chief, Otto Ruge, who had, rather courageously, spoken positively of young Quisling's military accomplishments during the trial.[247] Later in October, at the same time she wrote to the King, she also sent a letter to Prime Minister Gerhardsen, seeking to persuade him to use the government's influence to obtain clemency.[248] Another plea in quest of the same goal was penned to the commander-in-chief of Allied forces in Norway after the war, Sir Andrew Thorne. She later maintained that in her desperate effort she even drew up a letter to a "countryman" who would hardly have been sympathetic, Joseph Stalin. In the end, however, she rather wisely decided not to mail her letter to the Soviet dictator.[249]

Quisling's wife also endeavored unsuccessfully to obtain support for clemency by going in person to socially prominent individuals. Among these was the influential cultural and scientific personality, Dr. Johan Scharffenberg, a leading psychiatrist who had been an interested courtroom spectator during the Quisling trial. He actually agreed to meet with Quisling in prison.[250] But despite his later outspoken opposition to the death penalty, Scharffenberg insisted that he could do nothing on Quisling's behalf.[251] Although there is no additional source to verify this assertion, Maria Quisling also stated that she had a meeting with Bishop Berggrav.[252] If it actually took place, she must have received no encouragement whatsoever, because when she talked with her husband in prison on October 14, she vehemently advised him against seeking to arrange a meeting with Berggrav, emphasizing that it could only be damaging.[253]

Isolated as she was, with only a few friends for support, her campaign was an exercise in futility, although it obviously satisfied her emotional need to do all that was humanly possible. Her husband's most prominent followers were all imprisoned and could render no assistance. In the hostile postwar society, she had but a small coterie of friends, mostly female NS sympathizers or the wives of jailed NS members.[254]

From Norwegian officialdom there existed no possibility of any assistance or encouragement. Unknown to her, the Supreme Court panel, at the time it issued its opinion, had also added a formidable obstacle to any possible grant of mercy. When informing the King of their final decision, the five justices added the statement that the Supreme Court could find no reason to recommend clemency.[255] Their advice served as but one illustration of the obvious reality that there was no possibility of pardon whatsoever. Not only had Quisling legally been found guilty of treason in a court of law, but in addition the weight of public opinion was entirely in favor of the court's penalty being carried out. Norwegian society in 1945 simply would not have accepted a lesser sentence, either for Quisling or for others who received the supreme penalty at this time. Having experienced five years of occupation, during which Quisling collaborated with the Germans, popular opinion would have exploded in outrage had any attempt been made to grant clemency.

Like his wife, the most notorious prisoner at Møllergaten 19 was not at first aware of the Supreme Court's ruling. Not until five days after the justices had issued their decision did he hear the opinion read to him in the presence of his defense attorney and the prison director, at 1:05 p.m., October 18. He received a written copy when the oral presentation was concluded.[256]

He immediately sat down and wrote a letter to the King. But unlike his wife's earlier plea, this was not truly a request for clemency. In essence, as the contents revealed, this was his final position paper. The direct manner in which he condemned the legal procedures against him and his fellow NS members, the strong defense for the motivation of his actions during the war, and his refusal to indicate any error showed that he had little if any hope of clemency from Haakon VII. He had made the mental resolve to maintain the stature of the persecuted martyr who unflinchingly met his death, convinced that he had always acted unselfishly on behalf of his people. He voiced the complaint that he had been judged unfairly, and that if the sentence were executed, Norway would be guilty of a "miscarriage of justice". History, he declared, would pass severe judgement against the Norwegian people, while he would not be judged guilty if he suffered a martyr's death. The question was in the hands of the King and his government. He emphasized, however, that he was not seeking mercy for himself, but asked that mildness be shown his followers, who, he maintained, were being persecuted unfairly.[257]

Having adopted the martyr's mantle, he no longer had to concern himself with the ordinary preoccupations of the outside world. During his final days his thoughts were directed almost entirely toward the one person who remained uncritically loyal to the end, and who after his death would be among the small number of persons who would keep alive the ideal, unblemished Quisling image that for him had become reality – his faithful wife, Maria.

His consideration for her revealed a human side of his nature which had never been in evidence during the years when he strove to maintain the image of the serious-minded, dedicated *Fører*. He indicated his concern about what would happen to her when he was gone, and he did what little he could to try to aid her in the future. With no knowledge of how the financial expropriation decreed by the court would turn out, he could only ask his friends and relatives to provide Maria with help and guidance. In letters seeking such assistance, he openly revealed the strong feelings that he had for her. To his old friend, Vilhelm Ullmann, he declared his devotion to Maria: she was an exceptionally good person, and they loved each other deeply.[258] Similarly, in a letter to his brother Jørgen, he expressed admiration for his wife's fortitude during this difficult period. She had been to visit him that day, October 10, which was her birthday. It had been a sad day for her, but she managed to keep up a cheerful façade. She had been, he said, exceptionally brave and had been splendid toward him during this time, just as she always had been so marvelously faithful and full of loving care.[259]

It was natural that he placed his last writings in her charge. These included a series of commentaries which he wrote in his cell at Akershus during the period October 1–6. He entitled them "Universistic Aphorisms". They were published in an abbreviated form in 1980 as part of the fragmented reminiscences and letters which made up his wife's diary. Along with his pantheistic booklet from 1929 and the introduction to his philosophical work, which was read during his trial, this brief collection of aphorisms is all that has been published of his universistic philosophy.[260]

The religious, historical, philosophical, and scientific observations that he made in these commentaries, at times simplistic and occasionally incorrect, again revealed the difficulty of the task which he had assumed, as a twentieth century man, of trying to find a new, all-encompassing explanation for human existence. Yet because of the mystical element in his personality, he had to fulfill the need to create such a philosophical system this too was an essential part of his nature.

Faced with his pending execution, although the Supreme Court had not rendered its decision when he wrote these reflections, he understandably was preoccupied with questions concerning religion and death. He declared his faith in a coming religious and political revolution that would fulfill his fundamental ideas. The Old Testament, he predicted, would be eradicated from Christianity, supplanted entirely by the New Testament. But in addition the future would also witness the appearance of a "universistic testament" carrying the gospel of "God's Realm on Earth".[261] During this new historical epoch which "God's Realm on Earth" inaugurated, the world would become one.[262] He saw himself as the prophet for this final period of historical and religious development, having had the mission of establishing the "foundation" for this realm in Norway.[263]

The world, he maintained, was but in its initial phase of establishing this divine realm – only one small unit among the planets throughout the universe undergoing a process of divinely inspired transition in accordance with God's will, which permeated the cosmos.[264] He portrayed himself as a martyr, dying on behalf of his prophecy as had Christ and St. Olav. But death was not permanent, reincarnation would occur. In an undated letter, written to Maria from his death cell, he called on her to be steadfast in her faith: "Believe in God and believe in me."[265] Death would not separate them. He would always be with her until they met again.[266] For her part, she in turn accepted his religious belief as best she could.[267] From the available evidence, it appears that she was literally his only religious follower. Even more than in politics, his religious viewpoint was so unclear and mystical that it could only have meaning for its originator. It could never hope to attract a mass following.

When they met for the last time at Møllergaten 19, on Sunday, October 14, Vidkun and Maria Quisling both anticipated that the death sentence would soon be carried out, although she still continued to pursue her hopeless quest for clemency. Unknown to them both, he had but nine more days to live. With the acting prison director and a female constable present, they could not say all that they wished to each other. Nevertheless, their conversation, at times deliberately unclear, touched upon the matter that was uppermost in their minds, his pending execution. She encouraged him to be strong, and comforted him with the thought that he would again be with his mother, of whom he had been so fond. She persisted in keeping up a brave front, emphasizing that he should not worry about her – their friends would provide the necessary help that she needed. He in turn expressed the desire that his gravestone should only bear a simple inscription: "Vidkun Quisling".[268]

In his last letters to his wife, he continued to proclaim his love for her, the feeling that they would never be parted, and encouraging her to remain firm in her faith in God and in him.[269] As the letters reveal, he wrote to her with the recognition that the execution was inevitable, but with no knowledge of when it would be carried out. However, on Tuesday, October 23, the decision was made. The King, meeting in council with the government, rejected the petition for clemency and decreed that the execution should proceed.[270] Preparations were immediately made to have a firing squad carry out its task that very night.

The doomed man did not know until just hours before when his death would take place. In the early evening, at 6:00 p.m., Quisling received the news from the prison pastor that the execution had been set at five minutes past midnight. He asked to be allowed to say farewell to his wife, but in accordance with the rules affecting condemned prisoners who had been refused clemency, this request was denied him.[271] As the only alternative available, he had to resign himself to expressing his final words to Maria in writing. In this letter of farewell, he again encouraged her to be strong and to believe that his death had a deeper meaning, fulfilling God's will. He asked her to send greetings to his brother Jørgen and to others. Looking forward to his final resting place, he expressed the desire to be buried in the cemetery at Gjerpen, his father's parish in those years when the eldest Quisling son first made his reputation as an exceptionally able student. Above all, however, his attention in the letter was concentrated on Maria: "Remember our life together, and that we shall meet again. Keep my memory. Thank you for everything." His final thoughts, he lovingly declared, would be with her.[272]

During the late evening hours he prepared himself to meet the end in the company of the prison pastor.[273] But not even this, the final episode in his life's journey, was allowed to take place entirely according to plan. The execution was postponed for more than two hours in consideration of a foreign observer. The Danish government, anticipating the time when it would carry out similar executions of Danes convicted of treason and other criminal acts because of their collaboration with the Germans, sent a high police official, Aage Seidenfaden, to be present at Quisling's shooting. Seidenfaden's task was to gain experience in how such executions should take place, and to report his findings to the Danish Ministry of Justice. The plane carrying the Danish police chief could not touch down at the Oslo airport, however, due to fog, and was forced to land instead near Kristiansand in the extreme southern part of Norway. Because of this unforseen development, it took many hours for him to travel by car to Oslo over bad postwar roads. The execution was therefore delayed until his arrival. Having finally reached Oslo early in the morning of October 24, at 2:30 a.m. he clambered up the embankment to the stone walls of Akershus Castle, where Quisling would meet his fate, having passed through two military cordons.

The setting which the Dane found was highly dramatic, almost as if it had been designed for an execution. Indeed, Seidenfaden likened it to a film. With the fortress ramparts looming in the background, the night was dark and stormy. Withered leaves, torn from the branches of the surrounding tall trees, sailed through the air and covered the execution site.[274]

Quisling had not yet been brought to the place of execution when Seidenfaden arrived. Soon afterwards, however, the car carrying the condemned man pulled up a short distance away. In preparation for the end, his hands were already tied behind his back.[275] Back at the familiar site where so many of the highlights in his life had been celebrated, the final tragically short episode began. The former Minister President, upon emerging from the automobile, again proclaimed that he went to his death as an innocent man. He sent a last greeting to his wife.[276] Mercifully for him, the end came quickly. He was led to the place of execution – a small, open, wooden enclosure with three walls, built up against the stone rampart. He was bound upright, with a blindfold over his eyes. The firing squad of ten men marched in and made ready. Their target was a piece of white cloth, placed over the doomed man's heart. At 2:40 a.m. the soldiers took aim and fired. The noise from the ensuing volley reverberated through the late fall darkness, and in an instant the life of the most notorious figure in modern Norwegian history was snuffed out.[277]

In death as in life, Quisling remained a figure of controversy. This in large part was due to the manner in which the facts concerning his execution became available. Norwegian authorities, always reluctant to reveal personal information, were doubly so in this case, involving the death of someone as infamous as Quisling. The Ministry of Justice issued only a terse news release announcing his death. The statement, which also provided background information about how the petition for clemency had been denied, merely contained the time of execution by shooting, and when the next of kin had been informed.[278]

Such reticence allowed a fully constructed postwar myth to be created among the deceased NS *Fører*'s most loyal followers. It gained nourishment as the years went by following the execution, in particular when it was accepted by two foreign journalists, who wrote sensational accounts in their books of how Quisling met his death. The first was by an Englishman, Ralph Hewins, who wrote a largely uncritical popular biography of Quisling. He depicted the execution in terms of a Roman spectacle. According to his description, scores of spectators were allowed to gather along the ramparts to view the shooting, while Quisling was forced to stand waiting for their benefit, shivering in the cold night air. But even in death, Hewins asserted, Quisling showed his superiority over ordinary mortals by allegedly using his mathematical intelligence to balance his body in such a manner that he did not collapse when the bullets ended his life, but remained erect, apparently still alive, to the aghast amazement of the onlookers. In Hewins' account, the morbid spectacle continued even following the execution, with Quisling's body supposedly being placed on display at Møllergaten 19. Many "good Norwegians", maintained Hewins, came to view the corpse. They "prodded the body and made ribald remarks".[279]

Hewins' book aroused considerable debate and newspaper commentary in Norway not merely for its inaccurate description of Quisling's death, but for the many factual errors found throughout the biography as a whole. It was not, however, until the myth was repeated almost intact by a Danish writer, Thorkild Hansen, in a very detailed but controversial study of Knut Hamsun, that misconceptions concerning Quisling's death were challenged by eyewitness rebuttals. This was perhaps due to the fact that not only was Hansen's book extremely well written in a popular vein, and he therefore had greater impact than Hewins, but because it was published in Denmark and translated into Norwegian, it reached a much larger readership in Scandinavia.[280]

As a reaction to the fully flourishing myth, in the fall of 1978, following the publication of Hansen's Hamsun biography, a number of articles appeared in the Norwegian press which successfully torpedoed the myth, at least for the benefit of a Norwegian reading audience. In addition, Seidenfaden's report from October 1945 has later been made available for scholarly research by the Danish Ministry of Justice. Not only did these sources show that Quisling's execution was carried out quickly, but that like all mortals, he had collapsed immediately upon being shot. The two doctors present confirmed that eight bullets had pierced his heart. The military had professionally maintained tight security around Akershus Castle, allowing only a limited number of official observers to be present.[281] Furthermore, with no notice of the execution being issued until *after* it had been carried out, coupled with the rapid manner in which it was completed following the King's decision, and the early morning hour when it took place, few if any unauthorized persons knew when the death sentence would be enforced. The evidence released also showed that Quisling's corpse had not been put on public display. Following the execution, the body was placed in a casket, the lid was sealed, and the remains were driven to a garage at Møllergaten 19. Here the casket remained in the car under guard until about 6:00–7:00 a.m. The casket was then driven to the crematorium.[282]

Vidkun Quisling's biography does not fully end with a volley of rifle shots, followed by cremation, on October 24, 1945. The urn containing his ashes had a brief story of its own. For the time being, it remained in the possession of the police. The authorities were concerned that in the immediate postwar period, when emotions were still high because of what had taken place during the occupation, a Quisling grave might have become the site of possible demonstrations and desecrations if a private burial had been allowed. The urn therefore remained in official custody, although Maria Quisling made several unsuccessful appeals to be allowed to take possession of her late husband's ashes.[283] At the end of the 1950s, however, the government's position changed. On June 27, 1959, on the recommendation of the Minister of Justice, the government responded positively to the widow's petition.[284]

To her great satisfaction, she received the urn three days later, on June 30. On the next day, following a private service, it was interred in the family plot at Gjerpen. Quisling's last wish had thereby been fulfilled. But in understanding with the authorities, the site of his final resting place was kept secret.[285]

Although she had been a passive NS member since 1933, when her husband enrolled her in the party, Maria Quisling was never brought to trial after the war. Accusations against her were raised in 1946 by the police, but the court, in a pretrial inquiry, found no grounds for prosecution and ordered her to be released.[286] She eventually regained possession of the flat in Erling Skjalgssonsgate which she had shared for so many years with her husband. Here she lived for the rest of her years, surrounded by the paintings, pictures, furniture, and other memorabilia from her earlier life.

Almost thirty-five years after her husband's execution, Maria Quisling passed away on January 17, 1980. She was interred alongside him at Gjerpen. Only with the publication of her diary later in the same year did the location of the grave-site become public knowledge.[287] With her passing, the sad saga of Vidkun Quisling had reached its end.

Epilogue

No one shall go free, but neither shall anyone be punished without a hearing. We shall have a legal settlement. We do not use the Nazis' methods. Lynch justice, moreover, makes martyrs of the victims, and Nazis and war criminals do not deserve this.

The Home Front to the Nygaardsvold government,
October 9, 1944

As a prophet for the postwar period, Vidkun Quisling again proved to be a failure. None of the predictions for the future which he made during the war were fulfilled in the Norwegian society that emerged from five years of German occupation. The Minister President had always insisted that those Norwegians were deluded who believed that it would be possible to return to prewar conditions. The war, he maintained, was a crisis for both capitalism and democracy – neither would survive. The only choice lay between National Union and "Bolshevism", and cooperation with "Bolshevism" would lead inevitably to slavery. Those who cooperated as partners with the communists, he warned, always became their servants.[1]

Contrary to the Minister President's forecasts, the transition from war to peace took place in a remarkably uncomplicated manner which in no way corresponded to what he had predicted. He had always insisted that it would be impossible for his enemies in the long run to maintain their wartime cooperation. Following the war's conclusion, however, no significant disagreement arose between the government in exile and the Home Front leadership, nor did any friction occur between the Western Allies and the Russians over Norway's future.

At the end of the occupation, resumption of authority by Norwegian officials took place in a smooth manner, with the previously designated administrators immediately assuming their posts. The Home Front leadership only retained its control for a few days, resigning its provisional power on the arrival of Crown Prince Olav and a governmental delegation on May 13. The remainder of the Nygaardsvold government returned at the very end of May. On June 7, on the fortieth anniversary of Norway's emergence as a fully independent nation and on the fifth anniversary of his departure into exile, Haakon VII, the foremost symbol of resistance against the Germans and Quisling, stepped ashore in Oslo harbor to the greatest acclamation ever received by any Norwegian monarch. With the King's return a month after the occupation was over, the restoration of the constitutional monarchy was completed.

The resumption of parliamentary democracy took place in a similarly gradual fashion. Prime Minister Nygaardsvold had previously declared his government's intention of resigning once the war was over. He fulfilled this pledge on June 12. Two days later the *Storting* from 1940 reassembled as the nation's governmental authority, despite the element of disrepute it had gained from its considerations of the King's suspension during the difficult negotiating sessions with the *Reichskommissariat* in the summer of 1940. It approved the formation of an interim government of national unity under the leadership of the Labor party's Einar Gerhardsen. Gerhardsen, it may be recalled, had been one of Labor's strategists in the battle against NS in Oslo during the early 1930s. His government was a coalition of all the political parties that Quisling abhorred, from the Conservatives to the Communists. Its period in office, however, was short, serving only until a permanent government could be chosen which had popular legitimacy. On October 7 the first regular parliamentary elections were held, resulting in an absolute majority for the Labor party. This marked the beginning of a 20-year period during which Labor, the political organization which Quisling above all had regarded as his major opposition, would hold governmental power. The condemned prisoner therefore witnessed the fact that even before his execution, the parliamentary system, which he detested so much because it had denied him success, was functioning in the same manner as prior to the war. Unforeseen by him, the major difference from the prewar period was that the Labor party would for many years retain an absolute majority in the *Storting*.[2]

Instead of this orderly transition, Quisling had forecast that Norway would inevitably be subjected to a power struggle between the Western Allies and the Soviet Union, which he maintained would occur immediately following the war's conclusion. As a result of this confrontation, he had repeatedly insisted that Norway would fall victim to the onrushing Bolshevik hordes. The occupation of eastern Finnmark, he warned, was merely the beginning of a Communist takeover.[3]

In the face of such a dire prediction, the Allied powers' involvement in Norway in 1945 proved to be anticlimactic. Having received assurance that the British and American forces which had come to Norway following the German surrender, numbering at their maximum some 30,000, would leave the country in October, the Russians made preparations to withdraw from eastern Finnmark even earlier. Beginning in mid-September, the Red

Army units carried out their evacuation, and on September 26 the last Russian soldier crossed the border.[4] At that time Quisling's appeal had not yet come up before the Supreme Court.

The major legacy which the imprisoned ex-*Fører* left behind for postwar Norway to deal with was the great number of his discredited followers. They now faced, all of them individually, their day of reckoning. Long before the war was over, the Nygaardsvold government had declared that NS members would have to stand accountable for their actions once the occupation had ended. This was by no means only propaganda to frighten Quisling's adherents, or merely a statement of principle, perhaps to be implemented after the war. In cooperation with the Home Front leadership, preparation for the coming "legal settlement" (*rettsoppgjøret*) was planned systematically by Norwegian officials in London and Stockholm before the end of hostilities.

The process of dealing with NS went into effect as soon as the Home Front took control in May 1945. The more prominent party members were immediately rounded up and imprisoned. All persons affiliated with the party during the war were investigated in the course of an exhaustive legal examination. The entire process of investigating each individual suspected of treason proved to be extensive, much more so than Norwegian officials had originally anticipated. Almost 93,000 persons were investigated.[5] They included not solely NS members, but all persons under suspicion of illegal collaboration, including collaboration for the purpose of economic gain.

Considering the events of the past five years, in which NS as a party had served as an accomplice for the occupying power, the treatment the suspects received, with each case judged on its individual merits, was not severe. Slightly more than half of those investigated were either not brought to trial or were found innocent. Of the 46,085 judged guilty, the great majority, mostly passive NS members, did not receive prison sentences, but were fined and/or deprived of their civil rights for a limited period.[6]

Of the some 18,000 persons imprisoned,[7] few served long sentences. In 1948, when only some 3,200 remained interned, a law was passed which reduced the required period of incarceration prior to parole from two-thirds to one-half of the sentence. Three-fourths of the prisoners were thereupon released.[8] Those who had received sentences of more than eight years did not come under the provisions of this law. These persons, however, also escaped having to serve long sentences owing to the extensive granting of clemency by the government. Prisoners sentenced to 20-year terms served on the average 6 1/2 years, while those who received life imprisonment were incarcerated for an average of about nine years. The last four life-term prisoners received clemency and were released in November

1957, 12 1/2 years after the Second World War had come to its conclusion.[9]

The great majority of those who had held office under Quisling as NS ministers received either long-term or life imprisonment. Six were sentenced to life terms (Stang, Lippestad, Fuglesang, Hustad, Meidell, and Whist), while five received 20-year sentences (Fretheim, Von Hirsch, Skarphagen, Vassbotten, and Blehr). Irgens received the most lenient sentence, 15 years. Sverre Riisnæs, who could have expected to receive severe retribution, was declared incurably insane and thereby most probably avoided the death penalty.[10]

Two former ministers followed the NS *Fører* to face the firing squad – Hagelin and Skancke. These three were the only NS leaders executed for political treason. The remaining 22 Norwegians who were put to death had been associated with the State Police or the Gestapo, and had been found guilty of such crimes as torture, the killing of prisoners, or had caused the deaths of others under aggravating circumstances.[11]

Compared with other European countries that had been under German occupation, the treatment of collaborators in Norway was restrained. There did not occur the type of lynch justice that took place in countries such as France. The number of executions carried out was the lowest in any European society, and the legal process against persons suspected of treason compared favorably with those two countries whose experiences were most similar to Norway during the war, Denmark and the Netherlands.[12] This lack of severity in comparison with other societies was to a considerable degree due to the nature of the occupation which Norway had experienced. Despite its repressive, at times barbarous, character, the German occupation was far less severe than in most European countries, above all when compared with eastern Europe.

Beyond this, the restrained use of the death sentence can also in part be attributed to the natural antipathy to the application of the ultimate penalty that has been an ingrained part of Norwegian society since the second half of the nineteenth century. Although most Norwegians immediately after the war favored use of the death penalty, during the following years public opinion gradually reversed itself.[13] In June 1979 the ultimate step was taken. The death penalty was abolished entirely, being removed even from the military penal code, which had served as a major basis for Quisling's conviction. As a consequence of this legal change, had Vidkun Quisling been on trial today for the crimes that he stood accused of in 1945, he could not be condemned to death. Should such an extreme penalty again be required in the sentencing of some future Norwegian quisling, only retroactive legislation can make it possible.[14]

Although he lived to see that the events which took place immediately following the end of the war did not correspond with his assumptions, the former Minister President did not permit reality to influence his outlook. Having persuaded himself that he died in the cause of a prophetic mission, he met his death still convinced that the future would prove him correct. History, he so often repeated in the period before his execution, would judge him differently.

The course of history since 1945 did not bear out this contention. World War II was not the crisis for democracy and capitalism that he had predicted. As the rapid transition to postwar democracy illustrated, Norway's democratic traditions were strengthened by the country's five-year endurance of German occupation. Capitalism too survived the war quite well, although in a somewhat altered form. In the postwar period, the state assumed a greater role in regulating the economy. Capitalistic competition remained, but it was restricted to a certain degree by governmental rules and by state ownership of some segments of the economy. Norway, like the other Scandinavian countries, has maintained a mixed economy since 1945. Close interaction exists between the administration and various interest groups. The society is highly organized. Superficially, this may at first glance give it the appearance of being run according to the type of corporate system which Quisling favored. But the organizational structure of integrated interest groups is highly democratic in nature, and in no way resembles the fascist system that he wished to establish, in which a dictatorial state controlled and manipulated society.

The Second World War in Europe marked instead the death struggle for National Socialism, which was completely annihilated as a result of the outcome of the war. The groups throughout the continent which had been directly associated with Hitler's movement, including National Union, shared its fate. The tradition which Quisling's party had represented was so discredited that after 1945 it was impossible for any right-wing, nationalist, anti-socialist party to exist. When finally a radical party emerged to the right of the Conservatives in the 1970s, the Progress party (*Fremskrittspartiet*), it came into existence in complete adherence to democratic principles.

Vidkun Quisling therefore left behind no significant imprint on postwar Norwegian society. All of the goals which he had sought to realize as NS *Fører* and Minister President were forgotten, having never become part of the national consciousness. It was as if a slate had been wiped clean, eliminating in one stroke the programs which his administration had tried to carry out during the previous five years.

Since the end of the war not even Quisling's past adherents have made a serious attempt to revive his cause. Some may harbor resentment due to the treatment they experienced at the end of the occupation, but most appear to have turned their backs on the past, preferring instead to concentrate on the new lives which they created after the war.

Only one small group of former NS members made an organized effort in the postwar years to alter the discredited reputation of Vidkun Quisling's former movement. Consisting largely of middle-aged and elderly persons, it came into existence as the Association for Social Restoration (*Forbundet for Sosial Oppreisning*) in October 1949. During the 1950s and 1960s it worked without success to reverse the legal settlement against NS members. The group reorganized itself in the 1970s, and it now appears under the outwardly neutral title of Institute for Norwegian Occupation History. As the name indicates, it seeks through various publications to present a favorable historical interpretation of National Union and its *Fører*. Since 1952 this group of NS loyalists has issued its monthly newspaper, *Folk og Land* (*People and Country*). In the mid-1970s the paper had an average edition of approximately 2000 copies. As this relatively low number indicates, the irreconcilables, to their great disappointment, have not been able to gain the adherence of the vast majority of former NS members, who have avoided any association with the group. Because of its small size and the stigmatized past which it represents, it has had no political influence.[15]

In the 1970s a new neo-Nazi faction made its presence known. Because it seeks to take direct action and because of its extremist character, it has received considerable media attention, in contrast to the *Folk og Land* group, which for a long period was scarcely mentioned in the press. Under the title of Norwegian Front, the newcomers appear to have no direct ties to the older group of former NS members. Consisting of young activists with a strong admiration for Adolf Hitler and Nazism, it sought originally to win supporters through its vehement anti-communism. In the 1980s, now under the label National People's party, it is attempting to stir up resentment against immigrants, especially Pakistanis, but with little success. Although it calls itself a party, the group is but a sect. It has failed several times to obtain the minimum number of signatures needed to take part in elections. Its inability to gain followers is due not only to its racist, anti-democratic ideology, but also to several sensational acts of violence which, though not directly connected with the group, have discredited it. Although it does not officially identify itself with Quisling's political tradition, its attitude toward the NS past is positive. Most of its adherents, however, do not appear to have an NS background.

These two small factions, whose most noticeable feature so far is their insignificance, constitute the only recognizable links in post-1945 Norwegian society with Vidkun Quisling's heritage. For the overwhelming majority of citizens within his native country, his name today continues to have an odious connotation. It is therefore ironic that internationally only *his* name gains recognition among the political figures that modern Norwegian history has produced. In Norway as throughout the world, the name Quisling is a term for traitor. But it has not become a general term in Norway. It continues to be associated directly with the man who, at the most critical time in his country's modern existence, betrayed his social order. As a historical figure, Quisling is still very much alive in the nation's collective consciousness, representing a bitter memory from the immediate past.

Notes

Notes to Introduction

1. The two most useful studies on Quisling in Norwegian are Benjamin Vogt's brief biography, *Mennesket Vidkun og forræderen Quisling* (Oslo: Aschehoug, 1965), and Sverre Hartmann's chronologically more restricted coverage in *Fører uten folk* (rev. ed.; Oslo: Tiden Norsk Forlag, 1970). A fairly recent account by a prominent journalist, Per Øivind Heradstveit, entitled *Quisling. Hvem var han?* (Oslo: Hjemmenes forlag, 1976), provides little new information.

2. (London: W. H. Allen).

3. (Newton Abbot, Devon: David and Charles, 1971).

4. For a detailed and knowledgeable assessment of Hayes' study, see Hans Fredrik Dahl's review in *Historisk Tidsskrift* (*The Norwegian Historical Review*), Vol. 52, No. 1 (1973), pp. 90–96.

5. (Stuttgart: Deutsche Verlags-Anstalt, 1970).

Notes to Chapter I

1. Like many Norwegians, neither Quisling nor his father was very much concerned with spelling their names in a consistent manner. Unlike their father, Vidkun and his two brothers chose to spell their last name with a u rather than a v. Jon Laurits Qvisling sometimes spelled Jon with an added h and Laurits with a z rather than an s.

2. Jon Laurits Qvisling, *Fra mine unge aar. Erindringer og optegnelser.* (Skien: Erik St. Nilssens forlag, 1912), pp. 5 ff.

3. Jon Laurits Qvisling, *Gjerpens*

Prestegjelds og presters historie (Skien: Erik St. Nilssens forlag, 1905), p. 363.

4. Jon Laurits Qvisling, *Gjerpen. En bygdebok.* Vol. II: *Den historiske del.* (Kristiania: H. Aschehoug & Co., 1919), p. 146.

5. For a partial list of Pastor Qvisling's writings see Jon Laurits Qvisling, *Gjerpens Prestegjelds og presters historie*, pp. 360–363.

6. Benjamin Vogt, *Mennesket Vidkun og forræderen Quisling* (Oslo: H. Aschehoug & Co., 1965), pp. 25–27, and Sverre Hartmann, *Fører uten folk. Quisling som politisk og psykologisk problem* (Oslo: Tiden norsk forlag, 1959), pp. 53–54.

7. Hartmann, *ibid.* The exact date of the battle of Hafrsfjord is unknown.

8. Norway, Eidsivating lagstols landssvikavdeling, *Straffesak mot Vidkun Abraham Lauritz Jonssön Quisling* (Oslo: 1946), p. 328. Hereafter cited as *Straffesak.* Two earlier studies of Quisling, by Vogt and Hartmann, disagree over the degree of closeness that existed between Quisling's parents. Vogt depicts the marriage as unhappy, with Mrs. Qvisling leading a repressed life. See Vogt, *Mennesket Vidkun og forræderen Quisling*, pp. 25–26. Hartmann describes the relationship between Jon Laurits and his wife as considerate and loving, and he maintains that their children were brought up in a harmonious household. See Hartmann, *Fører uten folk*, p. 52. On the basis of what I have read, and also from what I learned when I visited Fyresdal in April 1983 and talked with persons who knew the family or belonged to it, I tend to feel that the atmosphere in which the Qvisling children were brought up was truly harmonious, in particular during the years at Gjerpen. See Vilhelm Ullman's testimony, August 25, 1945, *Straffesak*, p. 215; and Hartmann, *Fører uten folk*, p. 295, fn. 44.

9. Arnold Ræstad, "The Case Quis-

ling," unpublished MS (London: 1943), Oslo, Ministry of Foreign Affairs, *arkiv* #39, pp. 6–7.

10. *Straffesak*, p. 328.

11. Testimony of Vilhelm Ullmann, *ibid.*, p. 240

12. Vogt, *Mennesket Vidkun og forræderen Quisling*, p. 33.

13. *Straffesak*, p. 328.

14. Vogt, *Mennesket Vidkun og forraederen Quisling*, p. 35.

15. *Straffesak*, p. 328.

16. Vogt, *Mennesket Vidkun og forræderen Quisling*, p. 36.

17. *Ibid.*, p. 37.

18. Norway, Eidsivating lagstols landssvikavdeling, *Dokumenter i offentlig straffesak mot Vidkun Quisling. Tilleggshefte* (Oslo: 1945), p. 33. Hereafter cited as *Tilleggshefte*.

19. *Ibid.*

20. Vogt, *Mennesket Vidkun og forræderen Quisling*, p. 38.

21. Ræstad, "The Case Quisling," p. 11.

22. *Ibid.*

23. *Straffesak*, p. 328.

24. Ræstad, p. 11.

25. *Ibid.*, pp. 10–11.

26. *Straffesak*, p. 329.

27. Reidar Omang, *Stormfulle tider 1913–28*, Vol. II of *Norsk Utenrikstjeneste* (Oslo: Gyldendal, 1959), p. 164.

28. *Straffesak*, p. 329.

29. Quisling til Det kgl. Forsvarsdepartement, Petrograd, report #4, June 1, 1918. Riksarkivet, Generalstabens arkiv, Journalsaker 1166: Petrograd 1918. Hereafter cited as RA, GA, Journalsaker 1166.

30. *Ibid.*

31. Quisling to Det kgl. Forsvarsdepartement, report #12, October 23, 1918, RA, GA, Journalsaker 1166.

32. Vogt, *Mennesket Vidkun og forræderen Quisling*, p. 43.

33. See Magne Skodvin, *Striden om okkupasjonsstyret i Norge fram til 25. september 1940* (Oslo: Det Norske Samlaget, 1956), p. 334.

34. Vogt, *Mennesket Vidkun og forræderen Quisling*, pp. 49–50.

35. *Ibid*, p. 50; *Tilleggshefte*, p. 33.

36. Richard Andvord to Generalstabens

Avdeling E, Helsingfors, September 13, 1919, RA, GA, Journalsaker #1105.

37. RA, GA, Journalsaker #1105, #1102, #1106

38. *Ibid.* During his trial, Quisling related that he travelled widely in 1918 when he served as military attaché in Petrograd. He maintained he had been attached to Trotsky, and went so far as to declare that he advised Trotsky on how to defeat the Whites (*Straffesak*, p. 329). None of this has been substantiated.

39. *Straffesak*, p. 239.

40. Quisling to Generalstaben, Avdeling E, report #51, Helsinki, February 28, 1920, RA, GA, Journalsaker #1102.

41. Ræstad, "The Case Quisling," pp. 24–25.

42. Urbye's testimony, *Straffesak*, p. 239.

43. Ræstad, "The Case Quisling," p. 25.

44. *Ibid.*

45. Vogt, *Mennesket Vidkun og forræderen Quisling*, p. 54.

46. Jon Sørensen, *Fridtjof Nansens saga* (Oslo: Jacob Dybwads forlag, 1931), p. 265.

47. Vogt, *Mennesket Vidkun og forræderen Quisling*, p. 54.

48. *Straffesak*, p. 334.

49. Thomas Frank Johnson, *International Tramps: From Chaos to Permanent World Peace* (London: Hutchinson & Co., 1938), pp. 161–163.

50. *Ibid.*

51. Vogt, *Mennesket Vidkun og forræderen Quisling*, p. 54.

52. Sørensen, *Fridtjof Nansens saga*, p. 269.

53. Testimony of Halvor Hansson, August 25, 1945, *Straffesak*, p. 237. Quisling later made extensive use of pictures of this nature in his party's propaganda effort to discredit the Soviet Union.

54. Johnson, *International Tramps*, p. 165.

55. Vogt, *Mennesket Vidkun og forræderen Quisling*, p. 55.

56. Quisling to King Haakon VII, November 1, 1927, quoted in Hartmann, *Fører uten folk*, p. 87.

57. Vogt, *Mennesket Vidkun og forræderen Quisling*, p. 56.

58. *Ibid.* p. 57.

59. *Ibid.*

60. *Straffesak*, pp. 44–45.

61. *Ibid.*, p. 43.

62. Vogt, *Mennesket Vidkun og forræderen Quisling*, p. 56.

63. *Ibid.*, pp. 56–57, 74–75; Øistein Parmann, introduction to Maria Quisling, *Dagbok og andre efterlatte papirer*, Øistein Parmann, ed. (Oslo: Dreyers forlag, 1980), p. 19. Hereafter cited as Maria Quisling, *Dagbok*. See also Hans Fredrik Dahl *et al.*, *Den norske nasjonalsosialismen* (Oslo: Pax forlag, 1982), p. 37.

64. Maria Quisling, *Dagbok*, p. 17, p. 20; *Straffesak*, p. 7.

65. Maria Quisling, *ibid.*, pp. 20–21.

66. Benjamin Vogt was the first biographer to indicate that Quisling's marriage to Alexandra was not just pro forma. See "Quisling, Vidkun Abraham Lauritz Jonssøn," *Norsk biografisk leksikon*, Vol. XI p. 213; and *Mennesket Vidkun og forræderen Quisling*, pp. 57–58, 74–75. For what appears to be the most reliable account of Quisling's first marriage, see Øistein Parmann's introduction in Maria Quisling, *Dagbok*, pp. 18–21. Parmann's presentation is based on Alexandra's personal account, and agrees in most instances with a rather melodramatic series of three articles based on an interview with Alexandra that appeared in a woman's weekly, *Alle Kvinner*, August 26, September 2, and September 9, 1975.

67. Ræstad, "The Case Quisling," pp. 31–32; Hartmann, *Fører uten folk*, p. 86.

68. Hewins, *Quisling: Prophet without Honour*, pp. 67–68; "Gamle løgner blir som nye," *Folk og land*, December 1978.

69. Quisling, statement, May 31, 1945, University of Oslo, Historical Institute, Skodvin Collection, police reports, #124. My italics. University of Oslo, Historical Institute, Skodvin Collection hereafter cited as HI, Skodvin Collection.

70. See the illustrations in: Maria Quisling, *Dagbok*; Dahl, *et al*, *Den norske nasjonalsosialismen*, p. 37; and the series of articles in *Alle Kvinner*, August 26, September 2, and September 9, 1975.

71. *Straffesak*, p. 238.

72. Nansen to Quisling, October 17, 1923, *Tilleggshefte III*, p. 3.

73. *Ibid.*

74. Ernest E. Reynolds, *Nansen* (London: Geoffrey Bles, 1932), pp. 223–224.

75. Nansen to Quisling, October 17, 1923, *Tilleggshefte III*, p. 3.

76. *Studentene fra 1905*, quoted in *Straffesak*, p. 281.

77. Liv Nansen Høyer, *Nansen og verden* (Oslo: J. W. Cappelens forlag, 1955) pp. 225 ff.; Reynolds, *Nansen*, pp. 223–236.

78. Hayes, in *Quisling: The Career and Political Ideas of Vidkun Quisling 1887–1945*, pp. 32–33, maintains that Quisling was in charge of a lottery in Bulgaria on behalf of refugees, and more sketchily traces Quisling's alleged work in other parts of the Balkan area. However, none of the sources that Hayes cites appear to support his specific descriptions of Quisling's activity at this time.

79. Fridtjof Nansen, *Gjennom Armenia*, Vol. IV of *Fra Svalbard til Kaukasus*, ed. by Werner Werenskiold (Oslo: Jacob Dybwads forlag, 1941), pp. 6–7.

80. *Tilleggshefte*, p. 6.

81. Nansen, *Gjennom Armenia*, pp. 1–46.

82. *Ibid.*, pp. 46–210

83. Nansen, *Gjennom Kaukasus til Volga* (Oslo: Jacob Dybwads forlag, 1929), pp. 1 ff.

84. Translated by G. C. Wheeler (London: George Allen & Unwin, 1931), p. 7.

85. Reynolds, *Nansen*, p. 234.

86. *Ibid.*, p. 254.

87. Johnson, *International Tramps*, p. 327.

88. Nansen, letter of introduction for Quisling, June 16, 1926, *Straffesak*, p. 471; Nansen to Quisling, June 21, 1929, *Straffesak*, pp. 282–283.

89. *Straffesak*, p. 43.

90. *Ibid.*, p. 328. The one exception to this general rule was Frederik Prytz, and even Prytz at times held himself somewhat aloof from Quisling.

91. Unlike English, Norwegian, like most continental European languages, has an informal and a formal form for the personal pronoun you. Children, friends, and members of the family are addressed as *du*, persons with whom one has less personal ties are addressed as *De*. Although the formal use of *De* has declined greatly in Norway

during recent years, its usage was very strong during Quisling's lifetime.

92. Vogt, *Mennesket Vidkun og forræderen Quisling*, pp. 59–60

93. Nansen for Quisling, October 17, 1923, *Straffesak*, p. 282.

94. The letters are printed in *Tilleggshefte III*, pp. 3–4.

95. *Straffesak*, p. 283.

96. "Hvad Nansen mente om Quisling," *Tidens Tegn*, October 11, 1933.

97. Sigrun Nansen to Vidkun Quisling, July 19, 1937, Riksarkivet, Quislings arkiv, Box 11, Besvarte telegram folder.

98. *Straffesak*, p. 239.

99. Johnson, *International Tramps*, p. 165.

100. *Straffesak*, p. 241.

101. Sørensen, *Fridtjof Nansens saga*, p. 275; Wilhelm Keilhau, *I vår egen tid*, Vol. XI of *Det norske folks liv og historie*, eds. Edvard Bull, Haakon Shetelig, Wilhelm Keilhau, and Sverre Steen (Oslo: Aschehoug, 1938), p. 375.

102. *Straffesak*, p. 236, p. 238, p. 43.

103. Parliamentary debate, May 19, 1931, in *ibid.*, p. 473.

104. *Ibid.*, p. 475.

105. Letter from Tranmæl to *Stortingets presidentskap*, June 10, 1932, *Straffesak*, p. 483.

106. *Straffesak*, p. 475, p. 153.

107. *Ibid*, pp. 153–154.

108. Both Friis and Scheflo later rejoined the Labor party.

109. Friis to *Stortinget*, June 10, 1932, *Straffesak*, p. 150.; Scheflo to *Stortinget*, June 9, 1932, *Straffesak*, p. 151.

110. Friis to *Stortinget*, *ibid.*

111. Scheflo to *Stortinget*, June 9, 1932, *ibid.*, p. 151.

112. *Ibid.* The question of language reform was a very explosive political issue in Norway during the 1920s. The proponents of New Norwegian, patterned on the use of local dialects as opposed to the more formal written language which in part was similar to Danish, were enjoying a series of reform victories during this time. Quisling's interview was intended to allow the Communists to appeal to this influential segment of public opinion.

113. *Straffesak*, pp. 150–152.

114. *Ibid.*, p. 333, p. 152.

115. *Ibid.*, p. 333.

116. Prytz folder, *Quislings arkiv.* This folder was part of *Quislings arkiv* when the archive was located at *Universitetsbiblioteket*, where the author examined it in 1967. *Quislings arkiv* was subsequently moved to *Riksarkivet.* When the author next made use of the archive, in 1971, he was not able to find the Prytz folder.

117. Vogt, *Mennesket Vidkun og forræderen Quisling*, pp. 63–64.

118. Statement by Mrs. Maria Quisling to krim. konst. Erik Stai, June 23, 1945, HI, Skodvin Collection, police reports, #54.

119. See Vogt, *Mennesket Vidkun og forræderen Quisling*, pp. 44 ff. Quisling's statement that his political ideas dated back to 1918 is in *Straffesak*, p. 336.

120. *Ibid.*, p. 329.

121. Vogt, *Mennesket Vidkun og forræderen Quisling*, p. 65.

122. Ræstad, "The Case Quisling," p. 37.

123. *Ibid.*

124. Vogt, *Mennesket Vidkun og forræderen Quisling*, p. 64.

125. *Ibid.*, p. 66.

126. *Ibid.*, pp. 67–68.

127. *Ibid.*, p. 64.

128. *Ibid.*, pp. 67–68

129. Norway, Foreign Ministry, Folder Gruppe 5, Avdeling H, Administr. Ordn. Moskva 1927 – Jan. 1929.

130. Ivar Lykke to Benjamin Vogt, Oslo, June 11, 1927, *ibid.*

131. Urbye to the Foreign Ministry, June 3, 1927, Foreign Ministry, Folder Gruppe 5, Avdeling H, Administr. ordn, Moskva 1927 – Jan. 1929.

132. Urbye to the Foreign Ministry, June 9, 1927, *ibid.*

133. Statsråd-sekretariatet bifalt med kongelig resolusjon av 16. juni, 1927, *ibid.*

134. *Ibid.*

135. British Legation, Oslo, to The Royal Norwegian Ministry for Foreign Affairs, January 26, 1928, *ibid.*

136. Urbye to the Foreign Ministry, June 30, 1927, *ibid.*

137. *Ibid.*

138. Urbye to the Foreign Ministry, January 12, 1928, Norway, Foreign Ministry, Folder K5g 22a.

139. Ivar Lykke to the Norwegian Legation in Moscow, January 21, 1928, *ibid.*

140. Ræstad, "The Case Quisling," pp. 47–48.

141. *Ibid.*, p. 45; Benjamin Vogt, "Prytz, Anton Frederik Winter Jakhelln," *Norsk Biografisk Leksikon* (Oslo: H. Aschehoug & Co., 1923-), Vol. XI, p. 195.

142. Vogt, *ibid.*, pp. 195–196.

143. Vogt, *Mennesket Vidkun og forræderen Quisling*, p. 68.

144. *Ibid.*

145. Ræstad, "The Case Quisling," p. 45; Nordahl Grieg, *Hvordan en fører blir til,* reprint from *Veien Frem,* No. 5 (1936) (Oslo: Centrum forlag, 1945), p. 9; Vogt, *ibid.*, p. 69.

146. Vogt, "Prytz," p. 196.

147. Parliamentary debate of May 19, 1931, reprinted in *Straffesak,* pp. 475–476.

148. *Ibid.*, p. 476

149. Although not always accurate factually, Nordahl Grieg's brief polemical study of Quisling, *Hvordan en fører blir til,* at times provides keen insight into Quisling's personality. It discusses the impact of this event.

150. Urbye to the Foreign Ministry, August 23, 1928, Foreign Ministry, Gruppe Q 5, Avdeling H, Sak 1/27 Den administrative ordning ved Leg. Moskvas overtagelse av brit. interesser i Sovjet.

151. *Ibid.*

152. *Straffesak,* p. 43, p. 332; Harald Franklin Knudsen, *Jeg var Quislings sekretær* (Copenhagen: privately published, 1951), p. 40.

153. *Mennesket Vidkun og forræderen Quisling,* p. 70.

154. *Storting* debate of April 7, 1932, quoted in Oddvar Høidal, "Quislings stilling ved den norske legasjon i Moskva juni 1927 – desember 1929," *Historisk Tidsskrift,* Vol. 46, No. 2 (1974), p. 188.

155. Foreign Ministry, Gruppe H62, Avdeling D, Sak 1/28, Britisk U-båt L55; Sak 3/28, Britiske interesser . . .; Sak 2/28, Beskyttelse av kurder; Sak 5/27, Brit. Interesser i Moskva.

156. Gascoigne to Esmarch, Oslo, November 7, 1928, Foreign Ministry, Folder Gruppe 10, Avdeling H, Sak 2/28; Urbye to Foreign Ministry, Moscow, August 21, 1928, Foreign Ministry, Folder Gruppe 5,

Avdeling H, Administr, ordn. Moskva 1927-jan. 1929; Lindley to Esmarch, Oslo, August 29, 1929, Foreign Ministry, Folder Gruppe 10, Avdeling H, Sak 2/28; Wingfield to Mowinckel, Oslo, December 3, 1929, Foreign Ministry, Folder Gruppe 10, Avdeling H, Sak 2/28.

157. Vogt, *Mennesket Vidkun og forræderen Quisling,* p. 71.

158. Gudrun Ræder, *De uunværlige flinke* (Oslo: Gyldendal Norsk Forlag, 1975), p. 164.

159. *Ibid.*

160. *Straffesak,* p. 459.

161. *Ibid.*

162. Wingfield to Mowinckel, Oslo, December 3, 1929, Foreign Ministry, Folder Gruppe 10, Avdeling H, Sak 2/28; Lindley to Urbye, Oslo, August 24, 1929, Foreign Ministry, Folder Gruppe 5, Avdeling H, Administr. ordn. Moskva 1927-jan. 1929; Ræstad, "The Case Quisling," p. 41.

163. Not coincidentally, a book written by Thomas Frank Johnson, one of Quisling's associates in Nansen's relief activity, was entitled *International Tramps.*

Notes to Chapter II

1. Christian A. R. Christensen, *Fra verdenskrig til verdenskrig,* Vol. VIII of *Vårt folks historie,* Thorleif Dahl, Axel Coldevin, and Johan Schreiner eds. (Oslo: Aschehoug, 1961), pp. 172–198, 227–253.

2. *Ibid.*, p. 250; Edvard Bull, *Klassekamp og fellesskap 1920–1945,* Vol. XIII of *Norges historie,* Knut Mykland ed. (Oslo: J. W. Cappelens forlag, 1979), p. 18; Berge Furre, *Norsk historie 1905–1940* (Oslo: Det Norske Samlaget, 1971), p. 305.

3. Walter Galenson, "Scandinavia," in Walter Galenson, ed., *Comparative Labor Movements* (New York: Prentice-Hall, 1952), p. 141.

4. Arne Bergsgård, *Frå 17. mai til 9. april. Norsk historie 1814–1940* (Oslo: Det Norske Samlaget, 1958), p. 364.

5. *Ibid.*, pp. 371–372.

6. *Ibid.*, p. 358.

7. *Ibid.*

8. Hans Fredrik Dahl, "Fascismen i

Norge 1920–1940. Et overblikk," *Kontrast,* Vol. II, No. 3 (1966), p. 12.

9. See below, pp. 80–82.

10. Magnus Jensen, *Norges historie* (2 vols.; Oslo: Gyldendal Norsk Forlag, 1949), Vol. II, pp. 518–519. Not all segments of the Labor party accepted affiliation with the Comintern. In 1920 more moderate members of the party, proclaiming adherence to the idea of democratic elections rather than the possibility of revolutionary upheaval as a means of furthering the interests of the working class, seceded to form the Social Democratic party. Not long afterwards, the parent Labor party found its affiliation with the Third International to be anything but pleasant for its independent-minded leadership. Led by Martin Tranmæl, it proclaimed independence from the Comintern in 1923. However, those members of the Labor party who favored the ideal of undivided loyalty to the aspirations of international Communism promptly broke away to establish Norway's Communist party. As a result, for a short while there were three parties purporting to speak for the Norwegian working class. However, among these the Labor party predominated in terms of membership, votes obtained in elections, and parliamentary representation. In 1927 the Labor party and the Social Democrats reconciled their differences and were reunited. Once more, there was a unified Labor party. The Communist party, while strong at first following its secession from the Labor party, declined rapidly. Electing six representatives to the *Storting* in 1924, it saw its parliamentary delegation reduced by one half in 1927, and eliminated completely as a result of the 1930 election. The party was torn by dissension, with many of its leading figures rejoining the Labor party.

11. Christensen, *Fra verdenskrig til verdenskrig,* p. 252, pp. 293–294.

12. Arne Björnberg, *Parlamentarismens utveckling i Norge efter 1905* Skrifter utgivna av Statsvetenskapliga Föreningen i Uppsala, Vol. X (Uppsala and Stockholm: Statsvetenskapliga Föreningen, 1939), p. 327.

13. *Borgerlig* is a Norwegian political term which means non-socialist. I have chosen to employ it in this study because of its widespread usage in Norwegian politics.

Although similar to bourgeois in the Western European meaning of the word, *borgerlig* is not totally synonymous because within its Norwegian setting it is not restricted to urban residents or to members of the middle class. Adherents to all non-socialist political parties are, within the Norwegian political tradition, described as *borgerlig,* both by themselves and by their socialist opponents.

14. Jostein Nerbøvik, *Antiparlamentariske straumdrag i Noreg 1905–14* (Oslo: Universitetsforlaget, 1969), p. 69; Thomas Christian Wyller, *Christian Michelsen. Politikeren* (Oslo: Dreyers forlag, 1975) pp. 187–188.

15. Sørensen, *Fridtjof Nansens saga,* p. 242.

16. Nerbøvik, *Antiparlamentariske straumdrag i Noreg,* p. 118.

17. Bergsgård, *Frå 17. mai til 9. april,* p. 363.

18. *Ibid.*

19. See below, pp. 73–74.

20. Christensen, *Fra verdenskrig til verdenskrig,* p. 264.

21. As part of a process of "Norwegianization" (*fornorskning*), the name of the capital was changed from Kristiania to Oslo in 1925.

22. Hans Olaf Brevig, *NS – fra parti til sekt, 1933–37* (Oslo: Pax forlag, 1970), p. 13.

23. *Leidangen,* or *Ledingen,* are terms which are impossible to translate. Were one to do so, they would entirely lose character. They are the name for the naval militia established by the early Viking kings of Norway.

24. Brevig, *NS – fra parti til sekt,* p. 14.

25. *Ibid.*

26. Bergsgård, *Frå 17. mai til 9. april,* p. 359.

27. *Ibid.*

28. On the letterhead of its stationery the League used the slogan "Founded by Christian Michelsen and Fridtjof Nansen."

29. See below pp. 84–85 for a more detailed description of Quisling's affiliation with the Fatherland League.

30. Christian A. R. Christensen, *Okkupasjonsår og etterkrigstid,* Vol. IX of *Vårt folks historie,* Thorleif Dahl, Axel Coldevin, and Johan Schreiner, eds. (Oslo: Aschehoug, 1961), p. 81.

31. Dahl, "Fascismen i Norge 1920–40". *Kontrast*, Vol. II, No. 3, pp. 9–10.

32. Ulf Torgersen, "Våre helter og høvdinger," *ibid.*, p. 32; Hans Fredrik Dahl, "Den norske fascismen," *Dagbladet*, October 21, 1966. Although *Nationen* technically speaking was formally controlled by a leading agrarian interest group, the Farmers' Association (*Norges Bondelag*), the public in general regarded its views as being representative of the Agrarian party.

33. Torgersen, *ibid.*

34. Dahl, "Fascismen i Norge," *ibid.*, p. 12.

35. Bjørn Vidar Gabrielsen, "De gode middagers tid. Noen glimt av norsk mellomkrigsaktivisme," *ibid.*, p. 38.

36. *Ibid.*

37. Torgersen, "Våre helter og høvdinger," *ibid.*, p. 34.

38. *Ibid.*

39. *Ibid.*

40. *Ibid.*

41. *Ibid.*, p. 35.

42. Dahl, "Den norske fascismen," *Dagbladet*, October 21, 1966.

43. Nerbøvik, *Antiparlamentariske straumdrag i Noreg*, p. 145.

44. *Om at bebodde verdener finnes utenom jorden, og betydningen derav for vår livsanskuelse* (Oslo: privately published, 1929).

45. *Ibid.*, p. 18. Author's italics.

46. Birger Bergersen to Arnold Ræstad, March 23, 1943, in Ræstad, "The Case Quisling," p. 38.

47. Quoted in *Straffesak*, p. 280.

48. See the preface to *Universismen* in *Tilleggshefte*, pp. 44–45.

49. Maria Quisling, *Dagbok*, pp. 161–188. See below, pp. 765–766.

50. Ræstad, "The Case Quisling," p. 62.

51. Vogt, *Mennesket Vidkun og forræderen Quisling*, p. 88.

52. See above, p. 30.

53. "Politiske tanker ved Fridtjof Nansens død," *Tidens Tegn*, May 24, 1930.

54. *Ibid.*

55. *Ibid.*

56. *Ibid.*

57. Joakim Lehmkuhl, "Politiske tanker ved Fridtjof Nansens død," *Tidens Tegn*, May 29, 1930.

58. Captain Vidkun Quisling, "Nasjonal samling," *Tidens Tegn*, June 4, 1930.

59. See below, pp. 66–67.

60. *Russland og vi* (Oslo: Jacob Dybwads forlag, 1930).

61. *Ibid.*, p. 16.

62. *Ibid.*, p. 18.

63. *Ibid.*, p. 107.

64. *Ibid.*, p. 180.

65. *Ibid.*

66. *Ibid.*, p. 194.

67. *Ibid.*

68. In Norwegian elections each party submits a list of proposed representatives to the voters. However, only those candidates who are placed at the top of the list have any chance of being elected under ordinary circumstances. The number of representatives elected from each province (*fylke*) is fixed, with the allocation of seats being determined by proportional representation according to the percentage of the popular vote gained by the competing parties. Someone such as Prytz, appearing far down on the list of candidates, had no chance of being elected. Persons who were ranked so low on the list as he were used only for their symbolic value, in the hope that they might be able to attract voters through their affiliation with the party.

69. *Nationen*, October 6, 1930.

70. *Ibid.*

71. *Ibid.*

72. *Ibid.*

73. *Nationen*, October 18, 1930.

74. See above, p. 50.

75. Gabrielsen, "De gode middagers tid," *Kontrast*, Vol. II, No. 3, p. 39.

76. *Ibid.*; Hartmann, *Fører uten folk*, p. 209.

77. Realph Norland to Vidkun Quisling, January 20, 1931, Oslo, Riksarkivet, Quislings arkiv, Box 1, Fedrelandslaget folder. Quislings arkiv hereafter cited as QA.

78. "Fedrelandslagets beretning for året 1931," QA, Box 1, Fedrelandslaget folder.

79. *Tidens Tegn*, February 26, 1931.

80. Fedrelandslaget, "Til Storting og regjering," n. d., QA, Box 10, Brev m. v. 1930–1940 folder.

81. Christopher Borchgrevink to Quisling, January 2, 1931, QA, Box 1, Fedrelandslaget folder.

82. Oslo Fedrelandslag to Quisling,

April 26, 1931, *ibid.;* Oslo Fedrelandslag to "all nasjonalsinnet ungdom som skal avtjene sin verneplikt!", n.d., *ibid.* In the latter of these two documents, a propaganda appeal to potential recruits in the armed forces, Quisling is listed as a member of the executive committee. He contributed an aura of military support for this piece of propaganda by being titled according to his rank in the army reserve, that of major.

83. "Oprop fra aksjonskomiteen for 'Økonomisk Verneplikt,'" QA, Box 1, 1932 folder.

84. Gabrielsen, "De gode middagers tid," *Kontrast,* Vol. II, No. 3, p. 41.

85. Albert Balchen to Frederik Prytz, November 19, 1930, QA. This document was included in *Quislings arkiv* when the archive was part of Universitetsbibliotekets collections, but the author has not been able to locate the letter following the archive's transfer to Riksarkivet. Since the letter most likely is misplaced, it and similar documents whose location cannot be referred to by box number and folder title are simply cited under the general location QA.

86. Balchen to Prytz, January 16, 1931, QA, Box 1, 1932 folder; Quisling, draft version of *Redegjørelse for Nordiske Folkereisnings Retningslinjer,* QA, Box 1, 1932 folder.

87. Johan Throne Holst to Prytz, January 17, 1931, QA, Box 1, 1932 folder.

88. Nordiske Folkereisning i Norge to Herr . . . , n.d., QA, Box 1, 1932 folder.

89. *Ibid.*

90. *Ibid.*

91. Protocol of Nordiske Folkereisning's Central Committee meetings, March 17 – May 13, 1931, QA, Box 1, 1932 folder.

92. Hartmann, *Fører uten folk,* p. 114; Hans-Dietrich Loock, *Quisling, Rosenberg und Terboven: Zur Vorgeschichte und Geschichte der nationalsozialistischen Revolution in Norwegen* (Stuttgart: Deutsche Verlags-Anstalt, 1970), p. 63.

93. Nordiske Folkereisning i Norge, *Retningslinjer og lover vedtatt på konstituerende møte i Oslo 17. mars 1931* (Oslo: Det Mallingske Bogtrykkeri, 1931). Hereafter cited as *Retningslinjer.*

94. *Redegjørelse for Nordiske Folkereisnings Retningslinjer* (Oslo: Det Mallingske

Bogtrykkeri, 1931). Hereafter cited as *Redegjørelse.*

95. See above, pp. 69.

96. *Redegjørelse,* pp. 3–5.

97. *Ibid.,* p. 5.

98. *Ibid.*

99. *Ibid.,* p. 6.

100. *Ibid.*

101. *Ibid.*

102. *Ibid.*

103. *Ibid.,* p. 7.

104. *Retningslinjer,* p. 1.

105. *Ibid.*

106. *Ibid.,* p. 2.

107. *Ibid.,* p. 3.

108. *Ibid.,* pp. 3–4.

109. *Ibid.,* p. 4.

110. *Ibid.,* p. 5.

111. *Ibid.,* pp. 4–5.

112. *Ibid.,* p. 5.

113. *Ibid.,* pp. 6–7.

114. *Ibid.,* p. 8.

115. *Ibid.*

116. *Ibid.,* p. 9.

117. *Ibid.,* p. 12.

118. *Ibid.,* p. 10.

119. *Ibid.,* p. 11.

120. *Ibid.,* p. 12.

121. *Redegjørelse,* p. 7.

122. See below, pp. 187–188.

123. Protocol of Nordic Folk-Rising's Central Committee meetings, March 17 – May 13, 1931, QA, Box 1, 1932 folder.

124. *Ibid.*

125. *Ibid.;* Protocol of Nordic Folk-Rising's Central Committee meeting, June 10, 1931, QA, Box 1, 1932 folder.

126. Protocol of Nordic Folk-Rising's Central Committee meeting, March 17 – May 13, 1931, QA, Box 1, 1932 folder.

127. Loock, *Quisling, Rosenberg und Terboven,* p. 67. In 1975 a popular magazine published a short article which included a facsimile of Quisling's plan to have N.F.'s cells infiltrate the military. See *Nå,* No. 31, August 2, 1975, p. 24.

128. *Retningslinjer,* p. 11.

Notes to Chapter III

1. Bjørn Vidar Gabrielsen, *Menn og politikk. Senterpartiet 1920–1970* (Oslo: Aschehoug, 1970), pp. 68–70.

2. *Ibid.*, p. 69.

3. Protocol of the meeting of Nordic Folk-Rising Central Committee, May 13, 1931, QA, Box 1, 1932 folder.

4. Björnberg, *Parlamentarismens utveckling i Norge efter 1905*, p. 332.

5. Gabrielsen, *Menn og politikk*, p. 76.

6. *Straffesak*, p. 473.

7. Gabrielsen, *Menn og politikk*, p. 68, p. 78.

8. Brevig, *NS – fra parti til sekt*, pp. 16–17.

9. Hartmann, *Fører uten folk*, p. 122; Gabrielsen, *Menn og politikk*, p. 77.

10. Gabrielsen, *ibid.*, p. 76.

11. Hartmann, *Fører uten folk*, pp. 128–129.

12. *Arbeiderbladet*, May 11, 1931, in *ibid.*, p. 124.

13. *Storting* debate of May 19, 1931, quoted in *Straffesak*, p. 473.

14. See above, pp. 32–34.

15. *Storting* debate of May 19, 1931, *Straffesak*, 474.

16. *Ibid.*

17. *Ibid.*

18. *Ibid.*, p. 473.

19. *Ibid.*, p. 476.

20. See Lykke's defense of Quisling, *ibid.*, and the editorial in *Tidens Tegn*, "Vidkun Quisling," May 19, 1931.

21. Protocol of the meeting of Nordic Folk-Rising's Central Committee, May 13, 1931, QA, Box 1, 1932 folder. For Quisling's reference to Hambro, see *Nasjonal Samling, Rikspropagandaledelsen, Vidkun Quislings tale på førertinget 25. september 1942* (Oslo: Rikspropagandaledelsen, n.d.), p. 6.

22. "Forsvarsminister Quislings nye samfund," *Arbeiderbladet*, May 28, 1931.

23. "Den Quislingske 'folkereisning,'" *Arbeiderbladet*, June 6, 1931.

24. *Dagbladet*, June 5, 1931, quoted in *Arbeiderbladet*, *ibid.*

25. Protocol of the meeting of Nordic Folk-Rising's Central Committee, June 10, 1931, QA, Box 1, 1932 folder.

26. *Ibid.*

27. Nordic Folk-Rising in Norway to *Arbeidets frihet*, October 22, 1931, QA, Box 1, 1932 folder.

28. Christensen, *Okkupasjonsår og etterkrigstid*, p. 72.

29. *Ibid.*

30. Gabrielsen, *Menn og politikk*, p. 83.

31. Hartmann, *Fører uten folk*, p. 140.

32. Per Ole Johansen, *Menstadkonflikten 1931* (Oslo: Tiden Norsk Forlag, 1977), p. 133; Asbjørn Lindboe, *Fra de urolige tredveårene. Dagboknedtegnelser og kommentarer* (Oslo: Johan Grundt Tanum, 1965), p. 36.

33. Hartmann, *Fører uten folk*, p. 143.

34. *Arbeiderbladet*, June 12, 1931, quoted in *ibid.*, p. 300, fn. 129.

35. Gabrielsen, *Menn og politikk*, pp. 87–89; Lindboe, *Fra de urolige tredveårene*, pp. 48–49.

36. Lindboe, *ibid.*, p. 49.

37. *Ibid.*, pp. 49–50.

38. *Ibid.*, pp. 52–53.

39. *Ibid.*, p. 54.

40. *Ibid.*, p. 55.

41. Gabrielsen, *Menn og politikk*, pp. 94–95.

42. *Straffesak*, pp. 236–237.

43. Gabrielsen, *Menn og politikk*, p. 90; Lindboe, *Fra de urolige tredveårene*, p. 118.

44. Gabrielsen, *ibid.*, p. 97.

45. Police report of February 5, 1932, quoted in Hartmann, *Fører uten folk*, pp. 149–150.

46. "Den ondsinnede sladder om statsråd Quisling eftertrykkelig avlivet," *Tidens Tegn*, February 10, 1932; Vogt, *Mennesket Vidkun og forræderen Quisling*, p. 109.

47. "Overfallet," *Tidens Tegn*, February 6, 1932.

48. *Aftenposten*, February 5, 1932; *Arbeiderbladet*, February 5, 1932; quoted in Hartmann, *Fører uten folk*, p. 149.

49. "Overfallet," *Tidens Tegn*, February 6, 1932.

50. *Ibid.*

51. For one example, see Gabrielsen, *Menn og politikk*, pp. 96–97.

52. As late as the mid-1960s the author heard a number of versions of this story.

53. *Arbeiderbladet*, November 16, 1932, quoted in Hartmann, *Fører uten folk*, p. 222.

54. Politibetjent M. J. Krogh, "Overfall

på statsråd Quisling 2. febr. 1932," Rapport til Oslo politikammers opdagelsesavdeling, QA, Box 1, Div. Private saker folder; Mogens, *Tyskerne, Quisling og vi andre*, p. 46.

55. Report submitted by Professors Peter Bull and Francis Harbitz, quoted in "Den ondsinnede sladder om statsråd Quisling eftertrykkelig avlivet," *Tidens Tegn,* February 10, 1932.

56. *Ibid.*

57. Politibetjent M. J. Krogh, "Overfall på statråd Quisling 2. febr. 1932," Rapport til Oslo politikammers opdagelsesavdeling, QA, Box 1, Div. Private saker folder.

58. Hartmann, *Fører uten folk*, p. 222.

59. Per Larssen, Minister of Commerce, whose resignation did not meet with any opposition.

60. Hartmann, *Fører uten folk*, p. 171; Gabrielsen, *Menn og politikk*, p. 100.

61. Gabrielsen, *ibid.*

62. *Storting* debate of April 5, 1932, in Norway, *Kongeriket Norges enogåttiende ordentlige Stortings Forhandlinger*, 1932, syvende del (Oslo, 1932), p. 432. *Stortings Forhandlinger* hereafter cited as Stf.

63. *Ibid.*

64. *Storting* debate of April 7, 1932, Stf, p. 546.

65. *Ibid.*

66. *Ibid.*, p. 548.

67. *Ibid.*, pp. 548–549.

68. *Ibid.*, p. 554.

69. *Ibid.*, p. 559, p. 564.

70. Lindboe, *Fra de urolige tredveårene* p. 127.

71. *Ibid.*, pp. 126–127.

72. *Storting* debate of April 7, 1932, Stf, p. 563.

73. Vidkun Quisling, "P. M.", November 20, 1932, QA, Box 3, Hundseid-saken folder, p. 4.

74. *Ibid.*

75. Lindboe, *Fra de urolige tredveårene*, p. 128.

76. *Tidens Tegn*, April 12, 1932.

77. Vidkun Quisling, "P. M.", of November 20, 1932, QA, Box 3, Hundseid-saken folder, p. 4.

78. "Innstilling fra spesialkomiteen til undersøkelse av Quisling-saken," *Straffesak*, p. 478.

79. For a more detailed discussion of Quisling's involvement with the Commu-

nists and the Labor party in 1924–25, see above, pp. 32–34.

80. *Straffesak*, pp. 150–151, 483.

81. "Statsråd Quisling," *Tidens Tegn*, June 13, 1932.

82. "Stratsråd Quislings erklæring," *Tidens Tegn*, June 18, 1932.

83. "Innstilling fra spesialkomiteen til undersøkelse av Quisling-saken," *Straffesak*, p. 478.

84. *Ibid.*, pp. 482–483.

85. Håkon Meyer, *Et annet syn* (Oslo: Dreyers forlag, 1952), p. 70.

86. *Storting* debate of June 30, 1932, Stf, p. 2654.

87. *Ibid.*

88. Meyer, *Et annet syn*, p. 70.

89. "Innstilling fra spesialkomitéen til undersøkelse av Quisling-saken," *Straffesak*, p. 482.

90. "Mowinckel angriper skarpt forsvarsministeren," *Dagbladet*, evening ed., June 30, 1932.

91. "Statsministeren taler ut i Quisling-saken," *Nationen*, July 1, 1932.

92. "Statsraad Quislings tale i Stortinget i gaar," *Tidens Tegn*, July 1, 1932.

93. *Ibid.*

94. Gabrielsen, *Menn og politikk*, p. 108.

95. *ABC*, September 21, 1932.

96. *Dagbladet*, September 5, 1932, quoted in Hartmann, *Fører uten folk*, p. 192.

97. *Ibid.*, p. 193.

98. *Ibid.*

99. See below, p. 623.

100. *Arbeiderbladet*, October 1, 1932, quoted in Hartmann, *Fører uten folk*, p. 194.

101. ". . . my plan was to take up this case concerning Captain Kullmann, . . . first get it out of the way and then take up and get cleared out of the way the remainder of the entire case [the Labor party] and get cleaned out all this that was a cancer in our society." Quisling, defense statement, September 6, 1945, *Straffesak*, p. 336.

102. Hartmann, *Fører uten folk*, p. 195.

103. Norway, Defense Department, Memorandum to Justice Department, October 14, 1932, quoted in *ibid.*, p. 197.

104. *Ibid.*, p. 198.

105. Lindboe, *Fra de urolige tredve-årene*, p. 179.

106. *Arbeiderbladet*, October 17, 1932, cited in Hartmann, *Fører uten folk*, p. 199.

107. Vidkun Quisling, "Åpent brev til Aftenpostens politiske redaktør, herr Johs. Nesse," *Tidens Tegn*, October 26, 1932.

108. *Ibid.*

109. Johannes Nesse, "Åpent svar til statsråd Quisling," *Tidens Tegn*, October 27, 1932.

110. Lindboe, *Fra de urolige tredve-årene*, p. 186; Hartmann, *Fører uten folk*, p. 208.

111. The Constitution of 1814 had formally abolished titles of nobility. At the time of disestablishment there were but two titled families in Norway, Løvenskiold and Wedel-Jarlsberg.

112. Lindboe, *Fra de urolige tredve-årene*, pp. 186–188.

113. *Ibid.*, pp. 187–188.

114. *Ibid.*, p. 188.

115. *Ibid.*, p. 187.

116. "Veien som er stengt – og veien som er åpen," *Tidens Tegn*, December 2, 1932.

117. Lindboe, *Fra de urolige tredve-årene*, p. 189.

118. *Ibid.*, p. 188.

119. "En usmakelig manøver mot Quisling," *ABC*, December 8, 1932.

120. Lindboe, *Fra de urolige tredve-årene*, p. 188.

121. Vidkun Quisling, Memorandum to the Agrarian party's *Storting* delegation, March 24, 1933, QA, Box 3, Hundseid-saken folder; "En usmakelig manøver mot Quisling," *ABC*, December 8, 1932.

122. Lindboe, *Fra de urolige tredve-årene*, p. 189.

123. *Nationen*, November 16, 1932.

124. *Dagbladet*, November 16, 1932, quoted in Hartmann, *Fører uten folk*, p. 223.

125. *Arbeiderbladet*, November 17, 1932, quoted in Hartmann, *Fører uten folk*, pp. 223–225.

126. Lindboe, *Fra de urolige tredve-årene*, p. 190.

127. *Ibid.*, pp. 185–186.

128. "Quisling," *ABC*, December 15, 1932.

129. "Årsberetning for Oslo Fedre-landslag 1932," QA. As one example of the resolutions passed by the Fatherland League in support of Quisling, see Fatherland League, "Til Storting og Regjering!," spring 1932, QA, Box 10, Brev m. v. 1930–1940 folder.

130. "Årsberetning for Oslo Fedre-landslag 1932," *ibid.*; see also *ABC*, September 21, 1932.

131. Ida Blom, *Kampen om Eirik Raudes land* (Oslo: Gyldendal Norsk Forlag, 1973), pp. 269 ff.

132. Jens Hundseid to Frederik Wedel Jarlsberg, October 16, 1932, quoted in Hartmann, *Fører uten folk*, p. 192.

133. Lindboe, *Fra de urolige tredve-årene*, pp. 158 ff.

134. *Ibid.*, pp. 189–190.

135. Report from Attorney General Haakon Sund to the Department of Justice, November 18, 1932, quoted in Hartmann, *Fører uten folk*, pp. 234–238.

136. *Arbeiderbladet*, November 17, 1932, quoted in *ibid.*, p. 224.

137. *Tidens Tegn*, November 21, 1932.

138. Quisling, "P.M.", November 20, 1932, QA, Box 3, Hundseid-saken folder.

139. *Ibid.*

140. *Ibid.*

141. Lindboe, *Fra de urolige tredve-årene*, p. 180.

142. Hartmann, *Fører uten folk*, p. 228.

143. Lindboe, *Fra de urolige tredve-årene*, p. 181.

144. *Ibid.*, pp. 190–191.

145. Quisling to Hundseid, November 26, 1932, quoted in Hartmann, *Fører uten folk*, p. 230.

146. Lindboe, *Fra de urolige tredve-årene*, pp. 179–180; Hartmann, *ibid.*, p. 231; Gabrielsen, *Menn og politikk*, p. 113.

147. Gabrielsen, *ibid.*

148. Quisling, "P.M. vedr. behandlingen av Kullmann-saken," QA, Box 3, Hundseid-saken folder; Lindboe, *Fra de urolige tredveårene*, pp. 181–182.

149. Lindboe, *ibid.*, p. 182.

150. Quisling to Minister of Church and Education Nils Trædal, December 5, 1932, QA, Box 3, Hundseid-saken folder.

151. *Ibid.*

152. *Ibid.*

153. *Ibid.*

154. Lindboe, *Fra de urolige tredve-årene*, p. 181.

155. Quisling, "P.M. vedr. behandlingen av Kullmann-saken," March 2, 1933, QA, Box 3, Hundseid-saken folder.

156. *Ibid.*; Lindboe, *Fra de urolige tredveårene*, p. 183.

157. "Falske forhåpninger," *Tidens Tegn*, December 13, 1932.

158. "Hundseid mot Quisling," *Dagbladet*, December 13, 1932.

159. Lindboe, *Fra de urolige tredve-årene*, p. 184.

160. *Tidens Tegn*, December 15, 1932.

161. *Ibid.*; Quisling, "P.M. vedr. behandlingen av Kullmann-saken," March 2, 1933, QA, Box 3, Hundseid-saken folder.

162. Quisling, "P.M. vedr. behandlingen av Kullmann-saken," *ibid.*; Lindboe, *Fra de urolige tredveårene*, p. 184.

163. The memorandum was serialized in *Nationen*, February 28, March 1, March 2, March 3, 1933.

164. *Ibid.*

165. Lindboe, *Fra de urolige tredve-årene*, pp. 184–185; Hartmann, *Fører uten folk*, pp. 254–255.

166. "Statsraad Quisling imøtegaar riksadvokaten," *Nationen*, February 28, 1933; "Kullmann-sakens bakgrunn," *Tidens Tegn*, February 28, March 1, 1933.

167. Former Minister of Finance Jon Sundby, quoted in Hartmann, *Fører uten folk*, p. 173.

168. *Straffesak*, pp. 197–201; Christensen, *Okkupasjonsår og etterkrigstid*, pp. 103–108.

169. Bjørn Vidar Gabrielsen, "Røde og hvite garder i Norge," *Norsk militært Tidskrift*, Vol. 123, No. 2 (1964), p. 100.

170. *Ibid.*, p. 102.

171. *Ibid.*, p. 103.

172. Lindboe, *Fra de urolige tredve-årene*, p. 180.

173. *Ibid.*

174. *Straffesak*, p. 235.

Notes to Chapter IV

1. Christopher Borchgrevink, "Vidkun Quisling," *Tidens Tegn*, January 25, 1933.

2. *Ibid.*

3. *Storting* debate following the Speech from the Throne, January 31, 1933, quoted in *Straffesak*, p. 483.

4. Undated and untitled document, possibly authored by Hjort and Throne Holst, whose names appear on the top of page two. In QA, Box 3, Forarbeider til NS program folder. This sketch of a plan for a "national block" was quite probably drawn up prior to the fall of the Hundseid government, since it declared that the "national block" would support the government and cooperate with the Agrarian party.

5. Vogt, *Mennesket Vidkun og forræderen Quisling*, p. 114.

6. *Storting* finance debate, February 24, 1933, *Stortingstidende* 1933, pp. 623–624.

7. *Ibid.*, p. 624.

8. *Ibid.*

9. *Ibid.*, p. 623.

10. Lindboe, *Fra de urolige tredveårene*, p. 207.

11. "Statsråd Quisling uttrådt av Bondepartiet?," *Aftenposten*, February 25, 1933.

12. Quisling, "Klare linjer," *Nationen*, February 27, 1933.

13. *Ibid.*

14. *Ibid.*

15. Quisling, "Retningslinjer," *Tidens Tegn*, March 2, 1933.

16. *Ibid.*

17. *Ibid.*

18. *Ibid.*

19. "Foran høstens valg," *Tidens Tegn*, March 2, 1933.

20. Quisling, "P.M. vedr. behandlingen av Kullmann-saken," March 2, 1933, QA, Box 3, Hundseid-saken folder.

21. In addition to Quisling, the other signatories were Ragnar Hvoslef, Frederik Prytz, and Adolf F. Munthe. "Referat av møte i Den Nordiske Folkereisnings Politiske Komite 10. mars 1933," QA, Box 11, Opprettelsen av NS 1933 folder.

22. *Ibid.*

23. Quisling, undated memorandum, "Den politiske komite," QA, Box 11, Opprettelsen av NS 1933 folder.

24. Christopher Borchgrevink to Quisling, March 10, 1933, QA, Box 3, Forarbeider til NS-program folder; Borchgrevink to Quisling, April 29, 1933, QA, Box 3, Forarbeider til NS-program folder.

25. Joakim Lehmkuhl to Quisling, March 15, 1933, QA, Box 1, Fedrelandslaget folder.

26. Quisling to the Agrarian party's *Storting* delegation, March 24, 1933, QA, Box 3, Hundseid-saken folder.

27. *Ibid.*

28. Gabrielsen, *Menn og politikk*, pp. 121–122.

29. *Ibid.*, p. 121.

30. Kitty Engh, for the Agrarian party, to Quisling, April 5, 1933, QA, Box 3, 1933 avisutklipp etc. folder.

31. Gabrielsen, *Menn og politikk*, p. 122.

32. Johan B. Hjort, Memorandum of April 3, 1933, cited in Brevig, *NS – fra parti til sekt*, p. 28.

33. *Ibid.*

34. *Ibid.*, p. 29; Hjort, "P.M. angående *Tidens Tegn*," n.d., QA, Box 3, Forarbeider til NS-program folder.

35. Gabrielsen, *Menn og politikk*, p. 122.

36. "Jens Hundseid," *ABC*, March 2, 1933. Italics part of text.

37. Protocol of the meeting of Nordic Folk-Rising's Political Committee, April 26, 1933, QA, Box 11, Opprettelsen av NS 1933 folder.

38. Formal application for the establishment of *Det Norske Folkeparti*, to the Department of Justice, April 1933, QA, Box 2, NF's Arbeiderpolitikk folder. The document was never sent.

39. "Omrids til organisation," March 31, 1933, QA, Box 10, Quislings utkast til program for NS osv. folder.

40. Protocol of the meeting of Nordic Folk-Rising's Political Committee, April 26, 1933, QA, Box 11, Opprettelsen av NS 1933 folder.

41. Protocol of the meeting of Nordic Folk-Rising's Political Committee, May 1, 1933, *ibid.*

42. *Ibid.*

43. Jon Leirfall to Johan Mellbye, April 3, 1933, quoted in Gabrielsen, *Menn og politikk*, p. 122. Leirfall's italics.

44. Protocol of the meeting of Nordic Folk-Rising's Political Committee, May 1, 1933, QA, Box 11, Opprettelsen av NS 1933 folder.

45. "'Nasjonalpartiet' er stiftet," *Arbeiderbladet*, May 4, 1933.

46. *Nationen*, May 10, 1933.

47. Quisling to the Agrarian party's Board of Directors, May 5, 1933, QA, Box 2, NF's Arbeiderpolitikk Folder.

48. *Ibid.*

49. Hjort to Prytz, May 5, 1933, QA, Box 3, Hundseid-saken folder. In his well-written volume on the history of the Conservative party, Rolf Danielsen maintains that the creation of NS was an indication of the defeat and isolation of right-wing activism in Norway, and that the formation of NS occurred only after Quisling had failed to gain acceptance within established political groups. See Rolf Danielsen, *Borgerlig oppdemningspolitikk (1918–1940)*, Vol. II of Francis Sejersted, *Høyres historie* (Oslo: Cappelen, 1984), p. 203. While right-wing activism may have peaked with the parliamentary election of 1930, this did not become apparent until after the succeeding election. In the meantime, Quisling had been able to achieve prominent status. Because of his apparent value, he could have retained his ties with the Agrarian party and the Fatherland League had he desired to do so, but not under the absolute conditions that he demanded.

50. *Tidens Tegn*, June 3, 1927.

51. Hartmann, *Fører uten folk*, p. 269.

52. *Ibid.*

53. *Ibid.*, p. 270; Brevig, *NS – fra parti til sekt*, p. 31.

54. Hjort to Prytz, May 5, 1933, QA, Box 3, Hundseid-saken folder.

55. Hartmann, *Fører uten folk*, pp. 270–274.

56. *Ibid.*, p. 272; Brevig, *NS – fra parti til sekt*, p. 32.

57. Hartmann, *ibid.* pp. 272–273.

58. *Ibid.*, p. 273.

59. *Ibid.*

60. *Ibid.*, p. 313, fn. 275.

61. QA, Box 3, Hundseid-saken folder.

62. Protocol of Nordic Folk-Rising's Political Committee, May 13, 1933, QA, Box 11, Opprettelsen av NS 1933 folder.

63. Norway, Department of Justice, Justisdepartementets Protokoll, Journalnr. 2755–33 K2. Loock, in *Quisling, Rosenberg und Terboven*, p. 108, indicates that National Union's formal registration occurred a

month earlier, on June 28, 1933. As his source, Loock cites a party publication, *Nasjonal Samlings historiske kamp*. It was in National Union's interest to have its formal registration appear to have taken place as close as possible to the official, and incorrect, founding date of May 17, 1933. This source is therefore inaccurate.

64. *Tidens Tegn*, May 16, 1933.

65. Johannes Nesse to Quisling, May 15, 1933, QA, Box 2, dr. ing. Franz Lawaczeck folder.

66. *Nationen*, May 16, 1933.

67. The Radical People's party, previously known as the Labor Democrats, was a non-socialist reform party whose main strength was concentrated in the two eastern provinces of Oppland and Hedmark. Founded in 1906 by the radical reformer, Johan Castberg, the party came into its own in the decade following the dissolution of Norway's union with Sweden, thanks to the influence that Castberg exerted as a member of the Liberal cabinet headed by Gunnar Knudsen. However, its representation in parliament declined steadily during the 1920s and 1930s, and the party disintegrated after it failed to elect a single representative in the election of 1936.

68. This particular weakness was first commented on by Editor Nesse of *Aftenposten* in his refusal to publish the program; Nesse to Quisling, May 15, 1933, QA, Box 2, dr. ing. Franz Lawaczeck folder.

69. Nesse, *ibid.*, also noted this inconsistency in the program.

70. Even among Quisling's collaborators there was some confusion about the distinction he drew between a movement and a party. See Christopher Borchgrevink to Quisling, May 18, 1933, QA, Box 3, 1933 folder.

71. The statement concerning a "democratic elite government" was not included in the program which appeared in *Tidens Tegn*, but appeared in a special reprint edition which was longer and partly revised.

72. "Nasjonal opmarsj," *Tidens Tegn*, May 16, 1933.

73. Brevig, *NS – fra parti til sekt*, p. 33; Hartmann, *Fører uten folk*, pp. 276–277.

74. Joakim Lehmkuhl, "Et folkets diktatur," *ABC*, May 24, 1933.

75. *Ibid.*

76. Johan B. Hjort, "Fedrelandslaget og Quisling," *ABC*, June 1, 1933; *Tidens Tegn*, June 1, 1933.

77. *ABC*, June 1, 1933.

78. Quisling, "Nasjonal Samling," *Tidens Tegn*, June 3, 1933.

79. Adolf Egeberg, Jr., the first Secretary of National Union, in conversation with Sverre Hartmann, August 20, 1959, cited in Hartmann, *Fører uten folk*, pp. 277, 313, fn. 279.

80. Brevig, *NS – fra parti til sekt*, p. 44.

81. Hans Krag and Sam. Halvorsen, report to National Union's Finance Committee, October 23, 1933, QA.

82. National Union's Finance Committee to Quisling, n.d., QA, Box 10, Brev m.v. 1930–1940 folder. This document was probably written some time toward the end of October 1933.

83. *Ibid.*

84. *Ibid.*

85. *Ibid.*

86. Johan Faye, for *Norges Handels- og Sjøfartstidende*, to A/S Sporveis-Annonse (Walter Fürst), July 17, 1933, QA, Box 3, 1933 folder.

87. For further discussion of NS' press situation prior to the 1933 election, see below p. 229.

88. Thor Tharum to Quisling, July 17, 1933, quoted in Loock, *Quisling, Rosenberg und Terboven*, p. 110.

89. Ragnar Skancke to Quisling, September 24, 1933, QA, Box 4, Privat og politisk kamp, 1933–34 folder.

90. Hans Hanson, Jr., to Quisling, October 12, 1933, QA, Box 1, 1933 folder.

91. Martin Tveter to Quisling, March 6, 1934, QA, Box 4, Diverse-mindre viktige folder.

92. *Kongsemnerne*, Act III.

93. Interview with a former leading NS member, Oslo, May 31, 1967.

94. Brevig, *NS – fra parti til sekt*, p. 41.

95. *Ibid.*, p. 45.

96. *Ibid.*, pp. 40–41.

97. *Ibid.*, p. 40.

98. *Ibid.*, p. 42.

99. Stein Ugelvik Larsen, "Nazismen i Norge," in Bjarte Birkeland and Stein Ugelvik Larsen, eds., *Nazismen og norsk litteratur* (Bergen: Universitetsforlaget, 1975), p. 75.

100. *Ibid.*
101. Brevig, *NS – fra parti til sekt*, pp. 109–111; Larsen, *ibid.*
102. Brevig, *ibid.*, p. 42.
103. *Ibid.*, p. 105.
104. Bergsgård, *Frå 17. mai til 9. april.*, p. 374.
105. Kaare Frøland, *Krise og kamp. Bygdefolkets Krisehjelp – En kriseorganisasjon i norsk mellomkrigspolitikk* (Oslo and Bergen: Universitetsforlaget, 1962), pp. 92–105.
106. *Ibid.*, pp. 122–123.
107. Sverre Støstad, *Storting* debate of April 6, 1932, Stf, p. 463.
108. Frøland, *Krise og kamp*, pp. 132–133.
109. *Ibid.*, pp. 132 ff.
110. *Ibid.*, p. 167.
111. *Ibid.*, pp. 163–167.
112. *Ibid.*, pp. 168–169.
113. The agreement is printed in its entirety in *ibid.*, pp. 172–174.
114. *Bygdefolket*, August 19, 1933, quoted in *ibid.*, p. 181.
115. Frøland, *ibid.*, p. 184.
116. *Norske aviser 1763–1969* (Oslo: Universitetsbiblioteket, 1973), p. 381.
117. Quisling, "Nasjonal Samling," *Tidens Tegn*, June 3, 1933.
118. Quisling, "Nasjonal Samling," *Tidens Tegn*, May 16, 1933.
119. National Union's election program for 1933, QA, Box 3, 1933 folder.
120. Such statements appeared in most of Quisling's pronouncements during the election campaign of 1933. See, for example, Quisling's proclamation of National Union's founding in *Tidens Tegn*, May 16, 1933.
121. W. F. K. Christie, "Nasjonal Samling. Større styrke – ikke splittelse," *Tidens Tegn*, June 7, 1933; Quisling, "Nasjonal Samling," *Tidens Tegn*, June 3, 1933.
122. Quisling to the Agrarian party's parliamentary delegation, June 27, 1933, QA, Box 3, Hundseid-saken folder; "Quisling fremfører sine anklager mot Hundseid," *Nationen*, October 6, 1933; "Hundseid svarer Quisling," *Nationen*, October 7, 1933; "Quisling sendte anklageskrift til Bondepartiets stortingsgruppe," *Aftenposten*, October 6, 1933.
123. Frøland, *Krise og kamp*, p. 128.
124. "Nasjonal samling's første valgmøte i Oslo," *Nationen*, September 13, 1933; "Nationen skåner Quisling og overser Balchen," *Dagbladet*, October 14, 1933.
125. "Bonde Balchen avslører et Quislingsk falskneri," *Dagbladet*, October 13, 1933.
126. Johannes Nesse to Quisling, May 15, 1933, QA, Box 2, dr. ing. Franz Lawaczeck folder; Christie, "Nasjonal Samling. Større styrke, – ikke splittelse," *Tidens Tegn*, June 7, 1933.
127. "Den nye front," *Aftenposten*, morning edition, August 5, 1933.
128. Quisling, "N. S. Partimeddelelser," No. 3, August 9, 1933.
129. O. L. Bærøe and Harald Gram, for the Conservative party's Board of Directors, September 1, 1933, published in *Tidens Tegn*, September 2, 1933.
130. "Høire nekter å gå i listeforbund med Nasjonal samling," *Tidens Tegn*, August 30, 1933; "Listeforbund mellem Frisinnede, Bondepartiet, Nasjonal samling og Høire. Det frisinnede folkeparti retter en inntrengende henstilling til de andre partier," *Tidens Tegn*, September 1, 1933. "Samlet Front," *Tidens Tegn*, September 1, 1933; Sven Elvestad, "Det siste forsøk," *ibid.*
131. "Nasjonal Samling. Fra møtet i Hippodromen paa Vindern igaar kveld," *Nationen*, September 2, 1933.
132. "Hvad slags handling?" *Aftenposten*, September 2, 1933.
133. *Tidens Tegn*, September 6, 1933.
134. "Høire i Bergen beslutter listeforbund med Frisinnede folkeparti og Nasjonal samling," *Tidens Tegn*, September 9, 1933.
135. The Conservative party's national board of directors, press statement of September 18, 1933, published in *Tidens Tegn*, September 19, 1933.
136. *Ibid.*
137. "Kamp på to fronter," *Aftenposten*, September 15, 1933.
138. "Nasjonal samlings første valgmøte i Oslo," *Nationen*, September 13, 1933.
139. *Ibid.*
140. "Ut med sproget, hr. major!" *Aftenposten*, September 14, 1933.
141. "Listeforbund og flertallsregjering," *Tidens Tegn*, August 25, 1933.
142. "Svar og spørsmål til hr. Quisling," *ABC*, September 21, 1933.

143. Alexander Prebensen to Quisling, September 19, 1933, QA, Box 3, 1933 folder; "Svar og spørsmål til hr. Quisling," *ABC*, September 21, 1933.

144. *ABC*, *ibid*.; "Diktaturpartiet," *Aftenposten*, September 26, 1933. Although frowned upon, this practice was legal.

145. *Aftenposten*, *ibid*.

146. Quisling, "N. S. Partimeddelelser," No. 3, August 9, 1933.

147. *Ibid*.

148. "Statsråd Quisling trekker op sine politiske fremgangslinjer. Og holder kraftig opgjør med partipolitikken," *Tidens Tegn*, August 25, 1933; "Nasjonal Samling. Fra møtet i Hippodromen paa Vinderen igaar kveld," *Nationen*, September 2, 1933.

149. "Krisehjelpen og Quisling," *Aftenposten*, September 6, 1933.

150. "Svar og spørsmål til hr. Quisling," *ABC*, September 21, 1933.

151. "Statsråd Quisling trekker op sine politiske fremgangslinjer. Og holder kraftig opgjør med partipolitikken," *Tidens Tegn*, August 25, 1933.

152. "Politisk bigami," Arbeiderbladet, July 13, 1933.

153. "En skummel affære som må opklares," *Arbeiderbladet*, July 12, 1933; "Kortene på bordet," *Arbeiderbladet*, July 13, 1933.

154. "Rapport fra Nasjonal Samlings møte i Grünerløkkens skoles gymnastiksal fredag den 22. september 1933," QA, Box 3, 1933 folder; "Voldsomme optøier under Nasjonal Samlings møte på Grünerløkken," *Tidens Tegn*, September 23, 1933.

155. Letter of complaint from NS to the Oslo Police Chief, September 26, 1933, QA, Box 3, 1933 folder. The letter was not sent. "Voldsomme optøier under Nasjonal Samlings møte på Grünerløkken," *ibid*.

156. "Kommunistoptøier mot Quisling også i Kristiansand," *Tidens Tegn*, September 28, 1933.

157. "Brutalt overfall på Quisling igåraftes," *Tidens Tegn*, October 12, 1933.

158. Harry Høst, "Smuss og renselsesfest," *Tidens Tegn*, October 14, 1933.

159. Norway, Stortingets Kontor, *Stortingsvalget 1933*, Vol. IX, No. 26 of Norges Offisielle Statistikk (Oslo: H. Aschehoug and Co., for Stortingets Kontor, 1934), pp. 126–127.

160. *Ibid*., pp. 38–39.

161. *Ibid*., p. 67.

162. The four provinces were Oppland, Buskerud, Vestfold, and Telemark. Frøland, *Krise og kamp*, p. 280.

163. Stortingets Kontor, *Stortingsvalget 1933*, pp. 140–141.

164. Christensen, *Okkupasjonsår og etterkrigstid*, p. 86.

165. *Ibid*., p. 83.

166. *Ibid*., p. 87.

167. Stortingets Kontor, *Stortingsvalget 1933*, p. 159.

168. *Ibid*., p. 153.

169. *Ibid*.

170. Until 1952 Norwegian electoral law provided that two-thirds of all *Storting* representatives were to be elected from the rural districts in the provinces, one-third from the towns. The towns and provinces therefore formed separate election districts, with the eighteen provinces electing one hundred representatives and the eleven town districts electing the remaining fifty. Stortingets Kontor, *Stortingsvalget 1933*, passim.

171. Author's calculations, based on statistics in Stortingets Kontor, *ibid*., pp. 151–153.

172. Stortingets Kontor, *ibid*., p. 67.

173. *Straffesak*, p. 484.

174. Quisling, "Stenografisk referat av major Quislings foredrag den 26. oktober 1933," QA, Box 2, Quisling, uttalelser, foredrag, etc. – 1933–37 folder.

175. Dahl, "Fascismen i Norge 1920–40," *Kontrast*, Vol. II, No. 3, p. 15.

176. "I diktaturets skygge," *Aftenposten*, October 18, 1933.

177. "Aarsaken til nederlaget," *Tidens Tegn*, October 19, 1933.

178. Quisling, "Stenografisk referat av major Quislings foredrag den 26. oktober 1933," QA, Box 2, Quisling, uttalelser, foredrag, etc. – 1933–37 folder.

179. *Ibid*.

180. Stortingets Kontor, *Stortingsvalget 1933*, pp. 62–63.

181. Frøland, *Krise og kamp*, pp. 189–190.

182. Quisling to NS' organizational secretary, March 12, 1934, QA, Box 4, Den nasjonale Blokk folder.

183. Frøland, *Krise og kamp*, p. 190.

184. Steinar Klevar to Quisling, No-

vember 13, 1935, QA, Box 4, NS Korrespondanse 1933–36 folder.

185. Conversation with a former leading
NS member, Oslo, May 31, 1967.

186. Andreas Norland, *Hårde Tider.
Fedrelandslaget i norsk politikk* (Oslo:
Dreyers forlag, 1973), p. 222.

187. *Ibid.*, pp. 226–228.

188. *Tidens Tegn*, November 27, 1933.

189. Norland, *Hårde Tider*, p. 229.

190. Draft copy of a letter from Quisling to Harald Sverdrup-Thygeson, November 29, 1933, QA, Box 1, Fedrelandslaget
folder.

191. Quisling, "Fedrelandslaget som
politisk parti," *Tidens Tegn*, November 30,
1933.

192. Joakim Lehmkuhl, "Hr. Quisling
og Fedrelandslaget," *Tidens Tegn*, December 1, 1933; Quisling, "Fedrelandslaget.
Svar til ingeniør Lehmkuhl fra Vidkun Quisling," *Tidens Tegn*, December 2, 1933.

193. "Quisling," *ABC*, December 7,
1933.

194. Quisling, "Fedrelandslaget som
politisk parti," *Tidens Tegn*, November 30,
1933.

195. Norland, *Hårde tider*, pp. 224–
225.

Notes to Chapter V

1. Interview with a former member of
NS, Oslo, May 31, 1967.

2. NS' Finance Committee to Quisling,
n.d., QA, Box 10, Brev m.v. 1930–1940 folder.

3. Stenographic record of Quisling's
speech of October 26, 1933, QA, Box 2,
1933–1937 folder.

4. *Ibid.*

5. *Ibid.*

6. "Stor-Fosen gods solgt," *Aftenposten*,
September 8, 1933; Brevig, *NS – fra parti til
sekt*, p. 74.

7. See below, pp. 173ff. See also p. 797,
fn. 75.

8. Hjort to Quisling, November 4,
1933, QA.

9. Walter Fürst, "Årsakene til og følgene av N.S.' sammenbrudd," *Ragnarok*,
Vol. III, No. 3 (May 1937), pp. 66–70.

10. See for example Georg Vedeler to
Quisling, October 21, 1933, QA, Box 4,
Privat og politisk kamp 1933–34 folder; Ve-
deler to National Union's Central Office,
October 25, 1933, QA, Box 3, 1933 folder;
Leif Rabben to Quisling, November 18,
1933, QA, Box 3, 1933 folder; Eivind Kuls-
rud and Ragnar Møllhausen to Quisling,
November 11, 1933, QA, Box 3, 1933 fol-
der.

11. Hjort to Quisling, November 4,
1933, QA. See above, pp. 135–139, for discussion of Quisling's program of May 16,
1933.

12. Hans S. Jacobsen, "N.S. og dens
fremtidige politikk," October 27, 1933, QA,
Box 3, 1933 folder.

13. *Ibid.*

14. Jacobsen, "Vidkun Quisling og
N.S.," *Ragnarok*, Vol. III, No. 3, p. 61.

15. Norland, *Hårde tider*, pp. 228–229.
See above, p. 162.

16. See Jacob Thurmann Ihlen to Quisling, December 26, 1933, QA, Box 3, 1933
folder.

17. Vedeler to Quisling, December 7,
1933, QA, Box 3, Hundseid-saken folder.

18. Ihlen to Quisling, December 26,
1933, QA, Box 3, 1933 folder.

19. Hvoslef to Quisling, December 21,
1933, QA, Box 4, NS korrespondanse 1933–
1936 folder. See also Hvoslef to National
Union, December 21, 1933, QA, Box 4, NS
korrespondanse 1933–1936 folder.

20. Vedeler to Quisling, December 26,
1933, QA, Box 4, Forarbeide til N.S.P.
1934 folder.

21. Quisling's numerous drafts for a
new party program are located in QA, Box
4, Forarbeide til N.S.P. 1934 folder.

22. Vedeler to Quisling, January 2,
1934, QA, Box 4, Forarbeide til N.S.P.
1934 folder.

23. "Program for Nasjonal Samling,"
February 15, 1934.

24. Quisling to Trygve Roseth, March
5, 1934, QA, Box 5, 1934 korrespondanse
folder.

25. Quisling to Gunnar W. Lindblom,
April 28, 1934, QA, Box 4, Diverse –
mindre viktige folder.

26. Norland, *Hårde tider*, pp. 216–217.

27. Odin Augdahl to Hjort, February
18, 1934, QA, Box 5, 1933–36 korrespon-

danse til V. Q. folder; Ekko Kilberg to
Quisling, March 10, 1934, QA, Box 4, Di-
verse – mindre viktige folder; Quisling to
Kilberg, March 20, 1934, QA, Box 4, Di-
verse – mindre viktige folder; Ræstad, "The
Case Quisling," p. 99.

28. Norland, *Hårde tider*, p. 216.

29. See Quisling's correspondence in
QA for the period 1933–1934.

30. L. Andree Winciansen to Quisling,
July 10, 1934, QA, Box 8, Quislings private
korrespondanse folder; Finn Torjusen to
Quisling, July 10, 1934, QA, Box 4, NS
korrespondanse 1933–1936 folder; Winciansen to Quisling, July 15, 1934, QA, Box 4,
NS korrespondanse 1933–1936 folder.

31. Vedeler to Quisling, June 27, 1934,
QA, Box 4, NS korrespondanse 1933–1936
folder; Tormod B. Kværno to Quisling, August 17, 1934, QA, Box 8, Quislings private
korrespondanse folder.

32. Winciansen to Quisling, July 10,
1934, QA, Box 8, Quislings private korrespondanse folder; Torjusen to Fürst, July 10,
1934, QA, Box 4, NS korrespondanse 1933–
1936 folder.

33. Anna Stang Havstad to Quisling,
January 14, 1934, QA, Box 8, Quislings private korrespondanse folder; E. Bonnevie to
Quisling, February 3, 1934, QA, Box 5,
1934 korrespondanse folder; Lindblom to
Quisling, April 26, 1934, QA, Box 4, Diverse – mindre viktige folder.

34. Havstad to Quisling, January 14,
1934, *ibid.*

35. Norland, *Hårde tider*, p. 239.

36. Ida Blom, "Bønder og blokkfor-
handlinger 1933–1936," *Historisk Tidsskrift*,
Vol. 51, No. 4 (1972), p. 396. *Historisk
Tidsskrift* hereafter cited as HT.

37. See Blom, *ibid.*, p. 394, for the
prevalence of such viewpoints within the
Agrarian party.

38. *Ibid.*, p. 395.

39. *Ibid.*

40. *Ibid.*, p. 401.

41. Norland, *Hårde tider*, pp. 240–241.

42. *ABC*, March 8, 1933, quoted in
Norland, *ibid.*, p. 242.

43. Quisling to Vedeler, March 13,
1934, QA, Box 4, Den nasjonale Blokk folder.

44. Norland, *Hårde tider*, p. 239.

45. Brevig, *NS – fra parti til sekt*, p. 59;

Gabrielsen, *Menn og politikk*, p. 157; Blom,
"Bønder og blokkforhandlinger," HT, Vol.
51, No. 4, p. 400.

46. Vedeler to Quisling, February 28,
1934, QA, Box 4, Den nasjonale Blokk folder.

47. Hjort to Quisling, March 5, 1934,
ibid.

48. *Ibid.*

49. Hjort, "Forslag til avtale om opret-
telsen av et nasjonalt fellesråd," *ibid.*

50. Quisling to Vedeler, March 13,
1934, *ibid.*

51. *Ibid.*

52. Rolf Thommessen, on behalf of the
Independent People's party's national board
of directors, to National Union c/o Quisling, March 17, 1934, *ibid.*

53. NS and the Fatherland League to the
Agrarian party, draft copy, April 9, 1934,
ibid.

54. Hundseid, countersigned by Hans
Holten, on behalf of the Agrarian party's
executive committee, to National Union,
April 10, 1934, *ibid.*

55. Hans Holten, on behalf of the Agrarian party, to National Union, April 16,
1934, *ibid.*

56. Bernhard Kjelstrup, for the Independent People's party, to Quisling, May
4, 1934, *ibid.*

57. Brevig, *NS – fra parti til sekt*, p. 67;
Norland, *Hårde tider*, p. 244.

58. Norland, *ibid.*, pp. 244–245.

59. *Ibid.*, p. 246.

60. *Ibid.*, p. 245.

61. *Ibid.*, pp. 246–247.

62. *Ibid.*, p. 247.

63. Memorandum to the Conservative,
Liberal, and Agrarian party *Storting* delegations, n.d., QA, Box 4, Den nasjonale
Blokk folder. The document was not dated,
but Norland declares it was signed on June
16. Furthermore, Norland points out that
while the Agrarian party negotiators were
formally replaced by representatives from
the Farmers' Association when the petition
was being drawn up, nevertheless members
of the Agrarian *Storting* delegation took part
in the document's formulation. See Norland, *Hårde tider*, p. 247.

64. Norland, *ibid.*

65. See *Tidens Tegn* for the above dates
and *ABC* on June 14, 1934.

66. Blom, "Bønder og blokkforhandlinger," HT, Vol. 51, No. 4, p. 403.

67. O. K. Skuggevik, quoted in Blom, *ibid*, p. 404.

68. "Norges Bondelag krever en nasjonal samlings-regjering," *Tidens Tegn*, June 23, 1934.

69. Thoralv Klaveness to Quisling, July 9, 1934, QA, Box 8, Privat korrespondanse folder.

70. Chr. Jøranli, quoted by Ørnulf Lundesgaard in Lundesgaard to Quisling, June 28, 1934, QA, Box 11, Korr., avisutklipp, brosjyrer osv. folder.

71. Norland, *Hårde tider*, p. 246, p. 249.

72. "Avklaring," *Tidens Tegn*, June 27, 1934.

73. Thommessen to Quisling, June 27, 1934, QA, Box 4, Den nasjonale Blokk folder.

74. Thommessen, "Utkast til overenskomst," June 28, 1934, *ibid*.

75. Agreement between the representatives of the Agrarian party, the Fatherland League, the Independent People's party, and National Union, June 28, 1934, *ibid*. The agreement was signed by Nils Trædal and Gabriel Moseid on behalf of the Agrarian party; by Joakim Lehmkuhl, Ranik Halle, and Ole Sandberg on behalf of the Fatherland League; by Rolf Thommessen and R. F. Raeder on behalf of the Independent People's party; and by Vidkun Quisling, Frederik Prytz, and Tormod Hustad on behalf of National Union.

76. Thommessen, "Utkast til overenskomst," June 28, 1934, QA, Box 4, Den nasjonale Blokk folder.

77. Quisling, note concerning the result of the national block negotiations, n.d., *ibid*. The note was quite probably written at the end of June 1934.

78. Kjelstrup to Quisling, July 6, 1934, *ibid*.

79. Kjelstrup to the national block negotiators, September 14, 1934, *ibid*.

80. Thommessen, statement of August 14, 1934, quoted in Norland, *Hårde tider*, p. 250.

81. Norland, ibid.

82. Vedeler to Quisling, February 28, 1934, QA, Box 4, Den nasjonale Blokk folder; Aslak Bøe, for the Oslo organization of the Independent People's party, to National Union, September 5, 1934, QA, Box 4, Kommunevalget 1934 folder; Norland, *Hårde tider*, pp. 250–251.

83. Eyvind Mehle to Quisling, September 12, 1934, QA, Box 4, korrespondanse 1933–1936 folder.

84. Gabrielsen, *Menn og politikk*, p. 161.

85. Brevig, *NS – fra parti til sekt* p. 71; Gabrielsen, *ibid*., p. 160.

86. Kjelstrup, for the Independent People's party, confidential memorandum to members of the larger committee, September 14, 1936, QA, Box 4, Den nasjonale Blokk folder.

87. Norland, *Hårde tider*, pp. 255–258.

88. R. Hvoslef (?), for National Union, to the party's Oslo organization headed by R. Møllhausen, April 27, 1934, QA, Box 4, Den nasjonale Blokk folder. The signature on the document is not legible.

89. Haldis Neegaard Østbye to Quisling, August 27, 1934, *ibid*.

90. *Ibid*.

91. Norway, Det Statistiske Centralbyrå, *Kommunevalgene og ordførervalgene 1934*. (Oslo: 1935), pp. 24–25.

92. *Ibid*., pp. 28–29.

93. *Ibid*., pp. 24–25.

94. *Tidens Tegn*, September 12 and October 15, 1934. The official election statistics in *Kommunevalgene og ordførervalgene 1934* fail to indicate the joint lists of candidates presented by NS and the Independent People's party in Asker and Bærum, although such lists were presented to the voters. See *Asker og Bærum Budstikke* for the period prior to the election.

95. "Bonde Balchen avslører et Quislingsk falskneri," *Dagbladet*, October 13, 1933; "Nationen skåner Quisling og overser Balchen," *Dagbladet*, October 14, 1933.

96. "Frisinnede folkeparti, Nasjonal samling og Bondepartiet går sammen ved kommunevalget i Oslo," *Tidens Tegn*, September 12, 1934.

97. "En valgkandidat på den nasjonale fellesliste overfalt," *Tidens Tegn*, October 11, 1934.

98. Norway, Det Statistiske Centralbyrå, *Kommunevalgene 1931* (Oslo: 1932), p. 12: *Kommunevalgene og ordførervalgene 1934*, p. 11.

99. *Kommunevalgene og ordførervalgene 1934*, pp. 28–29.
100. *Ibid.*, p. 11.
101. *Ibid.*
102. Author's calculations based on statistics in *ibid.*, pp. 24–29.
103. *Kommunevalgene og ordførervalgene 1934*, pp. 28–29.
104. *Tidens Tegn*, October 20, 1934. In the local elections the voters had the opportunity of rearranging the ranking of the candidates on the party list which they voted for.
105. *Asker og Bærum Budstikke*, October 17, 1934.
106. *Kommunevalgene og ordførervalgene 1934*, p. 24. The four provinces were Østfold, Akershus, Oppland, and Hedemark.
107. Author's calculations based on statistics in *ibid.*, pp. 28–29.
108. National Union, Rikspropagandaledelsen, *NS årbok 1942* (Oslo: Blix forlag, 1943), p. 110.
109. *Kommunevalgene og ordførervalgene 1934*, p. 14. The one municipality in which an NS representative was selected mayor was Torpa *kommune* in Oppland. Since NS did not have a majority here, or anywhere else for that matter, the NS mayor was chosen because of personal considerations and not because he was an NS representative.
110. Norland, *Hårde tider*, pp. 214–215.
111. *Kommunevalgene og ordførervalgene 1934*, pp. 24–25, 28–29.
112. Harry Høst to Hjort, November 17, 1934, QA, Box 5, 1933–36 korrespondanse folder; Brevig, *NS – fra parti til sekt*, p. 51; Dahl, "Fascismen i Norge," *Kontrast*, Vol. II, No. 3, p. 16.
113. "Lover for Nasjonal Samling," paragraph 5; "Lover for Fylkesorganisasjonen (F.O.) av NS Hovedorganisasjon," paragraph 2; in Orvar Sæther, ed., *Vår Organisasjon: Nasjonal Samling, NS Ungdomsfylking* (Oslo: NSUF's Centralstyre, 1936), p. 15, p. 19.
114. Emil Rogge to Quisling, with enclosed press clipping, April 28, 1935, QA.
115. *Ibid.*
116. Haldis Neegaard Østbye, original MS of a NS history for the period 1933–

1940, QA. Letterheads on NS stationery located in QA also indicate the change of address.
117. National Union to Bjørnsgård, etc., May 25, 1934, QA, Box 5, 1934 korrespondanse folder; *Fritt Folk*, May 5, 1936.
118. "Lover for Nasjonal Samling," paragraph 3, Saether, *Vår organisasjon*, p. 13.
119. Kathrine Holter (KH) to Quisling, February 3, 1934, QA, Box 4, NS korrespondanse 1933–36 folder.
120. See above, p. 170.
121. Kilberg to Quisling, March 10, 1934, QA, Box 4, Diverse – mindre viktige folder; Quisling to Kilberg, March 20, 1934, QA, Box 4, Diverse – mindre viktige folder.
122. Quisling to Kilberg, *ibid.*
123. Brevig, *NS – fra parti til sekt*, p. 45.
124. Hjort to Quisling, March 13, 1936, QA, Box 6, Oslo-Akershus folder.
125. Brevig, *NS – fra parti til sekt*, p. 47.
126. Hjort to Quisling, March 13, 1936, QA, Box 6, Oslo-Akershus folder.
127. Quisling to the NS organization in Oslo, October 8, 1935, QA, Box 6, NSKO folder.
128. "Landshirdens ledelse og indeling," n.d., QA, Box 6, Rikshirden folder.
129. Brevig, *NS – fra parti til sekt*, p. 48.
130. Hans L'Orange, for the Organizational Division, to the NS organization in Akershus, in care of Hjort, December 2, 1935, QA.
131. *Ibid.*
132. L'Orange to all NS provincial organizations, January 5, 1934, QA, Box 5, 1934 korrespondanse folder.
133. Knut Geelmuyden to Hjort, January 14, 1934, QA, Box 4, NS korrespondanse 1933–1936 folder; Quisling to Vedeler, draft, n.d. (probably early 1934), QA, Box 4, NS korrespondanse 1933–1936 folder; Schröder-Nielsen to Quisling, January 23, 1934, QA, Box 5, 1934 korrespondanse folder; Quisling to Anders Brokstad, April 5, 1934, QA, Box 4, Diverse – mindre viktige folder; Brokstad to Quisling, September 14, 1936, QA, Box 4, NS korrespondanse 1933- 1936 folder; interview with a former

NS member May 31, 1967. See also *NS årbok 1942*, pp. 41 ff.

134. See *NS årbok 1942*, *ibid.*; Sæther, *Vår organisasjon*, pp. 19 ff.

135. Saether, *ibid.*, p. 9.

136. *Ibid.*, pp. 9–10, 56–57.

137. *Ibid.*, pp. 50–52.

138. *Ibid.*, p. 10.

139. The lists of newspapers which appear in *NS årbok 1942*, p. 111, and Brevig, *NS – fra parti til sekt*, p. 51, when combined provide a complete total of the number of NS publications.

140. Herlof Harstad, "Pressedirektiv IV" to all provincial press leaders and *førere*, November 10, 1934, QA, Box 5, 1934 korrespondanse folder. Eyvind Mehle served as Press Director before Harstad.

141. Brevig, *NS – fra parti til sekt*, p. 52; Østbye to Quisling, August 18, 1935, QA, Box 8, Quislings private korrespondanse folder.

142. Østbye, *ibid.*

143. *Norske aviser 1753–1969* (Oslo: Universitetsbiblioteket, 1973), p. 182.

144. *Ibid.*, pp. 331, 182, 370, 415, 167, 570, 435, 180; *Norsk bokfortegnelse 1936–1940* (Oslo: Universitetsbiblioteket, 1943), p. 349.

145. Brevig, *NS – fra parti til sekt*, p. 56; Stein Ugelvik Larsen, "The Social Foundations of Norwegian Fascism 1933–1945: An Analysis of Membership Data," in Stein Ugelvik Larsen, Bernt Hagtvet and Petter Myklebust, eds., *Who Were the Fascists: Social Roots of European Fascism* (Bergen: Universitetsforlaget, 1982), p. 619, fn. 12.

146. Meyer, *Et annet syn*, p. 68.

147. Brevig, *NS – fra parti til sekt*, pp. 36–37.

148. Quisling, "Hvorfor Stiklestad?", in Eyvind Mehle, ed., *Olavstanken. Fra Stiklestad til Stiklestad* (Oslo: Centralforlaget, 1944), p. 164.

149. *NS årbok 1942*, p. 22.

150. Lindboe, *Fra de urolige tredveårene*, pp. 211–212.

151. Østbye, MS of a history of NS, QA.

152. Østbye, for the NS Press and Propaganda Office, to all NS provincial, district, and league leaders, March 17, 1936, QA.

153. Østbye, for the NS Press and Pro-

paganda Office, to all NS provincial, district, and league leaders, April 4, 1936, QA.

154. Vidkun Quisling, *Quisling har sagt – citater fra taler og avisartikler* (Oslo: J. M. Stenersens forlag, 1940), Vol. I, pp. 48–49.

155. Østbye, MS of a history of NS, QA.

156. Hjort to Lunde, May 7, 1936, QA, Box 5, 1933–36 korrespondanse folder.

157. Lunde to Hjort, May 19, 1936, QA.

158. Dag O. Bruknapp, "Ideene splitter partiet. Rasespørsmålets betydning i NS's utvikling," in Rolf Danielsen and Stein Ugelvik Larsen, eds., *Fra idé til dom. Noen trekk fra utviklingen av Nasjonal Samling* (Bergen: Universitetsforlaget, 1976), p. 24.

159. *Ibid.*

160. Jacob D. Sømme, "Jon Alfred Hansen Mjøen," *Norsk biografisk leksikon* (Oslo: H. Aschehoug & Co., 1923-), Vol. IX, p. 255.

161. Bruknapp, "Ideene splitter partiet," *Fra idé til dom*, pp. 25–27; Brevig, *NS – fra parti til sekt*, p. 52.

162. Sømme, "Jon Alfred Hansen Mjøen," *Norsk biografisk leksikon*, Vol. IX. pp. 255–256.

163. Bruknapp, "Ideene splitter partiet," *Fra idé til dom*, p. 24.

164. M. Rabinowitz to the NS Executive Committee, April 24, 1934, QA, Box 4, Diverse – mindre viktige folder. See also Brevig, *NS – fra parti til sekt*, illustration #3, facsimile of *Nasjonal Samling*, No. 28, 1934.

165. Bruknapp, "Ideene splitter partiet," *Fra idé til dom*, pp. 22–23.

166. *Ibid.*, p. 22.

167. Brevig, *NS – fra parti til sekt*, pp. 52–53.

168. Østbye to Quisling, August 9, 1935, QA, Box 4, NS korrespondanse 1933–1936 folder.

169. Brevig, *NS – fra parti til sekt*, p. 36.

170. Bruknapp, "Ideene splitter partiet," *Fra idé til dom*, p. 23.

171. Brevig, *NS – fra parti til sekt*, p. 36.

172. Bruknapp, "Ideene splitter partiet," *Fra idé til dom*, pp. 28–29; Brevig, *NS – fra parti til sekt*, p. 52.

173. Bruknapp, *ibid.*, p. 29.

174. Harald Franklin Knudsen, *Jeg var Quislings sekretær* (Copenhagen: privately published, 1951), pp. 54–55.

175. Yngvar Ustvedt, *Verdensrevolusjonen på Hønefoss. En beretning om Leo Trotskijs opphold i Norge* (Oslo: Gyldendal norsk Forlag, 1974), p. 19.

176. Østbye to Quisling, August 9, 1935, QA, Box 4, NS korrespondanse 1933–1936 folder; Ustvedt, *ibid.*, pp. 92–93, 192.

177. Ustvedt, *ibid.*, pp. 85 ff.

178. *Ibid.*, p. 134.

179. *Ibid.*, p. 150.

180. Sømme, "Jon Alfred Hansen Mjøen," *Norsk biografisk leksikon*, Vol. IX, p. 256.

181. Quisling, *Russland og vi*, p. 107.

182. *Ibid.*, p. 108.

183. Bruknapp, "Ideene splitter partiet," *Fra idé til dom*, pp. 27–28.

184. *Straffesak*, p. 130.

185. Quisling, "Et varsko til alle nordmenn," *Fritt Folk*, October 11, 1936.

186. Hans S. Jacobsen to Quisling, March 1, 1935, QA, Box 7, Korrespondanse vedr. NS antibolsjevisme folder; Bruknapp, "Ideene splitter partiet," *Fra idé til dom*, p. 37.

187. Quisling, "Skal Norge innvikles i krigspolitikken?", Part I, *Tidens Tegn*, September 25, 1934.

188. *Ibid.*, Part II, September 27, 1934.

189. Østbye, MS of an NS history, QA.

190. Vedeler to Quisling, September 21, 1935, QA, Box 7, Korrespondanse vedr. NS antibolsjevisme folder; Sjur Fuhr to Quisling, November 4, 1935, QA, Box 8, Quislings private korrespondanse folder; Valdemar Hansteen to Martin Tveter, March 8, 1936, QA, Box 4, NS korrespondanse 1933–1936 folder.

191. Quisling's clippings are located in QA, Box 7, Avisutklipp, brosjyrer, og korr. 1933–1937 folder. Fascist literature addressed to Quisling is found in QA, Box 4, NS korrespondanse 1933–36 folder.

192. For his participation in the Fascist international, see "Et nytt verdensforbund," *Nasjonal Samling*, September 19, 1935; and Bruknapp, "Ideene splitter partiet," *Fra idé til dom*, p. 12.

193. "Et nytt verdensforbund," *ibid.*

194. *Ibid.*

195. Østbye, MS of a NS history, QA.

196. Vedeler to Quisling, September 21, 1935, QA, Box 7, Korrespondanse vedr. NS antibolsjevisme folder.

197. Bruknapp, "Ideene splitter partiet," *Fra idé til dom*, p. 37.

198. *Ibid.*, p. 25.

199. Blom, "Bønder og blokkforhandlinger 1933–1936," HT, Vol. 51, No. 4, p. 405.

200. Quisling, *Quisling har sagt*, Vol. I, p. 40.

201. Østbye, MS of a NS history, QA.

202. *Ibid.*

203. *Ibid.*

204. *Ibid.*

205. In the 1930s only the constitutions of the United States (1787) and Sweden (1809) had been in effect longer than the Norwegian constitution of 1814.

206. Quisling, open letter to King Haakon VII, August 20, 1936, printed in *Straffesak*, pp. 486–487.

207. *Ibid.*, p. 487.

208. Quisling, "Til Kongen fra Nasjonal Samling," *Fritt Folk*, August 21, 1936.

209. "Av Riksadvokatens uttalelse til Justisdepartementet om Quislings brev til Kongen," *Straffesak*, p. 488.

210. *Ibid.*

211. *Ibid.*

212. *Ibid.*

213. Quisling, open letter to King Haakon VII, August 20, 1936, printed in *Straffesak*, pp. 486–487. See also Meyer, *Et annet syn*, p. 68.

214. *Fritt Folk*, March 26, 1936.

215. Jacobsen, "Vidkun Quisling og N.S.," *Ragnarok*, Vol. III, No. 3, p. 61.

216. NS program of 1934, paragraph 22.

217. Jacobsen, "Vidkun Quisling og N.S.," *Ragnarok*, Vol. III, No. 3, p. 60.

218. *Ibid.*, p. 63.

219. *Ibid.*, p. 62.

220. *Ibid.*, p. 61; Bruknapp, "Ideene splitter partiet," *Fra idé til dom*, p. 15; Odin Augdahl, "Norges politiske partier," *Ragnarok* yearbook, 1936, p. 215.

221. Petition from forty NS members to Quisling, October 30, 1933, QA, Box 11, Opprettelsen av NS 1933 folder.

222. Winciansen to Quisling, July 10, 1934, QA, Box 8, Quislings private korrespondanse folder; Torjusen to Fürst, July 10,

1934, QA, Box 4, NS korrespondanse 1933–1936 folder.

223. Fürst to Møllhausen, October 4, 1934, and October 5, 1934, QA, Box 7, korrespondanse vedr. NS antibolsjevisme folder; "Vår propagandachef," *Nasjonal Samling*, October 10, 1934.

224. Bruknapp, "Ideene splitter partiet," *Fra idé til dom*, p. 15.

225. Jacobsen to Quisling, March 1, 1935, QA, Box 7, Korrespondanse vedr. NS antibolsjevisme folder.

226. Tveter to Eigil Lehmann, September 3, 1935, QA, Box 10, Brev m.v. 1930–1940 folder; Tveter to Gulbrand Lunde, November 29, 1935, printed in Bruknapp, "Ideene splitter partiet," *Fra idé til dom*, pp. 44–47.

227. Tveter to Quisling, March 6, 1934, QA, Box 4, Diverse – mindre viktige folder.

228. Hansteen to Tveter, March 8, 1936, QA, Box 3, 1933 folder.

229. Bruknapp, "Ideene splitter partiet," *Fra idé til dom*, pp. 19–20.

230. Tveter to Quisling, September 4, 1935, QA, Box 10, Brev. m.v. 1930–1940 folder.

231. Hansteen to Tveter, March 8, 1936, QA, Box 3, 1933 folder.

232. *Ibid.*; Bruknapp, "Ideene splitter partiet," *Fra idé til dom*, p. 21.

233. Bruknapp, *ibid.*, p. 20.

234. *Ibid.*, p. 22.

235. *Kommunevalgene og ordførervalgene 1934*, pp. 28–29.

236. Geelmuyden to Hjort, January 14, 1934, QA, Box 4, NS korrespondanse 1933–1936 folder; Quisling to Vedeler, draft copy, n.d., QA, Box 4, NS korrespondanse 1933–1936 folder; Bruknapp, "Ideene splitter partiet," *Fra idé til dom*, p. 21.

237. Tveter to Quisling, September 4, 1935, QA, Box 10, Brev m.v. 1930–1940 folder.

238. Tveter to Quisling, March 6, 1934, QA, Box 4, Diverse – mindre viktige folder.

239. *Ibid.*

240. Quisling to Tveter, March 7, 1934, QA.

241. Bruknapp, "Ideene splitter partiet," *Fra idé til dom*, p. 31.

242. Østbye to Quisling, August 9, 1935, QA, Box 4, NS korrespondanse 1933–1936 folder.

243. Quoted by Bruknapp, "Ideene splitter partiet," *Fra ide til dom*, p. 31.

244. Jørgen Quisling, "Kristendommen og den nytyske hedenskap," *Tidens Tegn*, August 15, 1935.

245. Tveter to Quisling, September 4, 1935, QA, Box 10, Brev m.v. 1930–1940 folder.

246. Jacobsen, "Vidkun Quisling og NS," *Ragnarok*, Vol. III, No. 3, pp. 58–59.

247. Vedeler to Quisling, September 9, 1935, QA, Box 7, Korrespondanse vedr. NS antibolsjevisme folder; Fuhr to Quisling, November 4, 1935, QA, Box 8, Quisling's private korrespondanse folder.

248. Tveter to Kjeld Stub, October 23–29, 1935, QA, Box 10, Brev m.v. 1930–1940 folder.

249. *Ibid.*

250. Tveter to Lunde, November 29, 1935, printed in Bruknapp, "Ideene splitter partiet," *Fra idé til dom*, pp. 44–47.

251. Bruknapp, *ibid.*, pp. 33–34

252. Hansteen to Tveter, March 8, 1936, QA, Box 3, 1933 folder; Bruknapp, *ibid.*, p. 34.

253. Bruknapp, *ibid.*, pp. 34–36.

254. Hansteen to Tveter, March 8, 1936, QA, Box 3, 1933 folder.

255. Vedeler to Quisling, March 11, 1936, QA, Box 4, NS korrespondanse 1933–1936 folder.

256. Bruknapp, "Ideene splitter partiet," *Fra idé til dom*, pp. 36–37.

257. Tveter, "Hvorfor jeg har forlatt Nasjonal Samling," November 20, 1935, QA, Box 10, Brev m.v. 1930–1940 folder.

258. Bruknapp, "Ideene splitter partiet," *Fra idé til dom*, p. 37.

259. Hjort to Quisling, July 19, 1936, QA.

260. Brevig, *NS – fra parti til sekt*, p. 102.

Notes to Chapter VI

1. Jens Jebsen to Quisling, August 11, 1936, QA, Box 4, NS korrespondanse 1933–36 folder; H. Henriksen to Quisling, September 30, 1936, QA, Box 6, Oslo-Akershus folder; Ørnulf Lundesgaard to Quisling,

October 6, 1936, QA, Box 4, NS korrespondanse 1933–36 folder; Sjur Fuhr to Quisling, November 19, 1936, QA, Box 7, Korrespondanse vedr. NS antibolsjevisme folder.

2. "Arbeidsplan for 1936," QA, Box 14, Propaganda 35–36 osv. folder; Gulbrand Lunde to all NS regional, district, and group leaders, January 2, 1936, QA.

3. *Ibid*. Fuglesang to all NS regional, district, and group leaders, January 6, 1936, QA, Box 14, Propaganda 35–36 osv. folder.

4. "Arbeidsplan for 1936," *ibid*.

5. *Fritt Folk*, April 27, 1936.

6. "Nasjonal Samling og stortingsvalget," *Fritt Folk*, April 27, 1936. Italics part of text.

7. Hjort, "Hvad Nasjonal Samling vil," *Tidens Tegn*, September 8, 1936.

8. Anders Lange, "Nasjonal splittelse"; Brynjulf Bjørset, "Hvad Nasjonal Samling vil – men ikke gjør," *Tidens Tegn*, September 9, 1936.

9. "De uavhengiges liste," *Tidens Tegn*, September 7, 1936.

10. Thomas Christian Wyller, "Hovedtrekk av Nasjonal Samlings ideer om stat og samfunn 1930–1940," *Statsvetenskaplig Tidskrift* (Lund, Sweden), Vol. LVI, No. 2 (1953), p. 222.

11. *Ibid*., pp. 223–225.

12. *Ibid*., p. 222.

13. Quisling, "Fritt Folk," *Fritt Folk*, March 26, 1936.

14. *Ibid*.

15. Hjort, "Et perverst samfund," *Fritt Folk*, March 26, 1936.

16. Quisling's speech at the *førerting*, September 25, 1942, printed in Quisling, *Mot nytt land. Artikler og taler av Vidkun Quisling 1941–1943*, Vol. IV of *Quisling har sagt* (Oslo: NS Rikspropagandaledelse, n.d.), pp. 126–127. Italics part of text.

17. Fuglesang to the Farmers' Association, April 2, 1936, quoted in Østbye, MS of a NS history, QA.

18. *Ibid*.

19. Berg Bondelag, Gjerpen Bondelag, Gransherad Bondelag, and Rakkestad Bondelag to Quisling, n.d., QA, Box 11, NS-anliggender 1936–1938 folder.

20. Quisling, "Uttalelse," August 27, 1936, QA, Box 11, NS-anliggender 1936–38 folder.

21. *Ibid*.

22. T. Dehli Laurantzen to Gulbrand Lunde, June 3, 1936, QA.

23. Victor Mogens, *Tyskerne, Quisling og vi andre* (Oslo: Utenriks-forlaget, 1945), p. 55.

24. "Voldsomme spetakler omkring N.S. møtet i Gjøvik igår," *Velgeren*, May 22, 1936; "Nazistene satte hele Gjøvik på ende igår," *Opland Arbeiderblad*, May 22, 1936.

25. Quisling to all NS provincial, district, and league leaders, January 3, 1936, QA, Box 14, Propaganda 35–36 osv. folder.

26. "Quislings forslag om et nordisk verdenssamband," *Fritt Folk*, June 30, 1936.

27. *Ibid*.

28. See the letters from Cecilie to Vidkun in QA, in particular in Box 4, NS korrespondanse 1933–36 folder.

29. "Quisling stilles i Oslo og Telemark," *Fritt Folk*, September 15, 1936.

30. Jens Rolfsen to Quisling, September 1, 1936, QA, Box 4, NS korrespondanse 1933–36 folder.

31. Interview with a former NS member, May 31, 1967.

32. Norway, Stortingets Kontor, *Stortingsvalget 1936*, Vol. IX, No. 107 of Norges offisielle statistikk (Oslo: H. Aschehoug & Co., for Stortingets Kontor, 1937), p. 131.

33. Sjur Fuhr to Quisling, November 19, 1936, QA, Box 7, korrespondanse vedr. NS antibolsjevisme folder. See also Steinar Klevar to Quisling, November 13, 1935, QA, Box 4, NS korrespondanse 1933–36 folder.

34. Leif Rabben to Quisling, May 27, 1936, QA, Box 8, Quisling's private korrespondanse folder; Anders Brokstad to Quisling, September 14, 1936, QA, Box 4, NS korrespondanse 1933–36 folder.

35. *Ibid*.

36. Konrad Sundlo to Quisling, April 2, 1936, QA, Box 14, Propaganda 35–36 osv. folder; Rabben to Quisling, May 27, 1936, QA, Box 8, Quisling's private korrespondanse folder.

37. Sundlo and Rabben, *ibid*.; Rolfsen to Quisling, September 1, 1936, QA, Box 4, NS korrespondanse, 1933–36 folder; S. Stephensen to Quisling, August 21, 1936, QA, Box 4, NS korrespondanse 1933–36 folder.

38. Lunde to Quisling, August 8, 1936, QA, Box 4, NS korrespondanse 1933–36 folder.

39. Jacobsen, "Vidkun Quisling og N.S.," *Ragnarok*, Vol. 3, No. 3, p. 61. See also Sjur Fuhr to Quisling, November 11, 1936, QA, Box 7, Korrespondanse vedr. NS antibolsjevisme folder.

40. Brokstad to Quisling, September 9, 1936, QA, Box 4, NS korrespondanse 1933–36 folder; Kaare Hovind to Quisling, January 9, 1937, QA, Box 4, NS korrespondanse 1933–36 folder.

41. Hovind, *ibid.*

42. Brokstad to Quisling, September 9, 1936, QA, Box 4, NS korrespondanse 1933–36 folder; Blomma Gulbrandsen to Quisling, August 10, 1936, QA, Box 4, NS korrespondanse 1933–36 folder.

43. Brokstad, *ibid.*; Lunde to Hjort, July 24 and August 10, 1936, QA; Lundesgaard to Quisling, October 10, 1936, QA, Box 4, NS korrespondanse 1933–36 folder.

44. Fuhr to Quisling, November 11, 1936, QA, Box 7, Korrespondanse vedr. NS antibolsjevisme folder.

45. Hovind to Quisling, January 9, 1937, QA, Box 4, NS korrespondanse 1933–36 folder.

46. J. B. Kolflaath to Quisling, October 23, 1936, QA, Box 8, Quislings private korrespondanse folder.

47. Hjort, "Hvad Nasjonal Samling vil," *Tidens Tegn*, September 8, 1936.

48. Quisling, "En varsko til alle nordmenn," *Fritt Folk*, October 14, 1936.

49. Stortingets Kontor, *Stortingsvalget 1936*, p. 107.

50. Rolfsen to Quisling, March 27, 1936, QA, Box 6, Oslo-Akershus folder; Hilmar Knutsen to Quisling, January 28, 1937, QA, Box 6, Oslo-Akershus folder; Brevig, *NS – Fra parti til sekt*, p. 84.

51. Hjort, "Hvad Nasjonal Samling vil," *Tidens Tegn*, September 8, 1936.

52. Anders Lange, "Nasjonal splittelse," and Brynjolf Bjørset, "Hvad Nasjonal Samling vil – men ikke gjør," *Tidens Tegn*, September 9, 1936. These two commentaries were in rebuttal to J. B. Hjort's article in the paper's previous edition.

53. Joakim Lehmkuhl in ABC, April 30, 1936, quoted in Norland, *Hårde tider*, p. 281.

54. Stortingets Kontor, *Stortingsvalget 1936*, pp. 32–129. In the 1936 election the Radical People's party's restricted its participation to Oppland province.

55. Quisling, "En varsko til alle nordmenn," *Fritt Folk*, October 14, 1936.

56. Helge Slettebøe to Quisling, October 22, 1936, QA, Box 10, Brev m.v. 1930–1940 folder.

57. Knut Hamsun, "Vidkun Quisling," *Fritt Folk*, October 17, 1936.

58. *Ibid.*

59. "I Quislings spor. Hvad man stemmer på," *Aftenposten*, October 19, 1936.

60. Fuglesang to Norsk Presseforbund, November 3, 1936, QA.

61. "NS er sikker på 10 mandater," *Samarbeid*, October 8, 1936.

62. Stortingets Kontor, *Stortingsvalget 1933*, p. 153; Stortingets Kontor, *Stortingsvalget 1936*, p. 133.

63. Det Statistiske Centralbyrå, *Kommunevalgene og ordførervalgene 1934*, p. 28; Stortingets Kontor, *Stortingsvalget 1936*, p. 132.

64. Steinar Klevar to Quisling, November 13, 1935, QA, Box 4, NS korrespondanse 1933–36 folder.

65. Stortingets Kontor, *Stortingsvalget 1933*, p. 151; Stortingets Kontor, *Stortingsvalget 1936*, p. 131.

66. Ragnar Skancke to Quisling, September 24, 1933, QA, Box 4, Privat og politisk kamp 1933–34 folder.

67. Stortingets Kontor, *Stortingsvalget 1933*, p. 152; Stortingets Kontor, *Stortingsvalget 1936*, p. 132.

68. Klevar to Quisling, November 13, 1935, QA, Box 4, NS korrespondanse 1933–36 folder; Brokstad to Quisling, September 9, 1936, QA, Box 4, NS korrespondanse 1933–36 folder.

69. Stortingets Kontor, *Stortingsvalget 1933*, p. 151; Stortingets Kontor, *Stortingsvalget 1936*, p. 131.

70. *Ibid.*, p. 152; *ibid.*, p. 132.

71. Stortingets Kontor, *Stortingsvalget 1936*, pp. 131–132.

72. *Ibid.*, p. 132.

73. *Ibid.*, pp. 34–129.

74. *Ibid.*, p. 139.

75. *Ibid.*, p. 139, p. 132.

76. Gabrielsen, "De gode middagers tid," *Kontrast*, Vol. II, No. 3, p. 42.

77. One partial exception to this pattern was the Community Party (*Samfundspartiet*), which stood for a radical change in the system of finances and the distribution of goods. It took part in its first national election in 1933, gaining one seat. Although its vote in 1936 increased to 3.1 per cent, its Storting representation remained limited to one. Like the Fatherland League and the Independent People's party, the Community Party failed to survive the war.

78. Quisling, "Til alle NS-folk," *Fritt Folk*, October 21, 1936.

79. Fuhr to Quisling, November 19, 1936, QA, Box 7, Korrespondanse vedr. NS antibolsjevisme.

80. Hovind to Quisling, January 9, 1937, QA, Box 4, NS korrespondanse 1933–36.

81. Quisling, "Til alle NS-folk," *Fritt Folk*, October 21, 1936.

82. *Ibid.*

83. *Ibid.*

Notes to Chapter VII

1. Hjort to Quisling, November 4, 1933, QA.

2. *Ibid.*

3. Ørnulf Lundesgaard to Quisling, March 5, 1937, QA, Box 4, 1933–36 korrespondanse folder; Brevig, *NS – fra parti til sekt*, p. 42.

4. Finn Solberg to Quisling, December 2, 1936, QA, Box 5, 1933–36 korrespondanse til V.Q. folder.

5. *Ibid.*

6. Hans L'Orange, for the Central Office's Organization Division, to NS in Akershus via J. B. Hjort, December 2, 1935, QA.

7. Solberg to Quisling, December 2, 1936, Box 5, 1933–36 korrespondanse til V.Q. folder.

8. Jens Rolfsen to Quisling, November 29, 1935, QA, Box 6, Strid mellom Oslo og Akershus fylkesorg. av NS folder; Hjort to the Central Office's Organizational Division, December 18, 1935, QA, Box 6, Strid mellom Oslo og Akershus fylkesorg. av NS folder.

9. L'Orange to Quisling, August 15, 1935, QA, Box 6, Strid mellom Oslo og Akershus fylkesorg. av NS folder; L'Orange, for the Central Office's Organizational Division to NS in Akershus via J. B. Hjort, December 2, 1935, QA; Hjort to the Central Office's Organizational Division, December 18, 1935, QA, Box 6, Strid mellom Oslo og Akershus fylkesorg. av NS folder.

10. L'Orange, for the Central Office's Organization Division, to NS in Akershus c/o J. B. Hjort, December 2, 1935, QA; Hjort to the Central Office's Organization Division, December 18, 1935, QA, Box 6, Strid mellom Oslo og Akershus fylkesorg. av NS folder.

11. Hjort to Fuglesang, May 5, 1936, QA.

12. Lunde to Hjort, May 19, 1936, QA; Lunde to Fuglesang, August 4, 1936, QA, Box 4, NS korrespondanse 1933–36 folder.

13. Hjort to Quisling, September 9, 1935, QA, Box 6, NSKO folder; Quisling to the provincial organization in Akershus, Hjort, the *Hird* office, and Fuglesang, October 8, 1935, QA, Box 6, NSKO folder.

14. Quisling, *ibid.*

15. Hjort to Orvar Sæther, March 14, 1936, QA, Box 5, 1933–36 korrespondanse til V.Q. folder; Solberg to Quisling, December 2, 1936, QA, Box 5, 1933–36 korrespondanse til V.Q. folder.

16. Hjort to Quisling, March 24, 1936, QA, Box 6, Oslo-Akershus folder; Knud Schnitler to Hjort, April 4, 1936, QA; Solberg to Quisling, *ibid.*

17. L'Orange to Quisling, August 15, 1935, QA, Box 6, Strid mellom Oslo og Akershus fylkesorg. av NS folder; Solberg to Quisling, *ibid.*

18. Hjort to Quisling, March 24, 1936, QA, Box 6, Oslo-Akershus folder; Solberg to Quisling, *ibid.*

19. Solberg, *ibid.*

20. Hjort to Quisling, April 17, 1936, QA.

21. Rolfsen to Quisling, March 27, 1936, QA; Hjort to Quisling, April 3, 1936, QA, Box 6, Oslo-Akershus folder; Roy Alex. Rossland to Hjort, April 3, 1936, QA, Box 6, Oslo-Akershus folder; Fuglesang to Quisling, April 3, 1936, QA, Box 6, Oslo-Akershus folder; Hjort to Quisling, April 4,

1936, QA; Schnitler to Hjort, April 4, 1936, QA.

22. Solberg to Quisling, December 2, 1936, QA, Box 5, 1933–36 korrespondanse til V.Q. folder.

23. Thorvald Meyer to Kramer, May 25, 1936, QA, Box 5, 1933–36 korrespondanse til V.Q. folder.

24. Kjell Gundersen to Quisling, March 25, 1936, QA, Box 10, Brev m.v. 1930–1940 folder.

25. Quisling to Hjort, April 3, 1936, QA, Box 6, Oslo-Akershus folder; Hjort to Quisling, April 3, 1936, Box 6, QA, Oslo-Akershus folder; Hjort to Quisling, April 4, 1936, QA.

26. Hjort to Quisling, March 25, 1936, QA, Box 6, Oslo-Akershus folder.

27. Hjort to Quisling, May 5, 1936, QA, Box 6, Oslo-Akershus folder; Hjort to Fuglesang, May 5, 1936, QA; Haldis Neegaard Østbye to Quisling, QA, Box 4, NS korrespondanse 1933–36 folder.

28. Rolfsen to Quisling, March 27, 1936, QA; Fuglesang to Quisling, April 3, 1936, QA, Box 6, Oslo-Akershus folder.

29. Ørnulf Lundesgaard to Quisling, April 24, 1936, QA, Box 4, NS korrespondanse 1933–36 folder.

30. Quisling, "Oppfordring til alle NS-folk," *Fritt Folk*, May 23, 1936.

31. *Ibid.*

32. Rolfsen to the NS Akershus organization, September 9, 1936, QA, Box 6, Oslo-Akershus folder.

33. Rolfsen to Quisling, March 16, 1936, QA, Box 6, Oslo-Akershus folder; Thomas Neumann to Quisling, May 28, 1936, QA, Box 14, Propaganda, 35–36 osv. folder.

34. Eleven former officers and members in the NS Oslo organization to Quisling, April 21, 1936, QA, Box 6, Oslo-Akershus folder.

35. Sigrid Mohn to Quisling, July 7, 1936, QA, Box 4, NS korrespondanse 1933–36 folder.

36. Rolfsen to Quisling, March 16, 1936, QA, Box 6, Oslo-Akershus folder; L'Orange to Quisling, April 20, 1936, QA, Box 6, Oslo-Akershus folder.

37. Herman Harris Aall to Quisling, July 7, 1936, QA; Th. Ellingsen to Quisling, July 31, 1936, QA.

38. Hjort to Quisling, June 3, 1936, QA.

39. Georg Vedeler to Quisling, June 29, 1936, QA.

40. Hjort to Quisling, June 29, 1936, QA; Herlof Harstad to Quisling, July 20, 1936, QA.

41. Vedeler to Quisling, June 29, 1936, QA.

42. *Ibid.*

43. Aall to Quisling, July 7, 1936, QA.

44. *Ibid.*

45. Hjort to Quisling, July 9, 1936, QA.

46. *Ibid.*

47. Aall to Quisling, July 7, 1936, QA.

48. Hjort to Quisling, July 9, 1936, QA.

49. Quisling received a letter from Aall dated July 7, 1936, plus the carbon copy of a letter sent to Hjort on July 10. Hjort sent a personal letter to Quisling on July 9, another which was co-signed by editor Herlof Harstad and *Fritt Folk*'s business manager, Arne Wiese, and Harstad sent another letter on his own on July 20. All are located in QA.

50. Formal statement by Quisling on October 27, 1936, QA. The statement was printed and distributed to party members.

51. *Ibid.*

52. *Ibid.*

53. Hjort to Quisling, October 27, 1936, QA; incomplete and undated letter from an anonymous *Fritt Folk* staff member to Quisling, QA, Box 5, 1933–36 korrespondanse til V.Q. folder.

54. Anders Brokstad to Quisling, September 14, 1936, QA, Box 4, NS korrespondanse 1933–36 folder; Lundesgaard to Quisling, October 6, 1936, QA, Box 4, NS korrespondanse 1933–36 folder.

55. Lunde to Hjort, July 24, 1936, QA; Lunde to Hjort, August 10, 1936, QA.

56. Hjort to Quisling, October 29, 1936, QA.

57. *Ibid.*

58. Hjort to Quisling, October 27, 1936, QA.

59. *Ibid.*

60. *Ibid.*

61. *Ibid.*

62. Hjort's recommendation for NS'

reorganization, October 27, 1936, QA, Box 5, 1933–36 korrespondanse til V.Q. folder.

63. Lunde to Quisling, August 8, 1936, QA, Box 4, NS korrespondanse 1933–36 folder; Lunde to Fuglesang, August 8, 1936, QA, Box 4, NS korrespondanse 1933–36; Hjort to Fuglesang, May 5, 1936, QA.

64. Hjort's recommendation for NS' reorganization, October 27, 1936, QA, Box 5, 1933–36 korrespondanse til V.Q. folder.

65. "Saken mot kamporganisasjonen henlagt," *Fritt Folk*, May 5, 1936; Kamporganisasjonen, "Skriftlig erklæring," QA.

66. Kamporganisasjonen, *ibid.*

67. J. S. Nissen to the Central Office's Organizational Division, Hans L'Orange, November 25, 1936, QA, Box 8, Quisling's private korrespondance folder.

68. L'Orange, for the Organizational Division, "Medlemmer av K.O. pr. 3/11–36," QA, Box 6, NSKO folder.

69. Hjort to Quisling, October 27, 1936, QA.

70. Five NS officers from Drammen *krets* to Quisling, November 29, 1936, QA, Box 10, Brev m.v. 1930–1940 folder.

71. Hjort to Quisling, October 31, 1933, QA.

72. *Ibid.*

73. Otto Sverdrup Engelschiøn to Quisling, November 2, 1936, QA, Box 5, 1933–36 korrespondanse til V.Q. folder.

74. Engelschiøn, *ibid*; O. A. Bachke to Quisling, November 22, 1936, QA, Box 5, 1933–36 korrespondanse til V.Q. folder.

75. Engelschiøn, *ibid.*

76. Hugo Borgen to Quisling, November 19, 1936, QA, Box 5, 1933–36 korrespondanse til V.Q. folder.

77. Hjort to Quisling, November 5, 1936, QA.

78. Sigfr. Nylander and Fuglesang, "Rapport til N S Fører ang. NSP A/S," January 20, 1937, QA, Box 5, 1933–36 korrespondanse til V.Q. folder.

79. Some twenty officers in the NS Women's Organization in Akershus to Quisling, November 9, 1936, QA, Box 14, NSK (1935–37) folder.

80. Sigurd Woxen to Quisling, January 2, 1937, QA.

81. Borgen to Quisling, November 19, 1936, QA,1933–36 korrespondanse til V.Q. folder.

82. Hjort to Quisling, November 19, 1936, QA.

83. "Lover for Nasjonal Samling," paragraph 5, section 3b, in Saether, *Vår organisasjon*, p. 15.

84. Hjort to Quisling, November 26, 1936, QA.

85. *Ibid.*

86. Hjort to members of the NS Council, December 23, 1936, QA.

87. *Ibid.*

88. *Ibid.*

89. Quisling to Hjort, December 28, 1936, QA, Box 6, Oslo-Akershus folder.

90. Quisling to Hjort, December 29, 1936, QA.

91. Hjort to Quisling, January 2, 1937, QA.

92. *Ibid.*

93. Woxen to Quisling, January 2, QA; Vedeler to Quisling, December 31, 1936, QA, Box 5, 1933–36 korrespondanse to V.Q. folder; Oliver Møystad to Quisling, QA, Box 4, NS korrespondanse 1933–36 folder.

94. Vedeler to Quisling, *ibid.*

95. Vedeler, *ibid.*; Woxen to Quisling, January 2, 1937, QA; Hektoen to Quisling, January 4, 1937, QA, Box 4, NS korrespondanse 1933–36 folder; Sigurd Stein to Quisling, January 5, 1936, QA, Box 5, 1933–36 korrespondanse til V.Q. folder; H. Naes and Sverre Johansen to Quisling, January 9, 1937, QA, Box 6, Oslo-Akershus folder.

96. Trygve Tellefsen to Quisling, January 4, 1937, QA, Box 4, NS korrespondanse 1933–36 folder; W. W. Valle and S. L. Lilleide to Quisling, n.d., but most probably shortly after January 16, 1937, QA, Box 5, 1933–36 korrespondanse til V.Q. folder; Brokstad to Quisling, January 24, 1937, QA, Box 4, NS korrespondanse 1933–36 folder.

97. Tellefsen, *ibid.*

98. Quisling to Woxen, February 4, 1937, quoted in Woxen to Quisling, February 13, 1937, QA, Box 4, NS korrespondanse 1933–36 folder.

99. Quisling to Hektoen, February 4, 1937, QA, Box 6, Hovedstyret folder.

100. Valle and Lilleide to Quisling, n.d., QA, Box 5, 1933–36 korrespondanse til V.Q. folder.

101. Hektoen to Quisling, January 4,

1937, QA Box 4, NS korrespondanse 1933–36 folder.

102. Valle and Lilleide to Quisling, n.d., QA, Box 5, 1933–36 korrespondanse til V.Q. folder.

103. National Union's bylaws, paragraph 5, section 2a, and paragraph 5, section 3c in Sæther, ed. *Vår organisasjon*, p. 15.

104. Quisling to Hektoen, February 4, 1937, QA, Box 6, Hovedstyret folder.

105. Naess and Johansen to Quisling, January 9, 1937, QA, Box 6, Oslo-Akershus folder; Hektoen to Quisling, January 4, 1937, QA, Box 4, NS korrespondanse 1933–36 folder; Woxen to Quisling, January 31, 1937, QA, Box 6, Hovedstyret folder.

106. Lundesgaard to Quisling, January 11, 1937, QA, Box 4, NS korrespondanse 1933–36 folder.

107. Finn Solberg, Berit Johansen and Knud Schnitler to Quisling, November 11, 1936, QA, Box 5, 1933–36 korrespondanse til V.Q. folder.

108. Quisling, "P.M. vedrørende eksklusjon av Arne Dolven, tidligere leder for NSUF i Akershus fylke," January 20, 1937, QA, Box 5, 1933–36 korrespondanse til V.Q. folder.

109. *Ibid.*

110. Hjort to members of the NS Council, December 23, 1936, QA.

111. Bjarne Gran to Quisling, January 8, 1937, QA, Box 5, 1933–36 korrespondanse til V.Q. folder.

112. Gran, *ibid.*; Arne S. to Brede, n.d., QA, Box 4, NS korrespondanse 1933–36 folder.

113. Hjort to Quisling, January 8, 1937, QA.

114. Arne Bech to Quisling, January 19, 1937, QA, Box 6, Oslo-Akershus folder.

115. Hjort to Quisling, January 8, 1937, QA; Gran to Quisling, January 8, 1937, QA, Box 5, 1933–36 korrespondanse til V.Q. folder; Kaare Soleng to Quisling, January 11, 1937, Box 5, QA, 1933–36 korrespondanse til V.Q. folder; Bech to Quisling, January 19, 1937, QA, Box 6, Oslo-Akershus folder.

116. Bech, *ibid.*; Soleng to Quisling, *ibid.*; Leif Ditlesen to Quisling, January 13, 1937, QA, Box 5, 1933–36 korrespondanse til V.Q. folder.

117. Quisling to Bech, January 11, 1937, QA, Box 6, Oslo-Akershus folder.

118. *Ibid.*

119. Bech to Quisling, January 19, 1937, QA, Box 6, Oslo-Akershus folder.

120. Hjort to Quisling, January 8, 1937, QA.

121. Quisling, "Hovedkontoret," January 9, 1937, QA, Box 6, Hovedstyret folder.

122. Quisling, "P.M. vedrørende eksklusjon av Arne Dolven, tidligere leder for NSUF i Akershus fylke," January 20, 1937 QA, Box 5, 1933–36 korrespondanse til V.Q. folder.

123. Quisling to members of the NS Council concerning *Fritt Folk*, January 20, 1937, QA, Box 5, 1933–36 korrespondanse til V.Q. folder.

124. *Ibid.*

125. Fuglesang and Nylander, "Rapport til NS Fører ang. NSP A/S," QA, Box 5, 1933–36 korrespondanse til V.Q. folder.

126. Hjort to Quisling, January 16, 1937, QA.

127. *Ibid.*

128. Quisling to Hjort, January 18, 1937, QA.

129. Hjort to Quisling, January 20, 1937, QA.

130. Hjort to Quisling, February 1, 1937.

131. Vedeler to Quisling, February 7, 1937, QA, Box 10, Brev m.v. 1930–1940 folder.

132. Vedeler, Ellen Schnitler, Sigurd Stinesen, *et al.* to Quisling, February 2, 1937, QA, Box 10, Brev m.v. 1930–1940 folder.

133. "Forrædere," *Nasjonal-Ungdommen*, February 15, 1937.

134. Hustad, "Renegater og provokatører," *ibid.*

135. Engelschiøn to Quisling, February 5, 1937, QA, Box 4, NS korrespondanse 1933–36 folder.

136. Hjort to Quisling, February 8, 1937, QA.

137. See Rolfsen to Quisling, March 27, 1936, QA, Box 6, Oslo-Akershus folder; Fuglesang to Quisling, April 3, 1936, QA, Box 6, Oslo-Akershus folder; Hilmar Knutsen to Quisling, January 28, 1937, QA, Box 6, Oslo-Akershus folder.

138. Sjur Fuhr to Quisling, February 15, 1937, QA, Box 11, NS-anliggender 1936–38 folder.

139. Hjort's importance for NS in the period 1933–36 was first emphasized in a scholarly work by Hans Olaf Brevig in *NS – fra parti til sekt*, pp. 41 ff.

140. Hustad, "Renegater og provokatører" *Nasjonal-Ungdommen*, February 15, 1937.

141. Quisling, "Til alle NS-folk," *Fritt Folk*, April 8, 1937.

142. Herlof Harstad, "Redaksjonsforholdene i *Fritt Folk*," March 31, 1937, QA.

143. Quisling, "Tåpelig aksjon mot Quisling," *Fritt Folk*, April 8, 1937.

144. *Ibid.*

145. Wiese to Quisling, April 10, 1937, QA.

146. Vogt, *Mennesket Vidkun og forræderen Quisling*, p. 182, p. 129.

147. *Ibid.*, p. 130.

148. Quisling, "Til alle NS-folk," *Fritt Folk*, April 8, 1937.

149. Th. Sørensen to Quisling, May 24, 1937, QA.

150. *Ibid.*

151. Sørensen to Herman Harris Aall, May 11, 1937, Oslo, Riksarkivet, Domsarkivet, Aallsaken, Folder #4, Korrespondanse med NS, Quisling og Hagelin før 9. april, document 1b. Domsarkivet hereafter cited as DA.

152. Aall to Sørensen, May 20, 1937, *ibid.*, document 1c.

153. Vedeler to Quisling, May 13, 1937, QA, Box 14, Propaganda 35–36 osv. folder.

154. *Ibid.*

155. *Fritt Folk*, June 3, 1937.

156. Jacobsen, "Vidkun Quisling og N.S.," *Ragnarok*, Vol. 3, No. 3 (May 1937), p. 65.

157. *Ibid.*, pp. 62–63.

158. Walter Fürst, "Årsakene til og følgene av N.S.' sammenbrudd," *Ragnarok*, *ibid.*, p. 66.

159. *Ibid.*, p. 69.

160. Stortingets Kontor, *Stortingsvalget 1936*, p. 109.

161. Brevig, *NS – fra parti til sekt*, p. 99.

162. Fuglesang, "Undergravningsarbeide," *Fritt Folk*, May 27, 1937.

163. Quisling, "Til alle NS-folk," *Fritt Folk*, April 8, 1937.

164. *Fritt Folk*, May 27, 1937.

165. Fuglesang, "Undergravningsarbeide," *Fritt Folk*, May 27, 1937.

166. "To møter," *Fritt Folk*, June 3, 1937.

167. Brevig, *NS – fra parti til sekt*, pp. 99–100. Hans-Dietrich Loock, citing Brevig's *cand. philol.* thesis (the pre-publication draft of Brevig's study), appears to have mistakenly regarded the departure of some 330 NS members from the party as a consequence of Hjort's resignation. Instead, this is the approximate number of persons who supported Wiesener's position on May 30, 1937. See Loock, *Quisling, Rosenberg und Terboven*, p. 153.

168. "To møter," *Fritt Folk*, June 3, 1937.

169. Albert Wiesener, "Nasjonal Samlings dilemma – Quisling eller saken," *Tidens Tegn*, June 1, 1937.

170. "Møtene i Oslo søndag," *Samarbeid*, June 3, 1937.

171. "Overveldende tillitsvotum til Nasjonal Samlings Fører," *Fritt Folk*, June 3, 1937.

172. *Ibid.*

173. *Ibid.*

174. "To møter," *Fritt Folk*, June 3, 1937; "NSK's protestskrivelse og appell," *Fritt Folk*, June 3, 1937; Vogt, *Mennesket Vidkun og forræderen Quisling*, p. 123.

175. Wiesener, "Nasjonal Samlings dilemma – Quisling eller saken," *Tidens Tegn*, June 1, 1937.

176. *Tidens Tegn*, June 1, 1937.

177. Wiesener, "Nasjonal Samlings dilemma – Quisling eller saken," *ibid.*

178. "Motpartens advokat," *Fritt Folk*, June 3, 1937.

179. "Quisling. Av Knut Hamsun," *Fritt Folk*, June 24, 1937.

180. Vedeler to Quisling, November 13, 1936, QA, Box 4, NS korrespondanse 1933–36 folder; Vedeler to Quisling, December 31, 1936, QA, Box 5, 1933–36 korrespondanse til V.Q. folder; Vedeler to Quisling, February 7, 1937, QA, Box 10, Brev m.v. 1930–1940 folder.

181. *Fritt Folk*, May 27, 1937.

182. Vedeler to Quisling, November 13,

1936, QA, Box 4, NS korrespondanse 1933–36 folder.

183. Wiesener, "Quisling eller saken," *Samarbeid*, June 3, 1937.

184. "Saker som ønskes fremmet på Riksmøtet," *Fritt Folk*, June 3, 1937.

185. "Årets Riksmøte henlagt til Hamar 2. 3. og 4. juli," *Fritt Folk*, June 10, 1937.

186. Ellen Schnitler to Quisling, June 17, 1937, QA, Box 8, Quislings private korrespondanse folder.

187. Vedeler, "Til Nasjonal Samlings fører Vidkun Quisling," *Samarbeid*, June 10, 1937.

188. Schnitler to Quisling, June 17, 1937, QA, Box 8, Quislings private korrespondanse folder.

189. "Til riksmøtets deltagere," *Samarbeid*, July 1, 1937.

190. "NS' 5. riksmøte det beste i bevegelsens historie," *Fritt Folk*, July 8, 1937.

191. *Ibid.*

192. *Ibid.*

193. *Ibid.*

194. *Ibid.*

195. "Riksmøtets Resultater," *Fritt Folk*, July 8, 1937.

196. Schnitler to Dora Bull, July 14, 1937, QA, Box 14, NSK (1935–37) folder.

197. *Ibid.*

198. *Ibid.*

199. Øyvor Hansson to Quisling, July 24, 1937, QA, Box 14, NSK (1935–37) folder.

200. Vedeler to Quisling, August 30, 1937, QA, Box 7, Korrespondanse vedr. NS antibolsjevisme folder.

201. Sigurd Stinesen and Georg Vedeler, "En redegjørelse," *Samarbeid*, September 9, 1937.

202. "Husk æresgaven til Quisling," *Fritt Folk*, July 8, 1937.

203. Schnitler to Dora Bull, July 14, 1937, QA, Box 14, NSK (1935–37) folder.

204. Arne Quisling to Vidkun Quisling, July 6, 1937, QA, Box 12, Brevordner påstemplet Hemmelig folder.

205. Vogt, *Mennesket Vidkun og forræderen Quisling*, pp. 130–131.

206. "Riksmøtets Resultater," *Fritt Folk*, July 8, 1937.

207. *Norske aviser 1763–1969*, p. 435, passim.

208. *Fritt Folk*, July 8, 1937.

209. Norway, Det Statistiske Centralbyrå, *Kommunevalgene og ordførervalgene 1937* (Oslo: H. Aschehoug, 1938), p. 26, p. 58.

210. *Ibid.*, p. 12.

211. *Ibid.*

212. *Ibid.*, p. 58.

213. *Ibid.*, pp. 58–59; "Oslo-Seieren," *Arbeiderbladet*, October 20, 1937.

214. *Kommunevalgene og ordførervalgene 1937*, pp. 12–13.

Notes to Chapter VIII

1. Jon Hvitsund to Christian Knudsen, October 25, 1939, QA, Box 8, Quislings private korrespondanse folder.

2. Haldis Neegaard Østbye, "Vidkun Quisling," in *Boken om Quisling* (Oslo: Blix forlag, 1940), pp. 83–84.

3. Østbye, manuscript of a history of NS, deposited in QA. Hereafter cited as Østbye MS.

4. Anton Beinset, "Ukens portrett," *Dagbladet*, December 3, 1938.

5. Skodvin, *Striden om okkupasjonsstyret*, p. 40; Berit Nøkleby, "Fra november til april – Sendemann Bräuers personlige politikk," Samtidshistorisk forskningsgruppe, *1940 – Fra nøytral til okkupert*, Norge og den 2. verdenskrig, Series (Oslo: Universitetsforlaget, 1969), p. 54.

6. See for example K. H. to Quisling, November 11, 1939, QA, Box 13, Brev 1938–1939 folder.

7. Aadahl to Quisling, March 8, 1939, QA, Box 13, Brev 1938–39 folder.

8. Norland, *Hårde tider*, p. 300.

9. Copy of telegram from Quisling to Hitler, April 20, 1939, DA, Quislingsaken, Folder #12. The undated copy of the original is located in QA, Box 8, Quislings private korrespondanse folder.

10. Østbye, "Vidkun Quisling," *Boken om Quisling*, pp. 83–84.

11. Quisling, "Oslo valgte Marx og mammon! Men...," *Fritt Folk*, October 23, 1937.

12. *Ibid.*

13. *Ibid.*

14. Fuglesang to Herman Harris Aall,

October 29, 1937, DA, Aallsaken, Folder #4 – Korrespondanse med NS, Quisling og Hagelin før 9. april, document #1f.

15. *Ibid.*

16. *Ibid.*

17. Quisling, "Oslo valgte Marx og mammon! Men . . .," *Fritt Folk*, October 23, 1937.

18. Fuglesang to Aall, October 29, 1937, DA, Aallsaken, Folder #4 – Korrespondanse med NS, Quisling og Hagelin før 9, april, document #1f.

19. Østbye MS, QA.

20. Anne Ljøstad to Hjort, April 4, 1936, QA, Box 6, Oslo-Akershus folder.

21. *Straffesak*, p. 191.

22. *Ibid.*

23. Fuglesang to Aall, June 22, 1937, DA, Aallsaken, Folder #4 – Korrespondanse med NS, Quisling og Hagelin før 9. april, document #1d.

24. *Ibid.*

25. *Ibid.*

26. Fuglesang to Aall, October 29, 1937, DA, *ibid.*, document #1f.

27. Loock, *Quisling, Rosenberg und Terboven*, pp. 153–154.

28. Dora Bull to Aall, December 21, 1938, DA, Quislingsaken, Folder #12.

29. Bull to Aall, February 13, 1939, *ibid.*

30. *Ibid.*

31. *Straffesak*, p. 192.

32. "Fritt Folk. Kort oversikt over stillingen idag med forslag til nytt budgett for drift som ukeblad," Oslo, August 31, 1937, QA.

33. Th. Sørensen to Aall, May 11, 1937, DA, Aallsaken, Folder #4 – Korrespondanse med NS, Quisling og Hagelin før 9. april, document #1b.

34. "Fritt Folk. Kort oversikt over stillingen idag med forslag til nytt budgett for drift som ukeblad," Oslo, August 31, 1937, QA.

35. Østbye MS, QA.

36. *Ibid.*; Fuglesang to Aall, October 29, 1937, DA, Aallsaken, Folder #4 – Korrespondanse med NS, Quisling og Hagelin før 9. april, document #1f.

37. Østbye MS, QA; testimony of John Thronsen, August 24, 1945, *Straffesak*, p. 192.

38. Bull to Aall, February 13, 1939, DA, Quislingsaken, Folder #12.

39. Østbye MS, QA.

40. Quisling, "Slutt op om 'Fritt Folk'!," *Fritt Folk*, January 8, 1938.

41. *Norske aviser 1763–1969*, p. 182.

42. "Confidential contract" between Quisling and John Thronsen, April 1, 1938, QA.

43. Quisling, "Slutt op om 'Fritt Folk'!," *Fritt Folk*, January 8, 1938.

44. *Ibid.*

45. Ellen Schnitler to Quisling, November 22, 1937, QA, Box 9, Quislings private korrespondanse før 9. april folder.

46. Lunde to Quisling, June 8, 1938, QA, Box 8, Quislings private korrespondanse folder.

47. *Ibid.*; *NS årbok 1942*, p. 115.

48. Hilmar Knutsen to Quisling, January 18, 1938, QA, Box 8, Quislings private korrespondanse folder.

49. Schnitler to Quisling, November 22, 1937, QA, Box 9, Quislings private korrespondanse før 9. april folder.

50. Fuglesang, minutes of the NS Council meeting for February 5, 1939, DA, Quislingsaken, Folder #12.

51. *Ibid.*

52. Bull to Aall, December 21, 1938, DA, Quislingsaken, Folder #12; Bull to Aall, February 13, 1939, DA, Quislingsaken, Folder #12.

53. Bull to Aall, December 21, 1938, *ibid.*

54. Fuglesang, minutes of the NS Council meeting for February 5, 1939, DA, Quislingsaken, Folder #12.

55. Fuglesang to Aall, May 24, 1938, DA, Aallsaken, Folder #4 – Korrespondanse med NS, Quisling og Hageling før 9. april, docs. #1k, #11. Fuglesang sent two letters to Aall concerning this subject, both dated May 24, 1938.

56. Norway, Department of Justice, Oslo, July 28, 1938, Journal number 3106–38 K2.

57. Trygve Tellefsen to Quisling, March 12, 1938, QA, Box 6, 1938–39 folder.

58. *NS årbok 1942*, p. 52.

59. Ellef Ringnes to Aall, December 20, 1938, Riksarkivet, Herman Harris Aalls privatarkiv, Folder #16 – Diverse korrespondanse.

60. S. L. Lilleide to Quisling, November 31, 1938, QA, Box 7, Korrespondanse vedr. NS antibolsjevisme folder.

61. Ringnes to Aall, December 20, 1938, Riksarkivet, Herman Harris Aalls privatarkiv, Folder #16 – Diverse korrespondanse.

62. Bull to Aall, February 13, 1939, DA, Quislingsaken, Folder #12; Chr. Jøranli to Quisling, May 9, 1939, QA, Box 8, Quislings private korrespondanse folder.

63. Ringnes to Aall, December 20, 1938, Riksarkivet, Herman Harris Aalls privatarkiv, Folder #16 – Diverse korrespondanse; Bull to Aall, December 21, 1938, DA, Quislingsaken, Folder #12; Bull to Aall, February 13, 1939, DA, Quislingsaken, Folder #12.

64. Bull to Aall, December 21, 1938, *ibid.*

65. Sundlo to National Union, January 13, 1939, QA, Box 8, Quislings private korrespondanse folder.

66. Chr. Jøranli to Quisling, May 8, 1939, QA, Box 8, Quislings private korrespondanse folder.

67. Fuglesang, minutes of the NS Council meeting for February 5, 1939, DA, Quislingsaken, Folder #12; *NS årbok 1942*, p. 31.

68. Quisling, "Stornordisk Fredssamband," *Fritt Folk*, March 11, 1937.

69. *Ibid.*

70. *Ibid.*

71. Quisling, "Et Stor-nordisk verdenssamband," *Stornordisk Samband*, Vol. I, No. 1 (July 1938), p. 3.

72. Quisling, "A Nordic World Federation," *British Union Quarterly*, Vol. I, No. 1 (January-April 1937), pp. 87–101.

73. Editor's comment, *ibid.*, p. 87.

74. Quisling, "A Nordic World Federation," *ibid.*, p. 100.

75. *Ibid.*, pp. 100–101.

76. Fuglesang to Aall, February 11, 1938, DA, Aallsaken, Folder #4 – Korrespondanse med NS, Quisling og Hagelin før 9. april, document #1h.

77. Editorial statement, *Stornordisk Samband*, Vol. I, No. 1 (July 1938), p. 1.

78. J. F. C. Fuller, "Erobringen av røde Spania," *Stornordisk Samband*, Vol. II, No. 1 (1939), pp. 3–12.

79. Quisling to Aall, August 2, 1939, DA, Quislingsaken, Folder #12; Aall to Quisling, August 8, 1939, DA, Quislingsaken, Folder #12; Quisling to Aall, August 15, 1939, DA, Quislingsaken, Folder #12.

80. Quisling, "Skal vi ta parti eller være nøitral?," *Tidens Tegn*, December 23, 1937.

81. *Ibid.*

82. Quisling, "Samlingen av alle tyskere," *Fritt Folk*, March 19, 1938.

83. *Ibid.*

84. *Ibid.*

85. *Ibid.*

86. *Ibid.*

87. *Fritt Folk*, January 22, 1938.

88. Quisling, "Nasjonalismens seiersgang," *Fritt Folk*, April 9, 1938.

89. *Ibid.*

90. *Ibid.*

91. "Den ensrettede verdenspresse – og den samvittighetsløse krigsagitasjon," *Fritt Folk*, October 1, 1938.

92. *Fritt Folk*, December 10, 1938.

93. *Ibid.*

94. Quisling, "Norge trekkes inn i krigen! Vekk med krigspolitikerne. Vi vil fred!," *Fritt Folk*, October 1, 1938.

95. Quisling, "Forsvars-spørsmålets kjerne," *Fritt Folk*, March 4, 1939.

96. Ole Kristian Grimnes, *Overfall*, Vol. I of *Norge i krig. Fremmedåk og frihetskamp 1940–1945*, Magne Skodvin, ed. (Oslo: Aschehoug, 1984), p. 17, p. 71.

97. *Fritt Folk*, March 4, 1939.

98. Quisling, "Skal vi ta parti eller være nøitral?," *Tidens Tegn*, December 23, 1937.

99. "Utsyn," *Stornordisk Samband*, Vol. I, Nov. 3 (October-November 1938), p. 93.

100. Gustav Smedal to Quisling, April 22, 1938, QA, Box 8, Quislings private korrespondanse folder; Quisling to Smedal, October 22, 1938, QA, Box 8, Quislings private korrespondanse folder.

101. Quisling to Fritz Clausen, October 12, 1938, QA, Box 13, Brev 1938–39 folder.

102. Quisling, "Den anglo-jødiske 'allianse'," *Fritt Folk*, August 20, 1938.

103. *Ibid.*

104. "Zions Vises Protokoller," *Fritt Folk*, October 23, 1937.

105. As an example, *Fritt Folk* explained Fiorello La Guardia's condemnation of Hitler's persecution of German Jews by maintaining that La Guardia was not Italian, but

rather Jewish. "Italiensk avstamning," *Fritt Folk*, March 11, 1937.

106. R. Thuland to Quisling, November 11, 1938, QA, Box 8, Quislings private korrespondanse folder.

107. Thuland to Quisling, December 27, 1938, QA, Box 13, Brev 1938–39 folder.

108. Thuland to Quisling, November 25, 1938, QA, Box 8, Quislings private korrespondanse folder; Beinset, "Ukens Portrett," *Dagbladet*, December 3, 1938; Bull to Aall, February 13, 1939, DA, Quislingsaken, Folder #12.

109. Beinset, *ibid*.

110. Thuland to Quisling, November 25, 1938, QA, Box 8, Quislings private korrespondanse folder.

111. Resolution of February 7, 1939, quoted in Østbye MS, QA.

112. Hjort, "Tyskland og dets venner," *Ragnarok*, 1938, pp. 239 ff.; Wiesener, "Tyskvennlighet igjen," *Ragnarok*, 1938, pp. 242 ff.

113. Dahl, *et al.*, *Den norske nasjonalsosialismen*, p. 73.

114. Quisling to Aall, December 12, 1938, DA, Quislingsaken, Folder #12; Quisling to the police chief in Drammen, December 7, 1938, QA, Box 10, Brev m.v. 1930–1940 folder; Sundlo to Quisling, December 18, 1938, QA, Box 8, Quislings private korrespondanse folder.

115. Hilmar Hansen, report from Norwegian Front's board of directors to Quisling, May 30, 1939, QA, Box 6, 1938–39 folder.

116. *Ibid*.

117. Norway, Stortinget, *Stortingsforhandlinger 1938*, April 5, 1938, p. 633.

118. *Ibid*., pp. 633–634.

119. *Ibid*.

120. Paul M. Hayes' statement that extension of the *Storting* period from three to four years was "unquestionably illegal" must no doubt be based on a misreading of the appropriate constitutional provisions. See Hayes, *Quisling: The Career and Political Ideas of Vidkun Quisling, 1887–1945*, pp. 121–122.

121. "Selvvalgt," *Dagbladet*, April 2, 1938; Arne Bergsgård, "Stortinget," *Dagbladet*, June 12, 1945.

122. *Stortingsforhandlinger 1938*, p. 633.

123. Quisling, "Stortingets statskupp," *Fritt Folk*, April 9, 1938.

124. *Ibid*.

125. Quisling, "Kampen mellem folket og partiveldet," *Fritt Folk*, February 18, 1939; Østbye to Aall, April 7, 1938, Riksarkivet, Herman Harris Alls privatarkiv, Plukk som er usorterte folder.

126. Quisling, "Vil Kongen nekte å åpne det ulovlige Storting?," *Fritt Folk*, December 2, 1939; *Straffesak*, p. 411.

127. Fuglesang, minutes of the NS Council meeting of February 5, 1939, DA, Quislingsaken, Folder #12.

128. Quisling, "Kampen mellem folket og partiveldet," *Fritt Folk*, February 18, 1939.

129. Quisling to Aall, August 15, 1939, DA, Quislingsaken, Folder #12.

130. Fuglesang to Aall, May 15, 1939, DA, Aallsaken, Folder #4 – Korrespondanse med NS, Quisling og Hagelin før 9. april, document #1p.

131. Quisling to Aall, August 15, 1939, DA, Quislingsaken, Folder #12.

132. Quisling, "Vil Kongen nekte å åpne det ulovlige Storting?," *Fritt Folk*, December 2, 1939.

133. Norway, Eidsivating Lagstols Landssvikavdeling, *Redegjørelse fra Vidkun Quisling i siktelse fremsatt i Olso Forhørsrett* (Oslo: 1945), p. 4.

134. Quisling, "Kampen mellem folket og partiveldet," *Fritt Folk*, February 18, 1939.

135. *Ibid*.

136. Fuglesang to Aall, May 24, 1938, DA, Aallsaken, Folder #4 – Korrespondanse med NS, Quisling og Hagelin før 9. april, document #11.

137. *Ibid*.

138. Anna Stang Havstad to Quisling, March 2, 1939, QA, Box 13, Brev 1938–39 folder.

139. Fuglesang to Aall, May 15, 1939, DA, Aallsaken, Folder #4 – Korrespondanse med NS, Quisling og Hagelin før 9. april, document #1p.

140. *Straffesak*, pp. 273–274, pp. 239–240.

141. *Ibid*., p. 274.

142. *Ibid*.

143. *Ibid*., p. 275.

144. Jøranli to Quisling, May 4, 1938,

QA, Box 11, NS-anliggender 1936–38 folder.

Notes to Chapter IX

1. QA, Box 7, Avisutklipp, brosjyrer, og korr. 1930–37 folder.
2. *Ibid.*; QA, Box 4, NS korrespondanse 1933–36 folder.
3. Max Pferdekämper to Heinrich Himmler, November 19, 1932, quoted in Hartmann, *Fører uten folk*, pp. 225–226.
4. Pferdekämper to Quisling, December 23, 1930, QA, Box 7, Avisutklipp, brosjyrer, og korr. 1930–37 folder.
5. Ludendorff Volkswarte-Verlag to Quisling, December 17, 1930, QA, Box 7, Avisutklipp, brosjyrer og korr. 1930–37 folder; Pferdekämper to Himmler, November 19, 1932, in Hartmann, *Fører uten folk*, pp. 225–226.
6. Pferdekämper to Himmler, November 19, 1932, *ibid.*
7. *Ibid.*
8. Pferdekämper to Himmler, December 13, 1932, Riksarkivet, police reports sorted by archivist Rolf Haffner, report #510.
9. Dr. Hans Keller to Quisling, May 17, 1935, QA, Box 4, Privat folder; Quisling to Keller, May 27, 1935, QA, Box 4, Privat folder.
10. Paul Wurm, for *Der Stürmer*, to Quisling, August 24, 1935, QA, Box 8, Quislings private korrespondanse folder.
11. Skodvin, *Striden om okkupasjonsstyret*, p. 24.
12. *Straffesak*, p. 139; Skodvin, *ibid.*
13. Skodvin, *ibid.*; Loock, *Quisling, Rosenberg und Terboven*, pp. 187–188.
14. Loock is somewhat in error when he identifies Aall as a historian. Although Aall wrote on historical subjects, he was not formally trained as a historian. See *Quisling, Rosenberg und Terboven*, p. 69.
15. Aall to Quisling, April 17, 1935, with an appended "plan for an inter–Germanic and Nordic daily published by National Union, Oslo," QA, Box 4, NS korrespondanse 1933–36 folder.
16. *Ibid.*

17. Aall to Quisling, April 17, 1935, QA, Box 4, NS korrespondanse 1933–36 folder.
18. Charles Stangeland to Aall, December 25, 1936, DA, Aallsaken, Folder #1 – Diverse før opprettelsen av Malmösentralen, document #2e.
19. Aall to Hans Dräger, November 16, 1937, DA, Aallsaken, Folder #1 – Diverse før opprettelsen av Malmösentralen.
20. Police interrogation of Fermann, June 8, 1945, Riksarkivet, Haffner compilation, document #32.
21. Aall to Th. Sørensen, May 20, 1937, DA, Aallsaken, Folder #4 – Korrespondanse med N.S., Quisling og Hagelin før 9. april, document #1c.
22. Fermann to Aall, December 29, 1938, Riksarkivet, Hermann Harris Aalls privatarkiv, Korrespondanse 1937–1942 folder.
23. Ellef Ringnes to Aall, December 20, 1938, Riksarkivet, Herman Harris Aalls privatarkiv, Folder #16 – Diverse korrespondanse.
24. Hartmann, *Fører uten folk*, p. 14; Victor Mogens, *Tyskerne, Quisling og vi andre* (Oslo: Utenriks-forlaget, 1945), p. 62.
25. Loock, *Quisling, Rosenberg und Terboven*, p. 195.
26. *Ibid.*
27. Fermann to National Union, December 20, 1938, QA, Box 7, Korr. vedr. NS antibolsjevisme folder; Loock, *ibid.*, p. 196.
28. Loock, *ibid.*
29. Fermann to National Union, December 20, 1938, QA, Box 7, Korr. vedr. NS antibolsjevisme folder.
30. Quisling, "Opfordring," appended to Quisling's letter to Fermann, January 5, 1939, QA, Box 7, Korr. vedr. NS antibolsjevisme folder.
31. *Ibid.*
32. Quisling to the Fichtebund, January 28, 1939, QA, Box 8, Quislings private korrespondanse folder.
33. Quisling to Franco, February 28, 1939, QA, Box 6, 1938–39 folder.
34. Quisling to Hitler, April 20, 1939, DA, Quislingsaken, Folder #12. An undated copy is located in QA, Box 8, Quislings private korrespondanse folder.

35. Quisling to Aall, April 22, 1939, DA, Quislingsaken, Folder #12.

36. Quisling to Aall, March 8, 1939, *ibid.*

37. F. Pampanzano to Quisling, March 6, 1939, QA, Box 6, 1938–39 folder.

38. Skodvin, *Striden om okkupasjonsstyret*, p. 24.

39. *Ibid.*, p. 40.

40. Nøkleby, "Fra november til april – sendemann Bräuers personlige politikk," *1940 – Fra nøytral til okkupert*, pp. 54–55.

41. Fermann to Aall, December 29, 1938, Riksarkivet, Herman Harris Aalls privatarkiv, Korrespondanse 1937–1942 folder.

42. Fermann to Aall, March 7, 1939, *ibid.*

43. Thronsen to Fermann, May 10, 1939, DA, Aallsaken, Folder #4 – Korrespondanse med NS, Quisling og Hagelin før 9. april folder, document #1n.

44. Quisling to Aall, January 31, 1939, DA, Quislingsaken, Folder #12.

45. Quisling, "Opfordring," appended to Quisling's letter to Fermann, January 5, 1939, QA, Box 7, Korr. vedr. NS antibolsjevisme folder.

46. Fuglesang to Aall, October 29, 1937, DA, Aallsaken, Folder #4 – Korrespondanse med NS, Quisling og Hagelin før 9. april, document #1f.

47. Quisling to Aall, January 31, 1939, DA, Quislingsaken, Folder #12.

48. Quisling to Aall, March 8, 1939, *ibid.*

49. Quisling to Aall, April 12, 1939, *ibid.*

50. Quisling to Aall, April 22, 1939, *ibid.*

51. *Ibid.*

52. Aall to Quisling, February 1, 1939, QA, Box 10, Brev m.v. 1930–1940 folder.

53. Skodvin, *Striden om okkupasjonsstyret*, p. 24.

54. Aall to Quisling, February 1, 1939, QA, Box 10, Brev m.v. 1930–1940 folder; Loock, *Quisling, Rosenberg und Terboven*, p. 188.

55. Police interrogation of Ellef Ringnes, July 17, 1945, DA, Quislingsaken, Folder #12; *Straffesak*, p. 192.

56. Ringnes to Aall, May 27, 1937, Riksarkivet, Herman Harris Aalls privatarkiv, Korrespondanse 1937–1942 folder;

Ringnes to Aall, December 20, 1938; Riksarkivet, Herman Harris Aalls privatarkiv, Folder #16 – Diverse korrespondanse; Fermann to Aall, February 22, 1939, QA, Box 8, Quislings private korrespondanse folder; Fermann to Aall, February 27, 1939, QA, Box 11, NS-anliggender 1936–38 folder.

57. Ringnes to Aall, May 27, 1937, Riksarkivet, Herman Harris Aalls privatarkiv, Korrespondanse 1937–1942 folder.

58. Ringnes to Aall, December 20, 1938, Riksarkivet, Herman Harris Aalls privatarkiv, Folder #16 – Diverse korrespondanse; Police interrogation of Ringnes, July 17, 1945, DA, Quislingsaken, Folder #12.

59. Ringnes to Aall, December 20, 1938, *ibid.*; Aall to Quisling, March 1, 1939, QA, Box 8, Quislings private korrespondanse folder.

60. For Ringnes' contact with the Propaganda Ministry, see Ringnes to Aall, May 27, 1937, Riksarkivet, Herman Harris Aalls privatarkiv, Korrespondanse 1937–1942 folder; Ringnes to Ernst Züchner, Riksarkivet, Herman Harris Aalls privatarkiv, Korrespondanse 1937–1942 folder; Ellef Ringnes, *Bak okkupasjonens kulisser* (Oslo: Heim og Samfund, 1950), p. 13.

61. Norway, Department of Justice and Police, *Om landssvikoppgjøret* (Oslo: 1962), p. 131. Loock states that Hagelin was born a number of years later, in 1888. See *Quisling, Rosenberg und Terboven*, p. 196.

62. Loock, *ibid.*

63. Police interrogation of Hagelin, June 5, 1945, Riksarkivet, Haffner compilation, document #28.

64. Hagelin to Quisling, July 18, 1937, QA, Box 11, Lykkønskninger 1917–1937 folder.

65. Police interrogation of Herman Harris Aall, February 27, 1947, DA, Aallsaken, Folder #19 – Rapporter.

66. Quisling to Hagelin, April 19, 1939, DA, Offentlig Straffesak mot Albert Viljam Hagelin, "Tilleggsutdrag i offentlig straffesak mot Albert Viljam Hagelin," stenciled manuscript (Oslo: n.d.), p. 1.

67. Fermann to Aall, January 29, 1939, Riksarkivet, Herman Harris Aalls privatarkiv, Korrespondanse 1937–1942 folder; Aall to Quisling, February 1, 1939, QA, Box 10, Brev m.v. 1930–1940 folder.

68. Loock, *Quisling, Rosenberg und Terboven*, p. 162.

69. Skodvin, *Striden om okkupasjonsstyret*, p. 24.

70. Loock, *Quisling, Rosenberg und Terboven*, pp. 165–168.

71. *Ibid.*, pp. 171–175, 181–186.

72. *Ibid.*, p. 197.

73. *Ibid.*

74. *Ibid.*, pp. 197–198. See also Skodvin, *Striden om okkupasjonsstyret*, pp. 24–25.

75. Skodvin, *ibid.*, pp. 24–25, p. 39.

76. Fermann to Aall, January 29, 1939, Riksarkivet, Herman Harris Aalls privatarkiv, Korrespondanse 1937–1942 folder.

77. Skodvin, *Striden om okkupasjonsstyret*, p. 26.

78. Hartmann, *Fører uten folk*, p. 20. Hartmann quotes the autobiographical data supplied by Quisling on pp. 20–23.

79. Skodvin, *Striden om okkupasjonsstyret*, p. 348, fn. 65; Loock, *Quisling, Rosenberg und Terboven*, p. 199.

80. Loock, *ibid.*, pp. 199–200; Skodvin, *ibid.*, p. 25.

81. Skodvin, *ibid.*, p. 26, p. 348, fn. 64.

82. Police interrogation of Aall, February 27, 1947, DA, Aallsaken, Folder #19 – Rapporter; Loock, *Quisling, Rosenberg und Terboven*, p. 200.

83. Excerpt from Rettsbok for Oslo Forhørsrett, Forhørsrettssak nr. 10272/46, May 11, 1946, Riksarkivet, Herman Harris Aalls privatarkiv.

84. Police interrogation of Aall, February 27, 1947, DA, Aallsaken, Folder #19 – Rapporter; Hartmann, *Fører uten folk*, p. 25.

85. Hartmann, *ibid.*, p. 36.

86. "Die Organisation der Zentrale in Malmö," signed by drs. De La Roche, Alwaz, and Hohenstein, June 8, 1939, DA, Aallsaken, Folder 2A – "Malmösentralen."

87. See Harmann, *Fører uten folk*, pp. 32 ff.

88. Police interrogation of Aall, February 27, 1947, DA, Aallsaken, Folder #19 – Rapporter.

89. Police interrogation of Gerdt August Wagner, February 17, 1947, DA, Aallsaken, Folder #19 – Rapporter; Record of payments made by the "Malmö central," DA, Aallsaken, Folder #3 – "Malmösentralen."

90. For a record of Aall's activity in Sweden, see DA, Aallsaken, Folder #2a – "Malmösentralen."

91. Hippel's statement of December 13, 1948, quoted in Hartmann, *Fører uten folk*, pp. 287–288, fn. 12; Rettsbok for Oslo Forhørsrett, Forhørsrettssak nr. 10272/46, May 11, 1946, Riksarkivet, Herman Harris Aalls privatarkiv, Korrespondanse 1940–1943 folder; Police interrogation of Aall, February 27, 1947, DA, Aallsaken, Folder #19 – Rapporter.

92. Police interrogation of Aall, February 27, 1947, *ibid.*

93. *Straffesak*, p. 215.

94. Hagelin to Aall, June 5, 1939, DA, Fermannsaken, Folder #23, document #9a.

95. Quisling to Aall, June 6, 1939, DA, Quislingsaken, Folder #12.

96. Aall to Hagelin, n.d. (probably June 6, 1939), DA, Fermannsaken, Folder #23, document #9a. Aall noted this brief message on the same letter he had received from Hagelin dated June 5. See above, footnote #94.

97. Hartmann, *Fører uten folk*, p. 47, p. 288, fn. 12.

98. See Erwin Lahousen's letter to Sverre Hartmann, October 4, 1947, in *ibid.*, pp. 292–293.

99. Quisling to Aall, July 19, 1939, DA, Quislingsaken, Folder #12; Quisling to Aall, August 2, 1939, DA, Quislingsaken, Folder #12; Aall to Quisling, August 8, 1939, DA, Quislingsaken, Folder #12; Quisling to Aall, August 15, 1939, DA, Quislingsaken, Folder #12.

100. Aall to Quisling, July 15, 1939, QA, Box 8, Quislings private korrespondanse folder; Quisling's receipts dated August 16, September 18, October 17, and November 10, 1939, DA, Aallsaken, Folder #3 – "Malmösentralen."

101. Police interrogation of Aall, February 27, 1947, DA, Aallsaken, Folder #19 – Rapporter. In Hippel's account of the meeting of June 9, only he, Quisling, and Hagelin are mentioned as being present. In another statement, occurring at an even earlier date than that which he made to the police on February 27, 1947, Aall similarly confirmed that Quisling had received 15,000

kroner in December 1939 so that he would work for "social individualism" through the press. See Rettsbok for Oslo Forhørsrett, Forhørsrettssak nr. 10272/46, May 11, 1946, Riksarkivet, Herman Harris Aalls privatarkiv, Korrespondanse 1940–1943 folder.

102. Loock, *Quisling, Rosenberg und Terboven*, pp. 200–201.

103. *Straffesak*, p. 212, p. 341.

104. Scheidt to Rosenberg, June 16, 1939, DA, Quislingsaken, Folder #7 – Straffesak – Etterforskning mot Quisling; Loock, *Quisling, Rosenberg und Terboven*, p. 201.

105. Loock, *ibid.*, p. 165.

106. Scheidt to Rosenberg, June 16, 1939, DA, Quislingsaken, Folder #7 – Straffesak – Etterforskning mot Quisling.

107. *Ibid.*

108. *Ibid.*

109. Police interrogation of Fermann, June 8, 1945, Riksarkivet, police reports, Haffner compilation, document #32.

110. *Straffesak*, p. 212, p. 342.

111. Police interrogation of Fermann, June 8, 1945, Riksarkivet, police reports, Haffner compilation, document #32.

112. Skodvin, *Striden om okkupasjonsstyret*, p. 26.

113. Arno Schickedanz to Hans-Heinrich Lammers, June 24, 1939, QA.

114. Quisling to Aall, June 28, 1939, DA, Quislingsaken, Folder #12.

115. *Ibid.*

116. *Ibid.*; Quisling to Aall, July 19, 1939, *ibid.*

117. Quisling to Aall, August 15, 1939, *ibid.*

118. Aall to Quisling, July 15, 1939, QA, Box 8, Quislings private korrespondanse folder; Quisling to Aall, July 19, 1939, DA, Quislingsaken, Folder #12; DA, Aallsaken, index to Folder #3–"Malmösentralen," items number 14, 15, 17, and 19.

119. Skodvin, *Striden om okkupasjonsstyret*, p. 27.

120. Loock, *Quisling, Rosenberg und Terboven*, p. 202.

121. Skodvin, *Striden om okkupasjonsstyret*, p. 27.

122. Loock, *Quisling, Rosenberg und Terboven*, pp. 202–203

123. Skodvin, *Striden om okkupasjonsstyret*, p. 27; Loock, *ibid.*, p. 203.

124. Loock, *ibid.*

125. *Ibid.*, pp. 202–203.

126. Skodvin, *Striden om okkupasjonsstyret*, pp. 27–28.

127. *Ibid.*, pp. 28–29.

128. Rosenberg, "Den politiske forberedelse til Norgesaksjonen," *Straffesak*, p. 28.

129. Quisling to Scheidt, July 24, 1939, DA, Quislingsaken, Folder #7 – Straffesak – Etterforskning mot Quisling; Police interrogation of Ralph Haldor Fossum, police reports, Haffner compilation, document #218; Fuglesang, testimony, August 24, 1945, *Straffesak*, pp. 190–191.

130. Loock, *Quisling, Rosenberg und Terboven*, p. 203.

131. Rosenberg, "Den politiske forberedelse til Norgesaksjonen," June 15, 1940, *Straffesak*, p. 28.

132. Loock, *Quisling, Rosenberg und Terboven*, pp. 203–204.

133. Quisling to Aall, September 18, 1939, Riksarkivet, Herman Harris Aalls privatarkiv, Løse dok. folder.

134. *Ibid.*

135. Police interrogation of Aall, February 27, 1947, DA, Aallsaken, Folder #19 – Rapporter; Quisling to Neville Chamberlain, October 11, 1939, DA, Quislingsaken, Folder #15.

136. Quisling to Chamberlain, October 11, 1939, *ibid.*

137. The British Legation, Oslo, to Quisling, October 21, 1939, *Straffesak*, p. 491.

138. Knudsen, *Jeg var Quislings sekretær*, p. 112; Ringnes, *Bak okkupasjonens kulisser*, p. 30.

139. For Quisling's private expressions of doubt concerning the Nazi-Soviet Pact, see Quisling to Aall, September 18, 1939, Riksarkivet, Herman Harris Aalls privatarkiv, Løse dok. folder; Skodvin, *Striden om okkupasjonsstyret*, p. 41.

140. Quisling, "Innkretsningspolitikken brutt," *Fritt Folk*, September 2, 1939.

141. Fr. Sejersted to Quisling, January 10, 1940, QA, Box 7, Korrespondanse vedr. NS antibolsjevisme folder.

142. Loock, *Quisling, Rosenberg und Terboven*, p. 218; Quisling's testimony, August 21, 1945, *Straffesak*, p. 64.

143. Skodvin, *Striden om okkupasjonsstyret*, p. 41.

144. Nøkleby, "Fra november til april – sendemann Bräuers personlige politikk," *1940 – Fra nøytral til okkupert*, p. 21; Skodvin, *ibid.*; Knut Johansen to the Attorney General (*Riksadvokaten*), June 4, 1945, DA, Quislingsaken, Folder #7 – Straffesak – Etterforskning mot Quisling.

145. Noack, report of December 8, 1939, in Ulrich Noack, *Norwegen zwischen Friedensvermittlung und Fremdherrschaft* (Krefeld: Verlag Aufbau der Mitte, 1952), p. 36.

146. Noack, "Bericht über die antirussischen Pläne Quislings," quoted in Skodvin, *Striden om okkupasjonsstyret*, p. 42.

147. Skodvin, *ibid.*

148. *Ibid.*; Quisling's testimony, September 7, 1945, *Straffesak*, p. 344.

149. According to Skodvin, *ibid.*, the first long discussion between Noack and Quisling occurred on December 4. The second followed on December 8, when Quisling, with Noack's help, drew up the details of his plan in German.

150. Quisling to Aall, December 5, 1939, in Hayes, *Quisling*, p. 159.

151. Quisling to Aall, December 7, 1939, in *ibid.*

152. Police interrogation of Aall, February 27, 1947, DA, Aallsaken, Folder #19 – Rapporter.

153. *Ibid.*

154. Skodvin, *Striden om okkupasjonsstyret*, p. 63.

155. *Ibid.*, pp. 67–68.

156. Excerpt from Schreiber's statement of May 5, 1946, in Loock, *Quisling, Rosenberg und Terboven*, p. 219. See also Skodvin, *ibid.*, p. 68.

157. Loock, *ibid.*

158. Skodvin, *Striden om okkupasjonsstyret*, p. 69.

159. Raeder to Vice-Admiral Kurt Assmann, January 10, 1944, quoted in *Straffesak*, p. 64. Also quoted in Carl-Axel Gemzell, *Raeder, Hitler und Skandinavien. Der Kampf für einen maritimen Operationsplan*, Bibliotheca Historica Lundensis, Vol. XVI (Lund, Sweden: Gleerups, 1965), p. 270, fn. 14.

160. See Loock, *Quisling, Rosenberg und Terboven*, p. 219, fn. 59.

161. Hermann Boehm, *Norwegen zwischen England und Deutschland. Die*

Zeit vor und während des Weltkrieges (Lippoldsberg: Klosterhaus Verlag, 1956), p. 52.

162. Rosenberg, diary entry of December 11, 1939, in Hans-Günther Seraphim, ed., *Das politische Tagebuch Alfred Rosenbergs aus den Jahren 1934/35 und 1939/40* (Göttingen: Musterschmidt Verlag, 1956), p. 91. Hereafter cited as *Tagebuch*. Abbreviated Norwegian translation in *Straffesak*, p. 36.

163. Rosenberg, diary entry of December 11, 1939, *ibid.*; Skodvin, *Striden om okkupasjonsstyret*, p. 30.

164. Rosenberg, diary entry of December 11, 1939, *ibid.*

165. *Ibid.*

166. Scheidt to Rosenberg, July 15, 1939, quoted in Skodvin, *Striden om okkupasjonsstyret*, p. 27; Hagelin to Scheidt, July 12, 1939, quoted in Skodvin, p. 28; Hagelin to Schickedanz, November 26, 1939, quoted in Loock, *Quisling, Rosenberg und Terboven*, p. 220.

167. Rosenberg, diary entry of December 11, 1939, in Seraphim, *Tagebuch*, p. 91; Quisling's testimony, August 21, 1945, *Straffesak*, p. 65. Hans Dietrich Loock presents the viewpoint that the navy was responsible for Quisling's journey to Germany in December 1939, and that Rosenberg's organization did not play any significant role in this context. See Loock, *Quisling, Rosenberg und Terboven*, p. 204, pp. 218–221. This interpretation is open to question. It appears instead that Rosenberg's Office of Foreign Affairs and the naval high command found each other in a matter of mutual interest, and they cooperated accordingly.

168. Protocol of the meeting in the naval high command, 12:00 noon, December 11, 1939, DA, Quislingsaken, Folder #7 – Straffesak – Etterforskning mot Quisling.

169. Hagelin to Schickedanz, November 20, 1939, quoted in Loock, *Quisling, Rosenberg und Terboven*, p. 220.

170. Protocol of the meeting in the naval high command, 12:00 noon, December 11, 1939, DA, Quislingsaken, Folder #7 – Straffesak – Etterforskning mot Quisling.

171. *Ibid.*

172. *Ibid.*

173. Rosenberg, diary entry of December 11, 1939, in *Straffesak*, p. 36. In the Seraphim edition of Rosenberg's diary the

major portion of the entry which deals with Raeder's reaction to Quisling's proposals and the upcoming meeting with Hitler is described as having been destroyed.

174. Raeder's conference with Hitler, December 12, 1939, printed in *Straffesak*, p. 38.

175. *Ibid.*

176. *Ibid.*

177. *Ibid.*

178. *Ibid.*

179. Rosenberg, diary entry of December 14, 1939, in *Straffesak*, p. 36.

180. *Ibid.*

181. Rosenberg's memorandum concerning the "visit of Minister Quisling – Norway," appended to Rosenberg's letter to Raeder, December 13, 1939, printed in *Straffesak*, p. 39.

182. *Ibid.*

183. *Ibid.*

184. *Ibid.*

185. *Ibid.*

186. Rosenberg to Raeder, December 13, 1939, DA, Quislingsaken, Folder #7 – Straffesak – Etterforskning mot Quisling.

187. Rosenberg, diary entry of December 14, 1939, in Seraphim, *Tagebuch*, p. 93.

188. Raeder to Vice-Admiral Kurt Assmann, January 10, 1944, in *Straffesak*, p. 51.

189. Loock, *Quisling, Rosenberg und Terboven*, pp. 223–224.

190. Rosenberg, diary entry of December 19, 1939, in Seraphim, *Tagebuch*, pp. 93–94.

191. *Ibid.*, p. 94.

192. General Alfred Jodl, diary entry, December 13, 1939, quoted in Loock, *Quisling, Rosenberg und Terboven*, p. 224; Raeder's memo to Vice-Admiral Kurt Assmann, January 10, 1944, in *Straffesak*, p. 51. The discrepancy between Jodl's date of entry and Quisling's visit on the 14th appears to be due to Jodl's failure to use the correct date. See Gemzell, *Raeder, Hitler und Skandinavien*, pp. 273–274, fn. 22; and Loock, pp. 223–224, fn. 78.

193. Nøkleby, "Fra november to april – sendemann Bräuers personlige politikk," *1940 – Fra nøytral til okkupert*, p. 22, p. 30.

194. *Ibid.*, pp. 55–56.

195. Skodvin, *Striden om okkupasjonsstyret*, p. 42; Nøkleby, *ibid.*, p. 56.

196. Skodvin, *ibid.*, p. 43

197. *Ibid.*, p. 34.

198. Skodvin, *Striden om okkupasjonsstyret*, pp. 43–44.

199. *Ibid.*, p. 44.

200. The exact chronology of Quisling's stay in Berlin, including his two meetings with Hitler, is difficult to establish because of the lack of consistency in German sources. The author has relied mainly on Rosenberg's diary entries, which were made at the time of the visit, plus Rosenberg's and Raeder's correspondence.

201. Rosenberg, diary entry of December 19, 1939, Seraphim, *Tagebuch*, p. 94.

202. *Ibid.*

203. Skodvin, *Striden om okkupasjonsstyret*, p. 34.

204. Schickedanz, memorandum to Lammers of December 21, 1939, containing a summary of their conversation of December 19, Seraphim, *Tagebuch*, p. 163.

205. Skodvin, *Striden om okkupasjonsstyret*, p. 34.

206. Rosenberg, diary entry of December 20, 1939, Seraphim, *Tagebuch*, p. 94.

207. *Ibid.*, pp. 94–95.

Notes to Chapter X

1. Skodvin, *Striden om okkupasjonsstyret*, p. 45.

2. Rosenberg, diary entry of January 2, 1940, Seraphim, *Tagebuch*, p. 95.

3. Skodvin, *Striden om okkupasjonsstyret*, p. 47.

4. Rosenberg, diary entry of January 7, 1940, Seraphim, *Tagebuch*, p. 96.

5. Loock, *Quisling, Rosenberg und Terboven*, p. 228.

6. Hagelin, *Aktennotiz* to Rosenberg, January 13, 1940, Appendix 9 to Rosenberg's "Die politische Vorbereitung der Norwegen-Aktion," June 15, 1940, University of Oslo, Historical Institute, Skodvin Collection. Hereafter cited as HI, Skodvin Collection.

7. Skodvin, *Striden om okkupasjonsstyret*, p. 46.

8. *Ibid.*, pp. 46–47.

9. *Ibid.*, p. 47; Loock, *Quisling, Rosenberg und Terboven*, pp. 227–228.

10. Skodvin, *ibid.*

11. Interrogation of Joachim von Ribbentrop, Nuremberg, August 15, 1945, *Straffesak*, p. 635.

12. Skodvin, *Striden om okkupasjonsstyret*, p. 48.

13. Bräuer, report to the Foreign Ministry, January 18, 1940, Nøkleby, "Fra november til april – sendemann Bräuers personlige politikk," *1940 – Fra nøytral til okkupert*, p. 57.

14. Bräuer, report to Grundherr, January 23, 1940, quoted in Skodvin, *Striden om okkupasjonsstyret*, p. 49.

15. Skodvin, *ibid.*, pp. 49–51.

16. *Ibid.*, p. 32, p. 34.

17. *Ibid.*, p. 35.

18. Rosenberg, diary entry of January 7, 1940, Seraphim, *Tagebuch*, p. 96.

19. Loock, *Quisling, Rosenberg und Terboven*, p. 229.

20. See below, pp. 358–359, for coverage of the *Altmark* incident.

21. Rosenberg, diary entry, February 19, 1940, Seraphim, *Tagebuch*, p. 102.

22. Olav Riste, "War Comes to Norway," in Olav Riste, Magne Skodvin, and Johannes Andenæs, *Norway and the Second World War* (Oslo: Johan Grundt Tanum, 1966), pp. 38–39.

23. Keitel's order of January 27, 1939, in *Straffesak*, p. 51. The document, as printed in *Straffesak*, is incorrectly dated January 23, 1939.

24. Magne Skodvin, "Norge i stormaktspolitikken opp til 9. april: Litteraturoversyn," *Historisk Tidsskrift*, Vol. 36, No. 6 (1952–53), p. 665.

25. Riste, "War Comes to Norway," *Norway and the Second World War*, pp. 14–18.

26. Nøkleby, "Fra november til april – sendemann Bräuers personlige politikk," *1940 – Fra nøytral til okkupert*, p. 42.

27. Riste, "War Comes to Norway," *Norway and the Second World War*, p. 20; note from the British Legation in Oslo to the Norwegian Foreign Ministry, March 2, 1940, Sweden, Foreign Ministry, *Förspelet till det tyska angreppet på Danmark och Norge den 9 april 1940* (Stockholm: 1947), pp. 121–122.

28. Halvdan Koht, *For fred og fridom 1939–1940* (Oslo: Tiden Norsk Forlag, 1957), p. 181.

29. Riste, "War Comes to Norway," *Norway and the Second World War*, pp. 20–21.

30. Loock, *Quisling, Rosenberg und Terboven*, p. 250; Riste, *ibid.*, p. 41.

31. Riste, *ibid.*

32. *Ibid.*, p. 43.

33. Quoted in *ibid.*

34. Ole Kristian Grimnes, *Overfall*, Vol. I of *Norge i krig. Fremmedåk og frihetskamp 1940–1945*, Magne Skodvin, ed. (Oslo: Aschehoug, 1984), p. 56; Loock, *Quisling, Rosenberg und Terboven*, p. 256.

35. Grimnes, *ibid.*, pp. 54–55; Magne Skodvin, "Norge i stormaktsstrategien. Frå Finlands-freden til 'Wilfred,'" *1940 – Fra nøytral til okkupert*, pp. 119–120; Loock, *ibid.* pp. 241–242.

36. Loock, *ibid.*, p. 243; Riste, "War Comes to Norway," *Norway and the Second World War*, p. 25.

37. Norway, Stortinget, *Innstilling fra Undersøkelseskommisjonen av 1945*, Vol. I, appendices, Vol. II (Oslo: 1947), pp. 242–243. *Innstilling fra Undersøkelseskommisjonen av 1945* hereafter cited as *Innstilling.*

38. Koht, *For fred og fridom*, p. 209.

39. Sverre Steen, review of Magne Skodvin, *Striden om okkupasjonsstyret*, *Historisk Tidsskrift*, Vol. 38, No. 1 (1957–1958), p. 57.

40. Skodvin, *Striden om okkupasjonsstyret*, pp. 9–10.

41. Rosenberg, "Den politiske forberedelse av Norgesaksjonen," *Straffesak*, p. 30.

42. Skodvin, *Striden om okkupasjonsstyret*, pp. 37–39.

43. *Ibid.*, pp. 66–67.

44. *Ibid.*, pp. 69–70

45. Rosenberg, diary entries, February 19, March 3, March 6, 1940, Seraphim, *Tagebuch*, pp. 102–104.

46. Rosenberg, diary entries, January 7, February 19, 1940, *ibid.*, p. 96, p. 102; Scheidt, report of February 21, 1940, DA, Quislingsaken, Folder #7 – Straffesak – Etterforskning mot Quisling, document #4; Skodvin, *Striden om okkupasjonsstyret*, pp. 38–39.

47. Rosenberg, "Den politiske forberedelse av Norgesaksjonen," June 15, 1940, *Straffesak*, p. 29.

48. Rosenberg, diary entry, January 19,

1940, Seraphim, *Tagebuch*, p. 97; Scheidt, report of February 21, 1940, DA, Quislingsaken, Folder #7 – Straffesak – Etterforskning mot Quisling, document #4.

49. Loock, *Quisling, Rosenberg und Terboven*, p. 229. Nicolai Plesner, a witness at Quisling's treason trial, testified that he exchanged 8,000 pounds into Norwegian currency for Hagelin in the period before the invasion. See *Straffesak*, p. 179.

50. Scheidt, report of February 21, 1940, DA, Quislingsaken, Folder #7 Straffesak – Etterforskning mot Quisling, document #4.

51. "Slutt op om den eneste VIRKELIG NASJONALE avis i vårt land FRITT FOLK," *Fritt Folk*, January 13, 1940.

52. Quisling to Aall, January 17, 1940, Riksarkivet, Herman Harris Aalls privatarkiv, Løse dok. folder.

53. "Fritt Folks opplag 25000," *Fritt Folk*, January 20, 1940.

54. Scheidt, report of February 21, 1940, DA, Quislingsaken, Folder #7 – Straffesak, Etterforskning mot Quisling, document #4.

55. Rosenberg, "Den politiske forberedelse av Norgesaksjonen," June 15, 1940, *Straffesak*, p. 30.

56. Contract between A/S Nasjonale Pressebyrå, represented by John Thronsen, and Fabritius Rotasjonstrykkeri A/S, represented by Hroar Scheibler, March 14, 1940, DA, Quislingsaken, Folder #17.

57. *Straffesak*, pp. 192–193.

58. *Fritt Folk*, April 1, 1940, ff.

59. Police interrogation of John Thronsen, August 1, 1945, DA, Quislingsaken, Folder #17.

60. *Fritt Folk*, February 17, 1940.

61. Police interrogation of John Thronsen, August 1, 1945, DA, Quislingsaken, Folder #17. Thronsen did not reveal the specific number of positions this included.

62. Skodvin, "Historisk innleiing," *Om landssvikoppgjøret*, p. 15.

63. "Quislings nyttårshilsen til NS," *Fritt Folk*, January 13, 1940.

64. Quisling, "Norges stilling," *Fritt Folk*, March 9, 1940.

65. *Ibid.*

66. *Ibid.*

67. Skodvin, *Striden om okkupasjonsstyret*, pp. 76–77.

68. Police interrogation of Aall, June 9, 1945, Riksarkivet, Haffner compilation, document #34; Skodvin, *ibid.*, p. 76.

69. Skodvin, *ibid.*

70. Rosenberg, diary entry of April 9, 1940, Seraphim, *Tagebuch*, pp. 104–105; Skodvin, *ibid.*, p. 77.

71. Rosenberg, diary entry of April 9, 1940, *ibid.*

72. Skodvin, *Striden om okkupasjonsstyret*, p. 77.

73. Interrogation of General Keitel at Nuremberg, August 15, 1945, *Straffesak*, pp. 643–644; Sverre Hartmann, "Quislings konferanse med den tyske overkommando 3. april i København," *Samtiden*, Vol. 65 (1956) p. 319.

74. Skodvin, *Striden om okkupasjonsstyret*, p. 77.

75. *Ibid.*; Hartmann, "Quislings konferanse med den tyske overkommando," *Samtiden*, Vol. 65, p. 320.

76. Excerpt from Jodl's diary, April 4, 1940, Stortingsarkivet, Undersøkelseskommisjonen av 1945s arkiv, Box 11, envelope 25. Stortingsarkivet, Undersøkelseskommisjonen av 1945s arkiv, hereafter cited as UKs arkiv.

77. Hartmann, "Quislings konferanse med den tyske overkommando," *Samtiden*, Vol. 65, p. 320; interrogation of General Keitel at Nuremberg, August 15, 1945, *Straffesak*, p. 641.

78. Police interrogation of Quisling, June 4, 1945, Riksarkivet, Haffner compilation, document #22a; *Straffesak*, p. 93.

79. Danish police interrogation of Fritz Clausen, n.d., DA, Quislingsaken, Folder #17.

80. See Jodl's diary entry for April 4, 1940, Uks arkiv, Box 11, envelope 25; Keitel's Nuremberg interrogation, August 15, 1945, *Straffesak*, p. 643; Rosenberg, "Den politiske forberedelse av Norgesaksjonen," June 15, 1940, *Straffesak*, p. 31; Hans Piekenbrock, statement of April 2, 1956, cited by Hartmann in "Quislings konferanse med den tyske overkommando," *Samtiden*, Vol. 65, pp. 319 ff.

81. "Dagsorden for N.S. Rådsmøte, søndag, 7. april 1940," DA, Fermannsaken, Folder #23, document #22.

82. Koht, *For fred og fridom*, p. 213, p. 216.

83. *Ibid.*, pp. 202 ff. The question of whether or not the Nygaardsvold government, in particular Foreign Minister Koht, reacted responsibly to warnings of a possible German attack has been the subject of considerable controversy in Norway since the end of the war. For a recent discussion of this question, see Grimnes, *Overfall*, pp. 66–72.

84. Koht, *ibid.*, p. 217.

85. *Ibid.*, p. 219.

86. Skodvin, *Striden om okkupasjonsstyret*, p. 79.

87. Author's copy of Quisling's "Landsmenn" proclamation, April 8, 1940. The proclamation is quoted in its entirety in Skodvin, *ibid.*, pp. 79–80.

88. Erik Anker Steen, *Norges sjøkrig* (7 vols.; Oslo: Gyldendal Norsk Forlag, 1954–1969), Vol. II, pp. 54–62; Ragnvald Roscher Nielsen, "Krigen i Norge april-juni 1940," *Norges krig 1940–1945* (3 vols.; Oslo: Gyldendal Norsk Forlag, 1947–1950), Vol. I, pp. 114–119.

89. Koht, *For fred og fridom*, p. 222; Christensen, *Okkupasjonsår og etterkrigstid*, p. 166.

90. Loock, in *Quisling, Rosenberg und Terboven*, p. 281, has pushed the time for the events of the morning of April 9 forward by one hour in his account of (1) the time when the government first assembled, (2) the arrival of the German squadron at the narrows in the Oslo fjord at Oscarsborg, and (3) Bräuer's meeting with Koht. Loock apparently has set the time for these events according to German time rather than Norwegian time.

91. Koht, *For fred og fridom*, p. 223.

92. Nøkleby, "Fra november til april – sendemann Bräuers personlige politikk," *1940 – Fra nøytral til okkupert*, pp. 62–64.

93. German ultimatum, April 9, 1940, in *Innstilling*, Vol. I, appendices, Vol. I, pp. 43–48.

94. Koht, *For fred og fridom*, pp. 224–225.

95. Skodvin, "Historisk innleiing," *Om landssvikoppgjøret*, pp. 8–9; Steen, review of Skodvin's *Striden om okkupasjonsstyret*, *Historisk Tidsskrift*, Vol. 38, No. 1, pp. 57–58.

96. Steen, *ibid.*, pp. 58–59.

97. Statement by Hans Joachim von Neuhaus, former German legation counsel in Oslo, April 22, 1946, UKs arkiv, Box 3, envelope 3; Skodvin, *Striden om okkupasjonsstyret*, p. 86.

98. Skodvin, *ibid.*, p. 63, pp. 69–70.

99. *Ibid.*, p. 67.

100. *Ibid.*, p. 71.

101. Steen, review of Skodvin's *Striden om okkupasjonsstyret*, *Historisk Tiddsskrift*, Vol. 38, No. 1, p. 60.

102. Skodvin, *Striden om okkupasjonsstyret*, p. 81.

103. *Ibid.*, p. 71.

104. *Ibid.*; Loock, *Quisling, Rosenberg und Terboven*, p. 285.

105. Police interrogation of Harald Franklin Knudsen, June 16, 1945, Riksarkivet, Haffner compilation, document #50.

106. Håkon Meyer, "9. april og Quislings statskupp," *Samtiden*, Vol. 81, No. 7 (1972), p. 452.

107. Skodvin, *Striden om okkupasjonsstyret*, p. 83.

108. Police interrogation of Harald Franklin Knudsen, June 16, 1945, Riksarkivet, Haffner compilation, document #50; Knudsen's testimony, August 24, 1945, *Straffesak*, pp. 194–196.

109. Knudsen's testimony, *ibid.*, p. 195.

110. Skodvin, *Striden om okkupasjonsstyret*, p. 72, p. 83.

111. Testimony of Bernhard Øivind Salbu, August 23, 1945, *Straffesak*, p. 169.

112. Knudsen, *Jeg var Quislings sekretær*, p. 128.

113. Skodvin, *Striden om okkupasjonsstyret*, p. 82.

114. Testimony of Gerhard Berghold, August 23, 1945, *Straffesak*, p. 146.

115. Quoted in Skodvin, *Striden om okkupasjonsstyret*, p. 72.

116. Quisling's testimony, August 21, 1945, *Straffesak*, p. 82.

117. Quisling's testimony, August 21, 1945, *ibid.*; Quisling's defense summation, September 7, 1945, *Straffesak*, p. 353.

118. *Straffesak*, pp. 82–83.

119. Testimony of Bjarne Knudsen, August 25, 1945, *ibid.*, p. 220.

120. *Ibid.*, p. 221; Skodvin, *Striden om okkupasjonsstyret*, p. 83.

121. Testimony of Colonel Hans Sommerfeldt Hiorth, August 23, 1945, *Straffesak*, pp. 154–155. The exact time of Quis-

ling's phone call to Elverum, like many of his actions on April 9, is difficult to determine. Skodvin surmises that the conversation with Colonel Hiorth at Elverum occurred as late as between 9:00 and 10:00 p.m., which was after Quisling had publicly proclaimed himself prime minister over the radio. Skodvin assumes this to be true because the Nygaardsvold government did not leave Hamar for Elverum until just before 8:00 p.m. See Skodvin, *Striden om okkupasjonsstyret*, pp. 101–102. However, already at the first *Storting* meeting held at Hamar, which began at 1:00 p.m., the announcement was made that the government and *Storting* might soon have to move to Elverum in order to avoid German capture. It is quite possible that Quisling, through contacts in the Defense Ministry or elsewhere, might have learned that such a move was contemplated, the confusion being what it was at the time. The war had not yet taught Norwegians the necessity of secrecy. Oslo radio on the morning of April 9 had announced the government's move to Hamar, giving the Germans full knowledge of its whereabouts. Furthermore, Colonel Hiorth based his conclusion that Quisling's call occurred between 5:00 and 6:00 p.m. not only on his own recollection, but also on the confirmation which he received from the officers who served with him at the time.

122. "Norsk politikk 9. april – 7. juni 1940," *Innstilling*, Vol. I, appendices, Vol. II, appendix no. 8, p. 260.

123. Skodvin, *Striden om okkupasjonsstyret*, p. 84.

124. Grimnes, *Overfall*, p. 110.

125. *Ibid.*; Skodvin, *Striden om okkupasjonsstyret*, pp. 84–85.

126. Testimony of Gerhard Berghold, August 23, 1945, *Straffesak*, p. 146; Skodvin, *ibid.*, p. 86.

127. Loock, *Quisling, Rosenberg und Terboven*, p. 288.

128. Skodvin, *Striden om okkupasjonsstyret*, pp. 85–86.

129. Quisling's radio proclamation of 7:32 p.m., April 9, 1940, *Aftenposten*, morning edition, April 10, 1940, in Norway, Eidsivating lagstols landssvikavdeling, *Dokumenter i offentlig straffesak mot Vidkun Quisling* (Oslo: 1945), pp. 22–23.

130. Quisling's radio proclamation of

10:00 p.m., April 9, 1940, Norway, Eidsivating lagstols landssvikavdeling, *Dokumenter i offentlig straffesak mot Vidkun Quisling*, Tillegshefte II (Oslo: 1945), pp. 4–5. See also Skodvin, *Striden om okkupasjonsstyret*, p. 9, p. 345, fn. 1.

131. Norway, Eidsivating lagstols landssvikavdeling, *Redegjørelse fra Vidkun Quisling i siktelse fremsatt i Oslo Forhørsrett 26. mai 1945* (Oslo: 1945), p. 7.

132. *Lofotposten*, April 10, 1940, quoted in Gunnleik Jensson, ed., *Norsk presse under hakekorset* (3 vols.; Oslo: Tell forlag, 1945–1946), Vol. I, p. 19; "Jonas Lie hjem fra fronten," *Dagbladet*, May 6, 1940; Skodvin, *Striden om okkupasjonsstyret*, pp. 164–165.

133. "Mysterium omkring regjeringen Quisling," *Adresseavisen*, April 11, 1940; telephone conversation between Sedlatzek [*sic.*], Trondheim, and the German legation in Stockholm, April 13, 1940, monitored by the Swedes, *Straffesak*, p. 508; Skodvin, *ibid.*, pp. 165–166.

134. Bjørn Bjørnsen, *Det utrolige døgnet* (Oslo: Gyldendal norsk Forlag, 1977), p. 278. See also Skodvin, *ibid.*, pp. 166–167.

135. Statement by Hans Joachim von Neuhaus, April 22, 1946, UKs arkiv, Box 3, envelope 3.

136. Bräuer to the Norwegian government, April 9, 1940, "Norsk politikk 9. april – 7. juni 1940," *Innstilling*, Vol. I, appendices, Vol. II, appendix 8, pp. 257–258.

137. *Ibid.*, p. 260, p. 264.

138. *Ibid.*, p. 258.

139. *Ibid.*, pp. 258–259.

140. *Ibid.*, p. 261.

141. *Ibid.*, p. 262.

142. *Ibid.*, p. 265.

143. Skodvin, *Striden om okkupasjonsstyret*, p. 86.

144. *Ibid.*, pp. 87–88.

145. *Ibid.*, p. 88.

146. *Ibid.*

147. Rosenberg, diary entry of April 9, 1940, Seraphim, *Tagebuch*, p. 104.

148. "Norsk politikk 9. april – 7. juni 1940," *Innstilling*, Vol. I, appendices, Vol. II, appendix 8, pp. 264–265, p. 272.

149. *Ibid.*, p. 273.

150. *Ibid.*

151. *Ibid.*, pp. 275–276.

152. *Ibid.*, p. 278.

153. *Ibid.*, p. 276.
154. Skodvin, *Striden om okkupasjons-styret*, p. 103, pp. 104–106.
155. *Ibid.*, p. 106.
156. *Ibid.*, p. 103.
157. "Norsk politikk 9. april – 7. juni 1940," *Innstilling*, Vol. I, appendices, Vol. II, appendix 8, p. 280.
158. Kjeld Stub Irgens, note from the summer of 1940, probably written in June, UKs arkiv, Box 3, envelope 1. Also quoted in Skodvin, *Striden om okkupasjonsstyret*, pp. 103–104.
159. "Norsk politikk 9. april – 7. juni 1940," *Innstilling*, Vol. I, appendices, Vol. II, appendix 8, p. 281.
160. Irgens, note from the summer of 1940, see fn. 158.
161. *Ibid.*
162. *Ibid.*; *Straffesak*, p. 84.
163. Quisling to Hitler, April 10, 1940, quoted in Skodvin, *Striden om okkupasjonsstyret*, p. 105. Norwegian translation in *Straffesak*, pp. 169–170.
164. Quoted in Skodvin, *ibid.*, p. 119. See also the testimony of Karl Jacob Lyche, August 23, 1945, *Straffesak*, p. 170.
165. Quisling's proclamation of April 10, 1940, appearing in *Aftenposten* and other Oslo papers, *Straffesak*, p. 506.
166. *Aftenposten*, April 11, 1940, morning edition, in *ibid.*, p. 507.
167. *Tidens Tegn*, April 13, 1940, in *ibid.*, p. 509.
168. *Aftenposten*, April 11, 1940, morning edition, in *ibid.*, p. 507.
169. *Nationen*, July 12, 1946; statement by Bernhard Salbu, May 30, 1945, Riksarkivet, police reports, Haffner compilation, document #7.
170. *Straffesak*, pp. 507–508.
171. "Norsk politikk 9. april – 7. juni 1940," *Innstilling*, Vol. I, appendices, Vol. II, appendix 8, p. 281.
172. Skodvin, *Striden om okkupasjonsstyret*, pp. 110–111.
173. "Norsk politikk 9. april – 7. juni 1940," *Instilling*, Vol. I, appendices, Vol. II, appendix 8, p. 282.
174. Harald Franklin Knudsen to Quisling, November 27, 1943, quoted in Skodvin, *Striden om okkupasjonsstyret*, pp. 372–373, fn. 42.
175. Skodvin, *ibid.*, pp. 170–171.

176. "Administrasjonsrådet," *Innstilling*, Vol. I, p. 129.
177. *Ibid.*
178. Skodvin, *Striden om okkupasjonsstyret*, pp. 99–100.
179. "Administrasjonsrådet," *Innstilling*, Vol. I, p. 144.
180. Quisling to Welhaven, April 12, 1945, DA, Quislingsaken, Folder #2.
181. Welhaven, statement of May 31, 1945, Riksarkivet, police reports, Haffner compilation, document #11.
182. "Administrasjonsrådet," *Innstilling*, Vol. I, pp. 129–130.
183. Statement by Rolf M. Thorsteinsen, July 24, 1945, Riksarkivet, police reports, Haffner compilation, document #86.
184. "Administrasjonsrådet," *Innstilling*, Vol. I, p. 130.
185. Knut Aagesen, "Fagopposisjonen av 1940," *1940 – Fra nøytral til okkupert*, p. 374.
186. "Statsminister Quislings mektige appell til det norske folk og den norske presse," *Fritt Folk*, April 13, 1940.
187. *Ibid.*
188. *Ibid.*
189. *Ibid.*
190. *Ibid.*
191. Skodvin, *Striden om okkupasjonsstyret*, p. 123.
192. *Aftenposten*, April 12, 1940, evening edition, *Straffesak*, p. 507.
193. Skodvin, *Striden om okkupasjonsstyret*, p. 123.
194. "Administrasjonsrådet," *Innstilling*, Vol. I, pp. 130–131.
195. Skodvin, *Striden om okkupasjonsstyret*, pp. 113–114.
196. Rosenberg, diary entry, April 11, 1940, Seraphim, *Tagebuch*, p. 105.
197. Telephone conversation between Hewel and Quisling, 5:21 p.m., April 11, 1940, monitored by Swedish intelligence, in *Straffesak*, p. 506.
198. *Ibid.*
199. Rosenberg, diary entry, April 11, 1940, Seraphim, *Tagebuch*, pp. 105–106.
200. *Ibid.*, p. 106; Skodvin, *Striden om okkupasjonsstyret*, p. 134.
201. Sverre Kjeldstadli, *Hjemmestyrkene. Hovedtrekk av den militaere motstanden under okkupasjonen* (Oslo: Aschehoug,

1959), p. 40; Skodvin, *Striden om okkupa-sjonsstyret*, p. 116.

202. Telephone conversation between *Sonderführer* Sedlatschek in Trondheim and the German legation, Stockholm, April 13, 1940, monitored by Swedish intelligence, *Straffesak*, p. 508. See also Kjeldstadli, *ibid.*

203. "Administrasjonsrådet," *Innstilling*, Vol. I, pp. 130–132.

204. Telephone conversation between Scheidt, Oslo, and Hagelin, Berlin, April 13, 1940, monitored by Swedish intelligence, quoted in Kjeldstadli, *Hjemmestyrkene*, p. 40.

205. Skodvin, *Striden om okkupasjonsstyret*, p. 117.

206. *Ibid.*, pp. 118–119; Kjeldstadli, *Hjemmestyrkene*, p. 39.

207. Skodvin, *ibid.*, p. 96, p. 118.

208. Rosenberg, diary entry, April 11, 1940, Seraphim, *Tagebuch*, pp. 105–106; Skodvin, *ibid.*, p. 115.

209. Rosenberg, "Notat ang. den norske handelsminister Hagelins besøk lørdag den 13. april 1940," DA, Quislingsaken, Folder #7 – Straffesak – Etterforskning mot Quisling; Skodvin, *ibid.*, pp. 133–134.

210. Rosenberg, *ibid.*

211. Skodvin, *Striden om okkupasjonsstyret*, p. 137.

212. Rosenberg, diary entry, December 14, 1939, Seraphim, *Tagebuch*, p. 93; Skodvin, *ibid.*, pp. 139–140.

213. Knudsen, *Jeg var Quislings sekretaer*, p. 145.

214. "Administrasjonsrådet," *Innstilling*, Vol. I, p. 130.

215. *Ibid.*, pp. 130–131.

216. *Ibid.*, p. 131.

217. *Ibid.*, p. 135.

218. *Ibid.*, p. 132.

219. Eivind Berggrav, *Da kampen kom. Noen blad fra startåret* (Oslo: Land og Kirke, 1945), p. 13.

220. "Administrasjonsrådet," *Innstilling*, Vol. I, p. 133; Nøkleby, "Fra november til april – sendemann Bräuers personlige politikk," *1940 – Fra nøytral til okkupert*, p. 65.

221. "Administrasjonsrådet," *ibid.*, pp. 135–138.

222. *Ibid.*, p. 138.

223. *Ibid.*, p. 139, pp. 141–143.

224. *Ibid.*, p. 143.

225. *Ibid.*, p. 145.

226. *Ibid.*

227. *Ibid.*, pp. 145–146.

228. Nøkleby, "Fra november til april – sendemann Bräuers personlige politikk," *1940 – Fra nøytral til okkupert*, p. 70.

229. Skodvin, *Striden om okkupasjonsstyret*, p. 96.

230. "Administrasjonsrådet," *Innstilling*, Vol. I, p. 147.

231. *Ibid.*, p. 148.

232. Paal Berg, diary entry, April 14, 1940, quoted in *ibid.*, pp. 148–149.

233. Nøkleby, "Fra november til april – sendemann Bräuers personlige politikk," *1940 – Fra nøytral til okkupert*, p. 66.

234. "Administratrasjonsrådet," *Innstilling*, Vol. I, p. 153.

235. *Ibid.*, p. 152.

236. Skodvin, *Striden om okkupasjonsstyret*, p. 143.

237. *Ibid.*, pp. 143–144.

238. Loock, *Quisling, Rosenberg und Terboven*, p. 318.

239. See *Straffesak*, pp. 87–89.

240. Skodvin, *Striden om okkupasjonsstyret*, p. 144.

241. "Administrasjonsrådet," *Innstilling*, Vol. I, pp. 155–156.

242. Loock, *Quisling, Rosenberg und Terboven*, pp. 313–314.

243. *Ibid.*, p. 320.

244. Skodvin, *Striden om okkupasjonsstyret*, p. 147.

245. Loock, *Quisling, Rosenberg und Terboven*, p. 320.

246. *Straffesak*, p. 88.

247. Loock, *Quisling, Rosenberg und Terboven*, p. 321.

248. "Administrasjonsrådet," *Innstilling*, Vol. I, p. 158.

249. *Straffesak*, pp. 88–89.

250. "Administrasjonsrådet," *Innstilling*, Vol. I, p. 158.

251. Paal Berg, diary entry, April 15, 1940, quoted in *ibid.*, p. 159.

252. Ferdinand Schjelderup, *Fra Norges kamp for retten. 1940 i Høyesterett* (Oslo: Grøndahl & Søns forlag, 1945), p. 50; *Innstilling, ibid.*, p. 159, p. 161.

253. *Innstilling, ibid.*, p. 157.

254. *Ibid.*, p. 161.

255. *Ibid.*, p. 160.

256. *Ibid.*, p. 159

257. Berggrav, *Da kampen kom*, pp. 26–27.

258. "Administrasjonsrådet," *Innstilling*, Vol. I, p. 160.

259. Trygve Iversen, "Rapport til Oslo Politikammer," April 15, 1945, quoted in *Straffesak*, p. 509.

260. Iversen, *ibid.*; "Administrasjonsrådet," *Innstilling*, Vol. I, pp. 160–161.

261. *Innstilling, ibid.*, p. 161.

262. *Ibid.*, pp. 162–163.

263. Quisling's speech is printed in its entirety in *ibid.*, pp. 163–164.

264. *Innstilling, ibid.*, p. 163

265. Schjelderup, *Fra Norges kamp for retten*, p. 53.

266. "Administrasjonsrådet," *Innstilling*, Vol. I, p. 159.

Notes to Chapter XI

1. Skodvin, *Striden om okkupasjonssty-ret*, pp. 145–146.

2. Nøkleby, "Fra november til april – sendemann Bräuers personlige politikk," *1940 – Fra nøytral til okkupert*, p. 67.

3. Skodvin, *Striden om okkupasjonssty-ret*, pp. 153–154. Habicht fell on the eastern front in the winter of 1943–44. Bräuer was somewhat more fortunate, being taken prisoner by the Russians. He was among the few German captives who survived Russian imprisonment, returning to Germany nine years after the conclusion of the war.

4. Berggrav, *Da kampen kom*, pp. 19–20.

5. Schjelderup, *Fra Norges kamp for retten*, pp. 77–78.

6. "Administrasjonsrådet," *Innstilling*, Vol. I, p. 168.

7. Skodvin, *Striden om okkupasjonssty-ret*, p. 188.

8. *Ibid.*, p. 189; Skodvin, "Historisk innleiing," *Om landssvikoppgjøret*, p. 10.

9. Jodl, diary entry, April 19, 1940, UKs arkiv, Box 11, envelope 25; Skodvin, *Striden om okkupasjonsstyret, ibid.*; Magne Skodvin, "Svar til Sverre Steen og Sverre Hartmann," *Historisk Tidsskrift*, Vol. 38, No. 2 (1957–1958), p. 190.

10. Loock, *Quisling, Rosenberg und Terboven*, p. 331.

11. Skodvin, *Striden om okkupasjonssty-ret*, p. 206; Loock, *ibid.*

12. Norway, Administrasjonsrådet, *Protokoll for møter i det Administrasjonsråd som er oppnevnt av Høyesterett mandag den 15. april* (Oslo: stenciled, n.d.), HI, Skodvin Collection, pp. 4–5. Hereafter cited as Administrasjonsrådet, *Protokoll*.

13. *Ibid.*, p. 6.

14. *Ibid.*, p. 9; Loock, *Quisling, Rosenberg und Terboven*, pp. 332–333.

15. Administrasjonsrådet, *ibid.*, p. 13; Schjelderup, *Fra Norges kamp for retten*, pp. 67–68.

16. Administrasjonsrådet, *ibid.*, pp. 12–13.

17. Loock, *Quisling, Rosenberg und Terboven*, p. 333.

18. Skodvin, "Historisk innleiing," *Om landssvikoppgjøret*, p. 24.

19. Bernard Øivind Salbu, statement of May 30, 1945, Riksarkivet, police reports, Haffner compilation, document #7; Harald Franklin Knudsen, statement of June 16, 1945, Riksarkivet, police reports, document #50; Skodvin, *Striden om okkupasjonsstyret*, p. 175.

20. Quisling, "La landet få fred," *Fritt Folk*, April 19, 1940, printed in *Straffesak*, pp. 510–511.

21. Skodvin, *Striden om okkupasjonssty-ret*, pp. 204–205.

22. *Ibid.*, pp. 207–208.

23. Administrasjonsrådet, *Protokoll*, April 19, 1940, p. 20; Skodvin, *ibid.*, p. 208.

24. Skodvin, *ibid.*

25. Quoted in *ibid.*

26. *Ibid.*, p. 209.

27. Magne Skodvin, "Norsk okkupasjonshistorie i europeisk samanheng," *Nordisk Tidskrift*, Vol. 27 (1951), p. 309.

28. Terboven was born on May 23, 1898. For additional biographical information, see Loock, *Quisling, Rosenberg und Terboven*, pp. 335–339, and Skodvin, *Striden om okkupasjonsstyret*, pp. 190–192.

29. Skodvin, *ibid.*, p. 190.

30. Skodvin, "Norsk okkupasjonshistorie i europeisk samanheng," *Nordisk Tidskrift*, Vol. 27, p. 309.

31. Skodvin, *Striden om okkupasjonssty-ret*, p. 192, p. 223.

32. *Ibid.*, p. 192.

33. *Ibid.*, p. 193.

34. *Ibid.*, pp. 193–196.
35. *Ibid.*, p. 255.
36. The *Führererlass* of April 24 is printed in its entirety in *ibid.*, pp. 196–198. For Terboven's agreement with Himmler, see Loock, *Quisling, Rosenberg und Terboven*, pp. 358–360.
37. Skodvin, *ibid.*, p. 197.
38. *Ibid.*, pp. 215–216.
39. *Ibid.*, pp. 216–223.
40. Dellbrügge's postwar statement to Undersøkelseskommisjonen av 1945. See Skodvin, *ibid.*, pp. 255–256.
41. Dellbrügge's postwar statement to Undersøkelseskommisjonen av 1945, HI, Skodvin Collection.
42. *Ibid.*, in Skodvin, *Striden om okkupasjonsstyret*, p. 256.
43. Dellbrügge, postwar statement to Undersøkelseskommisjonen av 1945, HI, Skodvin Collection.
44. Skodvin, *Striden om okkupasjonsstyret*, p. 256.
45. Skodvin, *ibid.*, pp. 257–258; Loock, *Quisling, Rosenberg und Terboven*, p. 367.
46. Rosenberg, diary entry, April 27, 1940, Seraphim, *Tagebuch*, p. 107.
47. Rosenberg, *ibid.*, pp. 107–108. See also Skodvin, *Striden om okkupasjonsstyret*, p. 226.
48. Rosenberg, *ibid.*, p. 108.
49. *Ibid.*
50. *Ibid.*
51. Rosenberg, diary entry, May 8, 1940, *ibid.*, p. 114.
52. Skodvin, *Striden om okkupasjonsstyret*, pp. 235–236.
53. *Ibid.*, pp. 236–237.
54. Rosenberg, diary entry, April 27, 1940, Seraphim, *Tagebuch*, p. 108.
55. Rosenberg, diary entry, May 7, 1940, *ibid.*, p. 111.
56. Skodvin, *Striden om okkupasjonsstyret*, p. 258.
57. During his treason trial, Quisling declared that Scheidt "wrote" one of the two letters, which was addressed to Hitler. When making this assertion, Quisling displayed a frequently employed tactic in his defense, attempting to make one of his advisers responsible for an act which he stood accused of having committed. Scheidt most probably assisted in translating the letter

into proper German, but its content clearly bears Quisling's stamp of authorship.
58. Quisling to Terboven, May 2, 1940, Norwegian translation in *Straffesak*, p. 92.
59. Quisling to Hitler, May 1, 1940, Norwegian translation in *ibid.*, pp. 92–93.
60. *Ibid.*
61. *Ibid.*
62. Quisling to Schickedanz, May 1, 1940, Norwegian translation, DA, Quislingsaken, Etterforskning mot Quisling, folder #7.
63. W. To Quisling, May 31, 1940, QA, Box 9, 9. april folder.
64. See for example Knut Hamsun's appeal entitled "Nordmenn!," *Fritt Folk*, May 4, 1940.
65. Rosenberg, diary entry, May 7, 1940, Seraphim, *Tagebuch*, pp. 111–112.
66. Rosenberg, diary entry, May 8, 1940, *ibid.*, p. 114.
67. Loock, *Quisling, Rosenberg und Terboven*, p. 369.
68. Skodvin, *Striden om okkupasjonsstyret*, p. 230.
69. *Straffesak*, p. 65.
70. Skodvin, *Striden om okkupasjonsstyret*, p. 231
71. Statement by Eberhard Günther Kern, June 15, 1945, HI, Skodvin Collection, police reports, #48.
72. Skodvin, *Striden om okkupasjonsstyret*, p. 231.
73. *Ibid.*, pp. 261–263.
74. Loock, *Quisling, Rosenberg und Terboven*, p. 349.
75. Skodvin, *Striden om okkupasjonsstyret*, pp. 232–233; Loock, *ibid.*, pp. 350–351.
76. Skodvin, *ibid.*, p. 238.
77. Statement by Carl Dietrich Hildisch, June 19, 1945, HI, Skodvin Collection, police reports, #52.
78. Boehm, *Norwegen zwischen England und Deutschland*, p. 95.
79. *Ibid.*, p. 96–97.
80. *Ibid.*, p. 98.
81. Skodvin, *Striden om okkupasjonsstyret*, p. 265.
82. *Ibid.*, pp. 262–263.
83. Loock, *Quisling, Rosenberg und Terboven*, pp. 378–379.
84. *Straffesak*, p. 89.
85. Skodvin, *Striden om okkupasjonsstyret*, p. 272.

86. *Straffesak*, pp. 89–91. See also Loock, *Quisling, Rosenberg und Terboven*, pp. 378–379.

87. Loock, *ibid.*, pp. 380–381.

88. "Administrasjonsrådet," *Innstilling*, Vol. I, p. 173.

89. Berggrav, *Da kampen kom*, p. 51.

90. Skodvin, *Striden om okkupasjonsstyret*, p. 389, fn. 2.

91. "Administrasjonsrådet," *Innstilling*, Vol. I, pp. 184–185; Schjelderup, *Fra Norges kamp for retten*, p. 94.

92. "Administrasjonsrådet," *ibid.*, pp. 180–182.

93. Loock, *Quisling, Rosenberg und Terboven*, p. 384, p. 396.

94. *Ibid.*, pp. 427–430.

95. *Ibid.*, p. 430.

96. Noack, memorandum of May 20, 1940, quoted in Loock, *Quisling, Rosenberg und Terboven*, p. 385; quoted in Schjelderup, *Fra Norges kamp for retten*, p. 106.

97. Loock, *ibid.*, pp. 385–386.

98. Noack, memorandum of May 20, 1940, quoted in "Administrasjonsrådet," *Innstilling*, Vol. I, pp. 182–183.

99. Administrasjonsrådet," *ibid.*, pp. 181 ff.

100. *Ibid.*, p. 185.

101. *Ibid.*, pp. 185–186; Loock, *Quisling, Rosenberg und Terboven*, pp. 392–394.

102. Dellbrügge, postwar statement to Undersøkelseskommisjonen av 1945, HI, Skodvin Collection.

103. Skodvin, *Striden om okkupasjonsstyret*, p. 391, fn. 49.

104. *Ibid.*, p. 274.

105. Persons sympathetic to NS have frequently suggested that the surrender of Norwegian army units in northern Norway constituted the establishment of de facto peace between Norway and Germany. This viewpoint has been advocated in order to absolve Quisling and his followers of any subsequent collaboration with the Germans. This interpretation is incorrect. In its final proclamation from northern Norway before going into exile, the government clearly stated its intent to continue the armed struggle. Norwegian naval forces followed the government to England, and during the course of the war a Norwegian air force and army units were created. Furthermore, the German government maintained that a state

of war still existed with Norway, as shown by its internment of Norwegian officers in 1943 and its seizure of Norwegian vessels as war prizes.

106. Haakon VII, proclamation of June 7, 1940, quoted in "Administrasjonsrådet," *Innstilling*, Vol. I, pp. 186–187.

107. Statement by Georg Wilhelm Müller, April 25, 1946, Stortingsarkivet, UKs arkiv, Box 14, envelope 16.

108. Skodvin, *Striden om okkupasjonsstyret*, p. 269, p. 271; Magne Skodvin, review of Thomas Christian Wyller, *Nyordning og motstand. Organisasjonenes politiske rolle under okkupasjonen*, in *Historisk Tidsskrift*, Vol. 39, No. 2 (1959–1960), p. 195.

109. *Ibid.*; Skodvin, "Historisk innleiing," *Om landssvikoppgjøret*, p. 10.

110. Skodvin, *Striden om okkupasjonsstyret*, p. 271.

111. Meyer, *Et annet syn*, p. 57.

112. Loock, *Quisling, Rosenberg und Terboven*, pp. 422–423.

113. "Jonas Lie hjem fra fronten," *Dagbladet*, May 6, 1940.

114. Skodvin, *Striden om okkupasjonsstyret*, p. 272; Loock, *Quisling, Rosenberg und Terboven*, pp. 430–433.

115. Knudsen, *Jeg var Quislings sekretaer*, pp. 156–157.

116. H. Waaler, "Tribunaltidens utskeielser," *Fritt Folk*, June 8, 1940.

117. Skodvin, *Striden om okkupasjonsstyret*, p. 272.

118. Skodvin, "Historisk innleiing," *Om landssvikoppgjøret*, pp. 15–16.

119. Helge Paulsen, "Reichskommissariat og 'motytelsene' under riksrådsforhandlingene," *1940 – Fra nøytral til okkupert*, p. 321.

120. Skodvin, "Historisk innleiing," *Om landssvikoppgjøret*, p. 14.

121. Administrasjonsrådet, *Protokoll*, July 19, 1940, p. 241.

122. Loock, *Quisling, Rosenberg und Terboven*, p. 444.

123. Sverre Steen, *Riksrådsforhandlingene*, Innstilling, Vol. I, appendix 9, p. 7.

124. Trygve Lie, *Med England i ildlinjen 1940–1942* (Oslo: Tiden Norsk Forlag, 1956), p. 28.

125. Statement by Ole F. Harbek, November 27, 1945, UKs arkiv, Box 1, envelope 16; statement by Andreas Moan, Sep-

tember 24, 1947, UKs arkiv, Box 23, envelope 8.

126. Harbek, *ibid.*; Moan, *ibid.*; Steen, *Riksrådsforhandlingene*, p. 118.

127. "Riksrådsforhandlingene," *Innstilling*, Vol. I, p. 242.

128. *Ibid.*, pp. 244 ff.

129. *Ibid.*, p. 245.

130. *Ibid.*, p. 252.

131. Steen,   *Riksrådsforhandlingene*, p. 80.

132. Skodvin, *Striden om okkupasjonsstyret*, p. 276. Loock, in *Quisling, Rosenberg und Terboven*, p. 437, fn. 153, states that the exact date of the meeting is unknown.

133. Telegram from Terboven to Bormann, June 29, 1940, quoted in Loock, *ibid.*, p. 480.

134. Loock, *ibid.*, pp. 437–438.

135. Steen, *Riksrådsforhandlingene*, p. 100.

136. *Ibid.*, p. 103.

137. Skodvin, *Striden om okkupasjonsstyret*, p. 306; Hagelin, memorandum of June 28, 1940, HI, Skodvin Collection.

138. "Riksrådsforhandlingene," *Innstilling*, Vol. I, pp. 254–255.

139. Fridtjof Heyerdahl, diary notations, end of June 1940, UKs arkiv, Box 23, envelope 9.

140. Steen, *Riksrådsforhandlingene*, pp. 102–103.

141. Quisling to Hitler, July 10, 1940, quoted in *Straffesak*, p. 67. See also Skodvin, *Striden om okkupasjonsstyret*, pp. 277–278.

142. Skodvin, *ibid.*, p. 278.

143. *Ibid.*

144. Loock, *Quisling, Rosenberg und Terboven*, p. 448.

145. Skodvin, *Striden om okkupasjonsstyret*, p. 279.

146. Loock, *Quisling, Rosenberg und Terboven*, pp. 449–450.

147. *Ibid.*, p. 448; Skodvin, *Striden om okkupasjonsstyret*, p. 279.

148. Loock, *ibid.*, pp. 448–449.

149. Hagelin, note of a conversation between Quisling, Dr. Stahlecker, and G. W. Müller, June 27, 1940, HI, Skodvin Collection.

150. Hagelin to Dellbrügge, July 6, 1940, *ibid.*; Hagelin to the *Reichskommissariat*, July 5, 1940, *ibid.*

151. Loock, *Quisling, Rosenberg und Terboven*, pp. 432–434.

152. *Ibid.*, p. 435.

153. *Ibid.*, pp. 436–437.

154. *Ibid.*, p. 437.

155. Boehm, *Norwegen zwischen England und Deutschland*, pp. 102–103. See also Skodvin, *Striden om okkupasjonsstyret*, pp. 280–281; and Loock, *Quisling, Rosenberg und Terboven*, p. 481.

156. Boehm, *ibid.*, p. 104

157. *Ibid.*; Helge Paulsen, "Terboven i konflikt med Kriegsmarine," *Motstandskamp, strategi og marinepolitikk*, Samtidshistorisk Forskningsgruppe, Norge og den 2. verdenskrig Series (Oslo: Universitetsforlaget, 1972), p. 70.

158. Loock, *Quisling, Rosenberg und Terboven*, p. 481.

159. Paulsen, "Terboven i konflikt med Kriegsmarine," *Motstandskamp, strategi og marinepolitikk*, p. 70–71.

160. Loock, *Quisling, Rosenberg und Terboven*, p. 482.

161. *Ibid.*

162. Skodvin, *Striden om okkupasjonsstyret*, p. 282.

163. Loock, *Quisling, Rosenberg und Terboven*, pp. 485–486.

164. Quisling to Hitler, July 10, 1940, *Straffesak*, pp. 66–68.

165. Loock states that the memorandum was sent to the Reich Chancellery already on July 8, 1940. See *Quisling, Rosenberg und Terboven*, p. 486.

166. Skodvin, *Striden om okkupasjonsstyret*, p. 283; Quisling's testimony, August 21, 1945, *Straffesak*, p. 68.

167. Paulsen, "Reichskommissariat og 'motytelsene' under riksrådsforhandlingene," *1940 – Fra nøytral til okkupert*, p. 294.

168. Skodvin, *Striden om okkupasjonsstyret*, p. 287.

169. Loock, *Quisling, Rosenberg und Terboven*, p. 488.

170. *Ibid.*, pp. 488–490.

171. Rosenberg to Hitler, July 21, 1940, in Steen, *Riksrådsforhandlingene*, appendix 1, pp. 203–211. See also Skodvin, *Striden om okkupasjonsstyret*, pp. 288–292; and Loock, *ibid.*, pp. 490–491.

172. Skodvin, *ibid.*, p. 292.

173. Loock, *Quisling, Rosenberg und Terboven*, p. 483.

174. Knudsen, *Jeg var Quislings sekretær*, pp. 157–158.

175. Paulsen, "Reichskommissariat og 'motytelsene,'" *1940 – Fra nøytral til okkupert*, pp. 320–321.

176. Loock, *Quisling, Rosenberg und Terboven*, p. 423.

177. Skodvin, *Striden om okkupasjonsstyret*, pp. 292–293.

178. Hagelin to Schickedanz, August 5, 1940, HI, Skodvin Collection.

179. Skodvin, *Striden om okkupasjonsstyret*, p. 293.

180. Loock, *Quisling, Rosenberg und Terboven*, pp. 501–504.

181. *Ibid.*, p. 506.

182. Scheidt, memorandum of September 4, 1940, concerning Quisling's August 16 discussion with Hitler, Seraphim, *Tagebuch*, pp. 178–179. Seraphim appears to have dated the meeting incorrectly, indicating that it took place on August 18, 1940. See Skodvin, *Striden om okkupasjonsstyret*, p. 294, and Loock, *Quisling, Rosenberg und Terboven*, p. 508.

183. Seraphim, *ibid.*, pp. 179–181.

184. "Orientering av Konr. Sundlo om den politiske situasjon i Norge pr. 18. august 1940," *Straffesak*, p. 514.

185. "Quisling hjemme igjen," *Fritt Folk*, August 21, 1940.

186. Skodvin, *Striden om okkupasjonsstyret*, p. 297.

187. Dellbrügge, postwar statement to Undersøkelseskommisjonen av 1945, HI, Skodvin Collection; Skodvin, *ibid.*, p. 269.

188. Paulsen, "Reichskommissariat og 'motytelsene,'" *1940 – Fra nøytral til okkupert*, p. 288.

189. *Ibid.*, pp. 336–337.

190. Loock, *Quisling, Rosenberg und Terboven*, p. 513.

191. Skodvin, *Striden om okkupasjonsstyret*, pp. 291–292.

192. Loock, *Quisling, Rosenberg und Terboven*, pp. 513–515.

193. See Skodvin, *Striden om okkupasjonsstyret*, pp. 299–300; and Loock, *ibid.*, p. 514.

194. Skodvin, *ibid.*, p. 300.

195. Quisling to Terboven, August 29, 1940, DA, Quislingsaken, folder #1.

196. *Ibid.* Minister President proved to be the title Quisling assumed when he again became head of a collaborationist government in February 1942.

197. *Ibid.*

198. Paulsen, "Reichskommissariat og 'motytelsene,'" *1940 – Fra nøytral til okkupert*, p. 323.

199. Loock, *Quisling, Rosenberg und Terboven*, pp. 506–508, p. 516.

200. Quisling to Terboven, August 29, 1940, DA, Quislingsaken, folder #1.

201. Loock, *Quisling, Rosenberg und Terboven*, p. 516.

202. *Ibid.*, pp. 516–517; Steen, *Riksrådsforhandlingene*, p. 142.

203. Loock, *ibid.*, p. 517; Skodvin, *Striden om okkupasjonsstyret*, pp. 302–303.

204. Quisling to Lammers, September 6, 1940, DA, Quislingsaken, folder #1.

205. Loock, *Quisling, Rosenberg und Terboven*, pp. 518–519.

206. The four candidates were Ellef Ringnes as Foreign Minister, Professor Ernst Selmer as Minister of Culture, Sigurd Johannessen as Trade Minister, and Rasmus Mork as Minister of Agriculture. Of the four, only Ringnes had previously been associated with NS, but he now belonged to the strong anti-Quisling faction centered around Victor Mogens of the Fatherland League.

207. For the complete list of the candidates proposed by Terboven on September 7, 1940, see Steen, *Riksrådsforhandlingene*, p. 146.

208. Loock, *Quisling, Rosenberg und Terboven*, p. 519, pp. 503–504.

209. Knudsen, *Jeg var Quislings sekretær*, pp. 165–166.

210. Skodvin, *Striden om okkupasjonsstyret*, p. 307.

211. Steen, *Riksrådsforhandlingene*, pp. 144–147.

212. *Ibid.*, p. 146.

213. For the most detailed examination of the State Council negotiations in September 1940, covering the period through September 14, see *ibid.*, pp. 144–174.

214. *Ibid.*, p. 168.

215. *Ibid.*, pp. 169–171.

216. Quisling to Terboven, September 9, 1940, DA, Quislingsaken, folder #1.
217. Quisling to Terboven, September 10, 1940, *ibid.*
218. *Ibid.*
219. Loock, *Quisling, Rosenberg und Terboven*, p. 533.
220. For a partisan account of the meeting, see Ringnes, *Bak okkupasjonens kulisser*, pp. 199–207.
221. Quisling to Terboven, September 10, 1940, DA, Quislingsaken, folder #1.
222. Ringnes, *Bak okkupasjonens kulisser*, pp. 205–207; G. W. Müller to Ringnes, June 12, 1947, quoted in Skodvin, *Striden om okkupasjonsstyret*, p. 401, fn. 40.
223. Quisling to Terboven, September 10, 1940, DA, Quislingsaken, folder #1.
224. Quoted in Loock, *Quisling, Rosenberg und Terboven*, p. 534.
225. *Ibid.*
226. Rosenberg, diary entry, September 12, 1940, Seraphim, *Tagebuch*, p. 118.
227. Rosenberg, diary entry, September 13, 1940, *ibid.*, p. 120.
228. Steen, *Riksrådsforhandlingene*, p. 177.
229. "D. Führer hat mir recht gegeben!" Rosenberg, diary entry, September 13, 1940, Seraphim, *Tagebuch*, p. 120.
230. *Ibid.*
231. Skodvin, *Striden om okkupasjonsstyret*, pp. 310–311.
232. Steen, *Riksrådsforhandlingene*, pp. 183–185.
233. *Ibid.*, p. 194.
234. Quoted in *ibid.*
235. Skodvin, *Striden om okkupasjonsstyret*, pp. 313–314.
236. *Ibid.*, p. 313.
237. Irgens, statement of June 12, 1946, UKs arkiv, Box 23, envelope 10.
238. Loock, *Quisling, Rosenberg und Terboven*, p. 537.
239. Skodvin, *Striden om okkupasjonsstyret*, p. 314.
240. *Ibid.*, p. 315.
241. *Ibid.*, pp. 315–321; Loock, *Quisling, Rosenberg und Terboven*, pp. 541–542.
242. Carlo Otte, statement, October 1945, UKs arkiv, Box 1, envelope 14.

Notes to Chapter XII

1. Printed in *Straffesak*, pp. 514–518.
2. *Ibid.*, p. 514.
3. *Ibid.*, p. 515.
4. *Ibid.*, pp. 515–517.
5. *Ibid.*, p. 517.
6. *Ibid.*, p. 518.
7. Terboven attempted to provide this step with a sheen of constitutionality by falsely declaring that the *Storting* had deposed the royal dynasty by a two–thirds majority. *Ibid.*, p. 517.
8. *Ibid.*, pp. 517–518.
9. *Ibid.*, p. 517. The nine NS members on the Council were Hagelin, Interior Department; Skancke, Church and Education Department; Lie, Police Department; Irgens, Maritime Department; Lunde, Propaganda and Culture Department; Professor Birger Meidell, Social Department; Sverre Riisnæs, Justice Department; Hustad, Labor Department; and Stang, Athletics Department. The latter's department was soon renamed the Department for Labor Service and Athletics.
10. *Ibid.*, pp. 514–518.
11. Interrogation of Quisling, July 28, 1945, HI, Skodvin Collection, police reports, #104; *Straffesak*, pp. 102–103.
12. *Ibid.*
13. Hagelin to the *Aussenpolitisches Amt*, September 24, 1940, Seraphim, *Tagebuch*, p. 185.
14. Carlo Otte, statement of October 1945, UKs arkiv, Box 1, envelope 14. See also Ringnes, *Bak okkupasjonens kulisser*, pp. 218–220.
15. Hans Dellbrügge to Helge Sivertsen, April 8, 1946, *ibid.*, Box 6, envelope 14.
16. Otte, statement of October 1945, *ibid.*, Box 1, envelope 14.
17. *Om landssvikoppgjøret*, pp. 136–139. The three were brought to trial after the war, charged with having aided the enemy by accepting appointments to the Commissarial Council. However, all were found to be innocent of the charge. Ravner and Sandberg were convicted by a lower court, but their convictions were overturned by the Supreme Court. Johannessen was found not guilty by a lower court.
18. Otte, statement of October 1945, UKs arkiv, Box 1, envelope 14.

19. *Ibid.*; Otte to Sandberg, April 18, 1941, HI, Skodvin Collection, 1941 folder.

20. Thomas Christian Wyller, *Nyordning og motstand. En framstilling og en analyse av organisasjonenes politiske funksjon under den tyske okkupasjon 25. 9. 1940 – 25. 9. 1942* (Oslo: Universitetsforlaget, 1958), pp. 3–4.

21. This is shown, for example, in Per Augdal's letter, for the Justice Department, to the Interior Department, April 1, 1941, HI, Skodvin Collection, 1941 folder. Accompanying this letter was the copy of a letter from Rudolf Schiedermair, head of the *Reichskommissariat*'s legal and administrative office, to Minister of Justice Sverre Riisnæs. Schiedermairs's letter emphasized the need for the departments to have prior approval from the *Reichskommissariat* before issuing decrees.

22. Irgens to A. V. Heiberg, October 11, 1945, quoted in *Irgens-saken* (Oslo: 1948), pp. 84–97. This book consists of excerpts from Irgens' postwar trial, plus newspaper accounts of the trial and statements by Swedish legal authorities. It is subjective, in favor of Irgens, and must be used with caution. The book's editor is unknown.

23. Bjarne Holst, for the Culture and Information Department, to Wessel Karlsen, NS' Lecture Organization, November 28, 1940, HI, Skodvin Collection, 1940 folder.

24. *Fritt Folk*, September 27, 1940.

25. Skodvin, *Striden om okkupasjonsstyret*, pp. 318–319.

26. *Ibid.*, p. 318.

27. *Ibid.*, p. 341.

28. Wyller, *Nyordning og motstand*, pp. 239–240.

29. Raeder to Boehm, October 1, 1940, quoted in Paulsen, "Terboven i konflikt med Kriegsmarine," *Motstandskamp, strategi og marinepolitikk*, p. 74.

30. *Ibid.*

31. Quisling, *Redegjørelse fra Vidkun Quisling*, p. 12.

32. Magne Skodvin, "Om 'statsakta' 1. februar 1942," lecture to Det Kongelige Norske Videnskabers Selskab, February 1, 1960.

33. Frau von Wangenheim, report of October 17, 1940, HI, Skodvin Collection, 1940 folder; Rosenberg to Lammers, October 22, 1940, with two reports from Hage-

lin, dated respectively September 24, 1940, and October 14, 1940, Seraphim, *Tagebuch*, pp. 183–190; Schreiber to Schickedanz, October 15, 1940, HI, Skodvin Collection, 1940 folder; Schickedanz to Quisling, October 18, 1940, HI, Skodvin Collection, 1940 folder.

34. Hagelin, report of October 14, 1940, Seraphim, *ibid.*, pp. 187–188.

35. *Ibid.*, p. 188.

36. *Ibid.*, p. 189.

37. *Ibid.*, p. 190.

38. *Ibid.*

39. Schreiber to Schickedanz, October 15, 1940, HI, Skodvin Collection, 1940 folder.

40. Rosenberg to Lammers, October 22, 1940, Seraphim, *Tagebuch*, pp. 183–184.

41. Schickedanz to Quisling, October 18, 1940, HI, Skodvin Collection, 1940 folder.

42. Police interrogation of Hagelin, November 1, 1945, *ibid.*

43. Quisling to Schickedanz, October 25, 1940, *ibid.*

44. Quisling, "Denkschrift über die Regelung der Verhältnisse Zwischen Norwegen and Deutschland," October 25, 1940, DA, Quislingsaken, folder #1.

45. *Ibid.* Quisling maintained during his postwar trial that he did not send this memorandum to Germany. See *Straffesak*, pp. 95–96. However, his letter to Schickedanz on October 25, 1940, indicates quite clearly that the memorandum was sent. In addition, Admiral Boehm also received a copy of the program, which Quisling wished to have forwarded to Hitler via Raeder. This too was sent. See Boehm, *Norwegen zwischen England und Deutschland*, p. 124.

46. Paulsen, "Terboven i konflikt med Kriegsmarine," *Motstandskamp, strategi og marinepolitikk*, p. 75.

47. Kjeldstadli, *Hjemmestyrkene*, p. 48.

48. Paulsen, "Terboven i konflikt med Kriegsmarine," *Motstandskamp, strategi og marinepolitikk*, p. 77.

49. Boehm to Raeder, "Gedanken zur politischen Lage," December 9, 1940, HI. Skodvin Collection, 1940 folder.

50. Paulsen, "Terboven i konflikt med Kriegsmarine," *Motstandskamp, strategi og marinepolitikk*, p. 77.

51. Boehm to Raeder, December 28, 1940, cited in *ibid.*, p. 78.

52. Raeder to Boehm, December 30, 1940, HI, Skodvin Collection, 1940 folder.

53. Paulsen, "Terboven i konflikt med Kriegsmarine," *Motstandskamp, strategi og marinepolitikk*, p. 77.

54. Raeder to Boehm, December 30, 1940, HI, Skodvin Collection, 1940 folder.

55. *Ibid*. See also Paulsen, "Terboven i konflikt med Kriegsmarine," *Motstandskamp, strategi og marinepolitikk*, pp. 77–79.

56. Raeder to Boehm, December 30, 1940, *ibid.*

57. Kjeldstadli, *Hjemmestyrkene*, p. 32; Paulsen, "Terboven i konflikt med Kriegsmarine," *Motstandskamp, strategi og marinepolitikk*, p. 80.

58. Quisling to Lammers, March 10, 1941, HI, Skodvin Collection, 1940 folder.

59. Magne Skodvin, "Det store fremstøt," *Norges krig*, Vol. II, p. 631.

60. Fuglesang to Skancke, August 2, 1940, QA.

61. Skodvin, "Historisk innleiing," *Om landssvikoppgjøret*, p. 14.

62. Skodvin, *ibid.*, p. 16.

63. "De nye," *Fritt Folk*, December 12, 1940.

64. Skodvin, "Det store fremstøt," *Norges krig*, Vol. II, p. 610. Aall's statement merely reflected the momentary optimism that existed within NS immediately after the establishment of the Commissarial Council. No such plebiscite was ever held.

65. Skodvin, *ibid.*

66. Tore Gjelsvik, *Hjemmefronten. Den sivile motstand under okkupasjonen 1940–1945* (Oslo: J. W. Cappelens forlag, 1977), p. 43. The major purpose of Goebbels' visit, however, was for him to obtain a personal impression of the situation in Norway for the Nazi leadership. See Skodvin, *ibid.*, p. 623.

67. Skodvin, *ibid.*, pp. 607–608; Gjelsvik, *ibid.*

68. Gjelsvik, *ibid.*

69. Skodvin, "Historisk innleiing," *Om landssvikoppgjøret*, p. 17.

70. Author's calculations based on statistics in *ibid.*, p. 16.

71. Skodvin, *ibid.*

72. *Ibid.*, p. 19, p. 20.

73. From the statistics provided in *ibid.*, the actual number aimed at was 95,450.

74. Based on statistics provided in Nordic Council, *Yearbook of Nordic Statistics, 1973* (Stockholm: 1974), p. 28, table 6.

75. The actual figure was 37.5 per cent. Author's calculation based on statistics in Skodvin, "Historisk innleiing," *Om landssvikoppgjøret*, p. 19.

76. Skodvin, *ibid.*, p. 16.

77. *Ibid.*

78. *Ibid.*, p. 17.

79. Norway, Statistisk Sentralbyrå, *Statistikk over landssvik 1940–1945*, Norges offisielle statistikk XI. 179. (Oslo: Statistisk Sentralbyrå, 1954), p. 10; *Om landssvikoppgjøret*, p. 463.

80. Skodvin, "Historisk innleiing," *Om landssvikoppgjøret*, p. 18.

81. "Jo sterkere NS er, jo ubryteligere er Norges stilling," *Fritt Folk*, August 25, 1941.

82. See below, pp. 605–608 for a detailed discussion of the different military units which Quisling promoted.

83. *Fritt Folk*, May 23, 1941; Skodvin, "Historisk innleiing," *Om landssvikoppgjøret*, pp. 20–21; Skodvin, "Det store fremstøt," *Norges krig*, Vol. II, p. 673.

84. *Fritt Folk*, November 11, 1940.

85. Hans Luihn, *De illegale avisene. Den frie, hemmelige pressen i Norge under okkupasjonen* (Oslo: Universitetsforlaget, 1960), pp. 52–53.

86. "Nasjonal Samlings Fører reiser kravet om en felles-europeisk jødelovgivning," *Fritt Folk*, March 29, 1941. *Fritt Folk* provided additional coverage of the anti-Semitic congress in its next issue.

87. *Morgenbladet*, September 6, 1941, in *Straffesak*, p. 539.

88. Chargé d'affaires Jens Bull, Stockholm, to the Norwegian Foreign Ministry, London, April 15, 1941, in Norway, Ministry of Foreign Affairs, *Norges forhold til Sverige under krigen 1940–45* (3 vols.; Oslo: Gyldendal Norsk Forlag, 1947–1950), Vol. II, p. 105.

89. See for example "Da Føreren igår talte til 'Fritt Folks' arbeidere og funksjonaerer," *Fritt Folk*, February 14, 1941.

90. Schjelderup, *Fra Norges kamp for retten*, p. 190.

91. *Om landssvikoppgjøret*, p. 155; Schjelderup, *ibid.*

92. *Om landssvikoppgjøret*, p. 154.

93. *Ibid.*

94. Skodvin, "Historisk innleiing," *ibid.*, p. 14.

95. Hans Clausen Korff, "Aktenvermerk," July 25, 1941, HI, Skodvin Collection, 1941 folder.

96. Carlo Otte to Erling Sandberg, April 18, 1941, *ibid.*

97. *Ibid.*

98. Korff, "Aktenvermerk," July 25, 1941, HI, Skodvin Collection, 1941 folder.

99. *Ibid.*

100. *NS årbok 1942*, p. iv.

101. *Om landssvikoppgjøret*, p. 140.

102. *NS årbok 1942*, pp. 35–40; *ibid.*

103. Quisling, "partiforordning" of July 31, 1941, QA.

104. Norway, Oslo Politikammer, DA, "Utdrag i sak for Eidsivating lagmannsrett: Påtalemyndigheten (aktor o.r. sakfører M. Dahl-Hansen) mot J. A. Lippestad (forsv. h.r. advokat Hans H. Schjøth)," mimeographed MS (3 vols. plus 2 vols. of addenda; Oslo: n.d.), Vol. I, pp. 4–6. Hereafter cited as DA, "Utdrag i sak . . . mot J. A. Lippestad."

105. *Om landssvikoppgjøret*, pp. 144–145.

106. *Ibid.*, p. 145.

107. *Ibid.*, p. 140.

108. *NS årbok 1942*, pp. 41 ff.

109. Gerhard Berghold, report of July 5, 1945, *Straffesak*, p. 595.

110. "Fylkesmennene og nyordningen av kommunene 1940," *Innstilling*, Vol. I, p. 343.

111. Norway, Department of Justice, DA, Offentlig straffesak mot Albert Viljam Hagelin, "Utdrag i Høyesterettssak S nr. 36/1946 mot Albert Viljam Hagelin," stenciled manuscript (Oslo: 1946), p. 122. Hereafter cited as Hagelinsaken.

112. Thorleif Dahl, for NS Personalkontor for Offentlig Tjeneste, directive of February 15, 1941, HI, Skodvin Collection, 1941 folder.

113. *Om landssvikoppgjøret*, p. 432.

114. Gjelsvik, *Hjemmefronten*, p. 29.

115. Lars L'Abée-Lund, "Politiet over og under jorden," *Norges krig*, Vol. III, pp. 278 ff.

116. *Ibid.*, p. 278.

117. NS program, February 1934, paragraph 4.

118. Serving in this capacity until the end of the war, Hundseid did not commit any overt acts of collaboration. He was brought to trial and convicted in 1946 because as a previous prime minister and party leader, he had presented a bad example by his failure to behave in a resolute manner against NS. His original sentence of twelve years was reduced to ten years by the Supreme Court. He was pardoned in 1949 after having been imprisoned for four years. Thereafter he lived in quiet retirement in Oslo until his death in 1965. See Gabrielsen, *Menn og politikk*, pp. 176–178.

119. "Fylkesmennene og nyordningen av kommunene 1940," *Innstilling*, Vol. I, p. 349.

120. *Ibid.*, p. 343.

121. *Ibid.*

122. *Ibid.*, pp. 343–344.

123. *Ibid.*, p. 348.

124. The Home Front leadership to Minister of Justice Terje Wold, September 15, 1943, in Norway, Stortinget, *Regjeringen og hjemmefronten under krigen. Aktstykker utgitt av Stortinget* (Oslo: Aschehoug, 1948), p. 297.

125. The Home Front leadership to Prime Minister Nygaardsvold, June 27, 1943, *ibid.*, p. 258.

126. Skodvin, "Historisk innleiing," *Om landsvikoppgjøret*, pp. 30–31.

127. "Høyesterett," *Innstilling*, Vol. I, p. 329.

128. *Ibid.*, pp. 329–330.

129. Schjelderup, *Fra Norges kamp for retten*, p. 212.

130. *Ibid.*, p. 219.

131. "Høyesterett," *Innstilling*, Vol. I, pp. 334–336.

132. *Ibid.*, p. 338; Gjelsvik, *Hjemmefronten*, p. 37.

133. Wyller, *Nyordning og motstand*, p. 14.

134. *Ibid.*, p. 244.

135. Skodvin, review of Wyller, *Nyordning og motstand*, *Historisk Tidsskrift*, Vol. 39, No. 2, (1959–1960), p. 194.

136. Wyller, *Nyordning og motstand*, pp. 248–249.

137. Gjelsvik, *Hjemmefronten*, p. 33.

138. *Ibid.*, pp. 33–34.

139. Thomas Christian Wyller, *Fra okkupasjonsårenes maktkamp. Nasjonal Samlings korporative nyordningsforsøk* (Oslo: Tanum, 1953), p. 85.

140. Gjelsvik, *Hjemmefronten*, p. 35.

141. For example, *Fritt Folk* at this time began to display a remarkable interest in American boxing matches. See the December 1940 sport sections of *Fritt Folk*.

142. Wyller, *Nyordning og motstand*, p. 249.

143. Schjelderup, *Fra Norges kamp for retten*, pp. 201–202.

144. Statement by Ingvald Strand, December 4, 1945, HI, Skodvin Collection, police reports, #353.

145. Schjelderup, *Fra Norges kamp for retten*, pp. 202–203; Wyller, *Nyordning og motstand*, p. 7.

146. Strand, statement of December 4, 1945, HI, Skodvin Collection, police reports, #353; Schjelderup, *ibid.*, p. 202.

147. Nils Trædal, statement of March 22, 1946, HI, Skodvin Collection, police reports, #477; Wyller, *Nyordning og motstand*, p. 8.

148. Wyller, *ibid.*, p. 7; Strand, statement of December 4, 1945, *ibid.*, police reports, #353.

149. Johan Mellbye, statement of November 27, 1945, *ibid.*, police reports, #348.

150. Gjelsvik, *Hjemmefronten*, pp. 31–32.

151. *Ibid.*, p. 32.

152. Wyller, *Nyordning og motstand*, pp. 11–12.

153. Aagesen, "Fagopposisjonen av 1940," *1940 – Fra nøytral til okkupert*, pp. 445–446.

154. *Ibid.*, p. 446.

155. Wyller, *Fra okkupasjonsårenes maktkamp*, p. 108; Meyer, *Et annet syn*, p. 220.

156. Aagesen, "Fagopposisjonen av 1940," *1940 – Fra nøytral til okkupert*, p. 448.

157. Halvard Olsen, "Rapport fra utvalget for fagforeningsspørsmål," April 8, 1942, HI, Skodvin Collection, 1942 folder; Meyer, *Et annet syn*, p. 223.

158. Quisling to Terboven, September 17, 1941, DA, Quislingsaken, folder #1.

159. Skodvin, "Historisk innleiing," *Om landssvikoppgjøret*, p. 29.

160. Statement by Rolf Jørgen Fuglesang, January 26, 1946, HI, Skodvin Collection, police reports, #398; Skodvin, "Historisk innleiing," *ibid.* pp. 28–29.

161. "Skrivelse til Høyesterettsadvokat A. V. Heiberg fra K. S. Irgens," October 11, 1945, *Irgens-saken*, p. 88.

162. Terboven to Irgens, May 13, 1941, partially quoted in *ibid.*, p. 82.

163. *Ibid.*

164. "Skrivelse til Høyesterettsadvokat A. V. Heiberg fra K. S. Irgens," October 11, 1945, *Irgens-saken*, p. 88.

165. *Ibid.*

166. Sigurd Johannessen, "Norges Fiskarlag under okkupasjonen," September 20, 1945, HI, Skodvin Collection, police reports, #380.

167. Wyller, *Fra okkupasjonsårenes maktkamp*, pp. 107–108.

168. Wyller, *Nyordning og motstand*, p. 10.

169. *Ibid.*

170. UKs arkiv, Box 14, envelope 18.

171. Wyller, *Nyordning og motstand*, pp. 14–16.

172. Skancke's letter of November 20, 1940, with accompanying declaration of loyalty, HI, Skodvin Collection, 1940 folder.

173. Gjelsvik, *Hjemmefronten*, p. 41; Wyller, *Nyordning og motstand*, p. 15.

174. Gjelsvik, *ibid.*

175. As opposed to the current condition of higher education, with universities located in Bergen, Trondheim, and Tromsø as well as Oslo, before 1946 Norway had only one university, the University of Oslo, which dated from 1811.

176. Didrik Arup Seip, *Hjemme og i fiendeland 1940–1945* (Oslo: Gyldendal Norsk Forlag, 1946), p. 255.

177. Sverre Steen, "Universitetet i ildlinjen," *Norges krig*, Vol. III, p. 135.

178. *Ibid.*, pp. 135–136.

179. Seip, *Hjemme og i fiendeland*, pp. 129–130.

180. Steen, "Universitetet i ildlinjen," *Norges krig*. Vol. III, pp. 142–143; Seip, *ibid.*, pp. 172–184.

181. Skodvin, "Historisk innleiing," *Om landssvikoppgjøret*, p. 22.

182. "Eden til Føreren hirdmønstringens høidepunkt," *Fritt Folk*, November 3, 1941.

183. Decree of January 23, 1941, co-signed Sjønne Melstrøm, QA.

184. Skodvin, "Det store fremstøt," *Norges krig*, Vol. II, pp. 634–635; Gjelsvik, *Hjemmefronten*, p. 43.

185. *Hirdmannen*, December 16, 1940.

186. G. W. Müller, "Norwegische Beobachtungen," December 5, 1940, HI, Skodvin Collection, 1940 folder; Gjelsvik, *Hjemmefronten*, p. 43.

187. Skodvin, "Det store fremstøt," *Norges krig*, Vol. II, pp. 635–636.

188. Jørgen Nordvik, "Provokasjon og retorsjon," in Sverre Riisnæs, *Den nye rettsstat på nasjonalsosialistisk grunn* (Oslo: Nasjonal Samlings Rikstrykkeri, 1941), pp. 17–19.

189. Müller, "Norwegische Beobachtungen," December 5, 1940, HI, Skodvin Collection, 1940 folder.

190. Skodvin, "Det store fremstøt," *Norges krig*, Vol. II, p. 635.

191. *Ibid.*, p. 624.

192. Gjelsvik, *Hjemmefronten*, pp. 43–44.

193. "Jo sterkere NS er, jo ubryteligere er Norges stilling," *Fritt Folk*, August 25, 1941.

194. Gjelsvik, *Hjemmefronten*, p. 44.

195. Müller, "Norwegische Beobachtungen," December 5, 1940, HI, Skodvin Collection, 1940 folder.

196. Skodvin, "Det store fremstøt," *Norges krig*, Vol. II, p. 637; Skodvin, "Historisk innleiing," *Om landssvikoppgjøret*, p. 22.

197. Skodvin, "Historisk innleiing," *ibid.*

198. Berggrav, *Da kampen kom*, p. 100.

199. *Ibid.*, pp. 101–103.

200. *Ibid.*, p. 109.

201. Einar Molland, "Kirkens kamp," *Norges krig*, Vol. III, pp. 38–40.

202. Berggrav, *Da kampen kom*, pp. 124 ff.; Molland, *ibid.*, pp. 43–44; Gjelsvik, *Hjemmefronten*, pp. 44–45.

203. The bishops' pastoral letter is printed in its entirety as an appendix to Berggrav's *Da kampen kom*.

204. *Ibid.*, p. 162.

205. Molland, "Kirkens kamp," *Norges krig*, Vol. III, p. 45.

Notes to Chapter XIII

1. Wyller, *Nyordning og motstand*, pp. 20–21; Gjelsvik, *Hjemmefronten*, pp. 46–47.

2. Skodvin, "Det store fremstøt," *Norges krig*, Vol. II, p. 646.

3. The protest letter of April 3, 1941, is quoted in its entirety in Wyller, *Nyordning og motstand*, pp. 23–26.

4. *Ibid.*, p. 27.

5. *Ibid.*

6. *Ibid.*

7. *Ibid.*

8. This protest, dated May 15, 1941, is quoted in its entirety in *ibid.*, pp. 29–33.

9. *Ibid.*, pp. 28–29.

10. Paul Frank, quoted in Skodvin, "Det store fremstøt," *Norges krig*, Vol. II, p. 651.

11. Wyller, *Nyordning og motstand*, p. 28.

12. *Ibid.*, pp. 35–36.

13. *Ibid.*, p. 34.

14. *Ibid.*, p. 33.

15. *Ibid.*, p. 37.

16. *Ibid.*

17. *Ibid.*, p. 53.

18. *Ibid.*, p. 39.

19. *Ibid.*, pp. 40–41.

20. *Ibid.*, p. 44.

21. *Ibid.*, p. 45.

22. *Ibid.*, pp. 47–48.

23. *Ibid.*, pp. 48–49.

24. *Ibid.*, p. 50.

25. *Ibid.*

26. Ferdinand Schjelderup, *På bred front* (Oslo: Grøndahl og Søns forlag, 1947), p. 84.

27. Gjelsvik, *Hjemmefronten*, p. 242, fn. 73.

28. A portion of the speech is quoted in Schjelderup, *På bred front*, pp. 84–86. See also Wyller, *Nyordning og motstand*, pp. 55–57.

29. Wyller, *ibid.*, p. 57, p. 313.

30. *Ibid.*, p. 56.

31. *Ibid.*, p. 60.

32. Skodvin, "Det store fremstøt," *Norges krig*, Vol. II, p. 651.

33. Wyller, *Nyordning og motstand*, p. 65.

34. Ole Kristian Grimnes, *Hjemmefrontens ledelse*, Samtidshistorisk Forskningsgruppe, Norge og den 2. verdenskrig Series (Oslo: Universitetsforlaget, 1977), p. 75; Wyller, *ibid.*, pp. 62–63.

35. Grimnes, *ibid.*, p. 76.

36. Wyller, *Nyordning og motstand*, p. 64.

37. *Ibid.*, pp. 66–67.

38. *Ibid.*, p. 69.

39. *Ibid.*, p. 71.

40. "Forordning om den civile undtagelsestilstand av 31. juli 1941," in *Norges krig*, Vol. II, p. 697.

41. Skodvin, "Det store fremstøt," *ibid.*, pp. 686–687.

42. *Fritt Folk*, September 4, 1941, quoted in *ibid.*, p. 688.

43. Kjeldstadli, *Hjemmestyrkene*, p. 121; Skodvin, *ibid.*, pp. 704–710.

44. Skodvin, *ibid.*, p. 696.

45. Gjelsvik, *Hjemmefronten*, p. 54.

46. *Ibid.*, p. 55; Skodvin, "Det store fremstøt," *Norges krig*, Vol. II, p. 692.

47. Gjelsvik, *ibid.*; Skodvin, *ibid.*, p. 694.

48. Gjelsvik, *ibid.*, p. 56.

49. Skodvin, "Det store fremstøt," *Norges krig*, Vol. II, pp. 696–698.

50. Gjelsvik, *Hjemmefronten*, p. 57.

51. Skodvin, "Det store fremstøt," *Norges krig*, Vol. II, pp. 703–704.

52. Luihn, *De illegale avisene*, p. 58.

53. *Ibid.*, p. 230.

54. Skodvin, "Det store fremstøt," *Norges krig*, Vol. II, p. 703.

55. Excerpt from the judgement against Odd Jarmann Fossum, *Om landssvikoppgjøret*, p. 165.

56. DA, "Utdrag i sak ... mot J. A. Lippestad," p. 29.

57. Gjelsvik, *Hjemmefronten*, p. 52, pp. 57–58.

58. Jens Berg, enclosure #3, Lars Evensen, report to Trygve Lie, May 5, 1942, *Regjeringen og hjemmefronten under krigen*, pp. 89–90, Grimnes, *Hjemmefrontens ledelse*, pp. 57–58, p. 76.

59. Hagelin to Quisling, September 10, 1941, UKs arkiv, Box 24, envelope 6.

60. DA, "Utdrag i sak ... mot Alf Whist," pp. 8–9.

61. Quisling to Terboven, September 17, 1941, DA, Quislingsaken, folder #1.

62. Steen, "Universitetet i ildlinjen," *Norges krig*, Vol. III, p. 152.

63. *Ibid.*, p. 148.

64. *Ibid.*, pp. 150–151.

65. *Ibid.*, p. 153.

66. *Ibid.*, p. 154.

67. *Ibid.*, pp. 156–157.

68. *Ibid.*, p. 155.

69. *Ibid.*, pp. 158 ff.

70. Skodvin, "Det store fremstøt," *Norges krig*, Vol. II, p. 711.

71. *Med England i ildlinjen 1940–1942*, p. 97.

72. Åsmund Sveen, report of March 14, 1941, for the Propaganda Division of Gulbrand Lunde's Culture and Public Information Department, forwarded to the *Reichskommissariat*, March 26, 1941, HI, Skodvin Collection, 1941 folder.

73. "Tyskland kan ikke overlate Norge til fienden," *Morgenbladet*, November 18, 1941.

74. "Jo sterkere NS er, jo ubryteligere er Norges stilling," *Fritt Folk*, August 25, 1941.

75. Christensen, *Okkupasjonsår og etterkrigstid*, p. 253.

76. "Førerens familiegravsted skjendet av jøssinger!," *Fritt Folk*, September 19, 1941.

77. Quisling, "Cirkulære om opprettelse av en politisk etterretningsavdeling ved Rikshirdstaben. Strengt fortrolig og kun til personlig orientering," May 7, 1941, *Straffesak*, p. 534.

78. Skodvin, "Historisk innleiing," *Om landssvikoppgjøret*, p. 14.

79. *Tilleggshefte II*, p. 14.

80. Grimnes, *Hjemmefrontens ledelse*, pp. 45 ff.

81. "Referat av opplysninger gitt Undersøkelseskommisjonen av rektor Magnus Jensen 28. april 1947," UKs arkiv, Box 10, envelope 8; Rolf Kluge, *Hjemmefrontledelsen tar form. Kretsen dannes*, Samtidshistorisk Forskningsgruppe, Norge og den 2. verdenskrig Series (Oslo: Universitetsforlaget, 1970), pp. 25–26; Wyller, *Nyordning og motstand*, p. 77.

82. "Regjeringen Nygaardsvolds virksomhet fra 7. juni 1940 til 25. juni 1945,"

Innstilling, Vol. 1, Part VI (published separately), p. 166; Wyller, *ibid.*, p. 81.

83. Ole Kristian Grimnes, "Litt om Kretsen og Hjemmefrontledelsen," *Motstandskamp, strategi og marinepolitikk*, pp. 118–124; Gunnar Jahn, report to Undersøkelseskommisjonen av 1945, May 24, 1947, UKs arkiv, Box 10, envelope 8.

84. "Regjeringen Nygaardsvolds virksomhet fra 7. juni 1940 til 25. juni 1945," *Innstilling*, Vol. I, Part VI, pp. 165–167; Kluge, *Hjemmefrontledelsen tar form*, pp. 11–12.

85. Helga Stene, "Et bortkommet blad i okkupasjonstidens historie," *Historisk Tidsskrift*, Vol. XLIV, No. 1 (1965), pp. 93–95; Gjelsvik, *Hjemmefronten*, p. 42.

86. "Referat av opplysninger gitt Undersøkelseskommisjonen av statsråd Jens Chr. Hauge 27. mars 1946, UKs arkiv, Box 9, envelope 22; "Regjeringen Nygaardsvolds virksomhet fra 7. juni 1940 til 25. juni 1945, *Innstilling*, Vol. I, Part VI, pp. 168–169, 173–174; Grimnes, *Hjemmefrontens ledelse*, p. 284; Skodvin, "Historisk innleiing," *Om landssvikoppgjøret*, p. 11.

87. Quisling, statement of July 28, 1945, HI, Skodvin Collection, 1942 folder.

88. Testimony of Gerhard Berghold, August 23, 1945, *Straffesak*, p. 147.

89. Skodvin, review of Wyller, *Nyordning og motstand*, *Historisk Tidsskrift*, Vol, 39, No. 2, pp. 192–193.

90. Paulsen, "Terboven i konflikt med Kriegsmarine," *Motstandskamp, strategi og marinepolitikk*, p. 84.

91. Scheidt to Schreiber, January 24, 1941; Schreiber to Schickedanz, February 14, 1941, HI, Skodvin Collection, 1940 folder.

92. Paulsen, "Terboven i konflikt med Kriegsmarine," *Motstandskamp, strategi og marinepolitikk*, p. 84.

93. Arnt Rishovd to Quisling, January 3, 1941, HI, Skodvin Collection, 1941 folder.

94. Sveen, report of March 14, 1941, for the Propaganda Division of Gulbrand Lunde's Culture and Public Information Department, *ibid.*

95. Quisling to Wegener, February 14, 1941, DA, Quislingsaken, folder #1.

96. *Ibid.*

97. Press division directive, 1:00 P.M.

but no date, HI, Skodvin Collection, 1941 folder.

98. Quisling to Lammers, March 10, 1941, *ibid.*, 1940 folder; Hagelin to Lammers, May 29, 1941, *Tillegsutdrag i Offentlig Straffesak mot A. V. Hagelin*, pp. 13–16.

99. Quisling, statement of July 28, 1945, HI, Skodvin Collection, 1942 folder; Quisling, statement of August 2, 1945, police report #105, HI, Skodvin Collection.

100. Kjeldstadli, *Hjemmestyrkene*, pp. 48–49; Paulsen, "Terboven i konflikt med Kriegsmarine," *Motstandskamp, strategi og marinepolitikk*, p. 80.

101. Kjeldstadli, *ibid.*, p. 49.

102. *Ibid.*; Skodvin, "Det store fremstøt," *Norges krig*, Vol. II, pp. 658–661.

103. Kjeldstadli, *ibid.*; Skodvin, *ibid.*, p. 661.

104. Paulsen, "Terboven i konflikt med Kriegsmarine," *Motstandskamp, strategi og marinepolitikk*, pp. 84–85; Skodvin, *ibid.*, p. 662.

105. Paulsen, *ibid.*, p. 85; Kjeldstadli, *Hjemmestyrkene*, p. 32.

106. Paulsen, *ibid.*; Skodvin, "Det store fremstøt," *Norges krig*, Vol. II, p. 665.

107. Kjeldstadli, *Hjemmestyrkene*, p. 33.

108. Paulsen, "Terboven i konflikt med Kriegsmarine," *Motstandskamp, strategi og marinepolitikk*, p. 86.

109. *Ibid.*, p. 85.

110. *Ibid.*, pp. 86–87.

111. Quisling himself alluded to such rumors in his letter to Dr. Lammers. Quisling to Lammers, March 10, 1941, HI, Skodvin Collection, 1940 folder. See also Skodvin, "Det store fremstøt," *Norges krig*, Vol. II, pp. 665–666.

112. Scheidt to Quisling, February 27, 1941, HI, Skodvin Collection, *ibid.*

113. Rosenberg, "Aktennotiz für den Führer," March 4, 1941, *ibid.*

114. Schickedanz to Lammers, March 5, 1941, *ibid.*, 1941 folder.

115. Skodvin, "Det store fremstøt," *Norges krig*, Vol. II, pp. 663–664; H. R. Trevor-Roper, *The Last Days of Hitler* (3rd ed.; New York: Collier Books, 1962), p. 191.

116. Quisling to Lammers, March 10, 1941, HI, Skodvin Collection, 1940 folder.

117. *Ibid.*

118. Lammers to Quisling, April 7, 1941, *ibid.*, 1941 folder.

119. Quoted in Skodvin, "Det store fremstøt," *Norges krig*, Vol. II, p. 668.

120. Paulsen, "Terboven i konflikt med Kriegsmarine," *Motstandskamp, strategi og marinepolitikk*, pp. 88–89.

121. *Ibid.*, p. 89.

122. *Ibid.*, p. 88. Boehm's and Schreiber's reports were dated April 7. Boehm, who forwarded the reports, made an addendum on April 8 which gave an optimistic and entirely illusory assessment of the significance of Quisling's assurance of April 8.

123. *Ibid.*, pp. 88–89.

124. Author unknown, report from Oslo of May 23, 1941, HI, Skodvin Collection, notes on microfilm, München, MA/11.

125. Hagelin to Lammers, May 29, 1941, HI, Skodvin Collection, 1941 folder.

126. *Ibid.*

127. Note of a conversation between Quisling and Wegener, May 29, 1941, HI, Skodvin Collection, notes on microfilm, München, MA/11.

128. Scheidt to Quisling, February 27, 1941, HI, Skodvin Collection, 1940 folder.

129. "De norske frivillige igår tatt i ed av Reichsführer SS Himmler," *Fritt Folk*, January 31, 1941.

130. "Den første avdeling av Norges SS oprettet med kst. statsråd JONAS LIE som sjef," *Fritt Folk*, May 23, 1941. The Norwegian SS, composed of NS members, took oaths of allegiance to Adolf Hitler and Quisling.

131. Scheidt, "Aktennotiz für Reichsleiter Rosenberg," May 30, 1941, HI, Skodvin Collection, 1941 folder.

132. *Ibid.*

133. Paulsen, "Terboven i konflikt med Kriegsmarine," *Motstandskamp, strategi og marinepolitikk*, pp. 89–90.

134. Hagelin to Scheidt, July 4, 1941, HI, Skodvin Collection, 1941, folder.

135. Quisling to Hitler, June 19, 1941, UKs arkiv, Box 24, envelope 6.

136. Scheidt to Hagelin, June 24, 1941, HI, Skodvin Collection, 1941 folder.

137. Hagelin to Scheidt, July 4, 1941, *ibid.*; Terboven to Hagelin, July 10, 1941, *ibid.*

138. Hans Clausen Korff, "Aktenvermerk über das Verhältnis zu den Staatsräten

und Nasjonal Samling," July 25, 1941, based on a discussion between Wegener, Otte, Korff, and Berghold, June 22, 1941. In *ibid.*

139. Terboven to Hagelin, July 10, 1941, *ibid.*

140. See below, pp. 606–607.

141. Skodvin, "Det store fremstøt," *Norges krig*, Vol. II, p. 684.

142. Quoted in *ibid.*, pp. 685–686.

143. Scheidt to Hagelin, June 24, 1941, HI, Skodvin Collection, 1941 folder.

144. Quisling to Lammers, August 2, 1941, DA, Quislingsaken, folder #1.

145. *Ibid.*

146. Lammers to Quisling, August 17, 1941, HI, Skodvin Collection, 1941 folder.

147. Paulsen, "Terboven i konflikt med Kriegsmarine," *Motstandskamp, strategi og marinepolitikk*, p. 90; Boehm, *Norwegen zwischen England und Deutschland*, p. 135.

148. Scheidt to Hagelin, August 19, 1941, HI, Skodvin Collection, 1941 folder.

149. Wegener, "Notat for herr Reichskommissar," Norwegian translation, September 1, 1941, DA, Quislingsaken, folder #1.

150. *Ibid.*

151. Hansteen had been a member of the Communist party before World War II, and had been given an honorary rank of colonel in the Red Army. However, he broke with the Communists after the beginning of the war because of the party's initial position of pro-German neutrality. He became the strongest and most forceful advocate of resistance within the LO leadership. Because of his critical references to Hansteen, one of the charges brought against Quisling when he was tried for treason was that of being an accessory to Hansteen's execution. See *Straffesak*, p. 5.

152. Wegener, "Notat for herr Reichskommissar," Norwegian translation, September 1, 1941, DA, Quislingsaken, folder #1.

153. Scheidt to Hagelin, September 6, 1941, HI, Skodvin Collection, 1941 folder.

154. Skodvin, *Striden om okkupasjonsstyret*, p. 378, fn. 66.

155. Boehm, *Norwegen zwischen England und Deutschland*, p. 140.

156. Dr. Alfred Huhnhäuser, quoted in Skodvin, "Det store fremstøt," *Norges krig*, Vol. II, p. 715.

157. Boehm, *Norwegen zwischen England und Deutschland*, p. 140.

158. Paulsen, "Terboven i konflikt med Kriegsmarine," *Motstandskamp, strategi og marinepolitikk*, p. 90; Boehm, *ibid.*, pp. 137–138.

159. Paulsen, *ibid.*, p. 91; Boehm, *ibid.*, p. 138.

160. Quoted in Boehm, *ibid.*, p. 139.

161. Wegener to Quisling, September 16, 1941, *Dokumenter i offentlig straffesak mot Vidkun Quisling*, pp. 60–61.

162. *Ibid.*

163. Quisling, memorandum of September 17, 1941, DA, Quislingsaken, folder #1.

164. *Ibid.*

165. "Skrivelse til Høyesterettsadvokat A. V. Heiberg fra K. S. Irgens, datert 11. oktober 1945," *Irgens-saken*, p. 89.

166. Quoted in Skodvin, "Det store fremstøt," *Norges krig*, Vol. II, p. 716.

167. *Ibid.*

168. "Skrivelse til Høyesterettsadvokat A. V. Heiberg fra K. S. Irgens, datert 11. oktober 1945," *Irgens-saken*, p. 89.

169. "Minister Fuglesang," *Fritt Folk*, September 26, 1941.

170. Fuglesang, statement of January 26, 1946, HI, Skodvin Collection, police reports, #398.

171. "Minister Lippestad," *Fritt Folk*, September 26, 1941.

172. Kjeldstadli, *Hjemmestyrkene*, pp. 53–54; Skodvin, "Det store fremstøt," *Norges krig*, Vol. II, p. 718.

173. *Ibid.*

174. Quoted in Skodvin, *ibid.*

175. Sverre Hartmann, "Lofot- og Vågsøyraidene margstjal Statsakten: En militærpolitisk studie," *Samtiden*, Vol. 64 (1955), p. 488; Boehm, *Norwegen zwischen England und Deutschland*, pp. 150–151; Skodvin, *Striden om okkupasjonsstyret*, pp. 340–341; Skodvin, *ibid.*, pp. 714–715.

176. Quisling to Wegener, November 8, 1941, HI, Skodvin Collection, 1941 folder.

177. Wegener indicates that the discussion between Quisling and Terboven took place some time in November, while Sverre Hartmann maintains that their meeting occurred at the less likely time of mid-December. See Boehm, *Norwegen zwischen England und Deutschland*, pp. 150–151; and Hartmann, "Lofot- og Vågsøyraidene marg-

stjal Statsakten," *Samtiden*, Vol. 64, pp. 492–493.

178. Hartmann, *ibid.*, p. 489, pp. 492–493; Boehm, *ibid.*, p. 151.

179. *Ibid.*

180. Skodvin, "Det store fremstøt," *Norges krig*, Vol. II, pp. 722–723; Christensen, *Okkupasjonsår og etterkrigstid*, p. 294.

181. Wyller, *Nyordning og motstand*, p. 90; Skodvin, *ibid.*, pp. 718–719; Kjeldstadli, *Hjemmestyrkene*, pp. 53–54.

182. *Fritt Folk*, December 15, 1941. Hagelin quoted in Skodvin, *ibid.*, p. 720.

183. Skodvin, "Norsk okkupasjonshistorie i europeisk samanheng," *Nordisk Tidskrift*, Vol. 27, pp. 313–314; Wyller, *Nyordning og motstand*, p. 90.

184. Kjeldstadli, *Hjemmestyrkene*, pp. 36–37; Paulsen, "Terboven i konflikt med Kriegsmarine," *Motstandskamp, strategi og marinepolitikk*, pp. 92–93.

185. Paulsen, *ibid.*, p. 93; Kjeldstadli, *ibid.*, p. 37.

186. Paulsen, *ibid.*, Kjeldstadli, *ibid.*, p. 54.

187. Paulsen, *ibid.*, pp. 93–94; Skodvin, "Norsk okkupasjonshistorie i europeisk samanheng," *Nordisk Tidskrift*, Vol. 27, p. 313.

188. Christensen, *Okkupasjonsår og etterkrigstid*, p. 298; Bull, *Klassekamp og fellesskap*, p. 427.

189. Skodvin, "Norsk okkupasjonshistorie i europeisk samanheng," *Nordisk Tidskrift*, Vol. 27, p. 314; Kjeldstadli, *Hjemmestyrkene*, p. 54.

190. Schreiber, "Aktennotiz," January 23, 1942, HI, Skodvin Collection, 1941 folder; Paulsen, "Terboven i konflikt med Kriegsmarine," *Motstandskamp, strategi og marinepolitikk*, p. 94, p. 97.

191. The earliest specific reference to Terboven's proposal dates from January 22. See Paulsen, *ibid.*, p. 95.

192. Quisling, undated document listing the dates and terms by which he would take over as head of government, HI, Skodvin Collection, 1942 folder. In addition, details of this plan were included in Schreiber's "Aktennotiz," January 23, 1942, HI, Skodvin Collection, 1941 folder. See also Paulsen, *ibid.*

193. Paulsen, *ibid.*

194. Magne Skodvin, unpublished MS

dealing with the background to Quisling's takeover as Minister President, HI, Skodvin Collection, 1942 folder. Hereafter referred to as Skodvin, MS.

195. Schreiber, "Aktennotiz," January 23, 1942, HI, Skodvin Collection, 1941 folder.

196. *Ibid.*; Paulsen, "Terboven i konflikt med Kriegsmarine," *Motstandskamp, strategi og marinepolitikk*, pp. 95–96.

197. Skodvin, MS; Louis Lochner, ed., *The Goebbels Diaries* (Garden City, N.Y.: Doubleday & Co., 1948), pp. 36–37.

198. Quisling to Terboven, January 26, 1942, DA, Quislingsaken, folder #1.

199. Skodvin, MS.

200. Quisling to Terboven, January 29, 1942, HI, Skodvin Collection, 1942 folder.

201. Terboven's discussion with Schiedermair was recorded by Swedish intelligence agents, who tapped the line. Stenographic copy in DA, Quislingsaken, Straffesak – Etterforskning mot Quisling, folder #7.

202. Wyller, *Nyordning og motstand*, p. 92.

203. Goebbels, diary entry of January 24, 1942, quoted in Kjeldstadli, *Hjemmestyrkene*, pp. 137–138.

Notes to Chapter XIV

1. Skodvin, "Det store fremstøt," *Norges krig*, Vol. II, p. 727.

2. Terboven and Schiedermair, telephone conversation, January 29, 1942, stenographic copy, DA, Quislingsaken, folder #7.

3. Skodvin, MS.

4. Statement by Birger Liljedahl Vassbotten, June 11, 1945, HI, Skodvin Collection, 1942 folder.

5. Quoted in Skodvin, "Det store fremstøt," *Norges krig*, Vol. II, p. 726.

6. "Petition" from the NS ministers to Quisling, January 31, 1942, HI, Skodvin Collection, 1942 folder.

7. Skodvin, "Det store fremstøt," *Norges krig*, Vol. II, pp. 727–728.

8. Berit Nøkleby, *Holdningskamp*, Vol. IV of *Norge i krig. Fremmedåk og frihets-*

kamp 1940–1945, Magne Skodvin, ed. (Oslo: Aschehoug, 1986), p. 16; Mogens, *Tyskerne, Quisling og vi andre*, p. 272.

9. Wyller, *Nyordning og motstand*, p. 92; Skodvin, "Det store fremstøt," *Norges krig*, Vol. II, pp. 729–730.

10. Boehm, *Norwegen zwischen England und Deutschland*, pp. 147–148.

11. Quisling, speech at Akershus Castle, February 1, 1942, in Vidkun Quisling, *Mot nytt land. Artikler og taler av Vidkun Quisling 1941–1943*, Haldis Neegaard Østbye, ed., (Oslo: Blix forlag, for NS Rikspropagandaledelsen, n.d.), pp. 64–66.

12. *Ibid.*, p. 76.

13. *Ibid.*, pp. 74–75.

14. *Ibid.*, p. 69.

15. *Ibid.*, p. 83.

16. *Fritt Folk*, May 26, 1942.

17. Quisling, *Mot nytt land*, p. 71.

18. *Straffesak*, p. 105.

19. Skodvin, "Det store fremstøt," *Norges krig*, Vol. II, p. 729.

20. Luihn, *De illegale avisene*, p. 86.

21. Skodvin, "Det store fremstøt," *Norges krig*, Vol. II, p. 731.

22. *Norges forhold til Sverige under krigen*, Vol. III, p. 346.

23. *Morgenbladet*, February 3, 1942, quoted in *Dokumenter i offentlig straffesak*, p. 67.

24. *Morgenbladet*, February 4, 1942, quoted in *ibid.*

25. Lochner, *The Goebbels Diaries*, p. 66.

26. Goebbels, diary notation of February 4, 1942, *ibid.*, p. 68.

27. Goebbels, diary notation of February 3, 1942, *ibid.*, p. 66.

28. Goebbels, diary notation of February 4, 1942, *ibid.*, p. 68.

29. Quoted in Kjeldstadli, *Hjemmestyrkene*, p. 138.

30. Skodvin, "Det store fremstøt," *Norges krig*, Vol. II, p. 731.

31. *Straffesak*, p. 103. See also Quisling's statement of August 2, 1945, HI, Skodvin Collection, police reports, #105.

32. Quisling's expectation to serve as regent is made in Schreiber's report of January 23, 1942. Although Schreiber refers to the body that would elect Quisling as being an archaic assembly made up of representatives from different social classes (*stenderforsam-*

ling), undoubtedly what Quisling had in mind was his long-planned corporative body. See Paulsen, "Terboven i konflikt med Kriegsmarine," *Motstandskamp, strategi og marinepolitikk*, p. 95; Boehm, *Norwegen zwischen England und Deutschland*, p. 145.

33. "Besuch des norwegischen Ministerpräsident Quisling in Berlin vom 12. bis 15. Februar 1942: Program," HI, Skodvin Collection, 1942 folder.

34. *Ibid.*

35. Wærmann, note of a conversation with Lammers, February 20, 1942, to Foreign Minister Ribbentrop, Auswärtiges Amt, HI, Skodvin Collection, 1942 folder. Lammers retained possession of the original copy of Quisling's memorandum.

36. "Memorandum om nyordningen i Norge," Norwegian translation, February 10, 1942, *Dokumenter i offentlig straffesak*, pp. 68–69.

37. *Ibid.*

38. *Ibid.*

39. Goebbels, diary notation, February 13, 1942, Lochner, *The Goebbels Diaries*, p. 83. The quote in German is from Kjeldstadli, *Hjemmestyrkene*, p. 142. Lochner translated this sentence as: "That, of course, is very childish."

40. "Besuch des norwegischen Ministerpräsident Quisling in Berlin vom 12. bis 15. Februar 1942: Program," HI, Skodvin Collection, 1942 folder.

41. Message from the Propaganda Ministry to Hans Moser, chief of the *Reichskommissariat*'s *Presse Abteilung*, February 14, 1942, HI, Skodvin Collection, 1942 folder.

42. "Besuch des norwegischen *Minister-präsident* Quisling in Berlin vom 12. bis 15. Februar 1942: Program," *ibid.*

43. "Ministerpresident Quisling i besøk hos storadmiral Raeder," *Fritt Folk*, February 18, 1942.

44. Raeder to Boehm, February 19, 1942, HI, Skodvin Collection, 1942 folder. See also Boehm, *Norwegen zwischen England und Deutschland*, pp. 152–153.

45. Boehm, *ibid.*, p. 153.

46. Wærmann, note of a conversation with Lammers, February 20, 1942, to Foreign Minister Ribbentrop, Auswärtiges Amt, HI, Skodvin Collection, 1942 folder.

47. Wyller, *Nyordning og motstand*, p. 93, pp. 98–99.

48. Quisling, *Redegjørelse fra Vidkun Quisling til siktelse fremsatt i Oslo Forhørsrett*, p. 13.

49. *Fritt Folk*, May 26, 1942.

50. Wyller, *Nyordning og motstand*, pp. 98–99.

51. "Memorandum om nyordningen i Norge," Norwegian translation, February 10, 1942, *Dokumenter i offentlig straffesak*, pp. 68–69.

52. Luihn, *De illegale avisene*, p. 86.

53. Johannes Ø. Dietrichson, "Trekk fra kampen om ungdomstjenesten," *Norges krig*, Vol. III, p. 111.

54. Law establishing *Norges Lærersamband*, published on the title page of *Norsk Skuleblad*, Vol. 9, No. 7 (February 14, 1942).

55. Wyller, *Nyordning og motstand*, pp. 100–103.

56. Quisling, *Mot nytt land*, pp. 70–71.

57. Magnus Jensen, "Kampen om skolen," *Norges krig*, Vol. III, p. 81.

58. *Ibid.*, p. 83.

59. Dietrichson, "Trekk fra kampen om ungdomstjenesten," *Norges krig*, Vol. III, p. 111.

60. Quoted in *ibid.*, p. 112.

61. Wyller, *Nyordning og motstand*, pp. 106–107.

62. *Ibid.*, p. 106.

63. Jensen, "Kampen om skolen," *Norges krig*, Vol. III, p. 82.

64. Wyller, *Nyordning og motstand*, p. 107; Gjelsvik, *Hjemmefronten*, pp. 68–69.

65. Quoted in Schjelderup, *På bred front*, p. 142.

66. Wyller, *Nyordning og motstand*, p. 109.

67. Quoted in *ibid.*, pp. 108–109.

68. *Ibid.*, p. 109. See also p. 341, fn. 40.

69. *Ibid.*, p. 111.

70. *Fritt Folk*, February 24, 1942, reprinted in "Utdrag i sak . . . mot J. A. Lippestad," pp. 45–46.

71. Jensen, "Kampen om skolen," *Norges krig*, Vol. III, p. 86.

72. *Ibid.*

73. *Ibid.*

74. *Ibid.*, pp. 86–87; Bull, *Klassekamp og fellesskap*, pp. 405–406.

75. Jensen, *ibid.*; Bull, *ibid.*, p. 406.

76. Dietrichson, "Trekk fra kampen om ungdomstjenesten," *Norges krig*, Vol. III, pp. 121–122.

77. Schjelderup, *På bred front*, p. 139.

78. Molland, "Kirkens kamp," *Norges krig*, Vol. III, p. 50.

79. The letter is quoted in its entirety in Schjelderup, *På bred front*, pp. 145–146.

80. Christensen, *Okkupasjonsår og etterkrigstid*, pp. 302–303.

81. Some speculation has occurred that Terboven's violent criticism of Berggrav in early 1942 was really a disguised attack against Falkenhorst. See Skodvin, "Det store fremstøt," *Norges krig*, Vol. II, pp. 729–730; and Wyller, *Nyordning og motstand*, p. 92. At present, however, there are no documentary sources to sustain such a conclusion. Terboven, as noted earlier, spent a good portion of his speech at Akershus Castle on February 1 denouncing Berggrav. Terboven had even earlier informed Goebbels of his plans to move against the Bishop. Goebbels, recalling the difficulties which the Nazi party had experienced in its confrontations with organized religious denominations in Germany, did not respond enthusiastically. See Goebbels, diary notations of January 27 and January 29, 1942, Lochner, *The Goebbels Diaries*, p. 52, pp. 55–56.

82. Molland, "Kirkens kamp," *Norges krig*, Vol. III, pp. 48–50.

83. *Ibid.*, pp. 50–51.

84. *Ibid.*, p. 51.

85. Schjelderup, *På bred front*, pp. 147–148.

86. *Ibid.*, p. 147; Molland, "Kirkens kamp," *Norges krig*, Vol. III, p. 51.

87. Molland, *ibid.*, pp. 51–52.

88. Gjelsvik, *Hjemmefronten*, p. 72.

89. Molland, "Kirkens kamp," *Norges krig*, Vol. III, p. 54.

90. *Ibid.*

91. *Ibid.*, p. 58.

92. *Ibid.*, p. 56.

93. *Ibid.*, p. 58. Even during his internment at his cabin, however, Berggrav succeeded in maintaining contact with the outside world through his police guards. Christensen, *Okkupasjonsår og etterkrigstid*, p. 307.

94. Molland, *ibid.*, p. 56.

95. Quoted in *ibid.*

96. Schjelderup, *På bred front*, p. 194.

97. Molland, "Kirkens kamp," *Norges krig*, Vol. III, p. 56.

98. *Ibid.*, pp. 67–68.

99. Quoted in Ferdinand Schjelderup, *Over bakkekammen 1943–1944* (Oslo: Gyldendal norsk Forlag, 1949), p. 15.

100. Quoted in *ibid.*, p. 16.

101. Molland, "Kirkens kamp," *Norges krig*, Vol. III, pp. 59–61.

102. Goebbels, diary notation, April 15, 1942, Lochner, *The Goebbels Diaries*, p. 170.

103. Gjelsvik, *Hjemmefronten*, p. 74.

104. Falkenhorst, weekly report to the *Oberkommando der Wehrmacht*, April 14, 1942, HI, Skodvin Collection, 1942 folder. Also quoted in Wyller, *Nyordning og motstand*, p. 125.

105. Wyller, *ibid.*

106. *Ibid.*, p. 112.

107. *Ibid.*, p. 113; Jensen, "Kampen om skolen," *Norges krig*, Vol. III, p. 88.

108. Skodvin, "Historisk innleiing," *Om landssvikoppgjøret*, p. 34; Jensen, *ibid.*, p. 87.

109. Magnus Jensen, *Fra 1905 til våre dager*, Vol. IV of *Norges historie* (3rd ed.; Oslo: Universitetsforlaget, 1965), p. 167. No female educators were arrested for public relations reasons.

110. Schjelderup, *På bred front*, pp. 196–201. At the largest concentration camp, where some 700 teachers were imprisoned at Jørstadmoen in eastern Norway, 28 to 30 gave in and joined the Teachers' Union. Previously five members of this group had submitted, including three who were ill. A smaller group of teachers, interned at Falstad in Trøndelag, were subjected to similar treatment. They held out until the end of April, when all but one gave in. This did not, however, influence the eventual outcome of the teachers' struggle. See Jensen, "Skolen i kamp," *Norges krig*, Vol. III, pp. 88–89.

111. Schjelderup, *ibid.*, pp. 202–213.

112. Skodvin, "Historisk innleiing," *Om landssvikoppgjøret*, p. 34.

113. Schjelderup, *På bred front*, p. 188.

114. Jensen, "Kampen om skolen," *Norges krig*, Vol. III, p. 93.

115. Irgens to A. V. Heiberg, October 11, 1945, *Irgens-saken*, pp. 91–92.

116. Kåre Norum's description of the

plight of the group of teachers who were first imprisoned at Grini, then transported to Jørstadmoen, and finally shipped aboard *Skjerstad* to Kirkenes. Quoted in Schjelderup, *På bred front*, p. 205. The entire report is quoted in Schjelderup, pp. 196–215.

117. Jensen, "Kampen om skolen," *Norges krig*, Vol. III, p. 94; Bull, *Klassekamp og fellesskap*, p. 407.

118. Jensen, *ibid.*

119. Living under difficult conditions, the teachers were put to work loading and unloading German ships at Kirkenes during the summer. In the fall, faced with having to spend a harsh Arctic winter under intolerable conditions, the group decided to give in and technically agreed to join the Teachers' Corporation. But by this time their retreat no longer had any symbolic importance. Quisling's entire offensive in 1942, not merely the campaign against the teachers, had ended in failure by the time the group returned from exile.

120. Skodvin, "Historisk innleiing," *Om landssvikoppgjøret*, p. 34.

121. Jensen, "Kampen om skolen," *Norges krig*, Vol. III, p. 98.

122. Christensen, *Okkupasjonsår og etterkrigstid*, p. 316; Jensen, *ibid.*, p. 86, pp. 96–97.

123. Quoted in Jensen, "Kampen om skolen," *Norges krig*, Vol. III, p. 98.

124. *Ibid.*

125. *Ibid.*, p. 99.

126. Quisling, trial testimony, August 24, 1945, *Straffesak*, p. 203.

127. Jensen, "Kampen om skolen," *Norges krig*, Vol. III, p. 99; Christensen *Okkupasjonsår og etterkrigstid*, p. 317.

128. Testimony of Josef Faaland, August 24, 1945, *Straffesak*, p. 202.

129. Altogether sixteen teachers from Stabekk School were arrested at this time. Four teachers from the school had previously been interned in March, with three being sent on the *Skjerstad* to Kirkenes. Testimony of Faaland, *ibid.*, pp. 202–203.

130. Jensen, "Kampen om skolen," *Norges krig*, Vol. III, p. 99; Christensen, *Okkupasjonsår og etterkrigstid*, p. 317.

131. Skodvin, "Historisk innleiing," *Om landssvikoppgjøret*, pp. 33–34.

132. Wyller, *Nyordning og motstand*, p. 110, pp. 132–133.

133. *Ibid.*, p. 110.

134. *Ibid.*, p. 132.

135. *Ibid.*, p. 131.

136. Schjelderup, *På bred front*, p. 166.

137. Wyller, *Nyordning og motstand*, p. 114.

138. Whist to Quisling, March 12, 1942, DA, "Utdrag i sak . . . mot Alf Larsen Whist," p. 15.

139. *Ibid.*, pp. 15–23.

140. Wyller, *Nyordning og motstand*, p. 117.

141. Carl T. Lohrbauer, "Skrivelse fra Innenriksdepartement, Foreningskontoret, til byråsjef Getz, Innenriksdepartement," January 21, 1942, DA, "Utdrag i sak . . . mot J. A. Lippestad," pp. 37–38.

142. Quisling, decree co-signed by Fuglesang appointing J. A. Lippestad in charge of preparation for Norway's Labor Corporation, March 16, 1942, in *ibid.*, p. 153.

143. Wyller, *Nyordning og motstand*, p. 117.

144. *Ibid.*, p. 120.

145. *Ibid.*, pp. 118–119; Skodvin, "Historisk innleiing," *Om landssvikoppgjøret*, p. 32.

146. Wyller, *ibid.*, pp. 119–120, p. 343, fn. 76.

147. *Ibid.*, pp. 120–121.

148. Lippestad to the NS Personnel Office, March 30, 1942, DA, "Utdrag i sak . . . mot J. A. Lippestad," pp. 55–56; Wyller, *ibid.*, p. 121.

149. Lippestad to the Culture and Public Information Department's Press Directorate, March 6, 1942, "Utdrag i sak . . . ," *ibid.*, pp. 48–49.

150. Wyller, *Nyordning og motstand*, p. 121.

151. *Ibid.*, p. 122.

152. Alf Ottesen, appendix 1 of a report by Lars Evensen to Trygve Lie, May 5, 1942, *Regjeringen og hjemmefronten under krigen*, p. 84.

153. Gjelsvik, *Hjemmefronten*, p. 74.

154. Wyller, *Nyordning og motstand*, pp. 126–127.

155. *Fritt Folk*, May 2, 1942, quoted in *ibid.*, p. 127.

156. Wyller, *ibid.*, pp. 130–131.

157. *Ibid.*, p. 127.

158. Jens Berg, appendix 3 of Lars Evensen's report to Trygve Lie, May 5, 1942, *Regjeringen og hjemmefronten under krigen*, p. 89.

159. Lippestad to *Abteilungsleiter* Fritz Johlitz in the *Reichskommissariat*'s *Abteilung Arbeit und Sozialwesen*, May 1, 1942, DA, "Utdrag i sak ... mot J. A. Lippestad," p. 58.

160. Quisling to Odd Fossum, May 5, 1942, *ibid.*, p. 61.

161. Wyller, *Nyordning og motstand*, pp. 135–136.

162. *Ibid.*, p. 117.

163. Boehm to Raeder, April 4, 1942, quoted in Paulsen, "Terboven i konflikt med Kriegsmarine," *Motstandskamp, strategi og marinepolitikk*, p. 98.

164. This undated memorandum received its final formulation by the end of March. Quoted in Boehm, *Norwegen zwischen England und Deutschland*, pp. 153–156. See also Paulsen, *ibid.*

165. Boehm, *ibid.*, p. 156; Paulsen, *ibid.*

166. Quisling to Hitler, "Memorandum angående Norges innen- og utenrikspolitiske stilling i dag," (Norwegian trans.), June 9, 1942, DA, Quislingsaken, folder #1; Skodvin, MS.

167. *Ibid.* It appears that Quisling took Terboven's initiative to begin peace negotiations quite seriously. Internal discussions took place within NS over what form a peace settlement should take. Frederik Prytz, now serving as Quisling's new Finance Minister, sent the draft of an 11 article proposed peace treaty to Hagelin for comment. A copy of the draft is located in HI, Skodvin Collection, 1942 folder.

168. Finance Minister Prytz and Labor Minister Hustad replied in separate memoranda dated June 1, 1942. Located in *ibid.* See also Wyller, *Nyordning og motstand*, p. 141.

169. Quisling to Hitler, "Memorandum angående Norges innen- og utenrikspolitiske stilling i dag," June 9, 1942, DA, Quislingsaken, folder #1.

170. *Ibid.*

171. The letter, dated June 22, 1942, was received by Quisling on the 29th. See Wyller, *Nyordning og motstand*, p. 348, fn. 37.

172. Lammers to Quisling, June 22, 1942, HI, Skodvin Collection, 1942 folder.

173. Lammers to Hagelin, June 22, 1942, *ibid.*

174. Gerhard Berghold, statement of July 5, 1945, *Straffesak*, p. 595.

175. Wyller, *Nyordning og motstand*, p. 143.

176. Quisling, *Mot nytt land*, p. 72.

177. Wyller, *Nyordning og motstand*, pp. 131–132.

178. *Ibid.*, pp. 142–143.

179. *Ibid.*, p. 144.

180. Wyller, *Fra okkupasjonsårenes maktkamp*, p. 159.

181. Quisling, *Mot nytt land*, p. 72.

182. Wyller, *Nyordning og motstand*, pp. 145–146.

183. *Ibid.*, p. 141, p. 144.

184. *Ibid.*, p. 145.

185. *Ibid.*, p. 144.

186. Thorleif Dahl to Frederik Prytz, August 8, 1942, quoted in *ibid.*

187. Wyller, *ibid.*

188. *Ibid.*, p. 146.

189. Draft proposal, "kunngjøring fra Ministerpresidenten om Rikstinget," *Om landssvikoppgjøret*, p. 168.

190. Wyller, *Nyordning og motstand*, p. 146.

191. *Ibid.*, pp. 136–139.

192. *Ibid.*, pp. 138–140.

193. *Ibid.*, p. 140.

194. *Ibid.*

195. See above, pp. 503–505.

196. Wyller, *Nyordning og motstand*, pp. 139–140.

197. Schjelderup, *På bred front*, pp. 281–282.

198. Wyller, *Nyordning og motstand*, pp. 148–149.

199. Jens Boyesen, "Fra yrkesorganisasjonenes kamp," *Norges krig*, Vol III, p. 302.

200. Wyller, *Nyordning og motstand*, p. 149.

201. *Ibid.*

202. *Ibid.*, pp. 149–150, p. 155.

203. *Ibid.*, p. 150.

204. Boyesen, "Fra yrkesorganisasjonenes kamp," *Norges krig*, Vol. III, pp. 302–303.

205. Wyller, *Nyordning og motstand*, p. 151.

206. *Ibid.*, pp. 151–152.

207. *Ibid.*, p. 152; Schjelderup, *På bred front*, pp. 284–285.

208. Wyller, *ibid.*, pp. 151–152.

209. *Ibid.*, p. 155.

210. *Ibid.*, p. 157.

211. *Ibid.*, p. 158.

212. *Ibid.*, p. 159.

213. DA, "Tilleggsutdrag i offentlig straffesak mot Albert Viljam Hagelin," stenciled (Oslo: n.d.), pp. 35–39.

214. Terboven to Hagelin, August 22, 1942, DA, "Utdrag i Høyesterettssak S nr. 36/1946 mot Albert Viljam Hagelin," stenciled (Oslo: 1946), pp. 1–2.

215. Wyller, *Nyordning og motstand*, p. 159.

216. *Ibid.*, pp. 160–162.

217. Lammers to Quisling, September 17, 1942, *Straffesak*, pp. 546–547.

218. Raeder to Boehm, October 23, 1942, quoted in Paulsen, "Terboven i konflikt med Kriegsmarine," *Motstandskamp, strategi og marinepolitikk*, p. 100.

219. *Ibid.*

220. Wyller, *Nyordning og motstand*, pp. 161–162.

221. *Ibid.*, pp. 152–153.

222. Quisling, "Organisering av et riksting. Tale i Universitetets gamle festsal 25. september 1942," *Mot nytt land*, pp. 132–133.

223. Wyller, *Nyordning og motstand*, p. 351, fn. 90.

224. Quisling, "Organisering av et riksting. Tale i Universitetets gamle festsal 25. september 1942," *Mot nytt land*, p. 122, pp. 138–139.

225. Quisling, "Vi må ta sikte på et Europa som ikke spiller sitt blod og sine krefter i innbyrdes strid, men utgjør en organisert enhet. Tale på Riksmøtet 25. [sic.] september 1942," *ibid.*, pp. 152–153. The speech was actually delivered on September 26.

226. Quoted in Wyller, *Nyordning og motstand*, p. 153.

227. Kjeldstadli, *Hjemmestyrkene*, pp. 146–147.

228. *Ibid.*, pp. 148–150.

229. *Ibid.*, pp. 148–149. See above, pp. 592–593.

230. *Ibid.*, p. 150.

Notes to Chapter XV

1. See for example Quisling's telegram to Terboven, ironically enough in response to the *Reichskommisar*'s congratulations on the first anniversary of Quisling's "takeover of power" as Minister President. Published in *Fritt Folk*, February 1, 1943.

2. Paulsen, "Terboven i konflikt med Kriegsmarine," *Motstandskamp, strategi og marinepolitikk*, pp. 108–111.

3. Rosenberg to Terboven, June 2, 1944, HI, Skodvin Collection, 1944 folder.

4. Terboven to Rosenberg, June 17, 1944, *ibid.*

5. Oskar Mendelsohn, *Jødenes historie i Norge gjennom 300 år*, Vol. II (Oslo: Universitetsforlaget, 1986), pp. 109–110; Wilhelm Arthur Konstantin Wagner, statement of June 23, 1945, *ibid.*, police reports, #76. See also Wagner's testimony of August 24, 1945, *Straffesak*, pp. 203–204.

6. Quisling, "Jødene må ut av Europa," *Fritt Folk*, December 7, 1942; Wagner, testimony, *ibid.*, p. 204; Quisling, testimony of August 22, 1945, *ibid.*, p. 130.

7. Mendelsohn, *Jødenes historie i Norge*, Vol. II, pp. 47–48, p. 50.

8. *Ibid.*, p. 48.

9. *Straffesak*, p. 377, pp. 548–549.

10. Karsten Meyer, letter of August 17, 1945, *ibid.*, p. 129.

11. "Lov om meldeplikt for jøder," *Fritt Folk*, November 19, 1942; *Straffesak*, p. 126, p. 377; Mendelsohn, *Jødenes historie i Norge*, Vol. II, pp. 96–97.

12. Mendelsohn, *ibid.*, p. 56, p. 57, p. 74, p. 84, p. 111.

13. *Ibid.*, p. 221; *Om landssvikoppgjøret*, p. 212. Irgens was the only member of Quisling's government who sought to sabotage the arrests. He tipped off the Home Front that the Jews were in danger. See Mendelsohn, *ibid.*, p. 221.

14. Asriel B. Hirsch, testimony of August 23, 1945, *Straffesak*, p. 160; Bull, *Klassekamp og fellesskap*, p. 399.

15. Schjelderup, *På bred front*, pp. 296–297; Gjelsvik, *Hjemmefronten*, p. 79.

16. Mendelsohn, *Jødenes historie i Norge*, Vol. II, pp. 184–185, p. 210.

17. *Ibid.*, p. 103. The letter is quoted in its entirety in *ibid.*, pp. 102–103. It was broadcast over London Radio, published in

the Swedish press, and referred to by the Swedish clergy. See *ibid.*, pp. 103–104.

18. Harold Flender, *Rescue in Denmark* (London: W. H. Allen, 1963), p. 192.

19. Meyer, letter of August 17, 1945, in *Straffesak*, p. 129; Franz Wendt, *Danmarks Historie 1939–1978*, special edition of *Danmarks Historie*, Vol. 14, Hal Koch and John Danstrup, eds. (Copenhagen: Politikens Forlag, 1978), p. 182; Flender, *ibid.*, pp. 171–172.

20. Mendelsohn, *Jødenes historie i Norge*, Vol. II, p. 123, p. 127, p. 320, p. 322. Quisling made a speech on December 6, 1942, in which he insisted that the only solution to the Jewish problem was to expel the Jews from Europe to another part of the world, preferably an island. His allusion was probably to Madagascar. Superficially this may give the impression that he did not have knowledge of the extermination process at this time. However, he would hardly have admitted in a public speech that the Germans were committing genocide.

21. Blehr, Proclamation of May 1, 1943, QA.

22. "En ny milepel passeres: Norges Næringssamband dannet," *Fritt Folk*, May 7, 1943.

23. Skodvin, "Historisk innleiing," *Om landssvikoppgjøret*, p. 32. A good example of how the Business Corporation failed to establish control over business activity is shown in its inability to take over effectively the Brewers' Association. See DA, "Utdrag i . . . sak mot Alf Larsen Whist," pp. 75–84, 109–110, 113–115.

24. Odd Melsom, "Grunnlaget for et Norges Arbeidssamband," *Fritt Folk*, December 1, 1942; "Ministerpresidenten hilser de norske arbeidere på Arbeidets Dag," *Fritt Folk*, May 2, 1944; "Ministerpresidenten gir arbeiderne sin støtte i deres bestrebelser med å danne et arbeidssamband," *Fritt Folk*, May 25, 1944.

25. See *Fritt Folk*, *ibid.*, May 2, 1944, and May 25, 1944. See also the excerpt from the verdict against Fossum in *Om landssvikoppgjøret*, p. 165.

26. Lippestad to *Arbeitungsleiter* Johlitz in the *Reichskommissariat*'s *Abteilung Arbeit und Sozialwesen*, April 6, 1943, DA, "Utdrag i sak . . . mot J. A. Lippestad," Vol. II, pp. 131–132.

27. Andenæs, *Det vanskelige oppgjøret*, p. 33.

28. Fuglesang and Sjønne Melstrøm, "Referat for Riks- og Landsledermøtet 28. 6. 1944 kl. 1800," in Referater fra Riks- og Landsledermøtene folder, QA.

29. Roald Dysthe, Statement of July 7, 1945, HI, Skodvin Collection, police reports, #174; "Direktør Alf Whist utnevnt . . ." *Fritt Folk*, November 11, 1941.

30. DA, "Utdrag i sak . . . mot Alf Larsen Whist," pp. 75–76; *Fritt Folk*, November 4, 1943.

31. Skodvin, *Striden om okkupasjonsstyret i Norge*, p. 334.

32. Tormod Hustad, statement of August 8, 1945, HI, Skodvin Collection, police reports, #229; *Om landssvikoppgjøret*, pp. 163–164.

33. Hustad, statement of August 8, 1945, *ibid.* In addition to Whist's inability to get along with Hustad, his relations with Eivind Blehr, the head of the Business Department, were equally strained because Blehr resented being under Whist's dominance in economic matters. See Whist to Quisling, May 10, 1944, DA, "Utdrag i sak . . . mot Alf Larsen Whist," pp. 120–123.

34. Hustad, statement of August 8, 1945, *ibid.*; Whist to Quisling, May 10, 1944, *ibid.*; *Om landssvikoppgjøret*, pp. 163–164.

35. Testimony of Johan Andreas Lippestad, DA, Offentlig straffesak mot Albert Viljam Hagelin, p. 106.

36. A good example of such resentment from Quisling's old guard is found in Ørnulf Lundesgaard's memo to Quisling, February 28, 1941, HI, Skodvin Collection, 1940 folder.

37. Hagelin, memorandum of March 27, 1943, QA, Box 9, Ty-Norge folder.

38. Quisling was not accompanied by any of his ministers during his meeting with Hitler on April 19, 1943. In the meeting of January 24, 1944, the Minister President brought with him Fuglesang, Jonas Lie, and Alf Whist. See *Fritt Folk*, April 21, 1943; *Fritt Folk*, January 25, 1944.

39. Hagelin to Lippestad, June 16, 1944, HI, Skodvin Collection, 1944 folder.

40. Prytz, memorandum of April 8, 1943, HI, Skodvin Collection, 1943 folder; letter co-signed Hagelin, Hustad, Lippestad,

Irgens, Skancke, Blehr, Fretheim, and Riisnæs, to Prytz, April 28, 1943, DA, Tilleggsutdrag fra offentlig straffesak mot A. V. Hagelin, pp. 69–71. Jonas Lie was absent from Oslo at the time the April 28 letter was sent, but he too supported the initiative against Prytz.

41. Prytz, memorandum of April 8, 1943, *ibid.*

42. Testimony of Olaf Ottesen Dahl, DA, Offentlig straffesak mot Albert Viljam Hagelin, pp. 134–138.

43. Hagelin, memorandum of August 2, 1943, HI, Skodvin Collection, 1943 folder.

44. *Ibid.*

45. Lammers to Hagelin, February 2, 1944, *ibid.*, 1944 folder; Lammers to Hagelin, May 2, 1944, *ibid.*, 1944 folder.

46. Hagelin to Lippestad, June 16, 1944, DA, "Utdrag i sak ... mot J. A. Lippestad," Tilleggsutdrag, Vol. II, pp. 42–43.

47. Quisling, testimony of August 22, 1945, *Straffesak*, pp. 111–112. See also Skodvin, "Norway under Occupation," *Norway and the Second World War*, p. 73.

48. *Morgenbladet*, January 14, 1941, in *Straffesak*, p. 528; *Morgenbladet*, March 9, 1943, in *Straffesak*, pp. 550–551; Fuglesang, testimony of August 24, 1945, *Straffesak*, p. 189.

49. *Morgenbladet*, January 14, 1941, *ibid.*

50. Sverre Riisnæs, *Nasjonal Samling og lovverket* (Oslo: Gunnar Stenersens forlag, 1942), pp. 32–33.

51. *Aftenposten*, January 14, 1941, in *Straffesak*, pp. 528–529.

52. Sverre Blindheim, *Nordmenn under Hitlers fane. Dei norske frontkjemparane* (Oslo: Noregs boklag, 1977), p. 12.

53. Quisling to Lammers, September 6, 1940, DA, Quislingsaken, folder #1.

54. Skodvin, "Historisk innleiing," *Om landssvikoppgjøret*, p. 24.

55. It is not possible to provide an exact number of how many Front Fighters fought on Germany's behalf during the war, but 6,000 appears to be a logical estimate. A total of 4,894 persons were tried after the war because they had served as Front Fighters. See *Om landssvikoppgjøret*, p. 194. In adddition, an estimated 1,000 died in battle. See Skodvin, "Historisk innleiing," *Om landssvikoppgjøret*, p. 20. This question is

not entirely settled, however. Magne Skodvin indicates that the total number was 5,000, but this appears to be too low. See "Historisk innleiing," *Om landssvikoppgjøret*, p. 20. On the other hand, Sverre Blindheim maintains that some 7,000 Norwegians fought for Hitler, but this figure appears to be inflated, even when due consideration is given for Blindheim's inclusion of some 350–400 women who joined the German Red Cross. See Blindheim, *Nordmenn under Hitlers fane*, p. 7, p. 101.

56. *Om landssvikoppgjøret*, p. 193.

57. Blindheim, *Nordmenn under Hitlers fane*, pp. 107–108. See *Fritt Folk*, August 21, 1943, for a representative advertisement in NS' main press organ which sought to recruit Norwegians for the *Kriegsmarine*.

58. Schjelderup, *På bred front*, p. 97.

59. Blindheim, *Nordmenn under Hitlers fane*, p. 192.

60. *Ibid.*, pp. 36–37.

61. *Om landssvikoppgjøret*, p. 193; Blindheim, *ibid.*, pp. 35–36.

62. Skodvin, "Historisk innleiing," *Om landssvikoppgjøret*, p. 21.

63. Blindheim, *Nordmenn under Hitlers fane*, pp. 39–42.

64. *Ibid.*, pp. 38–39, p. 44; Fuglesang, statement of June 13, 1945, HI, Skodvin Collection, police reports, #22b.

65. Skodvin, "Historisk innleiing," *Om landssvikoppgjøret*, p. 21.

66. *Ibid.*, p. 24; Blindheim, *Nordmenn under Hitlers fane*, pp. 66–67.

67. Blindheim, *ibid.*, p. 90.

68. *Ibid.*, p. 136.

69. Skodvin, "Historisk innleiing," *Om landssvikoppgjøret*, p. 22.

70. *Ibid.*; Blindheim, *Nordmenn under Hitlers fane*, p. 68.

71. Quisling, "partiforordning om Hirdplikt," February 25, 1943, QA.

72. From the statistics available, it appears that the *Hird* never numbered more than approximately 8,000 during the war. See Skodvin, "Historisk innleiing," *Om landssvikoppgjøret*, p. 22.

73. "Utdrag i sak ... mot J. A. Lippestad," DA, Vol. I, pp. 8–10; *Om landssvikoppgjøret*, pp. 158–159, p. 152.

74. *Om landssvikoppgjøret*, p. 152.

75. *Ibid.*, p. 158.

76. "Norges svar: til kamp mot bolsje

vismen ved alminnelig nasjonal arbeidsinnsats," *Fritt Folk*, February 23, 1943.

77. Kjeldstadli, *Hjemmestyrkene*, pp. 282–283.

78. *Morgenbladet*, February 25, 1943, in *Straffesak*, pp. 549–550.

79. "Føreren: Vår høyeste nasjonale plikt er å arbeide for en effektiv europeisk nyordning," *Fritt Folk*, February 23, 1943.

80. *Ibid.*

81. *Ibid.*

82. Lippestad, "Rundskriv fra Riksorganisasjonssjefen Lippestad til NS Fylkesførere og fylkesorganisasjonsledere," March 25, 1943, DA, "Utdrag i sak . . . mot J. A. Lippestad," Vol. II, pp. 122–124.

83. *Ibid.*; *Om landssvikoppgjøret*, pp. 158–159.

84. Alf Sanengen, "Kampen mot A-T og arbeidsmobiliseringen," *Norges krig*, Vol. III, p. 320.

85. "Den nasjonale arbeidsinnsats tjener bare nasjonale formål," *Fritt Folk*, April 21, 1943.

86. Schjelderup, *Over bakkekammen*, pp. 77–78; Sanengen, "Kampen mot A-T og arbeidsmobiliseringen," *Norges krig*, Vol. III, p. 320.

87. Grimnes, *Hjemmefrontens ledelse*, pp. 192–193.

88. Sanengen, "Kampen mot A-T og arbeidsmobiliseringen," *Norges krig*, Vol. III, p. 322.

89. Schjelderup, *Over bakkekammen*, pp. 82–83.

90. Grimnes, *Hjemmefrontens ledelse*, p. 193.

91. Kjeldstadli, *Hjemmefronten*, p. 280, Schjelderup, *Over bakkekammen*, p. 84.

92. Schjelderup, *ibid.*, pp. 169–170.

93. Molland, "Kirkens kamp," *Norges krig*, vol. III, pp. 64–65.

94. Gjelsvik, *Hjemmefronten*, p. 106.

95. DA, "Utdrag i sak . . . mot J. A. Lippestad," Tilleggsutdrag, Vol.II, p. 76.

96. Kjeldstadli, *Hjemmestyrkene*, p. 282.

97. Gjelsvik, *Hjemmefronten*, pp. 111–112; Sanengen, "Kampen mot A-T og arbeidsmobiliseringen," *Norges krig*, Vol. III, p. 322.

98. Jens Bull to Trygve Lie, July 8, 1944, *Regjeringen og hjemmefronten under krigen*, pp. 424–425.

99. Kjeldstadli, *Hjemmestyrkene*, p. 282.

100. Schjelderup, *Over bakkekammen*, pp. 211–212.

101. Kjeldstadli, *Hjemmestyrkene*, p. 261; Sverre Riisnæs, statement of June 13, 1945, HI, Skodvin Collection, police reports, #73.

102. Riisnaes, *ibid.*

103. *Ibid.*; Quisling, testimony of August 22, 1945, *Straffesak*, p. 131; Kjeldstadli, *Hjemmestyrkene*, p. 262.

104. *Straffesak*, pp. 23–24.

105. Kjeldstadli, *Hjemmestyrkene*, p. 261.

106. "Norge tilhører Europas antibolsjevikiske front – og alle som motarbeider den, setter sitt liv i fare," *Fritt Folk*, August 17, 1943; Kjeldstadli, *ibid.*

107. "På liv og død," *Fritt Folk*, August 17, 1943.

108. Schjelderup, *Over bakkekammen*, pp. 213–216: Lars L'Abée-Lund, "Politiet over og under jorden," *Norges krig*, Vol. III, pp. 279–280.

109. L'Abée-Lund, *ibid.*, p. 280; Grimnes, *Hjemmefrontens ledelse*, p. 212.

110. Kjeldstadli, *Hjemmestyrkene*, p. 263.

111. L'Abée-Lund, "Politiet over og under jorden," *Norges krig*, Vol. III, p. 280.

112. Schjelderup, *Over bakkekammen*, p. 213.

113. Kjeldstadli, *Hjemmestyrkene*, p. 259.

114. *Ibid.*, p. 260.

115. *Ibid.*, pp. 260–261.

116. Originally the Germans had intended to apprehend the officers at an earlier date, on August 5, but the arrests had to be postponed pending completion of German diplomatic negotiations with Sweden concerning troop transit privileges. See *Ibid.*, p. 260.

117. Falkenhorst, "Bekjentgjørelse," *Fritt Folk*, August 17, 1943.

118. "Norge tilhører Europas antibolsjevikiske front – og alle som motarbeider den, setter sitt liv i fare," *Fritt Folk*, *ibid.*

119. Schjelderup, *Over bakkekammen*, pp. 220–222.

120. "Skrivelse til Høyesterettsadvokat A. V. Heiberg fra K. S. Irgens," October 11, 1945, *Irgens-saken*, p. 92.

121. Goebbels, diary notation of September 17, 1943, Lochner, *The Goebbels Diaries*, p. 456.

122. Irgens to Quisling, August 31, 1943, HI, Skodvin Collection, 1943 folder. Although dated August 31, Irgens' protest letter was not forwarded to Quisling until September 10, 1943.

123. Irgens, memorandum of protest against the "Midlertidig lov om tiltak til opprettholdelse av ro og orden i krigstid av 14. august 1943," n.d., *ibid.*

124. *Ibid.*

125. "Skrivelse til Høyesterettsadvokat A. V. Heiberg fra K. S. Irgens," October 11, 1945, *Irgens-saken*, pp. 92–93; excerpt from Irgens court testimony, *Irgens-saken*, pp. 25–26.

126. Lippestad's testimony in DA, *Offentlig straffesak mot Albert Viljam Hagelin*, p. 107; Riisnæs, *Nasjonal Samling og lovverket*, pp. 69–70.

127. Excerpt from Irgens' court testimony in *Irgens-saken*, p. 26.

128. Steen, "Universitetet i ildlinjen," *Norges krig*, Vol. III, p. 171.

129. G. H. Monrad-Krohn, statement of June 10, 1945, HI, Skodvin Collection, police reports, #165.

130. *Ibid.*; Oddvar Munksgaard, *Gestapokameraten* (Oslo: Gyldendal Norsk Forlag, 1973), pp. 66–70.

131. Steen, "Universitetet i ildlinjen," *Norges krig*, Vol. III, p. 166.

132. Ragnar Skancke, statement of October 20, 1945, HI, Skodvin Collection, police reports, #333.

133. Monrad-Krohn, statement of June 30, 1945, *ibid.*, police reports, #165; Munksgaard, *Gestapokameraten*, p. 71.

134. Monrad-Krohn, *ibid.*

135. *Ibid.*

136. Steen, "Universitetet i ildlinjen," *Norges krig*, Vol. III, pp. 168–170.

137. *Ibid.*, p. 171.

138. *Ibid.*, pp. 173–174.

139. Adolf Hoel, statement, n.d., HI, Skodvin Collection, police reports, #334.

140. *Ibid.*

141. *Ibid.*; Steen, "Universitetet i ildlinjen," *Norges krig*, Vol. III, pp. 173–174.

142. "Utdrag av professor Adolf Hoels dagbok," HI, Skodvin Collection, police reports, #334. This excerpt from Hoel's diary,

along with two other documents drafted by Hoel, are listed under the same police report number.

143. Steen, "Universitetet i ildlinjen," *Norges krig*, Vol. III, pp. 174.

144. Schjelderup, *Over bakkekammen*, pp. 300–303; Steen, *ibid.*, pp. 174–175.

145. Steen, *ibid.*, pp. 178–179.

146. *Ibid.*, p. 179.

147. Rolf Holm, statement of December 3, 1945, HI, Skodvin Collection, police reports, #357.

148. "Utdrag av Sven Rachlev Dysthes forklaring 1.6.45," *ibid.*, police reports, #156; Steen, "Universitetet i ildlinjen," *Norges krig*, Vol. III, pp. 181–182.

149. "Utdrag av professor Adolf Hoels dagbok," HI, Skodvin Collection, police reports, #334.

150. *Ibid.*

151. Steen, "Universitetet i ildlinjen," *Norges krig*, Vol. III, pp. 181–182.

152. *Ibid.*, p. 182.

153. The Aula is no ordinary auditorium. It is one of the major symbols of Norwegian cultural achievement. In addition to serving as a center for concerts and recitals, the hall is often used for official ceremonies. Its walls are decorated with the frescos of Norway's greatest modern painter, Edvard Munch.

154. Steen, "Universitetet i ildlinjen," *Norges krig*, Vol. III, pp. 182–183.

155. Fritz Volberg, statement of September 1, 1945, HI, Skodvin Collection, police reports, #402; Kjeldstadli, *Hjemmestyrkene*, p. 266.

156. Steen, "Universitetet i ildlinjen," *Norges krig*, Vol. III, pp. 184–185.

157. *Ibid.*, p. 190.

158. *Ibid.*, p. 189.

159. *Norges forhold til Sverige under krigen 1940–45*, Vol. III, pp. 329–333; Schjelderup, *Over bakkekammen*, p. 305.

160. Volberg, statement of September 1, 1945, HI, Skodvin Collection, police reports, #402; Kjeldstadli, *Hjemmestyrkene*, p. 267.

161. Goebbels, diary notation of December 5, 1943, Lochner, *The Goebbels Diaries*, p. 542; diary notation of December 6, 1943, pp. 543–544.

162. Volberg, statement of September 1,

1945, HI, Skodvin Collection, police reports, #402.

163. Goebbels, diary notation of December 5, 1943, Lochner, *The Goebbels Diaries*, p. 542; *Norges forhold til Sverige under krigen*, Vol. III, p. 328.

164. Lochner, *ibid.*, p. 363.

165. Goebbels, diary notation of May 22, 1943, *ibid.*, p. 388; diary notation of September 23, 1943, *ibid.*, p. 475.

166. Goebbels, diary notation of May 22, 1943, *ibid.*

167. Goebbels, diary notation of December 6, 1943, *ibid.*, p. 544.

168. Volberg, statement of September 1, 1945, HI, Skodvin Collection, police reports, #402.

Notes to Chapter XVI

1. Kjeldstadli, *Hjemmestyrkene*, pp. 283–284.

2. *Ibid.*, p. 284.

3. Hans-Hendrik Neumann to Quisling, December 18, 1943, DA, Quislingsaken, folder #1.

4. Statement by Georg Wilhelm Müller, June 13, 1945, HI, Skodvin Collection, police reports, #45; statement by Herbert Noot, June 27, 1945, HI, Skodvin Collection, police reports, #89.

5. Neumann to Quisling, December 18, 1943, DA, Quislingsaken, folder #1.

6. *Ibid.*

7. Lammers to Quisling, January 11, 1944, HI, Skodvin Collection, 1944 folder.

8. Jonas Lie, note of January 21, 1944, *ibid.* Lie was part of the trio of NS ministers who accompanied Quisling, which also included Fuglesang and Alf Whist. See also Kjeldstadli, *Hjemmestyrkene*, p. 289.

9. Kjeldstadli, *ibid.*

10. Lie, note of January 21, 1944, HI, Skodvin Collection, 1944 folder.

11. Lie, note of January 22, 1944, in Kjeldstadli, *Hjemmestyrkene*, p. 289.

12. *Ibid.*

13. "Der Führer mottar Føreren i sitt hovedkvarter," *Fritt Folk*, January 25, 1944.

14. Jens Schive to Trygve Lie, March 6, 1944, with two reports from the resistance movement dated March 1, 1944, *Regjeringen og hjemmefronten under krigen*, p. 381.

15. Whist to Quisling, March 7, 1944, DA, "Utdrag i sak ... mot Alf Larsen Whist," pp. 100–106.

16. Kjeldstadli, *Hjemmestyrkene*, p. 288.

17. Sverre Riisnæs to Gottlob Berger, January 17, 1944, Norwegian translation, Resistance Museum, Akershus Castle, Oslo, Collections. The document is also quoted in its entirety in several printed sources, including Kjeldstadli, *Hjemmestyrkene*, pp. 287–288, and Gjelsvik, *Hjemmefronten*, pp. 146–148.

18. Kjeldstadli, *ibid.*, p. 261.

19. *Ibid.*, p. 286.

20. Gunnar Jahn, diary entry, January 22, 1944, quoted in Schjelderup, *Over bakkekammen*, p. 322.

21. *Ibid.*

22. Schjelderup, *ibid.*, p. 335.

23. Grimnes, *Hjemmefrontens ledelse*, p. 363, Kjeldstadli, *Hjemmestyrkene*, p. 289.

24. Directive drawn up by the Home Front in mid-February 1944 and broadcast over London Radio on March 15, 1944, quoted in Schjelderup, *Over bakkekammen*, pp. 339–340.

25. Schjelderup, *ibid.*, p. 338; Kjeldstadli, *Hjemmestyrkene*, p. 289.

26. Sanengen, "Kampen mot A-T og arbeidsmobiliseringen," *Norges krig*, Vol. III, p. 328; Grimnes, *Hjemmefrontens ledelse*, p. 364; Kjeldstadli, *Hjemmestyrkene*, p. 290. Kjeldstadli erroneously dates the issuance of the directive as March 26 rather than February 26, 1944. It is printed in a number of sources, including *Regjeringen og hjemmefronten under krigen*, pp. 381–382, and Schjelderup, *Over bakkekammen*, pp. 339–340.

27. For a detailed, but not impartial, account of how the A-T movement developed during its early prewar years, see the relevant sections in Walter Fyrst, *Min sti* (Oslo: privately published, 1981). Although he was associated with the Mogens faction which opposed Quisling during the spring and summer of 1940, Fürst rejoined NS in the fall. See pp. 179–181.

28. Kjeldstadli, *Hjemmestyrkene*, p.

439, fn. 56. See above, p. 428, for Fürst's dealings with the Administrative Council.

29. Statement by Magnus Hagem, September 22, 1945, HI, Skodvin Collection, police reports, #249.

30. Grimnes, *Hjemmefrontens ledelse*, p. 364; *Om landssvikoppgjøret*, p. 183; Riisnaes, *Nasjonal Samling og lovverket*, p. 30. A-T also included a women's group, but it was voluntary.

31. Hagem, statement of September 22, 1945, HI, Skodvin Collection, police reports, #249; Fyrst, *Min sti*, p. 175.

32. Hagem, *ibid.*

33. Sanengen, "Kampen mot A-T og arbeidsmobiliseringen," *Norges krig*, Vol. III, p. 326.

34. Gjelsvik, *Hjemmefronten*, p. 145.

35. Carl Frølich-Hanssen, statement of June 6, 1945, DA, Quislingsaken, folder #17; Dagny Egeberg-Holmsen, statement of June 23, 1945, DA, Quislingsaken, folder #17.

36. Gjelsvik, *Hjemmefronten*, pp. 145–146.

37. Kjeldstadli, *Hjemmestyrkene*, p. 440, fn. 64.

38. Sanengen, "Kampen mot A-T og arbeidsmobiliseringen," *Norges krig*, Vol. III, pp. 328–330.

39. Gjelsvik, *Hjemmefronten*, pp. 166–167.

40. *Fritt Folk*, March 24, 1944; Gjelsvik, *ibid.*, p. 167.

41. Gjelsvik, *ibid.*, pp. 167–168.

42. *Ibid.*, p. 155.

43. *Ibid.*

44. *Ibid.*, pp. 168–169.

45. *Ibid.*, p. 169; Grimnes, *Hjemmefrontens ledelse*, p. 364.

46. Grimnes, *ibid.*; Gjelsvik, *ibid.*, pp. 154–155; Kjeldstadli, *Hjemmestyrkene*, p. 290.

47. Grimnes, "Litt om Kretsen og om Hjemmefrontledelsen," *Motstandskamp, strategi og marinepolitikk*, p. 129.

48. *Ibid.*, p. 130; Grimnes, *Hjemmefrontens ledelse*, p. 397.

49. The Home Front's sabotage operation against the Oslo office of the Work Effort in April 1943 had been a relatively isolated incident. See above, pp. 610–611.

50. Ole Kristian Grimnes, "Sabotasjen i norsk og dansk motstandsbevegelse," *Motstandskamp, strategi og marinepolitikk*, p. 11.

51. *Ibid.*, pp. 13–14.

52. Grimnes, *Hjemmefrontens ledelse*, p. 362.

53. Gjelsvik, *Hjemmefronten*, pp. 154–155.

54. Kjeldstadli, *Hjemmestyrkene*, p. 294.

55. Müller, statement of June 13, 1945, HI, Skodvin Collection, police reports, #45; Kjeldstadli, *ibid.*, pp. 294–295.

56. "Skrivelse fra Arbeidsdirektoratet til Lippestad," May 8, 1944, DA, "Utdrag i sak . . . mot J. A. Lippestad," Vol. II, pp. 178–179.

57. Jens Schive to Trygve Lie, July 17, 1944, UKs arkiv, Box 14, envelope 33; Kjeldstadli, *Hjemmestyrkene*, pp. 294–295.

58. Herbert Noot, statement of June 27, 1945, HI, Skodvin Collection, police reports, #89; Lippestad to Karl A. Marthinsen, April 28, 1944, DA, "Utdrag i sak . . . mot J. A. Lippestad," Vol. II, p. 176.

59. "Norges nei til forræderiet i London," *Fritt Folk*, May 16, 1944.

60. Sanengen, "Kampen mot A-T og arbeidsmobiliseringen," *Norges krig*, Vol. III, pp. 334–335.

61. Grimnes, *Hjemmefrontens ledelse*, p. 364; E. Guldberg, "Rundskriv nr. 215 fra Direktoratet for Arbeidsformidling og Arbeidsløshetstrygd," DA, "Utdrag i sak . . . mot J. A. Lippestad," Tilleggsutdrag, Vol. II, pp. 28–32.

62. Guldberg, *ibid.*

63. Sanengen, "Kampen mot A-T og arbeidsmobiliseringen," *Norges krig*, Vol. III, p. 335.

64. "Registrering av alle menn i alderen 21–23 år," *Fritt Folk*, May 19, 1944.

65. Sanengen, "Kampen mot A-T og arbeidsmobiliseringen," *Norges krig*, Vol. III, p. 319.

66. *Ibid.*, p. 334.

67. Gjelsvik, *Hjemmefronten*, p. 170; Kjeldstadli, *Hjemmestyrkene*, pp. 295–296.

68. The directive is printed in its entirety in Sanengen, "Kampen mot A-T og arbeidsmobiliseringen," *Norges krig*, Vol. III, pp. 335–336.

69. *Ibid.*

70. Sanengen, *ibid.*, p. 337.

71. Gjelsvik, *Hjemmefronten*, p. 171; *ibid.*, p. 338.

72. Grimnes, "Sabotasjen i norsk og dansk motstandsbevegelse," *Motstandskamp, strategi og marinepolitikk*, p. 22; Gjelsvik, *ibid.*, pp. 171–172.

73. "Referat fra Riks- og Landsledermøtet 24. 5. 1944 kl. 1800," signed Rolf Jørgen Fuglesang and Sjønne Melstrøm, Referater fra Riks- og Landsledermøtene folder, QA.

74. Sanengen, "Kampen mot A-T og arbeidsmobiliseringen," *Norges krig*, Vol. III, pp. 338–339; Gjelsvik, *Hjemmefronten*, p. 172.

75. "Nasjonal arbeidsinnsats," *Fritt Folk*, May 26, 1944.

76. Gjelsvik, *Hjemmefronten*, pp. 172–173; Sanengen, "Kampen mot A-T og arbeidsmobiliseringen," *Norges krig*, Vol. III, pp. 339–340.

77. Kjeldstadli, *Hjemmestyrkene*, p. 298; Gjelsvik, *ibid.*, pp. 173–174; Sanengen, *ibid.*, pp. 340–342.

78. Gjelsvik, *ibid.*, pp. 174–175.

79. Home Front report of June 14, 1944, quoted in Jens Bull's memorandum to Trygve Lie, June 16, 1944, *Regjeringen og hjemmefronten under krigen*, p. 414.

80. Gjelsvik, *Hjemmefronten*, pp. 176–177.

81. Kjeldstadli, *Hjemmestyrkene*, p. 297. Author's italics.

82. *Ibid.*; *Om landssvikoppgjøret*, p. 157.

83. Sanengen, "Kampen mot A-T og arbeidsmobiliseringen," *Norges krig*, Vol. III, p. 343.

84. Gjelsvik, *Hjemmefronten*, p. 175.

85. Lippestad, "Skrivelse fra Lippestad til Næringsdepartementet," May 24, 1944, DA, "Utdrag i sak . . . mot J. A. Lippestad," Vol. II, pp. 186–187; Gjelsvik, *ibid.*

86. Sanengen, "Kampen mot A-T og arbeidsmobiliseringen," *Norges krig*, Vol. III, p. 343.

87. *Ibid.*, pp. 343–344; Gjelsvik, *Hjemmefronten*, pp. 177–178.

88. "Straffbar sympati," August 26, 1944.

89. *Ibid.*; Sanengen, "Kampen mot A-T og arbeidsmobiliseringen," *Norges krig*, Vol. III, p. 344.

90. Sanengen, *ibid.*, p. 346.

91. Gjelsvik, *Hjemmefronten*, p. 178, p. 261, fn. 456. The Home Front kept approximately 13,000 cards for the use of its operatives.

92. *Ibid.*, p. 178.

93. Schive to Trygve Lie, July 17, 1944, UKs arkiv, Box 14, envelope 33.

94. Kjeldstadli, *Hjemmestyrkene*, p. 297.

95. Sanengen, "Kampen mot A-T og arbeidsmobiliseringen," *Norges krig*, Vol. III, p. 348.

96. *Ibid.*; Gjelsvik, *Hjemmefronten*, p. 179.

97. Sanengen, *ibid.*; Kjeldstadli, *Hjemmestyrkene*, p. 301.

98. Gjelsvik, *Hjemmefronten*, pp. 178–179.

99. "Meddelelse fra Minister Alf. L. Whist," *Fritt Folk*, November 14, 1944.

100. Grimnes, *Hjemmefrontens ledelse*, p. 367.

101. *Ibid.*, pp. 368–369.

102. Schive, memorandum of June 16, 1944, *Regjeringen og hjemmefronten under krigen*, p. 414.

103. Tor Skjønsberg, quoted in Schive's memorandum of June 16, 1944, *ibid.*, pp. 418–419. Also quoted in Schjelderup, *Over bakkekammen*, p. 386.

104. Kjeldstadli, *Hjemmestyrkene*, p. 297; Christensen, *Okkupasjonsår og etterkrigstid*, p. 367.

105. Throughout his life Quisling expressed admiration for the manner in which the Bolsheviks maintained themselves in power which he had witnessed in Russia, a success that he in vain sought to emulate.

106. "I dag gjelder det for oss alle å holde fram med dobbelt kraft," *Fritt Folk*, September 5, 1944.

107. The "Warning" is quoted in Schjelderup, *Over bakkekammen*, pp. 243–247. See also Gjelsvik, *Hjemmefronten*, pp. 126–127.

108. Andreas Mohr, "Dere arbeider jo for tyskerne mens Norge og Tyskland er i krig," *Aftenposten*, November 20, 22, 1943, quoted in *Tilleggshefte*, p. 30. See also Gjelsvik, *ibid.*, p. 126.

109. DA, "Utdrag i sak . . . mot J. A. Lippestad," Vol. II, pp. 158–159.

110. Quisling to Tormod Hustad and all other ministers, October 10, 1942, DA,

Quislingsaken, Straffesak – Etterforskning mot Quisling, folder #7.

111. "Referat fra Riks- og Landsledermøtet, 7. 6. 44. kl. 1800," signed Rolf Jørgen Fuglesang and Sjønne Melstrøm, June 8, 1944, Referater fra Riks- og Landsledermøtene folder, QA.

112. The reports in the "Referater fra Riks- og Landsledermøtene" folder in QA constantly complained how difficult it was to provide protection for members of various NS organizations.

113. "Referat fra Riks- og Landsledermøtet, 24. 5. 44. kl. 1800," signed Rolf Jørgen Fuglesang and Sjønne Melstrøm, May 25, 1944, Referater fra Riks- og Landsledermøtene folder, QA.

114. Herman Harris Aall to Quisling, December 12, 1943, DA, Aallsaken, Diverse korrespondanse, folder #10.

115. "Det som skjedde på Stiklestad var fullbyrdelsen av det som begynte i Hafrsfjord," *Fritt Folk*, July 31, 1944.

116. Roald Dysthe, list of accusations to Hagelin, with copies to Quisling and the state prosecutor in Oslo, August 7, 1943, HI, Skodvin Collection, police reports, #10.

117. *Ibid.*; Schjelderup, *Over bakkekammen*, pp. 46–51.

118. Fuglesang to Aall, February 10, 1944, Riksarkivet, Herman Harris Aalls privat arkiv, Plukk som er usorterte.

119. See below, pp. 660–662.

120. Aall to Quisling, December 21, 1943, DA, Aallsaken, Diverse korrespondanse, folder #16; Fuglesang to Aall, February 10, 1944, Riksarkivet, Herman Harris Aalls privat arkiv, Plukk som er usorterte.

121. "Er det kommet rotter i huset?" *Nasjonal Ungdommen*, May 17, 1944.

122. Fuglesang, memorandum of January 16, 1945, QA.

123. Fuglesang to Klemens Dahlseide, June 5, 1944, QA; Dahlseide to Fuglesang, June 14, 1944, QA; Fuglesang, memorandum of January 16, 1945, QA.

124. Henrik Groth and Frits von der Lippe, "Kunsten i kamp," *Norges krig*, Vol. III, pp. 198–199.

125. Nøkleby, *Holdningskamp*, pp. 200–201.

126. *Om landssvikoppgjøret*, p. 150.

127. Hustad, statement of August 8,

1945, HI, Skodvin Collection, police reports, #229; Quisling to Hustad, January 11, 1944, HI, Skodvin Collection, 1944 folder.

128. *Ibid.*

129. Hustad, statement of August 8, 1945, *ibid.*

130. *Om landssvikoppgjøret*, p. 134.

131. Hustad, statement of August 8, 1945, HI, Skodvin Collection, police reports, #229.

132. Whist to Quisling, May 10, 1944, DA, "Utdrag i sak ... mot Alf Larsen Whist," pp. 120–123.

133. *Om landssvikoppgjøret*, p. 135.

134. Kjeldstadli, *Hjemmestyrkene*, p. 297.

135. Quisling to Whist, June 9, 1944, DA, "Utdrag i sak ... mot Alf Larsen Whist," pp. 127–128.

136. *Ibid.*

137. Lars Usterud Svendsen, statement of July 16, 1945, HI, Skodvin Collection, police reports, #234.

138. See above, pp. 489–490.

139. Svendsen, statement of July 16, 1945, HI, Skodvin Collection, police reports, #234; *Irgens-saken*, p. 14, pp. 106–108.

140. *Irgens-saken*, pp. 26–27, p. 107.

141. Quisling, statement of August 2, 1945, HI, Skodvin Collection, police reports, #105.

142. Jens Bull to the Norwegian Foreign Ministry, December 15, 1942, *Regjeringen og hjemmefronten under krigen*, p. 136.

143. Ernst Züchner, written statement of June 22, 1945, HI, Skodvin Collection, police reports, #61. See also *Straffesak*, pp. 603–604.

144. Magne Skodvin, "Norges plass i Hitlers militære planar," *Historisk Tidsskrift*, Vol. 35, No. 7 (1949–1951), p. 458.

145. Kjeldstadli, Hjemmestyrkene, pp. 192–194.

146. Jens Bull to Trygve Lie, April 14, 1944, with an appended communique from the Home Front, *Regjeringen og hjemmefronten under krigen*, p. 396.

147. *Straffesak*, p. 604.

148. "Strålende jubileumsmøte i Klingenberg i går," *Fritt Folk*, May 18, 1943.

149. "Vårt nasjonale Mål: Et fritt, stort

og lykkelig Norge," *Fritt Folk*, May 18, 1943.

150. *Ibid.*

151. *Straffesak*, p. 553.

152. *Ibid.*, pp. 553–554.

153. *Ibid.*, p. 553.

154. *Ibid.*, p. 554.

155. *Ibid.*

156. Sjønne Melstrøm, for the NS General Secretariat, to Per von Hirsch, Finance Department, October 6, 1943, HI, Skodvin Collection, 1943 folder.

157. "Takketelegram til der Führer fra ministerpresident Quisling," *Fritt Folk*, September 28, 1943.

158. *Ibid.*

159. "Norges nei til forræderiet i London," *Fritt Folk*, May 16, 1944.

160. "Ministerpresident Quisling: Enhver europeer bør være klar over hva saken gjelder," *Fritt Folk*, June 7, 1944.

161. "Verdensdelenes samling og kamp," August 26, 1944.

162. "NORGE er nyordningens basis i Norden," *Fritt Folk*, October 18, 1943.

163. "Det som skjedde på Stiklestad var fullbyrdelsen av det som begynte i Hafrsfjord," *ibid.*, July 31, 1944.

164. "NORGE er nyordningens basis i Norden," *ibid.*, October 18, 1943.

165. "Norges Nei til forræderiet i London," *ibid.*, May 16, 1944.

166. Statement by G. W. Müller, n.d., HI, Skodvin Collection, police reports, #401.

167. *Ibid.*; "Referat fra Riks- og Landsledermøtet 22. 11. 1944," signed Rolf Jørgen Fuglesang, November 24, 1944, Referater fra Riks- og Landsledermøtene folder, QA.

168. Fuglesang, statement of September 26, 1945, HI, Skodvin Collection, police reports, #403.

169. *Ibid.*; Müller, statement, n.d., HI, Skodvin Collection, police reports, #401.

170. See Dahl *et al.*, *Den norske nasjonalsosialismen*, pp. 182–183, for illustrations of Gimle.

171. HI, Skodvin Collection, police reports, #124; *Straffesak*, pp. 139–140.

172. *Straffesak*, p. 140.

173. Berit Nøkleby, *Nyordning*, Vol. II of *Norge i krig*, Magne Skodvin, ed. (Oslo: Aschehoug, 1985), p. 240; H. O. Christophersen, *Fra 9. april 1940 til kampåret*

1942, Vol. I of *Av nød til seier* (Oslo: Grøndahl & Søn forlag, 1977), p. 162.

174. *Straffesak*, p. 222.

175. Prytz to Quisling, with an enclosed letter from the Finance Department to Oslo's Tax Assessor, November 24, 1942, in *ibid.*, p. 549.

176. *Straffesak*, p. 223.

177. *Fritt Folk*, July 19, 1944.

178. *Straffesak*, p. 142.

179. *Ibid.*, pp. 224–230; Vidkun Quisling, *Vidkun Quislings bemerkninger til nytt i tiltalebeslutningen av 11-7-1945 i tilslutning til redegjørelse av 21-6-1945* (Oslo: 1945), pp. 22–23.

180. *Straffesak*, pp. 226–230.

181. "Ministerpresidenten kjøper del av gammel Asker-jord," news release for *Fritt Folk*, n.d., QA, Box 10, 1913–1943 folder.

182. *Straffesak*, pp. 140–141.

183. R. Skancke, countersigned Sigmund Feyling, to Quisling, "Avskrift av skjøte på eiendommen 'Moland' i Fyresdal, datert 16/5–1944," DA, Quislingsaken, Straffesak – Etterforskning mot Quisling, folder #7.

184. *Straffesak*, p. 145.

185. Gunvor to Vidkun, December 12, 1943, QA, Box 13, Brev 1938–39 folder; Agnes to Vidkun, December 20, 1943, QA, Box 12, Lykkønskinger 1942–45 folder.

186. See above, p. 590.

187. Finn Støren, memorandum of August 1943, DA, Størensaken, folder #29, doc. #2.

188. *Ibid.*

189. *Ibid.*

190. Prytz to Quisling, September 30, 1944, with an accompanying memorandum of September 28, 1944, DA, Quislingsaken, folder #1.

191. Støren, memorandum of August 1943, DA, Størensaken, folder #29, doc. #2.

192. Støren, "P.M. Norden september/oktober 1944," September 29, 1944, *ibid.*, doc. #12.

193. Støren, memorandum of August 1943, DA, *ibid.*, doc. #2.

194. Johan Stenersen to Quisling, March 1, 1943, QA, Box 9, Ty-Norge folder; Støren to Werner von Grundherr, June 12, 1944, HI, Skodvin Collection, 1944 folder; Støren to *Obersturmbannführer* von

Löw, August 30, 1944, DA, Størensaken, folder #29, doc. #8; Støren to *Standartenführer* Spaarman, August 30, 1944, HI, Skodvin Collection, 1944; Støren, "P.M. vedrørende mine forhandlinger i Berlin i begynnelsen av mars 1944," March 13, 1944, DA, Størensaken, folder #29, doc. #4; Støren, memorandum of September 21, 1944, DA, Størensaken, folder #29, doc. #10.

195. Støren, "P.M. vedrørende mine forhandlinger i Berlin i begynnelsen av mars 1944," *ibid.*

196. Støren to Grundherr, June 12, 1944, HI, Skodvin Collection, 1944 folder.

197. Støren, memorandum of September 21, 1944, DA, Størensaken, folder #29, doc. #10.

198. Støren to *Standartenführer* Spaarman, August 30, 1944, HI, Skodvin Collection, 1944 folder.

199. Støren, memorandum of September 21, 1944, DA, Størensaken, folder #29, doc. #10.

200. Skodvin, "Historisk innleiing," *Om landssvikoppgjøret*, p. 27.

201. Birger Liljedahl Vassbotten, statement of June 11, 1945, HI, Skodvin Collection, 1942 folder.

202. Prytz to Quisling, September 30, 1944, DA, Quislingsaken, folder #1.

203. Prytz to Quisling, September 25, 1944, as an attachment to Prytz to Quisling, September 30, 1944, *ibid.*

204. *Ibid.*

205. *Ibid.*

206. *Ibid.*

207. Støren, "P.M. Norden september/oktober 1944," DA, Størensaken, folder #29, doc. #12; *Om landssvikoppgjøret*, p. 130.

208. Støren, "P.M. Norden september/oktober 1944," *ibid.*

209. *Ibid.*

210. *Ibid.*

211. Skodvin, "Historisk innleiing," *Om landssvikoppgjøret*, p. 27; Skodvin "Om 'statsakta' 1. februar 1942," lecture to Det kongelige norske videnskabers selskab, February 1, 1960, HI, Skodvin Collection.

212. *Om landssvikoppgjøret*, p. 152.

213. Arne Dagfinn Dahl, "Frigjøringen av Finnmark," *Norges krig*, Vol. III, p. 572; Bull, *Klassekamp og fellesskap 1920–1945*, pp. 443–444; Berit Nøkleby, "Adjusting to

Allied Victory," in Henrik S. Nissen, ed., *Scandinavia during the Second World War* (Oslo and Minneapolis: Universitetsforlaget and The University of Minnesota Press, 1983), p. 308.

214. *Om landssvikoppgjøret*, p. 152.

215. *Norges forhold til Sverige under krigen*, Vol. III, p. 594.

216. Gjelsvik, *Hjemmefronten*, p. 207. In a later directive the Home Front reversed itself and urged the population to help the refugees from northern Norway. This in part was due to the resistance leadership's earlier lack of information concerning the plight of the deportees, but more significantly, the Home Front recognized that its initial instructions did not correspond with public opinion, which felt strong sympathy for the unfortunates driven from their homes in the north. See Grimnes, *Hjemmefrontens ledelse*, pp. 387–389.

217. *Om landssvikoppgjøret*, p. 152; Lippestad, statement of August 12, 1945, HI, Skodvin Collection, police reports, #558.

218. Carl Frølich-Hanssen, statement of June 25, 1945, DA, Quislingsaken, folder #17; Dagny Egeberg-Holmen, statement of June 23, 1945, DA, Quislingsaken, folder #17.

219. Lippestad, statement of August 12, 1945, HI, Skodvin Collection, police reports, #558.

220. *Ibid.*; Dahl, "Frigjøringen av Finnmark," *Norges krig*, Vol. III, p. 573.

221. Lippestad, *ibid.*; *Om landssvikoppgjøret*, pp. 152–153.

222. *Om landssvikoppgjøret*, *ibid.*

223. Quoted in Anders Ole Hauglid, Knut Erik Jensen, and Harry Westrheim, *Til befolkningen! Brannhøsten 1944 – Gjenreisingen etterpå* (Oslo: Universitetsforlaget, 1985), p. 44.

224. Gard Herbjørn Holtskog, statement of May 24, 1946, HI, Skodvin Collection, police reports, #558.

225. Hauglid, Jensen, and Westrheim, *Til befolkningen!*, pp. 45–46; Sverre Hartmann, *Nytt lys over kritiske faser i Norges historie under annen verdenskrig* (Oslo: Fabritius & Sønners forlag, 1965), pp. 188–189. Hitler's decree was formally issued on October 28, 1944.

226. Dahl, "Frigjøringen av Finnmark,"

Norges krig, Vol. III, pp. 580 ff.; Hauglid, Jensen, and Westrheim, *ibid.*, p. 91.

Notes to Chapter XVII

1. Author's interview with a leading NS member, Oslo, June 1, 1967.

2. Quisling, "Valget står mellem Nasjonal Samlings trange veg til nasjonal nyreising eller bolsjevismens brede veg til fordervelsen," *Fritt Folk*, January 2, 1945.

3. *Ibid.*

4. Quisling, New Year's telegrams to Hitler and Terboven, in *Fritt Folk*, Janaury 2, 1945.

5. Støren, "P.M. vedrørende Deutsches Volksopfer," January 17, 1945, DA, Størensaken, folder #29, doc. #14.

6. Lippestad's testimony, DA, Hagelinsaken, p. 110.

7. For Hagelin's resignation, see below pp. 679–680.

8. Støren, "P.M. vedrørende Deutsches Volksopfer," DA, Størensaken, folder #29, doc. #14.

9. Støren, "Redegjørelse til ministrene," February 2, 1945, *ibid.*, doc. #15.

10. *Ibid.*; Ole Brunæs, statement of November 1, 1951, HI, Skodvin Collection, January 1945 folder.

11. Støren, "Redegjørelse til ministrene," February 2, 1945, DA, Størensaken, folder #29, doc. #15; confidential report of February 9, 1945, DA, Quislingsaken, folder #2.

12. Brunæs, statement of November 1, 1951, HI, Skodvin Collection, January 1945 folder.

13. On one occasion following a Quisling visit, Hitler is reported to have said: "Man muss ja diese Gummischweinen ab und zu wieder aufpusten, damit sie stehen bleiben." The reference to *"Gummischweine"* was not restricted merely to Quisling, but was made with reference to all collaborationist leaders. See Ernst Züchner, statement of June 1945, *Dokumenter i offentlig straffesak*, p. 103.

14. *Fritt Folk*, Janaury 29, 1945. The communiqué appeared also in other Norwegian newspapers.

15. Brunæs, statement of November 1, 1951, HI, Skodvin Collection, January 1945 folder.

16. Støren, "Redegjørelse til ministrene," February 2, 1945, DA, Størensaken, folder #29, doc. #15.

17. *Ibid.*

18. "Meldungen aus Norwegen," No. 89, March 1, 1945, p. 6, Resistance Museum, Collections.

19. "Stortingsbygningen tilbakelevert til norske myndigheter," *Fritt Folk*, Febuary 2, 1945.

20. Støren, "Redegjørelse til ministrene," February 2, 1945, DA, Størensaken, folder #29, doc. #15.

21. Støren, "P.M. vedrørende Deutsches Volksopfer," January 17, 1945, *ibid.*, doc. #14.

22. Otte to Whist, February 12, 1945; Whist to Otte, February 24, 1945; Otte to Whist, March 3, 1945, DA, "Utdrag i sak ... mot Alf Larsen Whist," pp. 144–150, 153–155.

23. Ørnulf Lundesgaard, "P.M.," October 23, 1944, HI, Skodvin Collection, 1944 folder.

24. Otte, "Bericht. Politische Bereinigung der norwegischen Departments im Anfang des Jahres 1945," November 1945, *ibid.*, January 1945 folder.

25. Lundesgaard, "P.M.," October 23, 1944, *ibid.*, 1944 folder.

26. Otte, "Bericht. Politisches Bereinigung der norwegischen Departments im Anfang des Jahres 1945," November 1945, *ibid.*, January 1945 folder.

27. *Ibid.*

28. Thorleif Dahl's testimony, DA, Hagelinsaken, pp. 126–127.

29. Lippestad, statement of August 12, 1945, HI, Skodvin Collection, police reports, #558; *Om landssvikoppgjøret*, p. 152.

30. Lippestad's testimony, DA, Hagelinsaken, p. 110.

31. DA, Hagelinsaken, pp. 5–6.

32. *Ibid.*, p. 126.

33. *Om landssvikoppgjøret*, p. 134.

34. Lundesgaard, "P.M.," October 23, 1944, HI, Skodvin Collection, 1944 folder.

35. *Ibid.*

36. Ivar Elstad, statement of February 6, 1946, *ibid.*, police reports, #405.

37. *Ibid.*; Fuglesang, statement of February 7, 1946, *ibid.*, police reports, #409.

38. Elstad statement, *ibid.*; *Om landssvikoppgjøret*, p. 133.

39. *Om landssvikoppgjøret*, *ibid.*

40. *Ibid.*, pp. 131–132.

41. Kjeldstadli, *Hjemmestyrkene*, p. 225, pp. 324–325; Grimnes, "Sabotasjen i norsk og dansk motstandbevegelse," *Motstandskamp, strategi og marinepolitikk*, p. 15.

42. Grimnes, *ibid.*, pp. 15–16; Grimnes, *Hjemmefrontens ledelse*, p. 355.

43. Grimnes, *Hjemmefrontens ledelse*, pp. 359–360.

44. Quisling, "Valget står mellem Nasjonal Samlings trange veg til nasjonal nyreising eller bolsjevismens brede veg til fordervelsen," *Fritt Folk*, January 2, 1945.

45. Gjelsvik, *Hjemmefronten*, p. 214.

46. *Ibid.*, pp. 199–200.

47. Grimnes, *Hjemmefrontens ledelse*, pp. 404 ff.; Gjelsvik, *ibid.*, pp. 213–214.

48. Grimnes, *ibid.*, pp. 444–445.

49. *Ibid.*, pp. 446–447.

50. Report from Oslo, January 10, 1945, appended in Valentin Aass to Trygve Lie, January 22, 1945, *Regjeringen og hjemmefronten*, p. 517.

51. Jens Christian Hauge, "Fra krig til fred," *Norges krig*, Vol. III, p. 723.

52. *Om landssvikoppgjøret*, p. 208.

53. Gjelsvik, *Hjemmefronten*, pp. 219–220; *Norsk Tidend*, London, February 14, 1945.

54. Grimnes, *Hjemmefrontens ledelse*, p. 445; Gjelsvik, *ibid.*, p. 220.

55. *Aftenposten*, February 9–10, 1945, quoted in *Dokumenter i offentlig straffesak*, pp. 97–98.

56. *Redegjørelse fra Vidkun Quisling til siktelse fremsatt i Oslo forhørsrett*, p. 23.

57. Sverre Riisnæs, statement of June 13, 1945, HI, Skodvin Collection, police reports, #73.

58. *Aftenposten*, February 9, 1945, quoted in *Dokumenter i offentlig straffesak*, p. 98.

59. *Om landssvikoppgjøret*, p. 212. The formation of this staff, however, had no practical consequences. It simply came into existence as a result of the strong feeling that arose within NS following Marthinsen's assassination, insisting that some step be taken to prevent similar liquidations from happening in the future.

60. Gjelsvik, *Hjemmefronten*, p. 220.

61. Telegram from the Home Front to the government in London, received February 13, 1945, UKs arkiv, Box 13, envelope 16.

62. Grimnes, *Hjemmefrontens ledelse*, pp. 447–448.

63. Gjelsvik, *Hjemmefronten*, pp. 222–223.

64. Kjeldstadli, *Hjemmestyrkene*, p. 226.

65. Joseph Goebbels, *Final Entries, 1945: The Diaries of Joseph Goebbels*, ed. Hugh Trevor-Roper, trans. Richard Barry (New York: G. P. Putnam's Sons, 1978), p. 160.

66. Gjelsvik, *Hjemmefronten*, pp. 223–224.

67. Grimnes, *Hjemmefrontens ledelse*, p. 442.

68. "Ministerpresidenten besøker førermøtet på Jessheim," *Fritt Folk*, April 23, 1945.

69. "Meldungen aus Norwegen," No. 89, March 1, 1945, Resistance Museum, Collections.

70. Franz Böhme, "Betr.: Zusammenarbeit mit Nasjonal Samling," April 16, 1945, HI, Skodvin Collection, 1945 folders.

71. Gjelsvik, *Hjemmefronten*, p. 220.

72. See *ibid.*, p. 269, fn. 551.

73. The Home Front to Prime Minister Nygaardsvold, with accompanying proclamation, March 20, 1945, *Regjeringen og hjemmefronten under krigen*, pp. 550–551.

74. Prime Minister Nygaardsvold to the Home Front, April 17, 1945, *ibid.*, pp. 557–558.

75. Støren to Quisling, March 5, 1945, DA, Størensaken, folder #29, doc. #16.

76. *Ibid.*

77. *Ibid.*

78. "Ministerpresidenten besøker førermøtet på Jessheim," *Fritt Folk*, April 23, 1945.

79. Gjelsvik, *Hjemmefronten*, p. 220.

80. "Ministerpresidenten besøker førermøtet på Jessheim," *Fritt Folk*, April 23, 1945.

81. Einar Diesen, *Maidagene 45* (Oslo: Norsk Kunstforlag, 1977), p. 179.

82. Hauge, "Fra krig til fred," *Norges*

krig, Vol. III, p. 711; Christensen, *Okkupasjonsår og etterkrigstid*, p. 460.

83. Trygve Lie to Ambassador Hans Beck-Friis, April 12, 1942, *Norges forhold til Sverige under krigen*, Vol. III, pp. 310–312.

84. *Ibid.*, pp. 302–304.

85. Hauge, "Fra krig til fred," pp. 766–767; Christensen, *Okkupasjonsår og etterkrigstid*, p. 458; Hartmann, *Nytt lys over kritiske faser i Norges historie*, pp. 204–205.

86. Goebbels, *Final Entries*, p. 89.

87. "Fortrolig melding 19. April 1945 fra legasjonen i Stockholm til Utenriksdepartementet," *Norges forhold til Sverige under krigen*, Vol. III, p. 320.

88. Gjelsvik, *Hjemmefronten*, p. 230. Dr. Best did not, however, share the *Reichskommisar*'s desire for resistance, and had already committed himself to attempting to arrange a peaceful surrender in Denmark. See Hartmann, *Nytt lys over kritiske faser i Norges historie*, p. 197.

89. Quoted in Yngvar Ustvedt, *Den varme freden – den kalde krigen*, Vol. I of *Det skjedde i Norge* (Oslo: Gyldendal Norsk Forlag, 1978), p. 18.

90. Skodvin, *Striden om okkupasjonsstyret*, pp. 331–332. The exact time when this plan was under consideration is not known, but Skodvin assumes that it was in February-March, 1945. See *Striden om okkupasjonsstyret*, p. 405, fn. 14.

91. Quisling, statement of May 31, 1945, HI, Skodvin Collection, police reports, #124. Quisling at the time he gave this deposition to the police tried to deny that the idea of turning German soldiers into Norwegian citizens had originated with him, insisting instead that the Germans had proposed the scheme. This denial, however, was merely part of his general postwar strategy of evading responsibility whenever possible.

92. *Ibid.*

93. Hartmann, *Nytt lys over kritiske faser*, p. 199.

94. Knudsen, *Jeg var Quislings sekretær*, pp. 240–241.

95. Støren, "P.M. vedrørende situasjonen," April 6, 1945, DA, Størensaken, folder #29, doc. #17a.

96. Quisling's testimony of August 22, 1945, *Straffesak*, p. 108.

97. Ottar Lislegaard, testimony of August 24, 1945, *ibid.*, pp. 210–211.

98. Hauge, "Fra krig til fred," *Norges krig.*, Vol. III, p. 774; Gjelsvik, *Hjemmefronten*, p. 230.

99. Lislegaard, testimony of August 24, 1945, *Straffesak*, p. 211.

100. "Mob. plan for hirden 1945," in *Straffesak*, p. 109.

101. Lislegaard, testimony of August 24, 1945, *Straffesak*, p. 210.

102. Hauge, "Fra krig til fred," *Norges krig*, Vol. III, p. 741.

103. *Ibid.*, p. 774; Gjelsvik, *Hjemmefronten*, pp. 230–231.

104. Hauge, *ibid.*, pp. 774–775; The Home Front to Prime Minister Nygaardsvold, April 3, 1945, *Regjeringen og hjemmefronten under krigen*, p. 552.

105. Gjelsvik, *Hjemmefronten*, p. 231; Home Front report, author unknown, May 3, 1945, HI, Skodvin Collection, April 1945 folder.

106. Hauge, "Fra krig til fred," *Norges krig*, Vol. III, p. 768; Hartmann, *Nytt lys over kritiske faser*, p. 204.

107. Gjelsvik, *Hjemmefronten*, p. 230; Hauge, *ibid.*, p. 766.

108. Hartmann, *Nytt lys over kritiske faser*, p. 202.

109. Munksgaard, *Gestapo-kameraten*, p. 194. Although evidence suggests strongly that this incident took place, it needs to be noted that Munksgaard is the only source which specifically indicates that Quisling and Terboven met with the *Wehrmacht* command on Tuesday, May 1. Hartmann, in *Nytt lys over kritiske faser*, p. 202, mentions that Terboven was scheduled to confer with Böhme on Monday [*sic.*], May 1, but that Dönitz's order for Terboven and Böhme to meet with him at Flensburg arrived on the same date. Hauge, "Fra krig til fred," *Norges krig*, Vol. III, p. 770, similarly states that Dönitz sent this order on May 1. It is therefore plausible that Quisling and Terboven held a conference with Böhme at Lillehammer *before* the latter two departed for Germany because their meeting with Dönitz did not occur until May 3. Skodvin, in *Samtid og historie*, p. 159, appears to suggest that Terboven traveled to Germany already on April 30, 1945. If true, then neither he nor Quisling could have been at Lille-

hammer on May 1. This view disagrees with Hartmann and Hauge, who, as noted, show May 1 as the date on which Dönitz's order was issued. Since Hitler committed suicide on April 30, it does not appear likely that Terboven received an order from Dönitz to come to Flensburg already on the same day as *der Führer's* death.

110. Hartmann, *Nytt lys over kritiske faser*, p. 203.

111. Gjelsvik, *Hjemmefronten*, p. 231; Diesen, *Maidagene 45*, p. 229.

112. Hauge, "Fra krig til fred," *Norges krig*, Vol. III, p. 775.

113. "Utkast. Offisielt meddeles fra Ministerpresidentens Kansli [sic.]," May 2, 1945, HI, Skodvin Collection, 1942 folder.

114. *Ibid.*

115. Diesen, *Maidagene 45*, pp. 229–230.

116. "Plan om ny NS-regjering (Selmer Alm)" ca. May 1, 1945, HI, Skodvin Collection, May 1945 folder.

117. *Straffesak*, p. 232; Christensen, *Okkupasjonsår og etterkrigstid*, p. 468; Diesen, *Maidagene 45*, p. 229.

118. "PWIS Post Capitulation Planning. Utdrag." HI, Skodvin Collection, April 1945 folder; Hauge, "Fra krig til fred," *Norges krig*, Vol. III, p. 770.

119. "PWIS Post Capitulation Planning. Utdrag," *ibid.*

120. *Ibid.*; Hauge, "Fra krig til fred," *Norges krig*, Vol. III, p. 770.

121. Hauge, *ibid.*, p. 771.

122. Home Front report, author unknown, May 3, 1945, HI, Skodvin Collection, April 1945 folder; Diesen, *Maidagene 45*, p. 230.

123. *Ibid.*

124. Home Front report, author unknown, May 3, 1945, *ibid.*

125. Hauge, "Fra krig til fred," *Norges krig*, Vol. III, p. 776.

126. Home Front report, author unknown, May 3, 1945, HI, Skodvin Collection, April 1945 folder. See also Gjelsvik, *Hjemmefronten*, p. 270, fn. 571.

127. "På vårens og samfølelsens dag," *Fritt Folk*, May 1, 1945.

128. "Appell til alle medlemmer av Nasjonal Samling," *ibid.*, May 5, 1945.

129. "Regjeringens og partiets linje," *ibid.*, May 7, 1945.

130. Magne Skodvin, "Slutten sikker – dagen uviss," *Aftenposten*, May 5, 1970.

131. *Ibid.*

132. Secret Home Front report, May 6, 1945, HI, Skodvin Collection, May 1945 folder.

133. *Ibid.*

134. "Regjeringen vil opprettholde ro og orden med alle lovlige midler," *Fritt Folk*, May 7, 1945.

135. *Ibid.*

136. *Ibid.*

137. *Ibid.*

138. "Regjeringens og partiets linje," *ibid.*, May 7, 1945.

139. Home Front report, author unknown, May 3, 1945, HI, Skodvin Collection, 1945 folder.

140. "Møte på Oslo slott," *Fritt Folk*, May 7, 1945.

141. Hans S. Skarphagen, statement of February 9, 1946, HI, Skodvin Collection, police reports, #414.

142. *Ibid.*; Olaf Fermann, statement of February 11, 1946, *ibid.*, #413.

143. Arnvid Vassbotten, statement of February 9, 1946, HI, *ibid.*, #413; author's interview with a former prominent NS official, Oslo, May 30, 1967.

144. Statement by the Palace watchman, Paul Einar Iversen, June 21, 1945, HI, Skodvin Collection, police reports, #414.

145. See illustration in Hauge, "Fra krig til fred," *Norges krig*, Vol. III, p. 775.

146. Tor Arne Barstad, *Sabotasjen i Oslo-området 1944–45*, Samtidshistorisk Forskningsgruppe, Norge og den 2. verdenskrig Series (Oslo: Universitetsforlaget, 1975), pp. 141–142.

147. Quisling's handwritten draft, n.d., DA, Quislingsaken, Straffesak – Etterforskning mot Quisling, folder no. 7. This document is also printed in its entirety in *Straffesak*, p. 317.

148. *Ibid.*

149. Quisling's testimony, September 6, 1945, *Straffesak*, p. 317.

150. Quisling's testimony, *ibid.* Quisling's defense counsel more specifically declared that the draft was written at Gimle during the final unpleasant days before the capitulation." *Straffesak*, p. 421. This, in my opinion, is most probable.

151. Ragnar Skancke, statement, n.d.,

DA, Quislingsaken, folder 3 – Maria Quisling.

152. Christensen, *Okkupasjonsår og etterkrigstid*, p. 464.

153. Hauge, "Fra krig til fred," *Norges krig*, Vol. III, p. 786, p. 788. Jens Christian Hauge, the Milorg chief who after the war became Minister of Defense in Einar Gerhardsen's Labor government, provides in this essay a very good chronological account of the transition period from war to peace.

154. Quoted in *ibid.*, p. 787.

155. *Ibid.*, pp. 787–788; *Straffesak*, p. 421.

156. Quisling's defense statement, September 6, 1945, *Straffesak*, p. 327.

157. The scene was repeated on a smaller scale in all Norwegian towns and villages. For vivid descriptions and pictures of the atmosphere that existed in Oslo, see Hauge, "Fra krig til fred," *Norges krig*, Vol. III, pp. 784 ff.; Diesen, *Maidagene 45*; and Ustvedt, *Den varme freden, den kalde krigen*, pp. 33 ff.

158. Hauge, *ibid.*, p. 786.

159. *Ibid.*, p. 787.

160. Diesen, *Maidagene 45*, pp. 172–177, 232–234; Hauge, *ibid.*, pp. 788–789. For logistical reasons, however, the great majority of Grini prisoners did not leave camp until the next day.

161. Diesen, *ibid.*, pp. 235–242; Ustvedt, *Den varme freden – den kalde krigen*, p. 36.

162. Hauge, "Fra krig til fred," *Norges krig*, Vol. III, p. 790. According to the terms of the capitulation which Böhme received from an Allied military commission at Lillehammer on May 8, the *Wehrmacht* units were required to disarm themselves. This they carried out with exemplary discipline. See Hauge, pp. 803–808.

163. Harry Söderman, *Skandinaviskt mellanspel. Norska och danska trupper i Sverige* (Stockholm: Forum, 1945), pp. 296–297.

164. Hauge, "Fra krig til fred," *Norges krig*, Vol. III, p. 794.

165. *Ibid.*, pp. 802–803. One major exception to the general pattern of few private acts of retribution after the war involved Norwegian women who were believed to have had intimate relations with Germans during the occupation. Like similar incidents

in other liberated countries, such women sometimes had their hair shaved off and were subjected to additional indignities. See Ustvedt, *Den varme freden – den kalde krigen*, pp. 79–81.

166. Hauge, "Fra krig til fred," *Norges krig*, Vol. III, pp. 712–713.

167. Ustvedt, *Den varme freden – den kalde krigen*, pp. 37–38; Christensen, *Okkupasjonsår og etterkrigstid*, p. 474.

168. L'Abée-Lund, "Politiet over og under jorden," *Norges krig*, Vol. III, p. 290; author's interview with Sven Arntzen, Oslo, June 20, 1972; Kjell Sørhus and Rolf Ottesen, eds., *Milorg D 13 i kamp* (Oslo: Ernst G. Mortensens forlag, 1961), p. 281. Hereafter cited as *Milorg D 13 i kamp*.

169. Ustvedt, *Den varme freden – den kalde krigen*, p. 41; Diesen, *Maidagene 45*, p. 299; Hauge, "Fra krig til fred," *Norges krig*, Vol. III, p. 788.

170. Maria Quisling, statement, June 4, 1946, DA, Quislingsaken, folder 3 – Maria Quisling.

171. Hauge, "Fra krig til fred," *Norges krig*, Vol. III, p. 788; *Milorg D 13 i kamp*, p. 277; Ragnar Skancke, statement, n.d., DA, Quislingsaken, folder 3 – Maria Quisling; Fuglesang, statement, n.d., DA, Quislingsaken, folder 3 – Maria Quisling. Fuglesang maintained that some 400 men from the Ski Battalion came to Gimle, but this number appears to be too high.

172. Arntzen interview, June 20, 1972.

173. *Milorg D 13 i kamp*, pp. 277–283.

174. *Ibid.*, pp. 282–283. In addition to Foss, Quisling indicated to other persons on May 8 that he would refrain from attempting an armed defense. See Albert Kvaal, "dagbok-opptegnelse," May 11, 1945, DA, Quislingsaken, folder 15.

175. Maria Quisling, statement, June 4, 1946, DA, Quislingsaken, folder 3 – Maria Quisling.

176. *Ibid.*; *Milorg D 13 i kamp*, p. 283.

177. Kåre Norum, "Natten mellom 8. og 9. mai 1945 på Oslo Politistasjon," May 9, 1945, DA, Quislingsaken, folder 12; L'Abée-Lund, "Politiet over og under jorden," *Norges krig*, Vol. III, p. 290.

178. Arntzen interview, June 20, 1972.

179. Diesen, *Maidagene 45*, p. 275.

180. Norum, "Natten mellom 8. og 9.

mai 1945 på Oslo Politistasjon," May 9, 1945, DA, Quislingsaken, folder 12.

181. *Ibid.*

182. *Ibid.*; L'Abée-Lund, "Politiet over og under jorden," *Norges krig*, Vol. III, p. 290; Arntzen interview, June 20, 1972.

183. Norum, *ibid.*

184. Kvaal, "dagbok-opptegnelse," May 11, 1945, DA, Quislingsaken, folder 15.

185. Fuglesang, statement, n.d., DA, Quislingsaken, folder 3 – Maria Quisling.

186. Kvaal, "dagbok-opptegnelse," May 11, 1945, DA, Quislingsaken, folder 15; Norum, "Natten mellom 8. og 9. mai 1945 på Oslo Politistasjon," May 9, 1945, DA, Quislingsaken, folder 12; L'Abée-Lund, "Politiet over og under jorden," *Norges krig*, Vol. III, p. 290.

187. *Milorg D 13 i kamp*, pp. 282–283.

188. Kvaal, "dagbok-opptegnelse," May 11, 1945, DA, Quislingsaken, folder 15; Norum, "Natten mellom 8. og 9. mai 1945 på Oslo Politistasjon," May 9, 1945, DA, Quislingsaken, folder 12.

189. Norum, *ibid.*; L'Abée-Lund, "Politiet over og under jorden," *Norges krig*, Vol. III, p. 293.

190. Norum, *ibid.*; L'Abée-Lund, *ibid.*, p. 294.

191. Kvaal, "dagbok-opptegnelse," May 11, 1945, DA, Quislingsaken, folder 15.

192. Maria Quisling, statement, June 4, 1946, DA, Quislingsaken, folder 3 – Maria Quisling.

193. Norum, "Natten mellom 8. og 9. mai 1945 på Oslo Politistasjon," May 9, 1945, DA, Quislingsaken, folder 12; L'Abée-Lund, "Politiet over og under jorden," *Norges krig*, Vol. III, p. 294.

194. Jan Schjelderup Mathiesen, "Quisling arresteres og blir fengslet," *Verdens Gang*, October 30, 1973.

195. Diesen, *Maidagene 45*, p. 276; Norum, "Natten mellom 8. og 9. mai 1945 på Oslo Politistasjon," May 9, 1945, DA, Quislingsaken, folder 12.

196. Diesen, *ibid.*

197. *Ibid.*, p. 278; *Milorg D 13 i kamp*, p. 284; Mathiesen, "Quisling arresteres og blir fengslet," *Verdens Gang*, October 30, 1973. Some disagreement exists concerning exactly what Quisling brought with him to Møllergaten 19. Lars L'Abée-Lund has maintained that Quisling only carried with

him a blanket and a handbag, which contained toilet articles and a bottle of cognac. See L'Abée-Lund, "Ingen felle lagt for Quisling," *Dagbladet*, April 22, 1956; and Jan Schjelderup Mathiesen, "Ingen felle," *Verdens Gang*, November 17, 1973.

198. *Milorg D 13 i kamp*, p. 284. Question has been raised whether an arrangment actually had been agreed upon at the meeting with Dr. Foss on Tuesday, May 8, whereby Quisling would be interned. Quisling's NS defenders have later alleged that such an agreement had been made, and that Quisling was lured into a trap when he surrendered. As evidence, they point to the fact that the NS *Fører* and his ministers had packed their luggage at Gimle in preparation for internment. See Dahl, *et al.*, *Den norske nasjonalsosialismen*, p. 199. However, as noted above, the fact that the ministers at Gimle had expected negotiations to resume again on Wednesday, May 9, indicates that no final agreement had been reached during the previous day concerning Quisling's future arrangements after his surrender. Documents written at the time or shortly thereafter further show that those present at Gimle had not considered Foss' offer to have been authoritative, but at best the basis for further discussions. See Maria Quisling, statement, June 4, 1946, DA, Quislingsaken, folder 3 – Maria Quisling; and Norum, "Natten mellom 8. og 9. mai 1945 på Oslo Politistasjon," May 9, 1945, DA, Quislingsaken, folder 12. Fuglesang stated after the war that Quisling initially had expected to be interned in a manner other than "ordinary prison," but that he understood clearly following Lippestad's unsuccessful talks with Arntzen on the night of May 8–9 that imprisonment would occur under the strictest conditions. See Fuglesang, statement, n.d., DA, Quislingsaken, folder 3 – Maria Quisling.

199. Norum, *ibid.*; Diesen, *Maidagene 45*, p. 278; L'Abée-Lund, "Politiet over og under jorden," *Norges krig*, Vol. III, p. 294; Mathiesen, "Quisling arresteres og blir fengslet," *Verdens Gang*, October 30, 1973.

200. Norum, *ibid.*; L'Abée-Lund, *ibid.*

201. *Ibid.*

Notes to Chapter XVIII

1. Mathiesen, "Quisling arresteres og blir fengslet," *Verdens Gang*, October 30, 1973.
2. Andenæs, *Det vanskelige oppgjøret*, p. 79.
3. Mathiesen, "Quisling arresteres og blir fengslet," *Verdens Gang*, October 30, 1973.
4. Diesen, *Maidagene 45*, pp. 340–343; "Quisling i forhørsretten i dag," *Aftenposten*, evening edition, May 26, 1945.
5. Diesen, *ibid.*, pp. 344–345; *Aftenposten*, *ibid.*
6. Andenæs, *Det vanskelige oppgjøret*, pp. 84–87; Axel Hemming-Sjöberg, *Domen över Quisling* (Stockholm: Bokförlaget Natur och Kultur, 1946), pp. 491–492.
7. "Quisling avslører sine tyske herrer," *Aftenposten*, May 28, 1945.
8. *Ibid.*
9. See above, p. 1037.
10. "Quisling avslører sine tyske herrer," *Aftenposten*, May 28, 1945.
11. *Ibid.*
12. *Ibid.*
13. Mathiesen, "Quisling arresteres og blir fengslet," *Verdens Gang*, October 30, 1973.
14. Quisling, *Redegjørelse fra Vidkun Quisling til siktelse fremsatt i Oslo forhørsrett.* The document is also printed in *Straffesak*, pp. 570–591. Hereafter cited as *Redegjørelse*.
15. *Ibid.*, p. 2, p. 23.
16. *Ibid.*, pp. 3 ff.
17. *Ibid.*, pp. 10–11.
18. *Ibid.*, p. 7.
19. *Ibid.*, p. 1.
20. *Ibid.*, pp. 20–21.
21. *Ibid.*, pp. 18–19.
22. *Ibid.*, pp. 21–22.
23. *Ibid.*, pp. 1–2.
24. *Ibid.*, pp. 2–3.
25. *Ibid.*, pp. 24–25.
26. "Quisling i dødskogen på Trandum," *Aftenposten*, June 20, 1945.
27. *Ibid.*; Diesen, *Maidagene 45*, p. 349.
28. Dahl, et al., *Den norske nasjonalsosialismen*, p. 210.
29. "Quisling i dødsskogen på Trandum," *Aftenposten*, June 20, 1945.
30. The full indictment is printed in *Straffesak*, pp. 2–7.
31. Quisling, *Vidkun Quislings bemerkninger til nytt i tiltalebeslutningen av 11-7-1945 i tilslutning til redegjørelse av 21-6-1945.* Hereafter cited as *Vidkun Quislings bemerkninger.*
32. *Ibid.*, p. 3.
33. *Ibid.*
34. *Ibid.*, p. 5, p. 10, etc.
35. *Ibid.*, p. 3.
36. *Ibid.*, p. 6., p. 12.
37. *Ibid.*, p. 14, p. 17.
38. It is printed in its entirety in *Straffesak*, pp. 604–626.
39. Jan Schjelderup Mathiesen, "Fra forræderi og drap til tyverier," *Verdens Gang*, October 31, 1973.
40. *Straffesak*, p. 1.
41. *Ibid.*, p. 366.
42. Andenæs, *Det vanskelige oppgjøret*, pp. 79–82.
43. *Ibid.*, p. 82; Hemming-Sjöberg, *Domen över Quisling*, p. 490.
44. "Quislingsaken," *Bilder*, no. 8 (September 1945), p. 6.
45. Hemming-Sjöberg, *Domen över Quisling*, p. 492.
46. Quoted in *ibid.*
47. *Straffesak*, p. 8.
48. *Ibid.*, pp. 2–7.
49. *Ibid.*, pp. 2–3.
50. *Ibid.*, pp. 3–4.
51. *Ibid.*, pp. 4–5.
52. *Ibid.*, p. 5.
53. *Ibid.*; *Vidkun Quislings bemerkninger*, pp. 20–21.
54. *Straffesak*, pp. 5–6.
55. *Ibid.*, p. 24.
56. *Ibid.*, pp. 6–7.
57. *Ibid.*, p. 7.
58. *Ibid.*
59. *Ibid.*
60. *Ibid.*, p. 8.
61. *Ibid.*, p. 7.
62. *Ibid.*
63. *Ibid.*, pp. 8 ff.
64. *Ibid.*, p. 14.
65. *Ibid.*, p. 25.
66. *Ibid.*
67. *Ibid.*, pp. 25 ff.
68. *Ibid.*, pp. 59 ff.
69. *Ibid.*, pp. 62–63.
70. *Ibid.*, p. 63.

71. *Ibid.*, pp. 52–58.

72. *Ibid.*, pp. 59–60.

73. "Mobiliseringsoppgjøret 1940," September 28, 1939, in *Dokumenter i offentlig straffesak*, Tilleggshefte II, p. 4.

74. *Straffesak*, p. 45.

75. Testimony of Christian Laake, August 24, 1945, *ibid.*, pp. 214–215.

76. Testimony of Rasmus Hatledal, August 23, 1945, *ibid.*, pp. 164–165.

77. *Straffesak*, p. 76.

78. *Ibid.*, p. 76, p. 81.

79. *Ibid.*, pp. 76–77.

80. *Ibid.*, p. 78.

81. *Ibid.*, pp. 82–83.

82. *Ibid.*, p. 85.

83. *Ibid.*, p. 89.

84. *Ibid.*, p. 102.

85. *Ibid.*, p. 104.

86. *Ibid.*, p. 105.

87. *Ibid.*, p. 106.

88. *Ibid.*, p. 107–108.

89. *Ibid.*, p. 111–112.

90. *Ibid.*, p. 114.

91. *Ibid.*, p. 118.

92. *Ibid.*, pp. 119–121.

93. *Ibid.*, pp. 126–129.

94. *Ibid.*, p. 130.

95. *Ibid.*

96. *Ibid.*, pp. 130–131.

97. *Ibid.*, p. 133.

98. *Ibid.*, pp. 133–134.

99. *Ibid.*, pp. 135 ff.

100. *Ibid.*, p. 136–137.

101. *Vidkun Quislings bemerkninger*, pp. 23–24.

102. *Straffesak*, pp. 139 ff.

103. *Ibid.*, p. 142.

104. *Ibid.*, p. 144.

105. *Ibid.*, p. 278, p. 379.

106. *Ibid.*, p. 145.

107. Andenaes, *Det vanskelige oppgjøret*, pp. 88.

108. *Ibid.*

109. Among the less significant testimony for the prosecution was that provided by the following persons, in *Straffesak*: Sigrid Dagny Thoreid, pp. 166–167; Bernhard Øivind Salbu, pp. 168–169; Hartvig Kiran, p. 171; Thoralf Øksnevad, p. 171; Per Pavel Munthe, pp. 171–172; Wilhelm Carl Esser, pp. 205–206; Sofus Kahrs, pp. 208–209; Per Karlson, p. 209; and Orvar Saether, p. 212.

110. Testimony of Colonel Rasmus Hatledal and Lieutenant Colonel Harald Wrede-Holm, August 23, 1945, *ibid.*, pp. 161–166.

111. Testimony of Dr. Leo Eitinger and Asriel B. Hirsch, *ibid.*, pp. 157–161.

112. *Ibid.*, pp. 160–161.

113. Testimony of Eleonore Johanne Nielsen and Randi Riff Holst, August 23, 1945, *ibid.*, pp. 167–168, 169–170; and of Nicolai Plesner, August 24, 1945, *ibid.*, pp. 179–180.

114. *Ibid.*, pp. 180–188, 196–197, 241–242. When Hagelin later went on trial, which occurred after Quisling's execution, his memory had revived in a seemingly miraculous manner.

115. *Ibid.*, p. 192.

116. *Ibid.*, p. 193.

117. *Ibid.*, pp. 196–197.

118. Testimony of Egil Sundt, August 23, 1945, *ibid.*, pp. 155–156, and Christian Laake, August 24, 1945, pp. 214–215.

119. Testimony of Colonel Hans S. Hiorth, August 23, 1945, *ibid.*, pp. 154–155; Gunnar Schjelderup, August 24, 1945, pp. 172–173; and Bjarne Knudsen, August 25, 1945, pp. 220–222.

120. Testimony of Egil Sundt and Karl J. Lyche, August 23, 1945, *ibid.*, pp. 155–156, pp. 170–171.

121. Testimony of Petter Fredrik Broch, August 24, 1945, *ibid.*, pp. 175–179; Olaf Brinchmann-Hanssen, Paul Einar Iversen, Walther Salicath, Hans Bergsland Myhre, and Eilif Lie, August 25, 1945, *ibid.*, pp. 224–228, 229–231, p. 233.

122. *Straffesak*, p. 99.

123. Testimony of Paul Einar Iversen, August 25, 1945, *ibid.*, p. 226.

124. *Straffesak*, *ibid.*

125. Testimony of Rolf Jørgen Fuglesang and Bjørn Noreger, August 24, 1945, *ibid.*, pp. 188–191, 207–208; Fredrik Georg Nissen and Aksel Tostrup, August 25, 1945, *ibid.*, pp. 222–224, 228–229.

126. *Straffesak*, pp. 153–154. See above, pp. 32–34.

127. *Ibid.*, pp. 197–201.

128. *Ibid.*, pp. 235–238. Hansson's name is spelled incorrectly with one s in *ibid.*, pp. 236–238.

129. *Ibid.*, pp. 238–239.

130. Jan Schjelderup Mathiesen, "Sterke

prov for Quislings skyld," *Verdens Gang*, November 7, 1973.

131. *Straffesak*, p. 240.

132. *Ibid.*, p. 244.

133. *Ibid.*, p. 244, pp. 245–246.

134. *Ibid.*, p. 244.

135. *Ibid.*, pp. 244–245; Per Øivind Heradstveit, *Quisling. Hvem var han?* (Oslo: Hjemmets forlag, 1976), p. 18.

136. G. H. Monrad-Krohn, "Ad kasus major Vidkun Quisling," quoted in *Straffesak*, pp. 244–245. Quisling's health problem stemming from sciatica is indicated in a letter from his mother to his wife. See Anna Qvisling to Maria Quisling, May 15, 1930, Oslo University Library, Håndskriftavdelingen, MS fol. 3920 XII: 3. Letters between Vidkun and Maria Quisling in the period 1928–1930, located in Håndskriftavdelingen, similarly refer to the discomfort he experienced from sciatica.

137. *Straffesak*, p. 441.

138. *Ibid.*, p. 442

139. *Gåten Vidkun Quisling* (Oslo: H. Aschenhoug & Co.), p. 98.

140. *Ibid.*, p. 100.

141. To cite but two examples: Langfeldt deduced that Quisling in January 1940 was in a "psychotic phase." This view was based on testimony provided by Vilhelm Ullmann concerning *one conversation* which Quisling had with friends, extending over a two-hour period. During this time, according to Ullmann, Quisling was friendly and even-tempered except at one point when he made a number of wild accusations against the Labor party. *Ibid.*, pp. 81–83. Norway would have had an extraordinarily high rate of mental illness if everyone who made rash charges against the Labor party during the 1930s had been declared psychotic. Another sample of Langfeldt's use of debatable information occurred when he referred positively to firsthand knowledge of Dr. Johan Scharffenberg's assumption that Quisling was insane in the fall of 1942 when he had threatened two University deans (see above, p. 763). That Scharffenberg had reacted to this information by insisting Quisling be declared insane and interned, believing this to be possible, revealed perhaps as much concerning Scharffenberg's irrational condition at the time as it did Quisling's. *Ibid.*, pp. 10–13. Scharffenberg, however, despite his

strong feelings against the death penalty, did not publicly raise any objections to Quisling's execution in 1945 (see below, p. 763).

142. *Ibid.*, p. 100.

143. *På gjengrodde stier* (Oslo: Gyldendal Norsk Forlag, 1949). English translation: *On Over-Grown Paths* (New York: P. S. Eriksson, 1967).

144. Langfeldt, *Gåten Vidkun Quisling*, p. 100.

145. "Quisling har ikke svulst på hjernen," *Dagbladet*, August 29, 1945.

146. *Straffesak*, pp. 244–246.

147. *Ibid.*, pp. 246–247.

148. *Ibid.*, pp. 247–248.

149. *Ibid.*, p. 248.

150. Andenæs, *Det vanskelige oppgjøret*, p. 60; note written by an unknown NS prisoner at Akershus Castle, June 8, 1945, courtesy of Mrs. Åse Holtan, Brumunddal.

151. *Straffesak*, p. 248.

152. *Ibid.*, p. 250.

153. *Ibid.*, p. 269.

154. *Ibid.*

155. *Ibid.*, p. 271.

156. *Ibid.*, p. 272.

157. Andenæs, *Det vanskelige oppgjøret*, pp. 176–177.

158. *Straffesak*, p. 273.

159. *Ibid.*

160. "Quisling har ikke svulst på hjernen," *Dagbladet*, August 29, 1945.

161. *Straffesak*, p. 296.

162. *Ibid.*, pp. 278–279.

163. *Ibid.*, p. 284.

164. *Ibid.*, p. 290.

165. *Ibid.*, p. 299.

166. *Ibid.*, p. 297, p. 305.

167. *Ibid.*, pp. 305–306.

168. *Ibid.*, pp. 309–312.

169. *Ibid.*, pp. 314–315.

170. *Ibid.*, pp. 315–316.

171. *Ibid.*, p. 318.

172. *Ibid.*, p. 319.

173. *Ibid.*

174. *Ibid.*

175. *Ibid.*, p. 320.

176. *Ibid.*, pp. 320–321.

177. *Ibid.*, p. 320.

178. *Ibid.*, p. 322.

179. *Ibid.*, p. 324.

180. *Ibid.*, pp. 324–326.

181. Andenæs, *Det vanskelige oppgjøret*, p. 89.

182. *Straffesak*, p. 333; Hemming-Sjöberg, *Domen över Quisling*, pp. 432–433.

183. Hemming-Sjöberg, *ibid.*, p. 433.

184. *Straffesak*, p. 338.

185. *Ibid.*, p. 327.

186. *Ibid.*, p. 336.

187. *Ibid.*, pp. 344–345.

188. *Ibid.*, p. 364.

189. *Ibid.*

190. *Ibid.*, p. 365.

191. *Ibid.*, p. 366.

192. *Ibid.*

193. *Ibid.*

194. *Ibid.*, p. 377.

195. *Ibid.*

196. Hemming-Sjöberg, *Domen över Quisling*, p. 514.

197. *Straffesak*, p. 381.

198. *Ibid.*, p. 382.

199. Maria Quisling to King Haakon VII, October 9, 1945, quoted in Maria Quisling, *Dagbok*, p. 38.

200. *Dagbladet*, September 15, 1945. The paper incorrectly referred to September 10, 1945, as the Quislings' twenty third wedding anniversary.

201. *Straffesak*, p. 366.

202. *Ibid.*, p. 384.

203. *Ibid.*, pp. 383–384.

204. *Ibid.*, p. 384.

205. *Ibid.*, p. 387.

206. Jan Schjelderup Mathiesen, "Skarp prosedyre – for og mot – i Høyesterett," *Verdens Gang*, November 15, 1973.

207. *Straffesak*, pp. 388–393.

208. *Ibid.*, pp. 393–396.

209. *Ibid.*, pp. 396–397.

210. *Ibid.*, pp. 398–399.

211. *Ibid.*, pp. 399–400.

212. *Ibid.*, p. 400.

213. *Ibid.*, p. 388.

214. *Ibid.*, p. 400.

215. *Ibid.*, pp. 400 ff.

216. *Ibid.*, p. 418.

217. *Ibid.*, p. 422.

218. *Ibid.*, pp. 422–427.

219. *Ibid.*, pp. 427 ff.

220. *Ibid.*, p. 427.

221. *Ibid.*, p. 428.

222. *Ibid.*, p. 438.

223. *Ibid.*, p. 439.

224. *Ibid.*, p. 427.

225. *Ibid.*, p. 439.

226. *Ibid.*, p. 440.

227. *Ibid.*

228. *Ibid.*, pp. 440–441.

229. *Ibid.*, pp. 442–443.

230. *Ibid.*, p. 442.

231. *Ibid.*, p. 445.

232. *Ibid.*, p. 449.

233. *Ibid.*, p. 451.

234. *Ibid.*, p. 452.

235. *Ibid.*, p. 460.

236. Hemming-Sjöberg, *Domen över Quisling*, p. 476.

237. *Straffesak*, p. 460.

238. *Ibid.*, p. 461.

239. Not to be confused with Quisling's assistant defense attorney, Eilif Fougner.

240. Norges Høyesterett, sak L. nr. 26, S.nr. 77/1945: påtalemynmdigheten mot Vidkun Quisling, Kjennelse, DA, Quislingsaken, folder #5.

241. *Ibid.*

242. *Ibid.*

243. *Ibid.*

244. *Domen över Quisling*, p. 493.

245. Maria Quisling, *Dagbok*, p. 38.

246. Quoted in *ibid.*, pp. 39–40.

247. Quoted in *ibid.*, pp. 50–52.

248. Quoted in *ibid.*, pp. 40–41.

249. Maria Quisling, *Dagbok*, pp. 41–43. Copies of the letters to Thorne and Stalin have not been found.

250. *Ibid.*, p. 47; Martha Lien, police report, October 16, 1945, DA, Quislingsaken, Rettsbok i lagmannsrettssak #17 for 1945 – folder #6.

251. Maria Quisling, *ibid.*

252. *Ibid.*, p. 49.

253. Lien, police report, October 16, 1945, DA, Quislingsaken, Rettsbok i lagmannsrettssak #17 for 1945 – folder #6.

254. Constable Hegglund, police report, June 13, 1946, *ibid.*, folder #3 – Maria Quisling.

255. Paal Berg, Helge Klæstad, Emil Stang, Sigurd Fougner, and Henrik Bahr, to the King, October 13, 1945, *ibid*, folder #5.

256. Handwritten addendum to the Supreme Court opinion, illegible signature, Oslo Police Department, *ibid.*

257. Quisling to the King, October 18, 1945, quoted in Maria Quisling, *Dagbok*, pp. 53–56.

258. Quisling to Vilhelm Ullmann, October 13, 1945, in the possession of Dr. Viggo Ullmann, Lillehammer.

259. Quisling to Jørgen Quisling, October 10, 1945, in the possession of *ibid.*

260. Maria Quisling, *Dagbok*, pp. 162–188.

261. *Ibid.*, p. 163.

262. *Ibid.*, p. 164.

263. *Ibid.*, p. 171.

264. *Ibid.*, pp. 166 ff.

265. *Ibid.*, p. 188.

266. *Ibid.*, p. 191.

267. *Ibid.*, p. 62.

268. Lien, police report, October 16, 1945, DA, Quislingsaken, Rettsbok i lagmannsrettssak #17 for 1945 – folder #6.

269. Vidkun to Maria, October 15, October 17, October 18, 1945, quoted in Maria Quisling, *Dagbok*, pp. 58–60.

270. *Aftenposten*, October 24, 1945.

271. Aage Seidenfaden, "Beretning" to the Danish Ministry of Justice, October 27, 1945; in Copenhagen, Justitsministeriets arkiv. The author would like to express his thanks to Justitsministeriet for granting him access to this report.

272. Vidkun to Maria, October 23, 1945. The letter is shown in facsimile among the illustrations in Maria Quisling's *Dagbok*.

273. Maria Quisling, *Dagbok*, p. 63.

274. Seidenfaden, "Beretning," October 27, 1945. Seidenfaden later wrote an autobiography in which he repeated much of what he stated in his firsthand report of October 1945 concerning Quisling's execution. See *I politiets tjeneste* (Copenhagen: Gyldendal, 1955), pp. 124–126. Although on the whole quite reliable, the book is not as detailed as the report, and it contains a few minor inaccuracies.

275. Seidenfaden, "Beretning," *ibid.*; Harald Øie, "Slik ble Quisling henrettet," *Verdens Gang*, September 29, 1978.

276. Øie, *ibid.*; Seidenfaden, *ibid.*

277. Øie, *ibid.*; Seidenfaden, *ibid.*

278. "Quisling ble henrettet klokken 2.40 i natt," *Aftenposten*, October 24, 1945.

279. Hewins, *Quisling: Prophet without Honour*, p. 372.

280. Thorkild Hansen, *Processen mod Hamsun* (3 vols.; Copenhagen: Gyldendal, 1978), Vol. I, pp. 325–327. Hansen shortened his description of Quisling's execution slightly in the subsequent Norwegian edition. He at least appears to have recognized that Hewins' account of Quisling's corpse being put on display was incorrect, since this depiction was omitted entirely when the book was published in Norway. See Thorkild Hansen, *Prosessen mot Hamsun* (Oslo: Gyldendal norsk Forlag, 1978), pp. 307–308.

281. Seidenfaden, "Beretning," October 27, 1945; Øie, "Slik ble Quisling henrettet," *Verdens Gang*, September 29, 1978; "Dansk Quisling-rapport imøtegår Thorkild Hansen," *Ukens Nytt*, February 23, 1979; Sverre Hartmann, "Da eksekusjonen av Quisling ble utsatt," *Morgenbladet*, October 6, 1978. The articles in *Ukens Nytt* and by Hartmann use Seidenfaden as their main source.

282. Øie, *ibid.*; "Dansk Quisling-rapport imøtegår Thorkild Hansen," *Ukens Nytt*, *ibid.*

283. Maria Quisling to Minister of Justice Jens Haugland, May 21, 1959, quoted in Maria Quisling, *Dagbok*, pp. 157–158.

284. *Ibid.*, p. 153.

285. Maria Quisling to Arne Quisling, n.d., quoted in *ibid.*, pp. 153–156; Maria Quisling to Minister of Justice Jens Haugland, May 21, 1959, quoted in *ibid.*, pp. 157–158.

286. Stenographic record of the pre-trial proceedings, June 17, 1946, DA, Quislingsaken, folder #3 – Maria Quisling.

287. Øistein Parmann, Introduction to Maria Quisling, *Dagbok*, p. 22.

Notes to Epilogue

1. Quisling, "Valget står mellom Nasjonal Samlings trange veg til nasjonal nyreising eller bolsjevismens brede veg til fordervelsen," *Fritt Folk*, January 2, 1945.

2. Labor kept its absolute majority until 1961, and it retained control of the government, except for a few weeks in 1963, until 1965.

3. Quisling, "Valget står mellom Nasjonal Samlings trange veg til nasjonal nyreising eller bolsjevismens brede veg til fordervelsen," *Fritt Folk*, January 2, 1945; Quisling, "Regjeringen vil opprettholde ro og orden med alle lovlige midler," radio speech of May 5, 1945, printed in *Fritt Folk*, May 7, 1945.

4. Ustvedt, *Den varme freden – den kalde krigen*, p. 52, p. 102.

5. Statistisk Sentralbyrå, *Statistikk over landssvik 1940–1945*, pp. 13–14.

6. *Om landssvikoppgjøret*, p. 410.

7. *Ibid.*

8. Andenæs, *Det vanskelige oppgjøret*, p. 228.

9. *Ibid.*, pp. 229–230.

10. *Om landssvikoppgjøret*, pp. 127 ff.

11. Andenæs, *Det vanskelige oppgjøret*, p. 182. An additional twelve Germans were shot for war crimes, bringing the total number of executions in postwar Norway to 37.

12. *Ibid.*, pp. 168–171, p. 180.

13. *Ibid.*, pp. 182 ff.

14. *Ibid.*, pp. 185–189.

15. For a detailed examination of this group of irreconcilable former NS members, covering the period up to the mid-1970s, see Georg Øvsthus, "Dom og oppreisning," in *Fra idé til dom*, pp. 215–258.

Bibliography

I. Archival Sources

Justisdepartementet, Oslo
    Domsarkivet
        Dossiers on: Albert Viljam Hagelin
                    Johan Andreas Lippestad
                    Maria Quisling
                    Vidkun Quisling
                    Finn Støren
                    Alf Larsen Whist
                    Herman Harris Aall
Justitsministeriet, Copenhagen
    Justitsministeriets arkiv
        Aage Seidenfaden: "Beretning". October 27, 1945
Norges Hjemmefrontmuseum, Oslo
    Collections
    Meldungen aus Norwegen
Riksarkivet, Oslo
    Generalstabens arkiv
        Journalsaker: Petrograd 1918 #1166
                    Helsingfors 1919 #1105
                    Helsingfors 1920 #1102
                    Helsingfors 1921 #1106
    Quislings arkiv
Stortingsarkivet, Oslo
    Undersøkelseskommisjonen av 1945s arkiv
Universitetet i Oslo. Historisk Institutt
    Skodvin Collection
Universitetsbiblioteket, Oslo
    Manuscript Collection
Utenriksdepartementets arkiv, Oslo
    Gruppe 5, Avdeling H, Administr. Ordn. Moskva 1927 – Jan. 1929

Gruppe Q5, Avdeling H, Sak 1/27, Den administrative ordning ved Leg. Moskvas overtagelse av brit. interesser i Sovjet
Gruppe 10, Avdeling H, Sak 2/28
Gruppe H62, Avdeling D, Sak 5/27, Sak 1/28, Sak 2/28, Sak 3/28
Arkivnr. 39 – Arnold Ræstad: "The Case Quisling". Unpublished MS.

II. Printed Documents and Official Publications

Irgens-saken. Oslo: privately published, 1948.

Nordic Council. *Yearbook of Nordic Statistics, 1973.* Stockholm: 1974.

Norway. Administrasjonsrådet. *Protokoll for møter i det Administrasjonsråd som er oppnevnt av Høyesterett mandag den 15. april 1940.* Stenciled protocol in two volumes. Oslo: n.d.

Norway, Eidsivating Lagstols Landssvikavdeling. *Dokumenter i offentlig straffesak mot Vidkun Quisling.* With three appendices. Oslo: 1945.

———. Quisling, Vidkun. *Redegjørelse fra Vidkun Quisling til siktelse fremsatt i Oslo Forhørsrett.* Oslo: 1945.

———. *Vidkun Quislings bemerkninger til nytt i tiltalebeslutningen av 11-7-1945 i tilslutning til redegjørelse av 21-6-1945.* Oslo: 1945.

———. *Straffesak mot Vidkun Abraham Lauritz Jonssøn Quisling.* Oslo: 1946.

Norway. Forsvarsdepartementet. Krigshistoriske avdeling. Erik Anker Steen. *Norges sjøkrig 1940–1945.* Oslo: 1954–1969. 7 vols.

Norway. Justisdepartementet (Nasjonal Samling). Sverre Riisnæs. *Nasjonal Samling og lovverket.* Oslo: Gunnar Stenersens Forlag, 1942.

Norway. Justis- og Politidepartementet. *Om landssvikoppgjøret. Innstilling fra et utvalg nedsatt for å skaffe tilveie materiale til en innberetning fra Justisdepartementet til Stortinget.* Oslo: 1962.

Norway. Det Statistiske Centralbyrå. *Kommunevalgene og ordførervalgene 1934.* Oslo: 1935.

———. *Kommunevalgene og ordførervalgene 1937.* Oslo: 1938.

———. *Statistikk over landssvik 1940–1945.* Oslo: 1954.

Norway. Stortinget. *Kongeriket Norges ordentlige Stortings Forhandlinger.*

———. *Regjeringen og hjemmefronten under krigen. Aktstykker utgitt av Stortinget.* Oslo: 1948.

———. *Innstilling fra Undersøkelseskommisjonen av 1945.* Oslo: 1946–1947. 3 vols.

———. Sverre Steen. *Riksrådsforhandlingene.* Appendix 9, Vol. I, to *Innstilling fra Undersøkelseskommisjonen av 1945.* Oslo: 1947.

Norway. Stortingets Kontor. *Stortingsvalget 1933.* Oslo: 1934.

———. *Stortingsvalget 1936.* Oslo: 1937.

Norway. Universitetsbiblioteket. *Norsk bokfortegnelse 1936–1940.* Oslo: 1943.

———. *Norske aviser 1763–1969.* Oslo: 1973.

Norway. Det Kongelige Utenriksdepartementet. *Norges forhold til Sverige under krigen 1940–1945.* Oslo: 1947–1950. 3 vols.

Sweden. Kungliga Utrikesdepartementet. *Förspelet till det tyska angreppet på Danmark och Norge den 9 april 1940.* Handlingar rörande Sveriges politik under andra världskriget Series. Stockholm: 1947.

III. Newspapers and Periodicals

ABC
Aftenposten
Arbeiderbladet
Asker og Bærum Budstikke
Dagbladet
Fritt Folk
Nasjonal Samling
Nasjonal-Ungdommen
Nationen
Oslo-Pressen
Ragnarok
Samarbeid
Stornordisk Samband
Tidens Tegn
Verdens Gang

IV: Oral Interviews

The author interviewed a number of persons in Norway during the time when he researched this study. The interviews were conducted with individuals who knew Quisling personally, or who had firsthand knowledge of him. Among these were Quisling's acquaintances and family members, NS adherents from the 1930's and 1940's, and political opponents of Quisling, including some who held leading positions within the Home Front. These persons readily provided the author with interesting insights concerning his subject. However, except in a few instances, they have wished to remain anonymous and not be cited by name. The author has therefore chosen to use evidence obtained in this manner generally as background information. In the few instances when he does make direct use of interview material in the text, reference is made to the source in the relevant footnote citation.

V: Books and Articles

Aagesen, Knut. "Fagopposisjonen av 1940", pp. 357–59 in *1940 – Fra nøytral til okkupert*. Norge og den 2. verdenskrig Series, Samtidshistorisk Forskningsgruppe, eds. Oslo: Universitetsforlaget, 1969

Andenæs, Johannes, Olav Riste, and Magne Skodvin. *Norway and the Second World War*. Oslo: Johan Grundt Tanum Forlag, 1966

Andenæs, Johannes. *Det vanskelige oppgjøret*. Oslo: Tanum-Norli, 1980

Augdahl, Odin. "Norges politiske partier", *Ragnarok* yearbook, 1936

Barstad, Tor Arne. *Sabotasjen i Oslo-området 1944–45*. Norge og den 2. verdenskrig Series, Samtidshistorisk Forskningsgruppe, eds. Oslo: Universitetsforlaget, 1975

Berggrav, Eivind. *Da kampen kom. Noen blad fra startåret*. Oslo: Land og Kirke, 1945

Bergsgård, Arne. *Frå 17. mai til 9. april. Norsk historie 1814–1940*. Oslo: Det Norske Samlaget, 1958

Bjørneberg, Arne. *Parlamentarismens utveckling i Norge efter 1905*. Skrifter utgivna av Statsvetenskapliga Föreningen i Uppsala, Vol. X. Uppsala and Stockholm: Statsvetenskapliga Föreningen, 1939

Bjørnsen, Bjørn. *Det utrolige døgnet*. Oslo: Gyldendal Norsk Forlag, 1977

Blindheim, Svein. *Nordmenn under Hitlers fane. Dei norske frontkjemparane*. Oslo: Noregs Boklag, 1977

Blom, Ida. "Bønder og blokkforhandlinger 1933–1936". *Historisk Tidsskrift* (Norway), Vol. 51, No. 4 (1972), pp. 391–408

———. *Kampen om Eirik Raudes Land. Pressgruppepolitikk i Grønlands-spørsmålet 1921–1931*. Oslo: Gyldendal Norsk Forlag, 1973

Boehm, Hermann. *Norwegen zwischen England und Deutschland: die Zeit vor und während des Weltkrieges*. Lippoldsberg: Klosterhaus-Verlag, 1956. Norwegian edition: *Norge mellom England og Tyskland. Tiden før og under den annen verdenskrig*. Oslo: Store Bjørn, 1957

Boyesen, Jens. "Fra yrkesorganisasjonenes kamp", pp. 295–318 in Vol. III of *Norges krig 1940–1945*, Sverre Steen, ed. Oslo: Gyldendal Norsk Forlag, 1950

Brevig, Hans Olaf. *NS – fra parti til sekt 1933–37*. Oslo: Pax Forlag, 1970

Brøyn, Per. "Den svenske malmeksport fram til okkupasjonen av Narvik i april 1940 – med særlig tanke på utførselen til Tyskland", pp. 61–120 in *Mellom nøytrale og allierte*, Norge og den 2. verdenskrig Series, Samtidshistorisk Forskningsgruppe, eds. Oslo: Universitetsforlaget, 1968

Bruknapp, Dag O. "Ideene splitter partiet. Rasespørsmålets betydning i

NS's utvikling", pp. 9–47 in *Fra idé til dom. Noen trekk fra utviklingen av Nasjonal Samling*, Rolf Danielsen and Stein Ugelvik Larsen, eds. Bergen: Universitetsforlaget, 1976

Bull, Edvard. *Klassekamp og fellesskap 1920–1945*. Vol. 13 of *Norges historie*, Knut Mykland, ed. Oslo: J. W. Cappelens Forlag, 1979

Christensen, Christian A. R. *Fra verdenskrig til verdenskrig*. Vol. 8 of *Vårt folks historie*, Axel Coldevin, Thorleif Dahl, and Johan Schreiner, eds. Oslo: Aschehoug, 1961

———. *Okkupasjonsår og etterkrigstid*. Vol. 9 of *Vårt folks historie*, Axel Coldevin, Thorleif Dahl, and Johan Schreiner, eds. Oslo: Aschehoug, 1961

Christophersen, H. O. *Fra 9. april 1940 til kampåret 1942*. Vol. I of *Av nød til seier*. Oslo: Grøndahl & Søn Forlag, 1977

Dahl, Arne Dagfinn. "Frigjøringen av Finnmark", pp. 569–612 in Vol. III of *Norges krig 1940–1945*, Sverre Steen, ed. Oslo: Gyldendal Norsk Forlag, 1950

Dahl, Hans Fredrik. "Fascismen i Norge 1920–40. Et overblikk", *Kontrast*, Vol. II, No. 3 (October 1966), pp. 4–17

Dahl, Hans Fredrik, Bernt Hagtvet, and Guri Hjeltnes. *Den norske nasjonalsosialismen. Nasjonal Samling 1933–1945 i tekst og bilder*. Oslo: Pax Forlag, 1982

Danielsen, Rolf. *Borgerlig oppdemmingspolitikk 1918–1940*. Vol. II of *Høyres historie*, Francis Sejersted, ed. Oslo: J. W. Cappelens Forlag, 1984

Diesen, Einar. *Maidagene 45*. Oslo: Norsk Kunstforlag, 1982

Dietrichson, Johannes Ø. "Trekk fra kampen om ungdomstjenesten", pp. 111–126 in Vol. III of *Norges krig 1940–1945*, Sverre Steen, ed. Oslo: Gyldendal Norsk Forlag, 1950

Flender, Harold. *Rescue in Denmark*. London: W. H. Allen, 1963

Frøland, Kaare. *Krise og kamp. Bygdefolkets Krisehjelp – En kriseorganisasjon i norsk mellomkrigspolitikk*. Oslo: Universitetsforlaget, 1962

Fuller, J. F. C. "Erobringen av røde Spania", *Stornordisk Samband*, Vol. II, No. 1 (1939), pp. 3–12

Furre, Berge. *Norsk historie 1905–1940*. Oslo: Det Norske Samlaget, 1971

Fürst, Walter. "Årsakene til og følgene av N.S.' sammenbrudd", *Ragnarok*, Vol. 3, No. 3 (May 1937), pp. 66–70

——— (same author, but surname spelled Fyrst). *Min sti*. Oslo: privately published, 1981

Gabrielsen, Bjørn Vidar. "De gode middagers tid. Noen glimt av norsk mellomkrigsaktivisme", *Kontrast*, Vol. II, No. 3 (October 1966), pp. 37–42

——. *Menn og politikk. Senterpartiet 1920–1970.* Oslo: Aschehoug, 1970

——. "Røde og hvite garder i Norge", *Norsk militært tidsskrift*, Vol. 123, No. 2 (1964), pp. 90–105

Galenson, Walter. "Scandinavia", pp. 104–72 in *Comparative Labor Movements*, Walter Galenson, ed. New York: Prentice-Hall, 1952

Gemzell, Carl-Axel. *Raeder, Hitler und Skandinavien. Der Kampf für einen maritimen Operationsplan.* Bibliotheca Historica Lundensis, Vol. XVI. Lund, Sweden: Gleerups, 1965

Gjelsvik, Tore. *Hjemmefronten. Den sivile motstand under okkupasjonen 1940–45.* Oslo: J. W. Cappelens Forlag, 1977

Grieg, Nordahl. *Vidkun Quisling. Hvordan en fører blir til.* Reprint from *Veien Frem*, No. 5 (1936). Oslo: Centrums Forlag, 1945

Grimnes, Ole Kristian. *Hjemmefrontens ledelse.* Norge og den 2. verdenskrig Series, Samtidshistorisk Forskningsgruppe, eds. Oslo: Universitetsforlaget, 1977

——. "Litt om Kretsen og Hjemmefrontledelsen", pp. 118–137 in *Motstandskamp, strategi og marinepolitikk.* Norge og den 2. verdenskrig Series, Samtidshistorisk Forskningsgruppe, eds. Oslo: Universitetsforlaget, 1972

——. *Overfall.* Vol. I of *Norge i krig. Fremmedåk og frihetskamp 1940–1945*, Magne Skodvin, ed. Oslo: Aschehoug, 1984

——. "Sabotasjen i norsk og dansk motstandsbevegelse", pp. 9–36 in *Motstandskamp, strategi og marinepolitikk.* Norge og den 2. verdenskrig Series, Samtidshistorisk Forskningsgruppe, eds. Oslo: Universitetsforlaget, 1972

Groth, Henrik, and Frits von der Lippe. "Kunsten i kamp", pp. 195–214 in Vol. III of *Norges krig 1940–1945*, Sverre Steen, ed. Oslo: Gyldendal Norsk Forlag, 1950

Hamsun, Knut. *På gjengrodde stier.* Oslo: Gyldendal Norsk Forlag, 1949

Hansen, Thorkild. *Processen mod Hamsun.* Copenhagen: Gyldendal, 1978. 3 vols. Norwegian edition: *Prosessen mot Hamsun.* Oslo: Gyldendal Norsk Forlag, 1978

Hartmann, Sverre. *Fører uten folk. Quisling som politisk og psykologisk problem.* Oslo: Tiden Norsk Forlag, 1959. Revised edition: *Fører uten folk. Forsvarsminister Quisling – hans bakgrunn og vei inn i norsk politikk.* Oslo: Tiden Norsk Forlag, 1970

——. "Lofot- og Vågsøyraidene margstjal Statsakten. En militærpolitisk studie", *Samtiden*, Vol. 64 (1955), pp. 487–504

——. *Nytt lys over kritiske faser i Norges historie under annen verdenskrig.* Oslo: Fabritius & Sønners Forlag, 1965

——. "Quislings konferanse med den tyske overkommando: 3. april 1940 i København", *Samtiden*, Vol. 65 (1956), pp. 317–23

Hauge, Jens Christian. "Fra krig til fred", s. 711–824 in *Norges krig 1940–1945*. Vol. III, Sverre Steen, ed. Oslo: Gyldendal Norsk Forlag, 1950

Hauglid, Anders Ole, Knut Erik Jensen, and Harry Westrheim. *Til befolkningen! Brannhøsten 1944 – gjenreisingen etterpå*. Oslo: Universitetsforlaget, 1985

Hayes, Paul M. *Quisling: The Career and Political Ideas of Vidkun Quisling, 1887–1945*. Newton Abbot, Devon: David & Charles, 1971

Hemming-Sjöberg, Axel. *Domen över Quisling*. Stockholm: Bokförlaget Natur och Kultur, 1946

Heradstveit, Per Øyvind. *Quisling – hvem var han?* Oslo: Hjemmenes Forlag, 1976

Hewins, Ralph. *Quisling: Prophet without Honour*. London: W. H. Allen, 1965

Hjort, Johan Bernhard. "Tyskland og dets venner", *Ragnarok*, 1938, pp. 239–242

Høidal, Oddvar K. "Hjort, Quisling, and *Nasjonal Samling*'s Disintegration", *Scandinavian Studies*, Vol. 47, No. 4 (autumn 1975), pp. 467–97

——. "*Økonomisk Verneplikt* and *Nordiske Folkereisning*: Two Predecessors of *Nasjonal Samling*", *Scandinavian Studies*, Vol. 49, No. 4 (autumn 1977), pp. 367–411

——. "Quisling og Bondepartiet våren 1933", *Historisk Tidsskrift* (Norway), Vol. 57, No. 3 (1978), pp. 311–316

——. "Quislings stilling ved den norske legasjon i Moskva juni 1927 – desember 1929", *Historisk Tidsskrift* (Norway), Vol. 46, No. 2 (1974), pp. 185–190

——. "Vidkun Quisling's Decline as a Political Figure in Prewar Norway, 1931–1937", *The Journal of Modern History*, Vol. 43, No. 3 (September 1971), pp. 440–467

Høyer, Liv Nansen. *Nansen og verden*. Oslo: J. W. Cappelens Forlag, 1955

Jacobsen, Hans S. "Vidkun Quisling og N.S.", *Ragnarok*, Vol. 3, No. 3 (May 1937), pp. 57–65

Jensen, Magnus. *Fra 1905 til våre dager*. Vol. II of *Norges historie*. Oslo: Gyldendal Norsk Forlag, 1949. Vol. IV in 3rd. ed. Oslo: Universitetsforlaget, 1965

——. "Kampen om skolen", pp. 73–110 in Vol. III of *Norges krig 1940–1945*, Sverre Steen, ed. Oslo: Gyldendal Norsk Forlag, 1950

Jensson, Gunnleik. *Norsk presse under hakekorset*. Oslo: Tell Forlag, 1945–46. 3 vols

Johansen, Per Ole. *Menstadkonflikten 1931*. Oslo: Tiden Norsk Forlag, 1977

Johnson, Thomas Frank. *International Tramps: From Chaos to Permanent World Peace*. London: Hutchinson & Co., 1938

Keilhau, Wilhelm. *Vår egen tid*. Vol. XI of *Det norske folks liv og historie gjennem tidene*, Edvard Bull, Wilhelm Keilhau, Haakon Shetelig, and Sverre Steen, ed. Oslo: Aschehoug, 1938

Kjeldstadli, Sverre. *Hjemmestyrkene. Hovedtrekk av den militære motstanden under okkupasjonen*. Oslo: Aschehoug, 1959

Kluge, Rolf. *Hjemmefrontledelsen tar form. Kretsen dannes*. Norge og den 2. verdenskrig Series, Samtidshistorisk Forskningsgruppe, eds. Oslo: Universitetsforlaget, 1970

Knudsen, Harald Franklin. *Jeg var Quislings sekretær*. Copenhagen: privately published, 1951

Koht, Halvdan. *For fred og fridom i krigstid 1939–1940*. Oslo: Tiden Norsk Forlag, 1957

L'Abée-Lund, Lars. "Politiet over og under jorden". pp. 275–94 in Vol. III of *Norges krig 1940–1945*, Sverre Steen, ed. Oslo: Gyldendal Norsk Forlag, 1950

Langfeldt, Gabriel. *Gåten Vidkun Quisling*. Oslo: Aschehoug, 1969

Larsen, Stein Ugelvik. "Nazismen i Norge", pp. 73–96 in *Nazismen og norsk litteratur*, Bjarte Birkeland and Stein Ugelvik Larsen, eds. Oslo: Universitetsforlaget, 1975

––––––. "The Social Foundations of Norwegian Fascism 1933–1945: An Analysis of Membership Data", pp. 595–620 in *Who Were the Fascists: Social Roots of European Fascism*, Stein Ugelvik Larsen, Bernt Hagtvedt, and Jan Petter Myklebust, eds. Bergen: Universitetsforlaget, 1982

Lie, Trygve. *Med England i ildlinjen 1940–1942*. Oslo: Tiden Norsk Forlag, 1956

Lindboe, Asbjørn. *Fra de urolige tredveårene. Dagboksnedtegnelser og kommentarer*. Oslo: Johan Grundt Tanum, 1965

Lochner, Louis P., ed. *The Goebbels Diaries*. Garden City, N.Y.: Doubleday, 1948

Loock, Hans-Dietrich. *Quisling, Rosenberg und Terboven. Zur Vorgeschichte und Geschichte der nationalsozialistischen Revolution in Norwegen*. Stuttgart: Deutsche Verlags-Anstalt, 1970. Norwegian edition: *Quisling, Rosenberg og Terboven. Den nasjonalsosialistiske revolusjon i Norge – dens forhistorie og forløp*. Translated by Astrid and Einhart Lorenz. Oslo: Gyldendal Norsk Forlag, 1972

Luihn, Hans. *De illegale avisene. Den frie, hemmelige pressen i Norge under okkupasjonen*. Oslo: Universitetsforlaget, 1960

Mendelsohn, Oskar. *Jødenes historie i Norge gjennom 300 år*. Vol. II. Oslo: Universitetsforlaget, 1986

Meyer, Håkon. *Et annet syn*. Oslo: Dreyers Forlag, 1952

———. "9. april 1940 og Quislings statskupp", *Samtiden,* Vol. 81, No. 7 (1972), pp. 444–457

Mogens, Victor. *Tyskerne, Quisling og vi andre.* Oslo: Utenriks-forlaget, 1945

Molland, Einar. "Kirkens kamp", pp. 35–72 in Vol. III of *Norges krig 1940–1945,* Sverre Steen, ed. Oslo: Gyldendal Norsk Forlag, 1950

Munksgaard, Oddvar. *Gestapo-kameraten.* Oslo: Gyldendal Norsk Forlag, 1973

Nansen, Fridtjof. *Gjennom Armenia.* Vol. IV of *Fra Svalbard til Kaukasus,* Werner Werenskiold, ed. Oslo: Jacob Dybwads Forlag, 1941

———. *Gjennom Kaukasus til Volga.* Oslo: Jacob Dybwads Forlag, 1929

———. *Through the Caucasus to the Volga.* Translated by G. C. Wheeler. London: Allen & Unwin, 1931

Nasjonal Samling. Rikspropagandaledelsen. *NS Årbok 1942,* Willy Klevenberg, ed. Oslo: Blix Forlag, 1943

———. *Vidkun Quislings tale på førertinget, 25. september 1942.* Oslo: Rikspropagandaledelsen, n.d.

———. *Vidkun Quislings tale, 17. mai 1943.* Oslo: Rikspropagandaledelsen, n.d.

Nerbøvik, Jostein. *Antiparlamentariske straumdrag i Noreg 1905–14. Ein studie i motvilje.* Oslo: Universitetsforlaget, 1969

Noack, Ulrich. *Norwegen zwischen Friedensvermittlung und Fremdherrschaft.* Krefeld: Verlag Aufbau der Mitte, 1952

Nøkleby, Berit. "Adjusting to Allied Victory", pp. 279–323 in *Scandinavia during the Second World War,* Henrik S. Nissen, ed. Oslo and Minneapolis: Universitetsforlaget and The University of Minnesota Press, 1983

———. "Fra november til april – sendemann Brauers personlige politikk", pp. 7–88 in *1940 – Fra nøytral til okkupert.* Norge og den 2. verdenskrig Series, Samtidshistorisk Forskningsgruppe, eds. Oslo: Universitetsforlaget, 1969

———. *Holdningskamp.* Vol. IV of *Norge i krig. Fremmedåk og frihetskamp 1940–1945,* Magne Skodvin, ed. Oslo: Aschehoug, 1986

———. *Nyordning.* Vol. II of *Norge i krig. Fremmedåk og frihetskamp 1940–1945,* Magne Skodvin, ed. Oslo: Aschehoug, 1985

Nordiske Folkereisning i Norge. *Redegjørelse for Nordiske Folkereisnings Retningslinjer.* Oslo: Det Mallingske Bogtrykkeri, 1931

———. *Retningslinjer og lover vedtatt på konstituerende møte i Oslo 17. mars 1931.* Oslo: Det Mallingske Bogtrykkeri, 1931

Nordvik, Jørgen. "Provokasjon og retorsjon (gjengjeldelse). Et aktuelt strafferettsemne", pp. 15–19 in *Den nye rettsstat på nasjonalsosialistisk grunn.* Oslo: Nasjonal Samlings Rikstrykkeri, 1941

Norland, Andreas. *Hårde tider. Fedrelandslaget i norsk politikk.* Oslo: Dreyers Forlag, 1973

Omang, Reidar. *Stormfulle tider 1913–28.* Vol. II of *Norsk Utenrikstjeneste.* Oslo: Gyldendal norsk Forlag, 1959

Østbye, Haldis Neegaard. "Vidkun Quisling", pp. 43–96 in Ragnar Skancke, et al, *Boken om Quisling.* Oslo: Blix Forlag, 1940

Øvsthus, Georg. "Dom og oppreisning. Tidligere NS-medlemmers organiserte forsøk på å oppnå rehabilitering", pp. 215–258 in *Fra idé til dom. Noen trekk fra utviklingen av Nasjonal Samling,* Rolf Danielsen and Stein Ugelvik Larsen, eds. Bergen: Universitetsforlaget, 1976

Paulsen, Helge. "Reichskommisariat og 'motytelsene' under riksrådsforhandlingene", pp. 285–356 in *1940 – Fra nøytral til okkupert.* Norge og den 2. verdenskrig Series, Samtidshistorisk Forskningsgruppe, eds. Oslo: Universitetsforlaget, 1969

——. "Terboven i konflikt med Kriegsmarine", pp. 59–117, in *Motstandskamp, strategi og marinepolitikk.* Norge og den 2. verdenskrig Series, Samtidshistorisk Forskningsgruppe, eds. Oslo: Universitetsforlaget, 1972

Quisling, Maria: *Dagbok og andre efterlatte papirer.* Edited by Øistein Parmann. Oslo: Dreyers Forlag, 1980

Quisling, Vidkun. "A Nordic World Federation", *British Union Quarterly,* Vol. I, No. 1 (January–April 1937), pp. 87–101

——. *For Norges frihet og selvstendighet. Artikler og taler 9. april 1940 – 23. juni 1941.* Oslo: Gunnar Stenersens Forlag, 1942

——. "Hvorfor Stiklestad?", pp. 162–65 in *Olavstanken. Fra Stiklestad til Stiklestad,* Eivind Mehle, ed. Oslo: Centralforlaget, 1944

——. *Mot nytt land. Artikler og taler av Vidkun Quisling 1941–1943,* Haldis Neegaard Østbye, ed. Oslo: Blix Forlag, 1943

——. *Om at bebodde verdener finnes utenom jorden og betydningen derav for vår livsanskuelse.* Oslo: privately published, 1929

——. *Quisling har sagt. Citater fra taler og avisartikler.* Oslo: J. M. Stenersens Forlag, 1940

——. *Russland og vi.* Oslo: Jacob Dybwads Forlag, 1930. 2nd ed; Oslo: Blix Forlag, 1941

Qvisling, Jon Lauritz. *Fra mine unge aar. Erindringer og optegnelser.* Skien, Norway: Erik St. Nilssens Forlag, 1912

——. *Gjerpen. En bygdebok.* Vol. II: *Den historiske del.* Kristiania: Aschehoug, 1919

——. *Gjerpens Prestegjelds og presters historie.* Skien: Erik St. Nilssens Forlag, 1905

Ræder, Gudrun. *De uunnværlige flinke.* Oslo: Gyldendal Norsk Forlag, 1975

Reynolds, Ernest Edwin. *Nansen.* London: Geoffrey Bles, 1932

Riisnæs, Sverre. *Den nye rettsstat på nasjonalsosialistisk grunn*. Oslo: Nasjonal Samlings Rikstrykkeri, 1941

Ringnes, Ellef. *Bak okkupasjonens kulisser*. Oslo: Heim og Samfund, n.d.

Roscher Nielsen, Ragnvald. "Krigen i Norge april-juni 1940", pp. 87–452 in Vol. I of *Norges krig 1940–1945*, Sverre Steen, ed. Oslo: Gyldendal Norsk Forlag, 1947

Sæther, Orvar, ed. *Vår organisasjon. Nasjonal Samling, N S Ungdomsfylking*. Oslo: NSUF's Centralstyre, 1936

Sanengen, Alf. "Kampen mot A-T og arbeidsmobiliseringen", pp. 319–348 in Vol. III of *Norges krig 1940–1945*, Sverre Steen, ed. Oslo: Gyldendal Norsk Forlag, 1950

Schjelderup, Ferdinand. *Fra Norges kamp for retten. 1940 i Høyesterett*. Oslo: Grøndahl & Søns Forlag, 1945

———. *Over bakkekammen. 1943–1944*. Oslo: Gyldendal Norsk Forlag, 1949

———. *På bred front*. Oslo: Grøndahl & Søns Forlag, 1947

Seidenfaden, Aage. *I Politiets Tjeneste*. Copenhagen: Gyldendal, 1954

Seip, Didrik Arup. *Hjemme og i fiendeland 1940–45*. Oslo: Gyldendal Norsk Forlag, 1946

Seraphim, Hans-Günther, ed. *Das politische Tagebuch Alfred Rosenbergs aus den Jahren 1934/35 und 1939/40*. Vol. VIII of *Quellensammlung zur Kulturgeschichte*, Wilhelm Treue, ed. Göttingen: Musterschmidt-Verlag, 1956

Skodvin, Magne. "Det store fremstøt", pp. 573–734 in Vol. II of *Norges krig 1940–1945*, Sverre Steen, ed. Oslo: Gyldendal Norsk Forlag, 1948

———. "5. mai 1945: Slutten sikker – dagen uviss", pp. 156–63 in *Samtid og historie. Utvalde artiklar og avhandlingar*. Oslo: Det Norske Samlaget, 1975. Reprint from *Aftenposten*, May 5, 1970

———. "Norge i stormaktspolitikken opp til 9. april. Litteraturoversyn", *Historisk Tidsskrift* (Norway), Vol. 36, No. 6 (1952–53), pp. 638–672

———. "Norge i stormaktsstrategien. Frå Finlands-freden til 'Wilfred'", pp. 89–126 in *1940 – Fra nøytral til okkupert*. Norge og den 2. verdenskrig Series, Samtidshistorisk Forskningsgruppe, eds. Oslo: Universitetsforlaget, 1969

———. "Norges plass i Hitlers militære planer etter 7. juni 1940", *Historisk Tidskrift* (Norway), Vol. 35, No. 7 (1949–51), pp. 429–458

———. "Norsk okkupasjonshistorie i europeisk samanheng", *Nordisk Tidskrift* (Sweden), Vol. 27 (1951), pp. 308–320

———. Review of Thomas Christian Wyller, *Nyordning og motstand*, *Historisk Tidsskrift* (Norway), Vol. 39, No. 2 (1959–60), pp. 191–208

——. *Striden om okkupasjonsstyret i Norge fram til 25. september 1940*. Oslo: Det Norske Samlaget, 1956

——. "Svar til Sverre Steen og Sverre Hartmann", *Historisk Tidsskrift* (Norway), Vol. 38, No. 2 (1957–58), pp. 178–194

Söderman, Harry. *Skandinaviskt mellanspel. Norska och danska trupper i Sverige*. Stockholm: Forum, 1945

Sømme, Jacob D. "Mjøen, Jon Alfred Hansen", pp. 255–256 in *Norsk biografisk leksikon*, Vol. IX. Oslo: Aschehoug, 1923

Sørensen, Jon. *Fridtjof Nansens saga*. Oslo: Jacob Dybwads Forlag, 1931

Sørhus, Kjell, and Rolf Ottesen, eds. *Milorg D 13 i kamp*. Oslo: Ernst G. Mortensens Forlag, 1961

Steen, Sverre, and Sverre Hartmann. Review of Magne Skodvin, *Striden om okkupasjonsstyret i Norge fram til 25. september 1940, Historisk Tidsskrift* (Norway), Vol. 38, No. 1 (1957–58), pp. 49–86

Steen, Sverre. "Universitetet i ildlinjen", pp. 127–94 in Vol. III of *Norges krig 1940–1945*, Sverre Steen, ed. Oslo: Gyldendal Norsk Forlag, 1950

Stene, Helga. "Et bortkommet blad i okkupasjonstidens historie", *Historisk Tidsskrift* (Norway), Vol. 44, No. 1 (1965), pp. 92–96

Torgersen, Ulf. "Våre helter og høvdinger", *Kontrast*, Vol. II, No. 3 (October 1966), pp. 29–36

Trevor-Roper, Hugh R., ed. *Final Entries, 1945: The Diaries of Joseph Goebbels*. Translated by Richard Barry. New York: G. P. Putnam's Sons, 1978

——. *The Last Days of Hitler*. 3rd ed. New York: Collier Books, 1962

Ustvedt, Yngvar. *Den varme freden – den kalde krigen. Det skjedde i Norge*, Vol. I: 1945–52. Oslo: Gyldendal Norsk Forlag, 1978

——. *Verdensrevolusjonen på Hønefoss. En beretning om Leo Trotskijs opphold i Norge*. Oslo: Gyldendal Norsk Forlag, 1974

Vogt, Benjamin. "Prytz, Anton Frederik Winter Jakhelln", pp. 194–199 in *Norsk biografisk leksikon*, Vol. XI. Oslo: Aschehoug, 1923

——. *Mennesket Vidkun og forræderen Quisling*. Oslo: Aschehoug, 1965

——. "Quisling, Vidkun Abraham Lauritz Jonssøn", pp. 213–232 in *Norsk biografisk leksikon*, Vol. XI. Oslo: Aschehoug, 1923

Wendt, Frantz. *Danmarks Historie 1939–1978*. Special edition of *Danmarks Historie*, Vol. 14, Hal Koch and John Danstrup, eds. Copenhagen: Politikens Forlag, 1978

Wiesener, Albert. "Tyskvennlighet igjen", *Ragnarok*, 1938, pp. 242 ff

Wyller, Thomas Christian. *Christian Michelsen. Politikeren*. Oslo: Dreyers Forlag, 1975

——. *Fra okkupasjonsårenes maktkamp. Nasjonal Samlings korporative nyordningsforsøk*. Oslo: Tanum, 1953

―――. "Hovedtrekk av Nasjonal Samlings ideer om stat og samfunn 1930–40", *Statsvetenskaplig Tidskrift* (Sweden), Vol. 56, No. 2 (1953), pp. 212–255

―――. *Nyordning og motstand. En framstilling og en analyse av organisasjonenes politiske funksjon under den tyske okkupasjonen 25. 9. 1940–25. 9. 1942.* Oslo: Universitetsforlaget, 1958

Index

DATE DUE

DEC 1 2 1993			
ILL: N34295 4-08-98			

HIGHSMITH   # 45220

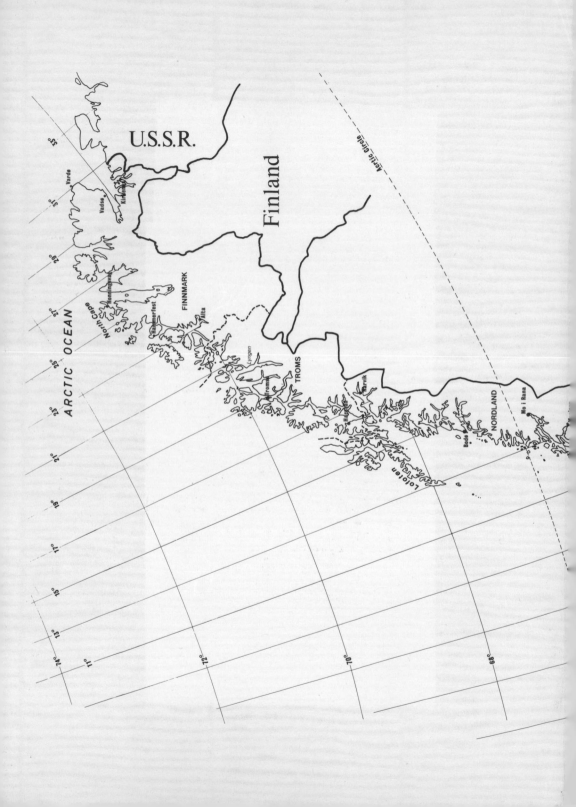